Alan Greenwood and his wife, Cleo, are the publishers of *Vintage Guitar* magazine, which they launched in 1986. *Vintage Guitar* is the largest monthly publication for guitar collectors, enthusiasts, and dealers. They also publish *Vintage Guitar®* Online at www.vintageguitar.com, and *The Official Vintage Guitar Magazine Price Guide*. His collection includes several vintage instruments from the '50s, '60s and '70s, as well as newer production and custom-made guitars and amps. He lives in Bismarck, North Dakota.

Gil Hembree began collecting guitars in 1966 as a college student working at Kitt's Music in Washington, DC. He holds a BSBA from American University and a MBA from Midwestern State University. He worked for General Motors Corporation in Flint and Detroit, Michigan for over 30 years as a Financial Administrator and Supervisor of Corporate Audit. During that time he played music semi-professionally and he has continued collecting guitars and amps. Since 1992 he has written for several guitar publications, and he is a contributing writer and a columnist ("401K Guitars") for *Vintage Guitar*. He has recently completed a new 352 page book, Gibson Guitars – Ted McCarty's Golden Era. It will be available March, 2007 and distributed by Hal Leonard Corporation to most music and book stores. Gil and his wife Jane live in Austin, Texas.

The Official Vintage Guitar® Magazine Price Guide

By Alan Greenwood and Gil Hembree

Vintage Guitar Books
An imprint of Vintage Guitar Inc., PO Box 7301, Bismarck, ND 58507, (701) 255-1197, Fax (701) 255-0250, publishers of *Vintage Guitar®* magazine and Vintage Guitar® Online at www.vintageguitar.com. Vintage Guitar is a registered trademark of Vintage Guitar, Inc.

ISBN-10: 1-884883-18-4
ISBN-13: 978-1-884883-18-7

Cover and Back photos: 1958 Gibson Les Paul Standard: Photo: Ward Meeker/ Doug Yellow Bird/VG Archive. 1957 Gibson Les Paul model: VG Archive. 1958 Gibson Les Paul model: VG Archive. Rickenbacker 362/12: VG Archive/ Dave Rogers. 1963 Fender Jazz Bass: VG Archive.

Cover Design: Doug Yellow Bird/Vintage Guitar, Inc.

Printed in the United States of America

EXCLUSIVELY DISTRIBUTED BY
HAL•LEONARD® CORPORATION
7777 W. BLUEMOUND RD. P.O. BOX 13819
MILWAUKEE, WISCONSIN 53213

V

Dave Belzer & Drew Berlin,
The Burst Brothers

IF YOU WANT THE BEST
BUY THE BEST
FROM THE BEST

THE HOLLYWOOD VINTAGE COLLECTION
7425 SUNSET BLVD., HOLLYWOOD, CA 90046
VINTAGE ROOM: 323.874.2302 STORE: 323.874.1060 FAX: 323.969.9783
EMAIL: GUITAR@VINTAGEGUITARS.NET

www.vintageguitars.net

TABLE OF CONTENTS

USING THE GUIDE

Understanding the Values

The values presented in *The Official Vintage Guitar Price Guide* are for excellent-condition, all-original instruments. Our definition of excellent condition allows for some wear, but the instrument should be well-maintained, with no significant blemishes, wear, repairs, or damage. All-original means the instrument has the parts and finish it had when it left the factory. Replacement parts and refinishes can greatly affect value, as can the appropriate case (or cover) in excellent condition. In many instances, a "wrong" case will not greatly affect value, but with the top-dollar collectibles, it can.

We use a range of excellent-condition values, as there is seldom agreement on a single price point for vintage and used instruments. A tighter range suggests there is a general consensus, while a wide range means the market isn't in strict agreement. A mint-condition instrument can be worth more than the values listed here, and anything in less-than-excellent condition will have a reduced value.

Repairs affect value differently. Some repair is necessary to keep an instrument in playable condition. The primary concern is the level of expertise displayed in the work and an amateurish repair will lower the value more than one that is obviously professional. A refinished guitar, regardless of the quality of the work, is generally worth 50% or less of the values shown in *The Guide*. A poorly executed neck repair or significant body repair can mean a 50% reduction in a guitar's value. A professional re-fret or minor, nearly invisible body repair will reduce a guitar's value by only 5%.

The values in the *The Guide* are for unfaded finishes. Slight color fade reduces the value by only 5%, but heavily faded examples can reduce the value by 25% to 50%.

Finding the Information

The table of contents shows the major sections and each is organized in alphabetical order by brand, then by model. In a few instances, there are separate sections for a company's most popular models, especially when there is a large variety of similar instruments. Examples include Fender's Stratocasters, Telecasters, Precision and Jazz basses, and Gibson's Les Pauls. The outer top corner of each page uses a dictionary-type header that tells the models or brands on that page. This provides a quick way to navigate each section. The index at the back shows the page numbers for each type of instrument, by brand, and is a great place to start when looking for a specific model or brand.

The Guide has excellent brand histories and in most cases the guitar section has the most detailed information for each brand. When possible, *The Guide* lists each model's years of availability and any design changes that affect values.

More information on many of the brands covered in *The Guide* is available in the pages of *Vintage Guitar* magazine and on the "Brand Pages" section of our website, www.vintage-guitar.com.

The authors of *The Guide* always appreciate your help, so if you find any errors, or have additional information on certain brands or models, we'd like to hear from you. We are especially looking for info on any brand not yet listed. Whatever you may have to contribute, feel free to drop us a line at al@vguitar.com.

New Retail Pricing Information

The Guide continues to add information on individual luthiers and smaller shops. It's difficult to develop values on used instruments produced by these builders because much of their output is custom work, production is low, and/or they haven't been producing for a period of time sufficient to see their instruments enter the used/resale market. To give you an idea about their instruments, we've developed five grades of retail values for new instruments. These convey only the prices charged by the builder, and are not indicative of the quality of construction. *The Guide* applies this scale to all builders and manufacturers of new instruments.

**The five retail-price grades are:
Budget - up to $250,
Intermediate - $251 to $1,000,
Professional - $1,001 to $3,000,
Premium - $3,001 to $10,000,
Presentation - more than $10,000.**

The Guide uses the terms "production" and "custom" to differentiate between builders who do true custom work versus those who offer standard production models. "Production" means the company offers specific models, with no variations. "Custom" means they do only custom orders, and "production/custom" indicates they do both. Here's an example:

Yellow Bird Guitars
1977-present. Luthier Doug Yellow Bird builds his professional-grade, custom, archtop guitars in Mandan, North Dakota. He also builds effects.

This tells who the builder is, the type of instruments they build, where they build them, how long they've been operating under that brand, that they do only custom work, and that they ask between $1,000 and $3,000 for their guitars (professional-grade).

We've applied the retail price grades and production and/or custom labels to most new-instrument manufacturers.

INTRODUCTION

As we were working on this newest edition of *The Official Vintage Guitar Price Guide*, *Vintage Guitar* magazine was celebrating 20 years of publication. As a hobby/avocation, guitar collecting has been around for a long time, and the last 20 years have been especially intense, as more buyers and sellers have entered the market and the profile and status of guitar collecting has been acknowledged. Today more than ever, knowing the relative value of an instrument is very important, and the *The Official Vintage Guitar Price Guide* has something for collectors of every style, taste, and level. In this 2007 Edition are values ranging from $25 for a 1970s Brentwood K-100 all the way to $415,000 for a 1959 Gibson Les Paul Standard. There are guitars almost two centuries old, and some models barely a year old.

In this Introduction, a lot of attention is given to electric guitars. In the older, more expensive segment of the market, electric guitars are hot, but sales figures for new guitars indicate electrics and acoustics are equally popular. Even though older, more expensive guitars get a lot of attention, we field just as many questions about models made in the 1990s and 2000s. This is particularly true of limited edition models. It has been said that we are in the second "golden era" of guitar building. Musicians love the newer models and there are many models made after 1990 that are sought-after in the market.

The Vintage Market

Vintage Guitar has been tracking guitar values since 1991, and in an effort to illustrate how collectible guitars have increased in value since that time, we developed "The 42-Guitar Index," which is comprised of excellent-condition instruments made in the 1960s or earlier (14 each from Fender, Gibson, and Martin – companies accepted as the top manufacturers of that era). When *VG* started the index, it included only guitars that had a unit value below $10,000 in 1991, with the average value being $3,660. That year, the 14 Gibsons had about the same total value as the 14 Fenders and the 14 Martins. The Index does not include the most expensive models like the '59 Gibson Les Paul Standard, nor does it include budget models like the Gibson Melody Maker.

Some may find it shocking that today the average value of an instrument in The Index is $19,706! As a percent of accumulative appreciation, the average value has increased 438% from

GUITAR DEALER PARTICIPANTS

The information refined on these pages comes from several sources, including the input of many knowledgeable guitar dealers. Without the help of these individuals, it would be very hard for us to provide the information here and in each issue of *Vintage Guitar* magazine. We deeply appreciate the time and effort they provide.

Andy Eder
Andy's Guitars

Bob Page
Buffalo Brothers

Norm Moren
Cold Springs Electrical Works

Stan Werbin & S.J. "Frog" Forgey
Elderly Instruments

Dave Belzer & Drew Berlin
Guitar Center

Vallis Kolbeck
GuitarVille (Seattle)

Kennard Machol & Leonard Coulson
Intermountain Guitar & Banjo

Jim Singleton
Jim's Guitars

Dave Hinson
Killer Vintage

Timm Kummer
Kummer's Vintage Instruments

Buzzy Levine
Lark Street Music

Larry Wexer
Laurence Wexer, Ltd.

Stan Jay
Mandolin Brothers

Bob November
McKenzie River Music

Lowell Levinger
Players Vintage Instruments

Mike Reeder
Mike's Music

Eliot Michael
Rumble Seat Music

Bruce Barnes & Kenny Rardin
Solidbodyguitar.com

Fred Oster
Vintage Instruments

Richard Friedman & David Davidson
We Buy Guitars

Nate Westgor
Willie's American Guitars

1991 to 2007. For that period, the average annual compounded percentage of return is 27% (the accumulative appreciation divided by 16 years). The average annual (non-compounded) rate of return is about 12% (each year-to-year annual percentage of improvement is added together and the sum is divided by 16 years). In other words, the value of The Index grew, on average, 12% each year. But, as you'll see in our graphs, much of that appreciation occurred recently.

We've discussed two ways to calculate return; the 27% compounded rate of return is larger than the 12% non-compounded rate for the same reason that a bank's savings account compounded interest rate is higher than it's annual interest rate. Compounded rates are higher because they take advantage of prior (compounding) appreciation. This may be too much information for some, but it's important to those who invest in guitars. As an investor, if you want to compare the guitar index rate of return with another investment, you should use the 12% average annual return. The 27% compound rate is a nice number, but in order to earn that return, you would have had to have owned all of the instruments in the index for the entire 16-year period.

Chart 1 is a trend-line chart showing the total value of The 42-Guitar Index for each year from 1991 to 2007. The average percent of annual improvement (non-compounded) in the 1990s was about 9%. There was no growth in the index in 2000 and '01. The slope of the line graph increased in '02 and the annual improvement from '02 to '06 was from 11% to 15%. The slope of the line graph increased dramatically in 2007 and the increase in value of the index from '06 to '07 was 54%. From late '05 to '07, precedent vintage-guitar values for many expensive instruments were disregarded and "speculative" prices became real prices for many of the guitars in The Index. As explained in the intro to *The Official Vintage Guitar Price Guide* 2006, speculative pricing became apparent in '05 and '06, and these aggressive

prices have been accepted in the marketplace.

While it is important to realize that The 42-Guitar Index is a good general analytical tool, the power of analysis is in the details. Every vintage guitar is different. No 1955 Fender Stratocaster is exactly like another 1955 Stratocaster. No vintage Les Paul is like another vintage Les Paul. They're all different. And of course, Les Pauls and Stratocasters are different guitars, as are ES-335s, SGs, Firebirds, Jazzmasters, and so on. The power of the *The Guide* is in the more than 500 pages of detail. We like to say, "We've done the work, so you won't have to," but the truth of the matter is that *The Guide* contains hundreds of pages of information that will help you develop your own conclusions.

THE 42 INDEX

FROM FENDER
1952 blond Precision Bass
1952 blond Esquire
1953 blond Telecaster
1956 sunburst Stratocaster
1958 sunburst Jazzmaster
1958 blond Telecaster
1960 sunburst Stratocaster
1961 sunburst, stack knob, Jazz Bass
1962 sunburst, 3-knob, Jazz Bass
1963 sunburst Telecaster Custom
1963 sunburst Esquire Custom

1964 Lake Placid Blue Jaguar
1964 sunburst Precision Bass
1966 Candy Apple Red Stratocaster
FROM GIBSON
1952 sunburst ES-5
1952 Les Paul Model
1954 Les Paul Jr.
1958 sunburst EB-2 Bass
1958 Les Paul Custom
1958 natural ES-335
1958 Super 400CES
1959 Les Paul Jr.
1959 J-160E
1961 sunburst ES-355
1961 Les Paul SG

1964 sunburst Thunderbird II Bass
1965 EB-3 Bass
1969 sunburst Citation
FROM MARTIN
1931 OM-28
1932 00-28 special order
1935 D-18
1944 scalloped-brace 000-28
1944 D-28
1950 D-28
1958 000-18
1959 D-18
1959 D-28E
1962 D-28
1967 GT-75
1968 000-18
1969 N-20
1969 D-45

#1 The 42 Guitar Index
1991 - 2007

Authors Alan Greenwood and Gil Hembree.

Chart 2 shows the changes in values of the three brands that make up The 42-Guitar Index – Fender, Gibson, and Martin. Some suspect there has been a relative softening in the Martin portion of the Index and indeed, Martin guitars in the Index have not shot up in value relative to Fenders and Gibsons. This is a new twist, but does not lead to any conclusions. Does Chart 2 suggest that Fenders and Gibsons are overpriced? Or does it suggest that Martins are undervalued? Are Martins a good buying opportunity?

As always, it's important to check the details. Within the Gibson and Fender indices, some electric guitar models are appreciating at amazing levels, while other Gibson and Fender models are appreciating at normal levels. So, one should always check specific model detail. Again, even though electric guitars in the index are performing exceptionally well, overall, acoustic guitars are just as popular as electric guitars; there is no demographic switch in the popularity of acoustic guitars versus electric guitars. It's true that the market for vintage Martins is a few years older than the market for vintage solidbodies. So is it possible that the older market is leveling off because of age? We don't think so, and any number of pro and con scenarios could be presented.

Chart 3 is new to the *The Guide*. It deals with a market basket of '70s vintage instruments. Instead of sticking with just the three brands in the 42 Index, we've included other cool brands like Guild, Gretsch, Rickenbacker, and Music Man. As with our other charts, Chart 3 is a general outlook, and should not replace examining individual models. Even within a certain model, specification changes in the 1970s are important. For example, early-'70s Strats had a four-bolt neck attachment,

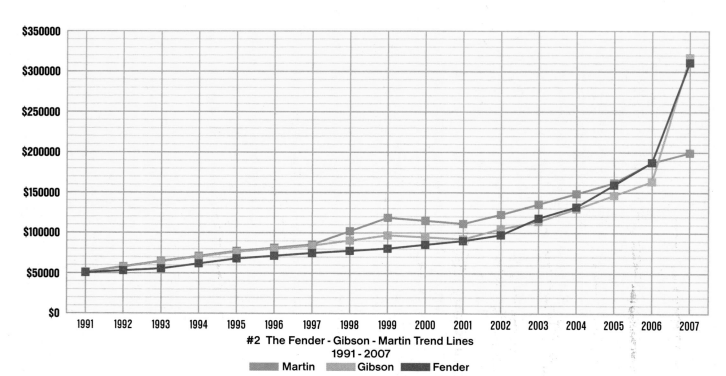

#2 The Fender - Gibson - Martin Trend Lines
1991 - 2007
Martin   Gibson   Fender

then Fender transitioned to a three-bolt attachment and uneven pickup polepieces, then came even polepieces with white plastic trim, and by '75 even polepieces with black-plastic trim. Also, many Stratocasters from the late '70s seem heavier than early-'70s models. All of these features are accepted differently in the market and selling prices have changed over time due to these variations. So Chart 3 is a good generalization, and if your interested in '70s models, you should dig into the details.

Chart 3 is made up of 14 guitars and basses. The Fender models are a '73 Jazz Bass with Walnut Brown finish, a '74 Strat with Walnut Brown finish, and a '73 Telecaster with standard natural finish. The Gibsons are a '76 Explorer with mahogany body and natural finish, a '76 Flying V with mahogany body, a '74 Les Paul Custom with two pickups and standard finish. The Martins are a '75 D-35, a '72 000-18, and a '72 D-18. From Rickenbacker, a '71 Model 4001 bass in Jetglo (black) finish, and a '77 Model 620 in Fireglo (red sunburst) finish. From other builders, a '75 Gretsch Chet Atkins Tennessean Model 7655, a '79 Guild Starfire IV, and a '77 Music Man Stingray bass with sunburst finish.

The trend line in Chart 3 is different from the trend line on Chart 1, even if at a glance they look similar. The 1970s index has a notable spike in the trend line in 2007, but it's nothing like

the spike in 2007 on Chart 1. Chart 3 doesn't have the plateau from 1999 to 2001 you see in Chart 1. In the early/mid '90s, instruments from the '70s were typically deemed inferior, and that translated to a smaller rate of increase during that period. In the early/mid '90s The 42-Guitar Index had consistent annual rate of appreciation of about 10% per year, where 1970s guitars had a rate that was about 3% to 6%. 1996 was the year '70s instruments began to get more respect in the market, and from '95 to '97 the '70s Index gained about 28%. From '03 to '07, the '70s Index had annual increases of about 10% per year. Using dollar value as a metric, it could be suggested that '70s guitars are twice as popular in this decade vs. the last.

Today's Market

What else is happening in the vintage guitar market in 2007? Well, Rickenbackers are coming out of the shadows, with Beatles-era modes being especially hot, as are the Rose-Morris series from the mid '60s. Full-body Rics – those made in the late 1950s and early '60s (and designated with an F suffix in their model names) – are also hot, as are Capri models made from 1958 to '60.

Danelectro Model 3412 Shorthorn six-string basses have significantly increased in value, as has the Model 4423 Long-

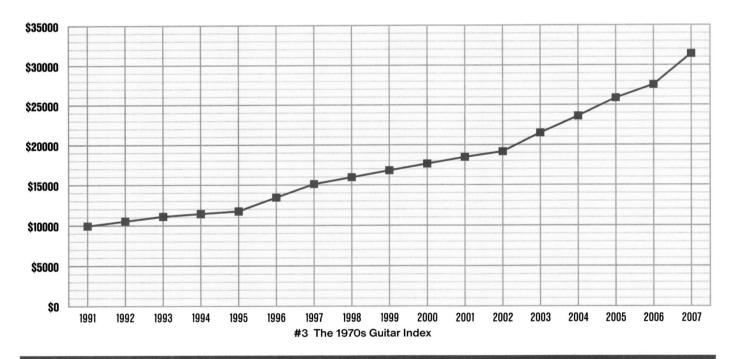

#3 The 1970s Guitar Index

BUILDER UPDATES AND CORRECTIONS

If you produce instruments for sale and would like to be included in the next *VG Price Guide*, send your infomation to al@vguitar.com. Include info on the types of instruments you build, model names and prices, yearly production, the year you started, where you are located and a short bio about yourself.

If you spot errors in the information about brands and models in this guide, or have information on a brand you'd like to see included, please contact us at the above email address. Your help is appreciated.

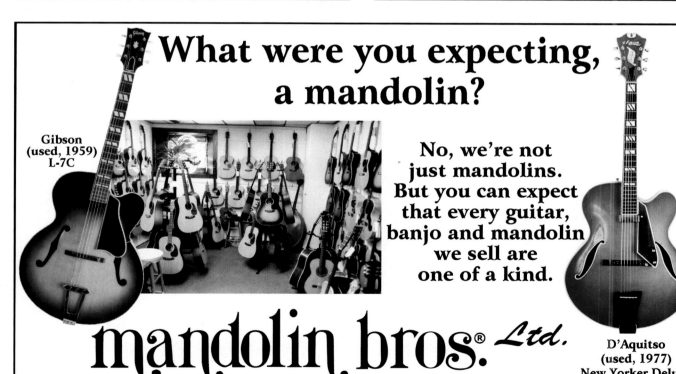

horn bass. The '70s Travis Bean TB-4000 (wedge V-body) Bass is in demand – and hard to find. Early/mid-'60s Gibson EB-3 models have picked up steam (the '65 EB-3 is included in The 42-Guitar Index).

Like most items listed in the 2007 Guide, amplifiers are showing increasing values, and demand remains strong for classic pre-CBS Fenders and 1960s/early-'70s Marshalls.

The "Effects" section of *The Guide* reflects a stable market, but some prestige brands like Foxx, Maestro, Mu-Tron, MXR, Pearl, Roland, Tycobrahe, Univox, and Vox have prices ranging from $600 to $1,000. Amongst guitar dealers, interest in effects has waned, but online auctions have taken up some of the slack. The average effect is about $50, and is easy to ship. That's a good fit – low cost and small size – for internet sales.

The mandolin market is supported mainly by bluegrass musicians who often like old Gibsons as well as newer brands like Dubenbostel, Gilchrist, and Monteleone.

As for steels and lap steel, Fender stand-up Stringmaster multi-neck models have became more popular and continue to hold their value. Lap steels, as instruments, are very popular as low-cost alternatives, and collectors love them because they are true "functional art."

We added the "Banjo" section in '06 at the request of readers. The high-end banjo market remains hot, including 1933-'39 Gibson Granada RB flathead models, and some '30s Gibson banjos fetch more than most vintage guitars. If you find an old banjo in a garage sale, check it out.

Our ukulele guru, Randy Klimpert, tells us the values of vintage ukes have maintained their upward trend as the instrument regains popularity and demand continues to exceed supply. With few manufacturers producing good-quality new models, even casual players must search for instruments of sufficient quality, which most often means "vintage." C.F. Martin and Kamaka ukuleles from all periods continue to set the standard. Uke fans can reach Randy at klimpert@earthlink.net.

Every section of the *The Guide* has hot items. Overall, most models listed increased in value from 2006 to '07. So it's up to you to search the pages and discover what's new and different. You'll find plenty, as nearly everything has changed. So enjoy the '07 *Guide*; sit back, flip through its pages, draw your own conclusions, and above all, enjoy the experience.

More Information

The official website of *Vintage Guitar* magazine, vintageguitar.com, is updated five times each week from the magazine's article archive. This ever-expanding resource includes interviews with noted guitarists, reviews of new gear and recordings, and historical information on many of the brands and models covered in this book. Of course, you can read more on classic guitars and your favorite players each month in *Vintage Guitar*.

If a model is missing from *The Guide*, or if you'd like something clarified, please drop a line to gil@vguitar.com. If you are a builder and would like to be included, want to correct your info, or have information on your favorite brand, drop a line to al@vguitar.com.

Acknowledgments

Compiling *The Official Vintage Guitar Price Guide* is a massive undertaking that requires the talents of many people. We use many sources to determine the values, but the vintage instrument dealers who give their time and expertise to provide market information play an important role. Many provide info on brands and models, and they are acknowledged on page XXIV.

Randy Klimpert provided the information and photos in the ukulele section. Many of the brand histories used in this edition are based on the work of longtime *VG* columnist Michael Wright.

Several people at *VG* played an important role, as well. Doug Yellow Bird designs the cover and inside pages. Jeanine Shea assists with proofreading and, with James Jiskra, compiles the ads and dealer directory. Ward Meeker selects all the photos. Wanda Huether and Jacob Strombeck entered much of the data. We thank all of them for their usual fine work.

We always welcome suggestions, criticisms, and ideas to improve future editions of *The Guide*. Contact us at Vintage Guitar, Inc., PO Box 7301, Bismarck, ND 58507, or by e-mail to gil@vguitar.com or al@vguitar.com.

Thank you,

Alan Greenwood and Gil Hembree

Guitars

Abel Axe

*1963 Airline Super III
Res-O-Glas*

A Fuller Sound

1998-present. Professional and premium grade, custom nylon and steel-string flat-tops built by Luthier Warren Fuller in Oakland, California.

Abel Axe

1994-present. Custom aircraft-grade aluminum body, wood neck, guitars built by twins Jim and Jeff Abel in Evanston, Wyoming. They offered the Abel Axe from '94-'96 and 2000-'01, and still do custom orders. They also made the Rogue Aluminator in the late '90s.

Axe

1994-1996. Offset double-cut aluminum body with dozens of holes in the body, wood neck, various colors by annodizing the aluminum body. Abel Axe logo on the headstock.

1994-1996	Non-trem model	$825	$925
1994-1996	Trem model	$850	$925

Abilene

Budget and intermediate grade, production, acoustic and electric guitars imported by Samick.

Acoustic Guitars

Recent import copies.

2000-2005	$70	$140

Electric Guitars

Solidbody and hollowbody electrics, designs often based on classic American models.

2000-2005	$60	$115

Abyss

1997-present. Luthier Kevin Pederson builds his premium grade, production/custom, hollowbody and solidbody guitars in Forest City, Iowa.

Acme

1960s. Imported copy electric guitar models for the student market.

Acoustic

Ca. 1965-ca. 1987, present. Mainly known for solidstate amps, the Acoustic Control Corp. of Los Angeles, California, did offer guitars and basses from around '69 to late '74. The brand was revived by Samick a few years ago on a line of amps.

Black Widow Guitar

1969-1970, 1972-1974. Both versions featured a unique black equal double-cut body with German carve, 2 pickups, a zero fret, and a protective spider design pad on back. The early version (called the AC500 Black Widow) had 22 frets, an ebonite 'board, and pickups with 1 row of adjustable polepieces. The later version was 24 frets, a rosewood 'board, and humbuckers with 2 rows of adjustable pole pieces (some '72s have the older style pickup). The jack and 4 control knobs were configured differently on the 2 versions, Acoustic outsourced the production of the guitars, possibly to Japan, but final 200 or so guitars

produced by Semie Moseley. The AC700 Black Widow 12-string was also available for '69-'70.

1969-1970	$850	$925
1972-1974	$825	$900

Agile

1985-present. Budget grade, production, acoustic and electric guitars imported by Rondo Music of Union, New Jersey. They also offer mandolins.

Solidbody Electrics

2000s	$125	$175

Aims

Ca. 1974-ca. 1976. Aims instruments, distributed by Randall Instruments in the mid-'70s, were copies of classic American guitar and bass models. Randall also offered a line of Aims amps during the same time.

Airline

Ca. 1958-1968, 2004-present. Airline originally was a brand used by Montgomery Ward on acoustic, electric archtop and solidbody guitars and basses, amplifiers, steels, and possibly banjos and mandolins. Instruments manufactured by Kay, Harmony and Valco. In '04, the brand was revived on a line of imported intermediate grade, production, reissues from Eastwood guitars (see that listing for new info).

Acoustic Archtops (lower end)

1950s	$175	$350
1960s	$175	$350

Acoustic Archtops (higher end)

1950s	$350	$500
1960s	$350	$500

Acoustic Res-O-Glas Resonator

Res-o-glas, coverplate with M-shaped holes, asymmetrical peghead.

1964	$700	$850

Amp-In-Case Model

1960s. Double-cut, single pickup, short scale guitar with amplifier built into the case, Airline on grille.

1960s	$325	$400

Electric Hollowbodies

1950s	Kay Barney Kessel		
	Artist copy	$600	$750
1960s	ES-175 copy	$450	$600
1960s	Harmony H-54		
	Rocket II copy	$250	$450
1960s	Harmony H-75 copy	$500	$650

Electric Res-O-Glas

Res-o-glas is a form of fiberglass. The bodies and sometimes the necks were made of this material.

1960s	Jack White's		
	Red Jetson style	$1,300	$2,000
1960s	Other style,		
	1 & 2 pu	$700	$900

Electric Res-O-Glas Resonator

Res-o-glas is a form of fiberglass. These models have resonator cones in the body.

1960s	$800	$950

MODEL YEAR	FEATURES	EXC. COND. LOW	HIGH
Electric Solidbodies (standard-lower end)			
1960s		$250	$600
Electric Solidbodies (deluxe-higher end)			
Appointments may include multiple pickups, block inlays, additional logos, more binding.			
1950s		$600	$900
1960s		$550	$650
Flat-Top (lower end, 13" body)			
1960s		$75	$150

Alamo

1947-1982. Founded by Charles Eilenberg, Milton Fink, and Southern Music, San Antonio, Texas, and distributed by Bruno & Sons. Alamo started out making radios, phonographs, and instrument cases. In '49 they added amplifiers and lap steels. From '60 to '70, the company produced beginner-grade solidbody and hollow-core body electric Spanish guitars. The amps were all-tube until the '70s. Except for a few Valco-made examples, all instruments were built in San Antonio.

MODEL YEAR	FEATURES	EXC. COND. LOW	HIGH
Electric Hollowbodies			
1960s		$225	$325
Electric Solidbodies			
1960s		$225	$325

Alamo Guitars

1999-present. The Alamo brand has been revived for a line of handcrafted, professional grade, production/custom, guitars by Alamo Music Products, which also offers Robin and Metropolitan brand guitars and Rio Grande pickups.

	FEATURES	EXC. COND. LOW	HIGH
Tonemonger			
1999-present. Ash or African Fakimba offset double cut solidbody, 3 single coils, tremolo.			
1999-2004		$575	$875

Alan Carruth

1970-present. Professional and premium grade, production/custom, classical and archtop guitars built by luthier Alan Carruth in Newport, New Hampshire. He also builds violins, harps and dulcimers. He started out building dulcimers and added guitars in '74.

Albanus

Late 1950s-1973. Luthier Carl Albanus Johnson built around 100 high quality archtop guitars in Chicago, Illinois. He died in '73. He also built violins.

Alberico, Fabrizio

1998-present. Luthier Fabrizio Alberico builds his premium grade, custom, flat-top and classical guitars in Cheltenham, Ontario.

Alembic

1969-present. Premium and presentation grade, production/custom, guitars, baritones, and 12-strings built in Santa Rosa, California. They also build basses. Established in San Francisco by Ron and Susan Wickersham, Alembic started out as a studio working with the Grateful Dead and other bands on a variety of sound gear. By '70 they were building custom basses, later adding guitars and cabinets. By '73, standardized models were being offered.

MODEL YEAR	FEATURES	EXC. COND. LOW	HIGH
California Special			
1988-present. Double-cut neck-thru solidbody, six-on-a-side tuners, various colors.			
1988-2000		$1,650	$1,900
Orion			
1990-present. Offset double-cut glued neck solidbody, various colors.			
1990-2000		$1,550	$1,700
Series I			
Early-1970s-present. Neck-thru, double-cut solidbody, bookmatched koa, black walnut core, 3 pickups, optional body styles available, natural.			
1970s		$2,750	$2,900

Alhambra

1930s. The Alhambra brand was most likely used by a music studio (or distributor) on instruments made by others, including Regal-built resonator instruments.

Allen Guitars

1982-present. Premium grade, production resonators, steel-string flat-tops, and mandolins built by Luthier Randy Allen, Colfax, California.

Alleva-Coppolo

1995-present. Professional and premium grade, custom/production, solidbody electric guitars built by luthier Jimmy Coppolo in Dallas, Texas, for '95-'97, and since in New York City. He also builds basses.

Aloha

1935-1960s. Private branded by Aloha Publishing and Musical Instruments Company, Chicago, Illinois. Made by others. There was also the Aloha Manufacturing Company of Honolulu which made musical instruments from around 1911 to the late '20s.

Alosa

1947-1958. Luthier Alois Sandner built these acoustic archtop guitars in Germany.

Alpha

1970s. One of the brand names of guitars built in the Egmond plant in Holland.

Alray

1967. Electrics and acoustics built by the Holman-Woodell guitar factory in Neodesha, Kansas, who also marketed similar models under the Holman brand.

1964 Alamo Fiesta I

Allen square-neck resophonic

Alvarez DY-91

1969 Ampeg
Dan Armstrong lucite

Alvarez

1965-present. Intermediate and professional grade, production, acoustic guitars imported by St. Louis Music. They also offer banjos and mandolins. Initially high-quality handmade guitars Yairi made by K. (Kazuo) Yairi were exclusively distributed, followed by lower-priced Alvarez line.

In '90 the Westone brand used on electric guitars and basses was replaced with the Alvarez name; these Alvarez electrics were offered until '02. Many Alvarez electric models designed by luthier Dana Sutcliffe; several models designed by Dan Armstrong.

Classic I, II, III
1994-1999. Designs based on classic solidbody American models.

MODEL YEAR	FEATURES	EXC. COND. LOW	HIGH
1994-1999		$100	$200

Flat-Top (lower end)
1966-present. Beginner-grade instruments, solid or laminate tops, laminate back and sides, little or no extra appointments. Some are acoustic/electric.

1970s		$75	$100
1980s		$80	$110
1990s		$85	$125

Flat-Top (mid-level)
1966-present. Solid tops, laminated back and sides, lower appointments such as bound 'boards and headstocks, nickel hardware and pearl inlay.

1970s		$125	$225
1980s		$125	$225
1990s		$125	$225

Flat-Top (mid-to-high-end)
1966-present. Solid spruce tops, solid mahogany or rosewood backs, laminated mahogany or rosewood sides, may have scalloped bracing, mid-level appointments like abalone headstock inlay, soundhole rosettes and herringbone body binding.

1970s		$225	$450
1980s		$225	$450
1990s		$225	$450

Flat-Top (high end)
1966-present. Solid rosewood and/or mahogany backs and sides, solid spruce tops, may have dovetail neck joint, highest appointments like abalone inlay and real maple binding.

1980s		$450	$600
1990s		$450	$600

Fusion Series (with piezo and EQ)
1981-present. Single-cut, acoustic/electrics with EQ and transducer/piezo pickups. Earlier models had spruce tops with spruce or mahogany back and sides. More recent models have maple tops, backs and sides.

1981-2000		$300	$375

Alvarez Yairi

1966-present. Alvarez Yairi guitars are handcrafted and imported by St. Louis Music.

Flat-Top (mid-level)
Solid top of cedar or spruce, depending on model, mid-level appointments.

MODEL YEAR	FEATURES	EXC. COND. LOW	HIGH
1970s		$300	$425
1980s		$325	$450
1990s		$350	$500
2000s		$375	$550

Flat-Top (higher-end)
Solid top of cedar or spruce, depending on model, higher-end appointments.

1970s		$500	$800
1980s		$550	$825
1990s		$650	$900
2000s		$700	$1,000

Flat-Top 9-String (DY-58)
Flat-top acoustic with 9 strings (doubles on the 3 high strings).

1989	Natural	$650	$900

Fusion Series (with piezo and EQ)
1998-2002. Piezo bridge with volume and tone controls, higher-end appointments.

1998-2002		$650	$900

Alvarez, Juan

1952-present. Professional and premium grade, production/custom, classical and flamenco guitars made in Madrid, Spain, origianlly by luthier Juan Alvarez Gil and now by son Juan Miguel Alvarez.

American Acoustech

1993-2001. Production steel string flat-tops made by Tom Lockwood (former Guild plant manager) and Dave Stutzman (of Stutzman's Guitar Center) as ESVL Inc. in Rochester, New York.

American Archtop Guitars

1995-present. Premium and presentation grade, custom 6- and 7-string archtops by luthier Dale Unger, in Stroudsburg, Pennsylvania.

American Conservatory (Lyon & Healy)

Late-1800s-early-1900s. Guitars and mandolins built by Chicago's Lyon & Healy and sold mainly through various catalog retailers. Mid-level instruments above the quality of Lyon & Healy's Lakeside brand, and generally under their Washburn brand.

Harp Guitar Style G2210
Early-1900s. Two 6-string necks with standard tuners, 1 neck fretless, rosewood back and sides, spruce top, fancy rope colored wood inlay around soundhole, sides and down the back center seam.

1917	Natural	$3,400	$3,800

Tenor Guitar
1920s. Four-string tenor, pear-shaped body.

1920s		$600	$700

MODEL YEAR	FEATURES	EXC. COND. LOW	HIGH

American Showster

1986-2004. Established by Bill Meeker and David Haines, Bayville, New Jersey, building guitars shaped like classic car tailfins or motorcycle gastanks. The Custom Series was made in the U.S.A., while the Standard Series (introduced in '97) was made in Czechoslovakia. They also made a bass.

AS-57 Classic (original '57)

1987-2004. Body styled like a '57 Chevy tail fin, basswood body, bolt-on neck, 1 humbucker or 3 single-coil pickups, various colors.

1987-2004		$2,000	$3,000

Ampeg

1949-present. Founded in '49 by Everett Hull as the Ampeg Bassamp Company in New York and has built amplifiers throughout its history. In '62 the company added instruments with the introduction of their Baby Bass and from '63 to '65, they carried a line of guitars and basses built by Burns of London and imported from England. In '66 the company introduced its own line of basses. In '67, Ampeg was acquired by Unimusic, Inc. From '69-'71 contracted with Dan Armstrong to produce lucite "see-through" guitars and basses with replaceable slide-in pickup design. In '71 the company merged with Magnavox. Beginning around '72 until '75, Ampeg imported the Stud Series copy guitars from Japan. Ampeg shut down production in the spring of '80. MTI bought the company and started importing amps. In '86 St. Louis Music purchased the company. In '97 Ampeg introduced new and reissue American-made guitar and bass models. They discontinued the guitar line in '01, but offered the Dan Armstrong guitar again starting in '05.

AMG1

1999-2001. Dan Amstrong guitar features, but with mahogany body with quilted maple top, 2 P-90-style or humbucker-style pickups.

1999-2001	Humbuckers, gold hardware	$950	$1,050
1999-2001	Kent Armstrong pickups	$450	$550
1999-2001	P-90s, standard hardware	$450	$550

Dan Armstrong Lucite Guitar

1969-1971. Clear plexiglas solidbody, with interchangable pickups, Dan Armstrong reports that around 9,000 guitars were produced, introduced in '69, but primary production was in '70-'71, reissued in '98.

1969-1971		$2,900	$3,600
1969-1971	Black smoke	$3,200	$3,900

Dan Armstrong Lucite Guitar Reissue

1998-2001, 2005-present. Produced by pickup designer Kent Armstrong (son of Dan Armstrong), offered in smoked (ADAG2) or clear (ADAG1). Latest version is Japanese-made.

1998-2001		$900	$1,300

Sonic Six (By Burns)

1964-1965. Solidbody, 2 pickups, tremolo, cherry finish, same as the Burns Nu-Sonic guitar.

1964-1965		$450	$550

Stud (GE-100/GET-100)

1973-1975. Import from Japan, double-cut, inexpensive materials, weight added for sustain, GET-100 included tremolo.

1973-1975		$300	$450

Heavy Stud (GE-150/GEH-150)

1973-1975. Import from Japan, single-cut body, weight added for sustain, single-coils or humbuckers (GEH).

1973-1975		$350	$450

Super Stud (GE-500)

1973-1975. Double-cut, weight added for sustain, top-of-the-line in Stud Series.

1973-1975		$375	$500

Thinline (By Burns)

1963-1964. Semi-hollowbody, 2 F-holes, 2 pickups, double-cut, tremolo, import by Burns of London, same as the Burns TR2 guitar.

1963-1964		$625	$700

Wild Dog (By Burns)

1963-1964. Solidbody, 3 pickups, shorter scale, tremolo, sunburst finish, import by Burns of London, same as the Burns Split Sound.

1963-1964		$625	$700

Wild Dog De Luxe (By Burns)

1963-1964. Solidbody, 3 pickups, bound neck, tremolo, sunburst finish, import by Burns of London, same as the Burns Split Sonic guitar.

1963-1964		$650	$750

Andersen Stringed Instruments

1978-present. Luthier Steve Andersen builds premium and presentation grade, production/custom flat-tops and archtops in Seattle, Washington. He also builds mandolins.

Andreas

1995-present. Luthier Andreas Pichler builds his aluminum-necked, solidbody guitars and basses in Dollach, Austria.

Angelica

Ca. 1967-1972. Entry-level guitars and basses imported from Japan.

Electric Solidbodies

1967-1972		$150	$200

Angus

1976-present. Professional and premium grade, custom-made steel and nylon string flat-tops built by Mark Angus in Laguna Beach, California.

Antares

1980s-1990s. Korean-made budget electric and acoustic guitars imported by Vega Music International of Brea, California.

1963 Ampeg Wild Dog Deluxe

Ampeg Dan Armstrong Plexi reissue

GUITARS

*Antique Acoustics
Blazer SJ*

Applause AE148

MODEL YEAR	FEATURES	EXC. COND. LOW	HIGH
Double Neck 6/4			
1990s. Cherry finish double-cut.			
1990s		$425	$500
Solidbodies			
1980s. Various models.			
1980s		$125	$200
1990s		$135	$210

Antique Acoustics

1970s-present. Luthier Rudolph Blazer builds production/custom flat-tops, 12 strings, and archtops in Tubingen, Germany.

Antonio Lorca

Intermediate and professional grade, production, classical guitars made in Valencia, Spain.

Apollo

Ca. 1967-1972. Entry-level guitars imported by St. Louis Music. They also offered basses and effects.

MODEL YEAR	FEATURES	EXC. COND. LOW	HIGH
Electric			
1967-1972. Japanese imports.			
1967-1972	Advanced model, 4 pickups	$175	$275
1967-1972	Standard model, less features	$125	$175

Applause

1976-present. Budget and intermediate grade, production, acoustic and acoustic/electric guitars. They also offer basses, mandolins and ukes. Kaman Music's entry-level Ovation-styled brand. The instruments were made in the U.S. until around '82, when production was moved to Korea.

On the U.S.-made guitars, the back of the neck was molded Urelite, with a cast aluminum neck combining an I-beam neck reinforcement, fingerboard, and frets in one unit. The Korean models have traditional wood necks.

MODEL YEAR	FEATURES	EXC. COND. LOW	HIGH
AA Models (acoustic)			
Laminate top, plastic or composition body. Specs and features can vary on AA Models.			
1976-1981	U.S.-made	$100	$150
1980s	Import	$80	$125
1990s	Import	$80	$135
AE Models (acoustic/electric)			
Laminate top, plastic or composition body. Specs and features can vary on AE Models.			
1976-1981	U.S.-made	$175	$225
1980s	Import	$150	$200
1990s	Import	$150	$225

Applegate

2001-present. Premium grade, production/custom, acoustic and classical guitars built by luthier Brian Applegate in Minneapolis, Minnesota.

Arbor

1983-present. Budget and intermediate grade, production, classical, acoustic, and solid and semi-

hollow body electric guitars imported by Musicorp (MBT). They also offer basses.

MODEL YEAR	FEATURES	EXC. COND. LOW	HIGH
Acoustic			
1980s		$75	$150
1990s		$75	$125
Electric			
1980s		$150	$225
1990s		$125	$175

Arch Kraft

1933-1934. Full-size acoustic archtop and flat-top guitars. Budget brand produced by the Kay Musical Instrument Company and sold through various distributors.

MODEL YEAR	FEATURES	EXC. COND. LOW	HIGH
Acoustic (Archtop or Flat-top)			
1933-1934		$275	$325

Aria Diamond

1960s. Brand name used by Aria in the '60s.

MODEL YEAR	FEATURES	EXC. COND. LOW	HIGH
Electric			
1960s. Various models and appointments in the '60s.			
1960s		$350	$550

Aria/Aria Pro II

1960-present. Budget and intermediate grade, production, electric, acoustic, acoustic/electric, and classical guitars. They also make basses, mandolins, and banjos. Aria was established in Japan in '53 and started production of instruments in '60 using the Arai, Aria, Aria Diamond, and Diamond brands. The brand was renamed Aria Pro II in '75. Aria Pro II was used mainly on electric guitars, with Aria used on others. Over the years, they have produced acoustics, banjos, mandolins, electrics, basses, amplifiers, and effects. Around '87 production of cheaper models moved to Korea, reserving Japanese manufacturing for more expensive models. Around '95 some models were made in U.S., though most contemporary guitars sold in U.S. are Korean. In '01, the Pro II part of the name was dropped altogether.

Early Arias don't have serial numbers or pot codes. Serial numbers began to be used in the mid '70s. At least for Aria guitars made by Matsumoku, the serial number contains the year of manufacture in the first one or two digits (Y##### or YY####). Thus, a guitar from 1979 might begin with 79####. One from 1981 might begin with 1#####. The scheme becomes less sure after 1987. Some Korean- made guitars use a serial number with year and week indicated in the first four digits (YYWW####). Thus 9628#### would be from the 28th week of 1996. However, this is not the case on all guitars, and some have serial numbers which are not date-coded.

Models have been consolidated by sector unless specifically noted.

MODEL YEAR	FEATURES	EXC. COND. LOW	HIGH

Acoustic Solid Wood Top
1960s-present. Steel string models, various appointments, generally mid-level imports.

| 1970-2005 | | $225 | $275 |

Acoustic Veneer Wood Top
1960s-present. Steel string models, various appointments, generally entry-level imports.

| 1970-2005 | | $125 | $200 |

Classical Solid Wood Top
1960s-present. Various models, various appointments, generally mid-level imports.

| 1970-2005 | | $200 | $250 |

Classical Veneer Wood Top
1960s-present. Various models, various appointments, generally entry-level imports.

| 1970-2005 | | $100 | $175 |

Fullerton Series
1995-2000. Various models with different appointments and configurations based on the classic offset double-cut soldibody.

| 1995-2000 | | $200 | $300 |

Herb Ellis (PE-175/FA-DLX)
1978-1987 (Model PE-175) and 1988-1993 (Model FA-DLX). Archtop hollowbody, ebony 'board, 2 humbuckers.

| 1977-1987 | | $400 | $600 |

Solidbody
1960s-present. Various models, various appointments, generally mid-level imports.

| 1980-1990 | | $250 | $350 |

Titan Artist TA Series
1967-present. Double cut, semi-hollow bodies, 2 pickups, various models.

| 1980-1990 | | $250 | $350 |

Armstrong, Rob

1971-present. Custom steel- and nylon-string flat-tops, 12 strings, and parlor guitars made in Coventry, England by luthier Rob Armstrong. He also builds mandolins and basses.

Arpeggio Korina

1995-present. Professional, premium and presentation grade, production/custom, korina wood solidbody guitars built by luthier Ron Kayfield in Pennsylvania.

58 Korina Reproduction V

| 1995 | | $825 | $900 |

Art & Lutherie

Budget and intermediate grade, production, steel- and nylon-string acoustic and acoustic/electric guitars. Founded by luthier Robert Godin, who also has the Norman, Godin, Seagull, and Patrick & Simon brands of instruments.

Flat-Top Models
Various models.

| 2000s | | $145 | $165 |

Artesano

Professional grade, production, classical guitars built in Valencia, Spain, and distributed by Juan Orozco. Orozco also made higher-end classical Orozco Models 8, 10 and 15.

Models 20 to 50
1980s. Classical solid tops.

| 1980s | | $225 | $300 |

Artinger Custom Guitars

1997-present. Luthier Matt Artinger builds his professional and premium grade, production/custom, hollow, semi-hollow, and chambered solidbody guitars in Emmaus, Pennsylvania. He also builds basses.

Asama

1970s-1980s. Some models of this Japanese line of solidbody guitars featured built-in effects. They also offered basses, effects, drum machines and other music products.

Ashborn

1848-1864. James Ashborn, of Wolcottville, Connecticut, operated one of the largest guitar making factories of the mid-1800s. Models were small parlor-sized instruments with ladder bracing and gut strings. Most of these guitars will need repair. Often of more interest as historical artifacts or museum pieces versus guitar collections.

Model 2
1848-1864. Flat-top, plain appointments, no position markers on the neck, identified by Model number.

| 1855 | Fully repaired | $450 | $650 |

Model 5
1848-1864. Flat-top, higher appointments.

| 1855 | Fully repaired | $1,350 | $1,500 |

Asher

1982-present. Luthier Bill Asher builds his professional grade, production/custom, solidbody electric guitars in Venice, California. He also builds lap steels.

Astro

1963-1964. The Astro AS-51 was a 1 pickup kit guitar sold by Rickenbacker. German luthier Arthur Strohmer also built archtops bearing this name.

Asturias

Professional and premium grade, production, classical guitars built on Kyushu island, in Japan.

Atkin Guitars

1993-present. Luthier Alister Atkin builds his production/custom steel and nylon string flat-tops in Canterbury, England. He also builds mandolins.

Atlas

Archtop guitars, and possibly other types, built in East Germany.

Aria Pro II Urchin Deluxe

Art & Lutherie Cedar

To get the most from this book, be sure to read "Using *The Guide*" in the introduction.

Babicz D'Esque

Baker RF

MODEL YEAR	FEATURES	EXC. COND. LOW	HIGH

Audiovox

Ca. 1935-ca. 1950. Paul Tutmarc's Audiovox Manufacturing, of Seattle, Washington, was a pioneer in electric lap steels, basses, guitars and amps.

Austin

1999-present. Budget and intermediate grade, production, acoustic, acoustic/electric, resonator, and electric guitars imported by St. Louis Music. They also offer basses, mandolins and banjos.

Acoustic Flat-Top
Various models.
1999-2005 $100 $130

Solidbody Electric
Various models.
1999-2005 $100 $150

Austin Hatchet

Mid-1970s-mid-1980s. Trademark of distributor Targ and Dinner, Chicago, Illinois.

Hatchet
1981. Travel guitar.
1981 $150 $180

Solidbody Electric
1970s-1980s. Various classic designs.
1980s $100 $160

Avalon

1920s. Instruments built by the Oscar Schmidt Co. and possibly others. Most likely a brand made for a distributor.

Avante

1997-present. Intermediate grade, production, imported shape cutaway acoustic baritone guitars designed by Joe Veillette and Michael Tobias and offered by MusicYo. Originally higher priced instruments offered by Alvarez, there was the baritone, a 6-string and a bass.

AV-2 Baritone
1997-present. Baritone guitar tuned B to B, solid spruce cutaway top, mahogany sides and back.
1997-2005 $275 $350

Avanti

1964-late 1960s. Italian-made guitar brand imported by European Crafts, of Los Angeles. Earlier models were plastic covered; later ones had paint finishes.

Electric Solidbody
1960s. Solidbody, 3 single-coils, dot markers.
1960s $150 $200

Aztec

1970s. Japanese-made copy guitars imported into Germany by Hopf.

Babicz

2004-present. Started by luthier Jeff Babicz and Jeff Carano, who worked together at Steinberger,

the company offers intermediate, professional, and premium grade, production/custom, acoustic and acoustic/electric guitars made in Poughkeepsie, New York, and overseas.

Bacon & Day

Established in 1921 by David Day and Paul Bacon, primarily known for fine quality tenor and plectrum banjos in the '20s and '30s. Purchased by Gretsch ca. '40.

Belmont
1950s. Gretsch era, 2 DeArmond pickups, natural.
1950s $1,275 $1,375

Dreadnought Flat-Top
1940s. Large B&D headstock logo, higher-end appointments.
1940s $1,600 $1,800

Ramona Archtop
1938-1940. Sunburst.
1938-1940 $650 $1,000

Senorita Guitar
1940. Sunburst, mahogany back and sides.
1940 $750 $1,200

Style B Guitar Banjo (Bacon)
1920s. 6-string guitar neck on a banjo-resonator body.
1920s $2,500 $2,800

Sultana I
1930s. Large 18 1/4" acoustic archtop, Sultana engraved on tailpiece, block markers, bound top and back, sunburst.
1938 $3,000 $4,000

Baker U.S.A.

1997-present. Professional and premium grade, production/custom, solidbody electric guitars. Established by master builder Gene Baker after working at the Custom Shops of Gibson and Fender, Baker produced solid- and hollowbody guitars in Santa Maria, California. They also built basses. Baker also produced the Mean Gene brand of guitars from '88-'90. In September '03, the company was liquidated and the Baker U.S.A. name was sold to Ed Roman. Gene Baker is no longer involved with Baker U.S.A.

B1/B1 Chambered/B1 Hollow
1997-present. Double-cut mahogany body, maple top, with a wide variety of options including chambered and hollowbody construction, set-neck.
1997-2003 $2,200 $2,700

BJ/BJ Hollow
1997-2003. Double-cut mahogany body, P-90-type pickups, several options available, set-neck.
1997-2003 $1,800 $2,200

BNT
1997-2000. Mahogany solidbody, maple top, neck-thru body, with various finishes and options.
1997-2000 $2,000 $2,500

MODEL YEAR	FEATURES	EXC. COND. LOW	HIGH

Baldwin

1965-1970. Founded in 1862, in Cincinnati, when reed organ and violin teacher Dwight Hamilton Baldwin opened a music store that eventually became one of the largest piano retailers in the Midwest. By 1965, the Baldwin Piano and Organ company was ready to buy into the guitar market but was outbid by CBS for Fender. Baldwin did procure Burns of London in September '65, and sold the guitars in the U.S. under the Baldwin name. Baldwin purchased Gretsch in '67. English production of Baldwin guitars ends in '70, after which Baldwin concentrates on the Gretsch brand.

Baby Bison (Model 560 by mid-1966)
1966-1970. Double-cut solidbody, V headstock, 2 pickups, shorter scale, tremolo, black, red or white finishes.

1965-1966		$700	$800
1966-1970	Model 560	$600	$700

Bison (Model 511 by mid-1966)
1965-1970. Double-cut solidbody, scroll headstock, 3 pickups, tremolo, black or white finishes.

1965-1966		$1,000	$1,200
1966-1970	Model 511	$900	$1,100

Double Six (Model 525 by mid-1966)
1965-1970. Offset double-cut solidbody, 12 strings, 3 pickups, green or red sunburst.

1965-1966		$1,300	$1,400
1966-1970	Model 525	$1,200	$1,300

G.B. 65
1965-1966. Baldwin's first acoustic/electric, single-cut D-style flat-top, dual bar pickups.

1965-1966		$700	$800

G.B. 66 De Luxe
1965-1967. Same as Standard with added density control on treble horn, golden sunburst.

1965-1967		$800	$900

G.B. 66 Standard
1965-1966. Thinline Electric archtop, dual Ultra-Sonic pickups, offset cutaways, red sunburst.

1965-1966		$750	$850

Jazz Split Sound/Split Sound (Model 503 mid-1966)
1965-1970. Offset double-cut solidbody, scroll headstock, 3 pickups, tremolo, red sunburst or solid colors.

1965-1966		$700	$800
1966-1970	Model 503	$650	$750

Marvin (Model 524 by mid-1966)
1965-1970. Offset double-cut solidbody, scroll headstock, 3 pickups, tremolo, white or brown finish.

1965-1966		$1,300	$1,400
1966-1970	Model 524	$1,100	$1,200

Model 706
1967-1970. Double-cut semi-hollowbody, scroll headstock, 2 pickups, 2 f-holes, no vibrato, red or golden sunburst.

1967-1970		$700	$800

Model 706 V
1967-1970. Model 706 with vibrato.

1967-1970		$750	$850

Model 712 R Electric XII
1967-1970. Double-sut semi-hollow body with regular neck, red or gold sunburst.

1967-1970		$600	$700

Model 712 T Electric XII
1967-1970. Model 712 with thin neck, red or gold sunburst.

1967-1970		$550	$750

Model 801 CP Electric Classical
1968-1970. Grand concert-sized classical with transducer based pickup system, natural pumpkin finish.

1968-1970		$700	$800

Nu-Sonic
1965-1966. Solidbody electric student model, 6-on-a-side tuners, black or cherry finish.

1965-1966		$450	$550

Vibraslim (Model 548 by late-1966)
1965-1970. Double-cut semi-hollowbody, 2 pickups, tremolo, 2 f-holes, red or golden sunburst. Notable spec changes with Model 548 in '66.

1965-1966		$800	$1,000
1966-1970	Model 548	$700	$900

Virginian (Model 550 by mid-1966)
1965-1970. Single-cut flat-top, 2 pickups (1 on each side of soundhole), scroll headstock, tremolo, natural.

1965-1966		$800	$1,000
1966-1970	Model 550	$750	$950

Ballurio

2000-present. Luthier Keith Ballurio builds his intermediate, professional, and premium grade, production/custom, solidbody and chambered guitars in Manassas, Virginia.

Baranik Guitars

1995-present. Premium grade, production/custom steel-string flat-tops made in Tempe, Arizona by luthier Mike Baranik.

Barclay

1960s. Thinline acoustic/electric archtops, solidbody electric guitars and basses imported from Japan. Generally shorter scale beginner guitars.

Electric Solidbody Guitars
1960s. Various models and colors.

1960s		$150	$225

Barcus-Berry

1964-present. Founded by John Berry and Les Barcus introducing the first piezo crystal transducer. Martin guitar/Barcus-Berry products were offered in the mid-'80s. They also offered a line of amps from around '76 to ca. '80.

2500 Model Series
Mid-1980s. Various acoustic and acoustic/electric models.

1980s		$225	$350

1967 Baldwin Baby Bison

Ballurio Stag

Bashkin Ballazza

1900 Bay State parlour guitar

MODEL YEAR	FEATURES	EXC. COND. LOW	HIGH

Barrington

1988-1991. Imports offered by Barrington Guitar Werks, of Barrington, Illinois. Models included solidbody guitars and basses, archtop electrics, and acoustic flat-tops. Barrington Music Products is still in the music biz, offering LA saxophones and other products.

BGW-800 (acoustic/electric)
1988-1991. Acoustic/electric, flat-top single-cut with typical round soundhole, opaque white.

1988-1991		$400	$450

BRG-883 T (solidbody)
1988-ca 1991. Barrington's line of pointy headstock, double-cut solidbodies, black.

1988-1991		$100	$150

Bartell of California

1964-1969. Founded by Paul Barth (Magnatone) and Ted Peckles. Mosrite-inspired designs.

Electric 12
1967. Mosrite-style body.

1967		$1,100	$1,300

Bartolini

1960s. European-made (likely Italian) guitars made for the Bartolini Accordion Company. Similar to Gemelli guitars, so most likely from same manufacturer. Originally plastic covered, they switched to paint finishes by the mid '60s.

Solidbody

1960s		$400	$475

Bashkin Guitars

1998-present. Luthier Michael Bashkin builds his premium grade, custom, steel-string acoustics in Fort Collins, Colorado.

Bauer, George

1894-1911. Luthier George Bauer built guitars and mandolins in Philadelphia, Pennsylvania. He also built instruments with Samuel S. Stewart (S.S. Stewart).

Baxendale & Baxendale

1975-present. Luthiers Scott Baxendale (father) and John Baxendale (son) build their professional and premium grade, custom, steel-string acoustic and solidbody electric guitars in Denver, Colorado. They were previously located in Tennessee and Texas.

Bay State

1865-ca.1910. Bay State was a trademark for Boston's John C. Haynes Co.

Parlor Guitar
1900s. Small parlor size, mahogany body with salt & pepper binding.

1900s		$900	$1,100

BC Rich

Ca. 1966/67-present. Budget, intermediate, and premium grade, production/custom, import and U.S.-made, electric and acoustic guitars. They also offer basses. Founded by Bernardo Chavez Rico in Los Angeles, California. As a boy he worked for his guitar-maker father Bernardo Mason Rico (Valencian Guitar Shop, Casa Rico, Bernardo's Guitar Shop), building first koa ukes and later, guitars, steel guitars and Martin 12-string conversions. He started using the BC Rich name ca. '66-'67 and made about 300 acoustics until '68, when first solidbody electric made using a Fender neck.

Rich's early models were based on Gibson and Fender designs. First production instruments were in '69 with 10 fancy Gibson EB-3 bass and 10 matching Les Paul copies, all carved out of single block of mahogany. Early guitars with Gibson humbuckers, then Guild humbuckers, and, from '74-'86, DiMarzio humbuckers. Around 150 BC Rich Eagles were imported from Japan in '76. Ca. '76 or '77 some bolt-neck guitars with parts made by Wayne Charvel were offered. Acoustic production ended in '82 (acoustics were again offered in '95).

For '83-'86 the BC Rich N.J. Series (N.J. Nagoya, Japan) was built by Masan Tarada. U.S. Production Series (U.S.-assembled Korean kits) in '84. From '86 on, the N.J. Series was made by Cort in Korea. Korean Rave and Platinum series begin around '86. In '87, Rich agrees to let Class Axe of ....New Jersey market the Korean Rave, Platinum and N.J. Series. Class Axe (with Neal Moser) introduces Virgin in '87 and in '88 Rave and Platinum names are licensed to Class Axe. In '89, Rico licensed the BC Rich name to Class Axe. Both imported and American-made BC Riches are offered during Class Axe management. In 2000, BC Rich became a division of Hanser Holdings.

During '90-'91, Rico begins making his upscale Mason Bernard guitars (approx. 225 made). In '94, Rico resumes making BC Rich guitars in California. He died in 1999.

First 340-360 U.S.-built guitars were numbered sequentially beginning in '72. Beginning in '74, serial numbers change to YYZZZ pattern (year plus consecutive production). As production increased in the late-'70s, the year number began getting ahead of itself. By '80 it was 2 years ahead; by '81 as much as 4 years ahead. No serial number codes on imports.

Assassin
1986-1998. Double-cut body, 2 humbuckers, maple thru-neck dot markers, various colors.

1986-1989	1st Rico era	$750	$850
1989-1993	Class Axe era, neck-thru	$700	$800
1994-1998	2nd Rico era USA, neck-thru	$700	$800

MODEL YEAR	FEATURES	EXC. COND. LOW	HIGH

B-28 Acoustic
Ca.1967-1982. Acoustic flat-top, hand-built, solid spruce top, rosewood back and sides, herringbone trim, pearl R headstock logo.

1970-1982		$400	$900

B-30 Acoustic
Ca.1967-1982. Acoustic flat-top.

1960s		$400	$900

B-38 Acoustic
Ca.1967-1982. Acoustic flat-top, cocobolo back and sides, herringbone trim.

1960s		$400	$900

B-41 Acoustic
1970s. Brazilian rosewood.

1970s		$1,400	$2,000

B-45 Acoustic
Hand-built, D-style rosewood body.

1970s		$1,900	$2,500

Beast (U.S.A. Custom Shop)
1999-present. Exaggerated four point cutaway body, flamed or quilted top.

1999-2003		$1,300	$1,500

Bich (U.S.A. assembly)
1978-1998. Four-point sleek body, came in Standard top or Supreme with highly figured maple body and active EQ.

1978-1979	Supreme	$1,600	$1,900
1980-1989	Standard	$1,100	$1,200
1980-1989	Supreme	$1,400	$1,600
1989-1993	Class Axe era	$800	$900
1994-1998	2nd Rico era USA bolt-on	$800	$900
1994-1998	2nd Rico era USA neck-thru	$1,000	$1,200

Bich 10-String
1978-present. Doubles on 4 low strings.

1978-1982		$2,300	$3,000

Black Hole
1988. Bolt neck, rosewood 'board, integrated pickup design, Floyd Rose.

1988		$200	$300

Body Art Collection
2003-present. Imports with different exotic graphics on different models issued each month from January '03 to March '04, 25th Anniversary model still available.

2003	Boris Beast	$125	$175
2003	Space Face Ironbird	$125	$175
2003	Torchy ASM	$125	$175
2004	40 Lashes Mockingbird	$175	$225
2004	Umethar Jr. V	$150	$175

Bronze Series
2001-present. Made in China. Includes 2 models; Mockingbird and Warlock.

2001-2005		$75	$175

Doubleneck Models
1980s. Doublenecks were sporadically made and specs (and values) may vary.

1980s	Bich	$2,500	$3,500
1980s	Eagle	$3,500	$4,000
1980s	Iron Bird custom order	$2,000	$2,500
1980s	Mockingbird	$3,500	$4,000
1980s	Seagull custom order	$3,500	$5,000

Eagle (USA)
1977-1996, 2000-2004. Curved double-cut solidbody, neck-thru. Models included are the Standard, Deluxe, Special and Supreme which is a highly figured, higher end model.

1977-1979	Standard	$2,000	$3,000
1977-1979	Supreme	$2,500	$3,500
1977-1982	Special	$1,300	$2,500
1980-1982	Standard, 3-on-a-side tuners	$1,400	$1,700
1980-1982	Supreme	$2,100	$2,700
2000-2004	Supreme	$2,000	$2,600

Elvira
2001. Elvira (the witch) photo on black Warlock body, came with Casecore coffin case.

2001		$400	$500

Exclusive EM1
1996-2004. Offset double-cut, bound top, 2 humbuckers.

1996-2004		$200	$250

Gunslinger
1987-1999. Inverted headstock, 1 (Gunslinger I) or 2 (Gunslinger II) humbuckers, recessed cutout behind Floyd Rose allows player to pull notes up 2 full steps.

1987-1989	Standard finish	$700	$800
1987-1989	Various graphic designs	$750	$850
1989-1993	Class Axe era	$600	$700
1994-1999	2nd Rico era, bolt-on	$600	$700
1994-1999	2nd Rico era, neck-thru	$600	$700

Ironbird
1983-2004. Pointy body and headstock.

1983-1984		$850	$950

Kerry King Wartribe1 Warlock
2004-present. Tribal Fire finish, 2 pickups.

2004-2005		$200	$225

Mockingbird
1976-present. Includes Standard and Supreme (fancier features) models, bolt or neck-thru.

1976	Earlier short horn	$2,500	$3,500
1976-1978	Supreme, short horn	$2,300	$3,300
1977-1978	Earlier short horn	$2,000	$3,000
1979-1983	Later long horn	$2,100	$2,400
1979-1983	Supreme	$2,400	$2,700
1984-1989	Last of 1st Rico era	$1,600	$2,400
1994-1999	2nd Rico era, bolt-on	$1,300	$1,700
1994-1999	2nd Rico-era, Supreme	$1,600	$2,000

Mockingbird Ice Acrylic
2004-present. See-thru acrylic body.

2004-2005		$200	$275

B.C. Rich Eagle Supreme

1979 B.C. Rich Mockingbird Deluxe

To get the most from this book, be sure to read "Using *The Guide*" in the introduction.

BC Rich Platinum Bich

Benedetto Bravo

Nighthawk
1978-ca.1982. Eagle-shaped body with bolt neck.

		LOW	HIGH
1978-1982		$700	$800

NJ Series
1983-present. Earlier models made in Japan. Made in Korea '86 forward. All NJ models fall within the same price range. Models include; Assassin, Beast, Bich, Ironbird, Mockingbird, Outlaw, ST III, Virgin, Warlock.

1983-1986		$350	$500
1987-1999		$275	$475
2000-2005		$275	$450

Phoenix
1977-ca.1982. Mockingbird-shaped with bolt neck.

1977-1982		$700	$800

Platinum Series
1986-present. Imported versions including Assassin, Beast, Bich, Ironbird, ST, Warlock.

1986-1999		$250	$375

Rave Series
1986-ca. 1990. Korean-made down-market versions of popular models.

1986-1990		$175	$200

Seagull/Seagull II/Seagull Jr.
1972-1977. Solidbody, neck-thru, 2 humbuckers, Seagull ('72-'75) is single-cut, II and Jr. ('75-'77) double-cut.

1972-1975	Initial design	$1,800	$2,800
1972-1975	Supreme	$2,300	$3,200
1975-1977	II & Jr.	$1,800	$2,800

Stealth I Series
1983-1989. Includes Standard (maple body, diamond inlays) and Series II (mahogany body, dot inlays), 2 pickups.

1983-1989	Series II	$1,200	$2,200
1983-1989	Standard	$1,200	$2,200

ST-III (U.S.A.-made)
1987-1998. Double-cut solidbody, hum/single/single or 2 humbucker pickups, Kahler tremolo.

1987-1989	Bolt-on	$600	$750
1987-1989	Neck-thru	$700	$850
1989-1993	Class Axe era	$600	$750
1994-1998	New Rico era, neck-thru & bolt-on	$600	$750

The Mag
2000. U.S. Handcrafted Series Mockingbird Acoustic Supreme, solid spruce top, quilt maple back and sides, pickup with preamp and EQ optional, dark sunburst.

2000		$850	$950

Warlock (USA)
1981-present. Four-point sleek body style with widow headstock.

1981-1989	Standard	$1,200	$1,450
1981-1989	Supreme	$1,500	$1,950
1994-1999	2nd Rico era, bolt-on	$950	$1,050
1994-1999	2nd Rico era, neck-thru	$1,050	$1,450

Warlock Ice Acrylic
2004-present. See-thru acrylic body.

2004-2005		$225	$300

Wave
1983. U.S.-made, very limited production based upon the Wave bass.

1983		$2,000	$2,500

Bear Creek Guitars
1995-present. Luthier Bill Hardin worked for OMI Dobro and Santa Cruz Guitar before introducing his own line of professional and premium grade, custom-made Weissenborn-style guitars, made in Kula, Hawaii. He also builds ukes.

Beardsell Guitars
1996-present. Production/custom flat-tops, classical and electric solidbody guitars built by luthier Allan Beardsell in Toronto, Ontario.

Behringer
1989-present. The German professional audio products company added budget, production, solidbody guitars in '03, sold in amp/guitar packages. They also offer effects and amps.

Beltona
1990-present. Production/custom metal body resonator guitars made in New Zealand by Steve Evans and Bill Johnson. Beltona was originally located in England. They also build ukes.

Beltone
1920s-1930s. Acoustic and resonator guitars made by others for New York City distributor Perlberg & Halpin. Martin did make a small number of instruments for Beltone, but most were student-grade models most likely made by one of the big Chicago builders. They also made mandolins.

Resonator Copy
1930s-1930s. Resonator copy but without a real resonator, rather just an aluminum plate on a wooden top, body mahogany plywood.

1938		$275	$425

Beltone (Import)
1950s-1960s. Japan's Teisco made a variety of brands for others, including the Beltone line of guitars, basses and amps. Carvin sold some of these models in the late 1960s. Italy's Welson guitars also marketed marble and glitter-finished guitars in the U.S. under this brand.

Benedetto
1968-present. Archtop guitars, violins and a few solidbodies hand-crafted by Robert Benedetto in East Stroudsburg, Pennsylvania. He is especially known for refining the 7-string guitar. From '99 to '06 he licensed the names of his standard models to Fender (see Benedetto FMIC); during that period, Benedetto only made special order instruments.

MODEL YEAR	FEATURES	EXC. COND. LOW	HIGH

Benny
1990s. Electric semi-hollow, 14 1/2" body, cutaway, chambered Sitka spruce top, natural.

1990s		$4,500	$6,000

Benny Deluxe
1990s. Electric semi-hollow, chambered spruce top, abalone inlays, deluxe version of the Benny, sunburst.

1990s		$5,500	$7,000

Cremona
1988-1991. Acoustic/electric archtop, single-cut, 17" body, natural.

1988-1991		$22,000	$27,000

Fratello
1988-1999. Acoustic archtop, single-cut, 17" body, blond or sunburst.

1980s		$11,000	$12,000
1990s		$11,000	$12,000

La Venezia
1990s. Acoustic archtop, single-cut, 17" body, sunburst.

1990s		$13,000	$15,000

Limelite Custom
1990s. Single-cut, neck pickup, select aged wood, blond.

1990s		$23,000	$28,000

Manhattan
1989-1999. Archtop with 16" body, neck pickup, blond.

1989-1999		$12,000	$13,000

Manhattan Custom
1990s. Carved 17" body, blond.

1990s		$14,000	$15,000

Benedetto (FMIC)
1999-2006. Premium and presentation, production/custom, acoustic and electric archtops. From '99 to '06, Bob Benedetto had an agreement with Fender (FMIC) to build Benedetto guitars under his guidance and supervision. The guitars were originally built in the FMIC Guild Custom Shop in Nashville, and later in Fender's Corona, California, facility.

Artist/Artist Award
2000-2003. Full body, rounded cutaway, single neck pickup, natural or sunburst.

2000-2003		$4,500	$5,000

Fratello
2000-2006. Single-cut archtop, block inlays, mini-humbucker.

2000-2003		$9,000	$11,000

Manhattan
2000-2006. 17" single-cut archtop (3" deep), suspended mini-humbucking pickup.

2000-2003		$10,000	$11,500

Benedict
1988-present. Founded by Roger Benedict. Professional and premium grade, production/custom, solid and semi-hollow body guitars built by luthier Bill Hager in Cedar, Minnesota. He also builds basses.

Bently
ca.1985-1998. Student and intermediate grade copy style acoustic and electric guitars imported by St. Louis Music Supply. Includes the Series 10 electrics and the Songwriter acoustics (which have a double reversed B crown logo on the headstock). St. Louis Music replaced the Bently line with the Austin brand.

Series 10 (Electric)
1980s. Electric solidbody guitars, various colors.

1980s		$80	$100

Songwriter Series (Acoustic)
1980s. Acoustic guitars, spruce top, mahogany, natural finish.

1980s		$50	$75

Berkowitz Guitars
1995-present. Luthier David D. Berkowitz builds his premium grade, custom/production, steel string and baritone guitars in Washington, DC.

Bernie Rico Jr. Guitars
Professional and premium grade, production/custom, solidbody electrics built by luther Bernie Rico, Jr., the son of BC Rich founder, in Hesperia, California. He also makes basses.

Bertoncini Stringed Instruments
1995-present. Luthier Dave Bertoncini builds his premium grade, custom, flat-top guitars in Olympia, Washington. He has also built solidbody electrics, archtops, mandolins and banjos.

Beyond The Trees
1976-present. Luthier Fred Carlson offers a variety of innovative designs for his professional and presentation grade, production/custom 6- and 12-string flat-tops in Santa Cruz, California. He also produces the Sympitar (a 6-string with added sympathetic strings) and the Dreadnautilus (a unique shaped headless acoustic).

Bigsby
1946-present. Pedal steel guitars, hollow-chambered electric Spanish guitars, electric mandolins, doublenecks, replacement necks on acoustic guitars, hand vibratos, all handmade by Paul Arthur Bigsby, machinist and motorcycle enthusiast (designer of '30s Crocker motorcycles), in Downey, California. Initially built for special orders.

Bigsby was a pioneer in developing pedal steels. He designed a hand vibrato for Merle Travis. In '48, his neck-through hollow electrics (with Merle Travis) influenced Leo Fender, and Bigsby employed young Semie Moseley. In '56, he designed the Magnatone Mark series guitars and 1 Hawaiian lap steel.

He built less than 50 Spanish guitars, 6 mandolins, 125 to 150 pedal steels and 12 or so neck replacements. SN was stamped on the end of fin-

1985 Bently Series 10 graphite

1952 Bigsby Grady Martin Doubleneck

Bischoff acoustic

Blueridge BR140

MODEL YEAR	FEATURES	EXC. COND. LOW	HIGH

gerboard: MMDDYY. In '65, the company was sold to Gibson president Ted McCarty who moved the tremolo/vibrato work to Kalamazoo. Bigsby died in '68. Fred Gretsch purchased the Bigsby company from Ted McCarty in '99. A solidbody guitar and a pedal steel based upon the original Paul Bigsby designs were introduced January, 2002. These were modeled on the 1963 Bigsby catalog, but look very similar to the typical Bigsby solidbodys made since the early 1950s. Early Bigsby guitars command high value on the collectible market.

Solidbody Guitars
Late-1940s-early-1950s, 2002. Solidbody, natural. Reissue offered in '02

1948-1952		$25,000	$35,000
2002	Reissue	$3,000	$3,500

Bil Mitchell Guitars
1979-present. Luthier Bil Mitchell builds his professional and premium grade, production/custom, flat-top and archtop guitars originally in Wall, New Jersey, and since '02 in Riegelsville, Pennsylvania.

Birdsong Guitars
2001-present. Luthiers Scott Beckwith and Jamie Hornbuckle build their professional grade, production/custom, solidbody guitars in Wimberley, Texas. They also build basses.

Bischoff Guitars
1975-present. Professional and premium-grade, custom-made flat-tops built by luthier Gordy Bischoff in Eau Claire, Wisconsin.

Bishline
1985-present. Luthier Robert Bishline, of Tulsa, Oklahoma, mainly builds banjos, but did build flat-tops and resonators in the past, and still does occasionally.

Black Jack
1960s. Violin-body hollowbody electric guitars and basses, possibly others. Imported from Japan by unidentified distributor. Manufacturers unknown, but some may be Arai.

Blackshear, Tom
1958-present. Premium and presentation grade, production, classical and flamenco guitars made by luthier Tom Blackshear in San Antonio, Texas.

Blade
1987-present. Intermediate and professional grade, production, solidbody guitars from luthier Gary Levinson and his Levinson Music Products Ltd. located in Switzerland. He also builds basses.

California Custom
1994-present. California Standard with maple top and high-end appointments.

1994-1999		$800	$1,000

California Deluxe/Deluxe
1994-1995. Standard with mahogany body and maple top.

1994-1995		$500	$800

California Hybrid
1998-1999. Standard with piezo bridge pickup.

1998-1999		$450	$650

California Standard
1994-present. Offset double-cut, swamp ash body, bolt neck, 5-way switch.

1994-1999		$300	$450

R 3
1988-1993. Offset double-cut maple solidbody, bolt maple neck, 3 single-coils or single/single/humbucker.

1988-1993		$400	$700

R 4
1988-1993. R 3 with ash body and see-thru color finishes.

1988-1992		$500	$800

Texas Series
2003-present. Includes Standard (3 single-coils) and Deluxe (gold hardware, single/single/hum pickups).

2003-2005	Deluxe	$550	$650
2003-2005	Special	$500	$600
2003-2005	Standard	$450	$550

Blanchard Guitars
1994-present. Luthier Mark Blanchard builds premium grade, custom steel-string and classical guitars originally in Mammoth Lakes, California, and since May '03, in northwest Montana.

Blue Star
1984-present. Luthier Bruce Herron builds his production/custom guitars in Fennville, Michigan. He also builds mandolins, lap steels, dulcimers and ukes.

Travelmaster
1990s. Various colors.

1990s		$150	$300

Bluebird
1920s-1930s. Private brand with Bluebird painted on headstock, built by the Oscar Schmidt Co. and possibly others. Most likely made for distributor.

13" Flat-Top
1930s.

1930s		$100	$150

Blueridge
Early 1980s-present. Intermediate and professional grade, production, solid-top acoustic guitars distributed by Saga. In '00, the product line was redesigned with the input of luthier Greg Rich (Rich and Taylor guitars).

BR-263
2000-present. 000 size flat-top, solid spruce top, Brazilian rosewood back and sides.

2000-2005		$1,300	$1,500

GUITARS

MODEL YEAR	FEATURES	EXC. COND. LOW	HIGH

Bluesouth

1991-present. Custom electric guitars built by luthier Ronnie Knight in Muscle Shoals, Alabama. He also built basses.

Boaz Elkayam Guitars

1985-present. Presentation grade, custom steel, nylon, and flamenco guitars made by luthier Boaz Elkayam in Chatsworth, California.

Bohmann

1878-ca. 1926. Acoustic flat-top guitars, harp guitars, mandolins, banjos, violins made in Chicago Illinois, by Joseph Bohmann (born 1848, in Czechoslovakia). Bohmann's American Musical Industry founded 1878. Guitar body widths are 12", 13", 14", 15". He had 13 grades of guitars by 1900 (Standard, Concert, Grand Concert sizes). Early American use of plywood. Some painted wood finishes. Special amber-oil varnishes. Tuner bushings. Early ovalled fingerboards. Patented tuner plates and bridge design. Steel engraved label inside. Probably succeeded by son Joseph Frederick Bohmann.

Ca. 1896 12" body faux rosewood, 13", 14" and 15" body faux rosewood birch, 12", 13", 14" and 15" body sunburst maple, 12", 13", 14" and 15" body rosewood. By 1900 Styles 0, 1, 2 and 3 Standard, Concert and Grand Concert maple, Styles 1, 2, 3, 4, 5, 6, 7, 8, 9, 10, 11 and 12 in Standard, Concert, and Grand Concert rosewood.

14 3/4" Flat-Top

Solid spruce top, veneered Brazilian rosewood back and sides, wood marquetry around top and soundhole, natural. Each Bohmann should be valued on a case-by-case basis.

1900		$1,100	$1,500

Bolin

1978-present. Professional and premium grade, production/custom, solidbody guitars built by luthier John Bolin in Boise, Idaho. Bolin is well-known for his custom work. His Cobra guitars are promoted and distributed by Sanderson Sales and Marketing as part of the Icons of America Series.

NS

1996-present. Slot-headstock, bolt-on neck, single-cut solidbody, Seymour Duncan passive pickups or EMG active, from '96 to the fall of 2001 custom-built serial numbers to 0050 then from the fall of '01 to the present production model build starting with SN 0051.

1996-2001	Custom-built	$1,500	$2,500
2001-2003	Standard production	$1,000	$1,500

Bolt

1988-1991. Founded by luthier Wayne Bolt and Jim Dala Pallu in Schnecksville, Pennsylvania, Bolt's first work was CNC machined OEM necks and bodies made for Kramer and BC Rich. In '90, they started building solidbody Bolt guitars, many

with airbrushed graphics. Only about 100 to 125 were built, around 40 with graphics.

Bond

1984-1985. Andrew Bond made around 1,400 Electraglide guitars in Scotland. Logo says 'Bond Guitars, London.'

ElectraGlide

1984-1985. Black carbon graphite 1-piece body and neck, double-cut, 3 single-coils (2 humbuckers were also supposedly available), digital LED controls that required a separate transformer.

1984-1985		$1,200	$1,400

Bourgeois

1993-1999, 2000-present. Luthier Dana Bourgeois builds his professional and premium grade, production/custom, acoustic and archtop guitars in Lewiston, Maine. Bourgeois co-founded Schoenberg guitars and built Schoenberg models from '86-'90. Bourgeois' 20th Anniversary model was issued in '97. Bourgeois Guitars, per se, went of business at the end of '99. Patrick Theimer created Pantheon Guitars, which included 7 luthiers (including Bourgeois) working in an old 1840s textile mill in Lewiston, Maine and Bourgeois models continue to be made as part of the Pantheon organization.

Country Boy

1990s-present. Pre-war D-style model designed for Ricky Skaggs with Sitka spruce top, select mahogany back and sides, Bourgeois script logo headstock inlay, individually labeled with a Ricky Skaggs label, natural.

1990s		$1,600	$2,000

Country Boy Deluxe

2000-present. Country Boy with Adirondack spruce top.

2000-2005		$1,800	$2,100

D - 20th Anniversary

1997. 20 made, bearclaw spruce top, rosewood back and sides, mother-of-pearl 'board, ornate abalone floral pattern inlay, abalone rosette and border, natural.

1997		$3,100	$3,300

JOM

1990s-present. Jumbo Orchestra Model flat-top, 15 5/8". Model includes one with cedar top, mahogany back and sides, and one with spruce top, Brazilian rosewood back and sides.

1990s	Brazilian rosewood	$2,900	$3,700
1990s	Indian rosewood	$1,900	$2,100
1990s	Mahogany	$1,100	$1,400

JR-A

1990s. Artisan Series, 15 5/8", spruce top, rosewood back and sides.

1990s		$700	$1,000

Martin Simpson

1997-2003. Grand auditorium with unusual cutaway that removes one-half of the upper treble bout, Englemann spruce top, Indian rosewood back and sides, natural.

1997-2003		$2,400	$2,500

Bolt Viper 100

Bourgeois D-150

To get the most from this book, be sure to read "Using *The Guide*" in the introduction.

GUITARS

Bown OM

Breedlove AD-25

MODEL YEAR	FEATURES	EXC. COND. LOW	HIGH

OM Soloist
1990s-present. Full-sized, soft cutaway flat-top, Adirondack spruce top, figured Brick Red Brazilian rosewood back and sides, natural.

1990s		$4,800	$5,000

Slope D
1993-present. D-size, 16", spruce top, mahogany back and sides.

1993-2004		$1,900	$2,100

Bown Guitars
1981-present. Luthier Ralph Bown builds custom steel-string, nylon-string, baritone, and harp guitars in Walmgate, England.

Bozo
1964-present. Bozo (pronounced Bo-zho) Padunovac learned instrument building in his Yugoslavian homeland and arrived in the United States in '59. In '64 he opened his own shop and has built a variety of high-end, handmade, acoustic instruments, many being one-of-a-kind. He has built around 570 guitars over the years. There were several thousand Japanese-made (K. Yairi shop) Bell Western models bearing his name made from '79-'80; most of these were sold in Europe. He currently builds premium and presentation grade, production/custom guitars in Lindenhurst, Illinois.

Acoustic 12-String
1970-1980s. Indian rosewood.

1970-1980s		$1,600	$2,400

Cutaway 12-String
1977-1998. Often old world Balkan ornamentation, generally Sitka spruce top, Indian rosewood back and sides, widow-style headstock, ornamentation can vary (standard or elaborate).

1977	Standard	$1,600	$2,400
1993	Elaborate	$3,500	$5,000
1998	Elaborate custom	$4,500	$6,000

Bradford
Mid-1960s. Brand name used by the W.T. Grant Company, one of the old Five & Ten style retail stores similar to F.W. Woolworth and Kresge. Many of these guitars and basses were made in Japan by Guyatone.

Acoustic Flat-Top
1960s. Various colors.

1960s		$100	$150

Electric Solidbody
1960s. Various colors.

1960s		$125	$175

Bradley
1970s. Budget Japanese copy models imported by Veneman's Music Emporium

Brawley Basses
Headquartered in Temecula, California, and designed by Keith Brawley, offering solidbody guitars made in Korea. They also made basses.

MODEL YEAR	FEATURES	EXC. COND. LOW	HIGH

Breedlove
1990-present. Founded by Larry Breedlove and Steve Henderson. Intermediate, professional, premium, and presentation grade, production/custom, steel and nylon string flat-tops built in Tumalo, Oregon and imported. They also build mandolins. Several available custom options may add to the values listed here.

AD20/SM (Atlas Series)
2004-present. Imported solid spruce top, solid mahogany back and sides, pinless bridge.

2004-2005		$250	$300

C1 (C10)
1990-2004. Shallow concert-sized flat-top, non-cut, solid spruce top, mahogany back and sides, natural.

1990-2004		$1,500	$1,800

C2 (C22)
1990-present. Highly figured walnut body with sitka spruce top, large sloping cutaway.

1990s		$1,800	$2,100

C5/Northwest
1995-present. Grand concert with large soft cutaway, sitka spruce top, figured myrtlewood body.

2000-2005		$2,200	$2,300

C15/R
1990-2004. Concert-size C1 with soft rounded cutaway, and optional cedar top and rosewood back and sides, gold tuners.

1990-2004		$1,800	$2,000

C-20
1990s-present. Concert series, mahgoany back and sides, sitka spruce top.

2000-2005		$1,800	$2,000

C25 Custom
1990s-present. Custom koa body, sitka spruce top.

2000-2005		$2,400	$2,600

CM
1990s-present. Unusual double-cut style, walnut body and top.

1990s		$3,700	$3,900

D20
2002-present. Sitka spruce top, mahogany body, non cut.

2002-2005		$1,900	$2,000

D25/R
2002-present. Cutaway, sitka spruce top, Indian rosewood back and sides.

2002-2005		$2,100	$2,200

Ed Gerhard
1997-present. Shallow jumbo, soft cut, Indian rosewood body.

1997-2005	Custom	$2,300	$2,500
1997-2005	Signature	$2,150	$2,250

J Series (Jumbo)
1990s-present. Spruce top, myrtlewood body.

2000-2005	J25	$2,500	$2,600

Myrtlewood Limited 01
Ca.1990s-2003. Acoustic/electric, D-size, solid spruce top, solid myrtlewood back and sides.

1995-2003		$1,650	$1,750

MODEL YEAR	FEATURES	EXC. COND. LOW	HIGH
N25E			
2000-present. Acoustic/electric version of N25.			
2000-2005		$1,700	$1,800
N25R			
2000-present. Classical, Western red cedar top, solid Indian rosewood back and sides.			
2000-2005		$1,800	$2,000
RD20 X/R			
1999. Indian rosewood back and sides, sitka spruce top, winged bridge, abalone soundhole rosette.			
1999		$1,650	$1,800
SC20			
1990-present. Limited edition, various woods.			
1990-2005		$1,600	$1,800
SC20-Z Custom			
Mid-size with deep body, flat-top, Zircote back and sides, sitka spruce top.			
1999		$1,700	$1,900
SC25			
1990-present. Limited edition, various woods.			
1990-2000		$1,800	$2,000
SJ20-12 W			
1990s-present. 12-string, walnut (W) back and sides.			
2000-2005		$1,600	$1,800

Brentwood

1970s. Student models built by Kay for store or jobber.

K-100

1970s. 13" student flat-top, K-100 label inside back, K logo on 'guard.

1970s		$25	$50

Brian Moore

1992-present. Founded by Patrick Cummings, Brian Moore and Kevin Kalagher in Brewster, New York; they introduced their first guitars in '94. Initially expensive custom shop guitars with carbon-resin bodies with highly figured wood tops; later went to all wood bodies cut on CNC machines. The intermediate and professional grade, production, iGuitar/i2000series was introduced in 2000 and made in Korea, but set up in the U.S. Currently the premium grade, production/custom, Custom Shop Series guitars are handcrafted in La Grange, New York. They also build basses and electric mandolins.

C-45

1999-2001. Solidbody, mahogany body, bolt neck, 2 P-90-type pickups, natural satin.

1999-2001		$850	$1,050

C-55/C-55P

1997-2004. Solidbody, burl maple body, bolt neck, currently produced as a limited edition. C-55P indicates Piezo option.

1997-2004		$850	$1,050

C-90/C-90P

1996-present. Solidbody, figured maple top, mahogany body, bolt neck, hum-single-hum pickups, red sunburst. C-90P has Piezo option.

1996-2004		$1,300	$1,500

DC-1/DC-1P

1997-present. Quilted maple top, 2 humbuckers, single-cut, gold hardware. DC-1P has Piezo option.

1997-1998		$1,700	$2,000

i1

2000-present. Double-cut solidbody, maple top, mahogany body.

2000-2005		$500	$800

iGuitar 2.13

2000-present. The iGuitar series are Korean-made and are the same as the i2000 Series models, but feature a 13 pin RMC system for access to digital guitar processors.

2000-2005		$900	$1,100

iGuitar 2P

2000-present. Single-cut solidbody, magnetic and piezo blend, maple top, Kalamta mahogany body and neck.

2000-2005		$550	$700

iGuitar 8.13/81.13

2000-present. Mahogany body, figured maple top, 2 humbuckers, 13-pin adapter.

2000-2005		$550	$700

MC1

1994-present. High-end model, quilted maple top, various pickup options including piezo and midi, gold hardware, currently produced as a limited edition-Should be evaluated on a case-by-case basis.

1990s		$2,000	$3,000

1990s Brian Moore MC/1

Brian Stone Classical Guitars

Luthier Brian Stone builds his classical guitars in Corvallis, Oregon.

Briggs

1999-present. Luthier Jack Briggs builds his professional and premium grade, production/custom, chambered and solidbody guitars in Raleigh, North Carolina.

Broman

1930s. The Broman brand was most likely used by a music studio (or distributor) on instruments made by others, including Regal-built resonator instruments.

Brook Guitars

1993-present. Simon Smidmore and Andy Petherick build their production/custom Brook steel-string, nylon-strings, and archtops in Dartmoor, England.

Bruné, R. E.

1966-present. Luthier Richard Bruné builds his premium and presentation grade, custom, classical and flamenco guitars in Evanston, Illinois. He also offers his professional and premium grade Model 20 and Model 30, which are handmade in a leading guitar workshop in Japan. Bruné's Guitars with Guts column appears quarterly in *Vintage Guitar* magazine.

Briggs Avatar

Burns Flyte

Burns Vitasonic

MODEL YEAR	FEATURES	EXC. COND. LOW	HIGH

Bruno and Sons

1834-present. Established in 1834 by Charles Bruno, primarily as a distributor, Bruno and Sons marketed a variety of brands, including their own. Currently part of Kaman Music.

Harp Guitar

1924		$2,000	$3,000

Hollowbody Electrics

1960s-1970s. Various imported models.

1960s		$150	$250

Parlor Guitar

1880-1920. Various woods used on back and sides.

1880-1920	Birch	$350	$500
1880-1920	Brazilian rosewood	$850	$1,100
1880-1920	Mahogany	$450	$700

Bunker

1961-present. Founded by guitarist Dave Bunker, who began building guitars with his father. He continued building custom guitars and basses while performing in Las Vegas in the '60s and developed a number of innovations. Around '92 Bunker began PBC Guitar Technology with John Pearse and Paul Chernay in Coopersburg, Pennsylvania, building instruments under the PBC brand and, from '94-'96, for Ibanez' USA Custom Series. PBC closed in '97 and Bunker moved back to Washington State to start Bunker Guitar Technology and resumed production of several Bunker models. In early 2002, Bunker Guitars became part of Maple Valley Tone Woods of Port Angeles, Washington. Currently Bunker offers intermediate, professional, and premium grade, production/custom, guitars and basses built in Port Angeles. Most early Bunker guitars were pretty much custom-made in low quantities.

Electric Solidbody or Archtop

1960-1990s. Various colors.

1990s		$900	$1,100

Burns

1960-1970, 1974-1983, 1992-present. Intermediate and professional grade, production, electric guitars built in England and Korea. They also build basses.

Jim Burns began building guitars in the late-'50s and established Burns London Ltd in '60. Baldwin Organ (see Baldwin listing) purchased the company in '65 and offered the instruments until '70. The Burns name was revived in '91 by Barry Gibson as Burns London, with Jim Burns' involvement, offering reproductions of some of the classic Burns models of the '60s. Jim Burns passed away in August '98.

Baby Bison

1965. Double-cut solidbody, scroll headstock, 2 pickups, shorter scale, tremolo.

1965		$800	$900

Bison

1964-1965. Double-cut solidbody, 3 pickups, tremolo, black or white, scroll-headstock, replaced flat headstock Black Bison. Has been reissued with both types of headstocks.

1964-1965		$1,200	$1,400
2000s	Reissue	$400	$475

Brian May Signature - Red Special

2001-2005. Replica of May's original 'Red Special' but with added whammy-bar, red finish. Korean-made.

2001-2005		$600	$650

Cobra

2004-present. Double-cut solid, 2 pickups.

2004-2005		$150	$175

Double Six

1964-1965. Solidbody 12-string, double-cut, 3 pickups, greenburst. Has been reissued.

1963-1965		$1,400	$1,500

Flyte

1974-1977. Fighter jet-shaped solidbody, pointed headstock, 2 humbucking pickups, silver, has been reissued.

1974-1977		$750	$900

GB 66 Deluxe

1965. Like 66 Standard, but with bar pickups and add Density control.

1965		$900	$1,000

GB 66 Deluxe Standard

1965. Offset double-cut, f-holes, 2 Ultra-Sonic pickups.

1965		$850	$950

Jazz

1962-1965. Offset double-cut solid, shorter scale, 2 pickups.

1962-1965		$650	$750

Jazz Split Sound

1962-1965. Offset double-cut solid, 3 pickups, tremolo, red sunburst.

1962-1965		$800	$1,000

Marquee

2000-present. Offset double-cut solid, 3 pickups, scroll headstock

2000-2005		$225	$275

Marvin

1964-1965. Offset double-cut solidbody, scroll headstock, 3 pickups, tremolo, white.

1964-1965		$1,500	$1,600

Nu-Sonic

1964-1965. Solidbody, 2 pickups, tremolo, white or cherry, has been reissued.

1964-1965		$550	$650

Sonic

1960-1964. Double shallow cut solid, 2 pickups, cherry.

1962-1964		$450	$550

Split Sonic

1962-1964. Solidbody, 3 pickups, bound neck, tremolo, red sunburst.

1962-1964		$850	$1,050

MODEL YEAR	FEATURES	EXC. COND. LOW	HIGH

Steer
2000-present. Semi-hollowbody, sound-hole, 2 pickups, non-cut and single-cut versions.

2000-2005		$350	$400

TR-2
1963-1964. Semi-hollow, 2 pickups, red sunburst.

1963-1964		$900	$1,100

Vibraslim
1964-1965. Double-cut, f-holes, 2 pickups, red sunburst.

1964-1965		$900	$1,100

Virginian
1964-1965. Burns of London model, later offered as Baldwin Virginian in '65.

1964-1965		$900	$1,100

Vista Sonic
1962-1964. Offset double-cut solid, 3 pickups, red sunburst.

1962-1964		$750	$850

Burns-Weill
1959. Jim Burns and Henry Weill teamed up to produce three solidbody electric and three solidbody bass models under this English brand.

Burnside
1987-1988. Budget solidbody guitars imported by Guild.

Solidbody Electric/Blade
1987-1988. Solidbody, fat pointy headstock.

1987-1988		$300	$400

Burny
1980s-present. Solidbody electric guitars from Fernandes and built in Japan, Korea or China.

Burton Guitars
1980-present. Custom classical guitars built by luthier Cynthia Burton in Portland, Oregon.

Buscarino Guitars
1981-present. Luthier John Buscarino builds his premium and presentation grade, custom archtops and steel-string and nylon-string flat-tops in Franklin, North Carolina.

Solidbody Electric - Custom-Built
1981-1990s.

1981-1990s		$1,350	$1,500

Byers, Gregory
1984-present. Premium grade, custom classical and Flamenco guitars built by luthier Gregory Byers in Willits, California.

C. Fox
1997-2002. Luthier Charles Fox built his premium grade, production/custom flat-tops in Healdsburg, California. In '02 he closed C. Fox Guitars and move to Portland, Oregon to build Charles Fox Guitars.

C. P. Thornton Guitars
2004-present. Luthier Chuck Thornton builds his professional and premium grade, production/custom, semi-hollow electric guitars in Turner, Maine. From '85 to '96 he built basses and guitars under the C. P. Thornton Basses brand.

CA (Composite Acoustics)
1999-present. Professional grade, production, carbon fiber composite guitars built in Lafayette, Louisiana.

Callaham
1989-present. Professional, production/custom, solidbody electric guitars built by luthier Bill Callaham in Winchester, Virginia. They also make tube amp heads.

Camelli (Italy)
1960s. Line of solidbody electrics from Italy.

Solidbody Electric

1960s		$325	$475

Campbell American Guitars
2005-present. Luthier Dean Campbell builds his intermediate and professional grade, production/custom, solidbody guitars in Pawtucket, Rhode Island. From '02 to '05, he built guitars under the Greene & Campbell brand.

Campellone
1978-present. Luthier Mark Campellone builds his premium grade, custom archtops in Greenville, Rhode Island. He also made electrics and basses in the '70s and '80s, switching to archtops around '90.

Deluxe
1990-present. 17", middle of the company product line, archtop, blond or sunburst.

1990-1995		$5,000	$5,500

Special
1994-present. 16" to 18" archtop, carved spruce top, carved flamed maple back, flamed maple sides, blond or sunburst.

1994-1999		$6,000	$6,800

Canvas
2004-present. Budget and intermediate grade, production, solid and semi-hollow body guitars imported from China by American Sejung Corp. They also offer basses.

Carbonaro
1974-present. Luthier Robert Carbonaro builds his premium grade, production/custom, archtop and flat-top guitars in Santa Fe, New Mexico.

Carl Fischer
1920s. Most likely a brand made for a distributor. Instruments built by the Oscar Schmidt Co. and possibly others.

Buscarino Virtuoso

Campbell American Precix

GUITARS

Carvin CT-6M

Chandler Lectra-Slide

MODEL YEAR	FEATURES	EXC. COND. LOW	HIGH

Carlos

ca.1976-late 1980s. Imported copies of classic American acoustics distributed by Coast Wholesale Music.

Model 240

1970s. D copy with mahogany (laminate?) back and sides, spruce top, natural.

1978		$150	$300

Model 275

1970s. D copy with rosewood (laminate?) sides and three-piece back, spruce top, natural.

1978		$200	$375

Carvin

1946-present. Intermediate and professional grade, production/custom, acoustic and electric guitars. They also offer basses and amps. Founded in Los Angeles by Hawaiian guitarist and recording artist Lowell C. Kiesel as the L.C. Kiesel Co. making pickups for guitars. Bakelite Kiesel-brand electric Hawaiian lap steels are introduced in early-'47. Small tube amps introduced ca. '47. By late-'49, the Carvin brand is introduced, combining parts of names of sons Carson and Gavin. Carvin acoustic and electric Spanish archtops are introduced in '54. Instruments are sold by mail-order only. The company relocated to Covina, California in '49 and to Escondido, California in '68. Two retail stores opened in Hollywood and Santa Ana, California in '91.

Approx. 2,000-4,000 guitars made prior to '70 with no serial number. First serial number appeared in '70, stamped on end of fingerboard, beginning with #5000. All are consecutive. Later SN on neck plates.

    Approximate SN ranges include:
    1970: First serial number #5000 to 10019 ('79).
    '80-'83: 10768 to 15919.
    '84-'87: 13666 to 25332.
    '88-'90: 22731 to 25683.
    '91-'94: 25359 to 42547.
    '95-'99: 45879 to 81427.
    '00-present: 56162 upward.

Acoustic/Electric AC/AE Series

1990s		$350	$700

Solidbody B/C/D Series (Mid-level)

1990s		$350	$700

Solidbody Carved-Top (Higher-End)

2000s		$800	$1,200

Solidbody DN/DB/DS Series (Doubleneck)

1975-1990s		$1,100	$1,500

Casa Montalvo

1987-present. Intermediate and professional grade, production/custom flamenco and classical guitars made in Mexico for George Katechis of Berkeley Musical Instrument Exchange.

MODEL YEAR	FEATURES	EXC. COND. LOW	HIGH

Casio

1987-1988. Digital guitars imported from Japan, plastic body, synthesizer features.

DG10

1987. Self-contained digital guitar.

1987		$100	$125

DG20

Midi-capable digital guitar.

1987		$200	$300

PG-300

1987. Similar to PG-380, but with less features.

1987		$300	$500

PG-310

1987. Similar to PG-380, but with less features.

1987		$400	$600

PG-380

1987. Guitar synth, double-cut, over 80 built-in sounds, midi controller capable.

1987		$600	$1,100

Champion

Ca. 1894-1897. Chicago's Robert Maurer built this brand of instruments under switching to the Maurer brand name around 1897.

Chandler

1984-present. Intermediate and professional grade, production/custom, solidbody electric guitars built by luthiers Paul and Adrian Chandler in Chico, California. They also build basses, laptops and pickups. Chandler started making pickguards and accessories in the '70s, adding electric guitars, basses, and effects in '84.

555 Model

1992-present. Sharp double-cut, 3 mini-humbuckers.

1990s	TV Yellow	$550	$650

Austin Special

1991-1999. Resembles futuristic Danelectro, lipstick pickups, available in 5-string version.

1991-1999		$550	$650

Austin Special Baritone

1994-1999. Nicknamed Elvis, gold metalflake finish, mother-of-toilet-seat binding, tremolo, baritone.

1994-1999		$550	$650

Metro

1995-2000. Double-cut slab body, P-90 in neck position and humbucker in the bridge position.

1994-2000		$550	$650

Telepathic

1994-2000. Classic single-cut style, 3 models; Basic, Standard, Deluxe.

1994-2000	Basic	$450	$550
1994-2000	Deluxe 1122 Model	$600	$700
1994-2000	Standard	$550	$650

Chapin

Professional and premium grade, production/custom, semi-hollow, solidbody, and acoustic electric guitars built by luthiers Bill Chapin and Fred Campbell in San Jose, California.

MODEL YEAR	FEATURES	EXC. COND. LOW	HIGH

Chapman

1970-present. Made by Emmett Chapman, the Stick features 10 strings and is played by tapping both hands. The Grand Stick features 12 strings.

Stick

10 or 12 strings, touch-tap hybrid electric instrument.

1970-1999	10-string	$1,250	$1,350
1970-1999	12-string	$1,400	$1,600
2000-2003	10-string	$1,300	$1,400

Charis Acoustic

1996-present. Premium grade, custom/production, steel-string guitars built by luthier Bill Wise in Bay City, Michigan.

Charles Fox Guitars

1968-present. Luthier Charles Fox builds his premium and presentation grade, custom, steel and nylon string guitars in Portland, Oregon. He also produced GRD acoustic and electric guitars for '78-'82 and C. Fox acoustic guitars for '97-'02. He also operates The American School of Lutherie in Portland.

Charles Shifflett Acoustic Guitars

1990-present. Premium grade, custom, classical, flamenco, resonator, and harp guitars built by luthier Charles Shifflett in High River, Alberta. He also builds basses and banjos.

Charvel

1976 (1980)-present. Intermediate and professional grade, production, solidbody electric guitars. They also build basses. Founded by Wayne Charvel as Charvel Manufacturing in '76, making guitar parts in Asuza, California. Moved to San Dimas in '78. Also in '78 Grover Jackson bought out Charvel. In '79 or early '80 Charvel branded guitars are introduced. U.S.-made to '85, a combination of imports and U.S.-made post-'85. Charvel also manufactured the Jackson brand.

Charvel licensed its trademark to IMC (Hondo) in '85. IMC bought Charvel in '86 and moved the factory to Ontario, California. On October 25, 2002, Fender Musical Instruments Corp. (FMIC) took ownership of Jackson/Charvel Manufacturing Inc.

Pre-Pro (Pre-Production) Charvels began in November 1980 and ran until sometime in 1981. These are known as 'non-plated' indicating pre-production versus a production neck plate. Production serialized neck plates are considered to be San Dimas models which have a Charvel logo, serial number, and a PO Box San Dimas notation on the neck plate. These Serialized Plated Charvels came after Pre-Pros. Late '81 and '82 saw the early serialized guitars with 21-fret necks; these are more valuable. During '82 the 22-fret neck was introduced. The so-called Soft Strat-, Tele-, Flying V-, and Explorer-style headstocks are associated with the early San Dimas Charvel models. In late '82 the pointy

headstock, called the Jackson style, was introduced. In '82 the Superstrat style with a neck plate was introduced. Superstrats with a Kahler tailpiece have a lower value than the Pre-Pro models (with Fender-style trem tailpiece).

Collectors of vintage Charvels look for the vintage Charvel 3-on-a-side logo. This is a defining feature and a cutoff point for valuations. Bogus builders are replicating early Charvels and attempting to sell them as originals so fakes can be a problem for Charvel collectors, so buyer beware.

Other electric guitar manufacturing info:

1986-1989	Japanese-made Models 1 through 8
1989-1991	Japanese-made 550 XL, 650 XL/ Custom, 750 XL (XL=neck-thru)
1989-1992	Japanese-made Models 275, 375, 475, 575
1990-1991	Korean-made Charvette models
1992-1994	Korean-made Models 325, 425

Early Charvel serial numbers (provided by former Jackson/Charvel associate Tim Wilson):
The first 500 to 750 guitars had no serial number, just marked "Made In U.S.A." on their neckplates. Five digit serial numbers were then used until November '81 when 4-digit number adopted, starting with #1001.

1981	1001-1095
1982	1096-1724
1983	1725-2938
1984	2939-4261
1985	4262-5303
1986	5304-5491

Pre-Pro

November 1980-1981. Pre-Pros came in different configurations of body styles, pickups, and finishes. There are five basic Pre-Pro formats: the Standard Body, the Bound Body, the Graphic Body, the Flamed Top, and the Matching Headstock. It is possible to have a combination, such as a Bound Body and Matching Headstock. Line items are based on body style and can feature any one of four neck/headstock-styles used: the so-called Tele-headstock, Strat-headstock, Flying V headstock, and Explorer headstock. Finishes included white, black, red, metallic Lake Placid Blue, and special graphics. All original parts adds considerable value and it is often difficult to determine what is original on these models, so expertise is required. An original Fender brass trem tailpiece, for example, adds considerable value. The Pre-Pro models were prone to modification such as added Kahler and Floyd Rose trems. Price ranges are wide because this is a relatively new market without mature pricing.

1980-1981	Bound body	$2,500	$5,000
1980-1981	Flamed Top Stained body	$2,500	$6,000
1980-1981	Graphic body	$2,500	$6,000
1980-1981	Matching Headstock and body	$2,500	$7,500
1980-1981	Standard body	$2,500	$4,000

Charles Fox steel-string

1986 Charvel Model 5

1987 Charvel Model 3

Charvel EVH

MODEL YEAR	FEATURES	EXC. COND. LOW	HIGH

San Dimas Serialized Plated
1981-1986, 1995-1997. U.S.-made with San Dimas neck plate, bolt neck, rounded headstock early production, pointy headstock later, reissued in mid-'90s.

1981-1982	Soft headstock	$2,500	$4,000
1982-1986	Pointy headstock	$1,500	$1,800
1995-1997	Soft headstock	$800	$1,000

275 Deluxe Dinky
1989-1991. Made in Japan, offset double-cut solidbody, 1 single-coil and one humbucker ('89), 3 stacked humbuckers ('90-'91), tremolo.

1989	1 single, 1 humbucker	$425	$550
1990-1991	Stacked humbuckers	$425	$550

325SL
1992-1994. Dot inlays.

1992-1994		$425	$550

325SLX
1992-1994. Surfcaster-like thinline acoustic/electric, dual cutaways, F-hole, on-board chorus, shark inlays, made in Korea.

1992-1994		$425	$550

375 Deluxe
1989-1992. Maple or rosewood 'board, dot inlays, single-single-humbucker.

1989-1992		$425	$550

475
1989-1992. Humbucker-single-single configuration, bolt-on neck, dot markers.

1989-1992		$400	$500

475 Deluxe/Special
1989-1992. Introduced as Special, changed to Deluxe, bound rosewood board, shark tooth inlays, 2 oval stacked humbuckers and 1 bridge humbucker.

1989-1992		$425	$550

525
1990s. Acoustic-electric, single-cut.

1990s		$425	$550

625-C12
1990s. Acoustic-electric cutaway 12-string.

1990s		$300	$350

625F/625ACEL
1990s. Acoustic-electric cutaway.

1990s		$300	$350

Avenger
1990-1991. Randy Rhoads-style batwing-shaped solidbody, 3 stacked humbuckers, tremolo, made in Japan.

1990-1991		$300	$375

Charvette
1989-1992. Charvette Series made in Korea, super-strat-style, model number series 100 through 300.

1990-1991		$175	$225

Custom Shop Kit
1976-1980. Includes kits that were built from after-market necks, bodies, and pickups. Most early-Charvel collectors do not consider these to be true Charvel branded instruments.

1976-1980		$500	$2,000

EVH Art Series/EVH-Guitars
Mid-2004. EVH guitars with hand stripe-work done by Edward Van Halen, classic early Charvel-Strat body with FMIC licensed Fender/Charvel headstock design, autographed by Ed, and sold in an on-line auction. These were the inspiration for the later Limited Edition EVH.

2004	Black w/yellow stripes	$10,000	$12,000
2004	Red w/black & white stripes	$10,000	$12,000
2004	White w/black stripes	$9,000	$11,000

Fusion Deluxe
1989-1991. Double-cut solidbody, tremolo, 1 humbucker and 1 single-coil pickup, made in Japan.

1988		$275	$425

Fusion Standard/AS FX 1
1993-1996. Double-cut solidbody, tremolo, 1 regular and 2 mini humbuckers, made in Japan, also named AS FX1.

1988		$350	$375

Model 1/1A/1C
1986-1989. Offset double-cut solidbody, bolt-on maple neck, dot inlays, 1 humbucker, tremolo, made in Japan. Model 1A has 3 single-coils. Model 1C has 1 humbucker and 2 single-coils.

1986-1989		$350	$375

Model 2
1986-1989. As Model 1, but with rosewood 'board.

1986-1989		$350	$375

Model 3/3A/3DR/3L
1986-1989. As Model 2, but with 1 humbucker, 2 single coils. Model 3A has 2 humbuckers. Model 3DR has 1 humbucker and 1 single-coil.

1986-1989		$400	$425

Model 4/4A
1986-1989. As Model 2, but with 1 regular humbucker and 2 stacked humbuckers mounted in the body (no pickguard), and with active electronics, shark-fin inlays. Model 4A has 2 regular humbuckers and dot markers.

1986-1989		$400	$425

Model 5/5A
1986-1989. As Model 4A, but is neck-thru construction, with JE1000TG active elctronics. Model 5A is single humbucker and single knob version of Model 5, limited production, made in Japan.

1986-1989		$400	$575

Model 6
1986-1989. As Model 4, but with shark's tooth 'board inlays, standard or various custom finishes.

1986-1989		$500	$625

Model 7
1988-1989. Single-cut solidbody, bound top, reversed headstock, 2 single-coils, made in Japan.

1988-1989		$500	$625

Model 88 LTD
1988. Double-cut solidbody, 1 slanted humbucker, shark fin inlay, 1000 built, made in Japan.

1988		$600	$700

MODEL YEAR	FEATURES	EXC. COND. LOW	HIGH

ST Custom
1990-1992. Offset double-cut ash solidbody, 2 single-coils and 1 humbucker, rosewood 'board, tremolo, made in Japan.

1990-1992		$350	$400

ST Deluxe
1990-1992. Same as ST Custom but with maple 'board.

1990-1992		$325	$375

Standard
2002-present. Typical offset double-cut Charvel body, 2 Seymour Duncan humbucker pickups, various opaque colors.

2002-2005		$225	$325

Star
1980-1981. The Star is considered by early-Charvel collectors to be Charvel's only original design with its unique four-point body.

1980-1981		$1,000	$6,000

Surfcaster
1991-1994. Offset double-cut, f-hole, various pickup options, bound body, tremolo, made in Japan.

1991-1993	1 single-coil, 1 humbucker	$750	$900
1991-1993	2 single-coils	$800	$1,000
1991-1993	3 single-coils	$850	$1,000
1991-1993	Optional custom color & features	$900	$1,200

Surfcaster 12
1991-1995. 12-string version of Surfcaster, no tremolo, made in Japan.

1991-1995		$850	$1,000

Surfcaster Double Neck
1992. Very limited production, 6/12 double neck, Charvel logo on both necks, black.

1992		$1,400	$2,000

Surfcaster HT (Model SC 1)
1992-1996. Made in Japan. Hard Tail (HT) non-tremolo version of Surfcaster, has single-coil and bridge humbucker.

1992-1996	Custom color & features	$800	$1,000
1992-1996	Standard colors & features	$750	$900

Chiquita
1979-present. Intermediate grade, production guitars made by Erlewine Guitars in Austin, Texas (see that listing). There was also a mini amp available.

Travel Guitar
1979-present. Developed by Mark Erlewine and ZZ Top's Billy Gibbons, 27" overall length solidbody.

1980s	Blond, natural or yellow	$275	$375
1980s	Red	$275	$325

Chrysalis Guitars
1998-present. Luthier Tim White builds his premium grade, production/custom Chrysalis Guitar System, which includes interchangeable components that can be quickly assembled into a full-size electric/acoustic guitar, in New Boston, New Hampshire. A variety of instruments may be created, including 6- and 12-string electrics and acoustics, electric and acoustic mandocello and acoustic basses.

Cipher
1960s. Solidbody electric guitars and basses imported from Japan by Inter-Mark. Generally strange-shaped bodies.

Electric Solidbody
Student-level import.

1960s		$150	$200

Citron
1995-present. Luthier Harvey Citron builds his professional and premium grade, production/custom solidbody guitars in Woodstock, New York. He also builds basses. In '75, Citron and Joe Veillette founded Veillette-Citron, which was known for handcrafted, neck-thru guitars and basses. That company closed in '83.

Custom-Made Electrics
2000s. A variety of solidbody and thin hollowbody mid- to high-end electrics.

2000s		$1,700	$2,700

Clifford
Clifford was a brand manufactured by Kansas City, Missouri instrument wholesalers J.W. Jenkins & Sons. First introduced in 1895, the brand also offered mandolins.

Coleman Guitars
1976-1983. Custom made presentation grade instruments made in Homosassa, Florida, by luthier Harry Coleman. No headstock logo, Coleman logo on inside center strip.

Flat-Top

1976-1983		$5,000	$15,000

Collings
1986-present. Professional, premium, and presentation grade, production/custom, flat-top, archtop and electric guitars built in Austin, Texas. They also build mandolins. Bill Collings started with guitar repair and began custom building guitars around '73. In '80, he relocated his shop from Houston to Austin and started Collings Guitars in '86.

00-41 (Brazilian rosewood)
2001. Premium Brazilian rosewood back and sides, Adirondack spruce top, abalone top purfling.

2001		$7,000	$8,000

000-1 (Mahogany)
1990s. Mahogany body, spruce top.

1990s	000-1	$2,500	$2,700
1990s	000-1A Adirondack	$2,900	$3,100

Chrysalis

Collings CJ

GUITARS

Collings OM2-H

Comins Chester Avenue

000-2H

1994-present. 15" 000-size, Indian rosewood back and sides, spruce top, slotted headstock, 12-fret neck, dot markers. AAA Koa back and sides in '96.

MODEL YEAR	FEATURES	EXC. COND. LOW	HIGH
1994-1995	Indian rosewood	$2,700	$3,500
1996	AAA Koa	$3,500	$4,000

000-41 (Indian rosewood)

1990s. Sitka spruce top, Indian rosewood sides and back, slotted headstock.

1999		$3,100	$3,300

C-10 (Mahogany)

1994-present. 000-size, spruce top, mahogany back and sides, natural.

1995		$2,700	$3,100

C-10 Deluxe

1994-present. Indian rosewood or flamed maple back and sides, natural.

1994-2002	Flamed maple	$2,700	$3,100
1994-2002	Indian rosewood	$2,700	$3,100

C-100 (Mahogany)

1986-1995. Quadruple 0-size, spruce top, mahogany back and sides, natural, replaced by CJ Jumbo.

1986-1995		$2,400	$2,700

CJ Jumbo (Indian rosewood)

1995-present. Quadruple 0-size, spruce top, Indian rosewood back and sides, natural.

1995-2001		$3,000	$3,200

D-1 Gruhn

1989. Short run for Gruhn Guitars, Nashville, Gruhn script logo on the headstock instead of Collings, signed by Bill Collins, Indian rosewood back and sides, sitka spruce top.

1989		$3,000	$4,000

D-1/D-1SB/D-1A Custom

1994-present. D-size, 15 5/8", spruce top, mahogany back and sides, natural. D-1SB is sunburst option. D-1A Custom upgrades to Adirondack spruce top and higher appointments, natural.

1995	D-1	$3,000	$3,200
1999-2002	D-1A Custom	$3,000	$4,000
2001	D-1SB	$3,000	$3,200

D-2 (Indian rosewood)

1986-1995. D-1 with Indian rosewood back and sides, natural.

1986-1995		$3,500	$4,000

D-2H (Indian rosewood)

1986-present. Dreadnought, same as D-2 with herringbone purfling around top edge.

1986-2001		$3,500	$4,000

D-2H/D-2HBZ (Brazilian rosewood)

1994-2001. Grade AA Brazilian rosewood, spruce top.

1994-2001		$5,200	$6,000

D-3

1990-present. Similar to D-2H but with abalone purfling/rosette.

1990s	Brazilian rosewood	$5,500	$6,500
2000s	Indian rosewood	$3,500	$4,000

OM-1/OM-1A

1994-present. Grand concert, sitka spruce top, mahogany back and sides, natural. OM-1A includes Adirondack spruce upgrade.

1990s	OM-1	$3,000	$3,200
1990s	OM-1A	$3,400	$3,500

OM-2H (Indian rosewood)

1990-present.

1990-2005		$3,000	$3,200

OM-2HAV (Brazilian rosewood)

1998. Adirondack spruce top, Brazilian rosewood back and sides, ivoroid-bound body.

1998		$5,500	$6,500

OM-3 (Brazilian rosewood)

1998. Brazilian rosewood back and sides, Adirondack spruce top, fancy rosette.

1998		$4,500	$5,500

OM-3 (Indian rosewood)

2002-present.

2002-2005		$2,500	$3,000

OM-3 (Maple)

Figured maple.

2003		$4,000	$4,500

OM-3HC (Indian rosewood)

1986. Single rounded cutaway, 15", spruce top, Indian rosewood back and sides, herringbone purfling.

1986		$4,000	$4,500

OM-42B (Brazilian rosewood)

2000. Brazilian rosewood back and sides, Adirondack spruce top, fancy rosette and binding.

2000		$7,000	$8,000

SJ

Spruce top, quilted maple back and sides or Indian rosewood (earlier option).

1990s	Indian rosewood	$3,500	$4,000
2003	Maple	$3,500	$4,000

SJ-41 (Brazilian rosewood)

1996. Cedar top, Brazilian rosewood back and sides.

1996		$7,000	$8,000

Comins

1992-present. Premium and presentation grade, custom archtops built by luthier Bill Comins in Willow Grove, Pennsylvania. He also offers a combo amp built in collaboration with George Alessandro.

Chester Avenue

1994-present. Electric archtop, solid spruce top and back, 17" or 18" cutaway, options can vary.

1994-1999	17"	$5,500	$6,000
1994-1999	18"	$6,000	$6,500

Classic

1995-present. Classic archtop jazz model, 17" cutaway, pickguard mounted neck pickup, block markers.

1995-1999		$4,500	$5,000

Parlor

1995-present. 14" archtop with viola styling, violin golden brown.

1995-1999		$3,000	$3,500

MODEL YEAR	FEATURES	EXC. COND. LOW	HIGH

Renaissance
1996-present. 17" archtop cutaway, carved European spruce top, solid curly maple back and sides, unique removable sound baffles, blond.

1996-1999		$5,500	$6,500

Concertone
Ca. 1914-1930s. Concertone was a brand made by Chicago's Slingerland and distributed by Montgomery Ward. The brand was also used on other instruments such as ukuleles.

Conklin
1984-present. Intermediate, professional and premium grade, production/custom, 6-, 7-, 8-, and 12-string solid and hollowbody electrics, by luthier Bill Conklin. He also builds basses. Originally located in Lebanon, Missouri, in '88 the company moved to Springfield, Missouri. Conklin instruments are made in the U.S. and overseas.

Conn Guitars
Ca.1968-ca.1978. Student to mid-quality classical and acoustic guitars, some with bolt-on necks, also some electrics. Imported from Japan by band instrument manufacturer and distributor Conn/Continental Music Company, Elkhart, Indiana.

Acoustic
1968-1978. Various models.

1968-1978		$100	$200

Classical
1968-1978. Various student-level models.

1968-1978		$100	$200

Solidbody Electric
1970s. Various models.

1970s.		$150	$200

Connor, Stephan
1995-present. Luthier Stephan Connor builds his premium grade, custom nylon-string guitars in Waltham, Massachusetts.

Conrad Guitars
Ca. 1968-1978. Mid- to better-quality copies of glued-neck Martin and Gibson acoustics and bolt-neck Gibson and Fender solidbodies. They also offered basses, mandolins and banjos. Imported from Japan by David Wexler and Company, Chicago, Illinois.

Acoustic 12-String
1970s. Dreadnought size.

1970s		$150	$200

Acoustical Slimline 12-String 40100
1970s. 2 DeArmond-style pickups, rosewood 'board, dot markers, sunburst.

1970s		$200	$300

Acoustical Slimline 40080/40085
1970s. 2 or 3 DeArmond-style pickups, rosewood 'board, block markers, sunburst.

1970s		$200	$300

Bison (40035/40030/40065/40005)
1970s. 1 thru 4 pickups available, rosewood 'board with dot markers, six-on-side headstock.

1970s		$175	$300

Bumper (40223)
1970s. Clear Lucite solidbody.

1974		$300	$400

De Luxe Folk Guitar
1970s. Resonator acoustic, mahogany back, sides and neck, Japanese import.

1974		$200	$300

Master Size 40178
1972-1977. Electric archtop, 2 pickups.

1972-1977		$200	$350

Violin-Shaped 12-String Electric 40176
1970s. Scroll headstock, 2 pickups, 500/1 control panel, bass side dot markers, sunburst.

1970s		$200	$300

Violin-Shaped Electric 40175
1970s. Scroll headstock, 2 pickups, 500/1 control panel, bass side dot markers, vibrato, sunburst.

1970s		$200	$350

White Styrene 1280 (solidbody)
1970s. Solid maple body covered with white styrene, 2 pickups, tremolo, bass side dot markers, white.

1970s		$200	$300

Contessa
1960s. Acoustic, semi-hollow archtop, solidbody and bass guitars made in Italy and imported by Hohner. They also made banjos.

Electric Solidbody
1967. Various models.

1967		$350	$450

Contreras
See listing for Manuel Contreras and Manuel Contreras II.

Coral
1967-1969. In '66 MCA bought Danelectro and in '67 introduced the Coral brand of guitars, basses and amps.

Firefly
1967-1969. Double-cut, f-holes, 2 pickups, with or without vibrato.

1967-1969		$550	$650

Hornet 2
1967-1969. Solidbody, 2 pickups, with or without vibrato.

1967-1969		$1,000	$1,600

Sitar
1967-1969. Six-string guitar with 13 drone strings and 3 pickups (2 under the 6 strings, 1 under the drones), kind of a USA-shaped body.

1967-1969		$2,000	$4,000

Córdoba
Line of classical guitars handmade in Portugal and imported by Guitar Salon International.

Conklin Jazz 8

1974 Conrad doubleneck

GUITARS

Corey James CJ Double

Cort Larry Coryell

MODEL YEAR	FEATURES	EXC. COND. LOW	HIGH
Classical			
2000s	Gipsy King	$900	$1,100
2000s	Higher-end	$500	$600
2000s	Mid-level	$300	$475
2000s	Student-level	$225	$275

Cordova

1960s. Classical nylon string guitars imported by David Wexler of Chicago.

Grand Concert Model WC-026

1960s. Highest model offered by Cordova, 1-piece rosewood back, laminated rosewood sides, spruce top, natural.

1963		$200	$400

Corey James Custom Guitars

2005-present. Luthier Corey James Moilanen builds his professional and premium grade, production/custom solidbody guitars in Davisburg, Michigan. He also builds basses.

Coriani, Paolo

1984-present. Production/custom nylon-string guitars and hurdy-gurdys built by luthier Paolo Coriani in Modeila, Italy.

Cort

1973-present. North Brook, Illinois-based Cort offers budget, intermediate and professional grade, production/custom, acoustic and solidbody, semi-hollow, hollow body electric guitars built in Korea. They also offer basses.

Cort was the second significant Korean private-label (Hondo brand was the first) to come out of Korea. Jack Westheimer, based upon the success of Tommy Moore and Hondo, entered into an agreement with Korea's Cort to do Cort-brand, private-label, and Epiphone-brand guitars.

Doubleneck

Cherry, 6/12 necks, double-cut solidbody.

1970s		$400	$600

Electric

1973-present. A variety of models were offered. These guitars were heavily distributed in the '80s. Currently, new Cort models sell from $85 and each model should be evaluated on a model-by-model basis. The 2000s included a Matt 'Guitar' Murphy signature model and a Jim Triggs electric archtop.

1973-1989		$250	$400
1990-1999		$150	$300
1996-2005	Larry Coryell	$350	$450
1998-2005	Matt Murphy Signature	$350	$450
2002-2005	Jim Triggs Archtop	$400	$450

Crafter

2000-present. Line of intermediate and professional grade, production, acoustic and acoustic/electric guitars from Hohner. They also offer mandolins and a bass.

Acoustic Flat-Top

2000-present. Various production models.

2000-2005		$150	$300

Crafter USA

1986-present. Crafter offers budget and intermediate grade, production, classical, acoustic, acoustic/electric, and electric guitars made in Korea. They also build basses and amps. From '72 to '86 they made Sungeum classical guitars.

Crafters of Tennessee

See listing under Tennessee.

Cranium

1996-present. Professional grade, production/custom, hollow, semi-hollow, and solidbody electrics built by luthier Wayne O'Connor in Peterborough, Ontario.

Crescent Moon

1999-present. Professional grade, production/custom, solidbody guitars and basses built by luthier Craig Muller in Baltimore, Maryland.

Crestwood

1970s. Copies of the popular classical guitars, flat-tops, electric solidbodies and basses of the era, imported by La Playa Distributing Company of Detroit.

Electric

1970s. Various models include near copies of the 335 (Crestwood model 2043, 2045 and 2047), Les Paul Custom (2020), Strat (2073), Jazzmaster (2078), Tele (2082), and the SG Custom (2084).

1970s		$250	$350

Cromwell

1935-1939. Budget model brand built by Gibson and distributed by mail-order businesses like Grossman, Continental, and Richter & Phillips.

Acoustic Archtops

1935-1939. Archtop acoustic, f-holes, pressed mahogany back and sides, carved and bound top, bound back, 'guard and 'board, no truss rod.

1935-1939		$700	$900
1935-1939	With 1930s era pickup	$1,500	$2,500

Acoustic Flat-Tops

1935-1939	G-2 (L-00)	$1,100	$1,300

Tenor Guitar (Flat-top)

1935-1939	GT-2	$700	$900

Crown

1960s. Violin-shaped hollowbody electrics, solidbody electric guitars and basses, possibly others. Imported from Japan.

Acoustic Flat-Top

1960s. 6-string and 12-string.

1960s		$75	$150

MODEL YEAR	FEATURES	EXC. COND. LOW	HIGH

Electric Archtops
Double pointed cutaways, 2 humbucking pickups, laminated top, full-depth body.

1960s		$350	$450

Electric Solidbody/Semi-hollow
1960s. Student-level Japanese import.

1960s	Pointy violin-shaped body	$250	$300
1960s	Standard body styles	$125	$175

Crucianelli
Early 1960s. Italian guitars imported into the U.S. by Bennett Brothers of New York and Chicago around '63 to '64. Accordion builder Crucianelli also made Imperial, Elite, PANaramic, and Elli-Sound brand guitars.

Cumpiano
1974-present. Professional and premium grade, custom steel-string and nylon-string guitars, and acoustic basses built by luthier William Cumpiano in Northampton, Massachusetts.

Custom
1980s. Line of solidbody guitars and basses introduced in the early '80s by Charles Lawing and Chris Lovell, owners of Strings & Things in Memphis, Tennessee.

Custom Kraft
Late-1960s. A house brand of St. Louis Music Supply, instruments built by Valco, Chicago. They also offered basses.

Sound Saturator
1960s. 12-string.

1960s		$275	$400

Super Zapp
1960s.

1960s		$275	$400

D'Agostino
1976-early 1990s. Acoustic and electric solidbody guitars and basses imported by PMS Music, founded in New York City by former Maestro executive Pat D'Agostino, his brother Steven D'Agostino, and Mike Confortti. First dreadnought acoustic guitars imported from Japan in '76. First solidbodies manufactured by the EKO custom shop beginning in '77. In '82 solidbody production moved to Japan. Beginning in '84, D'Agostinos were made in Korea. Overall, about 60% of guitars were Japanese, 40% Korean. They also had basses.

Acoustic Flat-Top
1976-1990. Early production in Japan, by mid-'80s, most production in Korea.

1970s		$150	$300

Electric Semi-Hollowbody
1981-early 1990s. Early production in Japan, later versions from Korea.

1980s		$225	$300

MODEL YEAR	FEATURES	EXC. COND. LOW	HIGH

Electric Solidbody
1977-early 1990s. Early models made in Italy, later versions from Japan and Korea.

1970s		$225	$300

Daily Guitars
1976-present. Luthier David Daily builds his premium grade, production/custom classical guitars in Sparks, Nevada.

Daion
1978-1985. Mid- to higher-quality copies imported from Japan. Original designs introduced in the '80s. They also had basses.

Acoustic Guitars
1978-1985. Various flat top models.

1978-1985		$250	$650

Electric Guitars
1978-1985. Various solid and semi-hollow body guitars.

1978-1985		$450	$800

Daisy Rock
2001-present. Budget and intermediate grade, production, full-scale and 3/4 scale, solidbody, semi-hollow, acoustic, and acoustic/electric guitars. Founded by Tish Ciravolo as a Division of Schecter Guitars, the Daisy line is focused on female customers. Initial offerings included daisy and heart-shaped electric guitars and basses.

Electric or Acoustic
2001-present. Various models and features.

2001-2005		$150	$200

D'Ambrosio
2001-present. Luthier Otto D'Ambrosio builds his premium grade, custom/production, acoustic and electric archtop guitars in Providence, Rhode Island.

Dan Armstrong
Dan Armstrong started playing jazz in Cleveland in the late-'50s. He moved to New York and also started doing repairs, eventually opening his own store on 48th Street in '65. By the late-'60s he was designing his Lucite guitars for Ampeg (see Ampeg for those listings). He moved to England in '71, where he developed his line of colored stomp boxes. He returned to the States in '75. Armstrong died in '04.

Wood Body Guitar
1973-1975. Sliding pickup, wood body, brown.

1973-1975		$3,500	$4,500

Danelectro
1946-1969, 1996-present. Founded in Red Bank, New Jersey, by Nathan I. (Nate or Nat) Daniel, an electronics enthusiast with amplifier experience. In 1933, Daniel built amps for Thor's Bargain Basement in New York. In '34 he was recruited by Epiphone's Herb Sunshine to build earliest Electar

1981 D'Agostino LP500

Daisy Rock Heartbreaker

Danelectro Convertible

Danelectro Guitarlin

amps and pickup-making equipment. From '35 to '42, he operated Daniel Electric Laboratories in Manhattan, supplying Epiphone. He started Danelectro in '46 and made his first amps for Montgomery Ward in '47. Over the years, Danelectro made amplifiers, solidbody, semi-hollow and hollowbody electric guitars and basses, electric sitar, and the Bellzouki under the Danelectro, Silvertone, and Coral brands. In '48, began supplying Silvertone amps for Sears (various coverings), with his own brand (brown leatherette) distributed by Targ and Dinner as Danelectro and S.S. Maxwell. He developed an electronic vibrato in '48 on his Vibravox series amps. In '50 he developed a microphone with volume and tone controls and outboard Echo Box reverb unit. In the fall of '54, Danelectro replaced Harmony as provider of Silvertone solidbody guitars for Sears.

Also in '54, the first Danelectro brand guitars appeared with tweed covering, bell headstock, and pickups under the pickguard. The Coke bottle headstock debuts as Silvertone Lightning Bolt in '54, and was used on Danelectros for '56 to '66. The company moved to Red Bank, New Jersey in '57, and in '58 relocated to Neptune, New Jersey. In '59, Harmony and Kay guitars replace all but 3 Danelectros in Sears catalog. In '66, MCA buys the company (Daniel remains with company), but by mid-'69, MCA halts production and closes the doors. Some leftover stock is sold to Dan Armstrong, who had a shop in New York at the time. Armstrong assembled several hundred Danelectro guitars as Dan Armstrong Modified with his own pickup design.

Rights to name acquired by Anthony Marc in late-'80s, who assembled a number of thinline hollowbody guitars, many with Longhorn shape, using Japanese-made bodies and original Danelectro necks and hardware. In '96, the Evets Corporation, of San Clemente, California, introduced a line of effects bearing the Danelectro brand. Amps and guitars, many of which were reissues of the earlier instruments, soon followed. In early 2003, Evets discontinued offering guitar and amps, but revived the guitar and bass line in '05.

MCA-Danelectro made guitars were called the Dane Series. Dane A model numbers start with an A (e.g. A2V), Dane B models start with a B (e.g. B3V), Dane C (e.g. C2N), and Dane D (e.g. D2N). The least expensive series was the A, going up to the most expensive D. All Dane Series instruments came with 1, 2 or 3 pickups and with hand vibrato options. The Dane Series were made from '67 to '69. MCA did carry over the Convertible, Guitarlin 4123, Long Horn Bass-4 and Bass-6 and Doubleneck 3923. MCA also offered the Bellzouki Double Pickup 7021. Each Dane Series includes an electric 12-string.

Baritone 6-String Reissue
1990s-2000s. Single cutaway, 6-string baritone tuning.

MODEL YEAR	FEATURES	EXC. COND. LOW	HIGH
1990s		$275	$475

Bellzouki
1961-1969. 12-string electric, teardrop-shaped body, single pickup, sunburst. Vincent Bell model has modified teardrop shape with 2 body points on both treble and bass bouts and 2 pickups.

MODEL YEAR	FEATURES	EXC. COND. LOW	HIGH
1960s	Single pickup	$800	$1,000
1960s	Vincent Bell, 2 pickups	$1,000	$1,200

Convertible
1959-1969, 1999-2000. Acoustic/electric, double-cut, guitar was sold with or without the removable single pickup.

1959-1969	Pickup installed	$500	$700
1959-1969	Acoustic, no pickup	$400	$500

Dane A Series
1967-1969. 1 and 2 pickup models, solid wood slab body, hard lacquer finish with 4 color options.

1967-1969		$450	$500

Dane B Series
1967-1969. 1 and 3 pickup models, semi-solid Durabody.

1967-1969		$500	$550

Dane C Series
1967-1969. 2 and 3 pickup models, semi-solid Durabody with 2-tone Gator finish.

1967-1969		$500	$550

Dane D Series
1967-1969. 2 and 3 pickup models, solid wood sculptured thinline body, 'floating adjustable pickguard-fingerguide', master volume with 4 switches.

1967-1969		$500	$550

Deluxe Double Pickup (6028)
Double-cut, 2 pointer knobs, 2 pickups, standard-size pickguard, master control knob, white (6026), dark walnut (6027), honey walnut (6028).

1960s		$800	$900

Deluxe Triple Pickup (6037)
Double-cut, 3 pointer knobs, 3 pickups, standard-size pickguard, master control knob, white (6036), dark walnut (6037), honey walnut (6038).

1960s		$1,100	$1,200

Doubleneck (3923)
1959-1969. A Shorthorn double-cut, bass and 6-string necks, 1 pickup on each neck, Coke bottle headstocks, white sunburst.

1959-1969		$1,500	$2,500

Electric Sitar
1967-1969. Traditional looking, oval-bodied sitar, no drone strings as on the Coral Sitar of the same period.

1967-1969		$1,000	$2,000

Guitaralin (4123)
1963-1969. The Longhorn guitar, with 2 huge cutaways, 32-fret neck, and 2 pickups.

1963-1969		$1,500	$2,400

Hand Vibrato Single Pickup (4011)
1960s. One pickup, double-cut, batwing headstock, simple design vibrato, black.

1960s		$400	$600

MODEL YEAR	FEATURES	EXC. COND. LOW	HIGH

Hand Vibrato Double Pickup (4021)
1960s. Two pickups, double-cut, batwing headstock, simple design vibrato, black.

| 1960s | | $600 | $700 |

Model C
1955-ca.1958. Single-cut, 1 pickup.

| 1955-1958 | | $500 | $600 |

Pro 1
1963-ca.1964. Odd-shaped double-cut electric with squared off corners, 1 pickup.

| 1963-1964 | | $600 | $700 |

Standard Single Pickup
1958-1967. A Shorthorn double-cut, 1 pickup, 2 regular control knobs, seal-shaped pickguard, Coke bottle headstock.

| 1958-1967 | | $600 | $700 |

Standard Double Pickup
1959-1967. A Shorthorn double-cut, 2 pickups, 2 stacked, concentric volume/tone controls, seal-shaped 'guard, Coke bottle headstock, black version of this guitar is often referred to as the Jimmy Page model because he occasionally used one.

| 1959-1967 | | $1,100 | $1,300 |

U-1
1956-ca.1960. Single-cut, 1 pickup, Coke bottle headstock.

| 1956-1960 | Custom color | $1,000 | $1,200 |
| 1956-1960 | Standard color | $600 | $900 |

U-1 '56 Reissue
1998-1999. Single-cut semi-hollow, masonite top and bottom, bolt-on neck, reissue of '56 U-1, with single 'lipstick tube' pickup, various colors.

| 1998-1999 | | $125 | $175 |

U-2
1956-1959. Single-cut, 2 pickups, stacked concentric volume/tone controls, Coke bottle headstock.

| 1956-1959 | Standard color | $800 | $1,100 |

U-2 '56 Reissue
1998-2003. 2 pickup U-1.

| 1998-2003 | | $175 | $225 |

U-3 '56 Reissue
1999-2003. Single-cut reissue of '56 U-3 with 3 'lipstick tube' pickups, various colors.

| 1999-2003 | | $200 | $275 |

D'Angelico

John D'Angelico built his own line of archtop guitars, mandolins and violins from 1932 until his death in 1964. His instruments are some of the most sought-after by collectors.

D'Angelico (L-5 Snakehead)
1932-1935. D'Angelico's L-5-style with snakehead headstock, his first model, sunburst.

| 1932-1935 | | $12,500 | $15,000 |

Excel/Exel (Cutaway)
1947-1964. Cutaway, 17" width, 1- and 3-ply bound f-hole, Larry Wexer noted from '50-'57, D'Angelico guitars suffer from severe binding problems and many have replaced bindings. Replaced bindings make the guitar non-original and these repaired guitars have lower values.

MODEL YEAR	FEATURES	EXC. COND. LOW	HIGH
1947-1949	Natural, non-original binding	$19,000	$24,000
1947-1949	Natural, original binding	$35,000	$45,000
1947-1949	Sunburst, non-original binding	$14,000	$18,000
1947-1949	Sunburst, original binding	$33,000	$42,000
1950-1959	Natural, non-original binding	$19,000	$24,000
1950-1959	Natural, original binding	$33,000	$42,000
1950-1959	Sunburst, non-original binding	$14,000	$18,000
1950-1959	Sunburst, original binding	$33,000	$42,000
1960-1964	Natural	$33,000	$42,000
1960-1964	Sunburst	$33,000	$42,000

Excel/Exel (Non-cutaway)
1936-1949. Non-cut, 17" width, 1- and 3-ply bound f-hole, natural finishes were typically not offered in the '30s, non-cut Excels were generally not offered after '49 in deference to the Excel cutaway.

1936-1939	Sunburst, straight f-hole	$17,000	$22,000
1938-1939	Sunburst, standard f-hole	$17,000	$22,000
1940-1949	Natural	$17,000	$22,000
1940-1949	Sunburst, standard f-hole	$15,000	$19,000

New Yorker (Cutaway)
1947-1964. Cutaway, 18" width, 5-ply-bound f-hole, New Yorker non-cut orders were overshadowed by the cut model orders starting in '47, all prices noted are for original bindings, non-original (replaced) bindings will reduce the value by 33%-50%.

1947-1949	Natural, 4 made	$61,000	$70,000
1947-1949	Sunburst	$48,000	$56,000
1950-1959	Natural	$60,000	$70,000
1950-1959	Sunburst	$48,000	$56,000
1960-1964	Natural	$60,000	$70,000
1960-1964	Sunburst	$48,000	$56,000

New Yorker (Non-cutaway)
1936-1949. Non-cut, 18" width, 5-ply-bound f-hole, New Yorker non-cut orders were overshadowed by the cut model orders starting in '47, all prices noted are for original bindings, non-original (replaced) bindings will reduce the value by 33%-50%.

1936-1939	Sunburst	$21,000	$25,000
1940-1949	Natural	$25,000	$29,000
1940-1949	Sunburst	$24,000	$28,000

New Yorker Special
1947-1964. Also called Excel New Yorker or Excel Cutaway New Yorker Cutaway, 17" width, New Yorker styling, prices are for original bindings, non-original (replaced) bindings reduce values by 33%-50%, not to be confused with D'Angelico Special (A and B style).

| 1947-1964 | Natural | $36,000 | $42,000 |
| 1947-1964 | Sunburst | $30,000 | $37,000 |

1957 Danelectro U-1

1960 D'Angelico New Yorker

D'Angelico New Yorker NYL-2

D'Aquisto custom oval-hole

MODEL YEAR	FEATURES	EXC. COND. LOW	HIGH

Special
1947-1964. Generally Style A and B-type instruments made for musicians on a budget, plain specs with little ornamentation, not to be confused with New Yorker Special.

1947-1964	Natural	$14,000	$16,000
1947-1964	Sunburst	$11,000	$13,000

Style A
1936-1945. Archtop, 17" width, unbound f-holes, block 'board inlays, multi-pointed headstock, nickel-plated metal parts.

1936-1939	Sunburst	$10,000	$12,000
1940-1945	Sunburst	$9,500	$11,000

Style A-1
1936-1945. Unbound f-holes, 17" width, arched headstock, nickel-plated metal parts.

1936-1939	Sunburst	$10,000	$12,000
1940-1945	Sunburst	$9,500	$11,000

Style B
1933-1948. Archtop 17" wide, unbound f-holes, block 'board inlays, gold-plated parts.

1936-1939	Sunburst	$11,000	$13,000
1940-1948	Sunburst	$10,000	$12,000

Style B Special
1933-1948. D'Angelico described variations from standard features with a 'Special' designation, Vintage dealers may also describe these instruments as 'Special'.

1936-1939	Sunburst	$13,000	$15,000
1940-1948	Sunburst	$13,000	$15,000

D'Angelico (Vestax)
1988-present. Premium and presentation grade, production/custom, archtop, flat-top, and solidbody guitars built by luthier Hidesato Shino and Vestax near Tokyo, Japan. Distributed in the U.S. by D'Angelico Guitars of America, in Westfield, New Jersey.

New Yorker NYL-2
17" single-cut archtop, spruce top, figured maple back and sides.

2000s	Natural	$2,400	$2,700

D'Angelico II
Mid-1990s. Archtops built in the U.S. and distributed by Archtop Enterprises of Merrick, New York.

Jazz Classic
1990s. Electric archtop, cutaway, carved spruce top, figured maple back and sides, single neck pickup, transparent cherry.

1990s		$4,000	$4,400

Daniel Friederich
1955-present. Luthier Daniel Friederich builds his custom/production, classical guitars in Paris, France.

D'Aquisto
1965-1995. James D'Aquisto apprenticed under D'Angelico until the latter's death, at age 59, in '64.

He started making his own brand instruments in '65 and built archtop and flat top acoustic guitars, solidbody and hollowbody electric guitars. He also designed guitars for Hagstrom and Fender. He died in '95, at age 59.

Avant Garde
1987-1994. 18" wide, non-traditional futuristic model, approximately 5 or 6 instruments were reportedly made, because of low production this pricing is for guidance only.

1990	Blond	$80,000	$125,000

Centura/Centura Deluxe
1994 only. 17" wide, non-traditional art deco futuristic archtop, approximately 10 made, the last guitars made by this luthier, due to the low production this pricing is for guidance only.

1994	Blond	$80,000	$100,000

Excel (Cutaway)
1965-1992. Archtop, 17" width, with modern thin-logo started in '81.

1965-1967	Blond	$53,000	$55,000
1965-1967	Sunburst	$45,000	$53,000
1968-1979	Blond	$43,000	$46,000
1968-1979	Sunburst	$33,000	$40,000
1980-1989	Blond	$53,000	$55,000
1980-1989	Sunburst	$40,000	$42,000
1990-1992	Blond	$53,000	$55,000
1990-1992	Sunburst	$40,000	$42,000

Excel (Flat-Top)
1980s. Flat-top, 16", flamed maple back and sides, Sitka spruce top, about 15 made, narrow Excel-style headstock, oval soundhole, D'Aquisto script logo on headstock.

1980s		$15,000	$20,000

Hollow Electric
Early model with bar pickup, D'Aquisto headstock, '70s model with humbuckers.

1965	Sunburst	$12,000	$14,000
1972	Sunburst	$12,000	$14,000

Jim Hall
Hollow-body electric, carved spruce top, 1 pickup.

1965	Laminate top	$12,000	$14,000
1978	Solid top	$12,000	$14,000

New Yorker Classic (Solidbody)
1980s. Only 2 were reported to be made, therefore this pricing is for guidance only.

1980s		$18,000	$20,000

New Yorker Deluxe (Cutaway)
1965-1992. Most are 18" wide.

1965-1967	Blond	$55,000	$65,000
1965-1967	Sunburst	$50,000	$65,000
1968-1979	Blond	$50,000	$55,000
1968-1979	Sunburst	$50,000	$53,000
1980-1989	Blond	$50,000	$55,000
1980-1989	Sunburst	$50,000	$53,000
1990-1992	Blond	$53,000	$55,000
1990-1992	Sunburst	$53,000	$55,000

New Yorker Special (7-String)
1980s. Limited production 7-string, single-cut.

1980s	Sunburst	$48,000	$50,000

The **Vintage Guitar Price Guide** shows low to high values for items in all-original excellent condition, and, where applicable, with original case or cover.

MODEL YEAR	FEATURES	EXC. COND. LOW	HIGH

New Yorker Special (Cutaway)
1966-1992. Most are 17" wide.

1966-1967	Blond	$55,000	$63,000
1966-1967	Sunburst	$50,000	$63,000
1970-1979	Blond	$45,000	$50,000
1970-1979	Sunburst	$45,000	$50,000
1980-1989	Blond	$47,000	$50,000
1980-1989	Sunburst	$47,000	$50,000
1990-1992	Blond	$53,000	$55,000
1990-1992	Sunburst	$53,000	$55,000

Solo/Solo Deluxe
1992-1993. 18" wide, non-traditional non-cut art deco model, only 2 reported made, because of low production this pricing is for guidance only.

1992-1993	Blond	$80,000	$100,000

D'Aquisto (Aria)
May 2002-present. Premium grade, production, D'Aquisto designs licensed to Aria of Japan by D'Aquisto Strings, Inc., Deer Park, New York.

DQ-CR
2002-present. Similar to D'Aquisto Centura.

2002-2005		$1,900	$2,300

Dauphin
1970s-present. Classical and flamenco guitars built in Spain.

Classical
Solid spruce top, rosewood back and sides.

1980-2000		$600	$900

Dave King Acoustics
1980-present. Premium grade, custom/production, acoustic and resonator guitars built by luthier Dave King in Reading, Berkshire, U.K.

Dave Maize Acoustic Guitars
1991-present. Luthier Dave Maize builds his professional and premium grade, production/custom, flat-tops in Cave Junction, Oregon. He also builds basses.

David Rubio
1960s-2000. Luthier David Spink built his guitars, lutes, violins, violas, cellos and harpsichords first in New York, and after '67, in England. While playing in Spain, he acquired the nickname Rubio, after his red beard. He died in '00.

David Thomas McNaught
1989-present. Professional, premium, and presentation grade, custom, solidbody guitars built by luthier David Thomas McNaught and finished by Dave Mansel in Locust, North Carolina. In '97, they added the production/custom DTM line of guitars.

Solidbody High-End
2000s. High-end solidbody with indepth inlay (rhino, moonscape), heavily figured wood, various styles.

2000s		$4,000	$6,000

Vintage Double-Cut
Classic/modern offset double-cut, figured maple top, 2 exposed humbuckers.

2002		$3,300	$3,600

Vintage Standard

2003		$3,300	$3,600

Davis, J. Thomas
1975-present. Premium and presentation grade, custom, steel-string flat-tops, 12-strings, classicals, archtops, Irish citterns and flat-top Irish bouzoukis made by luthier J. Thomas Davis in Columbus, Ohio.

Davoli
See Wandre listing.

de Jonge, Sergei
1972-present. Premium grade, production/custom classical and steel-string guitars built by luthier Sergei de Jonge originally in Oshawa, Ontario, and since '04 in Chelsea, Quebec.

De Paule Stringed Instruments
1969-1980, 1993-present. Custom steel-string, nylon-string, archtop, resonator, and Hawaiian guitars built by luthier C. Andrew De Paule in Eugene, Oregon.

David Thomas McNaught Vintage Doublecut

Dean
1976-present. Intermediate, professional and premium grade, production/custom, solidbody, hollowbody, acoustic, acoustic/electric, and resonator guitars made in the U.S., Korea, the Czech Republic and China. They also offer basses, banjos, mandolins, and amps. Founded in Evanston, Illinois, by Dean Zelinsky. Original models were upscale versions of Gibson designs with glued necks, fancy tops, DiMarzio pickups and distinctive winged headstocks (V, Z and ML), with production beginning in '77. In '80 the factory was relocated to Chicago. Dean's American manufacturing ends in '86 when all production shifts to Korea. In '91 Zelinsky sold the company to Tropical Music in Miami, Florida. For '93-'94 there was again limited U.S. (California) production of the E'Lite, Cadillac and ML models under the supervision of Zelinsky and Cory Wadley.

Korean versions were also produced. In '95, Elliott Rubinson's Armadillo Enterprises, of Clearwater, Florida, bought the Dean brand. In '97 and '98, Dean offered higher-end USA Custom Shop models. In '98, they reintroduced acoustics. In 2000, Zelinsky once again became involved in the company.

Baby ML
1982-1986. Downsized version of ML model.

1980s	Import	$375	$425
1980s	U.S.-made	$575	$725

Dean Baby ML

1983 Dean Bel Air

Dean Heirloom

MODEL YEAR	FEATURES	EXC. COND. LOW	HIGH
Baby V			
1982-1986. Downsized version of the V model.			
1980s	Import	$350	$400
1980s	U.S.-made	$500	$650
Baby Z			
1982-1986. Downsized version of the Z model.			
1980s	Import	$350	$400
1980s	U.S.-made	$550	$700
Bel Aire			
1983-1984. Solidbody, possibly the first production guitar with humbucker/single/single pickup layout, U.S.-made, an import model was introduced in '87.			
1980s	Import	$300	$350
1983-1984	U.S.-made	$550	$750
Budweiser Guitar			
Ca.1987. Shaped like Bud logo.			
1987		$550	$750
Cadillac (USA)			
1979-1985. Single long treble horn on slab body.			
1979-1985		$1,200	$1,300
Cadillac Deluxe (USA)			
1993-1994, 1996-1997. Made in U.S., single longhorn shape, various colors.			
1993-1994		$1,200	$1,600
1996-1997		$1,200	$1,600
Cadillac Reissue (Import)			
1992-1994. Single longhorn shape, 2 humbuckers, various colors.			
1992-1994		$400	$450
Cadillac Standard			
1996-1997. Slab body version.			
1996-1997		$1,200	$1,300
Dime O Flame (ML)			
2005-present. ML-body, Dimebuckers, burning flames finish, Dime logo on headstock.			
2005		$450	$550
Eighty-Eight			
1987-1990. Offset double-cut solidbody, import.			
1987-1990		$175	$275
E'Lite			
1978-1985, 1994-1996. Single-horn shape.			
1978-1985		$900	$1,000
1994-1996		$900	$1,000
E'Lite Deluxe			
Single-horn shape.			
1980s		$1,200	$1,600
Golden E'Lite			
Single pointy treble cutaway, fork headstock, gold hardware, ebony 'board, sunburst.			
1980		$1,200	$1,600
Hollywood Z (Import)			
1985-1986. Bolt-neck Japanese copy of Baby Z, Explorer shape.			
1985-1986		$175	$200
Jammer (Import)			
1987-1989. Offset double-cut body, bolt-on neck, dot markers, six-on-a-side tuners, various colors offered.			
1987-1989		$175	$225

MODEL YEAR	FEATURES	EXC. COND. LOW	HIGH
Mach I (Import)			
1985-1986. Limited run from Korea, Mach V with six-on-a-side tunes, various colors.			
1985-1986		$175	$225
Mach V (Import)			
1985-1986. Pointed solidbody, 2 humbucking pickups, maple neck, ebony 'board, locking trem, various colors, limited run from Korea.			
1985-1986		$175	$225
Mach VII (USA)			
1985-1986. Mach I styling, made in America, offered in unusual finishes.			
1985-1986		$1,000	$1,200
ML (Import)			
1983-1990. Korean-made.			
1983-1990		$425	$475
ML (ML Standard/US-made)			
1977-1986. There is a flame model and a standard model.			
1977-1986	Burst flamed top	$1,450	$1,600
1977-1986	Burst plain top	$1,400	$1,550
1977-1986	Common opaque finish	$800	$1,500
1977-1986	Less common finish	$1,500	$2,300
V Standard (USA)			
1977-1986. V body, there is a standard and a flame model offered.			
1977-1986	Burst flamed top	$1,450	$1,600
1977-1986	Burst plain top	$1,400	$1,550
1977-1986	Common opaque finish	$800	$1,500
1977-1986	Less common finish	$1,500	$2,300
Z Autograph (Import)			
1985-1987. The first Dean import from Korea, offset double-cut, bolt neck, dot markers, offered in several standard colors.			
1985-1987		$250	$350
Z Coupe/Z Deluxe (USA Custom Shop)			
1997-1998. Mahogany body offered in several standard colors, Z Deluxe with Floyd Rose tremolo.			
1997-1998		$1,100	$1,200
Z Korina (USA Custom Shop)			
1997-1998. Z Coupe with korina body, various standard colors.			
1997-1998		$1,200	$1,300
Z LTD (USA Custom Shop)			
1997-1998. Z Coupe with bound neck and headstock, offered in several standard colors.			
1997-1998		$1,200	$1,300
Z Standard (USA)			
1977-1986. Long treble cutaway solidbody, 2 humbuckers.			
1977-1983	Common finish	$800	$1,500
1977-1983	Less common finish	$1,500	$2,300

MODEL YEAR	FEATURES	EXC. COND. LOW	HIGH

Dean Markley

The string and pickup manufacturer offered a limited line of guitars and basses for a time in the '80s. They were introduced in '84.

DeArmond Guitars

1999-2004. Solid, semi-hollow and hollow body guitars based on Guild models and imported from Korea by Fender. They also offered basses. The DeArmond brand was originally used on pickups, effects and amps built by Rowe Industries.

Electric

1999-2004. Various import models, some with USA electronic components.

1999-2004	Jet Star (Polara style)	$200	$300
1999-2004	Starfire Special (Single cut)	$350	$450
1999-2004	Starfire (Double cut)	$450	$550
1999-2004	X155 (Duane Eddy style)	$500	$600
2000-2004	Baja Jet Baritone	$450	$550
2000-2004	M-75T (Bluesbird)	$350	$450

Dearstone

1993-present. Luthier Ray Dearstone builds his professional and premium grade, custom, archtop and acoustic/electric guitars in Blountville, Tennessee. He also builds mandolin family instruments and violins.

DeCava Guitars

1983-present. Professional and premium grade, production/custom, archtop and classical guitars built by luthier Jim DeCava in Stratford, Connecticut. He also builds ukes, banjos, and mandolins.

Decca

Mid-1960s. Acoustic, solid and hollow body guitars made in Japan by Teisco and imported by Decca Records, Decca headstock logo, student-level instruments. They also offered amps and a bass.

Acoustic Flat-Top

1960s. Decca label on the inside back.

1960s		$100	$175

DeGennaro

2003-present. Premium grade, custom/production, acoustic, archtop, semi-hollow and solidbody guitars built by luthier William Degennaro in Grand Rapids, Michigan. He also builds basses and mandolins.

Del Pilar Guitars

1956-1986. Luthier William Del Pilar made his classical guitars in Brooklyn, New York.

Classical (Mahogany)

1980s. Mahogany back and sides, spruce top, red and green rosette.

1980s		$1,400	$1,500

Classical (Rosewood)

1950s. Brazilian rosewood back and sides, cedar top, quilt rosette, 9-ply top binding.

1950s		$3,500	$4,000

Del Vecchio

1902-present. Casa Del Vecchio builds a variety of Spanish instruments including acoustic and resonator guitars in São Paulo, Brazil.

Dell'Arte

1997-present. Production/custom Maccaferri-style guitars from John Kinnard and Alain Cola. In '96, luthier John Kinnard opened a small shop called Finegold Guitars and Mandolins. In '98 he met Alain Cola, a long time jazz guitarist who was selling Mexican-made copies of Selmer/Maccaferri guitars under the Dell'Arte brand. Cola wanted better workmanship for his guitars, and in October '98, Finegold and Dell'Arte merged. As of May '99 all production is in California.

Anouman Custom

1990s		$1,200	$1,800

Delta Guitars

2005-present. Acoustic, acoustic/electric, and solidbody electric guitars from Musician's Wholesale America, Nashville, Tennessee.

Dennis Hill Guitars

1991-present. Premium and presentation grade, production/custom, classical and flamenco guitars built by luthier Dennis Hill in Panama City, Florida. He has also built dulcimers, mandolins, and violins.

Desmond Guitars

1991-present. Luthier Robert B. Desmond builds his premium grade, production/custom classical guitars in Orlando, Florida.

DeTemple

1995-present. Premium grade, production/custom, solidbody electric guitars built by luthier Michael DeTemple in Sherman Oaks, California. He also builds basses.

DeVoe Guitars

1975-present. Luthier Lester DeVoe builds his premium grade, production/custom flamenco and classical guitars in Nipomo, California.

Diamond

Ca. 1963-1964. Line of sparkle finish solidbody guitars made in Italy for the Diamond Accordion company.

Ranger

Ca. 1963-1964. Rangers came with 1, 2, 3, or 4 pickups, sparkle finish.

1960s	4 pickups	$500	$700

Dell'Arte Anouman Custom

DeVoe archtop

Dillion DSR 300

DiPinto Galaxie 4

MODEL YEAR	FEATURES	EXC. COND. LOW	HIGH

Dick, Edward Victor

1975-present. Luthier Edward Dick currently builds his premium grade, custom, classical guitars in Denver, Colorado (he lived in Peterborough and Ottawa, Ontario until '95). He also operates the Colorado School of Lutherie.

Dickerson

1937-1947. Founded by the Dickerson brothers in '37, primarily for electric lap steels and small amps. Instruments were also private branded for Cleveland's Oahu company, and for the Gourley brand. By '47, the company changed ownership and was renamed Magna Electronics (Magnatone).

Dillion

2000-present. Dillion, of Cary, North Carolina, offers intermediate grade, production, acoustic, acoustic/electric, hollow-body and solidbody guitars made in Korea and Vietnam. They also have basses and mandolins.

Electric Solidbodies

2000-present. Includes various models.

MODEL YEAR	FEATURES	EXC. COND. LOW	HIGH
2000-2005		$200	$450

Dillon

1975-present. Professional and premium grade, custom, flat-tops built by luthier John Dillon originally in Taos, New Mexico ('75-'81), then in Bloomsburg, Pennsylvania ('81-'01), and since 2001 back in Taos. He also builds basses.

DiPinto

1995-present. Intermediate and professional grade, production retro-vibe guitars from luthier Chris DiPinto of Philadelphia, Pennsylvania. He also builds basses. Until late '99, all instruments built in the U.S., since then all built in Korea.

Ditson

1916-1930. Ditson guitars were made by Martin and sold by the Oliver Ditson Company of Boston. The majority of production was from '16 to '22 with over 500 units sold in '21.

Concert Models

1916-1922. Similar in size to Martin size 0. Models include Style 1, Style 2 and Style 3.

MODEL YEAR	FEATURES	EXC. COND. LOW	HIGH
1916-1922	Style 1	$2,500	$6,000
1916-1922	Style 2	$3,500	$7,000
1916-1922	Style 3	$4,000	$8,000

Standard Models

1916-1922. Small body similar to Martin size 3, plain styling. Models include Style 1, Style 2 and Style 3.

MODEL YEAR	FEATURES	EXC. COND. LOW	HIGH
1916-1922	Style 1	$1,500	$3,000
1916-1922	Style 2	$2,000	$4,000
1916-1922	Style 3	$3,000	$6,000

Style 111 Dreadnought

Dreadnought-sized exceeding the Martin 000 size, initially intended to be a 6-string bass guitar, fan bracing on the top generally requires extensive restoration.

MODEL YEAR	FEATURES	EXC. COND. LOW	HIGH
1916-1922	.-	$4,000	$8,000

D'Leco Guitars

1991-present. Luthier James W. Dale builds his premium grade, production/custom archtops in Oklahoma City, Oklahoma.

DM Darling Guitars

2006-present. Luthier Denis Merrill builds his professional and premium grade, custom, acoustic, classical, resonator and solidbody guitars in Tacoma, Washington. From 1978 to '06 he built under his own name and Merrill Custom Shop. He also builds mandolin family instruments.

Dobro

1929-1942, ca. 1954-present. Currently, professional and premium grade, production, wood and metal body resophonic guitars offered by Gibson.

Founded 1929 in Los Angeles by John Dopyera, Rudy Dopyera, Ed Dopyera and Vic Smith (Dobro stands for "Dopyera Brothers"). Made instruments sold under the Dobro, Regal, Norwood Chimes, Angelus, Rex, Broman, Montgomery Ward, Penetro, Bruno, Alhambra, More Harmony, Orpheum, and Magn-o-tone brands.

Dobro instruments have a single cone facing outward with a spider bridge structure and competed with National products. Generally, model names are numbers referring to list price and therefore materials and workmanship (e.g., a No. 65 cost $65). Because of this, the same model number may apply to various different instruments. However, model numbers are never identified on instruments!

In '30, the company name was changed to Dobro Corporation, Ltd. In '32, Louis Dopyera buys Ted Kleinmeyer's share of National. Louis, Rudy and Ed now hold controlling interest in National, but in '32 John Dopyera left Dobro to pursue idea of metal resophonic violin. In December of '34 Ed Dopyera joins National's board of directors (he's also still on Dobro board), and by March of '35 Dobro and National have merged to become the National Dobro Corporation. Dobro moves into National's larger factory but continues to maintain separate production, sales and distribution until relocation to Chicago is complete. Beginning in early-'36 National Dobro starts relocating its offices to Chicago. L.A. production of Dobros continues until '37, after which some guitars continue to be assembled from parts until '39, when the L.A. operations were closed down.

All resonator production ended in '42. Victor Smith, Al Frost and Louis Dopyera buy the company and change the name to the Valco Manufacturing Company. The Dobro name does not appear when production resumes after World War II.

In mid-'50s - some sources say as early as '54 - Rudy and Ed Dopyera began assembling wood-bodied Dobros from old parts using the name DB Original. In about '59, some 12-fret DB Originals were made for Standel, carrying both DB Original and Standel logos. In around '61, production was moved to Gardena, California, and Louis Dopyera and Valco transferred the Dobro name to Rudy and Ed, who produce the so-called Gardena Dobros. At this time, the modern Dobro logo appeared with a lyre that looks like 2 back-to-back '6s'. Dobro Original debuts ca. '62. In late-'64 the Dobro name was licensed to Ed's son Emil (Ed, Jr.) Dopyera. Ed, Jr. designs a more rounded Dobro (very similar to later Mosrites) and has falling out with Rudy over it.

In '66 Semi Moseley acquires the rights to the Dobro brand, building some in Gardena, and later moving to Bakersfield, California. Moseley introduced Ed, Jr's design plus a thinline double-cutaway Dobro. Moseley Dobros use either Dobro or National cones. In '67 Ed, Sr., Rudy and Gabriella Lazar start the Original Music Instrument Company (OMI) and produce Hound Dog brand Dobros. In '68 Moseley goes bankrupt and in '70 OMI obtains the rights to the Dobro brand and begins production of OMI Dobros. In '75 Gabriella's son and daughter, Ron Lazar and Dee Garland, take over OMI. Rudy Dupyera makes and sells Safari brand resonator mandolins. Ed, Sr. dies in '77 and Rudy in '78. In '84 OMI was sold to Chester and Betty Lizak. Both wood and metal-bodied Dobros produced in Huntington Beach, California. Chester Lizak died in '92. Gibson purchased Dobro in '93 and now makes Dobros in Nashville, Tennessee.

Dobros generally feature a serial number which, combined with historical information, provides a clue to dating. For prewar L.A. guitars, see approximation chart below adapted from Gruhn and Carter's Gruhn's Guide to Vintage Guitars (Miller Freeman, 1991). No information exists on DB Originals.

Gardena Dobros had D prefix plus 3 digits beginning with 100 and going into the 500s (reportedly under 500 made). No information is available on Moseley Dobros.

OMI Dobros from '70-'79 have either D prefix for wood bodies or B prefix for metal bodies, plus 3 or 4 numbers for ranking, space, then a single digit for year (D XXXX Y or B XXX Y; e.g., D 172 8 would be wood body #172 from '78). For '80-'87 OMI Dobros, start with first number of year (decade) plus 3 or 4 ranking numbers, space, then year and either D for wood or B for metal bodies (8 XXXX YD or 8 XXX YB; e.g., 8 2006 5B would be metal body #2008 from '85). From '88-'92, at least, a letter and number indicate guitar style, plus 3 or 4 digits for ranking, letter for neck style, 2 digits for year, and letter for body style (AX XXXX NYYD or AX XXX NYYB).

L.A. Guitars (approx. number ranges, not actual production totals)

1929-30	900-2999
1930-31	3000-3999
1931-32	BXXX (Cyclops models only)
1932-33	5000-5599
1934-36	5700-7699

MODEL YEAR	FEATURES	EXC. COND. LOW	HIGH
Angelus			
1933-1937. Wood body, round or square neck, 2-tone walnut finish, continues as Model 19 in Regal-made guitars.			
1933-1937	Round neck	$800	$1,800
1933-1937	Square neck	$1,000	$2,000
Artist M-16			
1934-1935. German silver alloy body, engraved.			
1934-1935	H Square neck	$3,500	$3,900
1934-1935	M Round neck	$6,500	$7,000
Cyclops 45			
1932-1933. Bound walnut body, 1 screen hole.			
1932-1933	Round neck	$2,500	$3,500
1932-1933	Square neck	$2,500	$3,500
D-40 Texarkana			
1965-1967. Mosrite-era (identified by C or D prefix), traditional Dobro style cone and coverplate, dot inlays, Dobro logo on headstock, sunburst wood body. Red and blue finishes available.			
1965-1967	Sunburst, square neck	$1,200	$1,500
D-40E Texarkana			
1965-1967. D-40 electric with single pickup and 2 knobs.			
1965-1967		$1,400	$1,600
DM-33 California Girl/DM-33H			
1996-2004. Chrome-plated bell brass body, biscuit bridge, spider resonator, rosewood 'board. Girl or Hawaiian-scene (H) engraving.			
2000s		$1,400	$1,800
Dobro/Regal 46/47			
1935-1938 Dobro/Regal 46, renamed 47 1939-1942. Made by Regal of Chicago, aluminum body, round neck, 14 frets, slotted peghead, silver finish. Degraded finish was a common problem with the Dobro/Regal 47.			
1935-1938	Model 46	$1,200	$1,300
1939-1942	Model 47, degraded finish	$600	$800
1939-1942	Model 47, original finish	$1,900	$2,000
Dobro/Regal 62/65			
1935-1938 Dobro/Regal 62, continued as Dobro/Regal 65 for 1939-1942. Nickel-plated brass body, Spanish dancer etching, round or square neck. Note: Dobro/Regal 65 should not be confused with Dobro Model 65 which discontinued earlier.			
1935-1938	Model 62, round neck	$3,000	$3,600
1935-1938	Model 62, square neck	$2,000	$2,600
1939-1942	Model 65, round neck	$3,000	$3,600
1939-1942	Model 65, square neck	$2,000	$2,600
Dobro/Regal Tenor 27-1/2			
1930. Tenor version of Model 27.			
1930		$800	$900
Dobrolektric			
1998-2005. Resonator guitar with single-coil neck pickup, single-cut.			
1998-2005		$1,000	$1,150

Dobro DM-33H

1930s Dobro Model 45

Dobro Josh Graves signature model

Dobro Classic 60

MODEL YEAR	FEATURES	EXC. COND. LOW	HIGH
DS-33/Steel 33			
1995-2000. Steel body with light amber sunburst finish, resonator with coverplate, biscuit bridge.			
1995-2000		$1,200	$1,300
DW-90C			
2000s. Single sharp cutaway, wood body, metal resonator, F-hole upper bass bout.			
2000s		$1,400	$1,500
Hula Blues			
1980s-1990s. Dark brown wood body (earlier models have much lighter finish), painted Hawaiian scenes, round neck.			
1985-1990s		$900	$1,100
Josh Graves			
1996-present. Single bound ample body, spider cone, nickel plated.			
1996-2005		$2,400	$2,600
Leader 14M/14H			
1934-1935. Nickel plated brass body, segmented f-holes.			
1934-1935	H Square neck	$2,000	$3,000
1934-1935	M Round neck	$1,500	$2,500
Model 27 (OMI)			
1980s		$1,200	$1,300
Model 27 Cyclops			
1932-1933.			
1932-1933	Round neck	$1,600	$1,800
1932-1933	Square neck	$2,000	$2,500
Model 27 Deluxe			
1996-2005. Square neck.			
1996-2005		$1,500	$1,700
Model 27/27G			
1933-1937. Regal-made, wooden body.			
1933-1937	Round neck	$1,200	$1,500
1933-1937	Square neck	$2,000	$2,250
Model 33 (Duolian)			
1972. Only made in '72, becomes Model 90 in '73.			
1972		$1,100	$1,500
Model 33 H			
1973-1997 (OMI & Gibson). Same as 33 D, but with etched Hawaiian scenes, available as round or square neck.			
1980s	Round neck	$1,550	$1,700
1980s	Square neck	$1,550	$1,700
Model 36			
1932-1937. Wood body with resonator, round or square neck.			
1932-1937	Round neck	$1,500	$1,750
1932-1937	Square neck	$2,200	$2,600
Model 36 S			
1970-1980s. Chrome-plated brass body, square neck, slotted headstock, dot markers, engraved rose floral art.			
1970-1980s		$1,500	$1,600
Model 37			
1933-1937. Regal-made wood body, mahogany, bound body and 'board, round or square 12-fret neck.			
1933-1937	Round neck	$1,500	$2,000

MODEL YEAR	FEATURES	EXC. COND. LOW	HIGH
Model 37 Tenor			
1933-1937 (Regal). Tenor version of No. 37.			
1933-1937		$1,200	$1,800
Model 55/56 Standard			
1929-1931 Model 55 Standard, renamed 56 Standard 1932-1934. Unbound wood body, metal resonator, bound neck, sunburst.			
1929-1931	Model 55	$2,300	$2,500
1932-1934	Model 56	$2,300	$2,500
Model 60			
1933-1936. Similar to Model 66/66B.			
1933-1936	Round neck	$5,000	$5,500
1933-1936	Square neck	$7,000	$7,500
Model 60 Cyclops			
1932-1933.			
1932-1933		$4,700	$5,500
Model 60 Series			
1970-1993. Wood body (laminated maple) with Dobro resonator cone, model 60 until '73 when renamed 60 D, and various 60 model features offered, post-'93 was Gibson-owned production.			
1970-1973	Model 60	$1,000	$1,200
1973-1980s	Model 60 D	$1,000	$1,200
1980s	Model 60 DS	$1,100	$1,300
Model 65/66/66 B			
1920s-1930s. Wood body with sandblasted ornamental design top and back, metal resonator, sunburst. Model 66 B has bound top.			
1929-1931	Model 65	$3,000	$4,000
1932-1933	Model 66	$3,000	$4,000
1932-1933	Model 66 B	$3,000	$4,000
Model 66 Cyclops			
1978		$1,100	$1,300
Model 90 (Duolian) (OMI)			
1972-1993. Chrome-plated, f-holes, etched Hawaiian scene.			
1972-1993		$1,300	$1,500
Model 90 (Woodbody)/WB90 G / WB90 S			
1994-2005. Maple body with upper bout f-holes or sound holes, round neck, metal resonator with spider bridge, sunburst.			
1994-2005		$1,200	$1,500
Model 125 De Luxe			
1929-1934. Black walnut body, round or square neck, Dobro De Luxe engraved, triple-bound top, back and 'board, nickel-plated hardware, natural.			
1929-1934	Round neck	$6,000	$10,000
1929-1934	Square neck	$11,000	$15,000
Professional 15M/15H			
1934-1935. Engraved nickel body, round (M) or square (H) neck, solid peghead.			
1934-1935	H square neck	$3,200	$3,500
1934-1935	M round neck	$2,700	$3,000

Dodge

1996-present. Luthier Rick Dodge builds his intermediate and professional grade, production, solidbody guitars with changeable electronic modules in Tallahassee, Florida. He also builds basses.

MODEL YEAR	FEATURES	EXC. COND. LOW	HIGH

Domino

Ca. 1967-1968. Solidbody and hollowbody electric guitars and basses imported from Japan by Maurice Lipsky Music Co. of New York, New York, previously responsible for marketing the Orpheum brand. Models are primarily near-copies of EKO, Vox, and Fender designs, plus some originals. Models were made by Arai or Kawai. Earlier models may have been imported, but this is not yet documented.

Electric

1967-1968. Various models include the Baron, Californian, Californian Rebel, Dawson, and the Spartan.

1967-1968		$375	$475

Dommenget

1978-1985, 1988-present. Luthier Boris Dommenget (pronounced dommen-jay) builds his premium grade, custom/production, solidbody, flat-top, and archtop guitars in Balje, Germany. From '78 to '85 he was located in Wiesbaden, and from '88-'01 in Hamburg. He and wife Fiona also make pickups.

Don Musser Guitars

1976-present. Custom, classical and flat-top guitars built by luthier Don Musser in Cotopaxi, Colorado.

Doolin Guitars

1997-present. Luthier Mike Doolin builds his premium grade, production/custom acoustics featuring his unique double-cut in Portland, Oregon.

Dorado

Ca. 1972-1973. Six- and 12-string acoustic guitars, solidbody electrics and basses. Brand used briefly by Baldwin/Gretsch on line of Japanese imports.

Acoustic Flat-Top/Acoustic Dobro

1972-1973. Includes folk D, jumbo Western, and grand concert styles (with laminated (?) rosewood back and sides), and Dobro-style.

1970s	Higher-range models	$175	$250
1970s	Lower-range models	$75	$150
1970s	Mid-range models	$125	$200

Solidbody Electric

1972-1973. Includes Model 5985, a double-cuty with 2 P-90-style pickups.

1970s		$125	$225

Douglas Ching

1976-present. Luthier Douglas J. Ching builds his premium grade, production/custom, classical, acoustic, and harp guitars currently in Chester, Virginia, and previously in Hawaii ('76-'89) and Michigan ('90-'93). He also builds ukes, lutes and violins.

D'Pergo Custom Guitars

2002-present. Professional, premium, and presentation grade, production/custom, solidbody guitars built in Windham, New Hampshire. Every component of the guitars is built by D'Pergo.

Dragge Guitars

1982-present. Luthier Peter Dragge builds his custom, steel-string and nylon-string guitars in Ojai, California.

Dragonfly Guitars

1994-present. Professional grade, production/custom, sloped cutaway flat-tops, semi-hollow body electrics, and dulcitars built by luthier Dan Richter in Roberts Creek, British Columbia.

Drive

2000s. Student imports. Drive logo placed inside a rectangular border on the headstock.

DTM

1997-present. See David Thomas McNaught listing.

Duesenberg

1995-present. Professional and premium grade, production/custom, solid and hollow body electric guitars built by luthier Dieter Goelsdorf in Hannover, Germany. They also build basses. Rockinger had a Duesenberg guitar in the 1980s.

Dunwell Guitars

1996-present. Professional and premium grade, custom, flat-tops built by luthier Alan Dunwell in Nederland, Colorado.

Dupont

Luthier Maurice Dupont builds his classical, archtop, Weissenborn-style and Selmer-style guitars in Cognac, France.

Dyer

1910s-1925. Dyer was a house brand of William John Dyer's St. Paul, Minnesota, music store. The instruments were built by Knutsen. He also carried Stetson brand instruments made by the Larson Brothers.

Harp Guitar

1920s	Style 6	$5,300	$5,700

Dynacord

1950-present. Dynacord is a German company that makes audio and pro sound amps, as well as other electronic equipment. In 1966-'67 they offered solidbody guitars and basses from the Welson Company of Italy. They also had the Cora guitar and bass which is the center part of a guitar body with a tube frame in a guitar outline. They also offered tape echo machines.

Earthwood

1972-1985. Acoustic designs by Ernie Ball with input from George Fullerton. One of the first to offer acoustic basses.

1967 Domino Baron

Dunwell parlor guitar

Eastwood Airline

1982 EKO CO-2 Cobra

MODEL YEAR	FEATURES	EXC. COND. LOW	HIGH

Eastman

1992-present. Professional and premium grade, production, archtop and flat-top guitars mainly built in China, with some from Germany and Romania. Beijing, China-based Eastman Strings started out building violins and cellos. They added guitars in '02 and mandolins in '04.

Eastwood

1997-present. Mike Robinson's company imports budget and intermediate grade, production, solid and semi-hollowbody guitars, many styled after 1960s models. They also offer basses.

Airline J.B. Hutto Copy
2004. Supro/Airline copy, 6 knobs and switch on bass side of body, 1 knob near input jack on lower treble bout, 3 pickups, blue or white.

2004		$400	$500

Airline Jack White Copy
2004. Supro/Airline copy of Jack White's guitar, 4 knobs and toggle switch on treble side of body, block markers, 3 pickups, red or sunburst.

2004		$400	$500

Eaton, William

1976-present. Luthier William Eaton builds custom specialty instruments such as vihuelas, harp guitars, and lyres in Phoenix, Arizona. He is also the Director of the Robetto-Venn School of Luthiery.

Ed Claxton Guitars

1972-present. Premium grade, custom flat-tops made by luthier Ed Claxton, first in Austin, Texas, and currently in Santa Cruz, California.

Eduardo Duran Ferrer

1987-present. Luthier Eduardo Duran Ferrer builds his premium grade, classical guitars in Granada, Spain.

Egmond

1935-1972. Founded by Ulke Egmond, building acoustic, archtop, semi-hollow and solidbody guitars originally in Eindhoven, later in Best Holland. They also made basses. Egmond also produced instruments under the Orpheum (imported into U.S.) Rosetti (England), Miller, Wilson and Lion brand names.

Electric
1960s. Solid or semi-hollow bodies.

1960s		$300	$400

Ehlers

1985-present. Luthier Rob Ehlers builds his premium grade, production/custom, flat-top acoustic guitars in Oregon.

15 CRC
Cutaway, Western red cedar top, Indian rosewood back and sides.

1996		$2,800	$3,000

MODEL YEAR	FEATURES	EXC. COND. LOW	HIGH

15 SRC
Cutaway, European spruce top, Indian rosewood back and sides.

1998		$2,900	$3,100

16 BTM
European spruce top, mahogany back and sides, Troubadour peghead, black lacquer finish.

1998		$2,900	$3,100

16 SK Concert
16" lower bout, relatively small upper bout, small waist, European spruce top, flamed koa back and sides, diamond markers, natural.

1993		$2,400	$2,600

16 SM
European spruce top, mahogany back and sides.

1999		$2,400	$2,500

16 SSC
Cutaway, European spruce top, English sycamore back and sides.

1996		$3,000	$3,200

25 C
Limited Edition Anniversary Model, European spruce top, Indian rosewood back and sides, abalone top border.

2001		$3,900	$4,100

Eichelbaum Guitars

1994-present. Luthier David Eichelbaum builds his premium grade, custom, flat-tops in Santa Barbara, California.

EKO

1959-1985, 2000-present. Originally acoustic, acoustic/electric, electric thinline and full-size archtop hollowbody, solidbody electric guitars and basses built by Oliviero Pigini and Company in Recanati, Italy, and imported by LoDuca Brothers, Milwaukee, Radio and Television Equipment Company in Santa Ana, California and others.

First acoustic guitars followed by sparkle plastic-covered electrics by '62. Sparkle finishes are gone ca. '66.

Pigini dies ca. '67. LoDuca Bros. phases out in early-'70s. By '75 EKO offers some copy guitars and they purchased a custom shop to make other brands by '78.

Since about 2000, budget and intermediate grade, production, classical, acoustic, acoustic/electric, solidbody, solidbody, and hollowbody EKO guitars are again available and made in Asia. They also make basses and amps. They will soon have the Italian-made Vintage Series available.

Barracuda/Barracuda 12-String
1966-ca.1978. Double-cut semi-hollow, 2 pickups, 6- or 12-string.

1966-1978	6- and 12-string	$450	$550

Cobra I/II/III/XII
1966-1978. Double-cut solidbody, 2 knobs. Cobra I has 1 pickup, II 2 pickups and III 3 pickups. 12-string Cobra XII offered '67-'69, has 2 pickups.

1966-1978	Cobra I	$350	$400

MODEL YEAR	FEATURES	EXC. COND. LOW	HIGH
1966-1978	Cobra II	$400	$450
1966-1978	Cobra III	$450	$500
1967-1969	Cobra XII	$450	$500

Condor

1966-ca.1969. Double-cut solidbody with 3 or 4 pickups.

1966-1969		$500	$550

Dragon

1967-ca.1969. Single-cut archtop, 2 f-holes, 3 pickups, tremolo.

1967-1969		$500	$550

Flat-Top Acoustic

1960s. Various student-level flat-top acoustic models.

1960s		$200	$250

Florentine

1964-ca.1969. Double-cut archtop, 2 pickups.

1964-1969		$450	$550

Kadett/Kadett XII

1967-ca.1978. Double-cut solidbody with point on lower bass side of body, 3 pickups, tremolo. 12- string Kadett XII offered '68-'69.

1967-1978	Kadett	$450	$550
1968-1969	Kadett XII	$450	$550

Lancer

1967-ca.1969. Double-cut solidbody, 2 pickups.

1967-1969		$250	$350

Lark I/II

1970. Thin hollow cutaway, sunburst. Lark I has 1 pickup and Lark II 2.

1970	Lark I	$400	$450
1970	Lark II	$400	$450

Model 500/1 / 500/1V

1961-1964. Plastic covered solidbody, 1 pickup. 500/1 no vibrato, 1V with vibrato.

1961-1964	500/1	$300	$450
1961-1964	500/1V	$350	$500

Model 500/2 / 500/3V

1961-1964. Plastic covered solidbody, plastic sparkle finish. 500/2 no vibrato, 2 pickups. 3V with vibrato, 3 pickups.

1961-1964	500/2	$450	$650
1961-1964	500/3V	$550	$700

Model 500/4 / 500/4V

1961-1964. Plastic covered solidbody, 4 pickups. 500/4 no vibrato, 4V with vibrato.

1961-1964	500/4	$600	$750
1961-1964	500/4V	$650	$800

Model 540 (Classical)

1960s. Nylon-string classical guitar.

1960s		$200	$250

Model 700/3V

1961-1964. Map-shape/tulip-shape body, 3 pickups, vibrato, woodgrain plastic finish.

1961-1964		$900	$1,100

Model 700/4V

1961-1967. Map-shape/tulip-shape body, 4 pickups, multiple switches, vibrato.

1961-1967	Standard finish	$900	$1,100
1961-1967	Red, blue, silver sparkle	$1,100	$1,300

MODEL YEAR	FEATURES	EXC. COND. LOW	HIGH

Ranger 6/12

1967-ca.1982. D-size flat-top acoustic, large 3-point 'guard, dot inlays, EKO Ranger label. Ranger 12 is 12-string.

1967-1982	Ranger 12	$300	$450
1967-1982	Ranger 6	$250	$350

Rocket VI/XII (Rokes)

1967-ca.1969. Rocket-shape design, solidbody, 6-string, says Rokes on the headstock, Rokes were a popular English band that endorsed EKO guitars, marketed as the Rocket VI in the U.S.; and as the Rokes in Europe, often called the Rok. Rocket XII is 12-string.

1967-1969	Rocket VI	$600	$800
1967-1969	Rocket XII	$650	$800

El Degas

Early-1970s. Japanese-made copies of classic America electrics and acoustics, imported by Buegeleisen & Jacobson of New York, New York.

Solidbodies

Early-1970s. Copies of classic American models, including the Let's Play model.

1970s		$150	$250

Electar

See Epiphone listing.

Electra

1971-1984. Imported from Japan by St. Louis Music. Most instruments made by Matsumoku in Matsumoto, Japan. The Electra line replaced SLM's Japanese-made Apollo and U.S.-made Custom Kraft lines. First guitar, simply called The Electra, was a copy of the Ampeg Dan Armstrong lucite guitar and issued in '71, followed quickly by a variety of bolt-neck copies of other brands. In '75 the Tree-of-Life guitars debut with a leaf pattern carved into the top, and the Electra line expanded to 25 models. Open-book headstocks changed to wave or fan shape by '78. By around '81 ties with Matsumoku further solidified and decision eventually made to merge SLM's Electra brand with Matsumoku's Westone brand. Some Korean production begins in early-'80s. In the fall of '83, the Electra Brand becomes Electra Phoenix. By beginning of '84, the brand becomes Electra-Westone and by the end of '84 just Westone. Matsumoku-made guitars have serial number in which first 1 or 2 digits represent the year of manufacture. Thus a guitar with a serial number beginning in 0 or 80 would be from 1980.

Custom

1970s. Double-cut solidbody, 2 pickups, Custom logo on truss rod, cherry finish.

1970s		$400	$500

Elvin Bishop

1976-ca.1980. Double-cut semi-hollow body, tree-of-life inlay.

1976-1980		$700	$800

EKO 500/3V

1978 Electra MPC Standard

1981 Electra Outlaw

Elliot classical

MODEL YEAR	FEATURES	EXC. COND. LOW	HIGH

Flying Wedge
1970s. V body, six-on-a-side tuners.

1970s		$400	$500

MPC Outlaw
1976-1983. Has separate modules that plug in for different effects.

1976-1983		$500	$550
1976-1983	MPC plug in module	$50	$75

Omega
1976-ca. 1980. Single-cut solidbody, block inlays, Omega logo on truss rod, black with rosewood neck, or natural with figured top and maple neck.

1976-1980		$375	$500

Phoenix
1980-1984. Classic offset double-cut solidbody, Phoenix logo on headstock.

1980-1984		$250	$350

Rock
1971-1973. Single cut solidbody, becomes the Super Rock in '73.

1971-1973		$375	$525

Super Rock
1973-ca.1978. Renamed from Rock ('71-'73).

1973-1978		$375	$525

X145 60th Anniversary
1982. Classic offset double-cut only made one year, Anniversary plate on back of headstock, single/single/hum pickups.

1982		$250	$350

Electro
1964-1975. The Electro line was manufactured by Electro String Instruments and distributed by Radio-Tel. The Electro logo appeared on the headstock rather than Rickenbacker. Refer to the Rickenbacker section for models.

Elite
1960s. Guitars made in Italy by the Crucianelli accordion company, which made several other brands.

Elk
Late-1960s. Japanese-made by Elk Gakki Co., Ltd. Many were copies of American designs. They also offered amps and effects.

Elliott Guitars
1966-present. Premium and presentation grade, custom, nylon-string classical and steel-string guitars built by luthier Jeffrey Elliott in Portland, Oregon.

Elli-Sound
1960s. Guitars made in Italy by the Crucianelli accordion company, which made several other brands.

Emperador
1966-1992. Guitars and basses imported from Japan by Westheimer Musical Instruments.

Early models appear to be made by either Teisco or Kawai; later models were made by Cort.

Acoustic Archtop

1960s		$100	$200

Electric Solidbody

1960s		$100	$225

Encore
Late 1970s-present. Budget grade, production, classical, acoustic, and electric guitars imported by John Hornby Skewes & Co. in the U.K. They also offer basses.

English Electronics
1960s. Lansing, Michigan, company named after owner, some private branded guitars and amps by Valco (Chicago), many models with large English Electronics vertical logo on headstock.

Tonemaster
1965. National Val-Pro 84 with neck pickup and bridge mounted pickup, black.

1965		$650	$800

Epiphone
Ca. 1873-present. Budget, intermediate and professional grade, production, solidbody, archtop, acoustic, acoustic/electric, resonator, and classical guitars made in the U.S. and overseas. They also offer basses, amps, mandolins, ukes and banjos. Founded in Smyrna, Turkey, by Anastasios Stathopoulos and early instruments had his label. He emigrated to the U.S. in 1903 and changed the name to Stathoupoulo. Anastasios died in '15 and his son, Epaminondas ("Epi") took over. The name changed to House of Stathopoulo in '17 and the company incorporated in '23. In '24 the line of Epiphone Recording banjos debut and in '28 the company name was changed to the Epiphone Banjo Company. In '43 Epi Stathopoulo died and sons Orphie and Frixo took over. Labor trouble shut down the NYC factory in '51 and the company cut a deal with Conn/Continental and relocated to Philadelphia in '52. Frixo died in '57 and Gibson bought the company. Kalamazoo-made Gibson Epiphones debut in '58. In '69 American production ceased and Japanese imports began. Some Taiwanese guitars imported from '79-'81. Limited U.S. production resumed in '82 but sourcing shifted to Korea in '83. In '85 Norlin sold Gibson to Henry Juszkiewicz, Dave Barryman and Gary Zebrowski. In '92 Jim Rosenberg became president of the new Epiphone division.

AJ-500R (Flat-Top)
2004-present. Masterbuild Series, sloped shoulder D size, natural satin finish, solid spruce top, solid rosewood back and sides, pearl script logo.

2004-2005		$400	$425

Alley Cat
2000-present. Single cut small body archtop, I humbucker and 1 mini-humbucker.

2000-2005		$350	$400

GUITARS

MODEL YEAR	FEATURES	EXC. COND. LOW	HIGH
B.B. King Lucille			
1997-present. Laminated double-cut maple body, 2 humbuckers, Lucille on headstock.			
1997-2005		$500	$575
Barcelone (Classical)			
1963-1968. Highest model of Epiphone '60s classical guitars.			
1963-1964		$850	$950
1965-1968		$750	$850
Bard 12-String			
1962-1969. Flat-top, mahogany back and sides, natural or sunburst.			
1962-1964		$1,700	$2,100
1965-1966		$1,400	$1,700
1967-1969		$1,100	$1,400
Biscuit			
1997-2000, 2002-present. Wood body resonator, biscuit bridge, round neck.			
1997-2005		$300	$350
Blackstone			
1931-1950. Acoustic archtop, f-holes, sunburst.			
1933-1934	Masterbilt	$1,100	$1,400
1935-1937		$900	$1,200
1938-1939		$800	$1,100
1940-1941		$700	$1,000
1948-1949		$600	$1,000
Broadway (Acoustic)			
1931-1958. Non-cut acoustic archtop.			
1931-1938	Sunburst, walnut body	$2,700	$3,200
1939-1942	Sunburst, maple body	$2,700	$3,200
1946-1949	Natural	$2,700	$2,900
1946-1949	Sunburst	$2,400	$2,700
1950-1958	Sunburst	$2,300	$2,600
Broadway Regent (Acoustic Cutaway)			
1950-1958. Single-cut acoustic archtop, sunburst.			
1950-1958		$2,800	$3,200
Broadway (Electric)			
1958-1969. Gibson-made electric archtop, single-cut, 2 New York pickups (mini-humbucking pickups by '61), Frequensator tailpiece, block inlays, sunburst or natural finish with cherry optional in '67 only.			
1958-1959	Natural	$3,900	$4,300
1958-1959	Sunburst	$3,700	$4,100
1960-1964	Natural	$3,800	$4,000
1960-1964	Sunburst	$3,600	$3,900
1965	Natural	$3,700	$3,800
1965	Sunburst	$3,500	$3,600
1966-1967	Natural, cherry	$3,600	$3,700
1966-1967	Sunburst	$3,400	$3,500
1968-1969	Natural	$3,400	$3,600
1968-1969	Sunburst	$3,300	$3,400
Broadway Tenor			
1937-1953. Acoustic archtop, sunburst.			
1939		$1,000	$1,300
1950		$800	$1,100
Byron			
1949-ca.1955. Acoustic archtop, mahogany back and sides, sunburst.			
1949-1955		$350	$600

MODEL YEAR	FEATURES	EXC. COND. LOW	HIGH
Caiola Custom			
1963-1970. Introduced as Caiola, renamed Caiola Custom in '66, electric thinbody archtop, 2 mini-humbuckers, multi-bound top and back, block inlays, walnut or sunburst finish (walnut only by '68).			
1963-1964		$3,900	$4,400
1965		$3,700	$4,200
1966-1967		$3,500	$4,000
1968-1970		$3,400	$3,900
Caiola Standard			
1966-1970. Electric thinbody archtop, 2 P-90s, single-bound top and back, dot inlays, sunburst or cherry.			
1966-1967		$3,000	$3,600
1968-1970		$2,900	$3,400
Casino (1 Pickup)			
1961-1970. Thinline hollowbody, double-cut, 1 P-90 pickup.			
1961		$2,800	$3,000
1962-1964		$2,600	$2,800
1965-1966		$2,000	$2,600
1967-1968		$1,900	$2,500
1969-1970		$1,800	$2,300
Casino (2 Pickups)			
1961-1970. Two pickup (P-90) version. '61-'63 known as Keith Richards model, '64-'65 known as Beatles model.			
1961		$4,200	$5,000
1962-1964		$3,200	$4,200
1965-1966		$2,500	$3,200
1967-1970		$2,200	$3,100
Casino J.L. USA 1965			
2003. 1,965 made.			
2003		$1,800	$1,900
Casino Reissue			
1995-present. Sunburst.			
1995-1999		$450	$550
2000-2005		$425	$500
Century			
1939-1970. Thinline archtop, non-cut, 1 pickup, trapeze tailpiece, walnut finish, sunburst finish available in '58, Royal Burgundy available '61 and only sunburst finish available by '68.			
1949	Large rectangular pickup	$1,500	$2,000
1950	New York pickup	$1,500	$1,800
1951-1957	Sunburst	$1,400	$1,700
1958-1959	Sunburst, P-90 pickup	$1,600	$1,900
1960-1964	Sunburst, P-90 pickup	$1,500	$1,600
1965	Sunburst or cherry	$1,400	$1,500
1966-1967	Sunburst or cherry	$1,300	$1,400
1968-1970	Sunburst or cherry	$1,300	$1,400
Classic (Classical)			
1963-1970.			
1963-1964		$600	$700
1965-1970		$500	$600

Epiphone AJ-500R

1965 Epiphone Casino

1962 Epiphone Coronet

Epiphone Crestwood

MODEL YEAR	FEATURES	EXC. COND. LOW	HIGH

Collegiate
2004-2005. Les Paul-style body, 1 humbucker, various college graphic decals on body.

2004-2005		$200	$250

Coronet (Electric Archtop)
1939-1949. Electric archtop, laminated mahogany body, 1 pickup, trapeze tailpiece, sunburst, name continued as an electric solidbody in '58.

1939-1949		$1,200	$1,400

Coronet (Solidbody)
1958-1969. Solidbody electric, 1 New York pickup ('58-'59), 1 P-90 ('59-'69), cherry or black finish, Silver Fox finish available by '63, reintroduced as Coronet USA '90-'94, Korean-made '95-'98.

1958-1959		$2,000	$2,500
1960-1964		$1,900	$2,400
1966-1967		$1,500	$1,800
1968-1969		$1,400	$1,700

Coronet (Import)
1970s. Import electric, sunburst.

1970s		$350	$400

Coronet USA
1990-1994. Made in Nashville, reverse banana headstock, typical Coronet styled body, single-coil and humbucker.

1990-1994		$650	$800

Crestwood Custom
1958-1970. Solidbody, 2 New York pickups ('58-'60), 2 mini-humbuckers ('61-'70), symmetrical body and 3+3 tuners ('58-'62), asymmetrical and 1x6 tuners ('63-'70), slab body with no Gibson equivalent model.

1958-1960	Cherry, New York pickups, 3+3	$3,400	$3,900
1959-1960	Sunburst	$3,000	$3,500
1961-1962	Cherry, mini-humbuckers	$2,900	$3,600
1961-1962	White, mini-humbuckers	$3,500	$4,200
1963-1964	Cherry, 1x6	$2,900	$3,600
1963-1964	Pacific Blue, 1x6	$4,000	$7,000
1963-1964	White, 1x6	$3,400	$5,000
1965	Cherry	$2,700	$3,300
1965	Pacific Blue	$3,500	$6,000
1965	White	$3,200	$4,800
1966-1967	Cherry	$2,600	$3,200
1966-1967	Pacific Blue	$3,300	$5,000
1966-1967	White	$3,000	$3,500
1968-1970	Cherry, white	$2,600	$3,200

Crestwood Custom (Japan)
1970s.

1970s		$375	$425

Crestwood Deluxe
1963-1969. Solidbody with 3 mini-humbuckers, block inlay, cherry, white or Pacific Blue finish, 1x6 tuners.

1963-1964	Cherry	$4,100	$4,300
1963-1964	Pacific Blue	$4,700	$7,500
1963-1964	White	$4,600	$5,500
1965	Cherry	$4,000	$4,200
1965	Pacific Blue	$4,600	$6,500
1965	White	$4,500	$5,200
1966-1967	Cherry	$3,100	$3,700

MODEL YEAR	FEATURES	EXC. COND. LOW	HIGH
1966-1967	Pacific Blue	$3,700	$5,500
1966-1967	White	$3,500	$4,000
1968-1969	Cherry, white	$3,300	$3,700

De Luxe
1931-1957. Non-cut acoustic archtop, maple back and sides, trapeze tailpiece ('31-'37), frequensator tailpiece ('37-'57), gold-plated hardware, sunburst or natural finish.

1931-1934	Sunburst	$5,500	$6,000
1935-1939	Sunburst	$5,500	$5,900
1939	Natural, 1st year option	$6,200	$6,600
1940-1944	Natural	$6,000	$6,400
1940-1944	Sunburst	$5,500	$5,700
1945-1949	Natural	$5,300	$5,700
1945-1949	Sunburst	$4,700	$5,000
1950-1957	Natural	$5,000	$5,200
1950-1957	Sunburst	$4,000	$4,500

De Luxe Regent (Acoustic Archtop)
1948-1952. Acoustic cutaway archtop, high-end appointments, rounded cutaway, natural finish, renamed De Luxe Cutaway in '53.

1948-1952		$4,700	$6,000

De Luxe Cutaway/Deluxe Cutaway
1953-1970. Renamed from De Luxe Regent, cataloged Deluxe Cutaway by Gibson in '58, special order by '64 with limited production because acoustic archtops were pretty much replaced by electric archtops.

1953-1957	Epiphone NY-made	$4,500	$5,500
1958-1965	Gibson Kalamazoo, rounded cutaway	$5,000	$6,000
1965-1970	Special order only	$4,000	$6,000

De Luxe Electric (Archtop)
1954-1957. Single-cut electric archtop, 2 pickups, called the Zephyr De Luxe Regent from '48-'54. Produced with a variety of specs, maple or spruce tops, different inlays and pickup combinations.

1954-1957	Natural	$4,000	$5,000
1954-1957	Sunburst	$3,500	$4,500

Del Ray
1995-2000. Offset double-cut body, 2 blade humbuckers, dot markers, tune-o-matic, flamed maple top.

1995-2000		$300	$375

Devon
1949-1957. Acoustic archtop, non-cut, mahogany back and sides, sunburst finish, optional natural finish by '54.

1950-1953	Sunburst	$1,500	$2,000
1954-1957	Natural	$1,700	$2,200
1954-1957	Sunburst	$1,400	$1,800

Don Everly (SQ-180)
1997-2004. Jumbo acoustic reissue, large double 'guard, black gloss finish.

1997-2004		$500	$600

Dot (ES-335 Dot)/Dot Archtop
2000-present. Dot-neck ES-335.

2000-2005		$300	$350

The *Vintage Guitar Price Guide* shows low to high values for items in all-original excellent condition, and, where applicable, with original case or cover.

MODEL YEAR	FEATURES	EXC. COND. LOW	HIGH

Dot Studio
2004-present. Simplified Dot, 2 control knobs, black hardware.

2004-2005		$250	$275

Dwight
1963, 1967. Coronet labeled as Dwight for dealer, 75 made in '63 and 36 in '67, cherry.

1963		$1,900	$2,400
1967		$1,500	$1,800

EA/ET Series (Japan)
1970-1979. Production of the Epiphone brand was moved to Japan in '70. Models included the EA (electric thinline) and ET (electric solidbody).

1970-1975	ET-270	$275	$300
1970s	EA-250	$350	$450
1975-1979	ET-290	$350	$450

El Diablo
1994-1995. Offset double-cut acoustic/electric, onboard piezo and 3-band EQ, composite back and sides, spruce top, cherry sunburst.

1994-1995		$300	$350

Electar Model M
1935-1939. Epiphone's initial entry into the new electric guitar market of the mid-'30s, 14 3/4" laminate maple archtop, horseshoe pickup, trap door on back for electronics, Electar logo on headstock, oblong pickup replaces horseshoe in late-'37.

1935-1936	2 control knobs	$1,200	$1,400
1937-1939	3 control knobs	$1,200	$1,400

Electar Model M Tenor
1937-1939. 4-string electric tenor with Electar specs.

1937-1939	3 knobs, natural	$1,200	$1,400

Elitist Series
2003-present. Made in Japan, higher-grade series, using finer woods and inlays and U.S.-made Gibson pickups.

2003-2005	1961 SG Standard	$500	$550
2003-2005	1963 ES-335 Dot	$800	$850
2003-2005	Byrdland/L5	$1,000	$1,200
2003-2005	Casino	$950	$1,100
2005	Chet Atkins Country Gentleman	$950	$1,100
2003-2004	J-200	$950	$1,050
2003-2005	Les Paul Custom	$775	$800
2003-2005	Les Paul Standard	$700	$750
2003-2005	Les Paul Studio	$550	$600

Emperor (Acoustic Archtop)
1935-1957. Acoustic archtop, non-cut, maple back and sides, multi-bound body, gold-plated hardware, sunburst, optional natural finish by '39.

1935-1938	Sunburst	$7,000	$7,500
1939-1949	Natural	$7,500	$8,000
1939-1949	Sunburst	$6,500	$7,000
1950-1954	Natural	$6,000	$6,500
1950-1954	Sunburst	$5,500	$6,300

Emperor Regent
1948-1953. Acoustic archtop with rounded cutaway, renamed Emperor Cutaway in '53.

1948-1953	Natural	$8,000	$10,000
1948-1953	Sunburst	$7,500	$9,000

Emperor Cutaway
1953-1970 (Gibson-made 1958 on). Renamed from Emperor Regent, acoustic archtop, single-cut, maple back and sides, multi-bound body, gold-plated hardware, sunburst or natural finish.

1953-1957	Natural	$7,500	$9,500
1953-1957	Sunburst	$6,500	$8,500

Emperor Electric
1953-1957. Archtop, single-cut, 3 pickups, multibound body, sunburst, called the Zephyr Emperor Regent in '50-'53.

1953-1957		$4,300	$4,800

Emperor (Thinline Electric)
1958-1969. Single-cut, thinline archtop, 3 New York pickups in '58-'60, 3 mini-humbuckers '61 on, multibound, gold-plated hardware, sunburst or natural finish until '65 when only sunburst was made.

1958-1969	Natural	$12,000	$15,000
1958-1969	Sunburst	$11,000	$14,000
1960-1962	Natural	$11,000	$13,000
1960-1962	Sunburst	$10,000	$12,000
1963-1964	Special order only	$10,000	$12,000
1965-1968	Special order only	$8,000	$12,000

Emperor/Emperor II/Joe Pass Emperor II
1982-present. Single-cut archtop jazz guitar, 2 humbuckers, blocks, gold hardware. II added to name in '93, became Joe Pass Emperor II in '95, although his name was on the guitar as early as '91.

1982-2005		$500	$700

Entrada (Classical)
1963-1968. Classical, natural.

1963-1964		$600	$700
1965-1968		$500	$600

Espana (Classical)
1962-1968. Classical, maple back and sides, U.S.-made, natural, imported in '69 from Japan.

1962-1964		$700	$800
1965-1968		$600	$700

Exellente
1963-1969, 1994-1995. Flat-top, rosewood back and sides. Name revived on Gibson Montana insturment in '90s.

1963-1964		$6,500	$7,000
1965		$5,000	$5,500
1966-1967		$4,500	$5,000
1968-1969		$3,800	$4,500

1958 Korina Explorer
1998-present. Explorer with typical appointments, korina body. This guitar was produced with a variety of specs, ranging from maple tops to spruce tops, different inlay markers were also used, different pickup combinations have been seen, natural or sunburst finish.

1998-2005		$300	$400

Firebird
1995-2000. Two mini-humbuckers, Firebird Red, dot markers.

1995-2000		$350	$400

Firebird 300
1986-1988. Korean import, Firebird Red.

1986-1988		$250	$325

Epiphone Elitist Broadway

Epiphone Elitist '63 Dot

Epiphone Firebird

Epiphone FT-110

MODEL YEAR	FEATURES	EXC. COND. LOW	HIGH

Firebird 500
1986-1988. Korean import, Firebird Red.

| 1986-1988 | | $275 | $350 |

1963 Firebird VII/Firebird VII
2000-2005. Three mini-humbuckers, gold hardware, Maestro-style vibrato, block markers, Firebird Red, reverse body. 1963 added after first year.

| 2000-2005 | | $300 | $400 |

Flamekat
1999-2005. Archtop, flame finish, double dice position markers, 2 mini-humbuckers, Epiphone Bigsby.

| 1999-2003 | | $400 | $500 |

1958 Gothic Explorer/Flying V
2002-present. Flat black finish.

| 2002-2005 | | $300 | $400 |

1958 Korina Flying V
1998-present. Typical Flying V configuration, korina body.

| 1998-2005 | | $300 | $400 |

Flying V/'67 Flying V
1989-1998, 2003-2005. '67 or '58 specs, alder body, natural.

| 1989-1998 | '67 specs | $450 | $550 |
| 2003-2005 | '58 specs | $500 | $550 |

FT 30
1941-1949. Acoustic flat-top, brown stain, mahogany back and sides, reintroduced as Gibson-made FT 30 Caballero in '58.

| 1941-1949 | | $1,100 | $1,300 |

FT 30 Caballero
1958-1970. Reintroduced from Epiphone-made FT 30, Gibson-made acoustic flat-top, natural, all mahogany body, dot inlay, tenor available '63-'68.

1959		$950	$1,100
1960-1964		$650	$950
1965		$650	$800
1966-1967		$650	$725
1968-1970		$500	$700

FT 45
1941-1948. Acoustic flat-top, walnut back and sides, cherry neck, rosewood 'board, natural top, reintroduced as Gibson-made FT 45 Cortez in '58.

| 1941-1948 | | $1,400 | $1,500 |

FT 45 Cortez
1958-1969. Reintroduced from Epiphone-made FT 45, Gibson-made acoustic flat-top, mahogany back and sides, sunburst or natural top (sunburst only in '59-'62).

1958-1959	Sunburst	$1,300	$2,000
1960-1964	Sunburst or natural	$1,300	$1,800
1965	Sunburst or natural	$1,000	$1,500
1966-1967	Sunburst or natural	$950	$1,300
1968-1969	Sunburst or natural	$850	$1,100

FT 79
1941-1958. Acoustic 16" flat-top, square shoulder dreadnought, walnut back and sides until '49 and laminated maple back and sides '49 on, natural, renamed FT 79 Texan by Gibson in '58.

| 1941-1949 | Walnut back & sides | $3,100 | $3,300 |
| 1949-1958 | Laminated pressed maple body | $2,600 | $2,900 |

FT 79 Texan
1958-1970, 1993-1995. Renamed from Epiphone FT 79, Gibson-made acoustic flat-top, mahogany back and sides, sunburst or natural top, Gibson Montana made 170 in '93-'95.

1958-1959		$3,500	$3,800
1960-1964		$3,300	$3,600
1965		$2,800	$3,200
1966-1967		$2,500	$3,000
1968-1970		$2,200	$2,800

FT 85 Serenader 12-String
1963-1969. 12 strings, mahogany back and sides, dot inlay, natural.

1963-1964		$1,200	$1,600
1965-1966		$950	$1,300
1967-1969		$900	$1,100

FT 90 El Dorado
1963-1970. Dreadnought flat-top acoustic, mahogany back and sides, multi-bound front and back, natural.

1963-1964		$2,000	$2,800
1965		$1,900	$2,700
1966-1967		$1,800	$2,600
1968-1970		$1,700	$2,500

FT 95 Folkster
1966-1969. 14" small body, mahogany back and sides, natural, double white 'guards.

| 1966-1967 | | $650 | $725 |
| 1968-1969 | | $500 | $700 |

FT 98 Troubadour
1963-1969. 16" square shouldered drednought, maple back and sides, gold-plated hardware, classical width 'board.

| 1963-1964 | | $1,700 | $1,900 |
| 1965-1969 | | $1,500 | $1,700 |

FT 110
1941-1958. Acoustic flat-top, natural, renamed the FT 110 Frontier by Gibson in '58.

1941-1949	Square shoulder	$3,200	$3,700
1949-1954	Round shoulder	$3,000	$3,300
1954-1958	Mahogany neck	$2,900	$3,200

FT 110 Frontier
1958-1970, 1994. Renamed from FT 110, acoustic flat-top, natural or sunburst, Gibson Montana made 30 in '94.

1958-1959		$2,700	$3,200
1960-1964		$2,200	$3,000
1965		$2,100	$2,900
1966-1967		$2,000	$2,800
1968-1970	Maple	$1,900	$2,700

FT Series (Flat-Tops Japan)
1970s. In '70 Epiphone moved production to Japan. Various models were made, nearly all with bolt necks and small rectangular blue labels on the inside back.

1970s	FT 120	$50	$75
1970s	FT 130	$75	$100
1970s	FT 132, 133, 140	$100	$125
1970s	FT 135, 145, 146, 160N, 160 12-String	$175	$200
1970s	FT 150	$250	$300

MODEL YEAR	FEATURES	EXC. COND. LOW	HIGH
1970s	FT 155, 165 12-String, 350	$275	$325
1970s	FT 200 Monticello	$225	$250
1970s	FT 550, 565 12-String, 570SB SuperJumbo	$300	$350

G 310

1989-present. SG-style model with large 'guard and gig bag.

1989-2005		$100	$200

G 400

1989-present. SG-style, 2 humbuckers, crown inlays.

1989-2005		$300	$350

G 400 Custom

1998-2000, 2003-present. 3 humbucker version, gold harware, block inlays.

1998-2005		$400	$450

G 400 Deluxe

1999-present. Flame maple top version of 2 humbucker 400.

1999-2005		$375	$425

G 400 Limited Edition

2001-2002. 400 with Deluxe Maestro lyra vibrola, cherry red.

2001-2002		$450	$500

G 400 Tony Iommi

2003-present. SG-style model with cross 'board inlay markers, black finish.

2003-2005		$450	$500

G 1275 Custom Double Neck

1996-present. 6- & 12-string, SG-style alder body, maple top, mahogany neck, cherry red, set neck. Also offered as bolt-neck Standard for '96-'98.

1996-2005		$600	$800

Genesis

1979-1980. Double-cut solidbody, 2 humbuckers with coil-taps, carved top, red or black, available as Custom, Deluxe, and Standard models, Taiwan import.

1979-1980		$425	$600

Granada (Non-cutaway Thinbody)

1962-1969. Non-cut thinline archtop, 1 f-hole, 1 pickup, trapeze tailpiece, sunburst finish.

1962-1965		$900	$1,000
1966-1969		$600	$800

Granada (Cutaway)

1965-1970. Single-cut version.

1965-1966		$1,200	$1,300
1967-1970		$900	$1,100

Howard Roberts Standard

1964-1970. Single-cut acoustic archtop, bound front and back, cherry or sunburst finish, listed in catalog as acoustic but built as electric.

1964		$3,000	$3,500
1965-1967		$2,500	$3,000
1968-1970		$2,000	$3,000

Howard Roberts Custom

1965-1970. Single-cut archtop, bound front and back, 1 pickup, walnut finish (natural offered '66 only).

1965-1967		$3,000	$4,000
1968-1970		$2,500	$3,500

Howard Roberts III

1987-1991. Two pickups, various colors.

1987-1991		$575	$600

Joe Pass/Joe Pass Emperor II

1994-present. ES-175-style with rounded cutaway, block markers, 2 humbuckers, various colors.

1994-2004		$575	$600

Les Paul Black Beauty 3

1997-present. Classic styling with three gold plated pickups, black finish, block markers.

1997-2005		$450	$550

Les Paul Custom

1989-present. Various colors.

1989-2005		$425	$500

Les Paul Custom Plus (Flame Top)

1998-present. Flamed maple top version of 2 pickup Custom, gold hardware, sunburst.

1998-2005		$450	$550

Les Paul Deluxe

1998-2000. Typical mini-humbucker pickups.

1998-2000		$400	$450

Les Paul LP-100

1993-present. Affordable single-cut Les Paul, bolt-on neck.

1993-2005		$100	$200

Les Paul Sparkle L.E.

2001. Limited Edition LP Standard, silver, purple, red (and others) glitter finish, optional Bigsby.

2001		$425	$500

Les Paul Special

1994-2000. Double-cut, bolt neck.

1994-2000		$200	$250

Les Paul Special II

1996-present. Economical Les Paul, 2 pickups, single-cut, various colors.

1996-2005	Guitar only	$75	$150
1996-2005	Player Pack with amp	$100	$200

Les Paul Standard

1989-present. Solid mahogany body, carved maple top, 2 humbuckers.

1989-2005		$275	$375

Les Paul Standard Baritone

2004-2005. 27-3/4" long-scale baritone model.

2004-2005		$325	$400

Les Paul Standard Plus Top

2003-present. LP Standard figured curly maple sunburst top.

2003-2005		$300	$400

Les Paul Studio

1995-present. Epiphone's version of Gibson LP Studio.

1995-2000s		$300	$400

Les Paul Ultra

2005-present. LP Standard with chambered and contoured body, quilted maple top.

2005		$300	$400

Les Paul XII

1998-2000. 12-string solidbody, trapeze tailpiece, flamed maple sunburst, standard configuration.

1998-2000		$450	$550

Epiphone G-310

Epiphone Les Paul Special II

GUITARS

Epiphone Pro 2

1965 Epiphone Olympic

MODEL YEAR	FEATURES	EXC. COND. LOW	HIGH
Madrid (Classical)			
1962-1969. Classical, natural.			
1962-1964		$500	$550
1965-1969		$450	$500
Navarre			
1931-1940. Flat-top, mahogany back and sides, bound top and back, dot inlay, brown finish.			
1931-1937	Hawaiian, Masterbilt label	$1,750	$2,000
1938-1940	Hawaiian, standard label	$1,550	$1,800
Nighthawk Standard			
1995-2000. Epiphone's version of the Gibson Nighthawk, single-cut, bolt neck, figured top.			
1995-2000		$300	$375
Noel Gallagher Union Jack/Super Nova			
1997-2005. Limited edition, higher-end ES-335. Union Jack with British flag finish (introduced '99) or Supernova in solid blue.			
1997-2005		$500	$575
Olympic (Acoustic Archtop)			
1931-1949. Mahogany back and sides.			
1931-1939		$900	$1,000
1940-1949		$850	$1,000
Olympic Double (Solidbody)			
1960-1969. Slab body, the same as the mid-'60s Coronet, Wilshire and Crestwood Series, single-cut '60-'62, asymmetrical-cut '63-'70, 2 Melody Maker single-coils, vibrato optional in '64 and standard by '65.			
1960-1962	Sunburst, single-cut	$1,500	$2,300
1963-1964	Sunburst, double-cut	$1,200	$1,600
1965-1969	Cherry or sunburst	$800	$1,200
Olympic Single (Solidbody)			
1960-1970. Slab body, the same as the mid-'60s Coronet, Wilshire and Crestwood Series, single-cut '60-'62, asymmetrical double-cut '63-'70, 2 Melody maker single-coil pickups, vibrato optional in '64 and standard by '65.			
1960-1962	Sunburst, single-cut	$1,300	$1,900
1963-1964	Sunburst, double-cut	$900	$1,400
1965-1970	Cherry or sunburst	$650	$1,000
Olympic (3/4 Scale Solidbody)			
1960-1963. 22" scale, sunburst.			
1960-1963		$600	$1,300
Olympic Special (Solidbody)			
1962-1970. Short neck with neck body joint at the 16th fret (instead of the 22nd), single Melody Maker-style single-coil bridge pickup, small headstock, double-cut slab body, dot markers, Maestro or Epiphone vibrato optional '64-'65, slab body contour changes in '65 from symmetrical to asymmetrical with slightly longer bass horn, sunburst.			
1964	Symmetrical	$1,200	$1,500
1965	Asymmetrical	$750	$1,200
1966-1967		$650	$1,000
1968-1970		$550	$900

MODEL YEAR	FEATURES	EXC. COND. LOW	HIGH
PR-200 (EA-20)			
1992-2000. Imported dreadnought, spruce top, satin finish, mahogany back and sides, natural.			
1992-2000		$150	$225
PR-350			
1984-2000. Acoustic flat-top, mahogany body, also available with a pickup.			
1984-2000		$175	$250
PR-350 CE			
1989-2000. Cutaway 350, also available with a pickup.			
1989-2000		$250	$325
PR-600 ACS/ASB/N			
1980-1985. Import 000-size flat-top, glued bridge, dot markers, sunburst.			
1980-1985		$350	$400
PR-755S			
1980-1985. Flat-top, single-cut, solid spruce top, laminate rosewood body, set mahogany neck, block markers, gold hardware, natural.			
1980-1985		$275	$325
Pro 1			
1989-1996. Solidbody, double-cut, 1 single-coil and 1 humbucking pickup, bolt-on neck, various colors.			
1989-1996		$325	$400
Pro 2			
1995-1998. Higher-end Pro 1 with Steinberger DB bridge, set-neck, 2 humbuckers, various colors.			
1995-1998		$350	$400
Professional			
1962-1967. Double-cut, thinline archtop, 1 pickup, mahogany finish.			
1962-1964	With matching Professional Amp	$2,200	$2,400
1965	With matching Professional Amp	$1,900	$2,200
1966-1967	With matching Professional Amp	$1,800	$1,900
Recording A			
1928-1931. Standard 6-string or tenor 4-string model.			
1928-1931		$1,600	$2,600
Recording B			
1928-1931. Asymmetrical body, cutaway bouts, flat-top, arched back, laminated maple back.			
1928-1931		$2,300	$3,300
Recording C			
1928-1931.			
1928-1931		$2,800	$3,500
Recording D			
1928-1931.			
1928-1931		$3,300	$4,000
Recording E			
1928-1931.			
1928-1931		$4,500	$5,000

MODEL YEAR	FEATURES	EXC. COND. LOW	HIGH

Riviera
1962-1970, 1993-1994. Double-cut thinline archtop, 2 mini-humbuckers, Royal Tan standard finish changing to sunburst in '65, cherry optional by '66-'70, additional 250 were made in Nashville in '93-'94, a Riviera import was available in '82 and for '94-present.

1962-1964	Tan or custom cherry	$3,200	$3,700
1965	Sunburst or cherry	$2,900	$3,500
1966-1967	Burgundy Mist	$3,000	$3,700
1966-1967	Sunburst or cherry	$2,600	$3,300
1967-1968	Walnut	$2,500	$3,200
1968-1969	Sunburst or cherry	$2,300	$3,000

Riviera Reissue (Korea)
1993-present. Korean-made contemporary reissue, natural.

1993-2005		$375	$450

Riviera 12-String
1965-1970. Double-cut, 12 strings, thinline archtop, 2 mini-humbuckers, sunburst or cherry.

1965		$2,600	$3,000
1966-1967		$2,100	$2,600
1968		$2,100	$2,600

Riviera 12-String Reissue (Korea)
1997-2000. Korean-made reissue, natural.

1997-2000		$425	$650

Royal
1931-1935. 15 1/2" acoustic archtop, mahogany back and sides, dot markers, sunburst, bound top, back and neck, Masterbilt headstock logo.

1931-1935		$2,900	$3,100

S-900
1986-1989. Neck-thru-body, locking Bender tremolo system, 2 pickups with individual switching and a coil-tap control.

1986-1989		$350	$425

Seville EC-100 (Classical)
1938-1941, 1961-1969 (Gibson-made). Classical guitar, mahogany back and sides, natural, the '61-'63 version also available with a pickup.

1961-1964		$650	$750
1965-1969		$550	$650

SG Special
2000-present. SG body, dot markers, 2 open-coil humbuckers.

2000-2005	Guitar only	$75	$150
2000-2005	Players Pack with amp	$100	$200

Sheraton
1958-1970, 1993-1994. Double-cut thinline archtop, 2 New York pickups '58-'60, 2 mini-humbuckers '61 on, frequensator tailpiece, multi-bound, gold-plated hardware, sunburst or natural finish with cherry optional by '65, an additional 250 American-made Sheratons were built

1958-1959	Natural, New York pickups	$9,000	$10,000
1960	Natural, New York pickups	$8,000	$9,000
1961-1964	Natural, mini-humbuckers	$8,000	$9,000
1961-1964	Sunburst, mini-humbuckers	$7,200	$7,500
1965	Cherry	$6,300	$7,200
1965	Natural	$7,000	$8,000
1965	Sunburst	$6,200	$7,000
1966	Sunburst or cherry	$6,100	$6,700
1967	Sunburst or cherry	$5,300	$6,500
1968	Sunburst or cherry	$5,100	$6,000
1969	Sunburst	$4,500	$5,500
1993-1994	Model reintroduced	$450	$525

Sheraton (Japan)
1978-1983. Early reissue, not to be confused with Sheraton II issued in late-'90s, natural or sunburst.

1978-1983		$400	$500

Sheraton II (Reissue)
1997-present. Contemporary reissue, natural or sunburst.

1997-2005		$450	$525

Slasher
2001. Reverse offset double cut solidbody, bolt neck, six-on-a-side tuners, 2 pickups, dot markers.

2001		$275	$300

Sorrento (1 pickup)
1960-1970. Single-cut thinline archtop, 1 pickup in neck position, tune-o-matic bridge, nickel-plated hardware, sunburst, natural or Royal Olive finish, (cherry or sunburst by '68).

1960-1964		$1,700	$2,000
1965-1966		$1,600	$1,700
1967-1970		$1,500	$1,600

Sorrento (2 pickups)
1960-1970. Single-cut thinline archtop, 2 pickups, tune-o-matic bridge, nickel-plated hardware, sunburst, natural or Royal Olive finish, (cherry or sunburst by '68).

1960-1964		$2,300	$2,600
1965-1966		$2,100	$2,300
1967-1970		$1,700	$1,900

Sorrento (Reissue)
1997-2000.

1997-2000		$400	$475

Spartan
1934-1949. Acoustic archtop, multi-bound, trapeze tailpiece, sunburst.

1930s		$750	$1,100
1940s		$650	$900

Spider/The Spider
1997-2000. Wood body resonator, spider bridge, square neck.

1997-2000		$300	$350

Spirit
1979-1983. American-made electric solidbody, double-cut, carved top with 2 humbuckers, various colors.

1979-1983		$600	$750

Trailer Park Troubadour Airscreamer
2003-2005. Airstream trailer-shaped body, identifying logo on headstock.

2003-2005		$350	$400

1966 Epiphone Riviera

Epiphone Sheraton II

Epiphone Wilshire

Epiphone USA Map Guitar

MODEL YEAR	FEATURES	EXC. COND. LOW	HIGH
Triumph			

1931-1957. 15 1/4" '31-'33, 16 3/8" '33-'36, 17 3/8" '36-'57, walnut back and sides until '33, laminated maple back and sides '33, solid maple back and sides '34, natural or sunburst.

MODEL YEAR	FEATURES	EXC. COND. LOW	HIGH
1931-1932	Sunburst, laminated walnut body	$1,100	$1,700
1933	Sunburst, laminated maple body	$1,100	$1,700
1934-1935	Sunburst, solid maple body	$1,500	$1,800
1936-1940	Sunburst 17 3/8" body	$1,800	$2,400
1941-1949	Natural	$1,800	$2,400
1941-1949	Sunburst	$1,700	$2,200
1950-1957	Natural	$1,700	$2,200
1950-1957	Sunburst	$1,500	$1,800

Triumph Regent (Cutaway)

1948-1969. Acoustic archtop, single-cut, F-holes, renamed Triumph Cutaway in '53, then Gibson listed this model as just the Triumph from '58-'69.

1948-1952	Triumpt Regent , natural	$3,300	$3,500
1948-1952	Triumpt Regent , sunburst	$3,100	$3,300
1953-1957	Triumph Cutaway, natural	$3,200	$3,400
1953-1957	Triumph Cutaway, sunburst	$3,000	$3,200
1958-1959	Sunburst	$2,900	$3,100
1960-1964	Sunburst	$2,800	$3,000
1965	Sunburst	$2,300	$2,800
1966-1967	Sunburst	$2,200	$2,700
1968-1969	Sunburst	$2,200	$2,600

USA Map Guitar

1982-1983. Solidbody electric, mahogany body shaped like U.S. map, 2 pickups, American-made promotional model, natural.

1982-1983		$2,000	$2,500

Vee-Wee (Mini Flying V)

2003. Mini Flying V student guitar, Flying V shape with single bridge pickup, gig bag, solid opaque finish.

2003		$100	$125

Wildkat

2001-present. Thinline, single-cut, hollow-body, 2 P-90s, Bigsby tailpiece.

2001-2005		$300	$400

Wilshire

1959-1970. Double-cut solidbody, 2 pickups, tune-o-matic bridge, cherry.

1959	Symmetrical body	$4,500	$5,200
1960-1962	Thinner-style body, P-90s	$4,000	$4,700
1962	Mini-humbuckers	$3,800	$4,500
1963-1964	Asymmetrical body	$3,500	$4,000
1965-1966		$3,000	$3,500
1967-1970		$2,400	$3,000

Wilshire 12-String

1966-1968. Solidbody, 2 pickups, cherry.

1966-1967		$2,500	$3,000
1968		$2,400	$2,900

Wilshire II

1984-1985. Solidbody, maple body, neck and 'board, 2 humbuckers, 3-way switch, coil-tap, 1 tone and 1 volume control, various colors.

1984-1985		$225	$300

Windsor (1 Pickup)

1959-1962. Archtop, 1 or 2 pickups, single-cut thinline, sunburst or natural finish.

1959-1960	New York pickup, natural	$1,900	$2,100
1959-1960	New York pickup, sunburst	$1,800	$2,000
1961-1962	Mini-humbucker, natural	$1,900	$2,100
1961-1962	Mini-humbucker, sunburst	$1,800	$2,000

Windsor (2 Pickups)

1959-1962. Archtop, 1 or 2 pickups, single-cut thinline, sunburst or natural finish.

1959-1960	New York pickup, natural	$2,200	$2,500
1959-1960	New York pickup, sunburst	$2,100	$2,400
1961-1962	Mini-humbucker, natural	$2,200	$2,500
1961-1962	Mini-humbucker, sunburst	$2,100	$2,400

X-1000

1986-1989. Electric solidbody, Korean-made, various colors.

1986-1989		$225	$300

Zakk Wylde Les Paul Custom

2003-present. Bull's-eye graphic, block markers, split diamond headstock inlay.

2003-2005		$525	$625

Zenith

1931-1969. Acoustic archtop, bound front and back, f-holes, sunburst.

1931-1933		$900	$1,150
1934-1935	Larger 14 3/4" body	$900	$1,150
1936-1949	Still larger 16 3/8" body	$900	$1,150
1950-1957		$800	$1,050
1958-1959		$550	$950
1960-1964		$500	$900

Zephyr

1939-1957. Non-cut electric archtop, 1 pickup, bound front and back, blond or sunburst (first offered '53), called Zephyr Electric starting in '54.

1939-1940	Natural, 16 3/8", metal handrest pickup	$1,500	$2,000
1941-1943	Natural, no metal handrest	$1,500	$2,000
1944-1946	Natural, top mounted pickup	$1,500	$2,000
1947-1948	17 3/8", metal covered pickup	$1,500	$2,000
1949-1952	Natural, New York pickup	$1,500	$1,800

MODEL YEAR	FEATURES	EXC. COND. LOW	HIGH
1953-1957	Natural, New York pickup	$1,500	$1,700
1953-1957	Sunburst, New York pickup	$1,400	$1,600

Zephyr De Luxe (Non-cutaway)

1941-1954. Non-cut electric archtop, 1 or 2 pickups, multi-bound front and back, gold-plated hardware, natural or sunburst.

1941-1942	Natural	$2,500	$3,000
1945-1949	Natural, 1 pickup	$2,500	$3,000
1945-1949	Natural, 2 pickups	$2,700	$3,200
1950-1954	Natural, 2 pickups	$2,200	$2,700
1950-1954	Sunburst, 2 pickups	$2,000	$2,400

Zephyr De Luxe Regent (Cutaway)

1948-1954. Single-cut electric archtop, 1 or 2 pickups until '50, then only 2, gold-plated hardware, sunburst or natural finish. Renamed Deluxe Electric in '54.

1948-1949	Natural, 1 pickup	$3,200	$4,200
1948-1949	Natural, 2 pickups	$4,100	$5,100
1948-1949	Sunburst, 1 pickup	$3,000	$4,000
1948-1949	Sunburst, 2 pickups	$3,600	$4,600
1950-1954	Natural, 2 pickups	$4,000	$5,000
1950-1954	Sunburst, 2 pickups	$3,500	$4,500

Zephyr Cutaway

1954-1957. Cutaway version of Zephyr.

1954-1957	Natural	$2,700	$3,100
1954-1957	Sunburst	$2,500	$3,000

Zephyr Electric (Cutaway)

1958-1964. Gibson-made version, thinline archtop, single-cut, 2 pickups, natural or sunburst.

1958-1959	Natural	$2,600	$2,800
1958-1959	Sunburst	$2,400	$2,600
1960-1964	Natural	$2,400	$2,600
1960-1964	Sunburst	$2,200	$2,400

Zephyr Emperor Regent

1950-1954. Archtop, single rounded cutaway, multi-bound body, 3 pickups, sunburst or natural finish, renamed Emperor Electric in '54.

1950-1953	Natural	$4,000	$4,800
1950-1953	Sunburst	$3,800	$4,600

Zephyr Regent

1950-1953. Single-cut electric archtop, 1 pickup, natural or sunburst, called Zephyr Cutaway for '54-'57.

1950-1953	Natural	$1,500	$2,300
1950-1953	Sunburst	$1,400	$2,200

Erlewine

1979-present. Professional and premium grade, production/custom guitars built by luthier Mark Erlewine in Austin, Texas. Erlewine also produces the Chiquita brand travel guitar.

ESP

1983-present. Intermediate, professional, and premium grade, production/custom, Japanese-made solidbody guitars and basses. Hisatake Shibuya founded Electronic Sound Products (ESP), a chain of retail stores, in '75. They began to produce replacement parts for electric guitars in '83 and in '85 started to make custom-made guitars. In '87 a

factory was opened in Tokyo. In '86 ESP opened a sales office in New York, selling custom guitars and production models. In the '90s, ESP opened a California-based custom shop and in '96, they introduced the Korean-made LTD brand. Hisatake Shibuya also operated 48th Street Custom Guitars during the '90s but he closed that shop in 2003.

20th Anniversary

1995. Solidbody, double-cut, ESP95 inlaid at 12th fret, gold.

1995		$1,000	$1,100

Eclipse Custom/Custom T (Import)

1986-1988. Single-cut mahogany solidbody, earliest model with bolt dot marker neck, 2nd version with neck-thru design and blocks, the Custom T adds double locking tremolo.

1986-1987	Bolt, dots	$500	$550
1987-1988	Neck-through, Custom T	$500	$650
1987-1988	Neck-thru, blocks	$600	$650

Eclipse Deluxe

1986-1988. Single-cut solidbody, 1 single-coil and 1 humbucker, vibrato, black.

1986-1988		$400	$500

Horizon

1986, 1996-2001. Double-cut neck-thru, bound ebony 'board, 1 single-coil and 1 humbucker, buffer preamp, various colors, reintroduced '96-'01 with bolt neck, curved rounded point headstock.

1986		$400	$475
1996-2001		$250	$325

Horizon Classic (USA)

1993-1995. U.S.-made, carved mahogany body, set-neck, dot markers, various colors, optional mahogany body with figured maple top also offered.

1993-1995	Figured maple top	$1,100	$1,200
1993-1995	Standard mahogany body	$1,200	$1,400

Horizon Custom (USA)

1998-present. U.S. Custom Shop-made, mahogany body, figured maple top, bolt-on neck, mostly translucent finish in various colors.

1998-2005		$1,100	$1,200

Horizon Deluxe (Import)

1989-1992. Horizon Custom with bolt-on neck, various colors.

1989-1992		$600	$700

Hybrid I (Import)

1986 only. Offset double-cut body, bolt maple neck, dots, six-on-a-side tuners, vibrato, various colors.

1986		$300	$400

Hybrid II (Import)

Offset double-cut, rosewood 'board on maple bolt neck, lipstick neck pickup, humbucker at bridge, Hybrid II headstock logo.

1980s		$350	$450

LTD EC-1000

2002-present. Deluxe appointments including abalone inlays and figured-top, 2 humbuckers, Korean-made.

2002-2005		$650	$750

Epiphone Zephyr De Luxe Regent

ESP Eclipse II

ESP LTD Viper

1986 ESP Traditional

MODEL		EXC. COND.	
YEAR	FEATURES	LOW	HIGH

LTD EC-300
2002-2003. Single-cut solidbody, 2 humbuckers, Korean-made.
| 2000-2003 | | $300 | $400 |

LTD H-100
1998-present. Offset double-cut solidbody, 2 humbuckers, made in Korea.
| 1998-2005 | | $150 | $200 |

LTD Viper
2000-present. Double-cut solidbody, 2 humbuckers.
| 2000-2005 | | $300 | $400 |

Maverick/Maverick Deluxe
1989-1992. Offset double-cut, bolt maple or rosewood cap neck, dot markers, double locking vibrola, six-on-a-side tuners, various colors.
| 1989-1992 | | $300 | $400 |

Metal I
1986 only. Offset double-cut, bolt maple neck, rosewood cap, dots, various colors.
| 1986 | | $300 | $400 |

Metal II
1986 only. Single horn V body, bolt on maple neck with rosewood cap, dot markers, various colors.
| 1986 | | $325 | $425 |

Metal III
1986 only. Reverse offset body, bolt maple neck with maple cap, dot markers, gold hardware, various colors.
| 1986 | | $350 | $450 |

M-I Custom
1987-1994. Offset double-cut thru-neck body, offset block markers, various colors.
| 1987-1994 | | $600 | $700 |

M-I Deluxe
1987-1989. Double-cut solidbody, rosewood 'board, 2 single-coils and 1 humbucker, various colors.
| 1987-1989 | | $500 | $600 |

M-II
1989-1994, 1996-2000. Double-cut solidbody, reverse headstock, bolt-on maple or rosewood cap neck, dot markers, various colors.
| 1989-1994 | | $650 | $750 |

M-II Custom
1990-1994. Double-cut solidbody, reverse headstock, neck-thru maple neck, rosewood cap, dot markers, various colors.
| 1990-1994 | | $850 | $900 |

M-II Deluxe
1990-1994. Double-cut solidbody, reverse headstock, Custom with bolt-on neck, various colors.
| 1990-1994 | | $750 | $850 |

Mirage Custom
1986-1990. Double-cut neck-thru solidbody, 2-octave ebony 'board, block markers, 1 humbucker and 2 single-coil pickups, locking trem, various colors.
| 1986-1990 | | $600 | $700 |

Mirage Standard
1986 only. Single pickup version of Mirage Custom, various colors.
| 1986 | | $300 | $400 |

MODEL		EXC. COND.	
YEAR	FEATURES	LOW	HIGH

Phoenix
1987 only. Offset, narrow waist solidbody, thru-neck mahogany body, black hardware, dots.
| 1987 | | $450 | $550 |

Phoenix Contemporary
Late-1990s. 3 pickups vs. 2 on the earlier offering.
| 1998 | | $800 | $850 |

S-454/S-456
1986-1987. Offset double-cut, bolt maple or rosewood cap neck, dot markers, various colors.
| 1986-1987 | | $300 | $500 |

S-500
1991-1993. Double-cut figured ash body, bolt-on neck, six-on-a-side tuners, various colors.
| 1991-1993 | | $500 | $600 |

Traditional
1989-1990. Double-cut, 3 pickups, tremolo, various colors.
| 1989-1990 | | $500 | $600 |

Vintage/Vintage Plus S
1995-1998. Offset double-cut, bolt maple or rosewood cap neck, dot markers, Floyd Rose or standard vibrato, various colors.
| 1995 | 20th Anniversary Edition, gold | $750 | $900 |
| 1995-1998 | | $650 | $750 |

Espana
Early-1960s-early-1970s. Distributed by catalog wholesalers. Built in Sweden.
Classical
Early-1960s-early-1970s. Guitars with white spruce fan-braced tops with either walnut, mahogany, or rosewood back and sides.
| 1970s | | $100 | $175 |

EL-36
1969-early-1970s. Thin hollow double-cut, 2 pickups, natural.
| 1970s | | $150 | $225 |

Jumbo Folk
1969-early-1970s. Natural.
| 1970s | | $100 | $200 |

Essex (SX)
1985-present. Budget grade, production, electric and acoustic guitars imported by Rondo Music of Union, New Jersey. They also offer basses.
Solidbody Electric
1980s-1990s. Copies of classic designs like the Les Paul and Telecaster.
| 1980s | | $70 | $85 |

Este
1909-1939. Luthier Felix Staerke's Este factory built classical and archtop guitars in Hamburg, Germany. They also built high-end banjos. The plant ceased instrument production in '39 and was destroyed in WW II.

MODEL YEAR	FEATURES	EXC. COND. LOW	HIGH

Euphonon

Ca. 1933-1944. This Larson-made brand was intended to compete with the competition's new larger body, 14-fret, solid peghead (unslotted) models. Standard and dreadnought models were offered. Three models were offered ranging from the small 13 3/4" student model, to the top end 15" and 16" models. Ornamentation and features are as important as rosewood vs. mahogany. Euphonons with truss rods were marketed as Prairie State models.

Standard 13"-15"
1934-1944. Fancy binding.

Year	Features	Low	High
1934-1944		$8,000	$15,000
1934-1944	Brazilian rosewood	$15,000	$20,000

Standard 16"
1934-1944. Dreadnought with various features.

Year	Features	Low	High
1934-1944	D-46 appointments	$20,000	$30,000
1934-1944	Fancy binding	$15,000	$20,000
1934-1944	Pearl trim	$15,000	$25,000

Everett Guitars

1977-present. Luthier Kent Everett builds his premium grade, production/custom, steel-string and classical guitars in Atlanta, Georgia. From '01 to '03, his Laurel Series guitars were built in conjunction with Terada in Japan and set up in Atlanta. He has also built archtops, semi-hollow and solidbody electrics, resonators, and mandolins.

Evergreen Mountain

1971-present. Professional grade, custom, flat-top and tenor guitars built by luthier Jerry Nolte in Cove, Oregon. He also builds basses and mandolins and built over 100 dulcimers in the '70s.

Everly Guitars

1982-2001. Luthier Robert Steinegger built these premium grade, production/custom flat-tops in Portland, Oregon (also see Steinegger Guitars).

Excelsior

The Excelsior Company started offering accordions in 1924 and had a large factory in Italy by the late '40s. They started building guitars around '62, which were originally plastic covered, switching to paint finishes in the mid '60s. They also offered classicals, acoustics, archtops and amps. By the early '70s they were out of the guitar business.

Dyno & Malibu
1960s. Offset, double cut, 2 or 3 pickups, vibrato.

Year	Features	Low	High
1960s	Dyno I	$150	$175
1960s	Dyno II	$165	$200
1960s	Malibu I	$175	$225
1960s	Malibu II	$180	$250

Falk

Custom archtop guitars built by luthier Dave Falk in Independence, Missouri.

Farnell

1989-present. Luthier Al Farnell builds his professional grade, production, solidbody guitars in Ontario, California. He also offers his intermediate grade, production, C Series which is imported from China. He also builds basses.

Favilla

1890-1973. Founded by the Favilla family in New York, the company began to import guitars in 1970, but folded in '73. American-made models have the Favilla family crest on the headstock. Import models used a script logo on the headstock.

Acoustic Classical
1960s-1973. Various nylon-string classical models.

Year	Features	Low	High
1960s-1969		$300	$500
1970-1973	Import	$250	$400

Acoustic Flat-Top
1960s-1973. Various flat-top models, 000 to D sizes, mahogany to spruce.

Year	Features	Low	High
1960s-1969	USA made, Crest logo	$600	$750
1970-1973	Import, Script logo	$400	$500

Fender

1946 (1945)-present. Budget, intermediate, professional and premium grade, production/custom, electric, acoustic, acoustic/electric, classical, and resonator guitars built in the U.S. and overseas. They also build amps, basses, mandolins, bouzoukis, banjos, violins, and PA gear. Ca. 1939 Leo Fender opened a radio and record store called Fender Radio Service, where he met Clayton Orr 'Doc' Kauffman, and in '45 they started KF Company to build lap steels and amps. In '46 Kauffman left and Fender started the Fender Electric Instrument Company. By '50 Fender's products were distributed by F.C. Hall's Radio & Television Electronics Company (Radio-Tel, later owners of Rickenbacker). In '53 Radio-Tel is replaced by the Fender Sales Company which was ran by Don Randall.

In January '65 CBS purchased the company for $13 million and renamed it Fender Musical Instruments Corporation. The CBS takeover is synonymous with a decline in quality - whether true or not is still debated, but the perception persists among musicians and collectors, and Pre-CBS Fenders are more valuable. Fender experienced some quality problems in the late-'60s. Small headstock is enlarged in '65 and the 4-bolt neck is replaced by the 3-bolt in '71. With high value and relative scarcity of Pre-CBS Fenders, even CBS-era instruments are now sought by collectors. Leo Fender was kept on as consultant until '70 and went on to design guitars for Music Man and G&L.

Bill Schultz and Dan Smith were hired from Yamaha in '81. In '82 Fender Japan is established to produce licensed Fender copies for sale in Japan. Also in '82, the Fender Squier brand debuts on Japanese-made instruments for the European mar-

Everett Model O

Evergreen Mountain tenor guitar

GUITARS

Fender Avalon

Fender '51 NoCaster Relic

ket and by '83 they were imported into U.S. In '85, the company was purchased by an investor group headed by Bill Schultz but the purchase does not include the Fullerton factory. While a new factory was being established at Corona, California, all Fender Contemporary Stratocasters and Telecasters were made either by Fender Japan or in Seoul, Korea. U.S. production resumes in '86 with American Standard Stratocaster. The Fender Custom Shop, run by Michael Stevens and John Page, opens in '87. The Mexican Fender factory is established in '90. In '95, Fender purchased the Guild guitar company. On January 3, 2002, Fender Musical Instruments Corporation (FMIC) announced the sale of holdings in the company. FMIC recapitalized a minority portion of the common stock. The recapitalization partners included Roland Corporation U.S. (Los Angeles) and Weston Presidio, a private equity firm (San Francisco). As of January 1, 2003, Fred Gretsch Enterprises, Ltd granted Fender the exclusive rights to develop, produce, market and distribute Gretsch guitars worldwide. Around the same time, Fender also acquired the Jackson/Charvel Guitar Company. In October, '04, Fender acquired Tacoma Guitars. ....

Dating older Fender guitars is an imprecise art form at best. While serial numbers were used, they were frequently not in sequence, although a lower number will frequently be older than a substantially higher number. Often necks were dated, but only with the date the neck was finished, not when the guitar was assembled. Generally, dating requires triangulating between serial numbers, neck dates, pot dates, construction details and model histories.

From '50 through roughly '65, guitars had more-or-less sequential numbers in either 4 or 5 digits, though some higher numbers may have an initial 0 or - prefix. These can range from 0001 to 99XXX.

From '63 into '65, some instruments had serial numbers beginning with an L prefix plus 5 digits (LXXXXX). Beginning in '65 with the CBS take-over into '76, 6-digit serial numbers were stamped on F neckplates roughly sequentially from 10XXXX to 71XXXX. In '76 the serial number was shifted to the headstock decal. From '76-'77, the serial number began with a bold-face 76 or S6 plus 5 digits (76XXXXX).

From '77 on, serial numbers consisted of a 2-place prefix plus 5 digits (sometimes 6 beginning in '91): '77 (S7, S8), '78 (S7, S8, S9), '79 (S9, E0), '80-'81 (S9, E0, E1), '82 (E1, E2, E3), '84-'85 (E4), '85-'86 (no U.S. production), '87 (E4), '88 (E4, E8), '89 (E8, E9), '90 (E9, N9, N0), '91 (N0), '92 (N2).

Serial numbers on guitars made by Fender Japan consist of either a 2-place prefix plus 5 digits or a single prefix letter plus 6 digits: '82-'84 (JV), '83-'84 (SQ), '84-'87 (E), '85-'86+ (A, B, C), '86-'87 (F), '87-'88+ (G), '88-'89 (H), '89-'90 (I, J), '90-'91 (K), '91-'92 (L), '92-'93 (M).

Factors affecting Fender values: The sale to CBS in '65 is a major point in Fender instrument values as CBS made many changes that collectors feel affected quality. The '70s introduced the 3-bolt

neck and other design changes that aren't that popular with guitarists. Custom color instruments, especially Strats from the '50s and early-'60s, can be valued much more than the standard sunburst finishes. In '75 Fender dropped the optional custom colors and started issuing the guitars in a variety of standard colors. The various Telecaster and Stratocaster models are grouped under those general headings.

Avalon
1984-1995. Acoustic, 6-on-a-side tuners, mahogany neck, back and sides (nato after '93), spruce top, various colors.

MODEL YEAR	FEATURES	EXC. COND. LOW	HIGH
1984-1995		$300	$400

Broadcaster
Mid-1950-early-'51. For a short time in early-'51, before being renamed the Telecaster, models had no Broadcaster decal; these are called No-casters by collectors.

1950	Blond	$60,000	$85,000
1951	Clipped decal, "No Caster"	$40,000	$60,000

Broadcaster Leo Fender Custom Shop
1999 only. Leo Fender script logo signature replaces Fender logo on headstock, Custom Shop Certificate signed by Phyllis Fender, Fred Gretsch, and William Schultz, includes glass display case and poodle guitar case.

1999		$8,000	$10,000

'50s Relic/'51 No Caster Custom Shop
1996-present. Called the '50s Relic Nocaster for '96-'99, and '51 Nocaster in NOS, Relic, or Closet Classic versions at present, with the Relic Series being the highest offering.

1999-2004	Closet Classic	$1,700	$1,900

Bronco
1967-1980. Slab solidbody, 1 pickup, tremolo, red.

1967-1969		$800	$900
1970-1980		$700	$800

Bullet
1981-1983. Solidbody, came in 2- and 3-pickup versions (single-coil and humbucker), and single- and double-cut models, various colors. Becomes Squire Bullet in '85.

1981-1983	2 pickups	$300	$400
1981-1983	3 pickups	$375	$450

CG (Classical Guitar) Series
1995-2005. Various nylon-string classical acoustic and acoustic/electric models, label on the inside back clearly indicates the model number, back and sides of rosewood, mahogany or other woods.

1995-2005	Rosewood back and sides	$250	$300

Concert
1963-1970. Acoustic flat-top slightly shorter than King/Kingman, spruce body, mahogany back and sides (optional Brazilian or Indian rosewood, zebrawood or vermillion), natural, sunburst optional by '68.

1963-1965	Natural	$800	$1,000
1966-1968	Natural or sunburst	$700	$900
1969-1970	Natural or sunburst	$600	$800

MODEL YEAR	FEATURES	EXC. COND. LOW	HIGH
Concord			
1987-1992. Dreadnought flat-top, 6-on-a-side headstock, natural.			
1987-1992		$175	$275
Coronado I			
1966-1969. Thinline semi-hollowbody, double-cut, tremolo, 1 pickup, single-bound, dot inlay.			
1966-1967	Blue custom color	$1,100	$1,400
1966-1967	Cherry Red	$750	$1,000
1966-1967	Orange custom color	$1,100	$1,400
1966-1967	Sunburst	$750	$1,000
1966-1967	White (unfaded)	$1,000	$1,300
1968-1969	Sunburst	$650	$900
Coronado II			
1966-1969 (Antigua finish offered until '70). Thinline semi-hollowbody, double-cut, tremolo optional, 2 pickups, single-bound, block inlay, available in standard finishes but special issues offered in Antigua and 6 different Wildwood finishes (labeled on the pickguard as Wildwood I through Wildwood VI to designate different colors). Wildwood finishes were achieved by injecting dye into growing trees.			
1966-1967	Blue custom color	$1,400	$1,700
1966-1967	Cherry Red	$1,300	$1,400
1966-1967	Olympic White custom color	$1,300	$1,600
1966-1967	Orange custom color	$1,400	$1,700
1966-1967	Silver custom color	$1,400	$1,700
1966-1967	Sunburst	$1,300	$1,400
1966-1967	Wildwood (unfaded)	$1,500	$1,700
1967-1969	Antigua	$1,400	$1,700
1968-1969	Cherry Red	$1,200	$1,300
1968-1969	Orange custom color	$1,300	$1,600
1968-1969	Sunburst	$1,200	$1,300
1968-1969	Wildwood (unfaded)	$1,400	$1,500
1970	Antigua	$1,300	$1,500
Coronado XII			
1966-1969 (Antigua finish offered until '70). Thinline semi-hollowbody, double-cut, 12 strings, 2 pickups, block inlay, standard, Antigua and Wildwood finishes available.			
1966-1967	Cherry Red	$1,300	$1,400
1966-1967	Orange custom color	$1,400	$1,700
1966-1967	Sunburst	$1,300	$1,400
1966-1967	Wildwood	$1,400	$1,600
1968-1969	Antigua	$1,500	$1,700
1968-1969	Cherry Red	$1,200	$1,300
1968-1969	Orange custom color	$1,300	$1,600
1968-1969	Sunburst	$900	$1,200
1968-1969	Wildwood (unfaded)	$1,400	$1,500
Custom			
1969-1971. Six-string solidbody that used up parts from discontinued Electric XII, asymmetrical-cut, long			

MODEL YEAR	FEATURES	EXC. COND. LOW	HIGH
headstock, 2 split pickups, sunburst. Also marketed as the Maverick.			
1969-1971		$1,500	$1,700
Cyclone			
1998-present. Mexican import, solidbody, contoured offset waist, poplar body, various colors.			
1998-2005		$350	$400
D'Aquisto Elite			
1984, 1989-1994, 1994-2002. Part of Fender's Master Series, archtop, single-cut, glued neck, 1 pickup, gold-plated hardware, made in Japan until '94, in '94 the Fender Custom Shop issued a version that retailed at $6,000, various colors.			
1984		$2,000	$2,300
1989-1994		$2,000	$2,300
D'Aquisto Standard			
1984 (Serial numbers could range from 1983-1985). Part of Fender's Master Series, archtop, single-cut, glued neck, 2 pickups, made in Japan, various colors.			
1984		$1,800	$2,000
D'Aquisto Ultra			
1994-2000. USA Custom Shop, made under the supervision of James D'Aquisto, flamed maple back and sides, spruce top, ebony tailpiece, bridge and 'guard, all hand carved.			
1994-2000		$6,000	$7,000
Duo-Sonic			
1956-1969. Solidbody, 3/4-size, 2 pickups, Desert Sand ('56-'61), sunburst ('61-'63), blue, red or white after, short- and long-scale necks, short-scale necks listed here (see Duo-Sonic II for long-scale), reissued Mexican-made in '94.			
1956-1958	Maple neck	$1,200	$1,500
1959-1963	Rosewood 'board	$1,100	$1,400
1964-1965		$1,000	$1,300
1966-1969		$900	$1,100
Duo-Sonic II			
1965-1969. Solidbody, 2 pickups, blue, red or white, long-scale neck, though the long-scale neck Duo-Sonic was not known as the Duo-Sonic II until '65, we have lumped all long-scales under the II for the purposes of this Guide.			
1965-1969		$1,200	$1,700
Duo-Sonic Reissue			
1993-1997. Made in Mexico, black, red or white.			
1993-1997		$200	$250
Electric XII			

1965-1969. Solidbody, 12 strings, long headstock, 2 split pickups. Custom colors can fade or become darker; for example Lake Placid Blue changes to green. The price ranges below are for instruments that are relatively unfaded. Many older guitars have some color fade and minor fade is factored into these values. Each custom color should be evaluated on a case-by-case basis.

Custom color Fenders can be forged and bogus finishes have been a problem. As the value of custom color Fenders has increased, so has the problem of bogus non-original finishes. The prices in the Guide are for factory original finishes in excellent condition.

Fender Coronado II

Fender Cyclone

1970s Fender Electric XII

1962 Fender Esquire

MODEL YEAR	FEATURES	EXC. COND. LOW	HIGH

The prices noted do not take into account market factors such as fake instruments, which can have the effect of lowering a guitar's market value unless the guitar's provenance can be validated.

MODEL YEAR	FEATURES	EXC. COND. LOW	HIGH
1965-1966	Black, Blond	$3,000	$4,400
1965-1966	Blue Ice, Charcoal Frost, Dakota Red, Fiesta Red, Firemist Gold, Firemist Silver	$3,600	$5,200
1965-1966	Candy Apple Red, Olympic White	$3,200	$4,600
1965-1966	Foam Green	$4,000	$5,400
1965-1966	Lake Placid Blue	$3,200	$4,600
1965-1966	Ocean Turquoise, Sonic Blue, Teal Green	$3,700	$5,200
1965-1966	Sunburst, blocks	$2,300	$3,200
1965-1966	Sunburst, dots	$2,500	$3,400
1967-1969	Black, Blond	$2,700	$3,200
1967-1969	Blue Ice	$3,300	$3,800
1967-1969	Candy Apple Red	$2,900	$3,400
1967-1969	Charcoal Frost, Dakota Red, Fiesta Red, Firemist Gold, Firemist Silver	$3,300	$3,800
1967-1969	Foam Green, Ocean Turquoise, Sonic Blue, Teal Green	$3,400	$3,900
1967-1969	Lake Placid Blue	$2,900	$3,400
1967-1969	Olympic White	$2,900	$3,400
1967-1969	Sunburst	$2,100	$2,500

Esprit Elite

1983-1985. Part of the Master Series, made in Japan, double-cut, semi-hollow, carved maple top, 2 humbuckers, bound rosewood 'board, snowflake inlays, sunburst.

1983-1984		$1,100	$1,400

Esprit Standard

1983-1985. Part of the Master Series, made in Japan, double-cut, semi-hollow, carved maple top, 2 humbuckers, bound rosewood 'board, dot inlays, sunburst.

1983-1985		$1,000	$1,200

Esprit Ultra

1984. Part of the Master Series, made in Japan, double-cut, semi-hollow, carved spruce top, 2 humbuckers, bound rosewood 'board, split-block inlays, sunburst, gold hardware.

1984		$1,200	$1,500

Esquire

1950-1970. Ash body, single-cut, 1 pickup, maple neck, black 'guard '50-'54, white 'guard '54 on.

1950	Blond, black 'guard	$25,000	$30,000
1951	Blond, black 'guard	$23,000	$28,000
1952	Blond, black 'guard	$22,000	$30,000

MODEL YEAR	FEATURES	EXC. COND. LOW	HIGH
1953	Blond, black 'guard	$21,000	$29,000
1954	Blond, black 'guard	$20,000	$28,000
1954	Blond, white 'guard	$15,000	$22,000
1955	Blond, white 'guard	$14,500	$21,000
1956	Blond	$13,500	$20,000
1957	Blond	$13,000	$19,000
1958	Blond, backloader	$13,000	$18,000
1958	Blond, frontloader	$12,000	$17,000
1959	Blond, maple 'board	$13,000	$16,000
1959	Blond, rosewood 'board	$12,000	$15,000
1960	Blond	$11,000	$15,000
1960	Sunburst	$13,000	$16,000
1961	Blond	$10,000	$14,000
1961	Custom colors	$18,000	$23,000
1961	Sunburst	$12,000	$15,000
1962	Blond, curved 'board	$9,000	$12,000
1962	Blond, slab 'board	$9,500	$13,000
1962	Custom colors	$17,000	$22,000
1962	Sunburst	$10,500	$14,000
1963-1964	Blond	$9,000	$11,000
1963-1964	Burgundy Mist	$13,000	$16,000
1963-1964	Candy Apple Red	$12,000	$13,000
1963-1964	Lake Placid Blue	$12,000	$13,000
1963-1964	Olympic White	$11,000	$13,000
1965-1966	Blond	$7,500	$9,000
1965-1966	Olympic White	$9,000	$11,000
1967	Blond	$5,500	$6,500
1967	Blond, smuggler cavity	$5,000	$6,000
1967-1970	Blue Ice	$9,000	$11,000
1967-1970	Candy Apple Red	$7,500	$9,500
1967-1970	Lake Placid Blue	$7,500	$9,500
1967-1970	Olympic White	$7,500	$9,500
1967-1970	Sunburst	$6,500	$8,000
1968	Blond	$5,000	$6,000
1969	Blond	$4,500	$5,500
1970	Blond	$4,000	$4,800

Esquire Custom

1959-1970. Same as Esquire, but with bound alder sunburst body and rosewood 'board.

1959	Sunburst	$22,000	$26,000
1960	Custom colors	$31,000	$38,000
1960	Sunburst	$21,000	$25,500
1961-1962	Custom colors	$28,000	$34,000
1961-1962	Sunburst	$20,000	$24,000
1963-1964	Custom colors	$21,000	$26,000
1963-1964	Sunburst	$17,000	$21,000
1965-1966	Custom colors	$18,000	$22,000
1965-1966	Sunburst	$11,500	$14,000
1967	Sunburst	$10,000	$12,000
1968	Sunburst	$9,000	$11,000
1969	Sunburst	$8,000	$9,500
1970	Sunburst	$7,000	$8,000

MODEL YEAR	FEATURES	EXC. COND. LOW	HIGH

Esquire Custom (Import)
1983. Made in Japan with all the classic bound Esquire features, sunburst.

1983		$900	$1,000

Esquire Custom GT/Celtic/Scorpion
2003. Single-cut solidbody, 1 humbucker, 1 knob (volume), set-neck, solid colors.

2003		$250	$350

Esquire Custom Shop
Various colors.

1990s		$1,700	$2,200

Flame Elite
1984-1988. Part of the Master Series, made in Japan, neck-thru, offset double-cut, solidbody, 2 humbuckers, rosewood 'board, snowflake inlays.

1984-1988		$1,100	$1,400

Flame Standard
1984-1988. Part of the Master Series, made in Japan, neck-thru, offset double-cut, solidbody, 2 humbuckers, rosewood 'board, dot inlays.

1984-1988		$1,000	$1,200

Flame Ultra
1984-1988. Part of the Master Series, made in Japan, neck-thru, double-cut, solidbody, 2 humbuckers, rosewood 'board, split block inlays (some with snowflakes), gold hardware.

1984-1988		$1,200	$1,500

F-Series Dreadnought Flat-Top
1969-1981. The F-Series were Japanese-made flat-top acoustics, included were Concert- and Dreadnought-size instruments with features running from plain to bound necks and headstocks and fancy inlays, there was also a line of F-Series classical, nylon-string guitars. A label on the inside indicates the model. FC-20 is a classical with Brazilian rosewood. There was also an Asian (probably Korean) import Standard Series for '82-'90 where the models start with a F.

1969-1981	High-end solid top	$150	$250
1969-1981	Low-end laminated	$125	$150
1972-1981	FC-20 Classical	$175	$300

Gemini Series
1983-1990. Korean-made flat-tops, label on inside indicates model. I is classical nylon-string, II, III and IV are dreadnought steel-strings, there is also a 12-string and an IIE acoustic/electric.

1983-1987	Gemini II	$150	$175
1983-1988	Gemini I	$125	$150
1987-1990	Gemini III/IV	$175	$225

Harmony-Made Series
Early-1970s-mid-1970s. Harmony-made with white stencil Fender logo, mahogany, natural or sunburst.

1970s		$75	$150

Jag-Stang
1996-1998. Japanese-made, designed by Curt Cobain, body similar to Jaguar, tremolo, 1 pickup, oversize Strat peghead, Fiesta Red or Sonic Blue.

1996	1st issue, 50th Anniv. Label	$525	$600
1997-1998		$400	$575

Jaguar
1962-1975. Reintroduced as Jaguar '62 in '95-'99. Custom colors can fade and often the faded color has very little similarity to the original color. The values below are for an instrument that is relatively unfaded. Each custom color should be evaluated on a case-by-case basis. Custom color Fenders can be forged and bogus finishes have been a problem. As the value of custom color Fenders has increased, so has the problem of bogus non-original finishes. The prices in the Guide are for factory original finishes in excellent condition.

1962	Black	$3,700	$4,800
1962	Blond	$3,700	$4,900
1962	Burgundy Mist	$4,800	$6,300
1962	Dakota Red	$4,800	$6,300
1962	Daphne Blue	$4,500	$5,900
1962	Fiesta Red	$4,800	$6,300
1962	Foam Green	$5,200	$6,800
1962	Inca Silver	$4,500	$5,900
1962	Lake Pacid Blue	$4,100	$5,300
1962	Olympic White	$4,100	$5,300
1962	Shell Pink	$5,200	$6,800
1962	Sherwood Green	$4,800	$6,300
1962	Shoreline Gold	$4,800	$6,300
1962	Sonic Blue	$4,500	$5,900
1962	Sunburst	$3,100	$3,900
1962	Surf Green	$5,200	$6,800
1963-1964	Black	$3,500	$4,200
1963-1964	Blond	$3,500	$4,300
1963-1964	Burgundy Mist	$4,700	$5,900
1963-1964	Candy Apple Red	$3,700	$4,800
1963-1964	Dakota Red	$4,700	$5,900
1963-1964	Daphne Blue	$4,400	$5,500
1963-1964	Fiesta Red	$4,400	$5,500
1963-1964	Foam Green	$5,200	$6,500
1963-1964	Inca Silver	$4,400	$5,500
1963-1964	Lake Placid Blue	$3,700	$4,800
1963-1964	Olympic White	$3,700	$4,600
1963-1964	Sherwood Green	$4,400	$5,500
1963-1964	Shoreline Gold	$4,400	$5,500
1963-1964	Sonic Blue	$4,300	$5,400
1963-1964	Sunburst	$3,000	$3,500
1963-1964	Surf Green	$5,200	$6,500
1965	Sunburst	$2,700	$3,100
1965-1966	Black	$3,000	$4,000
1965-1966	Blond	$3,000	$4,100
1965-1966	Blue Ice	$4,000	$5,200
1965-1966	Candy Apple Red	$3,400	$4,400
1965-1966	Charcoal Frost	$4,000	$5,200
1965-1966	Dakota Red	$3,900	$5,100
1965-1966	Fiesta Red	$3,800	$5,000
1965-1966	Firemist Gold	$4,000	$5,200
1965-1966	Firemist Silver	$4,000	$5,200
1965-1966	Foam Green	$4,800	$6,300
1965-1966	Lake Placid Blue	$3,400	$4,400
1965-1966	Ocean Turquoise	$4,000	$5,200
1965-1966	Olympic White	$3,400	$4,400
1965-1966	Sonic Blue	$4,000	$5,200
1965-1966	Teal Green	$4,000	$5,200

Fender Flame Ultra

1962 Fender Jaguar

1965 Fender Jaguar

1959 Fender Jazzmaster

MODEL YEAR	FEATURES	EXC. COND. LOW	HIGH
1966	Sunburst, block markers	$2,400	$3,000
1966	Sunburst, dot markers	$2,700	$3,100
1967-1970	Black	$2,500	$3,000
1967-1970	Blond	$2,500	$3,000
1967-1970	Blue Ice	$3,000	$3,600
1967-1970	Candy Apple Red	$2,600	$3,200
1967-1970	Charcoal Frost	$3,000	$3,600
1967-1970	Dakota Red	$2,900	$3,500
1967-1970	Fiesta Red	$3,000	$3,600
1967-1970	Firemist Gold	$3,000	$3,600
1967-1970	Firemist Silver	$3,000	$3,600
1967-1970	Foam Green	$3,200	$4,000
1967-1970	Lake Placid Blue	$2,700	$3,200
1967-1970	Ocean Turquoise	$3,000	$3,700
1967-1970	Olympic White	$2,700	$4,200
1967-1970	Sonic Blue	$3,000	$3,700
1967-1970	Sunburst	$1,900	$2,100
1967-1970	Teal Green	$3,000	$3,700
1971-1975	Custom colors	$2,500	$3,000
1971-1975	Sunburst	$1,800	$1,900

Jaguar '62

1994-present. Reintroduction of Jaguar, Japanese-made until '99, then U.S.-made, basswood body, rosewood 'board, various colors.

MODEL YEAR	FEATURES	EXC. COND. LOW	HIGH
1994-1999	Import	$625	$725
1999-2005	U.S.A.-made	$975	$1,025

Jazzmaster

1958-1980. Contoured body, 2 pickups, rosewood 'board, clay dot inlay, reintroduced as Japanese-made Jazzmaster '62 in '96. Custom color Fenders can be forged and bogus finishes have been a problem. As the value of custom color Fenders has increased, so has the problem of bogus non-original finishes. The prices in the Guide are for factory original finishes in excellent condition.

MODEL YEAR	FEATURES	EXC. COND. LOW	HIGH
1958	Sunburst	$7,500	$8,000
1958	Sunburst, rare maple 'board	$8,500	$9,000
1959	Custom colors, includes rare	$13,000	$14,000
1959	Sunburst	$7,000	$8,000
1960	Black	$8,500	$9,000
1960	Blond	$8,500	$9,000
1960	Burgundy Mist	$11,000	$12,000
1960	Dakota Red	$11,000	$12,000
1960	Daphne Blue	$10,000	$11,000
1960	Fiesta Red	$11,000	$12,000
1960	Foam Green	$12,000	$13,000
1960	Inca Silver	$10,000	$12,000
1960	Lake Placid Blue	$9,500	$10,500
1960	Olympic White	$9,500	$10,500
1960	Shell Pink	$12,000	$13,000
1960	Sherwood Green	$11,000	$12,000
1960	Shoreline Gold	$11,000	$12,000
1960	Sonic Blue	$10,000	$11,000
1960	Sunburst	$6,500	$7,000
1960	Surf Green	$12,000	$13,000
1961	Black	$8,500	$9,000
1961	Blond	$8,500	$9,000

MODEL YEAR	FEATURES	EXC. COND. LOW	HIGH
1961	Burgundy Mist	$10,800	$11,500
1961	Dakota Red	$10,800	$11,500
1961	Daphne Blue	$9,800	$10,500
1961	Fiesta Red	$10,800	$11,500
1961	Foam Green	$11,300	$12,000
1961	Inca Silver	$9,800	$10,500
1961	Lake Placid Blue	$9,400	$10,000
1961	Olympic White	$9,400	$10,000
1961	Shell Pink	$11,300	$12,000
1961	Sherwood Green	$10,300	$11,000
1961	Shoreline Gold	$10,300	$11,000
1961	Sonic Blue	$9,800	$10,500
1961	Sunburst	$6,200	$6,600
1961	Surf Green	$11,300	$12,000
1962	Black	$8,000	$8,500
1962	Blond	$8,000	$8,500
1962	Burgundy Mist	$10,300	$11,000
1962	Dakota Red	$10,300	$11,000
1962	Daphne Blue	$10,300	$11,000
1962	Fiesta Red	$10,300	$11,000
1962	Foam Green	$11,300	$12,000
1962	Inca Silver	$10,300	$11,000
1962	Lake Placid Blue	$8,600	$9,200
1962	Olympic White	$8,600	$9,200
1962	Shell Pink	$11,300	$12,000
1962	Sherwood Green	$10,300	$11,000
1962	Shoreline Gold	$10,300	$11,000
1962	Sonic Blue	$9,400	$10,000
1962	Sunburst	$6,100	$6,500
1962	Surf Green	$11,300	$12,000
1963-1964	Black	$6,300	$6,700
1963-1964	Blond	$7,800	$8,400
1963-1964	Burgundy Mist	$10,300	$11,000
1963-1964	Candy Apple Red	$6,800	$7,200
1963-1964	Dakota Red	$10,300	$11,000
1963-1964	Daphne Blue	$9,400	$10,000
1963-1964	Fiesta Red	$10,300	$11,000
1963-1964	Foam Green	$11,000	$11,800
1963-1964	Inca Silver	$9,400	$10,000
1963-1964	Lake Placid Blue	$6,900	$7,300
1963-1964	Olympic White	$6,900	$7,300
1963-1964	Sherwood Green	$8,200	$8,700
1963-1964	Shoreline Gold	$8,200	$8,700
1963-1964	Sonic Blue	$7,500	$8,000
1963-1964	Sunburst	$4,700	$5,000
1963-1964	Surf Green	$11,000	$11,800
1965	Burgundy Mist	$7,500	$8,000
1965	Daphne Blue	$6,800	$7,300
1965	Sunburst	$4,000	$4,500
1965-1966	Black	$5,200	$5,500
1965-1966	Blond	$5,600	$6,000
1965-1966	Blue Ice	$6,800	$7,300
1965-1966	Candy Apple Red	$6,300	$6,700
1965-1966	Charcoal Frost	$6,800	$7,300
1965-1966	Dakota Red	$6,600	$7,000
1965-1966	Fiesta Red	$6,600	$7,000
1965-1966	Firemist Gold	$6,800	$7,300
1965-1966	Firemist Silver	$6,800	$7,300
1965-1966	Foam Green	$7,900	$8,400
1965-1966	Lake Placid Blue	$6,300	$6,700
1965-1966	Ocean Turquoise	$6,800	$7,300

MODEL YEAR	FEATURES	EXC. COND. LOW	HIGH
1965-1966	Olympic White	$6,000	$6,300
1965-1966	Sonic Blue	$6,800	$7,300
1965-1966	Teal Green	$6,900	$7,300
1966	Sunburst, block markers	$3,700	$3,900
1966	Sunburst, dot markers	$3,800	$4,000
1967	Sunburst	$3,700	$3,900
1967-1970	Blue Ice	$6,500	$7,000
1967-1970	Candy Apple Red	$6,000	$6,500
1967-1970	Charcoal Frost	$6,500	$7,000
1967-1970	Dakota Red	$6,300	$6,700
1967-1970	Fiesta Red	$6,300	$6,700
1967-1970	Firemist Gold	$6,500	$7,000
1967-1970	Firemist Silver	$6,500	$7,000
1967-1970	Foam Green	$7,500	$8,000
1967-1970	Lake Placid Blue	$6,000	$6,500
1967-1970	Ocean Turquoise	$6,500	$7,000
1967-1970	Olympic White	$6,000	$6,500
1967-1970	Sonic Blue	$6,500	$7,000
1967-1970	Teal Green	$7,900	$8,400
1968	Sunburst	$3,300	$3,500
1969	Sunburst	$3,000	$3,200
1970	Sunburst	$2,700	$2,900
1971-1975	Sunburst	$2,400	$2,500
1976-1980	Custom colors	$3,000	$3,500
1976-1980	Sunburst	$2,200	$2,300

Jazzmaster '62
1994-present. Japanese-made reintroduction of Jazzmaster, basswood body, rosewood 'board, U.S.-made from '99, various colors.

1994-1999	Import	$625	$725
1999-2005	U.S.A.-made	$975	$1,025

Jazzmaster The Ventures Limited Edition
1996. Japanese-made, ash body, 2 pickups, block inlay, transparent purple/black.

1996		$900	$1,100

Katana
1985-1986. Japanese-made wedge-shaped body, 2 humbuckers, set neck, triangle inlays, black.

1985-1986		$350	$450

Squier Katana
1985-1986. Korean-made version, 1 humbucker, bolt neck, dot inlays, black.

1985-1986		$250	$300

King
1963-1965. Full-size 15 5/8" wide acoustic, natural. Renamed Kingman in '65.

1963-1965		$1,000	$1,200

Kingman
1965-1971, 2006-present. Full-size 15 5/8" wide acoustic, slightly smaller by '70, offered in 3 Wildwood colors, referred to as the Wildwood acoustic which is a Kingman with dyed wood.

1965-1968		$900	$1,100
1969-1971		$800	$1,000

Lead I
1979-1982. Double-cut solidbody with 1 humbucker, maple or rosewood 'board, black or brown.

1979-1982		$375	$475

Lead II
1979-1982. Lead with 2 pickups, black or brown.

1979-1982		$425	$525

Lead III
1982. Lead with 2 split-coil humbuckers, 2 3-way switches, various colors.

1982		$525	$700

LTD
1969-1975. Archtop electric, single-cut, gold-plated hardware, carved top and back, 1 pickup, multi-bound, bolt-on neck, sunburst.

1969-1975		$4,000	$5,000

Malibu
1965-1971, 1983-1992, 2006-present. Flat top, spruce top, mahogany back and sides, black, mahogany or sunburst. Name used on Asian import model in '80s.

1965-1971		$575	$625

Marauder
1965 only. The Marauder has 3 pickups, and some have slanted frets, only 8 were made, thus it is very rare. 1st generation has hidden pickups, 2nd has exposed.

1965	1st generation	$7,000	$15,000
1965	2nd generation	$5,000	$10,000

Montego I/II
1968-1975. Electric archtop, single-cut, bolt-on neck, 1 pickup (I) or 2 pickups (II), chrome-plated hardware, sunburst.

1968-1975	I	$2,500	$3,000
1968-1975	II	$2,700	$3,200

Musiclander
1969-1972. Also called Swinger and Arrow, solidbody, 1 pickup, arrow-shaped headstock, no model name on peghead, red, white, and blue.

1969-1972		$1,300	$1,600

Musicmaster
1956-1980. Solidbody, 1 pickup, short-scale (3/4) neck, Desert Sand ('56-'61), sunburst ('61-'63), red, white or blue after. Regular-scale necks were optional and are called Musicmaster II from '64 to '69, after '69 II is dropped and Musicmaster continues with regular-scale neck.

1956-1959	Blond	$1,350	$1,600
1960-1964	Blond	$1,300	$1,500
1964-1969	Red, white, blue	$900	$1,100
1970-1980	Red, white, blue	$700	$750

Musicmaster II
1964-1969. Solidbody, 1 pickup, long regular-scale neck version of Musicmaster, red, white, or blue.

1964-1969		$725	$1,200

Mustang
1964-1982, 1997-1998. Solidbody, 2 pickups. Reissued as '69 Mustang in 1990s, name changed back to Mustang '97-'98. Dakota Red, Daphne Blue and Olympic White with Competition Red, Blue and Orange finishes added ca. '69-'72. Competition finishes featured a racing stripe on the front of the body.

1964-1965	Various colors	$1,400	$1,900
1966-1969	Various colors	$1,200	$1,700
1970-1979	Various colors	$1,000	$1,500
1980-1982	Various colors	$1,000	$1,300

Fender Marauder

1964 Fender Musicmaster

Fender Newporter

Fender Squier '51

MODEL YEAR	FEATURES	EXC. COND. LOW	HIGH

Mustang '69 Reissue
1994-1998. Japanese-made reissue of Mustang, blue or white.

1994-1998		$500	$550

Newporter
1965-1971, 1983-1992. Acoustic flat-top, mahogany back and sides. Name used on Asian import model in '80s.

1965-1968	Spruce top	$450	$550
1968-1971	Mahogany top	$350	$450

Palomino
1968-1971. Acoustic flat-top, spruce top, mahogany back and sides, triple-bound, black or mahogany.

1968-1971		$550	$600

Performer
1985-1986. Imported Swinger-like body design, 2 slanted humbuckers.

1985-1986		$900	$1,000

Prodigy
1991-1993. Electric solidbody, double-cut, chrome-plated hardware, 2 single-coil and 1 humbucker pickups, blue or black.

1991-1993		$400	$450

Redondo
1969-1971, 1983-1990. Mid-size flat-top, 14 3/8" wide, replaces Newport spruce top model. Name used on Asian import model in '80s.

1969-1971		$450	$550

Robben Ford
1989-1994. Symmetrical double-cut, 2 pickups, glued-in neck, solidbody with tone chambers, multi-bound, gold-plated hardware, sunburst. After '94 made in Fender Custom Shop.

1989-1994		$1,100	$1,500
1995	Custom Shop	$2,400	$2,700

Shenandoah 12-String
1965-1971. Acoustic flat-top, spruce top, mahogany back and sides.

1965-1968	Antigua	$900	$1,200
1965-1968	Blond	$650	$800
1969-1971	Antigua	$800	$1,100
1969-1971	Blond	$550	$750

Showmaster FMT (Custom Shop)
2000-present. Bound figured maple top (FMT), 2 single-coil pickups and a bridge position humbucker, maple neck, Custom Shop certificate.

2000s		$1,000	$1,300

Showmaster (Import)
2003-present. Off-set double-cut solidbody, set neck, various models.

2000s	3 single coils	$350	$425
2000s	Celtic, 1 bridge humbucker	$250	$325
2000s	HH, 2 humbuckers	$400	$475

Squier '51
2004-present. Korean-made, Strat-style body with a Tele-style neck, various colors.

2004-2005		$75	$125

MODEL YEAR	FEATURES	EXC. COND. LOW	HIGH

Squier Bullet
1985-1988. Fender Japan was established in '82, Squier production began in '83, production was shifted to Korea in '87.

1985-1988	Sunburst, humbuckers	$250	$325
1985-1988	White	$175	$275

Squier Stagemaster HH
1999-2002. 2 humbuckers.

1999-2002		$175	$185

Starcaster
1974-1980. Double-cut, thinline semi-hollowbody, 2 humbuckers, various colors. Fender currently uses the Starcaster name on a line of budget guitars sold through Costco stores.

1974-1980		$3,200	$3,800

Stratocaster
The following are all variations of the Stratocaster. The first five listings are for the main American-made models and the '85 interim production Japanese model. All others are listed alphabetically after that in the following order.

Stratocaster
Standard Stratocaster (includes "Smith Strat")
Standard Stratocaster (Japan)
American Standard Stratocaster
American Series Stratocaster
21st Century Limited Edition Stratocaster
25th Anniversary Stratocaster
35th Anniversary Stratocaster
40th Anniversary Stratocaster
'50s Stratocaster
50th Anniversary Stratocaster
'54 Stratocaster
'56 Stratocaster
'57 Stratocaster
'58 Stratocaster
'60 Stratocaster
'60s Stratocaster
'62 Stratocaster
'65 Stratocaster
'66 Stratocaster
'68 Stratocaster
'68 Reverse Strat Special
'69 Stratocaster
'72 Stratocaster
'70s Stratocaster
Acoustasonic Stratocaster
Aerodyne Stratocaster
Aluminum Stratocaster
American Classic Holoflake Stratocaster
American Classic Stratocaster
American Deluxe Stratocaster
American Deluxe Fat Stratocaster
Antigua Stratocaster
Big Apple Stratocaster
Big Block Stratocaster
Bill Carson Stratocaster
Blackie Stratocaster
Blue Flower Stratocaster

Bonnie Raitt Stratocaster
Bowling Ball/Marble Stratocaster
Buck Owens Ltd. Edition Telecaster
Buddy Guy Stratocaster
California Stratocaster
California Fat Stratocaster
Classic Player Stratocaster
Collector's Edition Stratocaster ('62 Reissue)
Contemporary Stratocaster
Crash Stratocaster
Deluxe Strat Plus
Deluxe Vintage Player '62 Stratocaster
Dick Dale Stratocaster
Elite Stratocaster
Eric Clapton Stratocaster
Eric Clapton Gold Leaf Stratocaster
Eric Johnson Stratocaster
Floyd Rose Classic Stratocaster
Foto Flame Stratocaster
Freddy Tavares Aloha Stratocaster
Gold Stratocaster
Gold Elite Stratocaster
Hank Marvin Stratocaster
Harley-Davidson 90th Anniversary
Hellecaster Stratocaster
Highway 1 Stratocaster/HSS
HM Stratocaster
Homer Haynes HLE Stratocaster
Hot Wheels Stratocaster
HRR Stratocaster
Ike Turner Tribute Stratocaster
Jeff Beck Stratocaster
Jimi Hendrix Monterey Pop Stratocaster
Jimi Hendrix Tribute Stratocaster
Jimi Hendrix Voodoo Stratocaster
Jimmy Vaughan Tex-Mex Stratocaster
John Mayer Stratocaster
Kon Tiki Stratocaster
Lone Star Stratocaster
Moto Limited Edition Stratocaster
Paisley Stratocaster
Playboy 40th Anniversary Stratocaster
Powerhouse/Powerhouse Deluxe Stratocaster
Richie Sambora Stratocaster
Roadhouse Stratocaster
Robert Cray Stratocaster
Robin Trower Signature Stratocaster
Roland Stratocaster (Mexico)
Rory Gallagher Tribute Stratocaster
Set-Neck Stratocaster
Short-Scale (7/8) Stratocaster
So-Cal Speed Shop L.E. Stratocaster
Splatter Stratocaster (Mexico)
Squier Stratocaster Standard
Squier II Stratocaster
Standard Stratocaster (Mexico)
Standard Fat Strat
Stevie Ray Vaughan Stratocaster
Stevie Ray Vaughan Tribute #1 Stratocaster
Strat Plus
Stratocaster HSS/HH
Stratocaster Junior
Stratocaster Special (Mexico)

Stratocaster XII
Stratacoustic
Stratosonic
Sub Sonic Stratocaster
Super/Deluxe Super Stratocaster
Tanqurey Tonic Stratocaster
Texas Special Stratocaster
The Strat
Tie-Dye Stratocaster
Tree of Life Stratocaster
Turquoise Sparkle Stratocaster
U.S. Ultra / Ultra Plus Stratocaster
Ventures Limited Edition Stratocaster
Walnut Stratocaster
Walnut Elite Stratocaster
Western Stratocaster
Yngwie Malmsteen Stratocaster

Stratocaster

1954-1981. Two-tone sunburst until '58, 3-tone after. Custom color finishes were quite rare in the '50s and early-'60s and are much more valuable than the standard sunburst finish. By the '70s, color finishes were much more common and do not affect the value near as much. In '75 Fender dropped the optional custom colors and started issuing the guitars in a variety of standard colors (sunburst, blond, white, natural, walnut and black).

Custom color Fenders can be forged and bogus finishes have been a problem. As the value of custom color Fenders has increased, so has the problem of bogus non-original finishes. The prices in the Guide are for factory original finishes in excellent condition. Many of the Fender custom colors have been included in the listings. One color, Shell Pink, is notable because many vintage authorities ask, "Does a Shell Pink Strat even exist?" An ultra-rare custom color should have strong documented provenance and be verifiable by at least one (preferable two or more) well-known vintage authorities.

Three-bolt neck '72-'81, otherwise 4-bolt. Unless noted, all Stratocasters listed have the Fender tremolo system. Non-tremolo models (aka hardtails) typically sell for less. Many guitarists feel the tremolo block helps produce a fuller range of sound. On average, many more tremolo models were made. One year, '58, seems to be a year where a greater percentage of non-tremolo models were made. Tremolo vs. non-tremolo valuation should be taken on a brand-by-brand basis; for example, a pre-'65 Gibson ES-335 non-tremolo model is worth more than a tremolo equipped model.

Fender USA '70s Stratocaster

1954 Fender Stratocaster

MODEL YEAR	FEATURES	EXC. COND. LOW	HIGH
1954	Sunburst	$55,000	$100,000
1955	Sunburst	$45,000	$80,000
1956	Blond, nickel hardware	$50,000	$70,000
1956	Mary Kaye, gold hardware	$53,000	$90,000
1956	Sunburst, alder body	$41,000	$65,000
1956	Sunburst, ash body	$44,000	$68,000

1956 Fender Stratocaster

1957 Fender Stratocaster

MODEL YEAR	FEATURES	EXC. COND. LOW	HIGH
1956	Sunburst, non-trem	$35,000	$60,000
1957	Blond, nickel hardware	$46,000	$70,000
1957	Custom colors	$50,000	$80,000
1957	Mary Kaye, gold hardware	$52,000	$85,000
1957	Sunburst, bakelite knobs	$40,000	$60,000
1957	Sunburst, plastic knobs	$38,000	$58,000
1958	Black	$36,000	$68,000
1958	Blond, nickel hardware	$37,000	$69,000
1958	Fiesta Red	$40,000	$68,000
1958	Mary Kaye, gold hardware	$43,000	$88,000
1958	Sunburst 2-tone	$35,000	$55,000
1958	Sunburst 2-tone, non-trem	$26,000	$47,000
1958	Sunburst 3-tone	$30,000	$53,000
1958	Sunburst 3-tone, non-trem	$24,000	$45,000
1959	Blond, nickel hardware	$32,000	$67,000
1959	Custom colors	$37,000	$80,000
1959	Mary Kaye, gold hardware	$40,000	$85,000
1959	Sunburst, maple 'board	$30,000	$53,000
1959	Sunburst, non-trem, slab	$23,000	$45,000
1959	Sunburst, slab 'board	$29,000	$52,000
1960	Black	$27,000	$52,000
1960	Blond	$28,000	$52,000
1960	Burgundy Mist	$32,000	$65,000
1960	Dakota Red	$32,000	$64,000
1960	Daphne Blue	$29,000	$59,000
1960	Fiesta Red	$32,000	$64,000
1960	Foam Green	$35,000	$70,000
1960	Inca Silver	$29,000	$59,000
1960	Lake Placid Blue	$27,000	$56,000
1960	Olympic White	$27,000	$56,000
1960	Shell Pink	$38,000	$75,000
1960	Sherwood Green	$31,000	$63,000
1960	Shoreline Gold	$31,000	$63,000
1960	Sonic Blue	$29,000	$59,000
1960	Sunburst	$25,000	$45,000
1960	Surf Green	$33,000	$66,000
1961	Black	$25,000	$49,000
1961	Blond	$26,000	$49,000
1961	Burgundy Mist	$30,000	$61,000
1961	Dakota Red	$30,000	$61,000
1961	Daphne Blue	$28,000	$58,000
1961	Fiesta Red	$30,000	$61,000
1961	Foam Green	$32,000	$64,000
1961	Inca Silver	$28,000	$58,000
1961	Lake Placid Blue	$26,000	$54,000
1961	Olympic White	$26,000	$54,000
1961	Shell Pink	$37,000	$72,000

MODEL YEAR	FEATURES	EXC. COND. LOW	HIGH
1961	Sherwood Green	$30,000	$61,000
1961	Shoreline Gold	$30,000	$61,000
1961	Sonic Blue	$28,000	$58,000
1961	Sunburst	$24,000	$44,000
1961	Surf Green	$32,000	$64,000
1962	Black, curve	$20,000	$34,000
1962	Black, slab	$24,000	$42,000
1962	Blond, curve	$20,000	$34,000
1962	Blond, slab	$25,000	$42,000
1962	Burgundy Mist, curve	$26,000	$44,000
1962	Burgundy Mist, slab	$29,000	$54,000
1962	Candy Apple Red, curve	$20,000	$34,000
1962	Candy Apple Red, slab	$22,000	$42,000
1962	Dakota Red, curve	$26,000	$44,000
1962	Dakota Red, slab	$29,000	$54,000
1962	Daphne Blue, curve	$24,000	$41,000
1962	Daphne Blue, slab	$27,000	$51,000
1962	Fiesta Red, curve	$26,000	$44,000
1962	Fiesta Red, slab	$29,000	$54,000
1962	Foam Green, curve	$28,000	$48,000
1962	Foam Green, slab	$31,000	$58,000
1962	Inca Silver, curve	$24,000	$41,000
1962	Inca Silver, slab	$27,000	$51,000
1962	Lake Placid Blue, curve	$22,000	$37,000
1962	Lake Placid Blue, slab	$26,000	$49,000
1962	Olympic White, curve	$22,000	$37,000
1962	Olympic White, slab	$26,000	$49,000
1962	Shell Pink, curve	$32,000	$57,000
1962	Shell Pink, slab	$36,000	$66,000
1962	Sherwood Green, curve	$26,000	$44,000
1962	Sherwood Green, slab	$29,000	$54,000
1962	Shoreline Gold, curve	$26,000	$44,000
1962	Shoreline Gold, slab	$29,000	$54,000
1962	Sonic Blue, curve	$24,000	$41,000
1962	Sonic Blue, slab	$27,000	$51,000
1962	Sunburst, curve	$19,000	$28,000
1962	Sunburst, slab	$23,000	$37,000
1962	Sunburst, slab, tortoise 'guard	$28,000	$39,000
1962	Surf Green, curve	$28,000	$48,000
1962	Surf Green, slab	$31,000	$58,000
1963	Black	$20,000	$34,000
1963	Blond	$20,000	$34,000
1963	Burgundy Mist	$26,000	$44,000
1963	Candy Apple Red	$22,000	$37,000
1963	Dakota Red	$27,000	$46,000

MODEL YEAR	FEATURES	EXC. COND. LOW	HIGH
1963	Daphne Blue	$24,000	$41,000
1963	Fiesta Red	$27,000	$46,000
1963	Foam Green	$28,000	$48,000
1963	Inca Silver	$24,000	$41,000
1963	Lake Placid Blue	$22,000	$38,000
1963	Olympic White	$22,000	$38,000
1963	Sherwood Green	$26,000	$44,000
1963	Shoreline Gold	$26,000	$44,000
1963	Sonic Blue	$24,000	$41,000
1963	Sunburst	$19,000	$28,000
1963	Surf Green	$28,000	$48,000
1964	Black	$19,000	$28,000
1964	Blond	$19,000	$28,000
1964	Burgundy Mist	$25,000	$37,000
1964	Candy Apple Red	$21,000	$31,000
1964	Dakota Red	$25,000	$37,000
1964	Daphne Blue	$23,000	$34,000
1964	Fiesta Red	$25,000	$37,000
1964	Foam Green	$27,000	$40,000
1964	Inca Silver	$23,000	$34,000
1964	Lake Placid Blue	$21,000	$31,000
1964	Olympic White	$21,000	$31,000
1964	Sherwood Green	$26,000	$39,000
1964	Shoreline Gold	$25,000	$37,000
1964	Sonic Blue	$23,000	$34,000
1964	Sunburst	$17,000	$24,000
1964	Surf Green	$26,000	$39,000
1965	Black	$15,000	$24,000
1965	Blond	$15,000	$24,000
1965	Blue Ice/Ice Blue	$20,000	$30,000
1965	Burgundy Mist	$22,000	$33,000
1965	Candy Apple Red	$17,000	$25,000
1965	Charcoal Frost	$20,000	$30,000
1965	Dakota Red	$19,000	$28,000
1965	Fiesta Red	$19,000	$28,000
1965	Firemist Gold	$20,000	$30,000
1965	Firemist Silver	$20,000	$30,000
1965	Foam Green	$23,000	$34,000
1965	Inca Silver	$20,000	$30,000
1965	Lake Placid Blue	$17,000	$25,000
1965	Ocean Turquoise	$20,000	$30,000
1965	Olympic White	$17,000	$25,000
1965	Sonic Blue	$20,000	$30,000
1965	Sunburst, F-plate	$12,000	$19,000
1965	Sunburst, green 'guard	$14,000	$21,000
1965	Sunburst, white 'guard	$13,000	$20,000
1965	Teal Green	$20,000	$30,000
1966	Black	$14,000	$20,000
1966	Blond	$14,000	$20,000
1966	Blue Ice/Ice Blue	$17,000	$25,000
1966	Candy Apple Red	$15,000	$22,000
1966	Charcoal Frost	$17,000	$25,000
1966	Dakota Red	$17,000	$25,000
1966	Fiesta Red	$17,000	$25,000
1966	Firemist Gold	$18,000	$27,000
1966	Firemist Silver	$18,000	$27,000
1966	Foam Green	$21,000	$31,000
1966	Lake Placid Blue	$15,000	$22,000
1966	Ocean Turquoise	$18,000	$27,000

MODEL YEAR	FEATURES	EXC. COND. LOW	HIGH
1966	Olympic White	$15,000	$22,000
1966	Sonic Blue	$17,000	$25,000
1966	Sunburst	$11,000	$14,000
1966	Teal Green	$20,000	$31,000
1967	Black	$13,000	$19,000
1967	Blond	$13,000	$19,000
1967	Blue Ice/Ice Blue	$17,000	$25,000
1967	Candy Apple Red	$14,000	$21,000
1967	Charcoal Frost	$17,000	$25,000
1967	Dakota Red	$16,000	$24,000
1967	Fiesta Red	$16,000	$24,000
1967	Firemist Gold	$17,000	$25,000
1967	Firemist Silver	$17,000	$25,000
1967	Foam Green	$18,000	$27,000
1967	Lake Placid Blue	$14,000	$21,000
1967	Ocean Turquoise	$17,000	$25,000
1967	Olympic White	$14,000	$21,000
1967	Sonic Blue	$17,000	$25,000
1967	Sunburst, maple cap	$10,500	$16,000
1967	Sunburst, rosewood cap	$9,500	$14,000
1967	Teal Green	$17,000	$25,000
1968	Black, maple cap	$13,000	$19,000
1968	Black, rosewood cap	$12,000	$18,000
1968	Blond, maple cap	$13,000	$19,000
1968	Blond, rosewood cap	$12,000	$18,000
1968	Blue Ice, maple cap	$17,000	$25,000
1968	Blue Ice, rosewood cap	$16,000	$24,000
1968	Candy Apple Red, maple cap	$14,000	$21,000
1968	Candy Apple Red, rosewood cap	$13,000	$19,000
1968	Charcoal Frost, maple cap	$17,000	$25,000
1968	Charcoal Frost, rosewood cap	$16,000	$24,000
1968	Dakota Red, maple cap	$16,000	$24,000
1968	Dakota Red, rosewood cap	$15,000	$22,000
1968	Fiesta Red, maple cap	$16,000	$24,000
1968	Fiesta Red, rosewood cap	$15,000	$22,000
1968	Firemist Gold, maple cap	$17,000	$25,000
1968	Firemist Gold, rosewood cap	$16,000	$24,000
1968	Firemist Silver, maple cap	$17,000	$25,000
1968	Firemist Silver, rosewood cap	$16,000	$24,000
1968	Foam Green, maple cap	$18,000	$27,000
1968	Foam Green, rosewood cap	$17,000	$25,000

1958 Fender Stratocaster Mary Kaye

1964 Fender Stratocaster

GUITARS

1965 Fender Stratocaster

1973 Fender Stratocaster
(hardtail)

MODEL YEAR	FEATURES	EXC. COND. LOW	HIGH
1968	Lake Placid Blue, maple cap	$14,000	$21,000
1968	Lake Placid Blue, rosewood cap	$13,000	$19,000
1968	Ocean Turquoise, maple cap	$17,000	$25,000
1968	Ocean Turquoise, rosewood cap	$16,000	$24,000
1968	Olympic White, maple cap	$14,000	$21,000
1968	Olympic White, rosewood cap	$13,000	$19,000
1968	Sonic Blue, maple cap	$17,000	$25,000
1968	Sonic Blue, rosewood cap	$16,000	$24,000
1968	Sunburst, maple cap	$9,000	$13,000
1968	Sunburst, rosewood cap	$8,000	$12,000
1968	Teal Green, maple cap	$17,000	$25,000
1968	Teal Green, rosewood cap	$16,000	$24,000
1969	Black, maple	$12,000	$18,000
1969	Black, rosewood cap	$11,000	$17,000
1969	Blond, maple cap	$12,000	$18,000
1969	Blond, rosewood cap	$11,000	$17,000
1969	Blue Ice, maple cap	$16,000	$24,000
1969	Blue Ice, rosewood cap	$15,000	$23,000
1969	Candy Apple Red, maple cap	$13,000	$20,000
1969	Candy Apple Red, rosewood cap	$12,000	$18,000
1969	Charcoal Frost, maple cap	$16,000	$24,000
1969	Charcoal Frost, rosewood cap	$15,000	$23,000
1969	Dakota Red, maple cap	$15,000	$23,000
1969	Dakota Red, rosewood cap	$14,000	$21,000
1969	Fiesta Red, maple cap	$14,000	$21,000
1969	Fiesta Red, rosewood cap	$15,000	$23,000
1969	Firemist Gold, maple cap	$16,000	$24,000
1969	Firemist Gold, rosewood cap	$15,000	$23,000
1969	Firemist Silver, maple cap	$16,000	$24,000
1969	Firemist Silver, rosewood cap	$15,000	$23,000
1969	Foam Green, maple cap	$17,000	$26,000

MODEL YEAR	FEATURES	EXC. COND. LOW	HIGH
1969	Foam Green, rosewood cap	$16,000	$24,000
1969	Lake Placid Blue, maple cap	$13,000	$20,000
1969	Lake Placid Blue, rosewood cap	$12,000	$18,000
1969	Ocean Turquoise, maple cap	$16,000	$24,000
1969	Ocean Turquoise, rosewood cap	$15,000	$23,000
1969	Olympic White, maple cap	$14,000	$21,000
1969	Olympic White, rosewood cap	$13,000	$19,000
1969	Sonic Blue, maple cap	$17,000	$25,000
1969	Sonic Blue, rosewood cap	$16,000	$24,000
1969	Sunburst, maple cap	$8,000	$12,000
1969	Sunburst, rosewood cap	$7,000	$11,000
1969	Teal Green, maple cap	$17,000	$25,000
1969	Teal Green, rosewood cap	$16,000	$24,000
1970	Black, maple cap	$12,000	$17,000
1970	Black, rosewood cap	$11,000	$15,000
1970	Blond, maple cap	$11,000	$15,000
1970	Blond, rosewood cap	$12,000	$17,000
1970	Blue Ice, maple cap	$13,000	$18,000
1970	Blue Ice, rosewood cap	$12,000	$17,000
1970	Candy Apple Red, maple cap	$12,000	$17,000
1970	Candy Apple Red, rosewood cap	$11,000	$15,000
1970	Charcoal Frost, maple cap	$13,000	$18,000
1970	Charcoal Frost, rosewood cap	$12,000	$17,000
1970	Dakota Red, maple cap	$13,000	$18,000
1970	Dakota Red, rosewood cap	$12,000	$17,000
1970	Fiesta Red, maple cap	$13,000	$18,000
1970	Fiesta Red, rosewood cap	$12,000	$17,000
1970	Firemist Gold, maple cap	$14,000	$19,000
1970	Firemist Gold, rosewood cap	$13,000	$18,000
1970	Firemist Silver, maple cap	$14,000	$19,000
1970	Firemist Silver, rosewood cap	$13,000	$18,000

The *Vintage Guitar Price Guide* shows low to high values for items in all-original excellent condition, and, where applicable, with original case or cover.

MODEL YEAR	FEATURES	EXC. COND. LOW	HIGH
1970	Foam Green, maple cap	$16,000	$22,000
1970	Foam Green, rosewood cap	$15,000	$21,000
1970	Lake Placid Blue, maple cap	$12,000	$17,000
1970	Lake Placid Blue, rosewood cap	$11,000	$15,000
1970	Ocean Turquoise, maple cap	$15,000	$21,000
1970	Ocean Turquoise, rosewood cap	$14,000	$20,000
1970	Olympic White, maple cap	$12,000	$17,000
1970	Olympic White, rosewood cap	$11,000	$15,000
1970	Sonic Blue, maple cap	$15,000	$21,000
1970	Sonic Blue, rosewood cap	$14,000	$20,000
1970	Sunburst, maple cap	$7,000	$10,000
1970	Sunburst, rosewood cap	$6,500	$9,000
1970	Teal Green, maple cap	$15,000	$21,000
1970	Teal Green, rosewood cap	$14,000	$20,000
1971	Black	$10,000	$14,000
1971	Blond	$10,000	$14,000
1971	Candy Apple Red	$10,000	$14,000
1971	Firemist Gold	$12,000	$17,000
1971	Firemist Silver	$12,000	$17,000
1971	Lake Placid Blue	$10,000	$14,000
1971	Ocean Turquoise	$12,000	$19,000
1971	Olympic White	$10,000	$14,000
1971	Sonic Blue	$12,000	$19,000
1971	Sunburst	$6,000	$9,000
1972	Black	$5,000	$7,000
1972	Blond	$5,000	$7,000
1972	Candy Apple Red	$5,000	$7,000
1972	Lake Placid Blue	$5,000	$7,000
1972	Olympic White	$5,000	$7,000
1972	Sonic Blue	$6,000	$8,000
1972	Sunburst	$3,000	$4,500
1973	Black	$4,000	$6,000
1973	Blond	$4,000	$6,000
1973	Candy Apple Red	$4,000	$6,000
1973	Lake Placid Blue	$4,000	$6,000
1973	Natural	$2,700	$3,500
1973	Olympic White	$4,000	$6,000
1973	Sunburst, non-trem	$2,700	$4,000
1973	Sunburst, trem	$3,000	$4,500
1973	Walnut	$2,700	$3,500
1974	Black	$3,500	$5,500
1974	Blond	$3,500	$5,500
1974	Natural	$2,700	$3,000
1974	Olympic White	$3,500	$5,500
1974	Sunburst, non-trem	$2,700	$4,000
1974	Sunburst, trem	$3,000	$4,500
1974	Walnut	$2,700	$3,000

MODEL YEAR	FEATURES	EXC. COND. LOW	HIGH
1975	Black	$2,600	$2,700
1975	Blond	$2,600	$2,700
1975	Natural	$2,100	$2,700
1975	Olympic White	$2,600	$2,700
1975	Sunburst, black parts	$2,100	$2,500
1975	Sunburst, white parts	$2,200	$2,600
1975	Walnut	$2,500	$2,700
1976	Black	$2,400	$2,600
1976	Blond	$2,400	$2,600
1976	Natural	$2,000	$2,500
1976	Olympic White	$2,400	$2,600
1976	Sunburst	$2,100	$2,500
1976	Walnut	$2,400	$2,600
1977	Black	$2,200	$2,300
1977	Blond	$2,200	$2,300
1977	Natural	$1,800	$2,100
1977	Olympic White	$2,200	$2,300
1977	Sunburst	$1,900	$2,100
1977	Walnut	$1,800	$2,100
1978	Antigua	$1,800	$2,200
1978	Black	$1,800	$2,200
1978	Blond	$1,800	$2,200
1978	Natural	$1,600	$2,000
1978	Olympic White	$1,800	$2,200
1978	Sunburst	$1,800	$2,100
1978	Walnut	$1,600	$2,000
1978	Wine	$1,700	$2,100
1979	Antigua	$1,700	$2,200
1979	Black	$1,700	$2,200
1979	Blond	$1,700	$2,200
1979	Natural	$1,500	$2,000
1979	Olympic White	$1,700	$2,200
1979	Sunburst	$1,600	$2,100
1979	Walnut	$1,500	$2,000
1979	Wine	$1,600	$2,100
1980	Antigua	$1,600	$2,100
1980	Black	$1,600	$2,100
1980	Natural	$1,400	$1,900
1980	Olympic White	$1,600	$2,100
1980	Sunburst	$1,500	$2,000
1980	Wine	$1,500	$2,000
1981	International colors	$1,400	$2,000
1981	Sunburst	$1,200	$1,500

Standard Stratocaster (includes "Smith Strat")

1981-1984. Replaces the Stratocaster. Renamed the American Standard Stratocaster for '86-'00 (see next listing). Renamed American Series Stratocaster in '00. From '81/'82 to mid-'83, 4 knobs same as regular Strat but with 4-bolt neck. In August '81, Dan Smith was hired by Bill Schultz and Fender produced an alder body, 4-bolt neck, 21-fret, small headstock Standard Stratocaster that has been nicknamed the Smith Strat (made from Dec. '81-'83). Mid-'83 to the end of '84 2 knobs and 'guard mounted input jack. Not to be confused with current Standard Stratocaster, which is made in Mexico.

1981	Smith Strat, 4-bolt, 3 knobs	$1,300	$1,600

1981 Fender Stratocaster

Fender American Series Stratocaster

GUITARS

*Fender American Vintage
'62 Stratocaster*

*Fender Custom Shop
'56 Stratocaster NOS*

MODEL YEAR	FEATURES	EXC. COND. LOW	HIGH
1982	Smith Strat, rare colors	$1,600	$2,000
1982	Smith Strat, various colors	$1,300	$1,600
1983	Smith Strat, various colors	$1,300	$1,600
1983-1984	Sunburst, 2-knob	$850	$900
1983-1984	Various colors, 2-knob	$750	$900

Standard Stratocaster (Japan)

1985. Interim production in Japan while the new Fender reorganized, standard pickup configuration and tremolo system, 3 knobs with switch, traditional style input jack, traditional shaped headstock, natural maple color.

1985	Black or red, white 'guard	$600	$700

American Standard Stratocaster

1986-2000. Fender's new name for the American-made Strat when reintroducing it after CBS sold the company. The only American-made Strats made in 1985 were the '57 and '62 models. See Stratocaster and Standard Stratocaster for earlier models, renamed American Series Stratocaster in 2000.

1986-1989	Various colors	$750	$875
1989	Mary Kaye Limited Edition	$875	$975
1990-1999	Various colors	$700	$750
1995	Limited Edition matching headstock	$900	$1,075

American Series Stratocaster

2000-present. Fender's updated standard production model, ash or alder body, rosewood 'board, dot markers, 3 staggered single-coil pickups, 5-way switch, hand polished fret edges.

2000-2005	Alder body	$625	$700
2000-2005	Ash body	$675	$750
2000-2005	Limited Edition colors	$700	$750
2000-2005	Limited Edition matching headstock	$950	$975
2000-2005	Ash body, hardtail	$625	$675

21st Century Limited Edition Stratocaster

2000. Custom Shop model, one of first 100 to leave Fender in 2000, certificate with CEO William C. Schultz, 21st logo on headstock.

2000		$1,100	$1,350

25th Anniversary Stratocaster

1979-1980. Has ANNIVERSARY on upper body horn, silver metallic or white pearlescent finish.

1979	White, 1st issue, flaking	$1,100	$1,300
1979	White, 1st issue, no flaking	$1,500	$1,600
1979-1980	Silver, faded to gold	$1,100	$1,300
1979-1980	Silver, unfaded	$1,500	$1,600

35th Anniversary Stratocaster

1989-1991. Custom Shop model, figured maple top, Lace Sensor pickups, Eric Clapton preamp circuit.

1989-1991		$2,200	$2,900

MODEL YEAR	FEATURES	EXC. COND. LOW	HIGH

40th Anniversary Stratocaster

1994 only. American Standard model (not Custom Shop model), plain top, appearance similar to a '54 maple-neck Stratocaster, sunburst. Not to be confused with the Custom Shop 40th Anniversary Diamond Edition.

1994		$1,300	$1,400

'50s Stratocaster Relic

1996-1999. Custom Shop model, reproduction of ca. '57 Strat with played-in feel, gold hardware is +$100, see-thru Mary Kaye ash body is +$100, replaced by '56 Strat.

1996-1999	Various colors	$1,300	$1,800

'50s Stratocaster (Import)

1991-present.

1991-2005		$450	$500

50th Anniversary Stratocaster

1995-1996. Custom Shop model, flame maple top, 3 vintage-style pickups, gold hardware, gold 50th Anniversary coin on back of the headstock, sunburst, 2500 made.

1995-1996		$1,400	$1,600

50th Anniversary Stratocaster Relic

1995-1996. Custom Shop Relic model, aged played-in feel, diamond headstock inlay, Shoreline Gold finish, 200 units planned.

1995-1996		$2,400	$2,700

'54 Stratocaster

1992-1998 (Custom Shop Classic reissue), 1997-present. Ash body, Custom '50s pickups, gold-plated hardware.

1992-1998	Various options	$1,500	$1,800

'54 Stratocaster FMT

1992-1998. Custom Classic reissue, Flame Maple Top, also comes in gold hardware edition.

1992-1998		$1,700	$1,800
1992-1998	Gold hardware option	$1,800	$1,900

'56 Stratocaster

1999-present. Custom Shop model, most detailed replica (and most expensive to date) of '56 Strat, including electronics and pickups, offered with rosewood or maple 'board, gold hardware is +$100.

1999-2005	Closet Classic	$1,700	$1,900
1999-2005	NOS	$1,600	$1,800
1999-2005	Relic	$1,900	$2,100

'57 Special Stratocaster

1992-1993. Custom Shop model, flamed maple top, birdseye maple neck, run of 60 made, sunburst.

1992-1993		$1,700	$1,900

'57 Stratocaster

Mid-1990s. Custom Shop model, replaced by the more authentic, higher-detailed '56 Custom Shop Stratocaster by '99, Custom Shop models can be distinguished by the original certificate that comes with the guitar.

1994-1996	Various colors	$1,200	$1,600

MODEL		EXC. COND.	
YEAR	FEATURES	LOW	HIGH

'57 Stratocaster (USA)

1982-present. U.S.A.-made at the Fullerton, California plant ('82-'85) and at the Corona, California plant ('85-present).

1982-1984	Various colors	$1,100	$1,200
1986-1989	Blond, ash body	$1,200	$1,300
1986-1989	Various colors	$1,100	$1,200
1990-1999	Blond, ash body	$1,200	$1,300
1990-1999	Various colors	$1,000	$1,100
2000-2005	Various colors	$900	$1,100

'57 Vintage Stratocaster (Japan)

1984-1985. Japanese-made, various colors.

| 1984-1985 | | $550 | $700 |

'58 Stratocaster

1996-1999. Custom Shop model, ash body, Fat '50s pickups, chrome or gold hardware (gold is +$100.), Custom Shop models can be distinguished by the original certificate that comes with the guitar.

| 1996-1999 | Various colors | $1,200 | $1,600 |

'58 Stratocaster (Dakota Red)

1996. Custom Shop model, run of 30 made in Dakota Red with matching headstock, maple neck, Texas special pickups, gold hardware.

| 1996 | | $1,500 | $1,800 |

'60 FMT Stratocaster

1997-1999. Custom Shop model, flame maple top.

| 1997-1999 | | $1,600 | $1,800 |

'60 Stratocaster

1992-present. Custom Shop model, '92-'99 version with Texas Special pickups, later version is more detailed replica (and most expensive to date) of '60 Strat, including electronics and pickups, gold hardware is +$100.

1992-1998	1st issue	$1,500	$1,700
1999-2005	Closet Classic	$1,700	$1,900
1999-2005	NOS	$1,600	$1,800
1999-2005	Relic	$1,900	$2,100
1999-2005	Various "rare" colors	$2,100	$2,400

'60s Stratocaster Relic

1996-1999. Custom Shop model, reproduction of '60s Strat with played-in feel, gold hardware is +$100, see-thru Mary Kaye ash body is +$100, replaced by '60 Relic.

| 1996-1999 | Various colors | $1,300 | $1,800 |

'60s Stratocaster (Japan)

1991-present. Made in Japan, basswood body, U-neck, rosewood 'board, trem, various colors.

| 1991-2005 | | $550 | $700 |

'62 Stratocaster (USA)

1982-present. Made at Fullerton plant ('82-'85) then at Corona plant ('86-present).

1982-1984	Various colors	$1,100	$1,200
1986-1989	Blond, ash body	$1,200	$1,300
1986-1989	Various colors	$1,100	$1,200
1990-1999	Blond, ash body	$1,200	$1,300
1990-2005	Various colors	$1,000	$1,100

'65 Stratocaster

2003-present. Custom Shop model, '65 small-headstock specs, rosewood or maple cap 'board, transition logo, offered in NOS, Relic, or Closet Classic versions.

2003-2005	Closet Classic	$1,700	$1,900
2003-2005	NOS	$1,600	$1,800
2003-2005	Relic	$1,900	$2,100

'66 Stratocaster

2004-present. Custom Shop model, offered in Closet Classic, NOS or Relic versions.

2004-2005	Closet Classic	$1,700	$1,900
2004-2005	NOS	$1,600	$1,800
2004-2005	Relic	$1,900	$2,100

'68 Stratocaster

1990s. Custom Shop model, Jimi Hendrix-style, maple cap neck.

| 1990s | | $1,600 | $1,900 |

'68 Stratocaster (Japan)

1994-1999. '68 specs including large headstock, part of Collectables Series, sunburst, natural, Olympic White.

| 1994-1999 | | $550 | $700 |

'68 Reverse Strat Special (USA)

2001-2002. With special reverse left-hand neck, large headstock (post-CBS style).

| 2001-2002 | | $750 | $1,100 |

'69 Stratocaster

1997-present. Custom Shop model, large headstock, U-shaped maple neck with rosewood or maple cap options, '69-style finish, gold hardware is +$100, since 2000, offered in NOS, Relic, or Closet Classic versions.

2000-2005	Closet Classic	$1,700	$1,900
2000-2005	NOS	$1,600	$1,800
2000-2005	Relic	$1,900	$2,100

'70s Stratocaster (Mexico)

1999-present. Made in Mexico, large headstock, white pickups and knobs, rosewood 'board.

| 1999-2005 | | $350 | $400 |

'72 Stratocaster (Japan)

1985-1996. Basswood body, maple 'board, large headstock.

| 1985-1996 | | $550 | $700 |

Acoustasonic Stratocaster

2003-present. Hollowed out alder Strat body with braceless graphite top, 3 in-bridge Fishman piezo pickups, acoustic sound hole.

| 2003-2005 | | $500 | $550 |

Aerodyne Stratocaster

2004-present. Strat with Aerodyne body profile, bound body, import.

| 200-2005 | | $450 | $500 |

Aluminum Stratocaster

1994-1995. Aluminum-bodied American Standard with anodized finish in blue marble, purple marble or red, silver and blue stars and stripes. Some with 40th Anniversary designation. There is also a Custom Shop version.

| 1994-1995 | Marble patterns | $1,700 | $2,500 |
| 1994-1995 | Red-silver-blue flag option | $1,800 | $2,600 |

Fender '60s Relic Stratocaster

1994 Fender Custom Shop Aluminum Stratocaster

GUITARS

*Fender Amerian
Deluxe Stratocaster*

Fender Buddy Guy Stratocaster

MODEL YEAR	FEATURES	EXC. COND. LOW	HIGH
American Classic Holoflake Stratocaster			
1992-1993. Custom Shop model, splatter/sparkle finish, pearloid 'guard.			
1992-1993		$1,500	$1,900
American Classic Stratocaster			
1992-1999. Custom Shop version of American Standard, 3 pickups, tremolo, rosewood 'board, nickel or gold-plated hardware, various colors.			
1992-1999	See-thru blond ash body	$1,400	$1,600
1992-1999	Various colors and options	$1,300	$1,500
American Deluxe Stratocaster			
1998-present. Made in USA, premium alder or ash body, noiseless pickups.			
1998-1999	Ash body, transparent finish	$900	$1,000
1998-1999	Various colors	$850	$900
2000-2005	Various colors	$850	$975
American Deluxe Fat Stratocaster			
1998-2003. Made in USA, Fender DH-1 bridge humbucker for fat sound, premium alder or ash body.			
1998-2003	Ash body, transparent finish	$900	$1,000
1998-2003	Various colors	$850	$900
Antigua Stratocaster			
2003. Japanese-made limited-edition reissue, '70s features and antigua finish.			
2003		$550	$700
Big Apple Stratocaster			
1997-2000. Two humbucking pickups, 5-way switch, rosewood 'board or maple neck, non-tremolo optional.			
1997-2000	Various colors	$750	$800
Big Block Stratocaster			
2005-present. Pearloid block markers inlays, black finish with matching headstock, single coil in neck and middle position, humbucker pickup in bridge position, vintage style tremolo.			
2005		$600	$650
Bill Carson Stratocaster			
1992. Based on the '57 Strat, birdseye maple neck, Cimarron Red finish, 1 left-handed and 100 right-handed produced, serial numbers MT000-MT100, made in Fender Custom Shop, and initiated by The Music Trader (MT) in Florida.			
1992		$2,000	$2,150
Blackie Stratocaster			
1987. Custom Shop model, recreation of Eric Clapton's Blackie Stratocaster, 12 made, includes letter of authentication, stenciled tweed case.			
1987		$2,400	$2,500
Blue Flower Stratocaster			
1988-1993, 2003-2004. Made in Japan, '72 Strat reissue with a reissue '68 Tele Blue Floral finish.			
1988-1993		$800	$1,200
Bonnie Raitt Stratocaster			
1995-2000. Alder body, often in blueburst, Bonnie Raitt's signature on headstock.			
1995-2000		$950	$1,000

MODEL YEAR	FEATURES	EXC. COND. LOW	HIGH
Bowling Ball/Marble Stratocaster			
Ca.1983-1984. Standard Strat with 1 tone and 1 volume control, jack on 'guard, called Bowling Ball Strat due to the swirling, colored finish.			
1983-1984		$2,000	$2,500
Buck Owens Ltd. Edition Telecaster			
1998-2002. Custom Shop model, red, white and blue sparkle finish, gold hardware, gold 'guard, rosewood 'board, by Fender Japan.			
1998-2002		$900	$1,000
Buddy Guy Stratocaster (Signature)			
1995-present. Maple neck, 3 Gold Lace Sensor pickups, ash body, signature model, blond or sunburst.			
1995-2005		$1,000	$1,200
Buddy Guy Stratocaster (Mexico)			
1996-present. Maple neck, polka-dot finish.			
1996-2005		$400	$475
California Stratocaster			
1997-1999. Made in the U.S., painted in Mexico, 2 pickups, various colors.			
1997-1999		$525	$700
California Fat Stratocaster			
1997-1998. Humbucker pickup in bridge position.			
1997-1998		$525	$700
Classic Player Stratocaster			
2000. Custom Shop model, Standard Stratocaster with useful 'player-friendly features' such as noiseless stacked single-coil pickups and factory Sperzel locking tuners, made in the Custom Shop, black, gold anodized 'guard.			
2000		$1,250	$1,350
Collector's Edition Stratocaster ('62 Reissue)			
1997. Pearl inlaid '97 on 12th fret, rosewood 'board, alder body, gold hardware, tortoise 'guard, nitro finish, sunburst, 1997 made.			
1997		$1,300	$1,500
Contemporary Stratocaster			
1989-1998. U.S.-made Custom Shop model, 7/8 scale body, hum/single/single pickups, various colors.			
1989-1998		$1,100	$1,400
Contemporary Stratocaster (Import)			
1985-1987. Import model used while the new Fender reorganized, black headstock with silver-white logo, black or white 'guard, 2 humbucker pickups or single-coil and humbucker, 2 knobs and slider switch.			
1985-1987		$325	$425
Crash Stratocaster			
2005. Master Built Custom Shop model, hand painted by John Crash Matos, approximately 50, comes with certificate, the original certificate adds value, the prices shown include the certificate.			
2005		$10,000	$14,000
Deluxe Strat Plus			
1987-1998. Three Lace Sensor pickups, Floyd Rose, alder (poplar available earlier) body with ash veneer on front and back, various colors, also see Strat Plus.			
1987-1998		$775	$825

The *Vintage Guitar Price Guide* shows low to high values for items in all-original excellent condition, and, where applicable, with original case or cover.

MODEL YEAR	FEATURES	EXC. COND. LOW	HIGH

Deluxe Vintage Player '62 Stratocaster

2005-2006. Design blends vintage and modern features based upon '62 specs including vintage style tuners, bridge and aged plastic parts. Updates include 3 Samarium Cobalt Noiseless pickups and Deluxe American Standard electronics, limited edition, Olympic White or Ice Blue

2005-2006		$1,000	$1,100

Dick Dale Stratocaster

1994-present. Custom Shop signature model, alder body, reverse headstock, sparkle finish.

1994-2005		$1,500	$1,900

Elite Stratocaster

1983-1984. The Elite Series feature active electronics and noise-cancelling pickups, push buttons instead of 3-way switch, Elite script logo on 4-bolt neck plate, various colors. Also see Gold Elite Stratocaster and Walnut Elite Stratocaster.

1983-1984	Standard colors	$975	$1,100
1983-1984	Stratoburst option(s)	$1,000	$1,250

Eric Clapton Stratocaster

1988-present. U.S.-made, '57 reissue features, active electronics.

1988-2005		$950	$1,000

Eric Clapton Stratocaster (CS)

2004. Custom Shop model, re-creation of Clapton's personal guitar, standard non-active single-coil pickups, black or blue finish.

2004		$1,700	$1,800

Eric Clapton Gold Leaf Stratocaster

2004. Custom Shop model, special build for Guitar Center, 50 made, 23k gold leaf finish/covering.

2004		$7,000	$8,000

Eric Johnson Stratocaster

2005. Custom Shop model, lightweight '57 spec body, '57 soft-v-neck profile, special design Custom Shop Eric Johnson pickups, vintage tremolo with 5-springs.

2005		$1,300	$1,400

Floyd Rose Classic Relic Stratocaster

1998-1999. Custom Shop model, late '60s large headstock, 1 humbucker and 1 Strat pickup.

1998-1999		$1,300	$1,700

Floyd Rose Classic Stratocaster

1992-1997. Two single-coils, bridge humbucker, Floyd Rose tremolo, various colors.

1992-1997		$725	$825

Foto Flame Stratocaster

1994-1996, 2000. Japanese-made Collectables model, alder and basswood body with Foto Flame (simulated woodgrain) finish on top cap and back of neck.

1994-1996		$500	$600
2000		$500	$600

Freddy Tavares Aloha Stratocaster

1993-1994. Custom Shop model, hollow aluminum body with hand engraved Hawaiian scenes, custom inlay on neck, 153 made.

1993-1994		$4,400	$5,300

Gold Stratocaster (CS)

1989. Custom Shop model, 500 made, gold finish with gold anodized and white 'guards included.

1989		$2,100	$2,200

Gold Stratocaster

1981-1983. Gold metallic finish, gold-plated brass hardware, 4-bolt neck, maple 'board, skunk strip, trem.

1989		$1,000	$1,500

Gold Elite Stratocaster

1983-1984. The Elite series feature active electronics and noise-cancelling pickups, the Gold Elite has gold hardware and pearloid tuner buttons, also see Elite Stratocaster and Walnut Elite Stratocaster.

1983-1984		$1,000	$1,300

Hank Marvin Stratocaster

1995-1996. Custom Shop model, Feista Red.

1995-1996		$1,400	$1,700

Harley-Davidson 90th Anniversary Stratocaster

1993. Custom Shop, 109 total made, Harley-Davidson and Custom Shop V logo on headstock (Diamond Edition, 40 units), 9 units produced for the Harley-Davidson company without diamond logo, 60 units were not Diamond Edition, chrome-plated engraved metal body, engraved 'guard, Custom Shop Certificate important attribute.

1993		$10,000	$12,000

Hellecaster Stratocaster

1997. Custom Shop model, gold sparkle 'guard, gold hardware, split single-coils, rosewood 'board.

1997		$1,300	$1,600

Highway 1 Stratocaster/HSS

2003-present. U.S.-made, alder body, satin lacquer finish, HSS version has humbucker/single/single pickups.

2003-2005		$450	$600

HM Stratocaster (USA/Import)

1988-1992 ('88 Japanese-made, '89-'90 U.S.- and Japanese-made, '91-'92 U.S.-made). Heavy Metal Strat, Floyd Rose, regular or pointy headstock, black hardware, 1 or 2 humbuckers, 1 single-coil and 1 humbucker, or 2 single-coils and 1 humbucker. Later models have choice of 2 humbuckers and 1 single-coil or 2 single-coils and 1 humbucker.

1988-1990	Bud Dry logo finish	$400	$525
1988-1990	Import	$275	$375
1989-1992	US	$400	$500

Homer Haynes HLE Stratocaster

1988-1989. Custom Shop model, '59 Strat basics with gold finish, gold anodized guard, and gold hardware, limited edition of 500.

1988-1989		$1,500	$1,900

Hot Wheels Stratocaster

2003. Custom Shop model commissioned by Hot Wheels, 16 made, orange flames over background, large Hot Wheels logo.

2003		$2,900	$3,500

Fender Dick Dale Stratocaster

Fender Highway 1 Stratocaster Stratocaster

GUITARS

*Fender Ike Turner
Tribute Stratocaster*

*Fender Jeff Beck
Stratocaster*

MODEL YEAR	FEATURES	EXC. COND. LOW	HIGH

HRR Stratocaster
1990-1995. Japanese-made, hot-rodded vintage-style Strat, Floyd Rose tremolo system, 3 pickups, maple neck, Foto Flame, black, Olympic White or sunburst.

1990-1995		$350	$500

Ike Turner Tribute Stratocaster
2005. Custom Shop model, 100 made, replica of Ike Turner's Sonic Blue Strat.

2005		$1,900	$2,000

Jeff Beck Stratocaster
1994-present. Alder body, Lace Sensor pickups, special designed tremolo, various colors but mostly Surf Green.

1994-2000	Rare color	$1,000	$1,400
1994-2005	Standard color	$950	$1,000

Jimi Hendrix Monterey Pop Stratocaster
1997-1998. Custom Shop model, near replica of Monterey Pop Festival sacrifice guitar, red psychedelic-style finish.

1997-1998		$7,000	$8,500

Jimi Hendrix Tribute Stratocaster
1997-2000. Left-handed guitar strung right-handed, maple cap neck, Olympic White finish.

1997-2000		$1,100	$1,300

Jimi Hendrix Voodoo Stratocaster
1998-2002. Right-handed body with reverse peghead, maple neck, sunburst, Olympic White, or black.

1998-2002		$1,200	$1,400

Jimmy Vaughan Tex-Mex Stratocaster
1997-present. Poplar body, maple 'board, Jimmy Vaughan signature on headstock, 3 Tex-Mex pickups, various colors.

1997-2005		$400	$500

John Mayer Stratocaster
2005. Custom Shop model alder body, special scooped mid-range pickups, vintage tremolo, special design gigbag with pocket for laptop computer.

2005		$1,100	$1,200

Kon Tiki Stratocaster
2003. Custom Shop model, limited run of 25, Tiki Green including Tike 3-color art work on headstock.

2003		$1,300	$1,500

Lone Star Stratocaster
1996-2000. Alder body, 1 humbucker and 2 single-coil pickups, rosewood 'board or maple neck, various colors.

1996-2000		$700	$800

Moto Limited Edition Stratocaster
1990s. Custom Shop model, pearloid cover in various colors, includes Certificate of Authenticity, not to be confused with white pearloid Moto Strat which is part of a guitar and amp set (as listed below).

1990s		$1,500	$1,700

Moto Set Stratocaster
1995-1996. Custom Shop set including guitar, case, amp and amp stand, white pearloid finish.

1995-1996		$3,800	$4,100
1995-1996	Red (few made)	$4,100	$4,300

MODEL YEAR	FEATURES	EXC. COND. LOW	HIGH

Paisley Stratocaster
1988-1995, 2003-2004. Japanese-made '72 Strat reissue with a reissue '68 Tele Pink Paisley finish.

1988-1995		$800	$1,200

Playboy 40th Anniversary Stratocaster
1994. Custom Shop model, nude Marilyn Monroe graphic on body.

1994		$6,000	$6,500

Powerhouse/Powerhouse Deluxe Stratocaster
1997-present. Import Standard Strat configuration with pearloid 'guard, various colors.

1997-2005		$425	$500

Richie Sambora Stratocaster
1993-2002. Alder body, Floyd Rose tremolo, maple neck, sunburst. There was also a cheaper Richie Sambora Standard Stratocaster in blue or white.

1993-2002	USA	$900	$1,100
1994-2002	Import	$350	$500

Roadhouse Stratocaster
1997-2000. U.S.-made, poplar body, tortoise shell 'guard, maple 'board, 3 Texas Special pickups, various colors.

1997-2000		$675	$800

Robert Cray Stratocaster
1991-present. Custom Shop signature model, rosewood 'board, chunky neck, lighter weight, non-tremolo, alder body, gold-plated hardware, various colors. There is also a chrome hardware Robert Cray Standard Stratocaster model.

1991-2005		$1,000	$1,200

Robin Trower Signature Stratocaster
2004. Custom Shop model, 100 made, large head-stock (post '65-era styling), with '70s logo styling, post '71 3-bolt neck, bullet truss rod, white.

2004		$2,100	$2,300

Roland Stratocaster (Mexico)
1998-present. Single synth pickup and 3 standard single-coil pickups, made in Mexico.

1998-2003		$450	$500

Rory Gallagher Tribute Stratocaster
2005. Custom Shop model, heavily distressed '61 model based on Gallagher's guitar, price includes the original Custom Shop certificate, a model without the certificate is worth less, Rory Gallagher logo signature on back of headstock.

2005		$2,100	$2,300

Set-Neck Stratocaster
1992-1999. Custom Shop model, mahogany body and figured maple top, 4 pickups, glued-in neck, active electronics, by '96 ash body.

1992-1999		$1,100	$1,400

Short-Scale (7/8) Stratocaster
1989-1995. Similar to Standard Strat, but with 2 control knobs and switch, 24" scale vs. 25" scale, sometimes called a mini-Strat, Japanese import, various colors.

1989-1995		$525	$600

MODEL YEAR	FEATURES	EXC. COND. LOW	HIGH

So-Cal Speed Shop L.E. Stratocaster

2005-2006. Limited edition for Musician's Friend, custom red, white, and black So-Cal paint job over basswood body and rosewood 'board, 1 humbucker, So-Cal Speed Shop decal.

2005-2006		$450	$475

Splatter Stratocaster (Mexico)

2003. Made in Mexico, splatter paint job, various color combinations, with gig bag.

2003		$250	$300

Squier Stratocaster Standard

1982-present. Low-cost Stratocaster Standard version of the Squier line. Fender Japan was established in '82 with Squier production beginning in '83. Production was shifted to Korea in '87 and later allocated to China, India (Squier II '89-'90) and Mexico.

1983-1989		$250	$350
1990-1999		$175	$275
2000-2005	Indonesia	$100	$125

Squier Stratocaster Standard (Affinity Series)

1997-present. Made in China.

1997-2005		$100	$125

Squier Stratocaster Standard (Double Fat Strat)

2000-present. Made in China, 2 humbucker pickups.

2000-2005		$125	$175

Squier Stratocaster Standard (Floyd Rose)

1995-1996. Floyd Rose tailpiece, fotoflame finish, large Fender script logo.

1995-1996		$300	$350

Squier II Stratocaster

1989-1990. Import from India.

1989-1990		$100	$125

Standard Stratocaster (Mexico)

1990-present. Fender Mexico started guitar production in '90. Not to be confused with the American-made Standard Stratocaster of '81-'84. High end of range includes a hard guitar case, while the low end of the range includes only a gig bag, various colors.

1990-1999		$250	$275
2000-2005		$250	$325

Standard Stratocaster Satin Finish

2003-present. Made in Mexico, poplar body, satin finish.

2003-2005		$250	$300

Standard Fat Strat

1999-2003. Mexican-made version.

1999-2003		$375	$400

Stevie Ray Vaughan Stratocaster

1992-present. U.S.-made, alder body, sunburst, gold hardware, SRV 'guard, lefty tremolot, Brazilian rosewood 'board (pau ferro by '93).

1992-2005		$1,000	$1,100

Stevie Ray Vaughan Tribute #1 Stratocaster

2004. Custom Shop model limited edition recreation of SRV's #1 made by Master Builder John Cruz in the Custom Shop, 100 made, $10,000 MSRP, in-

cludes flight case stenciled "SRV - Number One," and other goodies.

2004		$20,000	$25,000

Strat Plus

1987-1999. Three Lace Sensor pickups, alder (poplar available earlier) body, tremolo, rosewood 'board or maple neck, various colors. See Deluxe Strat Plus for ash veneer version.

1987-1999		$750	$900

Stratocaster HSS/HH

2004-present. Made in U.S., HSS has humbucker/single/single pickups, HH has 2 humbuckers.

2004-2005	Alder body	$650	$725
2004-2005	Ash body, transparent finish	$700	$750

Stratocaster Junior

2004-present. Import, short 22.7" scale, Alder body, non-trem hardtail bridge.

2004-2005		$200	$250

Stratocaster Special (Mexico)

1993-1995. A humbucker and a single-coil pickup, 1 volume, 1 tone.

1993-1995		$275	$325

Stratocaster XII

1988-1995. Alder body, maple neck, 21-fret rosewood 'board, 3 vintage Strat pickups, Japanese-made, various colors.

1988-1995		$600	$650

Stratacoustic

2000-2005. Thinline acoustic/electric, single-cut, spruce top, fiberglass body.

2000-2005		$200	$225

Stratosonic

2003. Stratocaster-style with 2 P-90 black soapbar pickups, wrap-around bridge tailpiece, transparent cherry finish.

2003		$700	$800

Sub Sonic Stratocaster

2000-2001. Baritone model tuned B-E-A-D-G-B, single-single-hum pickup configuration, Strat-styling.

2000-2001		$700	$900

Super/Deluxe Super Stratocaster

1997-2003. Import made in Mexico, part of Deluxe Series, Standard Strat features with maple neck.

1997-2003		$275	$300

Tanqurey Tonic Stratocaster

1988. Made for a Tanqurey Tonic liquor ad campaign giveaway in '88; many were given to winners around the country, ads said that they could also be purchased through Tanqurey, but that apparently didn't happen.

1988	Tanqurey Tonic Green	$900	$1,100

Texas Special Stratocaster

1991-1992. Custom Shop model, 50 made, state of Texas map stamped on neck plate, Texas Special pickups, maple fretboard, sunburst.

1991-1992		$1,700	$2,000

Fender Stevie Ray Vaughan Stratocaster

Fender Stratacoustic

Fender Tie-Dye Stratocaster

Fender Yngwie Malmsteen Stratocaster

MODEL YEAR	FEATURES	EXC. COND. LOW	HIGH

The Strat

1980-1983. Alder body, 4-bolt neck, large STRAT on painted peghead, gold-plated brass hardware, various colors.

1980-1983	Rare colors	$1,200	$1,500
1980-1983	Various common colors	$850	$1,200

Tie-Dye Stratocaster

2004-2005. Single-coil neck and humbucker bridge pickups, Band of Gypsies or Hippie Blue tie-dye pattern poly finish.

2004-2005	Band of Gypsies	$325	$375

Tree of Life Stratocaster

1993. Custom Shop model, 29 made, tree of life fretboard inlay, 1-piece quilted maple body.

1993		$7,000	$10,000

Turquoise Sparkle Stratocaster

2001. Custom Shop model, limited run of 75 for Mars Music, turquoise sparkle finish.

2001		$1,100	$1,300

U.S. Ultra / Ultra Plus Stratocaster

1990-1997. Alder body with figured maple veneer on front and back, single Lace Sensor pickups in neck and middle, double Sensor at bridge, ebony 'board, sunburst.

1990-1997		$875	$950

Ventures Limited Edition Stratocaster

1996. Japanese-made tribute model, matches Jazzmaster equivalent, black.

1996		$900	$1,000

Walnut Stratocaster

1981-1983. American black walnut body and 1-piece neck and 'board.

1981-1983		$1,600	$2,200

Walnut Elite Stratocaster

1983-1984. The Elite Series features active electronics and noise-cancelling pickups, Walnut Elite has a walnut body and neck, gold-plated hardware and pearloid tuner buttons. Also see Elite Stratocaster and Gold Elite Stratocaster.

1983-1984		$1,700	$2,300

Western Stratocaster

1995. Custom Shop model, only 5 made, featured in Fender Custom Shop book from the 1990s.

1995		$9,000	$12,000

Yngwie Malmsteen Stratocaster

1988-present. U.S.-made, maple neck, scalloped 'board, 3 single-coil pickups, blue, red, white.

1988-2001		$950	$1,100

TC-90

2004. Semi-hollow thinline, double-cut, Duncan SP-90 pickups stop bar and tune-o-matic tailpiece.

2004		$450	$475

Telecaster

The following are all variations of the Telecaster. The first five listings are for the main American-made models and the '85 interim production Japanese model. All others are listed alphabetically after that in the following order. Broadcaster and

MODEL YEAR	FEATURES	EXC. COND. LOW	HIGH

Nocaster models are under Broadcaster.
  Telecaster
  Standard Telecaster
  Standard Telecaster (Japan)
  American Standard Telecaster
  American Series Telecaster
  40th Anniversary Telecaster
  '50s Telecaster
  50th Anniversary Spanish Guitar Set
  50th Anniversary Telecaster
  '52 Telecaster
  '63 Telecaster
  '90s Telecaster Deluxe (Foto-Flame)
  Aerodyne Telecaster
  Albert Collins Telecaster
  Aluminum Telecaster
  American Classic Telecaster
  American Deluxe Power Telecaster
  American Deluxe Telecaster
  Antigua Telecaster
  Big Block Telecaster
  Black and Gold Telecaster
  Blue Flower Telecaster
  California Telecaster
  California Fat Telecaster
  Collector's Edition Telecaster
  Contemporary Telecaster
  Danny Gatton Telecaster
  Deluxe Nashville Telecaster
  Deluxe Telecaster
  Elite Telecaster
  Highway 1 Telecaster/Texas Telecaster
  HMT Telecaster
  James Burton Telecaster
  Jerry Donahue Telecaster
  John Jorgenson Telecaster
  Jr. Telecaster
  NHL Premier Edition Telecaster
  Paisley Telecaster
  Plus/Plus Deluxe Telecaster
  Rosewood Telecaster
  Set-Neck Telecaster
  Sparkle Telecaster
  Squier Telecaster
  Standard Telecaster (Mexico)
  Telecaster Custom
  '60s Telecaster Custom
  '62 Custom Telecaster
  '72 Telecaster Custom
  Telecaster Thinline
  '69 Telecaster Thinline
  '72 Telecaster Thinline
  '90s Telecaster Thinline
  Thinline Telecaster
  Texas Special Telecaster

Telecaster

1951-1982. See Standard Telecaster (following listing) for '82-'85, and American Standard Telecaster for '88-2000. Currently called American Series Telecaster.

1951	Blond, black 'guard	$32,000	$65,000

MODEL YEAR	FEATURES	EXC. COND. LOW	HIGH
1952	Blond, black 'guard	$30,000	$52,000
1953	Blond, black 'guard	$29,000	$51,000
1954	Blond, black 'guard	$28,000	$50,000
1954	Blond, white 'guard	$22,000	$37,000
1955	Blond, white 'guard	$21,000	$36,000
1956	Blond	$20,000	$35,000
1957	Blond	$19,000	$34,000
1957	Custom colors	$30,000	$52,000
1958	Black	$22,000	$37,000
1958	Blond, backloader	$18,000	$32,000
1958	Blond, top loader	$18,000	$32,000
1958	Fiesta Red	$27,000	$34,000
1958	Sunburst, backloader	$19,000	$24,000
1958	Sunburst, top loader	$18,000	$23,000
1959	Blond, maple	$18,000	$22,000
1959	Blond, slab	$17,000	$21,000
1959	Custom colors	$28,000	$35,000
1959	Sunburst, maple	$18,000	$23,000
1959	Sunburst, slab	$17,000	$22,000
1960	Blond	$11,000	$18,000
1960	Less common custom colors	$20,000	$34,000
1960	More common custom colors	$13,000	$22,000
1960	Sunburst	$13,000	$22,000
1961	Black	$13,000	$22,000
1961	Blond	$10,000	$17,000
1961	Burgundy Mist	$18,000	$30,000
1961	Dakota Red	$15,000	$25,000
1961	Daphne Blue	$15,000	$25,000
1961	Fiesta Red	$15,000	$25,000
1961	Foam Green	$19,000	$32,000
1961	Inca Silver	$16,000	$27,000
1961	Lake Placid Blue	$14,000	$23,000
1961	Olympic White	$13,000	$22,000
1961	Shell Pink	$19,000	$32,000
1961	Sherwood Green	$16,000	$27,000
1961	Shoreline Gold	$16,000	$27,000
1961	Sonic Blue	$17,000	$29,000
1961	Sunburst	$12,000	$20,000
1961	Surf Green	$19,000	$32,000
1962	Black, curved	$12,000	$20,000
1962	Black, slab	$13,000	$22,000
1962	Blond, curved	$9,000	$15,000
1962	Blond, slab	$9,500	$16,000
1962	Burgundy Mist, curved	$16,000	$27,000
1962	Burgundy Mist, slab	$17,000	$28,000
1962	Dakota Red, curved	$13,000	$22,000
1962	Dakota Red, slab	$14,000	$23,000
1962	Daphne Blue, curved	$14,000	$23,000

MODEL YEAR	FEATURES	EXC. COND. LOW	HIGH
1962	Daphne Blue, slab	$15,000	$25,000
1962	Fiesta Red, curved	$13,000	$22,000
1962	Fiesta Red, slab	$14,000	$23,000
1962	Foam Green, curved	$17,000	$28,000
1962	Foam Green, slab	$18,000	$30,000
1962	Inca Silver, curved	$15,000	$25,000
1962	Inca Silver, slab	$16,000	$27,000
1962	Lake Placid Blue, curved	$12,000	$20,000
1962	Lake Placid Blue, slab	$13,000	$22,000
1962	Olympic White, curved	$10,000	$18,000
1962	Olympic White, slab	$11,000	$19,000
1962	Shell Pink, curved	$17,000	$28,000
1962	Shell Pink, slab	$18,000	$30,000
1962	Sherwood Green, curved	$14,000	$23,000
1962	Sherwood Green, slab	$15,000	$25,000
1962	Shoreline Gold, curved	$14,000	$23,000
1962	Shoreline Gold, slab	$15,000	$25,000
1962	Sonic Blue, curved	$15,000	$25,000
1962	Sonic Blue, slab	$16,000	$27,000
1962	Sunburst, curved	$11,000	$17,000
1962	Sunburst, slab	$12,000	$18,000
1962	Surf Green, curved	$17,000	$28,000
1962	Surf Green, slab	$18,000	$30,000
1963	Black	$11,000	$20,000
1963	Blond	$10,000	$15,000
1963	Burgundy Mist	$15,000	$27,000
1963	Dakota Red	$13,000	$22,000
1963	Daphne Blue	$15,000	$23,000
1963	Fiesta Red	$13,000	$22,000
1963	Foam Green	$16,000	$28,000
1963	Inca Silver	$15,000	$25,000
1963	Lake Placid Blue	$12,000	$20,000
1963	Olympic White	$11,000	$18,000
1963	Sherwood Green	$14,000	$23,000
1963	Shoreline Gold	$14,000	$23,000
1963	Sonic Blue	$15,000	$25,000
1963	Sunburst	$11,000	$16,000
1963	Surf Green	$16,000	$28,000
1964	Black	$10,000	$19,000
1964	Blond	$8,000	$15,000
1964	Burgundy Mist	$14,000	$24,000
1964	Candy Apple Red	$11,000	$19,000
1964	Dakota Red	$12,000	$21,000
1964	Daphne Blue	$13,000	$22,000
1964	Fiesta Red	$12,000	$21,000
1964	Foam Green	$15,000	$25,000
1964	Inca Silver	$14,000	$24,000
1964	Lake Placid Blue	$11,000	$19,000
1964	Olympic White	$10,000	$19,000
1964	Sherwood Green	$13,000	$23,000
1964	Shoreline Gold	$13,000	$23,000
1964	Sonic Blue	$14,000	$24,000

1952 Fender Telecaster

1959 Fender Telecaster

GUITARS

1965 Fender Telecaster

1966 Fender Telecaster
(Lake Placid Blue)

MODEL YEAR	FEATURES	EXC. COND. LOW	HIGH
1964	Sunburst	$10,000	$18,000
1964	Surf Green	$15,000	$25,000
1965	Black	$10,000	$15,000
1965	Blond	$8,000	$12,000
1965	Blue Ice	$12,000	$18,000
1965	Candy Apple Red	$10,000	$15,000
1965	Charcoal Frost	$12,000	$18,000
1965	Dakota Red	$11,000	$17,000
1965	Fiesta Red	$11,000	$17,000
1965	Firemist Gold	$12,000	$19,000
1965	Firemist Silver	$12,000	$19,000
1965	Foam Green	$12,000	$19,000
1965	Lake Placid Blue	$10,000	$15,000
1965	Ocean Turquoise	$12,000	$19,000
1965	Olympic White	$9,000	$13,000
1965	Sonic Blue	$12,000	$19,000
1965	Sunburst	$9,000	$13,000
1965	Teal Green	$12,000	$19,000
1966	Black	$8,500	$12,000
1966	Blond	$8,000	$10,000
1966	Blue Ice	$10,700	$16,000
1966	Candy Apple Red	$8,600	$13,000
1966	Charcoal Frost	$10,700	$16,000
1966	Dakota Red	$9,500	$14,000
1966	Fiesta Red	$9,500	$14,000
1966	Firemist Gold	$10,700	$16,000
1966	Firemist Silver	$10,700	$16,000
1966	Foam Green	$11,000	$16,000
1966	Lake Placid Blue	$8,600	$13,000
1966	Ocean Turquoise	$10,700	$16,000
1966	Olympic White	$6,900	$13,000
1966	Sonic Blue	$10,700	$16,000
1966	Sunburst	$7,600	$11,000
1966	Teal Green	$10,700	$16,000
1967	Black	$6,000	$9,000
1967	Blond, maple cap	$5,200	$9,000
1967	Blond, rosewood cap	$4,800	$8,500
1967	Blond, smuggler cavity	$4,800	$8,500
1967	Blue Ice	$9,000	$13,500
1967	Candy Apple Red	$8,000	$12,000
1967	Charcoal Frost	$9,000	$13,500
1967	Dakota Red	$9,000	$13,500
1967	Fiesta Red	$8,500	$12,750
1967	Firemist Gold	$9,000	$13,500
1967	Firemist Silver	$9,000	$13,500
1967	Foam Green	$9,000	$13,500
1967	Lake Placid Blue	$8,000	$12,000
1967	Ocean Turquoise	$9,000	$13,500
1967	Olympic White	$8,000	$12,000
1967	Sonic Blue	$9,000	$13,500
1967	Sunburst	$7,200	$9,000
1967	Teal Green	$9,000	$13,500
1968	Black, maple cap	$6,000	$8,500
1968	Black, rosewood cap	$5,500	$8,000
1968	Blond, Bigsby	$4,600	$7,500
1968	Blond, maple cap	$5,200	$8,500
1968	Blond, rosewood cap	$4,800	$8,000

MODEL YEAR	FEATURES	EXC. COND. LOW	HIGH
1968	Blue Floral	$11,000	$14,000
1968	Blue Ice, maple cap	$9,000	$10,000
1968	Blue Ice, rosewood cap	$8,500	$9,500
1968	Candy Apple Red, maple cap	$8,000	$9,000
1968	Candy Apple Red, rosewood cap	$7,500	$8,500
1968	Charcoal Frost, maple cap	$9,000	$10,000
1968	Charcoal Frost, rosewood cap	$8,500	$9,500
1968	Dakota Red, maple cap	$9,000	$10,000
1968	Dakota Red, rosewood cap	$8,500	$9,500
1968	Fiesta Red, maple cap	$8,500	$9,500
1968	Fiesta Red, rosewood cap	$9,000	$10,000
1968	Firemist Gold, maple cap	$9,000	$10,000
1968	Firemist Gold, rosewood cap	$8,500	$9,500
1968	Firemist Silver, maple cap	$9,000	$10,000
1968	Firemist Silver, rosewood cap	$8,500	$9,500
1968	Foam Green, maple cap	$9,000	$11,000
1968	Foam Green, rosewood cap	$8,500	$10,500
1968	Lake Placid Blue, maple cap	$8,000	$9,000
1968	Lake Placid Blue, rosewood cap	$7,500	$8,500
1968	Ocean Turquoise, maple cap	$9,000	$11,000
1968	Ocean Turquoise, rosewood cap	$8,500	$10,500
1968	Olympic White, maple cap	$8,000	$9,000
1968	Olympic White, rosewood cap	$7,500	$8,500
1968	Pink Paisley	$11,000	$14,000
1968	Sonic Blue, maple cap	$9,000	$11,000
1968	Sonic Blue, rosewood cap	$8,500	$10,500
1968	Sunburst, Bigsby	$6,000	$8,000
1968	Sunburst, maple cap	$7,000	$9,000
1968	Sunburst, rosewood cap	$6,500	$8,500
1968	Teal Green, maple cap	$9,000	$11,000
1968	Teal Green, rosewood cap	$8,500	$10,500
1969	Black, maple cap	$5,000	$7,500
1969	Black, rosewood cap	$4,500	$7,000

The *Vintage Guitar Price Guide* shows low to high values for items in all-original excellent condition, and, where applicable, with original case or cover.

MODEL YEAR	FEATURES	EXC. COND. LOW	HIGH
1969	Blond, maple cap	$5,000	$7,500
1969	Blond, rosewood cap	$4,500	$7,000
1969	Blue Floral	$10,000	$13,000
1969	Blue Ice, maple cap	$8,000	$9,000
1969	Blue Ice, rosewood cap	$7,500	$8,500
1969	Candy Apple Red, maple cap	$7,000	$8,000
1969	Candy Apple Red, rosewood cap	$6,500	$7,500
1969	Charcoal Frost, maple cap	$8,000	$9,000
1969	Charcoal Frost, rosewood cap	$7,500	$8,500
1969	Dakota Red, maple cap	$8,000	$9,000
1969	Dakota Red, rosewood cap	$7,500	$8,500
1969	Fiesta Red, maple cap	$8,000	$9,000
1969	Fiesta Red, rosewood cap	$7,500	$8,500
1969	Firemist Gold, maple cap	$8,000	$9,000
1969	Firemist Gold, rosewood cap	$7,500	$8,500
1969	Firemist Silver, maple cap	$8,000	$9,000
1969	Firemist Silver, rosewood cap	$7,500	$8,500
1969	Foam Green, maple cap	$8,000	$9,000
1969	Foam Green, rosewood cap	$7,500	$9,500
1969	Lake Placid Blue, maple cap	$7,000	$8,000
1969	Lake Placid Blue, rosewood cap	$6,500	$7,500
1969	Ocean Turquoise, maple cap	$8,000	$10,000
1969	Ocean Turquoise, rosewood cap	$7,500	$9,500
1969	Olympic White, maple cap	$7,000	$8,000
1969	Olympic White, rosewood cap	$6,500	$7,500
1969	Pink Paisley	$10,000	$13,000
1969	Sonic Blue, maple cap	$8,000	$10,000
1969	Sonic Blue, rosewood cap	$7,500	$9,500
1969	Sunburst, maple cap	$6,000	$8,000
1969	Sunburst, rosewood cap	$5,500	$7,500
1969	Teal Green, maple cap	$8,000	$10,000
1969	Teal Green, rosewood cap	$7,500	$9,500

MODEL YEAR	FEATURES	EXC. COND. LOW	HIGH
1970	Black	$5,800	$6,500
1970	Blond	$4,200	$6,500
1970	Blond, Bigsby	$4,000	$6,200
1970	Blue Ice	$7,000	$8,000
1970	Candy Apple Red	$5,700	$7,500
1970	Charcoal Frost	$7,000	$8,000
1970	Dakota Red	$7,000	$8,000
1970	Fiesta Red	$7,000	$8,000
1970	Firemist Gold	$7,000	$8,000
1970	Firemist Silver	$7,000	$8,000
1970	Foam Green	$7,000	$9,000
1970	Lake Placid Blue	$5,700	$7,500
1970	Ocean Turquoise	$7,000	$9,000
1970	Olympic White	$5,700	$7,500
1970	Sonic Blue	$7,000	$9,000
1970	Sunburst	$5,000	$7,000
1970	Teal Green	$7,000	$9,000
1971	Black	$4,700	$5,500
1971	Blond	$3,600	$5,500
1971	Candy Apple Red	$4,700	$6,500
1971	Firemist Gold	$6,000	$7,000
1971	Firemist Silver	$6,000	$7,000
1971	Lake Placid Blue	$4,700	$6,500
1971	Ocean Turquoise	$6,000	$7,000
1971	Olympic White	$4,700	$5,500
1971	Sonic Blue	$6,000	$7,000
1971	Sunburst	$4,000	$6,000
1972	Black	$3,000	$4,500
1972	Blond	$3,000	$4,000
1972	Candy Apple Red	$4,000	$5,000
1972	Lake Placid Blue	$4,000	$5,000
1972	Olympic White	$4,000	$5,000
1972	Sonic Blue	$4,500	$5,500
1972	Sunburst	$3,500	$5,500
1973	Black	$3,000	$4,000
1973	Blond	$3,000	$3,500
1973	Candy Apple Red	$4,000	$4,500
1973	Lake Placid Blue	$4,000	$4,500
1973	Natural	$2,200	$3,500
1973	Olympic White	$4,000	$4,500
1973	Sunburst	$3,500	$5,000
1973	Walnut	$2,200	$3,500
1974	Black	$3,000	$4,000
1974	Blond	$3,000	$3,500
1974	Natural	$2,200	$3,500
1974	Olympic White	$4,000	$4,500
1974	Sunburst	$3,500	$5,000
1974	Walnut	$2,200	$3,500
1975	Black	$2,600	$2,700
1975	Blond	$2,100	$2,600
1975	Natural	$2,100	$2,700
1975	Olympic White	$2,600	$2,700
1975	Sunburst	$2,600	$2,700
1975	Walnut	$2,500	$2,700
1976	Black	$2,400	$2,600
1976	Blond	$2,100	$2,500
1976	Natural	$2,000	$2,500
1976	Olympic White	$2,400	$2,600
1976	Sunburst	$2,400	$2,600
1976	Walnut	$2,400	$2,600
1977	Black	$2,200	$2,300

1968 Fender Telecaster (Pink Paisley)

1972 Fender Telecaster

*Fender American Series
Telecaster*

Fender Albert Collins Telecaster

MODEL YEAR	FEATURES	EXC. COND. LOW	HIGH
1977	Blond	$1,900	$2,100
1977	Natural	$1,800	$2,100
1977	Olympic White	$2,200	$2,300
1977	Sunburst	$2,200	$2,300
1977	Walnut	$1,800	$2,100
1978	Antigua	$1,800	$2,200
1978	Black	$1,800	$2,200
1978	Blond	$1,800	$2,100
1978	Natural	$1,600	$2,000
1978	Olympic White	$1,800	$2,200
1978	Sunburst	$1,800	$2,200
1978	Walnut	$1,600	$2,000
1978	Wine	$1,700	$2,100
1979	Antigua	$1,700	$2,200
1979	Black	$1,700	$2,200
1979	Blond	$1,600	$2,100
1979	Natural	$1,500	$2,000
1979	Olympic White	$1,700	$2,200
1979	Sunburst	$1,700	$2,200
1979	Walnut	$1,500	$2,000
1979	Wine	$1,600	$2,100
1980	Antigua	$1,600	$2,100
1980	Black	$1,600	$2,100
1980	Blond	$1,500	$2,000
1980	Natural	$1,400	$1,900
1980	Olympic White	$1,600	$2,100
1980	Sunburst	$1,600	$2,100
1980	Wine	$1,500	$2,000
1981	International colors	$1,400	$2,000
1981	Sunburst	$1,200	$1,500

Standard Telecaster
1982-1984. See Telecaster for '51-'82, and American Standard Telecaster (following listing) for '88-2000. Not to be confused with the current Standard Telecaster, which is made in Mexico.

1982-1984	Blond	$1,300	$1,600
1982-1984	Jewel or various colors	$1,400	$2,000

Standard Telecaster (Japan)
1985. Interim production in Japan while the new Fender reorganized.

1985		$600	$700

American Standard Telecaster
1988-2000. Name used when Fender reissued the standard American-made Tele after CBS sold the company. The only American-made Tele available for '86 and '87 was the '52 Telecaster. See Telecaster for '51-'81, and Standard Telecaster for '82-'84. All '94 models have a metal 40th Anniversary pin on the headstock, but should not be confused with the actual 40th Anniversary Telecaster model (see separate listing), all standard colors, renamed the American Series Telecaster in 2000.

1988-1989		$750	$875
1990-1999		$700	$750

American Series Telecaster
2000-present. Current name for the regular U.S.-made Telecaster. See Telecaster for '51-'81, Standard Telecaster for '82-'84, and American Standard for '88-'99.

2000-2005		$625	$750

MODEL YEAR	FEATURES	EXC. COND. LOW	HIGH

40th Anniversary Telecaster
1988, 1999. Custom Shop model limited edition run of 300, 2-piece flamed maple top, gold hardware ('88), flamed maple top over ash body, gold hardware ('99).

1988	1st run, high-end	$3,500	$4,000
1999	2nd run, plain top	$1,300	$1,600

'50s Telecaster (Import)
1982-present.

1982-2005		$450	$500

50th Anniversary Spanish Guitar Set Custom Shop
1996. 50 sets made, Tele Prototype reproduction with similar era copy of woodie amp.

1996		$6,500	$9,000

50th Anniversary Telecaster
1995-1996. Custom Shop model, flame maple top, 2 vintage-style pickups, gold hardware, sunburst, gold 50th Anniversary coin on back of the headstock, 1250 made.

1995-1996		$1,400	$1,600

'52 Telecaster
1982-present. Ash body, maple neck or rosewood 'board.

1982-1999	Blond	$950	$1,100
1990-1999	Copper (limited number)	$950	$1,100
2000-2005		$1,000	$1,100

'63 Telecaster
1999-present. Custom Shop model, alder body (or blond on ash), original spec pickups, C-shaped neck, rosewood 'board.

1999-2005	Closet Classic	$1,700	$1,900
1999-2005	NOS	$1,500	$1,800

'90s Telecaster Deluxe (Foto-Flame)
1995-1998. Import, 1 Tele-style bridge pickup and 2 Strat-style pickups, rosewood 'board, Foto Flame '95-'97 and standard finishes '97-'98.

1995-1997	Foto-Flame	$500	$600
1997-1998	Standard finish	$450	$500

Aerodyne Telecaster
2004-present. Tele with Aerodyne body profile, bound body, import.

2004-2005		$450	$475

Albert Collins Telecaster
1990-present. U.S.-made Custom Shop signature model, bound swamp ash body, humbucker pickup in neck position.

1990-2005	Natural	$1,200	$1,300
1995	Silver sparkle	$1,300	$1,400

Aluminum Telecaster
1994-1995. Aluminum-bodied American Standard with anodized finish in blue marble, purple marble or red, silver and blue stars and stripes.

1994-1995	Marble patterns	$1,700	$2,500
1994-1995	Red-silver-blue flag option	$1,800	$2,600

American Classic Holoflake Telecaster
1996-1999. Custom Shop model, splatter/sparkle finish, pearloid 'guard.

1996-1999		$1,400	$1,900

MODEL YEAR	FEATURES	EXC. COND. LOW	HIGH

American Classic Telecaster
1996-1999. Custom Shop model, handcrafted version of American Standard, thin lacquer-finished ash body, maple or rosewood 'board, various options and colors, earlier versions had gold hardware and custom-color options.

1996-1999		$1,300	$1,400

American Deluxe Power Telecaster
1999-2001. With Fishman power bridge piezo pickups.

1999-2001		$1,200	$1,300

American Deluxe Telecaster
1998-present. Premium ash or alder body with see-thru finishes.

1998-1999	Alder	$825	$875
1998-1999	Ash	$850	$900
2000-2005	Ash	$850	$975

Antigua Telecaster
2003. Japanese-made limited-edition (400made) reissue, '70s features and antigua finish.

2003		$550	$700

Big Block Telecaster
2005-present. Pearloid block markers inlays, black finish with matching headstock, 3 single-coil pickups with the center pickup reverse wound, 5-way switch.

2005		$600	$650

Black and Gold Telecaster
1981-1982. Black finish, gold-plated brass hardware.

1981-1982		$1,100	$1,300

Blue Flower Telecaster
1986-1993, 2003-2004. Import, Blue Flower finish.

1986-1993	1st issue	$600	$1,200
2003-2004	2nd issue	$550	$650

Buck Owens Ltd. Edition Telecaster
1998-2002. Custom Shop model, red, white and blue sparkle finish, gold hardware, gold 'guard, rosewood 'board, by Fender Japan.

1998-2002		$900	$1,000

California Telecaster
1997-1998. Alder body, maple fretboard, sunburst, Tex-Mex Strat and Tele pickup configuration.

1997-1998		$525	$700

California Fat Telecaster
1997-1998. Alder body, maple fretboard, Tex-Mex humbucker and Tele pickup configuration.

1997-1998		$525	$700

Collector's Edition Telecaster
1998. Mid-1955 specs including white 'guard, offered in sunburst with gold hardware (which was an option in '55), 1,998 made.

1998		$1,300	$1,500

Contemporary Telecaster (Import)
1985-1987. Japanese-made while the new Fender reorganized, 2 or 3 pickups, vibrato, black chrome hardware, rosewood 'board.

1985-1987		$325	$425

Danny Gatton Telecaster
1990-present. Custom Shop model, like '53 Telecaster, maple neck, 2 humbuckers.

1990-2005		$1,700	$2,200

Deluxe Nashville Telecaster (Mexico)
1998-present. Made in Mexico, Tex-Mex Strat and Tele pickup configuration, various colors.

1998-2005		$500	$600

Deluxe Telecaster (USA)
1972-1981. Two humbucker pickups, various colors.

1972-1974		$2,500	$2,500
1975-1978		$2,000	$3,000
1978-1979	Antigua	$1,700	$2,200
1979-1981		$1,500	$2,000

Elite Telecaster
1983-1985. Two active humbucker pickups, 3-way switch, 2 volume knobs, 1 presence and filter controls, chrome hardware, various colors.

1983-1985		$950	$1,100

Highway 1 Telecaster/Texas Telecaster
2003-present. U.S.-made, alder body, satin lacquer finish, Texas version (introduced in '04) has ash body and Hot Vintage pickups.

2003-2005		$475	$600

HMT Telecaster
1990-1993. Japanese-made Metal-Rock Tele, available with or without Floyd Rose tremolo, 1 Fender Lace Sensor pickup and 1 DiMarzio bridge humbucker pickup, black.

1990-1993		$275	$375

James Burton Telecaster
1990-present. Ash body, 3 Fender Lace pickups, available in black with Gold Paisley, black with Candy Red Paisley, Pearl White, and Frost Red until '05. In '06 in black with red or blue flame-shaped paisley, or Pearl White.

1990-2005	Black and gold paisley, gold hardware	$1,000	$1,100
1990-2005	Black and red paisley, black hardware	$1,100	$1,200
1990-2005	Frost Red or Pearl White	$700	$800
2006	Paisley flames	$1,000	$1,100

Jerry Donahue Telecaster
1992-2001. Custom Shop model designed by Donahue, Tele bridge pickup and Strat neck pickup, birdseye maple neck and top, basswood body, gold hardware, passive circuitry, there was also a Japanese J.D. Telecaster.

1992-2001	Sunburst	$1,100	$1,300
1992-2001	Transparent Crimson or Sapphire Blue	$1,400	$1,700

John Jorgenson Telecaster
1998-2000. Custom Shop model, double-coil stacked pickups, sparkle or black finish, korina body.

1998-2000	Gold sparkle	$1,400	$1,900

Jr. Telecaster
1994, 1997-present. Custom Shop model, transparent blond ash body, 2 P-90-style pickups, set neck, 11 tone chambers, 100 made in '94, reintroduced in '97.

1994		$1,500	$1,800

Fender Highway 1 Texas Telecaster

Fender James Burton Telecaster

1965 Fender Telecaster Custom

Fender Standard Telecaster

MODEL YEAR	FEATURES	EXC. COND. LOW	HIGH

NHL Premier Edition Telecaster
1999-2000. Limited edition of 100 guitars with NHL hockey art logo on the top.

1999-2000		$1,300	$1,500

Paisley Telecaster
1986-1998, 2003-2004. Import, Pink Paisley finish.

1986-1989		$550	$750
1990-1998		$500	$600

Plus/Plus Deluxe Telecaster
1990-1997. Tele with Strat 3-pickup combination, Deluxe has added Strat-style tremolo system, various colors.

1990-1997		$750	$900

Rosewood Telecaster
1969-1972. Rosewood body and neck.

1969-1972		$6,000	$10,000

Rosewood Telecaster (Japan)
1986-1996. Japanese-made reissue, rosewood body and neck.

1986-1996		$2,000	$2,400

Set-Neck Telecaster
1990-1996. Glued-in neck, Custom Shop, 2 humbucking pickups, Set-Neck CA (Country Artist) has 1 humbucker and 1 Tele pickup, various colors.

1990-1996		$1,100	$1,400

Sparkle Telecaster
1993-1995. Custom Shop model, poplar body, white 'guard, sparkle finish: champagne, gold, silver.

1993-1995		$1,400	$1,600

Squier Telecaster
1983-present. Fender Japan was established in '82 with Squier production beginning in '83. Production was shifted to Korea in '87 and later allocated to China, India (Squier II '89-'90) and Mexico. This model is the low-cost version of the Telecaster for Squier.

1983-1984	Blond, 1st year '70s-style logo	$250	$350
1985-1989	Black or blond	$200	$300

Squier Telecaster Affinity
1998-present. Standard Telecaster styling, various colors.

1998-2005		$75	$125

Standard Telecaster (Mexico)
1990-present. Guitar production at the Mexico facility started in '91. High end of range includes a hard guitar case, while the low end of the range includes only a gig bag, various colors.

1990-1999		$250	$275
2000-2005		$260	$285

Telecaster Custom
1959-1972. Body bound top and back, rosewood 'board, 2 Tele pickups, see Telecaster Custom (2nd Edition) for the 1 Tele/1 humbucker version.

1959	Sunburst, maple	$27,000	$35,000
1960	Custom colors	$30,000	$65,000
1960	Sunburst	$23,000	$33,000
1961	Less common custom colors	$36,000	$60,000

MODEL YEAR	FEATURES	EXC. COND. LOW	HIGH
1961	More common custom colors	$24,000	$35,000
1961	Sunburst	$22,000	$32,000
1962	Less common custom colors	$35,000	$58,000
1962	More common custom colors	$23,000	$33,000
1962	Sunburst	$18,000	$30,000
1963	Less common custom colors	$30,000	$46,000
1963	More common custom colors	$18,000	$30,000
1963	Sunburst	$16,000	$26,000
1964	Less common custom colors	$30,000	$38,000
1964	More common custom colors	$17,000	$30,000
1964	Sunburst	$14,000	$24,000
1965	Less common custom colors	$22,000	$28,000
1965	More common custom colors	$15,000	$22,000
1965	Sunburst	$11,000	$19,000
1966	Less common custom colors	$20,000	$29,000
1966	More common custom colors	$14,000	$20,000
1966	Sunburst	$11,000	$14,000
1967	Less common custom colors	$18,000	$25,000
1967	More common custom colors	$13,000	$18,000
1967	Sunburst	$9,000	$14,000
1968	Less common custom colors	$17,000	$24,000
1968	More common custom colors	$12,000	$17,000
1968	Sunburst, maple cap	$9,000	$13,000
1968	Sunburst, rosewood cap	$8,000	$12,000
1969	Custom colors	$11,000	$25,000
1969	Sunburst	$7,000	$12,000
1970	Custom colors	$11,000	$21,000
1970	Sunburst	$6,500	$10,000
1971	Custom colors, 4-bolt	$10,000	$19,000
1971	Sunburst, 3-bolt	$3,000	$4,500
1971	Sunburst, 4-bolt	$6,000	$9,000
1972	Custom colors, 3-bolt	$4,000	$7,000
1972	Sunburst, 3-bolt	$3,000	$4,500

Telecaster Custom II
1972-1981. One humbucking and 1 Tele pickup, standard colors, see above for 2 Tele pickup version. Also called Custom Telecaster.

1972-1974		$2,500	$3,500
1975-1978		$2,000	$3,000
1979-1981		$1,500	$2,000

The *Vintage Guitar Price Guide* shows low to high values for items in all-original excellent condition, and, where applicable, with original case or cover.

MODEL YEAR	FEATURES	EXC. COND. LOW	HIGH

'60s Telecaster Custom
1997-1998. U.S. Custom Shop model, bound alder body, black or custom colors.

1997-1998		$1,300	$1,700

'62 Custom Telecaster (Import)
1984-1999. Made in Japan, bound top and back, rosewood 'board, sunburst or red.

1984-1999		$550	$700

'72 Telecaster Custom
1986-present. Import, 1 humbucker, 1 single-coil.

1986-1999	Japan	$550	$700
2000-2005	Mexico	$400	$600

Telecaster Thinline/Thinline II
1968-1980. Semi-hollowbody, 1 f-hole, 2 Tele pickups, ash or mahogany body, in late-'71 the tilt neck was added and the 2 Tele pickups were switched to 2 humbuckers.

1968	Less common custom colors	$8,000	$10,000
1968	More common custom colors	$7,500	$9,500
1968	Natural ash	$6,000	$7,500
1968	Natural mahogany	$6,000	$7,500
1968	Sunburst	$7,000	$9,000
1969	Less common custom colors	$7,800	$10,000
1969	More common custom colors	$7,300	$9,500
1969	Natural ash	$5,800	$7,500
1969	Natural mahogany	$5,800	$7,500
1969	Sunburst	$6,800	$9,000
1970	Less common custom colors	$7,500	$9,500
1970	More common custom colors	$7,000	$9,000
1970	Natural ash	$5,000	$7,000
1970	Natural mahogany	$5,500	$7,000
1970	Sunburst	$5,500	$8,500
1971	Custom colors, 3-bolt	$4,000	$6,000
1971	Custom colors, 4-bolt	$6,500	$7,500
1971	Natural ash, 3-bolt	$3,500	$4,500
1971	Natural ash, 4-bolt	$5,000	$6,000
1971	Natural mahogany, 3-bolt	$4,000	$5,000
1971	Natural mahogany, 4-bolt	$4,500	$5,500
1971	Sunburst, 3-bolt	$4,000	$5,000
1971	Sunburst, 4-bolt	$4,500	$5,500
1972-1974	Less common custom colors	$3,800	$4,800
1972-1974	Mahogany, humbuckers	$3,200	$3,800
1972-1974	More common custom colors	$3,200	$3,800
1972-1974	Natural ash, humbuckers	$3,000	$3,600
1972-1974	Sunburst, humbuckers	$3,000	$4,800

1975-1978	Blond, custom option	$2,500	$3,800
1975-1978	Natural ash, humbuckers	$2,000	$2,600
1975-1978	Sunburst, humbuckers	$2,000	$2,700

'69 Telecaster Thinline
1986-present. Import, 2 Tele pickups, natural.

1986-2005		$550	$700

'72 Telecaster Thinline
1988-present. Import, 2 humbuckers, f-hole.

1988-2005		$550	$700

'90s Telecaster Thinline
1997-2000. Bound semi-hollow ash body, f-hole, 2 single-coils.

1997-2000		$1,200	$2,000

Thinline Telecaster
1990s. Custom Shop model, gold sparkle.

1990s		$1,400	$1,700

Texas Special Telecaster
1991. Custom Shop model, 60 made, state of Texas outline on the 'guard, ash body with Texas Orange transparent finish, large profile maple neck.

1991		$1,800	$2,000

Toronado/Toronado Deluxe
1999-present. Contoured offset-waist body with 2 Atomic Humbucker pickups, offered in black, Arctic White, Candy Apple Red, and brown sunburst.

1999-2001	Atomic humbuckers	$400	$500
1999-2001	DE-9000 P-90s	$375	$475
2002-2005	GT with racing stripes, humbuckers	$450	$500

Villager 12-String
1965-1969. Acoustic flat top, spruce top, mahogany back and sides, 12 strings, natural.

1965-1969		$575	$750

Violin - Electric
1958-1976. Sunburst is the standard finish.

1958-1959	Natural, with bow	$1,500	$1,700
1960-1969	Natural, with bow	$1,400	$1,600
1970-1976	Natural, with bow	$1,200	$1,400

Wildwood
1963-1971. Acoustic flat top with Wildwood dyed top.

1966-1971	Various (faded)	$900	$1,000
1966-1971	Various (unfaded)	$1,200	$1,600

Will Ray Signature Jazz-A-Caster
1997. Made in the Fender Japan Custom Shop as one part of the three part 'Hellecasters' Series, Strat neck on a Tele body with 2 soap-bar Seymour Duncan Jazzmaster-style pickups, gold leaf finish, limited edition.

1997		$1,150	$1,300

Fernandes
1969-present. Established in Tokyo. Early efforts were classical guitars, but they now offer a variety of guitars and basses.

Electric Guitars
1969-present.

1969-2005	Standard models	$250	$350
1969-2005	Higher-end models	$350	$600

Fender '69 Telecaster Thinline

1974 Telecaster Thinline

First Act Lola

Floyd Rose Redmond

MODEL YEAR	FEATURES	EXC. COND. LOW	HIGH

FV-105RRR Randy Rhoads
1990s. Limited production Randy Rhoads, bold white polka dots on solid background.

1990s		$1,800	$2,000

Nomad Travel/Nomad Deluxe
1998-present. Unusual body style, extra large banana headstock, built-in effects, built-in amp and speaker. Deluxe models have added features. Standard discontinued in '05.

2000-2005	Deluxe	$250	$350
1998-2005	Standard	$150	$200

Fina
Production classical and steel-string guitars built at the Kwo Hsiao Music Wooden Factory in Huiyang City, Guang Dong, mainland China. They also build acoustic basses.

Fine Resophonic
1988-present. Professional and premium grade, production/custom, wood and metal-bodied resophonic guitars (including reso-electrics) built by luthiers Mike Lewis and Pierre Avocat in Vitry Sur Seine, France. They also build ukes and mandolins.

First Act
1995-present. Budget and professional grade, production/custom, acoustic, solid and semi-hollow body guitars built in China and in their Custom Shop in Boston. They also make basses, violins, and other instruments.

Flammang Guitars
1990-present. Premium grade, custom/production, steel string guitars built by luthier David Flammang in Greene, Iowa and previously in East Hampton and Higganum, Connecticut.

Flaxwood
2004-present. Professional grade, production/custom, solid and semi-hollow body guitars built in Finland, with bodies of natural fiber composites.

Fleishman Instruments
1974-present. Premium and presentation grade, custom flat-tops made by luthier Harry Fleishman in Sebastopol, California. He also offers basses and electric uprights. Fleishman is the director of Luthiers School International.

Fletcher Brock Stringed Instruments
1992-present. Custom flat-tops and archtops made by luthier Fletcher Brock originally in Ketchum, Idaho, and currently in Seattle, Washington. He also builds mandolin family instruments.

Flowers Guitars
Premium grade, custom, archtop guitars built by luthier Gary Flowers in Baltimore, Maryland.

Floyd Rose
2004-present. Floyd Rose, inventor of the Floyd Rose Locking Tremolo, introduced a line of intermediate and professional grade, production, solidbody guitars in January 2004.

Foggy Mountain
2005-present. Intermediate grade, production, steel and nylon string acoustic and acoustic/electric guitars imported from China.

Fontanilla Guitars
1987-present. Luthier Allan Fontanilla builds his premium grade, production/custom, classical guitars in San Francisco, California.

Fouilleul
1978-present. Production/custom, classical guitars made by luthier Jean-Marie Fouilleul in Cuguen, France.

Frame Works
1995-present. Professional grade, production/custom, steel- and nylon-string guitars built by luthier Frank Krocker in Burghausen, Germany. The instruments feature a neck mounted on a guitar-shaped frame. Krocker has also built traditional archtops, flat-tops, and classicals.

Framus
1946-1977, 1996-present. Professional and premium grade, production/custom, guitars made in Markneukirchen, Germany. They also build basses, amps, mandolins and banjos. Frankische Musikindustrie (Framus) founded in Erlangen, Germany by Fred Wilfer, relocated to Bubenreuth in '54, and to Pretzfeld in '67. Begun as an acoustic instrument manufacturer, Framus added electrics in the mid-'50s. Earliest electrics were mostly acoustics with pickups attached. Electric designs begin in early-'60s. Unique feature was a laminated maple neck with many thin plies. By around '64-'65 upscale models featured the organtone, often called a spigot, a spring-loaded volume control that allowed you to simulate a Leslie speaker effect. Better models often had mutes and lots of switches.

In the '60s, Framus instruments were imported into the U.S. by Philadelphia Music Company. Resurgence of interest in ca. '74 with the Jan Akkermann hollowbody followed by original mid-'70s design called the Nashville, the product of an alliance with some American financing.

The brand was revived in '96 by Hans Peter Wilfer, the president of Warwick, with production in Warwick's factory in Germany. Distributed in the U.S. by Dana B. Goods.

MODEL YEAR	FEATURES	EXC. COND. LOW	HIGH

Atilla Zoller AZ-10
Early-1960s-late-1970s. Single-cut archtop, 2 pickups, neck glued-in until the '70s, bolt-on after, sunburst. Model 5/65 (rounded cutaway) and Model 5/67 (sharp cutaway).

1960s	Model 5/65	$700	$800
1960s	Model 5/67	$700	$850

Big 18 Doubleneck
Late 1960s. Model 5/200 is a solidbody and Model 5/220 is acoustic.

1960s	Model 5/200	$700	$800
1960s	Model 5/220	$700	$800

Caravelle 5/117
Ca.1965-1977. Double-cut archtop, tremolo, 2 pickups, cherry or sunburst.

1960s		$600	$750

Jan Akkerman
1974-1977. Single-cut semi-hollowbody, 2 pickups, gold hardware.

1974-1977		$300	$500

Missouri 5/60 (E Framus Missouri)
Ca.1960-1977. Non-cut acoustic archtop until '65, single-cut archtop with 2 pickups after, natural or sunburst.

1960s		$400	$500

New Sound Series
1960s. Double-cut semi-hollowbody. Model 5/116 I has 2 pickups and Model 5/116 II has 3.

1960s	Model 5/115/54	$700	$850
1960s	Model 5/116/52	$650	$800

Sorella Series
Ca.1955-1977. Model 5/59 is single-cut acoustic archtop, Model 5/59/50 is electric 1-pickup, Model 5/59/52 is electric 2-pickup.

1959-1965	Model 5/59	$250	$450
1959-1966	Model 5/59/50	$300	$500
1959-1967	Model 5/59/52	$350	$550

Sorento
Ca.1965-1970. Oversized semi-hollowbody, single-cut, 2 pickups, organ effect, F-holes.

1960s	Model 5/112/52	$500	$600

Strato de Luxe Series
Ca.1964-1972. 1, 2, or 3 pickups, some models have gold hardware. Model 5/068 is 12-string, 2 pickups, tremolo.

1960s	Model 5/068	$600	$700
1960s	Model 5/168/52, 2 pus	$600	$700
1960s	Model 5/168/52, 3 pus	$650	$800

Strato Super
1960s. Economy version of Strato de Luxe.

1960s	Model 5/155/52	$400	$500

Studio Series
1960s. Model 5/51 is acoustic archtop, cutaway and Model 5/51E is electric, 1 pickup.

1960s	Model 5/51	$150	$400
1960s	Model 5/51E	$200	$450

Television Series
1960s. Offset double-cut, thinline hollowbody, cherry or sunburst. Model 5/118/52 has 2 pickups and Model 5/118/54 3 pickups.

1960s	Model 5/118/52	$600	$700
1960s	Model 5/118/54	$700	$800

Texan Series
1960s. Sunburst or natural, 6- or 12-string.

1960s	Natural, 12-string	$400	$500
1960s	Natural, 6-string	$300	$450
1960s	Sunburst, 12-string	$400	$500
1960s	Sunburst, 6-string	$300	$450

Fresher
1973-1985. The Japanese-made Fresher brand models were mainly copies of popular brands and were not imported into the U.S., but they do show up at guitar shows. They also made basses.

Solidbody Electric
1970s. Import from Japan.

1970s		$275	$375

Fritz Brothers
1988-present. Premium grade, production/custom, acoustic, semi-hollow, and solidbody guitars built by luthier Roger Fritz, originally in Mobile, Alabama, currently in Albion, California. He also builds basses.

Froggy Bottom Guitars
1970-present. Luthier Michael Millard builds his premium and presentation grade, production/custom flat-tops in Newfane, Vermont (until '84 production was in Richmond, New Hampshire).

Fukuoka Musical Instruments
1993-present. Custom steel- and nylon-string flat-tops and archtops built in Japan.

Futurama
1957-mid to late 1960s. Futurama was a brand name used by Selmer in the United Kingdom. Early instruments made by the Drevokov Cooperative in Czechoslovakia, models for '63-'64 made by Sweden's Hagstrom company. Some later '60s instruments may have been made in Japan. Hobbyists will recognize the brand name as Beatle George Harrison's first electric.

Futurama/Futurama II
1960s. Offset double-cut, 2- or 3-pickup versions available, large Futurama logo on headstock with the reverse capital letter F.

1960s		$350	$650

Fylde Guitars
1973-present. Luthier Roger Bucknall builds his professional and premium grade, production/custom acoustic guitars in Penrith, Cumbria, United Kingdom. He also builds basses, mandolins, mandolas, bouzoukis, and citterns.

Fritz Brothers Super Deluxe

Froggy Bottom Model K

G&L ASAT 3

G&L ASAT Z-3 Semi-Hollow

MODEL YEAR	FEATURES	EXC. COND. LOW	HIGH

G & L

1980-present. Intermediate and professional grade, production/custom, solidbody and semi-hollowbody electric guitars made in the U.S. and overseas. They also make basses. Founded by Leo Fender and George Fullerton following the severance of ties between Fender's CLF Research and Music Man. Company sold to John MacLaren and BBE Sound, when Leo Fender died in '91. In '98 they added their Custom Creations Department. In '03 G & L introduced the Korean-made G & L Tribute Series.

ASAT
1986-1998. Called the Broadcaster in '85. Two or 3 single-coil or 2 single-coil/1 humbucker pickup configurations until early-'90s, 2 single-coils after.

1986		$700	$850
1987	Leo Fender sig. on headstock	$750	$900
1988-1991	Leo Fender sig. on body	$850	$1,000
1992-1998		$600	$750

ASAT 20th Anniversary
2000. Limited Edition of 50, ash body, tinted bird-seye maple neck, 2-tone sunburst.

2000		$1,300	$1,500

ASAT '50
1999. Limited edition of 10.

1999		$1,000	$1,300

ASAT Blues Boy Limited Edition
1999. Limited edition of 20.

1999		$1,000	$1,400

ASAT Blues Boy Semi-Hollow Limited Edition
1999. Limited edition of 12, thin semi-hollow.

1999		$1,000	$1,300

ASAT Classic
1990-present. Two single-coil pickups, individually adjustable bridge saddles, neck-tilt adjustment and tapered string posts.

1990-1991	Signature on neck	$825	$1,000
1992-1997	3-bolt neck	$700	$900
1997-2005	4-bolt neck	$675	$875

ASAT Classic B-Bender
1997. 12 made with factory-original B-Bender.

1997		$1,000	$1,200

ASAT Classic Blues Boy
2001-present. Humbucker neck pickup, single-coil at bridge.

2001-2005		$700	$900

ASAT Classic Blues Boy Semi-Hollow
1997-present. Chambered Classic with F-holes.

1997-2005		$900	$1,000

ASAT Classic Commemorative
1991-1992. Leo Fender signature and birth/death dating.

1991-1992	Australian lacewood, 6 made	$3,800	$6,000
1991-1992	Cherryburst, 350 made	$2,200	$2,600

MODEL YEAR	FEATURES	EXC. COND. LOW	HIGH

ASAT Classic Custom
1996-1997, 2002-present.

1996-1997	1st version	$800	$950
2002-2005	2nd version, 4-bolt neck	$700	$750

ASAT Classic Custom Semi-Hollow
2002-present.

2002-2005		$700	$850

ASAT Classic Semi-Hollow
1997-present.

1997-2005		$700	$800

ASAT Classic Three
1998. Limited Edition of 100 units.

1998		$1,000	$1,400

ASAT Custom
1996. No pickguard, 25 to 30 made.

1996		$800	$900

ASAT Deluxe
1997-present. Two humbuckers, flamed maple top, bound body.

1997	3-bolt neck, less than 100 made	$1,000	$1,400
1997-2005	4-bolt neck	$950	$1,100

ASAT Deluxe Semi-Hollow
1997-present. Two humbuckers.

1997-2005		$1,000	$1,300

ASAT III
1988-1991, 1996-1998. Single-cut body, 3 single-coil pickups.

1988-1991	1st version, Leo era, 150 made	$950	$1,100
1996-1998	Post Leo era	$700	$850

ASAT Junior Limited Edition
1998-2002. Single-cut semi-hollowbody, 2 single-coil pickups, short run of 250 units.

1998-2002		$900	$1,100

ASAT S-3
1998-2000. Three soap-bar single-coil pickups, limited production.

1998-2000		$700	$900

ASAT Semi-Hollow
1997-present. Semi-hollow version of ASAT Special.

1997-2005		$700	$800

ASAT Special
1992-present. Like ASAT, but with 2 larger P-90-type pickups, chrome hardware, various colors.

1992-1997	3-bolt neck	$750	$800
1997-1999	4-bolt neck	$700	$750
2000-2005	4-bolt neck	$600	$650

ASAT Special Deluxe
2001-present. No 'guard version of the Special with figured maple top.

2001-2005		$800	$900

ASAT Z-2 Limited Edition
1999. Limited edition of 10 instruments, semi-hollow construction, natural ash, tortoise bound, engraved neckplate.

1999		$900	$1,100

MODEL YEAR	FEATURES	EXC. COND. LOW	HIGH

ASAT Z-3
1998-present. Three offset-style Z-3 high output pickups, sunburst.

1998-2005		$800	$1,000

ASAT Z-3 Semi-Hollow
1998-present. Semi-hollowbody-style, 3 offset-style Z-3 high output pickups.

1998-2005		$850	$1,050

Broadcaster
1985-1986. Solidbody, 2 single-coils with adjustable polepieces act in humbucking mode with selector switch in the center position, black parts and finish, name changed to ASAT in early-'86.

1985-1986	Signed by Leo, ebony board	$1,900	$2,400
1985-1986	Signed by Leo, maple board	$2,000	$2,500

Cavalier
1983-1986. Offset double-cut, 2 humbuckers, 700 made, sunburst.

1983-1986		$700	$1,000

Climax
1992-1996. Offset double-cut, bolt maple neck, six-on-a-side tuners, double locking vibrato, blue.

1992-1996		$700	$850

Climax Plus
1992-1996. Two humbuckers replace single-coils of the Climax, plus 1 single-coil.

1992-1996		$750	$900

Climax XL
1992-1996. Two humbuckers only.

1992-1996		$750	$900

Comanche V
1988-1991. Solidbody, 3 Z-shaped single-coil humbuckers, maple neck in choice of 3 radii, rosewood 'board, vibrato, fine tuners, Leo Fender's signature on the body, sunburst.

1988-1991		$850	$1,000

Comanche VI
1990-1991. Leo Fender's signature on the body, 6 mini-toggles.

1990-1991		$1,000	$1,300

Comanche (Reintroduced)
1998-present. Reissue with either swamp ash or alder body, bolt-on maple neck, 3 Z-coil pickups, standard or premium finish options.

1998-2005	Premium finish, flame top	$950	$1,100
1998-2005	Standard finish	$700	$850

Commemorative
1992-1997. About 350 made, Leo Fender signature on upper bass bout.

1992-1997	Sunburst	$2,000	$2,400

F-100 (Model I and II)
1980-1986. Offset double-cut solidbody, 2 humbuckers, natural. Came in a I and II model - only difference is the radius of the 'board.

1980-1986		$600	$850

F-100 E (Model I and II)
1980-1982. Offset double-cut solidbody, 2 humbuckers, active electronics, pre-amp, natural. Came in a

I and II model - only difference is the radius of the 'board.

1980-1982		$600	$850

G-200
1981-1982. Mahogany solidbody, maple neck, ebony 'board, 2 humbucking pickups, coil-split switches, natural or sunburst, 209 made.

1981-1982		$1,000	$1,300

GBL-LE (Guitars by Leo Limited Edition)
1999. Limited edition of 25, semi-hollowbody, 3 pickups.

1999		$1,000	$1,300

George Fullerton Signature
1995-present. Double-cut solidbody, sunburst.

1995-1997	3-bolt neck	$1,000	$1,300
1997-2005	4-bolt neck	$900	$1,200

HG-1
1982-1983. Offset double-cut, 1 humbucker, dot inlays. Very rare as most were made into HG-2s.

1982-1983		$1,900	$2,100

HG-2
1982-1984. 2-humbucker HG, body changes to classic offset double-cut in '84.

1982-1984		$1,000	$1,500

Interceptor
1983-1991. To '86 an X-shaped solidbody (about 70 made), either 3 single-coils, 2 humbuckers, or 1 humbucker and 2 single-coils, '87-'89 was an offset double-cut solidbody (about 12 made).

1983-1985	1st X-body	$1,200	$1,400
1985-1986	2nd X-body	$1,500	$1,700
1988-1991	Double-cut	$700	$900

Invader
1984-1991, 1998-present. Double-cut solidbody, 2 single-coil and 1 humbucker pickups.

1984-1991	1st version	$500	$700
1998-2003	2nd version	$800	$900

Invader Plus
1998-present. Two humbuckers and single blade pickup in the middle position.

1998-2005		$800	$900

John Jorgenson Signature Model ASAT
1995. About 190 made, Silver Metalflake finish.

1995		$900	$1,200

Legacy
1992-present. Classic double-cut configuration, various colors.

1992-1994	3-bolt neck, Duncan SSLs	$650	$800
1995-1997	3-bolt neck, Alnicos	$600	$750
1997-2005	4-bolt neck, Alnicos	$600	$700

Legacy Deluxe
2001-present. No 'guard, figured maple top.

2001-2005		$700	$850

Legacy HB
2001-present. One humbucker pickup at bridge position plus 2 single-coil pickups.

2001-2005		$600	$750

Legacy 2HB
2001-present. Two humbucker pickups.

2001-2003		$550	$700

G&L Tribute Invader

G&L Legacy

G&L Will Ray Signature Tribute

*Gallagher
Doc Watson*

MODEL YEAR	FEATURES	EXC. COND. LOW	HIGH
Legacy Special			
1993-present. Legacy with 3 humbuckers, various colors.			
1992-1997	3-bolt neck	$600	$700
1998-2005	4-bolt neck	$500	$600
Nighthawk			
1983. Offset double-cut solidbody, 3 single-coil pickups, 269 made, sunburst, name changed to Skyhawk in '84.			
1983		$650	$950
Rampage			
1984-1991. Offset double-cut solidbody, hard rock maple neck, ebony 'board, 1 bridge-position humbucker pickup, sunburst.			
1984-1991		$600	$800
Rampage (Reissue)			
2000. Limited Edition of 70 units, supplied with gig bag and not hard case, ivory finish.			
2000		$500	$700
S-500			
1982-present. Double-cut mahogany or ash solidbody, maple neck, ebony or maple 'board, 3 single-coil pickups, vibrato.			
1982-1987	No mini-toggle	$800	$900
1988-1991	Mini-toggle Leo's sig. on body	$850	$950
1992-1997	3-bolt neck	$650	$800
1997-2005	4-bolt neck	$600	$750
S-500 Deluxe			
2001-present. Deluxe Series features, including no 'guard and flamed maple top, natural.			
2001-2003		$700	$850
SC-1			
1982-1983. Offset double-cut solidbody, 1 single-coil pickup, tremolo, sunburst, 250 made.			
1982-1983		$500	$700
SC-2			
1982-1983. Offset double-cut solidbody, 2 MFD soapbar pickups, about 600 made.			
1982-1983	Shallow cutaways	$400	$600
1983	Deeper, pointed cutaways	$400	$500
SC-3			
1982-1991. Offset double-cut solidbody, 3 single-coil pickups, tremolo.			
1982-1983	Shallow cutaways	$500	$650
1984-1987	Deeper cutaways, no 'guard	$450	$600
1988-1991	Deeper cutaways, 'guard	$400	$550
Skyhawk			
1984-1991. Renamed from Nighthawk, offset double-cut, 3 single-coils, signature on headstock '84-'87, then on body '88-'91.			
1984-1987		$650	$700
1988-1991		$750	$800
Superhawk			
1984-1987. Offset double-cut, maple neck, ebony 'board, G&L or Kahler tremolos, 2 humbuckers, signature on headstock.			
1984-1987		$550	$700

MODEL YEAR	FEATURES	EXC. COND. LOW	HIGH
Will Ray Signature Model			
2002-present. Will Ray signature on headstock, 3 Z-coil pickups, Hipshot B-Bender.			
2002-2005		$900	$1,000

G.L. Stiles

1960-1994. Built by Gilbert Lee Stiles (b. October 2, 1914, Independence, West Virginia; d. 1994) primarily in the Miami, Florida area. First solidbody, including pickups and all hardware, built by hand in his garage. Stiles favored scrolls, fancy carving and walnut fingerboards. His later instruments were considerably more fancy and refined. He moved to Hialeah, Florida by '63 and began making acoustic guitars and other instruments. His acoustics featured double stressed (bent) backs for increased tension. He later taught for the Augusta Heritage Program and Davis and Elkins College in Elkins, West Virginia. Only his solidbodies had consecutive serial numbers. Stiles made approximately 1000 solidbodies and 500 acoustics.

Gabriel's Guitar Workshop

1979-present. Production/custom steel- and nylon-stringed guitars built by luthier Gabriel Ochoteco in Germany until '84 and in Brisbane, Australia since.

Gagnon

1998-present. Luthier Bill Gagnon builds his premium and presentation grade, production/custom, archtop guitars in Beaverton, Oregon.

Galanti

Ca.1962-ca.1967. Electric guitars offered by the longtime Italian accordion maker. They may have also offered acoustics.

Electric

1962-1967. Solidbody or hollowbody.

1962-1967		$400	$600

Galiano

New Yorkers Antonio Cerrito and Raphael Ciani offered guitars under the Galiano brand during the early part of the last century. They used the brand both on guitars built by them and others, including The Oscar Schmidt Company. They also offered mandolins.

Gallagher

1965-present. Professional and premium grade, production/custom, flat-top guitars built in Wartrace, Tennessee. J. W. Gallagher started building Shelby brand guitars in the Slingerland Drum factory in Shelbyville, Tennessee in '63. In '65 he and his son Don made the first Gallagher guitar, the G-50. Doc Watson began using Gallagher guitars in '68. In '76, Don assumed operation of the business when J. W. semi-retired. J. W. died in '79.

MODEL YEAR	FEATURES	EXC. COND. LOW	HIGH

71 Special
1970-present. Rosewood back and sides, spruce top, herringbone trim, bound ebony 'board, natural.

1970s		$1,600	$1,900

A-70 Ragtime Special
1978-present. Smaller auditorium/00 size, spruce top, mahogany back and sides, G logo, natural.

1980s		$1,600	$1,800

Custom 12-String
Introduced in 1965. Mahogany, 12-fret neck, natural.

1965		$1,000	$1,400

Doc Watson 12-String
1995-2000. Natural.

1995-2000		$1,500	$1,700

Doc Watson Model
1974-present. Spruce top, mahogany back and sides, scalloped bracing, ebony 'board, herringbone trim, natural.

1974-1979		$1,700	$2,000
1980-1989		$1,600	$1,800
1990-1999		$1,500	$1,700
2000-2005		$1,500	$1,700

Doc Watson Model (Cutaway)
1975-present. Spruce top, mahogany back and sides, scalloped bracing, ebony 'board, herringbone trim, natural.

1980s		$1,700	$2,000

G-45
1970-present. Mahogany back and sides, spruce top, ebony 'board, natural.

1980s		$1,000	$1,100

G-50
1980s-present. Mahogany back and sides, spruce top, ebony 'board, natural.

1980s		$1,100	$1,300

G-65
1980s-present. Rosewood back and sides, spruce top, ebony 'board, natural.

1980s		$1,400	$1,700

G-70
1978-present. Rosewood back and sides, herringbone purfling on top and soundhole, mother-of-pearl diamond 'board inlays, bound headstock, natural.

1980s		$1,500	$1,800

Gallagher, Kevin

1996. Kevin Gallagher, luthier, changed name brand to Omega to avoid confusion with J.W. Gallagher. See Omega listing.

Gallotone

1950s-1960s. Low-end foreign brand similar to 1950s Stellas, the Gallotone Champion, a 3/4 size student flat top, is associated with John Lennon as his early guitar.

Galloup Guitars

1994-present. Luthier Bryan Galloup builds his professional and premium grade, production/custom flat-tops in Big Rapids, Michigan. He also operates the Galloup School of Lutherie and The Guitar Hospital repair and restoration business.

Galveston

Budget and intermediate grade, production, imported acoustic, acoustic/electric, resonator and solidbody guitars. They also offer basses and mandolins.

Gamble & O'Toole

1978-present. Premium grade, custom classical and steel string guitars built by luthier Arnie Gamble in Sacramento, California, with design input and inlay work from his wife Erin O'Toole.

Ganz Guitars

1995-present. Luthier Steve Ganz builds his professional grade, production/custom classical guitars in Bellingham, Washington.

Garcia

Made by luthier Federico Garcia in Spain until late-1960s or very early-'70s when production moved to Japan.

Classical
1960s-1970s. Mid-level, '60s model is solid spruce top with solid mahogany, rosewood or walnut back and sides, '70s model is Spanish pine top with walnut back and sides.

1960s	Mahogany	$200	$250
1960s	Rosewood	$450	$550
1960s	Walnut	$250	$350
1970s	Spanish pine/walnut	$175	$225

Garrison

2000-present. Intermediate and professional grade, production, acoustic and acoustic/electric guitars designed by luthier Chris Griffiths using his Active Bracing System (a single integrated glass-fiber bracing system inside a solid wood body). He started Griffiths Guitar Works in 1993 in St. John's, Newfoundland, and introduced Garrison guitars in 2000.

G Series
2000-present.

2000-2005		$300	$550

Gemelli

Early 1960s-ca. 1966. European-made (likely Italian) guitars. Similar to Bartolini guitars, so most likely from same manufacturer. Originally plastic covered, they switched to paint finishes by around '65.

Giannini

1900-present. Classical, acoustic, and acoustic/electric guitars built in Salto, SP, Brazil near Sao Paolo. They also build violas, cavaquinhos and mandolins. Founded by guitar-builder Tranquillo Giannini, an Italian who traveled to Brazil in 1890 and discovered the exotic woods of Brazil. The

Ganz Gula

Garrison AG-600

MODEL YEAR	FEATURES	EXC. COND. LOW	HIGH

1965 Gibson B-25-12 N

company was producing 30,000 instruments a year by '30. They began exporting their acoustic instruments to the U.S. in '63. They added electric guitars in '60, but these weren't imported as much, if at all. Gianninis from this era used much Brazilian Rosewood.

Classical
Early-1970s. Nylon string import, small body.

1970s		$100	$300

CraViolia
1970s. Kidney bean-shaped rosewood body, acoustic, natural, line included a classical, a steel string, and a 12-string.

1972-1974		$275	$325

CraViolia 12-String
Early-1970s. Kidney bean-shaped body, 12 strings.

1972-1974		$300	$350

Gibson

1890s (1902)-present. Intermediate, professional, and premium grade, production/custom, acoustic and electric guitars made in the U.S. They also build basses, mandolins, amps, and banjos under the Gibson name. Gibson also offers instruments under the Epiphone, Kramer, Steinberger, Dobro, Tobias, Valley Arts, Slingerland (drums), Baldwin (pianos), Trace Elliot, Electar (amps), Maestro, Gibson Labs, Oberheim, and Echoplex brands.

Founded in Kalamazoo, Michigan by Orville Gibson, a musician and luthier who developed instruments with tops, sides and backs carved out of solid pieces of wood. Early instruments included mandolins, archtop guitars and harp guitars. By 1896 Gibson had opened a shop. In 1902 Gibson was bought out by a group of investors who incorporated the business as Gibson Mandolin-Guitar Manufacturing Company, Limited. The company was purchased by Chicago Musical Instrument Company (CMI) in '44. In '57 CMI also purchased the Epiphone guitar company, transferring production from Philadelphia to the Gibson plant in Kalamazoo. Gibson was purchased by Norlin in late-'69 and a new factory was opened in Nashville, Tennessee in '74. The Kalamazoo factory ceased production in '84. In '85, Gibson was sold to a group headed by Henry Juskewiscz. Gibson purchased the Flatiron Company in '87 and built a new factory in '89, moving acoustic instrument production to Bozeman, Montana.

The various models of Firebirds, Flying Vs, Les Pauls, SGs, and Super 400s are grouped together under those general headings. Custom Shop and Historic instruments are listed with their respective main model (for example, the '39 Super 400 Historical Collection model is listed with the Super 400s).

335 S Custom
1980-1981. Solidbody, 335-shaped, mahogany body, unbound rosewood 'board, 2 exposed Dirty Finger humbuckers, coil-tap, TP-6 tailpiece.

1980-1981	Sunburst	$825	$950

1981 Gibson 335S Deluxe

MODEL YEAR	FEATURES	EXC. COND. LOW	HIGH

335 S Deluxe
1980-1982. Same as 335 S Custom but with bound ebony 'board, brass nut.

1980-1982	Cherry	$825	$1,100
1980-1982	Silverburst	$900	$1,250
1980-1982	Sunburst	$825	$1,150

335 S Standard
1980-1981. Solidbody, 335-shaped, maple body and neck, 2 exposed split-coil humbuckers, stop tailpiece, no coil-tap, unbound 'board.

1980-1981	Sunburst	$800	$900

Advanced Jumbo
1936-1940. Dreadnought, 16" wide, round shoulders, Brazilian rosewood back and sides, sunburst, reintroduced '90-'97.

1936-1937		$45,000	$55,000
1938-1939		$40,000	$50,000
1940		$37,000	$47,000

Advanced Jumbo Reissue/AJ Special Edition
1990-1999, 2001-present. Issued as a standard production model, but soon available only as a special order for most of the '90s; currently offered as standard production. Renamed 1936 Advanced Jumbo for '97-'98. There were also some limited-edition AJs offered during the '90s.

1990-1999	Reissue	$1,500	$1,900
1995-1996	Special Ed. flamed maple	$1,900	$2,800
2001-2005	Reintroduced	$1,500	$1,900
2001-2005	Special Ed. Indian rosewood	$1,900	$2,800

B.B. King Commemorative ES-355 "Lucille"
2006. Limited edition of 80 guitars, price includes matching serial number/certificate number, matching B.B. King script logo case.

2006		$4,800	$5,500

B.B. King Custom
1980-1988. Lucille on peghead, 2 pickups, multi-bound, gold-plated parts, Vari-tone, cherry or ebony, renamed B.B. King Lucille in '88.

1980-1988		$1,800	$1,900

B.B. King Standard
1980-1985. Like B.B. King Custom, but with stereo electronics and chrome-plated parts, cherry or ebony.

1980-1985		$1,600	$1,800

B.B. King Lucille
1988-present. Introduced as B.B. King Custom, renamed B.B. King Lucille. Lucille on peghead, 2 pickups, multi-bound, gold-plated parts, Vari-tone, cherry or ebony.

1988-1999		$1,800	$1,900

B-15
1967-1971. Mahogany, spruce top, student model, natural finish.

1967-1969		$575	$725
1970-1971		$500	$600

MODEL YEAR	FEATURES	EXC. COND. LOW	HIGH

B-25
1962-1977. Flat-top, mahogany, bound body, cherry sunburst (natural finish is the B-25 N).

1962-1964		$1,200	$1,500
1965-1966		$950	$1,200
1967-1969		$900	$1,100
1970-1977		$700	$900

B-25 N
1962-1977. Flat-top, mahogany, bound body, natural (cherry sunburst finish is the B-25).

1962-1964		$1,250	$1,600
1965-1966		$1,100	$1,250
1967-1969		$1,000	$1,200
1970-1977		$800	$1,000

B-25 3/4
1962-1968. Short-scale version, flat-top, mahogany body, cherry sunburst (natural finish is the B-25 3/4 N).

1962-1964		$800	$1,100
1965-1966		$700	$850
1967-1968		$600	$800

B-25 N 3/4
1966-1968. Short-scale version, flat-top, mahogany body, natural (cherry sunburst finish is the B-25 3/4).

1966-1968		$750	$900

B-25-12
1962-1970. Flat-top 12-string version, mahogany, bound body, cherry sunburst (natural finish is the B-25-12 N).

1962-1964		$1,100	$1,500
1965-1966		$850	$1,200
1967-1968		$800	$1,000
1969-1970		$750	$900

B-25-12 N
1962-1977. Flat-top 12-string version, mahogany, bound body, natural (cherry sunburst is the B-25-12).

1962-1964		$1,200	$1,600
1965-1966		$950	$1,300
1967-1969		$900	$1,100
1970-1977		$800	$1,000

B-45-12
1961-1979. Flat-top 12-string, mahogany, round shoulders for '61, square after, sunburst (natural finish is the B-45-12 N).

1961-1962	Round shoulders	$1,900	$2,300
1962-1964	Square shoulders	$1,700	$2,100
1965-1966	Non-pin bridge introduced	$1,400	$1,700
1967-1969		$1,100	$1,400
1970-1979	Pin bridge reintroduced	$900	$1,100

B-45-12 N
1962-1979. Flat-top 12-string, mahogany, natural (cherry sunburst finish is the B-45-12).

1962-1964	Square shoulders	$1,800	$2,200
1965-1966	Non-pin bridge introduced	$1,500	$1,800
1967-1969		$1,200	$1,500
1970-1979	Pin bridge reintroduced	$1,000	$1,200

B-45-12 Limited Edition
1991-1992. Limited edition reissue with rosewood back and sides, natural.

1991-1992		$950	$1,200

Barney Kessel Custom
1961-1973. Double-cut archtop, 2 humbuckers, gold hardware, cherry sunburst.

1961-1962		$3,300	$4,000
1963-1964		$3,200	$3,900
1965-1966		$2,800	$3,300
1967-1969		$2,700	$3,000
1970-1973		$2,400	$2,700

Barney Kessel Regular
1961-1974. Double-cut archtop, 2 humbuckers, nickel hardware, cherry sunburst.

1961-1962		$2,900	$3,200
1963-1964		$2,800	$3,100
1965-1966		$2,600	$2,900
1967-1969		$2,500	$2,700
1970-1973		$2,100	$2,500

Blue Ridge
1968-1979, 1989-1990. Flat-top, dreadnought, laminated rosewood back and sides, natural finish, reintroduced for '89-'90.

1968-1969		$1,100	$1,200
1970-1979		$1,000	$1,100

Blue Ridge 12
1970-1978. Flat-top, 12 strings, laminated rosewood back and sides, natural finish.

1970-1978		$800	$900

Blueshawk
1996-2006. Small Les Paul single-cut-type body with f-holes, 2 single-coil hum cancelling Blues 90 pickups, 6-way Varitone rotary dial.

1996-2006		$650	$700

Byrdland
1955-1992. Thinline archtop, single-cut (rounded until late-'60, pointed '60-late-'69, rounded after '69, rounded or pointed '98-present), 2 pickups, now part of the Historic Collection.

1956-1957	Natural, P-90s	$9,500	$10,000
1956-1957	Sunburst, P-90s	$7,500	$8,000
1958-1959	Natural, PAFs	$12,000	$14,000
1958-1959	Sunburst, PAFs	$10,000	$12,000
1960-1962	Natural, PAFs	$10,000	$12,000
1960-1962	Sunburst, PAFs	$8,500	$11,000
1963-1964	Natural, pat #	$7,700	$10,500
1963-1964	Sunburst, pat #	$7,200	$10,000
1965-1966	Natural	$6,500	$8,000
1965-1966	Sunburst	$6,000	$7,000
1967-1969	Sunburst	$5,500	$6,200
1967-7669	Natural	$6,000	$6,700
1970-1992	Various colors	$4,000	$5,500

Byrdland Historic Collection
1993-present. Various colors.

1993-2005	Natural	$4,500	$5,500
1993-2005	Sunburst	$4,000	$5,000
1993-2005	Wine Red	$3,500	$4,000

Gibson B-45-12

1959 Gibson Byrdland

GUITARS

1957 Gibson C-2

1986 Gibson Corvus

MODEL YEAR	FEATURES	EXC. COND. LOW	HIGH

C-0 Classical
1962-1971. Spruce top, mahogany back and sides, bound top, natural.
| 1962-1964 | | $475 | $525 |
| 1965-1971 | | $350 | $450 |

C-1 Classical
1957-1971. Spruce top, mahogany back and sides, bound body, natural.
| 1957-1964 | | $600 | $700 |
| 1965-1971 | | $500 | $600 |

C-1 E Classical Electric
1960-1967. C-1 with ceramic bridge pickup, catalog notes special matched amplifier that filters out fingering noises.
| 1960-1964 | | $650 | $750 |
| 1965-1967 | | $550 | $650 |

C-1 S Petite Classical
1961-1966. Petite 13 1/4" body, natural spruce top, mahogany back and sides.
| 1961-1964 | | $500 | $550 |
| 1965-1967 | | $450 | $500 |

C-2 Classical
1960-1971. Maple back and sides, bound body, natural.
| 1960-1964 | | $700 | $800 |
| 1965-1971 | | $600 | $700 |

C-4 Classical
1962-1968. Maple back and sides, natural.
| 1962-1964 | | $850 | $950 |
| 1965-1968 | | $750 | $850 |

C-5 Classical
1957-1960. Rosewood back and sides, previously named GS-5 Classical in '54-'56.
| 1957-1960 | | $900 | $1,100 |

C-6 Classical
1958-1971. Rosewood back and sides, gold hardware, natural.
| 1958-1964 | | $1,300 | $1,600 |
| 1965-1971 | | $1,000 | $1,300 |

C-8 Classical
1962-1969. Rosewood back and sides, natural.
| 1962-1964 | | $1,500 | $2,000 |
| 1965-1969 | | $1,300 | $1,500 |

C-100 Classical
1971-1972. Slotted peghead, spruce top, mahogany back and sides, ebony 'board, Gibson Master Model label, non-gloss finish.
| 1971-1972 | | $300 | $400 |

C-200 Classical
1971-1972. C-100 with gloss finish.
| 1971-1972 | | $500 | $600 |

C-300 Classical
1971-1972. Similar to C-100, but with rosewood 'board, wider soundhole ring.
| 1971-1972 | | $550 | $650 |

C-400 Classical
1971-1972. Rosewood sides and back, spruce top, high-end appointments, chrome hardware.
| 1971-1972 | | $900 | $1,000 |

C-500 Classical
1971-1972. C-400 with gold hardware.
| 1971-1972 | | $1,000 | $1,200 |

CF-100
1950-1958. Flat-top, pointed cutaway, mahogany back and sides, bound body, sunburst finish.
| 1950-1958 | | $2,300 | $2,500 |

CF-100 E
1951-1958. CF-100 with a single-coil pickup.
| 1950-1958 | | $2,500 | $3,300 |

Challenger I
1983-1985. Single-cut Les Paul-shaped solidbody, 1 humbucker pickup, bolt-on maple neck with rosewood 'board and dot markers, silver finish standard.
| 1983-1985 | | $450 | $550 |

Challenger II
1983-1985. Single-cut Les Paul-shaped solidbody, 2 humbucker pickups, bolt-on maple neck with rosewood 'board and dot markers, various colors.
| 1983-1985 | | $500 | $600 |

Chet Atkins CE
1981-1995. CE stands for Classical Electric, single-cut, multi-bound body, rosewood 'board with standard width nut, gold hardware, various colors. In '95, the Atkins CE and CEC were consolidated into the Chet Atkins CE/CEC, with an ebony 'board with a standard (CE) and classical (CEC) nut. That model was discontinued in '06.
| 1981-1995 | | $900 | $1,000 |

Chet Atkins CEC
1981-1995. Same as CE but with ebony 'board and 2" classical width nut, black or natural.
| 1981-1995 | | $1,150 | $1,250 |

Chet Atkins Country Gentleman
1987-2005. Thinline archtop, single rounded cutaway, 2 humbuckers, multi-bound, gold hardware, Bigsby. Part of Gibson's Custom line.
| 1987-1995 | | $2,000 | $2,500 |

Chet Atkins SST
1987-2006. Steel string acoustic/electric solidbody, single-cut, bridge transducer pickup, active bass and treble controls, gold hardware.
| 1986-2001 | | $1,000 | $1,200 |

Chet Atkins SST-12
1990-1994. 12-string model similar to 6-string, mahogany/spruce body, preamp circuit controls single transducer pickup, natural or ebony finish.
| 1990-1994 | | $1,400 | $1,700 |

Chet Atkins Tennessean
1990-2005. Single rounded cutaway archtop, 2 humbuckers, f-holes, bound body. Part of Gibson's Custom line.
| 1990-2005 | | $1,400 | $1,500 |

Chicago 35
1994-1995. Flat-top dreadnought, round shoulders, mahogany back and sides, prewar script logo.
| 1994-1995 | factory electronics | $900 | $1,050 |

Citation
1969-1971. 17" full-depth body, single-cut archtop, 1 or 2 floating pickups, fancy inlay, natural or sunburst. Only 8 shipped for '69-'71, reissued the first time '79-'83 and as part of the Historic Collection in '93.
| 1969-1971 | | $13,000 | $23,000 |

MODEL YEAR	FEATURES	EXC. COND. LOW	HIGH

Citation (1st Reissue)
1979-1983. Reissue of '69-'71 model, reintroduced in '93 as part of Gibson's Historic Collection.

| 1979-1983 | Sunburst or natural | $12,000 | $15,000 |

Citation (2nd Reissue)
1993-present. Limited production via Gibson's Historic Collection, natural or sunburst.

| 1994-2003 | Natural | $12,000 | $13,500 |
| 1994-2003 | Sunburst | $12,000 | $13,500 |

CL-20/CL-20+
1997-1998. Flat-top, laminated back and sides, 4-ply binding with tortoiseshell appointments, abalone diamond inlays.

| 1997-1998 | | $1,000 | $1,100 |

CL-30 Deluxe
1997-1998. J-50 style dreadnought, solid spruce top, bubinga back and sides, factory electronics.

| 1997-1998 | | $800 | $950 |

CL-35 Deluxe Cutaway
1997-1988. Single cutaway CL-30.

| 1997-1998 | | $950 | $1,050 |

Corvus I
1982-1984. Odd-shaped solidbody with offset V-type cut, bolt maple neck, rosewood 'board, 1 humbucker, standard finish was silver gloss, but others available at an additional cost.

| 1982-1984 | | $400 | $500 |

Corvus II
1982-1984. Same as Corvus I, but with 2 humbuckers, 2 volume controls, 1 master tone control.

| 1982-1984 | | $450 | $550 |

Corvus III
1982-1984. Same as Corvus I, but with 3 single-coil pickups, master volume and tone control, 5-way switch.

| 1982-1984 | | $550 | $700 |

Crest Gold
1969-1971. Double-cut thinline archtop, Brazilian rosewood body, 2 mini-humbuckers, bound top and headstock, bound f-holes, gold-plated parts.

| 1969-1971 | | $3,500 | $5,500 |

Crest Silver
1969-1972. Silver-plated parts version of Crest.

| 1969-1972 | | $3,000 | $5,000 |

CS Series
2002-present. Scaled down ES-335 body style, made in Custom Shop.

2002-2005	CS-336 (plain top)	$1,500	$1,700
2002-2005	CS-336F (figured top)	$1,700	$1,900
2002-2003	CS-356 (plain top)	$1,900	$2,100
2002-2005	CS-356F (figured top)	$2,100	$2,300

Dove
1962-1996, 1999-2003. Flat-top acoustic, maple back and sides, square shoulders.

1962-1964	Natural	$5,000	$5,500
1962-1964	Sunburst	$4,500	$5,000
1965	Natural	$4,500	$5,000
1965	Sunburst	$4,200	$4,600
1966	Natural	$4,100	$4,500
1966	Sunburst	$3,800	$4,200
1967	Natural	$3,500	$4,000
1967	Sunburst	$3,300	$3,600
1968	Natural	$3,400	$3,900
1968	Sunburst	$3,200	$3,500
1969-1970	Natural	$2,100	$2,800
1969-1970	Sunburst	$2,000	$2,700
1971-1984	Natural	$2,000	$2,700
1971-1984	Sunburst	$1,900	$2,600
1984-1989	Various colors	$1,600	$1,900
1990-1996	Various colors	$1,500	$1,600
1999-2003	Reissue model	$2,000	$2,200

Dove Commemorative
1994-1996. Heritage or Antique Cherry finish.

| 1994-1996 | | $1,700 | $2,000 |

Doves In Flight
1996-present. Gibson Custom model, maple back and sides, doves in flight inlays.

| 1996-2005 | | $2,800 | $3,000 |

'60s Dove
1997-1999. Spruce top, maple back and sides, Dove appointments.

| 1997-1999 | | $1,600 | $1,800 |

EAS Deluxe
1992-1994. Single-cut flat-top acoustic/electric, solid flamed maple top, 3-band EQ.

| 1992-1994 | Vintage Cherry Sunburst | $850 | $950 |

EBS(F)-1250 Double Bass
1962-1970. Double-cut SG-type solidbody, double-neck with bass and 6-string, originally introduced as the EBSF-1250 because of a built-in fuzztone, which was later deleted, only 22 made.

1962-1964		$9,500	$12,500
1965-1966		$7,500	$10,000
1967-1969		$6,500	$8,000
1970		$5,000	$7,500

EC-10 Standard
1997-1998. Jumbo single-cut, on-board electronics, solid spruce top, maple back and sides.

| 1997-1998 | | $850 | $950 |

EC-20 Starburst
1997-1998. Jumbo single-cut, on-board electronics, solid spruce top, maple back and sides, renamed J-180 EC in '99.

| 1997-1998 | | $1,200 | $1,300 |

EC-30 Blues King Electro (BKE)
1997-1998. Jumbo single-cut, on-board electronics, solid spruce top, figured maple back and sides, renamed J-185 EC in '99.

| 1997-1998 | | $1,500 | $1,800 |

EDS-1275 Double 12
1958-1968, 1977-1990. Double-cut doubleneck with one 12- and one 6-string, thinline hollowbody until late-'62, SG-style solidbody '62 on.

1958-1959	Black or cherry	$16,000	$20,000
1958-1959	Sunburst	$16,000	$20,000
1958-1959	White	$16,000	$20,000
1960-1962	Black or cherry	$15,000	$19,000
1960-1962	Sunburst	$15,000	$19,000

Gibson Dove

Gibson Doves In Flight

1956 Gibson ES-5

1957 Gibson ES-5 Switchmaster

MODEL YEAR	FEATURES	EXC. COND. LOW	HIGH
1960-1962	White	$15,000	$19,000
1968	Black or cherry	$6,000	$9,000
1968	Jimmy Page exact specs	$9,000	$12,000
1968	White	$6,000	$9,000
1977-1979	Various colors	$2,800	$3,200
1980-1991	Various colors	$2,400	$2,600
1995-2000	Various colors	$2,000	$2,200

EDS-1275 Double 12 (Historic Collection)
1991-1994. Historic Collection reissue.

1991-1994	White	$2,000	$2,200

EDS-1275 Double 12 Centennial
1994. Guitar of the Month (May), gold medallion on back of headstock, gold hardware.

1994	Cherry	$2,000	$2,200

EMS-1235 Double Mandolin
1958-1968. Double-cut, doubleneck with 1 regular 6-string and 1 short 6-string (the mandolin neck), thinline hollowbody until late-1962, SG-style solidbody '62-'68, black, sunburst or white, total of 61 shipped.

1958-1961		$16,000	$20,000
1962-1964		$12,000	$16,000
1965-1968		$6,000	$12,000

ES-5
1949-1955. Single-cut archtop, 3 P-90 pickups, renamed ES-5 Switchmaster in '55.

1949-1955	Natural	$8,500	$12,000
1949-1955	Sunburst	$6,000	$10,000

ES-5 Switchmaster
1956-1962. Renamed from ES-5, single-cut (rounded until late-'60, pointed after) archtop, 3 P-90s until end of '57, humbuckers after, switchmaster control. The PAF pickups in this model are worth as much as the rest of the guitar. We have listed a non-original '58 with replaced pickups to demonstrate how value is reduced when the original PAFs are removed.

1956-1957	Natural, P-90s	$9,000	$10,000
1956-1957	Sunburst, P-90s	$8,000	$9,000
1957-1960	Natural, humbuckers	$14,000	$16,000
1957-1960	Natural, non-original pickups	$7,000	$8,000
1957-1960	Sunburst, humbuckers	$13,000	$15,000
1957-1960	Sunburst, non-original pickups	$6,000	$7,000
1960-1962	Pointed Florentine cutaway	$13,000	$15,000

ES-5/ES-5 Switchmaster Custom Shop Historic
1995-2002.

1995-2002	ES-5, P-90s, sunburst	$3,300	$4,000
1995-2002	Switchmaster, humbuckers, Wine Red	$3,300	$4,000
1995-2002	Switchmaster, natural option, humbuckers	$3,500	$4,500

MODEL YEAR	FEATURES	EXC. COND. LOW	HIGH
ES-100			

1938-1941. Archtop, 1 pickup, bound body, sunburst, renamed ES-125 in '41.

1938-1941		$1,000	$1,300

ES-120 T
1962-1970. Archtop, thinline, 1 f-hole, bound body, 1 pickup, sunburst.

1962-196		$900	$1,100
1966-1970		$800	$900

ES-125
1941-1943, 1946-1970. Archtop, non-cut, 1 pickup, sunburst, renamed from ES-100.

1941-1943	Blade pickup	$1,300	$1,500
1946-1950	1st non-adj., P-90s	$1,300	$1,600
1951-1964	Adj. P-90s with poles	$1,200	$1,500
1965-1970		$1,000	$1,400

ES-125 C
1966-1970. Wide body archtop, single pointed cutaway, 1 pickup, sunburst.

1966-1970		$1,000	$1,400

ES-125 CD
1966-1970. Wide body archtop, single-cut, 2 pickups, sunburst.

1966-1970		$1,500	$1,800

ES-125 D
1957. Limited production (not mentioned in catalog), 2 pickup version of thick body ES-125, sunburst.

1957		$1,500	$1,900

ES-125 T
1956-1969. Archtop thinline, non-cut, 1 pickup, bound body, sunburst.

1958-1959		$1,600	$1,900
1960-1964		$1,500	$1,800
1965-1969		$1,300	$1,600

ES-125 T 3/4
1957-1970. Archtop thinline, short-scale, non-cut, 1 pickup, sunburst.

1957-1964		$1,100	$1,200
1965-1970		$900	$1,100

ES-125 TC
1960-1970. Archtop thinline, single pointed cutaway, bound body, 1 P-90 pickup, sunburst.

1960-1964		$1,700	$2,000
1965-1966		$1,600	$1,700
1967-1970		$1,500	$1,600

ES-125 TD
1957-1963. Archtop thinline, non-cut, 2 pickups, sunburst.

1957-1963		$1,800	$2,100

ES-125 TDC or ES-125 TCD
1960-1971. Archtop thinline, single pointed cutaway, 2 P-90 pickups, sunburst.

1960-1964		$2,300	$2,600
1965-1966		$2,100	$2,300
1967-1971		$1,700	$1,900

ES-130
1954-1956. Archtop, non-cut, 1 pickup, bound body, sunburst, renamed ES-135 in '56.

1954-1956		$1,200	$1,500

MODEL YEAR	FEATURES	EXC. COND. LOW	HIGH

ES-135
1956-1958. Renamed from ES-130, non-cut archtop, 1 pickup, sunburst, name reused on a thin body in the '90s.

| 1956-1958 | | $1,200 | $1,500 |

ES-135 (Thinline)
1991-2002. Single-cut archtop, laminated maple body, 2 humbuckers or 2 P-90s, chrome or gold hardware, sunburst.

| 1991-2002 | Stoptail | $1,100 | $1,400 |
| 1991-2002 | Trapeze | $1,000 | $1,300 |

ES-137 Classic
2002-present. Thin-body electric single cut, large trapezoid inlays, 2 humbuckers, f-holes, gold hardware.

| 2002-2005 | | $1,000 | $1,200 |

ES-137 Custom
2002-present. Like Classic, but with split-diamond inlays and varitone.

| 2002-2005 | | $1,000 | $1,200 |

ES-137P
2002-2005. Like Classic, but with exposed humbuckers, chrome hardware and very small trapezoid inlays.

| 2002-2005 | | $800 | $900 |

ES-140 (3/4)
1950-1956. Archtop, single-cut, 1 pickup, bound body, short-scale.

| 1950-1956 | Natural option | $1,900 | $2,200 |
| 1950-1956 | Sunburst | $1,800 | $2,100 |

ES-140 3/4 T
1957-1968. Archtop thinline, single-cut, bound body, 1 pickup, short-scale, sunburst.

| 1956-1968 | | $1,800 | $2,100 |
| 1965-1968 | | $1,500 | $1,800 |

ES-140TN (3/4)
Natural finish option. Low run production, 57 made.

| 1956-1958 | | $1,800 | $2,500 |

ES-150
1936-1942, 1946-1956. Historically important archtop, non-cut, bound body, Charlie Christian bar pickup from '36-'39, various metal covered pickups starting in '40, sunburst.

1936-1939	Charlie Christian pickup	$3,800	$4,900
1940-1942	Metal covered pickup	$3,000	$3,900
1946-1956	P-90 pickup	$1,750	$1,900

ES-150 DC
1969-1975. Archtop, double rounded cutaway, 2 humbuckers, multi-bound.

| 1969-1975 | Cherry or walnut | $2,100 | $2,400 |
| 1969-1975 | Natural | $2,300 | $2,600 |

ES-165 Herb Ellis Model
1991-present. Single pointed cut hollowbody, 1 humbucker, gold hardware.

| 1991-2005 | | $1,700 | $2,000 |

ES-175
1949-1971. Archtop, single pointed cutaway, 1 pickup (P-90 from '49-early-'57, humbucker early-'57-'71), multi-bound.

| 1949-1951 | Natural | $4,000 | $5,000 |

MODEL YEAR	FEATURES	EXC. COND. LOW	HIGH
1949-1951	Sunburst	$3,500	$4,500
1952-1956	Natural, P-90	$3,500	$4,500
1952-1956	Sunburst, P-90	$3,000	$4,000
1957-1959	Natural, humbucker	$6,000	$7,000
1957-1959	Sunburst, humbucker	$5,500	$6,000
1960	Sunburst	$5,200	$5,800
1961	Sunburst	$5,000	$5,600
1962	Sunburst	$4,700	$5,200
1963	Sunburst	$4,500	$5,000
1964	Sunburst	$4,100	$4,600
1965	Sunburst	$3,500	$4,000
1966	Sunburst	$3,400	$3,900
1967-1969	Sunburst	$3,100	$3,600
1967-1969	Black	$4,500	$5,500
1970-1971	Various colors	$2,200	$3,000

ES-175 D
1951-present. Archtop, single-cut, 2 pickups (P-90s from '53-early-'57, humbuckers early-'57 on). Humbucker pickups were converted from PAF-stickers to Pat. No.-stickers in '62. Different models were converted at different times. An ES-175 model, made during the transitional time, with PAFs, will fetch more. In some of the electric-archtop models, the transition period may have been later than '62. Cataloged as the ES-175 Reissue in the '90s, Currently as the ES-175 under Gibson Custom.

1952-1956	Natural	$5,500	$7,000
1952-1956	Sunburst	$4,500	$6,000
1957-1959	Natural, humbuckers	$7,500	$9,000
1957-1959	Sunburst, humbuckers	$7,000	$8,000
1960	Natural	$6,500	$7,700
1960	Sunburst	$6,000	$7,200
1961	Natural	$6,400	$7,500
1961	Sunburst	$6,000	$7,000
1962	Natural	$6,200	$7,200
1962	Sunburst	$5,700	$6,700
1963	Natural	$5,900	$6,900
1963	Sunburst	$5,500	$6,500
1964	Natural	$5,500	$6,500
1964	Sunburst	$5,000	$6,000
1965	Natural	$4,000	$5,000
1965	Sunburst	$3,500	$4,500
1966	Natural	$3,800	$4,500
1966	Sunburst	$3,600	$4,200
1967-1969	Various colors	$3,300	$3,800
1970-1972	Various colors	$2,500	$3,000
1973-1979	Various colors	$2,400	$2,800
1980-1989	Various colors	$2,000	$2,400
1990-1999	Various colors	$2,000	$2,400
2000-2006	Various colors	$2,000	$2,300

ES-175 T
1976-1980. Archtop thinline, single pointed cutaway, 2 humbuckers, various colors.

| 1976-1980 | | $2,400 | $2,800 |

1962 Gibson ES-125TDC

1958 Gibson ES-175

Gibson ES-225 TDN

1959 Gibson ES-330 TD

MODEL YEAR	FEATURES	EXC. COND. LOW	HIGH
ES-175 CC			
1978-1979. 1 Charlie Christian pickup, sunburst or walnut.			
1978-1979		$2,900	$3,100
ES-225 T			
1955-1959. Thinline, single pointed cutaway, 1 P-90 pickup, bound body and neck.			
1955-1959	Natural	$1,800	$2,700
1955-1959	Sunburst	$1,600	$2,500
ES-225 TD			
1956-1959. Thinline, single-cut, 2 P-90s, bound body and neck.			
1956-1959	Natural	$2,000	$3,000
1956-1959	Sunburst	$1,900	$2,800
ES-250			
1939-1940. Archtop, carved top, special Christian pickup, multi-bound, high-end appointments.			
1939-1940	Natural,	$17,000	$21,000
1939-1940	Sunburst	$8,000	$11,000
ES-295			
1952-1958. Single pointed cutaway archtop, 2 pickups (P-90s from '52-late-'58, humbuckers after), gold finish, gold-plated hardware.			
1952-1957	P-90s	$7,800	$8,500
1957-1958	Humbuckers	$17,000	$20,000
ES-295 Reissue			
1990-1993. Gold finish, 2 P-90 pickups, Bigsby.			
1990-1993		$2,300	$2,600
ES-295 '52 Historic Collection			
1993-2000. Higher end reissue, Antique Gold finish, 2 P-90 pickups, Bigsby.			
1993-2000		$2,400	$2,600
ES-300			
1940-1942, 1945-1953. Archtop, non-cut, f-holes, had 4 pickup configurations during its run, sunburst or natural.			
1940	Natural, oblong diagonal pickup	$4,500	$5,000
1940	Sunburst, oblong diagonal pickup	$4,000	$4,500
1941-1942	Natural, 1 pickup	$3,500	$4,500
1941-1942	Sunburst, 1 pickup	$3,000	$3,500
1945-1948	Sunburst, 1 pickup	$2,900	$3,400
1949	Sunburst, 1 pickup	$2,900	$3,400
1949-1953	Sunburst, 2 pickups	$3,100	$3,700
ES-320 TD			
1971-1974. Thinline archtop, double-cut, 2 single-coil pickups, bound body, cherry, natural, or walnut.			
1971-1974		$900	$1,200
ES-325 TD			
1972-1978. Thinline archtop, double-cut, 2 mini-humbuckers, 1 f-hole, bound body, cherry or walnut.			
1972-1978		$1,000	$1,300
ES-330 T			
1959-1963. Double rounded cutaway, thinline, 1 pickup, bound body and neck, in the '60s came with either an original semi-hard case (better than chip board) or a hardshell case. Prices quoted are for hardshell case; approximately $100 should be deducted for the semi-hard case.			
1959-1961	Natural	$3,500	$5,000

MODEL YEAR	FEATURES	EXC. COND. LOW	HIGH
1959-1961	Sunburst	$2,800	$3,000
1962-1963	Cherry or sunburst	$2,600	$2,800
ES-330 TD			
1959-1972. Double rounded cutaway, thinline, 2 pickups, bound body and neck, in the '60s came with either an original semi-hard case (better than chip board) or a hardshell case. Prices noted for the hardshell case; approximately $100 should be deducted for the semi-hard case.			
1959-1960	Natural	$5,000	$6,000
1959-1960	Sunburst	$4,200	$5,000
1961	Cherry or sunburst	$4,200	$5,000
1962-1964	Cherry or sunburst	$3,200	$4,200
1965-1966	Cherry or sunburst	$2,500	$3,200
1967-1968	Burgundy Metallic (unfaded)	$2,400	$3,100
1967-1968	Cherry or sunburst	$2,200	$3,100
1968	Walnut option	$2,200	$3,000
1969-1972	Various colors, long neck	$2,200	$3,000
ES-333			
2003-2005. Economy ES-335, no 'guard, no headstock inlay, exposed coils, stencil logo.			
2003-2005		$775	$825
ES-335/ES-335 TD			
1958-1981. The original design ES-335 has dot 'board inlays and a stop tailpiece. Block inlays replaced dots in mid-'62, in late-'64 the stop tailpiece was replaced with a trapeze tailpiece. Replaced by the ES-335 DOT in '81.			
1958	Natural, unbound neck	$55,000	$75,000
1958	Natural, unbound neck, Bigsby	$45,000	$60,000
1958	Sunburst, bound neck	$37,000	$52,000
1958	Sunburst, bound neck, Bigsby	$32,000	$37,000
1958	Sunburst, unbound neck	$35,000	$50,000
1958	Sunburst, unbound neck, Bigsby	$30,000	$35,000
1959	Natural, bound neck	$65,000	$100,000
1959	Natural, bound neck, Bigsby	$47,000	$65,000
1959	Sunburst	$40,000	$55,000
1959	Sunburst, factory Bigsby	$34,000	$39,000
1960	Cherry, factory Bigsby	$20,000	$25,000
1960	Cherry, factory stop tail	$25,000	$38,000
1960	Natural, factory Bigsby	$30,000	$45,000
1960	Natural, factory stop tail	$40,000	$55,000
1960	Sunburst, factory Bigsby	$20,000	$25,000

MODEL YEAR	FEATURES	EXC. COND. LOW	HIGH
1960	Sunburst, factory stop tail	$25,000	$38,000
1961	Cherry, factory Bigsby	$20,000	$23,000
1961	Cherry, factory stop tail	$25,000	$33,000
1961	Sunburst, factory Bigsby	$20,000	$23,000
1961	Sunburst, factory stop tail	$25,000	$33,000
1962	Cherry, blocks, PAFs	$25,000	$30,000
1962	Cherry, blocks, pat. #	$23,000	$28,000
1962	Cherry, dots, PAFs	$25,000	$30,000
1962	Cherry, dots, pat. #	$20,000	$23,000
1962	Sunburst, blocks, PAFs	$25,000	$30,000
1962	Sunburst, blocks, pat. #	$23,000	$28,000
1962	Sunburst, dots, PAFs	$25,000	$30,000
1962	Sunburst, dots, pat. #	$23,000	$28,000
1962	Sunburst, vibrola tailpiece	$20,000	$23,000
1963-1964	Cherry, factory Bigsby	$19,000	$22,000
1963-1964	Cherry, factory stop tailpiece	$22,000	$27,000
1963-1964	Cherry, with Maestro	$19,000	$22,000
1963-1964	Sunburst, factory Bigsby	$19,000	$22,000
1963-1964	Sunburst, factory Maestro	$19,000	$22,000
1963-1964	Sunburst, factory stop tailpiec	$22,000	$27,000
1965	Cherry or sunburst, trapeze or tremolo	$7,000	$12,000
1965	With non-original stop tail added	$5,000	$6,000
1966	Burgundy Metallic (unfaded)	$6,000	$8,000
1966	Cherry or sunburst, non-original stiop tailpiece	$4,900	$5,100
1966	Cherry or sunburst, trapeze or tremolo	$5,500	$7,000
1966	Pelham Blue (unfaded)	$7,000	$9,000
1967	Burgundy Metallic (unfaded)	$5,500	$7,500
1967	Cherry or sunburst trapeze or tremelo	$5,000	$6,500

MODEL YEAR	FEATURES	EXC. COND. LOW	HIGH
1967	Pelham Blue (unfaded)	$6,500	$8,500
1968	Burgundy Metallic (unfaded)	$5,000	$5,500
1968	Cherry or sunburst trapeze or tremelo	$4,500	$5,300
1968	Pelham Blue (unfaded)	$6,000	$7,500
1969	Cherry or sunburst, trapeze or tremolo	$4,300	$4,700
1969	Walnut finish option	$3,500	$4,300
1970	Cherry or sunburst, trapeze or tremolo	$3,500	$4,300
1970	Walnut finish option	$3,000	$3,500
1971-1976	Cherry or sunburst, trapeze or tremolo	$3,300	$3,800
1971-1976	Walnut finish option	$2,800	$3,300
1977-1979	Various colors, coil tap	$2,000	$3,200
1980-1981	Various colors	$1,700	$2,500

ES-335 Dot
1981-1990. Reissue of 1960 ES-335 and replaces ES-335 TD. Name changed to ES-335 Reissue. Various color options including highly figured wood.

1981	Natural	$2,400	$2,700
1981-1990		$1,800	$2,400

ES-335 Reissue
1991-1997. Replaced the ES-335 DOT, dot inlays, various color options including highly figured wood. Renamed the 1959 ES-335 Dot Reissue in '98. A block inlay version, called the 1963 ES-335 Block Reissue also became available in '98.

1991-1997		$1,800	$2,100

ES-335 '59 Dot Reissue
1998-2000, 2002-present. Historical Series based upon 1959 ES-335 dot neck, figured maple top, nickel hardware.

1998-2005		$2,000	$2,700

ES-335 '63 Block Reissue
1998-2000, 2002-present. Historical Series based upon 1962 ES-335 with small block markers, maple top, nickel hardware.

1998-2005		$2,200	$2,700

ES-335 Artist
1981. Offset dot markers, large headstock logo, metal truss rod plate, gold hardware, 3 control knobs with unusual toggles and input specification.

1981		$2,300	$2,600

ES-335 Centennial
1994. Centennial edition, gold medallion in headstock, diamond inlay in tailpiece, cherry.

1994		$3,500	$4,000

1960 Gibson ES-335

Gibson ES-335 Dot Reissue

GUITARS

1960 Gibson ES-345TD

Gibson ES-355

MODEL YEAR	FEATURES	EXC. COND. LOW	HIGH
ES-335 Custom Shop			
1980s-1990s. Gibson Custom Shop logo on the back of the headstock, various color options including highly figured wood.			
1980s		$2,700	$3,000
1990s		$2,400	$3,000
ES-335 Dot CMT (Custom Shop)			
1983-1985		$2,700	$3,000
ES-335 Eric Clapton Crossroads '64 reissue			
2005. Reissue of EC's, with certificate.			
2005		$10,000	$12,000
ES-335 Jimmy Wallace Reissue			
1980	Blond	$2,700	$3,000
ES-335 Pro			
1979-1981. Two humbucking pickups with exposed coils, bound 'board, cherry or sunburst.			
1979-1981		$1,500	$2,000
ES-335 Showcase Edition			
1988. Guitar of the Month series, limited production, transparent white/beige finish, black gothic-style hardware, EMG pickups.			
1988		$2,000	$2,500
ES-335 Studio			
1986-1991. No f-holes, 2 Dirty Finger humbuckers, bound body, cherry or ebony.			
1986-1991		$1,300	$1,500
ES-335 TD CRR			
1979. Country Rock Regular, 2 stereo pickups, coil-tap, sunburst.			
1979		$2,400	$3,200
ES-335-12			
1965-1971. 12-string version of the 335.			
1965		$2,600	$3,000
1966-1967	Various colors	$2,100	$2,600
1968-1971		$2,100	$2,600
ES-336			
1996-1998. Custom Shop smaller sized ES-335 with smaller headstock, dot markers.			
1996-1998		$1,500	$1,800
ES-340 TD			
1968-1973. The 335 with a laminated maple neck, master volume and mixer controls, various colors.			
1968-1969		$2,700	$3,200
1970-1973		$2,500	$3,000
ES-345 TD			
1959-1983. The 335 with Vari-tone, stereo, 2 humbuckers, gold hardware, double parallelogram inlays, stop tailpiece '59-'64 and '82-'83, trapeze tailpiece '65-'82.			
1959	Cherry, Bigsby	$15,000	$20,000
1959	Cherry, stud tail	$20,000	$25,000
1959	Natural, Bigsby	$25,000	$35,000
1959	Natural, stud tail	$35,000	$45,000
1959	Sunburst, Bigsby	$15,000	$20,000
1959	Sunburst, stud tail	$20,000	$25,000
1960	Cherry, Bigsby	$12,000	$19,000
1960	Cherry, stud tail	$15,000	$24,000
1960	Natural, Bigsby	$17,000	$29,000
1960	Natural, stud tail	$25,000	$39,000

MODEL YEAR	FEATURES	EXC. COND. LOW	HIGH
1960	Sunburst, Bigsby	$12,000	$19,000
1960	Sunburst, stud tail	$15,000	$24,000
1961	Cherry, Bigsby	$10,000	$19,000
1961	Cherry, stud tail	$15,000	$24,000
1961	Sunburst, Bigsby	$10,000	$19,000
1961	Sunburst, stud tail	$15,000	$24,000
1962-1964	Bigsby	$7,000	$15,000
1962-1964	Stud tail	$14,000	$20,000
1965	Various colors	$4,000	$7,000
1966	Various colors	$3,500	$5,200
1967	Various colors	$3,400	$5,000
1968	Various colors	$3,300	$4,000
1969	Various colors	$2,900	$4,000
1970	Various colors	$2,600	$4,000
1971-1976	Various colors	$2,600	$3,300
1977-1979	Various colors	$2,300	$2,600
1980-1983	Various colors	$1,500	$2,300
ES-345 Reissue			
2002-present. ES-345 features with 6-position Varitone selector, gold hardware, stop tailpiece, various colors.			
2002-2005		$2,000	$2,200
ES-347 TD/ES-347 S			
1978-1993. 335-style with gold hardware, tune-o-matic bridge, 2 Spotlight double-coil pickups, coil-tap, bound body and neck, S added to name in '87.			
1978-1986		$1,900	$2,100
1987-1993		$1,900	$2,100
ES-350			
1947-1956. Originally the ES-350 Premier, full body archtop, single-cut, 1 P-90 pickup until end of '48, 2 afterwards.			
1947-1948	Natural, 1 pickup	$5,000	$7,000
1947-1948	Sunburst, 1 pickup	$4,500	$5,500
1949-1956	Natural, 2 pickups	$5,500	$7,500
1949-1956	Sunburst, 2 pickups	$5,000	$6,000
ES-350 T			
1955-1963. McCarty era, called the ES-350 TD in early-'60s, thinline archtop, single-cut (round '55-'60 and '77-'81, pointed '61-'63), 2 P-90 pickups '55-'56, humbuckers after, gold hardware.			
1956	Natural, P-90s	$6,500	$7,500
1956	Sunburst, P-90s	$4,500	$5,500
1957-1959	Natural, humbuckers	$10,000	$12,000
1957-1959	Sunburst, humbuckers	$8,000	$10,000
1960-1963	Natural	$8,000	$10,000
1960-1963	Sunburst	$6,000	$8,000
ES-350 T (2nd Issue)			
1977-1981. Norlin era, second issue of ES-350 T.			
1977-1981	Natural	$3,000	$4,500
1977-1981	Sunburst	$2,500	$4,000
ES-350 T Limited Edition Reissue			
1990s. Special medallion on back of headstock.			
1990s		$3,200	$3,400

MODEL YEAR	FEATURES	EXC. COND. LOW	HIGH

ES-350 Centennial
1994. ES-350 with all the Centennial Custom Shop appointments.

| 1994 | | $3,500 | $4,000 |

ES-355 TD
1958-1970. A 335-style with large block inlays, multi-bound body and headstock, 2 humbuckers, the 355 model was standard with a Bigsby, sideways or Maestro vibrato, non-vibrato models were an option. The prices shown assume a vibrato tailpiece, a factory stop tailpiece was considered an advantage and will fetch more. Early examples have factory Bigsby vibratos, early '60s have sideways vibratos, and late '60s have Maestro vibratos, cherry finish was the standard finish.

1958-1962	Cherry, PAFs, stop tail	$24,000	$28,000
1958-1962	Cherry, PAFs, vibrato	$20,000	$24,000
1963-1964	Cherry, pat. #, vibrato	$7,500	$10,000
1965	Burgundy Metallic (unfaded)	$6,500	$8,500
1965	Cherry or sunburst	$6,000	$7,800
1966	Burgundy Metallic (unfaded)	$5,500	$6,500
1966	Cherry or sunburst	$5,000	$6,000
1967	Burgundy Metallic (unfaded)	$4,700	$5,500
1967	Cherry or sunburst	$4,500	$5,000
1968-1970	Various colors	$4,000	$5,000

ES-355 TDSV
1959-1982. Stereo version of ES-355 with Vari-tone switch, a mono version was available but few were made, the 355 model was standard with a Bigsby, sideways or Maestro vibrato, non-vibrato models were an option. The prices shown assume a vibrato tailpiece. A factory stop tailpiece was considered an advantage and will fetch more, early examples have factory Bigsby vibratos, early-'60s have sideways vibratos and late-'60s have Maestro vibratos, cherry finish was standard, walnut became available in '69.

1959-1960	Bigsby	$13,000	$21,000
1961-1962	Sideways, late PAFs	$11,000	$21,000
1963-1964	Maestro, pat. #	$7,500	$9,000
1965	Burgundy Metallic (unfaded), Maestro	$6,500	$8,500
1965	Cherry or sunburst, Maestro	$6,000	$7,800
1966	Burgundy Metallic (unfaded) Maestro	$5,500	$6,500
1966	Cherry or sunburst, Maestro	$5,000	$6,000
1967	Cherry or sunburst, Maestro	$4,000	$5,000
1968	Various colors, Maestro	$4,000	$5,000

| 1969 | Various colors, Bigsby | $4,000 | $5,000 |
| 1970-1982 | Various colors, Bigsby | $3,500 | $3,800 |

ES-355 Centennial
1994. Custom Shop Guitar of the Month in June '94, high-end custom appointments, gold-plated hardware, sunburst.

| 1994 | | $3,500 | $4,000 |

ES-369
1982. A 335-style with 2 exposed humbucker pickups, coil-tap, sunburst.

| 1982 | | $1,300 | $1,700 |

ES-446
1999-2003. Single cut semi-hollow, 2 humbuckers, Bigsby, Custom Shop.

| 1999-2003 | Various colors | $1,600 | $1,900 |

ES-775
1990-1993. Single-cut hollowbody, 2 humbuckers, gold hardware, ebony, natural or sunburst.

| 1990-1993 | | $2,400 | $2,700 |

ES-Artist
1979-1985. Double-cut thinline, semi-hollowbody, no f-holes, 2 humbuckers, active electronics, gold hardware, ebony, fireburst or sunburst.

| 1979-1985 | | $2,300 | $2,600 |

EST-150 (Tenor)
| 1937-1940 | | $2,500 | $3,000 |

ETG-150 (Tenor)
1947-1942		$2,500	$3,000
1947-1964		$2,000	$2,500
1965-1971		$1,800	$2,000

Everly Brothers
1962-1972. Jumbo flat-top, huge double 'guard, star inlays, natural is optional in '63 and becomes the standard color in '68, reintroduced as the J-180 Everly Brothers in '86.

1962-1964	Black	$8,500	$9,500
1963	Natural option	$8,500	$9,500
1965-1966	Black	$6,500	$7,000
1967	Black	$6,000	$6,500
1968-1969	Natural replaces black	$4,000	$4,300
1970-1972	Natural	$3,500	$4,000

Explorer
1958-1959, 1963. Some '58s shipped in '63, korina body, 2 humbuckers. The Explorer market is a very specialized and very small market, with few genuine examples available and a limited number of high-end buyers. The slightest change to the original specifications can mean a significant drop in value. The narrow price ranges noted are for all original examples that have the original guitar case.

| 1958-1959 | | $165,000 | $210,000 |
| 1963 | | $140,000 | $165,000 |

Explorer (Mahogany body)
1976-1982. Mahogany body, 2 humbucking pickups.

| 1976-1982 | | $1,500 | $1,700 |

1967 Gibson Everly Brothers

1959 Gibson Explorer

1964 Gibson Firebird I

1965 Gibson Firebird III

MODEL YEAR	FEATURES	EXC. COND. LOW	HIGH

Explorer (Alder body)
1983-1989. Alder body, 2 humbuckers, maple neck, ebony 'board, dot inlays, triangle knob pattern, referred to as Explorer 83 in '83.

1983-1989	Custom colors limited run	$900	$1,300
1983-1989	Standard finishes	$700	$900

Explorer (Limited Edition Korina)
1976. Limited edition korina body replaces standard mahogany body, natural.

1976		$2,700	$3,500

Explorer Heritage
1983. Reissue of '58 Explorer, korina body, gold hardware, inked serial number, limited edition.

1983	Black	$2,500	$3,000
1983	Natural	$3,000	$3,500
1983	White	$2,500	$3,000

Explorer Korina
1982-1984. Korina body and neck, 2 humbucking pickups, gold hardware, standard 8-digit serial (versus the inked serial number on the Heritage Explorer of the same era).

1982-1984		$2,400	$3,000

Explorer '76/X-plorer
1990-present. Mahogany body and neck, rosewood 'board, dot inlays, 2 humbucking pickups, name changed to X-plorer in 2002.

1990-1999	Standard finish	$600	$900
1998	Sunburst or natural limited run	$1,000	$1,200
2000-2005	Various colors	$600	$800

Explorer 90 Double
1989-1990. Mahogany body and neck, 1 single-coil and 1 humbucker, strings-thru-body.

1989-1990		$550	$700

Explorer Centennial
1994 only. Les Paul Gold finish, 100 year banner inlay at 12th fret, diamonds in headstock and gold-plated knobs, Gibson coin in rear of headstock, only 100 made.

1994		$3,500	$4,000

Explorer CMT/The Explorer
1981-1984. Maple body, exposed-coil pickups, TP-6 tailpiece.

1981-1984		$800	$1,100

Explorer Gothic
1998-2003. Gothic Series with black finish and hardware.

1998-2003		$550	$900

Explorer II (E/2)
1979-1983. Five-piece maple and walnut laminate body sculptured like V II, ebony 'board with dot inlays, 2 humbucking pickups, gold-plated hardware, natural finish.

1979-1983	Figured maple top option	$1,400	$1,700

Explorer III
1984-1985. Alder body, 3 P-90 pickups, 2 control knobs.

1984-1985	Chrome hardware	$900	$1,000
1984-1985	Chrome hardware, locking trem	$800	$900

MODEL YEAR	FEATURES	EXC. COND. LOW	HIGH
1985	Black hardware, Kahler	$800	$900

F-25 Folksinger
1963-1971. 14-1/2" flat-top, mahogany body, most have double white 'guard, natural.

1963-1964		$1,100	$1,400
1965-1966		$1,000	$1,200
1967-1969		$900	$1,100
1970-1971		$800	$1,000

Firebird I
1963-1969. Reverse body and 1 humbucker '63-mid-'65, non-reversed body and 2 P-90s mid-'65-'69.

1963	Sunburst, reverse	$6,500	$7,500
1964	Cardinal Red, reverse	$7,000	$11,000
1964	Sunburst, reverse	$6,000	$7,000
1965	Cardinal Red, reverse	$6,500	$10,000
1965	Custom colors, non-reverse	$7,000	$8,000
1965	Sunburst, non-reverse, 2 P-90s	$3,100	$3,600
1965	Sunburst, reverse	$5,500	$6,500
1966-1967	Custom colors, non-reverse	$6,000	$7,000
1966-1967	Sunburst, non-reverse	$3,000	$3,400
1968-1969	Sunburst, non-reverse	$2,800	$3,200

Firebird 76
1976-1978. Reverse body, gold hardware, 2 pickups.

1976	Bicentennial White	$3,000	$3,500
1976	Black	$2,700	$3,000
1977-1978		$2,000	$2,700

Firebird I/ Firebird 76
1980-1982. Reintroduced Firebird 76 but renamed Firebird I.

1980-1982		$2,200	$2,700

Firebird I Custom Shop
1991-1992. Limited run from Custom Shop, reverse body, 1 pickup, gold-plated, sunburst.

1991-1992		$1,600	$2,200

Firebird I 1963 Reissue Historic Collection
1999-present. Neck-thru, reverse body, Firebird logo on 'guard.

1999-2005	Sunburst	$1,700	$1,800
2002	Blue Swirl limited edition	$1,900	$2,200

Firebird II/Firebird 2
1981-1982. Maple body with figured maple top, 2 full size active humbuckers, TP-6 tailpiece.

1981-1982		$1,700	$2,200

Firebird III
1963-1969. Reverse body and 2 humbuckers '63-mid-'65, non-reversed body and 3 P-90s mid-'65-'69.

1963	Cardinal Red	$13,000	$16,000
1963	Golden Mist	$13,000	$16,000
1963	Polaris White	$12,000	$15,000
1963	Sunburst	$8,000	$10,000

GUITARS

MODEL YEAR	FEATURES	EXC. COND. LOW	HIGH
1964	Cardinal Red, reverse	$12,000	$15,000
1964	Golden Mist, reverse	$12,000	$15,000
1964	Pelham Blue	$12,000	$15,000
1964	Polaris White, reverse	$11,000	$14,000
1964	Sunburst, reverse	$7,500	$9,500
1965	Frost Blue, non-reverse	$8,000	$12,000
1965	Frost Blue, reverse	$11,000	$14,000
1965	Inverness Green, non-reverse	$8,000	$12,000
1965	Iverness Green, reverse	$11,000	$14,000
1965	Sunburst, non-reverse, 3 P-90s	$3,600	$4,000
1965	Sunburst, reverse	$6,500	$9,000
1966-1967	Frost Blue	$8,000	$12,000
1966-1967	Pelham Blue	$8,000	$12,000
1966-1967	Sunburst, non-reverse	$3,400	$3,700
1968	Pelham Blue	$4,500	$7,000
1968	Sunburst	$3,100	$3,500
1969	Pelham Blue	$4,000	$6,000
1969	Sunburst	$3,000	$3,300

Firebird V

1963-1969,1994-present. Two humbuckers, reverse body '63-mid-'65, non-reversed body mid-'65-'69.

1963	Pelham Blue	$17,000	$21,000
1963	Sunburst	$11,000	$13,000
1964	Cardinal Red, reverse	$16,000	$20,000
1964	Sunburst, reverse	$10,000	$12,500
1965	Cardinal Red, reverse	$14,000	$18,000
1965	Sunburst, non-reverse	$4,400	$5,500
1965	Sunburst, reverse	$8,000	$10,000
1966-1967	Sunburst, non-reverse	$4,200	$5,200
1968	Sunburst	$4,000	$5,000
1969	Sunburst	$3,700	$4,500

Firebird V Celebrity Series

1990-1993. Reverse body, gold hardware, 2 humbuckers, various colors.

1990-1993		$1,300	$1,600

Firebird V Guitar Trader Reissue

1982. Guitar Trader commissioned Firebird reissue, only 15 made.

1982	Sunburst	$1,900	$2,400
1982	White	$2,400	$2,900

Firebird V Medallion

1972-1973. Reverse body, 2 humbuckers, Limited Edition medallion mounted on body.

1972-1973		$4,000	$4,500

Firebird V Reissue

1990- . Reverse body, two humbuckers.

1990-1999	Various colors	$1,100	$1,300

Firebird V-12

1966-1967. Non-reverse Firebird V-style body with standard six-on-a-side headstock and split diamond headstock inlay (like ES-335-12 inlay), dot markers, special twin humbucking pickups (like mini-humbuckers).

1966-1967	Custom colors	$8,000	$12,000
1966-1967	Sunburst	$4,700	$5,500

Firebird VII

1963-1969. Three humbuckers, reverse body '63-mid-'65, non-reversed body mid-'65-'69, sunburst standard.

1963		$15,000	$18,000
1964		$14,000	$17,000
1965	Reverse	$12,000	$15,000
1966-1967	Non-reverse	$5,500	$9,000
1968	Custom colors	$7,300	$10,300
1968	non-reverse	$5,000	$8,500
1969	non-reverse	$4,700	$6,700

Firebird VII (Historic/Custom Shop)

1997-present. Standard color is Vintage Sunburst, other colors available.

1997-2005	Custom colors	$3,000	$3,500
1997-2005	Sunburst	$2,600	$3,000

Firebird VII Centennial

1994 only. Headstock medallion, sunburst.

1994		$3,300	$4,000

Firebird VII reissue

2003-present. Reverse body, 3 mini-pickups, block markers, vibrola, matching headstock finish,

2000s	Blue Mist	$1,800	$1,900
2003-2005	Cherry (dark see-through)	$1,700	$1,800
2003-2005	Firebird Red	$1,500	$1,800
2003-2005	Sunburst	$1,400	$1,800

Firebird Studio

2004-present. Two humbuckers, dot markers, tune-o-matic and bar stoptail, reverse body.

2004-2005		$750	$850

FJ-N Jumbo Folk Singer

1963-1967. Square shoulders, jumbo flat-top, natural finish with deep red on back and sides.

1963-1964		$1,700	$1,900
1965-1967		$1,500	$1,700

Flamenco 2

1963-1967. Natural spruce top, 14 3/4", cypress back and sides, slotted headstock, zero fret.

1963-1964		$1,900	$2,100
1965-1967		$1,700	$1,900

Flying V

1958-1959, 1962-1963. Only 81 shipped in '58 and 17 in '59, guitars made from leftover parts and sold in '62-'63, natural korina body, string-thru-body design. As with any ultra high-end instrument, each instrument should be evaluated on a case-by-case basis. The Flying V market is a very specialized market, with few untouched examples available, and a limited number of high-end buyers. The price ranges noted are for all-original, excellent condition guitars with the original Flying V case. The slightest change to the original specifications can mean a significant drop in value.

1958-1959		$120,000	$140,000

1964 Gibson Firebird VII

1958 Gibson Flying V

1979 Gibson Flying V (mahogany)

1970s Gibson Heritage

MODEL YEAR	FEATURES	EXC. COND. LOW	HIGH

Flying V (Mahogany)
1966-1969, 1975-1980. Mahogany body, around 200 were shipped for '66-'70. Gibson greatly increased production of Flying Vs in '75. See separate listing for the '71 Medallion V version.

1966	Cherry or sunburst	$14,000	$15,000
1967-1969	Cherry or sunburst	$11,500	$13,000
1975	Various colors	$3,500	$3,900
1976	Various colors	$2,800	$3,500
1977	Various colors	$2,700	$2,800
1978	Various colors	$1,600	$2,700
1979	Silverburst	$3,400	$3,800
1979	Various colors	$2,500	$2,700
1980	Various colors	$2,500	$2,600

Flying V (Mahogany string-through-body)
1981-1982. Mahogany body, string-thru-body design, only 100 made, most in white, some red or black possible.

1981-1982	Black, red or white	$2,400	$2,600

Flying V Heritage
1981-1982. Limited edition based on '58 specs, korina body, 4 colors available.

1981-1982	Natural	$3,000	$4,000
1981-1982	Various colors	$3,000	$4,000

Flying V (Korina)
1983. Name changed from Flying V Heritage, korina body, various colors.

1983		$3,200	$3,500

Flying V '58/'59 Korina
1991-present. Based on '58/'59 Flying V, gold hardware, natural korina, Historic Collection.

1991-2005		$4,000	$6,000

Flying V Reissue/'67 Flying V/V Factor X
1990-present. Called Flying V Reissue first year, then '67 Flying V until '03, then V Factor X, mahogany body, X dropped in '05.

1990-2005	Rare colors	$1,000	$1,400
1990-2005	Various colors	$800	$975

Flying V '67
1997-2004. Korina body, '67 Flying V specs, natural or opaque colors, Historic Collection.

1997-2004	Red	$3,000	$3,500

Flying V '90 Double
1989-1990. Mahogany body, stud tailpiece, 1 single-coil and 1 double-coil humbucker, Floyd Rose tremolo, ebony, silver or white.

1989-1990		$700	$900

Flying V '98
1998. Mahogany body, '58 style controls, gold or chrome hardware.

1998		$950	$1,000

Flying V Centennial
1994 only. (see Explorer Centennial text)

1994		$3,500	$4,000

Flying V CMT/The V
1981-1985. Maple body with a curly maple top, 2 pickups, stud tailpiece, natural or sunburst.

1981-1985	Curly maple top	$1,200	$1,400

Flying V Custom (Limited Edition)
2002. Appointments similar to Les Paul Custom, including black finish, only 40 made.

2002		$3,500	$3,800

Flying V Designer Series
1983-1984. Custom paint finish.

1983-1984		$850	$950

Flying V Gothic/'98 Gothic
1998-2003. Satin black finish, black hardware, moon and star markers.

1998-2003		$550	$900

Flying V I/V '83/Flying V (no pickguard)
1981-1988. Introduced as Flying V I, then renamed Flying V '83 in 1983, called Flying V from '84 on. Alder body, 2 exposed humbuckers, maple neck, ebony 'board, dot inlays, black rings, no 'guard, ebony or ivory finish, designed for lower-end market.

1981-1988		$600	$800

Flying V II
1979-1982. Five-piece maple and walnut laminate sculptured body, ebony 'board with dot inlays, 2 V-shaped pickups (2 Dirty Fingers humbuckers towards end of run), gold-plated hardware, natural.

1979-1982		$1,400	$1,600

Flying V Lenny Kravitz
2002. Custom shop, 125 made.

2002		$2,500	$2,900

Flying V Medallion
1971. Mahogany body, stud tailpiece, numbered Limited Edition medallion on bass side of V, 350 made in '71 (3 more were shipped in '73-'74).

1971-1974		$5,500	$6,500

Flying V Primavera
1994. Primavera (light yellow/white mahogany) body, gold-plated hardware.

1994	Natural yellow/white	$1,500	$1,600
1994	Various special colors	$1,400	$1,500

Flying V Voodoo
2002-2003. Black finish, red pickups.

2002-2003		$1,000	$1,200

Hendrix Hall of Fame Flying V
Late-1991-1993. Limited Edition (400 made), numbered, black.

1991-1993		$2,200	$2,300

Hendrix Psychedelic Flying V
2005-present. Hand-painted 1967 Flying V replica, 300 made, includes certificate, instruments without the certificate are worth less than the amount shown.

2005		$8,000	$10,500

Lonnie Mack Flying V
1993-1994. Mahogany body with Lonnie Mack-style Bigsby vibrato, cherry.

1993-1994		$3,000	$3,500

Futura
1982-1984. Deep cutout solidbody, 2 humbucker pickups, gold hardware, black, white or purple.

1982-1984		$700	$750

MODEL YEAR	FEATURES	EXC. COND. LOW	HIGH

GB-1
1922-1923. Guitar-banjo, 6-string neck, walnut, renamed GB-5 in '23.

1920-1930s	Diamond flange	$1,500	$2,000
1920-1930s	Thick rim (Mastertone-style)	$1,500	$2,000

GB-3
1923-1931. Style 4 appointments, maple.

1920-1930s	Archtop (Mastertone-style)	$2,000	$2,500
1920-1930s	Two-piece flange	$2,000	$2,500

GB-4
1923-1931. Style 4 appointments, 14" rim.

1923-1931		$3,000	$4,000

Gospel
1973-1979. Flat-top, square shoulders, laminated maple back and sides, arched back, Dove of Peace headstock inlay, natural.

1973-1979		$800	$1,100

Gospel Reissue
1992-1997. Flat-top, laminated mahogany back and sides and arched back, natural or sunburst.

1992-1997		$1,000	$1,100

GS-1 Classical
1950-1956. Mahogany back and sides.

1950-1956		$900	$1,100

GS-2 Classical
1950-1956. Maple back and sides.

1950-1956		$900	$1,100

GS-5 Classical
1954-1956. Rosewood back and sides, renamed C-5 Classical in '57.

1954-1956		$1,400	$1,700

GS-35 Classical/Gut String 35
1939-1942. Spruce top, mahogany back and sides, only 39 made.

1939-1942		$2,000	$3,000

GS-85 Classical/Gut String 85
1939-1942. Rosewood back and sides.

1939-1942		$4,000	$6,000

GY (Army-Navy)
1918-1921. Slightly arched top and back, low-end budget model.

1918-1921	Sheraton Brown	$800	$1,100

Harley Davidson Limited Edition
1994-1995. Body 16" wide, flat-top, Harley Davidson in script and logo, 1500 sold through Harley dealers.

1994-1995	Black	$2,500	$3,000

Heritage
1964-1982. Flat-top dreadnought, square shoulders, rosewood back and sides (Brazilian until '67, Indian '68 on), bound top and back, natural finish.

1964	Brazilian rosewood	$2,000	$2,600
1965-1966	Brazilian rosewood	$1,600	$2,000
1967-1969	Brazilian rosewood	$1,500	$1,600
1969-1982	Indian rosewood	$1,300	$1,450

Heritage-12
1968-1970. Flat-top dreadnought, 12 strings, Indian rosewood back and sides, bound top and back, natural finish.

1968-1970		$1,250	$1,550

MODEL YEAR	FEATURES	EXC. COND. LOW	HIGH

HG-00 (Hawaiian)
1932-1942, 1991-present. Hawaiian version of L-00, 14 3/4" flat-top, mahogany back and sides, bound top, natural.

1932-1947		$2,500	$3,000

HG-20 (Hawaiian)
1929-1933. Hawaiian, 14 1/2" dreadnought-shaped, maple back and sides, round soundhole and 4 f-holes.

1929-1933		$2,500	$3,000

HG-22 (Hawaiian)
1929-1932. Dreadnought, 14", Hawaiian, round soundhole and 4 f-holes, white paint logo, very small number produced.

1929-1932		$3,000	$4,000

HG-24 (Hawaiian)
1929-1932. 16" Hawaiian, rosewood back and sides, round soundhole plus 4 f-holes, small number produced.

1929-1932		$5,000	$10,000

HG-Century (Hawaiian)
1937-1938. Hawaiian, 14 3/4" L-C Century of Progress.

1937-1938		$2,500	$3,500

Howard Roberts Custom
1974-1981. Full body single-cut archtop, soundhole, 1 humbucking pickup, chrome hardware, rosewood 'board, various colors.

1974-1981		$2,400	$2,600

Howard Roberts Artist
1976-1980. Full body single-cut archtop, soundhole, 1 humbucking pickup, gold hardware, ebony 'board, various colors.

1976-1980		$2,400	$2,600

Howard Roberts Artist Double Pickup
1979-1980. Two pickup version of HR Artist.

1979-1980		$2,400	$2,700

Howard Roberts Fusion
1979-1988. Single-cut, semi-hollowbody, 2 humbucking pickups, chrome hardware, ebony 'board, TP-6 tailpiece, various colors, renamed Howard Roberts Fusion IIL in '88.

1979-1988		$1,600	$1,700

Howard Roberts Fusion III
1991-present. Renamed from Howard Roberts Fusion IIL, same specs except for finger-style tailpiece and gold hardware, ebony or sunburst.

1991-2005		$1,600	$1,700

Hummingbird
1960-present. Flat-top acoustic, square shoulders, mahogany back and sides, bound body and neck.

1960	Cherry Sunburst, 156 shipped	$4,300	$4,700
1961-1962	Cherry Sunburst, 1000 shipped	$4,100	$4,300
1962-1963	Cherry Sunburst, maple option	$4,000	$4,100
1963-1964	Cherry Sunburst, 2700 shipped	$3,500	$4,000
1965-1966	Cherry Sunburst or natural	$3,300	$3,500

1974 Gibson Howard Roberts

Gibson Hummingbird

GUITARS

'40s Gibson J-45

1973 Gibson J-50 Deluxe

MODEL YEAR	FEATURES	EXC. COND. LOW	EXC. COND. HIGH
1967-1968	Screwed 'guard	$2,500	$3,300
1969	Natural or sunburst	$2,300	$2,500
1970	Natural or sunburst	$2,000	$2,300
1971-1980	Double X, block markers	$1,700	$2,000
1981-1983	Non-volute neck	$1,500	$1,700
1984	Double para. Markers	$1,200	$1,500
1985-1988	Single X	$1,300	$1,500
1989-1999	25 1/2" scale	$1,400	$1,600
2000-2005		$1,500	$1,700

Invader
1983-1988. Single cutaway solid mahogany body, two humbucker pickups, four knobs with three-way selector switch, stop tailpiece, bolt-on maple neck.

1983-1988		$475	$525

J-25
1983-1985. Flat-top, laminated spruce top, synthetic semi-round back, ebony 'board, natural or sunburst.

1983-1985		$400	$450

J-30
1985-1993. Dreadnought-size flat-top acoustic, mahogany back and sides, sunburst, renamed J-30 Montana in '94.

1985-1993		$800	$1,000

J-30 Montana
1994-1997. Renamed from J-30, dreadnought-size flat-top acoustic, mahogany back and sides, sunburst.

1994-1997		$900	$1,100

J-30 RCA Limited Edition
1991. Limited edition for RCA Nashville, RCA logo on headstock.

1991		$1,250	$1,350

J-40
1971-1982. Dreadnought flat-top, mahogany back and sides, economy satin finish.

1971-1982	Natural satin finish	$725	$800

J-45
1942-1982, 1984-1993, 1999-present. Dreadnought flat-top, mahogany back and sides, round shoulders until '68 and '84 on, square shoulders '69-'82, sunburst finish (see J-50 for natural version) then natural finish also available in '90s, renamed J-45 Western in '94, renamed Early J-45 in '97 then renamed J-45 in '99. The prices noted are for all-original crack free instruments. A single professionally repaired minor crack that is nearly invisible will reduce the value only slightly. Two or more, or unsightly repaired cracks will devalue an otherwise excellent original acoustic instrument. Repaired cracks should be evaluated on a case-by-case basis.

1942	Sunburst, banner logo	$5,500	$7,000
1943	Sunburst, banner logo	$4,800	$6,500
1944	Sunburst, banner logo	$4,700	$6,500
1945	Sunburst, banner logo	$4,600	$6,500

MODEL YEAR	FEATURES	EXC. COND. LOW	EXC. COND. HIGH
1945	Sunburst, rare maple body	$5,500	$6,500
1946	Sunburst, banner logo	$4,500	$6,500
1947	Sunburst	$4,400	$6,500
1948	Sunburst	$4,300	$6,500
1949	Sunburst	$4,200	$6,500
1950-1953	Sunburst	$4,200	$5,000
1954-1955	Sunburst	$4,200	$4,700
1956-1957	Sunburst	$3,600	$4,200
1958-1959	Sunburst	$3,200	$3,800
1960-1962	Sunburst	$3,000	$3,400
1963	Sunburst	$2,700	$3,200
1964	Sunburst	$2,600	$3,000
1965	Sunburst	$2,400	$2,800
1966	Sunburst	$2,200	$2,700
1967	Sunburst	$2,100	$2,200
1968	Black, round shoulders	$2,100	$2,200
1968	Sunburst, Gibson 'guard	$2,100	$2,200
1969	Sunburst, round shoulders	$2,100	$2,200
1969	Sunburst, square shoulders	$1,700	$1,800
1970	Sunburst, square shoulders	$1,600	$1,700
1971	Sunburst	$1,500	$1,600
1972	Sunburst	$1,400	$1,500
1973	Sunburst	$1,300	$1,400
1974	Sunburst	$1,200	$1,300
1975-1981	Sunburst	$1,000	$1,200
1984-1993	Various colors	$1,000	$1,200
1999-2005	Sunburst	$1,000	$1,200

J-45 Buddy Holly Limited Edition
1995. 250 made.

1995		$1,500	$1,700

J-45 Celebrity
1985. Acoustic introduced for Gibson's 90th anniversary, spruce top, rosewood back and sides, ebony 'board, binding on body and 'board, only 90 made.

1985		$1,700	$1,800

J-45 Rosewood
1999-present. Rosewood body, spruce top.

1999-2005		$1,600	$1,700

J-45 Western
1994-1997. Previously called J-45, name changed to Early J-45 in '97.

1994-1997		$1,000	$1,100

J-45/Early J-45
1997-1998. J-45 model name for '97 and '98.

1997-1998		$1,000	$1,100

J-50
1942, 1945-1981, 1990-1995, 1998-present. Dreadnought flat-top, mahogany back and sides, round shoulders until '68, square shoulders after, natural finish (see J-45 for sunburst version).

1945		$4,600	$6,500
1946		$4,500	$6,500
1947		$4,400	$6,500
1948		$4,300	$6,500

MODEL YEAR	FEATURES	EXC. COND. LOW	HIGH
1949		$4,200	$6,500
1950-1953		$4,200	$5,000
1954-1955		$4,200	$4,700
1956-1957		$3,600	$4,200
1958-1959		$3,200	$3,800
1960-1962		$3,000	$3,400
1963		$2,700	$3,200
1964		$2,600	$3,000
1965		$2,400	$2,800
1966		$2,300	$2,700
1967		$2,200	$2,500
1968	Sunburst, Gibson 'guard	$2,200	$2,500
1969	Round shoulders	$2,100	$2,200
1969	Square shoulders	$1,700	$1,800
1970	Square shoulders	$1,600	$1,700
1971		$1,500	$1,600
1972		$1,400	$1,500
1973		$1,300	$1,400
1974		$1,200	$1,300
1975-1981		$1,000	$1,200
1990-1995		$1,000	$1,200
1999-20005		$1,000	$1,200

J-55 (Reintroduced)
1973-1982. Flat-top, laminated mahogany back and sides, arched back, square shoulders, sunburst. See Jumbo 55 listing for '39-'43 version.

1973-1982		$800	$1,000

J-55 (Jumbo 55) Limited Edition
1994 only. 16" flat-top, spruce top, mahogany back and sides, 100 made, sunburst.

1994		$1,550	$1,700

J-60
1992-1999. Solid spruce top dreadnought, square shoulders, Indian rosewood back and sides, multiple bindings, natural or sunburst.

1992-1999		$1,200	$1,400

J-60 Curly Maple
1993 and 1996. Curly maple back and sides, limited edition from Montana shop, natural.

1993		$1,500	$2,100
1996		$1,500	$2,100

J-100
1970-1974, 1985-1997, 2003-present. Flat-top jumbo, multi-bound top and back, black 'guard, dot inlays, mahogany back and sides, '80s version has maple back and sides, dot inlays and tortoise shell 'guard, current model has maple back and sides, no 'guard, and J-200 style block inlays.

1972-1974	Mahogany	$1,300	$1,600
1985-1989	Maple	$1,300	$1,600
1990-1997		$1,250	$1,450

J-100 Xtra
1991-1997, 1999-2003. Jumbo flat-top, mahogany back and sides, moustache bridge, dot inlays, various colors, J-100 Xtra Cutaway also available, reintroduced in '99 with maple back and sides and single-bound body.

1991-1997		$1,200	$1,400

J-160E
1954-1979. Flat-top jumbo acoustic, 1 bridge P-90 pickup, tone and volume controls on front, sunburst finish, reintroduced as J-160 in '90.

1954-1960		$4,500	$6,500
1961		$5,000	$7,000
1962	Beatles' vintage June '62	$5,500	$8,000
1963		$4,000	$6,500
1964	Lennon's 2nd model	$5,500	$8,000
1965		$3,500	$4,000
1966		$3,300	$3,500
1967		$3,000	$3,300
1968		$2,800	$3,200
1969		$2,000	$2,800
1970		$1,600	$2,000
1971-1979		$1,400	$1,600

J-160E Reissue
1991-1997. Reintroduced J-160E with solid spruce top, solid mahogany back and sides.

1991-1997		$1,600	$2,000

J-160E John Lennon Peace Model
2002-present. Retro version of Lennons' stripped finish J-160E, natural finish with 'guard (unlike original Peace guitar that had the 'guard removed).

2002-2005		$1,100	$1,400

J-180/Everly Brothers/The Everly Brothers
1986-2005. Reissue of the '62-'72 Everly Brothers model, renamed The Everly Brothers ('92-'94), then The Everly ('94-'96), then back to J-180, black.

1986-2005		$1,400	$1,500

J-185
1951-1959. Flat-top jumbo, figured maple back and sides, bound body and neck.

1951-1956	Natural	$13,000	$14,000
1951-1956	Sunburst	$9,000	$11,000
1957-1959	Natural	$12,000	$13,000
1957-1959	Sunburst	$8,000	$9,000

J-185 Reissue
1990-1995, 1999-present. Flat-top jumbo, figured maple back and sides, bound body and neck, natural or sunburst, limited run of 100 between '91-'92.

1990-1995		$1,500	$1,750
1999-2005		$1,500	$1,750

J-185 EC
1999-present. Acoustic/electric, rounded cutaway, sunburst.

1999-2002		$1,500	$1,750

J-185-12
2000-2005. 12-string J-185, flamed maple sides and back.

2000-2005		$1,500	$1,750

J-200/SJ-200
1947-1996. Labeled SJ-200 until ca. '54. Super Jumbo flat-top, maple back and sides, see Super Jumbo 200 for '38-'42 rosewood back and sides model, called J-200 Artist for a time in the mid-'70s, renamed '50s Super Jumbo 200 in '97 and again renamed SJ-200 Reissue in '99, standard finish is sunburst.

1947-1949	Natural option	$15,000	$17,000

1956 Gibson J-160E

Gibson J-185 EC

GUITARS

1961 Gibson Johnny Smith

Gibson Johnny A Signature Series

MODEL YEAR	FEATURES	EXC. COND. LOW	HIGH
1947-1949	Sunburst	$14,000	$16,000
1950-1954	Natural option	$11,000	$13,000
1950-1954	Sunburst	$10,000	$11,000
1955-1959	Natural option	$10,000	$11,000
1955-1959	Sunburst	$9,500	$10,500
1960	Natural option	$9,000	$10,000
1960	Sunburst	$8,000	$9,000
1961	Natural option	$7,000	$9,000
1961	Sunburst	$6,000	$8,500
1962	Natural option	$7,000	$9,000
1962	Sunburst	$6,000	$8,500
1963	Natural option	$7,000	$9,000
1963	Sunburst	$6,000	$8,500
1964	Natural option	$6,700	$8,700
1964	Sunburst	$5,900	$8,400
1965	Natural or sunburst	$4,500	$6,000
1966	Natural or sunburst	$3,600	$4,500
1967-1969	Natural or sunburst	$3,500	$3,600
1970-1979	Natural or sunburst	$2,600	$3,000
1980-1989	Natural or sunburst	$2,500	$2,800
1990-1999	Natural or sunburst	$2,000	$2,500
2000s	Super J-200, natural	$1,500	$2,500

J-200 Celebrity
1985-1987. Acoustic introduced for Gibson's 90th anniversary, spruce top, rosewood back, sides and 'board, binding on body and 'board, sunburst, only 90 made.

1985-1987		$2,700	$3,000

J-200 Koa
1994. Figured Hawaiian Koa back and sides, spruce top, natural.

1994		$2,600	$2,800

J-250 R
1972-1973, 1976-1978. A J-200 with rosewood back and sides, sunburst, only 20 shipped from Gibson.

1972-1973		$2,600	$3,000
1976-1978		$2,600	$3,000

J-2000/J-2000 Custom/J-2000 R
1986, 1992-1999. Cutaway acoustic, rosewood back and sides (a few had Brazilian rosewood or maple bodies), ebony 'board and bridge, Sitka spruce top, multiple bindings, sunburst or natural, 28 made. Name changed to J-2000 Custom in '93 when it became available only on a custom-order basis.

1986	J-2000 R, rosewood	$2,700	$3,500
1986	J-2000, maple	$2,700	$3,500
1992	Rosewood	$2,700	$3,500
1993-1996	J-2000 Custom	$2,700	$3,500
1999	J-2000 Custom Cutaway	$3,400	$3,700

JG-0
1970-1972. Economy square shouldered jumbo, follows Jubilee model in '70.

1970-1972		$750	$850

JG-12
1970. Economy square shouldered jumbo 12-string, follows Jubilee-12 model in '70.

1970		$750	$850

Johnny A Signature Series
2003-present. Thinline semi-hollow, sharp double-cut, flamed maple top, humbucking pickups, Johnny A truss rod cover, gold plated hardware, Bigsby vibrato (part of his signature style), sunburst, includes certificate of authenticity.

2003-2005	Includes rare color option	$2,500	$3,400

Johnny Smith
1961-1989. Single-cut archtop, 1 humbucking pickup, gold hardware, multiple binding front and back, natural or sunburst.

1961-1962	$8,500	$9,000
1963-1964	$7,500	$8,500
1965-1966	$7,200	$7,500
1967-1969	$6,800	$7,400
1970-1979	$6,000	$7,000
1980-1989	$5,300	$6,000

Johnny Smith Double
1963-1989. Single-cut archtop, 2 humbucking pickups, gold hardware, multiple binding front and back, natural or sunburst.

1961-1962	$9,000	$9,500
1963-1964	$8,000	$9,000
1965-1966	$7,700	$8,000
1967-1969	$7,500	$8,000
1970-1979	$6,500	$7,500
1980-1989	$5,800	$6,500

Jubilee
1969-1970. Flat-top, laminated mahogany back and sides, single bound body, natural with black back and sides.

1969-1970	$750	$850

Jubilee Deluxe
1970-1971. Flat-top, laminated rosewood back and sides, multi-bound body, natural finish.

1970-1971	$900	$1,000

Jubilee-12
1969-1970. Flat-top, 12 strings, laminated mahogany back and sides, multi-bound, natural.

1969-1970	$750	$850

Jumbo
1934-1936. Gibson's first Jumbo flat-top, mahogany back and sides, round shoulders, bound top and back, sunburst, becomes the 16" Jumbo 35 in late-'36.

1934	$17,000	$20,000
1935	$16,000	$19,000
1936	$15,000	$18,000

Jumbo 35/J-35
1936-1942. Jumbo flat-top, mahogany back and sides, silkscreen logo, sunburst, reintroduced as J-35, square-shouldered dreadnought, in '83.

1936	$14,000	$15,000
1937	$12,000	$14,000
1938	$11,000	$13,000
1939	$9,500	$12,000
1940-1942	$9,000	$11,000

Jumbo 55/J-55

1939-1943. Flat-top dreadnought, round shoulders, mahogany back and sides, pearl inlaid logo, sunburst, reintroduced in '73 as J-55.

1939		$16,000	$19,000
1940-1943		$15,000	$18,000

Jumbo Centennial Special

1994. Reissue of 1934 Jumbo, natural, 100 made.

1994		$2,200	$2,300

Junior Pro

1987-1989. Single-cut, mahogany body, KB-X tremolo system 1 humbucker pickup, black chrome hardware, various colors.

1987-1989		$400	$450

Kalamazoo Award Model

1978-1981. Single-cut archtop, bound f-holes, multibound top and back, 1 mini-humbucker, gold-plated hardware, woodgrain 'guard with bird and branch abalone inlay, highly figured natural or sunburst.

1978-1981	Natural	$13,000	$14,000
1978-1981	Sunburst	$12,000	$13,000

L-0

1926-1933, 1937-1942. Acoustic flat-top, maple back and sides '26-'27, mahogany after.

1926-1933	Amber Brown	$2,500	$3,500
1937-1942	Various colors	$2,500	$3,500

L-00

1932-1946. Acoustic flat-top, mahogany back and sides, bound top to '36 and bound top and back '37 on.

1932-1939	Black or sunburst	$3,000	$4,000
1940-1946	Natural or sunburst	$3,000	$4,000

L-00/Blues King

1991-1997. Mahogany back and sides, spruce top, ebony or sunburst.

1991-1997		$1,100	$1,200

L-1 (Archtop)

1902-1925. Acoustic archtop, single-bound top, back and soundhole, name continued on flat-top model in '26.

1902-1907	Standard 12.5" body	$1,200	$1,300
1908-1925	Standard 13.5" body	$1,300	$1,500

L-1 (Flat-Top)

1926-1937. Acoustic flat-top, maple back and sides '26-'27, mahogany after.

1926-1927	13 1/2" maple body, 12 frets	$3,000	$4,000
1928-1930	13 1/2" mahogany body, 12 frets	$3,000	$4,000
1931	14 3/4" mahogany body	$3,000	$4,000
1932-1937	14 frets	$3,000	$4,000

L-2 (Archtop)

1902-1926. Round soundhole archtop, pearl inlay on peghead, 1902-'07 available in 3 body sizes: 12.5" to 16", '24-'26 13.5" body width.

1902-1907	Standard 12.5" body	$1,400	$1,500
1924-1926	Standard 13.5" body	$1,500	$1,600

L-2 (Flat-Top)

1929-1935. Acoustic flat-top, rosewood back and sides except for mahogany in '31, triple-bound top and back, limited edition model in '94.

1929-1930	Natural, 14 3/4" body, 13 frets	$5,300	$5,500
1931	Argentine Gray, 13 frets	$3,800	$5,000
1932-1933	Natural, 13 frets	$3,800	$5,000
1934-1935	Natural, 14 frets	$3,800	$5,000

L-2 1929 Reissue

1993.

1993		$1,900	$2,100

L-3 (Archtop)

1902-1933. Acoustic archtop, available in 3 sizes: 12 1/2", 13 1/2", 16".

1902-1907	Standard 12.5" body	$1,600	$1,700
1908-1926	Standard 13.5" body	$1,700	$1,800
1927-1929	Oval soundhole	$1,900	$2,100

L-4

1912-1956. Acoustic archtop, 16" wide.

1912-1927	Oval soundhole	$2,500	$3,000
1928-1934	Round soundhole	$2,500	$3,000
1935-1945	F-holes	$2,500	$3,000
1946-1956	Crown peghead inlay, triple bound	$2,200	$2,800

L-4 Special Tenor/Plectrum

Late-1920s. Limited edition 4-string flat-top.

1929		$2,300	$2,900

L-4 C/L-4 CN

1949-1971. Single-cut acoustic archtop.

1949-1959	Natural	$3,500	$4,200
1949-1960	Sunburst	$3,200	$4,000
1960-1964	Natural	$3,000	$3,700
1960-1964	Sunburst	$2,700	$3,400
1965-1966	Natural	$2,800	$3,100
1965-1966	Sunburst	$2,700	$3,000
1967-1969	Natural	$2,700	$3,000
1967-1969	Sunburst	$2,600	$2,900
1970-1971	Natural	$2,500	$2,900
1970-1971	Sunburst	$2,400	$2,800

L-4 CES

1958, 1969, 1986-present. Single pointed cutaway archtop, 2 humbuckers, gold parts, natural or sunburst, now part of Gibson's Custom Collection.

1958	Natural, PAF humbuckers	$11,000	$13,000
1958	Sunburst, PAF humbuckers	$10,000	$12,000
1969	Natural	$4,000	$6,000
1969	Sunburst	$3,000	$5,000
1986-1989	Natural or sunburst	$2,400	$3,000
1990-1999	Natural or sunburst	$2,400	$3,000
2000s	Natural or sunburst	$2,400	$3,000

L-4 A

2003-2005. 15 3/4" lower bout, mid-size jumbo, rounded cutaway, factory electronics with preamp.

2003-2005		$1,100	$1,200

1929 Gibson L-1

1915 Gibson L-4

1933 Gibson L-5

Gibson L-5 CT reissue

L-5

1922-1958. Acoustic archtop, non-cut, multiple bindings, Lloyd Loar label until '24, 17" body by '35, Master Model label until '27, sunburst with natural option later.

MODEL YEAR	FEATURES	EXC. COND. LOW	HIGH
1922-1924	Loar era	$50,000	$55,000
1924	Lloyd Loar signed (Mar-Dec)	$60,000	$65,000
1925-1927	Master Model label	$30,000	$40,000
1928	Last dot markers	$20,000	$30,000
1929	Early 1929	$13,000	$15,000
1929-1930	Block markers	$12,000	$13,000
1931-1932	Kaufman vibrola	$14,000	$16,000
1931-1932	Standard trapeze	$11,000	$12,000
1933-1934	16" body	$10,000	$12,000
1935-1940	17" body	$6,500	$8,000
1939-1940	Natural option	$7,500	$9,000
1946-1949	Natural option	$7,500	$8,500
1946-1949	Sunburst	$6,500	$7,000
1950-1958	Natural	$7,000	$8,500
1950-1958	Sunburst	$6,000	$7,000

L-5 '34 Non-Cutaway Historic

1994. 1934 specs including block pearl inlays, bound snakehead peghead, close grained solid spruce top, figured solid maple sides and back, Cremona Brown sunburst finish, replica Grover open back tuners.

1994		$5,000	$5,500

L-5 Premier/L-5 P

1939-1947. Introduced as L-5 Premier (L-5 P) and renamed L-5 C in '48, single rounded cutaway acoustic archtop.

1939-1940	Natural option	$18,000	$22,000
1939-1940	Sunburst	$15,000	$20,000

L-5 C

1948-1982. Renamed from L-5 Premier (L-5 P), single rounded cutaway acoustic archtop, sunburst.

1948	Natural	$14,000	$16,000
1948	Sunburst	$13,000	$15,000
1949	Natural	$13,000	$16,000
1949	Sunburst	$12,000	$15,000
1950-1959	Natural	$13,000	$14,000
1950-1959	Sunburst	$12,000	$13,000
1960-1962	Natural	$10,000	$12,000
1960-1962	Sunburst	$9,000	$11,000
1963-1964	Natural	$10,000	$12,000
1963-1964	Sunburst	$9,000	$11,000
1965-1966	Natural	$9,000	$11,000
1965-1966	Sunburst	$8,000	$10,000
1967-1969	Natural	$8,000	$10,000
1967-1969	Sunburst	$7,000	$9,000
1970-1972	Natural	$6,000	$8,000
1970-1972	Sunburst	$5,000	$7,000
1973-1975	Natural	$5,000	$6,000
1973-1975	Sunburst	$4,500	$5,500
1976-1982	Natural	$4,500	$5,500
1976-1982	Sunburst	$4,000	$5,000

L-5 CES

1951-present. Electric version of L-5 C, single round cutaway (pointed mid-'60-'69), archtop, 2 pickups (P-90s '51-'53, Alnico Vs '54-mid-'57, humbuckers after), now part of Gibson's Historic Collection.

MODEL YEAR	FEATURES	EXC. COND. LOW	HIGH
1951-1957	Natural, single coils	$22,000	$24,000
1951-1957	Sunburst, single coils	$18,000	$20,000
1958-1959	Natural, PAFs	$27,000	$35,000
1958-1959	Sunburst, PAFs	$22,000	$30,000
1960-1962	Natural, PAFs	$22,000	$30,000
1960-1962	Sunburst, PAFs	$17,000	$25,000
1963-1964	Natural, pat. #	$12,000	$17,000
1963-1964	Sunburst, pat. #	$9,000	$14,000
1965-1966	Natural	$7,300	$9,200
1965-1966	Sunburst	$6,300	$8,200
1967-1969	Natural	$7,000	$9,000
1967-1969	Sunburst	$6,000	$8,000
1970-1972	Natural	$5,600	$6,400
1970-1972	Sunburst	$5,500	$6,300
1973-1975	Natural	$5,400	$6,200
1973-1975	Sunburst	$5,300	$6,100
1976-1979	Natural	$5,400	$6,200
1976-1979	Sunburst	$5,300	$6,100
1980-1984	Kalamazoo made	$5,300	$6,200
1985-1992	Nashville made	$5,200	$6,100

L-5 CES Custom Shop Historic Collection

1990s. Historic Collection Series, sunburst.

1990s	100th Anniversary, black	$6,000	$6,500
1990s	Sunburst	$5,500	$6,000

L-5 CT (George Gobel)

1959-1961. Single-cut, thinline archtop acoustic, some were built with pickups, cherry, currently available in Gibson's Historic Collection.

1959-1961		$20,000	$22,000

L-5 CT Reissue

1998-present. Natural.

1998-2005		$5,000	$6,000

L-5 S

1972-1985, 2004-2005. Single-cut solidbody, multi-bound body and neck, gold hardware, 2 pickups (low impedance '72-'74, humbuckers '75 on), offered in natural, cherry sunburst or vintage sunburst. 1 humbucker version issued in '04 from Gibson's Custom, Art & Historic

1972-1974	Natural, gold hardware, low impedance pickups	$3,200	$3,600
1972-1974	Sunburst, low impedance pickups	$3,200	$3,600
1975-1980	Natural, gold hardware, humbuckers	$3,500	$4,500
1975-1980	Sunburst, humbuckers	$3,500	$4,500

L-5 Studio

1996-2000. Normal L-5 dual pickup features, marble-style 'guard, translucent finish, dot markers.

1996-2000		$1,900	$2,300

The *Vintage Guitar Price Guide* shows low to high values for items in all-original excellent condition, and, where applicable, with original case or cover.

MODEL YEAR	FEATURES	EXC. COND. LOW	HIGH

L-5 Wes Montgomery Custom Shop
1993-present. Various colors.

| 1993-1999 | | $5,500 | $6,000 |
| 2000-2005 | | $5,500 | $6,000 |

L-6 S
1973-1975. Single-cut solidbody, 2 humbucking pickups, stop tailpiece, cherry or natural, renamed L-6 S Custom in '75.

| 1973-1975 | | $725 | $850 |
| 1978-1979 | Silverburst option | $1,000 | $1,500 |

L-6 S Custom
1975-1980. Renamed from the L-6 S, single-cut solidbody, 2 humbucking pickups, stop tailpiece, cherry or natural.

| 1975-1980 | | $725 | $850 |

L-6 S Deluxe
1975-1981. Single-cut solidbody, 2 humbucking pickups, strings-thru-body design, cherry or natural.

| 1975-1981 | | $725 | $850 |

L-7
1932-1956. Acoustic archtop, bound body and neck, fleur-de-lis peghead inlay, 16" body '32-'34, 17" body X-braced top late-'34.

1932-1934	16" body	$2,800	$3,200
1935-1939	17" body, X-braced	$2,900	$3,300
1940-1950	Natural	$3,000	$3,600
1940-1950	Sunburst	$2,900	$3,200
1951-1956	Natural	$2,900	$3,200
1951-1956	Sunburst	$2,800	$3,000

L-7 C
1948-1972. Single-cut acoustic archtop, triple-bound top, sunburst or natural finish. Gibson revived the L-7 C name for a new acoustic archtop in 2002.

1948-1949	Natural	$4,900	$5,700
1948-1949	Sunburst	$4,300	$5,200
1950-1959	Natural	$4,800	$5,500
1950-1959	Sunburst	$4,200	$5,000
1960-1962	Natural	$3,500	$4,800
1960-1962	Sunburst	$3,300	$4,600
1963-1964	Natural	$3,300	$4,600
1963-1964	Sunburst	$3,000	$3,300
1965-1966	Natural	$3,000	$3,300
1965-1966	Sunburst	$3,000	$3,300
1967-1969	Natural	$3,000	$3,300
1967-1969	Sunburst	$2,900	$3,100
1970-1971	Natural	$3,000	$3,100
1970-1971	Sunburst	$2,900	$3,000

L-10
1923-1939. Acoustic archtop, single-bound body and 'board.

| 1923-1934 | Black, 16" body | $2,500 | $3,000 |
| 1935-1939 | Black or sunburst, 17" body, X-braced | $3,000 | $3,500 |

L-12
1930-1955. Acoustic archtop, single-bound body, 'guard, neck and headstock, gold-plated hardware, sunburst.

1930-1934	16" body	$3,200	$3,500
1935-1939	17" body, X-braced	$3,200	$3,500
1940-1941	Parallel top braced	$3,200	$3,500
1946-1949	Post-war	$3,000	$3,200
1950-1955		$2,800	$3,000

L-12 Premier/L-12 P
1947-1950. L-12 with rounded cutaway, sunburst.

| 1947-1950 | | $4,000 | $5,000 |

L-30
1935-1943. Acoustic archtop, single-bound body, black or sunburst.

| 1935-1943 | | $1,200 | $1,600 |

L-37
1937-1941. 14-3/4" acoustic archtop, flat back, single-bound body and 'guard, sunburst.

| 1937-1941 | | $1,200 | $1,600 |

L-48
1946-1971. 16" acoustic archtop, single-bound body, sunburst.

1946-1949		$1,000	$1,100
1950-1959		$950	$1,150
1960-1964		$900	$1,100
1965-1966		$800	$1,050
1967-1971		$700	$1,000

L-50
1932-1971. 14 3/4" wide acoustic archtop, flat or arched back, round soundhole or f-holes, pearl logo pre-war, decal logo post-war, sunburst.

1932-1934	14 3/4" body	$1,300	$1,500
1934-1943	16" body	$1,400	$1,600
1946-1949		$1,200	$1,400
1950-1959		$1,000	$1,400
1960-1964		$1,000	$1,400
1965-1966		$900	$1,150
1967-1971		$800	$1,100

L-75
1932-1939. 14 3/4" archtop with round soundhole and flat back, size increased to 16" with arched back in '35, small button tuners, dot markers, lower-end style trapeze tailpiece, pearl script logo, sunburst.

| 1932-1934 | 14 3/4" body | $1,900 | $2,200 |
| 1934-1939 | 16" body | $2,500 | $2,700 |

L-130
1999-2005. 14 7/8" lower bout, small jumbo, solid spruce top, solid bubinga back and sides, factory electronics with preamp.

| 1999-2005 | | $1,100 | $1,200 |

L-200 Emmylou Harris
2002-present. SJ-200/J-200 reissue, L-series smaller and thinner than standard jumbo body, solid Sitka spruce top, flamed maple sides and back, gold hardware, crest markers, natural or sunburst.

| 2002-2005 | | $1,200 | $1,300 |

L-C Century
1933-1941. Curly maple back and sides, bound body, white pearloid 'board and peghead (all years) and headstock (until '38), sunburst.

| 1933-1939 | | $4,000 | $5,000 |
| 1940-1941 | | $3,800 | $4,800 |

L-C Reissue
1994. Pearloid headstock and 'board.

| 1994 | | $2,300 | $2,450 |

LC-1 Cascade
2002-present. LC-Series acoustic/electric, advanced L-00-style, solid quilted maple back and sides.

| 2002-2005 | | $1,100 | $1,300 |

Gibson L-5 Wes Montgomery

Gibson L-50

GUITARS

Gibson Le Grande

Gibson Les Paul Neal Schon

MODEL YEAR	FEATURES	EXC. COND. LOW	HIGH

LC-3 Caldera
2003-2004. 14 3/4" flat-top, soft cutaway, solid cedar top, solid flamed Koa back and sides, fancy appointments.

2003-2004		$1,900	$2,000

Le Grande
1993-present. Electric archtop, 17", formerly called Johnny Smith.

1993-2005		$5,500	$6,500

Les Paul
Following are models bearing the Les Paul name, beginning with the original Les Paul Model. All others are listed alphabetically as follows:

Les Paul Model
'52 Les Paul Goldtop
'54 Les Paul Goldtop
'56 Les Paul Goldtop
'57 Les Paul Goldtop
'57/'58 Les Paul Jr.
'58 Les Paul Flametop/Reissue/Standard
'59 Les Paul Flametop/Reissue/Standard
'60 Corvette Les Paul
'60 Les Paul Flametop/Standard
Les Paul (All Maple)
Les Paul 25/50 Anniversary
Les Paul 25th Silver Anniversary (Guitar Center)
Les Paul 30th Anniversary
Les Paul 40th Anniversary
Les Paul 55
Les Paul Ace Frehley Signature
Les Paul Artisan
Les Paul Artist/L.P. Artist/Les Paul Active
Les Paul Bird's-Eye Standard
Les Paul Centennial
Les Paul Class 5
Les Paul Classic
Les Paul Classic Plus
Les Paul Classic Premium Plus
Les Paul Cloud 9 Series
Les Paul Custom
Les Paul Custom '54
Les Paul Custom 20th Anniversary
Les Paul Custom 35th Anniversary
Les Paul Custom Historic '54
Les Paul Custom Historic '57 Black Beauty
Les Paul Custom Historic '68
Les Paul Custom Lite
Les Paul Custom Music Machine
Les Paul Custom Plus
Les Paul Custom SG 30th Anniversary
Les Paul Dale Earnhardt
Les Paul Dale Earnhardt Intimidator
Les Paul DC Pro
Les Paul DC Standard
Les Paul DC Standard Plus
Les Paul DC Studio
Les Paul Deluxe
Les Paul Deluxe 30th Anniversary
Les Paul Deluxe Hall of Fame

Les Paul Deluxe Limited Edition
Les Paul Dickey Betts Goldtop
Les Paul Dickey Betts Red Top
Les Paul Elegant
Les Paul Gary Moore Model
Les Paul Guitar Trader Reissue
Les Paul Heritage 80
Les Paul Heritage 80 Award
Les Paul Heritage 80 Elite
Les Paul Indian Motorcycle
Les Paul Jim Beam
Les Paul Jimmy Page Signature
Les Paul Jimmy Page Signature Custom Shop
Les Paul Jimmy Wallace Reissue
Les Paul Joe Perry Signature
Les Paul Jr.
Les Paul Jr. 3/4
Les Paul Jr. Double Cutaway
Les Paul Jr. Special
Les Paul Jr. Tenor/Plectrum
Les Paul Jumbo
Les Paul KM (Kalamazoo Model)
Les Paul Leo's Reissue
Les Paul Limited Edition
Les Paul Melody Maker
Les Paul Music Machine 25th Anniversary
Les Paul Music Machine Brazilian Stinger
Les Paul Old Hickory
Les Paul Pee Wee
Les Paul Personal
Les Paul Pro Showcase Edition
Les Paul Pro-Deluxe
Les Paul Professional
Les Paul Recording
Les Paul Reissue Flametop
Les Paul Reissue Goldtop
Les Paul SG '61 Reissue
Les Paul SG Standard Reissue
Les Paul Signature
Les Paul SmartWood Standard
Les Paul SmartWood Studio
Les Paul Special
Les Paul Special (Reissue)
Les Paul Special 3/4
Les Paul Special Centennial
Les Paul Special Custom Shop
Les Paul Special Double Cutaway
Les Paul Special Tenor
Les Paul Spotlight Special
Les Paul Standard (Sunburst)
Les Paul Standard (SG body)
Les Paul Standard (reintroduced)
Les Paul Standard '58
Les Paul Standard '82
Les Paul Standard Lite
Les Paul Standard Plus
Les Paul Standard Premium Plus
Les Paul Standard Sparkle
Les Paul Strings and Things Standard
Les Paul Studio
Les Paul Studio Baritone
Les Paul Studio Custom
Les Paul Studio Gem

MODEL YEAR	FEATURES	EXC. COND. LOW	HIGH
Les Paul Studio Gothic			
Les Paul Studio Lite			
Les Paul Studio Plus			
Les Paul Studio Swamp Ash			
Les Paul Supreme			
Les Paul Tie Dye (St. Pierre)			
Les Paul Tie Dye Custom Shop			
Les Paul TV			
Les Paul TV 3/4			
Les Paul Ultima			
Les Paul Vixen			
Les Paul Voodoo/Voodoo Les Paul			
Les Paul XR-I/XR-II/XR-III			
Les Paul Zack Wylde Signature			
The Les Paul			
The Paul			
The Paul Firebrand Deluxe			
The Paul II			

Les Paul Model

1952-1958. The Goldtop, 2 P-90 pickups until mid-'57, humbuckers after, trapeze tailpiece until late-'53, stud tailpiece/bridge '53-mid-'55, Tune-o-matic bridge '55-'58, renamed Les Paul Standard in '58 All gold option add +10% if the neck retains 90% of the gold paint. All gold option with ugly green wear on the neck is equal to or below the value of a standard paint job. Some instruments had all mahogany bodies which did not have the maple cap. These instruments are of lower value than the standard maple on mahogany bodies. The all mahogany version, although more rare, has a 10% lower value. A factory installed Bigsby tailpiece will reduce value by 30%. A non-factory installed Bigsby will reduce value up to 50%.

1952	1st made, unbound neck	$26,000	$40,000
1952	5/8" knobs, bound neck	$23,000	$26,000
1953	1/2" knobs, trapeze tailpiece	$22,000	$24,000
1953	1/2" knobs, late-'53 stud tailpiece	$35,000	$70,000
1954	Stud tailpiece, wrap-around	$40,000	$80,000
1955	Stud tailpiece, wrap-around, early-'55	$40,000	$80,000
1955	Tune-o-matic tailpiece, late-'55	$55,000	$100,000
1956	Tune-o-matic tailpiece	$55,000	$100,000
1957	P-90s, early-'57	$55,000	$100,000
1957	PAF Humbuckers early-mid to late '57	$130,000	$175,000
1958	PAF Humbuckers	$130,000	$175,000

'52 Les Paul Goldtop

1998-2003. Goldtop finish, 2 P-90s, '52-style trapeze tailpiece/bridge.

1998-2003		$1,750	$1,950

'54 Les Paul Goldtop

1990s-present. Goldtop finish, 2 P-90s, '53-'54 stud tailpiece/bridge.

1997		$1,750	$1,950

'56 Les Paul Goldtop

1991-present. Renamed from Les Paul Reissue Goldtop. Goldtop finish, 2 P-90 pickups, now part of Gibson's Historic Collection.

1991-2005		$1,750	$1,950

'57 Les Paul Goldtop

1993-present. Goldtop finish, 2 humbuckers, now part of Gibson's Historic Collection.

1993-1999		$1,800	$2,000

'57/'58 Les Paul Jr.

1998-present. Historic Collection reissue of slab body, double-cut Les Paul Jr. Originally labeled '57, changed to '58 in early 2000s.

1998-2004		$1,550	$1,650

'58 Les Paul Flametop/Reissue/Standard

1996-1998, 2001-2004. Less top figure than '59 Reissue, also offered in plain top version ('94-'98), name changed to '58 Les Paul Reissue in '01, and '58 Les Paul Standard in '03, part of Gibson's Historic Collection, sunburst.

2001-2004		$2,700	$3,500

'59 Les Paul Flametop/Reissue/Standard

1991-present. Renamed from Les Paul Reissue Flametop, for 2000-'05 called the 1959 Les Paul Reissue, in '06 this model became part of Gibson's Vintage Original Spec series and is called the '59 Les Paul Standard. Flame maple top, 2 humbuckers, thick '59-style neck, sunburst finish, part of Gibson's Historic Collection, the original certificate authenticity adds value, an instrument without the matching certificate has less value. By '98 Gibson guaranteed only AAA Premium grade maple tops would be used.

1991-2006		$3,500	$4,500
2003	Brazilian rosewood fretboard	$6,500	$7,500
2003	Brazilian rosewood, Murphy aged	$7,500	$8,500

'60 Corvette Les Paul

1995-1996. Custom Shop Les Paul, distinctive Chevrolet Corvette styling from '60, offered in 6 colors.

1995-1996		$4,000	$5,700

'60 Les Paul Flametop/Standard

1991-present. Renamed from Les Paul Reissue Flametop, flame maple top, 2 humbuckers, thinner neck, sunburst finish, part of Gibson's Historic Collection, by 2006 this model was part of Gibson's 'Vintage Original Spec" series and was called the '60 Les Paul Standard.

1991-2006		$3,500	$4,500
2003	Brazilian rosewood fretboard	$6,500	$7,500
2003	Brazilian rosewood, Murphy aged	$7,500	$8,500

Les Paul (All Maple)

1984. Limited run, all maple body, Super 400-style inlay, gold hardware.

1984		$3,000	$3,400

1952 Gibson Les Paul Model

1957 Gibson Les Paul Model

Gibson Les Paul Class 5

1956 Gibson Les Paul Custom

MODEL YEAR	FEATURES	EXC. COND. LOW	HIGH

Les Paul 25/50 Anniversary
1978-1979. Regular model with 25/50 inlay on headstock, sunburst.

| 1978-1979 | Moderate flame | $2,200 | $2,700 |
| 1978-1979 | Premium flame | $2,700 | $3,700 |

Les Paul 25th Silver Anniversary (Guitar Center)
1978. Special order of 50 Les Paul Customs with metallic silver top, back, sides and neck, commissioned by Guitar Center of California, most have 25th Anniversary etched in tailpiece.

| 1978 | | $2,400 | $2,600 |

Les Paul 30th Anniversary
1982-1984. Features of a 1958 Les Paul Goldtop, 2 humbuckers, 30th Anniversary inlay on 19th fret.

| 1982-1984 | | $2,500 | $2,700 |

Les Paul 40th Anniversary (from 1952)
1991-1992. Black finish, 2 soapbar P-100 pickups, gold hardware, stop tailpiece, 40th Anniversary inlay at 12th fret.

| 1991-1992 | | $1,800 | $2,000 |

Les Paul 40th Anniversary (from 1959)
1999. Reissue Historic, highly figured.

| 1999 | | $3,300 | $3,800 |

Les Paul 55
1974, 1976-1981. Single-cut Special reissue, 2 pickups.

| 1974 | Sunburst | $1,400 | $1,600 |
| 1976-1981 | Sunburst or Wine Red | $1,200 | $1,400 |

Les Paul Ace Frehley Signature
1997-2001. Ace's signature inlay at 15th fret, 3 humbuckers, sunburst.

| 1997-2001 | | $2,900 | $3,100 |

Les Paul Artisan
1976-1982. Carved maple top, 2 or 3 humbuckers, gold hardware, hearts and flowers inlays on 'board and headstock, ebony, sunburst or walnut.

| 1976-1982 | | $2,200 | $3,000 |

Les Paul Artist/L.P. Artist/Les Paul Active
1979-1982. Two humbuckers (3 optional), active electronics, gold hardware, 3 mini-switches, multibound.

| 1979 | Sunburst | $1,600 | $1,800 |
| 1980-1982 | Ebony or sunburst | $1,500 | $1,700 |

Les Paul Bird's-Eye Standard
Birdseye top, gold hardware, 2 humbucking pickups.

| 1999 | Transparent amber | $1,900 | $2,200 |

Les Paul Centennial ('56 LP Standard Goldtop)
1994. Part of the Guitar of the Month program commemorating Gibson's 100th year, limited edition of 100, Goldtop Les Paul mahogany body with '56-style configuration, gold hardware, gold truss rod plate, gold medallion, engraved light-gold 'guard.

| 1994 | | $3,500 | $4,000 |

Les Paul Centennial ('59 LP Special)
1994. Part of the Guitar of the Month program commemorating Gibson's 100th year, limited edition, slab body Les Paul Special-style configuration, 100

made, gold hardware, P-90 pickups, gold medallion, commemorative engraving in 'guard, cherry.

| 1994 | | $3,500 | $4,000 |

Les Paul Class 5
2001-2005. Highly flamed or quilt top, or special finish, 1960 profile neck, weight relieved body, Burst Bucker humbucking pickups, several color options, Custom Shop.

| 2001-2005 | | $2,400 | $2,800 |
| 2001-2005 | Stars and Stripes, 50 made | $3,000 | $5,000 |

Les Paul Classic
1990-1998, 2001-present. Early models have 1960 on pickguard, 2 exposed humbucker pickups, Les Paul Model on peghead until '93, Les Paul Classic afterwards.

1990-1998	All gold neck and body	$1,600	$1,750
1990-1998	Various colors, plain top	$1,350	$1,550
2001-2005	Various colors	$1,350	$1,550

Les Paul Classic Plus
1991-1996, 1999-2000. Les Paul Classic with fancier maple top, 2 exposed humbucker pickups.

| 1991-1996 | Price depends on top figure | $1,700 | $2,100 |

Les Paul Classic Premium Plus
1993-1996, 2001-2002. Les Paul Classic with AAA-grade flame maple top, 2 exposed humbucker pickups.

| 1993-1996 | Price depends on top figure | $2,200 | $2,700 |

Les Paul Cloud 9 Series
2003. A special light weight Les Paul series run for three dealers, Music Machine, Dave's Guitar Shop, and Wildwood Guitars, '59 Les Paul body specs, CR series number series, '59 or '60 neck profile options, various colors, other reissue models available.

| 2003 | '52, '54, '56, '57, '58 models | $2,800 | $3,400 |
| 2003 | '59 or '60 models | $3,500 | $3,800 |

Les Paul Custom
1953-1963 (renamed SG Custom late-1963), 1968-present. Les Paul body shape except for SG body '61-'63, 2 pickups (3 humbuckers mid-'57-'63 and '68-'70, 3 pickups were optional various years after).

1954-1957	Single coils	$50,000	$55,000
1954-1957	Single coils, factory Bigsby	$40,000	$45,000
1957-1960	2 Humbuckers	$75,000	$110,000
1957-1960	2 Humbuckers, factory Bigsby	$70,000	$85,000
1957-1960	3 Humbuckers	$75,000	$110,000
1957-1960	3 Humbuckers, factory Bigsby	$70,000	$85,000
1961-1963	Black (option), SG body, factory stop tailpiece	$26,000	$36,000
1961-1963	Black (option), SG body, side-pull vibrato	$22,000	$30,000

MODEL YEAR	FEATURES	EXC. COND. LOW	HIGH
1961-1963	White, SG body, factory stop tailpiece	$25,000	$35,000
1961-1963	White, SG body, Maestro vibrola	$20,000	$23,000
1961-1963	White, SG body, Maestro, ebony block	$20,000	$23,000
1961-1963	White, SG body, side-pull vibrato	$15,000	$20,000
1968-1969	Black, 1-piece body	$8,000	$10,000
1968-1969	Black, 3-piece body	$6,000	$7,000
1970-1972	Volute, 2 pickups	$2,600	$3,000
1970-1972	Volute, 3 pickups	$3,000	$3,500
1973-1974	Volute, 2 pickups	$2,500	$3,000
1973-1974	Volute, 3 pickups	$3,000	$3,500
1975-1976	Maple fretboard option	$2,800	$3,300
1975-1976	Maple fretboard option, blond	$2,800	$3,300
1975-1976	Volute, 2 pickups, chrome hardware	$2,500	$3,000
1975-1976	Volute, 2 pickups, gold hardware	$2,550	$3,050
1975-1976	Volute, 3 pickups	$2,800	$3,300
1977-1978	Maple fretboard option, blond, 2 pickups	$2,800	$3,300
1977-1978	Volute, 2 pickups	$2,800	$3,000
1977-1978	Volute, 3 pickups	$2,700	$2,800
1979-1982	2 pickups	$2,300	$2,500
1979-1982	Silverburst, volute, 2 pickups	$2,500	$3,500
1983-1985	2 pickups	$2,200	$2,500
1983-1985	3 pickups	$2,400	$2,800
1986-1989	Various colors	$2,000	$2,300
1990-1999	Limited Edition color series	$2,000	$2,600
1990-1999	Various colors	$1,700	$2,000
2000-2006	Various colors	$1,700	$2,000

Les Paul Custom '54
1972-1973. Reissue of 1954 Custom, black finish, Alnico V and P-90 pickups.

1972-1973		$3,500	$4,400

Les Paul Custom 20th Anniversary
1974. Regular 2-pickup Custom, with 20th Anniversary inlay at 15th fret, black or white.

1974		$2,500	$3,500

Les Paul Custom 35th Anniversary
1989. Gold hardware, 3 pickups, carved, solid mahogany body and neck, 35th Anniversary inlay on headstock, black.

1989		$3,000	$3,500

Les Paul Custom Historic '54
1991-present. Historic Collection, 1954 appointments and pickup configuration, black, gold hardware.

1991-2005		$1,900	$2,200

Les Paul Custom Historic '57 Black Beauty/2-pickup
1991-present. Black finish, gold hardware, 2 humbucker pickups, part of Gibson's Historic Collection.

1991-2005		$1,750	$2,100

Les Paul Custom Historic '57 Black Beauty/3-pickup
1991-present. 3 humbucker version.

1991-2005		$1,750	$2,300

Les Paul Custom Historic '68
Historic Collection, ebony block marked fretboard, gold hardware, flamed maple top available, 2 pickups.

2000-2005		$2,000	$2,300

Les Paul Custom Lite
1987-1990. Full-thickness carved maple top, ebony 'board, pearl block position markers, gold hardware, PAF pickups, bound neck, headstock and body, black.

1987-1990		$1,400	$1,800

Les Paul Custom Lite (Show Case Ed.)
1988. Showcase Edition, only 200 made, gold top.

1988		$2,000	$2,500

Les Paul Custom Music Machine
2003. Custom run for dealer Music Machine with special serial number series, chambered body style for reduced body weight, quilt tops.

2003		$3,500	$3,800

Les Paul Custom Plus
1991-1998. Regular Custom with figured maple top, sunburst finish or colors.

1991-1998		$1,900	$2,100

Les Paul Custom SG 30th Anniversary
1991. 30th Anniversary limited edition of SG-style Les Paul Custom introduced in '61, Opaque TV Yellow finish including back of neck, typical split-diamond headstock inlay, block markers, tune-o-matic, gold hardware, 30th Anniversary logo.

1991		$2,300	$2,500

Les Paul Dale Earnhardt
1999. 333 made, Dale's image and large number 3 on the front and headstock, Dale Earnhardt signature script on fretboard, chrome hardware, several pieces of literature and an original certificate are part of the overall package, lack of an original matching serial number certificate will reduce the value, a lower serial number may add value.

1999		$3,000	$4,300

Les Paul Dale Earnhardt Intimidator
2000. 333 made, Dale's Goodwrench car on the front, The Intimidator inlay on the fretboard, includes certificate, chrome hardware.

2000		$3,000	$4,300

Les Paul DC Pro
1997-1998. Custom Shop, body like a '59 Les Paul Junior, carved highly figured maple top, various options.

1997-1998		$1,750	$1,900

Gibson Les Paul '57 Black Beauty

Gibson Les Paul DC Classic

Gibson Les Paul Deluxe

Gibson Les Paul Heritage 80

MODEL YEAR	FEATURES	EXC. COND. LOW	HIGH

Les Paul DC Standard

1998-1999, 2001-present. Offset double-cut, highly flamed maple top, mahogany set-neck, translucent lacquer finishes in various colors, typical Les Paul Model stencil logo on headstock and 'Standard' notation on truss rod cover, reintroduced as Standard Lite in '99 but without Les Paul designation on headstock or truss rod cover.

1998-1999		$1,150	$1,300

Les Paul DC Standard Plus

2001-present. Reintroduction of LP DC Standard, flamed top, gold hardware, cherry.

2001		$1,150	$1,300

Les Paul DC Studio

1997-1999. DC Series double-cut like late '50s models, carved maple top, 2 humbucker pickups, various colors.

1997-1999		$700	$750

Les Paul Deluxe

1969-1985. In 1969, the Goldtop Les Paul Standard was renamed the Deluxe. Two mini-humbuckers (regular humbuckers optional in mid-'70s). Mid-'70s sparkle tops, made at the request of the Sam Ash chain, are worth more than standard finishes. The market slightly favors the Goldtop finish, but practically speaking condition is more important than finish, such that all finishes fetch about the same amount (with the exception of the sparkle finish). Initially, the Deluxe was offered only as a Goldtop and the first year models are more highly prized than the others. Cherry sunburst was offered in '71, cherry in '71-'75, walnut in '71-'72, brown sunburst in '72-'79, natural in '75, red sparkle in '75 only, blue sparkle in '75-'77, wine red/see-thru red offered '75-'85. In '99, the Deluxe was reissued for its 30th anniversary.

1969	Goldtop	$3,700	$4,300
1970	Goldtop	$3,000	$3,800
1971-1975	Goldtop	$2,500	$3,500
1971-1975	Natural	$1,800	$2,000
1971-1975	Red (solid)	$2,000	$2,600
1971-1975	Sunburst	$2,000	$2,600
1971-1975	Wine	$2,000	$2,600
1975	Red sparkle, fewer made	$3,600	$4,500
1975-1977	Blue sparkle, more made	$2,600	$3,600
1976-1979	Various colors	$2,000	$3,000
1980-1985	Various colors	$2,000	$3,000

Les Paul Deluxe 30th Anniversary

1999. 30th Anniversary of the 1969 introduction of the Les Paul Deluxe, Limited Edition logo on the lower back of the headstock neck, Deluxe logo on truss rod cover, wine red.

1999		$1,550	$2,000

Les Paul Deluxe Hall of Fame

1991. All gold finish.

1991		$1,700	$2,000

Les Paul Deluxe Limited Edition

1999-2002. Limited edition reissue with Les Paul Standard features and Deluxe mini-humbuckers, black.

1999-2002		$1,700	$2,000

Les Paul Dickey Betts Goldtop

2001-2003. Aged gold top.

2001-2003		$5,000	$5,700

Les Paul Dickey Betts Red Top

2003. Transparent red, gold hardware.

2003		$2,600	$3,000

Les Paul Elegant

1996-present. Custom Shop, highly flamed maple top, abalone crown markers and Custom Shop headstock inlay.

1996-2000		$2,300	$2,600

Les Paul Gary Moore Model

2000-2002. Signature Series model, Gary Moore script logo on truss rod cover, flamed maple top.

2000-2002		$2,000	$2,100

Les Paul Guitar Trader Reissue

1982-1983. Special order flametop Les Paul by the Guitar Trader Company, Redbank, New Jersey. Approximately 47 were built, the first 15 guitars ordered received original PAFs, all were double black bobbins (except 1 Zebra and 1 double white), 3 of the guitars were made in the '60-style. The PAF equipped models were based on order date and not build date. The serial number series started with 9 1001 and a second serial number was put in the control cavity based upon the standard Gibson serial number system, which allowed for exact build date identification. Gibson's pickup designer in the early-'80s was Tim Shaw and the pickups used for the last 32 guitars have been nicknamed "Shaw PAFs." After Gibson's short run for Guitar Trader, 10 non-Gibson replica or bootleg Les Pauls were made. These GT bootleg guitars have a poorly done Gibson logo and other telltale issues.

1982-1983	Actual PAFs installed	$8,000	$8,500
1982-1983	Shaw PAFs	$4,500	$5,500
1983	"Bootleg" Les Paul	$1,500	$2,500

Les Paul Heritage 80

1980-1982. Copy of '59 Les Paul Standard, curly maple top, mahogany body, rosewood 'board, sunburst.

1980-1982		$2,000	$2,500

Les Paul Heritage 80 Award

1982. Ebony 'board, 1-piece mahogany neck, gold-plated hardware, sunburst.

1982		$2,500	$3,000

Les Paul Heritage 80 Elite

1980-1982. Copy of '59 Les Paul Standard, quilted maple top, mahogany body and neck, ebony 'board, chrome hardware, sunburst.

1980-1982		$2,000	$2,500

Les Paul Indian Motorcycle

2002. 100 made, has Indian script logo on fretboard and chrome cast war bonnet on the body, crimson red and cream white.

2002		$3,500	$4,000

Les Paul Jim Beam

2000. Jim Beam logo art on top of guitar, award-ribbon-style B Bean logo on headstock, white background with logo, JBLP serial number series, Custom Shop.

2000		$1,400	$1,600

MODEL YEAR	FEATURES	EXC. COND. LOW	HIGH

Les Paul Jimmy Page Signature

1995-1999. Jimmy Page signature on 'guard, mid-grade figured top, push-pull knobs for phasing and coil-tapping, Grover tuners, gold-plated hardware. This is not the '04 Custom Shop Jimmy Page Signature Series Les Paul (see separate listing).

1995	Highly figured, 1st year	$4,500	$5,200
1995	Low to moderate figure, 1st year	$4,000	$4,500
1996-1999	Highly figured	$4,000	$4,500
1996-1999	Low to moderate figure	$3,500	$4,000

Les Paul Jimmy Page Signature Custom Shop

2004. Introduced at the January '04 NAMM Show, 175 planned production, the first 25 were personally inspected, played-in, and autographed by Jimmy Page. Initial retail price for first 25 was $25,000, the remaining 150 instruments had an initial retail price of $16,400. Cosmetically aged by Tom Murphy to resemble Page's No. 1 Les Paul in color fade, weight, top flame, slab cut attribution on the edges, neck size and profile.

2004	1st 25 made	$20,000	$25,000
2004	Factory order 25-150	$12,000	$20,000

Les Paul Jimmy Wallace Reissue

1978-1997. Les Paul Standard '59 reissue with Jimmy Wallace on truss rod cover, special order by dealer Jimmy Wallace, figured maple top, sunburst.

1978-1983	Kalamazoo-made	$4,500	$5,000
1983-1989	Nashville-made	$4,000	$4,500
1990-1997		$4,000	$4,500

Les Paul Joe Perry Signature

1997-2001. Unbound slab body with push-pull knobs and Joe Perry signature below bridge, Bone-Yard logo model with typical Les Ppaul Standard bound body, configuration and appointments.

1997-2001	Bone-Yard option with logo	$2,000	$2,500
1997-2001	Unbound standard model	$1,700	$2,000

Les Paul Jr.

1954-1963, 1986-1992, 2001-2002, 2005-present. One P-90 pickup, single-cut solidbody '54-mid-'58, double-cut '58-early-'61, SG body '61-'63, renamed SG Jr. in '63, reintroduced as single-cut for '86-'92, reissued as the 1957 Les Paul Jr. Single Cutaway in '98. Headstock repair reduces the value by 40%-50%. Reinstalled tuners reduces the value by 5% to 10%. Replaced tuner buttons reduces the value by 5% to 10%. Current version from Musician's Friend.

1954	Sunburst, single-cut	$9,000	$15,000
1955	Sunburst, single-cut	$8,000	$14,000
1956	Sunburst, single-cut	$7,000	$13,000
1957	Sunburst, single-cut	$6,000	$12,000
1958	Sunburst, single-cut	$6,000	$11,000
1959	Cherry, double-cut	$5,000	$11,000
1960	Cherry, double-cut	$4,500	$10,000
1961	Cherry, double-cut	$4,400	$7,000
1961	Cherry, SG body	$4,000	$6,500
1962	Cherry, SG body	$3,000	$5,000
1963	Cherry, SG body	$2,500	$4,800
1986-1992	Sunburst, single-cut, tune-o-matic	$600	$1,000
2001-2005	Sunburst, single-cut, stop tailpiece	$475	$525

Les Paul Jr. 3/4

1956-1961. One P-90 pickup, short-scale, single-cut solidbody '54-mid-'58, double-cut '58-early-'61.

1956-1958	Sunburst, single-cut	$3,500	$4,000
1958-1961	Cherry, double-cut	$2,200	$3,000

Les Paul Jr. Double Cutaway

1986-1992, 1995-1996. Copy of '50s double-cut Jr., cherry or sunburst, reissued as the 1957 Les Paul Jr. Double Cutaway in '98.

1986-1992		$900	$1,000

Les Paul Jr. Special

1999-2004. Les Paul Jr. single-cut slab body with 2 P-90s (making it a Special) instead of the standard single P-90, double pickup controls, cherry, tinted natural or sunburst.

1999-2004		$775	$1,000

Les Paul Jr. Tenor/Plectrum

Late-1950s. Four string neck on Junior body, cherry.

1959		$3,000	$4,000

Les Paul Jumbo

1969-1970. Single rounded cutaway, flat-top dreadnought acoustic/electric, 1 pickup, rosewood back and sides, natural.

1969-1970		$2,500	$2,700

Les Paul KM (Kalamazoo Model)

1979. Regular Les Paul Standard with 2 exposed humbuckers, KM on headstock, sunburst, approximately 1500 were made in the Kalamazoo plant.

1979		$1,700	$2,500

Les Paul Leo's Reissue

1980-1985. Special order from Gibson's Nashville facility for Leo's Music, Oakland, California. Identified by serial number with L at the beginning, flamed maple top. About 800 guitars were made, with about 400 being exported to Japan. Kalamazoo-made Leo's have a 2nd serial number in the control cavity, Nashville-made Leo's do not have a 2nd serial number.

1980-1983	Kalamazoo-made, highly flamed	$5,000	$5,500
1980-1983	Kalamazoo-made, lower-level flame	$4,000	$4,500
1983-1985	Nashville-made	$4,000	$4,500

Les Paul Limited Edition (3-tone)

1997. Limited Edition stamped on the back of the headstock, Les Paul Standard configuration with cloud inlay markers, 2-piece 3-tone sunburst finish over non-figured maple top.

1997		$1,900	$2,200

Les Paul Melody Maker

2003-present. Slab body single-cut solidbody, P-90, dot markers.

2003-2005		$350	$375

Gibson Les Paul Jimmy Page Signature

1956 Gibson Les Paul Junior

Gibson Les Paul Recording

Gibson SG Standard Reissue

MODEL YEAR	FEATURES	EXC. COND. LOW	HIGH

Les Paul Music Machine 25th Anniversary
2002. Custom run for dealer Music Machine with special serial number series, 14 flame top and 14 quilt top instruments were produced, Music Machine 25th Anniversary logo on truss rod cover, special cherry sunburst finish.

2002	Flame top	$3,800	$4,200
2002	Quilt top	$4,000	$4,500

Les Paul Music Machine Brazilian Stinger
2003. Custom run for dealer Music Machine with special serial number series, Brazilian rosewood 'board, black stinger paint on back of neck-headstock, '59 or '60 reissue body and neck profile options, highly figured flame or quilt top options, other reissue options available.

2003	'54, '56 or '58, figured flame or quilt	$4,500	$5,500
2003	'54, '56 or '58, goldtop	$3,000	$3,800
2003	'59 or '60, figured flame or quilt	$7,000	$8,000
2003	'59 or '60, plain top	$3,500	$4,500

Les Paul Old Hickory
1998 only. Limited run of 200, tulip poplar body from The Hermitage, Custom-style trim.

1998		$2,500	$4,000

Les Paul Pee Wee
1999. 3/4" sized Les Paul Jr. style guitar, included battery-powered amp.

1999		$425	$475

Les Paul Personal
1969-1972. Two angled, low impedence pickups, phase switch, gold parts, walnut finish.

1970		$1,500	$2,000

Les Paul Pro Showcase Edition
1988. Goldtop 1956 specs, Showcase Edition decal, 200 made.

1988		$1,800	$1,850

Les Paul Pro-Deluxe
1978-1982. Two P-90 pickups, chrome-plated hardware, Pro engraved on truss rod cover, various colors.

1978-1982		$1,500	$2,000

Les Paul Professional
1969-1971, 1977-1979. Single-cut, 2 angled, low impedence pickups, carved top, walnut finish.

1969-1971		$1,500	$2,000

Les Paul Recording
1971-1980. Two angled, low impedence pickups, high/low impedence selector switch, various colors.

1971-1980		$1,500	$2,000

Les Paul Reissue Flametop
1983-1990. Flame maple top, 2 humbuckers, thicker '59-style neck, sunburst finish, renamed '59 Les Paul Flametop in '91.

1983-1990	Highly figured	$3,000	$4,000

Les Paul Reissue Goldtop
1983-1991. Goldtop finish, 2 P-100 pickups, renamed '56 Les Paul Goldtop in '91.

1983-1989		$1,500	$1,800
1990-1991		$1,500	$2,000

MODEL YEAR	FEATURES	EXC. COND. LOW	HIGH

Les Paul SG '61 Reissue
1993-2003. Renamed the Les Paul SG '61 Reissue from SG '62 reissue, early '60s Les Paul Standard SG specs with small guard, trapezoid markers, heritage cherry finish, by '03 the Les Paul script marking was not on the truss rod cover, renamed to SG '61 Reissue.

1993-2003		$1,000	$1,400

Les Paul SG Standard Reissue
2000-2004. Reissue of early-'60s specs including Deluxe Maestro vibrato with lyre tailpiece and Les Paul script truss rod logo, small pickguard, holly head veneer, rosewood 'board with tapezoid markers, available with stop bar tailpiece, extra slim low action '60 profile neck, small neck to body heel, standard color faded cherry, available in classic white or TV yellow, becomes the SG Standard reissue by 2005.

2000-2004		$2,000	$2,400

Les Paul Signature
1973-1978. Thin semi-hollowbody, double-cut, 2 low impedence pickups, f-holes, various colors.

1973-1978		$2,000	$3,400

Les Paul SmartWood Standard
1996-2002. Smartwood Series, figured maple top, mahogany body, Smartwood on truss rod cover, antique natural.

1996-2002		$950	$1,300

Les Paul SmartWood Studio
2002-present. Muiracatiara (Muir) top and mahogany back, Preciosa (Prec) 'board, Studio appointments including pearl-style dot markers.

2002-2005		$750	$950

Les Paul Special
1955-1959. Slab solidbody, 2 pickups (P-90s in '50s, P-100 stacked humbuckers on later version), single-cut until end of '58, double in '59, the '89 reissue is a single-cut, renamed SG Special in late-'59.

1955-1959	TV Yellow	$12,000	$19,000
1959	Cherry (mid- to late-'59)	$11,000	$13,000

Les Paul Special (Reissue)
1989-1998. Briefly introduced as Les Paul Junior II but name changed to Special in the first year, single-cut, 2 P-100 stacked humbucking pickups, tune-o-matic bridge, TV Yellow, in '90 there was a run of 300 with LE serial number, renamed Special SL in '98.

1989-1998		$650	$950

Les Paul Special 3/4
1959. Slab solidbody, 2 P-90 pickups, double-cut, short-scale, cherry finish, renamed SG Special 3/4 in late-'59.

1959		$7,500	$9,000

Les Paul Special Centennial
1994 only. 100 made, double-cut, cherry, 100 year banner at the 12th fret, diamonds in headstock and in gold-plated knobs, gold-plated Gibson coin in back of headstock.

1994		$3,000	$3,500

MODEL YEAR	FEATURES	EXC. COND. LOW	HIGH

Les Paul Special Custom Shop
1999-present. 1960 Special, offered in single- or double-cut version.

1999		$1,200	$1,400

Les Paul Special Double Cutaway
1976-1979, 1993-1998. Double-cut, 2 pickups (P-90s in '70s, P-100 stacked humbuckers in later version), various colors.

1976-1979		$1,300	$1,600
1993-1998		$1,100	$1,200

Les Paul Special Tenor
1959. Four-string electric tenor, LP Special body.

1959		$8,000	$15,000

Les Paul Spotlight Special
1983-1984. Curly maple and walnut top, 2 humbuckers, gold hardware, multi-bound top, Custom Shop Edition logo, natural or sunburst.

1983-1984		$3,000	$3,500

Les Paul Standard (Sunburst)
1958-1960, special order 1972-1975. Les Paul Sunbursts from '58-'60 should be individually valued based on originality, color and the amount and type of figure in the maple top, changed tuners or a Bigsby removal will drop the value. Approximately 15% came with the Bigsby tailpiece. The noted price ranges are guidance valuations. Each '58-'60 Les Paul Standard should be evaluated on a case-by-case basis. As is always the case, the low and high ranges are for an all original, excellent condition, undamaged guitar. About 70% of the '58-'60 Les Paul Standards have relatively plain maple tops. The majority of '58-'60 Les Paul Standards have moderate or extreme color fade.

Wider fret wire was introduced in early-'59. White bobbins were introduced in early- to mid-'59. Double ring Kluson Deluxe tuners were introduced in late-'60. It has been suggested that all '58-'60 models have 2-piece centerseam tops. This implies that 1-piece tops, 3-piece tops and off-centerseam tops do not exist.

Sunburst language includes terms such as: arching medullary grain, swirling medullary grain, ribbon-curl, chevrons, Honey-Amber, receding red aniline, pinstripe, bookmatched, double-white bobbins, zebra bobbins, black bobbins, fiddleback maple, sunburst finish, Honeyburst, lemon drop, quarter sawn, blistered figure, width of gradation, flat sawn, Teaburst, Bigsby-shadow, rift sawn, heel size, aged clear lacquer, 3-dimensional figure, intense fine flame, tag-shadow, red pore filler, Eastern maple fleck, medium-thick flame, shrunk tuners, wave and flame, flitch-matched, elbow discoloration, ambered top coat, natural gradation, grain orientation, script oxidation, asymmetrical figure Tangerineburst, Greenburst, and birdseye.

The bobbins used for the pickup winding were either black or white. The market has determined that white bobbin PAFs are the most highly regarded. Generally speaking, in '58 bobbins were black, in '59 the bobbin component transitioned to white and some guitars have 1 white and 1 black bobbin (aka zebra). In '60, there were zebras and double blacks returned.

Rather than listing separate line items for fade

MODEL YEAR	FEATURES	EXC. COND. LOW	HIGH

and wood, the Guide lists discounts and premiums as follows. The price ranges shown below are for instruments with excellent color, excellent wood, with the original guitar case. The following discounts and premiums should be considered.

An instrument with a plain top should be discounted about 50%.

An instrument with an average flame top should be discounted about 30%.

An instrument with moderate or total color fade should be discounted about 10%.

An instrument with a factory Bigsby should be discounted about 10%-15%.

Original jumbo frets are preferred over original small frets and are worth +10%.

An instrument with a non-original Les Paul case is worth $2,500 less.

1958	Highly flamed, strong color	$210,000	$365,000
1959	Highly flamed, strong color	$250,000	$415,000
1960	Highly flamed, strong color	$240,000	$415,000

Les Paul Standard (SG body)
1961-1963 (SG body those years). Renamed SG Standard in late-'63.

1961-1962	Cherry, side vibrola, PAFs	$19,000	$25,000
1962	Ebony block, SG, PAFs, deluxe vibrola	$25,000	$27,000
1962	Ebony block, SG, pat. #, deluxe vibrola	$20,000	$25,000
1963	Cherry, side vibrola, pat. #	$16,000	$20,000

Les Paul Standard (reintroduced then renamed)
1968-1969. Comes back as a goldtop with P-90s for '68-'69 (renamed Les Paul Deluxe, '69), available as special order Deluxe '72-'76.

1968	P-90s, small headstock	$9,000	$11,000
1968-1969	P-90s, large headstock	$7,000	$8,000

Les Paul Standard (reintroduced)
1976-present. Available as special order Deluxe '72-'76, reintroduced with 2 humbuckers '76-present.

1972-1974	Special order goldtop, P-90s	$4,500	$5,000
1972-1974	Special order sunburst, P-90s	$4,400	$4,900
1974-1975	Special order sunburst, humbuckers	$3,000	$4,200
1976	Sunburst, 4-piece pancake body	$2,500	$3,000
1976	Wine Red or natural	$2,500	$3,000
1977	Sunburst	$2,300	$2,500
1978	Natural	$2,400	$2,500

1960 Gibson Les Paul Standard

1962 Gibson Les Paul Standard

Gibson Les Paul Supreme

Gibson Les Paul
Studio Baritone

MODEL YEAR	FEATURES	EXC. COND. LOW	HIGH
1978	Sunburst	$2,300	$2,500
1979	Brown Sunburst	$2,300	$2,500
1979	Cherry Sunburst	$2,300	$2,500
1979	Goldtop	$2,400	$2,500
1979	Natural	$2,400	$2,500
1979	Wine Red	$2,300	$2,500
1980	Black	$2,300	$2,500
1980	Natural	$2,300	$2,500
1980	Sunburst	$2,300	$2,500
1980	Sunburst, mild flame	$2,400	$2,500
1980	Wine Red	$2,300	$2,500
1981	Sunburst	$2,300	$2,500
1981	Wine Red	$2,300	$2,500
1982	Black	$2,300	$2,500
1982	Brown Sunburst	$2,300	$2,500
1982	Candy Apple Red, gold hardware, LD	$2,300	$2,500
1982	Cherry Sunburst	$2,300	$2,500
1982	Goldtop	$2,400	$2,500
1982	Natural	$2,400	$2,500
1982	Wine Red	$2,300	$2,500
1983	Black	$2,200	$2,500
1983	Natural	$2,300	$2,500
1983	Sunburst	$2,200	$2,500
1984	Sunburst	$2,200	$2,500
1985	Black	$2,200	$2,500
1985	Sunburst	$2,200	$2,500
1985	Wine Red	$2,200	$2,500
1986	Sunburst	$2,000	$2,300
1987	Various colors	$2,000	$2,300
1988	Various colors	$2,000	$2,300
1989	Various colors	$2,000	$2,300
1990-1993	Limited Edition colors with sticker	$2,000	$2,600
1990-1999	Various colors	$1,700	$2,000
2000-2006	Various colors, includes figured wood	$1,600	$2,000

Les Paul Standard '58
1971-1975. Goldtop, called the '58, but set up like a '54 Goldtop with 2 soapbar pickups and stop tailpiece.

1971-1975		$3,500	$4,500

Les Paul Standard '82
1982. Standard 82 on truss rod cover, made in Kalamazoo, Made in USA stamp on back of the headstock, generally quilted maple tops.

1982		$2,600	$4,000

Les Paul Standard Lite
1999-2001. A member of DC body-style, renamed from DC Standard in '99, reintroduced as Les Paul Standard DC Plus in 2001, various translucent finishes, available in 2004 under this name also.

1999-2001		$1,000	$1,100

Les Paul Standard Plus
1995-1997, 2002-2003. Cherry sunburst standard with mid-level flame.

2002-2003		$1,900	$2,100

Les Paul Standard Premium Plus
2001-present. Premium plus flamed maple top.

2001-2005		$2,100	$2,600

Les Paul Standard Sparkle
2001. Sparkle holoflake top, reflective back, Standard logo on truss rod.

2001		$2,000	$2,500

Les Paul Strings and Things Standard
1975-1978. Special order flamed maple top Les Paul Standard model, built for Chris Lovell, owner of Strings and Things, a Gibson dealer in Memphis, approximately 28 were built, authentication of a Strings and Things Les Paul is difficult due to no diffinitive attributes, valuation should be on a case-by-case basis, sunburst.

1975-1978	2-piece top	$5,000	$7,000
1975-1978	3-piece top	$2,600	$3,100

Les Paul Studio
1983-present. Alder body, 2 humbuckers, various colors.

1983-1999		$850	$950
2000-2005		$850	$950

Les Paul Studio Baritone
2004-present. 28" baritone scale.

2004-2005		$1,000	$1,100

Les Paul Studio Custom
1984-1985. Alder body, 2 humbucking pickups, multibound top, gold-plated hardware, various colors.

1984-1985		$900	$1,000

Les Paul Studio Gem
1996-1998. Limited edition with Les Paul Studio features, but using P-90 pickups instead of humbucker pickups, plus trapezoid markers and gold hardware.

1996-1998		$900	$950

Les Paul Studio Gothic
2000-2001. Gothic Black.

2000-2001		$700	$750

Les Paul Studio Lite
1987-1998. Carved maple top, mahogany back and neck, 2 humbucker pickups, various colors.

1987-1998		$850	$925

Les Paul Studio Plus
2002-present. Two-piece AA flamed unbound top, gold hardware, Desert Burst or see-thru black.

2002-2005		$1,000	$1,100

Les Paul Studio Swamp Ash/Swamp Ash Studio
2004. Studio model with swamp ash body.

2004		$750	$800

Les Paul Supreme
2003-present. Highly figured AAAA maple top and back on translucent finishes only, custom binding, deluxe split style pearl inlay markers, chambered mahogany body, globe logo on headstock, solid colors available by '06.

2006	Solid colors	$2,000	$2,200
2003-2005	AAAA top	$2,200	$2,500

Les Paul Tie Dye (St. Pierre)
1996-1997. Hand colored by George St. Pierre, just over 100 made.

1996-1997		$2,500	$3,500

The *Vintage Guitar Price Guide* shows low to high values for items in all-original excellent condition, and, where applicable, with original case or cover.

MODEL YEAR	FEATURES	EXC. COND. LOW	HIGH
Les Paul Tie Dye Custom Shop			
2002. Limited series of one-off colorful finishes, Custom Shop logo.			
2002		$1,500	$3,000
Les Paul TV			
1954-1959. Les Paul Jr. with limed mahogany (TV Yellow) finish, single-cut until mid-'58, double-cut after, renamed SG TV in late-'59.			
1955	Single-cut	$9,000	$11,000
1956	Single-cut	$9,000	$11,000
1957	Single-cut	$9,000	$11,000
1958	Single-cut	$9,000	$11,000
1958-1959	Double-cut	$8,000	$9,500
Les Paul TV 3/4			
1954-1957. Limed mahogany (TV Yellow) Les Paul Jr. 3/4, short-scale, single-cut.			
1954-1957		$4,500	$5,500
Les Paul Ultima			
1996-2000. Custom Shop model, flame or quilted sunburst top, fancy abalone and mother-of-pearl tree of life, harp, or flame fingerboard inlay, multi abalone bound body.			
1996-2000		$5,000	$6,000
Les Paul Vixen			
2005-present. Les Paul Special single-cut slab body, dot markers, 2 humbuckers, 2 control knobs, wraparound bridge (not Tune-o-matic), various colors.			
2005-2006		$600	$700
Les Paul Voodoo/Voodoo Les Paul			
2004-2005. Single-cut, swamp ash body, 2 exposed humbuckers, black satin finish.			
2004-2005		$1,000	$1,200
Les Paul XR-I/XR-II/XR-III			
1981-1983. Basic model with Dirty Finger pickups, dot markers, Les Paul stencil logo on headstock, goldburst, silverburst, and cherryburst finishes.			
1981-1983	XR-I, goldburst	$750	$850
1981-1983	XR-II	$750	$850
1981-1983	XR-III	$750	$850
Les Paul Zack Wylde Signature			
2003-present. Custom shop, black and antique-white bullseye graphic finish.			
2003-2005	Black/white bullseye	$2,500	$2,800
2003-2005	Green Camo bullseye option	$2,500	$2,800
The Les Paul			
1976-1980. Figured maple top, 2 humbuckers, gold hardware, rosewood binding, 'guard, 'board, knobs, cover plates, etc., natural or rosewood finishing, natural only by '79.			
1976-1980	Natural or rosewood	$11,000	$13,000
The Paul			
1978-1982. Walnut body, 2 exposed humbuckers.			
1978-1982		$700	$750
The Paul Firebrand Deluxe			
1980-1982. Single-cut mahogany solidbody, rough natural finish, Gibson branded in headstock, 2 exposed humbuckers.			
1980-1982	Black	$600	$800

MODEL YEAR	FEATURES	EXC. COND. LOW	HIGH
1980-1982	Pelham Blue	$700	$950
1980-1982	Rough natural	$600	$850
The Paul II			
1996-1998. Mahogany body, 2 humbucking pickups, rosewood dot neck, renamed The Paul SL in '98.			
1996-1998		$550	$600
LG-0			
1958-1974. Flat-top acoustic, mahogany, bound body, rosewood bridge '58-'61 and '68-'74, plastic bridge '62-'67, natural.			
1958-1961	Rosewood bridge	$950	$1,100
1962-1964	Plastic bridge	$650	$950
1965-1966	Plastic bridge	$600	$800
1967-1969	Rosewood bridge	$600	$725
1970-1974		$500	$700
LG-1			
1943-1968. Flat-top acoustic, spruce top, mahogany back and sides, bound body, rosewood bridge '43-'61, plastic bridge after, examples seen to '74, sunburst.			
1943		$1,900	$2,100
1944		$1,800	$2,000
1945		$1,700	$1,900
1946		$1,600	$1,800
1947-1949		$1,400	$1,600
1950-1961		$1,300	$1,600
1962-1964		$850	$1,000
1965-1966		$800	$950
1967-1968		$750	$850
LG-2			
1942-1962. Flat-top acoustic, spruce top, mahogany back and sides (some with maple '43-'46), banner headstock '42-'46, bound body, X-bracing, sunburst finish, replaced by B-25 in '62.			
1942		$2,600	$3,300
1943		$2,500	$3,200
1944		$2,500	$3,100
1945		$2,400	$3,000
1946		$2,300	$2,700
1947-1949		$2,200	$2,600
1950-1955		$2,100	$2,300
1956-1961		$1,800	$2,200
1962	Adjustable bridge	$1,300	$1,800
LG-2 3/4			
1949-1962. Short-scale version of LG-2 flat-top, wood bridge, sunburst.			
1949-1962		$1,300	$2,500
LG-2 H			
1945-1955. Flat-top, Hawaiian, natural or sunburst.			
1944-1949		$2,200	$3,100
1950-1955		$1,800	$2,200
LG-3			
1942-1964. Flat-top acoustic, spruce top, mahogany back and sides, bound body, natural finish, replaced by B-25 N.			
1942		$2,900	$3,600
1943		$2,800	$3,500
1944		$2,700	$3,400
1945		$2,600	$3,200
1946		$2,400	$3,000

1950s Gibson Les Paul TV

1965 Gibson LG-1

Gibson Marauder

1970 Gibson Melody Maker

MODEL YEAR	FEATURES	EXC. COND. LOW	HIGH
1947-1949		$2,200	$2,800
1950-1955		$2,200	$2,400
1956-1961	Wood bridge	$1,900	$2,300
1962-1964	Plastic bridge	$1,400	$2,000

LG-12 (12-string)
1967-1973. 14-1/8" wide, mahogany back and sides, bound top, natural.

1967-1969	Adjustable saddle	$800	$950
1970-1974	Set saddle	$750	$850

M III Series
1991-1996. Double-cut solidbody with extra long bass horn, six-on-a-side tuners on a reverse pointy headstock, dot markers, reverse Gibson decal logo.

1991-1992	Deluxe	$1,500	$2,500

Mach II
1990-1991. Renamed from U-2, offset double-cut, 2 single coils and 1 humbucking pickup.

1990-1991		$600	$750

Map Guitar
1983, 1985. Body cutout like lower 48, 2 humbuckers, limited run promotion, '83 version in natural mahogany or red, white and blue, '85 version red, white and blue stars and stripes on a white background.

1983	Natural	$2,200	$3,000
1983	Red, white and blue	$2,400	$3,300

Marauder
1975-1980. Single-cut solidbody, pointed headstock, 2 pickups, bolt-on neck, various colors.

1975-1980		$575	$650

Melody Maker
1959-1971. Slab solidbody, 1 pickup, single-cut until '61, double '61-'66, SG body '66-'71, reintroduced as single-cut in '86-'93.

1959	Sunburst, single-cut	$1,900	$2,000
1960	Sunburst, single-cut	$1,600	$1,900
1961	Sunburst, single-cut	$1,500	$1,800
1962	Cherry, double-cut	$1,300	$1,600
1962	Sunburst, double-cut	$1,300	$1,600
1963	Cherry, double-cut	$1,100	$1,400
1964	Cherry, double-cut	$900	$1,200
1965-1966	Cherry, double cut	$850	$1,000
1966-1969	Blue or red, SG body	$1,000	$1,200
1968-1971	Walnut, SG body	$1,000	$1,200

Melody Maker 3/4
1959-1970. Short-scale version.

1959-1965	Melody Maker body	$600	$1,300
1966-1970	SG body	$650	$1,050

Melody Maker D
1960-1970. Two pickup version of Melody Maker, reintroduced as Melody Maker Double in '77.

1960	Sunburst, single-cut	$2,000	$2,300
1961	Sunburst, single-cut	$1,600	$2,000
1962	Cherry, double-cut	$1,500	$1,800

MODEL YEAR	FEATURES	EXC. COND. LOW	HIGH
1962	Sunburst, double-cut	$1,500	$1,800
1963	Cherry, double-cut	$1,400	$1,600
1964	Cherry, double-cut	$1,200	$1,400
1965-1966	Cherry, double-cut	$1,000	$1,100
1966-1969	Blue or red, SG body	$1,200	$1,400
1968-1970	Walnut, SG body	$1,200	$1,400

Melody Maker Double
1977-1983. Reintroduction of Melody Maker D, double-cut solidbody, 2 pickups, cherry or sunburst.

1977-1983		$700	$800

Melody Maker III
1967-1971. SG-style double-cut solidbody, 3 pickups, various colors.

1967-1969		$1,500	$1,700
1970-1971		$1,300	$1,500

Melody Maker 12
1967-1971. SG-style solidbody, 12 strings, 2 pickups, red, white or Pelham Blue.

1967-1969		$1,200	$1,400
1970-1971		$1,100	$1,400

MK-35
1975-1978. Mark Series flat-top acoustic, mahogany back and sides, black-bound body, natural or sunburst.

1975-1978		$700	$800

MK-53
1975-1978. Mark Series flat-top acoustic, maple back and sides, multi-bound body, natural or sunburst.

1975-1978		$775	$850

MK-72
1975-1978. Mark Series flat-top acoustic, rosewood back and sides, black-bound body, natural or sunburst.

1975-1978		$800	$950

MK-81
1975-1978. Mark Series flat-top acoustic, rosewood back and sides, multi-bound body, gold tuners, high-end appointments, natural or sunburst.

1975-1978		$850	$1,000

Moderne Heritage
1981-1983. Limited edition, korina body, 2 humbucking pickups, gold hardware.

1981-1983	Black or white	$2,300	$2,800
1981-1983	Natural	$3,000	$3,300

Nick Lucas
1928-1938. Flat-top acoustic, multi-bound body and neck, sunburst, reintroduced in '91 and '99. Also known as Nick Lucas Special and Gibson Special.

1928	Mahogany, 12-fret, 13 1/3"	$7,000	$10,000
1928	Rosewood, 12-fret, 13 1/2"	$8,000	$12,000
1929-1933	Rosewood, 13-fret, 14 3/4"	$9,000	$15,000
1934-1938	Maple, 14-fret, 14 3/4"	$8,000	$11,000

MODEL YEAR	FEATURES	EXC. COND. LOW	HIGH

Nick Lucas Reissue
1991-1992, 1999-2004. Limited edition flat-top acoustic, sunburst.

| 1991-1992 | | $1,600 | $1,700 |
| 1999-2004 | | $1,800 | $2,000 |

Nighthawk Custom
1993-1998. Flame maple top, ebony 'board, gold hardware, fireburst, single/double/mini pickups.

| 1993-1998 | | $1,000 | $1,100 |

Nighthawk Special
1993-1998. Single-cut solidbody, figured maple top, double-coil and mini-pickup or with additional single-coil options, dot marker inlay, cherry, ebony or sunburst.

| 1993-1998 | | $550 | $750 |

Nighthawk Standard
1993-1998. Single-cut solidbody, figured maple top, 2 or 3 pickups, double-parallelogram inlay, amber, fireburst or sunburst.

| 1993-1998 | | $850 | $950 |

Nouveau NV6T-M
1986-1987. A line of Gibson flat-tops with imported parts assembled and finished in the U.S., acoustic dreadnought, bound maple body, natural.

| 1986-1987 | | $400 | $450 |

Q-100
1985-1986. Offset double-cut solidbody, Kahler trem, 6-on-a-side tuners, 1 humbucker, black hardware.

| 1985-1986 | | $350 | $400 |

Q-200/Q2000
1985-1986. Like Q-100, but with 1 single-coil and 1 humbucker, black or chrome hardware.

| 1985-1986 | | $400 | $450 |

Q-300/Q3000
1985-1986. Like Q-100, but with 3 single-coils, black or chrome hardware.

| 1985-1986 | | $450 | $500 |

RD Artist
1978-1982. Double-cut solidbody, 2 humbuckers, TP-6 tailpiece, active electronics, ebony 'board, block inlays, gold-plated parts, various colors, called just RD (no Artist) in '81 and '82.

| 1978-1982 | | $1,200 | $1,800 |

RD Custom
1977-1979. Double-cut solidbody, 2 humbuckers, stop tailpiece, active electronics, dot inlays, maple 'board, chrome parts, natural or walnut.

| 1977-1979 | | $1,200 | $1,400 |

RD Standard
1977-1979. Double-cut solidbody, 2 humbuckers, stop tailpiece, rosewood 'board, dot inlays, chrome parts, natural, sunburst or walnut.

| 1977-1979 | | $1,100 | $1,300 |

Roy Smeck Radio Grande Hawaiian
1934-1939. Dreadnought acoustic flat-top, rosewood back and neck, bound body and neck, natural.

| 1934-1939 | | $8,000 | $12,000 |

Roy Smeck Radio Grande Hawaiian Reissue
1996. Part of Smart Wood Series, Grenadillo back and sides.

| 1996 | | $2,400 | $2,500 |

Roy Smeck Stage Deluxe Hawaiian
1934-1942. Dreadnought acoustic flat-top, mahogany back and sides, bound body, natural.

| 1934-1942 | | $6,000 | $7,500 |

S-1
1976-1980. Single-cut solidbody, pointed headstock, 3 single-coil pickups, similar to the Marauder, various colors.

| 1976-1980 | | $600 | $800 |

SG
Following are the various guitars, listed alphabetically, bearing the SG name:

SG '61 Reissue
2003-present. Renamed from Les Paul SG '61 Reissue, no Les Paul script on truss rod, small 'guard, stop bar tailpiece (no Deluxe Maestro vibrato), '60 slim-taper neck profile.

| 2003-2006 | | $1,300 | $1,400 |

SG '62 Reissue/SG Reissue
1986-1991. Trapezoid markers, stop bar, 2 humbuckers, called SG Reissue '86-'87, SG '62 Reissue '88-'91. Reintroduced as Les Paul SG '61 Reissue for '93-'03 and SG '61 Reissue '03-present, cherry.

| 1986-1991 | | $1,200 | $1,400 |

SG '62 Reissue Showcase Edition
1988. Guitar of the Month, bright blue opaque finish, 200 made.

| 1988 | | $1,200 | $1,400 |

'63 Corvette Sting Ray
1995-1996. SG-style body carved to simulate split rear window on '63 Corvette, Sting Ray inlay, 150 instruments built, offered in black, white, silver or red, Custom Shop.

| 1995-1996 | Black | $3,000 | $3,700 |

SG Classic
1999-present. Late '60s SG Special style, large pickguard, black soap-bar single-coil P-90s, dot markers, stop bar tailpiece, cherry or ebony stain. Offered by Musician's Friend since '03.

| 1999-2005 | | $550 | $650 |

SG Custom
1963-1980. Renamed from Les Paul Custom, 3 humbuckers, vibrato, made with Les Paul Custom plate from '61-'63 (see Les Paul Custom), white finish until '68, walnut and others after.

1963	White, pat. #	$12,000	$18,000
1964	White	$11,000	$17,000
1965	White	$10,000	$11,000
1966	White	$9,000	$11,000
1967	White	$9,000	$11,000
1968	White	$8,000	$9,000
1969-1970	Walnut, Lyre	$7,000	$7,500
1969-1970	White, Lyre	$7,500	$8,000
1970-1973	Walnut	$4,000	$7,000
1970-1973	White option	$4,500	$7,500

1977 Gibson RD Custom

1976 Gibson S-1

1963 Gibson SG Custom

Gibson SG Pete Townshend Signature

MODEL YEAR	FEATURES	EXC. COND. LOW	HIGH
1974-1976	Various colors	$2,300	$2,700
1977-1980	Various colors	$2,000	$2,400

SG Custom '67 Reissue/Les Paul SG '67 Custom

1991-1993. The SG Custom '67 Reissue has a wine red finish, the Les Paul SG '67 Custom ('92-'93) has a wine red or white finish.

1991-1993		$1,800	$1,900

SG Custom Reissue

1999-present. 1961 specs, SG body style, 3 humbuckers, Deluxe Maestro vibrato or stud with tune-o-matic bridge, white.

1999-2005		$1,700	$2,400

SG Deluxe

1971-1972, 1980-1985, 1998-1999. The '70s models were offered in natural, cherry or walnut finishes, reintroduced in '98 with 3 Firebird mini-humbucker-style pickups in black, Ice Blue or red finishes.

1971-1972	Cherry	$1,500	$1,800
1971-1972	Natural or walnut	$1,300	$1,600
1980-1985	Various colors	$825	$1,100
1998-1999	Various colors	$925	$1,100

SG Exclusive

1979. SG with humbuckers, coil-tap and rotary control knob, block inlay, pearl logo (not decal), black/ebony finish.

1979		$1,500	$1,700

SG Firebrand

1980-1982. Double-cut mahogany solidbody, rough natural finish, Gibson branded in headstock, 2 exposed humbuckers, Firebrand logo on The SG (Standard) model.

1980-1982		$750	$900

SG Gothic

2000-2003. SG Special with satin black finish, moon and star marker on 12th fret, black hardware.

2000-2003		$550	$900

SG I

1972-1977. Double-cut, mahogany body, 1 mini-humbucker (some with SG Jr. P-90), cherry or walnut.

1972-1977		$850	$950

SG II

1972-1976. 2 mini-humbuckers (some in '75 had regular humbuckers), cherry or walnut.

1972-1976		$1,000	$1,300

SG III

1972-1974. The sunburst version of the II, some shipped as late as '79.

1972-1974		$1,000	$1,300

SG Jr.

1963-1971, 1991-1994. One pickup, solidbody. Prices are for an unfaded finish, cherry finish faded to brown reduces the value by 30%.

1963	Cherry	$2,500	$4,500
1963	White	$3,500	$6,500
1964	Cherry	$2,400	$3,200
1964	White	$3,300	$5,000
1965	Cherry	$2,300	$2,900
1965	Pelham Blue	$5,000	$7,000
1965	White	$3,000	$4,000
1966	Cherry	$2,000	$2,600

MODEL YEAR	FEATURES	EXC. COND. LOW	HIGH
1966	White	$2,800	$3,500
1967	Cherry	$2,000	$2,500
1967	White	$2,800	$3,100
1968	Cherry	$2,000	$2,200
1968	White	$2,800	$3,000
1969	Cherry	$2,000	$2,200
1970	Cherry	$1,500	$2,000
1971	Cherry or walnut	$1,200	$1,500
1991-1994	Various colors	$600	$650

SG Les Paul Custom

1986-1992. 3 humbuckers, called the SG '62 Custom in '86 and SG '90 Les Paul Custom in '90-'92 and SG '67 Custom Shop (300 made) towards the end of its run.

1986-1989	Antique Ivory	$1,800	$2,000
1990-1992	White	$1,800	$2,000
1992	Burgundy	$1,800	$2,000

SG Les Paul Custom 30th Anniversary

1991. SG body, 3 humbuckers, gold hardware, TV Yellow finish, 30th Anniversary on peghead.

1991		$1,800	$2,000

SG Music Machine Stinger

2003. Custom run for dealer Music Machine, special serial number series, SG Custom with 2 pickups and SG Standard models available, black stinger paint job on neck/headstock, various colors.

2003	SG Custom	$2,800	$3,000
2003	SG Standard	$2,400	$2,600

SG Pete Townshend Signature (Historic/ Custom Shop)

2000-2003. SG Special with '70 specs, large 'guard, 2 cases, cherry red.

2000-2003	Includes certificate	$2,000	$2,300

SG Platinum

2005. A mix of SG Special and SG Standard specs, platinum paint on the body, back of neck, and headstock, no crown inlay, Gibson stencil logo, exposed humbucker pickups, large plantium-finish 'guard, special plantium colored Gibson logo guitar case.

2005		$875	$950

SG Pro

1971-1973. Two P-90 pickups, tune-o-matic bridge, vibrato, cherry, mahogany or walnut.

1971-1973	Cherry	$1,300	$1,600
1971-1973	Mahogany or walnut	$1,200	$1,500

SG Special

1959-1978, 1985-present. Rounded double-cut for '59-'60, switched to SG body early-'61, 2 P-90s '59-'71, 2 mini-humbuckers '72-'78, 2 regular humbuckers on current version, reintroduced in '85. Prices are for an unfaded finish, cherry finish faded to brown reduces the value by 20%-30%. Instruments with stop tailpieces vs. Maestro tailpiece have the same value.

1959	Cherry, slab, high neck pickup	$10,000	$12,000
1960	Cherry, slab, lower neck pickup	$10,000	$12,000
1961	Cherry, SG body	$6,000	$10,000
1962	Cherry	$5,000	$6,000
1962	White	$6,000	$8,000

MODEL YEAR	FEATURES	EXC. COND. LOW	HIGH
1963	Cherry	$4,300	$5,000
1963	White	$5,000	$6,000
1964	Cherry	$4,000	$4,500
1964	White	$4,800	$5,800
1965	Cherry	$3,800	$4,300
1965	White	$4,400	$5,400
1966	Cherry, large 'guard	$3,000	$3,500
1966	Cherry, small 'guard	$3,500	$4,000
1966	White, large 'guard	$3,500	$4,000
1966	White, small 'guard	$4,000	$4,500
1967	Cherry	$2,500	$3,000
1967	White	$3,000	$3,500
1968-1971	Cherry	$2,400	$2,800
1972-1975	Cherry or walnut	$1,300	$1,600
1976-1978	Cherry or walnut	$1,100	$1,400
1985-1999	Various colors	$725	$800
2000-2005	Common colors	$700	$800

SG Special Faded/Faded SG Special
2002-present. Aged worn cherry finish.

2002-2005	Half moon markers	$600	$650

SG Standard
1963-1981, 1983-present. Les Paul Standard changes to SG body, 2 humbuckers, some very early models have optional factory Bigsby. Prices are for an unfaded finish, a cherry finish faded to brown reduces the value by 30% or more.

1963	Cherry, small 'guard, deluxe vibrato	$18,000	$25,000
1964	Cherry, small 'guard, deluxe vibrato	$18,000	$25,000
1964	Pelham Blue, small 'guard, deluxe vibrato	$20,000	$30,000
1965	Cherry, small 'guard, deluxe vibrato	$14,000	$17,000
1965	Pelham Blue, small 'guard, deluxe vibrato	$15,000	$20,000
1966	Cherry, large 'guard	$4,500	$6,500
1967	Burgundy Metallic	$5,000	$7,000
1967	Cherry	$4,000	$6,500
1967	White	$5,000	$7,000
1968	Cherry, engraved lyre	$4,000	$6,000
1969	Engraved lyre, 1-piece neck	$4,000	$5,000
1969	Engraved lyre, 3-piece neck	$3,000	$4,000
1970	Cherry, non-lyre tailpiece	$2,500	$3,000
1970	Engraved lyre, 3-piece neck	$3,000	$3,800
1970	Walnut, non-lyre tailpiece	$2,000	$2,500

MODEL YEAR	FEATURES	EXC. COND. LOW	HIGH
1971	Cherry, non-lyre tailpiece	$2,200	$2,500
1971	Engraved lyre, 3-piece neck	$2,750	$3,300
1972-1975	New specs, block markers	$1,700	$2,000
1976-1981	New color line-up	$1,500	$1,700
1983-1987		$800	$1,100
1988-1999	New specs	$950	$1,150
2000-2005	Black	$800	$900
2000-2005	Cherry or sunburst	$900	$1,050

SG Standard Angus Young Signature
2000-present. Late-'60s specs with large 'guard, Deluxe Maestro lyre vibrato with Angus logo, late-'60s style knobs, Angus logo on headstock, aged cherry finish.

2000-2005		$1,700	$1,825

SG Standard Celebrity Series
1991-1992. SG Standard with large 'guard, gold hardware, black finish.

1991-1992		$1,400	$1,500

SG Standard Korina
1993-1994. Korina version of SG Standard, limited run, natural.

1993-1994		$1,800	$2,100

SG Standard Reissue
2004-present. Reissue of near '63-'64 specs with Deluxe Maestro lyre vibrato and small 'guard, also offered with stop bar tailpiece, cherry finish, '60 slim taper neck, smooth neck heel joint, trapezoid markers, unmarked truss rod cover without Les Paul designation, formerly called Les Paul SG Standard Reissue, by 2005 part of Gibson's 'Vintage Original Spec' Custom Shop series.

2004-2006		$2,000	$2,400

SG Supreme
2004-present. '57 humbuckers, flamed maple top, split-diamond markers, various colors.

2004		$1,225	$1,350
2005-2006		$1,300	$1,350

SG Tommy Iommi Signature (Historic/ Custom Shop)
2001-2003. Signature humbuckers without poles, cross inlays, ebony or wine red.

2001-2003		$2,200	$3,000

SG TV
1959-1968. Les Paul TV changed to SG body, double rounded cutaway solidbody for '59-'60, SG body '61-'68, 1 pickup, limed mahogany (TV yellow) finish. Prices are for unfaded finish, a faded finish reduces the value by 20%-30%.

1959-1961	TV Yellow, slab body	$8,000	$9,500
1961-1963	White, SG body	$3,500	$4,500

SG Voodoo/Voodoo SG
2004-2005. Black satin finish.

2004-2005		$1,000	$1,200

SG-90 Double
1988-1990. SG body, updated electronics, graphite reinforced neck, 2 pickups, cherry, turquoise or white.

1988-1990		$575	$625

1965 Gibson SG Standard

Gibson SG Tony Iommi Signature

1983 Gibson The SG

Gibson Songwriter Deluxe

MODEL YEAR	FEATURES	EXC. COND. LOW	HIGH

SG-90 Single

1988-1990. SG body, updated electronics, graphite reinforced neck, 1 humbucker pickup, cherry, turquoise or white.

| 1988-1990 | | $525 | $575 |

SG-100

1971-1972. Double-cut solidbody, 1 pickup, cherry or walnut.

| 1971-1972 | Melody Maker pickup | $750 | $1,200 |
| 1971-1972 | P-90 pickup option | $750 | $1,200 |

SG-200

1971-1972. Two pickup version of SG-100 in black, cherry or walnut finish, replaced by SG II.

| 1971-1972 | Melody Maker pickups | $950 | $1,400 |

SG-250

1971-1972. Two-pickup version of SG-100 in cherry sunburst, replaced by SG III.

| 1971-1972 | Melody Maker pickups | $1,100 | $1,500 |

SG-400/SG Special 400

1985-1987. SG body with 3 toggles, 2 knobs (master volume, master tone), single-single-humbucker pickupst, available with uncommon opaque finishes.

| 1985-1987 | | $700 | $800 |

SG-R1/SG Artist

1980-1982. Active RD-era electronics. SG style but thicker body, no 'guard, ebony 'board, black finish, dot markers, renamed SG Artist in '81.

| 1980 | SG-R1 | $1,000 | $1,100 |
| 1981-1982 | SG Artist | $1,000 | $1,100 |

SG-X (All American)

1995-1999. Renamed the SG-X in '98, previously part of the all American series, SG body with single bridge humbucker, various colors.

| 1995-1999 | | $600 | $800 |

The SG

1979-1983. Normal SG specs, solid walnut body and neck, ebony 'board, 2 humbuckers, model name logo on truss rod.

| 1979-1983 | | $750 | $900 |

SJ (Southern Jumbo)

1942-1969,1991-1996. Flat-top, sunburst standard, natural optional starting in '54 (natural finish version called Country-Western starting in '56), round shoulders (changed to square in '62), catalog name changed to SJ Deluxe in '70, refer to that listing.

1942-1944		$5,500	$6,000
1948-1949		$4,900	$5,500
1950-1953		$4,500	$4,900
1954-1956	Natural option	$4,000	$4,700
1954-1956	Sunburst	$3,800	$4,500
1956-1961	Round shoulder	$3,300	$3,800
1962-1964	Square shoulder	$3,000	$3,300
1965-1966		$2,600	$2,900
1967-1968		$2,200	$2,700
1969	Below belly bridge	$2,100	$2,200

SJ Deluxe (Southern Jumbo)

1970-1978. SJ name changed to SJ Deluxe in catalog, along with a series of engineering changes.

1970-1971	Non-adj. saddle	$1,500	$1,700
1972-1973	Unbound 'board	$1,100	$1,500
1974-1978	4-ply to binding	$900	$1,100

SJ (Southern Jumbo) Reissue

2003. Sunburst.

| 2003 | | $1,400 | $1,600 |

SJ-100 1939 Centennial

1994. Acoustic flat-top, limited edition, sunburst

| 1994 | | $1,600 | $1,900 |

SJ-200 Ray Whitley/J-200 Custom Club

1994-1995. Based on Ray Whitley's late-1930s J-200, including engraved inlays and initials on the truss rod cover, only 37 made, one of the limited edition models the Montana division released to celebrate Gibson's 100th anniversary.

| 1994-1995 | | $7,000 | $9,000 |

SJN (Country-Western)

1956-1969. Flat-top, natural finish version of SJ, round shoulders '56-'62, square shoulders after that, called the SJN in '60 and '61, the SJN Country Western after that, catalog name changed to SJN Deluxe in '70, refer to that listing.

1956-1961	Round shoulders	$3,500	$4,000
1962-1964	Square shoulders	$3,100	$3,500
1965-1966	Square shoulders	$2,800	$3,100
1967-1968	Square shoulders	$2,300	$2,800
1969	Below belly bridge	$1,900	$2,300

SJN Deluxe (Country-Western Jumbo)

1970-1978. SJN name changed to SJN Deluxe in catalog, along with a series of engineering changes.

1970-1971	Non-adj. saddle	$1,700	$1,900
1972-1973	Unbound 'board	$1,200	$1,700
1974-1978	4-ply to binding	$1,000	$1,200

Sonex-180 Custom

1980-1982. Two Super humbuckers, coil-tap, maple neck, ebony 'board, single-cut, body of Multi-Phonic synthetic material, various colors.

| 1980-1982 | | $600 | $700 |

Sonex-180 Deluxe

1980-1984. Hardwood neck, rosewood 'board, single-cut, body of Multi-Phonic synthetic material, 2 pickups, no coil-tap, various colors.

| 1980-1984 | | $500 | $600 |

Songbird Deluxe

1999-2003. Square shoulder flat top, Indian rosewood back and sides and 'board, on-board electronics.

| 1999-2003 | | $1,300 | $1,400 |

Songwriter Deluxe

2003-present. Square shoulder flat top, Indian rosewood back and sides, on-board electronics.

| 2003-2005 | Cutaway | $1,300 | $1,350 |
| 2003-2005 | Non-cutaway | $1,250 | $1,300 |

Spirit I

1982-1988. Double rounded cutaway, 1 pickup, chrome hardware, various colors.

| 1982-1988 | | $450 | $500 |

MODEL YEAR	FEATURES	EXC. COND. LOW	HIGH

Spirit II XPL
1985-1987. Double-cut solidbody, Kahler tremolo, 2 pickups, various colors.

1985-1987		$550	$600

SR-71
1987-1989. Floyd Rose tremolo, 1 humbucker, 2 single-coil pickups, various colors, Wayne Charvel designed.

1987-1989		$550	$600

Star
1992. Star logo on headstock, star position markers, single sharp cutaway flat-top, sunburst.

1992		$1,200	$1,500

Style O
1902-1925. Acoustic archtop, oval soundhole, bound top, neck and headstock, various colors.

1910-1925		$4,000	$4,500

Style U Harp Guitar
1902-1939. Acoustic 6-string, with 10 or 12 sub-bass strings, maple back and sides, bound soundhole, black.

1915-1919		$5,500	$6,500

Super 300 (Non-Cutaway)
1948-1955. Acoustic archtop, non-cut, bound body, neck and headstock, sunburst.

1948-1949		$4,500	$6,500
1950-1955		$4,000	$6,000

Super 300 C (Cutaway)
1954-1958. Acoustic archtop, rounded cutaway, bound body, neck and headstock, sunburst with natural option.

1954-1957	Sunburst	$4,000	$7,500

Super 400
1934-1941; 1947-1955. Acoustic archtop, non-cut, multi-bound, f-holes, sunburst (see Super 400 N for natural version).

1934	Super L-5 Deluxe (intro. Model)	$30,000	$40,000
1934-1935		$14,000	$16,000
1936-1941		$11,500	$14,500
1947-1949		$10,000	$13,500
1950-1955		$9,000	$13,000

Super 400 N
1940, 1948-1955. Natural finish version of Super 400, non-cut, acoustic archtop.

1940		$11,000	$15,000
1948-1949		$10,000	$11,000
1950-1955		$9,000	$10,000

Super 400 P (Premier)
1939-1941. Acoustic archtop, single rounded cutaway, '39 model 'board rests on top, sunburst finish.

1939		$30,000	$35,000
1940-1941		$25,000	$34,000

Super 400 PN (Premier Natural)
1939-1940. Rounded cutaway, '39 'board rests on top, natural finish.

1939		$41,000	$46,000
1940		$36,000	$41,000

Super 400 C
1948-1982. Introduced as Super 400 Premier, acoustic archtop, single-cut, sunburst finish (natural is called Super 400 CN).

1948-1949		$12,000	$15,000
1950-1959		$11,000	$14,000
1960-1962		$10,000	$13,000
1963-1964		$10,000	$12,000
1965-1966		$9,000	$10,000
1967-1969		$7,500	$9,000
1970-1974		$5,500	$8,000
1975-1979		$4,500	$7,000
1980-1982		$4,500	$6,800

Super 400 CN
1950-1987. Natural finish version of Super 400 C.

1950-1959		$13,000	$16,000
1960-1962		$12,000	$15,000
1963-1964		$12,000	$14,000
1965-1966		$10,000	$12,000
1967-1969		$9,000	$11,000

Super 400 CES
1951-present. Electric version of Super 400 C, archtop, single-cut (round '51-'60 and '69-present, pointed '60-'69), 2 pickups (P-90s '51-'54, Alnico Vs '54-'57, humbuckers '57 on), sunburst (natural version called Super 400 CESN), now part of Gibson's Historic Collection.

1951-1953	P-90s	$13,000	$18,000
1954-1956	Alnico Vs	$14,000	$20,000
1957-1959	PAFs	$25,000	$29,000
1960	PAFs	$20,000	$28,000
1961-1962	PAFs, sharp cut intro.	$15,000	$20,000
1963-1964	Pat. #	$13,000	$15,000
1965-1966		$9,500	$12,000
1967-1969		$7,500	$9,500
1970-1974		$6,500	$8,500
1975-1979		$6,000	$7,500
1980-1987		$6,000	$7,000

Super 400 CESN
1952-present. Natural version of Super 400 CES, now part of Gibson's Historic Collection.

1952-1953	P-90s	$24,000	$26,000
1954-1956	Alnico Vs	$24,000	$26,000
1957-1959	PAFs	$30,000	$35,000
1960	PAFs	$26,000	$34,000
1961-1962	PAFs, sharp cut intro.	$21,000	$29,000
1963-1964	Pat. #	$15,000	$21,000
1965-1966		$12,000	$15,000
1967-1969		$11,000	$12,500
1970-1974		$8,000	$11,000
1975-1979		$7,500	$8,500
1980-1987		$6,500	$8,000

'39 Super 400
1993-2000. Reissue of non-cut '39 version. Part of Gibson's Historic Collection, various colors.

1993-1995		$6,000	$7,000

Gibson Style U

1959 Gibson Super 400 CES

Gibson Tal Farlow

Gibson Trini Lopez Standard

MODEL YEAR	FEATURES	EXC. COND. LOW	HIGH

Super Jumbo 100
1939-1943. Jumbo flat-top, mahogany back and sides, bound body and neck, sunburst, reintroduced as J-100 with different specs in '84.

| 1939-1941 | Stairstep peghead | $24,000 | $29,000 |
| 1941-1943 | Standard peghead | $20,000 | $25,000 |

Super Jumbo/Super Jumbo 200
1938-1947. Initially called Super Jumbo in '38 and named Super Jumbo 200 in '39. name then changed to J-200 (see that listing) by '47 (with maple back and sides) and SJ-200 by the '50s. Named for super large jumbo 16 7/8" flat-top body, double braced with rosewood back and sides, sunburst finish.

| 1938-1939 | | $50,000 | $65,000 |
| 1940-1942 | | $50,000 | $60,000 |

Super V CES
1978-1993. Archtop, L-5 with a Super 400 neck, natural or sunburst.

| 1978-1993 | | $5,500 | $6,500 |

Tal Farlow
1962-1971, 1993-present. Full body, single-cut archtop, 2 humbuckers, triple-bound top, reintroduced '93, now part of Gibson's Historic Collection.

1962-1964	Viceroy Brown	$8,000	$10,000
1965-1966	Viceroy Brown	$7,500	$8,500
1967-1969	Viceroy Brown	$6,500	$7,500
1970-1971	Viceroy Brown	$5,000	$6,500
1993-1999	Cherry or Viceroy Brown	$2,800	$3,000
1993-1999	Natural, figured wood	$3,100	$3,300

TG-0 (L-0 based)
1927-1933. Acoustic tenor based on L-0, mahogany body, light amber.

| 1927-1933 | | $1,200 | $1,400 |

TG-0 (LG-0 based)
1960-1974. Acoustic tenor based on LG-0, mahogany body, natural.

1960-1964		$600	$750
1965-1966		$550	$650
1967-1969		$500	$550
1970-1974		$400	$500

TG-00 (L-00 based)
1932-1943. Tenor flat-top based on L-00.

| 1932-1943 | | $1,100 | $1,500 |

TG-1/L-1 Tenor/L-4 Tenor (and Plectrum)
1927-1937. Acoustic flat-top, tenor or plectrum guitar based on L-1, mahogany back and sides, bound body, sunburst.

| 1927-1933 | | $2,000 | $2,500 |
| 1934-1937 | | $1,500 | $2,200 |

TG-7
1934-1940. Tenor based on the L-7, sunburst.

| 1934-1940 | | $1,500 | $2,200 |

TG-25/TG-25 N
1962-1970. Acoustic flat-top, tenor guitar based on B-25, mahogany back and sides, natural or sunburst.

1962-1964		$700	$800
1965-1966		$600	$700
1967-1970		$500	$600

TG-50
1934-1958. Acoustic archtop, tenor guitar based on L-50, mahogany back and sides, sunburst.

1934-1940		$1,100	$1,400
1947-1949		$1,000	$1,300
1950-1958		$900	$1,200

Trini Lopez Deluxe
1964-1970. Double pointed cutaway, thinline archtop, 2 humbuckers, triple-bound, sunburst.

1964		$3,500	$4,500
1965-1966		$3,000	$4,000
1967-1970		$2,800	$3,000

Trini Lopez Standard
1964-1970. Double rounded cutaway, thinline archtop, 2 humbuckers, tune-o-matic bridge, trapeze tailpiece, single-bound, cherry, sparkling burgundy and Pelham Blue finishes.

1964	Cherry	$3,000	$4,000
1965-1966	Cherry	$2,400	$3,000
1965-1966	Sparkling Burgundy	$2,600	$3,300
1967-1970	Cherry	$2,300	$2,600
1967-1970	Sparkling Burgundy	$2,500	$2,900

U-2
1987-1989. Double-cut, 1 humbucker and 2 single-coil pickups, ebony or red, renamed Mach II in '90-'91.

| 1987-1991 | | $750 | $850 |

U-2 Showcase Edition
1988. November 1988 Guitar of the Month series, 250 made.

| 1988 | | $850 | $950 |

US-1/US-3
1986-1991. Double-cut maple top with mahogany back, 3 humbucker pickups (US-1), or 3 P-90s (US-3), standard production and Custom Shop.

| 1986-1991 | | $650 | $750 |

Victory MV II (MV 2)
1981-1984. Asymetrical double-cut with long horn, 3-way slider, maple body and neck, rosewood 'board, 2 pickups.

| 1981-1984 | | $700 | $1,100 |

Victory MV X (MV 10)
1981-1984. 3 humbuckers, 5-way switch, various colors.

| 1981-1984 | | $1,000 | $1,300 |

XPL Custom
1985-1986. Explorer-like shape, exposed humbuckers, locking tremolo, bound maple top, sunburst or white.

| 1985-1986 | | $600 | $700 |

Giffin
1977-1988, 1997-present. Professional and premium grade, production/custom, hollow-, semi-hollow-, and solidbody guitars built by luthier Roger Giffin in West San Fernando Valley, California. For '77-'88, Giffin's shop was in London. From '88 to '93, he worked for the Gibson Custom Shop in California as a Master Luthier. In '97, Giffin

MODEL YEAR	FEATURES	EXC. COND. LOW	HIGH

set up shop in Sweden for a year, moving back to California in the Spring of '98. He also built small numbers of instruments during '67-'76 and '94-'96 (when he had a repair business).

Micro Series

1997. Double-cut with long, sharp bass horn, bolt-on neck, quilted maple top over ash body, relatively small and light body, single and humbucker pickups.

1997		$650	$800

Model T

2000s. Double-cut solidbody, 1 bridge position P-90.

2000s		$550	$650

Gigliotti

2000-present. Premium grade, production/custom, electric guitars with a metal plate top and tone chambers and designed by Patrick Gigliotti in Tacoma, Washington.

GS

2004-present. Offset double-cut solidbody, 3 pickups, custom made to order.

2004-2005		$1,800	$1,900

Gila Eban Guitars

1979-present. Premium grade, custom, classical guitars built by luthier Gila Eban in Riverside, Connecticut.

Gilbert Guitars

1965-present. Custom classical guitars by luthiers John Gilbert and William Gilbert in Paso Robles, California. Son William has handled all production since 1991.

Girl Brand Guitars

1996-present. Premium-grade, production/custom, guitars built by luthier Chris Larsen in Tucson, Arizona.

Crossroadsgirl

2004. Single-cut, semi-hollow, 2 single-coils, various artistic custom option finishes and appointments.

2004		$1,500	$2,000

Gitane

2003-present. Classic Selmer-Maccaferri style jazz guitars made in China for Saga.

Gittler

1974-ca.1985. Minimalistic electric guitar designed by Allan Gittler, consisting basically of a thin rod with frets welded to it. A total of 560 were built, with Gittler making the first 60 in the U.S. from '74 to the early '80s. The remainder were made around '85 in Israel by the Astron corporation under a licensing agreement. Three Gittler basses were also built. Gittler emigrated to Israel in the early '80s and changed his name to Avraham Bar Rashi. He died in 2002. An U.S.-made Gittler is the only musical instrument in the Museum of Modern Art in New York.

Metal Skeleton Gittler

1971-1999.

1971-1982		$2,000	$3,500
1982-1999		$1,700	$1,900

Glendale

2004-present. Professional grade, production/custom, solidbody guitars built by luthier Dale Clark in Arlington, Texas.

GLF

1991-1997. Solidbody electric guitars built by luthier Kevin Smith in Minnesota. In '97 he started building his ToneSmith line of guitars.

Godin

1987-present. Intermediate and professional grade, production, solidbody electrics and nylon and steel string acoustic/electrics from luthier Robert Godin. They also build basses and mandolins. Necks and bodies are made in La Patrie, Quebec with final assembly in Berlin, New Hampshire. Godin is also involved in the Seagull, Norman, Art & Lutherie, and Patrick & Simon brand of guitars.

Acousticaster 6

1987-present. Thin line single-cut chambered maple body, acoustic/electric, maple neck, 6-on-a-side tuners, spruce top.

1987-1999		$450	$525
2000-2005		$475	$550

Acousticaster 6 Deluxe

1994-present. Acousticaster 6 with mahogany body.

1994-2005		$500	$650

Artisan ST I/ST I

1992-1998. Offset double-cut solidbody, birdseye maple top, 3 pickups.

1992-1998		$500	$600

Flat Five X

2002-2004. Single-cut, semi-hollow with f-holes, 3-way pickup system (magnetic to transducer).

2002-2004		$700	$800

G-1000/G-2000

1993-1996		$200	$325

Glissentar A11

2000-2004. Electric/acoustic nylon 11-string, solid cedar top, chambered maple body, fretless, natural.

2000-2004		$500	$600

Jeff Cook Signature

1994-1995. Quilted maple top, light maple back, 2 twin rail and 1 humbucker pickups.

1994-1995		$550	$650

LG/LGT

1995-present. Single-cut carved slab mahogany body, 2 Tetrad Combo pickups ('95-'97) or 2 Duncan SP-90 pickups ('98-present), various colors, satin lacquer finish. LGT with tremolo.

1997-2005		$300	$400

Gigliotti Special

Gittler

60s Goya Rangemaster

Goodall Standard

MODEL YEAR	FEATURES	EXC. COND. LOW	HIGH

LGX/LGXT/LGX-SA

1996-present. Single-cut maple-top carved solid-body, 2 Duncan humbuckers, various quality tops offered. LGXT with tremolo.

1997-2005	AA top	$700	$900
1997-2005	AAA top	$1,000	$1,200
1997-2005	Standard top	$600	$800
2000s	SA synth access	$1,000	$1,100

Montreal

2004-present. Chambered body carved from solid mahogany, f-holes, 2 humbuckers, saddle transducer, stereo mixing output.

2004-2005		$850	$950

Multiac Series

1994-present. Single-cut, thinline electric with solid spruce top, RMC Sensor System electronics, available in either nylon string or steel string versions, built-in EQ, program up/down buttons.

1994-2005	Nylon, classical	$800	$850
1994-2005	Steel string	$825	$875
2000-2005	Jazz SA	$850	$900

Radiator

1999-present. Single-cut, dual pickup, pearloid top, dot markers.

1999-2005		$225	$275

Solidac - Two Voice

2000-present Single-cut, 2-voice technology for electric or acoustic sound.

2000-2005		$300	$425

TC Signature

1980s-1999. Single-cut, quilted maple top, 2 Tetrad Combo pickups.

1990s		$550	$650

Golden Hawaiian

1920s-1930s. Private branded lap guitar most likely made by one of the many Chicago makers for a small retailer, publisher, cataloger, or teaching studio.

Guitars

1920s	Sunburst	$300	$500
1930s	Sunburst	$300	$500

Goodall

1972-present. Premium grade, custom flat-tops and nylon-strings, built by luthier James Goodall originally in California and, since '92, in Kailua-Kona, Hawaii.

Acoustic

1980s. Full-size, various models.

1980s		$2,000	$3,500

Gordon-Smith

1979-present. Intermediate and professional grade, production/custom, semi-hollow and solidbody guitars built by luthier John Smith in Partington, England.

Electric Guitars

2000s		$400	$800

MODEL YEAR	FEATURES	EXC. COND. LOW	HIGH

Gould Musical Instruments

Wholesale-importer owned by the Gould family since 1964, Rochester, Minnesota. Student-level imports.

Acoustic

1980s. D-size, laminated (WRM41) or solid wood top (WRM41ST).

1980s	WRM41	$75	$150
1980s	WRM41ST	$125	$175

Electric

1980s. Various models including Nighthawk, Snowbird, Warlock and Starfire.

1980s		$100	$175

Gower

1955-1960s. Built in Nashville by Jay Gower, later joined by his son Randy. Gower is also associated with Billy Grammer and Grammer guitars.

G-55-2 Flat-Top

1960s. Square shoulder-style flat-top, triple abalone rosette, abalone fretboard trim, small block markers, natural.

1960s		$1,200	$1,500

G-65 Flat-Top

1960s. Square shoulder-style flat-top, lower belly bridge with pearl dots on bridge, dot markers, sunburst.

1960s		$800	$1,200

Solidbody Electric

1960s. Mosrite influenced odd-shaped body, 2 single-coils, bolt neck, Bigsby bridge.

1960s		$500	$800

Goya

1955-present. Brand initially used by Hershman Musical Instrument Company of New York City, New York, in mid-'50s for acoustic guitars made in Sweden by Levin, particularly known for its classicals. From '58 to '61 they imported Hagstrom- and Galanti-made electrics labeled as Goya.

By '63 the company had become the Goya Musical Instrument Corporation, marketing primarily Goya acoustics. Goya was purchased by Avnet, Inc., prior to '66, when Avnet purchased Guild Guitars. In '69, Goya was purchased by Kustom which offered the instruments until '71. Probably some '70s guitars were made in Japan. The brand name was purchased by C.F. Martin in the mid-'70s, with Japanese-made acoustic guitars, solidbody electric guitars and basses, banjos and mandolins imported in around '78 and continuing through the '80s. The brand is currently used on Korean-made acoustic and acoustic/electric guitars, banjos and mandolins.

Classical

1955-1980s. Various models low- to high-end. Kustom ownership (imports) in the '70s and Martin ownership (Asia imports) in the '80s.

1955-1959		$175	$750
1960s		$150	$700
1970s		$75	$250
1980s		$75	$250

MODEL YEAR	FEATURES	EXC. COND. LOW	HIGH

Folk

1960-1980s. Various models low- to high-end. Kustom ownership (imports) in the '70s and Martin ownership (Asia imports) in the '80s.

1955-1959		$175	$750
1960s		$150	$700
1970s		$75	$250
1980s		$75	$250

Model 80/Model 90

1959-1962. Single-cut body, replaceable modular pickup assembly, sparkle top.

1959-1962		$750	$850

Panther S-3

1960s. Double-cut solidbody, 3 pickups, Panther S-3 Goya logo, volume and tone knobs with 6 upper bass bout switches, bolt-on neck.

1960s		$450	$600

Rangemaster

1967-1969. Double-cut with 2 offset double-coil pickups and lots of buttons, made by EKO, sunburst.

1967-1969		$450	$600

Graf, Oskar

1970-present. Luthier Oskar Graf builds his premium grade, production/custom flat-top, classical, and flamenco guitars in Clarendon, Ontario. He also builds basses and lutes.

Grammer

1965-1970. Founded by Bill Grammer then sold to Ampeg.

G-10

1965-1970. Solid Brazilian rosewood back and sides, solid spruce top, large crown-shaped bridge, pearl dot markers, natural.

1965-1970		$1,200	$1,600

G-20

1965-1970. Natural.

1965-1970		$1,200	$1,600

G-30

1965-1970. Natural.

1965-1970		$1,200	$1,600

G-58

1965-1970. Top-of-the-line Grammer, Brazilian rosewood back and sides, Adirondack spruce top.

1965-1970		$2,000	$2,300

S-30

1965-1970. Solid spruce top, solid ribbon mahogany back and sides.

1965-1970		$1,000	$1,200

Granada

1970s-1980s. Japanes-made acoustic, electric solid, semi-hollow and hollowbody guitars, many copies of classic American models. They also offered basses.

Solidbodies

Various copy models.

1970s		$200	$300

Granata Guitars

1989-present. Luthier Peter Granata builds his professional grade, custom, flat-top and resonator guitars in Oak Ridge, New Jersey.

Graveel

Production/custom, solidbody guitars built by luthier Dean Graveel in Indianapolis, Indiana.

GRD

1978-1982. High-end acoustic and electric guitars produced in Charles Fox's Guitar Research & Design Center in Vermont. GRD introduced the original thin-line acoustic-electric guitar to the world at the '78 Winter NAMM show.

Greco

1960s-present. Brand name used in Japan by Fuji Gen Gakki, maker of many Hoshino/Ibanez guitars; thus often Greco guitars are similar to Ibanez. During the '70s the company sold many high-quality copies of American designs, though by '75 they offered many weird-shaped original designs, including the Iceman and carved people shapes. By the late-'70s they were offering neck-through-body guitars. Currently owned by Kanda Shokai and offering solidbody, hollowbody and acoustic guitars.

Electric Archtop

1960s		$250	$600

Electric Solidbody

1960s		$250	$700

Electric Violin-Shape

1960s. Beatles violin-shape copy.

1960s		$250	$450

Folk 12-String

1960s		$175	$250

Green, Aaron

1990-present. Premium and presentation grade, custom, classical and flamenco guitars built by luthier Aaron Green in Waltham, Massachusetts.

Greene & Campbell

2002-2005. Luthier Dean Campbell builds his intermediate and professional grade, production/custom, solidbody guitars in Westwood, Massachusetts. Founding partner Jeffrey Greene left the company in '04; Greene earlier built guitars under his own name. In '05, Campbell changed the name to Campbell American Guitars.

Greene, Jeffrey

2000-2002. Professional grade, production/custom, electric solidbody guitars built by luthier Jeffrey Greene in West Kingston, Rhode Island. He went to work with Dean Campbell building the Greene & Campbell line of guitars.

1974 Grammer S-20

Green Concert Classical

GUITARS

Greenfield Philmore

1966 Gretsch Anniversary

Greenfield Guitars

1997-present. Premium grade, production/custom, flat-top, classical, and electric archtop guitars built by luthier Michael Greenfield in Montreal, Quebec.

Gretsch

1883-present. Currently Gretsch offers intermediate, professional, and premium grade, production, acoustic, solidbody, hollowbody, double neck, resonator and Hawaiian guitars. They also offer basses, amps and lap steels.

Previous brands included Gretsch, Rex, 20th Century, Recording King (for Montgomery Ward), Dorado (Japanese imports).

Founded by Friedrich Gretsch in Brooklyn, New York, making drums, banjos, tambourines, and toy instruments which were sold to large distributors including C. Bruno and Wurlitzer. Upon early death of Friedrich, son Fred Gretsch, Sr. took over business at age 15. By the turn of the century the company was also making mandolins. In the '20s, they were distributing Rex and 20th Century brands, some made by Gretsch, some by others such as Kay. Charles "Duke" Kramer joined Gretsch in '35. In '40 Gretsch purchased Bacon & Day banjos. Fred Gretsch, Sr. retired in '42 and was replaced by sons Fred, Jr. and Bill. Fred departs for Navy and Bill runs company until his death in '48, when Fred resumes control. After the war the decision was made to promote the Gretsch brand rather than selling to distributors, though some jobbing continues. Kramer becomes Chicago branch manager in '48.

In '67 Baldwin of Cincinnati buys Gretsch. During '70-'72 the factory relocates from Brooklyn to Booneville, Arkansas and company headquarters moves to Cincinnati. A '72 factory fire drastically reduces production for next two years. In '78 Baldwin buys Kustom amps and sells Gretsch to Kustom's Charlie Roy, and headquarters are moved to Chanute, Kansas. Duke Kramer retires in '80. Guitar production ends '80-'81. Ca. '83 ownership reverts back to Baldwin and Kramer was asked to arrange the sale of the company. In '84 Fred Gretsch III was contacted and in '85 Gretsch guitars came back to the Gretsch family and Fred Gretsch Enterprises, Ltd (FGE). Initial Gretsch Enterprise models were imports made by Japan's Terada Company. In '95, some U.S.-made models were introduced.

As of January 1, 2003, Fred Gretsch Enterprises, Ltd granted Fender Musical Instruments Corporation the exclusive rights to develop, produce, market and distribute Gretsch guitars worldwide where FMIC is responsible for all aspects of the Gretsch stringed instrument product lines and brands, including development of new products. Fred Gretsch consulted during the changeover and on product development and quality control.

12-String Electric Archtop (6075/6076)

1967-1972. 16" double-cut, 2 Super Tron pickups, 17" body option available, sunburst (6075) or natural (6076).

MODEL YEAR	FEATURES	EXC. COND. LOW	HIGH
1967-1972	Natural	$2,000	$2,300
1967-1972	Sunburst	$1,900	$2,200

12-String Flat-Top (6020)

1969-1972. 15 1/5" body, mahogany back and sides, spruce top, slotted headstock, dot markers.

1969-1972		$750	$900

Anniversary (6124/6125)

1958-1971, 1993-1999. Single-cut hollowbody archtop, 1 pickup (Filtron '58-'60, Hi-Lo Tron '61 on), bound body, named for Gretsch's 75th anniversary. 6124 is 2-tone greeen with 2-tone tan an option, 6125 sunburst. Model numbers revived in '90s.

1958-1959	Green 2-tone	$2,100	$2,300
1958-1959	Sunburst	$1,900	$2,100
1960-1961	2-tone green or tan	$2,000	$2,200
1960-1961	Sunburst	$1,900	$2,000
1962-1964	2-tone green or tan	$1,800	$2,150
1962-1964	Sunburst	$1,500	$1,800
1965-1966	Various colors	$1,300	$1,700
1967-1969	Various colors	$1,200	$1,500
1970-1971	Various colors	$1,100	$1,400

Anniversary (G6117/G6118)

1993-present. 2 pickup like Double Anniversary, 6118 in 2-tone green with (T) or without Bigsby, 6117 is sunburst.

1993-2005	Various colors	$1,100	$1,400

Astro-Jet (6126)

1965-1967. Solidbody electric, double-cut, 2 pickups, vibrato, 4/2 tuner arrangement, red top with black back and sides.

1965-1967		$1,400	$1,600

Atkins Axe (7685/7686)

1976-1980. Solidbody electric, single pointed cutaway, 2 pickups, ebony stain (7685) or red rosewood stain (7686), called the Super Axe with added on-board effects.

1976-1980		$1,200	$1,400

Atkins Super Axe (7680/7681)

1976-1981. Single pointed cutaway solidbody with built-in phaser and sustain, five knobs, three switches, Red Rosewood (7680) or Ebony (7681) stains.

1976-1981		$1,700	$2,100

Bikini (6023/6024/6025)

1961-1962. Solidbody electric, separate 6-string and bass neck-body units that slide into 1 of 3 body butterflies - 1 for the 6-string only (6023), 1 for bass only (6024), 1 for double neck (6 and bass - 6025). Components could be purchased separately.

1961-1962	6023/6024, single neck	$700	$1,000
1961-1962	6025, double neck	$1,600	$1,800

Black Falcon (I) G7593BK

1993-1998, 2003-2005. G63136BK with Bigsby and standard f-holes. Came back in '03 as Black Falcon I with wire handle Gretsch Bigsby tailpiece.

1993-1998		$1,650	$2,100

MODEL YEAR	FEATURES	EXC. COND. LOW	HIGH

Black Falcon G6136BK/TBK/DSBK
1992-1997, 2003-present. Black version of Falcon, single-cut, 2.75" body, oversize f-holes, G tailpiece, DSBK with DynaSonic pickups replaces Filter'Tron BK in '06. Had the Limited Edition 1955 designation for '96-'97. Bigsby-equipped TBK offered '04-present.

1992-1997		$1,650	$2,100

Black Falcon G7594BK
1992-1998. Black version of G7594 Falcon, double-cut, 2" thick body, Bigsby.

1992-1998		$1,650	$2,100

Black Hawk (6100/6101)
1967-1972. Hollowbody archtop, double-cut, 2 pickups, G tailpiece or Bigsby vibrato, bound body and neck, sunburst (6100) or black (6101).

1967-1969	6100, sunburst	$1,900	$2,300
1967-1969	6101, black	$1,800	$2,200
1970-1972	6100, sunburst	$1,800	$2,200
1970-1972	6101, black	$1,700	$2,100

Bo Diddley (6138)
2000-present. Reproduction of rectangle-shaped, semi-hollow guitar originally made for Diddley by Gretsch, Firebird Red.

2000-2005		$1,450	$1,600

Brian Setzer Nashville (G6120SSL, etc.)
1993-present. Hollowbody electric, double-cut, 2 Alnico PAF Filtertron pickups, based on the classic Gretsch 6120, formerly called the Brian Setzer Signature.

1993-2005	Western Orange	$1,800	$1,950

Broadkaster (Hollowbody)
1975-1980. Double-cut archtop, hollowbody, 2 pickups, natural or sunburst.

1975-1977	7603, Bigsby, natural	$1,100	$1,200
1975-1977	7604, Bigsby, sunburst	$1,000	$1,200
1975-1977	7607, G tailpiece, natural	$1,000	$1,100
1975-1977	7608, G tailpiece, sunburst	$900	$1,100
1977-1980	7609, red	$900	$1,100

Broadkaster (Solidbody)
1975-1979. Double-cut, maple body, 2 pickups, bolt-on neck, natural (7600) or sunburst (7601).

1975-1979		$650	$800

BST 1000 Beast
1979-1980. Single-cut solidbody, bolt-on neck, mahogany body, available with 1 pickup in walnut stain (8210) or red stain (8216) or 2 pickups in walnut (7617, 8215, 8217) or red stain (8211).

1979-1980		$550	$600

BST 2000 Beast
1979. Symmetrical double-cut solidbody of mahogany, 2 humbucking pickups, bolt-on neck, walnut stain (7620 or 8220) or red stain (8221).

1979		$600	$650

BST 5000 Beast
1979-1980. Asymmetrical double-cut solidbody, neck-thru, walnut and maple construction, 2 humbucker pickups, stud tailpiece, natural walnut/maple (8250).

1979-1980		$650	$700

Burl Ives (6004)
1949-1955. Flat-top acoustic, mahogany back and sides, bound body, natural top (6004).

1949-1955		$500	$650

Chet Atkins Country Gentleman (6122/7670)
1957-1981. Hollowbody, single-cut to late-'62 and double after, 2 pickups, painted f-holes until '72, real after, mahogany finish (6122). Model number changes to 7670 in '71.

1957-1960		$6,000	$8,000
1961		$5,500	$6,500
1962		$5,500	$6,500
1962-1963	George Harrison specs	$8,000	$12,000
1964		$4,200	$5,000
1965		$3,300	$4,900
1966		$3,200	$4,000
1967-1970		$2,800	$3,700
1971-1981	#7670	$2,300	$2,800

Chet Atkins Hollowbody (6120)
1954-1964. Archtop electric, single-cut to '61, double after, 2 pickups, vibrato, f-holes (real to '61 and fake after), G brand on top '54-'56, orange finish (6120). Renamed Chet Atkins Nashville in '64.

1954-1956		$9,000	$15,000
1957-1959		$7,000	$13,000
1960		$6,500	$7,000
1961		$6,000	$6,500
1961-1964		$3,500	$4,000

Chet Atkins Junior
1970. Archtop, single-cut, 1 pickup, vibrato, open f-holes, double-bound body, orange stain.

1970		$1,150	$1,250

Chet Atkins Nashville (6120/7660)
1964-1980. Replaced Chet Atkins Hollowbody (6120), electric archtop, double-cut, 2 pickups, amber red (orange). Renumbered 7660 in '71, reissued in '90 as the Nashville 6120.

1964		$3,500	$4,000
1965-1968		$2,800	$3,500
1969-1970		$2,500	$3,400
1971	#7660	$2,200	$3,200
1972	#7660	$1,900	$2,700
1973-1977	#7660	$1,800	$2,500
1978-1980	#7660	$1,400	$2,300

Chet Atkins Solidbody (6121)
1955-1963. Solidbody electric, single-cut, maple or knotty pine top, 2 pickups, Bigsby vibrato, G brand until '57, multi-bound top, brown mahogany, orange finish (6121).

1955-1956		$8,700	$10,200
1957	G brand	$8,500	$10,000
1957	No G brand	$7,000	$8,500
1958-1959		$6,500	$7,000
1960		$6,100	$6,500
1961-1963		$5,500	$6,100

Gretsch G6136TBK Black Falcon

Gretsch Chet Atkins 6120

1963 Gretsch Corvette

1966 Gretsch Country Club

Chet Atkins Tennessean (6119/7655)

1958-1980. Archtop electric, single-cut, 1 pickup until '61 and 2 after, vibrato. Renumbered as the 7655 in '71.

YEAR	FEATURES	LOW	HIGH
1958		$3,000	$4,000
1959		$3,000	$3,700
1960-1961	1 pickup	$3,000	$3,500
1961-1964	2 pickups	$2,900	$3,300
1965		$2,700	$3,100
1966-1967		$2,500	$3,000
1968-1970		$2,200	$2,700
1971-1972	#7655	$2,000	$2,400
1973-1980	#7655	$2,000	$2,200

Clipper (6185/6186/6187/7555)

1958-1975. Archtop electric, single-cut, sunburst, 1 pickup (6186) until '72 and 2 pickups (6185) from '72-'75, also available in 1 pickup natural (6187) from '59-'61.

YEAR	FEATURES	LOW	HIGH
1958-1961	#6186	$1,100	$1,400
1959-1961	#6187	$1,200	$1,500
1962-1967	#6186	$950	$1,100
1968-1971	#6186	$850	$950
1972-1975	#7555	$1,000	$1,200

Committee (7628)

1977-1980. Neck-thru electric solidbody, double-cut, walnut and maple body, 2 pickups, 4 knobs, natural.

YEAR	FEATURES	LOW	HIGH
1977-1980		$750	$900

Constellation

1955-1960. Renamed from Synchromatic 6030 and 6031, archtop acoustic, single-cut, G tailpiece, humped block inlay.

YEAR	FEATURES	LOW	HIGH
1955-1956		$2,000	$2,500
1957-1958		$1,900	$2,400
1959-1960		$1,700	$2,200

Convertible (6199)

1955-1958. Archtop electric, single-cut, 1 pickup, multi-bound body, G tailpiece, renamed Sal Salvadore in '58.

YEAR	FEATURES	LOW	HIGH
1955-1958		$3,000	$3,700

Corsair

1955-1960. Renamed from Synchromatic 100, archtop acoustic, bound body and headstock, G tailpiece, available in sunburst (6014), natural (6015) or burgundy (6016).

YEAR	FEATURES	LOW	HIGH
1955-1959		$850	$1,100
1960-1965		$750	$1,000

Corvette (Hollowbody)

1955-1959. Renamed from Electromatic Spanish, archtop electric, 1 pickup, f-holes, bound body, Electromatic on headstock, non-cut, sunburst (6182), natural or Jaguar Tan (6184), and ivory with rounded cutaway (6187).

YEAR	FEATURES	LOW	HIGH
1955-1959	6182, sunburst	$1,200	$1,500
1955-1959	6184, Jaguar Tan	$1,500	$1,800
1955-1959	6184, natural	$1,500	$1,800
1957-1959	6187, ivory	$1,500	$1,800

Corvette (Solidbody)

1961-1972, 1976-1978. Double-cut slab solidbody. Mahogany 6132 and cherry 6134 1 pickup for '61-'68. 2 pickup mahogany 6135 and cherry 7623 available by '63-'72 and '76-'78. From late-'61 through '63 a Twist option was offered featuring a red candy stripe 'guard. Platinum gray 6133 available for '61-'63 and the Gold Duke and Silver Duke sparkle finishes were offered in '66.

YEAR	FEATURES	LOW	HIGH
1961-1962	Mahogany, cherry	$900	$1,000
1961-1963	Platinum gray	$1,300	$1,600
1961-1963	Twist 'guard	$1,500	$1,800
1963-1965	Custom color	$1,100	$1,300
1963-1965	Mahogany, cherry, 1 pickup	$800	$900
1963-1965	Mahogany, cherry, 2 pickups	$1,000	$1,200
1966	Gold Duke	$1,300	$1,600
1966	Silver Duke	$1,300	$1,600
1966-1968	Mahogany, cherry, 1 pickup	$600	$800
1966-1968	Mahogany, cherry, 2 pickups	$900	$1,100
1969-1972	Mahogany, cherry, 2 pickups	$800	$1,000
1976-1978	7623, 2 pickups	$600	$750

Country Club

1954-1981. Renamed from Electro II Cutaway, archtop electric, single-cut, 2 pickups (Filter Trons after '57), G tailpiece, multi-bound, various colors.

YEAR	FEATURES	LOW	HIGH
1954-1956	Cadillac Green or natural	$3,800	$4,400
1954-1956	Sunburst	$2,800	$3,400
1957-1958	Cadillac Green or natural	$4,300	$4,900
1957-1958	Sunburst	$3,100	$3,800
1959	Cadillac Green or natural	$4,300	$4,700
1959	Sunburst	$3,000	$3,500
1960	Cadillac Green	$4,000	$4,600
1960	Sunburst	$2,900	$3,500
1961	Natural	$3,800	$4,300
1961	Sunburst	$2,800	$3,300
1962	Cadillac Green or natural	$3,500	$4,000
1962-1963	Sunburst	$2,700	$3,200
1964	Cadillac Green	$3,300	$4,000
1964	Sunburst	$2,700	$2,800
1965-1967	Sunburst or walnut	$2,400	$2,600
1970-1972	Various colors	$2,200	$2,400
1973-1981	Various colors	$2,000	$2,200

Country Club 1955 (G6196-1955)(FGE)

1995-1999. U.S.-made reissue of Country Club, single-cut, 2 DeArmond pickups, hand-rubbed lacquer finish.

YEAR	FEATURES	LOW	HIGH
1995-1999		$2,700	$2,900

Country Roc (7620)

1974-1978. Single-cut solidbody, 2 pickups, belt buckle tailpiece, western scene fretboard inlays, G brand, tooled leather side trim.

YEAR	FEATURES	LOW	HIGH
1974-1978		$1,900	$2,200

Deluxe Chet (7680/7681)

1972-1974. Electric archtop with rounded cutaway, Autumn Red (7680) or brown walnut (7681) finishes.

YEAR	FEATURES	LOW	HIGH
1972-1974		$2,300	$2,800

Deluxe Flat-Top (7535)

1972-1978 16" redwood top, mahogany back and sides.

MODEL YEAR	FEATURES	EXC. COND. LOW	HIGH
1972-1978		$1,700	$2,000

Double Anniversary Mono (6117/6118)

1958-1976. Archtop electric, single-cut, 2 pickups, stereo optional until '63, sunburst (6117) or green 2-tone (6118). Reissued in '93 as the Anniversary 6117 and 6118.

1958-1960	Green 2-tone	$2,900	$3,100
1958-1960	Sunburst	$2,700	$2,800
1960-1961	Green 2-tone	$2,600	$2,900
1960-1961	Sunburst	$2,500	$2,800
1962-1964	Green 2-tone	$2,400	$2,800
1962-1964	Sunburst	$2,100	$2,400
1963	Tan 2-tone	$2,400	$2,800
1965-1966	Various colors	$1,700	$2,100
1967-1969	Various colors	$1,600	$2,000
1970-1974	Various colors	$1,500	$1,700
1975-1976	Various colors	$1,400	$1,600

Double Anniversary Stereo (6111/6112)

1961-1963. One stereo channel/signal per pickup, sunburst (6111) or green (6112).

1961-1963	Green	$2,900	$3,200
1961-1963	Sunburst	$2,700	$3,000

Duane Eddy 6210DE

1997-2002. Import, 6120 style, 2 DeArmond single coils, Bigsby, orange.

1997-2002		$2,000	$2,200

Duo-Jet (6128)

1953-1971. Solidbody electric, single-cut until '61, double after, 2 pickups. black (6128) with a few special ordered in green, sparkle finishes were offered '63-'66, reissued in '90.

1953-1956	Black	$5,000	$6,300
1956-1957	Cadillac Green	$10,000	$11,000
1957	Black	$4,900	$5,700
1958-1960	Black	$4,600	$5,500
1961-1964	Black	$4,200	$4,800
1963-1966	Sparkle-gold, champagne, burgundy or tangerine	$4,500	$5,000
1964-1966	Silver sparkle	$4,500	$5,000
1965-1967	Black	$3,300	$3,900
1968-1971	Black	$2,400	$3,300

Duo-Jet Reissue (G6128)

1990-present. Reissue of the '50s solidbody, black, optional Bigsby (G6128T).

1990-2005		$1,200	$1,400

Duo-Jet Tenor

1959-1960. Electric tenor, 4 strings, block inlays, black.

1959-1960		$2,400	$3,500

Eldorado (6038/6039)

1959-1968. The smaller 17" version, named Fleetwood from '55 to '58, sunburst (6038) or natural (6039).

1960-1963	Natural	$1,900	$2,300
1960-1963	Sunburst	$1,700	$2,100
1964-1965	Natural	$1,700	$2,100

MODEL YEAR	FEATURES	EXC. COND. LOW	HIGH
1964-1965	Sunburst	$1,500	$1,900
1966-1968	Natural	$1,600	$2,000
1966-1968	Sunburst	$1,500	$1,800

Eldorado (6040/6041)

1955-1970, 1991-1997. This is the larger 18" version, renamed from Synchromatic 400, archtop acoustic, single-cut, triple-bound fretboard and peghead, sunburst (6040) or natural (6041). Reintroduced in '91, made by Heritage in Kalamazoo, as the G410 Synchromatic Eldorado in sunburst or natural (G410M).

1955-1959	Natural	$2,700	$3,100
1955-1959	Sunburst	$2,500	$2,800
1960-1963	Natural	$2,300	$2,700
1960-1963	Sunburst	$2,100	$2,400
1964-1965	Natural	$2,000	$2,400
1964-1965	Sunburst	$1,800	$2,200
1966-1967	Natural	$1,900	$2,300
1966-1967	Sunburst	$1,700	$2,100
1968-1969	Sunburst	$1,600	$2,000
1991-1997	Natural	$1,800	$2,200
1991-1997	Sunburst	$1,500	$1,900

Electro Classic (6006/6495)

1969-1973. Classical flat-top with piezo pickup.

1969-1970	#6006	$700	$1,000
1971-1973	#6495	$600	$1,000

Electro II Cutaway (6192/6193)

1951-1954. Archtop electric, single-cut, Melita bridge by '53, 2 pickups, f-holes, sunburst (6192) or natural (6193). Renamed Country Club in '54.

1951-1954	Natural	$3,300	$4,200
1951-1954	Sunburst	$2,300	$3,200

Electromatic Spanish (6185/6185N)

1940-1955. Hollowbody, 17" wide, 1 pickup, sunburst (6185) or natural (6185N). Renamed Corvette (hollowbody) in '55.

1940-1949	Sunburst	$1,300	$1,500
1950-1955	Natural	$1,750	$1,950
1950-1955	Sunburst	$1,300	$1,500

Fleetwood (6038/6039)

1955-1958. Named Synchronmatic prior to '55, sunburst (6038) or natural (6039). Renamed Eldorado in '59, available by custom order.

1955-1968		$2,500	$2,800

Folk/Folk Singing (6003/7505/7506)

1963-1975. Lower-model of Gretsch flat-tops, 14 1/4", mahogany back and sides. Renamed from Jimmie Rodgers model, renamed Folk Singing in '63.

1963-1965		$600	$900
1966-1969		$500	$800
1970-1975		$450	$700

Golden Classic (Hauser Model/Model 6000)

1961-1969. Grand Concert body size, nylon-string classical, 14 1/4" spruce top, mahogany back and sides, multiple inlaid sound hole purfling, inlaid headstock.

1961-1969		$500	$1,000

1959 Gretsch Double Anniversary

1956 Gretsch Duo Jet

Gretsch Monkees

Gretsch Rancher

MODEL YEAR	FEATURES	EXC. COND. LOW	HIGH

Grand Concert (6003)
1955-1959. Lower-model of Gretsch flat-tops, 14 1/4", mahogany back and sides. Renamed from Model 6003 and renamed Jimmie Rodgers in '59.

1955-1959		$450	$700

Jet Fire Bird (6131)
1955-1971. Solidbody electric, single-cut until '61, double '61-'71, 2 pickups, black body with red top, reissued in '90.

1955-1956		$4,800	$5,200
1957		$4,600	$5,100
1958-1960		$4,300	$4,800
1961-1964		$3,600	$4,500
1965-1967		$2,600	$3,700
1968-1971	Super Trons	$2,000	$2,600

Jet Firebird Reissue (G6131/G6131T)
1989-1997, 2003-present. Based on single-cut '58 specs, red top, 2 FilterTrons, thumbprint markers, gold hardware for '91-'05, currently chrome. Bigsby available (T). Non-Bigsby 6131 ends in '05. DynaSonic-equipped TDS starts in '05.

2003-2005		$1,200	$1,400

Jimmie Rodgers (6003)
1959-1962. 14" flat-top with round hold, mahogany back and sides, renamed from Grand Concert and renamed Folk Singing in '63.

1959-1962		$500	$700

Jumbo Synchromatic (125F)
1947-1955. 17" flat-top, triangular soundhole, bound top and back, metal bridge anchor plate, adjustable wood bridge, natural top with sunburst back and sides or optional translucent white-blond top and sides.

1947-1955	Natural	$2,000	$3,000
1947-1955	White-blond	$2,100	$3,500

Model 25 (Acoustic)
1933-1939. 16" archtop, no binding on top or back, dot markers, sunburst.

1933-1939		$650	$800

Model 30 (Acoustic)
1939-1949. 16" archtop, top binding, dot markers, sunburst.

1939-1949		$700	$900

Model 35 (Acoustic)
1933-1949. 16" archtop, single-bound top and back, dot markers, sunburst.

1933-1949		$800	$1,000

Model 50/50R (Acoustic)
1936-1939. Acoustic archtop, F-holes. Model 50R has round soundhole.

1936-1939		$900	$1,200

Model 65 (Acoustic)
1933-1939. Archtop acoustic, bound body, amber.

1933-1939		$1,000	$1,300

Model 6003
1951-1955. 14 1/4", mahogany back and sides, renamed Grand Concert in '55.

1951-1954		$500	$700

MODEL YEAR	FEATURES	EXC. COND. LOW	HIGH

Monkees
1966-1969. Hollowbody electric, double-cut, 2 pickups, Monkees logo on 'guard, bound top, f-holes and neck, vibrato, red.

1966-1969		$1,900	$2,400

New Yorker
Ca.1949-1970. Archtop acoustic, f-holes, sunburst.

1949-1951		$750	$900
1952-1954		$700	$850
1955-1959		$650	$800
1960-1965		$600	$750
1966-1970		$550	$700

Ozark/Ozark Soft String (6005)
1965-1968. 16" classical, rosewood back and sides.

1965-1968		$700	$1,200

Princess (6106)
1963. Corvette-type solidbody double-cut, 1 pickup, vibrato, gold parts, colors available were white/grape, blue/white, pink/white, or white/gold, often sold with the Princess amp.

1963		$1,900	$2,300

Rally (6104/6105)
1967-1969. Archtop, double-cut, 2 pickups, vibrato, racing strip on truss rod cover and pickguard, green or yellow.

1967-1969		$1,800	$2,200

Rambler (6115)
1957-1961. Small body electric archtop, single-cut, 1 pickup, G tailpiece, bound body and headstock.

1957-1961		$1,400	$1,700

Rancher
1954-1980. Flat-top acoustic, triangle soundhole, Western theme inlay, G brand until '61 and '75 and after, golden red (orange), reissued in '90.

1954-1955	G brand	$4,000	$4,700
1956-1957	G brand	$4,000	$4,700
1958-1961	G brand	$3,500	$4,200
1962-1964	No G brand	$3,000	$3,700
1965-1966	No G brand	$2,500	$3,200
1967-1969	No G brand	$2,000	$2,700
1970-1974	No G brand	$1,900	$2,200
1975-1980	G brand	$1,900	$2,200

Roc I/Roc II (7635/7621)
1974-1976. Electric solidbody, mahogany, single-cut, Duo-Jet-style body, 1 pickup (7635) or 2 pickups (7621), bound body and neck.

1974-1976	Roc I	$900	$1,100
1974-1977	Roc II	$1,000	$1,500

Roc Jet
1969-1980. Electric solidbody, single-cut, 2 pickups, adjustamatic bridge, black, cherry, pumpkin or walnut.

1970-1972		$1,500	$2,100
1973-1976		$1,400	$1,900
1977-1980		$1,000	$1,500

The *Vintage Guitar Price Guide* shows low to high values for items in all-original excellent condition, and, where applicable, with original case or cover.

MODEL YEAR	FEATURES	EXC. COND. LOW	HIGH

Round-Up (6130)
1954-1960. Electric solidbody, single-cut, 2 pickups, G brand, belt buckle tailpiece, maple, pine, knotty pine or orange. Reissued in '90.

1954-1956	Knotty pine (2 knots)	$15,000	$18,000
1954-1956	Knotty pine (4 knots)	$18,000	$23,000
1954-1956	Mahogany (few made)	$9,500	$13,000
1954-1956	Maple	$9,500	$13,000
1954-1956	Pine	$10,000	$14,000
1957-1960	Orange	$9,000	$13,000

Round-Up Reissue (G6121/G6121W)
1989-1995, 2003-present. Based on the '50s model, Western Orange, G brand.

1989-1995	$1,300	$1,500
2003-2005	$1,300	$1,500

Sal Fabraio (6117)
1964-1968. Double-cut thin electric archtop, distinctive cats-eye f-holes, 2 pickups, sunburst, ordered for resale by guitar teacher Sal Fabraio.

1964-1968	$2,100	$2,400

Sal Salvador (6199)
1958-1968. Electric archtop, single-cut, 1 pickup, triple-bound neck and headstock, sunburst.

1958-1959	$3,300	$3,500
1960-1962	$3,000	$3,200
1963-1964	$2,400	$2,600
1965-1966	$2,200	$2,500
1967-1968	$2,000	$2,300

Sho Bro (Hawaiian/Spanish)
1969-1978. Flat-top acoustic, multi-bound, resonator, lucite fretboard, Hawaiian version non-cut, square neck and Spanish version non- or single-cut, round neck.

1969-1978	Hawaiian	$750	$1,000
1969-1978	Spanish	$750	$1,000

Silver Classic (Hauser Model/Model 6001)
1961-1969. Grand Concert body size, nylon-string classical. Similar to Golden Classic but with less fancy appointments.

1961-1969	$400	$700

Silver Falcon G6136SL (1955)
1993-1999, 2003-present. Silver version of White Falcon G6136 with G tailpiece. Had the 1955 designation in the '90s.

1995-1999	$2,000	$2,500

Silver Falcon G7594SL
1995-1999. Silver version of G7594 White Falcon, double-cut, 2" thick body, Bigsby.

1995-1999	$1,900	$2,400

Silver Jet (6129)
1954-1963. Solidbody electric, single-cut until '61, double '61-'63, 2 pickups, Duo-Jet with silver sparkle top, reissued in '90. Optional sparkle colors were offered but were not given their own model numbers; refer to Duo-Jet listing for optional colors.

1954-1956	Silver	$8,000	$10,500
1957	Silver	$8,800	$9,800

MODEL YEAR	FEATURES	EXC. COND. LOW	HIGH
1958-1960	Silver	$6,500	$8,800
1961-1963	Silver, double-cut	$6,000	$8,000

Silver Jet 1957 Reissue (G6129-1957)
1990-present. Reissue of single-cut '50s Silver Jet, silver sparkle.

1990-2006	$1,200	$1,500

Songbird (Sam Goody 711)
1967-1968. Standard body thinline double cutaway with G soundholes, offered by Sam Goody of New York.

1967-1968	$1,900	$2,400

Southern Belle (7176)
1983. Electric archtop, walnut, Country Gentleman parts from the late-'70s assembled in Mexico and marketed as Southern Belle.

1983	$1,100	$1,300

Sparkle Jet
1994-present. Electric solidbody, single-cut, 2 pickups, Duo-Jet with sparkle finish.

1995-2005	$1,300	$1,500

Streamliner Double Cutaway (6102/6103)
1968-1973. Reintroduced from single-cut model, electric archtop, double-cut, 2 pickups, G tailpiece, cherry or sunburst.

1968-1969	$1,500	$2,000
1970-1973	$1,400	$1,900

Streamliner Single Cutaway (6189/6190/6191)
1955-1959. Electric archtop, single-cut, maple top, G tailpiece, 1 pickup, multi-bound, Bamboo Yellow (6189), sunburst (6190), or natural (6191), name reintroduced as a double-cut in '68.

1955-1959	$2,100	$2,500

Sun Valley (6010/7515/7514)
1959-1977. Flat-top acoustic, laminated Brazilian rosewood back and sides, multi-bound top, natural or sunburst.

1959-1964	$800	$1,300
1965-1969	$700	$1,200
1970-1977	$600	$1,000

Super Chet (7690/7690-B/7691/7691-B)
1972-1980. Electric archtop, single rounded cutaway, 2 pickups, gold hardware, mini control knobs along edge of 'guard, Autumn Red or walnut.

1972-1976	$2,900	$3,500
1977-1980	$2,500	$3,000

Supreme (7545)
1972-1978. Flat-top 16", spruce top, mahogany or rosewood body options, gold hardware.

1972-1978	Mahogany	$1,300	$1,600
1972-1979	Rosewood	$1,700	$2,000

Synchromatic (6030/6031)
1951-1954. 17" acoustic archtop, becomes Constellation in '55.

1951-1955	$1,700	$2,000

Synchromatic (6038/6039)
1951-1955. 17" acoustic archtop, single-cut, G tailpiece, multi-bound, sunburst (6038) or natural (6039), renamed Fleetwood in '55.

1951-1955	Sunburst	$1,900	$2,200

1954 Gretsch Roundup (6130)

1954 Gretsch Silver Jet

1940s Gretsch
Synchromatic 400

Gretsch White Falcon 6136T

MODEL YEAR	FEATURES	EXC. COND. LOW	HIGH

Synchromatic 75
1939-1949. Acoustic archtop, f-holes, multi-bound, large floral peghead inlay.

1939-1949		$1,200	$1,500

Synchromatic X75F
1947-1949. Acoustic flat-top, maple back and sides, triangular soundhole, sunburst, renamed Synchromatic Sierra in '49.

1947-1949		$1,200	$1,500

Synchromatic 100
1939-1955. Renamed from No. 100F, acoustic archtop, double-bound body, amber, sunburst or natural, renamed Corsair in '55.

1939-1949	Natural	$1,400	$1,700
1939-1949	Sunburst	$1,000	$1,400
1950-1955	Sunburst	$1,000	$1,300

Synchromatic 160 (6028/6029)
1939-1943, 1947-1951. Acoustic archtop, catseye soundholes, maple back and sides, triple-bound, natural or sunburst.

1939-1943	Sunburst	$1,300	$1,700
1947-1951	Sunburst	$1,200	$1,400
1948-1951	Natural	$1,400	$1,700

Synchromatic 200
1939-1949. Acoustic archtop, cats-eye soundholes, maple back and sides, multi-bound, gold-plated hardware, amber or natural.

1939-1949		$2,000	$2,200

Synchromatic 300
1939-1955. Acoustic archtop, cats-eye soundholes until '51 and f-holes after, multi-bound, natural or sunburst.

1939-1949	Natural	$2,500	$3,000
1939-1949	Sunburst	$2,200	$2,700
1950-1955	Natural	$2,200	$2,700
1950-1955	Sunburst	$2,000	$2,500

Synchromatic 400
1940-1955. Acoustic archtop, cats-eye soundholes until '51 and f-holes after, multi-bound, gold hardware, natural or sunburst.

1940-1949	Natural	$6,000	$6,500
1940-1949	Sunburst	$5,500	$6,000
1950-1955	Natural	$5,500	$6,000
1950-1955	Sunburst	$5,000	$5,500

Synchromatic 400F/6042 Flat Top
1947-1955. 18" flat top, renamed 6042 in the late '40s.

1947-1948	400F	$4,500	$5,500
1949-1959	6042	$4,000	$5,000

Synchromatic Limited (G450/G450M)
1997. Acoustic archtop, hand carved spruce (G450) or maple (G450M) top, floating pickup, sunburst, only 50 were to be made.

1997	Maple	$1,300	$1,500
1997	Spruce	$1,200	$1,400

Synchromatic Sierra
1949-1955. Renamed from Synchromatic X75F (see below), acoustic flat-top, maple back and sides, triangular soundhole, sunburst.

1949-1955		$1,200	$1,500

MODEL YEAR	FEATURES	EXC. COND. LOW	HIGH

TK 300 (7624/7625)
1977-1981. Double-cut maple solidbody, 1 humbucker, bolt-on neck, six-on-a-side tuners, hockey stick headstock, Autumn Red or natural.

1977-1981		$600	$800

Town and Country (6021)
1954-1959. Renamed from Jumbo Synchromatic 125 F, flat-top acoustic, maple back and sides, triangular soundhole, multi-bound.

1954-1959		$2,000	$2,300

TW300T (Traveling Wilburys)
1988-1990. Promotional guitar, solidbody electric, single-cut, 1 and 2 pickups, 6 variations, graphics.

1988-1990		$300	$325

Van Eps 7-String (6079/6080)
1968-1978. Electric archtop, single-cut, 2 pickups, 7 strings, sunburst or walnut.

1968-1978		$2,500	$3,000

Viking (6187/6188/6189)
1964-1975. Electric archtop, double-cut, 2 pickups, vibrato, sunburst (6187), natural (6188) or Cadillac Green (6189).

1964-1967	Cadillac Green	$2,900	$3,500
1964-1967	Natural	$2,900	$3,500
1964-1967	Sunburst	$2,700	$3,300
1968-1970	Cadillac Green	$2,300	$2,900
1968-1970	Natural	$2,300	$2,900
1968-1970	Sunburst	$2,300	$2,700
1971-1972	Various colors	$2,100	$2,300
1973-1975	Various colors	$2,000	$2,100

Wayfarer Jumbo (6008)
1969-1971. Flat-top acoustic dreadnought, non-cut, maple back and sides, multi-bound.

1969-1971		$800	$1,200

White Falcon Mono (6136/7595)
1955-1981. Includes the single-cut 6136 of '55-'61, the double-cut 6136 of '62-'70, and the double-cut 7594 of '71-'81.

1955	Single-cut 6136	$24,000	$25,000
1956		$22,000	$23,000
1957		$22,000	$23,000
1958		$22,000	$23,000
1959-1961		$22,000	$23,000
1962-1963	Double-cut 6136	$9,000	$10,000
1964		$8,000	$9,000
1965		$6,500	$8,500
1966		$6,500	$8,000
1967-1969		$5,500	$7,500
1970		$4,500	$6,000
1971-1972	Model 7594	$4,500	$5,900
1973-1979		$4,000	$5,600
1980-1981		$3,500	$5,300

White Falcon Stereo (6137/7595)
1958-1981. Features Project-O-Sonic Stereo, includes Includes the single-cut 6137 of '58-'61, the double-cut 6137 of '62-'70, and the double-cut 7595 of '71-'81.

1958	Early stereo specs	$24,000	$28,000
1959-1961	Single-cut 6137	$22,000	$26,000
1962-1963	Double-cut 6137	$11,000	$15,500
1964		$9,000	$14,000

MODEL YEAR	FEATURES	EXC. COND. LOW	HIGH
1965		$7,000	$10,000
1966		$7,000	$9,000
1967-1969		$6,000	$8,500
1970		$5,000	$6,500
1971-1972	Model 7595	$5,000	$6,400
1973-1979		$4,600	$6,400
1980-1981		$4,000	$6,100

White Falcon G6136-1955 Custom USA

1995-1999. U.S.-made, single-cut, DynaSonic pick-ups, gold sparkle appointments, rhinestone embedded knobs, white. In '04, Current U.S. model called G6136CST is released. The import White Falcon has sometimes been listed with the 1955 designation and is not included here.

1995-1999		$4,000	$5,700

White Falcon G7593/G7593 I

1993-present. G6136 with added Bigsby. Currently sold as G7593 White Falcon I.

1991-2005		$2,300	$2,600

White Falcon I/G6136

1991-present. Single-cut, white, 2.75" thick body, Cadillac G tailpiece. Called the White Falcon I for '91-'92 (not to be confused with current White Falcon I G7593). See Black and Silver Falcons under those listings.

1991-2005		$2,300	$2,600

White Falcon II/G7594

1991-present. Double-cut, white, 2" thick body, Bigsby. Called the White Falcon II for '91-'92, the G7594 for '93-ca. '02, and White Falcon II G7594 since.

1991-2005		$2,200	$2,500

White Penguin (6134)

1955-1964. Electric solidbody, single-cut until '62, double '62-'64, 2 pickups (DeArmond until '58 then Filter Tron), fewer than 100 made, white, gold sparkle bound, gold-plated parts. More than any other model, there seems a higher concern regarding forgery.

1956-1958		$80,000	$105,000
1959-1960		$75,000	$90,000
1961-1962		$75,000	$80,000
1962-1964		$65,000	$75,000

White Penguin G6134

1996-present. White, single-cut, metalflake binding, gold hardware, jeweled knobs, Cadillac G tailpiece.

1996-2005		$3,000	$3,200

Greven

1969, 1975-present. Luthier John Greven builds his premium grade, production/custom, acoustic guitars in Portland, Oregon.

Griffin String Instruments

1976-present. Luthier Kim Griffin builds his professional and premium grade, production/custom, parlor, steel-string, and classical guitars in Greenwich, New York.

Grimes Guitars

1974-present. Premium and presentation grade, custom, flat-tops, nylon-strings, archtops, semi-hollow electrics made by luthier Steve Grimes originally in Port Townsend, Washington, and since '82 in Kula, Hawaii.

Groove Tools

2002-2004. Korean-made, production, intermediate grade, 7-string guitars that were offered by Conklin Guitars of Springfield, Missouri. They also offered basses.

Grosh, Don

1993-present. Professional and premium grade, production/custom, solid and semi-hollow body guitars built by luthier Don Grosh in Santa Clarita, California. He also builds basses. Grosh worked in production for Valley Arts from '84-'92. Guitars generally with bolt necks until '03 when set-necks were added to the line.

Classical Electric

1990s. Single-cut solidbody with nylon strings and piezo-style hidden pickup, highly figured top.

1990s		$1,300	$1,600

Custom S Bent Top

Offset double-cut, figured maple carved top, 2 pickups.

2003		$1,300	$1,600

Custom T Carve Top

Single-cut, figured maple carved top, 2 pickups.

2003		$1,300	$1,600

Retro Classic

1993-present. Offset double-cut, 3 pickups.

2001		$1,300	$1,600

Retro Vintage T

1993-present. Single-cut, black 'guard.

2001		$1,300	$1,600

Gruen Acoustic Guitars

1999-present. Luthier Paul Gruen builds his professional grade, custom steel-string guitars in Chapel Hill, North Carolina. His speciality is his E.Q. model, which features 5 soundholes, 4 of which can be plugged with wooden stoppers to give different tonal balances.

Gruggett

Mid 1960s-present. In the 1960s, luthier Bill Gruggett worked with Mosrite and Hallmark guitars as well as building electric guitars under his own name in Bakersfield, California. He still makes his Stradette model for Hallmark guitars.

Guernsey Resophonic Guitars

1989-present. Production/custom, resonator guitars built by luthier Ivan Guernsey in Marysville, Indiana.

Gretsch White Penguin

Grosh Retro Classic

GUITARS

Guild D-35

*1969 Guild D-40
Bluegrass Jubilee*

MODEL YEAR	FEATURES	EXC. COND. LOW	HIGH

Guild

1952-present. Professional and premium grade, production/custom, acoustic, acoustic/electric, hollowbody and semi-hollowbody guitars. Founded in New York City by jazz guitarist Alfred Dronge, employing many ex-Epiphone workers. The company was purchased by Avnet, Inc., in '66 and the Westerly, Rhode Island factory was opened in '68. Hoboken factory closed in '71 and headquarters moved to Elizabeth, New Jersey. Company was Guild Musical Instrument Corporation in '86 but was in bankruptcy in '88. Purchased by Faas Corporation, New Berlin, Wisconsin, which became the U.S. Musical Corporation. The brand was purchased by Fender Musical Instrument Corporation in '95. The Guild Custom Shop opened in Nashville in '97. The Guild Custom Shop remains in Nashville, while all other Guild U.S. production has been moved to Corona, California.

A-50
1994-1996. Original A-50 models can be found under the Cordoba A-50 listing, the new model drops the Cordoba name, size 000 flat top, spruce top, Indian rosewood body.

1994-1996		$1,000	$1,200

Aragon F-30
1954-1986. Acoustic flat-top, spruce top, laminated maple arched back (mahogany back and sides by '59), reintroduced as just F-30 in '98.

1954-1959		$1,200	$1,700
1960-1969		$1,100	$1,600
1970-1986		$800	$1,500

Aragon F-30 NT
1959-1985. Natural finish version of F-30.

1959-1969		$1,200	$1,800
1970-1985		$900	$1,600

Aragon F-30 R
1973-1995. Rosewood back and sides version of F-30, sunburst.

1973-1979		$950	$1,650

Aristocrat M-75
1955-1963, 1967-1968. Electric archtop, single-cut, 2 pickups, blond or sunburst, name changed to Bluesbird M-75 in '68.

1955-1959		$2,900	$3,200
1960-1963		$2,400	$2,900
1967-1968		$1,500	$2,500

Aristocrat M-75 Tenor
Mid-late 1950s. Tenor version of 6-string Aristocrat electric, dual soapbar pickups, 4 knobs.

1950s		$2,900	$3,200

Artist Award
1961-1999. Renamed from Johnny Smith Award, single-cut electric archtop, floating DeArmond pickup (changed to humbucker in '80), multi-bound, gold hardware, sunburst or natural.

1961-1969		$4,500	$6,000
1970-1979		$4,200	$5,000
1980-1989		$3,800	$4,700
1990-1999		$3,500	$4,500

MODEL YEAR	FEATURES	EXC. COND. LOW	HIGH

Artist F-312 12-String
1963-1973. Flat-top, rosewood back and sides, spruce top, no board inlay (but some in '72 may have dots).

1964-1968	Brazilian rosewood	$2,500	$3,000
1969-1973	Indian rosewood	$1,400	$2,000

Bluegrass D-25/D-25 M
1968-1999. Flat-top, mahogany top until '76, spruce after, mahogany back and sides, various colors, called Bluegrass D-25 M in late-'70s and '80s, listed as D-25 in '90s.

1968-1979		$750	$950
1980-1989		$725	$850
1990-1999		$675	$800

Bluegrass D-25-12
1987-1992, 1996-1999. 12-string version of D-25.

1987-1992		$700	$850
1996-1999		$700	$800

Bluegrass D-35
1966-1988. Acoustic flat-top, spruce top and mahogany back and sides, rosewood 'board and bridge, natural.

1966-1969		$825	$1,000
1970-1979		$775	$950
1980-1988		$750	$900

Bluegrass F-47
1963-1976. 16" narrow-waist style, mahogany sides and back, acoustic flat-top, spruce top, mahogany back and sides, bound rosewood 'board and bridge, natural.

1963-1969		$1,500	$2,500
1970-1976		$1,400	$2,200

Bluegrass Jubilee D-40
1963-1992. Acoustic flat-top, spruce top, mahogany back and sides, rosewood 'board and bridge, natural. Has been reissued.

1963-1969		$1,200	$2,000
1970-1979		$1,150	$1,800
1980-1992		$1,100	$1,600

Bluegrass Jubilee D-40 C
1975-1991. Acoustic flat-top, single Florentine cutaway, mahogany back and sides, rosewood 'board and bridge, natural.

1975-1979		$1,050	$1,800
1980-1991		$1,000	$1,600

Bluegrass Jubilee D-44
1965-1972. Acoustic flat-top, spruce top, pearwood back and sides, ebony 'board, rosewood bridge.

1965-1969		$1,200	$2,000
1970-1972		$1,100	$1,800

Bluegrass Jubilee D-44 M
1971-1979. Acoustic flat top, spruce top, maple back & sides, ebony fingerboard, rosewood bridge.

1971-1979		$1,200	$2,000

Bluegrass Special D-50
1963-1993. Acoustic flat-top, spruce top, rosewood back and sides, ebony fretboard, multi-bound.

1963-1968	Brazilian rosewood	$3,000	$3,800
1969-1979		$2,100	$2,400
1980-1993		$1,100	$1,600

MODEL YEAR	FEATURES	EXC. COND. LOW	HIGH

Blues 90

Ca. 1997-present. Single-cut with 2 P-90 style pickups.

1997-1998		$1,000	$1,300

Bluesbird M-75 (Hollowbody)

1968-1970. Reintroduced from Aristocrat M-75, thinbody electric archtop of maple, spruce or mahogany, single-cut, 2 pickups, reintroduced as a solidbody in '70.

1968-1970		$1,500	$2,400

Bluesbird M-75 (Solidbody)

1970-1978. Solidbody version of hollowbody Bluesbird M-75, mahogany body, rounded cutaway, 2 pickups.

1970-1978		$1,300	$1,500

Bluesbird (Reintroduced)

1998-2004. AAA flamed top.

1998-2001		$1,200	$1,350
2002-2004		$1,100	$1,300

Brian May BHM-1

1984-1987. Electric solidbody, double-cut, vibrato, 3 pickups, bound top and back, red or green, Brian May Pro, Special and Standard introduced in '94.

1984-1987		$2,200	$2,600

Brian May Pro

1994-1995. Electric solidbody, double-cut, vibrato, 3 pickups, bound top and back, various colors.

1994-1995		$1,900	$2,200

CA-100 Capri

1956-1973. Acoustic archtop version of CE-100, sharp Florentine cutaway, solid spruce top, laminated maple back and sides, rosewood 'board and bridge, nickel-plated metal parts, natural or sunburst.

1956-1959		$1,100	$1,800
1960-1969		$1,100	$1,800
1970-1973		$1,100	$1,800

Capri CE-100

1956-1985. Electric archtop, single Florentine cutaway, 1 pickup (2 pickups by '83), maple body, Waverly tailpiece, sunburst, in '59-'82 CE-100 D listed with 2 pickups.

1956-1959		$1,400	$2,000
1960-1969		$1,200	$1,700
1970-1979		$1,100	$1,600
1980-1985		$1,100	$1,400

Capri CE-100 D

1956-1982. Electric archtop, single Florentine cutaway, 2 pickups, maple body, sunburst, Waverly tailpiece (D dropped, became the Capri CE-100 in '83).

1956-1959		$1,700	$2,300
1960-1969		$1,400	$2,000
1970-1979		$1,300	$1,900
1980-1982		$1,200	$1,700

Capri CE-100 T Tenor

1950s. Electric-archtop Capri 4-string tenor guitar, sunburst.

1956		$1,400	$2,000

Cordoba A-50

1961-1972. Acoustic archtop, lowest-end in the Guild archtop line, named Granda A-50 prior to '61.

1961-1972		$600	$650

Cordoba T-50 Slim

1961-1973. Thinbody version of Cordoba X-50.

1961-1973		$950	$1,400

Cordoba X-50

1961-1970. Electric archtop non-cut, laminated maple body, rosewood 'board, 1 pickup, nickel-plated parts.

1961-1970		$950	$1,400

Custom F-412 12-String

1968-1986. Special order only from '68-'74, then regular production, 17" wide body 12-string version of F-50 flat-top, spruce top, maple back and sides, arched back, 2-tone block inlays, gold hardware, natural finish.

1968-1969		$1,800	$2,400
1970-1979		$1,600	$2,200
1980-1986		$1,500	$1,900

Custom F-512 12-String

1968-1986, 1990. Rosewood back and sides version of F-412.

1968-1969		$1,900	$2,500
1970-1979		$1,700	$2,300
1980-1986		$1,600	$2,000

Custom F-612 12-String

1972-1973. Acoustic 12-string, similar to Custom F-512, but with 18" body, fancy mother-of-pearl inlays, and black/white marquee body, neck and headstock binding..

1972-1973	Brazilian rosewood	$3,000	$3,700
1972-1973	Indian rosewood	$2,100	$2,700

Custom Shop 45th Anniversary

1997. Built in Guild's Nashville Custom Shop, all solid wood, spruce top, maple back and sides, with high-end appointments.

1997	Natural, Gold hardware	$2,200	$2,500

D-4 Series

1991-2002. Dreadnought flat-top, mahogany sides, dot markers.

1991-2002	6-String	$500	$550
1992-1999	12-String	$625	$700

D-6 (D-6 E/D-6 HG/D-6 HE)

1992-1995. Flat-top, 15 3/4", mahogany back and sides, natural satin non-gloss finish, options available.

1992-1995		$600	$700

D-15 Mahogany Rush

1983-1988. Dreadnought flat-top, mahogany body and neck, rosewood 'board, dot inlays, stain finish.

1983-1988		$650	$750

D-16 Mahogany Rush

1984-1986. Like D-15, but with gloss finish.

1984-1986		$700	$800

D-17 Mahogany Rush

1984-1988. Like D-15, but with gloss finish and bound body.

1984-1988		$750	$850

D-25

2003. Solid mahogany body. Refer to Bluegrass D-25 for earlier models.

2003		$500	$550

1970s Guild Bluesbird

Guild Brian May Pro

1997 Guild D-55

*Guild Duane Eddy
Deluxe DE-500*

MODEL YEAR	FEATURES	EXC. COND. LOW	HIGH

D-30
1987-1999. Acoustic flat top, spruce-top, laminated maple back and solid maple sides, rosewood 'board, multi-bound, various colors.

1987-1989		$900	$1,000
1990-1999		$800	$950

D-40
1999-2003. Solid spruce top, mahogany back and sides, rosewood' board. See earlier models under Bluegrass Jubilee D-40.

1999-2000		$850	$1,000

D-46
1980-1985. Dreadnought acoustic, ash back, sides and neck, spruce top, ebony 'board, ivoroid body binding.

1980-1985		$950	$1,100

D-60
1987-1990, 1998-2000. Renamed from D-66, rosewood back and sides, 15 3/4", scalloped bracing, multi-bound top, slotted diamond inlay, G shield logo.

1987-1990		$1,600	$1,700
1998-2000		$1,500	$1,600

D-64
1984-1986. Maple back and side, multi-bound body, notched diamond inlays, limited production.

1984-1986		$1,300	$1,550

D-66
1984-1987. Amber, rosewood back and sides, 15 3/4", scalloped bracing, renamed D-60 in '87.

1984-1987		$1,500	$1,600

D-70
1981-1985. Dreadnought acoustic, spruce top, Indian rosewood back and sides, multi-bound, ebony 'board with mother-of-pearl inlays.

1981-1985		$1,950	$2,150

D-212 12-String
1981-1983. 12-string version of D-25, laminated mahogany back and sides, natural, sunburst or black, renamed D-25-12 in '87, reintroduced as D-212 '96-present.

1981-1983	Sunburst	$750	$900

D-412 12-String
1990-1997. Dreadnought, 12 strings, mahogany sides and arched back, satin finished, natural.

1990-1997		$850	$1,050

DCE True American
1993-2000. Cutaway flat-top acoustic/electric, 1 with mahogany back and sides, 5 with rosewood.

1993-2000	DCE1	$650	$750
1994-2000	DCE5	$675	$775

Del Rio M-30
1959-1964. Flat-top, 15", all mahogany body, satin non-gloss finish.

1959-1964		$700	$950

Detonator
1987-1990. Electric solidbody, double-cut, 3 pickups, bolt-on neck, Guild/Mueller tremolo system, black hardware.

1987-1990		$425	$525

Duane Eddy Deluxe DE-500
1962-1974, 1984-1987. Electric archtop, single rounded cutaway, 2 pickups (early years and '80s version have DeArmonds), Bigsby, master volume, spruce top with maple back and sides, available in blond (BL) or sunburst (SB).

1962	Natural	$6,200	$7,200
1962	Sunburst	$5,200	$6,200
1963	Natural	$6,000	$7,000
1963	Sunburst	$5,000	$6,000
1964	Natural	$5,800	$6,800
1964	Sunburst	$4,800	$5,800
1965	Natural	$5,300	$6,300
1965	Sunburst	$4,300	$5,300
1966	Natural	$4,700	$5,700
1966	Sunburst	$4,000	$5,000
1967-1969	Various colors	$3,500	$4,700
1970-1974	Various colors	$3,300	$4,200
1984-1987	Natural or sunburst	$3,300	$3,700

Duane Eddy Standard DE-400
1963-1974. Electric archtop, single rounded cutaway, 2 pickups, vibrato, natural or sunburst, less appointments than DE-500 Deluxe.

1963	Natural	$4,400	$5,000
1963	Sunburst	$3,900	$4,200
1964	Natural	$4,300	$4,800
1964	Sunburst	$3,600	$4,100
1965	Natural	$4,000	$4,400
1965	Sunburst	$3,200	$3,800
1966	Natural	$3,500	$4,000
1966	Sunburst	$3,000	$3,500
1967-1969	Various colors	$2,500	$3,300
1970-1974	Various colors	$2,400	$2,900

DV Series
1992-1999. Acoustic flat-top, spruce top, solid mahogany or rosewood back and sides, ebony or rosewood 'board and bridge, mahogany neck, satin or gloss finish.

1993-1999	DV-52, rosewood, satin	$950	$1,050
1993-1999	DV-72, limited edition	$1,200	$1,800
1996-1999	DV-6, mahogany, satin	$750	$850

Economy M-20
1958-1965, 1969-1973. Mahogany body, acoustic flat-top, natural or sunburst satin finish.

1958-1965		$800	$900
1969-1973		$600	$800

F-4 CEHG
1992-2002. High Gloss finish, single-cut flat-top, acoustic/electric.

1992-2002		$850	$900

F-5 CE
1992-2001. Acoustic/electric, single cutaway, rosewood back and sides, dot inlays, chrome tuners.

1992-2001		$975	$1,100

MODEL YEAR	FEATURES	EXC. COND. LOW	HIGH

F-30 R-LS
1990s. Custom Shop model, other F-30 models are listed under Aragon F-30 listing, rosewood sides and back, bearclaw spruce top, limited production.

1990s		$1,100	$1,300

F-45 CE
1983-1992. Acoustic/electric, single pointed cutaway, active EQ, preamp, spruce top, mahogany back and sides, rosewood 'board, natural finish.

1983-1992		$900	$1,000

F-47 RCE Grand Auditorium
1999-2003. Cutaway acoustic/electric, solid spruce top, solid maple back and sides, block inlays.

1999-2003		$1,300	$1,400

F-50
2002-present. Jumbo, solid spruce top, solid curly maple sides, arched laminated curly maple back, mahogany neck, abalone rosette.

2002-2005		$1,000	$1,025

F-65 CE
1992-2001. Acoustic/electric, single cutaway, rosewood back and sides, block inlay, gold tuners.

1992-2001		$1,350	$1,450

F-212 12-String
1964-1982. Acoustic flat-top jumbo, 12 strings, spruce top, mahogany back and sides.

1964-1969		$1,200	$1,700
1970-1979		$1,000	$1,200
1980-1982		$900	$1,100

F-212 XL 12-String
1966-1986. Acoustic flat-top, 17" body, 12 strings, spruce top, mahogany back and sides, ebony fingerboard.

1966-1969		$1,300	$1,800
1970-1979		$1,100	$1,300
1980-1986		$1,000	$1,200

F-412
2002-present. Solid spruce top, solid maple back and sides, block inlays, 12-string. See Custom F-412 for earlier models.

2002-2005		$1,000	$1,200

Freshman M-65
1958-1973. Electric archtop, single-cut, mahogany back and sides, f-holes, 1 single-coil (some with 2), sunburst or natural top.

1958-1959		$1,050	$1,300
1960-1969		$1,000	$1,200
1970-1973		$950	$1,100

Freshman M-65 3/4
1958-1973. Short-scale version of M-65, 1 pickup.

1958-1959	Natural or sunburst	$950	$1,150
1960-1969	Cherry, natural or sunburst	$900	$1,000
1970-1973	Cherry or sunburst	$850	$950

FS-46 CE
1983-1986. Flat-top acoustic/electric, pointed cutaway, black, natural or sunburst.

1983-1986		$625	$725

G-5P
1988-ca.1989. Handmade in Spain, cedar top, gold-plated hardware.

1988-1989		$575	$625

G-37
1973-1986. Acoustic flat-top, spruce top, laminated maple back and sides, rosewood 'board and bridge, sunburst or natural top.

1973-1986		$900	$1,000

G-41
1974-1978. Acoustic flat-top, spruce top, mahogany back and sides, rosewood 'board and bridge, 20 frets.

1975-1978		$850	$1,000

G-75
1975-1977. Acoustic flat-top, 3/4-size version of D-50, spruce top, rosewood back and sides, mahogany neck, ebony 'board and bridge.

1975-1977		$850	$1,200

G-212 12-String
1974-1983. Acoustic flat-top 12-string version of D-40, spruce top, mahogany back and sides, natural or sunburst.

1974-1983		$900	$1,200

G-212 XL 12-String
1974-1983. Acoustic flat-top, 12 strings, 17" version of G-212.

1974-1983		$1,000	$1,300

G-312 12-String
1974-1987. Acoustic flat-top 12-string version of the D-50, spruce top, rosewood back and sides.

1974-1987		$1,100	$1,700

George Barnes AcoustiLectric
1962-1972. Electric archtop, single-cut, solid spruce top, curly maple back and sides, multi-bound, 2 humbuckers, gold-plated hardware, sunburst or natural finish.

1962-1972		$3,000	$3,500

GF-30
1987-1991. Acoustic flat-top, maple back, sides and neck, multi-bound.

1987-1991		$900	$950

GF-50
1987-1991. Acoustic flat-top, rosewood back and sides, mahogany neck, multi-bound.

1987-1991		$950	$1,100

GF-60R
1987-1991. Jumbo size, rosewood sides and back, diamond markers.

1987-1991		$1,050	$1,200

Granda A-50 (Acoustic Archtop)
1956-1960. Lowest-end acoustic archtop in the Guild line, renamed Cordoba A-50 in '61.

1956-1960		$650	$700

Granda X-50
1954-1961. Electric archtop, non-cut, laminated all maple body, rosewood 'board and bridge, nickel-plated metal parts, 1 pickup, sunburst. Renamed Cordoba X-50 in '61.

1955-1959		$1,000	$1,500
1960-1961		$950	$1,400

GV Series
1993-1995. Flat-top, rosewood back and sides, various enhancements.

1993-1995	GV-52, jumbo, rosewood	$875	$925

Guild F212

Guild George Barnes AcoustiLectric

*1955 Guild
Manhattan X-175*

*1964 Guild
Jet Star S-50*

MODEL YEAR	FEATURES	EXC. COND. LOW	HIGH
1993-1995	GV-70, abalone soundhole ring	$925	$975
1993-1995	GV-72, herringbone, extra trim	$975	$1,025

Jet Star S-50

1963-1970. Electric solidbody, double-cut, mahogany or alder body, 1 pickup, vibrato optional by '65, asymmetrical headstock until '65, reintroduced as S-50 in '72-'78 with body redesign.

1963-1965	3-on-side tuners, single-coil	$850	$1,300
1966-1970	6-in-line tuners, single-coil	$650	$1,100
1972-1973	Single-coil	$550	$800
1974-1978	Humbucker	$600	$850

JF-30

1987-2004. Jumbo 6-string acoustic, spruce top, laminated maple back, solid maple sides, multi-bound.

1987-1999		$900	$1,000
2000-2004		$850	$1,000

JF-30 E

1994-2004		$1,000	$1,200

JF-30-12

1987-2004. 12-string version of the JF-30.

1987-1999		$1,000	$1,200

JF-50 R

1987-1988. Jumbo 6-string acoustic, rosewood back and sides, multi-bound.

1987-1988		$1,100	$1,600

JF-55

1989-2000. Jumbo flat-top, spruce top, rosewood body.

1989-2000		$1,500	$1,700

JF-55-12

1991-2000. 12-string JF-55.

1991-2000		$1,550	$1,700

JF-65 (R)(M)

1987, 1997-2001. Renamed from Navarre F-50, Jumbo flat-top acoustic, spruce top, R has rosewood back and sides (only offered in '87, reintroduced as JF-55 in '89) and M has maple.

1987	Maple	$1,500	$1,700
1987	Rosewood	$1,600	$1,900
1997-2001	Maple	$1,500	$1,700

JF-65-12

1987-2001. 12-string, version of maple JF-65.

1987-2001		$1,200	$1,300

JF-65R-12

1987. Rosewood body version of JF-65-12.

1987		$1,300	$1,400

Johnny Smith Award

1956-1961, 2004-present. Single-cut electric archtop, floating DeArmond pickup, multi-bound, gold hardware, sunburst or natural, renamed Artist Award in '61.

1956-1961		$5,000	$7,500

Liberator Elite

1988. Limited Edition, top-of-the-line, set-neck, offset double-cut solidbody, 2-piece figured maple top, mahogany body, rising-sun inlays, 3 active Bartolini

MODEL YEAR	FEATURES	EXC. COND. LOW	HIGH
pickups, 2 knobs and 4 toggles, last of the Guild solidbodies.			
1988		$900	$1,100

M-80 CS

1975-1984. Solidbody, double-cut, 2 pickups, has M-80 on truss rod cover, called just M-80 from '80-'84.

1975-1984		$700	$750

Manhattan X-170 (Mini-Manhattan X-170)

1985-2002. Called Mini-Manhattan X-170 in '85-'86, electric archtop hollowbody, single rounded cutaway, maple body, f-holes, 2 humbuckers, block inlays, gold hardware, natural or sunburst.

1985-1989		$1,350	$1,450
1990-2002		$1,400	$1,500

Manhattan X-175 (Sunburst)

1954-1985. Electric archtop, single rounded cutaway, laminated spruce top, laminated maple back and sides, 2 pickups, chrome hardware, sunburst.

1954-1959		$2,100	$2,400
1960-1969		$2,000	$2,200
1970-1985		$1,700	$1,900

Manhattan X-175 B (Natural)

1954-1976. Natural finish X-175.

1954-1959		$2,300	$2,600
1960-1969		$2,200	$2,500
1970-1976		$1,900	$2,200

Mark I

1961-1972. Classical, Honduras mahogany body, rosewood 'board, slotted headstock.

1961-1969		$300	$500
1970-1973		$275	$400

Mark II

1961-1987. Like Mark I, but with spruce top and body binding.

1961-1969		$425	$550
1970-1979		$400	$525
1980-1987		$375	$500

Mark III

1961-1987. Like Mark II, but with Peruvian mahogany back and sides and floral soundhole design.

1961-1969		$650	$750
1970-1979		$600	$700
1980-1987		$500	$600

Mark IV

1961-1985. Like Mark III, but with flamed pearwood back and sides (rosewood offered in '61, maple in '62).

1961-1969	Pearwood	$850	$950
1970-1979	Pearwood	$750	$850
1980-1985	Pearwood	$700	$800

Mark V

1961-1987. Like Mark III, but with rosewood back and sides (maple available for '61-'64.

1961-1968	Brazilian rosewood	$1,500	$2,500
1969-1979	Indian rosewood	$1,100	$1,200
1980-1987	Indian rosewood	$1,000	$1,100

Mark VI

1962-1973. Rosewood back and sides, spruce top, wood binding.

1962-1968	Brazilian rosewood	$1,800	$2,900
1969-1973	Indian rosewood	$1,400	$1,500

The Official Vintage Guitar Magazine Price Guide 2007   **Guild** Mark VII Custom — **Guild** Savoy A-150 (Natural)   **137**

GUITARS

MODEL YEAR	FEATURES	EXC. COND. LOW	HIGH

Mark VII Custom
1968-1973. Special order only, spruce top, premium rosewood back and sides, inlaid rosewood bridge, engraved gold tuners.

| 1962-1968 | Brazilian rosewood | $2,200 | $3,300 |
| 1969-1973 | Indian rosewood | $1,600 | $1,800 |

Navarre F-48
1972-1975. 17", mahogany, block markers.

| 1972-1975 | | $1,100 | $1,300 |

Navarre F-50 R/F-50 R
1965-1987, 2002-present. Rosewood back and side version of F-50, renamed JF-65 R in '87. Reissued in '02.

1965-1968	Brazilian rosewood	$3,500	$4,000
1969-1975	Indian rosewood	$2,200	$2,600
1976-1979		$2,000	$2,300
1980-1987		$1,900	$2,100

Navarre F-50/F-50
1954-1986, 1994-1995, 2002-present. Acoustic flat-top, spruce top, curly maple back and sides, rosewood 'board and bridge, 17" rounded lower bout, laminated arched maple back, renamed JF-65 M in '87. Reissued in '94 and in '02.

1954-1956		$3,200	$3,400
1957-1962	Pearl block markers added	$2,600	$2,900
1963-1969	Ebony 'board added	$2,400	$2,900
1970-1975		$2,200	$2,600
1976-1979		$1,800	$2,200
1980-1986		$1,700	$2,200
1994-1995		$1,500	$1,700

Nightbird
1985-1987. Electric solidbody, single sharp cutaway, tone chambers, 2 pickups, multi-bound, black or gold hardware, renamed Nightbird II in '87.

| 1985-1987 | | $1,400 | $1,600 |

Nightbird I
1987-1988. Like Nightbird but with chrome hardware, less binding and appointments, 2 pickups, coil-tap, phaser switch.

| 1987-1988 | | $1,200 | $1,400 |

Nightbird II
1987-1992. Renamed from Nightbird, electric solidbody, single sharp cut, tone chambers, 2 pickups, multi-bound, black hardware, renamed Nightbird X-2000 in '92.

| 1987-1992 | | $1,400 | $1,550 |

Nightbird X-2000
1992-1996. Renamed from Nightbird II.

| 1992-1996 | | $1,300 | $1,400 |

Polara S-100
1963-1970. Electric solidbody, double-cut, mahogany or alder body, rosewood 'board, 2 single coil pickups, built-in stand until '70, asymmetrical headstock, in '70 Polara dropped from title (see S-100), renamed back to Polara S-100 in '97.

| 1963-1964 | 2 pickups | $1,200 | $1,600 |
| 1965-1970 | 3 pickups | $1,100 | $1,300 |

Roy Buchanan T-200
1986. Single-cut solidbody, 2 pickups, pointed six-on-a-side headstock, poplar body, bolt-on neck, gold and brass hardware.

| 1986 | | $600 | $650 |

S-60/S-60 D
1976-1981. Double-cut solidbody, 1 pickup, all mahogany body, rosewood 'board. Renamed S-60 D in '77 with 2 DiMarzio pickups.

| 1976 | S-60 | $400 | $500 |
| 1977-1981 | S-60 D | $500 | $600 |

S-65 D
1980-1981. Electric solidbody, double-cut, 3 DiMarzio pickups, rosewood 'board.

| 1980-1981 | | $500 | $600 |

S-90
1972-1977. Double-cut SG-like body, 2 humbuckers, dot inlay, chrome hardware.

| 1972-1977 | | $650 | $750 |

S-100
1970-1978, 1994-1996. S-100 Standard is double-cut solidbody, 2 humbuckers, block inlays. Deluxe of '72-'75 had added Bigsby. Standard Carved of '74-'77 has acorns and oakleaves carved in the top.

1970-1978	Standard	$1,000	$1,200
1972-1975	Deluxe	$1,000	$1,200
1974-1977	Standard Carved	$1,000	$1,200

S-100 Reissue
1994-1997. Renamed Polara in '97.

| 1994-1997 | | $700 | $850 |

S-261
Ca.1985. Double-cut, maple body, black Kahler tremolo, 1 humbucker and 2 single-coil pickups, rosewood 'board.

| 1985 | | $450 | $600 |

S-275
1982-1983. Offset double-cut body, 2 humbuckers, bound figured maple top, sunburst or natural.

| 1982-1983 | | $500 | $700 |

S-280 Flyer
1983-1984. Double-cut poplar body, 2 humbuckers or 3 single-coils, maple or rosewood neck, dot markers.

| 1983-1984 | | $500 | $700 |

S-281 Flyer
1983-1988. Double-cut poplar body S-280 with locking vibrato, optional pickups available.

| 1983-1988 | | $500 | $700 |

S-300 Series
1976-1983. Double-cut mahogany solidbody with larger bass horn and rounded bottom, 2 humbuckers. S-300 A has ash body, D has exposed DiMarzio humbuckers.

1976-1983	S-300	$850	$1,100
1977-1982	S-300 D	$850	$950
1977-1983	S-300 A	$950	$1,000

Savoy A-150 (Natural)
1958-1973. Natural finish, acoustic archtop version of X-150, available with floating pickup.

| 1958-1961 | | $1,500 | $1,700 |

Guild Mark V

1976 Guild S-100

Guild Starfire II

Guild Starfire IV

MODEL YEAR	FEATURES	EXC. COND. LOW	HIGH

Savoy A-150 (Sunburst)
1958-1973. Sunburst, acoustic archtop version of X-150, available with floating pickup.

| 1958-1961 | | $1,400 | $1,600 |

Savoy X-150
1954-1965, 1998-2005. Electric archtop, single rounded cutaway, spruce top, maple back and sides, rosewood 'board and bridge, 1 single-coil pickup, sunburst, blond or sparkling gold finish.

1954	Sunburst	$1,500	$2,100
1955-1959	Sunburst	$1,500	$2,000
1960-1961	Sunburst	$1,400	$1,900

Slim Jim T-100
1958-1973. Electric archtop thinline, single-cut, laminated all-maple body, rosewood 'board and bridge, Waverly tailpiece, 1 pickup, natural or sunburst.

1958-1960		$1,150	$1,400
1961-1969		$1,000	$1,100
1970-1973		$900	$1,000

Slim Jim T-100 D
1958-1973. Semi-hollowbody electric, single Florentine cutaway, thinline, 2-pickup version of the T-100, natural or sunburst.

1958-1959		$1,250	$1,600
1960-1969		$1,200	$1,300
1970-1973		$1,100	$1,200

Songbird S-4
1987-1991. Designed by George Gruhn, flat-top, mahogany back, spruce top, single pointed cutaway, pickup with preamp, multi-bound top, black, natural or white.

| 1987-1991 | | $800 | $900 |

Standard F-112 12-String
1968-1982. Acoustic flat-top, spruce top, mahogany back, sides and neck.

1968-1969		$1,150	$1,450
1970-1979		$950	$1,150
1980-1982		$850	$1,050

Starfire I
1960-1964. Electric archtop, single-cut thinline, laminated maple or mahogany body, bound body and neck, 1 pickup.

| 1960-1961 | Starfire Red | $1,100 | $1,300 |
| 1962-1964 | | $1,000 | $1,200 |

Starfire II
1960-1976, 1997-2001. Electric archtop, single-cut thinline, laminated maple or mahogany body, bound body and rosewood neck, 2 pickups.

1960-1961	Sunburst	$1,400	$1,600
1962	Emerald Green	$1,600	$2,800
1962-1966	Special color options	$1,400	$2,800
1962-1966	Sunburst, Starfire Red	$1,300	$1,750
1967-1969	Sunburst, Starfire Red	$1,200	$1,650
1970-1975	Sunburst, Starfire Red	$900	$1,250
1997-2001	Reissue model	$1,000	$1,150

MODEL YEAR	FEATURES	EXC. COND. LOW	HIGH

Starfire III
1960-1974, 1997-2005. Electric archtop, single-cut thinline, laminated maple or mahogany body, bound body and rosewood neck, 2 pickups, Guild or Bigsby vibrato, Starfire Red.

1960-1961		$1,500	$1,700
1962-1966		$1,400	$1,850
1967-1969		$1,300	$1,750
1970-1974		$1,000	$1,350
1997-2005	Reissue model	$1,100	$1,250

Starfire IV
1963-1987, 1991-2005. Thinline, double-cut semi-hollowbody, laminated maple or mahogany body, f-holes, 2 humbuckers, rosewood 'board, cherry or sunburst.

1963-1966		$2,000	$2,200
1967-1969		$1,900	$2,100
1970-1975		$1,800	$2,000
1976-1979		$1,600	$1,800
1980-1987		$1,400	$1,600
1991-2005	Reissue model	$1,000	$1,200

Starfire IV Special (Custom Shop)
2001-2002. Nashville Custom Shop.

| 2001-2002 | | $2,000 | $2,200 |

Starfire V
1963-1973, 1999-2002. Same as Starfire IV but with block markers, Bigsby and master volume, natural or sunburst finish, reissued in '99.

1963-1966		$2,200	$2,500
1967-1969		$2,000	$2,300
1970-1973		$1,800	$2,100

Starfire VI
1964-1979. Same as Starfire IV but with higher appointments such as ebony 'board, pearl inlays, Guild/Bigsby vibrato, natural or sunburst.

1964-1966		$2,900	$3,500
1967-1969		$2,800	$3,300
1970-1975	Sunburst or blond	$2,700	$3,200
1976-1979		$2,600	$3,000

Starfire XII
1966-1973. Electric archtop, 12-string, double-cut, maple or mahogany body, set-in neck, 2 humbuckers, harp tailpiece.

1966-1967		$2,000	$2,400
1968-1969		$1,900	$2,200
1970-1973		$1,800	$2,000

Stratford A-350
1956-1973. Acoustic archtop, single rounded cutaway, solid spruce top with solid curly maple back and sides, rosewood 'board and bridge (changed to ebony by '60), sunburst.

1956-1959		$2,300	$2,600
1960-1965		$2,200	$2,500
1966-1969		$2,100	$2,400
1970-1973		$2,000	$2,300

Stratford A-350B
1956-1973. A-350 in blond/natural finish option.

1956-1959		$2,500	$2,800
1960-1965		$2,400	$2,700
1966-1969		$2,300	$2,600
1970-1973		$2,200	$2,500

MODEL YEAR	FEATURES	EXC. COND. LOW	HIGH

Stratford X-350
1954-1965. Electric archtop, single rounded cutaway, laminated spruce top with laminated maple back and sides, rosewood 'board, 6 push-button pickup selectors, sunburst finish (natural finish is X-375).

1953-1959		$2,600	$3,200
1960-1965		$2,500	$2,900

Stratford X-375/X-350 B
1954-1965. Natural finish version of X-350, renamed X-350 B in '58.

1953-1959	X-375	$2,800	$3,400
1960-1965	X-350 B	$2,700	$3,100

Stuart A-500
1956-1969. Acoustic archtop single-cut, 17" body, A-500 sunburst, available with Guild logo, floating DeArmond pickup.

1956-1959		$2,500	$2,800
1960-1965		$2,400	$2,700
1966-1969		$2,300	$2,600

Stuart A-550/A-500 B
1956-1969. Natural blond finish version of Stuart A-500, renamed A-500 B in '60.

1956-1959		$2,700	$3,000
1960-1965		$2,600	$2,900
1966-1969		$2,500	$2,800

Stuart X-500
1953-1995. Electric archtop, single-cut, laminated spruce top, laminated curly maple back and sides, 2 pickups, sunburst.

1953-1959		$3,000	$3,400
1960-1964		$2,800	$3,200
1965-1969		$2,600	$3,000
1970-1979		$2,400	$2,800
1980-1995		$2,200	$2,600

Stuart X-550/X-500 B
1953-1995. Natural blond finish Stuart X-500, renamed X-500 B in '60.

1953-1959		$3,200	$3,700
1960-1964		$3,000	$3,500
1965-1969		$2,800	$3,300
1970-1979		$2,600	$3,100
1980-1995		$2,400	$2,900

Studio 301/ST301
1968-1970. Thinline, semi-hollow archtop Starfire-style but with sharp horns, 1 pickup, dot inlays, cherry or sunburst.

1968-1969	Single-coil	$1,000	$1,200
1970	Humbucker	$1,100	$1,300

Studio 302/ST302
1968-1970. Like Studio 301, but with 2 pickups.

1968-1969	Single-coils	$1,200	$1,400
1970	Humbuckers	$1,300	$1,500

Studio 303/ST303
1968-1970. Like Studio 301, but with 2 pickups and Guild/Bigsby.

1968-1969	Single-coils	$1,200	$1,400
1970	Humbuckers	$1,300	$1,500

Studio 402/ST402
1969-1970. Inch thicker body than other Studios, 2 pickups, block inlays.

1969-1970	Humbuckers	$1,400	$1,600
1969-1970	Single-coils	$1,500	$1,700

T-250
1986-1988. Single-cut body and pickup configuration with banana-style headstock.

1986-1988		$600	$700

Thunderbird S-200
1963-1968. Electric solidbody, offset double-cut, built-in rear guitar stand, AdjustoMatic bridge and vibrato tailpiece, 2 humbucker pickups until changed to single-coils in '66.

1963-1965	Humbuckers	$3,500	$5,000
1966-1968	Single-coils	$2,500	$4,500

Troubador F-20
1956-1987. Acoustic flat-top, spruce top with maple back and sides (mahogany '59 and after), rosewood 'board and bridge, natural or sunburst.

1956-1959		$750	$850
1960-1969		$700	$800
1970-1979		$650	$750
1980-1987		$600	$700

TV Model D-55/D-65/D-55
1968-1987, 1990-present (special order only for 1968-1973). Dreadnought acoustic, spruce top, rosewood back and sides, scalloped bracing, gold-plated tuners, renamed D-65 in '87. Reintroduced as D-55 in '90.

1968-1969		$2,400	$2,700
1970-1975		$2,200	$2,600
1976-1979		$1,800	$2,200
1980-1987		$1,700	$2,200
1990-1999		$1,500	$1,700
2000-2003		$1,500	$1,700

Valencia F-40
1954-1963. Acoustic flat-top, rounded lower bout, spruce top, maple back and sides, rosewood 'board and bridge, sunburst finish. Renamed F-47 in '63.

1954-1956		$2,000	$2,400
1957-1962		$1,700	$2,200

X-79 Skyhawk
1981-1986. Four-point solidbody, 2 pickups, coil-tap or phase switch, various colors.

1981-1986		$700	$800

X-80 Skylark/Swan
1982-1986. Solidbody with 2 deep cutaways, banana-style 6-on-a-side headstock, renamed Swan in '85.

1983-1986		$700	$800

X-88 Flying Star Motley Crue
1984-1986. Pointy 4-point star body, rocketship meets spearhead headstock on bolt neck, 1 pickup, optional vibrato.

1984-1986		$600	$700

X-92 Citron
1984. Electric solidbody, detachable body section, 3 pickups.

1984		$600	$700

Guild Stratford X-375

Guild X-88D Flying Star

Guild X-700 Stuart

1966 Guyatone Lafayette

MODEL YEAR	FEATURES	EXC. COND. LOW	HIGH
X-100/X-110			

1953-1954. Guild was founded in 1952, so this is a very early model, 17" non-cut, single-coil soapbar neck pickup, X-100 sunburst finish, X-110 natural blond finish.

MODEL YEAR	FEATURES	EXC. COND. LOW	HIGH
1953-1954	X-100	$1,200	$1,600
1953-1954	X-110	$1,400	$1,800
X-160 Savoy			

1989-1993. No Bigsby, black or sunburst.

1989-1993		$1,100	$1,400
X-161/X-160B Savoy			

1989-1993. X-160 Savoy with Bigsby, black or sunburst.

1989-1993		$1,300	$1,500
X-200/X-220			

1953-1954. Electric archtop, spruce top, laminated maple body, rosewood 'board, non-cut, 2 pickups. X-200 is sunburst and X-220 blond.

1953-1954	X-200	$1,500	$2,200
1953-1954	X-220	$1,700	$2,400
X-300/X-330			

1953-1954. No model name, non-cut, 2 pickups, X-300 is sunburst and X-330 blond. Becomes Savoy X-150 in '54.

1953-1954	X-300	$1,500	$2,200
1953-1954	X-330	$1,700	$2,400
X-400/X-440			

1953-1954. Electric archtop, single-cut, spruce top, laminated maple body, rosewood 'board, 2 pickups, X-400 in sunburst and X-440 in blond. Becomes Manhattan X-175 in '54.

1953-1954	X-400	$2,100	$2,500
1953-1954	X-440	$2,300	$2,700
X-600/X-660			

1953. No model name, single-cut, 3 pickups, X-600 in sunburst and X-660 in blond. Becomes Statford X-350 in '54.

1953	X-600	$2,900	$3,200
1953	X-660	$3,200	$3,700
X-700			

1994-present. Rounded cutaway, 17", solid spruce top, laminated maple back and sides, gold hardware, natural or sunburst.

1994-2000		$2,000	$2,300

Guillermo Roberto Guitars

2000-present. Professional grade, solidbody electric bajo quintos made in San Fernando, California.

Gurian

1965-1981. Luthier Michael Gurian started making classical guitars on a special order basis, in New York City. In '69, he started building steel-string guitars as well. 1971 brought a move to Hinsdale, Vermont, and with it increased production.

MODEL YEAR	FEATURES	EXC. COND. LOW	HIGH
CL Series			

1970s. Classical Series, mahogany (M), Indian rosewood (R), or Brazilian rosewood (B).

1970s	CLB, Brazilian rosewood	$1,700	$1,900
1970s	CLM, mahogany	$1,200	$1,400
1970s	CLR, Indian rosewood	$1,400	$1,600
FLC			

1970s. Flamenco guitar, yellow cedar back and sides, friction tuning pegs.

1970s		$1,300	$1,500
J3R3H			

1970s. Jumbo, Indian rosewood sides and back, 3-piece back, herringbone trim.

1970s		$1,400	$1,900
JM/JMR			

1970s. Jumbo body, mahogany (JM) or Indian Rosewood (JMR), relatively wide waist (versus D-style or SJ-style).

1970s	JM	$1,300	$1,600
1970s	JMR	$1,700	$1,800
S2M			

1970s. Size 2 guitar with mahogany back and sides.

1970s		$1,200	$1,400
S2R/S2R3H			

1970s. Size 2 with Indian rosewood sides and back, R3H has 3-piece back and herringbone trim.

1970s	S2R	$1,400	$1,600
1970s	S2R3H	$1,700	$1,900
S3M			

Mahogany.

1970s		$1,400	$1,600
S3R/S3R3H			

1970s. Size 3 with Indian Rosewood, S3R3H has has 3-piece back and herringbone trim.

1970s	S3R	$1,500	$1,700
1970s	S3R3H	$1,800	$2,000

Guyatone

1933-present. Made in Tokyo by Matsuki Seisakujo, founded by Hawaiian guitarists Mitsuo Matsuki and Atsuo Kaneko (later of Teisco). Guya brand Rickenbacker lap copies in '30s. After a hiatus for the war ('40-'48), Seisakujo resumes production of laps and amps as Matsuki Denki Onkyo Kenkyujo. In '51 the Guyatone brand is first used on guitars, and in '52 they changed the company name to Tokyo Sound Company. Guyatones are among the earliest U.S. imports, branded as Marco Polo, Winston, Kingston and Kent. Other brand names included LaFayette and Bradford. Production and exports slowed after '68.

Electric Hollowbody Archtops

Various models.

1950s		$250	$500
1960s		$250	$500

Electric Solidbody

Various models.

1950s		$250	$500
1960s		$250	$500

MODEL		EXC. COND.	
YEAR	FEATURES	LOW	HIGH

Hagenlocher, Henner

1996-present. Luthier Henner Hagenlocher builds his premium grade, custom, nylon-string guitars in Granada, Spain.

Hagstrom

1958-1983, 2004-present. Intermediate, professional, and premium grade, production/custom, solidbody, semi-hollowbody and acoustic guitars made in the U.S. and imported. Founded by Albin Hagström of Älvdalen, Sweden, who began importing accordions in 1921 and incorporated in '25. The name of the company was changed to A.B. Hagström, Inc. in '38, and an American sales office was established in '40. Electric guitar and bass production began in '58 with plastic-covered hollowbody De Luxe and Standard models. The guitars were imported into the U.S. by Hershman Music of New York as Goya 90 and 80 from '58-'61. Bass versions were imported in '61. Following a year in the U.S., Albin's son Karl-Erik Hagström took over the company as exclusive distributor of Fender in Scandinavia; he changed the U.S. importer to Merson Musical Instruments of New York (later Unicord in '65), and redesigned the line. The company closed its doors in '83. In 2004 American Music & Sound started manufacturing and distributing the Hagstrom brand under license from A.B. Albin Hagstrom.

Corvette/Condor

1963-1967. Offset double-cut solidbody, 3 single-coils, multiple push-button switches, spring vibrato, called the Condor on U.S. imports.

1963-1967		$900	$1,100

D'Aquisto Jimmy

1969, 1976-1979. Designed by James D'Aquisto, electric archtop, f-holes, 2 pickups, sunburst, natural, cherry or white. The '69 had dot inlays, the later version had blocks. From '77 to '79, another version with an oval soundhole (no f-holes) was also available.

1976-1979		$1,100	$1,500

Deluxe

2004-present. Carved single cut mahogany body, set-neck, 2 humbuckers, sparkle tops or sunburst.

2004-2005		$400	$500

F-300

2004-present. Offset double cut alder body, three single-coils, sparkle top, sunburst, or solid colors.

2004-2005		$300	$325

H-12 Electric/Viking XII

1965-1967. Double-cut, 2 pickups, 12 strings.

1965-1967		$550	$750

H-22 Folk

1965-1967. Flat-top acoustic.

1965-1967		$400	$500

Impala

1963-1967. Two-pickup version of the Corvette, sunburst.

1963-1967		$750	$900

Model I

1965-1971. Small double-cut solidbody, 2 single-coils, early models have plastic top.

1965-1971	Rare finish	$600	$750
1965-1971	Standard finish	$550	$600

Model II/F-200 Futura/H II

1965-1972, 1975-1976. Offset double-cut slab body with beveled edge, 2 pickups, called F-200 Futura in U.S., Model II elsewhere, '75-'76 called H II. F-200 reissued in 2004.

1965-1972		$600	$650

Model III/F-300 Futura/H III

1965-1972, 1977. Offset double-cut slab body with beveled edge, 3 pickups, called F-300 Futura in U.S., Model III elsewhere, '77 called H III.

1965-1972		$650	$750
1977		$650	$750

Super Swede

1979-1983, 2004-present. Glued-in neck upgrade of Swede, '04 version is maple top upgrade of Swede.

1979-1983		$950	$1,050
2004-2005	Re-issue	$450	$500

Swede

1970-1982, 2004-present. Bolt-on neck, single-cut solidbody, black, cherry or natural, '04 version is set-neck.

1979-1982		$750	$850

Viking/V1/Viking II/VII

1965-1968, 1972-1979, 2004-present. Double-cut thinline, 2 f-holes, also advertised as the V-1.

1965-1968		$700	$850
1972-1979		$500	$700

Hallmark

1965-1967, 2004-present. Imported and U.S.-made, intermediate and premium grade, production/custom, guitars from luthiers Bob Shade and Bill Gruggett, and located in Greenbelt, Maryland. They also make basses. The brand was originally founded by Joe Hall in Arvin, California, in '65. Hall had worked for Semie Moseley (Mosrite) and had also designed guitars for Standel in the mid-'60s. Bill Gruggett, who also built his own line of guitars, was the company's production manager. Joe Hall estimates that less than 1000 original Hallmark guitars were built. The brand was revived by Shade in '04.

Sweptwing

1965-1967. Pointed body, sorta like a backwards Flying V.

1965-1967		$450	$600

Hamer

1974-present. Intermediate, professional and premium grade, production/custom, electric guitars made in the U.S. and overseas. Hamer also makes basses and the Slammer line of instruments. Founded in Arlington Heights, Illinois, by Paul Hamer and Jol Dantzig. Prototype guitars built in early-'70s were on Gibson lines, with first production guitar, the Standard (Explorer shape),

Hagstrom HL-550

Hallmark Sweptwing Custom

Hamer Artist Custom

Hamer Monaco III

MODEL YEAR	FEATURES	EXC. COND. LOW	HIGH

introduced in '75. Hamer was puchased by Kaman Corporation (Ovation) in '88. The Illinois factory was closed and the operations were moved to the Ovation factory in Connecticut in '97.

Artist/Archtop Artist/Artist Custom

1995-present. Similar to Sunburst Archtop with semi-solid, f-hole design, named Archtop Artist, then renamed Artist (with stop tailpiece)/Artist Custom in '97.

1995-2005	Sunburst	$1,000	$1,400

Blitz

1982-1984 (1st version), 1984-1990 (2nd version). Explorer-style body, 2 humbuckers, three-on-a-side peghead, dot inlays, choice of tremolo or fixed bridge, second version same except has angled six-on-a-side peghead and Floyd Rose tremolo.

1982-1984	3-on-a-side peghead	$650	$900
1984-1990	6-on-a-side peghead	$650	$750

Californian

1987-1997. Solidbody double cut, bolt neck, 1 humbucker and 1 single-coil, Floyd Rose tremolo.

1987-1989		$650	$900
1990-1997		$650	$750

Californian Custom

1987-1997. Downsized contoured body, offset double-cut, neck-thru-body, optional figured maple body, Duncan Trembucker and Trem-single pickups.

1987-1989		$650	$900
1990-1997		$650	$750

Californian Elite

1987-1997. Downsized contoured body, offset double-cut, optional figured maple body, bolt-on neck, Duncan Trembucker and Trem-single pickups.

1987-1989		$750	$1,000
1990-1997		$750	$850

Centaura

1989-1995. Contoured body of alder or swamp ash, offset double-cut, bolt-on neck, 1 humbucker and 2 single-coil pickups, Floyd Rose tremolo, sunburst.

1989-1995		$750	$800

Chaparral

1985-1987 (1st version), 1987-1994 (2nd version). Contoured body, offset double-cut, glued maple neck, angled peghead, 1 humbucker and 2 single-coils, tremolo, second version has bolt neck with a modified peghead.

1985-1987	Set-neck	$750	$800
1987-1994	Bolt neck	$500	$650

Daytona

1993-1997. Contoured body, offset double-cut, bolt maple neck, dot inlay, 3 single-coils, Wilkinson VSV tremolo.

1993-1997		$700	$750

Diablo

1992-1997. Contoured alder body, offset double-cut, bolt maple neck, rosewood 'board, dot inlays, reversed peghead '92-'94, 2 pickups, tremolo.

1992-1997		$550	$650

DuoTone

1993-2003. Semi-hollowbody, double-cut, bound top, glued-in neck, rosewood 'board, 2 humbuckers, EQ.

1993-2003		$500	$600

Echotone Custom

2000-2002. Thinline semi-hollow archtop, f-holes, 2 humbuckers, trapezoid inlays, gold hardware.

2000-2002		$300	$450

Eclipse

1994-2003. Asymmetrical double-cut slab mahogany body, glued neck, three-on-a-side peghead, rosewood 'board, dot inlays, 2 Duncan Mini-Humbuckers, cherry.

1994-2003		$700	$950

FB I

1986-1987. Reverse Firebird-style body, glued-in neck, reverse headstock, 1 pickup, rosewood 'board with dot inlays, also available in non-reverse body.

1986-1987		$500	$600

FB II

1986-1987. Reverse Firebird-style, glued-in neck, ebony 'board with boomerang inlays, angled headstock, 2 humbuckers, Floyd Rose tremolo, also available as a 12-string.

1986-1987		$600	$650

Korina Standard

1995-1996. Limited run, Korina Explorer-type body, glued-in neck, angled peghead, 2 humbuckers.

1995-1996		$1,050	$1,200

Maestro

1990. Offset double-cut, 7 strings, tremolo, bolt-on maple neck, 3 Seymour Duncan rail pickups.

1990		$750	$1,000

Miller Music Guitar

1985-1986. Miller (Beer) Music graphic art (white letters on red background), shaped like Miller bottle label. There was a matching bass. Trapezoid-shaped Miller Genuine Draft guitars and basses were offered in '87.

1985-1986		$1,100	$1,300

Mirage

1994-1998. Double-cut carved figured koa wood top, transparent flamed top, initially with 3 single-coil pickups, dual humbucker option in '95.

1994-1998		$1,050	$1,200

Monaco Elite

2003-present. Single-cut solidbody, 2 humbuckers, 3-in-a-line control knobs, tune-o-matic-style bridge, mother-of-pearl inlaid 'victory' position markers, carved flamed maple cap over mahogany body, flamed maple sunburst.

2003-2005		$1,250	$1,400

Phantom A5

1982-1884, 1985-1986 (2nd version). Contoured offset double-cut, glued neck, 3-on-a-side peghead, 1 triple-coil and 1 single-coil pickup, second version same but with 6-on-a-side peghead and Kahler tremolo.

1982-1984		$550	$700

MODEL YEAR	FEATURES	EXC. COND. LOW	HIGH

Phantom GT
1984-1986. Contoured body, offset double-cut, glued-in fixed neck, six-on-a-side peghead, 1 humbucker, single volume control.

1984-1986		$450	$600

Prototype
1981-1985. Contoured mahogany body, double-cut with 1 splitable triple-coil pickup, fixed bridge, three-on-a-side peghead, Prototype II has extra pickup and tremolo.

1981-1985		$800	$900

Scarab I
1984-1986. Multiple cutaway body, six-on-a-side peghead, 1 humbucker, tremolo, rosewood or ebony 'board, dot inlays.

1984-1986		$500	$650

Scarab II
1984-1986. Two humbucker version of the Scarab.

1984-1986		$550	$700

Scepter
1986-1990. Futuristic-type body, ebony 'board with boomerang inlays, angled six-on-a-side peghead, Floyd Rose tremolo.

1986-1990		$900	$1,100

Special
1980-1983 (1st version), 1984-1985 (Floyd Rose version), 1992-1997 (2nd version). Double-cut solidbody, flame maple top, glued neck, 3-on-a-side peghead, 2 humbuckers, Rose version has mahogany body with ebony 'board, the second version is all mahogany and has tune-o-matic bridge, stop tailpiece and Duncan P-90s, cherry red.

1980-1983	1st version	$800	$900
1984-1985	With Floyd Rose	$750	$850
1992-1997	2nd version	$700	$800

Special FM
1993-1997. Special with flamed maple top, 2 humbuckers, renamed the Special Custom in '97.

1993-1999		$1,000	$1,100

Standard
1974-1985, 1995-1999. Futuristic body, maple top, bound or unbound body, glued neck, angled headstock, either unbound neck with dot inlays or bound neck with crown inlays, 2 humbuckers. Reissued in '95 with same specs but unbound mahogany body after '97. Higher dollar Standard Custom still available.

1974-1975	Pre-production, about 20 made	$2,500	$4,000
1975-1977	Production, about 50 made, PAFs	$2,300	$3,000
1977-1979	Dimarzio PAF-copies	$2,100	$2,500
1980-1985		$1,900	$2,300
1995-1999		$1,300	$1,500

Stellar 1
1999-2000. Korean import, double-cut, 2 humbuckers.

1999-2000		$150	$200

Steve Stevens I
1984-1992. Introduced as Prototype SS, changed to Steve Stevens I in '86, contoured double-cut, six-on-a-side headstock, dot or crown inlays, 1 humbucker and 2 single-coil pickups.

1984-1992		$700	$800

Steve Stevens II
1986-1987. One humbucker and 1 single-coil version.

1986-1987		$700	$750

Studio
1993-present. Double-cut, flamed maple top on mahogany body, 2l humbuckers, cherry or natural.

1993-2005		$950	$1,000

Sunburst
1977-1983, 1990-1992. Double-cut bound solidbody, flamed maple top, glue-in neck, bound neck and crown inlays optional, 3-on-a-side headstock, 2 humbuckers.

1977-1979		$1,500	$1,700
1980-1983	Arlington Heights built	$1,400	$1,600
1990-1992		$1,200	$1,300

Sunburst (import)
1997-present. Import version of Sunburst, flat or arch top, 2 pickups.

1997-2005		$200	$250

Sunburst Archtop
1991-present. Sunburst model with figured maple carved top, 2 humbuckers, offered under various names:

Standard - unbound neck and dot inlays, tune-o-matic and stop tailpiece '91-'93.

Custom - a Standard with bound neck and crown inlays '91-'93.

Archtop - bound neck with crown inlays '94-'97.

Studio Custom - bound neck with crown inlays '97-present.

Studio - unbound body, by '95 stud wrap-around tailpiece '93-present.

Archtop GT - Gold top with P-90 soapbar-style pickups '93-'97.

1991-1997		$1,000	$1,400

T-51
1993-1997. Classic single-cut southern ash body, 2 single-coils.

1993-1997		$700	$800

T-62
1991-1995. Classic offset double-cut solidbody, tremolo, pau ferro 'board, Lubritrak nut, locking tuners, 3-band active EQ, various colors.

1991-1995		$700	$800

TLE
1986-1992. Single-cut mahogany body, maple top, glued neck, 6-on-a-side headstock, rosewood 'board, dot inlays, 3 pickups.

1986-1992		$750	$850

TLE Custom
1986-1992. Bound, single-cut solidbody with maple top, glued-in neck, angled headstock, ebony 'board with boomerang inlays, 3 pickups.

1986-1992		$750	$850

Hamer Standard Flametop

Hamer Scarab

GUITARS

Harmony Buck Owens

Harmony H-82G Rebel

MODEL YEAR	FEATURES	EXC. COND. LOW	HIGH

Vector

1982-1985. V-style body (optional flame maple top), 3-on-a-side peghead, rosewood 'board, 2 humbuckers, Sustain Block fixed bridge (Kahler or Floyd Rose tremolos may also be used).

1982-1985	Regular top	$500	$800
1982-1985	Maple top	$700	$1,000

Harmony

1892-1976, late 1970s-present. Huge, Chicago-based manufacturer of fretted instruments, mainly budget models under the Harmony name or for many other American brands and mass marketers. Harmony was at one time the largest guitar builder in the world. In its glory days, Harmony made over one-half of the guitars built in the U.S., with '65 being their peak year. But by the early-'70s, the crash of the '60s guitar boom and increasing foreign competition brought an end to the company.

The Harmony brand appeared on Asian-built instruments starting in the late '70s to the '90s with sales mainly is mass-retail stores. In 2000, the Harmony brand was distributed by MBT International. In '02, former MBT International marketing director Alison Gillette announced the launch of Harmony Classic Reissue Guitars and Basses.

Many Harmony guitars have a factory order number on the inside back of the guitar which often contains the serial number. Most older Harmony acoustics and hollowbodies have a date ink-stamped inside the body. DeArmond made most of the electronic assemblies used on older Harmony electrics, and they often have a date stamped on the underside.

Archtone H1215/H1215 Tenor
1950s. Lower-end archtop, sunburst.

1950-1960s	4-string tenor	$350	$600
1950-1960s	6-string	$150	$200

Blond H62
1950s-1960s. Thin body, dual pickup archtop, curly maple back and sides, spruce top, blond.

1950s		$550	$800
1960s		$450	$700

Brilliant Cutaway H1310/H1311
1962-1965. 16 1/2" body (Grand Auditorium), acoustic archtop cutaway, block markers, sunburst.

1962-1965		$525	$575

Broadway H954
1930s-1971. 15-3/4" body, acoustic archtop, dot markers, sunburst.

1960s		$250	$325

Buck Owens
Acoustic flat-top, red, white and blue.

1969		$600	$800

Cremona
1930s-1952. Full-size archtop line, Harmony and Cremona logo on headstock, natural. Cutaways became available in '53.

1940s		$250	$350

Espanada H63/H64
1950s-1960s. Thick body, single-cut, jazz-style double pickups, black finish with white appointments.

1950s		$550	$800
1960s		$450	$700

Grand Concert H165
1960s. Flat-top, all mahogany body.

1960s		$250	$300

H72/H72V Double Cutaway Hollowbody
1966-1971. Two pickups, multiple bindings, cherry red, H72V has Bigsby.

1966-1971		$350	$450

H73 Double Cutaway Hollowbody
Double cutaway, 2 pickups.

1960s		$350	$450

H75 Double Cutaway Hollowbody
1960-1970. Three pickups, multi-bound body, 3-part f-holes, block inlays, bolt neck, brown sunburst.

1960-1970		$350	$450

H76 Double Cutaway Hollowbody
Late-1960s. Three pickups, Bigsby vibrato tailpiece, sunburst.

1960s		$600	$700

H77 Double Cutaway Hollowbody
1964-1970. Same as H75, but in cherry sunburst.

1964-1970		$600	$700

H78 Double Cutaway Hollowbody
Late-1960s. Three pickups, Bigsby vibrato tailpiece, cherry.

1960s		$600	$700

H79 Double Cutaway Hollowbody 12-String
1966-1970. Unique slotted headstock, cherry finish.

1966-1970		$700	$800

H4101/Flat Top tenor guitar

1950-1970s		$350	$400

Hollywood H37/H39/H41
Auditorium-sized 15 3/4" non-cut electric archtop, H37 has a single pickup and bronze finish, H39 has a single pickup and brown mahogany shaded finish, H41 has dual pickups and brown finish.

1960s		$300	$350

Lone Ranger
1950-1951. Lone Ranger headstock stencil, Lone Ranger and Tonto stencil on brown body. This model was first introduced in 1936 as the Supertone Lone Ranger with same stencil on a black body.

1950-1951		$300	$325

Master H945
1965-1966. 15" (Auditorium) acoustic archtop, block markers, music note painted logo on headstock, sunburst.

1965-1966		$250	$350

Meteor H70/H71
1958-1966. Single rounded cutaway 2" thin body, 2 pickups, 3-part f-holes, block inlays, bolt neck, H70 sunburst, H71 natural (ended '65), lefty offered '65-'66, reintroduced as H661 and H671 (without Meteor name) in '72-'74.

1958-1966	H70	$350	$650
1958-1965	H71	$400	$700

MODEL YEAR	FEATURES	EXC. COND. LOW	HIGH

Monterey H950/H952/H1325/H1456/H1457/H6450

1930s-1974. Line of Auditorium and Grand Auditorium acoustic archtop models.

1950s	H952 Colorama	$175	$375
1960s		$125	$300
1970s	H6450	$100	$225

Patrician

1932-1973. Model line mostly with mahogany bodies and alternating single/double dot markers (later models with single dots), introduced as flat-top, changed to archtop in '34. In '37 line expanded to 9 archtops (some with blocks) and 1 flat-top. Flat-tops disappeared in the '40s, with various archtops offered up to '73.

1940s-1973	Archtop	$300	$350

Rebel H81

1968-1971. Single pickup version of Rebel, brown sunburst.

1968-1971		$225	$300

Rebel H82/H82G

Listed as a new model in 1971. Thin body, hollow tone chamber, double-cut, 2 pickups, H82 sunburst, H82G greenburst avacado shading (renumbered as H682 and H683 in '72).

1970s	H82	$300	$350
1970s	H82G	$350	$375

Rocket H53/H54/H56/H59

1959-1973. Single-cut, F-holes, dot inlays, 2-tone brown sunburst ('59-'62) or red sunburst ('63 on), came with 1 pickup (Rocket I H53 '59-'71), 2 pickups (Rocket II H54 has 2 pickups, Rocket VII H56 has 2 pickups and vibrato, Rocket III H59 has 3 pickups. Rockets were single-cut, brown sunburst in the early-'60s and double-cut red sunburst in the early-'70s.

1959-1973	1 pickup	$275	$375
1959-1973	2 pickups	$300	$475
1959-1973	3 pickups	$575	$675

Silhouette De Luxe Double H19

1964-1967. Double-cut solidbody, deluxe pickups, block markers, advanced vibrato, sunburst.

1964-1967		$425	$500

Silhouette H14/H15/H17

1964-1967. Double-cut solidbody, H14 single pickup, H15 dual pickup, H17 dual with vibrato (offered until '66).

1965-1966	H17	$250	$350
1965-1967	H14	$175	$225
1965-1967	H15	$225	$325

Singing Cowboys H1057

Western chuck-wagon scene stencil top, Singing Cowboys stenciled on either side of upper bouts, brown background versus earlier Supertone version that had black background.

1950s		$300	$325

Sovereign Jumbo Deluxe H1266

1960s-1970s. Jumbo nearly D-style, 16" wide body with out-size 'guard, natural.

1960s		$550	$600
1970s		$475	$550

Sovereign Jumbo H1260

1960s-1970s. Jumbo shape, 16" wide body, natural.

1960s		$500	$550
1970s		$425	$500

Sovereign Western Special Jumbo H1203

1960s-1970s. 15" wide body, 000-style.

1960s		$550	$600

Stratotone Deluxe Jupiter H49

1958-1968. Single-cut, tone chamber construction, 2 pickups, bound spruce top, curly maple back and 6 control knobs.

1958-1968		$450	$550

Stratotone Mars Electric H45/H46

1958-1968. Single-cut, tone chamber construction, H45 with 1 pickup and sunburst finish, H46 with 2 pickups.

1958-1968		$250	$375

Stratotone Mercury Electric H47/H48

1958-1968. Single-cut, tone chamber construction, H47 with 1 pickup, block inlay and curly maple sunburst top, H48 is the same with a blond top.

1958-1968		$325	$425

TG1201 Tenor

Spruce top, two-on-a-side tuners, Sovereign model tenor, natural

1950s		$350	$400

Harptone

1893-ca. 1975. The Harptone Manufacturing Corporation was located in Newark, New Jersey. They made musical instrument cases and accessories and got into instrument production from 1934 to '42, making guitars, banjos, mandolins, and tiples. In '66 they got back into guitar production, making the Standel line from '67 to '69. Harptone offered flat-tops and archtops under their own brand until the mid-'70s when the name was sold to the Diamond S company, which owned Micro-Frets.

E-6N

D-style body, spruce top and mahogany back and sides, unique Harptone headstock, natural.

1970s		$900	$1,100

Harwood

Harwood was a brand introduced in 1885 by Kansas City, Missouri instrument wholesalers J.W. Jenkins & Sons (though some guitars marked Harwood, New York). May have been built by Jenkins until circa 1905, but work was later contracted out to Harmony.

Parlor guitars

Slotted headstocks, most had mahogany bodies, some with Brazilian rosewood body, considered to be well made.

1890s	Brazilian rosewood	$950	$1,100
1890s	Mahogany	$400	$600

Hascal Haile

Late 1960s-1986. Luthier Hascal Haile started building acoustic, classical and solidbody guitars in Tompkinsville, Kentucky, after retiring from furniture making. He died in '86.

Harmony Rocket

1957 Harmony Stratotone Newport

Hayman 3030

Heit Deluxe

MODEL YEAR	FEATURES	EXC. COND. LOW	HIGH

Hayes Guitars

1993-present. Professional and premium grade, production/custom, steel and nylon string guitars made by luthier Louis Hayes in Paonia, Colorado.

Hayman

1970-1973. Solid and semi-hollow body guitars and basses developed by Jim Burns and Bob Pearson for Ivor Arbiter of the Dallas Arbiter Company and built by Shergold in England.

Haynes

1865-early 1900s. The John C. Haynes Co. of Boston also made the Bay State brand.
Parlor Guitar
1900s-1920s. Small 12 1/2" parlor guitar with typical narrow bouts, spruce top, Brazilian rosewood back and sides, multicolored wood marquetry trim, natural.

1910		$500	$1,000

Heartfield

1989-1994. Founded as a joint venture between Fender Musical Instrument Corporation (U.S.A.) and Fender Japan (partnership between Fender and distributors Kanda Skokai and Yamano Music) to build and market more advanced designs (built by Fuji Gen-Gakki). First RR and EX guitar series and DR Bass series debut in '90. Talon and Elan guitar series and Prophecy bass series introduced in '91. The brand was dead by '94.
Elan
1989-1994. Carved-style bound double-cut body, flamed top, 2 humbuckers, offset headstock.

1989-1994		$400	$550

EX
1990-1994. 3 single-coils, Floyd Rose tremolo.

1990-1994		$300	$350

Talon
1989-1994. Offset double-cut, wedge-triangle headstock, dot markers, hum/single/hum pickups.

1989-1994		$300	$350

Heiden Stringed Instruments

1974-present. Luthier Michael Heiden builds his premium grade, production/custom, flat-top guitars in Chilliwack, British Columbia. He also builds mandolins.

Heit Deluxe

Ca. 1967-1970. Imported from Japan by unidentified New York distributor. Many were made by Teisco, the most famous being the Teisco V-2 Mosrite copy. They also had basses.
Acoustic Archtop
1967-1970. Various models.

1967-1970		$125	$200

Electric Solidbody
1967-1970. Various models.

1967-1970		$125	$200

MODEL YEAR	FEATURES	EXC. COND. LOW	HIGH

Hemken, Michael

1993-present. Luthier Michael Hemken builds his premium grade, custom, archtops in St. Helena, California.

Heritage

1985-present. Professional, premium, and presentation grade, production/custom, hollow, semi-hollow, and solidbody guitars built in Kalamazoo, Michigan. They have also made banjos, mandolins, flat-tops, and basses in the past.

Founded by Jim Deurloo, Marvin Lamb, J.P. Moats, Bill Paige and Mike Korpak, all former Gibson employees who did not go to Nashville when Norlin closed the original Gibson factory in '84.
Eagle
1986-present. Single rounded cutaway semi-hollowbody, mahogany body and neck, 1 jazz pickup, f-holes, sunburst or natural.

1986-1999		$1,500	$1,700
2000-2005		$1,600	$1,900

Eagle Custom
Eagle with custom inlays.

2001		$2,100	$2,400

Gary Moore Model
1989-1991. Single-cut solidbody, 2 pickups, chrome hardware, sunburst.

1989-1991		$1,500	$1,900

Golden Eagle
1985-present. Single-cut hollowbody, back inlaid with mother-of-pearl eagle and registration number, multi-bound ebony 'board with mother-of-pearl cloud inlays, bound f-holes, gold-plated parts, ebony bridge inlaid with mother-of-pearl, mother-of-pearl truss rod cover engraved with owner's name, 1 Heritage jazz pickup, multi-bound curly maple 'guard.

1985-1999		$2,300	$2,600
2000-2005		$2,500	$2,800

H-140 CM/Goldtop
1985-2005. Single pointed cutaway solidbody, bound curly maple ('85-'04) or solid gold top ('94-'05), 2 humbuckers, chrome parts.

1985-2004	CM maple top	$725	$800
1994-2005	Goldtop	$725	$800

H-147
1990-1991. Single-cut solidbody, 2 humbuckers, mahogany body, mother-of-pearl block inlays, black with black or gold hardware.

1990-1991		$750	$850

H-150 C/H-150 CM
1985-present. Single rounded cutaway solidbody, curly maple top, 2 pickups, chrome parts, cherry sunburst.

1985-1999		$825	$875
2000-2005		$925	$975

H-157 Ultra
Single-cut solidbody, large block markers, highly figured maple top.

1993-1994		$1,250	$1,350

MODEL YEAR	FEATURES	EXC. COND. LOW	HIGH

H-204 DD
1986-1989. Single-cut solidbody of mahogany, curly maple top, 1-piece mahogany neck, 22-fret rosewood 'board.

1986-1989		$500	$600

H-207 DD
1986-1989. Double-cut solidbody of mahogany, curly maple top, 1-piece mahogany neck, 22-fret rosewood 'board.

1986-1989		$500	$600

H-357
1989-1994. Asymmetrical solidbody, neck-thru.

1989-1994		$2,000	$2,100

H-535
1987-present. Double-cut semi-hollowbody archtop, rosewood 'board, 2 humbucker pickups.

1987-1999		$1,000	$1,100
1987-1999	Flamed maple top	$1,100	$1,200
2000-2005		$1,200	$1,300

H-550
1990-present. Single-cut hollow body, laminated maple top and back, multiple bound top, white bound 'guard, f-holes, 2 humbuckers.

1990-2005		$2,100	$2,300

H-555
1989-present. Like 535, but with maple neck, ebony 'board, pearl and abalone inlays, gold hardware.

1989-2005		$1,500	$1,700

H-575
1987-present. Single sharp cut hollow body, solid maple top and back, cream bound top and back, wood 'guard, f-holes, 2 humbuckers.

1987-2005		$1,400	$1,500

H-576
1990-2004. Single rounded cut hollow body, laminated maple top and back, multiple bound top, single bound back and f-holes and wood 'guard, 2 humbuckers.

1990-2004		$1,200	$1,400

HFT-445
1987-2000. Flat-top acoustic, mahogany back and sides, spruce top, maple neck, rosewood 'board.

1987-2000		$600	$800

Johnny Smith
1989-2001. Custom hand-carved 17" hollowbody, single-cut, f-holes, 1 pickup.

1989-2001	Optional colors	$3,000	$3,300
1989-2001	Sunburst	$2,700	$3,000

Millennium Eagle 2000
2000-present. Single-cut semi-solidbody, multiple bound curly maple top, single-bound curly maple back, f-holes, 2 humbuckers.

2000-2005		$1,600	$1,900

Millennium SAE
2000-present. Single-cut semi-solidbody, laminated arch top, single cream bound top and back, f-holes, 2 humbuckers.

2000-2005		$1,000	$1,200

Parsons Street
1989-1992. Offset double-cut, curly maple top on mahogany body, single/single/hum pickups, pearl block markers, sunburst or natural.

1989-1992		$700	$800

Roy Clark
1992-present. Thinline, single-cut semi-hollow archtop, gold hardware, 2 humbuckers, block markers, cherry sunburst.

1992-2005		$1,700	$1,900

SAE Custom
1992-2000. Single-cut maple semi-hollow body, f-holes, 2 humbuckers and 1 bridge pickup.

1992-2000		$1,000	$1,100

Super Eagle
1988-present. 18" body, single-cut electric archtop, 2 humbuckers.

1989-2005	Optional colors	$2,700	$2,900
1989-2005	Sunburst	$2,500	$2,700

Sweet 16
1987-present. Single-cut maple semi-hollowbody, spruce top, 2 pickups, pearl inlays.

1987-2005	Optional colors	$2,400	$2,700
1987-2005	Sunburst	$2,100	$2,500

Hermann Hauser
Born in 1882, Hauser started out building zithers and at age 23 added classical guitars and lutes, most built in his shop in Munich, Germany. He died in 1952. His son and grandson, Hermann II and III, continued the tradition. Instruments should be evaluated on a case by case basis.

Classical Guitars

1920s		$5,000	$25,000

Model I
1930s. Classical, Brazilian rosewood sides and back, wood purflings, fancy rosette, inside-back label signed by maker, prices vary depending on the instrument.

1930s		$20,000	$25,000

Hermann Hauser II
Born in 1911 and the son of Hermann Hauser I, he built between 500 and 600 classical guitars in Germany during his career. He died in 1988.

Classical guitar (high-end)

1970s	Various models	$10,000	$45,000

Hermann Hauser III
1988-present. Hermann III started build guitars in '74, and took over the family business upon the death of his father in '88. He continues to build classical guitars in Munich, Germany.

Hess
1872-ca. 1940. Located in Klingenthal, Germany, Hess built acoustic and harp guitars, as well as other stringed instruments and accordians.

Hewett Guitars
1994-present. Luthier James Hewett builds his professional and premium grade, custom/production, steel string, archtop jazz, solidbody and harp guitars in Panorama Village, Texas.

Heritage Johnny Smith

1937 Herman Hauser

GUITARS

Hoffman Concert 12

1967 Höfner Committee

MODEL YEAR	FEATURES	EXC. COND. LOW	HIGH

Hill Guitar Company

1972-1980, 1990-present. Luthier Kenny Hill builds his professional and premium grade production/custom, classical and flamenco guitars in Felton, California and Michoacan, Mexico.

Hirade Classical

1968-present. Professional grade, production, solid top, classical guitars built in Japan by Takamine. The late Mass Hirade was the founder of the Takamine workshop. He learned his craft from master luthier Masare Kohno. Hirade represents Takamine's finest craftsmanship and material.

H-5
Solid cedar top, laminate rosewood body.

1980s		$900	$1,100

H-8
1989-1996. Solid spruce top, solid rosewood body.

1989-1996		$1,200	$1,400

HD-5C
Solid cedar top, rosewood laminate body, cutaway, pickup and preamp.

1980s		$1,000	$1,200

Hoffman Guitars

1971-present. Premium grade, custom flat-tops and harp guitars built by luthier Charles Hoffman in Minneapolis, Minnesota.

Höfner

1887-present. Budget, intermediate, and professional grade, production, archtop, acoustic, and classical guitars built in Germany and the Far East. They also produce basses and bowed-instruments. Founded by Karl Hofner in Schonbach, Germany. The company was already producing guitars when sons Josef and Walter joined the company in 1919 and '21 and expanded the market worldwide. They moved the company to Bavaria in '50 and to Hagenau in '97.

Beatle Electric Model 459TZ
1966-1967. Violin-shaped 500/1 body, block-stripe position markers, transistor-powered flip-fuzz and treble boost, sunburst.

1966-1967		$1,600	$1,700

Beatle Electric Model 459VTZ
1966-1967. Violin-shaped 500/1 body, same as Model 459TZ except with vibrato tailpiece, sunburst.

1966-1967		$1,600	$1,700

Beatle Electric Model G459TZ Super
1966-1967. Violin-shaped 500/1 body, deluxe version of Model 459TZ, including flamed maple sides, narrow grain spruce top, gold hardware, elaborate inlays and binding, natural blond.

1966-1967		$1,800	$1,900

Beatle Electric Model G459VTZ Super
1966-1967. Violin-shaped 500/1 body, same as G459VTZ Super but with vibrato tailpiece, narrow grain spruce top, gold hardware, natural blond.

1966-1967		$1,800	$1,900

MODEL YEAR	FEATURES	EXC. COND. LOW	HIGH

Club Model 126
1954-1970. Mid-sized single-cut solidbody, dot markers, flamed maple back and sides, spruce top, sunburst. Listed with Hofner Professional Electric Series.

1954-1970		$700	$900

Committee Model 4680 Thin Electric
1961-1968. Thinline single-cut archtop, 2 pickups, split-arrowhead markers, no vibrato, sunburst.

1961-1968		$1,400	$1,600

Deluxe Model 176
1964-1983. Double-cut, 3 pickups, polyester varnished sunburst finish, vibrola tailpiece, similar to Model 175 polyester varnished red and gold version.

1964-1983		$600	$700

Galaxy Model 175
1963-1966. Double-cut, 3 pickups, red and gold vinyl covering, fancy red-patch 'guard, vibrola, similar to Model 176 polyester varnished sunburst version.

1963-1966	Red and gold vinyl	$1,300	$1,500
1963-1966	Sunburst	$1,200	$1,400

Golden Hofner
1959-1963. Single-cut archtop, blond, 2 pickups, f-holes.

1959-1963		$1,300	$2,500

Jazzica Custom
2000-present. Full body, single soft cutaway, acoustic/electric archtop, carved German spruce top, sunburst.

2000-2005		$1,700	$1,800

Model 172 II (R) (S) (I)
1962-1963. Double-cut body, polyester varnished wood (S) or scruff-proof red (R) or white (I) vinyl, 2 pickups, vibrato.

1962-1963		$450	$550

Model 173 II (S) (I)
1962-1963. Double-cut body, polyester varnished wood (S) or scruffproof vinyl (I), 3 pickups, vibrato.

1962-1963	Gold foil vinyl	$450	$550
1962-1963	White vinyl	$450	$550

Model 178
1967-ca. 1969. Offset double cut solidbody, 2 pickups with an array of switches and push button controls, fancy position markers, vibrola, sunburst. 178 used on different design in the '70s.

1967-1969		$500	$600

Model 180 Shorty Standard
1982. Small-bodied, single-cut, solidbody, 1 pickup, travel guitar, the Shorty Super had a built-in amp and speaker.

1982		$300	$400

Model 456 (Acoustic archtop)
1951-1950s. Full body acoustic archtop, f-holes, laminated maple top, sides, back, large pearloid blocks, two color pearloid headstock laminate.

1950s		$600	$700

Model 457 President
1959-1972. Single-cut thinline archtop, 2 pickups, non-vibrato.

1959-1972		$700	$1,000

MODEL YEAR	FEATURES	EXC. COND. LOW	HIGH

Model 470SE2 Electric Archtop
1961-1993. Large single rounded cutaway electric archtop on Hofner's higher-end they call "superbly flamed maple (back and sides), carved top of best spruce," 2 pickups, 3 control knobs, gold hardware, pearl inlay, natural finish only.

1961-1993		$1,200	$1,300

Model 471SE2 Electric Archtop
1969-1977. Large single pointed cutaway electric archtop, flamed maple back and sides, spruce top, black celluloid binding, ebony 'board, pearl inlays, sunburst version of the 470SE2.

1969-1977		$1,200	$1,300

Model 490 Acoustic
Late 1960s. 16" body, 12-string, spruce top, maple back and sides, dot markers, natural.

1960s		$275	$350

Model 490E Acoustic Electric
Late 1960s. Flat-top 12-string with on-board pickup and 2 control knobs.

1960s		$400	$500

Model 491 Flat-Top
1960s-1970s. Slope shoulder body style, spruce top, mahogany back and sides, shaded sunburst.

1970s		$400	$450

Model 492 Acoustic
Late 1960s. 16" body, 12-string, spruce top, mahogany back and sides, dot markers.

1960s		$500	$550

Model 492E Acoustic Electric
Late 1960s. Flat-top 12-string with on-board pickup and 2 control knobs.

1960s		$550	$600

Model 496 Jumbo Flat-Top
1960s. Jumbo-style body, selected spruce top, flamed maple back and sides, gold-plated hardware, vine pattern 'guard, sunburst.

1960s		$950	$1,100

Model 514-H Classical Concert
1960s. Concert model, lower-end of the Hofner classical line, natural.

1960s	.	$250	$300

Model 4575VTZ/Verythin (Professional Extra Thin)
1960s. Extra-thinline acoustic, double-cut with shallow rounded horns, 2 or 3 pickups, vibrato arm, treble boost and flip-fuzz, straight-line markers. The Verythin Standard was reintroduced in '01.

1960s	2 pickups	$700	$800
1960s	3 pickups	$800	$900

Model 4578TZ President
1959-1970. Double-cut archtop.

1959-1965		$750	$950
1966-1970		$650	$850

Model 4600/V2 (Professional Extra Thin)
1968-1970. Thinline acoustic, double-cut, 2 pickups, vibrato arm, dot markers, sunburst.

1968-1970		$600	$800

Senator (Acoustic archtop)
1958-1960s. Floating pickup option available, full body archtop, f-holes, made for Selmer, London.

1958-1960		$500	$700

Verythin Standard
2000-present. Update of the 1960s Verythin line.

2000-2005	Reissue Verythin	$800	$950

Hohner
1857-present. Budget and intermediate grade, production, acoustic and electric guitars. They also have basses, ukes and mandolins. Matthias Hohner, a clockmaker in Trossingen, Germany, founded Hohner in 1857, making harmonicas. Hohner has been offering guitars and basses at least since the early '70s. HSS was founded in 1986 as a distributor of guitars and other musical products. By 2000, Hohner was also offering the Crafter brands of guitars.

Alpha Standard
Designed by Klaus Scholler, solidbody, stereo outputs, Flytune tremolo.

1987		$225	$300

G 2T/G 3T Series
1980s-1990s. Steinberger-style body, 6-string, neck-thru, locking tremolo.

1980-1990s		$200	$300

Jacaranda Rosewood Dreadnought
Flat-top acoustic.

1978		$250	$350

Jack
1987-1990s. Mate for Jack Bass. Headless, tone circuit, tremolo, 2 single-coils and 1 humbucker.

1987-1992		$200	$300

L 59/L 75 Series
Late-1970s-1980s. Classic single-cut solidbody, 2 humbuckers, glued neck, sunburst, 59 has upgrade maple body with maple veneer top.

1970s		$275	$325

Miller Beer Guitar
Solidbody, shaped like Miller beer logo.

1985		$300	$350

Professional
1980s. Single-cut solidbody, maple neck, extra large 'guard, natural.

1980s		$250	$300

Professional Series - TE Custom
1980s-1990s. Single-cut solidbody, bolt neck.

1980-1990s		$1,000	$1,400

Professional Series - TE Prinz
Late 1980s-early 1990s. Based on Prince's No. 1 guitar, 2 single-coils, bolt neck, Professional The Prinz headstock logo, natural.

1989-1990		$1,000	$1,400

SE 35
1989-mid-1990s. Semi-hollow thinline, 2 humbuckers, natural.

1989		$350	$450

SG Lion
1980s-1990s. Offset double-cut, pointy headstock, glued neck.

1980-1990s		$200	$300

Höfner Verythin

Hohner G3T Headless

Hohner ST Custom

1978 Hondo II Longhorn

MODEL YEAR	FEATURES	EXC. COND. LOW	HIGH

ST Series
1986-1990s. Includes the bolt neck ST 57, ST Special, ST Special S, Viper I, Viper II (snakeskin finish option), ST Victory, ST Metal S, and the ST Custom.

1986-1992		$150	$250

Standard Series - EX Artist
1970s-1980s. Solidbody, 2 humbuckers, gold hardware, neck-thru, solid maple body, rosewood 'board, tremolo.

1970-1980s		$200	$300

Standard Series - RR Custom
1970s-1980s. Randy Rhoads V body, 2 humbuckers, chrome hardware, glued neck, mahogany body, rosewood 'board, tremolo.

1970-1980s		$200	$300

Standard Series - SR Heavy
1970s-1980s. Hybrid body, 2 humbuckers, neck-thru, solid maple body, rosewood 'board, tremolo.

1970-1980s		$200	$300

Holiday
Student-level, private-branded similar to Stella but may have solid tops.

Hollenbeck Guitars
1970-present. Luthier Bill Hollenbeck builds his premium grade, production/custom, hollow and semi-hollow body acoustics and electric guitars in Lincoln, Illinois.

Holman
1966-1968. Built by the Holman-Woodell guitar factory in Neodesha, Kansas. The factory was started to build guitars for Wurlitzer, but that fell through by '67.

Hondo
1969-1987, 1991-present. Budget grade, production, imported acoustic, classical and electric guitars. They also offer basses and mandolins. Originally imported by International Music Corporation (IMC) of Fort Worth, Texas, founded by Jerry Freed and Tommy Moore and named after a small town near San Antonio, Texas. Early pioneers of Korean guitarmaking, primarily targeted at beginner market. Introduced their first electrics in '72. Changed brand to Hondo II in '74. Some better Hondos made in Japan '74-'82/'83. In '85 IMC purchases major interest in Jackson/Charvel, and the Hondo line was supplanted by Charvels. 1987 was the last catalog before hiatus. In '88 IMC was sold and Freed began Jerry Freed International and in '91 he revived the Hondo name. Acquired by MBT International in '95.

Acoustic Flat-Top
1969-1987, 1991-present.

1970s		$125	$250

Electric Hollowbody
1969-1987, 1991-present.

1980s		$225	$400

MODEL YEAR	FEATURES	EXC. COND. LOW	HIGH

Electric Solidbody
1969-1987, 1991-present.

1969-1987		$225	$500
1991-1999		$125	$350
2000s		$50	$100

Longhorn 6/12 Doubleneck Copy
1970s-1980s. Copy of Danelectro Longhorn 6/12 Doubleneck guitar, Dano coke bottle-style headstock, white sunburst.

1980s		$650	$800

Longhorn Copy
Ca. 1978-1980s. Copy of Danelectro Long Horn guitar, Dano Coke bottle-style headstock, brown-copper.

1970s		$350	$450

M 16 Rambo-Machine Gun
1970s-1980s. Machine gun body-style, matching machine gun-shaped guitar case, black or red.

1970-1980s		$400	$600

Hopf
1906-present. Intermediate, professional, premium, and presentation grade, production/custom, classical guitars made in Germany. They also make basses, mandolins and flutes.

The Hopf family of Germany has a tradition of instrument building going back to 1669, but the modern company was founded in 1906. Hopf started making electric guitars in the mid-'50s. Some Hopf models were made by others for the company. By the late-'70s, Hopf had discontinued making electrics, concentrating on classicals.

Explorer Standard
1960s. Double-cut semi-hollow, sharp horns, center block, 2 mini-humbuckers.

1960s		$450	$500

Saturn Archtop
1960s. Offset cutaway, archtop-style soundholes, 2 pickups, white.

1960s		$500	$900

Super Deluxe Archtop
1960s. Archtop, 16 3/4", catseye soundholes, carved spruce top, flamed maple back and sides, sunburst.

1960s		$600	$1,000

Horabe
Classical and Espana models made in Japan.

Model 25 Classical
Solid top.

1960s		$450	$600

Model 40 Classical
Solid cedar top, rosewood back and sides.

1960s		$650	$800

Model 60 Classical
1980s. German spruce top, solid Indian rosewood rims.

1980s		$850	$1,200

MODEL YEAR	FEATURES	EXC. COND. LOW	HIGH

Howe-Orme

1897-ca. 1910. Elias Howe and George Orme built a variety of mandolin family instruments and guitars and received many patents for their designs. Many of their guitars featured detachable necks.

Hoyer

1874-present. Intermediate grade, production, flat-top, classical, electric, and resonator guitars. They also build basses. Founded by Franz Hoyer, building classical guitars and other instruments. His son, Arnold, added archtops in the late-1940s, and solidbodies in the '60s. In '67, Arnold's son, Walter, took over, leaving the company in '77. The company changed hands a few times over the following years. Walter started building guitars again in '84 under the W.A. Hoyer brand, which is not associated with Hoyer.

Junior

Early-1960s. Solidbody with unusual sharp horn cutaway, single neck pickup, bolt-on neck, dot markers, Arnold Hoyer logo on headstock, shaded sunburst.

1960s		$500	$550

Soloist Electric

Single-cut archtop, 2 pickups, teardrop f-holes, sunburst.

1960-1962		$500	$600

Humming Bird

1947-ca.1968. Japanese manufacturer. By 1968 making pointy Mosrite inspirations. Probably not imported into the U.S.

Electric Solidbody

1950s		$125	$300

Humphrey, Thomas

1970-present. Premium and presentation grade, custom, nylon-string guitars built by luthier Thomas Humphrey in Gardiner, New York. In 1996 Humphrey began collaborating with Martin Guitars, resulting in the Martin C-TSH and C-1R. Often the inside back label will indicate the year of manufacturer.

Classical

1976-1984. Brazilian or Indian rosewood back and sides, spruce top, traditionally-based designs evolved over time with Millenium becoming a benchmark design in 1985, values can increase with new designs. Valuations depend on each specific instrument and year and type of construction, price ranges are guidance only; each instrument should be evaluated on a case-by-case basis.

1976-1984		$6,000	$8,000

Millennium (Classical)

1985-present. Professional performance-grade high-end classical guitar with innovative taper body design and elevated 'board, tops are generally spruce (versus cedar) with rosewood back and sides.

1995-2005		$9,000	$14,000

Huss and Dalton Guitar Company

1995-present. Luthiers Jeff Huss and Mark Dalton build their professional and premium grade flat-tops and banjos in Staunton, Virginia.

CM Custom

1995-present. 15 1/4" lower bout, soft cutaway, sitka spruce top, mahogany back and sides.

1995-2005		$2,400	$2,600

OM

1997-present. 15 1/8" lower bout, sitka spruce top, Indian rosewood back and sides, fancy inlay markers.

1997-2005		$2,000	$2,200

Ibanez

1932-present. Budget, intermediate, and professional grade, production/custom, acoustic and electric guitars. They also make basses, amps, mandolins, and effects.

Founded in Nagoya, Japan, by Matsujiro Hoshino as book and stationary supply, started retailing musical instruments in 1909. He began importing instruments in '21. His son Yoshitaro became president in '27 and began exporting. Manufacturing of Ibanez instruments began in '32. The company's factories were destroyed during World War II, but the business was revived in '50. Junpei Hoshino, grandson of founder, became president in '60; a new factory opened called Tama Seisakusho (Tama Industries). Brand names by '64 included Ibanez, Star, King's Stone, Jamboree and Goldentone, supplied by 85 factories serving global markets. Sold acoustic guitars to Harry Rosenblum of Elger Guitars ('59-ca.'65) in Ardmore, Pennsylvania, in early-'60s. Around '62 Hoshino purchased 50% interest in Elger Guitars, and ca. '65 changed the name to Ibanez.

Jeff Hasselberger headed the American guitar side beginning '73-'74, and the company headquarters were moved to Cornwells Heights, Pennsylvania in '74. By '75 the instruments are being distributed by Chesbro Music Company in Idaho Falls, Idaho, and Harry Rosenblum sells his interest to Hoshino shortly thereafter. Ca. '81, the Elger Company becomes Hoshino U.S.A. An U.S. Custom Shop was opened in '88. Most glued-neck guitars from '70s are fairly rare.

Dating: copy guitars begin ca. '71. Serial numbers begin '75 with letter (A-L for month) followed by 6 digits, the first 2 indicating year, last 4 sequential (MYYXXXX). By '88 the month letter drops off. Dating code stops early-'90s; by '94 letter preface either F for Fuji or C for Cort (Korean) manufacturer followed by number for year and consecutive numbers (F4XXXX=Fuji, C4XXXX=Cort, 1994).

470S/S470

1992-present. Offset double-cut mahogany solidbody, single-single-hum pickups until about '95 (470 S), hum-single-hum (S470) afterwards.

1992-2005		$400	$500

Hoyer archtop

Huss and Dalton TD-R

*Ibanez AR-1200
Doubleneck Arist*

1977 Ibanez Artist Professional

MODEL YEAR	FEATURES	EXC. COND. LOW	HIGH

540S/Pro 540S/Saber 540S
1987-1994. Offset double-cut solidbody, maple neck, rosewood 'board, dots, single-single-hum pickups, called the Pro 540 in '87, the Saber 540S in '88, there was also a double humbucker model (541S-HH).

| 1987-1994 | | $550 | $600 |

540SFM/S540FM
1991-1998. Solidbody, flame maple top, maple neck, rosewood 'board, single-single-hum pickups until '94 (540SFM), hum-single-hum (S540FM) afterwards.

| 1991-1998 | | $650 | $800 |

540SLTD/S540LTD
1989-1998. Offset double-cut mahogany solidbody, maple neck, bound rosewood 'board, sharktooth inlays, hum-single-hum pickups, model changed to S540LTD in '94.

| 1989-1998 | | $650 | $800 |

AE40
1994. Acoustic/electric, single-cut, flame maple.

| 1994 | | $325 | $375 |

AH10 (Allan Holdsworth)
1985-1987. Offset double-cut solidbody, bolt neck, bridge humbucker, dots, various colors.

| 1985-1987 | | $400 | $500 |

AM100 Stagemaster
1983-1984, 1989-1990. Small double cut semi-hollow body, 2 humbuckers. Model name used again, without "Stagemaster" in '89-'90.

| 1983-1984 | | $650 | $800 |

AM50 Stagemaster
1983-1984. Small double cut semi-hollow body, 2 humbuckers, no pickguard.

| 1983-1984 | | $650 | $750 |

AM70
1985-1987. Small double-cut semi-hollow body, f-holes, 2 humbuckers.

| 1985-1987 | | $700 | $800 |

AM75/AM75T
1985-1987. Small double cut semi hollow body, vibrato, 2 humbuckers.

| 1985-1987 | | $750 | $850 |

Artcore Electric Hollowbody (China)
2002-present. Artcore semi-hollow and hollow body models, glued mahogany necks, rosewood 'boards, 2 Artcore medium output pickups, f-holes.

| 2002-2005 | | $125 | $200 |

Artcore United Electric Hollowbody (China/Japan)
2002-present. Body made in China and assembled in Japan, 2 Artcore medium output pickups, f-holes with binding.

| 2002-2005 | | $400 | $500 |

Artist 2640/AR1200 Doubleneck
1977-1984. Double cut solidbody, set 6/12 necks, 4 humbuckers, gold hardware. Called 2640 until '79 when changed to AR1200.

| 1977-1984 | | $1,100 | $1,400 |

Artist AR100
1979-1984. Set neck double cut maple top solidbody, 2 humbuckers.

| 1979-1984 | | $550 | $700 |

MODEL YEAR	FEATURES	EXC. COND. LOW	HIGH

Artist AS100/AS100
1979-1982, 1989-1990. Double cut set neck semi-hollow body, sunburst, dots, replaced Artist 2629. Artist dropped from name when it becomes hollow body archtop in '82.

| 1979-1982 | Semi-hollow body | $900 | $1,200 |

Artist AS200/AS200
1979-1981. Double cut flame maple semi-hollow body, block markers, gold hardware, 2 humbuckers, replaced Artist 2630. Artist dropped from name when model becomes hollowbody archtop in '82.

| 1979-1981 | Semi-hollow body | $1,200 | $1,300 |

Artist Model 2612
1974-1975. Rounded double-cut solidbody, black finish, birch top, gold hardware, bound rosewood 'board, 2 humbuckers, fleur-de-lis inlay.

| 1974-1975 | | $800 | $900 |

Artist Model 2613
1974-1975. Natural version of 2612.

| 1974-1975 | | $800 | $900 |

Artist Model 2617
1976-1980. Pointed double-cut natural ash solidbody, set-neck, German carved top, spilt block inlays, bound ebony 'board, 2 humbuckers, later would evolve into the Professional model.

| 1976-1980 | | $1,100 | $1,200 |

Artist Model 2618
1976-1979. Like 2617, but with maple and mahogany body and dot markers. Becomes AR200 in '79.

| 1976-1979 | | $900 | $1,000 |

Artist Model 2619
1976-1979. Like 2618, but with split block markers. Becomes AR300 in '79.

| 1976-1979 | | $900 | $1,000 |

Artist Model 2630 Artist Deluxe
1976-1979. Double cut semi-hollow body, sunburst, name changed to AS200 in '79.

| 1976-1979 | | $1,100 | $1,300 |

AS50 Artstar
1998-1999. Laminated maple body, bound rosewood 'board, dot inlays, 2 humbuckers.

| 1998-1999 | | $700 | $850 |

AS80 Artstar
1994-2002. Double cut semi-hollow body, dot markers, chrome hardware.

| 1994-2002 | | $600 | $700 |

AW300
1996-1998. Grand concert size flat-top, solid spruce top, mahogany body, bound rosewood 'board.

| 1996-1998 | | $275 | $350 |

AX Series
2001-present. Double-cut solidbody, 2 humbuckers, bolt neck, 6 and 7-string models.

| 2001-2005 | | $150 | $200 |

Blazer Series
1980-1982, 1997-1998. Offset double-cut, 10 similar models in the '80s with different body woods and electronic configurations. Series name returns on 3 models in late '90s.

| 1980-1982 | Various models | $250 | $450 |

MODEL YEAR	FEATURES	EXC. COND. LOW	HIGH

Bob Weir Model 2681
1975-1980, 1995. Double-cut solidbody of carved solid ash, maple neck, ebony 'board with tree-of-life inlay, gold-plated Super 70 pickups, produced in limited numbers. Reintroduced as a limited run in '95.

1975-1980		$1,800	$2,100

Bob Weir Standard Model 2680
1976-1980. Double-cut solidbody of carved solid ash, maple neck, ebony 'board, dot markers, gold-plated Super 70 pickups, production model.

1976-1980		$900	$1,100

Concert CN200 Custom
1978-1979. Carved maple top, mahogany body, 7 layer black/white binding, bolt-on neck, gold hardware, block inlays, 2 Super 80 pickups.

1978-1979		$350	$450

Concert CN250
1978-1979. Like CN200 but with vine inlay.

1978-1979		$400	$500

Concord 673
1974-1978. D-style flat-top, laminated spruce top, laminated maple and jacaranda body, maple 'board, natural finish, gold tuners. Just the 637 for '74-'75, Concord added to name in '76.

1974-1978		$300	$425

Destroyer II DT400/DT500
1980-1984. Basswood body, set-neck, 2 pickups, cherry sunburst. Model changed to DT500 in '82.

1980-1984		$500	$600

Destroyer II DT555 Phil Collen
1983-1987. Bound basswood solidbody, 3 humbuckers, vibrato, black.

1983-1987		$700	$800

Destroyer DTX120
2000-2004. DT250 Destroyer II reissue, 2 humbuckers.

2000-2004		$275	$350

EG80 Star
1957-1961. Single cut set neck solidbody, 1 oval pickup, large 'guard.

1957-1961		$200	$350

EX Series
1988-1993. Double cut solidbodies with long thin horns, various models, all models may not be included.

1991-1993	EX370	$225	$275
1992-1993	EX1700	$225	$275
1992-1993	EX3700FM maple top	$250	$325

FA-100
1978-1982. Hollowbody, single-cut, 2 pickups, f-holes, block inlays.

1978-1982		$1,000	$1,100

FG-360S
1973-1974. Single-cut solidbody, bolt neck, trapezoid markers, maple top, sunburst.

1973-1974		$400	$500

GAX70
1998-present. Symmetrical double-cut, 2 humbuckers, set neck, dot markers.

1998-2005		$150	$225

GAX75
2001-present. GAX70 with Downshifter bridge.

2001-2005		$150	$225

George Benson GB10
1977-present. Single-cut, laminated spruce top, flame maple back and sides, 2 humbuckers, 3-piece set-in maple neck, ebony 'board.

1977-1979	Blond	$1,900	$2,200
1977-1979	Sunburst	$1,800	$2,000
1980-1989	Blond	$1,800	$2,000
1980-1989	Sunburst	$1,700	$1,800
1990-2005	Blond	$1,700	$1,800
1990-2005	Sunburst	$1,600	$1,700

George Benson GB100 Deluxe
1993-1996. GB-10 with flamed maple top, pearl binding, sunburst finish 'guard, pearl vine inlay tailpiece, gold hardware.

1993-1996		$2,500	$2,800

George Benson GB20
1978-1982. Larger than GB10, laminated spruce top, flame maple back and sides.

1978-1982		$1,700	$1,900

Iceman 2663/2663 TC/2663 SL
1975-1978. The original Iceman Series models, called the Flash I, II and III respectively, I has 2 humbuckers, II (TC) and III (SL) have 1 triple-coil pickup.

1975-1978		$650	$800

Iceman IC200
1978-1980. Continuation of 2 humbucker Iceman 2663, 555 made.

1978-1980		$750	$850

Iceman IC250
1978-1979. Flame maple top, 64 made.

1978-1979		$950	$1,200

Iceman IC300
1995-2003. Reintroduced line, made in Korea, standard model without tremolo.

1995-2003		$350	$450

Iceman IC300 (Korina)
1978-1979. Korina finished ash body, engraved twin Super 80 pickups, 137 made.

1978-1979		$750	$800

Iceman IC350
1995-1996. Reintroduced Korean version with tremolo, black.

1995-1996		$350	$450

Iceman IC400
1978-1979, 1981-1982. Mahogany body, maple top, set neck, 2 pickups, parallelogram inlays in first version, blocks in second.

1978-1982		$850	$1,000

Iceman IC-400 CS
1981 only. 28 made.

1981		$950	$1,000

Iceman IC500
1994. Limited production primarily for Japanese domestic market.

1994		$900	$950

Ibanez Destroyer II

Ibanez George Benson GB10

Ibanez JEM 777

1988 Ibanez Maxxas

MODEL YEAR	FEATURES	EXC. COND. LOW	HIGH

Iceman PS10 Paul Stanley
1978-1981. Limited edition Paul Stanley model, abalone trim, Stanley's name engraved at 21st fret, reissued in '95 with upgraded model names.

1978-1981	Korina finish	$2,500	$3,500
1978-1981	Sunburst or black	$2,500	$3,500

Iceman PS10 II Paul Stanley
1995-1996. Reissue of original PS-10

1995-1996	Black	$1,300	$1,600

IMG-2010 Guitar Controller MIDI
1985-1987. Similar to Roland GR-707, slim triangle-wedge body with treble horn.

1985-1987		$400	$550

JEM 77 Series
1988-1999, 2003-present. Basswood body, monkey grip handle, 3 pickups, 'board with tree of life or pyramids inlay, finishes include floral pattern or multicolor swirl. Current version has dot inlays and solid finish. The JEM 77BRMR Bad Horsie was introduced in 2005 with a mirror finish.

1980s	Floral	$1,400	$2,000
1980s	Multicolor	$1,400	$2,000
2005	77BRMR "Bad Horsie"	$1,500	$1,900

JEM 555
1994-2000. Basswood, dots and vine inlay, 3 pickups.

1994-2000		$575	$650

JEM 777 Series
1987-1996. Basswood body, monkey grip 3 pickups, pyramids or vine inlay.

1987	LG Loch Ness Green, limited edition	$1,300	$1,600
1988-1989	SK Shocking Pink, pyramids	$1,000	$1,400
1988-1996	DY Desert Sun Yellow, pyramids	$1,000	$1,400
1989-1993	VBK black, vines	$1,000	$1,400
1989-1993	VDY yellow, vines	$1,000	$1,600
1989-1993	White	$1,000	$1,600
1991	BF Blue Floral	$1,000	$1,400

JEM 10th Anniversary
1996. Limited Edition signature Steve Vai model, bolt neck, vine metal 'guard, vine neck inlays and headstock art.

1996		$1,400	$2,000

JEM 90th Anniversary
1997. Limited Edition signature Steve Vai model, textured silver finish, chrome 'guard.

1997		$1,400	$2,000

JEM Y2KDNA (limited edition)
2000. Red Swirl marble finish using Steve Vai's blood in the paint.

2000		$3,500	$4,000

Joe Pass Model JP20
1981-1990. Full body, single-cut, 1 pickup, abalone and pearl split block inlay, JP inlay on headstock.

1981-1990	Sunburst	$1,800	$1,900

MODEL YEAR	FEATURES	EXC. COND. LOW	HIGH

Joe Satriani JS100
1994-present. Offset double cut basswood body, 2 humbuckers, vibrato, red, black, white or custom finish.

1994-2005	Custom finish	$525	$725
1994-2005	Standard finish	$400	$550

Joe Satriani Y2K
2000. Clear see-thru plexi-style body.

2000		$1,900	$2,300

JPM100 John Petrucci/JPM100P3
1996-1999. Offset double-cut solidbody, 2 pickups, available in multi-color art finish.

1996-1999		$1,700	$2,000

Lee Ritenour LR10
1981-1987. Flame maple body, bound set neck, Quick Change tailpiece, 2 pickups, dark red sunburst, foam-filled body to limit feedback.

1981-1987		$900	$1,100

M340
1978-1979. Flat-top, spruce top, flamed maple back and sides, maple 'board.

1978-1979		$400	$450

Maxxas
1987-1988. Solidbody (MX2) or with internal sound chambers (MX3, '88 only), 2 pickups, all-access neck joint system.

1987-1988	MX2	$850	$1,000
1988	MX3	$1,000	$1,350

Model 1453
1971-1973. Copy of classic single-cut hollowbody, replaced by Model 2355 in '73.

1971-1973		$1,000	$1,200

Model 1912
1971-1973. Double-cut semi-hollow body, sunburst finish.

1971-1973		$1,000	$1,200

Model 2020
1970. Initial offering of the copy era, offset double-cut, 2 unusual rectangular pickups, block markers, raised nailed-on headstock logo, sunburst.

1970		$500	$750

Model 2240M
Early 1970s. Thick hollowbody electric copy, single pointed cutaway, double-parallelogram markers, 2 humbuckers, natural finish.

1971-1973		$1,300	$1,400

Model 2336 Les Jr.
1974-1976. Copy of classic slab solidbody, TV Lime.

1974-1976		$500	$600

Model 2340 Deluxe '59er
1974-1977. Copy of classic single-cut solidbody, flametop, Hi-Power humbuckers.

1974-1977		$600	$800

Model 2341 Les Custom
1974-1977. Copy of classic single-cut solidbody.

1974-1977		$600	$800

Model 2342 Les Moonlight/Sunlight Special
1974-1977. Copy of classic slab solidbody, black (Moonlight) or ivory (Sunlight).

1974-1977		$550	$650

MODEL YEAR	FEATURES	EXC. COND. LOW	HIGH

Model 2343 FM Jr.
1974-1976.

1974-1976		$500	$600

Model 2344
1974-1976. Copy of classic Double-cut solidbody.

| 1974-1976 | | $400 | $450 |

Model 2345
1974-1976. Copy of classic sharp double-cut solidbody, set neck, walnut or white, vibrato, 3 pickups.

| 1974-1976 | | $600 | $700 |

Model 2346
1974. Copy of classic sharp double-cut solidbody, vibrato, set neck, 2 pickups.

| 1974 | | $600 | $700 |

Model 2347
1974-1976. Copy of classic sharp double-cut solidbody, set-neck, 1 pickup.

| 1974-1976 | | $500 | $600 |

Model 2348 Firebrand
1974-1977. Copy of classic reverse solidbody, mahogany body, bolt neck, 2 pickups.

| 1974-1977 | | $650 | $700 |

Model 2350 Les
1971-1977. Copy of classic single-cut solidbody, bolt neck, black, gold hardware, goldtop version (2350G Les) also available. A cherry sunburst finish (2350 Les Custom) was offered by '74.

| 1971-1977 | | $600 | $700 |

Model 2351
1974-1977. Copy of classic single-cut solidbody, gold top, 2 pickups.

| 1974-1977 | | $600 | $700 |

Model 2351DX
1974-1977. Copy of classic single-cut solidbody, gold top, 2 mini-humbuckers.

| 1974-1977 | | $600 | $650 |

Model 2352 Telly
1974-1978. Copy of early classic single-cut solidbody, 1 bridge pickup, white finish.

| 1974-1978 | | $500 | $700 |

Model 2352CT
1974-1978. Copy of classic single-cut solidbody, single-coil bridge and humbucker neck pickup.

| 1974-1978 | | $500 | $700 |

Model 2352DX Telly
1974-1978. Copy of classic single-cut solidbody, 2 humbuckers.

| 1974-1978 | | $500 | $700 |

Model 2354
1974-1977. Copy of classic sharp double-cut solidbody, 2 humbuckers, vibrato.

| 1974-1977 | | $500 | $700 |

Model 2354S
1972-1977. Stop tailpiece version of 2354.

| 1972-1977 | | $500 | $700 |

Model 2355/2355M
1973-1977. Copy of classic single-cut hollowbody, sunburst or natural maple (M).

| 1973-1977 | | $1,300 | $1,400 |

Model 2356
1973-1975. Copy of classic double pointed cutaway hollowbody, bowtie markers, sunburst. There was another Model 2356 in '74, a copy of a different hollowbody.

| 1973-1975 | | $800 | $1,100 |

Model 2363R
1973-1974. Cherry finish copy of classic varitone double-cut semi-hollow body.

| 1973-1974 | | $1,000 | $1,100 |

Model 2364 Ibanex
1971-1973. Dan Armstrong see-thru Lucite copy, 2 mounted humbuckers.

| 1971-1973 | | $750 | $800 |

Model 2368 Telly
1974-1978. Copy of classic single-cut thinline, chambered f-hole body, single coil pickup, mahogany body.

| 1974-1978 | | $500 | $700 |

Model 2368F
1973-1974. Classic single-cut black 'guard copy.

| 1973-1974 | | $550 | $700 |

Model 2370
1972-1977. Sunburst version of Model 2363R.

| 1972-1977 | | $1,000 | $1,100 |

Model 2372 Les Pro/2372DX Les Pro
1972-1977. Copy of classic single-cut solidbody, bolt neck, low impedance pickups, DX with gold hardware available for '73-'74.

| 1972-1977 | | $600 | $700 |

Model 2374 Crest
1974-1976. Copy of classic double-cut semi-hollow body, walnut finish.

| 1974-1976 | | $900 | $1,100 |

Model 2375 Strato
1971-1978. Copy of classic offset double-cut solidbody, 3 single-coils, sunburst.

| 1971-1978 | | $500 | $600 |

Model 2375ASH Strato
1974-1978. 2375 with ash body.

| 1974-1978 | | $550 | $700 |

Model 2375WH/N/BK Strato
1974-1978. 2375 in white (WH), natural (N), and black (BK) finishes.

| 1974-1978 | | $500 | $600 |

Model 2377
1974-1975. Copy of classic double sharp-cut solidbody, short production run, dot markers.

| 1974-1975 | | $450 | $500 |

Model 2380
1973-1977. Copy of classic double-cut solidbody with low impedence pickups, small block markers.

| 1973-1977 | | $600 | $700 |

Model 2383
1974-1976. Copy of classic double sharp cut solidbody, white or walnut, 3 humbuckers, gold hardware.

| 1974-1976 | Walnut | $500 | $700 |
| 1974-1976 | White | $650 | $750 |

1970 Ibanez Model 2020

Ibanez Model 2375

Ibanez Model 2384

Ibanez Model 2387 Rocket Roll

MODEL YEAR	FEATURES	EXC. COND. LOW	HIGH
Model 2384 Telly			
1974-1976. Copy of classic single-cut, f-holes, 2 humbuckers, ash body.			
1974-1976		$500	$700
Model 2387 Rocket Roll/Rocket Roll Sr.			
1975-1977. Copy of classic v-shpaed solidbody, set-neck, dot markers, gold-covered pickups.			
1975-1977		$1,100	$1,400
Model 2390			
1974-1976. Copy of classic double-cut semi-hollow body, maple 'board, walnut finish.			
1974-1976		$900	$1,000
Model 2395			
1974-1976. Natural finished 2390.			
1974-1976		$900	$1,000
Model 2397			
1974-1976. Double-cut semi-hollow body, low impedance electronics, trapezoid markers, goldtop.			
1974-1976		$900	$1,000
Model 2399DX Jazz Solid			
1974-1976. Single-cut solidbody, sunburst, set-neck, gold hardware.			
1974-1976		$700	$900
Model 2401 Signature			
1974-1976. Double-cut semi-hollow archtop, gold top, bolt neck.			
1974-1976		$900	$1,000
Model 2402/2402DX Double Axe			
1974-1977. Double sharp cut solidbody 6/12 double-neck, cherry or walnut, DX model has gold hardware and white finish.			
1974-1977		$1,300	$1,500
Model 2404 Double Axe			
1974-1977. Double sharp cut solidbody guitar/bass doubleneck copy, walnut, white available '75 only.			
1974-1977		$1,300	$1,500
Model 2405 Custom Agent			
1974-1977. Single-cut solidbody, set neck, scroll headstock, pearl body inlay, 2 humbuckers.			
1974-1977		$1,400	$1,500
Model 2406 Double Axe			
1974-1977. Double sharp cut solidbody doubleneck, two 6-strings, cherry or wlanut.			
1974-1977		$1,300	$1,500
Model 2407 Strato Jazz			
1974-1976. Offset double-cut solidbody double-neck.			
1974-1976		$1,200	$1,400
Model 2451			
1974-1977. Single-cut solidbody, maple 'board, black or natural, set neck.			
1974-1977		$700	$900
Model 2453 Howie Roberts			
1974-1977. Single-cut archtop, round soundhole, maple body, set neck, rosewood 'board, block markers, 1 pickup, gold hardware, burgundy or sunburst.			
1974-1977		$1,000	$1,100
Model 2454			
1974-1977. Copy of classic double-cut semi-hollow body, set-neck, small block markers, cherry finish over ash.			
1974-1977		$900	$1,000

MODEL YEAR	FEATURES	EXC. COND. LOW	HIGH
Model 2455			
1974-1977. Copy of classic single-cut archtop, 2 pickups, natural.			
1974-1977		$1,200	$1,700
Model 2459 Destroyer			
1975-1977. Korina finished mahogany body.			
1975-1977		$900	$1,200
Model 2460			
1975-1977. Copy of classic single-cut archtop, natural.			
1975-1977		$1,000	$1,600
Model 2461			
1975-1977. Copy of classic single-cut archtop, laminated spruce top, curly maple body, set-neck, ebony 'board, pearl blocks, 2 pickups, gold hardware, sunburst or natural.			
1975-1977		$1,400	$1,800
Model 2464			
1975-1977. Copy of classic single-cut thinline arcthop, natural.			
1975-1977		$1,300	$1,600
Model 2469 Futura			
1976-1977. Korina finished furturistic model copy.			
1976-1977		$1,100	$1,600
Model 600 Series			
1974-1978. Copy era acoustic flat-tops with model numbers in the 600 Series, basically copies of classic American square shoulder dreadnoughts. Includes the 683, 684, 693, and the six-on-a-side 647; there were 12-string copies as well.			
1974-1978		$500	$700
Model 700 Series			
1974-1977. Upgraded flat-top models such as the Brazilian Scent 750, with more original design content than 600 Series.			
1974-1977		$500	$700
Musician MC Series			
1978-1982. Solidbodies, various models.			
1978-1980	MC-500 Carved Top	$900	$1,500
1978-1980	Neck-thru body	$700	$900
1978-1982	Bolt neck	$600	$800
Performer PF100 Standard			
1978-1979. Single cut solidbody, plain birch top, mahogany body, bolt neck, dot inlays, 2 humbuckers.			
1978-1979		$350	$450
Performer PF200 Custom			
1978-1979. Maple top PF100.			
1978-1979		$350	$500
Performer PF300			
1978-1980. Single cut solidbody, maple top, mahogany body, set neck, 2 humbuckers, Tri-Sound.			
1978-1980		$500	$600
Performer PF400			
1978-1979. Single cut solidbody, flame maple top, alder body, set neck, block inlays, 2 humbuckers, Tri-Sound.			
1978-1979		$500	$650
PF Performance Series Acoustics			
1987-present. Line of mostly dreadnought size flat-tops, various models.			
1987-1998	PF-10	$200	$300
1987-1998	PF1012 12-string	$350	$400

MODEL YEAR	FEATURES	EXC. COND. LOW	HIGH

PM20 Pat Metheny

1997-1999. Double-cut semi-hollow body, f-holes, 1 pickup, rosewood 'board.

1997-1999		$900	$1,000

PM100 Pat Metheny

1996-present. Double-cut semi-hollow body, f-holes, 2 pickups, ebony 'board.

1996-2005		$1,000	$1,100

Pro Line PL1770/PLZ1770

1985-1987. Alder solidbody, ebony 'board, hum/single/single pickups, locking trem, Z added in '87.

1985-1987		$350	$450

Pro Line PL2550/PLZ2550

1985-1987. Alder solidbody, neck-thru body, hum/single/single pickups, locking trem, Z added in '87.

1986-1987		$450	$550

Pro Line PR1660

1985. Randy Rhoads-style body, 2 humbuckers.

1985		$300	$400

RG220

1994-1999. Offset double-cut solidbody, 2 humbuckers.

1998-1999		$250	$300

RG270

1994-2002. Offset double-cut solidbody, 2 humbuckers.

1994-2002		$250	$300

RG320

1998-2000. Offset double-cut solidbody, 2 humbuckers.

1998-2000		$250	$300

RG350DX

1998-2001. Offset double-cut solidbody, hum/single/hum pickups.

1998-2001		$250	$300

RG470

1993-2002. Double long pointy cut basswood solidbody, hum/single/hum pickups, dot markers.

1993-2002		$300	$400

RG520QS

1997-2002. Offset double-cut mahogany solidbody, quilt top, 2 humbuckers, dot markers.

1997-2002		$450	$550

RG550/RG550 DX

1987-1993, 1997-2002. Pointy headstock, long thin horn double-cut solidbody, hum/single/hum pickups. Roadstar Deluxe series until '91, than RG series.

1987-1993		$550	$650
1997-2002		$550	$600

RG560/RG565

1988-1992. Offset double cut, single/single/hum pickups, Roadstar Deluxe series until '91, than RG series.

1988-1992		$500	$550

RG570

1989-1992, 1996-2002. Offset double cut, hum/single/hum pickups, Roadstar Deluxe series until '91, than RG series.

1996-2002		$500	$550

RG760

1989-1992. Offset double cut, shark tooth inlays, single/single/hum pickups mounted in body. Roadstar Deluxe series until '91, than RG series.

1989-1992		$450	$550

RG770

1990-1993. Hum/single/hum version of RG760. Roadstar Deluxe series until '91, than RG series.

1990-1993		$450	$550

RG1200

1992. Offset double-cut, hum/single/hum pickups, flame maple top.

1992		$500	$650

RG7620/RG7621

1997-2000. 7-string models in the RG Series, 7621, available '98 only, had fixed bridge.

1997-2000		$550	$650

RGT42

2002-2004. Offset double cut, 2 humbuckers, dot markers.

2002-2004		$400	$450

Roadstar/Roadstar II Series

1983-1985. Various offset double-cut solidbodies, says Roadstar II on headstock.

1983-1985		$275	$500

Roadstar Standard Series

1986-1988. Various offset double-cut solidbodies, says Roadstar II on headstock.

1986-1987	RG120/135/140	$275	$300
1987	RG240		
	(more features)	$300	$325
1987	RG250 (flame maple)	$325	$350

Roadstar Deluxe Series

1986-1991. Offset double cut basswood (or maple top) solidbodies, various models, higher appointments than original series, but still says Roadstar II on headstock.

1986	RG530		
	(2 hum, maple)	$400	$550
1986-1887	RG440 (h\s\s)	$450	$650
1986-1987	RG410 (1 hum)	$350	$500
1986-1987	RG420 (2 hum)	$400	$550
1986-1987	RG430 (3 SC)	$450	$650

Roadster

1979-1983. Offset double-cut, maple 'board, bolt neck, replaced by Roadstar series in '83.

1979-1983		$325	$375

Rocket Roll II RR550

1982-1984. Flying V body, six-on-side headstock, pearloid blocks, cherry sunburst, maple top, set neck.

1982-1984		$800	$1,000

RT Series

1992-1993. Offset double-cut, bolt neck, rosewood 'board, dot markers, hum/single/hum pickups. 150 has lower pickup quality, 650 has flamed top.

1992-1993	RT150	$275	$325
1992-1993	RT420	$325	$375
1992-1993	RT450	$375	$450
1992-1993	RT650	$450	$500

Ibanez PF 1055

Ibanez RT 650

Ibanez UV777

J Frog Vampira 900

MODEL YEAR	FEATURES	EXC. COND. LOW	HIGH

RX20/GRX20
1994-present. Offset double cut maple solidbody, 2 humbuckers, maple 'board, became the agathis or alder body, rosewood 'board GRX in '98.

| 1994-2005 | | $175 | $225 |

Studio ST300
1978-1980. Maple/ash body, active tone system, tri-sound switch, natural, gold hardware, 2 humbuckers.

| 1978-1980 | | $550 | $700 |

Studio ST50 Jr.
1979-1981. Set-neck, small offset sharp double-cut mahogany solidbody, 2 exposed pickups.

| 1979-1981 | | $450 | $550 |

Talman TC420
1995-1997. Offset double cut, bolt neck, 2 humbuckers, dot markers.

| 1995-1997 | | $400 | $450 |

Talman TC620
1995-1996. 2 stacked P-90 style pickups, BP version was black with pearloid 'guard.

| 1995-1996 | | $300 | $400 |

Talman TC630
1995-1997. 3 lipstick pickups, dot markers.

| 1995-1997 | | $450 | $550 |

Universe UV7/7P/77
1990-1997. Basswood 7-strings, hum/single/hum pickups. The '90-'93 white 7P and multi-colored 77 have pyramid inlays, the black '90-'97 7 has dots.

| 1990-1993 | 7P | $1,000 | $1,100 |
| 1990-1997 | 7 and 77 | $1,200 | $1,300 |

Universe UV777 Series
1991-1993. Basswood 7-string, pyramid inlays, maple 'board, hum/single/hum pickups.

| 1991-1993 | UV777GR | $1,900 | $2,100 |

USRG-10 (U.S.A.)
1994-1995. RG style guitars built in the U.S. by PBC Guitar Technology.

| 1994-1995 | | $850 | $900 |

V300
1978-1991. Vintage Series acoustic dreadnought, spruce top, mahogany back and sides, sunburst or various colors.

| 1978-1991 | | $300 | $350 |

Ibanez, Salvador
1875-1920. Salvador Ibanez was a Spanish luthier who operated a small guitar-building workshop. In the early 1900s he founded Spain's largest guitar factory. In 1929 Japan's Hoshino family began importing Salvador Ibanez guitars. Demand for the Salvador Ibanez guitars became so great that the Hoshino family began building their own guitars, which ultimately became known as the Ibanez brand. Guitars from 1875-1920 were mostly classical style and often can be identified by a label on the inside back which stipulates Salvador Ibanez.

Ignacio Rozas
1987-present. Luthier Ignacio M. Rozas builds his classical and flamenco guitars in Madrid, Spain. He also offers factory-made guitars built to his specifications.

MODEL YEAR	FEATURES	EXC. COND. LOW	HIGH

Imperial
Ca.1963-ca.1970. Imported by the Imperial Accordion Company of Chicago, Illinois. Early guitars made in Italy by accordion builder Crucianelli. By ca. '66 switched to Japanese guitars. They also made basses.

Electric Solidbody
1963-1968. Italian-made until '66, then Japanese-made, includes the Tonemaster line.

| 1963-1968 | | $150 | $250 |

Infeld
2003-present. Solidbody guitars and basses offered by string-maker Thomastik-Infeld of Vienna.

Infinox
1980s. Infinox by JTG, of Nashville, offered a line of 'the classic shapes of yesterday and the hi tech chic of today'. Classic shapes included copies of many classic American solidbody designs with the block letter Infinox by JTG logo on headstock, special metallic grafteq paint finish, space-age faux graphite-feel neck, Gotoh tuning machines, Gotoh locking nut tremolo with fine tuners, all models with 1 or 2 humbucker pickups.

Interdonati
1930s. Guitars built by luthier Philip Interdonati, of Staten Island, New York, originally professional grade, luthier's label is on the inside back.

Size 000 Flat-Top

| 1930s | | $3,500 | $7,500 |

Italia
1999-present. Intermediate grade, production, solid, semi-solid, and hollow body guitars designed by Trevor Wilkinson and made in Korea. They also build basses.

J Burda Guitars
Flat-top guitars built by luthier Jan Burda in Berrien Springs, Michigan.

J. Frog Guitars
1978-present. Professional and premium grade, production/custom, solidbody guitars made in Las Vegas, Nevada by Ed Roman.

J.B. Player
1980s-present. Budget and intermediate grade, production, imported acoustic, acoustic/electric, and solidbody guitars. They also offer basses, banjos and mandolins. Founded in United States. Moved production of guitars to Korea but maintained a U.S. Custom Shop. MBT International/ Musicorp took over manufacture and distribution in '89.

MODEL YEAR	FEATURES	EXC. COND. LOW	HIGH

J.R. Zeidler Guitars

1977-present. Luthier John Zeidler builds his premium and presentation grade, custom, flat-top, 12-string, and archtop guitars in Wallingford, Pennsylvania. He also builds mandolins.

Auditorium Cutaway

Introduced in 1982. Sitka or Adirondack spruce top, Indian rosewood sides, gold hardware.

1990s		$4,500	$5,500

Concert

1990s. Spruce top, Indian rosewood back and sides, the name does not denote the size, which approximates 00 Grand Concert.

1990s		$5,500	$6,000

J.T. Hargreaves Basses & Guitars

1995-present. Luthier Jay Hargreaves builds his premium grade, production/custom, classical and steel string guitars in Seattle, Washington. He also builds basses.

Jack Daniel's

2004-present. Acoustic and electric guitar models, some with custom Jack Daniel's artwork on the body and headstock, built by Peavey for the Jack Daniel's Distillery. There is also an amp model and a bass.

Jackson

1980-present. Currently Jackson offers intermediate, professional, and premium grade, production, electric guitars. They also offer basses. In '78 Grover Jackson bought out Charvel Guitars and moved it to San Dimas. Jackson made custom-built bolt-on Charvels. In '82 the pointy, tilt-back Jackson headstock became standard. The Jackson logo was born in '80 and used on a guitar designed as Randy Rhoad's first flying V. Jacksons were neck-through construction.

The Charvel trademark was licensed to IMC in '85. IMC moved the Jackson factory to Ontario, California in '86. Grover Jackson stayed with Jackson/Charvel until '89 (see Charvel). On October 25, 2002, Fender Musical Instruments Corp (FMIC) took ownership of Jackson/Charvel Manufacturing Inc.

DR3

1996-2001. Dinky Reverse, double-cut solidbody, reverse headstock, triangle markers, 2 humbuckers, locking vibrato, made in Japan, flamed maple top available.

1996-2001		$300	$400

DR5

1996 only. Offset double-cut solidbody, 2 Kent Armstrong humbuckers, rosewood 'board, dot markers.

1996		$300	$400

JSX94

1994-1995. Offset double-cut solidbody, single/single/hum, rosewood 'board, dot markers.

1994-1995		$250	$350

KE2 USA Kelly

1998-present. Alder solidbody, flame maple top, neck-thru.

1998-2005		$1,000	$1,200

Kelly Custom

1984-early 1990s. Solidbody, Kahler tremolo, 2 humbuckers, ebony 'board with shark's tooth inlays, bound neck and headstock.

1984-1993		$800	$1,000

Kelly Pro

1994-1995. Pointy-cut solidbody, neck-thru, 2 humbuckers, bound ebony 'board, sharkfin inlays.

1994-1995		$600	$800

Kelly Standard

1993-1995. Pointy cutaway solidbody, bolt neck, 2 humbuckers, dot markers.

1993-1995	Bolt-on	$500	$700

Kelly XL

1994-1995. Pointy cutaway solidbody, bolt neck, 2 humbuckers, bound rosewood 'board, sharkfin inlays.

1994-1995		$600	$800

King V (KV2)

2003-present. King V Pro reissue, neck-thru, sharkfin markers, Floyd Rose, U.S.-made.

2003-2005		$600	$700

King V Pro

1993-1995. Soft V-shaped neck-thru solidbody, sharkfin markers, 2 humbuckers.

1993-1995		$500	$700

King V STD

1993-1995. Bolt neck version of King V.

1993-1995		$300	$350

Phil Collen

1989-1991, 1993-1995. Offset double-cut maple neck-thru solidbody, six-on-a-side tuners, 1 volume, bound ebony 'board, U.S.-made, early version has poplar body, 1 humbucker; later version with basswood body, 1 single-coil and 1 humbucker.

1993-1995		$1,000	$1,200

Phil Collen PC1 (U.S.A.)

1996-present. Quilt maple top, bolt-on maple neck, maple board, koa body '96-'00, mahogany body '01-present, 1 humbucker and 1 single coil '96-'97, humbucker, stacked humbucker, and single coil '98-present.

1996-2005		$1,100	$1,300

Phil Collen PC3 (Import)

1996-2001. Downscale version of Collen model, poplar body, bolt neck, humbucker\single\single.

1996-2001		$450	$525

PS Performers Series

1995-2003. Some with PS model number on truss rod cover.

1995-2001	PS3 Rhoads body	$175	$275
1995-2003	PS2 Dinky body h/s/h	$175	$225
1995-2001	PS4 Dinky body h/s/h	$200	$275
1995-2001	PS7 h/s/s	$200	$275
1997-2001	PS6/PS6T Kelly body	$200	$250

Jack Daniel's USA Custom

Jackson Phil Collen

Jackson Randy Rhoads

James Tyler Studio Elite

Randy Rhoads (U.S.A.)

1983-present. V-shaped neck-thru solidbody, 2 humbuckers, originally made at San Dimas plant, serial numbers RR 0001 to RR 1929, production moved to the Ontario plant by '87, serial numbers RR 1930 to present in sequential order.

MODEL YEAR	FEATURES	EXC. COND. LOW	HIGH
1983	Early serial #, no trem	$2,200	$2,700
1983-1986	Kahler trem	$1,400	$1,600
1983-1986	Rose trem or string-thru	$1,700	$2,200
1987-1989	Early Ontario-built	$1,300	$1,500
1990-1999	Ontario-built	$1,100	$1,300
2000-2002		$900	$1,100
2002-2005	FMIC, RR5	$700	$900

Randy Rhoads (Import)

1992-present. Bolt neck import version, includes Randy Rhoads EX, RR3.

1992-2005		$325	$375

Randy Rhoads Custom Shop

1999. U.S.-made Custom Shop, special features.

1999		$1,100	$1,200

Randy Rhoads Custom Shop RR1T

2002 only. U.S.-made Custom Shop, only 50 made, Randy Rhoads body.

2002		$1,400	$1,600

Randy Rhoads Limited Edition

1992 only. Shark fin-style maple neck-thru body, gold hardware, white with black pinstriping, block inlays, six-on-a-side tuners, U.S.-made, only 200 built.

1992		$1,400	$1,500

San Dimas Serialized Plated

1980-1982. Various custom-built solidbody models, values vary depending on each individual instrument. The values are true for so-called "Serialized Plated" with Jackson neck plate, Jackson logo and serial number.

1980-1982		$3,000	$5,000

Soloist

1984-1990. Double-cut, neck-thru, string-thru solidbody, 2 humbuckers, bound rosewood 'board, U.S.-made, replaced by the Soloist USA in '90.

1984-1986	San Dimas-built	$1,300	$1,600
1986-1990	Ontario-built	$1,100	$1,400

Soloist Custom

1993-1995. Double-cut, neck-thru solidbody, 1 humbucker and 2 single-coils, bound ebony 'board, shark's tooth inlays, U.S.-made.

1993-1995		$900	$1,100

Soloist Student J1 (U.S.A.)

1984-1999. Double-cut neck-thru solidbody, Seymour Duncan single-single-hum pickups, rosewood 'board, dot inlays, no binding.

1984-1986	San Dimas-built	$750	$900
1986-1999	Ontario-built	$700	$850

Soloist USA

1990-1995. Replaces Soloist, sharkfin markers, single-single-hum.

1990-1995		$1,000	$1,100

Surfcaster SC1

1998-2001. Jackson logo on headstock, Charvel Surfcaster styling.

MODEL YEAR	FEATURES	EXC. COND. LOW	HIGH
1998-2001		$700	$750

Warrior USA

1990-1992. Four point neck-thru solidbody, 1 humbucker and 1 single-coil, triangle markers, active electronics, U.S.-made, the Warrior Pro was Japanese version.

1990-1992	Red	$1,100	$1,300

Warrior Pro (Import)

1990-1992. Japanese version.

1990-1992		$275	$350

Y2KV Dave Mustaine Signature

2000-2002. V-shaped body, shark tooth markers, neck-thru, 2 humbuckers.

2000-2002		$1,700	$2,500

Jackson-Guldan/Jay G Guitars

1920s-1960s. The Jackson-Guldan Violin Company, of Columbus, Ohio, mainly built inexpensive violins, violas, cellos, etc. but also offered acoustic guitars in the 1950s and early '60s, some of which were distributed by Wards. Their sales flyers from that era state - Made in America by Jackson-Guldan Craftsman. Very similar to small (13"-14") Stella economy flat-tops. Jay G name with quarter-note logo is sometimes on the headstock. They also offered lap steels and small tube amps early on.

Jacobacci

1930s-1994. Founded in France by Italian Vincent Jacobacci and originally building basso-guitars, banjos, and mandolins. Sons Roger and Andre joined the company and encouraged pop to add lapsteels and electric and regular acoustic guitars around '52. The guitars are sometimes labeled as Jaco and, from ca. '54 to ca. '66, as Jaco Major. In '58 the company introduced aluminum neck models, and in '59 their first solidbodies. In the '60s they also made instruments branded Royal, Texas, Ohio, Star and made instruments for Major Conn and other companies. By the mid '60s, they were producing mainly jazz style guitars.

James R. Baker Guitars

1996-present. Luthier James R. Baker builds his premium grade, custom, archtops in Shoreham, New York.

James Tyler

Early 1980s-present. Luthier James Tyler builds his professional and premium grade, custom/production, solidbody guitars in Van Nuys, California, and also has a model built in Japan. He also builds basses.

Janofsky Guitars

1978-present. Production classical and flamenco guitars built by luthier Stephen Janofsky in Amherst, Massachusetts.

MODEL YEAR	FEATURES	EXC. COND. LOW	HIGH

Jaros

1995-present. Professional and premium grade, production/custom, solidbody and acoustic/electric guitars originally built by father and son luthiers Harry and Jim Jaros in Rochester, Pennsylvania. In '01 Ed Roman in Las Vegas, bought the brand. He sold it in '04 to Dave Weiler in Nashville.

Jasmine

1994-present. Budget and intermediate grade, production, steel and classical guitars offered by Takamine Jasmine or Jasmine by Takamine. Student level instruments.

Jay Turser

1997-present. Budget and intermediate grade, production, imported acoustic, acoustic/electric, electric and resonator guitars. They also offer basses and amps. Designed and developed by Tommy Rizzi for Music Industries Corp.

JD Bluesville

2005-present. John Schappell and luthier Davis Millard build their professional grade, custom/production, solidbody electric guitars in Allentown, Pennsylvania.

Jeff Traugott Guitars

1991-present. Premium and presentation grade, custom, flat-top, nylon-string, and acoustic/electric guitars built by luthier Jeff Traugott, in Santa Cruz, California.

Jeremy Locke Guitars

1985-present. Premium grade, production/custom, classical and flamenco guitars built by luthier Jeremy Locke in Coomera, South East Queensland, Australia.

Jeronimo Pena Fernandez

1967-present. Luthier Jeronimo Pena Fernandez started building classical guitars in Marmolejo, Spain, in the '50s. In '67, he went full-time and soon became well-known for his fine work. He is now retired, but still builds a few guitars a year.

Classical

Brazilian rosewood back and sides, cedar top, full-size classical guitar, higher-end luthier.

1960-1990s .		$5,000	$8,000

Jerry Jones

1981-present. Intermediate grade, production, semi-hollow body electric guitars and sitars from luthier Jerry Jones, built in Nashville, Tennessee. They also build basses. Jones started building custom guitars in '81, and launched his Danelectro-inspired line in '87.

Electric Models

Various models include Baritone 6-string ('89-present); Electric Sitar ('90-present) with buzz-bar sitar bridge, individual pickup for sympathetic strings and

custom color gator finish; Longhorn Guitarlin ('89-'00, '05-present) with large cutaway Guitarlin-style body, 24 frets in '89 and 31 after; and the Neptune 12-string ('81-present) single-cut with 3 pickups.

1990s	Baritone 6-string	$550	$650
1990s	Electric Sitar	$600	$700
1990s	Longhorn Guitarlin	$600	$700
1990s	Neptune Electric 12-string	$600	$750

Jersey Girl

1991-present. Premium grade, production/custom, solidbody guitars made in Japan. They also build effects.

JET

1998-present. Premium grade, custom/production, chambered solidbody electric guitars built by luthier Jeffrey Earle Terwilliger in Raleigh, North Carolina.

Jewel

1920s. Instruments built by the Oscar Schmidt Co. and possibly others. Most likely a brand made for a distributor.

JG Guitars

1991-present. Luthier Johan Gustavsson builds his premium and presentation grade, production/custom, solidbody electric guitars in Malmö, Sweden.

Jim Redgate Guitars

1992-present. Luthier Jim Redgate builds his premium grade, custom, nylon-string classical guitars in Belair, Adelaide, South Australia.

John Le Voi Guitars

1970-present. Production/custom, gypsy jazz, flat-top, and archtop guitars built by luthier John Le Voi in Lincolnshire, United Kingdom. He also builds mandolin family instruments.

John Price Guitars

1984-present. Custom classical and flamenco guitars built by luthier John Price in Australia.

Johnson

Mid-1990s-present. Budget, intermediate and professional grade, production, acoustic, classical, acoustic/electric, resonator and solidbody guitars imported by Music Link, Brisbane, California. Johnson also offers basses, amps, mandolins, ukuleles and effects.

Jon Kammerer

1995-present. Luthier Jon Kammerer builds his professional grade, custom, acoustic and electric guitars in Keokuk, Iowa. He also builds the Sinister Custom Shop Bass for Sinister Guitars.

Jaros Bluesman Plus

Jerry Jones Electric Sitar

GUITARS

Kalamazoo KG--14

Kathy Wingert flat-top

MODEL YEAR	FEATURES	EXC. COND. LOW	HIGH

Jones

See TV Jones listing.

Jordan

1981-present. Professional and premium grade, custom, flat-top and archtop guitars built by luthier John Jordan in Concord, California. He also builds electric violins and cellos.

Jose Oribe

1962-present. Presentation grade, production, classical, flamenco, and steel-string acoustic guitars built by luthier Jose Oribe in Vista, California.

Jose Ramirez

1882-present. Professional, premium, and presentation grade, custom/production, classical guitars built by luthier José Ramirez IV in Madrid, Spain. The company was founded by his great-grandfather.

K & S

1992-1998. Hawaiian-style and classical guitars distributed by George Katechis and Marc Silber and handmade in Paracho, Mexico. A few 16" wide Leadbelly Model 12-strings were made in Oakland, California by luthier Stewart Port. K & S also offered mandolins, mandolas and ukes. In '98, Silber started marketing guitars under the Marc Silber Guitar Company brand and Katechis continued to offer instruments under the Casa Montalvo brand.

Kakos, Stephen

1972-present. Luthier Stephen Kakos builds his premium grade, production/custom, classical guitars in Mound, Minnesota.

Kalamazoo

1933-1942, 1965-1970. Budget brand built by Gibson. Made flat-tops, solidbodies, mandolins, lap steels, banjos and amps. Name revived for a line of amps, solidbodies and basses in '65-'67.

KG-1/KG-1 A

1965-1969. Offset double-cut (initial issue) or SG-shape (second issue), 1 pickup, Model 1 A with spring vibrato, red, blue or white.

1965-1969		$200	$300

KG-2/KG-2 A

1965-1970. Offset double-cut (initial shape) or SG-shape, 2 pickups, Model 2 A with spring vibrato, red, blue or white.

1965-1970		$325	$450

KG-11

1933-1941. Flat-top, all mahogany, 14" with no 'guard, sunburst.

1933-1941		$600	$900

KG-14

1936-1940. Flat-top L-0-size, mahogany back and sides, with 'guard, sunburst.

1936-1940		$800	$1,000

MODEL YEAR	FEATURES	EXC. COND. LOW	HIGH

KG-16

1939-1940. Gibson-made archtop, small body, f-hole.

1939-1940		$650	$750

KG-21

1936-1941. Early model 15" archtop (bent, not curved), dot markers, bound top, sunburst.

1936-1941		$650	$750

KG-31

1935-1940. Archtop L-50-size, 16" body, non-carved spruce top, mahogany back and sides.

1935-1940		$700	$800

KG-32

1939-1942. Archtop, 16" body.

1939-1942		$725	$825

KTG-14 Tenor

1936-1940. Flat-top L-0-size tenor, mahogany back and sides, bound top, sunburst.

1936-1940		$350	$500

Kamico

Brand started in 1947. Flat-top acoustic guitars. Low-end budget brand made by Kay Musical Instrument Company and sold through various distributors.

Acoustic Flat-Tops

1940s. Various models.

1940s		$200	$250

Kapa

Ca. 1962-1970. Begun by Dutch immigrant and music store owner Kope Veneman in Hyattsville, Maryland whose father had made Amka guitars in Holland. Kapa is from K for Kope, A for son Albert, P for daughter Patricia, and A for wife Adeline. Crown shield logo from Amka guitars.

The brand included some Hofner and Italian imports in '60. Ca. '66 Kapa started offering thinner bodies. Some German Pix pickups ca. '66. Thinlines and Japanese bodies in '69. Kapa closed shop in '70 and the parts and equipment were sold to Micro-Frets and Mosrite. Later Veneman was involved with Bradley copy guitars imported from Japan. Approximately 120,000 Kapa guitars and basses were made.

Electric Guitars

1962-1970. Various models include Challenger with 3-way toggle from '62-'66/'67 and 2 on/off switches after; Cobra with 1 pickup; Continental and Continental 12-string; Minstrel and Minstrel 12-string with teardrop shape, 3 pickups; and the Wildcat, mini offset double-cut, 3 pickups and mute.

1962-1970	Various models	$300	$600

Kasha

1967-1997. Innovative classical guitars built by luthier Richard Schneider in collaboration with Dr. Michael Kasha. Schneider also consulted for Gibson and Gretsch. Schneider died in '97.

MODEL YEAR	FEATURES	EXC. COND. LOW	HIGH

Kathy Wingert Guitars

1996-present. Luthier Kathy Wingert builds her premium grade, production/custom, flat-tops in Rancho Palos Verdes, California.

Kawai

1927-present. Kawai is a Japanese piano and guitar maker. They started offering guitars around '56 and they were imported into the U.S. carrying many different brand names, including Kimberly and Teisco. In '67 Kawai purchased Teisco. Odd-shaped guitars were offered from late-'60s through the mid-'70s. Few imports carrying the Kawai brand until the late-'70s; best known for high quality basses. By '90s they were making plexiglass replicas of Teisco Spectrum 5 and Kawai moon-shaped guitar. Kawai quit offering guitars and basses around 2002.

Acoustic Hollowbody Archtops
1956-2002.

1956-2002		$250	$300

Electric Archtops
1956-2002.

1956-2002	Various	$250	$400

Kay

Ca. 1931 (1890)-present. Originally founded in Chicago, Illinois as Groehsl Company (or Groehsel) in 1890, making bowl-backed mandolins. Offered Groehsl, Stromberg, Kay Kraft, Kay, Arch Kraft brand names, plus made guitars for S.S.Maxwell, Old Kraftsman (Spiegel), Recording King (Wards), Supertone (Sears), Silvertone (Sears), National, Dobro, Custom Kraft (St.Louis Music), Hollywood (Shireson Bros.), Oahu and others.

In 1921 the name was changed to Stromberg-Voisinet Company. Henry Kay "Hank" Kuhrmeyer joined the company in '23 and was secretary by '25. By the mid-'20s the company was making many better Montgomery Ward guitars, banjos and mandolins, often with lots of pearloid.

First production electric guitars and amps are introduced with big fanfare in '28; perhaps only 200 or so made. Last Stromberg instruments seen in '32. Kuhrmeyer becomes president and the Kay Kraft brand was introduced in '31, probably named for Kuhrmeyer's middle name, though S-V had used Kay brand on German Kreuzinger violins '28-'36. By '34, if not earlier, the company is changed to the Kay Musical Instrument Company. A new factory was built at 1640 West Walnut Street in '35. The Kay Kraft brand ends in '37 and the Kay brand is introduced in late-'36 or '37. Violin Style Guitars and upright acoustic basses debut in '38. In '40 the first guitars for Sears, carrying the new Silvertone brand, are offered.

Kamico budget line introduced in '47 and Rex flat-tops and archtops sold through Gretsch in late-'40s. Kuhrmeyer retires in '55 dies a year later. New gigantic factory in Elk Grove Village, Illinois opens in '64. Seeburg purchased Kay in '66 and sold

it to Valco in '67. Valco/Kay went out of business in '68 and its assets were auctioned in '69. The Kay name went to Sol Weindling and Barry Hornstein of W.M.I. (Teisco Del Rey) who began putting Kay name on Teisco guitars. By '73 most Teisco guitars are called Kay. Tony Blair, president of Indianapolis-based A.R. Musical Enterprises Inc. (founded in '73) purchased the Kay nameplate in '79 and currently distributes Kay in the U.S. Currently Kay offers budget and intermediate grade, production, acoustic, semi-hollow body, solidbody, and resonator guitars. They also make amps, basses, banjos, mandolins, ukes, and violins.

Barney Kessel Artist
1957-1960. Single-cut, 15 1/2" body, 1 (K6701) or 2 (K6700) pickups, Kelvinator headstock, sunburst or blond.

1957-1960		$1,200	$1,500

Barney Kessel Pro
1957-1960. 13" hollowbody, single-cut, Kelvinator headstock, ebony 'board with pearl inlays, white binding, 1 or 2 pickups, sunburst.

1957-1960		$1,500	$1,700

K20
1939-1942. 16" archtop, solid spruce top, maple back and sides, sunburst.

1939-1942		$250	$300

K22
1950s. Flat-top similar to Gibson J-100 17", spruce top, mahogany back and sides.

1955-1959		$400	$600

K26
1955-1959. Flat-top, block markers, natural.

1955-1959		$500	$700

K44
1947-1951. Non-cut archtop, solid spruce top, 17" curly maple veneered body, block markers, sunburst.

1947-1951		$400	$500

K45
1952-1954. Non-cut archtop, 17" body, engraved tortoiseshell-celluloid headstock, large block markers, natural.

1952-1954		$450	$550

K46
1947-1951. Non-cut archtop, solid spruce top, 17" curly maple-veneered body, double-eighth note headstock inlay, sunburst.

1947-1951		$475	$600

K48 Artist
1947-1951. Non-cut archtop, 17" solid spruce top with figured maple back and sides, split block inlays, sunburst or black.

1947-1951		$900	$1,200

K48/K21 Jazz Special
Late-1960s. Slim solidbody with 3 reflective pickups, garden spade headstock, fancy position Circle K headstock logo.

1968	White	$400	$500

Kathy Wingert 00 Cutaway

1957 Kay Barney Kessel

K100 Vanguard

Kay 573 Speed Demon

MODEL YEAR	FEATURES	EXC. COND. LOW	HIGH

K100 Vanguard
1961-1966. Offset double-cut slab solidbody, genuine maple veneered top and back over hardwood body, sunburst.

1961-1966		$125	$175

K102 Vanguard
1961-1966. Double pickup version of the K100, sunburst.

1961-1966		$150	$200

K161 Thin Twin "Jimmy Reed"
1952-1958. Cutaway semi-hollow, 2 pickups, birds-eye maple, often called the Jimmy Reed, sunburst.

1952-1958		$500	$650

K300 Double Cutaway Solid Electric
1962-1966. Two single-coils, block inlays, some with curly maple top and some with plain maple top, natural.

1962-1966		$500	$600

K535
1961-1965. Thinline double-cut, 2 pickups, vibrato, sunburst.

1961-1965		$500	$600

K571/K572/K573 Speed Demon
1961-1965. Thinline semi-acoustic/electric, single pointed cutaway, some with Bigsby vibrato, with 2 (K571), 2 (K572) or 3 (K573) pickups. There was also a Speed Demon solidbody.

1961-1965	K571	$350	$450
1961-1965	K572	$450	$550
1961-1965	K573	$500	$650

K592
1962-1966. Thinline semi-acoustic/electric, double Florentine cut, 2 or 3 pickups, Bigsby vibrato, pie-slice inlays, cherry.

1962-1966		$500	$650

K671/K672 Swingmaster
1961-1965. Single rounded cutaway semi-hollow-body, with 1 (K671) or 2 (K672) pickups.

1961-1965	K671	$600	$750
1961-1965	K672	$700	$800

K1160 Standard
1957-1964. Small 13" (standard) flat-top, laminated construction.

1957-1964		$50	$75

K1961/K1962/K1963
1960-1965. Part of Value Leader line, thinline single-cut, hollowbody, identified by single chrome-plated checkered, body-length guard on treble side, laminated maple body, maple neck, dot markers, sunburst, with 1 (K1961), 2 (K1962) or 3 (K1963) pickups.

1960-1965	K1961	$400	$500
1960-1965	K1962	$500	$550
1960-1965	K1963	$500	$650

K1982/K1983 Style Leader/Jimmy Reed
1960-1965. Part of the Style Leader mid-level Kay line. Sometimes dubbed Jimmy Reed of 1960s. Easily identified by the long brushed copper dual guardplates on either side of the strings. Brown or gleaming golden blond (natural) finish, laminated curly maple body, simple script Kay logo, with 2 (K1982) or 3 (K1983) pickups.

MODEL YEAR	FEATURES	EXC. COND. LOW	HIGH
1960-1965	K1982	$500	$575
1960-1965	K1983	$500	$650

K3500 Student Concert
1966-1968. 14 1/2" flat-top, solid spruce top, laminated maple back and sides.

1966-1968		$75	$100

K5113 Plains Special
1968. Flat-top, solid spruce top, laminated mahogany back and sides.

1968		$150	$200

K5160 Auditorium
1957-1965. Flat-top 15" auditorium-size, laminated construction.

1957-1965		$100	$150

K6100 Country
1950s-1960s. Jumbo flat-top, spruce x-braced top, mahogany back and sides, natural.

1957-1962		$350	$450

K6116 Super Auditorium
1957-1965. Super Auditorium-size flat-top, laminated figured maple back and sides, solid spruce top.

1957-1965		$200	$250

K6120 Western
1960s. Jumbo flat-top, laminated maple body, pin-less bridge, sunburst.

1962		$175	$225

K6130 Calypso
1960-1965. 15 1/2" flat-top with narrow waist, slotted headstock, natural.

1960-1965		$250	$300

K6533/K6535 Value Leader
1961-1965. Value Leader was the budget line of Kay, full body archtop, sunburst, with 1 (K6533) or 2 (K6535) pickups.

1961-1965	K6533	$250	$300
1961-1965	K6535	$250	$300

K7000 Artist
1960-1965. Highest-end of Kay classical series, fan bracing, spruce top, maple back and sides.

1960-1965		$400	$450

K7010 Concerto
1960-1965. Entry level of Kay classical series.

1960-1965		$75	$150

K7010 Maestro
1960-1965. Middle level of Kay classical series.

1960-1965		$225	$275

K8110 Master
1957-1960. 17" master-size flat-top which was largest of the series, laminated construction.

1957-1960		$150	$200

K8127 Solo Special
1957-1965. Kay's professional grade flat-top, narrow waist jumbo, block markers.

1957-1965		$450	$550

K8995 Upbeat
1958-1960. Less expensive alternative to Barney Kessel Jazz Special, 2 pickups, sunburst.

1958-1960		$850	$1,000

The *Vintage Guitar Price Guide* shows low to high values for items in all-original excellent condition, and, where applicable, with original case or cover.

MODEL YEAR	FEATURES	EXC. COND. LOW	HIGH

Kay Kraft

Ca.1931-1937. First brand name of the Kay Musical Instrument Company as it began its transition from Stromberg-Voisinet Company to Kay (see Kay for more info).

Kay Kraft Recording King

1931-1937		$400	$600

Kel Kroydon (by Gibson)

1930-1933. Private branded budget level instruments made by Gibson. They also had mandolins and banjos. The name has been revived on a line of banjos by Tom Mirisola and made in Nashville.

KK-1

1930-1933. 14 3/4" L-0 sytle body, colorful parrot stencils on body.

1930-1933		$2,000	$2,500

Keller Custom Guitars

1994-present. Professional grade, production/custom, solidbody guitars built by luthier Randall Keller in Mandan, North Dakota.

Keller Guitars

1975-present. Premium grade, production/custom, flat-tops made by luthier Michael L. Keller in Rochester, Minnesota.

Ken Franklin

2003-present. Luthier Ken Franklin builds his premium grade, production/custom, acoustic guitars in Ukiah, California.

Kendrick

1989-present. Premium grade, production/custom, solidbody guitars built in Texas. Founded by Gerald Weber in Pflugerville, Texas and currently located in Kempner, Texas. Mainly known for their handmade tube amps, Kendrick added guitars in '94 and also offers speakers and effects.

Kent

1961-1969. Imported from Japan by Buegeleisen and Jacobson of New York, New York. Manufacturers unknown but many early guitars and basses were made by Guyatone and Teisco.

Acoustic Flat-Tops

1962-1969.

1962-1969		$125	$150

Acoustic/Electric Guitars

1962-1969.

1962-1969		$175	$225

Electric 12-String

1960s. Thinline electric, double pointy cutaways, 12 strings, slanted dual pickup, sunburst.

1965-1969		$300	$450

Semi-Hollow Electric

1960s. Thinline electric, offset double pointy cutaways, slanted dual pickups, various colors.

1962-1969		$300	$450

Solidbody Electrics

1962-1969. Models include Polaris I, II and III, Lido, Copa and Videocaster.

1962-1969		$150	$350

Kevin Ryan Guitars

1989-present. Premium grade, custom, flat-tops built by luthier Kevin Ryan in Westminster, California.

Kiesel

See Carvin.

Kimberly

Late-1960s-early-1970s. Private branded import made in the same Japanese factory as Teisco.

May Queen

1960s. Same as Teisco May Queen with Kimberly script logo on headstock and May Queen Teisco on the 'guard.

1960s		$450	$600

Kingsley

1960s. Early Japanese imports, Teisco-made.

Soldibody Electric

1960s. Four pickups with tremolo.

1960s		$300	$400

Kingslight Guitars

1980-present. Luthier John Kingslight builds his premium grade, custom/production, steel string guitars in Portage, Michigan (in Taos, New Mexico for '80-'83). He also builds basses.

Kingston

Ca. 1958-1967. Guitars and basses imported from Japan by Jack Westheimer and Westheimer Importing Corporation of Chicago, Illinois. Early examples made by Guyatone and Teisco.

Electric

1958-1967. Various models include: B-1, soldbody, 1 pickup; B-2T/B-3T/B-4T, solidbodies, 2/3/4 pickups and tremolo; SA-27, thin hollowbody, 2 pickups, tremolo.

1958-1967		$150	$400

Kinscherff Guitars

1990-present. Luthier Jamie Kinscherff builds his premium grade, production/custom, flat-top guitars in Austin, Texas.

Kleartone

1930s. Private brand made by Regal and/or Gibson.

Small flat top

1930s		$600	$900

Klein Acoustic Guitars

1972-present. Luthiers Steve Klein and Steven Kauffman build their production/custom, premium and presentation grade flat-tops in Sonoma, California. They also build basses.

1964 Kent No. 540

Ken Franklin Madison

GUITARS

1977 Kramer 650G

Koll Duo Glide

MODEL			EXC. COND.	
YEAR		FEATURES	LOW	HIGH

Klein Electric Guitars

1988-present. Steve Klein added electrics to his line in '88. In '95, he sold the electric part of his business to Lorenzo German, who continues to produce professional grade, production/custom, solidbody guitars in Linden, California. He also builds basses.

Klira

1887-1980s. Founded by Johannes Klira in Schoenbach, Germany, mainly made violins, but added guitars in the 1950s. The guitars of the '50s and '60s were original designs, but by the '70s most models were similar to popular American models. The guitars of the '50s and '60s were aimed at the budget market, but workmanship improved with the '70s models. They also made basses.

Hollowbody Electrics

1960s		$250	$400

Solidbody Electrics

1960s		$200	$400

Knutsen

1890s-1920s. Luthier Chris J. Knutsen of Tacoma and Seattle, Washington, experimented with and perfected Hawaiian and harp guitar models. He moved to Los Angeles, California around 1916, where he also made steels and ukes.

Convertible

1909-1914. Flat-top model with adjustable neck angle that allowed for a convertible Hawaiian or Spanish setup.

1909-1914		$2,500	$4,000

Harp Guitar

1900s. Normally 11 strings with fancy purfling and trim.

1900-1910		$6,500	$7,000

Knutson Luthiery

1981-present. Professional and premium grade, custom, archtop and flat-top guitars built by luthier John Knutson in Forestville, California. He also builds basses and mandolins.

Kohno

1960-present. Luthier Masaru Kohno built his classical guitars in Tokyo, Japan. When he died in '98, production was taken over by his nephew, Masaki Sakurai.

Classical

Brazilian rosewood back and sides, spruce top.

1970s		$2,800	$3,200

Koll

1990-present. Professional and premium grade, custom/production, solidbody, chambered, and archtop guitars built by luthier Saul Koll, originally in Long Beach, California, and since '93, in Portland, Oregon. He also builds basses.

Kona

1910s-1920s, 2001-present. Acoustic Hawaiian guitars sold by C.S. Delano and others, with later models the Herman Weissenborn Co. Weissenborn appointments in line with style number, with thicker body and solid neck construction. Since '01, the Kona name is now used on an import line of budget grade, production, acoustic and electric guitars and basses.

Style 3

1920s	Koa	$3,500	$4,000

Style 4

1920s	Brown koa	$3,800	$4,400

Koontz

1970-late 1980s. Luthier Sam Koontz started building custom guitars in the late '50s. Starting in '66 Koontz, who was associated with Harptone guitars, built guitars for Standel. In '70, he opened his own shop in Linden, New Jersey, building a variety of custom guitars. Koontz died in the late '80s. His guitars varied greatly and should be valued on a case-by-case basis.

Kramer

1976-1990, 1995-present. Currently Kramer offers budget and intermediate grade, production, imported acoustic, acoustic/electric, semi-hollow and solidbody guitars. They also offer basses, amps and effects.

Founded by New York music retailer Dennis Berardi, ex-Travis Bean sales rep Gary Kramer and ex-Norlin executive Peter LaPlaca. Initial financing provided by real estate developer Henry Vaccaro. Parent company named BKL Corporation (Berardi, Kramer, LaPlaca), located in Neptune City, New Jersey. The first guitars were designed by Berardi and luthier Phil Petillo and featured aluminum necks with wooden inserts on back to give them a wooden feel. Guitar production commenced in late-'76.

Control passed to Guitar Center of Los Angeles for '79-'82, which recommended a switch to more economical wood necks. Aluminum necks were phased out during the early-'80s, and were last produced in '85. In '89, a new investment group was brought in with James Liati as president, hoping for access to Russian market, but the company went of business in late-'90.

In '95 Henry Vaccaro and new partners revived the company and designed a number of new guitars in conjunction with Phil Petillo. However, in '97 the Kramer brand was sold to Gibson. In '98, Henry Vaccaro released his new line of aluminum-core neck, split headstock guitars under the Vacarro brand.

Non-U.S.-made models include the following lines: Aerostar, Ferrington, Focus, Hundred (post-'85 made with 3 digits in the 100-900), Showster, Striker, Thousand (post-'85 made with 4 digits in the 1000-9000), XL (except XL-5 made in '80s). **Serial numbers for import models include:**

MODEL YEAR	FEATURES	EXC. COND. LOW	HIGH

Two alpha followed by 4 numbers: for example AA234l with any assortment of letters and numbers.

One alpha followed by 5 numbers: for example B23412.

Five numbers: for example 23412.

Model number preceeding numbers: for example XL1-03205.

The notation "Kramer, Neptune, NJ" does indicate U.S.A.-made production.

Most post-'85 Kramers were ESP Japanese-made guitars. American Series were ESP Japanese components that were assembled in the U.S.

The vintage/used market makes value distinctions between U.S.-made and import models.

Headstock and logo shape can help identify U.S. versus imports as follows:

Traditional or Classic headstock with capital K as Kramer: U.S.A. '81-'84.

Banana (soft edges) headstock with all caps KRAMER: U.S.A. American Series '84-'86.

Pointy (sharp cut) headstock with all caps KRAMER: U.S.A. American Series '86-'87.

Pointy (sharp cut) headstock with downsized letters Kramer plus American decal: U.S.A. American Series '87-'94.

Pointy (sharp cut) headstock with downsized letters Kramer but without American decal, is an import.

250-G Special
1977-1979. Offset double-cut, tropical woods, aluminum neck, dot markers, 2 pickups.

1977-1979		$450	$575

350-G Standard
1976-1979. Offset double-cut, tropical woods, aluminum neck, tuning fork headstock, ebonol 'board, zero fret, 2 single coils, dot inlays. The 350 and 450 were Kramer's first models.

1976-1979		$600	$775

450-G Deluxe
1976-1980. Like 350-G, but with block inlays, 2 humbuckers. Became the 450G Deluxe in late '77 with dot inlays.

1976-1980		$700	$900

650-G Artist
1977-1980. Aluminum neck, ebonol 'board, double-cut solidbody, 2 humbuckers.

1977-1980		$900	$1,150

Baretta
1984-1990. Offset double-cut, banana six-on-a-side headstock, 1 pickup, Floyd Rose tremolo, black hardware, U.S.A.-made.

1984	1st style, larger headstock	$1,200	$1,600
1984-1985	2nd style, angled headstock	$600	$800
1985-1987	3rd style, ESP neck	$400	$625
1985-1987	With graphics	$450	$725
1988-1990	Standard opaque	$600	$800
1988-1990	With graphics	$650	$900
1990	Baretta III hybrid	$500	$700

Baretta II/Soloist
1986-1990. Soloist sleek body with pointed cutaway horns.

1986-1990		$350	$500

Classic Series
1986-1987. Solidbody copies of the famous Southern California builder, including offset contoured double-cut (Classic I) and slab body single-cut designs (Classic II and Classic III).

1986-1987	Classic I	$425	$650
1986-1987	Classic II	$400	$625
1986-1987	Classic III	$400	$600

Condor
1985-1986. Futuristic 4-point body with large upper bass horn and lower treble horn.

1985-1986		$350	$600

DMZ Custom Series
1978-1991. Solidbody double-cut with larger upper horn, bolt-on aluminum T-neck, slot headstock, models include the 1000 (super distortion humbuckers), 2000 (dual-sound humbuckers), 3000 (3 SDS single-coils), 6000 (dual-sound humbuckers, active DBL).

1978-1991	DMZ-1000	$575	$775
1978-1991	DMZ-2000	$625	$825
1978-1991	DMZ-3000	$500	$700
1978-1991	DMZ-6000	$700	$900

Duke Custom/Standard
1981-1982. Headless aluminum neck, 22-fret neck, 1 pickup, Floyd Rose tremolo.

1981-1982		$550	$600

Duke Special
1982-1985. Headless aluminum neck, two pickups, tuners on body.

1982-1985		$600	$650

Eliot Easton Pro I
1987-1988. Designed by Elliot Easton, offset double-cut, six-on-a-side headstock, Floyd Rose tremolo, 2 single-coils and 1 humbucker.

1987-1988		$475	$700

Eliot Easton Pro II
1987-1988. Same as Pro I, but with fixed-bridge tailpiece, 2 single-coils.

1987-1988		$400	$600

Ferrington
1985-1990. Acoustic-electric, offered in single- and double-cut, bolt-on electric-style neck, transducers, made in Korea.

1985-1990		$350	$550

Focus/F Series (Import)
1983-1989. Kramer introduced the Focus series as import copies of their American-made models like the Pacer, Baretta, Vanguard (Rhoads-V), and Voyager (star body). Model numbers were 1000-6000, plus the Focus Classic I, II, and III. Most models were offset, double-cut solidbodies. In '87 the Focus line was renamed the F-Series. In '88 a neck-through body design, which is noted as NT, was introduced for a short time. The Classic series was offered with over a dozen color options.

1983	Focus 4000, Pacer	$250	$375

1979 Kramer DMZ-2000

Kramer Elliot Easton Pro

GUITARS

Kramer Focus

1980 Kramer Gene Simmons Axe

MODEL YEAR	FEATURES	EXC. COND. LOW	HIGH
1983-1984	Focus 1000, Pacer Special	$225	$325
1983-1987	Focus 2000, Pacer Imperial	$225	$350
1983-1987	Focus 3000, Pacer Deluxe	$250	$350
1983-1987	Focus 6000, Pacer Custom	$250	$375
1984-1986	Focus 1000, Baretta	$325	$450
1984-1986	Focus 4000, Vanguard	$250	$375
1986-1987	Focus 5000, Voyager	$250	$375
1987-1988	Focus 1000/F1000	$300	$400
1987-1989	Focus Classic I, 3 pickups	$225	$350
1987-1989	Focus Classic II	$220	$345
1987-1989	Focus Classic III	$225	$325
1988	Focus 1000/F1000 NT	$375	$500
1988	Focus 2000/F2000 NT	$275	$400
1988-1989	Focus 2000/F2000	$200	$300
1988-1989	Focus 3000/F3000	$225	$325
1988-1989	Focus 6000/F6000	$225	$350
1989	Focus 1000/F1000	$300	$400

Gene Simmons Axe

1980-1981. Axe-shaped guitar, aluminum neck, 1 humbucker, slot headstock, stop tailpiece, 25 were made.

1980-1981		$2,500	$3,500

Gorky Park (Import)

1986-1989. Triangular balalaika, bolt-on maple neck, pointy droopy six-on-a-side headstock, 1 pickup, Floyd Rose tremolo, red with iron sickle graphics, tribute to Russian rock, reissued in late-'90s.

1986-1989		$400	$700

Hundred Series

1988-1990. Import budget line, most with offset double-cut 7/8th solidbody.

1988-1989	615, bound 610	$275	$400
1988-1990	110, 1 pickup	$200	$300
1988-1990	120	$250	$375
1988-1990	210, 2 pickups	$225	$350
1988-1990	220	$250	$375
1988-1990	310, 3 pickups	$225	$350
1988-1990	410	$225	$350
1988-1990	420, V-body	$275	$400
1988-1990	610, sleek body, 3 pickups	$250	$375
1988-1990	620	$250	$375
1989-1990	111, 2 pickups	$225	$325
1989-1990	112, carved 111	$250	$350
1989-1990	612	$250	$375
1989-1990	710	$250	$400
1989-1990	720, revised 710	$250	$400

Liberty '86 Series

1986-1987. Offset double cut arched-top solidbody, pointy head, 2 humbuckers, black, white or flame-maple bound body.

1986-1987	Black or white	$450	$650
1986-1987	Flame maple	$550	$750

Metalist/Showster Series

1989-1990. Korean-made offset double-cut solid-body, metal trim in body design, pointy droopy six-on-a-side headstock, various pickup options, Floyd Rose.

1989-1990		$375	$500

Nightswan

1987-1990. Offset double-cut, six-on-a-side head-stock, 2 Duncan humbuckers, Floyd Rose tremolo, blue metallic.

1987-1990		$550	$850

Pacer Series

1981-1987. Offset double-cut, six-on-a-side head-stock, various pickup options, bolt-on maple neck.

1981-1986	Custom	$450	$675
1982	Special, 1 pickup	$400	$600
1982-1984	Pacer, 2 pickups	$450	$650
1982-1985	Carerra, 2 pickups	$475	$675
1982-1987	Imperial	$425	$625
1983-1986	Deluxe	$450	$650
1987	Custom II	$425	$650

Paul Dean

1986-1988. Offset double cut, neck-thru, hum/single/single pickups, droopy pointy head.

1986-1988		$650	$1,000

ProAxe (U.S.A.)

1989-1990. U.S.A.-made, offset double-cut, sharp pointy headstock, dot markers, 2 or 3 pickups, smaller 7/8ths size body, 3 models offered with slightly different pickup options. The model was discontinued when Kramer went out of business in 1990.

1989-1990	Deluxe	$575	$875
1989-1990	Special	$550	$850
1989-1990	Standard	$525	$825

Richie Sambora

1987-1989. Designed by Sambora, mahogany offset double-cut, maple neck, pointy droopy six-on-a-side headstock, gold hardware, Floyd Rose, 3 pickups, 2 coil-taps.

1987-1989		$600	$900

Ripley Series

1984-1987. Offset double-cut, banana six-on-a-side headstock, 22 frets, hexophonic humbucking pickups, panpots, dual volume, Floyd Rose tremolo, black hardware, stereo output, pointy droopy headstock in '87.

1984-1987		$350	$550

Savant/Showster Series

1989-1990. Offset double-cut solidbody, pointy headstock, various pickup options.

1989-1990		$325	$450

Stagemaster Series (Import)

1983-1987. Offset double-cut neck-thru solidbody models, smaller 7/8th body, built by ESP in Japan.

1983-1987	Custom/Custom I	$525	$750
1983-1987	Deluxe/Deluxe I	$525	$725
1983-1987	Imperial	$500	$700
1983-1987	Special	$450	$650
1983-1987	Standard/Standard I	$475	$700
1987	Deluxe II	$425	$625

MODEL YEAR	FEATURES	EXC. COND. LOW	HIGH

Striker Series (Import)

1984-1989. Korean imports, offset doube-cut, various pickup options, series included Striker 100, 200, 300, 400, 600 and 700 Bass.

1984-1989	100ST, 1 pickup	$175	$225
1984-1989	200ST, 2 pickups	$200	$250
1984-1989	300ST, 3 pickups	$200	$250
1985-1989	400ST, Rhoads-body	$200	$250
1985-1989	500ST, Star-body	$225	$275
1986-1989	600ST, 3 pickups	$250	$300
1988-1989	605ST, 3 pickups, bound	$275	$325

Sustainer

1989. Offset double-cut solidbody, reverse pointy headstock, Floyd Rose tremolo.

1989		$500	$800

Vanguard Series

1981-1986, 1999-present. U.S.-made or American Series (assembled in U.S.). V shape, 1 humbucker, aluminum (Special '81-'83) or wood (Custom '81-'83) neck. Added for '83-'84 were the Imperial (wood neck, 2 humbuckers) and the Headless (alum neck, 1 humbucker). For '85-'86, the body was modified to a Jackson Randy Rhoads style V body, with a banana headstock and 2 humbuckers. In '99 this last design was revived as an import.

1981-1983	Custom	$450	$650
1981-1983	Special	$400	$600
1983-1984	Imperial, wood neck	$425	$625
1985-1986	Rhoads V-body	$425	$650

Voyager

1982-1985. Wood neck, classic headstock, rosewood 'board, 1 pickup (2 optional), Floyd Rose tremolo, black.

1982-1985	Imperial	$450	$675

XKG-10

1980-1981. Aluminum neck, V-shaped body.

1980-1981		$500	$600

XKG-20

1980-1981. More traditional double-cut body with small horns.

1980-1981		$475	$575

XL Series

1980-1981 and 1987-1990. The early-'80s U.S.-made models were completely different than the late-'80s model. The late-'80s models were inexpensive imports.

1980-1981	XL-5, 2 humbuckers, aluminum neck	$600	$800
1987-1990	XL-1, 2 pickups, wood neck	$100	$150
1987-1990	XL-6, 3 pickups, wood neck	$100	$150
1989	XL-2, 2 humbuckers, wood neck	$100	$150
1989	XL-3, 3 pickups, wood neck	$100	$150

ZX Aero Star Series (Import)

1986-1989. Offset double-cut solidbodies, pointy six-on-a-side headstock. Models include the 1 humbucker ZX-10, 2 humbucker ZX-20, 3 single coil ZX-30, and hum/single/single ZX-30H.

1986-1989		$100	$125

Kramer-Harrison, William

1977-present. Luthier William Kramer-Harrison builds his premium grade, custom, classical and flat-top guitars in Kingston, New York.

Kubicki

1973-present. Kubicki is best known for their Factor basses, but did offer a few guitar models in the early '80s. See Bass section for more company info.

Kustom

1968-present. Founded by Bud Ross in Chanute, Kansas, and best known for the tuck-and-roll amps, Kustom also offered guitars from '68 to '69. See Amp section for more company info.

Electric Hollowbody

1968-1969. Hollowed-out 2-part bodies; includes the K200A (humbucker, Bigsby), the K200B (single-coils, trapeze tailpiece), and the K200C (less fancy tuners), various colors.

1960s		$775	$875

Kyle, Doug

1990-present. Premium grade, custom, Selmer-style guitars made by luthier Doug Kyle in England.

L Benito

2001-present. Professional grade, steel and nylon string acoustics from luthier Lito Benito and built in Chile.

La Baye

1967. Designed by Dan Helland in Green Bay, Wisconsin and built by the Holman-Woodell factory in Neodesha, Kansas. Introduced at NAMM and folded when no orders came in. Only 45 prototypes made. A few may have been sold later as 21st Century. They also had basses.

2x4 6-String

1967. Narrow plank body, controls on top, 2 pickups, tremolo, 12-string version was also made.

1967		$1,200	$1,500

La Mancha

1996-present. Professional and premium grade, production/custom, classical guitars made in Mexico under the supervision of Kenny Hill and Gil Carnal and distributed by Jerry Roberts of Nashville.

Style F Classical

1996-present. Solid cedar top, solid rosewood back and sides.

1996-2005		$1,900	$2,100

Kramer Vanguard

1967 La Baye 2x4

MODEL		EXC. COND.	
YEAR	FEATURES	LOW	HIGH

La Patrie

Production, classical guitars. Founded by luthier Robert Godin, who also has the Norman, Godin, Seagull, and Patrick & Simon brands of instruments.

La Scala

Ca. 1920s-1930s. La Scala was another brand of the Oscar Schmidt Company of New Jersey, and was used on guitars, banjos, and mandolins. These were often the fanciest of the Schmidt instruments. Schmidt made the guitars and mandolins; the banjos were made by Rettberg & Lang.

Lace Music Products

1979-present. Intermediate and professional, production, electric guitars from Lace Music Products, a division of Actodyne General Inc. which was founded by Don Lace Sr., inventor of the Lace Sensor Pickup. In '96 Lace added amplifiers and in 2001 they added guitars. In '02, they also started offering the Rat Fink brand of guitars.

Lacey Guitars

1974-present. Luthier Mark Lacey builds his premium and presentation archtops and flat-tops in Nashville, Tennessee.

Lado

1973-present. Founded by Joe Kovacic, Lado builds professional and premium grade, production/custom, solidbody guitars in Lindsay, Ontario. Some model lines are branded J. K. Lado. They also build basses.

Lafayette

Ca. 1963-1967. Sold through Lafayette Electronics catalogs. Early Japanese-made guitars and basses from pre-copy era, generally shorter scale beginner instruments. Many made by Guyatone, some possibly by Teisco.

Acoustic Thinline Archtop

1963-1967. Various models.

1963-1967		$150	$250

Lakeside (Lyon & Healy)

Early-1900s. Mainly catalog sales of guitars and mandolins from the Chicago maker. Marketed as a less expensive alternative to the Lyon & Healy Washburn product line.

Harp Guitar - Jumbo Style G3740

Early-1900s. Spruce top, rosewood finished birch back and sides, two 6-string necks with standard tuners, 1 neck is fretless without dot markers, rectangular bridge.

1917	Natural	$2,000	$3,000

Lakewood

1986-present. Luthier Martin Seeliger builds his professional and premium grade, production/custom, steel and nylon string guitars in Giessen, Germany. He also builds mandolins.

MODEL		EXC. COND.	
YEAR	FEATURES	LOW	HIGH

Langejans Guitars

1971-present. Premium grade, production/custom, flat-top, 12-string, and classical guitars built by luthier Delwyn Langejans in Holland, Michigan.

Larrivee

1968-present. Professional and premium grade, production/custom, acoustic, acoustic/electric, and classical guitars built in Vancouver, British Columbia and, since '01, in Oxnard, California. Founded by Jean Larrivee, who apprenticed under Edgar Monch in Toronto. He built classic guitars in his home from '68-'70 and built his first steel string guitar in '71. Moved company to Victoria, BC in '77 and to Vancouver in '82. In '83, he began building solidbody electric guitars until '89, when focus again returned to acoustics.

Up to 2002, Larrivee used the following model designations: 05 Mahogany Standard, 09 Rosewood Standard, 10 Deluxe, 19 Special, 50 & 60 Standard (unique inlay), 70 Deluxe, and 72 Presentation. Starting in '03 designations used are: 01 Parlor, 03 Standard, 05 Select Mahogany, 09 Rosewood Artist, 10 Rosewood Deluxe, 19 California Anniv. Special Edition Series, 50 Traditional Series, 60 Traditional Series, E = Electric, R = Rosewood.

00-10

2000s. 00-size 14" lower bout, spruce top, rosewood back and sides, gloss finish.

2000s		$1,500	$1,600

C-10 Deluxe

Late-1980s-1990s. Sitka spruce top, Indian rosewood back and sides, sharp cutaway, fancy binding.

1980s		$1,600	$2,000

C-72 Cutaway Presentation

Spruce top, Indian rosewood back and sides, sharp cutaway, ultra-fancy abalone and pearl hand-engraved headstock.

1990s	Mermaid headstock	$2,600	$3,000

C-72 Presentation

Spruce top, Indian rosewood back and sides, non-cut Style D, ultra-fancy abalone and pearl hand-engraved headstock.

1990s	Jester headstock	$2,100	$2,600

D-10 Deluxe

1990s-present. Spruce top, rosewood rims, abalone top and soundhole trim.

1995-2005		$1,700	$2,000

D-70 Deluxe

1992		$1,600	$2,000

D-Style Classical

1970s. Rosewood body, unicorn inlays.

1970s		$2,100	$2,300

J-05 12

2000s. Jumbo acoustic-electric 12-string, spruce top, mahogany back and sides.

2000s		$1,200	$1,400

JV-05 Mahogany Standard

2000s		$1,100	$1,200

Lace Twister

Larrivee L-19

MODEL YEAR	FEATURES	EXC. COND. LOW	HIGH

L-0 Standard Series
1980s-1990s. Models include L-03 (satin finish), L-05 (mahogany) and L-09 (Indian rosewood).

1980s	L-05	$800	$1,100
1983-1987	L-09	$1,000	$1,500
1990s	L-03	$700	$800

L-72 Presentation Custom
Mid- to late-1990s. Spruce top, Indian rosewood rims, ornate vase and vine inlays.

1996		$3,100	$3,500

Parlor Walnut
Early 2000s. Spruce top, solid walnut back and sides.

2002		$500	$600

RS-4 CM Carved Top
1988-1989. Carved top solidbody, curly maple top, single-single-humbucker pickups, sunburst or translucent finishes.

1988-1989		$950	$2,000

Larson Brothers (Chicago)
Late 1890s-1944. Chicago's Carl and August Larson built guitars under a variety of names, (refer to Stetson, Maurer and Prairie State listings).

Laskin
1973-present. Luthier William "Grit" Laskin builds his premium and presentation grade, custom, steel-string, classical, and flamenco guitars in Toronto, Ontario. Many of his instruments feature extensive inlay work.

Laurie Williams Guitars
1983-present. Luthier Laurie Williams builds his premium and presentation grade, custom/production, steel string, classical and archtop guitars on the North Island of New Zealand. He also builds mandolins.

Leach Guitars
1980-present. Luthier Harvey Leach builds his professional and premium grade, custom, flattops, archtops, and solidbody electrics and travel guitars in Cedar Ridge, California. He also builds basses.

Lehmann Stringed Instruments
1971-present. Luthier Bernard Lehmann builds his professional and premium grade, production/custom, flat-top, archtop, classical and Gypsy guitars in Rochester, New York. He also builds lutes, vielles and rebecs.

Lehtela
1993-present. Professional and premium grade, custom/production, acoustic, acoustic/electric, archtop, and solidbody guitars built by luthier Ari Lehtela in Charlotte, North Carolina. He also builds basses.

Les Stansell Guitars
1980-present. Luthier Les Stansell builds his premium grade, custom, nylon-string guitars in Pistol River, Oregon.

Levin
1900-1973. Founded by Herman Carlson Levin and located in Gothenburg, Sweden, Levin was best known for their classical guitars, which they also built for other brands, most notably Goya from ca. 1955 to the mid '70s. They also built mandolins and ukes.

Linc Luthier
Professional and premium grade, custom/production, electric and acoustic guitars built by luther Linc Luthier in Upland, California. He also builds basses and double-necks.

Lindberg
Ca. 1950s. Line of guitars produced by Hoyer for Germany's Lindberg music store.

Lindert
1986-present. Luthier Chuck Lindert makes his intermediate and professional grade, production/custom, Art Deco-vibe electric guitars in Chelan, Washington.

Line 6
1996-present. Professional grade, production, imported solidbody and acoustic modeling guitars able to replicate the tones of a variety of instruments. Line 6 also builds effects and amps.

Lion
1960s. One of the brand names of guitars built for others by Egmond in Holland.

Loar
2005-present. Professional grade, production, imported archtop acoustic guitars designed by Greg Rich for The Music Link, which also has Johnson and other brands of intruments.

Lollar
1979-present. Luthier Jason Lollar builds his premium grade, production/custom, solidbody and archtop guitars in Vashon, Washington.

Lopez, Abel Garcia
1985-present. Luthier Abel Garcia Lopez builds his premium grade, custom, classical guitars in Mexico.

Loprinzi
1972-present. Professional and premium grade, production/custom, classical and steel-string guitars built in Clearwater, Florida. They also build ukes.

Founded by Augustino LoPrinzi and his brother

Larson Brothers Euphanon

Line 6 Variax 700N

Lowden D-32

Manuel Contreras II Double Top

MODEL		EXC. COND.	
YEAR	FEATURES	LOW	HIGH

Thomas in New Jersey. The guitar operations were taken over by AMF/Maark Corp. in '73. LoPrinzi left the company and again started producing his own Augustino Guitars, moving his operations to Florida in '78. AMF ceased production in '80, and a few years later, LoPrinzi got his trademarked name back.

Classical
Various models.

1970s	Brazilian rosewood	$1,300	$1,700
1970s	Indian rosewood	$1,000	$1,300
1970s	Mahogany	$500	$900

Lord
Mid-1960s. Acoustic and solidbody electric guitars imported by Halifax.

Acoustic
Various models.

1960s		$100	$200

Lotus
Late-1970s-present. Budget grade acoustic and electric guitars imported originally by Midco International, of Effingham, Illinois, and most recently by Musicorp. They also make basses, banjos and mandolins.

Louis Panormo
Early to mid-1800s. Spanish guitars made in London, England by luthier Louis (Luis) Panormo. He was born in Paris in 1784, and died in 1862.

Lowden
1973-present. Luthier George Lowden builds his premium and presentation grade, production/custom, steel and nylon string guitars in Downpatrick, Northern Ireland. From '80 to '85, he had some models made in Japan.

Flat-Tops
2000s. Standard models include D, F, O, and S sizes and models 10 thru 32.

2000s	12-string	$1,300	$1,800
2000s	Premium 6-string	$1,900	$2,200
2000s	Standard 6-string	$1,200	$1,600

LSR Headless Instruments
1988-present. Professional and premium grade, production/custom, solidbody headless guitars made in Las Vegas, Nevada by Ed Roman. They also make basses.

LTD
1995-present. Intermediate grade, production, Korean-made solidbody guitars offered by ESP. They also offer basses. See ESP for models.

Lucas Custom Instruments
1989-present. Premium and presentation grade, production/custom, flat-tops built by luthier Randy Lucas in Columbus, Indiana.

MODEL		EXC. COND.	
YEAR	FEATURES	LOW	HIGH

Lucas, A. J.
1990-present. Luthier A. J. Lucas builds his production/custom, classical and steel string guitars in Lincolnshire, England.

Lyle
Ca. 1969-1980. Imported by distributor L.D. Heater of Portland, Oregon. Generally higher quality Japanese-made copies of American designs by unknown manufacturers, but some early ones, at least, were made by Arai and Company. They also had basses.

Acoustic
1969-1980. Various models.

1969-1980		$150	$200

Electric
1969-1980. Various copy models include double-cut semi-hollow A-790, and the sharp double-cut solidbodies S750 (1 pickup) and S-760 (2 pickups).

1970s	A-790	$200	$275
1970s	S-750	$150	$200
1970s	S-760	$175	$225

Lyon & Healy
In the 1930s, Lyon & Healy was an industry giant. It operated a chain of music stores, and manufactured harps (their only remaining product), pianos, Washburn guitars and a line of brass and wind instruments. See Washburn, American Conservatory, Lakeside, and College brands.

Lyra
1920s. Instruments built by the Oscar Schmidt Co. and possibly others. Most likely a brand made for a distributor.

Lyric
1996-present. Luthier John Southern builds his professional and premium grade, custom, semi-hollow and solidbody guitars in Tulsa, Oklahoma. He also builds basses.

M. Campellone Guitars
See listing under Campellone Guitars

Maccaferri
1923-1990. Built by luthier and classical guitarist Mario Maccaferri (b. May 20, 1900, Cento, Italy; d. 1993, New York) in Cento, Italy; Paris, France; New York, New York; and Mount Vernon, New York. Maccaferri was a student of Luigi Mozzani from '11 to '28. His first catalog was in '23, and included a cutaway guitar. He designed Selmer guitars in '31. Maccaferri invented the plastic clothespin during World War II and used that technology to produce plastic ukes starting in '49 and Dow Styron plastic guitars in '53. He made several experimental plastic electrics in the '60s and plastic violins in the late-'80s.

MODEL YEAR	FEATURES	EXC. COND. LOW	HIGH

Plastic (Dow Styron)

1950s. Plastic construction, models include Deluxe (archtop, crown logo), Islander (Islander logo), TV Pal (4-string cutaway) and Showtime (Showtime logo).

1950s	Deluxe	$200	$275
1950s	Islander	$200	$225
1950s	Showtime	$200	$225
1950s	TV Pal	$150	$175

Madeira

Late-1970s. Imports serviced and distributed exclusively by Guild Guitars.

Acoustic Dreadnought

1970s. Acoustic dreadnoughts all with spruce top, models include A-7 (brown mahogany, lowest model), A-12A (12-string, mahogany), A-14 (mahogany), A-14-12 (12-string, mahogany), A-15B (mahogany, all black finish), A-16 (rosewood), A-17M (maple), A-25 (mahogany), A-30M (maple), A-35 (rosewood), A-75 (rosewood) and P-300 (maple).

1970s	A-12A	$300	$350

Magnatone

Ca. 1937-1971. Founded as Dickerson Brothers in Los Angeles, California and known as Magna Electronics from '47, with Art Duhamell president. Brands include Dickerson, Oahu (not all), Gourley, Natural Music Guild, Magnatone. In '59 Magna and Estey merged and in '66 the company relocated to Pennsylvania. In '71, the brand was taken over by a toy company.

Cyclops

1930s. Dobro-made resonator guitar.

1930s	Round neck	$1,500	$1,700
1930s	Square neck	$1,900	$2,100

Tornado

1965-1966. Offset double-cut body, 3 DeArmond pickups, vibrato.

1965-1966		$600	$700

Typhoon

1965-1966. Double-cut solidbody, 3 DeArmond pickups, vibrato.

1965-1966		$500	$600

Zephyr

1965-1966. Double-cut with 2 DeArmond single-coil pickups, metallic finish, vibrato.

1965-1966		$500	$550

Magno-Tone

1930s. Brand most likely used by a music studio (or distributor) on instruments made by others, including Regal-built resonator instruments.

Mai Kai

1910s. Line of Hawaiian guitars built in Los Angeles by the Shireson Brothers.

Mako

1985-1989. Line of budget to lower-intermediate solidbody guitars from Kaman (Ovation, Hamer). They also offered basses and amps.

Solidbodies

1985-1989	Various models	$175	$275

Manuel Contreras

1962-1994. Luthier Manuel Gonzalez Contreras worked with José Ramírez III, before opening his own shop in Madrid, Spain, in '62.

Guitarra de Estudio

1970s. Designed as a student model, but with solid cedar top and solid mahogany back and sides.

1970s	$500	$600

Manuel Contreras II

1986-present. Professional grade, production/custom, nylon-string guitars made in Madrid, Spain, by luthier Pablo Contreras, son of Manuel.

C5

2000s. Solid close-grained cedar top, Indian rosewood back and sides.

2000s	$700	$1,000

Manuel Rodriguez and Sons, S.L.

1905-present. Professional, premium, and presentation grade, custom flat-top and nylon-string guitars from Madrid, Spain.

Manuel Velázquez

1933-present. Luthier Manuel Velázquez has built his classical guitars in Puerto Rico ('72-'82), New York City, Virginia, and Florida. His son and daughter now build guitars with him.

Manzanita Guitars

1993-present. Custom, steel-string, Hawaiian, and resonator guitars built by luthiers Manfred Pietrzok and Moritz Sattler in Rosdorf, Germany.

Manzer Guitars

1976-present. Luthier Linda Manzer builds her premium and presentation grade, custom, steel-string, nylon-string, and archtop guitars in Toronto, Ontario.

Maple Lake

2003-present. Intermediate grade, production, flat-top and acoustic/electric imported guitars from luthier Abe Wechter. Wechter also builds guitars under his own name.

Mapson

1995-present. Luthier James L. Mapson builds his premium and presentation grade, production/custom, archtops in Santa Ana, California.

Marc Silber Guitar Company

1998-present. Intermediate and professional grade, production, flat-top, nylon-string, and Hawaiian guitars designed by Marc Silber and made in Mexico. These were offered under the K & S Guitars and/or Silber brands for 1992-'98. Silber also has ukuleles.

Maccaferri G-40

Maple Lake 2611c

Marchione Neck-Through

1935 Martin O-15

MODEL YEAR	FEATURES	EXC. COND. LOW	HIGH

Marchione Guitars

1993-present. Premium and presentation grade, custom, archtops and solidbodies built by Stephen Marchione originally in New York City, but currently in Houston, Texas.

Marcia

1920s. Instruments built by the Oscar Schmidt Co. and possibly others. Most likely a brand made for a distributor.

Marco Polo

1960-ca. 1964. Imported from Japan by Harry Stewart and the Marco Polo Company of Santa Ana, California. One of the first American distributors to advertise inexpensive Japanese guitars and basses. Manufacturers unknown, but some acoustics by Suzuki, some electrics by Guyatone.

Acoustic Hollowbody Guitars

1960-1964. Various models.

1960s		$100	$200

Mark Wescott Guitars

1980-present. Premium grade, custom, flat-tops, built by luthier Mark Wescott in Marmora, New Jersey.

Marling

Ca. 1975. Budget line guitars and basses marketed by EKO of Recanati, Italy; probably made by them, although possibly imported.

Acoustic Guitars

1975. Includes the steel-string S.110, and the dreadnoughts W.354 Western, and W.356 Western.

1975		$75	$100

Electric Guitars

1975. Includes the E.400 (semi-acoustic/electric), E.490 (solidbody), E.480 (single-cut-style), and the 460 (Manta-style).

1975		$100	$175

Martelle

1934. Private brand attributed to Gibson and some to Kay.

De Luxe

1934. Gibson 12-fret round shoulder Jumbo construction, mahogany back and sides, sunburst, Hawaiian or Spanish option.

1934		$8,500	$9,000

Martin

1833-present. Intermediate, professional, premium, and presentation grade, production/custom, acoustic, acoustic/electric, archtop and resonator guitars. Founded in New York City by Christian Frederick Martin, former employee of J. Staufer in Vienna, Austria. Moved to Nazareth, Pennsylvania in 1839. Early guitars were made in the European style, many made with partners John Coupa, Charles Bruno and Henry Schatz. Scalloped X-bracing was introduced in the late-1840s. The

dreadnought was introduced in 1916 for the Oliver Ditson Company, Boston; and Martin introduced their own versions in 1931.

Martin model size and shape are indicated by the letter prefix (e.g., 0, 00, 000, D, etc.); materials and ornamentation are indicated by number, with the higher the number, the fancier the instrument (e.g., 18, 28, 35, etc.). Martin offered electric thinline guitars from '61-'68 and electric solidbodies from '78-'82. The Martin Shenandoah was made in Asia and assembled in U.S. Japanese Martin Sigma ('72-'73) and Korean Martin Stinger ('85 on) imported solidbodies.

0-15

1935, 1940-1943, 1948-1961. All mahogany, unbound rosewood 'board, slotted peghead and 12-fret neck until '34, solid peghead and 14-fret neck thereafter, natural mahogany.

1935	2 made, maple/birch	$2,400	$2,900
1940-1943		$2,000	$2,300
1948-1949		$1,800	$2,100
1950-1959		$1,600	$1,900
1960-1961		$1,500	$1,700

0-15 T

1960-1963. Tenor with Style 15 appointments, natural mahogany.

1960-1963		$950	$1,150

0-16

1961 only. Six made.

1961		$1,800	$2,150

0-16 NY

1961-1995. Mahogany back and sides, 12 frets, slotted peghead, unbound extra-wide rosewood 'board, natural.

1961-1969		$1,600	$2,150
1970-1979		$1,400	$1,900
1980-1989		$1,300	$1,800
1990-1995		$1,300	$1,800

0-17

1906-1917, 1929-1948, 1966-1968. First version has mahogany back and sides, 3 black soundhole rings, rosewood bound back, unbound ebony 'board, 12 frets, slotted peghead. Second version ('29 and on) is all mahogany, 3 white-black-white soundhole rings, top bound until '30, thin black backstripe, 12 frets and slotted peghead until '34, solid peghead and 14 frets thereafter, natural mahogany.

1906-1917	Gut braces	$1,800	$2,400
1929-1934	Bar frets, 12 fret-style	$2,400	$2,600
1934-1939	T-frets, 14 fret-style	$2,700	$3,000
1940-1945		$2,500	$2,700
1946-1948		$2,300	$2,500
1966-1968	7 made	$1,900	$2,300

0-17 H

1930, 1935-1941. Hawaiian, mahogany back and sides, 12 frets clear of body, natural.

1930	60 made	$2,400	$2,600
1935-1941		$2,700	$3,000

0-17 S

Early 1930s. Limited production style 17 with spruce top, unique 'guard.

MODEL YEAR	FEATURES	EXC. COND. LOW	HIGH
1931		$3,800	$4,200

0-17 T

1932-1960. Mahogany back and sides, tenor, natural.

1932-1949		$1,400	$1,600
1950-1960	Mahogany	$1,300	$1,500

0-18

1898-1996. Rosewood back and sides until 1917, mahogany back and sides after, Adirondack spruce top until 1946, slotted peghead and 12 frets until 1934, solid peghead and 14 frets after 1934, braced for steel strings in 1923, improved neck in late-1934, non-scalloped braces appear late-'44, natural.

1898-1917	Brazilian rosewood	$2,600	$3,000
1918-1922	Mahogany, gut braces	$2,400	$2,900
1923-1939	Steel braces	$3,200	$3,500
1940-1944	Scalloped braces	$3,000	$3,300
1945-1949		$2,700	$3,000
1950-1959		$2,300	$2,700
1960-1969		$2,200	$2,700
1970-1979		$1,900	$2,200
1980-1990s		$1,000	$1,700

0-18 G

1960s. Special order classical nylon-string model, natural.

1961		$1,500	$2,000

0-18 K

1918-1935. Hawaiian, all koa wood, braced for steel strings in 1923, T-frets and steel T-bar neck in late-1934, natural.

1918-1922		$2,700	$3,300
1923-1927	Steel braces	$2,900	$3,500
1928-1935		$3,000	$3,500

0-18 T

1929-1995. Mahogany body, spruce top, tenor, natural.

1929-1939		$1,600	$2,100
1940-1959		$1,500	$2,000
1960-1964		$1,400	$1,600
1965-1969		$1,300	$1,500
1970-1979		$1,200	$1,300
1980-1989		$1,100	$1,200
1990-1995		$1,000	$1,100

0-21

1898-1948. Rosewood back and sides, Adirondack spruce top until 1946, 12 frets, braced for steel strings in 1923, T-frets and steel T-bar neck in late-1934, non-scalloped braces in late-1944, natural.

1898-1926	Gut braces	$3,500	$4,800
1927-1943	Steel braces	$4,000	$5,800
1944-1948	Non-scalloped	$3,000	$4,300

0-26

1850-1890. Rosewood back and sides, ivory-bound top, rope-style purfling.

1850-1890		$3,700	$5,000

0-27

1850-1898. Rosewood back and sides, ivory-bound top.

1850-1898		$4,000	$5,200

0-28

1870s-1931, 1937 (6 made), 1969 (1 made). Brazilian rosewood back and sides, braced for steel strings in 1923, herringbone binding until 1937, natural.

1870-1927		$4,500	$5,500
1928-1931		$5,500	$6,500

0-28 Ian Anderson

2004. Adirondack spruce top, scalloped bracing, Indian rosewood sides and back, slotted headstock, gloss natural finish, limited edition 87 made.

2004		$2,900	$3,000

0-28 K

1917-1931, 1935. Hawaiian, all koa wood, braced for steel strings in '23, natural.

1917	Spruce top option	$5,500	$6,500
1917-1924	Figured koa	$5,500	$6,500
1925-1931	Steel braces	$6,000	$7,500

0-28 T

1930-1931. Tenor neck.

1930-1931		$3,300	$3,800

0-30

1899-1921. Brazilian rosewood back and sides, ivory-bound body, neck and headstock.

1899-1921		$5,000	$6,000

0-42

1870s-1942. Brazilian rosewood back and sides, 12 frets, natural.

1890-1926	Gut braces	$12,000	$15,000
1927-1930	Steel braces	$15,000	$17,000

0-45

1904-1939. Brazilian rosewood back and sides, natural, special order only for '31-'39.

1904-1928	Gut braces	$35,000	$40,000
1929-1930	Steel braces	$40,000	$50,000

00-16 C

1962-1977, 1980-1981. Classical, mahogany back and sides, 5-ply bound top, satin finish, 12 frets, slotted peghead, natural.

1962-1969		$1,100	$1,200
1970-1977		$900	$1,100
1980-1981	2 made	$900	$1,100

00-17

1908-1917, 1930-1960, 1982-1988, 2000-2003. Mahogany back and sides, 12 frets and slotted headstock until '34, solid headstock and 14 frets after '34, natural mahogany, reissued in 2000 with a high gloss finish.

1908-1917	Limited production	$2,100	$2,700
1930-1939		$2,700	$3,300
1940-1944		$2,500	$3,200
1945-1949		$2,400	$2,600
1950-1960		$2,000	$2,400
2000-2003	Reissue model	$1,000	$1,100

00-17 H

1934-1935. Hawaiian set-up, mahogany body, no binding.

1934-1935		$2,700	$3,000

1936 Martin 0-17

1923 Martin 0-21

1936 Martin 00-18 sunburst

Martin 00-18V

MODEL YEAR	FEATURES	EXC. COND. LOW	HIGH

00-18

1898-1995. Rosewood back and sides until 1917, mahogany after, braced for steel strings in 1923, improved neck in late-1934, war-time design changes 1942-1946, non-scalloped braces in late-1944, Adirondack spruce top until 1946, natural.

1898-1917	Rosewood	$4,500	$5,000
1918-1922	Mahogany	$4,000	$4,500
1923-1939	Steel braces in '23	$5,200	$5,500
1934-1939	Sunburst option	$5,000	$6,000
1940-1941		$5,000	$5,200
1942-1943	Ebony rod	$4,700	$5,000
1944	Scalloped braces early '44	$4,500	$4,700
1944-1946	Non-scalloped	$3,500	$3,800
1946	Steel bar neck	$3,400	$3,700
1947-1949		$3,000	$3,600
1950-1952		$2,800	$3,300
1953-1959		$2,400	$2,800
1960-1962		$2,300	$2,600
1963-1965		$2,100	$2,300
1966	Black guard late '66	$2,100	$2,300
1966	Tortoise guard early '66	$2,000	$2,200
1967		$1,900	$2,200
1968		$1,700	$2,200
1969		$1,600	$2,200
1970-1979		$1,400	$1,700
1980-1989		$1,200	$1,500
1990-1995		$1,100	$1,300

00-18 C

1962-1995. Renamed from 00-18 G in '62, mahogany back and sides, classical, 12 frets, slotted headstock, natural.

1962-1969		$1,200	$1,500
1970-1979		$1,000	$1,200

00-18 E

1959-1964. Flat top Style 18, single neck pickup and 2 knobs, heavier bracing, natural.

1959-1964		$2,500	$3,000

00-18 G

1936-1962. Mahogany back and sides, classical, natural, renamed 00-18 C in '62.

1936-1939		$1,700	$2,600
1940-1949		$1,600	$2,400
1950-1962		$1,500	$1,800

00-18 Gruhn Limited Edition

1995. Sitka spruce top, C-shaped neck profile, 25 made.

1995		$1,500	$1,600

00-18 H

1935-1941. Hawaiian, mahogany back amd sides, 12 frets clear of body, natural. The Price Guide is generally for all original instruments. The H conversion is an exception, because converting from H (Hawaiian-style) to 00-18 specs is considered by some to be a favorable improvement and something that adds value.

1935-1941		$4,500	$5,000
1935-1941	Converted to Spanish	$5,000	$5,500

MODEL YEAR	FEATURES	EXC. COND. LOW	HIGH

00-18 SH Steve Howe

1999-2000. Limited edition run of 250.

1999-2000		$2,500	$2,600

00-18 V

2003-present. Mahogany back and sides, spruce top, Vintage Series.

2003-2005		$1,450	$1,550

00-21

1898-1996. Brazilian rosewood back and sides, changed to Indian rosewood in 1970, dark outer binding, unbound ebony 'board until 1947, rosewood from 1947, slotted diamond inlays until 1944, dot after, natural.

1898-1926	Gut braces	$6,500	$7,000
1927-1931	Steel braces in '27	$8,000	$8,500
1932-1939		$7,500	$8,300
1934-1939	Sunburst option	$7,500	$8,500
1940-1944	Scalloped braces	$6,800	$8,000
1944-1949	Non-scalloped	$4,400	$5,400
1950-1959		$4,200	$5,200
1960-1965		$4,000	$5,000
1966-1969	Brazilian rosewood, black guard	$3,800	$4,800
1970-1996	Indian rosewood	$1,700	$1,900

00-21 Custom

2005-2006. Custom order size 00 style 21, Brazilian rosewood sides and back.

2005-2006		$2,600	$3,200

00-21 H

Special order limited production Hawaiian.

1914	1 made	$6,500	$7,000
1952	1 made	$6,500	$7,000
1955	1 made	$6,500	$7,000

00-21 NY

1961-1965. Brazilian rosewood back and sides, no inlay, natural.

1961-1965		$4,000	$5,000

00-28

1898-1941, 1958 (1 made), 1977 (1 made), 1984 (2 made). Brazilian rosewood back and sides, changed to Indian rosewood in 1977, herringbone purfling through 1941, white binding and unbound 'board after 1941, no inlays before 1901, diamond inlays from 1901-'41, dot after, natural.

1898-1924	Gut braces	$8,000	$12,000
1925-1931	Steel braces in '25	$10,000	$15,000
1932-1941	Special order	$10,000	$15,000
1958-1969	Special order	$3,400	$3,600

00-28 C

1966-1995. Renamed from 00-28 G, Brazilian rosewood back and sides, changed to Indian rosewood in '70, classical, 12 frets, natural.

1966-1969	Brazilian rosewood	$3,300	$4,200
1970-1979	Indian rosewood	$1,700	$1,900

00-28 G

1936-1962. Brazilian rosewood back and sides, classical, natural, reintroduced as 00-28 C in '66.

1936-1939		$4,500	$5,500
1940-1949		$4,000	$5,000
1951-1962		$3,000	$4,000

The Vintage Guitar Price Guide shows low to high values for items in all-original excellent condition, and, where applicable, with original case or cover.

MODEL YEAR	FEATURES	EXC. COND. LOW	HIGH

00-28 K Hawaiian
1919-1921, 1926-1933. Koa back and sides, Hawaiian set-up.

| 1919-1921 | 34 made | $6,700 | $7,000 |
| 1926-1933 | 1 made per year | $8,000 | $9,000 |

00-37 K2 Steve Miller
2001. All koa 12-fret style 00. The 00-37K SM has a spruce top. 68 made of each version

| 2001 | | $4,400 | $4,700 |

00-40 H
1928-1939. Hawaiian, Brazilian rosewood back and sides, 12 frets clear of body, natural. H models are sometimes converted to standard Spanish setup, in higher-end models this can make the instrument more valuable to some people.

| 1928-1939 | | $15,000 | $18,000 |
| 1928-1939 | Converted to Spanish | $15,000 | $20,000 |

00-40 K
Few were made (only 6), figured koa, natural.

| 1918 | 1 made | $20,000 | $23,000 |
| 1930 | 5 made | $20,000 | $23,000 |

00-42
1898-1942, 1973 (one made), 1994-1996. Brazilian rosewood back and sides, Indian rosewood in 1973, pearl top borders, 12 frets, ivory bound peghead until 1918, ivoroid binding after 1918, natural.

1898-1926	Gut braces	$15,000	$20,000
1927-1942	Steel braces	$20,000	$25,000
1973	1 made	$2,500	$3,500
1994-1996		$2,000	$3,000

00-42 K
1919. Koa body, 1 made.

| 1919 | | $20,000 | $25,000 |

00-44 Soloist/Olcott-Bickford Artist Model
1913-1939. Custom-made in small quantities, Brazilian rosewood, ivory or faux-ivory-bound ebony 'board.

| 1913-1939 | | $25,000 | $45,000 |

00-45
1904-1938, 1970-1995. Brazilian rosewood back and sides, changed to Indian rosewood in '70, 12 frets and slotted headstock until '34 and from '70 on 14 frets, and solid headstock from '34-'70, natural.

| 1904-1927 | Gut braces | $40,000 | $50,000 |
| 1928-1938 | Steel braces | $45,000 | $60,000 |

00-45 K
1919. Koa body, 1 made.

| 1919 | | $30,000 | $50,000 |

00-45 S Limited Edition
2003. 1902 vintage-pattern with fancy inlays, 00 size style 45, 50 made.

| 2003 | | $11,500 | $12,500 |

00-45 Stauffer Commemorative Limited Edition
1997. Stauffer six-on-a-side headstock, 45-style appointments, 00-size body, Sitka spruce top, Brazilian rosewood back and sides.

| 1997 | | $8,000 | $10,000 |

000-1 R
1996-2002. Solid spruce top with laminated Indian rosewood sides.

| 1996-2002 | | $700 | $900 |

000-15 Auditorium
1997-present. All solid wood mahogany body, dot markers, natural.

| 1997-2005 | | $500 | $600 |

000-16
1989-1995. Acoustic, mahogany back and sides, diamonds and squares inlaid, name changed to 000-16 T Auditorium in '96, sunburst.

| 1989-1995 | | $1,100 | $1,200 |

000-16 T
1996-1999. All solid wood mahogany back and sides, higher appointments than 000-15.

| 1996-1999 | | $850 | $1,000 |

000-18
1911-present (none in 1932-1933). Rosewood back and sides until '17, mahogany back and sides from '17, longer scale in '24-'34, 12 frets clear of body until '33, changed to 14 frets in '34. Improved neck late-'34, war-time changes '41-'46, non-scalloped braces in late-'44, sswitched from Adirondack spruce to Sitka spruce top in '46 (though some Adirondack tops in '50s and '60s), natural. Now called the 000-18 Auditorium.

1924-1927	Gut/nylon braces, 12-fret	$7,000	$11,000
1928-1931	Steel braces, 12-fret	$9,000	$13,000
1934-1939	24.5" scale, 14-fret clear	$10,000	$12,500
1934-1939	Sunburst option	$12,000	$16,000
1940-1941	Natural	$8,500	$10,500
1942-1944	Scalloped braces	$7,500	$9,000
1942-1944	Sunburst option	$8,500	$11,500
1944-1946	Non-scalloped	$4,500	$6,500
1944-1946	Sunburst option	$6,000	$7,300
1947-1949	Natural	$4,200	$6,000
1947-1949	Sunburst option	$5,900	$7,200
1950-1952	Natural	$4,000	$5,000
1953-1959		$3,700	$4,500
1960-1962		$3,000	$3,500
1963-1965		$2,900	$3,400
1966	Black guard late '66	$2,500	$3,000
1966	Tortoise guard early '66	$2,600	$3,200
1967	Last of Maple bridgeplate	$2,500	$3,100
1968		$2,300	$3,000
1969		$1,700	$2,300
1970-1979		$1,500	$1,800
1980-1989		$1,300	$1,600
1990-1999		$1,200	$1,400
2000-2005		$1,150	$1,250

000-18 WG Woody Guthrie
1999. Signed label including artwork and model identification.

| 1999 | | $1,800 | $1,900 |

Martin 00-21GE

1937 Martin 000-18

1953 Martin 000-21

1957 Martin 000-28

MODEL YEAR	FEATURES	EXC. COND. LOW	HIGH
000-21			

1902-1924 (22 made over that time), 1931(2), 1938-1959, 1965 (1), 1979 (12). Brazilian rosewood back and sides, changed to Indian rosewood in '70, natural.

MODEL YEAR	FEATURES	LOW	HIGH
1902-1937	Low production mostly gut	$13,000	$20,000
1938-1941	Pre-war specs	$15,000	$20,000
1942-1944	Ebony rod, scalloped braces	$10,000	$15,000
1944-1946	Non-scalloped	$7,000	$8,300
1947-1949	Herringbone, non-scalloped	$6,500	$6,800
1950-1959		$5,500	$6,000
1965	1 made	$5,000	$6,000
1979	12 made	$1,900	$2,500

000-28

1902-present. Brazilian rosewood back and sides, changed to Indian rosewood in '70, herringbone purfling through '41, white binding and unbound 'board after '41, no inlays before '01, slotted diamond inlays from '01-'44, dot after, 12 frets until '32, 14 frets '31 on (both 12 and 14 frets were made during '31-'32), natural.

MODEL YEAR	FEATURES	LOW	HIGH
1902-1927	Gut/nylon braces	$20,000	$28,000
1928-1931	Steel braces	$25,000	$35,000
1933		$25,000	$35,000
1934-1939		$30,000	$35,000
1940-1941		$25,000	$33,000
1942-1944	Scalloped braces	$20,000	$26,000
1944-1946	Herringbone, non-scalloped	$15,000	$21,000
1947-1949	Start of non-herringbone '47	$10,000	$12,000
1950-1952		$9,000	$10,000
1953-1958	Last of Kluson early '58	$8,000	$9,500
1958-1959	Grover tuners late '58	$7,000	$9,000
1960-1962		$6,500	$7,500
1963-1965		$5,000	$6,000
1966	Black guard late '66	$4,800	$5,600
1966	Tortoise guard early '66	$4,900	$5,700
1967	Last of maple bridgeplate	$4,800	$5,600
1968	Rosewood bridgeplate	$4,600	$5,500
1969	Last of Brazilian rosewood	$4,500	$5,000
1970-1979	Indian rosewood	$2,000	$2,600
1980-1989	Indian rosewood	$1,600	$2,100
1990-1999	Indian rosewood	$1,500	$2,100
2000-2005		$1,500	$1,800

000-28 C

1962-1969. Brazilian rosewood back and sides, classical, slotted peghead, natural.

MODEL YEAR	FEATURES	LOW	HIGH
1962-1969		$3,700	$4,700

000-28 EC Eric Clapton Signature

1996-present. Sitka spruce top, Indian rosewood back and sides, herringbone trim, natural.

MODEL YEAR	FEATURES	LOW	HIGH
1996-1999		$2,200	$2,300
2000-2005		$2,150	$2,300

000-28 ECB Eric Clapton Brazilian

2003. Limited edition, 2nd edition of EC Signature Series with Brazilian rosewood.

MODEL YEAR	FEATURES	LOW	HIGH
2003		$6,000	$6,500

000-28 G

1937-1955. Special order, very limited production.

MODEL YEAR	FEATURES	LOW	HIGH
1937-1940	3 made	$8,000	$10,000
1946-1949	10 made	$6,000	$8,000
1950-1955	4 made	$5,000	$6,000

000-28 Golden Era

1996 only. Sitka spruce top, rosewood back and sides, scalloped braces, herringbone trim, 12-fret model, natural.

MODEL YEAR	FEATURES	LOW	HIGH
1996		$2,900	$3,200

000-28 H

2000-2001. Herringbone top trim.

MODEL YEAR	FEATURES	LOW	HIGH
2000-2001		$1,700	$1,800

000-28 HB Brazilian 1937 reissue

1997. Pre-war specs including scalloped bracing, Brazilian rosewood.

MODEL YEAR	FEATURES	LOW	HIGH
1997		$5,400	$5,600

000-28 K

1921. Non-catalog special order model, only 2 known to exist, koa top, back and sides.

MODEL YEAR	FEATURES	LOW	HIGH
1921		$20,000	$30,000

000-41

1996. Custom shop style 000-41.

MODEL YEAR	FEATURES	LOW	HIGH
1996		$2,500	$3,000

000-42

1918, 1921-1922, 1925, 1930, 1934, 1938-1943. Brazilian rosewood back and sides, natural.

MODEL YEAR	FEATURES	LOW	HIGH
1918-1934	Special order	$35,000	$45,000
1938-1943		$40,000	$50,000

000-42 EC Eric Clapton

1995. Style 45 pearl-inlaid headplate, ivoroid bindings, Eric Clapton signature, 24.9" scale, flat top, sunburst top price is $8320 ('95 price), only 461 made.

MODEL YEAR	FEATURES	LOW	HIGH
1995		$8,000	$8,800

000-45

1906, 1911-1914, 1917-1919, 1922-1942, 1971-1993. Brazilian rosewood back and sides, changed to Indian rosewood in '70, 12-fret neck and slotted headstock until '34 (but 7 were made in '70 and 1 in '75), 14-fret neck and solid headstock after '34, natural.

MODEL YEAR	FEATURES	LOW	HIGH
1906-1919		$50,000	$70,000
1922-1927	Gut braces	$70,000	$80,000
1928-1929	Steel braces	$65,000	$85,000
1930-1933		$70,000	$90,000
1934-1936	14 frets, C.F.M. inlaid	$85,000	$100,000
1937-1939		$80,000	$95,000
1940-1942		$80,000	$90,000

MODEL YEAR	FEATURES	EXC. COND. LOW	HIGH

000-45 JR Jimmie Rodgers Golden Era
1997. Adirondack spruce top, Brazilian rosewood back and sides, scalloped high X-braces, abalone trim, natural, 100 made.

1997		$9,500	$11,000

000C Series
1996-present. French-style small soft cutaway (like vintage Selmer), models include; 000C-1E (mahogany body) and 000C-16RGTE (premium, rosewood body).

1996-2000	000C-1E	$1,000	$1,100
2001-2005	000C-16 RGTE	$1,000	$1,100

000C-16
1990-1995. Cutaway acoustic, mahogany back and sides, diamonds and squares inlay, name changed to 000-C16T Auditorium in '96.

1990-1995		$1,025	$1,150

000CXE
2002-present. Acoustic-electric, rounded cutaway, high pressure laminated body, black finish.

2002-2005		$450	$475

000CDB Dion The Wanderer
2002. Only 57 made, cutaway acoustic/electric, gloss black finish, Sitka spruce top, scalloped bracing, mahagony sides and back, slotted diamond and square markers, Dion logo on headstock.

2002		$2,100	$2,200

000-ECHF Bellezza Nera
2005. Limited edition Eric Clapton and Hiroshi Fujiwara Black Beauty Model, 476 made, Italian Alpine spruce top, Indian rosewood sides and back, black finish.

2005		$2,950	$3,250

0000-18 Gruhn 35th Anniversary Model
2005. Limited production 0000-size, Golden Era 18 styling.

2005		$2,500	$2,750

0000-28 Series
1997-2000. Several models, jumbo-size 0000 cutaway body, models include; H (herringbone trim), Custom (Indian rosewood, sitka spruce top), H-AG (Arlo Guthrie 30th anniversary, Indian rosewood back and sides, only 30 made), H Custom Shop (herringbone).

1997-2000	0000-28 H	$1,900	$2,400
1998	0000-28 Custom	$2,800	$3,000
1999	0000-28 H-AG	$3,800	$4,200
2000	0000-28 H Custom Shop	$1,700	$1,900

0000-38 Series
1997-2002. 0000-size, rosewood sides and back, replaced M-38.

1997-2002		$1,700	$2,100

1-17
1906-1917 (1st version), 1931-1934 (2nd version). First version has spruce top, mahogany back and sides, second version has all mahogany with flat natural finish.

1906-1917		$1,500	$1,700
1930-1934		$1,700	$1,900

1-17P
1928-1931. Mahogany back and sides, plectrum neck, 272 made.

1928-1931		$2,000	$2,500

1-18
1899-1927. Brazilian rosewood or mahogany back and sides.

1918-1927	Mahogany	$2,200	$2,500

1-21
1860-1926. Initially offered in size 1 in the 1860s, ornate soundhole rings.

1860-1899		$3,500	$4,500
1900-1926		$3,500	$4,500

1-26
1850-1890. Rosewood back and sides, ivory-bound top, rope-style purfling.

1850-1890		$3,500	$4,500

1-27
1880-1907.

1880-1907		$4,000	$5,000

1-28
1880-1923. Style 28 appointments including Brazilian rosewood back and sides.

1880-1923		$4,200	$5,200

1-30
1860s. Size 1 Style 30 with pearl soundhole trim, cedar neck.

1860s		$5,000	$6,000

1-42
1858-1919. Rosewood back and sides, ivory-bound top and 'board.

1858-1919		$8,000	$14,000

1-45
1904-1919. Only 6 made, slotted headstock and Style 45 appointments.

1904-1919		$20,000	$24,000

2-15
1939-1964. All mahogany body, dot markers.

1939	Special order	$1,300	$1,600

2-17
1910, 1922-1938. 1910 version has spruce top, mahogany back and sides. '22 on, all mahogany body, no body binding after '30.

1910	6 made	$1,400	$1,700
1922-1930		$1,600	$1,900

2-17 H
1927-1931. Hawaiian, all mahogany, 12 frets clear of body.

1927-1931		$1,600	$1,900

2-20
1855-1899. Rare style only offered in size 2.

1855-1899		$2,500	$3,000

2-21
1885-1929. Rosewood back and sides, herringbone soundhole ring.

1855-1929		$3,300	$4,300

2-24
1857-1898.

1857-1898		$3,400	$4,400

Martin 000-45 JR

Martin 0000-28

Martin D12-28

Martin DC-1E

MODEL YEAR	FEATURES	EXC. COND. LOW	HIGH
2-27			
1857-1907. Brazilian rosewood back and sides, pearl ring, zigzag back stripe, ivory bound ebony 'board and peghead.			
1857-1899		$3,800	$4,500
1900-1907		$3,800	$4,500
2-28 T			
1929-1930. Tenor neck, Brazilian rosewood back and sides, herringbone top purfling.			
1929-1930		$2,000	$2,500
2-30			
1902-1921. Similar to 2-27.			
1902-1921	7 made	$4,000	$4,500
2-34			
1870-1898. Similar to 2-30.			
1870-1898		$4,000	$4,500
2-44			
1940. Style 44, Olcott-Bickford Soloist custom order, only 4 made.			
1940		$20,000	$24,000
2 1/2-17			
1856-1897, 1909-1914. The first Style 17s were small size 2 1/2 and 3, these early models use Brazilian rosewood.			
1856-1897		$2,000	$2,500
1909-1914		$1,600	$1,900
2 1/2-18			
1865-1923. Parlor-size body with Style 18 appointments.			
1865-1898		$2,200	$2,700
1901-1917	Brazilian rosewood	$2,200	$2,700
1918-1923	Mahogany	$2,000	$2,200
2 1/2-42			
Style 42 size 2 1/2 with Brazilian rosewood.			
1880s		$8,000	$12,000
3-17			
1856-1897, 1908 (one made). The first Style 17s were small size 2 1/2 and 3. The early models use Brazilian rosewood, spruce top, bound back, unbound ebony 'board.			
1856-1889	Brazilian rosewood	$1,800	$2,000
1890-1897		$1,700	$2,000
1908	1 made	$1,300	$1,700
5-15			
2005-present. Sapele or mahogany body, shorter scale.			
2005		$600	$700
5-15 T			
1949-1963. All mahogany, non-gloss finish, tenor neck.			
1949-1963		$1,100	$1,500
5-17 T			
1927-1949. All mahogany, tenor neck.			
1927-1949		$1,200	$1,600
5-18			
1898-1989. Rosewood back and sides (changed to mahogany from 1917 on), 12 frets, slotted headstock.			
1918-1922	Gut braces, mahogany	$1,900	$2,100
1923-1939	Steel braces in '23	$2,200	$2,400
1940-1944		$2,100	$2,300

MODEL YEAR	FEATURES	EXC. COND. LOW	HIGH
1945-1949		$2,000	$2,200
1950-1959		$1,900	$2,100
1960-1969		$1,600	$1,900
1970-1989		$1,000	$1,500
5-21 T			
1926-1928. Tenor guitar with 21-styling.			
1926-1928		$2,200	$2,400
5-28			
2001-2002. Special edition, 1/2-size parlor guitar size 15 with Terz tuning, Indian rosewood back and sides.			
2001-2002		$2,100	$2,250
7-28			
1980-1995, 1997-2002. 7/8-body-size of a D-model, Style 28 appointments.			
1980-1995		$2,100	$2,400
1997-2002		$2,100	$2,400
Alternative II Resophonic			
2004-present. Textured aluminum top, matching headstock overlay, high pressure laminate sides and back, spun aluminum cone resonator, Fishman pickup.			
2004-2005		$700	$750
Alternative X Midi			
2001-present. Thin 00-size body, solid aluminum top, laminate back and sides, Stratabond aluminate neck, black micarta 'board, micro-dot markers. Roland GK Midi pickup with 13-pin output, additional Fishman Prefix Pro pickup and preamp system, requires Roland GA-20 (or substitute) Midi interface.			
2001-2005		$725	$825
ASD-41 Australian Series			
2005. Tasmanian Blackwood sides and back, Sitka spruce top, Australian theme appointments and label.			
2005		$4,500	$5,000
C-1			
1931-1942. Acoustic archtop, mahogany back and sides, spruce top, round hole until '33, f-holes appear in '32, bound body, sunburst.			
1931-1933	Round, 449 made	$2,000	$2,400
1932-1942	F-hole, 786 made	$2,000	$2,400
C-2			
1931-1942. Acoustic archtop, Brazilian rosewood back and sides, carved spruce top, round hole until '33, f-holes appear in '32, zigzag back stripe, multi-bound body, slotted-diamond inlay, sunburst.			
1931-1933	Round, 269 made	$3,000	$4,000
1932-1942	F-hole, 439 made	$3,000	$4,000
C-2 Conversion			
1931-1942. The VG Price Guide lists original, excellent condition instruments. A C-2 Conversion is an exception. The C-2 archtop was generally less popular than a flat-top with similar appointments. C series archtops and H series Hawaiians converted to Spanish setup flat-tops have more appeal to some players and collectors. The C-2 Conversion requires removal of the arched top and installation of a high quality spruce top. Appointments may vary.			
1931-1942	High-end appointments	$6,000	$12,000

MODEL YEAR	FEATURES	EXC. COND. LOW	HIGH

C-3
1931-1934. Archtop, Brazilian rosewood back and sides, round soundhole until early '33, f-holes after.

| 1931-1933 | Round, 53 made | $5,000 | $7,000 |
| 1933-1934 | F-hole, 58 made | $5,000 | $7,000 |

CEO Series
2000s. Chief Executive Officer C.F. Martin IV special editions.

| 2001-2002 | CEO-4R, rosewood | $1,700 | $1,800 |
| 2002 | CEO-5, bearclaw top | $1,800 | $1,900 |

Cowboy Series
2001-present. Inside label identifies model number. Models include Cowboy II (2001, 500 made), Cowboy III ('03, 750 made), and Cowboy IV ('05-'06, 250 made), Cowboy V ('06, 500).

| 2001-2005 | | $400 | $450 |

C-TSH (Humphrey/Martin)
Late-1990s. Designed by high-end classical guitar luthier Thomas Humphrey for Martin, based on his Millenium model, arched Englemann spruce top, rosewood back and sides.

| 1998 | | $2,000 | $2,300 |

Custom Ne Plus Ultra
2005. Very fancy appointments, 0000 M-size body, rhinestone on pearloid peghead.

| 2005 | | $3,800 | $4,200 |

Custom OM-45 Deluxe
1998-1999. Limited custom shop run of 14, Adirondack spruce and typical Style 45 appointments.

| 1998-1999 | | $10,000 | $14,000 |

D-1
1992-2005. Name first used for the prototype of the D-18, made in 1931, revived for current model with mahogany body, A-frame bracing, available as an acoustic/electric.

| 1992-2005 | | $700 | $900 |

D12-18
1973-1995. Mahogany back and sides, 12 strings, 14 frets clear of body, solid headstock.

1973-1979		$1,100	$1,600
1980-1989		$1,000	$1,450
1990-1995		$900	$1,300

D12-20
1964-1991. Mahogany back and sides, 12 strings, 12 frets clear of body, slotted headstock.

1964-1969		$1,200	$1,800
1970-1979		$1,100	$1,500
1980-1991		$1,000	$1,400

D12-28
1970-present. Indian rosewood back and sides, 12 strings, 14 frets clear of body, solid headstock.

| 1970-1979 | | $1,700 | $2,000 |
| 1980-2005 | | $1,500 | $1,700 |

D12-35
1965-1995. Brazilian rosewood back and sides, changed to Indian rosewood in '70, 12 strings, 12 frets clear of body, slotted headstock.

| 1965-1969 | Brazilian rosewood | $3,500 | $4,500 |
| 1970-1979 | Indian rosewood | $1,700 | $2,000 |

MODEL YEAR	FEATURES	EXC. COND. LOW	HIGH
1980-1989		$1,500	$1,700
1990-1995		$1,500	$1,700

D12-45
1970s. Special order instrument, not a standard catalog item, with D-45 appointments, Indian rosewood.

| 1970-1979 | | $5,000 | $6,500 |

D12XM
1999-2000. 12-string version of the DXM.

| 1999-2000 | | $350 | $425 |

D-15
1997-present. All mahogany body.

| 1997-2005 | | $500 | $600 |

D-16 A
1987-1990. North American ash back and sides, solid spruce top, scalloped bracing, rosewood 'board and bridge, solid mahogany neck.

| 1987-1990 | | $1,000 | $1,200 |

D-16 GT/GTE/D-16 RGT
1999-present. D-16 T specs, GT with glossy top and mahogany back and sides, RGT with satin top and rosewood back and sides.

1999-2003	GTE	$1,000	$1,050
1999-2005	Mahogany, gloss	$725	$775
1999-2005	Rosewood, satin	$775	$825

D-16 H
1991-1995. Full-size dreadnought, mahogany back and sides with satin finish, herringbone marquetry, vintage X-bracing, scalloped braces, optional acoustic pickup or active preamp system, replaced by D-16 T in '96.

| 1991-1995 | | $1,000 | $1,200 |

D-16 M
1986, 1988-1990. Mahogany back and sides, non-gloss satin finish.

| 1988-1990 | | $750 | $850 |

D-16 T
1995-2002. Solid spruce top, solid mahogany back and sides, scalloped braces, satin finish.

| 1995-2002 | | $875 | $925 |

D-16 TR
1995-2002. Indian rosewood version of 16 T.

| 1995-2002 | | $1,200 | $1,300 |

D-17
2000-2005. All solid mahogany back, sides and top, natural brown mahogany finish.

| 2000-2005 | | $775 | $900 |

D-18
1932-present. Mahogany back and sides, spruce top, black back stripe, 12-fret neck, changed to 14 frets in '34.

1932-1933	12-fret neck	$27,000	$30,000
1934-1936	14-fret neck	$26,000	$27,000
1937-1939		$24,000	$25,000
1940-1941		$18,500	$20,000
1942-1944	Scalloped braces	$14,000	$15,000
1944-1946	Non-scalloped	$7,500	$9,500
1947-1949		$6,500	$8,000
1950-1952		$5,500	$7,000
1953-1959		$4,500	$6,000
1960-1962		$3,300	$5,000

Martin Cowboy IV

Martin D-18

Martin D-18V

Martin D-25 K2

MODEL YEAR	FEATURES	EXC. COND. LOW	HIGH
1963-1965		$3,200	$4,000
1966	Black guard late '66	$2,800	$3,300
1966	Tortoise guard early '66	$2,900	$3,500
1967	Last of maple bridgeplate	$2,800	$3,400
1968	Rosewood bridgeplate	$2,500	$3,300
1969		$1,700	$2,300
1970-1979		$1,500	$1,800
1980-1989		$1,300	$1,600
1990-1999		$1,200	$1,400
2000-2005		$1,100	$1,200

D-18 Andy Griffith
2003. D-18 specs with bear claw spruce top, Andy's script signature on 18th fret.

2003		$2,200	$2,500

D-18 DC David Crosby
2002. David Crosby signature at 20th fret, Adirondack spruce top, quilted mahogany back and sides, 250 made.

2002		$2,200	$2,500

D-18 E
1958-1959. D-18 factory built with DeArmond pickups which required ladder bracing (reducing acoustic volume and quality).

1958-1959		$3,000	$3,500

D-18 GE Golden Era
1995. Part of the Golden Era Series, copy of '37 D-18, 272 made.

1995		$2,100	$2,300

D-18 LE
1986-1987. Limited Edition, quilted or flamed mahogany back and sides, scalloped braces, gold tuners with ebony buttons.

1986-1987		$1,800	$2,000

D-18 MB
1990. Limited Edition Guitar of the Month, flame maple binding, Engelmann spruce top signed by shop foremen, X-brace, total of 99 sold.

1990		$1,700	$1,900

D-18 S
1967-1993. Mahogany back and sides, 12-fret neck, slotted headstock, majority of production before '77, infrequent after that.

1967-1969		$1,900	$2,300
1970-1979		$1,600	$1,900
1980-1993		$1,600	$1,900

D-18 V (Vintage)
1992. Guitar of the Month, low-profile neck, scalloped braces, bound, total of 218 sold.

1992		$1,700	$1,900

D-18 VE
2005-present. D-18 V with Fishman Ellipse.

2005		$1,450	$1,650

D-18 VM/V
1996-present. 14-fret vintage series, mahogany body, M dropped from name in '99.

1996-2005		$1,400	$1,600

MODEL YEAR	FEATURES	EXC. COND. LOW	HIGH

D-18 VMS
1996-2002. VM with 12-fret neck and slotted headstock.

1996-2002		$1,800	$1,900

D-19
1977-1988. Deluxe mahogany dreadnought, optional mahogany top, multi-bound but unbound rosewood 'board.

1977-1988		$1,400	$1,700

D-21
1955-1969. Brazilian rosewood back and sides, rosewood 'board, chrome tuners.

1955-1958	Klusons to early '58	$6,300	$6,900
1958-1959	Grover tuners late '58	$6,000	$6,800
1960-1962		$5,500	$6,600
1963-1965		$5,300	$6,500
1966-1967		$4,500	$6,000
1968-1969		$4,300	$5,500

D-25 K
1980-1989. Dreadnought-size with koa back and sides and spruce top.

1980-1989		$1,600	$1,750

D-25 K2
1980-1989. Same as D-25K, but with koa top and black 'guard.

1980-1989		$1,700	$1,850

D-28
1931-present. Brazilian rosewood back and sides (changed to Indian rosewood in '70), '36 was the last year for the 12-fret model, '44 was the last year for scalloped bracing, '47 was the last year herringbone trim was offered, natural. Ultra high-end D-28 Martin guitar (pre-'47) valuations are very sensitive to structural and cosmetic condition. Finish wear and body cracks for ultra high-end Martin flat tops should be evaluated on a case-by-case basis. Small variances within the 'excellent condition' category can lead to notable valuation differences.

1931-1932		$70,000	$85,000
1933		$69,000	$82,000
1934	14-fret neck	$68,000	$80,000
1935-1936		$65,000	$75,000
1937-1938		$48,000	$60,000
1939		$38,000	$53,000
1940-1941		$36,000	$40,000
1942-1944	Scalloped braces	$32,000	$37,000
1944-1946	Herringbone, non-scalloped	$21,000	$23,000
1947-1949	Non-herringbone starting '47	$10,000	$12,000
1950-1952		$9,000	$10,000
1953-1958	Klusons to early '58	$8,000	$9,500
1958-1959	Grover tuners late '58	$7,000	$9,000
1960-1962		$5,200	$7,300
1963-1965		$5,000	$6,100
1966	Black guard late '66	$4,800	$6,000

MODEL YEAR	FEATURES	EXC. COND. LOW	HIGH
1966	Tortoise guard early '66	$4,900	$6,100
1967	Last of maple bridgeplate	$4,800	$5,900
1968	Rosewood bridgeplate	$4,600	$5,800
1969	Last of Brazilian rosewood	$4,500	$5,300
1970-1979	Indian rosewood	$2,000	$2,300
1980-1989		$1,600	$2,000
1990-1999		$1,400	$1,900
2000-2005		$1,400	$1,700

D-28 (1935 Special)
1993. Guitar of the Month, 1935 features, Indian rosewood back and sides, peghead with Brazilian rosewood veneer.

1993		$1,700	$2,300

D-28 50th Anniversary
1983. Stamped inside 1833-1983 150th Anniversary, Indian rosewood back and sides.

1983		$1,700	$2,100

D-28 CW/CWB Clarence White
2002-2004. CW has Indian rosewood back and sides, the CWB Brazilian, only 150 CWBs were to be built.

2002-2004	CW	$1,900	$2,200
2002-2004	CWB	$4,000	$4,400

D-28 DM Del McCourey Signature
2003. Limited edition of 115 instruments, natural.

2003		$2,400	$2,800

D-28 E
1959-1964. Electric, Brazilian rosewood back and sides, 2 DeArmond pickups, natural.

1959-1964		$3,500	$4,000

D-28 GE Golden Era
1999-2002. GE (Golden Era), Brazilian rosewood, herringbone trim.

1999-2002		$6,500	$7,500

D-28 LSH
1991. Guitar of the Month, Indian rosewood back and sides, herringbone trim, snowflake inlay, zigzag back stripe.

1991		$1,850	$2,100

D-28 Marquis
2004-present. D-28 reissue with specs designed to be close to the original.

2004-2005		$1,800	$2,600

D-28 P
1988-1990. P stands for low-profile neck, Indian rosewood back and sides.

1988-1990		$1,200	$1,500

D-28 S
1954-1993. Rosewood back and sides, 12-fret neck.

1960-1965	Special order	$6,000	$7,000
1966-1969	Brazilian rosewood	$6,000	$7,000
1970-1993	Indian rosewood	$2,200	$2,700

D-28 V
1983-1985. Brazilian rosewood back and sides, Limited Edition, herringbone trim, slotted diamond inlay.

1983-1985		$4,500	$5,000

D-2832 Shenandoah
1984-1992. Dreadnought acoustic, Thinline pickup, spruce top, V-neck, laminated rosewood sides, 3-piece rosewood back.

1984-1992		$750	$800

D-3-18
1991. Sitka spruce top, 3-piece mahogany back, 80-piece limited edition.

1991		$1,600	$2,100

D-35
1965-present. Brazilian rosewood back and sides, changed to Indian rosewood in '70, 3-piece back, natural with sunburst option.

1965		$4,200	$5,500
1966		$4,000	$5,000
1967		$3,500	$4,800
1968		$3,500	$4,700
1969	Brazilian rosewood	$3,500	$4,100
1970-1979	Indian rosewood	$1,700	$2,100
1980-1989		$1,500	$1,800
1990-1999		$1,500	$1,800
2000-2005		$1,500	$1,800

D-35 Ernest Tubb
2003. Indian rosewood back and sides, special inlays, 90 built.

2003		$2,400	$2,600

D-35 S
1966-1993. Brazilian rosewood back and sides, changed to Indian rosewood in '70, 12-fret neck, slotted peghead.

1966-1969	Brazilian rosewood	$4,000	$4,500
1970-1979	Indian rosewood	$2,000	$2,400
1980-1989		$2,000	$2,300
1990-1993		$2,000	$2,200

D-35 V Brazilian 20th Anniversary
1984.

1984		$3,700	$3,900

D-3532 Shenandoah
1984-1993. Dreadnought acoustic, spruce top, V-neck, laminated rosewood sides, 3-piece rosewood back.

1984-1993		$700	$800

D-37 K
1980-1995. Dreadnought-size, koa back and sides, spruce top.

1980-1995		$2,100	$2,300

D-37 K2
1980-1995. Same as D-37 K, but has a koa top and black 'guard.

1980-1995		$2,100	$2,300

D-40
1997-2005. Rosewood back and sides, hexagon inlays.

1997-2005		$2,200	$2,400

D-40 BLE
1990. Limited Edition Guitar of the Month, Brazilian rosewood back and sides, pearl top border except around 'board.

1990		$8,800	$9,500

1966 Martin D-35

Martin D-35 Ernest Tubb

1997 Martin D-45

Martin D-45 Mike Longworth

MODEL YEAR	FEATURES	EXC. COND. LOW	HIGH

D-41

1969-present. Brazilian rosewood back and sides for the first ones in '69 then Indian rosewood, bound body, scalloped braces, natural.

1969	Brazilian rosewood	$10,000	$15,000
1970-1979	Indian rosewood	$2,800	$3,500
1980-1989		$2,500	$3,100
1990-1999		$2,300	$3,000
1990-1999	Sunburst option	$2,600	$3,200
2000-2005		$2,300	$2,700

D-41 BLE

1989. Limited Edition Guitar of the Month, Brazilian rosewood back and sides, pearl top border except around 'board.

1989		$3,200	$3,800

D-41GJ George Jones

2001. Style 41 appointments, limited edition of 100, label signed by the Opossum.

2001		$3,200	$3,500

D-42

1996-present. Dreadnought, Indian rosewood back and sides, spruce top, pearl rosette and inlays, snowflake 'board inlays, gold tuners, gloss finish.

1996-2005		$2,900	$3,300

D-42 K/D-42 K2

2000-present. K has koa back and sides, the all koa body K2 was discontinued in '05.

2000-2005	D-42 K	$3,000	$3,500
2000-2005	D-42 K2	$3,000	$3,700

D-42 LE

1988 only. D-42-style, limited edition (75 sold), scalloped braces, low profile neck.

1988		$2,300	$2,500

D-42 V

1985. Vintage Series, 12 made, Brazilian rosewood, scalloped braces.

1985		$8,000	$9,000

D-45

1933-1942 (96 made), 1968-present. Brazilian rosewood back and sides, changed to Indian rosewood during '69. The pre-WW II D-45 is one of the holy grails. A pre-war D-45 should be evaluated on a case-by-case basis. The price ranges are for all-original guitars in excellent condition and are guidance pricing only. These ranges are for a crack-free guitar. Unfortunately, many older acoustics have a crack or two and this can make ultra-expensive acoustics more difficult to evaluate than ultra-expensive solidbody electrics. Technically, a repaired body crack makes a guitar non-original, but the vintage market generally considers a professionally repaired crack to be original. Crack width, length and depth can vary, therefore extra attention is suggested.

1936	Only 2 made	$245,000	$260,000
1937	Only 2 made	$225,000	$235,000
1938	Only 9 made	$215,000	$225,000
1939	Only 14 made	$200,000	$210,000
1940	Only 19 made	$190,000	$200,000
1941	Only 24 made	$190,000	$200,000
1942	Only 19 made	$175,000	$190,000

MODEL YEAR	FEATURES	EXC. COND. LOW	HIGH
1968	Brazilian rosewood	$30,000	$40,000
1969		$28,000	$38,000
1970-1974	Indian rosewood, 105 made	$6,500	$7,000
1975-1979		$6,500	$7,000
1980-1989		$5,000	$6,000
1990-1999		$4,500	$5,000
2000-2005		$4,500	$5,000

D-45 (1939 Reissue)

High-grade spruce top, figured Brazilian rosewood back and sides, high X and scalloped braces, abalone trim, natural, gold tuners.

1992		$10,500	$12,500

D-45 100th Anniversary LE

1996. Limited edition, 1896-1996 C.F. Martin Commemorative Anniversary Model label.

1996		$6,400	$6,600

D-45 200th Anniversary (C.F. Martin Sr. Deluxe)

1996 only. Commemorative model for C.F. Martin Sr.'s birth in 1796, Brazilian Deluxe Edition, natural.

1996		$12,000	$14,000

D-45 Brazilian

1994. Brazilian rosewood.

1994		$10,000	$11,000

D-45 Custom

Various options and models, Brazilian rosewood back and sides.

1991-1992		$7,000	$14,000

D-45 Deluxe

1993 only. Guitar of the Month, Brazilian rosewood back and sides, figured spruce top, inlay in bridge and 'guard, tree-of-life inlay on 'board, pearl borders and back stripe, gold tuners with large gold buttons, total of 60 sold.

1993		$14,000	$18,000

D-45 Gene Autry

1994 only. Gene Autry inlay (2 options available), natural.

1994		$15,000	$20,000

D-45 Mike Longworth Commemorative Edition

2005. East Indian rosewood back and sides, Adirondack spruce top, 91 made, label signed by Mike's wife Sue and C.F. Martin IV.

2005		$8,000	$9,000

D-45 S

1969-1993. Brazilian rosewood back and sides, 12-fret neck, S means slotted peghead, only 50 made.

1988-1993		$7,000	$9,000

D-45 Steven Stills Signature

2002. Limited edition of 91.

2002		$12,000	$14,000

D-45 V

1983-1985. Brazilian rosewood back and sides, scalloped braces, snowflake inlay, natural, name revived in '99.

1983-1985		$10,000	$12,500

MODEL YEAR	FEATURES	EXC. COND. LOW	HIGH

D-45 VR
1997-Present. Scalloped braces, high X-bracing, vintage aging toner, snowflake inlay, name changed to D-45 V in '99.
| 1997-2005 | | $5,000 | $5,500 |

D-50/D-50K/D-50K2
2003. Ultra high-end D-style solid Koa top, back and side, ultra fancy appointments, 5 made.
| 2003 | | $30,000 | $34,000 |

D-62
1989-1995. Dreadnought, flamed maple back and sides, spruce top, chrome-plated enclosed Schaller tuners.
| 1989-1995 | | $1,700 | $2,000 |

D-62 LE
1986. Flamed maple back and sides, spruce top, snowflake inlays, natural, Guitar of the Month October '86.
| 1986 | | $1,900 | $2,200 |

D-76
1975-1976. Limited Edition, Indian rosewood back and sides, 3-piece back, herringbone back stripe, pearl stars on 'board, eagle on peghead, only 200 made in '75 and 1,976 made in '76.
| 1976 | | $2,900 | $3,100 |

DC-1/DC-1 E
1995-2005. Cutaway D-1, all solid wood, mahogany back and sides, spruce top. Transducer pickup E available '97-'05, regular model ended in '00.
| 1995-2005 | | $650 | $850 |

DC-16 GTE Premium
2003-present. Rounded cutaway, all solid wood, gloss finish top, satin finish mahogany back and sides.
| 2003-2005 | | $1,000 | $1,100 |

DM
1990-present. Solid sitka spruce top, laminated mahogany back and sides, dot markers, natural satin.
| 1990-2000s | | $575 | $650 |

DM-12
1996-present. 12-string, laminated mahogany back and sides, herringbone rosette.
| 1996-2005 | | $600 | $675 |

DVM Veterans
2002-present. D-style, spruce top, rosewood back and sides, special veterans ornamentation.
| 2002-2005 | | $1,750 | $1,850 |

DXM
1998-present. Wood composite mahogany laminate D body, solid wood neck, decal rosette, screened headstock logo, unique DX bracing.
| 1998-2001 | | $350 | $400 |

E-18
1979-1982. Offset double-cut, maple and rosewood laminate solidbody, 2 DiMarzio pickups, phase switch, natural.
| 1979-1982 | | $650 | $750 |

EM-18
1979-1982. Offset double-cut, maple and rosewood laminate solidbody, 2 exposed-coil humbucking pickups, coil split switch.
| 1979-1982 | | $650 | $750 |

EMP-1
1998-1999. Employee series designed by Martin employee team, cutaway solid spruce top, ovangkol wood back and sides with rosewood middle insert (D-35-style insert), on-board pickup.
| 1998-1999 | | $1,800 | $2,200 |

F-1
1940-1942. Mahogany back and sides, carved spruce top, multi-bound, f-holes, sunburst.
| 1940-1942 | 91 made | $2,000 | $2,200 |

F-2
1940-1942. Rosewood back and sides, carved spruce top, multi-bound, f-holes.
| 1940-1942 | 46 made | $2,500 | $3,500 |

F-7
1935-1942. Brazilian rosewood back and sides, f-holes, carved top, back arched by braces, multi-bound, sunburst top finish.
| 1935-1942 | | $7,000 | $10,000 |

F-9
1935-1941. Highest-end archtop, Brazilian rosewood, Martin inlaid vertically on headstock, 7-ply top binding, 45-style back strip, sunburst.
| 1935-1941 | | $11,000 | $15,000 |

F-50
1961-1965. Single-cut thinline archtop with laminated maple body, 1 pickup.
| 1961-1965 | | $1,100 | $1,500 |

F-55
1961-1965. Single-cut thinline archtop with laminated maple body, 2 pickups.
| 1961-1965 | | $1,200 | $1,600 |

F-65
1961-1965. Electric archtop, double-cut, f-holes, 2 pickups, square-cornered peghead, Bigsby, sunburst.
| 1961-1965 | | $1,400 | $1,800 |

GT-70
1966-1968. Electric archtop, bound body, f-holes, single-cut, 2 pickups, tremolo, burgundy or black finish.
| 1966-1968 | | $1,100 | $1,400 |

GT-75
1966-1968. Electric archtop, bound body, f-holes, double-cut, 2 pickups, tremolo, burgundy or black finish.
| 1966-1968 | | $1,400 | $1,600 |

Hawaiian X
2002-2004. Hawaiian scene painted on top, similar to the Cowboy guitar model, limited edition of 500.
| 2002-2004 | | $750 | $850 |

HD-28 BLE
1990. Guitar of the Month, Brazilian rosewood back and sides, herringbone soundhole ring, low profile neck (LE), chrome tuners, aging toner finish.
| 1990 | | $4,000 | $5,000 |

HD-28 Custom 150th Anniversary
1983. 150th Anniversary, Martin Custom Shop, Indian rosewood sides and back, "1833-1983 150th Year" stamped on inside backstrip.
| 1983 | | $2,600 | $2,800 |

1963 Martin F-65

1966 Martin GT-75

To get the most from this book, be sure to read "Using **The Guide**" in the introduction.

Martin HD-28

Martin J-40

MODEL YEAR	FEATURES	EXC. COND. LOW	HIGH

HD-28 GM LSH
1994. Grand Marquis, Guitar of the Month, rosewood back and sides, large soundhole with double herringbone rings, snowflake inlay in bridge.

1994		$2,500	$3,000

HD-28 KM Keb Mo Signature Edition
2001. 252 made.

2001		$2,000	$2,500

HD-28 LE
1985. Guitar of the Month, rosewood back and sides, scalloped bracing, herringbone top purfling, diamonds and squares 'board inlay, V-neck.

1985		$2,500	$3,000

HD-28 MP
1990. Bolivian rosewood back and sides, scalloped braces, herringbone top purfling, zipper back stripe, low profile neck.

1990		$1,500	$2,000

HD-28 P
1987-1989. Rosewood back and sides, scalloped braces, herringbone, low profile neck (P), zigzag back stripe.

1987-1989		$1,500	$2,000

HD-28 Standard Series
1976-present. Indian rosewood back and sides, scalloped bracing, herringbone purfling.

1976-1979		$2,100	$2,400
1980-1989		$1,700	$2,100
1990-1999		$1,600	$1,900
2000-2005		$1,600	$1,800

HD-28 VS
1996-present. Slotted headstock, Indian rosewood sides and back.

1996-2005		$2,000	$2,300

HD-28 V/VR
1996-present. 14-fret vintage series, rosewood body, R dropped from name in '99.

1996-2005		$2,000	$2,100

HD-282 R
1994 only.

1994		$1,500	$1,800

HD-35
1978-present. Indian rosewood back and sides, herringbone top trim, zipper back stripe.

1978-1979		$1,900	$2,200
1980-1989		$1,900	$2,200
1990-1999		$1,900	$2,200
2000-2005		$1,900	$2,300

HD-35 P
1987-1989. HD-35 with low profile neck.

1987-1989		$1,500	$2,000

HD-40 MK Mark Knopfler Edition
2001-2002. Limited edition of 251 made, Mark Knopfler signature inlay 20th fret, herringbone trim, fancy marquetry soundhole rings.

2001-2002		$2,500	$3,000

HD-40 Tom Petty SE
2004-present. Indian rosewood sides and back, high-end appointments, 274 made, inside label with signature.

2004-2005		$3,500	$4,000

HJ-28
1992, 1996-2000. Guitar of the Month in '92, regular production starts in '96. Jumbo, non-cut, spruce top, Indian rosewood sides and back, herringbone top purfling, with or without on-board electronics.

1996-2000		$1,700	$1,800

HOM-35
1989. Herringbone Orchestra Model, Guitar of the Month, scalloped braces, 3-piece Brazilian rosewood back, bookmatched sides, 14-fret neck, only 60 built.

1989		$4,500	$5,500

HPD-41
1999-2001. Like D-41, but with herringbone rosette, binding.

1999-2001		$3,100	$3,200

J-1 Jumbo
1997-2002. Jumbo body with mahogany back and sides.

1997-2002		$700	$875

J12-16 GT
2000-present. 16" jumbo 12-string, satin solid mahogany back and sides, gloss solid spruce top.

2000-2005		$800	$850

J12-40
1985-1996. Called J12-40 M from '85-'90, rosewood back and sides, 12 strings, 16" jumbo size, 14-fret neck, solid peghead, gold tuners.

1996		$1,600	$1,900

J12-65
1985-1995. Called J12-65M for '84-'90, Jumbo style 65 12-string, spruce top, figured maple back and sides, gold tuning machines, scalloped bracing, ebony 'board, tortoiseshell-style binding, natural.

1985-1995		$1,600	$1,900

J-15
1999-present. Jumbo 16" narrow-waist body, solid mahogany top, sides, and back satin finish.

1999-2005		$500	$550

J-18/J-18M
1987-1996. J-size body with Style 18 appointments, natural, called J-18M for '87-'89.

1987-1996		$1,350	$1,400

J-40
1990-present. Called J-40 M from '85-'89, Jumbo, Indian rosewood back and sides, triple-bound 'board, hexagonal inlays.

1990-2005		$1,800	$2,200

J-40 Custom
1993-1996. J-40 with upgrades including abalone top trim and rosette.

1993-1996		$2,700	$2,900

J-40 M
1985-1989. Jumbo, Indian rosewood back and sides, triple-bound 'board, hexagonal inlays, name changed to J-40 in '90.

1985-1989		$1,900	$2,200

J-41 Special
2004-present. East Indian rosewood back and sides, Style 45 snowflake inlays.

2004-2005		$2,350	$2,450

MODEL YEAR	FEATURES	EXC. COND. LOW	HIGH

J-65/J-65 E/J-65 M
1985-1995. Jumbo acoustic featuring maple back and sides, gold-plated tuners, scalloped bracing, ebony 'board, tortoise shell-style binding.

| 1985-1995 | | $1,900 | $2,200 |

LX Series
2003-present. Little Martin Series travel guitars.

| 2003-2005 | | $200 | $275 |

M-21 Custom
December 1984. Guitar of the Month, low profile neck M-Series, Indian rosewood back and sides, special ornamentation.

| 1984 | | $1,700 | $2,100 |

M-35 SC Shawn Colvin
2002. 120 made, M (0000) size, mahogany sides, 3-piece mahogany/rosewood back, Fishman pickup/preamp, Shawn Colvin & C.F.M. III signed label.

| 2002 | | $1,600 | $1,700 |

M-36
1978-1997. Indian rosewood back and sides, bound 'board, low profile neck, multi-bound, white-black-white back stripes.

| 1978-1997 | | $1,500 | $1,800 |

M-38
1977-1996. Indian rosewood back and sides, multi-bound, low profile neck, gold-plated tuners, stained top.

| 1977-1996 | | $1,900 | $2,100 |

MC-16 GTE
2002-2004. Acoustic/electric, M-size single cut, gloss finish solid spruce top, satin finish solid mahogany sides and back.

| 2002-2004 | | $900 | $1,000 |

MC-28
1981-1996. Rosewood back and sides, single-cut acoustic, oval soundhole, scalloped braces, natural.

| 1981-1996 | | $1,700 | $2,100 |

MC-68
1985-1995. Auditorium-size acoustic, rounded cut-away, maple back and sides, gold tuners, scalloped bracing, ebony 'board, tortoiseshell-style binding, natural or sunburst.

| 1985-1995 | | $2,000 | $2,400 |

MTV-1 Unplugged
1996. Body is 1/2 rosewood and 1/2 mahogany, scalloped bracing, MTV logo on headstock.

| 1996 | | $1,400 | $1,650 |

N-10
1968-1995. Classical, mahogany back and sides, fan bracing, wood marquetry soundhole ring, unbound rosewood 'board, 12-fret neck and slotted peghead from '70.

1968-1969	Short-scale	$1,300	$1,500
1970-1979	Long-scale	$1,200	$1,400
1980-1989	Long-scale	$1,200	$1,400
1990-1995	Long-scale	$1,200	$1,400

N-20
1968-1995. Classical, Brazilian rosewood back and sides (changed to Indian rosewood in '69), multi-bound, 12-fret neck, solid headstock (changed to slotted in '70), natural.

| 1968-1969 | Brazilian rosewood, short-scale | $3,000 | $3,500 |

1970-1979	Indian rosewood, long-scale	$1,400	$1,800
1980-1989	Long-scale	$1,400	$1,800
1990-1995	Long-scale	$1,400	$1,800

OM-18
1930-1934. Orchestra Model, mahogany back and sides, 14-fret neck, solid peghead, banjo tuners (changed to right-angle in '31).

| 1930-1933 | Natural | $25,000 | $30,000 |
| 1934 | Sunburst option | $27,000 | $32,000 |

OM-18 GE Golden Era 1930/Special Edition GE
2003-present. Mahogany back and sides, Brazilian rosewood purfling and binding.

| 2003-2005 | | $1,800 | $1,900 |

OM-18 V
1999-present. Vintage features.

| 1999-2005 | | $1,550 | $1,800 |

OM-18 VLJ/OMC-18 VLJ
2002. 133 made.

| 2002 | | $2,200 | $3,000 |

OM-21 Standard Series
1992-1997. Triple 0-size, 15 1/8", spruce top, rosewood back and sides, natural.

| 1992-1997 | | $1,400 | $1,500 |

OM-28
1929-1933. Orchestra Model, Brazilian rosewood back and sides, 14-fret neck, solid peghead, banjo tuners (changed to right-angle in '31), reintroduced with Indian rosewood in '90.

| 1929-1930 | Small guard, banjo tuners | $40,000 | $50,000 |
| 1931-1933 | Large guard | $35,000 | $44,000 |

OM-28 Marquis
2005-present. Orchestra Model, pre-war appointments, spruce top, ebony 'board and bridge, East Indian rosewood back, sides and headplate.

| 2005 | | $2,700 | $2,800 |

OM-28 PB Perry Bechtel
1993. Guitar of the Month, signed by Perry Bechtel's widow Ina, spruce top, Indian rosewood back and sides, zigzag back stripe, chrome tuners, V-neck, only 50 made.

| 1993 | | $4,500 | $5,000 |

OM-28 Reissue
1990-1996. Indian rosewood back and sides.

| 1990-1996 | | $1,900 | $2,200 |

OM-28 VR
1990-1996. Orchestra Model, reintroduced OM-28 with rosewood back and sides.

| 1990-1996 | | $1,900 | $2,200 |

OM-42 PS Paul Simon
1997. Bookmatched sitka spruce top, Indian rosewood back and sides, 42- and 45-style features, low profile PS neck, 500 made.

| 1997 | | $4,000 | $4,200 |

OM-42 Reissue
1999-present. Indian rosewood back and sides, Style 45 snowflake inlays, rounded neck profile.

| 1999-2005 | | $2,900 | $3,300 |

Martin OM-21 Standard Series

Martin OM-42

1937 Martin R-18

Maton MS500/12

MODEL YEAR	FEATURES	EXC. COND. LOW	HIGH

OM-45 Deluxe (special)
1999. 4 made on special order, highly figured Brazilian rosewood.

1999		$13,000	$18,000

OM-45 Deluxe Reissue
1994.

1994		$4,000	$4,300

OM-45 Deluxe/OM-45
1930-1933. OM-style, 45 level appointments with pearl inlay in 'guard and bridge, only 14 OM-45 Deluxe instruments made. Regular OM-45 with normal 45-style appointments. Condition is critically important on this or any ultra high-end instrument, minor flaws are critical to value.

1930	OM-45 Deluxe	$235,000	$250,000
1930-1933	OM-45	$150,000	$160,000

OMC-16RE Aura
2005-present. Orchestra Model cutaway, solid East Indian rosewood back and sides, spruce top, gloss body, pearl rosettes, bound body and 'board.

2005		$1,200	$1,300

OMC-28
1990. Guitar of the Month with rounded cutaway, gold tuners, low profile neck, pearl Martin script logo in headstock, label signed by C.F. Martin IV.

1990		$1,800	$2,100

OMC-28 Laurence Juber
2004. 133 made.

2004		$2,700	$2,800

R-17
1934-1942. All mahogany, arched top and back, 3-segment f-holes (changed to 1-segment in '37), 12-fret neck, sunburst.

1934-1942	940 made	$1,500	$2,000

R-18
1933-1942. Spruce arched top (carved top by 1937), mahogany back and sides, 14-fret neck, bound top, sunburst.

1933-1942	1,928 made	$2,200	$2,500

R-18 T
1934-1941. Tenor archtop, sunburst, 14 3/8" lower bout, 2 f-holes, dot markers.

1934-1941		$1,500	$1,800

SPD-16 Series
1996-2004. D-16 Series Special models.

1996-2000	SPD-16 T mahogany	$950	$1,100
1996-2000	SPD-16R/TR Rosewood	$1,350	$1,500
1996-2000	SPDC-16R/TR Cutaway	$1,350	$1,525
2000-2004	SPD-16 K Koa	$1,350	$1,475

Stauffer
1830s-ca.1850s. One of C.F. Martin's earliest models, distinguished by the scrolled, six-on-a-side headstock, ornamentation varies from guitar to guitar.

1830s	Plain, no ivory	$4,000	$7,000
1830s	Very fancy, ivory board and bridge	$7,000	$30,000

Maruha
Japanese-made acoustic, classical, archtop and solidbody guitars, often copies of American brands. Probably not imported into the U.S.

Marvel
Ca. 1950s- ca. 1960s. Brand name used for budget guitars and basses marketed by Peter Sorkin Company in New York, New York. Sorkin manufactured and distributed Premier guitars and amplifiers made by its Multivox subsidiary. Marvel instruments were primarily beginner-grade. Brand disappears by mid-'60s.

Electric Solidbody Guitars
1950s-mid-1960s. Various models.

1950s		$150	$250

Masaki Sakurai
See Kohno brand.

Mason
1936-1939. Henry L. Mason on headstock, wholesale distribution, similar to Gibson/Cromwell, pressed wood back and sides.

Student/Intermediate Student
1936-1939. Various flat-top and archtop student/ budget models.

1936-1939		$350	$750

Mason Bernard
1990-1991. Founded by Bernie Rico (BC Rich founder). During this period BC Rich guitars were liscensed and controlled by Randy Waltuch and Class Axe. Most Mason models were designs similar to the BC Rich Assassin, according to Bernie Rico only the very best materials were used, large MB logo on headstock. Around 225 guitars were built bearing this brand.

MB-1/MB-2 Assassin

1990-1991		$550	$700

Maton
1946-present. Intermediate and professional grade, production/custom, acoustic, acoustic/electric, hollow body and solidbody guitars built in Box Hill, Victoria, Australia. Founded by Bill May and his brother Reg and still run by the family. Only available in USA since '82.

Mauel Guitars
1995-present. Luthier Hank Mauel builds his premium grade, custom, flat-tops in Auburn, California.

Maurer
1897-1944. Robert Maurer built instruments under his own name and the Champion brand in his Chicago-based woodworking shop. He sold the shop to the Larson Brothers in 1900, but the Maurer name was retained. The Larsons offered low-end and high quality Maurer models. They also branded instruments for various retailers.

MODEL YEAR	FEATURES	EXC. COND. LOW	HIGH

13" Acoustic Flat-Top (Standard)
Early-1900s. Rosewood back and sides, spruce top, 12 3/4", made by Larson Brothers of Chicago.

1910		$3,000	$4,000

13" Higher-End Flat-Top (Brazilian)
Early-1900s. Spruce top, 13 5/8", Brazilian rosewood back and sides, high-end pearl appointments, slotted headstock.

1910	Natural	$5,000	$8,000

14" Flat-Top (Brazilian)
1920s-1930s. Mid-sized (about 14") with Brazilian rosewood back and sides, attractive appointments.

1920s	Abalone trim	$8,000	$20,000

14" Flat-Top (Mahogany)
1920s-1930s. Mid-sized (about 14") with mahogany back and sides, standard appointments.

1930s		$2,500	$3,500

15" High-end Flat-Top (Brazilian)
Early-1900s. Brazilian rosewood back and sides, tree of life inlay, 15", pearl-bound.

1920s		$9,000	$12,000

McAlister Guitars
1997-present. Premium grade, custom, flat-tops built by luthier Roy McAlister in Watsonville, California.

McCollum Guitars
1994-present. Luthier Lance McCollum builds his premium grade, custom, flat-top and harp guitars in Colfax, California.

McCurdy Guitars
1983-present. Premium grade, production/custom, archtops built by luthier Ric McCurdy originally in Santa Barbara, California and, since '91, New York, New York.

McGill Guitars
1976-present. Luthier Paul McGill builds his premium grade, production/custom, classical, resonator, and acoustic/electric guitars in Nashville, Tennessee.

McGlynn Guitars
2005-present. Luthier Michael J. McGlynn builds his premium and presentation grade, custom, solidbody guitars in Henderson, Nevada.

MCI, Inc
1967-1988. MusiConics International (MCI), of Waco, Texas, introduced the world to the Guitorgan, invented by Bob Murrell. Later, they also offered effects and a steel guitar. In the '80s, a MIDI version was offered. MCI was also involved with the Daion line of guitars in the late '70s and early '80s.

GuitOrgan B-35
1970s (ca. 1976-1978?). Duplicated the sounds of an organ and more. MCI bought double-cut semi-hollow body guitars from others and outfitted them with lots of switches and buttons. Each fret has 6 segments that correspond to an organ tone. There was also a B-300 and B-30 version, and the earlier M-300 and 340.

1970s		$1,300	$1,700

McInturff
1996-present. Professional and premium grade, production/custom, solidbody guitars built by luthier Terry C. McInturff originally in Holly Springs, North Carolina, and since '04, in Moncure, North Carolina. McInturff spent 17 years during guitar repair and custom work before starting his own guitar line.

Monarch
Offset double cutaway contoured mahogany solidbody, set-neck, single-single-hum pickups, transparent cherry.

2000s		$1,400	$1,500

Taurus Custom
Flame maple top, chambered mahogany body, matching flamed maple headstock, abalone slash inlays, gold hardware.

2000s		$2,300	$2,500

Taurus Standard
Single-cut, carved flamed maple top on chambered mahogany body, dual humbucker pickups, gold hardware.

1996-2005	Sunburst	$1,900	$2,200

McPherson Guitars
1981-present. Premium grade, production, flat-tops built by luthier Mander McPherson in Sparta, Wisconsin.

Mean Gene
1988-1990. Heavy metal style solidbodies made by Gene Baker, who started Baker U.S.A. guitars in '97, and Eric Zoellner in Santa Maria, California. They built around 30 custom guitars.

Megas Guitars
1989-present. Luthier Ted Megas builds his premium grade, custom, archtop and solidbody guitars, originally in San Franciso, and currently in Portland, Oregon.

Melancon
Professional and premium grade, custom/production, solid and semi-hollow body guitars built by luthier Gerard Melancon in Thibodaux, Louisiana. They also build basses.

Mello, John F.
1973-present. Premium grade, production/custom, classical and ftat-top guitars built by luthier John Mello in Kensington, California.

Melophonic
1960s. Brand built by the Valco Company of Chicago.

McCollum harp guitar

Megas Athena solidbody

GUITARS

Metropolitan Glendale Deluxe

Michael Lewis San Rafael

MODEL YEAR	FEATURES	EXC. COND. LOW	HIGH

Resonator Guitar
Valco-made.

| 1965 | | $600 | $800 |

Melville Guitars
1988-present. Luthier Christopher Melville builds his premium grade, custom, flat-tops in Milton, Queensland, Australia.

Mercurio
2002-2005. Luthier Peter Mercuio built his custom/production solidbody guitars, featuring his interchangeable PickupPak system to swap pickups, in Chanhassen, Minnesota.

Mermer Guitars
1983-present. Luthier Richard Mermer builds his premium grade, production/custom, steel-string, nylon-string, and Hawaiian guitars in Sebastian, Florida.

Merrill Brothers
1998-present. Premium grade, production/custom, steel-string and harp guitars built by luthiers Jim and Dave Merrill in Williamsburg, Virginia.

Mesrobian
1995-present. Luthier Carl Mesrobian builds his professional and premium grade, custom, archtop guitars in Salem, Massachusetts.

Messenger
1967-1968. Built by Musicraft, Inc., originally of 156 Montgomery Street, San Francisco, California. The distinguishing feature of the Messengers is a metal alloy neck which extended through the body to the tailblock, plus mono or stereo outputs. Sometime before March '68 the company relocated to Astoria, Oregon. Press touted "improved" magnesium neck, though it's not clear if this constituted a change from '67. Brand disappears after '68. They also made basses.

Electric Hollowbody Archtop
1967-1968. Symmetrical double-cut body shape, metal neck with rosewood 'boards, stereo.

| 1967-1968 | Rojo Red | $2,200 | $2,800 |

Metropolitan
1995-present. Professional and premium grade, production/custom, retro-styled solidbodies designed by David Wintz reminiscent of the '50s National Res-o-glas and wood body guitars. They feature full-scale set-neck construction and a wood body instead of Res-o-glas. Wintz also makes Robin and Alamo brand instruments.

Glendale Custom
1997-present. Single-cut, African fakimba body, set-neck, 2 pickups, various colors.

| 1997-2005 | | $1,400 | $1,700 |

Glendale Custom Acoustic
1997-2004. Single-cut, African fakimba body, set-neck, 3 pickups including piezo.

| 1997-2004 | | $1,900 | $2,300 |

Glendale Deluxe
1997-present. Single-cut, African fakimba body, set-neck, 2 pickups, dot markers.

| 1997-2005 | | $800 | $1,100 |

Glendale Super Acoustic
1997-2004. Single-cut, flamed maple top, 3 pickups including piezo, gold hardware.

| 1997-2004 | | $2,900 | $3,400 |

Tanglewood Custom
1996-present. Map-shape basswood body, German body carve front and back, 2 humbuckers, bound ebony 'board, butterfly inlays, various colors.

| 1996-2005 | | $1,400 | $1,700 |

Tanglewood Custom Acoustic
1996-2004. Tanglewood Custom with added piezo bridge pickup, various colors.

| 1996-2004 | | $1,900 | $2,300 |

Tanglewood Deluxe
1996-present. Similar to Custom, but with unbound rosewood 'board, dot inlays, German body carve on top only.

| 1996-2005 | | $800 | $1,100 |

Westport Custom
1997-present. Single-cut, 3 pickups, art deco design, African fakimba body, set-neck, various colors.

| 1997-2005 | | $1,400 | $1,700 |

Westport Custom Acoustic
1997-2004. Single-cut, 3 pickups, art deco design, African fakimba body, set-neck.

| 1997-2004 | | $1,900 | $2,300 |

Westport Deluxe
1997-present. Single-cut, 2 humbuckers.

| 1997-2005 | | $800 | $1,000 |

Westport Super Acoustic
1997-2004. Single-cut, 3 pickups with piezo, art deco design, Africa fakimba body, set-neck.

| 1997-2004 | | $3,100 | $3,500 |

Miami
1920s. Instruments built by the Oscar Schmidt Co. and possibly others. Most likely a brand made for a distributor.

Michael Dunn Guitars
1968-present. Luthier Michael Dunn builds his production/custom Maccaferri-style guitars in New Westminster, British Columbia. He also offers a harp uke and a Weissenborn- or Knutsen-style Hawaiian guitar, and has built archtops.

Michael Kelly
2000-present. Intermediate and professional grade, production, acoustic, solidbody and archtop guitars imported by Elite Music Brands of Clearwater, Florida. They also offer mandolins and basses.

MODEL YEAR	FEATURES	EXC. COND. LOW	HIGH

Michael Lewis Instruments

1992-present. Luthier Michael Lewis builds his premium and presentation grade, custom, archtop guitars in Grass Valley, California. He also builds mandolins.

Michael Menkevich

1970-present. Luthier Michael Menkevich builds his professional and premium grade, production/custom, flamenco and classical guitars in Elkins Park, Pennsylvania.

Segovia

Solid cedar top, solid Indian rosewood back and sides, Spanish cedar neck.

1990s		$2,200	$2,500

Michael Silvey Custom Guitars

2003-present. Solidbody electric guitars built by Michael Silvey in North Canton, Ohio.

Michael Thames

1972-present. Luthier Michael Thames builds his premium grade, custom/production, classical guitars in Taos, New Mexico.

Classical

1990s. Solid cedar top, solid Indian rosewood back and sides, mahogany neck.

1995		$3,400	$3,600

Michael Tuttle

2003-present. Professional and premium grade, custom, solid and hollow body guitars built by luthier Michael Tuttle in Saugus, California. He also builds basses.

Microfrets

1967-1975, 2004-present. Professional grade, production, electric guitars built in Myersville, Maryland. They also build basses. Founded by Ralph S. Jones, Sr. in Frederick, Microfrets offered over 20 models of guitars that sported innovative designs and features, with pickups designed by Bill Lawrence. The brand was revived, again in Frederick, by Will Meadors and Paul Rose in '04.

Serial numbers run from about 1000 to about 3800. Not all instruments have serial numbers, particularly ones produced in '75. Serial numbers do not appear to be correlated to a model type, but are sequential by the general date of production.

Instruments can be identified by body styles as follows; Styles 1, 1.5, 2, and 3. An instrument may be described as a Model Name and Style Number (for example, Covington Style 1). Style 1 has a wavey-shaped pickguard with control knobs mounted below the guard and the 2-piece guitar body has a particle board side gasket. Style 1.5 has the same guard and knobs, but no side body gasket. Style 2 has an oblong pickguard with top mounted control knobs and a pancake style seam between the top and lower part of the body. Style 3 has a seamless

2-piece body and a Speedline neck.

Baritone Signature

1971. Baritone version of Signature Guitar, sharply pointed double-cut, with or without f-holes, single- or double-dot inlays.

1971		$600	$700

Baritone Stage II

1971-ca. 1975. Double-cut, 2 pickups.

1971-1975		$600	$700

Calibra I

1969-1975. Double-cut, 2 pickups, f-hole.

1969-1975		$500	$600

Covington

1967-1969. Offset double-cut, 2 pickups, f-hole.

1967-1969		$800	$900

Golden Comet

1969-1971. Double-cut, 2 pickups, f-hole.

1969-1971		$600	$700

Golden Melody

1969-1971, 2004-present. Offset double-cut, 2 pickups, f-hole, M-shaped metal design behind tailpiece.

1969-1971		$800	$900

Huntington

1969-1975. Double-cut, 2 pickups.

1969-1975		$800	$900

Orbiter

1967-1969. Odd triple cutaway body, thumbwheel controls on bottom edge of 'guard.

1967-1969		$800	$900

Plainsman

1967-1969. Offset double-cut, 2 pickups, f-hole, thumbwheel controls on bottom edge of 'guard.

1967-1969		$900	$1,000

Signature

1967-1969. Double-cut, 2 pickups.

1967-1969		$700	$850

Spacetone

1969-1971, 2004-present. Double-cut semi-hollow body, 2 pickups.

1969-1971		$700	$850

Stage II

1969-1975. Offset double-cut, 2 pickups.

1969-1975		$700	$850

Swinger

1971-1975. Offset double-cut, 2 pickups.

1971-1975		$800	$900

Wanderer

1969. Double-cut, 2 pickups.

1969		$600	$700

Mike Lull Custom Guitars

1995-present. Professional and premium grade, production/custom, guitars built by luthier Mike Lull in Bellevue, Washington. He also builds basses.

Milburn Guitars

1990-present. Luthiers Orville and Robert Milburn build their premium grade, custom, classical guitars in Sweet Home, Oregon.

1972 Microfrets Calibra I

Mike Lull SX

Monteleone Eclipse

Moonstone Eagle

MODEL YEAR	FEATURES	EXC. COND. LOW	HIGH

Miller
1960s. One of the brand names of guitars built for others by Egmond in Holland.

Minarik
Luthier M.E. Minarik builds his professional and premium grade, custom/production, solid and chambered body guitars in Van Nuys, California.

Minerva
1930s. Resonator and archtop guitars sold through catalog stores, likely made by one of the big Chicago builders of the era.

Mirabella
1997-present. Professional and premium grade, custom archtops, flat-tops, hollowbody, and solidbody guitars built by luthier Cristian Mirabella in Babylon, New York. He also builds mandolins and ukes.

Mitre
1983-1985. Bolt neck, solidbody guitars made in Aldenville (or East Longmeadow), Massachusetts, featuring pointy body shapes, 2 humbuckers, active or passive electronics and with or without trems. They also offered a bass.

MJ Guitar Engineering
1993-present. Professional and premium grade, production/custom, hollow-body, chambered and solidbody guitars built by luthier Mark Johnson in Rohnert Park, California. He also builds basses.

Mobius Megatar
2000-present. Professional grade, production, hybrid guitars designed for two-handed tapping, built in Mount Shasta, California. Founded by Reg Thompson, Henri Dupont, and Traktor Topaz in '97, they released their first guitars in '00.
True Tapper
2000-present. Similar to Chapman Stick, 2 pickups.

2000-2005		$600	$800

Modulus
1978-present. Founded by Geoff Gould in the San Francisco area, currently built in Novato, California. Modulus currently offers professional grade, production/custom, solidbody electric guitars. They also build electric basses.
Genesis 2/2T
1996-present. Double-cut, long extended bass horn alder body, bolt-on carbon fiber/red cedar neck, hum-single-single pickups, locking vibrato (2T model).

1996-2005		$1,100	$1,300

Moll Custom Instruments
1996-present. Luthier Bill Moll builds his professional and premium grade, archtops in Springfield, Missouri. He has also built violins, violas and cellos.

MODEL YEAR	FEATURES	EXC. COND. LOW	HIGH

Monrad, Eric
1993-present. Premium, custom, flamenco and classical guitars built by luthier Eric Monrad in Healdsburg, California.

Montalvo
See listing under Casa Montalvo.

Montaya
Late-1980s. Montaya Hyosung 'America' Inc., Korean acoustic and electric import copies.

Monteleone
1976-present. Presentation grade, production/custom, archtop guitars built by Luthier John Monteleone in Islip, New York.
Eclipse
17" electric archtop, natural orange.

1991-1992		$14,000	$18,000

OM-42
1970s. Styled like an old Martin OM, spruce top, Brazilian rosewood back.

1975		$10,000	$14,000

Radio City
18" acoustic archtop cutaway, art deco fretboard inlays, golden blond.

1996		$19,000	$22,000

Monty
1980-present. Luthier Brian Monty builds his professional and premium grade, production, archtop, semi-hollow, solidbody, and flatop guitars originally in Lennoxville, Quebec, and currently in Anne de Prescott, Ontario.

Moon (Japan)
1979-present. Professional and premium grade, production/custom, guitars made in Japan. They also build basses.

Moon (Scotland)
1979-present. Intermediate, professional and premium grade, production/custom, acoustic and electric guitars built by luthier Jimmy Moon in Glasgow, Scotland. They also build mandolin family instruments.

Moonstone
1972-present. Professional, premium, and presentation grade production/custom flat-top, solid and semi-hollow electric guitars, built by luthier Steve Helgeson in Eureka, California. He also builds basses. Higher unit sales in the early-'80s. Some models have an optional graphite composite neck built by Modulus.
Eclipse Standard
1979-1983. Figured wood body, offset double-cut, neck-thru, dot markers, standard maple neck, natural finish.

1979-1983		$1,800	$2,300

MODEL YEAR	FEATURES	EXC. COND. LOW	HIGH

Explorer
1980-1983. Figured wood solidbody, neck-thru, standard maple neck, natural finish.

1980-1983		$1,800	$2,300

Flaming V
1980-1984. Figured wood body, V-shaped, neck-thru, standard maple neck, natural finish.

1980-1984		$1,800	$2,300

M-80
1980-1984. Figured wood double-cut semi-hollow body, standard maple or optional graphite neck, natural finish.

1980s	Optional graphite neck	$2,500	$3,500
1980s	Standard maple neck	$2,000	$2,500

Vulcan Deluxe
1979-1983. Figured maple carved-top body, offset double-cut, diamond markers, standard maple neck, natural finish.

1979-1983		$2,200	$2,500

Vulcan Standard
1979-1983. Mahogany carved-top body, offset double-cutaway, dot markers, standard maple neck, natural finish.

1979-1983		$2,100	$2,400

Morales
Ca.1967-1968. Guitars and basses made in Japan by Zen-On, not heavily imported into the U.S., if at all.

Solidbody Electric Guitars
1967-1968. Various models.

1967-1968		$150	$250

More Harmony
1930s. Private branded by Dobro for Dailey's More Harmony Music Studio. Private branding for catalog companies, teaching studios, publishers, and music stores was common for the Chicago makers. More Harmony silk-screen logo on the headstock.

More Harmony Dobro
1930s. 14" wood body with upper bout f-holes and metal resonator.

1930s	Sunburst	$800	$1,800

Morgaine Guitars
1994-present. Luthier Jorg Tandler builds his professional and premium grade, production/custom electrics in Germany.

Morgan Monroe
1999-present. Intermediate grade, production, acoustic, acoustic/electric and resonator guitars made in Korea and distributed by SHS International of Indianapolis, Indiana. They also offer mandolins, basses, banjos, and fiddles.

Morris
1967-present. Intermediate, professional and premium grade, production, acoustic guitars imported by Moridaira of Japan. Morris guitars were first imported into the U.S. from the early '70s to around '90. They are again being imported into the U.S. starting in 2001.

000 Copy
1970s. Brazilian rosewood laminate body, import.

1970s		$350	$450

D-45 Copy
1970s. Brazilian laminate body.

1970s		$450	$600

Mortoro Guitars
1992-present. Luthier Gary Mortoro builds his premium grade, custom, archtop guitars in Miami, Florida.

Mosrite
The history of Mosrite has more ups and downs than just about any other guitar company. Founder Semie Moseley had several innovative designs and had his first success in 1954, at age 19, building doubleneck guitars for super picker Joe Maphis and protégé Larry Collins. Next came the Ventures, who launched the brand nationally by playing Mosrites and featuring them on album covers. At its '60s peak, the company was turning out around 1,000 guitars a month. The company ceased production in '69, and Moseley went back to playing gospel concerts and built a few custom instruments during the '70s.

In the early-'80s, Mosrite again set up shop in Jonas Ridge, North Carolina, but the plant burned down in November '83, taking about 300 guitars with it. In early-'92, Mosrite relocated to Booneville, Arkansas, producing a new line of Mosrites, of which 96% were exported to Japan, where the Ventures and Mosrite have always been popular.

Semie Moseley died, at age 57, on August 7, '92 and the business carried on until finally closing its doors in '93. The Mosrite line has again been revived, offering intermediate and premium grade, production, reissues.

Throughout much of the history of Mosrite, production numbers were small and model features often changed. As a result, exact production dates are difficult to determine.

Brass Rail
1970s. Double-cut solidbody, has a brass plate running the length of the 'board.

1970s		$850	$950

Celebrity 1
Late-1960s-1970s. Thick hollowbody, 2 pickups.

1970s	Sunburst	$1,100	$1,200

Celebrity 2 Standard
Late-1960s-1970s. Thin hollowbody, 2 pickups, in the '70s, it came in a Standard and a Deluxe version.

1970s		$900	$1,100

Moonstone M-80

'60s Mosrite Celebrity

Mosrite Ventures

1976 Mossman Southwind

MODEL YEAR	FEATURES	EXC. COND. LOW	HIGH
Celebrity 3			
Late-1960s. Thin hollowbody, double-cut, 2 pickups, f-holes.			
1960s		$900	$1,100
Combo Mark 1			
1966-1968. Bound body, 1 f-hole.			
1966-1968		$1,700	$1,800
Custom-Built			
1950s. Pre-production custom instruments hand-built by Semie Moseley, guidance pricing only, each instrument will vary.			
1950s		$5,000	$15,000
D-100 Californian			
1960s. Double-cut, resonator guitar with 2 pickups.			
1967		$900	$1,200
D-40 Resonator Guitar			
1960s.			
1960s		$800	$900
Joe Maphis Mark 1			
1960s. Semi-hollow double-cut, 2 single-coils, spruce top, walnut back, rosewood 'board.			
1960s	Natural	$1,800	$2,500
Joe Maphis Mark XVIII			
1960s. 6/12 doubleneck, double-cut, 2 pickups on each neck, Moseley tremolo on 6-string.			
1960s		$3,800	$4,200
Mosrite 1988			
1988-early-1990s. Has traditional Mosrite body styling, Mosrite pickups and bridge.			
1988		$650	$900
Octave Guitar			
1965. 14" scale, 1 pickup, Ventures Mosrite body style, single neck pickup, very few made.			
1965		$5,000	$7,000
Ventures (Jonas Ridge/Boonville)			
1982-1993. Made in Jonas Ridge, NC or Booneville, AR, classic Ventures styling.			
1982-1993		$1,800	$2,400
Ventures 12-String			
1966-1968. Double-cut solidbody, 12 strings.			
1966-1968		$3,000	$3,500
Ventures Mark V			
1963-1968. Double-cut solidbody.			
1963-1968		$2,000	$2,500
Ventures Model			
1963-1968. Double-cut solidbody, triple-bound body '63, no binding after, Vibramute for '63-'64, Moseley tailpiece '65-'68.			
1963	Blue or red, bound	$6,000	$7,300
1963	Sunburst, bound	$5,500	$6,800
1964	Blue or red, Vibramute	$5,200	$6,800
1964	Sunburst, Vibramute	$5,200	$6,300
1965	Blue, red, sunburst, Moseley tailpiece	$4,000	$4,700
1965	Blue, red, sunburst, Vibramute	$5,000	$6,200
1966	Moseley tailpiece	$3,700	$4,000
1967	Moseley tailpiece	$3,400	$3,700
1968	Moseley tailpiece	$2,800	$3,400

Mossman

1965-present. Professional and premium grade, production/custom, flat-top guitars built in Sulphur Springs, Texas. They have also built acoustic basses. Founded by Stuart L. Mossman in Winfield, Kansas. In '75, fire destroyed one company building, including the complete supply of Brazilian rosewood. They entered into an agreement with C.G. Conn Co. to distribute guitars by '77. 1200 Mossman guitars in a Conn warehouse in Nevada were ruined by being heated during the day and frozen during the night. A disagreement about who was responsible resulted in cash flow problems for Mossman. Production fell to a few guitars per month until the company was sold in '86 to Scott Baxendale. Baxendale sold the company to John Kinsey and Bob Casey in Sulphur Springs in '89.

MODEL YEAR	FEATURES	EXC. COND. LOW	HIGH
Flint Hills			
1970-mid-1980s. Flat-top acoustic, rosewood back and sides.			
1970-1979		$1,700	$1,900
Golden Era			
D-style, vine inlay and other high-end appointments, Indian rosewood sides and back.			
1977		$2,900	$3,100
Great Plains			
1970-mid-1980s. Flat-top, Indian rosewood, herringbone trim.			
1970-1979		$1,700	$1,900
Southwind			
1976-ca. 1986, mid-1990s-2002. Flat-top, abalone trim top.			
1976-1979		$1,900	$2,100
Tennessee			
1975-1979. D-style, spruce top, mahogany back and sides, rope marquetry purfling, rope binding.			
1975-1979		$1,100	$1,300
Tennessee 12-String			
1975-1979.			
1975-1979		$1,100	$1,300
Winter Wheat			
1976-1979, mid-1990s-present. Flat-top, abalone trim, natural finish.			
1976-1979		$1,900	$2,100
Winter Wheat 12-String			
1976-1979. 12-string version of Winter Wheat, natural.			
1976-1979		$1,900	$2,100

Mozart

1930s. Private brand made by Kay.

Hawaiian (square neck)

1930s. Spruce top, solid mahogany sides and back, pealoid overlay on peghead with large Mozart inscribed logo, small jumbo 15 1/2" body.

1935-1939		$800	$850

The Vintage Guitar Price Guide shows low to high values for items in all-original excellent condition, and, where applicable, with original case or cover.

GUITARS

Mozzani

Built in shops of Luigi Mozzani (b. March 9, 1869, Faenza, Italy; d. 1943) who opened lutherie schools in Bologna, Cento and Rovereto in 1890s. By 1926 No. 1 and 2 Original Mozzani Model Mandolin (flat back), No. 3 Mandola (flat back), No. 4 6-String Guitar, No. 5 7-, 8-, and 9-String Guitars, No. 6 Lyre-Guitar.

Murph

1965-1966. Mid-level electric semi-hollow and solidbody guitars built by Pat Murphy in San Fernado, California. Murph logo on headstock.

Electric Solidbody

Model Year	Features	Exc. Cond. Low	High
1965-1966		$650	$850

Electric XII

1965-1966		$700	$900

Music Man

1972-present. Professional grade, production, solidbody guitars built in San Luis Obispo, California. They also build basses. Founded by ex-Fender executives Forrest White and Tom Walker in Orange County, California. Music Man originally produced guitar and bass amps based on early Fender ideas using many former Fender employees. They contracted with Leo Fender's CLF Research to design and produce a line of solidbody guitars and basses. Leo Fender began G & L Guitars with George Fullerton in '82. In '84, Music Man was purchased by Ernie Ball and production was moved to San Luis Obispo.

Axis

1996-present. Offset double-cut solidbody, figured maple top, basswood body, 2 humbucker pickups, Floyd Rose.

1996-2005		$1,200	$1,300

Edward Van Halen

1990-1995. Basswood solidbody, figured maple top, bolt-on maple neck, maple 'board, binding, 2 humbuckers, named changed to Axis.

1990-1995		$2,000	$2,500

Sabre I

1978-1982. Offset double-cut solidbody, maple neck, 2 pickups, Sabre I comes with a flat 'board with jumbo frets.

1978-1982		$850	$1,000

Sabre II

1978-1982. Same as Sabre I, but with an oval 7 1/2" radius 'board.

1978-1982		$850	$1,000

Silhouette

1986-present. Offset double-cut, contoured beveled solidbody, various pickup configurations.

1987-2005		$1,000	$1,100

Steve Morse Model

1987-present. Solidbody, 4 pickups, humbuckers in the neck and bridge positions, 2 single-coils in the middle, special pickup switching, 6-bolt neck mounting, maple neck.

1987-2005		$1,050	$1,150

Stingray I

1976-1982. Offset double-cut solidbody, flat 'board radius.

1976-1979		$900	$1,100
1980-1982		$900	$1,100

Stingray II

1976-1982. Offset double-cut solidbody, rounder 'board radius.

1976-1979		$900	$1,100
1980-1982		$900	$1,100

Musicvox

1996-present. Intermediate grade, production, Korean-made retro-vibe guitars and basses from Matt Eichen of Cherry Hill, New Jersey.

Electric Guitars

1996-2005	Spaceranger, 2 pickups	$225	$275

Nady

1976-present. Wireless sound company Nady Systems offered guitars and basses with built-in wireless systems for 1985-'87. Made by Fernandes in Japan until '86, then by Cort in Korea.

Lightning/Lightning I

1985-1987. Double-cut, neck-thru, solidbody, 24 frets, built-in wireless, labeled as just Lightning until cheaper second version came out in '86.

1985	Fernandes	$650	$750
1986-1987	Cort	$600	$700

Lightning/Lightning II

1986-1987. Cheaper, bolt-neck version of the Lightning I.

1986-1987	Cort	$350	$550

Napolitano Guitars

1993-present. Luthier Arthur Napolitano builds his professional and premium grade, custom, archtop guitars in Allentown, New Jersey.

Nashguitars

2001-present. Luthier Bill Nash builds his professional grade, production/custom, solidbody electric guitars in Olympia, Washington. He also builds basses.

Timewarp Models

2001-present. Various aged solidbody models.

2001-2005	E Series	$300	$500
2001-2005	S Series	$500	$700
2001-2005	T Series	$400	$600

Nashville Guitar Company

1985-present. Professional and premium grade, custom, flat-top guitars built by luthier Marty Lanham in Nashville, Tennessee. He has also built banjos.

Custom Slide

Weissenborn Hawaiian copy with hollow neck, natural koa.

1997		$3,300	$3,500

Music Man Silhouette

1985 Nady Lightning

National Bel-Aire

1949 National California

National

Ca. 1927-present. Founded in Los Angeles, California as the National String Instrument Corporation by John Dopyera, George Beauchamp, Ted Kleinmeyer and Paul Barth. In '29 Dopyera left to start the Dobro Manufacturing Company with Rudy and Ed Dopyera and Vic Smith. The Dobro company competed with National until the companies reunited. Beauchamp and Barth then left National to found Ro-Pat-In with Adolph Rickenbacker and C.L. Farr (later becoming Electro String Instrument Corporation, then Rickenbacher). In '32 Dopyera returns to National and National and Dobro start their merger in late-'33, finalizing it by mid-'34. Throughout the '30s, National and Dobro maintained separate production, sales and distribution. National Dobro moved to Chicago, Illinois in '36. In Chicago, archtop and flat top bodies are built primarily by Regal and Kay; after '37 all National resonator guitar bodies made by Kay. L.A. production is maintained until around '37, although some assembly of Dobros continued in L.A. (primarily for export) until '39 when the L.A. offices are finally closed. By ca. '39 the Dobro brand disappears.

In '42, the company's resonator production ceased and Victor Smith, Al Frost and Louis Dopyera buy the company and change name to Valco Manufacturing Company. Post-war production resumes in '46. Valco is purchased by treasurer Robert Engelhardt in '64. In '67, Valco bought Kay, but in '68 the new Valco/Kay company went out of business. In the Summer of '69 the assets, including brandnames, were auctioned off and the National and Supro names were purchased by Chicago-area distributor/importer Strum 'N Drum (Noble, Norma brands). The National brand is used on copies in early- to mid-'70s, and the brand went into hiatus by the '80s.

In '88 National Resophonic Guitars is founded in San Luis Obispo, California, by Don Young, with production of National-style resonator guitars beginning in '89 (see following). In the '90s, the National brand also resurfaces on inexpensive Asian imports.

National Resonator guitars are categorized by materials and decoration (from plain to fancy): Duolian, Triolian, Style 0, Style 1, Style 2, Style 3, Style 4, Don #1, Style 97, Don #2, Don #3, Style 35.

National guitars all have serial numbers which provide clues to date of production. This is a complex issue. This list combines information included in George Gruhn and Walter Carter's Gruhn's Guide to Vintage Guitars, which was originally provided by Bob Brozman and Mike Newton, with new information provided by Mike Newton.

Pre Chicago numbers

A101-A450	1935-1936

Chicago numbers

A prefix (some may not have the prefix)	1936-mid-1997
B prefix	Mid-1937-1938

MODEL YEAR	FEATURES	EXC. COND. LOW	HIGH
C prefix		Late-1938-1940	
G prefix up to 200		Ea. 1941-ea. 1942	
G suffix under 2000		Ea. 1941-ea. 1942	
G suffix 2000-3000s (probably old parts)		1943-1945	
G suffix 4000s (old parts)		Late 1945-mid-1947	
V100-V7500		1947	
V7500-V15000		1948	
V15000-V25000		1949	
V25000-V35000		1950	
V35000-V38000		1951	
X100-X7000		1951	
X7000-X17000		1952	
X17000-X30000		1953	
X30000-X43000		1954	
X43000-X57000		1955	
X57000-X71000		1956	
X71000-X85000		1957	
X85000-X99000		1958	
T100-T5000		1958	
T5000-T25000		1959	
T25000-T50000		1960	
T50000-T75000		1961	
T75000-T90000		1962	
G100-G5000		1962	
T90000-T99000		1963	
G5000-G15000		1963	
G15000-G40000		1964	
1 prefix		1965-ea. 1968	
2 prefix		Mid-1968	

Aragon De Luxe

1939-1942. Archtop with resonator (the only archtop resonator offered), spruce top and maple back and sides, light brown.

1939-1942		$8,000	$14,000

Bel-Aire

1953-1961. Single pointed cut archtop, 2 pickups until '57, 3 after, master tone knob and jack, bound body, sunburst.

1953-1961		$900	$1,500

Bluegrass 35

1963-1965. Acoustic, non-cut single-cone resonator, Res-O-Glas body in Arctic White.

1963-1965		$900	$2,000

Bobbie Thomas

Ca.1967-1968. Double-cut thinline hollowbody, bat-shaped F-holes, 2 pickups, Bobbie Thomas on 'guard, vibrato.

1967-1968		$400	$600

Bolero

1956-1957. Les Paul-shape, control knobs mounted on 'guard, single pickup, trapeze tailpiece, sunburst.

1956-1957		$700	$800

California

1949-1955. Electric hollowbody archtop, multi-bound, F-holes, trapeze tailpiece, 1 pickup, natural.

1949-1955		$750	$850

MODEL YEAR	FEATURES	EXC. COND. LOW	HIGH

Club Combo
1952-1955, 1959-1961. Electric hollowbody archtop, 2 pickups, rounded cutaway.

1952-1961		$700	$975

Don Style 1
1934-1936. Plain body with engraved borders, pearl dot inlay, 14 frets, single-cone, silver (nickel-plated).

1934-1936		$8,000	$10,000

Don Style 2
1934-1936. Geometric Art Deco body engraving, 14 frets, single-cone, fancy square pearl inlays and pearloid headstock overlay, silver (nickel-plated).

1934-1936		$10,000	$20,000

Don Style 3
1934-1936. Same as Style 2 but more elaborate floral engravings, fancy pearl diamond inlays, 14 frets, single-cone, silver (nickel-plated), only a very few made.

1934-1936		$11,000	$35,000

Duolian
1930-1939. Acoustic steel body, frosted paint finish until '36, mahogany-grain paint finish '37-'39, round neck, square neck available in '33, 12-fret neck until '34 then 14-fret.

1930-1934	Round neck, 12 frets	$3,000	$4,500
1935-1939	Round neck, 14 frets	$2,700	$4,000

El Trovador
1933 only. Wood body, 12 frets.

1933		$2,500	$3,000

Electric Spanish
1935-1938. 15 1/2" archtop with Pat. Appl. For bridge pickup, National crest logo, fancy N-logo 'guard, black and white art deco, sunburst, becomes New Yorker Spanish '39-'58.

1935-1938		$1,000	$1,200

Estralita
1934-1942. Acoustic with single-cone resonator, f-holes, multi-bound, 14-fret, mahogany top and back, shaded brown.

1934-1942		$700	$850

Glenwood
1954-1958. Les Paul-shaped solidbody, wood body, not fiberglass, single-cut, multi-bound, 2 pickups, natural, renamed Glenwood Deluxe with Bigsby in '59.

1954-1958		$1,250	$1,500

Glenwood 95
1962-1964. Glenwood 98 without third bridge-mount pickup.

1962-1964	Vermillion Red/Flame Red	$2,500	$2,800

Glenwood 98
1964-1965. USA map-shaped solidbody of molded Res-O-Glas, 2 regular and 1 bridge pickups, vibrato, pearl white finish.

1964-1965	Pearl White	$3,000	$3,200

Glenwood 99
1962-1965. USA map-shaped solidbody of molded Res-O-Glas, 2 regular and 1 bridge pickups, butterfly inlay.

1962-1963	Snow White	$3,500	$3,700
1964-1965	Sea Foam Green	$4,000	$4,300

Glenwood Deluxe
1959-1961. Renamed from Glenwood, Les Paul-shaped solidbody, wood body, not fiberglass, multi-bound, 2 pickups, factory Bigsby, vibrato, natural.

1959-1961		$1,500	$1,800

Model 1155
1948-1961. Flat top acoustic with Gibson body, mahogany back and sides, bolt-on neck.

1948-1961		$1,000	$2,100

N-600 Series
1968. Offset double-cut solidbody, 1, 2, and 3 pickup models, with and without vibrato.

1968		$450	$650

N-800 Series
1968. Double-cut semi-hollow body, various models with or without Bigsby.

1968	No Bigsby	$650	$750
1968	With Bigsby	$750	$850

Newport 82
1963-1965. Renamed from Val-Pro 82, USA map-shaped Res-O-Glas, 1 pickup, red finish.

1963-1965	Pepper Red	$1,500	$1,600

Newport 84
1963-1965. Renamed from Val-Pro 84, USA map-shaped Res-O-Glas, 1 regular and 1 bridge pickup, Sea Foam Green finish.

1963-1965	Sea Foam Green	$1,700	$1,800

Newport 88
1963-1965. Renamed from Val-Pro 88, USA map-shaped Res-O-Glas, 2 regular and 1 bridge pickup, black finish.

1963-1965	Raven Black	$1,800	$1,900

Pro Dual Pickup
1960s. Non-catalog Jetson-style res-o-glas type body, National logo, 2 pickups, red.

1960s		$1,100	$1,200

Reso-phonic
1956-1964. Pearloid-covered, single-cut semi-solid-body acoustic, single resonator, maroon or white, also a non-cut, square neck version was offered, which is included in these values.

1956-1964	Round neck	$1,750	$2,000
1956-1964	Square neck	$1,000	$1,100

Rosita
1933-1939. Plywood body by Harmony, plain metal resonator, plain appointments.

1933-1939		$1,000	$1,400

Silvo (Electric Hawaiian)
1937-1941. Nickel-plated metal body flat-top, small upper bout, f-holes, square neck, multiple straight line body art over dark background, Roman numeral parallelogram markers, National badge headstock logo, Silvo name on coverplate.

1937-1941	Silver	$3,500	$4,100

1955 National Debonaire

1933 National El Trovador

1930s National Style N

National Triolian

MODEL YEAR	FEATURES	EXC. COND. LOW	HIGH

Studio 66
1961-1964. Electric solidbody of Res-O-Glas, single-cut, 1 pickup, renamed Varsity 66 in '65.

| 1961-1962 | Sand Buff, bridge pickup | $1,000 | $1,400 |
| 1963-1964 | Jet Black, neck pickup | $1,000 | $1,400 |

Style O
1930-1942. Acoustic single-cone brass body (early models had a steel body), Hawaiian scene etching, 12-fret neck '30-'34, 14-fret neck '35 on, round (all years) or square ('33 on) neck.

1930-1934	Round neck, 12-fret	$3,500	$4,500
1933-1942	Square neck	$3,000	$4,000
1935-1942	Round neck, 14-fret	$3,500	$4,500

Style 1 Tricone
1927-1943. German silver body tricone resonator, ebony 'board, mahogany square (Hawaiian) or round (Spanish) neck, plain body, 12-fret neck until '34, 14-fret after.

| 1927-1932 | Round neck | $5,000 | $7,000 |
| 1928-1932 | Square neck | $3,000 | $4,000 |

Style 1 Tricone Plectrum
1928-1935. 26" scale versus the 23" scale of the tenor.

| 1928-1935 | | $2,500 | $3,500 |

Style 1 Tricone Tenor
1928-1935. Tenor, 4 strings, 23" scale, square neck is Hawaiian, round neck is Spanish.

| 1928-1935 | | $2,500 | $3,500 |

Style 2 Tricone
1927-1942. German silver body tricone resonator, wild rose engraving, square (Hawaiian) or round (Spanish) neck, 12-fret neck until '34, 14-fret after.

| 1930s | Round neck | $7,000 | $9,000 |
| 1930s | Square neck | $4,000 | $6,000 |

Style 2 Tricone Plectrum
1928-1935. 26" scale versus the 23" scale of the tenor.

| 1928-1935 | | $2,700 | $4,000 |

Style 2 Tricone Tenor
1928-1935. Tenor.

| 1928-1935 | | $2,700 | $4,000 |

Style 3 Tricone
1928-1941. German silver body tricone resonator, lily-of-the-valley engraving, square (Hawaiian) or round (Spanish) neck, 12-fret neck until '34, 14-fret after, reintroduced with a nickel-plated brass body in '94.

1930s	Round neck	$15,000	$17,000
1930s	Square neck	$6,000	$7,500
1940-1941	Square neck	$5,000	$6,500

Style 3 Tricone Plectrum
1928-1935. 26" scale versus the 23" scale of the tenor.

| 1928-1935 | | $4,500 | $5,500 |

Style 3 Tricone Tenor
1928-1939.

| 1928-1939 | | $4,500 | $5,500 |

Style 4 Tricone
1928-1940. German silver body tricone resonator, chrysanthemum etching, 12-fret neck until '34, 14-fret after, reissued in '95 with same specs.

| 1930s | Round neck | $25,000 | $27,000 |
| 1930s | Square neck | $7,500 | $8,500 |

Style 35
1936-1942. Brass body tricone resonator, sandblasted minstrel and trees scene, 12 frets, square (Hawaiian) or round (Spanish) neck.

| 1936-1942 | Round neck | $25,000 | $35,000 |
| 1936-1942 | Square neck | $15,000 | $17,000 |

Style 97
1936-1940. Nickel-plated brass body tricone resonator, sandblasted scene of female surfrider and palm trees, 12 frets, slotted peghead.

| 1930s | Round neck | $15,000 | $25,000 |
| 1930s | Square neck | $7,000 | $10,000 |

Style N
1930-1931. Nickel-plated brass body single-cone resonator, plain finish, 12 frets.

| 1930-1931 | | $7,000 | $8,000 |

Triolian
1928-1941. Single-cone resonator, wood body replaced by metal body in '29, 12-fret neck and slotted headstock '28-'34, changed to 14-fret neck in '35 and solid headstock in '36, round or square ('33 on) neck available.

| 1928-1936 | Various colors | $3,000 | $3,800 |
| 1936-1937 | Fake rosewood grain finish | $2,200 | $3,000 |

Triolian Tenor
1928-1936. Tenor, metal body.

| 1928-1936 | | $1,300 | $2,000 |

Trojan
1934-1942. Single-cone resonator wood body, F-holes, bound top, 14-fret round neck.

| 1934-1942 | | $800 | $1,000 |

Val-Pro 82
1962-1963. USA map-shaped Res-O-Glas, 1 pickup, Vermillion Red finish, renamed Newport 82 in '63.

| 1962-1963 | | $1,250 | $1,600 |

Val-Pro 84
1962-1963. USA map-shaped Res-O-Glas, 1 regular and 1 bridge pickup, snow white finish, renamed Newport 84 in '63.

| 1962-1963 | | $1,500 | $1,900 |

Val-Pro 88
1962-1963. USA map-shaped Res-O-Glas, 2 regular and 1 bridge pickup, black finish, renamed Newport 88 in '63.

| 1962-1963 | | $1,900 | $2,100 |

Varsity 66
1964-1965. Renamed from Studio 66 in '64, molded Res-O-Glas, 1 pickup, 2 knobs, beige finish.

| 1964-1965 | | $1,000 | $1,400 |

Westwood 72
1962-1964. USA map-shaped solid hardwood body (not fiberglas), 1 pickup, Cherry Red.

| 1962-1964 | | $1,250 | $1,500 |

MODEL YEAR	FEATURES	EXC. COND. LOW	HIGH

Westwood 75

1962-1964. USA map-shaped solid hardwood body (not fiberglas), 1 regular and 1 bridge pickup, cherry-to-black sunburst finish.

| 1962-1964 | | $1,500 | $1,800 |

Westwood 77

1962-1965. USA map-shaped solid hardwood body (not fiberglas), 2 regular and 1 bridge pickup.

| 1962-1963 | Blond-Ivory | $1,500 | $1,800 |

National Reso-Phonic

1988-present. Professional and premium grade, production/custom, single cone, acoustic-electric, and tricone guitars (all with resonators), built in San Luis Obispo, California. They also build basses and ukes. McGregor Gaines and Don Young formed the National Reso-Phonic Guitar Company with the objective of building instruments based upon the original National designs.

Reso-Lectric

1990-present. Thin single-cut body with single-cone resonator, maple veneer top, lipstick neck pickup until '96 when changed to P-90 and added saddle transducer.

| 1993-1996 | Lipstick pickup | $800 | $1,000 |
| 1997-2005 | P-90 | $1,200 | $1,300 |

Neubauer

1966-1990s. Luthier Helmut Neubauer built his acoustic and electric archtop guitars in Bubenreuth, Germany.

New Orleans Guitar Company

1992-present. Luthier Vincent Guidroz builds his premium grade, production/custom, solid and semi-hollow body guitars in New Orleans, Louisiana.

Nickerson Guitars

1983-present. Luthier Brad Nickerson builds his professional and premium grade, production/custom, archtop and flat-top guitars in Northampton, Massachusetts.

Nielsen

2004-present. Premium grade, custom/production, archtop guitars built by luthier Dale Nielsen in Duluth, Minnesota.

Nioma

1930s. Brand most likely used by a music studio (or distributor) on instruments made by others, including Regal-built resonator instruments.

Noble

Ca. 1950-ca. 1969. Instruments made by others and distributed by Don Noble and Company of Chicago. Plastic-covered guitars made by EKO debut in '62. Aluminum-necked Wandré guitars added to the line in early-'63. By ca. '65-'66 the brand is owned by Chicago-area importer and distributor

Strum 'N Drum and used mainly on Japanese-made solidbodies. Strum 'N Drum bought the National brand name in '69 and imported Japanese copies of American designs under the National brand and Japanese original designs under Norma through the early '70s. The Noble brand disappears at least by the advent of the Japanese National brand, if not before.

Norma

Ca.1965-1970. Imported from Japan by Strum 'N Drum, Inc. of Chicago (see Noble brand info). Early examples were built by Tombo, most notably sparkle plastic covered guitars and basses.

Electric Solidbody

1965-1970s. Type of finish has affect on value. Various models include; EG-350 (student double-cut, 1 pickup), EG-403 (unique pointy cutaway, 2 pickups), EG-400 (double-cut, 2 pickups), EG-450 (double-cut, 2 split-coil pickups), EG-421 (double-cut, 4 pickups), EG-412-12 (double-cut, 12-string).

| 1965-1968 | Blue, red, gold sparkle | $350 | $550 |
| 1965-1970 | Non-sparkle | $200 | $350 |

Norman

1972-present. Intermediate grade, production, acoustic and acoustic/electric guitars built in LaPatrie, Quebec. Norman was the first guitar production venture luthier Robert Godin was involved with. He has since added the Seagull, Godin, and Patrick & Simon brands of instruments.

Northworthy Guitars

1987-present. Professional and premium grade, production/custom, flat-top and electric guitars built by luthier Alan Marshall in Ashbourne, Derbyshire, England. He also builds basses and mandolins.

Norwood

1960s. Budget guitars imported most likely from Japan.

Electric Solidbodies

1960s. Offset double-cut body, 3 soapbar-style pickups, Norwood label on headstock.

| 1960s | | $150 | $200 |

Novax Guitars

1989-present. Luthier Ralph Novak builds his fanned-fret professional and premium grade, production/custom, solidbody and acoustic guitars in San Leandro, California. He also builds basses.

Nyberg Instruments

1993-present. Professional grade, custom, flat-top and Maccaferri-style guitars built by luthier Lawrence Nyberg in Hornby Island, British Columbia. He also builds mandolas, bouzoukis and citterns.

National Val-Pro 82

Novax Charlie Hunter

GUITARS

O'Hagan Twenty-Two

1999 Olson SJ

MODEL		EXC. COND.	
YEAR	FEATURES	LOW	HIGH

Oahu

1926-1985, present. The Oahu Publishing Company and Honolulu Conservatory, based in Cleveland, Ohio was active in the sheet music and student instrument business in the '30s. An instrument, set of instructional sheet music, and lessons were offered as a complete package. Lessons were often given to large groups of students. Instruments, lessons, and sheet music could also be purchased by mail order. The Oahu Publishing Co. advertised itself as The World's Largest Guitar Dealer. Most '30s Oahu guitars were made by Kay with smaller numbers from the Oscar Schmidt Company.

Guitar Models from the Mid-'30s include: 71K (jumbo square neck), 72K (jumbo roundneck), 68B (jumbo, vine body decoration), 68K (deluxe jumbo square neck), 69K (deluxe jumbo roundneck), 65K and 66K (mahogany, square neck), 64K and 67K (mahogany, roundneck), 65M (standard-size, checker binding, mahogany), 53K (roundneck, mahogany), 51 (black, Hawaiian scene, pearlette 'board), 51K (black, pond scene decoration), 52K (black, Hawaiian scene decoration), 50 and 50K (student guitar, brown). The brand has been revived on a line of tube amps.

Round Neck 14" Flat-Top
1930s. Spruce top, figured maple back and sides, thin logo.

1932		$1,000	$1,500

Style 50K Student Guitar
Student-size guitar, brown finish.

1935		$200	$300

Style 65M
Standard-size mahogany body, checker binding, natural brown.

1933-1935		$350	$550

Style 68K De Luxe Jumbo
Hawaiian, 15.5" wide, square neck, Brazilian back and sides, spruce top, fancy pearl vine inlay, abalone trim on top and soundhole, rosewood pyramid bridge, fancy pearl headstock inlay, butterbean tuners, ladder-braced, natural. High-end model made for Oahu by Kay.

1935		$4,100	$4,500

Odessa

1981-1990s. Budget guitars imported by Davitt & Hanser (BC Rich). Mainly acoustics in the '90s, but some electrics early on.

O'Hagan

1979-1983. Designed by clarinetist and importer Jerol O'Hagan in St. Louis Park, Minnesota. Primarily neck-thru construction, most with German-carved bodies. In '81 became Jemar Corporation and in '83 it was closed by the I.R.S., a victim of recession.

SN=YYM(M)NN (e.g., 80905, September '80, 5th guitar); or MYMNNN (e.g., A34006, April 1983, 6th guitar). Approximately 3000 total instruments were made with the majority being

NightWatches (approx. 200 Twenty Twos, 100-150 Sharks, 100 Lasers; about 25 with birdseye maple

Electric
1979-1983. Models include; Laser (solidbody, double-cut, maple or walnut body, set-thru neck, 3 single-coil Schaller pickups), Shark (Explorer-looking solidbody) and Twenty Two (V, 2 humbuckers).

1979-1983		$350	$550

Ohio

1959-ca. 1965. Line of electric solidbodies and basses made by France's Jacobacci company, which also built under its own brand. Sparkle finish, bolt-on aluminum necks, strings-thru-body design.

Old Kraftsman

Ca. 1930s-ca. 1960s. Brandname used by the Spiegel catalog company for instruments made by other American manufacturers, including Regal, Kay and even Gibson. The instruments were of mixed quality, but some better grade instruments were comparable to those offered by Wards.

Archtops
1930s-1960s. Various models.

1930s	17", Stauffer-style		
	headstock	$500	$650
1950s		$350	$500
1960s		$350	$400

Thin Twin Jimmy Reed Model

1950s		$550	$700

OLP (Officially Licensed Product)

Intermediate grade, production, guitars based on higher dollar guitar models officially licensed from the original manufacturer. OLP logo on headstock. They also offer basses.

Musicman

2000s		$450	$650

Olson Guitars

1977-present. Luthier James A. Olson builds his presentation grade, custom, flat-tops in Circle Pines, Minnesota.

Omega

1996-present. Luthier Kevin Gallagher builds his premium grade, custom/production acoustic guitars in East Saylorsburg, Pennsylvania.

Oncor Sound

1980-ca. 1981. This Salt Lake City-based company made both a guitar and a bass synthesizer.

Opus

1972-Mid 1970s. Acoustic and classical guitars, imported from Japan by Ampeg/Selmer. In '75-'76, Harmony made a line of acoustics with the Opus model name.

MODEL YEAR	FEATURES	EXC. COND. LOW	HIGH

Orpheum

1897-1942, 1944-early 1970s, 2001-present. Intermediate grade, production, acoustic and resonator guitars. They also offer mandolins. Orpheum originally was a brand of Rettberg and Lange, who made instruments for other companies as well. William Rettberg and William Lange bought the facilities of New York banjo maker James H. Buckbee in 1897. Lange went out on his own in '21 to start the Paramount brand. He apparently continued using the Orpheum brand as well. He went out of business in '42. In '44 the brand was acquired by New York's Maurice Lipsky Music Co. who used it primarily on beginner to medium grade instruments, which were manufactured by Regal, Kay, and United Guitar (and maybe others). In the early '60s Lipsky applied the brand to Japanese and European (by Egmond) imports. Lipsky dropped the name in the early '70s. The brand was revived in '01 by Tacoma Guitars.

Cutaway Thin Electric (Kay Thin Twin K-161)

Introduced 1952-1953 by Kay and also sold as the Orpheum Cutaway Thin Electric, 2 tube/bar pickups, 4 knobs, block markers, curly maple top and back, mahogany sides, natural.

1953		$550	$700

Orpheum Special (Regal-made)

1930s. Slot head, Dobro-style wood body, metal resonator, sunburst.

1930s		$900	$1,200

Ultra Deluxe Professional Cutaway Model 899

1950s. 17" cutaway, 2 pickups, 2 knobs, maple back and sides, top material varies, dot markers, finishes as follows: E-C copper, E-G gold, E-G-B gold-black sunburst, E-B blond curly maple, E-S golden orange sunburst.

1950s	All finishes	$1,300	$1,900

Orville by Gibson

1984-1993. Orville by Gibson and Orville guitars were made by Japan's Fuji Gen Gakki for Gibson. Basically the same models except the Orville by Gibson guitars had real Gibson USA PAF '57 Classic pickups and a true nitrocellulose lacquer finish. The Orville models used Japanese electronics and a poly finish. Some Orvilles were made in Korea and are of a lower quality. These Korean guitars had the serial number printed on a sticker. Prices here are for the Orville by Gibson models.

Electric Guitars

1990s	ES-175	$800	$1,100
1990s	ES-335	$600	$900
1990s	Flying V	$500	$900
1990s	Les Paul Custom	$500	$1,000
1990s	Les Paul Jr. dlb.cut.	$400	$700
1990s	Les Paul Standard	$700	$900
1990s	Les Paul Studio J.P.	$700	$900

Oscar Schmidt

1879-1938, 1979-present. Budget and intermediate grade, production, acoustic, acoustic/electric, and electric guitars distributed by U.S. Music Corp. (Washburn, Randall, etc.). They also offer mandolins, banjos, ukes and the famous Oscar Schmidt autoharp.

The original Oscar Schmidt Company, Jersey City, New Jersey, offered banjo mandolins, tenor banjos, guitar banjos, ukuleles, mandolins and guitars under their own brand and others (including Sovereign and Stella). By the early 1900s, the company had factories in the U.S. and Europe producing instruments. Oscar Schmidt was also an early contributor to innovative mandolin designs and the company participated in the '00-'30 mandolin boom. The company hit hard times during the Depression and was sold to Harmony by the end of the '30s. In '79, Washburn acquired the brand and it is now part of U.S. Music.

Stella Model No. 501D

1921	Decalcomania top	$150	$300

Otwin

1950s-1960s. A brand used on electric guitars made by the Musima company of East Germany. Musima also produced guitars under their own brand.

Outbound Instruments

1990-2002. Intermediate grade, production, travel-size acoustics from the Boulder, Colorado-based company.

Ovation

1966-present. Intermediate and professional grade, production, acoustic and acoustic/electric guitars built in the U.S. They also build basses and mandolins.

Ovation's parent company, helicopter manufacturer Kaman Corporation, was founded in 1945 by jazz guitarist and aeronautical engineer Charles Huron Kaman in Bloomfield, Connecticut. In the '60s, after losing a government contract, Kaman began looking to diversify. When offers to buy Martin and Harmony were rejected, Kaman decided to use their helicopter expertise (working with synthetic materials, spruce, high tolerances) and designed, with the help of employee and violin restorer John Ringso, the first fiberglass-backed (Lyracord) acoustic guitars in '65. Production began in '66 and the music factory moved to New Hartford, Connecticut, in '67. Early input was provided by fingerstyle jazz guitarist Charlie Byrd, who gave Kaman the idea for the name Ovation. C. William Kaman II became president of the company in '85. Kaman Music purchased Hamer Guitars in '88, and Trace Elliot amplifiers (U.K.) in '90.

Adamas 1587

1979-1998. Carbon top, walnut, single-cut, bowl back, binding, mini-soundholes.

1979-1998	Black Sparkle	$1,600	$1,900

Oscar Schmidt OE

Otwin Deluxe

Ovation Adamas 1687

Ovation Breadwinner

MODEL YEAR	FEATURES	EXC. COND. LOW	HIGH

Adamas 1597
1998-1999. Carbon birch composite top, on-board electronics.

| 1998-1999 | Black | $900 | $1,000 |

Adamas 1687
1977-1998. Acoustic/electric, carbon top, non-cut, bowl back, mini-soundholes.

| 1977-1998 | Sunburst | $1,800 | $1,900 |

Adamas II 1881 NB-2
1993-1998. Acoustic/electric, single-cut, shallow bowl.

| 1993-1998 | Brown | $1,600 | $1,900 |

Anniversary Electric 1657
1978. Deep bowl, acoustic/electric, abalone inlays, gold-plated parts, carved bridge, for Ovation's 10th anniversary. They also offered an acoustic Anniversary.

| 1978 | | $600 | $800 |

Balladeer 1111
1968-1983, 1993-2000. Acoustic, non-cut with deep bowl, bound body, natural top, later called the Standard Balladeer.

| 1976-1983 | Natural | $350 | $450 |

Balladeer Artist 1121
1968-1990. Acoustic, non-cut with shallow bowl, bound body.

| 1968-1990 | Natural | $400 | $500 |

Balladeer Classic 1122
1970s. Classical shallow-bowl version of Concert Classic, nylon strings, slotted headstock.

| 1970s | | $325 | $425 |

Balladeer Custom 1112
1976-1990. Acoustic, deep bowl, diamond inlays.

| 1976-1990 | Natural | $425 | $550 |

Balladeer Custom 12-String Electric 1655/1755
1982-1994. 12-string version of Balladeer Custom Electric.

| 1982-1994 | Sunburst | $425 | $550 |

Balladeer Custom Electric 1612/1712
1976-1990. Acoustic/electric version of Balladeer Custom, deep bowl.

| 1976-1990 | Natural | $425 | $550 |

Balladeer Standard 1661/1761
1982-2000. Acoustic/electric, deep bowl, rounded cutaway.

| 1982-2000 | | $550 | $650 |

Breadwinner 1251
1971-1983. Axe-like shaped single-cut solidbody, 2 pickups, textured finish, black, blue, tan or white.

| 1971-1983 | | $750 | $850 |

Celebrity CC-57
1990-1996. Laminated spruce top, shallow bowl, mahogany neck.

| 1990-1996 | Black | $200 | $300 |

Celebrity CK-057
2002-2004. Acoustic/electric rounded cutaway, shallow back.

| 2002-2004 | | $400 | $450 |

Celebrity CS-257 (Import)
1992-2005. Super shallow bowl back body, single-cut, Adamas soundholes, alternating dot and diamond markers, made in Korea.

| 1992-2005 | Black | $300 | $400 |

Classic 1613/1713
1971-1993. Acoustic/electric, non-cut, deep bowl, no inlay, slotted headstock, gold tuners.

| 1971-1993 | Natural | $500 | $600 |

Classic 1663/1763
1982-1998. Acoustic/electric, single-cut, deep bowl, cedar top, EQ, no inlay, slotted headstock, gold tuners.

| 1982-1998 | | $600 | $700 |

Classic 1863
1989-1998. Acoustic/electric, single-cut, shallow bowl, no inlay, cedar top, EQ, slotted headstock, gold tuners.

| 1989-1998 | | $600 | $700 |

Collectors Series
1982-present. Limited edition, different model featured each year and production limited to that year only, the year designation is marked at the 12th fret, various colors (each year different).

| 1982-2004 | | $600 | $900 |

Concert Classic 1116
1974-1990. Deep-bowl nylon string classical, slotted headstock.

| 1974-1990 | | $350 | $500 |

Contemporary Folk Classic Electric 1616
1974-1990. Acoustic/electric, no inlay, slotted headstock, natural or sunburst.

| 1974-1990 | Natural | $300 | $450 |

Country Artist Classic Electric 1624
1971-1990. Nylon strings, slotted headstock, standard steel-string sized neck to simulate a folk guitar, on-board electronics.

| 1971-1990 | | $300 | $450 |

Country Artist Electric 1624
1971-1990. Acoustic/electric nylon string, non-cut, shallow bowl, slotted headstock, no inlay, chrome tuners.

| 1971-1990 | | $400 | $600 |

Country Artist Classic Electric 6773
1995-present. Classic electric nylon string, soft-cut, solid spruce top, slotted headstock, Ovation pickup system.

| 1995-2005 | | $400 | $600 |

Custom Legend 1117
1970s. Non-electrical 2nd generation Ovation, higher-end with abalone inlays and gold hardware, open V-bracing pattern. Model 1117-4, natural.

| 1970s | | $550 | $650 |

Custom Legend 1569
1980s. Rounded cutaway acoustic/electric, super shallow bowl, gloss black finish.

| 1980s | | $625 | $675 |

Custom Legend 1619/1719
1974-present. Acoustic/electric 2nd generation Ovation, electric version of model 1117, higher-end with abalone inlays and gold hardware, open V-bracing pattern.

| 1974-2005 | | $650 | $850 |

MODEL YEAR	FEATURES	EXC. COND. LOW	HIGH

Custom Legend 1959
1980-present. Acoustic/electric, abalone top border, 'board binding, abalone floral inlay, gold tuners, natural or sunburst.

| 1980s | | $750 | $850 |

Custom Legend 1959-12
1980s. Acoustic/electric 12-string, deep bowl, AAA sitka spruce top, abalone inlay.

| 1980s | | $750 | $850 |

Deacon 1252
1973-1980. Axe-shaped solidbody electric, active electronics, diamond fret markers.

| 1973-1980 | Sunburst | $600 | $700 |

Deacon 12-String 1253
1975. Axe-shaped solidbody, diamond inlay, 2 pickups. only a few made.

| 1975 | | $600 | $700 |

Eclipse
1971-1973. Thinline double cut acoustic-electric archtop, 2 pickups.

| 1971-1973 | | $500 | $600 |

Elite 1718
1982-1997. Acoustic/electric, non-cut, deep bowl, solid spruce top, Adamas-type soundhole, volume and tone controls, stereo output.

| 1982-1997 | Sunburst | $750 | $850 |

Elite 1758
1990-1998. Acoustic/electric, non-cut, deep bowl.

| 1990-1998 | | $750 | $900 |

Elite 1768
1990-1998. Acoustic/electric, cutaway, deep bowl.

| 1990-1998 | Natural | $750 | $900 |

Elite 1868
1983-present. Acoustic/electric, cutaway, shallow bowl.

| 1983-2005 | Sunburst | $750 | $900 |

Elite 5858
1991. Super shallow bowl, single cutaway, Adamas-style soundhole, gold hardware, on-board factory OP24 pickup.

| 1991 | | $900 | $1,100 |

Elite Doubleneck
1989-1990s. Six- and 12-string necks, can be ordered with a variety of custom options.

| 1989 | | $800 | $1,100 |

Folklore 1614
1972-1983. Acoustic/electric, 12-fret neck on full-size body, wide neck, on-board electronics.

| 1972-1983 | | $600 | $700 |

Glen Campbell 12-String 1118 (K-1118)
1968-1982. Acoustic, 12 strings, shallow bowl version of Legend, gold tuners, diamond inlay.

| 1968-1982 | | $600 | $700 |

Glen Campbell Artist Balladeer 1127
1968-1990. Acoustic, shallow bowl, diamond inlay, gold tuners.

| 1968-1990 | Natural | $500 | $600 |

Hurricane 12-String K-1120
1968-1969. ES-335-style electric semi-hollowbody, double-cut, 12 strings, F-holes, 2 pickups.

| 1968-1969 | | $500 | $600 |

Josh White 1114
1967-1970, 1972-1983. Designed by and for folk and blues singer Josh White, has wide 12-fret to the body neck, dot markers, classical-style tuners.

| 1967-1970 | | $600 | $700 |
| 1972-1983 | | $500 | $600 |

Legend 1117
1972-1999. Deep bowl acoustic, 5-ply top binding, gold tuners, various colors (most natural).

| 1972-1999 | | $500 | $600 |

Legend 12-String 1866
1989-present. Acoustic/electric, cutaway, 12 strings, shallow bowl, 5-ply top binding.

| 1989-2005 | Black | $650 | $750 |

Legend 1717
1990-1998. Acoustic/electric, 5-ply top binding, various colors.

| 1990-1998 | | $650 | $750 |

Legend 1869
1994. Acoustic/electric, cutaway, super shallow bowl.

| 1994 | Natural | $700 | $800 |

Legend Cutaway 1667
1982-1996. Acoustic/electric, cutaway, deep bowl, abalone, gold tuners.

| 1982-1986 | | $650 | $750 |

Legend Electric 1617
1972-1998. Acoustic/electric, deep bowl, abalone, gold tuners, various colors.

| 1972-1998 | | $500 | $600 |

Pacemaker 12-String 1115/1615
1968-1982. Originally called the K-1115 12-string, Renamed Pacemaker in '72.

| 1968-1982 | | $650 | $750 |

Patriot Bicentennial
*1976. Limited run of 1776 guitars, Legend Custom model with drum and flag decal and "1776*1976" decal on lower bout.*

| 1976 | | $750 | $900 |

Pinnacle
1990-1992. Spruce or sycamore top, broad leaf pattern rosette, mahogany neck, piezo bridge pickup.

| 1990-1992 | Sunburst | $450 | $550 |

Pinnacle Shallow Cutaway
1990-1994. Pinnacle with shallow bowl body and single-cut.

| 1990-1994 | Sunburst | $500 | $600 |

Preacher 1281
1975-1982. Solidbody, mahogany body, double-cut, 2 pickups.

| 1975-1982 | | $600 | $700 |

Preacher 12-String 1285
1975-1983. Double-cut solidbody, 12 strings, 2 pickups.

| 1975-1983 | | $600 | $700 |

Preacher Deluxe 1282
1975-1982. Double-cut solidbody, 2 pickups with series/parallel pickup switch and mid-range control.

| 1975-1982 | | $550 | $650 |

Ovation Hurricane

Ovation K-1360

Ovation Tornado

*Pantheon Bourgeois
Vintage Dreadnought*

MODEL YEAR	FEATURES	EXC. COND. LOW	HIGH

Thunderhead 1460
1968-1972. Double-cut, 2 pickups, gold hardware, phase switch, master volume, separate tone controls, pickup balance/blend control, vibrato.

1968-1972		$500	$600

Tornado 1260
1968-1973. Same as Thunderhead without phase switch, with chrome hardware.

1968-1973		$450	$550

UK II 1291
1980-1982. Single-cut solidbody, 2 pickups, body made of Urelite on aluminum frame, bolt-on neck, gold hardware.

1980-1982		$700	$850

Ultra GS
1985. Double-cut solidbody electrics, 1, 2, or 3 pickups.

1985		$200	$300

Viper 1271
1975-1982. Single-cut, 2 single-coil pickups.

1975-1982		$500	$600

Viper III 1273
1975-1982. Single-cut, 3 single-coil pickups.

1975-1982		$550	$650

Viper EA 68
1994-present. Thin acoustic/electric, single-cut mahogany body, spruce top over sound chamber with multiple upper bout soundholes.

1994-2005		$550	$650

P. W. Crump Company
1975-present. Luthier Phil Crump builds his custom flat-top guitars in Arcata, California. He also builds mandolin-family instruments.

Pagan
Guitars made in Germany and imported into the U.S. by a guitar shop.

Palen
1998-present. Premium grade, production/custom, archtop guitars built by luthier Nelson Palen in Beloit, Kansas.

Palmer
Early 1970s-present. Budget and intermediate grade, production acoustic, acoustic/electric and classical guitars imported from Europe and Asia. They also have offered electrics.

Panache
2004-present. Budget grade, production, solidbody electric and acoustic guitars imported from China.

PANaramic
1961-1963. Guitars and basses made in Italy by the Crucianelli accordion company and imported by PANaramic accordion. They also offered amps made by Magnatone.

Pantheon Guitars
2000-present. Patrick Theimer created Pantheon which offers premium grade, production/custom, flat-tops built by seven luthiers (including Dana Bourgeois) working in an old 1840s textile mill in Lewiston, Maine.

Paolo Soprani
Early 1960s. Italian plastic covered guitars with pushbutton controls made by the Polverini Brothers.

Paramount
1920s-1942, Late 1940s. The William L. Lange Company began selling Paramount banjos, guitar banjos and mandolin banjos in the early 1920s, and added archtop guitars in '34. The guitars were made by Martin and possibly others. Lange went out of business by '42; Gretsch picked up the Paramount name and used it on acoustics and electrics for a time in the late '40s.

GB
1920s-1930s. Guitar banjo.

1920s		$1,500	$1,900

Style C
1930s. 16" acoustic archtop, maple back and sides.

1930s		$600	$800

Style L
1930s. Small body with resonator, limited production to about 36 instruments.

1930s		$2,500	$3,500

Parker
1992-present. U.S.-made and imported intermediate, professional, and premium grade, production/custom, solidbody guitars featuring a thin skin of carbon and glass fibers bonded to a wooden guitar body. In '05, they added wood body acoustic/electrics. They also build basses. Located northwest of Boston, Parker was founded by Ken Parker and Larry Fishman (Fishman Transducers). Korg USA committed money to get the Fly Deluxe model into production in July '93. Parker added a Custom Shop in '03 to produce special build instruments and non-core higher-end models that were no longer available as a standard product offering. In early '04, Parker was acquired by U.S. Music Corp.

Concert
1997 only. Solid sitka spruce top, only piezo system pickup, no magnetic pickups, transparent butterscotch.

1997		$1,300	$1,500

Fly
1993-1994. There are many Parker Fly models, the model simply called Fly is similar to the more common Fly Deluxe, except it does not have the Fishman piezo pickup system.

1993-1994		$1,100	$1,400

MODEL		EXC. COND.	
YEAR	FEATURES	LOW	HIGH

Fly Artist
1998-1999. Solid sitka spruce top, vibrato, Deluxe-style electronics, transparent blond finish.

1998-1999		$1,700	$1,800

Fly Classic
1996-1998, 2000-present. One-piece Honduras mahogany body, basswood neck, electronics same as Fly Deluxe.

1996-2005		$1,000	$1,300

Fly Deluxe
1993-present. Poplar body, basswood neck, 2 pickups, Fishman bridge transducer, '93-'96 models were offered with or without vibrato, then non-vibrato discontinued. The Deluxe normally came with a gig bag, but also offered with a hardshell case, which would add about $50 to the values listed.

1993-2005		$900	$1,200

Fly Maple Classic
2000. Classic with maple body (vs. mahogany), transparent butterscotch.

2000		$1,400	$1,500

Fly Supreme
1996-1999. One-piece flame maple body, electronics same as the Fly Deluxe, includes hard molded case.

1990s	Highly flamed butterscotch	$2,000	$2,300

NiteFly/NiteFly NFV1/NFV3/NFV5
1996-1999. Three single-coil pickup NiteFly, Fishman piezo system, bolt neck, maple body for '96-'98, ash for '99. Called the NiteFly in '96, NiteFly NFV1 ('97-'98), NiteFly NFV3 ('98), NiteFly NFV5 ('99).

1996-1999		$500	$700

NiteFly/NiteFly NFV2/NFV4/NFV6/SA
1996-present. Two single-coil and 1 humbucker pickup NiteFly, Fishman piezo system, bolt neck, maple body for '96-'98, ash for '99-present. Called the NiteFly in '96, NiteFly NFV2 ('97-'98), NiteFly NFV4 ('98), NiteFly NFV6 ('99), NiteFly SA ('00-present).

1996-2003		$400	$500

P Series
2000-2003. Various models include P-38 (ash body, bolt maple neck, rosewood 'board, vibrato, piezo bridge pickup and active Parker Alnico humbucker and 2 single-coils, gig bag); P-40 (as P-38, but with pickups mounted on body, no 'guard); P-44 (mahogany body, flamed maple top, piezo bridge pickup and 2 special Parker humbuckers).

2000-2003		$400	$500

Tulipwood Limited Edition
1998. Limited build of 35 guitars, standard Deluxe features with tulipwood body.

1998		$1,300	$1,500

Patrick Eggle Guitars
1991-present. Founded by Patrick Eggle and others in Birmingham, England, building solid and semi-solid body electric guitars. They also builds basses. In '95, Eggle left the company to build acoustics.

Patrick James Eggle
2001-present. Eggle cofounded the Patrick Eggle Guitar company in '91 building solidbodies. In '95, he left to do repairs and custom work. In '01 he opened a new workshop in Bedforshire, England, building professional and premium grade, production/custom, archtop and flatop guitars. He has since relocated to Hendersonville, North Carolina.

Paul Reed Smith
1985-present. Intermediate, professional and premium grade, production/custom, solid and semi-hollow body guitars made in the U.S. and imported. They also build basses. Paul Reed Smith built his first guitar in '75 as an independent study project in college and refined his design over the next 10 years building custom guitars. After building two prototypes and getting several orders from East Coast guitar dealers, Smith was able to secure the support necessary to start PRS in a factory on Virginia Avenue in Annapolis, Maryland. On '95, they moved to their current location on Kent Island in Stevensville. In 2001 PRS introduced the Korean-made SE Series.

10th Anniversary
1995. Only 200 made, offset double-cut, carved maple figured top, mahogany body, ebony 'board, mother-of-pearl inlays, abalone purfling, gold McCarty pickups, either 22-fret wide-fat or wide-thin mahogany neck, 10th Anniversary logo.

1995		$5,300	$6,000

513 Rosewood
Dec.2003-present. Brazilian rosewood neck, newly developed PRS pickup system with 13 sound settings, hum-single-hum pickups.

2003-2005		$3,400	$3,500

Artist II/Artist 22
1993-1995. Curly maple top, mahogany body and neck, maple purfling on rosewood 'board, inlaid maple bound headstock, abalone birds, 22 frets, gold hardware, short run of less than 500 instruments.

1993-1995		$2,000	$3,000

Artist III
1996-1997. Continuation of the 22-fret neck with some changes in materials and specs, figured maple tops, short run of less than 500 instruments.

1996-1997	Black Cherry	$2,000	$3,000

Artist IV
1996. Continuation of the 22-fret neck with some upgrades in materials and specs, short run of less than 70 instruments.

1996		$3,000	$4,000

Artist Limited
1994-1995. Like the Artist II with 14-carat gold bird inlays, abalone purfling on neck, headstock and truss rod cover, Brazilian rosewood 'board, 165 made.

1994-1995		$3,000	$4,000

Patrick James Eggle Etowah

Parker PM-10N

PRS CE 22 Maple Top

PRS Custom 24 Brazilian

Artist/Artist I/Artist 24

1991-1994. Carved maple top, offset double-cut mahogany body, 24-fret neck, bird markers, less than 500 made. A different Custom 24 Artist package was subsequently offered in the 2000s.

MODEL YEAR	FEATURES	EXC. COND. LOW	HIGH
1991-1994		$3,000	$4,000

CE 22

1994-present. Double-cut carved alder (1995) or mahogany (post 1995) body, bolt-on maple neck with rosewood 'board, dot inlays, 2 humbuckers, chrome hardware, translucent colors, options include vibrato and gold hardware and custom colors.

1994-2005	Alder, standard features	$1,100	$1,400
1994-2005	Alder, upgrade options	$1,200	$1,500

CE 22 Maple Top

1994-present. CE 22 with figured maple top, upgrade options included gold hardware, custom colors or 10 top.

1994-1995	Standard features	$1,200	$1,600
1994-1995	Upgrade options	$1,300	$1,700
1996-2005	Standard features	$1,200	$1,500
1996-2005	Upgrade options	$1,300	$1,600

CE 24 (Classic Electric, CE)

1988-present. Double-cut alder body, carved top, 24-fret bolt-on maple neck, 2 humbuckers, dot inlays, upgrade options included gold hardware, custom colors or 10 top.

1988-1991	Standard features, rosewood board	$1,400	$2,000
1988-1991	Upgrade, rosewood board	$1,500	$2,200
1992-1995	Standard features	$1,200	$1,500
1992-1995	Upgrade options	$1,300	$1,600
1996-2005	Standard features	$1,100	$1,400
1996-2005	Upgrade options	$1,200	$1,500

CE 24 Maple Top (CE Maple Top)

1989-present. CE 24 with figured maple top, 24-fret 'board, upgrade options may include any or all the following: gold hardware, custom colors or 10 top.

1988-1991	Standard features	$1,500	$2,100
1988-1991	Upgrade options	$1,600	$2,300
1992-1995	Standard features	$1,200	$1,600
1992-1995	Upgrade options	$1,300	$1,700
1996-1999	Standard features	$1,100	$1,500
1996-1999	Upgrade options	$1,200	$1,600
2000-2005	Standard features	$1,200	$1,500
2000-2005	Upgrade options	$1,300	$1,600

Custom (Custom 24/PRS Custom)

1985-present. Double-cut solidbody, curly maple top, mahogany back and neck, pearl and abalone moon inlays, 24 frets, 2 humbuckers, tremolo, options include quilted or 10 Top, bird inlays, and gold hardware.

1985	Standard features	$4,000	$9,000
1985	Upgrade options	$5,000	$10,000
1986	Standard features	$3,700	$5,000
1986	Upgrade options	$4,300	$5,500
1987	Standard features	$3,200	$4,500
1987	Upgrade options	$3,500	$5,000
1988	Standard features	$2,600	$3,800
1988	Upgrade options	$2,700	$4,000

MODEL YEAR	FEATURES	EXC. COND. LOW	HIGH
1989-1991	Standard features	$2,500	$3,100
1989-1991	Upgrade options, rosewood board	$2,600	$3,200
1992-1995	Standard features	$1,900	$2,200
1992-1995	Upgrade options	$2,000	$2,400
1996-2004	Standard features	$1,800	$1,900
1996-2004	Upgrade options	$1,900	$2,000
2005	20th Anniversary Custom 24	$1,900	$2,500

Custom 22

1993-present. Custom 22 with flamed or quilted maple top on mahogany body, 22-fret set-neck, upgrade option is gold hardware, normally the quilt top is higher than flamed top.

1993-1995	Standard features	$1,900	$2,200
1993-1995	Upgrade options	$2,000	$2,400
1996-2005	Standard features	$1,800	$1,900
1996-2005	Upgrade options	$1,900	$2,000

Custom 22 (Brazilian)

2003-2004. Limited run of 500 with Brazilian rosewood 'board, figured 10 top, pearl bird inlays.

2003-2004		$2,200	$2,400

Custom 22/12

December 2003-present. 12-string version, flame or quilt maple top, hum/single/hum pickups.

2003-2005		$2,500	$3,000

Custom 24 (Brazilian)

2003-2004. Limited run with Brazilian rosewood 'board, figured 10 top, pearl bird inlays.

2003-2004		$2,200	$2,400

Custom 24 (Walnut)

1992. Seamless matched walnut over mahogany, 3 made.

1992		$5,000	$5,500

Dave Navaro Signature

2005-present. Carved maple top, bird inlays, trem, white

2005		$2,000	$2,100

Dragon I

1992. 22 frets, PRS Dragon pickups, wide-fat neck, gold hardware, 'board inlay of a dragon made of 201 pieces of abalone, turquoise and mother-of-pearl, limited production of 50 guitars.

1992		$16,000	$25,000

Dragon II

1993. 22 frets, PRS Dragon pickups, wide-fat neck, gold hardware, 'board inlay of a dragon made of 218 pieces of gold, coral, abalone, malachite, onyx and mother-of-pearl, limited production of 100 guitars.

1993		$12,000	$20,000

Dragon III

1994. Carved maple top, mahogany back, 22 frets, PRS Dragon pickups, wide-fat neck, gold hardware, 'board inlay of a dragon made of 438 pieces of gold, red and green abalone, mother-of-pearl, mammoth ivory, and stone, limited production of 100 guitars.

1994		$15,000	$20,000

Dragon 2000

1999-2000. Three-D dragon inlay in body versus neck inlay of previous models, limited production of 50 guitars.

1999-2000		$10,000	$18,000

MODEL YEAR	FEATURES	EXC. COND. LOW	HIGH

Dragon 2002
2002. Limited edition of 100 guitars, ultra-inlay work depicting dragon head on the guitar body.

2002		$10,000	$17,000

EG II
1991-1995. Double-cut solidbody, bolt-on neck, 3 single-coils, single-single-hum, or hum-single-hum pickup options, opaque finish.

1991-1995		$1,100	$1,300

EG II Maple Top
1991-1995. EG II with flamed maple top, chrome hardware.

1991-1995		$1,200	$1,500

EG 3
1990-1991. Double-cut solidbody, bolt-on 22-fret neck, 3 single-coil pickups.

1990-1991	Flamed 10 top	$1,300	$1,500
1990-1991	Opaque finish	$1,100	$1,300

EG 4
1990-1991. Similar to EG 3 with single-single-hum pickup configuration, opaque finish.

1990-1991		$1,100	$1,300

Golden Eagle
1997-1998. Very limited production, eagle head and shoulders carved into lower bouts, varied high-end appointments.

1997-1998		$17,000	$23,000

Limited Edition
1989-1991, 2000. Double-cut, semi-hollow mahogany body, figured cedar top, gold hardware, less than 300 made. In '00, single-cut, short run of 5 antique white and five black offered via Garrett Park Guitars.

1989-1991	Various colors	$2,200	$2,500
2000	White	$2,500	$3,000

McCarty Model
1994-present. Mahogany body with figured maple top, upgrade options may include a 10 top, gold hardware, bird inlays.

1994-1995	Standard features	$1,700	$1,800
1994-1995	Upgrade options	$1,800	$2,000
1996-2005	Standard features	$1,600	$1,800
1996-2005	Upgrade options	$1,700	$1,900

McCarty Archtop (Spruce)
1998-2000. Deep mahogany body, archtop, spruce top, 22-fret set-neck.

1998-2000	Chrome hardware	$1,900	$2,100
1998-2000	Gold hardware	$2,000	$2,200

McCarty Archtop Artist
1998-2002. Highest grade figured maple top and highest appointments, gold hardware.

1998-2002		$4,000	$5,000

McCarty Archtop II (Maple)
1998-2000. Deep mahogany body, archtop, figured maple top, 22-fret set-neck.

1998-2000	Flamed 10 top, chrome hardware	$2,300	$2,800
1998-2000	Flamed 10 top, gold hardware	$2,400	$3,000
1998-2000	Quilted 10 top	$2,400	$3,000

McCarty Hollowbody (Spruce)
2000-present. Similar to Hollowbody I with less appointments.

2000-2005	Standard features	$1,900	$2,100
2000-2005	Upgrade options	$2,000	$2,200

McCarty Hollowbody II (Maple)
1998-present. Medium deep mahogany hollowbody, figured maple top, 22-fret set-neck, chrome hardware.

1998-2005	Standard features	$2,200	$2,400
1998-2005	Upgrade options	$2,300	$2,600

McCarty Hollowbody/Hollowbody I
1998-present. Medium deep mahogany hollowbody, spruce top, 22-fret set-neck, chrome hardware.

1998-2005	Standard features	$1,900	$2,100
1998-2005	Upgrade options	$2,000	$2,200

McCarty Model (Brazilian)
2003-2004. Limited run with Brazilian rosewood 'board.

2003-2004		$2,400	$2,500

McCarty Soapbar (Maple)
1998-present. Soapbar with figured maple top option, nickel hardware.

1998-2005		$1,700	$1,800

McCarty Soapbar/Soapbar Standard
1998-present. Solid mahogany body, P-90-style soapbar pickups, 22-fret set-neck, nickel-plated hardware, upgrade options may include gold hardware and bird inlays.

1998-1999	Standard features	$1,500	$1,700
1998-1999	Upgrade options	$1,600	$1,800
2000-2005	Standard features	$1,600	$1,700
2000-2005	Upgrade options	$1,700	$1,800

McCarty Standard
1994-present. McCarty Model with carved mahogany body but without maple top, nickel-plated hardware, upgrade options may include gold hardware and bird inlays.

1994-1995	Standard features	$1,500	$1,800
1994-1995	Upgrade options	$1,600	$1,900
1996-2005	Standard features	$1,400	$1,700
1996-2005	Upgrade options	$1,500	$1,800

Metal
1985-1986. Solid mahogany body with custom 2-color striped body finish and graphics, 24-fret set-neck, nickel hardware, 2 humbuckers.

1985-1986		$4,000	$8,500

Modern Eagle
2004-present. Higher-end model based on Private Stock innovations, standard PRS double-cut, flying eagle markers, satin nitrocellulose finish, Brazilian rosewood neck.

2004-2005		$4,000	$4,500

Private Stock Program
April 1996-present. One-off custom instruments based around existing designs such as the McCarty Model. Values may be somewhat near production equivalents or they may be higher. The Private Stock option was reintroduced by 2003 and a '03 typical offering might retail at about $7,500, but a '03 Santana I Private Stock might retail at over $15,000, so each

PRS McCarty

PRS Metal

PRS Santana SE

Pawar Stage

MODEL YEAR	FEATURES	EXC. COND. LOW	HIGH

guitar should be evaluated on a case-by-case basis.

| 1996-2005 | Hollowbody, typical specs | $7,000 | $9,000 |
| 1996-2005 | Solidbody, typical specs | $7,000 | $9,000 |

PRS Guitar

1985-1986. Set-neck, solid mahogany body, 24-fret 'board, 2 humbuckers, chrome hardware, renamed Standard from '87-'98 then Standard 24 from '98.

1984-1985	Preproduction with provenance	$15,000	$40,000
1985	Sunburst and optional colors	$5,000	$15,000
1986	Sunburst and optional colors	$4,000	$9,000

Rosewood Ltd.

1996. Mahogany body with figured maple top, 1-piece rosewood neck with ultra-deluxe tree-of-life neck inlay, gold hardware.

| 1996 | | $9,000 | $12,000 |

Santana

1995-1998. Mahogany body, slightly wider lower bout than other models, figured maple top, 24-fret set-neck, symmetric Santana headstock, unique body purfling, chrome and nickel-plated hardware, limited production special order.

| 1995-1998 | | $5,000 | $6,000 |

Santana II

1998-present. Three-way toggle replaces former dual mini-switches, special order.

| 1998-2005 | | $3,500 | $4,000 |

Santana III

2001-present. Less ornate version of Santana II.

| 2001-2005 | | $2,300 | $2,500 |

Santana SE

2001-present. Solid mahogany body, set mahogany neck, 2 humbuckers, thin diagonal line position markers.

| 2001-2005 | | $300 | $350 |

SE EG

December 2003-present. 3 single-coils, SE logo on headstock, 2 knobs, set-neck.

| 2003-2005 | | $300 | $350 |

SE Soapbar/Soapbar II

Dec.2003-present. Single-cut, soapbar pickups. Replaced by Soapbar II with classic PRS double-cut introduced in early-'05.

| 2003-2004 | Single-cut | $300 | $350 |
| 2005 | Double-cut | $275 | $325 |

Signature/PRS Signature

1987-1991. Solid mahogany body, figured maple top, set-neck, 24 frets, hand-signed signature on headstock, limited run of 1,000.

| 1987-1991 | | $5,000 | $6,000 |

Single Cut

2000-2004, 2005-present. Single-cut mahogany body, maple top, 22-fret 'board, upgrade options may include either or all of the following: 10 top flamed maple, gold hardware, bird inlays.

| 2000-2005 | Standard features | $1,800 | $2,400 |
| 2000-2005 | Upgrade options | $1,900 | $2,500 |

MODEL YEAR	FEATURES	EXC. COND. LOW	HIGH

Special

1987-1990, 1991-1993. Similar to Standard with upgrades, wide-thin neck, 2 HFS humbuckers. From '91-'93, a special option package was offered featuring a wide-thin neck and high output humbuckers.

| 1987-1990 | Solid color finish | $2,500 | $3,500 |
| 1991-1993 | Special order only | $3,000 | $3,500 |

Standard

1987-1998. Set-neck, solid mahogany body, 24-fret 'board, 2 humbuckers, chrome hardware. Originally called the PRS Guitar from '85-'86 (see that listing), renamed Standard 24 from '98.

1987-1989	Sunburst and optional colors	$2,300	$3,300
1990-1991	Last Brazilian board	$1,700	$2,000
1992-1995		$1,500	$1,800
1995-1998		$1,400	$1,700

Standard 22

1994-present. 22-fret Standard.

1994-1995		$1,400	$1,800
1995-1999		$1,300	$1,700
2000-2005		$1,300	$1,700

Standard 24

1998-present. Renamed from Standard, solid mahogany body, 24-fret set-neck.

| 1998-1999 | | $1,300 | $1,700 |
| 2000-2005 | | $1,300 | $1,700 |

Studio

1988-1991. Standard model variant, solid mahogany body, 24-fret set-neck, chrome and nickel hardware, single-single-hum pickups, special Studio package offered '91-'96.

| 1988-1991 | | $1,600 | $1,800 |

Studio Maple Top

1990-1991. Mahogany solidbody, bird 'board inlays, 2 single-coil and 1 humbucking pickups, tremolo, transparent finish.

| 1990-1991 | | $1,800 | $2,200 |

Swamp Ash Special

1996-present. Solid swamp ash body, 22-fret bolt-on maple neck, 3 pickups, upgrade options available.

| 1996-2005 | Figured maple neck option | $1,500 | $1,900 |

Tremonti SE (Import)

2002-2004, 2005-present. Single-cut, contoured mahogany body, 2 humbuckers, stop tailpiece.

| 2002-2005 | | $375 | $475 |

Pawar

1999-present. Founded by Jay Pawar, Jeff Johnston and Kevin Johnston in Willoughby Hills, Ohio, Pawar builds professional and premium grade, production/custom, solidbody guitars that feature the Pawar Positive Tone System with over 20 single coil and humbucker tones.

Stage Turn of the Century

1999-present. Chambered swamp ash double-cut solidbody, figured maple top, bass-side scroll horn, set-neck.

| 2000 | | $1,100 | $1,500 |

MODEL YEAR	FEATURES	EXC. COND. LOW	HIGH

PBC Guitar Technology

See Bunker Guitars for more info.

Peavey

1965-present. Headquartered in Meridan, Mississippi, Peavey builds budget, intermediate, professional, and premium grade, production/custom, acoustic and electric guitars. They also build basses, amps, PA gear, effects and drums. Hartley Peavey's first products were guitar amps. He added guitars to the mix in '78.

Axcelerator/AX
1994-1998. Offset double-cut swamp ash or poplar body, bolt-on maple neck, dot markers, AX with locking vibrato, various colors.

1994-1998		$275	$325

Cropper Classic
1995-2005. Single-cut solidbody, 1 humbucker and 1 single coil, figured maple top over thin mahogany body, transparent Onion Green.

1995-2005		$425	$500

Defender
1994-1995. Double-cut, solid poplar body, 2 humbuckers and 1 single-coil pickup, locking Floyd Rose tremolo, metallic or pearl finish.

1994-1995		$150	$200

Destiny
1989-1992. Double-cut, mahogany body, maple top, neck-thru-bridge, maple neck, 3 integrated pickups, double locking tremolo.

1989-1992		$300	$400

Destiny Custom
1989-1992. Destiny with figured wood and higher-end appointments, various colors.

1989-1992		$400	$550

Detonator AX
1995-1998. Double-cut, maple neck, rosewood 'board, dot markers, hum/single/hum pickups, black.

1995-1998		$200	$300

EVH Wolfgang
1996-2004. Offset double-cut, arched top, bolt neck, stop tailpiece or Floyd Rose vibrato, quilted or flamed maple top upgrade option.

1996-2004	Flamed maple	$800	$1,200
1996-2004	Standard top	$700	$1,050

EVH Wolfgang Special
1997-2004. Offset double-cut lower-end Wolfgang model, various opaque finishes, flamed top optional.

1997-2004	Flamed maple top	$600	$650
1997-2004	Standard finish	$500	$550

Falcon/Falcon Active/Falcon Custom
1987-1992. Double-cut, 3 pickups, passive or active electronics, Kahler locking vibrato.

1987-1992	Custom color	$300	$350
1987-1992	Standard color	$200	$300

Firenza
1994-1999. Offset double-cut, bolt-on neck, single-coil pickups.

1994-1999		$250	$300

Firenza AX
1994-1999. Upscale Firenza Impact with humbucking pickups.

1994-1999		$300	$375

Generation S-1/S-2
1988-1994. Single-cut, maple cap on mahogany body, bolt-on maple neck, six-on-a-side tuners, active single/hum pickups, S-2 with locking vibrato system.

1988-1994		$225	$300

Horizon/Horizon II
1983-1985. Extended pointy horns, angled lower bout, maple body, rear routing for electronics, 2 humbucking pickups. Horizon II has added blade pickup.

1983-1985		$150	$250

Hydra Doubleneck
1985-1989. Available as a custom order, 6/12-string necks each with 2 humbuckers, 3-way pickup select.

1985-1989		$150	$250

Impact 1/Impact 2
1985-1987. Offset double-cut, Impact 1 has higher-end synthetic 'board, Impact 2 with conventional rosewood 'board.

1985-1987		$200	$300

Mantis
1984-1989. Hybrid X-shaped solidbody, 1 humbucking pickup, tremolo, laminated maple neck.

1984-1989		$175	$250

Milestone 12-String
1985-1986. Offset double-cut, 12 strings.

1985-1986		$175	$275

Milestone/Milestone Custom
1983-1986. Offset double-cut solidbody.

1983-1986		$100	$200

Mystic
1983-1989. Double-cut, 2 pickups, stop tailpiece initially, later Power Bend vibrato, maple body and neck.

1983-1989		$150	$225

Nitro I Active
1988-1990. Active electronics.

1988-1990		$225	$300

Nitro I/II/III
1986-1989. Offset double-cut, banana-style headstock, 1 humbucker (I), 2 humbuckers (II), or single/single/hum pickups (III).

1986-1989	Nitro I	$150	$225
1986-1989	Nitro II	$175	$250
1986-1989	Nitro III	$200	$275

Odyssey
1990-1994. Single-cut, figured carved maple top on mahogany body, humbuckers.

1990-1994		$400	$550

Odyssey 25th Anniversary
1990. Single-cut body, limited production.

1990		$550	$700

Omniac JD USA
2005-present. Jerry Donahue-designed single-cut solidbody, 2 single-coils.

2005		$700	$750

Peavey Generation EXP

Peavey Omniac JD USA

GUITARS

Peavey Predator Plus

Pedro de Miguel classical

MODEL YEAR FEATURES	EXC. COND. LOW	HIGH
Patriot		
1983-1987. Double-cut, single bridge humbucker.		
1983-1987	$150	$200
Patriot Plus		
1983-1987. Double-cut, 2 humbucker pickups, bi-laminated maple neck.		
1983-1987	$175	$225
Patriot Tremolo		
1986-1990. Double-cut, single bridge humbucker, tremolo, replaced the standard Patriot.		
1986-1990	$175	$225
Predator Series		
1985-1988, 1990-present. Double-cut poplar body, 2 pickups until '87, 3 after, vibrato.		
1985-1988	$125	$175
1990-2005	$100	$125
Raptor I/Plus/Plus TK/Plus EXP		
1997-present. Offset double-cut solidbody, 3 pickups.		
1997-2005	$90	$110
Razer		
1983-1989. Double-cut with arrowhead point for lower bout, 2 pickups, 1 volume and 2 tone controls, stop tailpiece or vibrato.		
1983-1989	$300	$400
Reactor		
1993-1999. Classic single-cut style, 2 single-coils.		
1993-1999	$275	$325
Rotor Series		
2004-present. Classic futuristic body, elongated upper treble bout/lower bass bout, 2 humbuckers.		
2004-2005 Rotor EX	$300	$325
2004-2005 Rotor EXP	$350	$425
T-1000 LT		
1992-1994. Double-cut, 2 single-coils and humbucker with coil-tap.		
1992-1994	$225	$250
T-15		
1981-1983. Offset double-cut, bolt-on neck, dual ferrite blade single-coil pickups, natural.		
1981-1983	$125	$200
T-15 Amp-In-Case		
1981-1983. Amplifier built into guitar case and T-15 guitar.		
1981-1983	$250	$275
T-25		
1979-1985. Synthetic polymer body, 2 pickups, cream 'guard, sunburst finish.		
1979-1985	$175	$225
T-25 Special		
1979-1985. Same as T-25, but with super high output pickups, phenolic 'board, black/white/black 'guard, ebony black finish.		
1979-1985	$175	$225
T-26		
1982-1986. Same as T-25, but with 3 single-coil pickups and 5-way switch.		
1982-1986	$200	$250
T-27		
1981-1983. Offset double-cut, bolt-on neck, dual ferrite blade single-coil pickups.		
1981-1983	$225	$250

MODEL YEAR FEATURES	EXC. COND. LOW	HIGH
T-30		
1982-1985. Short-scale, 3 single-coil pickups, 5-way select, by '83 amp-in-case available.		
1982-1985	$225	$250
T-60		
1978-1988. Contoured offset double-cut, ash body, six-in-line tuners, 2 humbuckers, thru-body strings, by '87 maple bodies, various finishes.		
1978-1988 Black	$250	$300
1978-1988 Natural	$250	$300
1978-1988 Red, sunburst, white	$275	$325
Tracer Custom		
1989-1990. Tracer with 2 single/hum pickups and extras.		
1989-1990	$150	$200
Tracer/Tracer II		
1987-1994. Offset scooped double-cut with extended pointy horns, poplar body, 1 pickup, Floyd Rose.		
1987-1994	$150	$200
Vandenberg Quilt Top		
1989-1992. Vandenberg Custom with quilted maple top, 2 humbuckers, glued-in neck, quilted maple top, mahogany body and neck.		
1989-1992	$800	$1,200
Vandenberg Signature		
1988-1992. Double-cut, reverse headstock, bolt-on neck, locking vibrato, various colors.		
1988-1992	$450	$575
Vortex I/Vortex II		
1986. Streamlined Mantis with 2 pickups, 3-way, Kahler locking vibrato. Vortex II has Randy Rhoads Sharkfin V.		
1986	$275	$325
V-Type Series		
2004-present. Offset double-cut solidbody, pointed reverse 6-on-a-side headstock, 2 humbuckers.		
2004-2005	$325	$375

Pedro de Miguel

1991-present. Luthiers Pedro Pérez and Miguel Rodriguez build their professional and premium grade, custom/production, classical guitars in Madrid, Spain. They also offer factory-made instruments built to their specifications.

Pegasus Guitars and Ukuleles

1977-present. Premium grade, custom steel-string guitars built by luthier Bob Gleason in Kurtistown, Hawaii, who also builds ukulele family instruments.

Penco

Ca. 1974-1978. Generally high quality Japanese-made copies of classic American acoustic, electric and bass guitars. Probably (though not certainly) imported into Philadelphia during the copy era. Includes dreadnought acoustics with laminated woods, bolt-neck solidbody electric guitars and basses, mandolins and banjos.

MODEL YEAR	FEATURES	EXC. COND. LOW	HIGH

Acoustic Flat-Top
1974-1978. Various models.

1974-1978		$150	$225

Electric Solidbody
1974-1978. Various copies.

1974-1978		$200	$275

Pensa (Pensa-Suhr)
1982-present. Premium grade, production/custom, solidbody guitars built in the U.S. They also build basses. Rudy Pensa, of Rudy's Music Stop, New York City, started building Pensa guitars in '82. In '85 he teamed up with John Suhr to build Pensa-Suhr instruments. Name changed back to Pensa in '96.

Classic
1992-Ca. 1998. Offest double-cut, 3 single-coils, gold hardware.

1992-1998		$1,500	$1,700

MK 1 (Mark Knopfler)
1985-present. Offset double-cut solidbody, carved flamed maple bound top, 3 pickups, gold hardware, dot markers, bolt-on neck.

1985-2005		$1,600	$1,800

Suhr Custom
1985-1989. Two-piece maple body, bolt-on maple neck with rosewood 'board, custom order basis with a variety of woods and options available.

1985-1989	Flamed maple top	$1,600	$1,800

Suhr Standard
1985-1991. Double-cut, single/single/hum pickup configuration, opaque solid finish normally, dot markers.

1985-1991		$1,400	$1,600

Perlman Guitars
1976-present. Luthier Alan Pearlman builds his premium grade, custom, steel-string and classical guitars in San Francisco, California.

Perry Guitars
1982-present. Premium grade, production/custom, classical guitars built by luthier Daryl Perry in Winnipeg, Manitoba. He also builds lutes.

Petillo Masterpiece Guitars
1965-present. Luthiers Phillip J. and David Petillo build their intermediate, professional and premium grade, custom, steel-string, nylon-string, 12-string, resonator, archtop, and Hawaiian guitars in Ocean, New Jersey.

Petros Guitars
1992-present. Premium grade, production/custom, flat-top, 12-string, and nylon-string guitars built by father and son luthiers Bruce and Matthew Petros in Kaukauna, Wisconsin.

Apple Creek
1992-1999.

1992-1999		$2,500	$3,300

Phantom Guitar Works
1992-present. Intermediate grade, production/custom, classic Phantom, and Teardrop shaped solid and hollowbody guitars assembled in Clatskanie, Oregon. They also offer basses and the MandoGuitar. Phantom was established by Jack Charles, former lead guitarist of the band Quarterflash. Some earlier guitars were built overseas.

Pieper
2005-present. Premium grade, custom, solidbody guitars built by luthier Robert Pieper in New Haven, Connecticut. He also builds basses.

Pimentel and Sons
1951-present. Luthiers Lorenzo Pimentel and sons build their professional, premium and presentation grade, flat-top, jazz, cutaway electric, and classical guitars in Albuquerque, New Mexico.

Flamenco
1960s. Spruce top, cyprus back and sides.

1960s		$1,000	$1,300

W1 Classical
1970s. Cedar top, walnut back and sides.

1970s		$900	$1,000

Player
1984-1985. Player guitars featured interchangable pickup modules that mounted through the back of the guitar. They offered a double-cut solidbody with various options and the pickup modules were sold separately. The company was located in Scarsdale, New York.

MDS-1B
1984-1985. Offset double-cut, bolt neck, 1, 2 or 3 pickups, Player headstock logo.

1984-1985	1 pickup	$200	$250
1984-1985	2 pickups	$400	$450
1984-1985	3 pickups	$550	$650

Pleasant
Late 1940s-ca.1966. Solidbody electric guitars, obviously others, Japanese manufacturer, probably not imported into the U.S.

Electric Solidbodies
1940s-1966. Various models.

1950-1966		$125	$200

Prairie State
Late 1920s-ca. 1940. Larson Brothers brand, basically a derivative of Maurer & Company, but advertised as "a new method of guitar construction." The Prairie State equivalent models were slightly more expensive than the Maurer models (on average 5% to 10% more). Prairie State guitars were also promoted "reinforced with steel" and "the tube or support near the top withstands the strain of the strings, leaving the top or sound-board free and resilient." One or more steel tubes are noticable running from the neck block to the tail block, when looking through the round soundhole. These gui-

Petros Prairie FS

Phantom Deluxe

1959 Premier Custom

Premier Deluxe E-621

MODEL YEAR	FEATURES	EXC. COND. LOW	HIGH

tars were advertised as being suitable for playing steel (high nut and steel strings). Steel strings were the rage in the 1920s (re: Martin finally converting all guitar models to steel strings by 1928).

1932 Prairie State Catalog Models - description and prices:
Style 225 Concert $65.00
Style 425 Auditorium $70.00
Style 426 Style 425 Steel $70.00
Style 427 Reinforced Neck $75.00
Style 428 Style 427 Steel $75.00
Style 235 Concert with trim $80.00
Style 335 Grand Concert + trim $83.00
Style 435 Auditorium with trim $85.00
Style 340 Grand Concert fancy $90.00
Style 350 Grand Concert fancy $97.00
Style 440 Auditorium fancy trim $93.00
Style 450 Auditorium fancy trim $100.00

Mid-Size Mid to High End Flat-Top
15" spruce X-braced top, Brazilian rosewood back and sides, solid headstock, mid- to high-end appointments.

1920s		$7,000	$10,000

Small Higher-End Flat-Top
Spruce top, 13 5/8" scale, Brazilian rosewood back and sides, high-end pearl appointments, slotted headstock, natural.

1920s		$5,000	$7,000

Premier

Ca.1938-ca.1975, 1990s-present. Budget and intermediate grade, production, import guitars. They also offer basses.

Brands originally offered by Premier include Premier, Multivox, Marvel, Belltone and Strad-O-Lin. Produced by Peter Sorkin Music Company in Manhattan, New York City, New York, who began in Philadelphia, relocating to NYC in '35. First radio-sized amplifiers and stick-on pickups for acoustic archtops were introduced by '38. After World War II, they set up the Multivox subsidiary to manufacture amplifiers ca. '46. First flat-top with pickup appeared in '46.

Most acoustic instruments made by United Guitar Corporation in Jersey City, New Jersey. Ca. '57 Multivox acquires Strad-O-Lin. Ca.'64-'65 their Custom line guitars are assembled with probably Italian bodies and hardware, Japanese electronics, possibly Egmond necks from Holland. By ca. '74-'75, there were a few Japanese-made guitars, then Premier brand goes into hiatus.

The rights to the Premier brand are held by Entertainment Music Marketing Corporation in New York. The Premier brand reappears on some Asian-made solidbody guitars and basses beginning in the '90s.

Bantam Custom
1950s-1960s. Model below Special, single-cut archtop, dot markers, early models with white potted pickups, then metal-covered pickups, and finally Japanese-made pickups (least valued).

1950-1960s		$600	$750

MODEL YEAR	FEATURES	EXC. COND. LOW	HIGH

Bantam Deluxe
1950s-1960s. Single-cut archtop, fully bound, sparkle knobs, early models with white potted pickups, then metal-covered pickups, and finally Japanese-made pickups (least valued), block markers, single or double pickups (deduct $100 for single pickup instrument).

1950-1960s	Blond	$1,300	$1,500
1950-1960s	Sunburst	$1,200	$1,400

Bantam Special
1950s-1960s. Model below Deluxe, single-cut archtop, dot markers, early models with white potted pickups, then metal-covered pickups, and finally Japanese-made pickups (least valued), single or double pickup models offered (deduct $100 for single pickup instrument).

1950-1960s		$750	$800

Custom Solidbody
1958-1970. Notable solidbody bass scroll cutaway, various models with various components used, finally import components only.

1958-1970	1 pickup	$400	$500
1958-1970	2 pickups	$500	$600
1958-1970	3 pickups	$650	$750

Deluxe Archtop
1950s-1960s. Full body 17 1/4" archtop, square block markers, single-cut, early models with white potted pickups, later '60s models with metal pickups.

1950-1960s	Blond	$1,200	$1,600
1950-1960s	Sunburst	$1,200	$1,400

Semi-Pro 16" Archtop
1950s-early-1960s. Thinline electric 16" archtop with 2 1/4" deep body, acoustic or electric.

1950-1960s	Acoustic	$700	$750
1950-1960s	Electric	$800	$850

Semi-Pro Bantam Series
1960s. Thinline electric archtop with 2 3/4" deep body, offered in cutaway and non-cut models.

1960s		$300	$400

Special Archtop
1950s-1960s. Full body 17 1/4" archtop, less fancy than Deluxe, single-cut, early models with white potted pickups, '60s models with metal pickups.

1950-1960s		$850	$950

Studio Six Archtop
1950s-early-1960s. 16" wide archtop, single pickup, early pickups white potted, changed later to metal top.

1950-1960s		$550	$600

Prestige

Intermediate, professional, and premium grade, production/custom, acoustic, solidbody and hollowbody guitars from Vancouver, British Columbia. They also offer basses.

Queen Shoals Stringed Instruments

1972-present. Luthier Larry Cadle builds his production/custom, flat-top, 12-string, and nylon-string guitars in Clendenin, West Virginia.

MODEL YEAR	FEATURES	EXC. COND. LOW	HIGH

Queguiner, Alain

1982-present. Custom flat-tops, 12 strings, and nylon strings built by luthier Alain Queguiner in Paris, France.

R.C. Allen

1951-present. Luthier R. C. "Dick" Allen builds professional and premium grade, custom hollowbody and semi-hollowbody guitars in El Monte, California. He has also built solidbody guitars.

Rahan

1999-present. Professional grade, production/custom, solidbody guitars built by luthiers Mike Curd and Rick Cantu in Houston, Texas.

Rahbek Guitars

2000-present. Professional and premium grade, production/custom, solidbody electrics built by luthier Peter Rahbek in Copenhagen, Denmark.

Raimundo

1970s-present. Intermediate, professional and premium grade flamenco and classical guitars made in Valencia, Spain, by luthiers Antonio Aparicio and Manual Raimundo.

RainSong

1991-present. Professional grade, production, all-graphite and graphite and wood acoustic guitars built in Woodinville, Washington. The guitars were developed after years of research by luthier engineer John Decker with help from luthier Lorenzo Pimentel, engineer Chris Halford, and sailboard builder George Clayton. The company was started in Maui, but has since moved to Woodinville.

Ramirez

1882-present. Founded by José Ramírez, the company is now in its fourth generation of family ownership in Madrid, Spain.

1A
Classical.

1960s		$4,000	$5,500
1970s		$4,000	$5,500
1990s		$4,500	$5,500

De Camera
1980s. Classical, cedar top, Brazilian rosewood back and sides.

1980s		$4,500	$5,500

Flamenco
European spruce top, cyprus back and sides.

1920s		$4,500	$6,000
1960-1969		$4,000	$5,500
1970-1979		$4,000	$5,500

R4 Classical
1995-2000s. All solid wood, Western red cedar top, rosewood back and sides.

1995-2002		$1,500	$2,000

Randy Reynolds Guitars

1996-present. Luthier Randy Reynolds builds his premium grade, production/custom classical and flamenco guitars in Colorado Springs, Colorado.

Randy Wood Guitars

1968-present. Premium grade, custom/production, archtop, flat-top, and resonator guitars built by luthier Randy Woods in Bloomingdale, Georgia. He also builds mandolins and banjos.

Rarebird Guitars

1978-present. Luthier Bruce Clay builds his professional and premium grade, production/custom, acoustic, electric solidbody and hollowbody guitars and mini guitars, originally in Arvada, Colorado, but since '05 in Santa Fe, New Mexico. He also builds basses.

Rat Fink

2002-present. Lace Music Products, the makers of the Lace Sensor pickup, offered the intermediate grade, production, guitars and basses, featuring the artwork of Ed "Big Daddy" Roth until '05. They continue to offer amps.

Recording King

1936-1941. Brand name used by Montgomery Ward for instruments made by various American manufacturers, including Kay, Gibson and Gretsch. Generally mid-grade instruments. M Series are Gibson-made archtops.

Carson Robison/Model K
1936-1939. Flat-top, 14 3/4", mahogany back and sides, renamed Model K in early-'38.

1936-1939		$1,200	$1,400

Kay 17" flat top.
1940-1941. Large jumbo, 17" lower bout, pearloid veneer peghead, large Recording King logo.

1940-1941		$800	$1,100

M-2
1936-1941. Gibson-made archtop with carved top and F-holes, maple back and sides.

1936-1941		$800	$1,100

M-3
1936-1941. Gibson-made archtop, F-holes, maple back and sides, carved top.

1936-1941		$1,000	$1,500

M-4
1936-1941. Gibson-made archtop, f-holes, maple back and sides, rope-checkered binding, flying bat wing markers.

1936-1941		$1,300	$1,800

M-5
1936-1941. Gibson-made archtop with F-holes, maple back and sides, trapeze tailpiece, checkered top binding.

1936-1938	16" body	$1,300	$1,800
1939-1941	17" body	$1,400	$1,900

Rainsong WS1000

Rat Fink RF3

Recording King (TML) Cowboy

Renaissance Model T

M-6
1938-1939. M-5 with upgraded gold hardware.

MODEL YEAR	FEATURES	EXC. COND. LOW	HIGH
1938-1939		$1,500	$2,000

Ray Whitley
1939-1940. High-quality model made by Gibson, round shoulder flat-top, mahogany or Brazilian rosewood back and sides, 5-piece maple neck, Ray Whitley stencil script peghead logo, pearl crown inlay on peghead, fancy inlaid markers.

1939-1940		$16,000	$21,000

Recording King (TML)
2005-present. Budget grade, production, acoustic cowboy stenciled guitars designed by Greg Rich for The Music Link, which also offers Johnson and other brand instruments. They also have banjos.

Regal
Ca. 1884-1966, 1987-present. Intermediate and professional grade, production, acoustic and wood and metal body resonator guitars. They also build basses.

Originally a mass manufacturer founded in Indianapolis, Indiana, the Regal brand was first used by Emil Wulschner & Son. In 1901 new owners changed the company name to The Regal Manufacturing Company. The company was moved to Chicago in '08 and renamed the Regal Musical Instrument Company. Regal made brands for distributors and mass merchandisers as well as marketing its own Regal brand. Regal purchased the Lyon & Healy factory in '28. Regal was licensed to co-manufacture Dobros in '32 and became the sole manufacturer of them in '37 (see Dobro for those instruments). Most Regal instruments were beginner-grade; however, some very fancy archtops were made during the '30s. The company was purchased by Harmony in '54 and absorbed. From '59 to '66, Harmony made acoustics under the Regal name for Fender. In '87 the Regal name was revived on a line of resonator instruments by Saga.

Concert Folk H6382
1960s. Regal by Harmony, solid spruce top, mahogany back and sides, dot markers, natural.

1960s		$250	$350

Deluxe Dreadnought H6600
1960s. Regal by Harmony, solid spruce top, mahogany back and sides, bound top and back, rosewood 'board, dot markers, natural.

1960s		$250	$375

Dreadnought 12-String H1269
1960s. Regal by Harmony, solid spruce top, 12-string version of Deluxe, natural.

1960s		$250	$350

Esquire
1940s. 15 1/2" acoustic archtop, higher-end appointments, fancy logo art and script pearl Esquire headstock logo and Regal logo.

1940s	Natural	$1,300	$1,400

Marveltone
1930s. 00-size fancy flat-top, rosewood sides and back, slotted headstock.

1930s		$2,900	$3,100

Model 27
1933-1942. Birch wood body, mahogany or maple, 2-tone walnut finish, single-bound top, round or square neck.

MODEL YEAR	FEATURES	EXC. COND. LOW	HIGH
1933-1942		$1,000	$1,500

Model 45
1933-1937. Spruce top and mahogany back and sides, bound body, square neck.

1933-1937		$1,500	$1,800

Model 55 Standard
1933-1934. Regal's version of Dobro Model 55 which was discontinued in '33.

1933-1934		$1,200	$1,500

Model 75
1939-1940. Metal body, square neck.

1939-1940		$2,000	$3,000

Model TG 60 Resonator Tenor Guitar
1930s. Wood body, large single cone biscuit bridge resonator, 2 upper bout metal ports, 4-string tenor.

1930s		$1,400	$1,600

Parlor (small body) Guitar
1920s. Slotted headstock, birch sides and back, spruce top.

1920s		$250	$300

RD-45
1994-present. Standard style Dobro model with wood body, metal resonator, dual screen holes.

1994-2005		$225	$275

Spirit Of '76
1976. Red-white-blue, flat-top.

1976		$350	$400

Reliance
1920s. Instruments built by the Oscar Schmidt Co. and possibly others. Most likely a brand made for a distributor.

Renaissance
1978-1980. Plexiglass solidbody electric guitars and basses. Founded in Malvern, Pennsylvania, by John Marshall (designer), Phil Goldberg and Daniel Lamb. Original partners gradually leave and John Dragonetti takes over by late-'79. The line is redesigned with passive electronics on guitars, exotic shapes, but when deal with Sunn amplifiers falls through, company closes. Brandname currently used on a line of guitars and basses made by Rick Turner in Santa Cruz, California.

Fewer than 300 of first series made, plus a few prototypes and several wooden versions; six or so prototypes of second series made. SN=M(M)YYXXXX: month, year, consecutive number.

Electric Plexiglas Solidbody
1978-1980. Models include the SPG ('78-'79, DiMarzio pickups, active electronics), T-200G ('80, Bich-style with 2 passive DiMarzio pickups), and the S-200G ('80, double-cut, 2 DiMarzio pickups, passive electronics).

1978-1980		$600	$800

MODEL YEAR	FEATURES	EXC. COND. LOW	HIGH

Renaissance Guitars

1994-present. Professional grade, custom, semi-acoustic flat-top, nylon-string and solidbody guitars built by luthier Rick Turner in Santa Cruz, California. He also builds basses.

Model 1/Model One Lindsey Buckingham

1996-present. Originally built for Buckingham in '79, with 1 humbucker or will added piezo, soft cutaway old-style body.

1996-2005		$2,500	$3,200

Model T

1996-present. Mahogany, fade-away single-cut, Kay Kraft-style body, bolt-on neck, horseshoe pickup.

1996-2005		$800	$1,000

RS-6

1997-present. Acoustic/electric, solid cedar top, semi-hollow rosewood body, no soundhole, bolt maple neck.

1997-2005	Natural	$1,100	$1,300

Reuter Guitars

1984-present. Professional and premium grade, custom, flat-top, 12-string, resonator, and Hawaiian guitars built by luthier John Reuter, the Director of Training at the Roberto-Venn School of Luthiery, in Tempe, Arizona.

Reverend

1996-present. Intermediate grade, production, guitars built in Warren, Michigan, by luthier Joe Naylor, who also founded Naylor Amps. They also built basses, amps and effects in the past.

Semi-Hollow Electric

1997-present. Offset double-cut semi-hollowbody, bolt maple neck, various pickup options. Models include Avenger, Commando, Hitman, Rocco, Slingshot and Spy. By '04 the Workhorse Series included the Avenger TL, Commando, and Slingshot Custom, which were all factory-direct instruments.

1997-2003	Various models and options	$550	$750
2004-2005	Workhorse Series	$400	$500

Rex

1930s-1940s, 1960s. Generally beginner-grade guitars made by Harmony and Kay and sold through Fred Gretsch distributors. In the '60s, there were Italian-made electrics bearing the Rex brand. They also had amps.

Acoustic Flat-Top

1940s. Various models.

1940s		$275	$350

Ribbecke Guitars

1972-present. Premium and presentation grade, custom thinline, flat-top, and archtop guitars built by luthier Tom Ribbecke in Healdsburg, California.

Rich and Taylor

1993-1996. Custom acoustic and electric guitars and banjos from luthiers Greg Rich and Mark Taylor (Crafters of Tennessee).

Richard Schneider

1960s-1997. Luthier Richard Schneider built his acoustic guitars in Washington state. Over the years, he collaborated with Dr. Michael A. Kasha on many guitar designs and innovations. Originally from Michigan, he also was involved in designing guitars for Gretsch and Gibson. He died in early '97.

Richter Mfg.

1930s. One of many Chicago makers of the era.

Small 13"

1930s. Typical small 13" lower bout body, slotted headstock, decalmania art over black finish, single dot markers.

1930s		$375	$450

Rick Turner

1979-1981, 1990-present. Rick Turner has a long career as a luthier, electronics designer and innovator. He also makes the Renaissance line of guitars in his shop in Santa Cruz, California.

Rickenbacker

1931-present. Professional and premium grade, production/custom, acoustic and electric guitars built in California. They also build basses. Founded in Los Angeles as Ro-Pat-In by ex-National executives George Beauchamp, Paul Barth and National's resonator cone supplier Adolph Rickenbacher. Rickenbacher was born in Basel, Switzerland in 1886, emigrated to the U.S. and moved to Los Angeles in 1918, opening a tool and die business in '20.

In the mid-'20s, Rickenbacher began providing resonator cones and other metal parts to George Beauchamp and Louis Dopyera of National String Instrument Corporation and became a shareholder in National. Beauchamp, Barth and Harry Watson came up with wooden "frying pan" electric Hawaiian lap steel for National in '31; National was not interested, so Beauchamp and Barth joined with Rickenbacher as Ro-Pat-In (probably for ElectRO-PATent-INstruments) to produce Electro guitars. Cast aluminum frying pans were introduced in '32. Some Spanish guitars (flat-top, F-holes) with Electro pickups were produced beginning in '32.

Ro-Pat-In changes their name to Electro String Instrument Corporation in '34, and brand becomes Rickenbacher Electro, soon changed to Rickenbacker, with a "k." Beauchamp retires in '40. There was a production hiatus during World War II. In '53, Electro was purchased by Francis Cary Hall (born 1908), owner of Radio and Television Equipment Company (Radio-Tel) in Santa Ana, California (founded in '20s as Hall's Radio Service, which

Reverend Warhawk 290

Rick Turner Model One

Rickenbacker 325

Rickenbacker 330

began distributing Fender instruments in '46). The factory was relocated to Santa Ana in '62 and the sales/distribution company's name is changed from Radio-Tel to Rickenbacker Inc. in '65.

1950s serial numbers have from 4 to 7 letters and numbers, with the number following the letter indicating the '50s year (e.g., NNL8NN would be from '58). From '61 to '86 serial numbers indicate month and year of production with initial letter A-Z for the year A=1961, Z=1986) followed by letter for the month A-M (A=January) plus numbers as before followed by a number 0-9 for the year (0=1987; 9=1996). To avoid confusion, we have listed all instruments by model number. For example, the Combo 400 is listed as Model 400/Combo 400.

Electro ES-16
1964-1971. Double-cut, set neck, solidbody, 3/4 size, 1 pickup. The Electro line was manufactured by Rickenbacker and distributed by Radio-Tel. The Electro logo appears on the headstock.

MODEL YEAR	FEATURES	EXC. COND. LOW	HIGH
1964-1971		$800	$1,000

Electro ES-17
1964-1975. Cutaway, set neck, solidbody, 1 pickup.

1964-1969		$800	$1,300
1970-1975		$700	$1,000

Electro Spanish (Model B Spanish)
1935-1943. Small guitar with a lap steel appearance played Spanish-style, hollow bakelite body augmented with 5 chrome plates, called the Model B ca. '40.

1935-1936		$3,000	$4,500
1938-1939		$2,900	$4,200
1940-1943		$2,800	$4,000

Model 220 Hamburg
1992-1997. Solidbody.

1992-1997		$675	$800

Model 230 GF
1992.

1992		$1,200	$1,800

Model 230 Hamburg
1983-1991. Solidbody, offset double-cut, 2 pickups, dot inlay, rosewood 'board, chrome-plated hardware.

1983-1991		$650	$725

Model 250 El Dorado
1983. Deluxe version of Hamburg, gold hardware, white binding.

1983-1992		$500	$600

Model 260 El Dorado
1992-1997.

1992-1997		$600	$700

Model 270
1964-1970.

1964-1970		$1,700	$3,000

Model 310
1958-1970, 1981-1985. Two-pickup version of Model 320.

1960-1971		$2,500	$7,500
1981-1985		$900	$1,500

Model 315
1958-1974. Two-pickup version of Model 325.

MODEL YEAR	FEATURES	EXC. COND. LOW	HIGH
1960-1974		$2,500	$7,500

Model 320
1958-1992. Short-scale hollowbody, 3 pickups, f-holes optional in '61 and standard in '64 and optional again in '79.

1960-1971		$4,000	$10,500
1981-1995		$900	$1,500

Model 325
1958-1975, 1985-1992. This was a low production model, with some years having no production. In the mid-'60s, the 325 was unofficially known as the John Lennon Model due to his guitar's high exposure on the Ed Sullivan Show and in the Saturday Evening Post.

1958-1960	John Lennon specs	$15,000	$35,000
1959-1960		$12,000	$24,000
1961-1963		$12,000	$24,000
1964-1965	Fireglo or black	$10,000	$12,000
1966	Fireglo or black	$8,500	$10,500
1966	Mapleglo	$8,500	$10,500
1967-1968		$8,250	$10,000
1970-1979		$1,500	$2,000
1981-1995		$1,000	$1,500

Model 325 JL
1989-1993. John Lennon Limited Edition, 3 vintage Ric pickups, vintage vibrato, maple body; 3/4-size rosewood neck, a 12-string and a full-scale version are also available.

1989-1993		$2,000	$2,800

Model 325/12V63
1985-1986		$1,700	$2,200
1999		$1,600	$2,100

Model 325C58
2002-present. Copy of the '58 model that John Lennon saw in Germany.

2002-2004		$1,350	$2,100
2005-2006	Hamburg	$1,750	$2,100

Model 325C64
2002-present. Copy of the famous '64 model.

2002-2005		$2,000	$2,200

Model 325V59
1984-2001. Reissue of John Lennon's modified '59 325, 3 pickups, short-scale.

1984-2001		$1,500	$2,000

Model 325V63
1984-2001. Reissue of John Lennon's '63 325.

1987-2001		$1,400	$2,100

Model 330
1958-present. Thinline hollowbody, 2 pickups, slash soundhole, natural or sunburst.

1958-1960	Capri	$4,000	$8,500
1961-1965	330-style body	$2,700	$4,500
1965-1970	330-style body	$2,500	$3,500
1971-1979		$1,200	$1,400
1990-1989		$1,100	$1,300
1990-1999		$1,100	$1,200
2000-2005		$900	$1,000

MODEL YEAR	FEATURES	EXC. COND. LOW	HIGH

Model 330 F
1958-1969. F-style.

1958-1961	Thick version	$4,000	$8,500
1961-1964	Thin version	$3,500	$4,500
1965-1969	Thin version	$2,500	$3,500

Model 330/12
1965-present. Thinline, 2 pickups, 12-string version of Model 300.

1964		$3,200	$4,500
1965-1970	330-style body	$3,000	$3,500
1971-1979		$1,000	$1,400
1980-1989		$1,000	$1,300
1990-1999		$1,000	$1,200
2000-2005		$950	$1,050

Model 330S/12
1964 (1 made)-1965 (2 made).

1964-1965		$3,500	$4,000

Model 331 Light Show
1970-1975. Model 330 with translucent top with lights in body that lit up when played, needed external transformer. The first offering's design, noted as Type 1, had heat problems and a fully original one is difficult to find. The 2nd offering's design, noted as Type 2, was a more stable design and is more highly valued in the market.

1970-1971	Type 1 1st edition	$10,000	$19,000
1972-1975	Type 2 2nd edition	$15,000	$23,000

Model 335
1961-1970. Thinline, 330-style body, 2 pickups, vibrato, Fireglo. Called the 330VB from '85-'97.

1961-1970		$2,500	$4,500

Model 335 Capri
1958-1960. Thinline, 2 pickups, vibrato. The Capri Model name is technically reserved for the '58 to mid-'60s vintage, these models had a 2" depth. Ca. mid-'60 the body depth was reduced to 1 1/2", Autumnglo, Fireglo or Mapleglo. Rickenbacker dropped the Capri name in '60.

1958-1960		$4,000	$8,500

Model 335 F
1958-1969. F-style.

1958-1961	Thick version	$4,000	$8,500
1961-1964	Thin version	$4,000	$5,000
1965-1969	Thin version	$2,500	$4,500

Model 336/12
1966-1974. Like 300-12, but with 6-12 converter comb, 330-style body.

1966-1974		$2,500	$4,500

Model 340
1958-present. Thin semi-hollowbody, thru-body maple neck, 2 single-coil pickups, sharp point horns, very limited production '58-'65, with first notable volume of 45 units starting in '66.

1958-1960	Capri	$4,000	$8,500
1961-1965	330-style body	$3,500	$4,500
1966-1970	330-style body	$2,500	$3,500
2000-2005		$650	$800

Model 340 F
1958-1969. F-style.

1958-1961	Thick version	$4,000	$8,500

Model 340/12
1965-1990s. 330-style body.

1965-1970		$2,500	$4,500
1971-1980		$900	$1,400

Model 345
1961-1974. Thinline 330-345 series, version with 3 pickups and vibrato tailpiece, in the mid-'60s Jetglo Black was a very unusual color, caution advised.

1961-1965	330-style body	$3,500	$4,500
1965-1969	330-style body	$2,500	$3,500
1970-1974	2 humbuckers, slant frets	$1,000	$1,100

Model 345 Capri
1958-1960. Thinline 330-345 series, version with 3 pickups and vibrato tailpiece. The Capri Model name is technically reserved for the '58 to mid-'60s vintage, these models had a 2" depth. Body depth was reduced to 1 1/2" ca. mid-'60 and Capri name was dropped.

1958-1960		$4,000	$8,500

Model 345 F
1958-1969. F-style.

1958-1961	Thick version	$4,000	$8,500

Model 350 Liverpool
1983-1997. Thinline, 3 pickups, vibrato, no soundhole.

1983-1989		$1,000	$1,300
1990-1997		$1,000	$1,250

Model 350 SH
1988-1990. Susanna Hoffs limited edition.

1988-1990		$2,000	$4,000

Model 350V63 Liverpool
1994-present. Like 355 JL, but without signature.

1994-2005		$1,200	$1,350

Model 350/12V63 Liverpool
1994-present. 12-string 350V63.

1994-2005		$1,100	$1,450

Model 355 JL
1989-1993. John Lennon model, signature and drawing on 'guard.

1989-1993		$2,200	$3,200

Model 355/12 JL
1989-1993. 12-string 355 JL, limited production.

1989-1993		$1,700	$2,500

Model 360/360 VB
1958-present. Deluxe thinline, 2 pickups, slash soundhole, bound body until '64.

1958-1960	Capri	$4,000	$8,500
1961-1964	360-style body, OS	$3,200	$4,500
1964-1970	NS, more common	$2,000	$3,100
1971-1973		$1,500	$3,100
1974-1977		$1,300	$1,900
1978-1979		$1,200	$1,700
1980-1983		$1,000	$1,400
1984-1989	360 VB with vibrato	$1,100	$1,300
1990-1994		$1,000	$1,200
1995-1999		$950	$1,150
1995-1999	Rare colors	$1,150	$2,000
2000-2005		$950	$1,100

Rickenbacker 331 Light Show

Rickenbacker 360

1967 Rickenbacker 365

Rickenbacker 366/12 Convertible

MODEL YEAR	FEATURES	EXC. COND. LOW	HIGH
Model 360/12			
1964-present. Deluxe thinline, 2 pickups, 12-string version of Model 360, Rick-O-Sound stereo.			
1964	NS (introduced)	$4,500	$11,000
1964	OS, less common	$10,000	$25,000
1965	NS, more common	$4,000	$8,000
1965	OS, less common	$10,000	$25,000
1965-1966	Harrison exact specs, OS	$19,000	$25,000
1966-1969	NS, more common	$3,500	$5,500
1966-1969	OS, less common	$4,000	$7,500
1970-1979		$2,500	$3,000
1980-1999		$1,300	$2,000
2000-2005		$1,000	$1,300
Model 360 F			
1959-1972. F-style.			
1959-1961	Thick version	$4,000	$8,500
1961-1964	Thin version	$3,500	$4,500
Model 360 CW			
2000. Carl Wilson Limited Edition, 6-string, includes certificate, 500 made.			
2000		$2,200	$2,600
Model 360/12 CW			
2000. 12-string version of 360 CW.			
2000		$2,200	$2,600
Model 360 Tuxedo			
1987 only. Tuxedo option included white body, white painted fretboard, and black hardware.			
1987		$1,200	$1,800
Model 360/12 Tuxedo			
1987 only. 12-string version of 360 Tuxedo.			
1987		$1,400	$2,000
Model 360 WB			
1984-1998. Double bound body, 2 pickups, vibrato optional (VB).			
1984-1990		$1,400	$1,800
1991-1998	Non-vibrato WB	$1,100	$1,300
1991-1998	Vibrato option WBVB	$1,100	$1,300
Model 360/12 WB			
1984-1998. 12-string version of 360 WB.			
1984-1998		$1,500	$3,000
Model 360/12C63			
2004-present. More exact replica of the Harrison model.			
2004-2005		$2,300	$2,600
Model 360V64			
1991-2003. Reissue of '64 Model 360 old style body without vibrola, has binding with full length inlays.			
1991-1999		$1,800	$2,200
2000-2003		$1,800	$2,200
Model 360/12V64			
1985-2003. Deluxe thinline with '64 features, 2 pickups, 12 strings, slanted plate tailpiece.			
1985-2003	Black and less common colors	$2,200	$2,500
1985-2003	Common colors	$2,000	$2,300
Model 362/12			
1975-1992. Doubleneck 6 & 12, 360 features.			
1975-1992		$3,700	$5,500

MODEL YEAR	FEATURES	EXC. COND. LOW	HIGH
Model 365			
1958-1974. Deluxe thinline, 2 pickups, vibrato, called Model 360 WBVB from '84-'98.			
1958-1960	Capri	$4,000	$8,500
1961-1963		$3,000	$4,500
1965-1969	NS, more common	$3,000	$3,500
1965-1969	OS, less common	$3,000	$5,500
1970-1974		$2,200	$3,000
Model 365 F			
1959-1972. Thin full-body (F designation), 2 pickups, Deluxe features.			
1959-1961	Thicker body	$4,000	$8,500
1961-1964	Thinner body	$4,500	$8,500
Model 366/12 Convertible			
1966-1974. Two pickups, 12 strings, comb-like device that converts it to a 6-string, production only noted in '68, perhaps available on custom order basis.			
1966-1968	OS	$4,000	$4,500
Model 370			
1958-1990, 1994-present. Deluxe thinline, 3 pickups. Could be considered to be a dealer special order item from '58-'67 with limited production ('58=0, '59=4, '60=0, '61=3, '62-'67=0, then started more regularly in '68).			
1958-1960	Capri	$4,000	$8,500
1961-1966		$3,500	$4,500
1968-1969		$3,000	$3,500
1970-1979		$2,200	$3,000
1980-2005		$1,000	$1,400
Model 370 F			
1959-1972. F-style, 3 pickups, Deluxe features.			
1959-1961	Thicker body	$3,300	$8,500
1961-1964	Thinner body	$3,300	$8,500
Model 370 WB			
1984-1998. Double bound body, 3 pickups, vibrato optional (VB).			
1984-1989		$1,600	$2,000
1990-1998		$1,300	$1,500
Model 370/12			
1965-1990, 1994-present. Not regular production until '80, deluxe thinline, 3 pickups, 12 strings. Could be considered to be a dealer special order item in the '60s and '70s with limited production.			
1966	Special order	$4,000	$5,000
1980-1990		$2,100	$2,500
1994-2005		$1,000	$1,400
Model 370/12 RM			
1988. Limited Edition Roger McGuinn model, 1000 made, higher-quality appointments.			
1988		$3,500	$4,400
Model 375			
1958-1974. Deluxe thinline, 3 pickups, vibrato, called Model 370 WBVB from '84-'98.			
1958-1960	Capri	$4,000	$8,500
1961-1964		$3,500	$4,500
1965-1969		$3,000	$3,500
1970-1974		$2,200	$3,000
Model 375 F			
1959-1972. F-style, 2 pickups.			
1959-1961	Thicker body	$4,000	$8,500

MODEL YEAR	FEATURES	EXC. COND. LOW	HIGH

Model 380 L Laguna
1996-2005. Semi-hollow, oil-finished walnut body, Maple neck and 'board, 2 humbuckers, PZ saddle pickups optional.

1996-2005		$900	$1,600
1996-2005	PZ option	$1,300	$1,700

Model 381
1958-1963, 1969-1974. Double-cut archtop, 2 pickups, slash soundhole, solid 'guard, reintroduced in '69 with double split-level 'guard.

1958-1963	Light sporadic production	$4,000	$8,500
1969-1974	Various colors, some rare	$3,500	$6,500

Model 381 JK
1988-1997. John Kay model, 2 humbucking pickups, active electronics, stereo and mono outputs.

1988-1997		$2,700	$4,000

Model 381V68
1987-1990. Renamed V69 in '91.

1987-1990		$1,750	$1,900

Model 381V69
1991-present. Reissue of vintage 381, originally called 381V68.

1987-2005		$1,850	$1,950

Model 381/12V69
1987-present. Reissue of 381/12, deep double-cut body, sound body cavity, catseye soundhole, triangle inlays, bridge with 12 individual saddles. Finishes include Fireglo, Mapleglo and Jetglo.

1987-2005		$1,750	$2,000

Model 400/Combo 400
1956-1958. Double-cut tulip body, neck-thru, 1 pickup, gold anodized 'guard, 21 frets, replaced by Model 425 in '58. Available in black (216 made), blue turquoise (53), Cloverfield Green (53), Montezuma Brown (41), and 4 in other custom colors.

1956-1958	Black	$3,000	$3,500
1956-1958	Other colors	$3,500	$4,500

Model 420
1965-1983. Non-vibrato version of Model 425, single pickup.

1965-1968		$1,000	$1,400
1969-1983		$900	$1,100

Model 425/Combo 425
1958-1973. Double-cut solidbody, 1 pickup, sunburst.

1958-1959	425 Cresting Wave	$2,000	$2,500
1960		$1,400	$1,600
1961-1966		$1,300	$1,500
1968		$1,100	$1,300
1969-1973		$1,000	$1,200

Model 430
1971-1982. Style 200 body, natural.

1971-1982		$675	$800

Model 450/Combo 450
1957-1984. Replaces Combo 450, 2 pickups (3 optional '62-'77), tulip body shape '57-'59, cresting wave body shape after.

1957-1958	450 Tulip body (Combo)	$3,500	$4,500

1960	Cresting Wave, flat body	$3,400	$3,700
1961	Cresting Wave, super slim	$3,300	$3,500
1962		$2,000	$3,000
1963		$1,800	$2,500
1964		$1,700	$2,300
1965		$1,600	$2,100
1966		$1,600	$2,100
1970-1979		$1,100	$1,400
1980-1984		$900	$1,200

Model 450/12
1964-1985. Double-cut solidbody, 12-string version of Model 450, 2 pickups.

1964		$1,700	$2,300
1965		$1,600	$2,100
1966		$1,500	$2,000
1967-1969		$1,400	$1,900
1970-1979		$900	$1,400
1980-1985		$900	$1,400

Model 450V63
1999-2001. Reissue of '63 450.

1999-2001		$1,200	$1,500

Model 456/12 Convertible
1968-1978. Double-cut solidbody, 2 pickups, comb-like device to convert it to 6-string.

1968-1969		$1,600	$2,000
1970-1978		$1,400	$1,600

Model 460
1961-1985. Double-cut solidbody, 2 pickups, neck-thru-body, deluxe trim.

1961-1965		$2,000	$2,800
1966-1969		$1,400	$2,000
1970-1979		$1,000	$1,800
1980-1985		$1,000	$1,800

Model 480
1973-1984. Double-cut solidbody with long thin bass horn in 4001 bass series style, 2 pickups, cresting wave body and headstock, bolt-on neck.

1973-1979		$925	$1,150
1980-1983		$925	$1,150

Model 481
1973-1983. Cresting wave body with longer bass horn, 2 humbuckers (3 optional).

1973-1983		$1,125	$1,575

Model 483
1973-1979. Cresting wave body with longer bass horn, 3 humbuckers.

1973-1979		$975	$1,200

Model 600/Combo 600
1954-1966. Modified double-cut.

1954-1957	Blond/white	$2,500	$4,500
1956-1958	OT/Blue Turquoise	$2,500	$4,500
1966		$1,300	$1,500

Model 610
1985-1991. Cresting-wave cutaway solidbody, 2 pickups, trapeze R-tailpiece, Jetglo.

1985-1991		$675	$775

Model 610/12
1988-1997. 12-string version of Model 610.

1988-1997		$725	$850

Rickenbacker Combo 400

Rickenbacker 610

Rickenbacker Model 625

Rickenbacker 660 TP

MODEL YEAR	FEATURES	EXC. COND. LOW	HIGH
Model 615			
1962-1966, 1969-1977. Double-cut solidbody, 2 pickups, vibrato.			
1962-1965		$1,900	$2,400
1966-1969		$1,800	$2,300
1970-1977		$1,300	$1,800
Model 620			
1974-present. Double-cut solidbody, deluxe binding, 2 pickups, neck-thru-body.			
1974-1979		$1,100	$1,300
1980-1989		$1,100	$1,250
1990-1999		$1,000	$1,200
2000-2005		$1,000	$1,200
Model 620/12			
1981-present. Double-cut solidbody, 2 pickups, 12 strings, standard trim.			
1981-1989		$1,100	$1,300
1990-1999		$1,000	$1,200
2000-2005		$1,000	$1,200
Model 625			
1962-1977. Double-cut solidbody, deluxe trim, 2 pickups, vibrato.			
1962-1965		$3,500	$4,500
1966-1969		$2,500	$3,000
1970-1977		$2,000	$2,500
Model 650/Combo 650			
1957-1959. Standard color, 1 pickup.			
1957-1959		$2,500	$4,500
Model 650 A Atlantis			
1991-2004. Cresting wave solidbody, neck-thru, 2 pickups, chrome hardware, turquoise.			
1991-2004		$800	$925
Model 650 C Colorado			
1993-present. Maple neck and body, neck-thru, 2 pickups.			
1993-2005		$800	$925
Model 650 D Dakota			
1993-present. Tulip-shaped neck-thru solidbody, single pickup, chrome hardware, walnut oil-satin finish.			
1993-2005		$800	$925
Model 650 E Excalibur/F Frisco			
1991-2003. African Vermilion, gold hardware, gloss finish. Name changed to Frisco in '95.			
1991-2003		$800	$925
Model 650 S Sierra			
1993-present. Tulip-shaped neck-thru solidbody, single pickup, gold hardware, walnut oil-satin finish.			
1993-2005		$800	$925
Model 660			
1998-present. Cresting wave maple body, triangle inlays, 2 pickups.			
1998-2005		$1,100	$1,300
Model 660/12			
1998-present. 12-string 660.			
1990-2000s		$1,600	$1,800
Model 660/12 TP			
1991-1998. Tom Petty model, 12 strings, cresting wave body, 2 pickups, deluxe trim, limited run of 1000.			
1991-1998		$2,400	$3,100

MODEL YEAR	FEATURES	EXC. COND. LOW	HIGH
Model 800/Combo 800			
1954-1966. Offset double-cut, 1 horseshoe pickup until late-'57, second bar type after, called the Model 800 in the '60s.			
1954-1959	Blond/white	$2,500	$4,500
1954-1959	Blue or green	$2,500	$4,500
1966		$2,500	$4,500
Model 850/Combo 850			
1957-1959. Extreme double-cut, 1 pickup until '58, 2 after, various colors, called Model 850 in the '60s.			
1957-1959		$2,500	$4,500
Model 900			
1957-1980. Double-cut tulip body shape, 3/4 size, 1 pickup. Body changes to cresting wave shape in '69.			
1957-1960		$1,500	$2,000
1961-1968		$1,500	$2,000
Model 950/Combo 950			
1957-1980. Like Model 900, but with 2 pickups, 21 frets. Body changes to cresting wave shape in '69.			
1957-1960		$1,700	$2,100
1961-1964		$1,700	$2,100
1965-1980		$1,600	$2,000
Model 1000			
1957-1970. Like Model 900, but with 18 frets. Body does not change to cresting wave shape.			
1956-1960		$1,500	$1,800
1961-1966		$1,500	$1,800
1967-1970		$1,400	$1,700
Model 1993/12 RM			
1964-1967. Export 'slim-line' 12-string model made for English distributor Rose-Morris of London, built along the lines of the U.S. Model 360/12 but with small differences that are considered important in the vintage guitar market.			
1964	Flat tailpiece	$10,000	$25,000
1965-1967	R tailpiece	$4,500	$11,000
Model 1996 RM			
1964-1967. Rose-Morris import, 3/4 size built similiarly to the U.S. Model 325.			
1964-1967	Black	$10,000	$12,000
1964-1967	FG and MG	$4,500	$11,000
Model 1997 PT			
1987-1988. Pete Townsend Signature Model, semi-hollowbody, single f-hole, maple neck, 21-fret rosewood 'board, 3 pickups, Firemist finish, limited to 250 total production.			
1987-1988		$3,700	$4,400
Model 1997 RM			
1964-1967. Export 'slim-line' model made for English distributor Rose-Morris of London, built along the lines of the U.S. Model 335, but with small differences that are considered important in the vintage guitar market, 2 pickups, vibrola tailpiece. Rose-Morris export models sent to the USA generally had a red-lined guitar case vs. the USA domestic blue-lined guitar case.			
1964-1967		$3,700	$5,300
Model 1997 RM Reissue			
1987-2002. Reissue of '60s Rose-Morris model, but with vibrola (VB) or without.			
1987-2002		$950	$1,250

The *Vintage Guitar Price Guide* shows low to high values for items in all-original excellent condition, and, where applicable, with original case or cover.

MODEL YEAR	FEATURES	EXC. COND. LOW	HIGH

Model 1997 SPC
1993-2002. 3 pickup version of reissue.

1993-2002		$1,100	$1,400

Model 1998 RM
1964-1967. Export 'slim-line' model made for English distributor Rose-Morris of London, built along the lines of a U.S. Model 345 but with small differences that are considered important in the vintage guitar market, 3 pickups, vibrola tailpiece.

1964-1967		$4,000	$5,800

RKS
2003-present. Professional and premium grade, production/custom, electric hollowbody and solidbody guitars designed by Ravi Sawhney and guitarist Dave Mason and built in Thousand Oaks, California. They also build basses.

Robert Cefalu
1998-present. Luthier Robert Cefalu builds his professional grade, production/custom, acoustic guitars in Buffalo, New York. The guitars have an RC on the headstock.

Robert Guitars
1981-present. Luthier Mikhail Robert builds his premium grade, production/custom, classical guitars in Summerland, British Columbia.

Robertson Guitars
1995-present. Luthier Jeff Robertson builds his premium grade, production/custom flat-top guitars in South New Berlin, New York.

Robin
1982-present. Professional and premium grade, production/custom, guitars from luthier David Wintz and built in Houston, Texas. Most guitars were Japanese-made until '87; American production began in '88. Most Japanese Robins were pretty consistent in features, but the American ones were often custom-made, so many variations in models exist. They also make Metropolitan (since '96) and Alamo (since '00) brand guitars.

Avalon Classic
1994-present. Single-cut, figured maple top, 2 humbuckers.

1994-2004		$1,000	$1,400

Medley Special
1992-1995. Ash body, maple neck, rosewood 'board, 24 frets, various pickup options.

1992-1995		$450	$600

Medley Standard
1985-present. Offset double-cut swamp ash solidbody, bolt neck, originally with hum-single-single pickups, but now also available with 2 humbuckers.

1985-1987	Japan-made	$400	$500
1988-2005	U.S.-made	$600	$700

Octave
1982-1990s. Tuned an octave above standard tuning, full body size with 15 1/2" short-scale bolt maple neck. Japanese-made production model until '87, U.S.-made custom shop after.

1990s	With original case	$600	$800

Raider I/Raider II/Raider III
1985-1991. Double-cut solidbody, 1 humbucker pickup (Raider I), 2 humbuckers (Raider II), or 3 single-coils (Raider III), maple neck, either maple or rosewood 'board, sunburst.

1985-1991	1 pickup	$400	$450
1985-1991	2 pickups	$450	$500
1985-1991	3 pickups	$475	$525

Ranger Custom
1982-1986, 1988-present. Swamp ash bound body, bolt-on maple neck, rosewood or maple 'board, 2 single coils and 1 humbucker, orange, made in Japan until '86, U.S.-made after.

1982-1986	Japan	$400	$500
1988-2005	U.S.-made	$800	$1,000

RDN-Doubleneck Octave/Six
1982-1985. Six-string standard neck with 3 pickups, 6-string octave neck with 1 pickup, double-cut solidbody.

1982-1985	With original case	$600	$750

Savoy Deluxe/Standard
1995-present. Semi-hollow thinline single cut archtop, 2 pickups, set neck.

1995-2005		$1,200	$1,300

Soloist/Artisan
1982-1986. Mahogany double-cut solidbody, carved bound maple top, set neck, 2 humbuckers. Renamed Artisan in '85. Only about 125 made in Japan.

1982-1986		$450	$600

Wrangler
1995-2002. Classic '50s single-cut slab body, 3 Rio Grande pickups, opaque finish.

1995-2002		$450	$750

Robinson Guitars
2002-present. Premium and presentation grade, custom/production, steel string guitars built by luthier Jake Robinson in Kalamazoo, Michigan.

Rogands
Late 1960s. Produced by France's Jacobacci company and named after brothers Roger and Andre. Short-lived brand; the brothers made instruments under several other brands as well.

Rogue
2001-present. Budget and intermediate grade, production, acoustic, resonator and sitar guitars. They also offer amps, mandolins, banjos, effects, ukes and basses.

Roland
Best known for keyboards, effects, and amps, Roland offered synthesizer-based guitars and basses from 1977 to '86.

RKS solidbody

Robin Ranger Custom

GUITARS

Roman Pearlcaster

Running Dog Concert

MODEL YEAR	FEATURES	EXC. COND. LOW	HIGH

GR-707 Synth Guitar
1983-1986. Slab-wedge asymmetrical body, bass bout to headstock support arm, 2 humbucker pickups, multi-controls.

| 1983-1986 | Silver | $1,200 | $1,300 |

GS-500 Synth Guitar/Module
1977-1986. Snyth functions in a single-cut solidbody guitar. The GS-300 was the same electronics in a classic offset double-cut body.

| 1977-1986 | Sunburst | $800 | $1,100 |

Roman & Lipman Guitars
1989-2000. Production/custom, solidbody guitars made in Danbury, Connecticut by Ed Roman. They also made basses.

Roman Abstract Guitars
1989-present. Professional and premium grade, production/custom, solidbody guitars made in Las Vegas, Nevada by Ed Roman.

Roman Centurion Guitars
2001-present. Premium and presentation grade, custom guitars made in Las Vegas, Nevada by Ed Roman.

Roman Pearlcaster Guitars
1999-present. Professional and premium grade, production/custom, solidbody guitars made in Las Vegas, Nevada by Ed Roman.

Roman Quicksilver Guitars
1997-present. Professional and premium grade, production/custom, solid and hollow-body guitars made in Las Vegas, Nevada by Ed Roman.

Roman Vampire Guitars
2004-present. Professional and premium grade, production/custom, solidbody guitars made in Las Vegas, Nevada by Ed Roman.

Rono
1967-present. Luthier Ron Oates builds his professional and premium grade, production/custom, flat-top, jazz, Wiesenborn-style, and resonator guitars in Boulder, Colorado. He also builds basses and mandolins.

Rosetti
1950s-1960s. Guitars imported into England by distributor Rosetti, made by Holland's Egmond, maybe others.

Roudhloff
1810s-1840s. Luthier Francois Roudhloff built his instruments in France. Labels could state F. Roudhloff-Mauchand or Roudhloff Brothers. Valuation depends strongly on condition and repair. His sons built guitars under the D & A Roudhloff label.

MODEL YEAR	FEATURES	EXC. COND. LOW	HIGH

Small Brazilian
1977 1840s. Solid spruce top, laminated Brazilian sides and back.

| 1840s | | $2,000 | $3,000 |

Rowan
1997-present. Professional and premium grade, production/custom, solidbody and acoustic/electric guitars built by luthier Michael Rowan in Garland, Texas.

Royal
ca. 1954-ca. 1965. Line of jazz style guitars made by France's Jacobacci company, which also built under its own brand.

Royden Guitars
1996-present. Professional grade, production/custom, flat-tops and solidbody electrics built by luthier Royden Moran in Peterborough, Ontario.

RS Guitarworks
1994-present. Professional grade, production/custom, solid and hollowbody guitars built by luthier Roy Bowen in Winchester, Kentucky.

Rubio, German Vasquez
1993-present. Luthier German Vasquez Rubio builds his professional and premium grade, production/custom classical and flamenco guitars in Los Angeles, California.

Ruck, Robert
1966-present. Premium grade, custom classical and flamenco guitars built by luthier Robert Ruck originally in Kalaheo, Hawaii, and currently in Eugene, Oregon.

Custom Classical
1966-present. Premium grade classical with solid spruce top and solid rosewood back and sides.

| 1990s | | $6,000 | $9,000 |

Running Dog Guitars
1994-present. Luthier Rick Davis builds his professional and premium grade, custom flat-tops in Richmond, Vermont.

Rustler
1993-ca. 1998. Solidbody electrics with hand-tooled leather bound and studded sides and a R branded into the top, built by luthier Charles Caponi in Mason City, Iowa.

RVC Guitars
1999-present. Professional and premium grade, production/custom, solidbody guitars made in Las Vegas, Nevada by Ed Roman.

RWK
1991-present. Luthier Bob Karger builds his intermediate grade, production/custom, solidbody electrics and travel guitars in Highland Park, Illinois.

MODEL		EXC. COND.	
YEAR	FEATURES	LOW	HIGH

Ryder

1963. Made by Rickenbacker, the one guitar with this brand was the same as their solidbody Model 425.

S. B. Brown Guitars

1994-present. Custom flat-tops made by luthier Steve Brown in Fullerton, California.

S. B. MacDonald Custom Instruments

1988-present. Professional and premium grade, custom/production, flat-top, resonator, and solidbody guitars built by luthier Scott B. MacDonald in Huntington, New York.

S. Yairi

Ca. 1965-1980s. Steel string folk guitars and classical nylon string guitars by master Japanese luthier Sadao Yairi, imported by Philadelphia Music Company of Limerick, Pennsylvania. Early sales literature called the brand Syairi. Most steel string models have dreadnought bodies and nylon-string classical guitars are mostly standard grand concert size. All models are handmade. Steel string Jumbos and dreadnoughts have Syairi logo on the headstock, nylon-classical models have no logo. The Model 900 has a solid wood body, others assumed to have laminate bodies.

S.D. Curlee

1975-1982. Founded in Matteson, Illinois by music store owner Randy Curlee, after an unsuccessful attempt to recruit builder Dan Armstrong. S.D. Curlee guitars were made in Illinois, while S.D. Curlee International instruments were made by Matsumoku in Japan. The guitars featured mostly Watco oil finishes, often with exotic hardwoods, and unique neck-thru-bridge construction on American and Japanese instruments. These were the first production guitars to use a single-coil pickup at the bridge with a humbucker at the neck, and a square brass nut. DiMarzio pickups. Offered in a variety of shapes, later some copies. Approximately 12,000 American-made basses and 3,000 guitars were made, most of which were sold overseas. Two hundred were made in '75-'76; first production guitar numbered 518.

Electric Solidbody

1975-1982. Models include the '75-'81Standard I, II and III, '76-'81? International C-10 and C-11, '80-'81 Yanke, Liberty, Butcher, Curbeck, Summit, Special, and the '81-'82 Destroyer, Flying V.

1975-1982		$400	$600

S101

2002-present. Budget and intermediate grade, production, classical, acoustic, resonator, solid and semi-hollow body guitars imported from China by American Sejung Corp. They also offer basses, mandolins, and banjos.

Sadowsky

1980-present. Professional and premium grade, production/custom, solidbody, archtop, and electric nylon-string guitars built by luthier Roger Sadowsky in Brooklyn, New York. He also builds basses and amps. In '96, luthier Yoshi Kikuchi started building Sadowsky Tokyo instruments in Japan.

T Custom

1990-2000s		$1,800	$2,000

Vintage Style

Swamp ash body, Barden pickups, vintage-style gears, bridge, control plate and 'guard, sunburst.

1982-1987		$1,200	$1,600

Saga

Saga Musical Instruments, of San Francisco, California distributes a wide variety of instruments and brands, occasionally including their own line of solidbody guitars called the Saga Gladiator Series (1987-'88, '94-'95). In the 2000s, Saga also offered component kits ($90-$130) that allowed for complete assembly in white wood.

Sahlin Guitars

1975-present. Luthier Eric Sahlin builds his premium grade, custom, classical and flamenco guitars in Spokane, Washington.

Samick

1958-2001, 2002-present. Budget, intermediate and professional grade, production, imported acoustic and electric guitars. They also offer basses, mandolins, ukes and banjos. Samick also distributes Abilene and Silvertone brand instruments.

Samick started out producing pianos, adding guitars in '65 under other brands. In '88 Samick greatly increased their guitar production. The Samick line of 350 models was totally closed out in 2001. A totally new line of 250 models was introduced January 2002 at NAMM. All 2002 models have the new compact smaller headstock and highly styled S logo.

Sammo

1920s. Labels in these instruments state they were made by the Osborne Mfg. Co. with an address of Masonic Temple, Chicago, Illinois. High quality and often with a high degree of ornamentation. They also made ukes and mandolins.

Sand Guitars

1979-present. Luthier Kirk Sand opened the Guitar Shoppe in Laguna Beach, California in 1972 with James Matthews. By '79, he started producing his own line of premium grade, production/custom-made flat-tops.

Sandoval Engineering

1979-present. Luthier Karl Sandoval builds his premium grade, custom, solidbody guitars in Santa Fe Springs, California.

1976 S.D. Curlee Standard

Sadowsky Vintage Style

GUITARS

Santa Cruz H13

Schecter Jazz Elite

MODEL YEAR	FEATURES	EXC. COND. LOW	HIGH

Sano

1944-ca. 1970. Sano was a New Jersey-based accordion company that imported Italian-made solid and semi-hollow body guitars for a few years, starting in 1966. They also built their own amps and reverb units.

Santa Cruz

1976-present. Professional, premium and presentation grade, production/custom, flat-top, 12-string, and archtop guitars from luthier Richard Hoover in Santa Cruz, California. They also build a mandocello. Founded by Hoover, Bruce Ross and William Davis. Hoover became sole owner in '89. Custom ordered instruments with special upgrades may have higher values than the ranges listed here.

Archtop
Early 1980s-2004. Originally called the FJZ, but by mid-'90s, called the Archtop, offering 16", 17" and 18" cutaway acoustic/electric models, often special order. Spruce top, curly maple body, ebony 'board, floating pickup, f-holes, sunburst or natural. Many custom options available.

1980-2004		$4,000	$7,000

D 12-Fret
1994-present. 15 1/2" scale, 12-fret neck, slotted headstock, round shoulders, spruce top, mahogany back and sides, notch diamond markers, herringbone trim and rosette, natural. Special order models will vary in value and could exceed the posted range.

1994-2005		$2,500	$2,700

D Koa
1980s-1990s. Style D with koa back and sides.

1990s		$2,400	$2,600

D PW
2001-present. Pre-war D-style.

2001-2005		$1,650	$1,800

F
1976-present. 15 7/8" scale with narrow waist, sitka spruce top, Indian rosewood back and sides, natural.

1976-2005		$2,400	$2,600

F46R
1980s. Brazilian rosewood, single-cut.

1980s		$4,000	$4,400

FS (Finger Style)
1988-present. Single-cut, cedar top, Indian rosewood back and sides, mahogany neck, modified X-bracing.

1988-2005		$2,500	$2,700

H/H13
1976-present. Parlor size acoustic, offered in cutaway and non-cut versions, and options included koa, rosewood or maple, special inlays, slotted headstock, and shallow or deep bodies.

1976-1999		$2,200	$2,500
2000-2005		$1,900	$2,100

MODEL YEAR	FEATURES	EXC. COND. LOW	HIGH

OM (Orchestra Model)
1987-present. Orchestra model acoustic, sitka spruce top, Indian rosewood (Brazilian optional) back and sides, herringbone rosette, scalloped braces.

1987-1999	Brazilian rosewood	$4,500	$4,800
1987-2005	Indian rosewood	$1,800	$2,200

Tony Rice
1976-present. Dreadnought-size, Indian rosewood body (Brazilian optional until Tony Rice Professional model available), sitka spruce top, solid peghead, zigzag back stripe, pickup optional.

1976-1999		$2,300	$2,500
2000-2005		$1,900	$2,100

Tony Rice Professional
1997-present. Brazilian rosewood back and sides, carved German spruce top, zigzag back stripe, solid peghead.

1997-2004		$4,500	$4,800

Vintage Artist Custom
1992-2004. Martin D-42 style, mahogany body, Indian rosewood back and sides, sitka spruce top, zigzag back stripe, solid peghead, scalloped X-bracing, pickup optional.

1992-2004		$2'900	$3,200

VJ (Vintage Jumbo)
2000-present. 16" scale, round shouldered body, sitka spruce, figured mahogany back and sides, natural.

2000-2005		$2,100	$2,500

Sawchyn Guitars

1972-present. Professional and premium grade, production/custom, flat-top and flamenco guitars and mandolins built by luthier Peter Sawchyn in Regina, Saskatchewan.

Schaefer

1997-present. Premium grade, production/custom electric archtops handcrafted by luthier Edward A. Schaefer, who was located in Fort Worth, Texas, until '03 and is currently in Duluth, Minnesota.

Schecter

1976-present. Intermediate, professional and premium grade, production/custom, acoustic and electric guitars. They also offer basses. Guitar component manufacturer founded in California by four partners (David Schecter's name sounded the best), started offering complete instruments in '79. The company was bought out and moved to Dallas, Texas in the early '80s. By '88 the company was back in California and in '89 was purchased by Hisatake Shibuya. Schecter Custom Shop guitars are made in Burbank, California and their Diamond Series is made in South Korea.

Diamond Series
1997-present. Korea-made models, many body style series with names as C, S, Tempest, 00, 007, PT, Hellcat, Ultra, Banshee, Hellraiser, Blackjack, Omen, Damien, Aviation, Semi/Hollow, Baritones, and Double Neck.

1997-2000	A1/A7	$300	$400

MODEL YEAR	FEATURES	EXC. COND. LOW	HIGH
1997-2001	Model 007	$275	$300
1997-2004	Avenger	$300	$500
1997-2005	007 Elite	$350	$375
1997-2005	Hellcat	$250	$275
2000-2005	Omen 7	$250	$275
2001-2004	Tempest Special	$300	$350
2004	Jazz Elite	$250	$300

Genesis

1985-late 1980s. Offset double-cut, bolt neck, single-single-hum pickups, dot markers.

1980s		$250	$300

Scheerhorn

1989-present. Professional and premium grade, custom, resonator and Hawaiian guitars built by luthier Tim Scheerhorn in Kentwood, Michigan.

Schoenberg

1986-present. Premium grade, production/custom, flat-tops offered by Eric Schoenberg of Tiburon, California. From '86-'94 guitars made to Schoenberg's specifications by Martin. From '86-'90 constructed by Schoenberg's luthier and from '90-'94 assembled by Martin but voiced and inlaid in the Schoenberg shop. Current models made to Schoenberg specs by various smaller shops.

Schon

1986-1991. Designed by guitarist Neal Schon, early production by Charvel/Jackson building about 200 in the San Dimas factory. The final 500 were built by Larrivee in Canada. Leo Knapp also built custom Schon guitars from '85-'87, and '90s custom-made Schon guitars were also available.

Standard (Canadian-made)

1987-1991. Made in Canada on headstock.

1987-1991		$350	$450

Standard (U.S.A.-made)

1986 only. San Dimas/Jackson model, single-cut, pointy headstock shape, Made in U.S.A. on headstock.

1986		$2,000	$2,500

Schramm Guitars

1990-present. Premium grade, production/custom, classical and flamenco guitars built by luthier David Schramm in Clovis, California.

Schroder Guitars

1993-present. Luthier Timothy Schroeder builds his premium grade, production/custom, archtops in Northbrook, Illinois.

Schwartz Guitars

1992-present. Premium grade, custom, flat-top guitars built by luthier Sheldon Schwartz in Concord, Ontario.

ScoGo

2001-present. Professional and premium grade, production/custom, solidbody guitars built by luthier Scott Gordon in Parkesburg, Pennsylvania.

Scorpion Guitars

1998-present. Professional and premium grade, custom, solidbody guitars made in Las Vegas, Nevada by Ed Roman.

Seagull

1982-present. Intermediate grade, production, acoustic and acoustic/electric guitars built in Canada. Seagull was founded by luthier Robert Godin, who also has the Norman, Godin, and Patrick & Simon brands of instruments.

Artist Mahogany Folk

1997-2003. Small body 14 3/4" lower bout, cedar top, mahogany back and sides, script Artist logo on headstock.

1997-2003		$375	$425

M6 Cedar GT

2003-present. Cedar top, mahogany back and sides.

2003-2005		$250	$300

S6+ Folk

1993-present. Wild cherry back and sides, cedar top,

1993-2005		$275	$350

Sebring

1980s-mid-1990s. Entry level Korean imports distributed by V.M.I. Industries.

Seiwa

Early 1980s. Entry-level to mid-level Japanese electric guitars and basses, logo may indicate Since 1956.

Sekova

Mid-1960s-mid-1970s. Entry level instruments imported by the U.S. Musical Merchandise Corporation of New York.

Selmer

1932-1952. France-based Selmer & Cie was primarily a maker of wind instruments when they asked Mario Maccaferri to design a line of guitars for them. The guitars, with an internal sound chamber for increased volume, were built in Mante La Ville. Both gut and steel string models were offered. Maccaferri left Selmer in '33, but guitar production continued, and the original models are gradually phased out. In '36, only the 14 fret oval model is built. Production is stopped for WWII and resumes in '46, finally stopping in '52. Less than 900 guitars are built in total.

Classique

1942. Solid Rosewood back and sides, no cutaway, solid spruce top, round soundhole, classical guitar size, possibly only 2 built.

1942		$5,500	$7,000

Schon Standard

1968 Sekova Grecian

*Sheppard Minstral
Grand Concert*

Sho-Bro resonator

MODEL YEAR	FEATURES	EXC. COND. LOW	HIGH

Concert
1932-1933. For gut strings, cutaway, laminated Indian rosewood back and sides, internal resonator, spruce top with D hole, wide walnut neck, ebony 'board, only a few dozen built.

| 1932-1933 | | $16,000 | $20,000 |

Eddie Freeman Special
1933. For steel strings, 4 strings, laminated Indian rosewood back and sides, cutaway, no internal resonator, solid spruce top, D hole, black and white rosette inlays, walnut 12 fret neck, ebony 'board, 640mm scale, approx. 100 made.

| 1933 | | $5,500 | $8,000 |

Espagnol
1932. For gut strings, laminated Indian rosewood back and sides, no cutaway, internal resonator, solid spruce top, round soundhole, wide walnut neck, ebony 'board, only a few made.

| 1932 | | $8,000 | $10,000 |

Grand Modele 4 Cordes
1932-1933. For steel strings, 4 string model, laminated back and sides, cutaway, internal resonator, solid spruce top, D hole, walnut neck, ebony 'board, 12 fret, 640mm scale, 2 or 3 dozen made.

| 1932-1933 | | $9,000 | $13,000 |

Harp Guitar
1933. For gut strings, solid mahogany body, extended horn holding 3 sub bass strings, 3 screw adjustable neck, wide walnut neck, ebony 'board, only about 12 built.

| 1933 | | $13,000 | $15,000 |

Hawaienne
1932-1934. For steel strings, 6 or 7 strings, laminated back and sides, no cutaway, internal resonator, solid spruce top, D hole, wide walnut neck, ebony 'board, 2 or 3 dozen built.

| 1932-1934 | | $18,000 | $25,000 |

Modele "Jazz"
1936-1942, 1946-1952. For steel strings, laminated Indian rosewood back and sides (some laminated or solid mahogany), cutaway, solid spruce top, small oval soundhole, walnut neck, ebony 'board (latest ones with rosewood necks), 14 fret to the body, 670mm scale. Production interrupted for WWII.

| 1936-1952 | | $23,000 | $27,000 |

Modeles de Transition
1934-1936. Transition models appearing before 14 fret oval hole model, some in solid maple with solid headstock, some with round soundhole and cutaway, some 12 fret models with oval hole.

| 1934-1936 | | $16,000 | $18,000 |

Orchestre
1932-1934. For steel strings, laminated back and sides, cutaway, internal resonator, solid spruce top, D hole, walnut neck, ebony 'board, about 100 made.

| 1932-1934 | | $26,000 | $30,000 |

MODEL YEAR	FEATURES	EXC. COND. LOW	HIGH

Tenor
1932-1933. For steel strings, 4 strings, laminated back and sides, internal resonator, solid spruce top, D hole, walnut neck, ebony 'board, 12 fret, 570mm scale, 2 or 3 dozen built.

| 1932-1933 | | $5,000 | $8,000 |

Serge Guitars
1995-present. Luthier Serge Michaud builds his production/custom, classical, steel-string, resophonic and archtop guitars in Breakeyville, Quebec.

Sexauer Guitars
1967-present. Premium and presentation grade, custom, steel-string, 12-string, nylon-string, and archtop guitars built by luthier Bruce Sexauer in Petaluma, California.

Shanti Guitars
1985-present. Premium and presentation grade, custom, steel-string, 12-string, nylon-string and archtop guitars built by luthier Michael Hornick in Avery, California.

Shelley D. Park Guitars
1991-present. Luthier Shelley D. Park builds her professional grade, custom, nylon- and steel-string guitars in Vancouver, British Columbia.

Shelton-Farretta
1967-present. Premium grade, production/custom, flamenco and classical guitars built by luthiers John Shelton and Susan Farretta originally in Portland, Oregon, and since '05 in Alsea, Oregon.

Sheppard Guitars
1993-present. Luthier Gerald Sheppard builds his premium grade, production/custom, steel-string guitars in Kingsport, Tennessee.

Shergold
1968-1992. Founded by Jack Golder and Norman Houlder, Shergold originally made guitars for other brands like Hayman and Barnes and Mullins. In '75, they started building guitars and basses under their own name. By '82, general guitar production was halted but custom orders were filled through '90. In '91, general production was again started but ended in '92 when Golder died.

Sherwood
c.1950s. Private brand made by Chicago manufacturerers such as Kay.

Shifflett
1990-present. Luthier Charles Shifflett builds his premium grade, production/custom, flat-top, classical, flamenco, resophonic, and harp guitars in High River, Alberta. He also builds basses and banjos.

MODEL YEAR	FEATURES	EXC. COND. LOW	HIGH

Sho-Bro

1969-1978. Spanish and Hawaiian style resonator guitars made by Sho-Bud in Nashville, Tennessee and distributed by Gretsch. Designed Shot Jackson and Buddy Emmons.

Grand Slam

1978. Acoustic, spruce top, mahogany neck, jacaranda sides and back, and mother-of-pearl inlays, abalone soundhole purfling.

1970s		$450	$550

Resonator

1972-1978. Flat-top style guitar with metal resonator with 2 small circular grilled soundholes.

1972-1978		$650	$750

Siegmund Guitars & Amplifiers

1993-present. Luthier Chris Siegmund builds his professional, premium, and presentation grade, custom/production, archtop, solidbody, and resonator guitars in Los Angeles, California. He founded the company in Seattle, moving it to Austin, Texas for '95-'97. He also builds effects pedals and amps.

Sigma

1970-present. Budget and intermediate grade, production, import acoustic guitars distributed by C.F. Martin Company.

DR Series

1970-2003. Various dreadnought models.

1970-1996	DR-28H	$325	$400
1970-1996	DR-35H	$350	$425
1970-2003	DR-41	$375	$450

GCS-6

Grand concert semi-narrow waist body, laminated spruce top, mahogany back and sides, natural.

1994		$150	$200

Signet

1972-Mid 1970s. Acoustic flat-top guitars, imported from Japan by Ampeg/Selmer.

Silber

1992-1998. Solid wood, steel-string guitars designed by Marc Silber, made in Paracho, Mexico, and distributed by K & S Music. Silber continues to offer the same models under the Marc Silber Music brand.

Silvertone

1941-ca. 1970, present. Brand of Sears instruments which replaced their Supertone brand in '41. The Silvertone name was used on Sears phonographs, records and radios as early as the 'teens, and on occasional guitar models. When Sears divested itself of the Harmony guitar subsidiary in '40 it turned to other suppliers including Kay. In '40 Kay-made archtops and Hawaiian electric lap steels appeared in the catalog bearing the Silvertone brand, and after '41-'42, all guitars, regardless of manufacturer, were called Silvertone.

Sears offered Danelectro-made solidbodies in the fall of '54. Danelectro hollowbodies appeared in '56. By '65, the Silvertones were Teisco-made guitars from W.M.I., but never sold through the catalog. First imports shown in catalog were in '69. By '70, most guitars sold by Sears were imports and did not carry the Silvertone name. Currently, Samick offers a line of amps under the Silvertone name.

Amp-In-Case

The 1-pickup guitar, introduced in 1962, came with a smaller wattage amp without tremolo. The 2-pickup model, introduced in '63, came with a higher-watt amp with tremolo and better quality Jensen speaker. Gray tolex covered the guitar-amp case.

1960s	1 pickup	$350	$425
1960s	2 pickups	$450	$525

Belmont

1950s. Single-cut solidbody, double pickup, black.

1958		$400	$450

Espanada

Bigsby, 2 pickups, black.

1960s		$300	$475

Estrelita

Semi-hollowbody archtop, 2 pickups, black, Harmony-made.

1960s		$350	$550

Gene Autry Melody Ranch

1941-1955. 13" Harmony-made acoustic, Gene Autry signature on belly, cowboy roundup stencil, same as earlier Supertone Gene Autry Roundup.

1941-1955		$250	$450

Meteor

Single-cut, 1 pickup, sunburst.

1955		$250	$375

Student-level 13" Flat-Top

Harmony-made, 13" lower bout.

1960s		$50	$75

Ultra Thin Professional

1960s. Harmony-made, thin hollow cutaway, 3 pickups, Bigsby tailpiece.

1960s		$550	$750

Simon & Patrick

1985-present. Intermediate and professional grade, production, acoustic and acoustic/electric guitars built in Canada. Founded by luthier Robert Godin and named after his sons. He also produces the Seagull, Godin, and Norman brands of instruments.

Singletouch

Luthier Mark Singleton builds his professional and premium grade, custom/production, solid and semi-hollow body guitars in Phillips Ranch, California. He also builds basses.

Skylark

1981. Solidbody guitars made in Japan and distributed by JC Penney. Two set-neck models and one bolt-neck model were offered. Most likely a one-time deal as brand quickly disappeared.

Siegmund Outcaster

'60s Silvertone semi-hollow-body

Smart J-2

Specimen Products Maxwell

MODEL YEAR	FEATURES	EXC. COND. LOW	HIGH

Slammer

1990-present. Budget and intermediate grade, production, guitars imported by Hamer. They also offer basses. Originally Slammers were upscale copies of Hamer models made in Korea. In '96, production of a more budget line was switched to Indonesia.

Slammer Series (import)

1995-2005	Various models	$175	$325

Slingerland

1930s-mid-1940s. The parent company was Slingerland Banjo and Drums, Chicago, Illinois. The company offered other stringed instruments into the '40s. They also marketed the May Bell brand. The guitars were made by other companies. Slingerland Drums is now owned by Gibson.

Nitehawk

1930s. 16" archtop, Nitehawk logo on headstock, fancy position neck markers.

1930s		$550	$700

Songster Archtop/Flat-Top

1930s.

1930s	Archtop	$500	$650
1930s	Flat-Top	$1,100	$1,100

Smart Musical Instruments

1986-present. Luthier A. Lawrence Smart builds his professional and premium grade, custom, flat-top guitars in McCall, Idaho. He also builds mandolin-family instruments.

Smith, George

1959-present. Custom classical and flamenco guitars built by luthier George Smith in Portland, Oregon.

Smith, Lawrence K.

1989-present. Luthier Lawrence Smith builds his professional and premium grade, production/custom, flat-top, nylon-string, and archtop guitars in Thirrow, New South Wales, Australia.

Somervell

1979-present. Luthier Douglas P. Somervell builds his premium and presentation grade, production/custom, classical and flamenco guitars in Brasstown, North Carolina.

Somogyi, Ervin

1971-present. Luthier Ervin Somogyi builds his presentation grade, production/custom, flat-top, flamenco, and classical guitars in Oakland, California.

SonFather Guitars

1994-present. Luthier David A. Cassotta builds his production/custom, flat-top, 12-string, nylon-string and electric guitars in Rocklin, California.

Sorrentino

1930s. Private brand made by Epiphone and distributed by C.M.I. Quality close to similar Epiphone models.

Arcadia

1930s. Lower-end f-hole acoustic archtop similar to Epiphone Blackstone.

1930s		$500	$750

Southwell Guitars

1983-present. Premium grade, custom, nylon-string guitars built by luthier Gary Southwell in Nottingham, England.

Sovereign

Ca. 1899-1938. Sovereign was originally a brand of The Oscar Schmidt Company of Jersey City, New Jersey, and used on guitars, banjos and mandolins starting in the very late 1800s. In the late '30s, Harmony purchased several trade names from the Schmidt Company, including Sovereign and Stella. Sovereign then ceased as a brand, but Harmony continued using it on a model line of Harmony guitars.

Specimen Products

1984-present. Luthier Ian Schneller builds his professional and premium grade, production/custom, aluminum and wood body guitars in Chicago, Illinois. He also builds basses, ukes, amps and speaker cabs.

Spector/Stuart Spector Design

1975-1990 (Spector), 1991-1998 (SSD), 1998-present (Spector SSD). Known mainly for basses, Spector offered U.S.-made guitars during '75-'90 and '96-'99, and imports for '87-'90 and '96-'99. Since 2003, they again offer U.S.-professional grade, production, solidbody guitars. See Bass Section for more company info.

St. Blues

1980-1986, 2005-present. Luthier Thomas Beard builds his intermediate and professional grade, production/custom, imported and U.S. assembled, solidbody guitars in Memphis, Tennessee.

St. George

Mid to late 1960s. Early Japanese brand imported possibly by Buegeleisen & Jacobson of New York, New York.

St. Moritz

1960s. Guitars and basses imported from Japan by unidentified distributor. Manufacturers unknown, but some appear to be either Teisco or Kawai. Generally shorter scale beginner guitars, some with interesting pickup configurations.

MODEL		EXC. COND.	
YEAR	FEATURES	LOW	HIGH

Stahl

1900-1941. William Stahl ran a publishing company in Milwaukee and sold instruments from a variety of builders under his own name. By at least 1906, some of his better instruments were coming from the Larson Brothers of Chicago. The guitars listed here were built by the Larsons and valuation is based on style number.

Style 4 Flat-Top
1930s. Mahogany body.

1930s		$3,000	$4,000

Style 5 Flat-Top
1930s. Mahogany body.

1930s		$3,000	$4,000

Style 6 Orchestra Special Flat-Top
1930s. Rosewood body.

1929-1930		$5,000	$7,500

Style 7 Special Solo Flat-Top
1930s. 13 1/2" scale, choice rosewood body, white spruce top, fancy appointments.

1930s		$5,500	$8,000

Style 8 Special Solo Flat-Top
1930s. Choicest rosewood body, finest white spruce top, fancy appointments.

1930s		$6,500	$9,000

Style 9 Artist Special Flat-Top
1930s. Choicest rosewood body, finest white spruce top, fancy appointments.

1930s		$7,500	$10,000

Stambaugh

1995-present. Luthier Chris Stambaugh builds his professional grade, custom/production, solidbody guitars in Stratham, New Hampshire. He also builds basses.

Standel

1952-1974, 1997-present. Amp builder Bob Crooks offered instruments under his Standel brand 3 different times during the '60s. In '61 Semie Moseley, later of Mosrite fame, made 2 guitar models and 1 bass for Standel, in limited numbers. Also in '61, Standel began distributing Sierra steels and Dobro resonators, sometimes under the Standel name. In '65 and '66 Standel offered a guitar and a bass made by Joe Hall, who also made the Hallmark guitars. In '66 Standel connected with Sam Koontz, who designed and produced the most numerous Standel models (but still in relatively small numbers) in Newark, New Jersey. These models hit the market in '67 and were handled by Harptone, which was associated with Koontz. By '70 Standel was out of the guitar biz. See Amp section for more company info.

Custom Deluxe Solidbody 101/101X
1967-1968. Custom with better electronics, 101X has no vibrato, sunburst, black, pearl white and metallic red.

1967-1968		$1,100	$1,300

Custom Deluxe Thin Body 102/102X
1967-1968. Custom with better electronics, 102X has no vibrato, offered in sunburst and 5 solid color options.

1967-1968		$1,300	$1,500

Custom Solidbody 201/201X
1967-1968. Solidbody, 2 pickups, vibrola, 2 pointed cutaways, headstock similar to that on Fender XII, 201X has no vibrato, sunburst, black, pearl white and metallic red.

1967-1968		$900	$1,100

Custom Thin Body 202/202X
1967-1968. Thin body, headstock similar to that on Fender XII, 202X has no vibrato, offered in sunburst and 5 solid color options.

1967-1968		$1,000	$1,200

Starfield

1992-1993. Solidbody guitars from Hoshino (Ibanez) made in the U.S. and Japan. U.S. guitars are identified as American models; Japanese ones as SJ models. Hoshino also used the Starfield name on a line of Japanese guitars in the late '70s. These Starfields had nothing to do with the '90s versions and were not sold in the U.S.

Starforce

Ca. 1989. Import copies from Starforce Music/ Starforce USA.

Stars

Intermediate grade, production, solidbody guitars made in Korea.

Stauffer

1800s. Old World violin and guitar maker, Georg Stauffer. Valid attributions include "signed or labeled by the maker" indicating the guitar was actually made by Stauffer, as opposed to "attributed to Stauffer or one of his contemporaries." See Martin for listing.

Stefan Sobell Musical Instruments

1982-present. Premium grade, production/custom, flat-top, 12-string, and archtop guitars built by luthier Stefan Sobell in Hetham, Northumberland, England. He also builds mandolins, citterns and bouzoukis.

Steinberger

1979-present. Currently Steinberger offers budget, intermediate, and professional grade, production, electric guitars. They also offer basses. Founded by Ned Steinberger, who started designing NS Models for Stuart Spector in '76. In '79, he designed the L-2 headless bass. In '80, the Steinberger Sound Corp. was founded. Steinberger Sound was purchased by the Gibson Guitar Corp. in '87, and in '92, Steinberger relocated to Nashville, Tennessee.

1968 Standel 510

Stefan Sobell Model 1

Stella/Harmony

1952 Stromberg Master 400

MODEL YEAR	FEATURES	EXC. COND. LOW	HIGH

Headless model codes for '85-'93 are:
First letter is X for bass or G for guitar.
Second letter is for body shape: M is regular offset double-cut guitar body; L is rectangle body; P is mini V shaped body.
Number is pickup designation: 2 = 2 humbuckers, 3 = 3 single coils, 4 = single/single/humbucker.
Last letter is type of tremolo: S = S-Trem tremolo; T = Trans-Trem which cost more on original retail.

Steinegger
1976-present. Premium grade, custom steel-string flat-top guitars built by luthier Robert Steinegger in Portland, Oregon.

Stella
Ca. 1899-1974, present. Stella was a brand of the Oscar Schmidt Company which started using the brand on low-mid to mid-level instruments in the very late 1800s. Oscar Schmidt produced all types of stringed instruments and was very successful in the 1920s. Company salesmen reached many rural areas and Stella instruments were available in general stores, furniture stores, and dry goods stores, ending up in the hands of musicians such as Leadbelly and Charlie Patton. Harmony acquired the Stella brand in '39 and built thousands of instruments with that name in the '50s and '60s. Harmony dissolved in '74. The Stella brand has been reintroduced by MBT International.

00 Style
Early-1900s. Oak body flat-top.

1908		$750	$1,000

Harp Guitar
Early-1900s.

1915		$2,000	$2,500

Singing Cowboy
Late-1990s. Copy of Supertone (black background)/ Silvertone/Harmony Singing Cowboy, import with laminated wood construction and ladder bracing.

2000	Stencil over black	$50	$75

Stetson
1910s-1925. Stetson was a house brand of William John Dyer's St. Paul, Minnesota, music store. The guitars were built by Chicago's Larson Brothers. He also carried Dyer brand instruments made by Knutsen.

Small Higher-End Flat-Top

1910s		$3,300	$4,000

Stevenson
1999-present. Professional grade, production/ custom, solidbody electric guitars built by luthier Ted Stevenson in Lachine, Quebec. He also builds basses and amps.

Stonetree
1996-present. Luthier Scott Platts builds his professional and premium grade, custom/production, solidbody and chambered electric guitars in Saratoga, Wyoming. He also builds basses.

Strad-O-Lin
Ca.1920s-ca.1960s. The Strad-O-Lin company was operated by the Hominic brothers in New York, primarily making mandolins for wholesalers. Around '57 Multivox/Premier bought the company and also used the name on guitars, making both electrics and acoustics. Premier also marketed student level guitars under the U.S. Strad brand.

Stratospere
1954-ca. 1958. Solidbody electrics made in Springfield, Missouri by brothers Claude and Russ Deaver, some featuring fanned frets.

Electric Guitar

1954-1958		$1,000	$2,000

Stromberg
1906-1955, 2001-present. Intermediate and professional grade, production, archtop guitars imported by Larry Davis.

Founded in Boston by master luthier Charles Stromberg, a Swedish immigrant, building banjos and drums. Son Harry joined the company in 1907and stayed until '27. Son Elmer started in 1910 at age 15. The shop was well known for tenor banjos, but when the banjo's popularity declined, they began building archtop orchestra model guitars. The shop moved to Hanover Street in Boston in '27 and began producing custom order archtop guitars, in particular the 16" G-series and the Deluxe. As styles changed the G-series was increased to 17 3/8" and the 19" Master 400 model was introduced in '37. Stromberg designs radically changed around '40, most likely when Elmer took over guitar production. Both Charles and Elmer died within a few months of each other in '55.

Larry Davis of WD Music Products revived the Stromberg name and introduced a series of moderately priced jazz guitars in June, 2001. The models are crafted by a small Korean shop with component parts supplied by WD.

Deluxe
1927-1955. Non-cut, 16" body to '34, 17 3/8" body after '35, also sometimes labeled Delux.

1927-1930		$10,000	$11,000
1931-1955		$12,000	$13,000

G-1
1927-1955. Non-cut, 16" body to '35, 17 3/8" body after '35, sunburst.

1927-1955		$10,000	$11,000

G-3
Early 1930s. Archtop, 16 3/8", 3 segment F-holes, ladder bracing, gold hardware, engraved tailpiece, 8-ply 'guard, 5-ply body binding, laminate maple back, fancy engraved headstock with Stromberg name, less

MODEL YEAR	FEATURES	EXC. COND. LOW	HIGH

total refinement than higher-end Stromberg models.

| 1927-1935 | | $11,000 | $12,000 |

Master 300

1937-1955. 19" non-cut.

| 1937-1955 | Natural | $35,000 | $40,000 |
| 1937-1955 | Sunburst | $30,000 | $35,000 |

Master 400

1937-1955. 19" top-of-the-line non-cut, the most common of Stromberg's models.

| 1937-1955 | Natural | $50,000 | $65,000 |
| 1937-1955 | Sunburst | $45,000 | $55,000 |

Master 400 Cutaway

1949. Only 7 cutaway Strombergs are known to exist.

| 1949 | Natural | $80,000 | $90,000 |

Stromberg-Voisinet

1921-ca.1932. Marketed Stromberg (not to be confused with Charles Stromberg of Boston) and Kay Kraft brands, plus guitars of other distributors and retailers. Stromberg was the successor to the Groehsl Company (or Groehsel) founded in Chicago, Illinois in 1890; and the predecessor to the Kay Musical Instrument Company. In 1921, the name was changed to Stromberg-Voisinet Company. Henry Kay "Hank" Kuhrmeyer joined the company in '23 and was secretary by '25. By the mid-'20s, the company was making many better Montgomery Ward guitars, banjos and mandolins, often with lots of pearloid.

Joseph Zorzi, Philip Gabriel and John Abbott left Lyon & Healy for S-V in '26 or '27, developing 2-point Venetian shape, which was offered in '27. The first production of electric guitars and amps was introduced with big fanfare in '28; perhaps only 200 or so made. The last Stromberg acoustic instruments were seen in '32. The Kay Kraft brand was introduced by Kuhrmeyer in '31 as the company made its transition to Kay (see Kay).

Archtop Deluxe

1920s-1930s. Venetian cutaways, oval soundhole, decalomania art on top, trapeze tailpiece, light sunburst. Later offered under the Kay-Kraft brand.

| 1930s | | $500 | $650 |

Archtop Standard

1920s-1930s. Venetian cutaways, oval soundhole, no decalomania art, plain top, trapeze tailpiece, light sunburst. Later offered under the Kay-Kraft brand.

| 1930s | | $450 | $600 |

Stuart Custom Guitars

2004-present. Professional and premium grade, production/custom, solid and semi-hollow body guitars built by luthier Fred Stuart in Riverside, California. Stuart was a Senior Master Builder at Fender. He also builds pickups.

Suhr Guitars

1997-present. Luthier John Suhr builds his professional and premium grade, production/custom, solidbody electrics in Lake Elsinore, California. He

also builds basses. He previously built Pensa-Suhr guitars with Rudy Pensa in New York.

Superior Guitars

1987-present. Intermediate grade, production/custom Hawaiian, flamenco and classical guitars made in Mexico for George Katechis Montalvo of Berkeley Musical Instrument Exchange. They also offer mandolin-family instruments.

Supersound

1958. England's Jim Burns first production brand, about 20 short scale, single-cut solidbodies were produced bearing this name.

Supertone

1914-1941. Brand used by Sears, Roebuck and Company for instruments made by various American manufacturers, including especially its own subsidiary Harmony (which it purchased in 1916). When Sears divested itself of Harmony in '40, instruments began making a transition to the Silvertone brand. By '41 the Supertone name was gone.

Acoustic Flat-Top (13" Wide, Non-Stencil)

| 1930s | | $150 | $250 |

Acoustic Flat-Top (High-End Appointments)

| 1920s | Pearl trim 00-42 likeness | $1,300 | $2,200 |
| 1920s | Pearl trim, Lindbergh model | $1,300 | $1,800 |

Gene Autry Roundup

1932-1939. Harmony made acoustic, Gene Autry signature on belly, cowboy roundup stencil, 13" body until '35, then 14".

| 1932-1939 | | $250 | $400 |

Lone Ranger

1936-1941. Black with red and silver Lone Ranger and Tonto stencil, silver-painted fretboard, 13 1/2" wide. "Hi-Yo Silver" added in '37, changed to "Hi-Ho Silver" in '38.

| 1936-1941 | | $250 | $375 |

Singing Cowboys

1938-1943. Stencil of guitar strumming cowboys around chuck wagon and campfire, branded Silvertone after '41.

| 1938-1943 | | $250 | $375 |

Supertone Wedge

1930s. Triangle-shaped wedge body, laminate construction, blue-silver Supertone label inside sound chamber, art decals on body.

| 1930s | | $250 | $300 |

Supro

1935-1968, 2004-present. Budget brand of National Dobro Company. Some Supro models also sold under the Airline brand for Montgomery Ward.

In '42 Victor Smith, Al Frost and Louis Dopyera bought National and changed the name to Valco

Suhr Standard

Supro Folkstar

1965 Supro S-555

1958 Supro Dual-Tone

MODEL YEAR	FEATURES	EXC. COND. LOW	HIGH

Manufacturing Company. Valco Manufacturing Company name changed to Valco Guitars, Inc., in '62. Company treasurer Robert Engelhardt bought Valco in '64. In '67 Valco bought Kay and in '68 Valco/Kay went out of business. In the summer of '69, Valco/Kay brands and assets were sold at auction and the Supro and National names purchased by Chicago-area importer and distributor Strum N' Drum (Norma, Noble). TIn the early-'80s, ownership of the Supro name was transferred to Archer's Music, Fresno, California. Some Supros assembled from new-old-stock parts. Amp builder Bruce Zinky revived the Supro name for a guitar and amp model.

Belmont

1955-1964. For '55-'60, 12" wide, single-cut, 1 neck pickup, 2 knobs treble side in 'guard, reverse-stairs tailpiece, No-Mar plastic maroon-colored covering. For '60, size increased to 13 1/2" wide. For '62-'64, Res-o-glas fiberglas was used for the body, a slight cutaway on bass side, 1 bridge pickup, 2 knobs on opposite sides. Polar White.

1955-1962	Black or white No-Mar	$750	$1,000
1961-1964	Polar White Res-o-glas	$1,100	$1,400

Bermuda

1962 only. Slab body (not beveled), double pickups, dot markers, cherry glass-fiber finish.

1962		$1,100	$1,300

Collegian Spanish

1939-1942. Metal body, 12 frets. Moved to National line in '42.

1939-1942		$1,150	$1,350

Coronado/Coronado II

1961-1967. Listed as II in '62 15 1/2" scale, single-cut thinline, 2 pickups with 4 knobs and slider, natural blond spruce top. Changed to slight cutaway on bass side in '62 when renamed II.

1961-1962	Blond, natural spruce top	$1,200	$1,400
1963-1967	Black fiberglass	$1,500	$1,900

Dual-Tone

1954-1966, 2004-present. The Dual Tone had several body style changes, all instruments had dual pickups. '54, 11 1/4" body, No Mar Arctic White plastic body ('54-'62). '55, 12" body. '58, 13" body. '60, 13 1/2" body. '62, Res-o-glas Ermine White body, light cutaway on bass side.

1954-1961	Arctic White No-Mar	$900	$1,200
1962-1964	Ermine White Res-o-glas	$1,000	$1,300

Folk Star/Vagabond

1964-1967. Molded Res-o-glas body, single-cone resonator, dot inlays, Fire Engine Red. Name changed to Vagabond in '66.

1964-1967		$750	$900

Kingston

1962-1963. Double-cut slab body, bridge pickup, glass-fiber sand finish, similar to same vintage Ozark.

1962-1963		$500	$600

Martinique

1962-1967. Single-cut, 13 1/2" wide, 2 standard and 1 bridge pickups, 6 knobs on bass side, 1 knob and slider on treble side, block markers, cataloged as "Supro's finest electric," Val-Trol script on 'guard, Bigsby vibrato tailpiece, blue or Ermine White Polyester Glas.

1962-1967		$2,000	$2,300

Ozark

1952-1954, 1958-1967. Non-cut, 1 pickup, dot inlay, white pearloid body, name reintroduced in '58 as a continuation of model Sixty with single-cut, Dobro tailpiece.

1952-1954	White pearloid	$600	$1,000
1958-1961	Red	$600	$1,000
1962-1967	Jet Black or Fire Bronze	$600	$1,000

Ranchero

1948-1960. Full body electric archtop, neck pickup, dot markers, bound body, sunburst.

1948-1960		$600	$700

Sahara

1960-1964. 13 1/2" body-style similar to Dual-Tone, single pickup, 2 knobs, Sand-Buff or Wedgewood Blue.

1960-1964		$850	$950

Silverwood/Val-Trol

1960-1962. Single-cut, 13 1/2" wide, 2 standard and 1 bridge pickups, 6 knobs on bass side, 1 knob and slider on treble side, block markers, cataloged as "Supro's finest electric", natural blond, Val-Trol script on 'guard, renamed Martinique in '62.

1960-1962		$1,500	$2,000

Sixty

1955-1958. Single-cut, single pickup, white No-Mar, becomes Ozark in '58.

1955-1958		$500	$600

Special 12

1958-1960. Single-cut, replaces Supro Sixty, neck pickup 'guard mounted.

1958-1960		$500	$600

Strum 'N' Drum Solidbody

1970s. Student-level import, 1 pickup, large Supro logo on headstock.

1970s		$250	$350

Super

1958-1964. 12" wide single-cut body style like mid-'50s models, single bridge pickup, short-scale, ivory.

1958-1964		$500	$550

Super Seven

1965-1967. Offset double-cut solidbody, short scale, middle pickup, Calypso Blue.

1965-1967		$400	$450

Suprosonic 30

1963-1967. Introduced as Suprosonic, renamed Suprosonic 30 in '64, double-cut, single neck pickup, vibrato tailpiece, more of a student model, Holly Red.

1963-1967		$550	$650

MODEL YEAR	FEATURES	EXC. COND. LOW	HIGH

Tremo-Lectric
1965. Fiberglas hollowbody, 2 pickups, unique built-in electric tremolo (not mechanical), Wedgewood Blue finish, multiple controls associated with electric tremolo.

1965		$1,500	$2,000

White Holiday/Holiday
1963-1967. Introduced as Holiday, renamed White Holiday in '64, fiberglas double-cut, vibrato tailpiece, single bridge pickup, Dawn White.

1963-1967		$850	$950

Suzuki Takeharu
See listing for Takeharu.

SX
See listing for Essex.

T. H. Davis
1976-present. Professional and premium grade, custom, steel string and classical guitars built by luthier Ted Davis in Loudon, Tennessee. He also builds mandolins.

Tacoma
1995-present. Intermediate, professional, and premium grade, production, acoustic guitars produced in Tacoma, Washington. They also build acoustic basses and mandolins. In October, '04, Fender acquired Tacoma.

C-1C/C-1CE Chief
1997-present. Cutaway flat-top with upper bass bout soundhole, solid cedar top, mahogany back and sides, rosewood 'board. Sides laminated until 2000, solid after, CE is acoustic/electric.

1997-2005		$400	$500
1997-2005	Fishman electronics	$550	$650

CB-10E4 Thunderchief
2000-present. 17 3/4 flat-top, solid spruce top, solid mahogany back, laminated mahogany sides, rounded cutaway, bolt-on neck, natural satin finish, factory Fishman Prefix Plus pickup system (E4), dot markers.

2000-2005		$700	$750

DM Series
1997-present. Dreadnought, solid spruce top, mahogany back and sides, satin finish, natural. Models include DM-8, -9, -10 and -14.

1997-2005	DM-9, DM-10	$350	$500

DR Series
1997-present. Dreadnought, solid sitka spruce top, solid rosewood back and sides, natural. Models include DR-20 (non-cut, herringbone trim, abalone rosette), DR-8C (cutaway), and DR-38.

1997-2003	DR-20	$675	$775
2000-2003	DR-38	$1,025	$1,100
1997-2002	DR-8C	$625	$725

JK-50CE4 Jumbo Koa
1997-2003. Jumbo cutaway, 17" lower bout, sitka spruce top, figured koa back and sides.

1997-2003		$1,100	$1,300

MODEL YEAR	FEATURES	EXC. COND. LOW	HIGH

JR-14C Jumbo Rosewood
Late-1990s. Jumbo cutaway, 16 5/8" lower bout, gloss spruce top, satin rosewood body.

1998		$950	$1,050

P-1/P-2 Papoose
1995-present. Travel-size mini-flat-top, all solid wood, mahogany back and sides (P-1) or solid rosewood (P-2), cedar top, natural satin finish.

1995-2005	P-1	$200	$350
1995-2002	P-2	$250	$400

Parlor Series
1997-2003. Smaller 14 3/4" body, solid spruce top, various woods for back and sides.

1997-2003	PK-30 Koa	$950	$1,100
1997-2003	PK-40 Rosewood	$1,000	$1,100

PM-15
1997-1998. Solid spruce top, solid mahogany back and sides.

1997-1998		$500	$600

PM-20
1997-2003. Solid spruce top, solid mahogany back and sides, gloss finish.

1997-2003		$650	$700

Takamine
1962-present. Intermediate and professional grade, production, steel- and nylon-string, acoustic and acoustic/electric guitars. They also make basses. Takamine is named after a mountain near its factory in Sakashita, Japan. Mass Hirade joined Takamine in '68 and revamped the brand's designs and improved quality. In '75, Takamine began exporting to other countries, including U.S. distribution by Kaman Music (Ovation). In '78, Takamine introduced acoustic/electric guitars. They offered solidbody electrics and some archtops for '83-'84.

Acoustic Electric Cutaways (laminate)
All laminate (plywood) construction, cutaway, standard features, pickup and preamp.

1980s		$250	$400
1990s		$250	$400

Acoustic Electrics (laminate construction)
All laminate (plywood) construction, non-cut, standard features, pickup and preamp.

1980s		$250	$400
1990s		$250	$400

Acoustic Electrics (solid top)
Solid wood top, sides and back can vary, cutaway, standard features, preamp and pickup.

1980s		$450	$900
1990s		$450	$900

Classical Guitars (solid top)
Solid wood (often cedar) top, classical, sides and back can vary.

1980s		$450	$600
1990s		$450	$600

Tacoma RM6C

1984 Takamine Wave

Taku Sakashta Indian

Taylor Baby

MODEL YEAR	FEATURES	EXC. COND. LOW	HIGH

Collectors (limited edition)

Each year a different limited edition collector's guitar is issued. '97 - solid top, koa body, cutaway, natural finish, preamp and pickup. '98 - solid top, rosewood body, cutaway, natural finish, preamp and pickup. '99 - solid top, rosewood body, cutaway, natural finish, preamp and pickup. '00 - solid top, rosewood body, cutaway, natural finish, preamp and pickup. '01 - solid top, rosewood body, cutaway, natural finish, preamp and pickup.

1990s		$950	$1,100

Takeharu (by Suzuki)

Mid-1970s. Classical guitars offered by Suzuki as part of their internationally known teaching method (e.g. Violin Suzuki method), various sized instruments designed to eliminate the confusion of size that has been a problem for classroom guitar programs.

Taku Sakashta Guitars

1994-present. Premium and presentation grade, production/custom, archtop, flat-top, 12-sting, and nylon-string guitars, built by luthier Taku Sakashta in Sebastopol, California.

Tama

Ca. 1959-1967, 1974-1979. Hoshino's (Ibanez) brand of higher-end acoutic flat-tops made in Japan. Many of the brand's features would be transferred to Ibanez's Artwood acoustics.

Tanara

2000s. Student-level models imported by Chesbro, inside label identifies model and country of origin.

Taylor

1974-present. Intermediate, professional, premium, and presentation grade, production/custom, steel- and nylon-string, acoustic and acoustic/electric guitars built in El Cajon, California. They have also built basses. Founded by Bob Taylor, Steve Schemmer and Kurt Listug in Lemon Grove, California, the company was originally named the Westland Music Company, but was soon changed to Taylor (Bob designed the guitars and it fit on the logo). Taylor and Listug bought out Schemmer in '83.

Bob Taylor was the first commercially successful guitar maker to harness CAD/CAM CNC technology for acoustic guitars. The CNC technology allowed Taylor to build a less expensive guitar model without resorting to offshore manufacturing. Taylor's CNC-based intermediate priced all wood acoustic was the Model 410. Soon other builders followed Bob Taylor's lead.

310

1998-present. D-style solid spruce top, sapele-mahogany back and sides.

1998-2005		$700	$900

MODEL YEAR	FEATURES	EXC. COND. LOW	HIGH

310ce

1998-present. 310 with Venetian cutaway, on-board electronics.

1998-2005		$1,000	$1,100

312ce

1998-present. Grand Concert Venetian cutaway, solid spruce top, sapele-mahogany back and sides, on-board electronics.

1998-2005		$800	$1,000

314

1998-present. Mid-size Grand Auditorium-style, solid spruce top, sapele-mahogany back and sides.

1998-2005		$800	$900

314ce

1998-present. 314 with Venetian cutaway, on-board electronics.

1998-2005		$1,100	$1,200

314cek

2000. Limited edition 314 with flamed koa body.

2000		$1,000	$1,200

315ce

1998-present. Jumbo-style Venetian cutaway, solid spruce top, sapele-mahogany back and sides, on-board electronics.

1998-2005		$1,000	$1,100

355 12-String

1998-present. Jumbo 12-string, solid spruce top, sapele-mahogany back and sides.

1998-2005		$900	$1,000

355ce 12-String

1998-present. 355 with cutaway, on-board electronics.

1998-2005		$950	$1,050

410

1991-present. D-style, solid spruce top, mahogany back and sides until '98, African ovangkol back and sides after '98.

1991-2003		$1,000	$1,100

410ce

1991-present. 410 with cutaway, on-board electronics.

1991-2005		$1,100	$1,200

412

1991-1998. Solid spruce top, grand concert, mahogany back and sides until '98, African ovangkol back and sides after '98.

1991-1998		$900	$1,000

412ce

1998-present. Cutaway electric version replaced the 412 in '98.

1998-2005		$1,100	$1,200

414

1998-present. Solid sitka spruce top, grand auditorium, ovangkol back and sides, pearl dot inlays, natural.

1998-2005		$1,100	$1,200

414ce

1998-present. 414 with cutaway, on-board electronics.

1998-2005		$1,150	$1,250

MODEL YEAR	FEATURES	EXC. COND. LOW	HIGH

415

1998-present. Solid sitka spruce top, jumbo, ovangkol back and sides, pearl dot inlays.

| 1998-2005 | | $1,000 | $1,100 |

420

1990-1997. D-style, sitka spruce top, maple back and sides, natural.

| 1990-1997 | | $1,000 | $1,100 |

422 K

1991-1998. Grand concert, solid koa construction, satin natural finish.

| 1991-1998 | | $900 | $1,000 |

450 12-String

1996-1997. Dreadnought 12-string, satin finish.

| 1996-1997 | | $1,000 | $1,100 |

455 12-String

2001-present. Solid Sitka spruce top, ovangkol back and sides, dot markers.

| 2001-2005 | | $1,100 | $1,200 |

455ce 12-String

2001-present. 455 with cutaway, on-board electronics.

| 2001-2005 | | $1,200 | $1,300 |

455ce LTD 12-String

2001. Limited edition.

| 2001 | | $1,400 | $1,500 |

510

1978-present. All solid wood dreadnought, spruce top, mahogany back and sides.

| 1978-1979 | | $1,350 | $1,400 |
| 1980-2005 | | $1,200 | $1,300 |

510 Limited

2002. Limited edition.

| 2002 | | $1,300 | $1,400 |

510ce

1978-present. 510 with cutaway, on-board electronics.

| 1978-1979 | | $1,500 | $1,600 |
| 1980-2005 | | $1,400 | $1,500 |

512

1978-2000. Solid Engelmann spruce top, grand concert, solid American mahogany back and sides, dot markers.

| 1978-2000 | | $1,300 | $1,400 |

512ce

1978-present. 512 with cutaway, on-board electronics.

| 1978-2005 | | $1,600 | $1,800 |

512NG Nanci Griffith

1996-1997. Model 512ce with sunburst finish.

| 1996-1997 | | $1,700 | $1,900 |

514c

1990-1998. Venetian cutaway, grand auditorium, solid spruce or solid red cedar top, mahogany back and sides, no electronics, natural.

| 1990-1998 | | $1,600 | $1,800 |

514ce

1998-present. 514c with on-board electronics.

| 1998-2005 | | $1,600 | $1,800 |

555 12-String

1978-present. Solid sitka spruce top, jumbo, solid mahogany back and sides, higher-end appointments.

| 1994-2005 | | $1,800 | $1,900 |

555ce 12-String

1994-present. 555 with cutaway, on-board electronics.

| 1994-2005 | | $1,900 | $2,000 |

610

1978-1998. Solid spruce top, dreadnought, solid maple back and sides, generally with amber stained finishes.

| 1978-1998 | | $1,400 | $1,600 |

610ce

1998-present. 610 with cutaway, on-board electronics.

| 1998-2005 | | $1,500 | $1,700 |

612

1984-1998. Solid spruce top, grand concert, solid maple back and sides, generally with amber stained finishes.

| 1984-1998 | | $1,600 | $1,800 |

612ce

1998-present. 612 with cutaway, on-board electronics.

| 1998-2005 | | $1,700 | $1,900 |

614

1978-1998. Solid spruce top, grand auditorium, solid maple back and sides, generally with amber stained finishes.

| 1978-1998 | | $1,700 | $1,900 |

614ce

1998-present. 614 with cutaway, on-board electronics.

| 1998-2005 | | $1,800 | $2,000 |

615

1981-1998. Jumbo, spruce top, flamed maple back and sides, non-cut.

| 1981-1998 | | $1,800 | $2,000 |

655

1978-present. Solid spruce top, jumbo, solid maple back and sides, generally with Amber stained finishes.

| 1978-2005 | | $1,700 | $1,900 |

655 12-String

1978-1991, 1996-present. Solid spruce top, solid maple back and sides, generally with amber stained finishes.

| 1978-2005 | | $1,700 | $1,900 |

655ce 12-String

1998-present. 655 with cutaway, on-board electronics.

| 1998-2005 | | $1,800 | $2,000 |

710

1977-present. Dreadnought-size, rosewood back and sides, spruce top.

| 1977-2005 | | $1,700 | $1,900 |

710BR

1990s. Model 710 with Brazilian rosewood.

| 1990s | | $2,700 | $2,800 |

Taylor 310ce

Taylor 655

Taylor 712

Taylor 912ce

MODEL YEAR	FEATURES	EXC. COND. LOW	HIGH

710ce L30 Commemorative
2004. 30th Anniversary Limited Edition, Englemann spruce top, Indian rosewood body, on-board electronics, 30th Anniversary script logo on headstock, single-cut.

| 2004 | | $1,900 | $2,100 |

712
1984-present. Grand Concert small body, solid wood, non-cut, rosewood back and sides, spruce top, cedar soundboard.

| 1984-2005 | | $1,400 | $1,500 |

712ce
2000-present. 712 with cutaway, on-board electronics.

| 2000-2005 | | $1,500 | $1,600 |

714
1996-present. 15 7/8" lower bout, grand auditorium, solid red cedar top, solid Indian rosewood back and sides.

| 1996-2005 | | $1,600 | $1,800 |

714ce
1998-present. 714 with cutaway, on-board electronics.

| 1998-2005 | | $1,700 | $1,900 |

755 12-String
1990-1998. D-style, 12 strings, solid spruce top, rosewood back and sides, natural.

| 1990-1998 | | $1,600 | $1,800 |

810
1975-present. Classic original Taylor dreadnought design - early model.

| 1975-2005 | | $1,400 | $1,700 |

810ce
1998-present. 810 with cutaway, on-board electronics.

| 1998-2003 | Brazilian rosewood option | $3,100 | $3,600 |
| 1998-2005 | Indian rosewood | $1,450 | $2,000 |

814
2005-present. Cutaway, grand auditorium, rosewood back and sides, spruce top.

| 2005 | | $2,150 | $2,250 |

815
Jumbo, solid sitka spruce top, Indian rosewood back and sides.

| 1970s | | $2,200 | $2,300 |

815c
1993-1998. Cutaway jumbo, no electronics, solid sitka spruce top, Indian rosewood back and sides.

| 1993-1998 | | $1,700 | $2,100 |

815ce
1998-present. 815c with on-board electronics.

| 1998-2005 | | $1,800 | $2,200 |

855 12-String
1993-present. Jumbo 12-string, solid sitka spruce top, rosewood back and sides, natural.

| 1993-2005 | | $1,700 | $2,100 |

910
1977-present. Dreadnought, maple back and sides until change to Indian rosewood in '86, spruce top, wide abalone-style rosette.

| 1986-2005 | | $2,000 | $2,500 |

910ce
1998-present. 910 with cutaway, on-board electronics.

| 1998-2005 | | $2,100 | $2,600 |

912c
1993-2002. Grand concert, rosewood back and sides, abalone.

| 1993-2002 | | $2,400 | $2,600 |

914ce
2002-present. 914c with on-board electronics.

| 2002-2005 | | $2,500 | $2,700 |

Baby
1996-present. Solid spruce top, 3/4 dreadnought, mahogany laminated back and sides until '99, sapele laminate after.

| 1996-2005 | | $225 | $275 |

Baby Mahogany (M)
1998-present. Solid mahogany top version of Baby, mahogany laminated back and sides until '99, sapele laminate after.

| 1998-2005 | | $250 | $350 |

Baby Rosewood
2000-2003. Laminated Indian rosewood back and sides version, solid sitka spruce top

| 2000-2003 | | $275 | $375 |

Big Baby
2000-present. 15/16"-size dreadnought, solid sitka spruce top, sapele-mahogany laminated back and sides, satin finish, gig bag.

| 2000-2005 | | $300 | $400 |

Dan Crary Signature Model
1986-2000. Dreadnought, Venetian cutaway, thin spruce top, Indian rosewood back and sides, Crary signature on headstock.

| 1986-2000 | | $1,300 | $1,500 |

LKSM6/12 Leo Kottke
1997-present. Jumbo 17" body, 6- or 12-string, rounded cutaway, sitka spruce top, mahogany back and sides, gloss finish, Leo Kottke signature.

| 1997-2005 | 12-string | $1,800 | $1,900 |
| 1997-2005 | 6-string | $1,600 | $1,700 |

GSGW
2001. Limited production of 100 guitars, grand concert size, spruce top, Zircote back and sides.

| 2001 | | $3,500 | $4,000 |

GSST
2000. Limited production.

| 2000 | | $4,000 | $4,500 |

K10
1983-present. Acoustic dreadnought, koa back and sides, spruce top, distinctive binding.

| 1983-2005 | | $1,900 | $2,100 |

K14c
1998-2002. 15 3/4" lower bout grand auditorium, solid cedar top, solid flamed koa body, gloss finish.

| 1998-2002 | | $2,100 | $2,300 |

K20
1983-1992. Non-cut D-style, koa top/back/sides, abalone rosette.

| 1983-1992 | | $1,300 | $1,500 |

MODEL YEAR	FEATURES	EXC. COND. LOW	HIGH

K20c
1998-2002. Cutaway K20.

1998-2002		$1,800	$2,000

K20ce
2001-present. Special order only by 2004, on-board electronics.

2001-2005		$1,900	$2,100

K55 12-String
2001-prresent. Jumbo size 12-string, spruce top, koa back and sides.

2001-2005		$2,200	$2,300

NS Series
2002-present. Nylon Strung series, models include NS42ce, NS44 (ovangkol body), NS62ce (maple body) and NS74. All models were cutaway electric (ce) by '04.

2002-2005	NS42ce	$1,100	$1,200
2002-2003	NS44	$1,000	$1,100
2002-2005	NS62ce	$1,000	$1,100
2002-2003	NS74	$1,000	$1,100

PS Presentation Limited
2003. Engleman spruce top, quilted maple back and sides.

2003		$3,900	$4,100

PS12c
1996-2004. Presentation Series grand concert 15" lower bout, solid Englemann spruce top, solid AAA flamed koa back and sides, fancy 'Byzantine' vine inlay on fretboard.

1996-2004		$5,000	$5,500

PS14BZ Special Edition
1996. Presentation Series special edition with Englemann spruce top, Brazilian rosewood back and sides, abalone trim.

1996		$4,500	$5,000

PS14c
2000. Presentation Series special edition with spruce top, AAA koa back and sides.

2000		$5,000	$5,500

PS15
1996-present. Solid Engelmann spruce top, jumbo, Brazilian rosewood back and sides, scalloped X-bracing, high-end appointments.

1996-2005		$5,000	$5,500

T5 Series
2005-present. hollow thinline body, sapele back and sides, spruce, maple, or koa tops, Custom models have gold hardware and Artist inlays, Standard is chrome with micro-dots.

2005	Custom (flamed maple)	$2,500	$2,700
2005	Custom (koa top)	$2,850	$3,000
2005	Custom (spruce top)	$2,400	$2,500
2005	Standard (maple top)	$2,400	$2,500
2005	Standard (spruce top)	$2,000	$2,100

MODEL YEAR	FEATURES	EXC. COND. LOW	HIGH

W10
1998-present. Claro walnut back and sides, dreadnought, optional tops include sitka spruce, Western red cedar, or claro walnut.

1998-2005		$1,400	$1,600

W14ce
2000-present. Claro walnut back and sides, grand auditorium, red cedar top, on-board electronics.

2000-2005		$1,700	$2,000

XX-RS 20th Anniversary
1994. Grand Auditorium 15 3/4" lower bout, spruce top, Indian rosewood back and sides.

1994		$2,500	$2,700

XXV-RS 25th Anniversary
1999-2000. D-size, spruce top, sapele back and sides.

1999-2000		$2,100	$2,200

XXX-KE 30th Anniversary
2004. Limited edition, Englemann spruce top, highly figured koa sides and back, slotted headstock, fancy appointments.

2004		$3,000	$3,200

Teisco
1946-1974, 1994-present. Founded in Tokyo, Japan by Hawaiian and Spanish guitarist Atswo Kaneko and electrical engineer Doryu Matsuda, the original company name was Aoi Onpa Kenkyujo; Teisco was the instrument name. Most imported into U.S. by Chicago's W.M.I. Corporation and Jack Westheimer beginning ca. '63-'64, some early ones for New York's Bugeleisen and Jacobson. Brands made by the company include Teisco, Teisco Del Rey, Kingston, World Teisco, Silvertone, Kent, Kimberly and Heit Deluxe.

In '56, the company's name was changed to Nippon Onpa Kogyo Co., Ltd., and in '64 the name changed again to Teisco Co., Ltd. In January '67, the company was purchased by Kawai. After '73, the brand was converted to Kay in U.S.; Teisco went into hiatus in Japan until being revived in the early-'90s with plexiglass reproductions of the Spectrum 5 (not available in U.S.). Some older Teisco Del Rey stock continued to be sold in U.S. through the '70s.

Electrics

1966-1969	1, 2, or 3 pickups	$100	$400
1966-1969	4 pickups or special finishes	$400	$550
1966-1969	Spectrum V	$400	$550
1968-1969	May Queen, black	$500	$600
1968-1969	May Queen, red	$600	$700

Tele-Star
1965-ca.1972. Imported from Japan by Tele-Star Musical Instrument Corporation of New York, New York. Primarily made by Kawai, many inspired by Burns designs, some in cool sparkle finishes. They also built basses.

Taylor NS62ce

Teisco Spectrum 5

Timtone SH2

Tokai Talbo

MODEL YEAR	FEATURES	EXC. COND. LOW	HIGH
Electrics			
1966-1969	1, 2, or 3 pickups	$125	$275
1966-1969	4 pickups or special finishes	$300	$400
1966-1969	Amp-in-case	$175	$275
1969-1970	Double neck 6/4	$500	$650

Tennessee

1970-1993, 1996-present. Luthier Mark Taylor builds his professional and premium grade, production/custom, acoustic guitars in Old Hickory, Tennessee. He also builds mandolins, banjos and the Tut Taylor brand of resophonic guitars. Mark and his father Robert "Tut" Taylor started making the Tennessee brand of acoustic and resophonic guitars, banjos, and mandolins in '71. In '77, Tut left the company and Mark continued on as Crafters of Tennessee. In '93, Mark and Greg Rich started building instruments as Rich and Taylor. In '96, Mark resumed production under the Tennessee brand.

Texas

1959-ca. 1965. Line of aluminum neck electric solidbodies and basses made by France's Jacobacci company, which also built under its own brand. One, 2, or 3 pickups.

TheDon

Guitars made in Germany and imported into the U.S. by a guitar shop.

Thomas Rein

1972-present. Luthier Thomas Rein builds his premium grade, production/custom, classical guitars in St. Louis, Missouri.

Thompson Guitars

1980-present. Luthier Ted Thompson builds his professional and premium grade, production/custom, flat-top, 12-string, and nylon-string guitars in Vernon, British Columbia.

Thorn Custom Guitars

2000-present. Professional and premium grade, custom/production, solid and hollowbody electrics built by luthiers Bill Thorn and his sons Bill, Jr. and Ron in Glendale, California. They started Thorn Custom Inlay in the early '90s to do custom inlay work for other builders. In '00, they added their own line of guitars.

Threet Guitars

1990-present. Premium grade, production/custom, flat-tops built by luthier Judy Threet in Calgary, Alberta.

Tilton

1850s-late 1800s. Built by William B. Tilton, of New York City. He was quite an innovator and held several guitar-related patents. He also built banjos.

MODEL YEAR	FEATURES	EXC. COND. LOW	HIGH
Parlor			
1890s. Parlor guitar with various woods.			
1850s	Brazilian, fancy binding	$2,200	$2,800
1860s	Brazilian, fancy binding	$2,200	$2,800
1890s	Diagonal grain spruce top, Brazilian	$1,500	$2,200
1890s	Pearl trim, Brazilian	$3,500	$4,500
1890s	Standard grain spruce top, Brazilian	$1,500	$2,000

Timeless Instruments

1980-present. Luthier David Freeman builds his professional, premium and presentation grade, custom, flattop, 12-string, nylon-string, and resonator guitars in Tugaske, Saskatchewan. He also builds mandolins and dulcimers.

Timm Guitars

1997-present. Professional grade, custom, flat-top, resonator and travel guitars built by luthier Jerry Timm in Auburn, Washington.

Timtone Custom Guitars

1993-2006. Luthier Tim Diebert built his premium grade, custom, solidbody, chambered-body and acoustic guitars in Grand Forks, British Columbia. He also built basses and lap steels.

Tippin Guitar Co.

1978-present. Professional, premium and presentation grade, production/custom, flat-top guitars built by luthier Bill Tippin in Marblehead, Massachusetts.

Tobias

1977-present. Known mainly for basses, Tobias did offer guitar models in the '80s. See Bass Section for more company info.

TogaMan GuitarViol

2003-present. Premium grade, production/custom, bow-playable solidbody guitars built by luthier Jonathan Wilson in San Fernando, California.

Tokai

1947-present. Japan's Tokai Company started out making a keyboard harmonica that was widely used in Japanese schools. In '65, they started producing acoustic guitars, followed shortly by electrics. In the late '60s, Tokai hooked up with Tommy Moore, a successful instrument merchandiser from Fort Worth, Texas, and by '70 they were producing private label and OEM guitars, sold in the U.S. under the brands of various importers. By the '70s, the Tokai name was being used on the instruments. Today Tokai continues to offer electrics, acoustics, and electric basses made in Japan and Korea.

MODEL YEAR	FEATURES	EXC. COND. LOW	HIGH

ASD 403 Custom Edition
Classic offset double-cut solidbody, single-single-hum pickups, locking tremolo.

1980s		$550	$700

AST 56
Classic offset double-cut solidbody style, 3 single-coils.

1980s		$550	$700

ATE 52
Classic single-cut solidbody style, 2 single-coils.

1980s		$550	$700

Love Rock
1977-1980s. Classic single-cut solidbody style, 2 humbuckers, figured tops at the high end.

1980s		$550	$1,000

Tom Anderson Guitarworks
1984-present. Professional and premium grade, production/custom, solidbody, semi-solidbody and acoustic guitars built by luthier Tom Anderson in Newbury Park, California.

Classic
1984-present. Double-cut solidbody, classic 3 pickup configuration, colors and appointments can vary.

1984-2005		$1,400	$1,600

Cobra
1993-present. Single-cut solid mahogany body with figured maple top.

1993-2005		$1,700	$1,800

Drop Top
1992-present. Double-cut solidbody, single-single-hum pickups, various specs.

1992-2005		$1,600	$1,800

Hollow Classic
1996-present. Ash double-cut with tone chambers, 3 pickups.

1996-2005		$1,500	$1,800

TommyHawk
1993-2005. Acoustic travel guitars built by luthier Tom Barth in Succasunna, New Jersey. They also offered a full-scale acoustic/electric model. Barth died in '05.

Tonemaster
1960s. Guitars and basses, imported from Italy, with typical '60s Italian sparkle plastic finish and push-button controls, bolt-on neck.

ToneSmith
1997-present. Luthier Kevin Smith builds his professional and premium grade, production/custom, semi-hollow body guitars in Rogers, Minnesota. He also builds basses. He previously built GLF brand guitars and built the line of Vox USA guitars from '98-'01.

Tony Nobles
1990-present. Professional and premium grade, custom, acoustic and electric guitars built by luthier Tony Nobles in Wimberley, Texas. Tony writes a monthly repair article for *Vintage Guitar* magazine.

Tony Vines Guitars
1989-present. Luthier Tony Vines builds his premium and presentation grade, custom/production, steel string guitars in Kingsport, Tennessee.

Torres (Antonio de Torres Jurado)
19th Century luthier most often associated with the initial development of the Classical Spanish guitar.

Toyota
1972-?. Imported from Japan by Hershman of New York, New York. At least 1 high-end acoustic designed by T. Kurosawa was ambitiously priced at $650.

Traphagen, Dake
1972-present. Luthier Dake Traphagen builds his premium grade, custom, nylon-string guitars in Bellingham, Washington.

Traugott Guitars
1991-present. Premium grade, production/custom, flat-top and acoustic/electric guitars built by luthier Jeff Traugott in Santa Cruz, California.

Traveler Guitar
1992-present. Intermediate grade, production, travel size electric, acoustic, classical and acoustic/electric guitars made in Redlands, California. They also make basses.

Travis Bean
1974-1979, 1999. Aluminum-necked solidbody electric guitars and basses. The company was founded by motorcycle and metal-sculpture enthusiast Travis Bean and guitar repairman Marc McElwee in Southern California; soon joined by Gary Kramer (see Kramer guitars). Kramer left Travis Bean in '75 and founded Kramer guitars with other partners. Guitar production began in mid-'76. The guitars featured carved aluminum necks with three-and-three heads with a T cutout in the center and wooden 'boards. Some necks had bare aluminum backs, some were painted black. A total of about 3,650 instruments were produced. Travis Bean guitar production was stopped in the summer of '79.

Serial numbers were stamped on headstock and were more-or-less consecutive. These can be dated using production records published by Bill Kaman in Vintage Guitar magazine. Original retail prices were $895 to $1195.

The company announced renewed production in '99 with updated versions of original designs and new models, but it evidently never got going.

Tom Anderson Drop Top

Tony Nobles Exhibition

Travis Bean TB-1000 Artist

Triggs San Salvador

MODEL YEAR	FEATURES	EXC. COND. LOW	HIGH

TB-500
Aluminum neck, T-slotted headstock, double-cut, 2 single coils mounted in 'guard, 2 controls, dot markers, white.

| 1975-1976 | | $2,000 | $3,000 |

TB-1000 Artist
1974-1979. Aluminum neck, T-slotted headstock, double-cut archtop, 2 humbuckers, 4 controls, block inlays.

| 1974-1979 | | $2,000 | $3,000 |

TB-1000 Standard
1974-1979. Similar to TB-1000 Artist, but with dot inlays.

| 1974-1979 | | $2,000 | $3,000 |

TB-3000 Wedge
1976-1979. Aluminum neck with T-slotted head-stock, triangle-shaped body, 2 humbucking pickups, 4 controls, block markers on 'board.

| 1976-1979 | | $3,000 | $4,000 |

Triggs
1992-present. Luthiers Jim Triggs and his son Ryan build their professional and premium grade, production/custom, archtop, flat-top, and solidbody guitars originally in Nashville Tennessee, and, since '98, in Kansas City, Kansas. They also build mandolins.

Acoustic/Electric Archtop
1992-present. Various archtop cutaway models.

1992-2005	Byrdland 17"	$2,500	$3,500
1992-2005	Excel 17"	$5,500	$6,500
1992-2005	Jazzmaster	$2,500	$3,500
1992-2005	New Yorker 18"	$6,500	$7,500
1992-2005	Stromberg Master 400	$7,000	$8,500

Trinity River
Acoustic and resonator guitars from Stenzler Musical Instruments of Ft. Worth, Texas. They also offer basses, mandolins, and fiddles.

True North Guitars
1994-present. Luthier Dennis Scannell builds his premium grade, custom, flat-tops in Waterbury, Vermont.

True Tone
1960s. Guitars, basses and amps retailed by Western Auto, manufactured by Chicago guitar makers like Kay. The brand was most likely gone by '68.

Double Cutaway Electric Archtop (K592)
1960s. Made by Kay and similar to their K592 double-cut thinline acoustic, 2 pickups, Bigsby tailpiece, burgundy red.

| 1960s | | $500 | $650 |

Fun Time
Early- to mid-1960s. Student 13" flat-top, painted 5-point 'guard, red sunburst finish.

| 1960s | | $50 | $75 |

MODEL YEAR	FEATURES	EXC. COND. LOW	HIGH

Imperial Deluxe
Mid-1960s. Harmony-made (Rocket), 3 pickups, trapeze tailpiece, 6 control knobs, block markers, sunburst.

| 1960s | | $575 | $675 |

Jazz King (K573 Speed Demon)
1960s. Kay's K573 Speed Demon, 3 pickups, thinline archtop electric with F-hole, eighth note art on 'guard, sunburst.

| 1960s | | $500 | $650 |

Rock 'n Roll Electric (K100)
1960s. Kay's K100, slab body, single pickup, but with a bright red multiple lacquer finish.

| 1960s | | $125 | $175 |

Solidbody (K300 Kay)
1960s. Made by Kay and similar to their K300, double-cut, dual pickups and vibrola arm, red.

| 1960s | | $450 | $550 |

Speed Master (K6533 Value Leader Archtop)
1960s. Made by Kay and similar to their K6533 full-body electric archtop Value Leader line, eighth note art 'guard, sunburst.

| 1960s | | $250 | $300 |

Western Spanish Auditorium
Early- to mid-1960s. 15" flat-top, laminate construction, celluloid 'guard, sunburst.

| 1960s | | $175 | $225 |

Tucker
2000-present. Founded by John N. "Jack" Tucker, John Morrall, and David Killingsworth, Tucker builds professional and premium grade, production/custom, albizzia wood solidbody guitars in Hanalei, Hawaii. They also build basses.

Tut Taylor
Line of professional and premium grade, production/custom, resophonic guitars built by luthier Mark Taylor of Crafters of Tennessee in Old Hickory, Tennessee. Brand named for his father, dobro artist Tut Taylor. Taylor also builds the Tennessee line of guitars, mandolins and banjos and was part of Rich and Taylor guitars for '93-'96.

TV Jones
1993-present. Professional and premium grade, production/custom, hollow, chambered, and solid body guitars built by luthier Thomas Vincent Jones originally in California, now in Poulsbo, Washington. The instruments have either Jones or TV Jones inlaid on the headstock. He also builds pickups.

U. A. C.
1920s. Instruments built by the Oscar Schmidt Co. and possibly others. Most likely a brand made for a distributor.

MODEL YEAR	FEATURES	EXC. COND. LOW	HIGH

Unique Guitars

2003-present. Professional and premium grade, production/custom, solidbody guitars built by luthier Joey Rico in California. He also builds basses. Joey is the son of Bernie Rico, the founder of BC Rich guitars.

Univox

1964-1978. Univox started out as an amp line and added guitars around '68. Guitars were imported from Japan by the Merson Musical Supply Company, later Unicord, Westbury, New York. Many if not all supplied by Arai and Company (Aria, Aria Pro II), some made by Matsumoku.

Univox Lucy ('69) first copy of lucite Ampeg Dan Armstrong. Generally mid-level copies of American designs.

Acoustic Flat-Top
1969-1978. Various models.

1970s		$100	$225

Bi-Centennial
1976. Offset double-cut, heavily carved body, brown stain, 3 humbucker-style pickups.

1976		$550	$900

Electric Hollowbody
Various models.

1970s		$300	$500

Electric Solidbody
Includes Flying V, Mosrite and Hofner violin-guitar copies.

1970s		$250	$550

Guitorgan FSB C-3000
1970s. Double-cut semi-hollow body, multiple controls, Guitorgan logo on headstock, footpedal.

1970s		$1,100	$1,300

USA Custom Guitars

1999-present. Professional and premium grade, custom/production, solidbody electric guitars built in Tacoma, Washington. USA also does work for other luthiers.

Vaccaro

1997-2002. Founded by Henry Vaccaro, Sr., one of the founders of Kramer Guitars. They offered intermediate and professional grade, production/custom, aluminum-necked guitars designed by Vaccaro, former Kramer designer Phil Petillo, and Henry Vaccaro, Jr., which were made in Asbury Park, New Jersey. They also built basses.

Valco

Valco, from Chicago, was a big player in the guitar and amplifier business. Their products were private branded for other companies like National, Supro, Airline, Oahu, and Gretsch.

Valencia

1985-present. Budget grade, production, classical guitars imported by Rondo Music of Union, New Jersey.

Valley Arts

Ca. 1977-present. Professional and premium grade, production/custom, semi-hollow and solidbody guitars built in Nashville, Tennessee. They also make basses. Valley Arts originally was a Southern California music store owned by partners Al Carness and Mike McGuire where McGuire taught and did most of the repairs. Around '77, McGuire and Valley Arts started making custom instruments on a large scale. By '83, they opened a separate manufacturing facility to build the guitars. In '92 Samick acquired half of the company with McGuire staying on for a year as a consultant. Samick offered made-in-the-U.S. production and custom models under the Valley Arts name. In '02, Valley Arts became a division of Gibson Guitar Corp., which builds the guitars in Nashville. Founders Carness and McGuire are back with the company. They reintroduced the line in January, '03

California Pro (U.S.-made)
1983-2002. Double-cut body, six-on-a-side tuners, single/single/hum pickups, 2 knobs and switch, various colors, serial number begins with CAL.

1983-2002		$550	$650

Optek Fretlight (U.S.-made)
Double-cut body, about 126 LED lights in fretboard controlled by a scale/chord selector, black opaque.

1990		$500	$600

Standard Pro (U.S.-made)
1990-1993. Double-cut body, six-on-a-side tuners, single/single/hum pickups, 2 knobs and switch, black opaque, serial number begins with VA.

1990-1993		$500	$600

Vantage

1977-present. Budget and intermediate grade, production, acoustic and electric guitars. They also build basses. Instruments from Japan from '77-'90 and from Korea from '90-present.

Vega

1903-1980s, 1989-present. The name Vega means star and a star logo is often seen on the original Vega guitars. The original Boston-based company was purchased by C.F. Martin in '70 and used on imports. In '80, Martin sold the Vega trademark to Korea's Galaxy Trading Company. The Deering Banjo Company, in Spring Valley, California acquired the brand in '89 and uses it (and the star logo) on a line of banjos.

C Series Archtop
1930-1950s. Several different C-model numbers, mid-level archtops including carved solid tops with bookmatched figured maple backs, natural or sunburst.

1930s	Higher models (C-56)	$1,100	$1,800
1930s	Lower models	$850	$1,100
1940s		$850	$1,100
1950s	Cutaway	$950	$1,200

Valencia JF

1970 Univox Lucy

'05 Veleno Original

Veillette Acoustic 12

MODEL YEAR	FEATURES	EXC. COND. LOW	HIGH

Duo-Tron Electric Archtop
1940s-1950s. Mid-level large body non-cut archtop, single pickup, block markers, natural or sunburst.

| 1940s | | $1,400 | $2,100 |
| 1950s | | $1,400 | $2,000 |

FT-90 Flat-Top
1960s. 15" body with narrow waist, dot markers, Vega logo, natural.

| 1960s | | $450 | $550 |

O'Dell
1950s. Full body, single cut, acoustic-electric, 1 pickup, tailpiece controls.

| 1950s | Sunburst | $1,100 | $1,800 |

Parlor Guitar
Early-1900s. Small parlor-sized instrument, Brazilian rosewood back and sides, styles vary, fancy appointments associated with higher-end models, including binding, purfling and inlays.

| 1900s | Mid-level | $1,300 | $1,600 |
| 1910s | Higher-end | $2,500 | $3,500 |

Profundo Flat-Top
1940s-1950s. Flat-top D-style body, spruce top, mahogany or rosewood back and sides.

| 1940s-50s | Mahogany | $1,000 | $1,500 |
| 1940s-50s | Rosewood | $2,500 | $3,500 |

Solidbody Electric (Import)
1970s-1980s. Solidbody copies of classic designs, Vega script logo on headstock, bolt-on necks.

| 1970s | | $225 | $350 |

Vega, Charles
1993-present. Luthier Charles Vega builds his premium, production/custom, nylon-string guitars in Baltimore, Maryland.

Veillette
1991-present. Luthiers Joe Veillette (of Veillette-Citron fame) and Martin Keith build their professional grade, production/custom, acoustic, acoustic/electric, electric 6- and 12-string and baritone guitars in Woodstock, New York. They also build basses and mandolins.

Veillette-Citron
1975-1983. Founded by Joe Veillette and Harvey Citron who met at the New York College School of Architecture in the late '60s. Joe took a guitar building course from Michael Gurian and by the Summer of '76, he and Harvey started producing neck-thru solidbody guitars and basses. Veillette and Citron both are back building instruments.

Velázquez
1948-1972. Manuel Velázquez, New York, New York, gained a reputation as a fine repairman in the late 1940s. He opened his 3rd Avenue guitar building shop in the early 1950s. By the mid-1950s he was considered by some as being the finest American builder of classical guitars. Velázquez left New York in 1972 and moved to Puerto Rico. He continued building guitars for the Japanese

market. He returned to the United States in 1982. By the 2000s he built instruments with this son and daughter.

Professional-grade Classical
1950s-1960s. Brazilian rosewood sides and back.

| 1950-1960s | | $5,000 | $15,000 |

Veleno
1967, 1970-1977, 2003-present. Premium and presentation grade, production/custom, all-aluminum electric solidbody guitars built by luthier John Veleno in St. Petersburg, Florida. First prototype in '67. Later production begins in late-'70 and lasts until '75 or '76. The guitars were chrome or gold-plated, with various anodized colors. The Traveler Guitar was the idea of B.B. King; only 10 were made. Two Ankh guitars were made for Todd Rundgren in '77. Only one bass was made. Approximately 185 instruments were made up to '77 and are sequentially numbered. In 2003, John Veleno reintroduced his brand.

Original (Aluminum Solidbody)
1973-1976. V-headstock, chrome and aluminum.

| 1973-1976 | | $8,000 | $9,000 |

Traveler Guitar
1973-1976. Limited production of about a dozen instruments, drop-anchor-style metal body.

| 1973-1976 | | $10,000 | $13,000 |

Vengeance Guitars & Graphix
2002-present. Luthier Rick Stewart builds his professional and premium grade, custom/production, solidbody guitars in Arden, North Carolina. He also builds basses.

Ventura
1970s. Acoustic and electric guitars imported by C. Bruno Company, mainly copies of classic American models. They also offered basses.

Hollowbody Electric Guitars
| 1970s | Natural or Sunburst | $450 | $550 |

Versoul, LTD
1989-present. Premium grade, production/custom steel-string flat-top, acoustic/electric, nylon-string, resonator, solidbody, and baritone guitars built by luthier Kari Nieminen in Helsinki, Finland. He also builds basses and sitars.

Victor Baker Guitars
1998-present. Professional and premium grade, custom, carved archtop, flat-top and solidbody electric guitars built by luthier Victor Baker in Philadelphia, Pennsylvania.

Victor Guitars
2004-present. Luthier Edward Victor Dick builds his premium grade, production/custom, steel-string acoustics in Denver, Colorado.

MODEL YEAR	FEATURES	EXC. COND. LOW	HIGH

Victoria

1920s. Instruments built by the Oscar Schmidt Co. and possibly others. Most likely a brand made for a distributor.

Viking Guitars

1998-present. Professional and premium grade, custom, solidbody guitars made in Las Vegas, Nevada by Ed Roman.

Vincente Tatay

1894-late 1930s. Classical guitars built by luthier Vicente Tatay and his sons in Valencia, Spain.

Vinetto

2003-present. Luthier Vince Cunetto builds his professional grade, production/custom, solid, chambered and semi-hollow body guitars in St. Louis, Missouri.

Vivi-Tone

1933-ca. 1936. Founded in Kalamazoo, Michigan, by former Gibson designer Lloyd Loar, Walter Moon and Lewis Williams, Vivi-Tone built acoustic archtop guitars as well as some of the earliest electric solidbodies. They also built amps, basses and mandolins.

Guitar

1930s. Deep archtop-style body with F-holes on the backside and magnetic bridge pickup.

1930s	Rare model	$4,500	$5,000
1930s	Standard model, sunburst	$2,500	$3,000

Vox

1957-1972, 1982-present. Name introduced by Jennings Musical Instruments (JMI) of England. First Vox products were amplifiers brought to the market in '58 by Tom Jennings and Dick Denny. Guitars were introduced in '61, with an Echo Unit starting the Vox line of effects in '63.

Guitars and basses bearing the Vox name were offered from '61-'69 (made in England and Italy), '82-'85 (Japan), '85-'88 (Korea), and for '98-2001 (U.S.). Vox products are currently distributed in the U.S. by Korg USA. Special thanks to Jim Rhoads of Rhoads Music in Elizabethtown, Pennsylvania, for help on production years of these models.

Ace

1967 Late 1960s. Offset double cut solidbody, 2 single-coils, Ace logo.

1967-1968		$800	$1,000

Apollo

1967-1968. Single sharp cutaway, 1 pickup, distortion, treble and bass booster, available in sunburst or cherry.

1967-1968		$750	$900

Bobcat

1963-1968. Double-cut semi-hollowbody style, block markers, 3 pickups, vibrato, 2 volume and 2 tone controls.

1963-1968		$900	$1,000

Bossman

1967-1968. Single rounded cutaway, 1 pickup, distortion, treble and bass booster, available in sunburst or cherry.

1967-1968		$600	$700

Bulldog

1966. Solidbody double-cut.

1966		$850	$1,050

Delta

1967-1968. Solidbody, 2 pickups, distortion, treble and bass boosters, vibrato, 1 volume and 2 tone controls, available in white only.

1967-1968		$1,100	$1,400

Folk XII

1966-1969. Dreadnought 12-string flat-top, large 3-point 'guard, block markers, natural.

1966-1969		$450	$550

Guitar-Organ

1966. Standard Phantom with oscillators from a Continental organ installed inside. Plays either organ sounds, guitar sounds, or both. Weighs over 20 pounds.

1966		$1,500	$2,000

Mando Guitar

1966. Made in Italy, 12-string mandolin thing.

1966		$1,400	$1,600

Mark III

1998-2001. Teardrop reissue, 2 single-coils, fixed bridge or Bigsby.

1998-2001		$675	$750

Mark IX

1965-1966. Solidbody teardrop-shaped, 9 strings, 3 pickups, vibrato, 1 volume and 2 tone controls, sunburst.

1965		$1,000	$1,200

Mark VI

1965-1967. Teardrop-shaped solidbody, 3 pickups, vibrato, 1 volume and 2 tone controls.

1964-1965	England, white, Brian Jones model	$3,300	$3,900
1965-1967	Italy, sunburst	$1,100	$1,300

Mark VI Reissue

1998-2001. Actually, this is a reissue of the original Phantom VI (Vox couldn't use that name due to trademark reasons).

1998-2001		$750	$850

Mark XII

1965-1967. Teardrop-shaped solidbody, 12 strings, 3 pickups, vibrato, 1 volume and 2 tone controls, sunburst. Reissued for '98-'01.

1965-1967		$1,200	$1,500

Phantom VI

1962-1967. Five-sided body, 6 strings, 3 pickups, vibrato, 1 volume and 2 tone controls.

1962-1964	English-made	$2,100	$2,300
1965-1967	Italian-made	$1,400	$1,600

Phantom XII

1964-1967. Five-sided body, 12 strings, 3 pickups, vibrato, 1 volume and 2 tone controls.

1964	English-made	$2,200	$2,400
1965-1967	Italian-made	$1,600	$1,800

Vox Mark VI

Vox Phantom XII

GUITARS

1965 Wandré Model Karak

Warrior Z Knight

MODEL YEAR	FEATURES	EXC. COND. LOW	HIGH

Spitfire
1965-1967. Solidbody double-cut, 3 pickups, vibrato tailpiece.

| 1965-1967 | | $500 | $600 |

Starstream
1967-1968. Teardrop-shaped hollowbody, 2 pickups, distortion, treble and bass boosters, wah-wah, vibrato, 1 volume and 2 tone controls, 3-way pickup selector, available in cherry or sandburst.

| 1967-1968 | | $1,100 | $1,300 |

Starstream XII
1967-1968. 12 string Starstream.

| 1967-1968 | | $1,100 | $1,350 |

Stroller
1961-1966. Made in England, solidbody, single bridge pickup, Hurricane-style contoured body, dot markers, red.

| 1961-1966 | | $350 | $500 |

Student Prince
1965-1967. Mahogany body thinline archtop electric, 2 knobs, dot markers, made in Italy.

| 1965-1967 | | $400 | $505 |

Super Ace
1963-1965. Solidbody double-cut.

| 1963-1965 | | $350 | $500 |

Super Lynx
1965-1967. Similar to Bobcat but with 2 pickups and no vibrola, double-cut, 2 pickups, adjustable truss rod, 2 bass and 2 volume controls.

| 1965-1967 | | $700 | $800 |

Super Lynx Deluxe
1965-1967. Super Lynx with added vibrato tailpiece.

| 1965-1967 | | $750 | $850 |

Super Meteor
1965-1967. Solidbody double-cut.

| 1965-1967 | | $350 | $500 |

Tempest XII
1965-1967. Solidbody double-cut, 12 strings, 3 pickups.

| 1965-1967 | | $600 | $700 |

Thunder Jet
1960s-style with single pickup and vibrato arm.

| 1960s | | $600 | $700 |

Tornado
1965-1967. Thinline archtop, single pickup, dot markers, sunburst.

| 1965-1967 | | $350 | $450 |

Typhoon
1965-1967. Hollowbody single-cut, 2 pickups, 3-piece laminated neck.

| 1965-1967 | | $400 | $550 |

Ultrasonic
1967-1968. Hollowbody double-cut, 2 pickups, distortion, treble and bass boosters, wah-wah, vibrato, 1 volume and 2 tone controls, 3-way pickup selector, available in sunburst or cherry.

| 1967-1968 | | $750 | $900 |

Viper
1968. Double-cut, thinline archtop electric, built-in distortion.

| 1968 | | $1,100 | $1,200 |

MODEL YEAR	FEATURES	EXC. COND. LOW	HIGH

Walker

1994-present. Premium and presentation grade, production/custom, flat-top and archtop guitars built by luthier Kim Walker in North Stonington, Connecticut.

Wandre (Davoli)

Ca. 1956/57-1969. Solidbody and thinline hollowbody electric guitars and basses created by German-descended Italian motorcycle and guitar enthusiast, artist, and sculptor from Milan, Italy, Wandre Pioli. Brands include Wandre (pronounced Vahn-dray), Davoli, Framez, JMI, Noble, Dallas, Avalon, Avanti I and others. Until '60, they were built by Pioli himself; from '60-'63 built in Milan by Framez; '63-'65 built by Davoli; '66-'69 built in Pioli's own factory.

The guitars originally used Framez pickups, but from '63 on (or earlier) they used Davoli pickups. Mostly strange shapes characterized by neck-thru-tailpiece aluminum neck with plastic back and rosewood 'board. Often multi-color and sparkle finishes, using unusual materials like linoleum, fiberglass and laminates, metal bindings. Often the instruments will have numerous identifying names but usually somewhere there is a Wandre "blob" logo.

Distributed early on in the U.K. by Jennings Musical Industries, Ltd. (JMI) and in the U.S. by Don Noble and Company. Model B.B. dedicated to Brigitte Bardot. Among more exotic instruments were the minimalist Krundaal Bikini guitar with a built-in amplifier and attached speaker, and the "pogo stick" Swedenbass. These guitars are relatively rare and highly collectible. In '05, the brand was revived on a line of imported intermediate grade, production, solidbodies from Eastwood guitars.

Metal Solidbody

| 1960s | | $1,500 | $4,500 |

Warren

2005-present. Luthier Don Warren builds his professional and premium grade, custom/production, solidbody electric guitars in Latham, New York.

Warrior

1995-present. Professional, premium, and presentation grade, production/custom, acoustic and solidbody electric guitars built by luthier J.D. Lewis in Roseville, Georgia. Warrior also builds basses.

Washburn (Lyon & Healy)

1880s-ca.1949. Washburn was founded in Chicago as one of the lines for Lyon & Healy to promote high quality stringed instruments, ca. 1880s. The rights to manufacture Washburns were sold to J.R. Stewart Co. in '28, but rights to Washburn name were sold to Tonk Brothers of Chicago. In the Great Depression (about 1930), J.R. Stewart Co. was hit

MODEL YEAR	FEATURES	EXC. COND. LOW	HIGH

hard and declared bankruptcy. Tonk Brothers bought at auction all Stewart trade names, then sold them to Regal Musical Instrument Co. Regal built Washburns by the mid-'30s. The Tonk Brothers still licensed the name. These Washburn models lasted until ca. '49. In '74 the brand resurfaced.

Model 1897
High-end appointments, plentiful pearl, 18 frets, slightly larger than parlor size, natural.

1910		$2,500	$3,800

Model 1915
Brazilian rosewood back and sides.

1928		$2,000	$2,500

Model 5257 Solo
1930s. Jumbo size body, rosewood back and sides, natural.

1930s		$5,500	$6,000

Model 5265 Tenor
1920s. Pear-shaped mahogany body, 4-string tenor.

1920s		$550	$650

Parlor Guitar
Early-1900s. Lower-end, small 12"-13" body, plain appointments.

1900s		$500	$600

Style 188
Rosewood back and sides with full pearl 'board inlaid with contrasting colored pearl, pearl on edges and around soundhole.

1890s		$4,000	$4,800

Style A
1920s. Smaller body, rosewood back and sides, top stencil decoration, natural.

1920s		$3,000	$3,500

Washburn
1974-present. Budget, intermediate, professional, and premium grade, production/custom, acoustic and electric guitars made in the U.S., Japan, and Korea. They also make basses, amps, banjos and mandolins.

Originally a Lyon & Healy brand, the Washburn line was revived in '74, promoted by Beckman Musical Instruments. Beckman sold the rights to the Washburn name to Fretted Instruments, Inc. in '76. Guitars originally made in Japan and Korea, but production moved back to U.S. in '91. Currently Washburn is part of U.S. Music.

Washington
Washington was a brand manufactured by Kansas City, Missouri instrument wholesalers J.W. Jenkins & Sons. First introduced in 1895, the brand also offered mandolins.

Watkins/WEM
1957-present. Watkins Electric Music (WEM) was founded by Charlie Watkins. Their first commercial product was the Watkins Dominator (wedge Gibson stereo amp shape) in '57. They made the Rapier line of guitars and basses from

the beginning. Watkins offered guitars and basses up to '82.

Wayne
1998-present. Professional and premium grade, production/custom, solidbody guitars built by luthiers Wayne and Michael (son) Charvel in Paradise, California. They also build lap steels.

Webber
1988-present. Professional grade, production/custom flat-top guitars built by luthier David Webber in North Vancouver, British Columbia.

Weber
1996-present. Premium grade, production/custom, carved-top acoustic and resonator guitars built by luthier Bruce Weber and his Sound To Earth, Ltd. company, originally in Belgrade, Montana, and since '04, in Logan, Montana. They also build mandolins.

Webster
1940s. Archtop and acoustic guitars, most likely built by Kay or other mass builder.

Model 16C
1940s. Acoustic archtop.

1940s		$500	$600

Wechter
1984-present. Intermediate, professional and premium grade, production/custom, flat-top, 12-string, resonator and nylon-string guitars from luthier Abe Wechter in Paw Paw, Michigan. He also offers basses. The Elite line is built in Paw Paw, the others in Asia. Until '94 he built guitars on a custom basis. In '95, he set up a manufacturing facility in Paw Paw to produce his new line and in '00 he added the Asian guitars. In '04, he added resonators designed by Tim Scheerhorn. Wechter was associated with Gibson Kalamazoo from the mid-'70s to '84. He also offers the Maple Lake brand of acoustics.

Weissenborn
1910s-1937, present. Hermann Weissenborn was well-established as a violin and piano builder in Los Angeles by the early 1910s. Around '20, he added guitars, ukes and steels to his line. Most of his production was in the '20s and '30s until his death in '37. He made tenor, plectrum, parlor, and Spanish guitars, ukuleles, and mandolins, but is best remembered for his koa Hawaiian guitars that caught the popular wave of Hawaiian music. That music captivated America after being introduced to the masses at San Francisco's Panama Pacific International Exposition which was thrown in '15 to celebrate the opening of the Panama Canal and attended by more than 13 million people. He also made instruments for Kona and other brands. The Weissenborn brand has been revived on a line of reissue style guitars.

Wayne Exotic Rock Legend

1930s Weissenborn

Weissenborn Style 1 tenor

Worland Jumbo

MODEL YEAR	FEATURES	EXC. COND. LOW	HIGH
Spanish Acoustic			
1920s. High-end Spanish set-up, rope binding, koa top, sides and back, limited production.			
1920s		$4,300	$5,300
Style #1 Hawaiian			
Koa, no binding, 3 wood circle soundhole inlays.			
1926		$2,800	$3,500
Style #2 Hawaiian			
Koa, black celluloid body binding, white wood 'board binding, rope soundhole binding.			
1926		$3,000	$4,000
Style #3 Hawaiian			
Koa, rope binding on top, 'board, and soundhole.			
1925		$3,500	$5,000
Style #4 Hawaiian			
Koa, rope binding on body, 'board, headstock and soundhole.			
1927		$4,500	$6,500
Tenor			
1920		$1,700	$2,000

Welker Custom

Professional and premium grade, production/custom, archtop and flat-top guitars built by luthier Fred Welker in Nashville, Tennessee.

Wendler

1999-present. Intermediate and professional grade, production/custom, solidbody, electro-acoustic guitars from luthier Dave Wendler of Ozark Instrument Building in Branson, Missouri. He also builds basses and amps. In '91, Wendler patented a pickup system that became the Taylor ES System.

Westbury-Unicord

1978-ca. 1983. Imported from Japan by Unicord of Westbury, New York. High quality original designs, generally with 2 humbuckers, some with varitone and glued-in necks. They also had basses.

Westone

1970s-1990, 1996-2001. Made by Matsumoku in Matsumoto, Japan and imported by St. Louis Music. Around '81, St. Louis Music purchased an interest in Matsumoku and began to make a transition from its own Electra brand to the Westone brand previously used by Matsumoku. In the beginning of '84, the brand became Electra-Westone with a phoenix bird head surrounded by circular wings and flames. By the end of '84 the Electra name was dropped, leaving only Westone and a squared-off bird with W-shaped wings logo. Electra, Electra-Westone and Westone instruments from this period are virtually identical except for the brand and logo treatment. Many of these guitars and basses were made in very limited runs and are relatively rare.

From '96 to '01, England's FCN Music offered Westone branded electric and acoustic guitars. The electrics were built in England and the acoustics came from Korea. Matsumoku-made guitars feature a serial number in which the first 1 or 2 digits represent the year of manufacture. Electra-Westone guitars should begin with either a 4 or 84.

Weymann

1864-1940s. H.A. Weymann & Sons was a musical instrument distributor located in Philadelphia that marketed various stringed instruments, but mainly known for banjos. Some guitar models made by Regal and Vega, but they also built their own instruments.

Parlor

1904-ca. 1920. Small 14 5/8" body parlor-style, fancy pearl and abalone trim, fancy fretboard markers, natural.

1910		$3,000	$3,500

Style 24

1920s. Mid-size body, 12-fret, slotted peghead, made by Vega for Weymann, mahogany sides and back, natural.

1920s		$800	$850

Wilkanowski

Early-1930s-mid-1940s. W. Wilkanowski primarily built violins. He did make a few dozen guitars which were heavily influenced by violin design concepts and in fact look very similar to a large violin with a guitar neck.

Violin-Shaped Acoustic

1930-1945. Violin brown.

1930-1945		$15,000	$22,000

Wilkins

1984-present. Custom guitars built by luthier Pat Wilkins in Van Nuys, California. Wilkins also does finish work for individuals and a variety of other builders.

William Hall and Son

William Hall and Son was a New York City based distributor offering guitars built by other luthiers in the mid to late 1800s.

Wilson

1960s. One of the brand names of guitars built for others by Egmond in Holland.

Wilson Brothers Guitars

2004-present. Intermediate and professional grade, production, imported electric and acoustic guitars. They also build basses. Founded by Ventures guitarist Don Wilson. VCM and VSP models made in Japan; VM electrics in Korea; VM acoustic in China.

Ventures Model VM Electrics

2004-present. Wilson Brothers and The Ventures Model logos on the headstock, various models made in Korea.

2004-2005 VM-65		$200	$250

MODEL YEAR	FEATURES	EXC. COND. LOW	HIGH

Windsor

Ca. 1890s-ca. 1914. Brand used by Montgomery Ward for flat top guitars and mandolins made by various American manufacturers, including Lyon & Healy and, possibly, Harmony. Generally beginner-grade instruments.

Acoustic Flat-Top
1890s-1914.

1900s		$200	$325

Winston

Ca. 1963-1967. Imported from Japan by Buegeleisen and Jacobson of New York. Manufacturers unknown, but some are by Guyatone. Generally shorter scale beginner guitars. They also had basses.

Worland Guitars

1997-present. Professional grade, production/custom, flat-top, 12-string, and harp guitars built by luthier Jim Worland in Rockford, Illinois.

WRC Music International

1989-mid-1990s. Guitars by Wayne Richard Charvel, who was the original founder of Charvel Guitars. He now builds Wayne guitars with his son Michael.

Wright Guitar Technology

1993-present. Luthier Rossco Wright builds his unique intermediate grade, production, travel/practice steel-string and nylon-string guitars in Eugene, Oregon.

Wurlitzer

Wurlitzer marketed a line of American-made guitars in the 1920s. They also offered American- and foreign-made guitars starting in '65. The American ones were built from '65-'66 by the Holman-Woodell guitar factory in Neodesha, Kansas. In '67, Wurlitzer switched to Italian-made Welson guitars.

Model 2077 (Martin 0-K)
1920s. Made by Martin for Wurlitzer who had full-line music stores in most major cities. Size 0 with top, back and sides made from koa wood, limited production of about 28 instruments.

1922	Natural	$4,500	$5,500

Model 2090 (Martin 0-28)
1920s. Made by Martin for Wurlitzer who had full-line music stores in most major cities. Size 0 with appointments similar to a similar period Martin 0-28, limited production of about 11 instruments, Wurlitzer branded on the back of the headstock and on the inside back seam, Martin name also branded on inside seam.

1922	Natural	$6,500	$8,000

Wild One "Stereo"
1960s. Two pickups, various colors.

1967		$500	$800

Xaviere

Imtermediate and professional grade, prodution, solid and semi-hollow body guitars from Guitar Fetish, which also has GFS pickups.

Yamaha

1946-present. Budget, intermediate, professional, and presentation grade, production/custom, acoustic, acoustic/electric, and electric guitars. They also build basses, amps, and effects. The Japanese instrument maker was founded in 1887. Began classical guitar production around 1946. Solidbody electric production began in '66; steel string acoustics debut sometime after that. Production shifted from Japan to Taiwan (Yamaha's special-built plant) in the '80s, though some high-end guitars still made in Japan. Some Korean production began in '90s.

Serialization patterns:

Serial numbers are coded as follows:

H = 1, I = 2, J = 3, etc., Z = 12

To use this pattern, you need to know the decade of production.

Serial numbers are ordered as follows: Year/Month/Day/Factory Order

Example: NL 29159 represents a N=1987 year, L=5th month or May, 29=29th day (of May), 159=159th guitar made that day (the factory order). This guitar was the 159 guitar made on May 29, 1987.

AE-11
1966-1974. Single-cut, arched top, glued neck, 2 pickups, natural.

1966-1974		$700	$1,100

AE-12
1973-1977. Single-cut thinline archtop.

1973-1977		$700	$1,100

AE-18
1973-1977. AE-12 with upgrade inlays and gold hardware.

1973-1977		$800	$1,100

AE-500
1998-2000. Solidbody with rounded cutaway horn, 2 humbuckers, pearloid guard, dot markers.

1998-2000		$300	$375

AE-1200
1985-1992. Full body electric archtop, cherry sunburst.

1985-1992		$800	$1,100

APX-4
1992-1995. Acoustic/electric cutaway flat-top.

1992-1995		$350	$500

APX-7
1987-1994. Acoustic/electric, 2 pickups, mono 2-way, gold hardware.

1987-1994		$350	$500

APX-10
1987-1994. Acoustic/electric flat-top cutaway, 2 pickups, stereo 2-way. Called APX-10T if ordered with rosewood back and sides.

1987-1994		$475	$550

Wright Guitar Technology SoloEtte

Xaviere XV-700

GUITARS

Yamaha RGX Standard

Yamaha SA-2000

MODEL YEAR	FEATURES	EXC. COND. LOW	HIGH

APX-20
1987-1994. Acoustic/electric single-cut flat-top, solid spruce top, sycamore back and sides, 2 pickups, stereo 2-way, abalone inlays.

1987-1994		$475	$550

DW-8 VRS
1999-2002. Dreadnought flat-top, sunburst, solid spruce top, higher-end appointments like abalone rosette and top purfling.

1999-2002		$500	$600

Eterna Acoustic
1983-1994. Folk style acoustics, there were 4 models.

1983-1994		$250	$350

FG Series Flat-Tops
1970-1994. Economy market, laminated sides and back, a 12 suffix indicates 12-string, CE indicates on-board electronics, many models are D-style bodies.

1970s	FG-110	$200	$250
1970s	FG-260-12, mahogany	$200	$250
1970s	FG-310, mahogany	$225	$275
1970s	FG-340, mahogany	$225	$275
1973	FG-1500, Brazilian rosewood	$400	$500
1980s	FG-210-12	$200	$250
1980s	FG-335 II	$225	$275
1983-1994	FG-345	$225	$275
1983-1994	FG-412-12SB, sunburst	$250	$350
1983-1994	FG-512-12, natural	$250	$350
1984-1994	FG-410, acoustic	$250	$350
1984-1994	FG-410CE, electric	$350	$450
1984-1994	FG-411-12, acoustic, mahogany	$250	$350
1984-1994	FG-411CE-12, electric	$350	$450
1984-1994	FG-430A	$250	$350
1984-1994	FG-750S, mahogany	$250	$350

G-245S
1981-1985. Classical, solid spruce top, rosewood back and sides.

1981-1985		$350	$450

G-255S
1981-1985. Classical, spruce top, Indian rosewood back and sides.

1981-1985		$400	$500

GC Series
1983-1996. Classical guitars, '70s made in Japan, '80s made in Taiwan.

1983-1994	GC-30	$500	$750
1980s	GC-6D	$500	$650

Image Custom
1989-1992. Electric double-cut, flamed maple top, active circuitry, LED position markers.

1989-1992		$400	$500

L Series Flat-Tops
1984-1996. Solid wood, custom hand-built.

1984-1996	L-10A, Indian rosewood	$800	$1,000
1984-1996	L-8	$500	$700

Pacifica
1989-present. Offset double-cut with longer horns, dot markers, various models.

1989-1999	Mid-line models	$150	$200
2000-2005	Mid-line models	$150	$175

RGX Series
1988-1989. Bolt-on neck for the 600 series and neck-thru body designs for 1200 series, various models include 110 (1 hum), 211 (hum-single), 220 (2 hums), 312 (hum-single-single), 603 (3 singles), 612 (hum-single-single), 620 (2 hums), 1203S (3 singles), 1212S (hum-single-single), 1220S (2 hums).

1988-1989	Various models	$250	$350

RGZ-312
1989-1992. Offset double-cut solid body, bolt neck, 2 single-coils and 1 humbucker, dot markers.

1989-1992		$300	$400

RGZ-820R
1993-1994. Blues Saraceno Signature Model, bolt neck, 2 humbuckers, dot markers.

1993-1994		$400	$550

SA Series (Super Axe)
1966-1994. Full-size and thinline archtop models.

1966-1970s	SA-30T	$700	$775
1966-1970s	SA-50T, natural, figured maple	$725	$875
1979-1984	SA-2000	$975	$1,100
1980s	SA-1300, sunburst, dots	$575	$700
1980s	SA-700	$850	$950

SBG-200
1983-1992. Solidbody, glued neck, unbound, dot inlays on rosewood 'board, gold hardware, white top.

1983-1992		$350	$550

SBG-500
1981-1992. Electric, laminated body, set-in neck, 2 pickups, Tune-O-Matic bridge, sunburst or burgundy finish.

1981-1992		$450	$650

SBG-2000
1980-1992. Electric, double-cut beveled body, set-neck, 2 pickups.

1980-1992		$450	$650

SBG-2100
1984-1992. Double-cut solidbody, set-neck.

1984-1992		$450	$650

SE-250
1986-1992. Electric, offset double-cut, 2 pickups.

1986-1992		$250	$350

SE-350H
1986-1992. Solidbody, offset double-cut, 2 humbuckers.

1986-1992		$250	$350

SG-20
1972-1973. Bolt-on neck, slab body, single-cut, 1 pickup.

1972-1973		$350	$500

MODEL YEAR FEATURES	EXC. COND. LOW	HIGH

SG-3
1965-1966. Early double-cut solidbody with sharp horns, bolt neck, 3 hum-single pickup layout, large white guard, rotor controls, tremolo.

| 1965-1966 | $950 | $1,200 |

SG-5/SG-5A
1966-1971. Asymmetrical double-cut solidbody with extended lower horn, bolt neck, 2 pickups, chrome hardware.

| 1966-1971 | $950 | $1,200 |

SG-7/SG-7A
1966-1971. Like SG-5, but with gold hardware.

| 1966-1971 | $1,000 | $1,500 |

SG-30/SG-30A
1973-1976. Slab katsura wood (30) or slab maple (30A) solidbody, bolt-on neck, 2 humbuckers, dot inlays.

| 1973-1976 | $400 | $550 |

SG-35/SG-35A
1973-1976. Slab mahogany (35) or slab maple (35A) solidbody, bolt-on neck, 2 humbuckers, parallelogram inlays.

| 1973-1976 | $450 | $600 |

SG-40
1972-1973. Bolt-on neck, carved body, single-cut.

| 1972-1973 | $450 | $600 |

SG-45
1972-1976. Glued neck, single-cut, bound flat-top.

| 1972-1976 | $500 | $700 |

SG-50
1974-1976. Slab katsura wood solidbody, glued neck, 2 humbuckers, dot inlays, large 'guard.

| 1974-1976 | $500 | $700 |

SG-60
1972 only. Bolt-on neck, carved body, single-cut.

| 1972 | $500 | $600 |

SG-60T
1973 only. SG-60 with large cast vibrato system.

| 1973 | $550 | $650 |

SG-65
1972-1976. Glued neck, single-cut, bound flat-top.

| 1972-1976 | $600 | $700 |

SG-70
1974-1976. Slab maple solidbody, glued neck, 2 humbuckers, dot inlays, large 'guard.

| 1974-1976 | $600 | $700 |

SG-80
1972 only. Bolt-on neck, carved body, single-cut.

| 1972 | $500 | $650 |

SG-80T
1973. SG-60 with large cast vibrato system.

| 1973 | $550 | $700 |

SG-85
1972-1976. Glued neck, single-cut, bound flat-top.

| 1972-1976 | $600 | $700 |

SG-90
1974-1976. Carved top mahogany solidbody, glued neck, elevated 'guard, bound top, dot inlays, chrome hardware.

| 1974-1976 | $700 | $750 |

SG-175
1974-1976. Carved top mahogany solidbody, glued neck, elevated 'guard, abalone bound top, abalone split wing or pyramid inlays, gold hardware.

| 1974-1976 | $800 | $900 |

SG-500
1976-1978. Carved unbound maple top, double pointed cutaways, glued neck, 2 exposed humbuckers, 3-ply bound headstock, bound neck with clay split wing inlays, chrome hardware. Reissued as the SBG-500 (800S in Japan) in '81.

| 1976-1978 | $675 | $875 |

SG-700
1976-1978. Carved unbound maple top, double pointed cutaways, glued neck, 2 humbuckers, 3-ply bound headstock, bound neck with clay split wing inlays, chrome hardware.

| 1976-1978 | $750 | $850 |

SG-700S
1999-2001. Set neck, mahogany body, 2 humbuckers with coil tap.

| 1999-2001 | $750 | $850 |

SG-1000/SBG-1000
1976-1983 ('84 in Japan). Carved maple top, double pointed cutaways, glued neck, 2 humbuckers, 3-ply bound headstock, unbound body, bound neck with clay split wing inlays, gold hardware. Export model name changed to SBG-1000 in '80.

| 1976-1979 | SG-1000 | $750 | $850 |
| 1980-1983 | SBG-1000 | $750 | $850 |

SG-1500
1976-1979. Carved maple top, double pointed cutaways, laminated neck-thru-body neck, laminated mahogany body wings, 2 humbuckers, 5-ply bound headstock and body, bound neck with dot inlays, chrome hardware. Name used on Japan-only model in the '80s.

| 1976-1979 | $850 | $950 |

SG-2000/SG-2000S
1976-1980 (1988 in Japan). Carved maple top, double pointed cutaways, laminated neck-thru-body neck, laminated mahogany body wings, 2 humbuckers, 5-ply bound headstock and body, bound neck with abalone split wing inlays, gold hardware. In '80, the model was changed to the SBG-2000 in the U.S., and the SG-2000S everywhere else except Japan (where it remained the SG-2000). Export model renamed SBG-2100 in '84.

| 1976-1980 | $900 | $1,000 |

SG-2100S
1983. Similar to SG-2000 with upgrades such as the pickups.

| 1983 | $1,000 | $1,100 |

SG-3000/SBG-3000/Custom Professional
1982-1992. SG-2000 upgrade with higher output pickups and abalone purfling on top.

| 1982-1992 | $1,000 | $1,100 |

Yamaha SG-30

Yamaha SG-1500

Yanuziello electric

Zemaitis S22 Metal-Front

MODEL YEAR	FEATURES	EXC. COND. LOW	HIGH

SHB-400
1981-1985. Solidbody electric, set-in neck, 2 pickups.

1981-1985		$400	$500

SJ-180
1983-1994. Student Jumbo, entry level Folk Series model, laminated top.

1983-1994		$100	$150

SJ-400S
1983-1994. Student Jumbo Folk Series model, solid wood top.

1983-1994		$200	$300

SSC-500
1983-1992. Solidbody electric, 3 pickups, set-in neck.

1983-1992 .		$400	$500

Weddington Classic
1989-1992. Electric solidbody, redesigned set-in neck/body joint for increased access to the higher frets.

1989-1992		$400	$500

Yanuziello Stringed Instruments
1980-present. Production/custom resonator and Hawaiian guitars built by luthier Joseph Yanuziello, in Toronto, Ontario.

Yosco
1900-1930s. Lawrence L. Yosco was a New York City luthier building guitars, round back mandolins and banjos under his own brand and for others.

Zeiler Guitars
1992-present. Custom flat-top, 12-string, and nylon-string guitars built by luthier Jamon Zeiler in Cincinnati, Ohio.

MODEL YEAR	FEATURES	EXC. COND. LOW	HIGH

Zemaitis
1960-1999, 2004-present. Professional, premium, and presentation grade, custom/production, electric guitars. Tony Zemaitis (born Antanus Casimere Zemaitis) began selling his guitars in 1960. He emphasized simple light-weight construction and was known for hand engraved metal front guitars. The metal front designs were originally engineered to reduce hum, but they became popular as functional art. Each hand-built guitar and bass was a unique instrument. Ron Wood was an early customer and his use of a Zemaitis created a demand for the custom-built guitars. Approximately 6 to 10 instruments were built each year. Tony retired in '99, and passed away in '02 at the age of 67. In '04, Japan's Kanda Shokai Corporation, with the endorsement of Tony Zemaitis, Jr., started building the guitars again. KSC builds the higher priced ones and licenses the lower priced guitars to Greco.

Celebrity association with Zemaitis is not uncommon. Validated celebrity provenance may add 25% to100% (or more) to a guitar's value. Tony Zemaitis also made so-called student model instruments for customers with average incomes. These had wood tops instead of metal or pearl. Some wood top instruments have been converted to non-Zemaitis metal tops, which are therefore not fully original Zemaitis instruments.

Acoustic Models

1965	12-string, 1st year	$22,000	$26,000
1970s	6-string	$15,000	$17,000
1980s	12-string, D-hole	$13,000	$16,000
1980s	12-string, heart-hole	$24,000	$29,000
1980s	6-string, D-hole	$13,000	$15,000
1980s	6-string, heart-hole	$19,000	$29,000

MODEL YEAR	FEATURES	EXC. COND. LOW	HIGH
Electric Models			
1980-1990s	Student model, wood top	$12,000	$19,000
1980s	Disc-front	$20,000	$35,000
1980s	Metal-front	$25,000	$35,000
1980s	Pearl-front	$30,000	$40,000
1994	"Black Pearl", very few made	$34,000	$39,000
1995	Disc-front 40th Anniversary	$29,000	$39,000

Zen-On

1946-ca.1968. Japanese manufacturer. By '67 using the Morales brand name. Not heavily imported into the U.S., if at all (see Morales).

Acoustic Hollowbody
1946-1968. Various models.

1950s		$150	$250

Electric Solidbody
1960s. Teisco-era and styling.

1960s		$150	$250

Zeta

1982-present. Zeta has made solid, semi-hollow and resonator guitars, many with electronic and MIDI options, in Oakland, California over the years, but currently only offer basses, amps and violins.

Zim-Gar

1960s. Imported from Japan by Gar-Zim Musical Instrument Corporation of Brooklyn, New York. Manufacturers unknown. Generally shorter scale beginner guitars.

Electric Solidbody

1960s		$150	$250

Zimnicki, Gary

1980-present. Luthier Gary Zimnicki builds his professional and premium grade, custom, flat-top, 12-string, nylon-string, and archtop guitars in Allen Park, Michigan.

Zion

1980-present. Professional and premium grade, production/custom, semi-hollow and solidbody guitars built by luthier Ken Hoover, originally in Greensboro, North Carolina, currently in Raleigh.

Classic
1989-present. Double-cut solidbody, six-on-a-side headstock, opaque finish, various pickup options, dot markers.

1989-2005	Custom quilted top	$700	$800
1989-2005	Opaque finish	$500	$600

Graphic
1980s-1994. Double-cut basswood body, custom airbrushed body design, bolt-on neck, Green Frost Marble finish.

1990		$850	$950

Radicaster
1987-present. Double-cut basswood body, graphic finish, bolt-on neck, various pickup configurations, marble/bowling ball finish.

1987-2005		$650	$800

The Fifty
1994-present. Single-cut ash solidbody, 2 single coils, bolt-on neck.

1994-2005	Custom figured top	$700	$800
1994-2005	Natural, plain top	$550	$650

Zolla

1979-present. Professional grade, production/custom, electric guitars built by luthier Bill Zolla in San Diego, California. Zolla also builds basses, necks and bodies.

Zon

1981-present. Currently luthier Joe Zon only offers basses, but he also built guitars from '85-'91. See Bass Section for more company info.

ZZ Ryder

Solidbody electric guitars from Stenzler Musical Instruments of Ft. Worth, Texas. They also offer basses.

Zeta MIDI guitar

Zion Primera

Basses

Alamo Titan

Alembic Distillate

MODEL YEAR	FEATURES	EXC. COND. LOW	HIGH

A Basses

1976-2002. Luthier Albey Balgochian built his professional grade, solidbody basses in Waltham, Massachusetts. Sports the A logo on headstock.

Solidbody Basses

1990s		$800	$1,100

Acoustic

Ca. 1965-ca. 1987. Mainly known for solidstate amps, the Acoustic Control Corp. of Los Angeles, did offer guitars and basses from around '69 to late '74. The brand was revived a few years ago by Samick for a line of amps.

Black Widow Bass

1969-1970, 1972-1974. Around '69 Acoustic offered the AC600 Black Widow Bass (in both a fretted and fretless version) which featured an unique black equal double-cut body with German carve, an Ebonite 'board, 2 pickups, each with 1 row of adjustable polepieces, a zero fret, and a protective "spider design" pad on back. Also available was the AC650 short-scale. The '72-'74 version had the same body design, but had a rosewood 'board and only 1 pickup with 2 rows of adjustable pole pieces (the '72s had a different split-coil pickup with 4 pole pieces, 2 front and 2 back). Acoustic outsourced the production of the basses, possibly to Japan, but at least part of the final production was by Semie Moseley.

1972-1974		$850	$925

Aims

Ca. 1974-ca. 1976. Aims instruments, distributed by Randall Instruments in the mid-'70s, were copies of classic American guitar and bass models. Randall also offered a line of Aims amps during the same time.

Airline

1958-1968, 2004-present. Brand for Montgomery Ward. Built by Kay, Harmony and Valco. In '04, the brand was revived on a line of reissues from Eastwood guitars.

Electric Solidbody Bass

1958-1968	Various models	$200	$300

Pocket 3/4 Bass (Valco/National)

1962-1968. Airline brand of double-cut 'Pocket Bass,' short-scale, 2 pickups, 1 acoustic bridge and 1 neck humbucker, sunburst and other colors.

1962-1968		$650	$750

Alamo

1947-1982. Founded by Charles Eilenberg, Milton Fink, and Southern Music, San Antonio, Texas. Distributed by Bruno & Sons.

Eldorado Bass (Model 2600)

1965-1966. Solidbody, 1 pickup, angular offset shape, double-cut.

1965-1966		$200	$250

MODEL YEAR	FEATURES	EXC. COND. LOW	HIGH

Titan Bass

1963-1970. Hollowbody, 1 pickup, angular offset shape.

1963-1970		$200	$250

Alembic

1969-present. Professional, premium, and presentation grade, production/custom, 4-, 5-, and 6-string basses built in Santa Rosa, California. They also build guitars. Established in San Francisco as one of the first handmade bass builders. Alembic basses come with many options concerning woods (examples are maple, bubinga, walnut, vermilion, wenge, zebrawood), finishes, inlays, etc., all of which affect the values listed here. These dollar amounts should be used as a baseline guide to values for Alembic.

Anniversary Bass

1989. 20th Anniversary limited edition, walnut and vermillion with a walnut core, 5-piece body, 5-piece neck-thru, only 200 built.

1989		$2,000	$2,200

Custom Shop Built Bass

1969-present. Various one-off and/or custom built instruments. Each instrument should be evaluated individually. Prices are somewhat speculative due to the one-off custom characteristics and values can vary greatly.

1978	Dragon Doubleneck	$8,000	$9,000
2000	Stanley Clarke Custom	$3,000	$5,000
2004	Dragon 4-string, 4 made	$4,000	$4,500

Distillate Bass

1979-1991. Exotic woods, active electronics.

1979-1991	Distillate 4	$1,400	$1,800
1979-1991	Distillate 5	$1,600	$2,100

Elan Bass

1985-1996. Available in 4-, 5-, 6- and 8-string models, 3-piece thru-body laminated maple neck, solid maple body, active electronics, solid brass hardware, offered in a variety of hardwood tops and custom finishes.

1985-1996	Elan 4	$1,300	$1,700
1985-1996	Elan 5	$1,500	$2,000

Epic Bass

1993-present. Mahogany body with various tops, extra large pointed bass horn, maple/walnut veneer set-neck, available in 4-, 5-, and 6-string versions.

1993-1999	4-string	$1,000	$1,200
1993-1999	5-string	$1,200	$1,300
1993-1999	6-string	$1,300	$1,400
2000-2004	4-string	$1,000	$1,200
2000-2004	5-string	$1,200	$1,300
2000-2004	6-string	$1,300	$1,400

Essence Bass

1991-present. Mahogany body with various tops, extra large pointed bass horn, walnut/maple laminate neck-thru.

1991-1999	Essence 4	$1,400	$1,600

BASSES

MODEL YEAR	FEATURES	EXC. COND. LOW	HIGH
1991-1999	Essence 5	$1,500	$1,700
1991-1999	Essence 6	$1,600	$1,800
2000-2004	Essence 4	$1,400	$1,600
2000-2004	Essence 5	$1,500	$1,700
2000-2004	Essence 6	$1,600	$1,800

Exploiter Bass

1980s. Figured maple solidbody 4-string, neck-thru, transparent finish.

1984-1988		$1,400	$2,000

Persuader Bass

1983-1991		$1,000	$1,300

Series I Bass

1971-present. Mahogany body with various tops, maple/purpleheart laminate neck-thru, active electronics, available in 3 scale lengths and with 4, 5 or 6 strings.

1971-1979	Medium- or long-scale	$5,500	$6,000
1971-1979	Short-scale	$5,500	$6,000
1980-1989	Medium- or long-scale	$5,500	$6,000
1980-1989	Short-scale	$5,500	$6,000
1990-2000	All scales, highly figured top	$5,500	$6,000

Series II Bass

Generally custom-made option, each instrument valued on a case-by-case basis, guidance pricing only.

1971-2000		$6,500	$7,000

Spoiler Bass

1981-1999. Solid mahogany body, maple neck-thru, 4 or 6 strings, active electronics, various high-end wood options.

1981-1986	6-string	$1,700	$2,000
1981-1999	4-string	$1,500	$1,800

Stanley Clarke Signature Standard Bass

1990-present. Neck-thru-body, active electronics, 24-fret ebony 'board, mahogany body with maple, bubinga, walnut, vermilion, or zebrawood top, 4-, 5-, and 6-string versions.

1990-2000	All scales	$2,000	$2,200

Alleva-Coppolo

1995-present. Luthier Jimmy Coppolo builds his professional and premium grade, custom/production, solidbody basses in Dallas, Texas, for '95-'97, and since in New York City. He also builds guitars.

Alvarez

1965-present. Imported by St. Louis Music, they offered electric basses from '90 to '02 and acoustic basses in the mid-'90s.

Electric Bass (mid-level)

1990s	Hollowbody	$250	$400
1990s	Solidbody	$200	$350

American Conservatory (Lyon & Healy)

Late-1800s-early-1900s. Mainly catalog sales guitars and mandolins from the Chicago maker. Mid-level Lyon & Healy offering, above their Lakeside brand, and generally under their Washburn brand.

MODEL YEAR	FEATURES	EXC. COND. LOW	HIGH

Monster Bass G2740

Early-mid-1900s. Six-string acoustic flat-top, spruce top, birch back and sides with rosewood stain, natural. Their catalog claimed it was "Indespensable to the up-to-date mandolin and guitar club."

1917		$3,500	$5,000

American Showster

1986-2004. Established by Bill Meeker and David Haines, Bayville, New Jersey. They also made guitars.

AS-57-B Bass

1987-1997. Bass version of AS-57 with body styled like a '57 Chevy tail fin.

1987-1997		$2,000	$3,000

Ampeg

1949-present. Ampeg was founded on a vision of an amplified bass peg, which evolved into the Baby Bass. Ampeg has sold basses on and off throughout its history.

AEB-1 Bass

1966-1967. F-holes through the body, fretted, scroll headstock, pickup in body, sunburst. Reissued as the AEB-2 for '97-'99.

1966-1967		$2,200	$2,600

ASB-1 Devil Bass

1966-1967. Long-horn body, fretted, triangular f-holes through the body, fireburst.

1966-1967		$2,500	$3,500

AUB-1 Bass

1966-1967. Same as AEB-1, but fretless, sunburst. Reissued as the AUB-2 for '97-'99.

1966-1967		$1,900	$2,100

AUSB-1 Devil Bass

1966-1967. Same as ASB-1 Devil Bass, but fretless.

1966-1967		$2,500	$3,500

BB-4 Baby Bass

1962-1971. Electric upright slim-looking bass that is smaller than a cello, available in sunburst, white, red, black, and a few turquoise. Reissued as the ABB-1 Baby Bass for '97-'99.

1962-1971	Solid color	$2,400	$3,100
1962-1971	Sunburst	$2,300	$2,700

BB-5 Baby Bass

1964-1971. Five-string version.

1964-1971	Sunburst	$2,500	$3,300

Dan Armstrong Lucite Bass

1969-1971. Clear solid lucite body, did not have switchable pickups like the Lucite guitar.

1969-1971		$1,700	$2,900

Dan Armstrong Lucite Bass Reissue

1998-2001. Lucite body, Dan Armstrong Ampeg block lettering on 'guard.

1998-2001		$725	$825

GEB-101 Little Stud Bass

1973-1975. Import from Japan, offset double-cut solidbody, two-on-a-side tuners, 1 pickup.

1973-1975		$300	$450

Alembic Series I

1960s Ampeg Dan Armstrong

Applause AE-40

1976 Aria Mach 1

MODEL YEAR	FEATURES	EXC. COND. LOW	HIGH

GEB-750 Big Stud Bass
1973-1975. Import from Japan, similar to Little Stud, but with 2 pickups.

1973-1975		$375	$500

Andreas
1995-present. Aluminium-necked, solidbody guitars and basses built by luthier Andreas Pichler in Dollach, Austria.

Angelica
1967-1975. Student and entry-level basses and guitars imported from Japan.
Electric Solidbody Bass
Japanese imports.

1970s	Various models	$100	$150

Apollo
Ca. 1967-1972. Entry-level basses imported from Japan by St. Louis Music. They also had guitars and effects.
Electric Hollowbody Bass
Japanese imports.

1970s		$100	$200

Applause
1976-present. Intermediate grade, production, acoustic/electric basses. They also offer guitars, mandolins and ukes. Kaman Music's entry-level Ovation-styled brand. The instruments were made in the U.S. until around '82, when production was moved to Korea.

Arbor
1983-present. Budget grade, production, solidbody basses imported by Musicorp (MBT). They also offer guitars.
Electric Bass

1983-1999	Various models	$150	$200
2000-2005	Various models	$75	$125

Aria/Aria Pro II
1960-present. Budget and intermediate grade, production, acoustic, acoustic/electric, solidbody, hollowbody and upright basses. They also make guitars, mandolins, and banjos. Originally branded as Aria; renamed Aria Pro II in '75; both names used over the next several year; in '01, the Pro II part of the name was dropped altogether.
Electric Bass

1980s	Various models	$250	$350

Armstrong, Rob
1971-present. Custom basses made in Coventry, England, by luthier Rob Armstrong. He also builds mandolins, flat-tops, and parlor guitars.

Artinger Custom Guitars
1997-present. Professional and premium grade, production/custom, basses built by luthier Matt Artinger in Emmaus, Pennsylvania. He also builds

MODEL YEAR	FEATURES	EXC. COND. LOW	HIGH

builds hollow, semi-hollow, and chambered solidbody guitars.

Asama
1970s-1980s. Japanese line of solidbody basses. They also offered guitars, effects, drum machines and other music products.

Audiovox
Ca. 1935-ca. 1950. Paul Tutmarc's Audiovox Manufacturing, of Seattle, Washington, was a pioneer in electric lap steels, basses, guitars and amps. Tutmarc is credited with inventing the electric bass guitar in '35, which his company started selling in the late '30s.

Austin
1999-present. Budget and intermediate grade, production, basses imported by St. Louis Music. They also offer guitars, mandolins and banjos.

Avante
1997-present. Shape cutaway acoustic bass designed by Joe Veillette and Michael Tobias originally offered by Alvarez. Currently only a lower-priced baritone is offered by MusicYo. They also offer guitars.

Baldwin
1965-1970. The giant organ company got into guitars and basses in '65 when it bought Burns Guitars of England and sold those models in the U.S. under the Baldwin name.
Bison Bass
1965-1970. Scroll headstock, 3 pickups, black or white finishes.

1965-1966		$900	$1,200
1966-1970	Model 516	$900	$1,100

Baby Bison Bass
1965-1970. Scroll head, 2 pickups, black, red or white finishes.

1965-1966		$700	$800
1966-1970	Model 560	$600	$700

G.B. 66 Bass
1965-1966. Bass equivalent of G.B. 66 guitar, covered bridge tailpiece.

1965-1966		$750	$850

Jazz Split Sound Bass
1965-1970. Offset double-cut solidbody, 2 pickups, red sunburst.

1965-1966	Long-scale	$700	$800
1966-1970	Short-scale	$650	$750

Nu-Sonic Bass
1965-1966. Bass version of Nu-Sonic.

1965-1966		$600	$700

Shadows Bass/Shadows Signature
1965-1970. Named after Hank Marvin's backup band, solidbody, 3 slanted pickups, white finish.

1965-1966	Shadows	$1,300	$1,400
1966-1970	Shadows Signature	$1,000	$1,100

MODEL YEAR	FEATURES	EXC. COND. LOW	HIGH
Vibraslim Bass			
1965-1970. Thin body, scroll head, 2 pickups, sunburst.			
1965-1966		$800	$900
1966-1970	Model 549	$700	$800

Barclay

1960s. Generally shorter-scale, student-level imports from Japan. They also made guitars.

MODEL YEAR	FEATURES	EXC. COND. LOW	HIGH
Electric Solidbody Bass			
1960s	Various models	$125	$175

Bass Collection

1985-1992. Mid-level imports from Japan, distributed by Meisel Music of Springfield, New Jersey. Sam Ash Music, New York, sold the remaining inventory from '92 to '94.

MODEL YEAR	FEATURES	EXC. COND. LOW	HIGH
SB300 Series			
1985-1992. Offset double-cut, bolt neck, ash or alder body, models include 300, 301 (fretless) and 302 (5-string).			
1985-1992		$300	$600
SB400/SB500 Series			
1985-1992. Offset double-cut, bolt neck, basswood body, active electronics, models include 401, 402 (fretless), 405 (5-string) and 501 (alder body).			
1985-1992		$400	$650
SB600 Series			
1985-1992. Offset double-cut, bolt neck, maple/walnut body, active electronics.			
1985-1992		$450	$700

BC Rich

1966-present. Budget, intermediate, and premium grade, production/custom, import and U.S.-made basses. They also offer guitars.

Many BC Rich models came in a variety of colors. For example, in '88 they offered black, Competition Red, metallic red, GlitteRock White, Ultra Violet, and Thunder Blue. Also in '88, other custom colors, graphic features, paint-to-match headstocks, and special inlays were offered.

MODEL YEAR	FEATURES	EXC. COND. LOW	HIGH
Bich Bass			
1976-1998. Solidbody, neck-thru, 2 pickups.			
1976-1983		$1,100	$1,200
1984-1993		$800	$1,200
1994-2004	New Rico-era	$800	$900
Bich Supreme 8-String Bass			
Late-1970s-early-1980s.			
1978-1982		$1,700	$1,900
Eagle Bass (U.S.A. assembly)			
1977-1996. Curved double-cut, solidbody, natural.			
1977-1979		$2,000	$2,500
1980-1982		$1,400	$1,700
Gunslinger Bass			
1987-1999. Inverted headstock, 1 humbucker.			
1987-1989		$700	$800
1990-1999		$600	$700

MODEL YEAR	FEATURES	EXC. COND. LOW	HIGH
Ironbird Bass			
1984-1998. Kinda star-shaped, neck-thru, solidbody, 2 pickups, active electronics, diamond inlays.			
1980s		$850	$950
Mockingbird Bass			
1976-present.			
1976	USA, short-horn	$2,000	$3,000
1977-1978	USA, short-horn	$1,500	$2,500
1979-1983	USA, long-horn	$1,500	$2,300
1984-1989	End 1st Rico-era	$1,300	$2,100
1994-2004	New Rico-era	$1,300	$1,700
Nighthawk Bass			
1979-ca.1980. Bolt-neck.			
1978-1982		$700	$800
NJ Bass Series			
1983-present. Various models include Beast, Eagle, Innovator, Mockingbird, Virgin and Warlock.			
1983-1986		$350	$500
1987-1999		$275	$475
2000-2005		$275	$450
Platinum Bass Series			
1986-present. Imported versions including Eagle, Mockingbird, Beast, Warlock.			
1986-1999		$250	$375
Seagull/Seagull II Bass			
1972-1977. Solidbody, single cut to '75, double Seagull II after.			
1972-1975	Initial design	$1,300	$2,300
1976-1977	Seagull II	$1,300	$2,300
Son Of A Rich Bass			
1977-ca.1981. Basically a bolt neck Bich, U.S. made.			
1977-1981		$850	$1,000
ST-III Bass			
Available in bolt neck and non-bolt neck (1986 price at $999 & $1299 respectively), black hardware, P-Bass/J-Bass pickup configuration, 2 tone controls, 1 volume control, jumbo frets, ebony 'board.			
1987-1989	Bolt-on	$600	$750
1987-1989	Neck-thru	$700	$850
1989-1998		$600	$750
Warlock Bass (U.S.A.)			
1981-present. Introduced in '81 along with the Warlock guitar, USA-made, standard bolt-on model, maple body and neck, rosewood 'board, 22/accyruzer jumbo frets, Badass II low profile bridge by '88.			
1981-1989		$800	$1,000
Wave Bass			
1980s		$1,500	$2,000

Benedict

1988-present. Founded by Roger Benedict. Professional and premium grade, production/custom, solidbody basses built by luthier Bill Hager in Cedar, Minnesota. They also build guitars.

Bernie Rico Jr. Guitars

Professional and premium grade, production/custom, solidbody basses built by luthier Bernie Rico, Jr. in Hesperia, California. His father founded BC Rich guitars. He also makes guitars.

BC Rich NJ Series Virgin

1988 BC Rich Bich Bass

Birdsong Corto

1979 Carvin LB-50

MODEL YEAR	FEATURES	EXC. COND. LOW	HIGH

Birdsong Guitars

2001-present. Luthiers Scott Beckwith and Jamie Hornbuckle build their intermediate and professional grade, production/custom, solidbody basses in Wimberley, Texas. They also build guitars.

Black Jack

1960s. Entry-level and mid-level imports from Japan. They also offered guitars.

Electric Solidbody Bass

1960s	Various models	$100	$175

Blade

1987-present. Intermediate and professional grade, production, solidbody basses from luthier Gary Levinson's Levinson Music Products Ltd. in Switzerland. He also builds guitars.

Bradford

1960s. House brand of W.T. Grant department store, often imported. They also offered guitars.

Electric Solidbody Bass

1960s	Various models	$100	$175

Brawley Basses

Solidbody bass guitars designed by Keith Brawley and made in Korea. The company was headquartered in Temecula, California. They also made guitars.

Brian Moore

1992-present. Brian Moore added basses in '97. Currently they offer professional grade, production, solidbody basses. They also build guitars and mandolins.

Brice

1985-present. Budget grade, production, electric and acoustic basses imported by Rondo Music of Union, New Jersey.

BSX Bass

1990-present. Luthier Dino Fiumara builds his professional and premium grade, production/custom, acoustic, solidbody, semi-solid upright basses in Aliquippa, Pennsylvania.

Bunker

1961-present. Luthier Dave Bunker builds intermediate, professional, and premium grade, production/custom, basses in Port Angeles, Washington. He also builds guitars.

Burns

1960-1970, 1974-1983, 1992-present. Intermediate and professional grade, production, basses built in England and Korea. They also build guitars.

Nu-Sonic Bass

1964-1965		$700	$800

Scorpion

2003-present. Double-cut scorpion-like solidbody.

2003-2005		$350	$400

Burns-Weill

1959. Jim Burns and Henry Weill teamed up to produce three solidbody electrics and three solidbody basses under this English brand.

C. P. Thornton Basses

1985-1996. Solidbody basses and guitars built by luthier Chuck Thornton. He currently builds guitars under the C. P. Thornton Guitars brand in Turner, Maine.

Campellone

1978-present. Archtop guitar builder Mark Campellone, of Greenville, Rhode Island, built basses in the '70s.

Canvas

2004-present. Budget and intermediate grade, production, solidbody basses made in China. They also offer guitars.

Carvin

1946-present. Intermediate and Professional grade, production/custom, acoustic and electric basses. They also build guitars and amps.

AC Series Acoustic Electric

1996-present. 4- and 5-string acoustic/electrics.

1996-2004		$400	$650

Solidbody Electric Basses

1960s-2005		$350	$600

Chandler

1984-present. Premium grade, production/custom, solidbody 12-string electric basses built by luthiers Paul and Adrian Chandler in Chico, California. They also build guitars, laptops and pickups.

Charles Shifflett Acoustic Guitars

1990-present. Luthier Charles Shifflett builds his premium grade, custom, acoustic basses in High River, Alberta. He also builds flat-top, classical, flamenco, resophonic, and harp guitars, and banjos.

Charvel

1978-present. U.S.-made from '78 to '85 and a combination of imports and U.S.-made post-'85. They also build guitars.

Early Pre-Pro Basses

1980-1981. Pre-mass production basses, made Nov. '80 to '81. Refer to Charvel guitar section for details.

1980-1981	All models	$1,000	$3,000

San Dimas Serialized Plated

1981-1982. Soft headstock early models.

1981-1982	Soft headstock	$1,000	$3,000

MODEL YEAR	FEATURES	EXC. COND. LOW	HIGH

850 XL Bass
1988-1991. Four-string, neck-thru-body, active electronics.

1988-1991		$375	$475

CX-490 Bass
1991-1994. Double-cut, 4-string, bolt neck, red or white.

1991-1994		$225	$275

Eliminator Bass
1990-1991. Offset double-cut, active electronics, bolt neck.

1990-1991		$250	$300

Fusion Bass
1989-1991. 4- and 5-string models, active circuitry.

1989-1991	IV	$300	$400
1989-1991	V	$400	$600

Model 1 Bass
1986-1989. Double-cut, bolt neck, 1 pickup.

1986-1989		$350	$375

Model 2 Bass
1986-1989. Double-cut, bolt neck, 2 pickups.

1986-1989		$350	$375

Model 3 Bass
1986-1989. Neck-thru-body, 2 single-coil pickups, active circuitry, master volume, bass and treble knobs.

1986-1989		$400	$425

Model 5 Bass
1986-1989. Double-cut, P/J pickups.

1986-1989		$400	$575

SB-4 Bass
1990s. Offset double cut solid, long bass horn, 2 pickups.

1990s		$300	$350

Star Bass
1980-1981. Unique 4-point solidbody, 1 pickup, considered by Charvel collectors to be Charvel's only original early design.

1980-1981		$1,000	$3,000

Surfcaster Bass
1991-1994. Semi-hollow, lipstick tube pickups.

1991-1994		$800	$1,000

Cipher
1960s. Student market basses imported from Japan. They also made guitars.

Electric Solidbody Bass
1960s. Japanese imports.

1960s		$150	$200

Citron
1995-present. Luthier Harvey Citron (of Veillette-Citron fame) builds his professional and premium grade, production/custom basses in Woodstock, New York. He also builds solidbody guitars.

Clevinger
1982-present. Established by Martin Clevinger, Oakland, California. Mainly specializing in electric upright basses, but has offered bass guitars as well.

Upright Solidbody Electric Bass
1982-present. Straight vertical-shaped compact body, several options available that can increase values, black.

1982-1999		$1,700	$2,500

College Line
One of many Lyon & Healy brands, made during the era of extreme design experimentation.

Monster Bass (Style 2089)
Early-1900s. 22" lower bout, flat-top guitar/bass, natural.

1915		$4,000	$5,000

Conklin
1984-present. Intermediate, professional, and premium grade, production/custom basses from luthier Bill Conklin, of Springfield, Missouri. Conklin also offers guitars. Conklin instruments are made in the U.S. and overseas.

M.E.U. (Mobile Electric Upright) Bass
1995-present. Cello-style hollowbody, played in an upright position, 4-string or 5-string option.

1995-2004	4-string	$1,150	$1,350

Conrad
Ca.1968-1978. Student and mid-level copy basses imported by David Wexler, Chicago, Illinois. They also offered guitars, mandolins and banjos.

Model 40096 Acoustical Slimline Bass
1970s. 2 pickups.

1970s		$200	$300

Model 40177 Violin-Shaped Bass
1970s. Scroll headstock, 2 pickups.

1970s		$225	$425

Model 40224 Bumper Bass
1970s. Ampeg Dan Armstrong lucite copy.

1970s		$225	$325

Professional Bass
1970s. Offset double-cut.

1970s		$175	$250

Professional Bison Bass
1970s. Solidbody, 2 pickups.

1970s		$175	$250

Contessa
1960s. Acoustic, semi-hollow archtop, solidbody and bass guitars made in Germany. They also made banjos.

Coral
1967-1969. In '66 MCA bought Danelectro and in '67 introduced the Coral brand of guitars, basses and amps. The line included several solid and semi-solidbody basses.

Solidbody Bass
1967-1969. Includes the 4-string Deluxe Bass D2N4 and Wasp 2B4, and the 6-string Wasp 2B6, all offset double-cut, 2 pickup solidbodies.

1967-1969		$550	$650

Conklin Groove Tools 4

Cort Curbow 4-string

BASSES

Cort GB-3

1968 Custom Kraft Bone Buzzer

MODEL		EXC. COND.	
YEAR	FEATURES	LOW	HIGH

Corey James Custom Guitars

2005-present. Professional and premium grade, production/custom solidbody basses built by luthier Corey James Moilanen in Davisburg, Michigan. He also builds guitars.

Cort

1973-present. North Brook, Illinois-based Cort offers intermediate and professional grade, production, acoustic and solidbody electric basses built in Korea. They also offer guitars.

Electric Solidbody Bass

1973-1999	Various models	$150	$325

Crafter

2000-present. Intermediate grade, production, acoustic/electric bass from Hohner. They also offer guitars.

Crafter USA

1986-present. Intermediate grade, production, solidbody basses made in Korea. They also build guitars and amps.

Crestwood

1970s. Imported by La Playa Distributing Company of Detroit. Product line includes copies of the popular classical guitars, flat-tops, electric solidbodies and basses of the era.

Electric Bass

1970s. Includes models 2048, 2049, 2079, 2090, 2092, 2093, and 2098.

1970s		$150	$275

Crown

1960s. Violin-shaped hollowbody electrics, solidbody electric guitars and basses, possibly others. Imported from Japan.

Electric Solidbody Bass

Japanese imports.

1960s		$100	$275

Cumpiano

1974-present. Professional and premium grade, custom steel-string and nylon-string guitars, and acoustic basses built by luthier William Cumpiano in Northampton, Massachusetts.

Custom

1980s. Line of solidbody guitars and basses introduced in the early-'80s by Charles Lawing and Chris Lovell, owners of Strings & Things in Memphis.

Custom Kraft

Late-1960s. A house brand of St. Louis Music Supply, instruments built by Valco, Chicago, Illinois. They also offered guitars.

MODEL		EXC. COND.	
YEAR	FEATURES	LOW	HIGH

Bone Buzzer Model 12178

Late 1960s. Symmetrical double-cut thin hollow body, lightning bolt f-holes, 4-on-a-side tuners, 2 pickups, sunburst or emerald sunburst.

1968		$275	$400

D'Agostino

1976-early 1990s. Import company established by Pat D'Agostino. Solidbodies imported from EKO Italy '77-'82, Japan '82-'84, and in Korea for '84 on. Overall, about 60% of guitars and basses were Japanese, 40% Korean.

Electric Solidbody Bass

1970s	Various models	$225	$350

Daion

1978-1985. Higher quality copy basses imported from Japan. Original designs introduced in '80s. They also had guitars.

Electric Basses

1978-1985	Various models	$450	$800

Daisy Rock

2001-present. Budget and intermediate grade, production, full-scale and 3/4 scale, solidbody, semi-hollow, and acoustic/electric basses. Founded by Tish Ciravolo as a Division of Schecter Guitars, initial offerings included daisy and heart-shaped electric guitars and basses.

Danelectro

1946-1969, 1997-present. Danelectro offered basses throughout most of its early history. In '96, the Evets Corporation, of San Clemente, California, introduced a line of Danelectro effects; amps, basses and guitars, many reissues of earlier instruments, soon followed. In early '03, Evets discontinued the guitar, bass and amp lines, but revived the guitar and bass line in '05.

Model 1444L Bass

Ca.1958-ca.1964. Masonite body, single-cut, 2 pickups, copper finish.

1958-1962		$750	$900
1963-1964		$650	$800

Model 3412 Shorthorn Bass

1958-ca.1966. Coke bottle headstock, 1 pickup, copper finish.

1958-1959		$750	$900
1960-1962		$700	$850
1963-1964		$650	$800
1965-1966		$600	$750

Model 3612 Shorthorn 6-String Bass

1958-ca.1966. Coke bottle headstock, 1 pickup, copper finish.

1958-1962		$1,400	$2,000
1963-1964		$1,200	$1,800
1965-1966		$1,000	$1,600

Model 4423 Longhorn Bass

1958-ca.1966. Coke bottle headstock, 2 pickups, copper finish.

1958-1959		$1,700	$2,700

MODEL YEAR	FEATURES	EXC. COND. LOW	HIGH
1960-1962		$1,600	$2,600
1963-1964		$1,500	$2,500
1965-1966		$1,500	$2,400

'58 Longhorn Bass Reissue/Longhorn Pro

1997-2003. Reissues of classic Longhorn bass.

| 1997-2003 | | $225 | $275 |

UB-2 6-String Bass

Ca.1956-ca.1959. Single-cut, 2 pickups.

| 1956-1959 | | $1,500 | $2,500 |

Dave Maize Acoustic

1991-present. Luthier Dave Maize builds his premium grade, production/custom, acoustic basses in Cave Junction, Oregon. He also builds flat-tops.

Dean

1976-present. Intermediate and professional grade, production, solidbody, hollowbody, acoustic, and acoustic/electric, basses made overseas. They also offer guitars, banjos, mandolins, and amps.

Baby ML Bass

1982-1986. Downsized version of ML. U.S.-made.

| 1982-1986 | | $350 | $400 |

Mach V Bass

1985-1986. U.S.-made pointed solidbody, 2 pickups, rosewood 'board.

| 1985-1986 | | $600 | $800 |

ML Bass

1977-1986. Futuristic body style, fork headstock, U.S.-made.

| 1977-1983 | U.S.A.-made | $1,400 | $1,500 |
| 1984-1986 | Korean import | $400 | $450 |

Dean Markley

The string and pickup manufacturer offered a limited line of guitars and basses for a time in the late 1980s.

DeArmond

1999-2004. Electric basses based on Guild models and imported from Korea by Fender. They also offered guitars.

Decca

Mid-1960s. Solidbody basses imported from made in Japan by Teisco and imported by Decca Records, Decca headstock logo, student-level instruments. They also offered guitars and amps.

DeGennaro

2003-present. Professional and premium grade, custom/production, solidbody basses built by luthier William Degennaro in Grand Rapids, Michigan. He also builds guitars and mandolins.

DeTemple

1995-present. Premium grade, production/custom, solidbody electric basses built by luthier Michael DeTemple in Sherman Oaks, California. He also builds guitars.

Dillon

1975-present. Professional and premium grade, custom, acoustic basses built by luthier John Dillon in Taos, New Mexico. He also builds guitars.

Dingwall

1988-present. Luthier Sheldon Dingwall, Saskatoon, Canada, started out producing guitar bodies and necks, eventually offering complete guitars and basses. Currently Dingwall offers professional to premium grade, production/custom 4-, 5-, and 6-string basses featuring the Novax Fanned-Fret System.

DiPinto

1995-present. Intermediate and professional grade, production retro-vibe basses from luthier Chris DiPinto of Philadelphia, Pennsylvania. He also builds guitars. Until late '99, all instruments built in the U.S., since then built in Korea and the U.S.

Domino

Ca. 1967-1968. Imported from Japan by Maurice Lipsky Music of New York, mainly copies, but some original designs. They also offered guitars.

Electric Bass

1967-1968. Includes the Beatle Bass and Fireball Bass, a Vox Phantom IV copy.

| 1967-1968 | | $150 | $400 |

Dorado

Ca. 1972-1973. Name used briefly by Baldwin/Gretsch on line of Japanese guitar and bass imports.

Electric Solidbody Bass

Japanese imports.

| 1970s | | $100 | $175 |

Dragonfly

1994-present. Professional grade, production/custom, acoustic basses built by luthier Dan Richter in Roberts Creek, British Columbia. He also builds guitars and dulcitars.

Duesenberg

1995-present. Professional grade, production/custom, hollow and semi-hollow basses built by luthier Dieter Goelsdorf in Hannover, Germany. They also build guitars.

Earthwood

1972-1985. Acoustic designs by Ernie Ball with input from George Fullerton. One of the first to offer acoustic basses.

Acoustic Bass

1972-1985. Big bodied acoustic bass alternative between Kay double bass and solidbody Fender bass.

| 1972-1985 | | $1,100 | $1,500 |

DiPinto Belvedere

1983 Earthwood Acoustic Bass

Eastwood Rocket

1967 Epiphone Embassy

MODEL YEAR	FEATURES	EXC. COND. LOW	HIGH

Eastwood
1997-present. Budget and intermediate grade, production, imported solid and semi-hollowbody basses, many styled after 1960s models. They also offer guitars.

EKO
1959-1985, 2000-present. Built by the Oliviero Pigini Company, Italy. Original importers included LoDuca Brothers, Milwaukee, Wisconsin. Since about 2000, production, acoustic and electric EKO basses are again available and made in Italy and China. They also make guitars and amps.

Cobra II Bass
1967-ca.1969. Offset double-cut solidbody, 2 pickups.

1967-1969		$350	$450

Kadett Bass
1967-1978. Red or sunburst.

1967-1978		$425	$525

Model 1100/2 Bass
1961-1966. Jaguar-style plastic covered solidbody, 2 pickups, sparkle finish.

1961-1966		$500	$600

Model 995/2 Violin Bass
1966-ca.1969.

1966-1969		$400	$500

Rocket IV/Rokes Bass
1967-early-1970s. Rocket-shape design, solidbody, says Rokes on the headstock, the Rokes were a popular English band that endorsed EKO guitars. Marketed as the Rocket IV in the U.S. and as the Rokes in Europe. Often calle d the Rok. Sunburst, 1 pickup.

1967-1971		$500	$800

Electra
1971-1984. Imported basses from Japan by St. Louis Music. They also offered guitars.

Electric Solidbody Bass
Japanese imports, various models.

1970s		$250	$500

MPC Outlaw Bass
1970s. Has 2 separate modules that plug in for different effects, neck-thru-body.

1970s		$500	$550

Emperador
1966-1992. Student-level basses imported by Westheimer Musical Instruments. Early models appear to be made by either Teisco or Kawai; later models were made by Cort. They also had guitars.

Electric Solidbody Bass
Japanese imports, various models.

1960s		$100	$200

Encore
Late 1970s-present. Budget grade, production, solidbody basses imported by John Hornby Skewes & Co. in the U.K. They also offer guitars.

MODEL YEAR	FEATURES	EXC. COND. LOW	HIGH

Hollowbody Bass
1960s. Copy model, greenburst.

1960s		$300	$400

Engelhardt
Engelhardt specializes in student acoustic basses and cellos and is located in Elk Grove Village, Illinois.

EM-1 Maestro Bass
A popular school model upright acoustic bass, spruce top, curly maple back, rosewood trimmings, 3/4 size, sunburst.

1970s		$500	$650

Supreme Bass
Professional quality 3/4 size upright bass, spruce top, curly maple back, ebony trimmings.

1970		$1,000	$1,200

Epiphone
1928-present. Epiphone didn't add basses until 1959, after Gibson acquired the brand. The Gibson Epiphones were American-made until '69, then all imports until into the '80s, when some models were again made in the U.S. Currently Epiphone offers intermediate and professional grade, production, acoustic and electric basses.

B-5 Acoustic Bass Viol
1950s. 3/4-size laminate construction.

1950s		$3,000	$4,000

EB-0 Bass
1998-present. SG body style, single pickup, bolt-on neck.

1998-2004		$175	$250

EB-3 Bass
1999-present. SG body style, 2 pickups.

1999-2005		$275	$350

EBM-4 Bass
1991-1998. Alder body, maple neck, split humbucker, white.

1991-1998		$225	$275

Elitist Series Basses
2003-present. Higher-end appointments such as set-necks and USA pickups.

2003-2005 EB-3		$650	$750

Embassy Deluxe Bass
1963-1969. Solidbody, double-cut, 2 pickups, tune-o-matic bridge, cherry finish.

1963-1964		$1,550	$1,800
1965-1966		$1,450	$1,700
1967-1969		$1,250	$1,600

Explorer Korina Bass
2000-2001. Made in Korea, Gibson Explorer body style, genuine korina body, set neck, gold hardware.

2000-2001		$400	$450

Les Paul Special Bass
1997-present. LP Jr.-style slab body, single-cut, bolt neck, 2 humbuckers.

1997-2004		$300	$350

MODEL YEAR	FEATURES	EXC. COND. LOW	HIGH

Newport Bass
1961-1970. Double-cut solidbody, 1 pickup (2 pickups optional until '63), two-on-a-side tuners until '63, four-on-a-side after that, cherry.

1961-1962		$1,500	$2,000
1963-1964		$1,450	$1,700
1965-1966		$1,350	$1,600
1967-1969		$1,150	$1,500
1970		$1,100	$1,250

Rivoli Bass (1 pickup)
1959-1970. ES-335-style semi-hollowbody bass, two-on-a-side tuners, 1 pickup (2 in '70), reissued in '94 as the Rivoli II.

1959		$2,600	$2,900
1960		$2,400	$2,700
1961		$2,000	$2,400
1964		$1,700	$2,400
1965		$1,600	$2,300
1966		$1,500	$2,200
1967-1969		$1,400	$2,200
1970		$1,200	$1,700

Rivoli Bass (2 pickups)
1970 only. Double pickup Epiphone version of Gibson EB-2D.

1970	Sunburst	$1,800	$2,000

Thunderbird IV Bass
1997-present. Reverse-style mahogany body, 2 pickups, sunburst.

1997-2002		$325	$475

Viola Bass
1990s-present. Beatle Bass 500/1 copy, sunburst.

1990-2000s		$350	$450

ESP
1975-present. Intermediate, professional, and premium grade, production/custom, electric basses. Japan's ESP (Electric Sound Products) made inroads in the U.S. market with mainly copy styles in the early '80s, mixing in original designs over the years. In the '90s, ESP opened a California-based Custom Shop. They also build guitars.

B-1 Bass
1990s. Vague DC-style slab solidbody with bolt-on neck, ESP and B-1 on headstock.

1990s		$500	$600

Horizon Bass
1987-1993. Offset double-cut solidbody, 4- and 5-string versions, active electronics, 34" scale

1987-1993	4-string	$600	$700

Essex (SX)
1985-present. Budget grade, production, electric basses imported by Rondo Music of Union, New Jersey. They also offer guitars.

Electric Solidbody Basses

1990s		$70	$85

Evergreen Mountain
1971-present. Professional grade, custom, acoustic basses built by luthier Jerry Nolte in Cove, Oregon. He also builds guitars and mandolins.

MODEL YEAR	FEATURES	EXC. COND. LOW	HIGH

Farnell
1989-present. Luthier Al Farnell builds his professional grade, production, solidbody basses in Ontario, California. He also offers his intermediate grade, production, C Series which is imported from China. He also builds guitars.

Fender
1946-present. Intermediate, professional, and premium grade, production/custom, electric and acoustic basses made in the U.S. and overseas. Leo Fender is the father of the electric bass. The introduction of his Precision Bass in late '51 changed forever how music was performed, recorded and heard. Leo followed with other popular models of basses that continue to make up a large part of Fender's production. Please note that all the variations of the Jazz and Precision Basses are grouped under those general headings.

Ashbory
2003-present. Unique-shaped travel bass, Ashbory logo on body, Fender logo on back of headstock, previously sold under Fender's DeArmond brand.

2005		$150	$175

Bass V
1965-1970. Five strings, double-cut, 1 pickup, dot inlay '65-'66, block inlay '66-'70.

1965	Black, blond	$2,900	$3,300
1965	Blue Ice, Charcoal Frost, Firemist Gold, Firemist Silver, Inca Silver, Ocean Turquoise, Sonic Blue, Teal Green	$3,700	$4,300
1965	Burgundy Mist	$4,000	$4,600
1965	Candy Apple Red, Lake Placid Blue, Olympic White	$3,200	$3,600
1965	Dakota Red, Fiesta Red	$3,400	$4,000
1965	Foam Green	$4,200	$4,800
1965	Sunburst	$2,600	$3,000
1966	Sunburst	$1,900	$2,200
1966	Sunburst, dot inlay	$2,000	$2,300
1966-1967	Black, blond	$2,100	$2,400
1966-1967	Blue Ice, Charcoal Frost, Firemist Gold, Firemist Silver, Ocean Turquoise, Sonic Blue, Teal Green	$2,800	$3,300
1966-1967	Candy Apple Red, Lake Placid Blue	$2,400	$2,800
1966-1967	Dakota Red, Fiesta Red	$2,600	$3,000
1966-1967	Foam Green	$3,200	$3,700
1966-1967	Olympic White	$2,300	$2,700
1967	Sunburst, block inlay	$1,900	$2,200
1968-1970	Black, blond	$1,700	$2,100

ESP Surveyor II

1966 Fender Bass V

Fender Bass VI reissue

1967 Fender Coronado II

MODEL YEAR	FEATURES	EXC. COND. LOW	HIGH
1968-1970	Blue Ice, Charcoal Frost, Firemist Gold, Firemist Silver, Ocean Turquoise, Sonic Blue, Teal Green	$2,300	$2,800
1968-1970	Candy Apple Red	$1,900	$2,400
1968-1970	Lake Placid Blue, Olympic White	$1,900	$2,300
1968-1970	Dakota Red, Fiesta Red	$2,200	$2,600
1968-1970	Sunburst	$1,600	$2,000

Bass VI

1961-1975. Six strings, Jazzmaster-like body, 3 pickups, dot inlay until '66, block inlay '66-'75. Reintroduced as Japanese-made Collectable model '95-'98.

MODEL YEAR	FEATURES	EXC. COND. LOW	HIGH
1961-1962	Black, blond	$8,500	$9,000
1961-1962	Burgundy Mist, Dakota Red, Fiesta Red, Sherwood Green, Shoreline Gold	$11,000	$12,000
1961-1962	Daphne Blue, Inca Silver, Sonic Blue	$10,000	$11,000
1961-1962	Foam Green, Surf Green	$12,000	$13,000
1961-1962	Lake Placid Blue, Olympic White	$9,500	$10,000
1961-1962	Shell Pink	$13,000	$15,000
1961-1962	Sunburst	$5,000	$6,000
1963-1964	Black, blond	$6,500	$7,500
1963-1964	Burgundy Mist, Dakota Red, Fiesta Red, Sherwood Green, Shoreline Gold	$8,500	$10,000
1963-1964	Candy Apple Red, Lake Placid Blue, Olympic White	$7,000	$8,000
1963-1964	Sonic Blue, Daphne Blue, Inca Silver	$8,000	$9,000
1963-1964	Foam Green, Surf Green	$9,000	$10,000
1963-1964	Sunburst	$3,500	$4,500
1965	Black, blond	$4,500	$5,500
1965	Blue Ice, Candy Apple Red, Charcoal Frost, Lake Placid Blue, Olympic White	$5,000	$6,000
1965	Candy Apple Red, Lake Placid Blue	$4,500	$5,000
1965	Dakota Red, Fiesta Red, Firemist Gold, Firemist Silver, Ocean Turquoise, Sonic Blue	$6,000	$7,000

MODEL YEAR	FEATURES	EXC. COND. LOW	HIGH
1965	Foam Green, Teal Green	$6,500	$7,500
1965	Sunburst	$3,400	$3,700
1966	Black, blond	$4,200	$5,200
1966	Blue Ice/Ice Blue, Candy Apple Red, Charcoal Frost, Lake Placid Blue, Olympic White	$4,800	$5,800
1966	Dakota Red, Fiesta Red, Firemist Gold, Firemist Silver, Ocean Turquoise, Sonic Blue	$5,800	$6,800
1966	Foam Green, Teal Green	$6,300	$7,300
1966	Sunburst, block inlay	$3,200	$3,300
1966	Sunburst, dot inlay	$3,300	$3,600
1967-1969	Black, blond	$3,200	$4,200
1967-1969	Blue Ice/Ice Blue, Candy Apple Red, Charcoal Frost, Lake Placid Blue, Olympic White	$3,800	$4,800
1967-1969	Dakota Red, Fiesta Red, Firemist Gold, Firemist Silver, Ocean Turquoise, Sonic Blue	$4,800	$5,800
1967-1969	Foam Green, Teal Green	$5,300	$6,300
1967-1969	Sunburst	$2,900	$3,200
1970-1971	Black, blond	$2,900	$3,200
1970-1971	Candy Apple Red, Lake Placid Blue, Olympic White	$3,500	$3,800
1970-1971	Firemist Gold, Firemist Silver, Ocean Turquoise, Sonic Blue	$4,500	$4,800
1970-1971	Sunburst	$2,600	$2,900
1972-1974	Black, blond	$2,600	$2,900
1972-1974	Candy Apple Red, Lake Placid Blue, Olympic White	$3,200	$3,500
1972-1974	Natural, Walnut	$2,100	$2,400
1972-1974	Sunburst	$2,300	$2,600
1975	Black, blond	$2,500	$2,700
1975	Natural, Walnut	$1,900	$2,100
1975	Olympic White	$2,700	$3,000
1975	Sunburst	$2,100	$2,300

Bass VI Reissue

1995-1998. Import, sunburst.

1995-1998		$1,000	$1,300

BG-29 Bass

1995-present. Acoustic flat-top bass, single-cut, two-on-a-side tuners, Fishman on-board controls, black.

1995-2000		$325	$400

MODEL YEAR	FEATURES	EXC. COND. LOW	HIGH

Bullet Bass (B30, B34, B40)

1982-1983. Alder body, 1 pickup, offered in short- and long-scale, red or walnut. U.S.-made, replaced by Japanese-made Squire Bullet Bass.

1982-1983		$300	$400

Squire Bullet Bass

1980s. Japanese-made, Squire-branded, replaces Bullet Bass, black.

1980s		$175	$275

Coronado I Bass

1966-1970. Thinline, double-cut, 1 pickup, dot inlay, sunburst and cherry red were the standard colors, but custom colors could be ordered.

1966-1970	Cherry red, sunburst	$750	$1,000
1966-1970	Other custom colors	$1,000	$1,400
1966-1970	White custom color	$1,000	$1,300

Coronado II Bass

1967-1972. Two pickups, block inlay, sunburst and cherry red standard colors, but custom colors could be ordered. Only Antigua finish offered from '70 on.

1967-1969	Cherry red, sunburst	$1,000	$1,400
1967-1969	Other custom colors	$1,300	$1,700
1967-1969	White custom color	$1,100	$1,500
1970-1972	Antigua only	$1,200	$1,500

HM Bass IV

1989-1991. Japanese-made, 4 strings, basswood body, no 'guard, 3 Jazz Bass pickups, 5-way switch, master volume, master TBX, sunburst.

1989-1991		$350	$650

HM Bass V

1989-1991. Five-string version of HM, sunburst.

1989-1991		$350	$650

Jazz Bass

The following are variations of the Jazz Bass. The first four listings are for the main U.S.-made models. All others are listed alphabetically after that in the following order:

Jazz Bass
Standard Jazz Bass
American Standard Jazz Bass
American Series Jazz Bass
American Series Jazz Bass V
50th Anniversary American Standard Jazz Bass
'62 Jazz Bass
'64 Jazz Bass (Custom Shop)
'75 Jazz Bass American Vintage Series
Aerodyne Jazz Bass
American Deluxe Jazz Bass
American Deluxe Jazz V Bass
Custom Classic Jazz Bass
Deluxe Jazz Bass (active)
Deluxe Jazz Bass V (active)
Foto Flame Jazz Bass
Geddy Lee Signature Jazz Bass
Gold Jazz Bass
Highway 1 Jazz Bass

Jazz Bass Special (Import)
Jazz Plus Bass
Jazz Plus V Bass
Marcus Miller Signature Jazz Bass
Noel Redding Signature Jazz Bass
Reggie Hamilton Jazz Bass
Squire Jazz Bass
Standard Jazz Bass (later model)
Standard Jazz Fretless Bass (later model)
Standard Jazz V Bass (later model)
Ventures Limited Edition Jazz Bass
Victor Baily Jazz Bass

Jazz Bass

1960-1981. Two stack knobs '60-'62, 3 regular controls '62 on. Dot markers '60-'66, block markers from '66 on. Rosewood 'board standard, but maple available from '68 on. With the introduction of vintage reissue models in '81, Fender started calling the American-made version the Standard Jazz Bass. That became the American Standard Jazz Bass in '88 and then became the American Series Jazz Bass in 2000.

The custom colors listing are for unfaded or very slightly faded examples. Moderately faded examples will approximate values somewhat below the low end of the value range. A heavily faded example will be worth much less than the ranges shown, even if otherwise in excellent, original condition. Fade does not always mean lighter tint. A heavily faded bass will have a different tint than an unfaded one (for example, a heavily faded Lake Placid Blue can turn dark green) and will fetch values slightly higher than a standard sunburst example. Custom color Fenders can be forged and bogus finishes have been a problem. The prices in the Guide are for factory original finishes in excellent condition.

Post '71 Jazz Bass values are affected more by condition than color or neck option. The Jazz Bass was fitted with a 3-bolt neck or bullet rod in late-'74. Prices assume a 3-bolt neck starting in '75.

1960	Black, blond	$23,000	$30,000
1960	Burgundy Mist, Dakota Red, Fiesta Red, Sherwood Green, Shoreline Gold	$30,000	$39,000
1960	Daphne Blue, Inca Silver, Sonic Blue	$28,000	$36,000
1960	Foam Green, Surf Green	$32,000	$42,000
1960	Lake Placid Blue, Olympic White	$26,000	$34,000
1960	Shell Pink	$37,000	$48,000
1960	Sunburst	$18,000	$23,000
1961-1962	Stack knob, black, blond	$21,000	$27,000
1961-1962	Stack knob, Burgundy Mist, Dakota Red, Fiesta Red, Sherwood Green, Shorline Gold	$28,000	$36,000

1961 Fender Jazz Bass

1972 Fender Jazz Bass

1975 Fender Jazz Bass

Fender Aerodyne Jazz Bass

MODEL YEAR	FEATURES	EXC. COND. LOW	HIGH
1961-1962	Stack knob, Daphne Blue, Inca Silver, Sonic Blue	$26,000	$33,000
1961-1962	Stack knob, Foam Green, Surf Green	$30,000	$38,000
1961-1962	Stack knob, Lake Placid Blue, Olympic White	$24,000	$32,000
1961-1962	Stack knob, Shell Pink	$35,000	$40,000
1961-1962	Stack knob, sunburst	$16,000	$18,000
1962	3 knob, black, blond	$14,000	$19,000
1962	3 knob, Burgundy Mist, Dakota Red, Fiesta Red, Sherwood Green, Shoreline Gold	$20,000	$26,000
1962	3 knob, Daphne Blue, Inca Silver, Sonic Blue	$18,000	$24,000
1962	3 knob, Foam Green, Surf Green	$22,000	$28,000
1962	3 knob, Lake Placid Blue, Olympic White	$16,000	$22,000
1962	3 knob, Shell Pink	$22,000	$29,000
1962	3 knob, sunburst	$13,000	$15,000
1963-1964	Black, blond	$13,000	$18,000
1963-1964	Burgundy Mist, Dakota Red, Fiesta Red, Sherwood Green	$19,000	$25,000
1963-1964	Candy Apple Red	$16,000	$21,000
1963-1964	Daphne Blue, Inca Silver, Sonic Blue	$17,000	$23,000
1963-1964	Foam Green	$21,000	$27,000
1963-1964	Lake Placid Blue, Olympic White	$15,000	$21,000
1963-1964	Shoreline Gold	$18,000	$25,000
1963-1964	Sunburst	$12,000	$14,000
1963-1964	Surf Green	$21,000	$28,000
1965	Black, blond	$10,000	$13,000
1965	Blue Ice, Charcoal Frost, Fiesta Red, Firemist Gold, Firemist Silver, Ocean Turquoise, Sonic Blue, Teal Green	$13,000	$16,000
1965	Candy Apple Red, Lake Placid Blue, Olympic White	$11,000	$14,000
1965	Dakota Red	$12,000	$15,000
1965	Foam Green	$14,000	$17,000
1965	Sunburst	$7,500	$10,000

MODEL YEAR	FEATURES	EXC. COND. LOW	HIGH
1966	Blocks, Candy Apple Red	$8,500	$10,500
1966	Blocks, Olympic White, match headstock	$10,000	$13,000
1966	Blocks, Sonic Blue	$10,000	$13,000
1966	Blocks, sunburst	$6,000	$8,000
1966	Charcoal Frost, Fiesta Red, Firemist Gold, Firemist Silver, Ocean Turquoise, Teal Green	$12,000	$15,000
1966	Dakota Red	$11,000	$14,000
1966	Dots, black, blond	$9,000	$12,000
1966	Dots, Blue Ice, Sonic Blue	$12,000	$15,000
1966	Dots, Candy Apple Red	$10,000	$13,000
1966	Dots, Foam Green	$13,000	$16,000
1966	Dots, Olympic White	$10,000	$13,000
1966	Dots, Sonic Blue	$12,000	$15,000
1966	Dots, sunburst	$7,500	$9,000
1966	Lake Placid Blue	$8,500	$10,500
1966	Lake Placid Blue, matching headstock	$10,000	$13,000
1967	Less common custom colors	$9,000	$14,000
1967	More common custom colors	$8,000	$10,000
1967	Sunburst	$5,000	$7,500
1968	Less common custom colors	$8,500	$13,500
1968	More common custom colors	$7,500	$9,500
1968	Sunburst	$4,500	$7,000
1969	Less common custom colors	$6,000	$13,000
1969	More common custom colors	$4,500	$9,000
1969	Sunburst	$4,500	$7,000
1970	Less common custom colors	$5,000	$6,000
1970	More common custom colors	$4,000	$4,500
1970	Sunburst	$3,500	$4,000
1971	Less common custom colors	$4,500	$5,500
1971	More common custom colors	$3,500	$4,000
1971	Sunburst	$3,000	$3,500
1972	Custom colors	$3,000	$4,000
1972	Sunburst	$2,700	$3,200
1973	Custom colors	$2,700	$4,000
1973	Sunburst	$2,500	$2,900
1974	Custom colors	$2,500	$3,500
1974	Sunburst, 4-bolt neck	$2,300	$2,700

MODEL YEAR	FEATURES	EXC. COND. LOW	HIGH
1975-1977	Black, blond, white, 3-bolt neck	$2,100	$2,800
1975-1977	Natural, Walnut, 3-bolt neck	$1,600	$2,300
1975-1977	Sunburst, 3-bolt neck	$1,900	$2,600
1978-1979	Sunburst	$1,600	$2,100
1978-1979	Various colors, 3-bolt neck	$1,500	$2,200
1980	Sunburst	$1,500	$2,100
1980	Various colors, 3-bolt neck	$1,500	$2,100
1981	Black	$1,300	$1,600
1981	Black and Gold Collector's Edition	$1,400	$2,000
1981	International colors	$1,400	$2,000
1981	Sunburst	$1,300	$1,600

Standard Jazz Bass

1981-1985. Replaced Jazz Bass ('60-'81) and replaced by the American Standard Jazz Bass in '88. Name now used on import version.

1981-1982	Rare colors	$1,600	$2,000
1981-1982	Various colors	$1,300	$1,600
1982-1984	Top mounted input jack	$850	$900
1985	Japan import	$600	$700

American Standard Jazz Bass

1988-2000. Replaced Standard Jazz Bass ('81-'88) and replaced by the American Series Jazz Bass in '00. Various colors.

1988-1989		$750	$875
1990-1999		$700	$750

American Series Jazz Bass

2000-present. Replaces American Standard Jazz Bass.

2000-2004		$750	$975

American Series Jazz Bass V

2000-present. Five-string version.

2000-2004		$750	$975

50th Anniversary American Standard Jazz Bass

1996. Regular American Standard with gold hardware, 4- or 5-string, gold 50th Anniversary commemorative neck plate, rosewood 'board, sunburst.

1996		$700	$750

'62 Jazz Bass

1982-present. U.S.A.-made, reissue of '62 Jazz Bass.

1982-1985	Standard colors	$1,100	$1,200
1986-1989	Standard colors	$1,100	$1,200
1990-1999	Rare colors	$1,200	$1,300
1990-1999	Standard colors	$1,000	$1,100
2000-2003	Standard colors	$1,000	$1,100

'64 Jazz Bass (Custom Shop)

2000-present. Alder body, rosewood 'board, tortoise shell 'guard.

2000-2004	Closet Classic option	$1,700	$1,900
2000-2004	N.O.S option	$1,600	$1,800
2000-2004	Relic option	$1,900	$2,100

'75 Jazz Bass American Vintage Series

1994-present. Maple neck with black block markers.

1994-2003		$1,300	$1,400

Aerodyne Jazz Bass

2003-present. Bound basswood body, P/J pickups, Deluxe Series.

2003-2004		$450	$500

American Deluxe Jazz Bass

1998-present. Made in the U.S.A., active electronics, alder or ash body. Alder body colors - sunburst or transparent red, ash body colors - white, blond, transparent teal green or transparent purple.

1998-1999		$850	$900
2000-2004		$850	$975

American Deluxe Jazz V Bass

1998-present. Five-string model, various colors.

1998-1999		$875	$925
2000-2004		$875	$1,000

Custom Classic Jazz Bass

2001-present. Slightly slimmer waist, deeper cutaways, maple or rosewood 'board, block inlays.

2001-2005		$950	$1,050

Deluxe Jazz Bass (active)

1995-present. Made in Mexico, active electronics, various colors.

1995-2004		$400	$500

Deluxe Jazz Bass V (active)

1995-present. Made in Mexico, various colors.

1995-2004		$425	$525

Foto Flame Jazz Bass

1994-1996. Japanese import, alder and basswood body with Foto Flame figured wood image.

1994-1996		$500	$600

Geddy Lee Signature Jazz Bass

1998, 2004. Limited run import in '98, part of Artist Series in '04.

1998	Black	$550	$600
2004	Artist Series	$675	$750

Gold Jazz Bass

1981-1984. Gold finish and gold-plated hardware.

1981-1984		$1,000	$1,300

Highway 1 Jazz Bass

2003-present. U.S.-made, alder body, satin lacquer finish.

2003-2004		$475	$600

Jazz Bass Special (Import)

1984-1991. Japanese-made, Jazz/Precision hybrid, Precision-shaped basswood body, Jazz neck (fretless available), 2 P/J pickups.

1984-1991		$450	$500

Jazz Plus Bass

1990-1994. Alder body, 2 Lace Sensors, active electronics, rotary circuit selector, master volume, balance, bass boost, bass cut, treble boost, treble cut, various colors.

1990-1994		$750	$900

Jazz Plus V Bass

1990-1994. Five-string version.

1990-1994		$775	$925

Fender American Jazz

Fender '62 Jazz Bass

Fender Reggie Hamilton Jazz

1971 Fender Mustang Bass

MODEL YEAR	FEATURES	EXC. COND. LOW	HIGH

Marcus Miller Signature Jazz Bass
1998-present. Japanese import, sunburst.

1998-2004		$575	$625

Noel Redding Signature Jazz Bass
1997. Limited Edition import, artist signature on 'guard, sunburst, rosewood 'board.

1997		$575	$650

Reggie Hamilton Jazz Bass
2005-present. Alder body, C-profile neck, passive/active switch and pan control.

2005		$625	$675

Squire Jazz Bass
1980s-present. Jazz bass import, without cover plates, various colors.

1980s		$175	$275
1990s		$175	$275
2000s		$125	$150

Standard Jazz Bass (later model)
1988-present. Imported from various countries. Not to be confused with '81-'88 American-made model with the same name.

1988-1999		$250	$325
2000-2004		$275	$325

Standard Jazz Fretless Bass (later model)
1994-present. Fretless version.

1994-2004		$275	$350

Standard Jazz V Bass (later model)
1998-present. 5-string, import model.

1998-2004		$300	$350

Ventures Limited Edition Jazz Bass
1996. Made in Japan, part of Ventures guitar and bass set, dark purple.

1996		$875	$1,000

Victor Baily Jazz Bass
2001-present. Koa, rosewood and mahogany body, fretless with white fret markers.

2001-2005		$1,075	$1,125

JP-90 Bass
1990-1994. Two P/J pickups, rosewood fretboard, poplar body, black or red.

1990-1994		$475	$525

Musicmaster Bass
1970-1983. Shorter scale, solidbody, 1 pickup. various colors.

1970-1983		$575	$700

Mustang Bass
1966-1982. Shorter scale, solidbody, 1 pickup, offered in standard and competition colors, (competition colors refer to racing stripes on the body).

1966-1969		$1,100	$1,300
1970-1979		$1,000	$1,100
1980-1982		$850	$1,000

Performer Bass
1985-1986. Swinger-like body style, active electronics, various colors.

1985-1986		$900	$1,000

MODEL YEAR	FEATURES	EXC. COND. LOW	HIGH

Precision Bass

The following are variations of the Precision Bass. The first four listings are for the main U.S.-made models. All others are listed alphabetically after that in the following order:

Precision Bass
Standard Precision Bass
American Standard Precision Bass
American Series Precision Bass
40th Anniversary Precision Bass (Custom Shop)
50th Anniversary American Standard Precision Bass
50th Anniversary Precision Bass
'51 Precision Bass
'55 Precision Bass (Custom Shop)
'57 Precision Bass
'57 Precision Bass (Import)
'59 Precision Bass (Custom Shop)
'62 Precision Bass
'62 Precision Bass (Import)
American Deluxe Precision Bass
American Deluxe Precision V Bass
Big Block Precision Bass
Deluxe P-Bass Special
Elite I Precision Bass
Elite II Precision Bass
Foto Flame Precision Bass
Gold Elite I Precision Bass
Gold Elite II Precision Bass
Highway 1 Precision Bass
Precision Bass Jr.
Precision Bass Lyte
Precision Bass Special
Precision U.S. Deluxe/Plus Deluxe Bass
Precision U.S. Plus/Plus Bass
Squire Precision Bass Special
Squire Precision V Bass Special
Standard Precision Bass (later model)
Sting Precision Bass
Walnut Precision Bass Special
Walnut Elite I Precision Bass
Walnut Elite II Precision Bass

Precision Bass
1951-1981. Slab body until '54, 1-piece maple neck standard until '59, optional after '69., rosewood 'board standard '59 on (slab until mid-'62, curved after), blond finish standard until '54, sunburst standard after that (2-tone '54-'58, 3-tone after '58). Replaced by the Standard Precision Bass in '81-'85, then the American Standard Precision in '88-'00. Renamed American Series Precision Bass in '00. Unlike the Jazz and Telecaster Basses, the Precision was never fitted with a 3-bolt neck or bullet rod.

The custom colors listings are for unfaded or very slightly faded examples. Moderately faded examples will approximate values somewhat below the low end of the value range. Fade does not always mean lighter tint. A heavily faded example will be worth much less than the ranges shown, even if otherwise in excellent, original condition. A heavily faded bass will have a different tint than an unfaded one (for example, a heavily faded Lake Placid Blue can turn dark green), and will fetch values slightly higher than a standard sunburst example.

Custom color Fenders can be forged and bogus finishes have been a problem. The prices in the Guide are for factory original finishes in excellent condition.

MODEL YEAR	FEATURES	EXC. COND. LOW	HIGH
1951	Butterscotch blond, slab body	$24,000	$30,000
1952	Butterscotch blond, slab body	$23,000	$29,000
1953	Butterscotch blond, slab body	$21,000	$27,000
1954	Blond, slab body	$19,000	$25,000
1955	Blond, contour body	$17,000	$23,000
1956	Blond, contour body	$16,000	$22,000
1956	Sunburst	$15,000	$21,000
1957	Blond, last full year	$16,000	$22,000
1957	Sunburst, anodized guard late '57	$15,000	$21,000
1957	Sunburst, white guard early '57	$15,000	$21,000
1958	Blond option	$15,000	$21,000
1958	Sunburst, anodized guard	$15,000	$21,000
1959	Blond	$13,000	$19,000
1959	Sunburst	$11,000	$17,000
1959	Sunburst, anodized guard	$13,000	$19,000
1960	Blond	$13,000	$16,000
1960	Sunburst	$10,000	$13,000
1961	Black	$13,000	$16,500
1961	Blond (see-thru)	$13,000	$16,000
1961	Burgundy Mist, Sherwood Green, Shoreline Gold, Dakota Red, Fiesta Red	$19,000	$22,000
1961	Daphne Blue, Inca Silver, Sonic Blue	$18,000	$21,000
1961	Foam Green, Surf Green	$20,000	$23,000
1961	Lake Placid Blue, Olympic White	$17,000	$20,000
1961	Shell Pink	$22,000	$25,000
1961	Sunburst, slab rosewood	$10,000	$11,000
1962	Curved, black, blond	$11,200	$12,700
1962	Curved, Burgundy Mist, Dakota Red, Fiesta Red, Sherwood Green, Shoreline Gold	$15,000	$17,000
1962	Curved, Daphne Blue, Inca Silver, Sonic Blue	$13,700	$16,000

MODEL YEAR	FEATURES	EXC. COND. LOW	HIGH
1962	Curved, Foam Green, Surf Green	$15,900	$18,000
1962	Curved, Lake Placid Blue, Olympic White	$13,300	$15,000
1962	Curved, Shell Pink	$16,700	$19,000
1962	Curved, sunburst	$7,500	$8,500
1962	Slab, black	$13,000	$16,500
1962	Slab, blond	$13,000	$16,000
1962	Slab, Burgundy Mist, Dakota Red, Fiesta Red, Sherwood Green, Shoreline Gold	$19,000	$22,000
1962	Slab, Daphne Blue, Inca Silver	$18,000	$21,000
1962	Slab, Foam Green, Surf Green	$20,000	$23,000
1962	Slab, Lake Placid Blue, Olympic White, Sonic Blue	$17,000	$20,000
1962	Slab, Shell Pink	$22,000	$25,000
1962	Slab, sunburst	$10,000	$11,000
1963-1964	Blond, black	$11,200	$12,700
1963-1964	Burgundy Mist, Candy Apple Red, Daphne Blue, Sherwood Green, Shoreline Gold	$15,000	$17,000
1963-1964	Dakota Red, Foam Green, Sonic Blue	$13,700	$16,000
1963-1964	Fiesta Red, Surf Green	$15,900	$18,000
1963-1964	Inca Silver, Lake Placid Blue	$13,300	$15,000
1963-1964	Olympic White	$16,700	$19,000
1963-1964	Sunburst	$7,500	$8,500
1965	Black, blond	$7,800	$9,700
1965	Blue Ice, Charcoal Frost, Fiesta Red, Firemist Gold, Firemist Silver, Ocean Turquoise, Sonic Blue, Teal Green	$9,500	$12,000
1965	Candy Apple Red, Lake Placid Blue, Olympic White	$8,500	$10,500
1965	Dakota Red	$9,000	$11,300
1965	Foam Green	$10,200	$12,700
1965	Sunburst	$6,000	$7,500
1966	Black, blond	$7,000	$7,800
1966	Candy Apple Red, Lake Placid Blue, Olympic White	$8,000	$8,500
1966	Dakota Red	$8,500	$9,000

1953 Fender Precision Bass

1962 Fender Precision Bass (Shoreline Gold)

1978 Fender Precision Bass (Antigua)

Fender '51 Precision Bass

MODEL YEAR	FEATURES	EXC. COND. LOW	HIGH
1966	Firemist Gold, Blue Ice, Teal Green, Sonic Blue, Ocean Turquoise, Firemist Silver, Fiesta Red, Charcoal Frost	$9,000	$9,500
1966	Foam Green	$9,500	$10,200
1966	Sunburst	$5,500	$6,000
1967-1969	Black, blond	$5,000	$7,000
1967-1969	Blue Ice, Charcoal Frost, Fiesta Red, Firemist Gold, Firemist Silver, Ocean Turquoise, Sonic Blue, Teal Green	$7,000	$9,000
1967-1969	Candy Apple Red, Lake Placid Blue, Olympic White	$6,000	$8,000
1967-1969	Dakota Red	$6,500	$8,500
1967-1969	Foam Green	$7,500	$9,500
1967-1969	Sunburst	$3,500	$5,500
1970	Black, blond	$3,100	$5,000
1970	Candy Apple Red, Lake Placid Blue	$3,500	$6,000
1970	Firemist Gold, Firemist Silver, Ocean Turquoise, Sonic Blue	$4,300	$7,000
1970	Olympic White	$3,400	$6,000
1970	Sunburst	$3,000	$3,500
1971	Black, blond	$2,500	$3,100
1971	Candy Apple Red, Lake Placid Blue	$2,800	$3,500
1971	Firemist Gold, Firemist Silver, Ocean Turquoise, Sonic Blue	$3,300	$4,300
1971	Olympic White	$2,700	$3,400
1971	Sunburst	$2,400	$3,000
1972	Black, blond	$2,200	$3,000
1972	Candy Apple Red, Lake Placid Blue	$2,700	$3,200
1972	Olympic White	$2,500	$3,100
1972	Sonic Blue	$3,000	$4,000
1972	Sunburst	$2,200	$2,900
1973	Black, blond	$2,100	$2,900
1973	Candy Apple Red, Lake Placid Blue	$2,600	$3,100
1973	Natural, Walnut	$1,800	$2,100
1973	Olympic White	$2,400	$3,000
1973	Sunburst	$2,100	$2,800
1974	Black, blond, Olympic White	$2,000	$2,800
1974	Natural, Walnut	$1,700	$2,000
1974	Sunburst	$2,000	$2,700
1975-1977	Black, blond, Olympic White	$1,800	$2,500
1975-1977	Natural	$1,500	$2,000
1975-1977	Sunburst	$1,800	$2,400
1975-1977	Walnut	$1,500	$1,800

MODEL YEAR	FEATURES	EXC. COND. LOW	HIGH
1978-1979	Antigua, black, blond, Olympic White	$1,500	$2,100
1978-1979	Natural, Walnut	$1,300	$1,900
1978-1979	Sunburst	$1,500	$2,000
1978-1979	Wine	$1,500	$2,000
1980	Black, Olympic White, Wine	$1,400	$2,000
1980	Natural	$1,300	$1,800
1980	Sunburst	$1,400	$1,900
1981	Black & gold, International colors	$1,400	$2,000
1981	Black, Sunburst, White	$1,200	$1,500

Standard Precision Bass

1981-1985. Replaces Precision Bass, various colors. Replaced by American Standard Precision '88-'00. The Standard name is used on import Precision model for '88-present.

1981-1984		$850	$1,500
1985	Japan import	$600	$700

American Standard Precision Bass

1988-2000. Replaces Standard Precision Bass, replaced by American Series Precision in '00.

1988-1989	Blond, gold hardware	$875	$975
1988-1989	Various colors	$750	$875
1990-2000	Various colors	$700	$750

American Series Precision Bass

2000-present. Replaces American Standard Precision Bass, various colors.

2000-2004		$750	$975

40th Anniversary Precision Bass (Custom Shop)

1991. 400 made, quilted amber maple top, gold hardware.

1991		$1,300	$1,400

50th Anniversary American Standard Precision Bass

1996. Regular American Standard with gold hardware, 4- or 5-string, gold 50th Anniversary commemorative neck plate, rosewood 'board, sunburst.

1996		$700	$750

50th Anniversary Precision Bass

2001. Commemorative certificate with date and serial number, butterscotch finish, ash body, maple neck, black 'guard.

2001		$825	$900

'51 Precision Bass

2003-present. Import from Japan, does not include pickup or bridge covers as part of the package, blond or sunburst.

2003		$225	$275

'55 Precision Bass (Custom Shop)

2003-present. 1955 specs including oversized 'guard, 1-piece maple neck/fretboard, preproduction bridge and pickup covers, single-coil pickup. Offered in N.O.S., Closet Classic or highest-end Relic.

2003	Closet Classic option	$1,700	$1,900
2003	N.O.S. optioin	$1,600	$1,800
2003	Relic option	$1,900	$2,100

MODEL YEAR	FEATURES	EXC. COND. LOW	HIGH

'57 Precision Bass
1982-present. U.S.-made reissue, various colors.
1982-1989		$1,100	$1,200
1990-1999		$1,000	$1,100

'57 Precision Bass (Import)
1984-1986. Foreign-made, black.
1984-1986		$450	$650

'59 Precision Bass (Custom Shop)
2003-present. Custom Shop built with late-'59 specs, rosewood 'board.
2003	Closet Classic option	$1,700	$1,900
2003	N.O.S. option	$1,600	$1,800
2003	Relic option	$1,900	$2,100

'62 Precision Bass
1982-present. U.S.A.-made reissue of '62 Precision, alder body.
1982-1989	Mary Kaye Blond, gold hardware	$1,200	$1,300
1982-1999	Standard colors	$1,100	$1,200
1990-1999	Rare colors	$1,200	$1,300
1999	Mars Music custom color	$1,200	$1,300
2000-2003	Standard colors	$1,000	$1,100

'62 Precision Bass (Import)
1984-1986. Foreign-made, black.
1984-1986		$550	$700

American Deluxe Precision Bass
1998-present. Made in U.S.A., active electronics, alder or ash body. Alder body colors - sunburst or transparent red. Ash body colors - white blond, transparent teal green or transparent purple.
1998-1999		$850	$900
2000-2004		$850	$975

American Deluxe Precision V Bass
1999-present. 5-string version.
1998-1999		$900	$950

Big Block Precision Bass
2005-present. Pearloid block markers, black finish with matching headstock, 1 double Jazz Bass humbucker, bass and treble boost and cut controls.
2005		$600	$650

Deluxe P-Bass Special
1995-present. Made in Mexico, P/J pickups, Jazz Bass neck.
1995-2003		$375	$400

Elite I Precision Bass
1983-1985. The Elite Series feature active electronics and noise-cancelling pickups, ash body, 1 pickup, various colors.
1983-1985		$900	$1,025

Elite II Precision Bass
1983-1985. Ash body, 2 pickups, various colors.
1983-1985		$975	$1,100

Foto Flame Precision Bass
1994-1996. Made in Japan, simulated woodgrain finish, natural or sunburst.
1994-1996		$500	$600

Gold Elite I Precision Bass
1983-1985. The Elite Series feature active electronics and noise-cancelling pickups, gold-plated hardware version of the Elite Precision I, 1 pickup.
1983-1985		$900	$1,100

Gold Elite II Precision Bass
1983-1985. Two pickup version.
1983-1985		$1,000	$1,300

Highway 1 Precision Bass
2003-present. U.S.-made, alder body, satin lacquer finish.
2003-2004		$475	$600

Precision Bass Jr.
2004-present. 3/4 size.
2004		$275	$325

Precision Bass Lyte
1992-2001. Japanese-made, smaller, lighter basswood body, 2 pickups, sunburst.
1992-2001		$575	$625

Precision Bass Special
1980-1983, 1997-1998. Active electronics, gold-plated brass hardware, 1 split-coil pickup. '90s version similar, but with chrome hardware and made in Mexico.
1997-1998	Mexico	$375	$475

Precision U.S. Deluxe/Plus Deluxe Bass
1991-1994. P-style bass with P-bass and Jazz bass pickups, concentric knobs, no 'guard models available, various colors.
1991-1994		$650	$700

Precision U.S. Plus/Plus Bass
1989-1992. P-style bass with P- and J-bass pickup, model variations, black.
1989-1992		$650	$700

Squire Precision Bass Special
1999-present. Agathis body, P/J pickups.
1999-2004		$150	$175

Squire Precision V Bass Special
2000-present. 5-string version.
2000-2004		$155	$200

Standard Precision Bass (later model)
1987-present. Traditional style, import, currently made in Mexico. Not to be confused with '81-'85 American-made model with the same name.
1987-1999		$250	$325

Sting Precision Bass
2001-present. 2-tone sunburst, 1 single-coil, Sting's signature.
2001-2004		$500	$600

Walnut Precision Bass Special
1980-1983. Precision Bass Special with a walnut body, natural.
1980-1983		$1,200	$1,800

Walnut Elite I Precision Bass
1983-1985. The Elite Series feature active electronics and noise-cancelling pickups. Walnut body, 1 pickup, rosewood 'board, natural.
1983-1985		$1,200	$1,800

Walnut Elite II Precision Bass
1983-1985. Two-pickup version.
1983-1985		$1,500	$2,000

1983 Fender Elite II Precision

Fender Standard Precision Bass

1968 Fender Telecaster Bass (Paisley)

1981 G&L L-1000

MODEL YEAR	FEATURES	EXC. COND. LOW	HIGH

Prodigy/Prodigy Active Bass
1992-1995. Poplar body, 1 J- and 1 P-style pickup, active.

1992-1995		$400	$450

Stu Hamm Urge Bass (U.S.A.)
1992-1999. Contoured Precision-style body with smaller wide treble cutaway, J and P pickups, various colors.

1992-1999		$850	$1,000

Stu Hamm Urge II Bass (U.S.A.)
1999-present. Made in the U.S.A.

1999-2004		$850	$1,000

Telecaster Bass
1968-1979. Slab solidbody, 1 pickup, fretless option '70, blond and custom colors available (Pink Paisley or Blue Floral '68-'69).

1968	Black	$2,100	$3,000
1968	Blond	$2,000	$2,700
1968	Blue Floral, Paisley	$4,800	$6,500
1968	Lake Placid Blue	$4,000	$5,500
1969	4-bolt, single-coil	$2,000	$2,600
1970	4-bolt, single-coil	$1,900	$2,500
1971	4-bolt, single-coil	$1,800	$2,400
1972	4-bolt, single-coil	$1,700	$2,300
1973-1974	3-bolt, humbucker	$1,600	$2,200
1975-1976	3-bolt, humbucker	$1,500	$2,100
1977-1979	3-bolt, humbucker	$1,200	$1,700

Fernandes
1969-present. Intermediate and professional grade, production, solidbody basses. Established '69 in Tokyo. Early efforts were classical guitars, but they now offer a variety of guitars and basses.

Electric basses

1969-2005	Higher-end models	$350	$500
1969-2005	Standard models	$250	$350

Fina
Production acoustic basses built at the Kwo Hsiao Music Wooden Factory in Huiyang City, Guang Dong, mainland China. They also build guitars.

First Act
1995-present. Budget and professional grade, production/custom, basses built in China and their Custom Shop in Boston. They also make guitars, violins, and other instruments.

Fleishman Instruments
1974-present. Premium and presentation grade, acoustic and solidbody basses made by luthier Harry Fleishman in Sebastopol, California. He also offers electric uprights, designed by him and built in China. Fleishman also designs basses for others and is the director of Luthiers School International. He also builds guitars.

Fodera
1983-present. Luthiers Vinnie Fodera and Joseph Lauricella build their premium grade, production/custom, solidbody basses in Brooklyn, New York.

Framus
1946-1975, 1996-present. Professional and premium grade, production/custom, basses made in Germany. They also build guitars and amps. Distributed in the U.S. by Dana B. Goods.

Atlantic Bass Model 5/140
1960s. Single-cut thinline with f-holes, 2 pickups, sunburst or blackrose.

1960s		$300	$500

Atlantic Bass Model 5/143
1960s. Offset double-cut thinbody with f-holes, 2 pickups, 4-on-a-side keys.

1960s		$400	$600

Atlantic Bass Model 5/144
1960s. Double-cut thinbody with f-holes, ES-335 body style, 2 pickups. Becomes Model J/144 in '70s.

1960s		$450	$650

Charavelle 4 Bass Model 5/153
1960s. Double-cut thinline with f-holes, 335-style body, 2 pickups, sunburst, cherry red or Sunset.

1960s		$500	$700

De Luxe 4 Bass Model 5/154
1960s. Double-cut thinline with sharp (acute) hornes and f-holes, 2 pickups, mute, sunburst or natural/blond. 2nd most expensive in Framus bass lineup in the mid-'60s, although not as famous as the Stone/Bill Wyman bass.

1960s		$600	$700

Electric Upright Bass
1950s. Full-scale neck, triangular body, black.

1958		$1,500	$2,000

Star Bass Series (Bill Wyman)
1959-1968. Early flyer says, "Bill Wyman of the Rolling Stones prefers the Star Bass." The model name was later changed to Framus Stone Bass. Single-cut semi-hollow body, 5/149 (1 pickup) and 5/150 (2 pickups), sunburst.

1959-1965	Model 5/150	$650	$750
1960s	Model 5/149	$600	$700

Strato De Luxe Star Bass Model 5/165
Ca. 1964-ca. 1972. Offset double-cut solidbody, 2 pickups, sunbust. There was also a gold hardware version (5/165 gl) and a 6-string (5/166).

1960s		$500	$650

Strato Star Bass Series
Ca. 1963-ca. 1972. Double-cut solidbody, 5/156/50 (1 pickup) or 5/156/52 (2 pickups), beige, cherry or sunburst.

1960s	Model 5/156/50	$400	$450
1960s	Model 5/156/52	$450	$500

T.V. Star Bass
1960s. Offset double-cut thinbody with f-holes, 2 pickups, short-scale, sunburst or cherry red. Most expensive of the '60s Framus basses, although not as popular as the Bill Wyman 5/150 model.

1960s		$500	$700

Triumph Electric Upright
1956-1960. Solidbody bean pole electric bass, small body, long neck, slotted viol peghead, gold or black.

1956-1960		$1,500	$2,100

MODEL YEAR	FEATURES	EXC. COND. LOW	HIGH
Upright Bass Viol			
1946	Carved top	$3,000	$5,000

Fresher

1973-1985. Japanese-made, mainly copies of popular brands and not imported into the U.S., but they do show up at guitar shows. They also made guitars.

Solidbody Electric Bass

1970s		$250	$350

Fritz Brothers

1988-present. Luthier Roger Fritz builds his premium grade, production/custom, semi-hollow body basses in Albion, California. He also builds guitars.

Fylde

1973-present. Luthier Roger Bucknall builds his professional and premium grade, production/custom acoustic basses in Penrith, Cumbria, United Kingdom. He also builds guitars, mandolins, mandolas, bouzoukis, and citterns.

G & L

1980-present. Intermediate and professional grade, production/custom, electric basses made in the U.S. In '03, G & L introduced the Korean-made G & L Tribute Series. A Tribute logo is clearly identified on the headstock. They also build guitars.

ASAT Bass

1989-present. Single-cut, solidbody, active and passive modes, 2 humbucking pickups, various colors.

1989-1991	About 400 made	$600	$750
1992-2003		$500	$650

ASAT Commemorative Bass

1991-1992. About 150 made, 4-string ASAT commemorating Leo Fender's life.

1991-1992		$1,300	$1,600

ASAT Semi-Hollow Bass

2001-present. Semi-hollowbody style on ASAT bass.

2001-2003		$650	$800

Climax Bass

1992-1996. Single active humbucker MFD pickup.

1992-1996		$550	$600

El Toro Bass

1983-1991. Double-cut, solidbody, 2 active, smaller, humbucker pickups, sunburst.

1983-1991		$600	$900

Interceptor Bass

1984-1991. Sharp pointed double-cut, solidbody, 2 active, smaller humbucker pickups, sunburst.

1984-1991		$700	$1,000

JB-2 Bass

2001-present. Alder body, 2 Alnico V pickups.

2001-2003		$500	$700

L-1000 Bass

1980-1994. Offset double-cut, solidbody, 1 pickup, various colors.

1980-1994		$500	$700

L-1500 Bass/L-1500 Custom Bass

1997-present.

1997-2003		$600	$700

L-1505 Bass

1998-present. Five-string version, single MFD humbucker pickup.

1998-2003		$600	$700

L-2000 Bass

1980-present. Offset double-cut solidbody, 2 pickups, active electronics. Originally, the L-2000 was available with active (L-2000E) or passive (L-2000) electronics.

1980-1982		$750	$850
1983-1991	Leo signature	$700	$800
1992-2003		$600	$700

L-2000 Fretless Bass

1980-1998. Fretless version.

1980-1982		$800	$900

L-2000(E) Bass

1980-1982. Offset double-cut, solidbody, 2 pickups, active electronics. Originally, the L-2000 was available with active (L-2000E) or passive (L-2000) electronics.

1980-1982		$700	$850

L-2000 Custom Bass

1997. Ash top, wood-grain binding upgrade.

1997		$700	$850

L-2500 Bass

1997-present. Five-string, dual MFD humbucker pickups, figured tops can vary.

1997-2003		$600	$850

L-2500 Custom Bass

1997. Ash top, wood-grain binding upgrade.

1997		$700	$900

L-5000 Bass

1988-1992. Offset double-cut, solidbody, G & L Z-shaped split-humbucking pickup, 5 strings, approximately 400 made.

1988-1992		$550	$650

L-5500 Bass

1993-1997. Alder body, 5-string.

1993-1997		$600	$750

L-5500 Custom Bass

1997. Ash top, wood-grain binding upgrade.

1997		$650	$700

LB-100 Bass

1993-2000. Follow-up to earlier Legacy Bass.

1993-2000		$450	$600

Legacy Bass

1992-1993. Offset double-cut solidbody, 1split-coil pickup, renamed LB-100 in '93.

1992-1993		$600	$700

Lynx Bass

1984-1991. Offset double-cut, solidbody, 2 single-coil pickups, black.

1984-1991		$650	$800

SB 1 Bass

1982-2000. Solidbody, maple neck, body and 'board, split-humbucker pickup, 1 tone and 1 volume control.

1982-1984	1 J-style pickup	$500	$550
1985-2000	1 P-style pickup	$525	$575

1981 G&L L-1000

1983 G&L SB-1

G&L SB-2

Gibson EB-1

MODEL YEAR	FEATURES	EXC. COND. LOW	HIGH

SB 2 Bass

1982-present. Maple neck with tilt adjustment, 1 split-coil humbucking and 1 single-coil bridge pick-ups.

1982-1984	2 P-style pickups	$525	$575
1985-2003	1 P- and 1 J-style pickups	$550	$600

G.L. Stiles

1960-1994. Built by Gilbert Lee Stiles primarily in the Miami, Florida area. He also built guitars.

Electric Solidbody Bass

1970s	Various models	$350	$450

Galveston

Budget and intermediate grade, production, imported acoustic, acoustic/electric and solidbody basses. They also offer guitars and mandolins.

Electric Solidbody Basses

2000s	Various models	$75	$125

Gibson

1902-present. Professional grade, production, U.S.-made electric basses. Gibson got into the electric bass market with the introduction of their Gibson Electric Bass in '53 (that model was renamed the EB-1 in '58 and reintroduced under that name in '69). Many more bass models followed. Gibson's custom colors can greatly increase the value of older instruments. Custom colors offered from '63 to '69 are Cardinal Red, Ember Red, Frost Blue, Golden Mist Metallic, Heather Metallic, Inverness Green, Kerry Green, Pelham Blue Metallic, Polaris White, Silver Mist Metallic.

20/20

1987-1988. Designed by Ned Steinberger, slim-wedge Steinberger style solidbody, 2 humbucker pickups, 20/20 logo on headstock, Luna Silver or Ferrari Red finish.

1987-1988		$1,000	$1,200

Electric Bass (EB-1)

1953-1958. Introduced as Gibson Electric Bass in '53, but was called the EB-1 by Gibson in its last year of '58, thus, the whole line is commonly called the EB-1 by collectors, reissued in '69 as the EB-1 (see EB-1 listing), brown.

1953-1958		$4,000	$5,000

EB Bass

1970 only. Renamed from Melody Maker Bass, SG body, 1 humbucker pickup.

1970		$1,000	$1,200

EB-0 Bass

1959-1979. Double-cut slab body with banjo-type tuners in '59 and '60, double-cut SG-type body with conventional tuners from '61 on, 1 pickup. Faded custom colors are of less value.

1959-1960	Cherry, slab body	$3,700	$4,500
1961	Cherry, SG body	$1,800	$2,200
1962	Cherry	$1,700	$2,000
1963-1964	Cherry	$1,650	$1,900
1965	Cherry	$1,550	$1,800

MODEL YEAR	FEATURES	EXC. COND. LOW	HIGH
1966	Cherry	$1,500	$1,700
1967	Cherry	$1,450	$1,700
1968	Black	$1,400	$1,700
1968	Burgundy Metallic	$1,600	$1,900
1968	Cherry	$1,400	$1,700
1968	Pelham Blue	$1,700	$2,200
1969	Cherry	$1,350	$1,650
1969	Pelham Blue	$1,700	$2,200
1970-1971	Cherry	$1,300	$1,600
1972-1974	Cherry	$1,000	$1,500
1975-1979	Cherry	$1,000	$1,300

EB-0 F Bass

1962-1965. EB-0 with added built-in fuzz, cherry.

1962		$1,700	$2,000
1963-1964		$1,650	$1,900
1965		$1,550	$1,800

EB-0 L Bass

1969-1979. 34.5 inch scale version of the EB-0, various colors.

1969		$1,350	$1,650
1970-1971		$1,300	$1,450
1972-1979		$1,000	$1,300

EB-1 Bass

1969-1972. The Gibson Electric Bass ('53-'58) is often also called the EB-1 (see Electric Bass). Violin-shaped mahogany body, 1 pickup, standard tuners.

1969-1972		$1,700	$2,000

EB-2 Bass

1958-1961, 1964-1972. ES-335-type semi-hollowbody, double-cut, 1 pickup, banjo tuners '58-'60 and conventional tuners '60 on.

1958	Sunburst, banjo tuners	$3,000	$3,500
1959	Natural, banjo tuners	$3,500	$4,000
1959	Sunburst, banjo tuners	$2,600	$2,900
1960	Sunburst, banjo tuners	$2,400	$2,700
1961	Sunburst, conventional tuners	$2,000	$2,400
1964	Sunburst	$1,700	$2,400
1965	Sunburst	$1,600	$2,300
1966	Cherry	$1,500	$2,200
1966	Sunburst	$1,500	$2,200
1967-1969	Sparkling Burgundy	$1,600	$2,300
1967-1969	Sunburst	$1,400	$2,200
1970-1972	Sunburst	$1,200	$1,500

EB-2 D Bass

1966-1972. Two-pickup version of EB-2, cherry, sunburst, or walnut.

1966	Cherry, sunburst	$2,300	$2,800
1967-1969	Cherry, sunburst	$2,200	$2,700
1967-1969	Sparkling Burgundy	$2,300	$2,800
1970-1972	Sunburst	$1,800	$2,000

EB-3 Bass

1961-1979. SG-style solidbody, 2 humbuckers, solid peghead '61-'68 and '72-'79, slotted peghead '69-'71, cherry to '71, various colors after.

1961		$2,500	$3,600
1962		$2,200	$3,500

MODEL YEAR	FEATURES	EXC. COND. LOW	HIGH
1963		$2,100	$3,400
1964		$2,100	$3,300
1965		$2,000	$3,200
1965	Jack Bruce exact specs	$3,000	$5,000
1966		$2,000	$3,100
1967-1968		$2,000	$3,000
1969		$1,900	$2,300
1970-1971		$1,800	$1,900
1972-1974		$1,700	$1,800
1975-1979		$1,300	$1,700

EB-3 L Bass

1969-1972. 34.5" scale version of EB-3, cherry, natural, or walnut.

1969		$1,800	$2,300
1970-1971		$1,700	$1,900
1972		$1,600	$1,800

EB-4 L Bass

1972-1975. SG-style, 1 humbucker, 34.5" scale, cherry or walnut.

1972-1975		$1,500	$1,800

EB-6 Bass

1960-1966. Introduced as semi-hollowbody 335-style 6-string with 1 humbucker, changed to SG-style with 2 pickups in '62.

1960-1961	Sunburst, 335-style	$7,500	$9,500
1962-1964	Cherry, SG-style	$8,500	$12,000
1965-1966	Cherry, SG-style	$7,000	$9,000

EB-650 Bass

1991-1993. Semi-acoustic single cut, maple neck, laminated maple body with center block, 2 TB Plus pickups.

1991-1993		$950	$1,100

EB-750

1991-1993. Like EB-650, but with Bartolini pickups and TCT active eq.

1991-1993		$1,050	$1,200

Explorer Bass

1984-1987. Alder body, 3-piece maple neck, ebony 'board, dot inlays, 2 humbuckers, various colors.

1984-1987		$900	$1,200

Flying V Bass

1981-1982 only. Solidbody, Flying V body.

1981-1982	Blue stain or ebony	$2,800	$3,200
1981-1982	Silverburst	$3,400	$3,800

Gibson IV Bass

1986-1988. Mahogany body and neck, double-cut, 2 pickups, black chrome hardware, various colors.

1986-1988		$500	$600

Gibson V Bass

1986-1988. Double-cut, 5 strings, 2 pickups.

1986-1988		$600	$750

Grabber Bass (G-1)

1974-1982. Double-cut solidbody, 1 pickup, bolt maple neck, maple 'board, various colors.

1974-1982		$700	$975

Grabber III Bass (G-3)

1975-1982. Double-cut solidbody, 3 pickups, bolt maple neck, maple 'board, nickel-plated hardware, various colors.

1975-1982		$800	$1,100

Les Paul Bass

1970-1971. Single-cut solidbody, 2 pickups, walnut finish, renamed Les Paul Triumph Bass '71-'79.

1970-1971		$1,400	$1,600

Les Paul Deluxe Plus LPB-2 Bass

1991-1998. Upgraded Les Paul Special LPB-1 bass, with carved maple top, trapezoid inlays, TCT active eq and Bartolini pickups. Flame maple top Premium version offered '93-'98.

1991-1998		$900	$1,000

Les Paul Signature Bass

1973-1979. Double-cut, semi-hollowbody, 1 pickup, sunburst or gold (gold only by '76). Name also used on LPB-3 bass in '90s.

1973-1975	Sunburst	$2,700	$3,600
1973-1979	Gold	$2,600	$3,600

Les Paul Special LPB-1 Bass

1991-1998. 2 TB-Plus pickups, ebony 'board, dots, slab mahogany body, active electronics, also available as 5-string.

1991-1998		$650	$750

Les Paul Special V Bass

1993-1996. Single-cut slab body, 5-string, 2 pickups, dot markers, black/ebony.

1993-1996		$650	$750

Les Paul Standard LPB-3 Bass

1991-1995. Like Les Paul Deluxe LPB-2 Bass, but with TB Plus pickups. Flame maple top Premium version offered '93-'95.

1991-1995		$1,000	$1,100

Les Paul Triumph Bass

1971-1979. Renamed from Les Paul Bass.

1971-1979	Various colors	$1,200	$1,600
1973-1974	White optional color	$1,500	$1,800

Melody Maker Bass

1967-1970. SG body, 1 humbucker pickup.

1967-1970		$1,000	$1,200

Q-80 Bass

1986-1988. Victory Series body shape, 2 pickups, bolt neck, black chrome hardware, renamed Q-90 in '88.

1986-1988		$550	$700

Q-90 Bass

1988-1992. Renamed from Q-80, mahogany body, 2 active humbuckers, maple neck, ebony 'board.

1988-1992		$550	$700

RD Artist Bass

1977-1982. Double-cut solid maple body, laminated neck, 2 pickups, active electronics, string-thru-body, block inlays, various colors.

1977-1982		$850	$1,000

RD Artist Custom Bass

1977-1982. Custom option with bound top, low production.

1977-1982	Sunburst, mild figure	$950	$1,200

RD Standard Bass

1977-1979. Double-cut, solid maple body, laminated neck, 2 pickups, regular electronics, string-thru-body, dot inlays, various colors.

1977-1979		$850	$1,000

Gibson Melody Maker

1978 Gibson RD Artist

Gibson SG Bass reissue

1965 Gibson Thunderbird IV

MODEL YEAR	FEATURES	EXC. COND. LOW	HIGH

Ripper Bass
1974-1982. Introduced as L-9 S Bass in '73, double-cut solidbody, glued neck, 2 pickups, string-thru-body, various colors.

1974-1982		$800	$900

SB Series Bass
1971-1978. Various models include 300 (30" scale, 1 pickup), 350 (30" scale, 2 pickups), 400 (34" scale, 1 pickup), 450 (34" scale, 2 pickups). From '75 to '78 the 450 was special order only.

1971-1973	SB-300	$600	$900
1971-1973	SB-400	$600	$900
1972-1974	SB-350	$650	$950
1972-1974	SB-450	$650	$950
1975-1978	SB-450 special order	$650	$950

SG Reissue Bass
2005-present. 2 pickups, '60's specs, mahogany body and neck.

2005		$725	$775

Thunderbird II Bass
1963-1969. Reverse solidbody until '65, non-reverse solidbody '65-'69, 1 pickup, custom colors available, reintroduced with reverse body for '83-'84.

1963	Sunburst, reverse	$7,500	$9,000
1964	Pelham Blue, reverse	$7,500	$8,000
1964	Sunburst, reverse	$6,500	$7,000
1965	Cardinal Red, non-reverse	$5,000	$6,000
1965	Inverness Green, non-reverse	$5,000	$6,000
1965	Sunburst, non-reverse	$3,400	$4,000
1965	Sunburst, reverse	$4,800	$6,500
1966	Cardinal Red, non-reverse	$4,500	$5,800
1966	Sunburst, non-reverse	$3,200	$3,800
1967	Cardinal Red, non-reverse	$4,300	$5,600
1967	Sunburst, non-reverse	$3,000	$3,600
1968	Cardinal Red, non-reverse	$4,100	$5,400
1968	Sunburst, non-reverse	$2,700	$3,300
1969	Sunburst, non-reverse	$2,600	$3,100

Thunderbird IV Bass
1963-1969. Reverse solidbody until '64, non-reverse solidbody '65-'69, 2 pickups, custom colors available, reintroduced with reverse body for '86-present (see Thunderbird IV Bass Reissue).

1963	Sunburst, reverse	$8,000	$11,000
1964	Frost Blue, reverse	$11,000	$22,000
1964	Pelham Blue, reverse	$10,000	$20,000
1964	Sunburst, reverse	$6,500	$8,500
1965	Cardinal Red, non-reverse	$7,000	$20,000
1965	Inverness Green, non-reverse	$7,000	$20,000
1965	Sunburst, reverse	$6,000	$7,000
1965-1966	Sunburst, non-reverse	$4,500	$6,000
1966	White, non-reverse	$6,000	$7,000
1967	Sunburst non-reverse	$3,700	$4,700
1968	Sunburst, non-reverse	$3,500	$4,500
1969	Sunburst, non-reverse	$3,200	$4,200

Thunderbird IV Bass (Reissue)
1987-present. Has reverse body and 2 pickups, sunburst.

1987-1990		$1,300	$1,500
1991-2002		$1,100	$1,400
1991-2002	Rare color	$1,400	$1,600

Thunderbird 76 Bass
1976 only. Reverse solidbody, 2 pickups, rosewood 'board, various colors.

1976		$2,600	$2,900

Thunderbird 79 Bass
1979 only. Reverse solidbody, 2 pickups, sunburst.

1979		$1,900	$2,300

Victory Artist Bass
1981-1985. Double-cut, solidbody, 2 humbuckers and active electronics, various colors.

1981-1985		$650	$800

Victory Custom Bass
1982-1984. Double-cut, solidbody, 2 humbuckers, passive electronics, limited production.

1982-1984		$650	$800

Victory Standard Bass
1981-1986. Double-cut, solidbody, 1 humbucker, active electronics, various colors.

1981-1986		$600	$750

Godin
1987-present. Intermediate and professional grade, production, solidbody electric and acoustic/electric basses from luthier Robert Godin. They also build guitars and mandolins.

Godlyke
2006-present. Professional and premium grade, production, solidbody basses from effects distributor Godlyke.

Gold Tone
1993-present. Wayne and Robyn Rogers build their intermediate grade, production/custom acoustic basses in Titusville, Florida. They also offer lap steels, mandolins, banjos and banjitars.

Goya
1955-present. Originally imports from Sweden, brand later used on Japanese and Korean imports. They also offered basses, mandolins and banjos.

Electric Solidbody Bass

1960s	Various models	$350	$500

MODEL		EXC. COND.	
YEAR	FEATURES	LOW	HIGH

Graf, Oskar

1970-present. Luthier Oskar Graf builds his premium grade, production/custom upright solidbody and acoustic basses in Clarendon, Ontario. He also builds guitars and lutes.

Granada

1970s-1980s. Japanese-made electric basses, most being copies of classic American models. They also offered guitars.

Greco

1960s-present. Currently owned by Kanda Shokai, of Japan, and offering solidbody basses. They also offer guitars. Early bass models were copies of popular brands, but by the '70s original designs appear.

Beatle Bass Copy

1970s		$250	$500

Gretsch

1883-present. Intermediate and professional grade, production, solidbody, hollow body, and acoustic/electric basses. Gretsch came late to the electric bass game, introducing their first models in the early '60s.

Bikini Doubleneck Bass

1961-1962. Solidbody electric, separate 6-string and bass-neck body units that slid into 1 of 3 body "butterflies"--1 for the 6-string only (6023), 1 for bass only (6024), 1 for doubleneck (6 and bass-6025). Components could be purchased separately. Prices here are for bass neck and 1 body.

1961-1962		$700	$1,000

Broadkaster Bass (7605/7606)

1975-1979. Double-cut solidbody, 1 pickup, bolt-on maple neck, natural (7605) or sunburst (7606).

1975-1979		$650	$800

Committee Bass (7629)

1977-1980. Double-cut walnut and maple soldibody, neck-thru, 1 pickup, natural.

1977-1980		$750	$900

G6072 Long Scale Hollow Body Bass

1998-present. Reissue of the '68 double-cut hollowbody, 2 pickups, sunburst, gold hardware.

1998-2002		$1,100	$1,250

Model 6070/6072 Bass

1968-1971 (1972 for 6070). Country Gentleman thinline archtop double-cut body, fake f-holes, 1 pickup (6070) or 2 (6072), gold hardware.

1968-1972	Model 6070	$1,200	$1,500
1968-1971	Model 6072	$1,300	$1,600

Model 6071/6073 Bass

1968-1971 (1972 for 6071). Single-cut hollowbody, fake f-holes, 1 pickup (6071) or 2 (6073), padded back, red mahogany.

1968-1972	Model 6071	$1,100	$1,400
1968-1971	Model 6073	$1,200	$1,500

Model 7615 Bass

1972-1975. Offset double-cut solidbody, slotted bass horn (monkey grip), large polished rosewood 'guard covering most of the body, 2 pickups, dot markers, brown mahogany finish. Only bass offered in Gretsch catalog for this era.

1972-1975		$800	$1,000

TK 300 Bass (7626/7627)

1976-1981. Double-cut solidbody, 1 pickup, Autumn Red Stain or natural.

1976-1981		$550	$700

Groove Tools

2002-2004. Korean-made, production, intermediate grade, solidbody basses that were offered by Conklin Guitars of Springfield, Missouri. They also had guitars.

GT Bass

2002-2004. Offset double-cut with large bass horn, bolt-on neck, clear hard finish, models include GT-4 (4-string), GT-5 (5-string) and GT-7 (7-string).

2002-2004	GT-4	$300	$400
2002-2004	GT-5	$300	$400
2002-2004	GT-7	$400	$600

Grosh, Don

1993-present. Professional grade, production/custom, solidbody basses built by luthier Don Grosh in Santa Clarita, California. He also builds guitars.

Guild

1952-present. Guild added electric basses in the mid-'60s and offered them until '02.

Ashbory Bass

1986-1988. 18" scale, total length 30", fretless, silicone rubber strings, active electronics, low-impedance circuitry.

1986-1988		$650	$700

B-4 E Bass

1993-1999. Acoustic/electric single-cut flat-top, mahogany sides with arched mahogany back, multibound, gold hardware until '95, chrome after.

1993-1999		$750	$850

B-30 E Bass

1987-1999. Single-cut flat-top acoustic/electric, mahogany sides, arched mahogany back, multi-bound, fretless optional.

1987-1999		$1,200	$1,400

B-50 Acoustic Bass

1976-1987. Acoustic flat-top, mahogany sides with arched mahogany back, spruce top, multi-bound, renamed B-30 in '87.

1976-1987		$1,200	$1,400

B-301/B-302 Bass

1976-1981. Double-cut solidbody, chrome-plated hardware. Models include B-301 (mahogany, 1 pickup), B-301 A (ash, 1 pickup), B-302 (mahogany, 2 pickups), B-302 A (ash, 2 pickups), and B-302 AF (ash, fretless).

1976-1981	B-301	$500	$600
1976-1981	B-302	$550	$650

Grosh J-5

Guild Ashbory

Guild SB-602

Hagstrom 8-string

MODEL YEAR	FEATURES	EXC. COND. LOW	HIGH
1977-1981	B-301 A	$550	$650
1977-1981	B-302 A	$550	$700
1977-1981	B-302 AF	$500	$700

B-500 Acoustic Bass
1992-1993. Acoustic/electric flat-top, round soundhole, single-cut, solid spruce top, maple back and sides, dark stain, limited production.

1992-1993		$1,200	$1,400

Jet Star Bass
1964-1970 (limited production '68-'70). Offset double-cut solidbody, short treble horn, 1 pickup, 2-on-a-side tuners '64-'66 and 4 in-line tuners '66-'70.

1964-1966	2 on side tuners	$850	$1,300
1967-1970	4 in-line	$650	$1,100

JS I/JS II Bass
1970-1976. Double-cut solidbody, 1 pickup (JS I) or 2 (JS II), mini-switch, selector switch, renamed JS Bass 2 in '73 with carved oak leaf design available.

1970-1976	JS I	$600	$850
1970-1976	JS II	$700	$950

M-85 I/M-85 II Bass (Semi-hollow)
1967-1972. Single-cut semi-hollowbody, 1 pickup (M-85 I) or 2 (M-85 II).

1967-1972	M-85 I	$1,200	$1,600
1967-1972	M-85 II	$1,400	$1,800

M-85 I/M-85 II BluesBird Bass (Solidbody)
1972-1976. Single-cut soldibody archtop, Chesterfield headstock inlay, cherry mahogany, 1 humbucker pickup (I) or 2 (II).

1972-1973	M-85 I	$900	$1,200
1972-1976	M-85 II	$1,100	$1,400

MB-801 Bass
1981-1982. Double-cut solidbody, 1 pickup, dot inlays.

1981-1982		$500	$650

SB-601/SB-602/SB-602 V Pilot Bass
1983-1988. Offset double-cut solidbody, bolt-on neck, poplar body. Models include SB-601 (1 pickup), SB-602 (2 pickups or fretless) and SB-602 V (2 pickups, 5-string).

1983-1988	SB-601	$450	$600
1983-1988	SB-602	$500	$700
1983-1988	SB-602 V	$550	$700
1983-1988	SB-602, fretless	$500	$675

Starfire Bass
1965-1975. Double-cut semi-hollow thinbody, 1 pickup, mahogany neck, chrome-plated hardware, cherry or sunburst.

1965-1969	Single-coil	$1,400	$1,600
1970-1975	Humbucker	$1,200	$1,500

Starfire II Bass
1965-1978. Two-pickup version of Starfire Bass.

1965-1969	2 single-coils	$1,600	$1,800
1970-1978	2 humbuckers	$1,500	$1,700

X-701/X-702 Bass
1982-1984. Body with 4 sharp horns with extra long bass horn, 1 pickup (X-701) or 2 (X-702), various metallic finishes.

1982-1984	X-701	$800	$900
1982-1984	X-702	$900	$1,000

Guyatone
1933-present. Large Japanese maker which also produced instruments under the Marco Polo, Winston, Kingston, Kent, LaFayette, and Bradford brands.

Electric Solidbody Bass

1960s	Various models	$300	$450

Hagstrom
1921-1983, 2004-present. This Swedish guitar company first offered electric basses in '61.

8-String Bass
1967-1969. Double-cut solidbody, 2 pickups, various colors.

1967-1969		$1,300	$1,500

F-100 B Bass
1970s. Offset double-cut solidbody, 1 pickup, Fender style headstock.

1970s		$550	$700

Model I B Bass
1965-1966, 1971-1973. Double-cut solidbody, 2 pickups, red.

1965-1966		$550	$600

Model II B/F-400 Bass
1965-1970. Offset double-cut solidbody, 2 pickups, sunburst, called F-400 in U.S., II B elsewhere.

1965-1970		$600	$650

Swede Bass
1971-1976. Single-cut solidbody, block inlays, 2 pickups, cherry.

1971-1976		$700	$1,000

Swede 2000 Bass (with synth)
1977. Circuitry on this Swede bass connected to the Ampeg Patch 2000 pedal so bass would work with various synths.

1977		$750	$950

V-IN Bass/Concord Bass
1970s. Bass version of V-IN guitar, 335-style body, 2 pickups, sunburst.

1970s		$600	$1,000

Hallmark
1965-1967, 2004-present. Imported, intermediate grade, production, basses. Hallmark is located in Greenbelt, Maryland. They also make guitars. The brand was originally founded by Joe Hall in Arvin, California, in '65.

Hamer
1975-present. Intermediate and professional grade, production/custom, acoustic and electric basses. Founded in Arlington Heights, Illinois, by Paul Hamer and Jol Dantzig, Hamer was purchased by Kaman in '88. They also build guitars.

8-String Short-Scale Bass
1978-1993. Double cut solidbody, 1 or 2 pickups, 30.5" scale.

1978-1993		$1,400	$1,500

MODEL YEAR	FEATURES	EXC. COND. LOW	HIGH

12-String Acoustic Bass
1985-present. Semi-hollow, long scale, single cut, soundhole, 2 pickups. Import XT model added in the 2000s.

1985-2005		$1,500	$2,000

12-String Short-Scale Bass
1978-1996. Four sets of 3 strings - a fundamental and 2 tuned an octave higher, double cut maple and mahogany solidbody, 30.5" scale.

1978-1996		$1,500	$2,000

Blitz Bass
1982-1990. Explorer-style solidbody, 2 pickups, bolt-on neck.

1982-1984	1st edition	$650	$900
1984-1990		$650	$750

Chaparral Bass
1986-1995, 2000-present. Solidbody, 2 pickups, glued-in neck, later basses have bolt-on neck.

1986-1987	Set-neck	$750	$800
1987-1995	Bolt-on neck	$500	$650

Chaparral Max Bass
1986-1995. Chaparral Bass with figured maple body, glued-in neck and boomerang inlays.

1986-1995		$550	$700

Chaparral 5-String Bass
1987-1995. Five strings, solidbody, 2 pickups, glued-in neck, later basses have 5-on-a-side reverse peghead.

1987-1995		$500	$700

Chaparral 12-String Bass
1992-present. Long 34" scale 12-string, offset double cut. Import XT model added in '01.

1992-2005		$1,500	$2,000

Cruise Bass
1982-1990, 1995-1999. J-style solidbody, 2 pickups, glued neck ('82-'90) or bolt-on neck ('95-'99), also available as a 5-string.

1982-1990	Set-neck	$500	$700
1995-1999	Bolt-on neck	$500	$600

Cruise Bass 5
1982-1989. Five-string version, various colors.

1982-1989		$550	$700

FBIV Bass
1985-1987. Reverse Firebird shape, 1 P-Bass Slammer and 1 J-Bass Slammer pickup, mahogany body, rosewood 'board, dots.

1985-1987		$550	$650

Standard Bass
1975-1984. Explorer-style bound body with 2 humbuckers.

1975-1979		$850	$950
1980-1984		$700	$850

Velocity 5
2002-present. Offset double-cut, long bass horn, active, 1 humbucker.

2002-2004		$150	$175

Harmony
1892-1976. Harmony once was one of the biggest instrument makers in the world, making guitars and basses under their own brand and for others.

H-22 Bass
Early-1960s-1970s. Single- or double-cut, sunburst.

1960-1970s		$300	$500

Rocket Bass
1960s-1970s. First models single-cut, later models double-cut, similar to Rocket guitar.

1960-1970s		$350	$500

Hartke
Hartke offered a line of wood and aluminum-necked basses from 2000 to '03.

Electric Bass

2000-2003		$100	$200

Hayman
1970-1973. Solid and semi-hollow body guitars and basses developed by Jim Burns and Bob Pearson for Ivor Arbiter of the Dallas Arbiter Company and built by Shergold in England.

Heartfield
1989-1994. Distributed by Fender, imported from Japan. They also offered guitars.

DR-4 Bass
1989-1994. Double-cut solidbody, graphite reinforced neck, 2 single-coils, 4 strings, available in 5- and 6-string models.

1989-1994		$225	$375

Heit Deluxe
Ca. 1967-1970. Imported from Japan, many were made by Teisco. They also had guitars.

Höfner
1887-present. Professional grade, production, basses. They also offer guitars and bowed instruments. Hofner basses, made famous in the U.S. by one Paul McCartney, are made in Germany.

JB-59 Upright Jazz Bass
Electric solidbody, 3/4-size, solid mahogany, pickup, preamp.

1980s		$1,100	$1,500

Model 185 Solid Bass
1962-ca. 1970. Classic offset double-cut solidbody, 2 double-coil pickups.

1960s		$400	$500

Model 500/1 Beatle Bass
1956-present. Semi-acoustic, bound body in violin shape, glued-in neck, 2 pickups, sunburst, currently listed as the 500/1 50th Anniversary.

1956-1959		$3,300	$4,100
1960-1961		$3,500	$4,200
1960-1961	Lefty	$4,000	$5,000
1962		$3,500	$4,200
1962	Lefty	$4,000	$5,000
1963		$3,300	$4,100
1963	Lefty	$5,000	$6,000
1964		$3,200	$4,000
1964	Lefty	$4,000	$5,000
1965		$2,900	$3,800

Harmony H-22

Hamer Blitz

BASSES

1963 Höfner 500/1

'80s Hondo H 1181

MODEL YEAR	FEATURES	EXC. COND. LOW	HIGH
1965	Lefty	$3,600	$4,000
1966		$2,500	$3,000
1966	Lefty	$2,800	$3,500
1967		$2,000	$2,300
1967	Lefty	$2,100	$2,400
1968-1969	Blade pickup	$1,700	$2,000
1968-1969	Lefty, blade pickup	$1,800	$2,100
1970-1973		$1,700	$2,000
1970-1973	Lefty	$1,800	$2,100
1974-1979		$1,500	$1,800

Model 500/1 1964-1984 Bass Reissue
1984. '1964-1984' neckplate notation.

1984		$1,700	$2,000

'63 Model 500/1 Beatle Bass Reissue
1994-present. Right- or left-handed.

1990-2004		$1,500	$1,800

Model 500/2 Bass
1965-1970. Similar to the 500/1, but with 'club' body Hofner made for England's Selmer, sunburst. Club Bass has been reissued.

1965-1970		$1,700	$2,000

Model 500/3 Senator
1962. Sunburst.

1962		$1,700	$1,900

Model 500/5 Bass
1959-1979. Single-cut body with Beatle Bass-style pickups, sunburst.

1960s		$1,900	$2,100

Model (G)5000/1 Super Beatle (G500/1) Bass
1968-present. Bound ebony 'board, gold-plated hardware, natural finish, the version with active circuit is called G500/1 Super Beatle, reissued in '94

1968-1975		$1,500	$1,800

President Bass
Made for England's Selmer, single-cut archtop, 2 pickups, sunburst.

1961-1962		$1,700	$2,000
1963-1965		$1,600	$1,900
1966-1967		$1,300	$1,700
1968-1969		$1,200	$1,600
1970-1972		$1,100	$1,400

Hohner
1857-present. Intermediate and professional grade, production, solidbody basses. Hohner has been offering basses at least since the early '70s. They also offer guitars, banjos, mandolins and ukes.

Electric Basses

1980-2000		$250	$400

Hondo
1969-1987, 1991-present. Budget grade, production, imported acoustic and electric solidbody basses. They also offer guitars and mandolins.

Electric Solidbody Bass

1970-1990s	Various models	$125	$250

MODEL YEAR	FEATURES	EXC. COND. LOW	HIGH

H 1181 Longhorn Bass
Ca. 1978-1980s. Copy of Danelectro Longhorn Bass, 1 split pickup.

1970-1980s		$425	$550

Hopf
1906-present. From the mid-'50s to the late-'70s, Hopf offered electric basses made in their own factory and by others. Hopf currently mainly offers classical guitars and mandolins.

Hoyer
1874-present. Intermediate grade, production, electric basses. They also build guitars.

Ibanez
1932-present. Intermediate and professional grade, production, solidbody basses. They also have guitars, amps, and effects.

Axstar 50 AXB Bass
1986-1987. Headless solidbody, 1-piece maple neck, rosewood 'board, 2 humbuckers.

1986-1987		$275	$325

Axstar 60 AXB Bass
1986-1987. Headless solidbody, 1-piece maple neck, ebony 'board, 2 low impedance pickups.

1986-1987		$400	$450

Axstar 65 AXB Bass
1986-1987. Five-string version of the 60 AXB.

1986-1987		$400	$450

Axstar 1000 AXB Bass
1986-1987. Headless alder solidbody, 1-piece maple neck-thru-body, ebony 'board, 2 low impedance pickups.

1986-1987		$450	$500

BTB500 Series Bass
1999-2000. Offset double-cut ash solidbody, 2 pickups, extra long bass horn, dot markers, natural walnut.

1999-2000		$500	$600

Destroyer X Series Bass
1983-1986. Futuristic-style body, P- and J-style pickups, dot markers, X Series notation on headstock, bolt neck.

1983-1986		$400	$450

Model 2030 Bass
1970-1973. First copy era bass, offset double-cut, sunburst.

1970-1973		$450	$600

Model 2353 Bass
1974-1976. Copy model, offset double-cut, 1 pickup, black.

1974-1976		$450	$600

Model 2364B Bass
1971-1973. Dan Armstrong see-thru Lucite copy with 2 mounted humbucker pickups, clear finish.

1971-1973		$500	$600

Model 2365 Bass
1974-1975. Copy model, Offset double-cut, rosewood 'board, pearloid block markers, sunburst.

1974-1975		$450	$600

MODEL YEAR	FEATURES	EXC. COND. LOW	HIGH

Model 2366B/2366FLB Bass
1974-1975. Copy model, offset double-cut, 1 split-coil pickup, sunburst, FLB fretless model.

1974-1975		$450	$600

Model 2385 Bass
1974-1975. Copy model, offset double-cut, 1 pickup, ash natural finish.

1974-1975		$450	$600

Model 2388B Bass
1974-1976. Ric 4001 copy.

1974-1976		$450	$600

Musician EQ Bass
1978-1979. Offset double-cut solidbody, 2 pickups, EQ, ash and mahogany body, ebony 'board, dot inlays, became the MC900.

1978-1979		$500	$600

Musician MC800 Bass
1979-1980. Offset double-cut solidbody, 2 pickups, laminated neck.

1979-1980		$450	$550

Musician MC900 Bass
1979-1980. MC800 with on-board 3-band EQ.

1979-1980		$500	$600

Newport Bass
1974-1975. Copy model, cresting wave body, blond.

1974-1975		$600	$700

PL 5050 Bass
Ca. 1985-ca. 1988. Part of the Pro Line Series.

1985-1988		$350	$450

Roadstar II Bass
1982-1987. Solidbody basses, various models and colors.

1982-1987		$250	$400

Rocket Roll Bass
1974-1976. Korina solidbody, V-shape, natural.

1974-1976		$900	$1,100

SB-900 Bass
1990-1993. Ultra slim solidbody.

1990-1993		$350	$450

SR-400 Bass
1993-present. Offset double-cut solidbody, long bass horn, 2 pickups.

1993-2003		$300	$400

SR-405 Bass
1994-present. 5-string SR-400.

1994-2003		$300	$400

SR-500 Bass
1993-present. Offset double-cut, long bass horn, active pickups, bolt neck.

1993-2005		$350	$450

SR-505 Bass
1993-present. 5-string SR 500.

1993-2005		$350	$450

SR-885 Bass
1991-2003. Offset double-cut solidbody, 5-string, 2 humbuckers.

1991-2003		$300	$450

Imperial
Ca.1963-ca.1970. Imported by the Imperial Accordion Company of Chicago, Illinois. Early guitars and basses made in Italy, but by ca. '66 Japanese-made.

Electric Solidbody Bass
1960s	Various models	$150	$225

Hollowbody Bass
1960s. Hollowbody with sharp double-cuts.

1960s		$225	$275

Infeld
2003-present. Solidbody guitars and basses offered by string-maker Thomastik-Infeld of Vienna.

Italia
1999-present. Intermediate grade, production, solid and semi-solidbody basses designed by Trevor Wilkinson and made in Korea. They also build guitars.

J.B. Player
1980s-present. Intermediate grade, production, imported, acoustic/electric and solidbody basses. They also offer guitars, banjos and mandolins.

J.T. Hargreaves
1995-present. Luthier Jay Hargreaves builds his premium grade, production/custom, acoustic basses, in Seattle, Washington. He also builds guitars.

Jackson
1980-present. Intermediate, professional, and premium grade, production, solidbody basses. They also offer guitars. Founded by Grover Jackson, who owned Charvel.

Concert C5P 5-String (Import)
1998-2000. Bolt neck, dot inlay, chrome hardware.

1998-2000		$150	$200

Concert Custom Bass (U.S.-made)
1984-1995. Neck-thru Custom Shop bass.

1984-1989		$700	$875
1990-1995		$550	$775

Concert EX 4-String (Import)
1992-1995. Bolt neck, dot inlay, black hardware.

1992-1995		$250	$350

Concert V 5-String (Import)
1992-1995. Bound neck, shark tooth inlay.

1992-1995		$450	$550

Concert XL 4-String (Import)
1992-1995. Bound neck, shark tooth inlay.

1992-1995		$350	$450

Kelly Pro Bass
1994-1995. Pointy-cut bouts, neck-thru solidbody, shark fin marker inlays.

1994-1995		$600	$800

Ibanez SR-500

J.T. Hargreaves Jayhawk

Jay Turser JTB-2

'60s Kay bass

MODEL YEAR	FEATURES	EXC. COND. LOW	HIGH

Piezo Bass
1986. Four piezo electric bridge pickups, neck-thru, active EQ, shark tooth inlays. Student model has rosewood 'board, no binding. Custom Model has ebony 'board and neck and headstock binding.

1986		$400	$500

Jay Turser
1997-present. Intermediate grade, production, imported semi-hollow and solidbody basses. They also offer guitars and amps.

Jerry Jones
1981-present. Intermediate grade, production, semi-hollow body electric basses from luthier Jerry Jones, and built in Nashville, Tennessee. They also build guitars and sitars.

Neptune Longhorn 4 Bass
1988-present. Based on Danelectro longhorn models, 4-string, 2 lipstick-tube pickups, 30" scale.

1988-2000		$450	$500

Neptune Longhorn 6 Bass
1988-present. 6-string version.

1988-2000		$525	$600

Johnson
Mid-1990s-present. Budget and intermediate grade, production, solidbody and acoustic basses imported by Music Link, Brisbane, California. They also offer guitars, amps, mandolins and effects.

Juzek
Violin maker John Juzek was originally located in Prague, Czeckoslovakia, but moved to West Germany due to World War II. Prague instruments considered by most to be more valuable. Many German instruments were mass produced with laminate construction and some equate these German basses with the Kay laminate basses of the same era. Juzek still makes instruments.

Kalamazoo
1933-1942, 1965-1970. Kalamazoo was a brand Gibson used on one of their budget lines. They also used the name on electric basses, guitars and amps from '65 to '67.

Electric Bass
1965-1967	Bolt-on neck	$200	$450

Kapa
Ca. 1962-1970. Kapa was founded by Kope Veneman in Maryland and offered basses and guitars.

Electric Bass
1962-1970	Various models	$275	$500

Kawai
1927-present. Japanese instrument manufacturer Kawai started offering guitars under other brandnames around '56. There were few imports carrying the Kawai brand until the late-'70s; best known for

MODEL YEAR	FEATURES	EXC. COND. LOW	HIGH

high quality basses. Kawai quit offering guitars and basses around 2002.

Electric Bass
1960s	Various models	$200	$350
1970s	Various models	$200	$350
1980s	Various models	$300	$400

Kay
Ca. 1931-present. Currently, budget and intermediate grade, production, imported solidbldy basses. They also make amps, guitars, banjos, mandolins, ukes, and violins. Kay introduced upright acoustic laminate basses and 3/4 viols in '38 and electric basses in '54.

C1 Concert String Bass
1938-1967. Standard (3/4) size student bass, laminated construction, spruce top, figured maple back and sides, shaded light brown.

1938-1949		$2,700	$3,000
1950-1959		$2,500	$2,700
1960-1967		$2,300	$2,500

Jazz Special Electronic Bass
1960-1964		$500	$550

M-1 (Maestro) String Bass
1952-late-1960s. Standard (3/4) size bass, laminated construction, spruce top and curly maple back and sides. Model M-3 is the Junior (1/4) size bass, Model M-1 B has a blond finish, other models include the S-51 B Chubby Jackson Five-String Bass and the S-9 Swingmaster.

1952-1959		$2,500	$2,800
1960-1967		$2,300	$2,500

M-5 (Maestro) String Bass
1957-late-1960s. Five strings.

1957-1967		$3,000	$3,500

Semi-hollowbody Basses
1954-1966. Single or double cut, 1 or 2 pickups.

1954-1966	1 pickup	$300	$400
1954-1966	2 pickups	$400	$550

Solidbody Basses
1965-1968. Single or double cut, 1 or 2 pickups.

1965-1968	1 pickup	$300	$400
1965-1968	2 pickups	$400	$550

Ken Smith
See listing under Smith.

Kent
1961-1969. Basses and guitars imported from Japan by Buegeleisen and Jacobson of New York, New York. Manufacturers unknown but many early instruments by Guyatone and Teisco.

Electric Solidbody Bass
1962-1969. Import models include 628 Newport, 634 Basin Street, 629, and 635.

1961-1969	Century Red	$150	$350

Semi-Hollow Electric Bass
1960s. Offset soft cutaway, single pickup, 2 control knobs.

1961-1969	Sunburst	$250	$350

MODEL		EXC. COND.	
YEAR	FEATURES	LOW	HIGH

Kingslight Guitars

1980-present. Luthier John Kingslight builds his premium grade, custom/production, acoustic basses in Portage, Michigan (in Taos, New Mexico for '80-'83). He also builds guitars.

Kingston

Ca. 1958-1967. Imported from Japan by Westheimer Importing Corp. of Chicago. Early examples by Guyatone and Teisco. They also offered guitars.

Electric Solidbody Bass

1960s	Various models	$125	$300

Klein Acoustic Guitars

1972-present. Luthiers Steve Klein and Steven Kauffman build their production/custom, premium and presentation grade acoustic basses in Sonoma, California. They also build guitars.

Klein Electric Guitars

1988-present. Lorenzo German produces his professional grade, production/custom, basses in Linden, California. He also builds guitars.

Klira

Founded in 1887 in Schoenbach, Germany, mainly making violins, but added guitars and basses in the 1950s. The instruments of the '50s and '60s were aimed at the budget market, but workmanship improved with the '70s models.

Beatle Bass Copy

1960s. Beatle Bass 500/1 copy, sunburst.

1960s		$350	$500

Knutson Luthiery

1981-present. Professional grade, custom, electric upright basses built by luthier John Knutson in Forestville, California. He also builds guitars and mandolins.

Koll

1990-present. Professional and premium grade, custom/production, solidbody and chambered basses built by luthier Saul Koll, originally in Long Beach, California, and since '93, in Portland, Oregon. He also builds guitars.

Kona

2001-present. Budget grade, production, acoustic and electric basses made in Asia. They also offer guitars, amps and mandolins.

Kramer

1976-1990, 1995-present. Budget grade, production, imported solidbody basses. They also offer guitars. Kramer's first guitars and basses featured aluminum necks with wooden inserts on back. Around '80 they started to switch to more economical wood necks and aluminum necks were last produced in '85. Gibson acquired the brand in '97.

250-B Special Bass

1977-1979. Offset double-cut, aluminum neck, Ebonol 'board, zero fret, 1 single-coil, natural.

1977-1979		$400	$500

350-B Standard Bass

1976-1979. Offset double-cut, aluminum neck, Ebonol 'board, tropical woods, 1 single-coil, dots.

1976-1979		$550	$700

450-B Deluxe Bass

1976-1980. As 350-B, but with 2 single-coils and blocks.

1976-1980		$650	$850

650-B Artist Bass

1977-1980. Double-cut, birdseye maple/burled walnut, aluminum neck, zero fret, mother-of-pearl crowns, 2 humbuckers.

1977-1980		$850	$1,100

Aero Star ZX Series Bass

1986-1989. Various models include ZX-70 (offset double-cut solidbody, 1 pickup).

1986-1989	ZX-70 (Import)	$100	$125

DMZ 4000 Bass

1978-1982. Bolt-on aluminum neck, slot headstock, double-cut solidbody, active EQ and dual-coil humbucking pickup, dot inlay.

1978-1981		$550	$700
1982	Bill Wyman-type	$650	$900

DMZ 4001 Bass

1979-1980. Aluminum neck, slot headstock, double-cut solidbody, 1 dual-coil humbucker pickup, dot inlay.

1979-1980		$500	$600

DMZ 5000 Bass

1979-1980. Double-cut solidbody, aluminum neck, slotted headstock, 2 pickups, crown inlays.

1979-1980		$550	$700

DMZ 6000B Bass

1979-1980. Double-cut, aluminum neck, slotted headstock, 2 pickups, crown inlays.

1979-1980		$625	$800

Duke Custom/Standard Bass

1981-1983. Headless, aluminum neck, 1 humbucker.

1981-1983		$525	$550

Duke Special Bass

1982-1985. Headless, aluminum neck, 2 pickups, with frets or fretless.

1982-1985		$550	$600

Ferrington KFB-1/KFB-2 Acoustic Bass

1987-1990. Acoustic/electric, bridge-mounted active pickup, tone and volume control, various colors. KFB-1 has binding and diamond dot inlays; the KFB-2 no binding and dot inlays. Danny Ferrington continued to offer the KFB-1 after Kramer closed in '90.

1987-1990		$350	$500

Focus 7000 Bass

1985-1987. Offset double-cut solidbody, P and double J pickups, Japanese-made.

1985-1987		$250	$375

Ken Smith Black Tiger

'80s Kramer Duke Standard

BASSES

BASSES

1980 Kramer XL-8

1990 Kubicki Ex Factor 4

MODEL YEAR	FEATURES	EXC. COND. LOW	HIGH

Focus 8000 Bass
1985-1987. Offset double-cut solidbody, Japanese-made.

1985-1987		$275	$400

Focus K-77 Bass
1984. Offset double-cut solidbody, 1 pickup, Japanese-made.

1984		$225	$375

Focus K-88 Bass
1984. Two pickup Focus.

1984		$225	$375

Forum Series Bass
1987-1990. Japanese-made double-cut, 2 pickups, neck-thru (I & III) or bolt-neck (II & IV).

1987-1990	Forum I	$500	$750
1987-1990	Forum II	$400	$650
1987-1990	Forum III	$300	$400
1987-1990	Forum IV	$250	$350

Gene Simmons Axe Bass
1980-1981. Axe-shaped bass, slot headstock.

1980-1981		$2,500	$3,500

Hundred Series Bass
1988-1990. Import budget line, 7/8th solidbody.

1988-1990	710	$200	$325
1988-1990	720	$225	$350

Pacer Bass
1982-1984. Offset double-cut solidbody, red.

1982-1984		$400	$600

Pioneer Bass
1981-1986. First wood neck basses, offset double cut, JBX or PBX pickups, dots, '81-'84 models with soft headstocks, later '84 on with banana headstocks.

1981-1986	Double J, 2 JBX	$450	$650
1981-1986	Imperial, JBX & PBX	$400	$600
1981-1986	Special, 1 PBX	$375	$575
1982-1984	Carrera, JBX & PBX	$450	$650

Ripley Four-String Bass
1985-1987. Four-string version.

1985-1987		$300	$500

Ripley Five-String Bass
1984-1987. Offset double-cut, 5 strings, stereo, pan pots for each string, front and back pickups for each string, active circuitry.

1984-1987		$400	$600

Stagemaster Custom Bass
1981-1985, 1987-1990. First version had an aluminum neck (wood optional). Later version was neck-thru-body, bound neck, either active or passive pickups.

1981-1985	Imperial	$450	$650
1981-1985	Special	$400	$600
1981-1985	Standard	$425	$625
1987-1990	Reintroduced models	$400	$600

Striker 700 Bass
1985-1989. Offset double-cut, Korean-import, 1 pickup until '87, 2 after. Striker name was again used on a bass in '99.

1985-1987	1 pickup	$175	$225
1988-1989	2 pickups	$200	$250

MODEL YEAR	FEATURES	EXC. COND. LOW	HIGH

Vanguard Bass
1981-1984. V-shaped body.

1983-1984	Standard, wood neck	$400	$600

Vanguard Special Bass
1981-1983. V-shaped body, aluminum neck.

1981-1983		$350	$550

XKB-10 (Wedge) Bass
1980-1981. Wedge-shaped body, aluminum neck.

1980-1981		$500	$600

XKB-20 Bass
1981. 2nd version, more traditional double cut body.

1981		$475	$575

XL Bass Series
1980-1981. Odd shaped double-cut solidbody, aluminum neck.

1980-1981	XL-9 4-string	$625	$800
1981	XL-24 4-string	$700	$900
1981	XL-8 8-string	$700	$900

KSD
2003-present. Intermediate grade, production, imported bass line designed by Ken Smith (see Smith listing) and distributed by Brooklyn Gear.

Kubicki
1973-present. Professional and premium grade, production/custom, solidbody basses built by luthier Phil Kubicki in Santa Barbara, California. Kubicki began building acoustic guitars when he was 15. In '64 at age 19, he went to work with Roger Rossmeisl at Fender Musical Instrument's research and development department for acoustic guitars. Nine years later he moved to Santa Barbara, California, and established Philip Kubicki Technology, which is best known for its line of Factor basses and also builds acoustic guitars, custom electric guitars, bodies and necks, and mini-guitars and does custom work, repairs and restorations.

Ex Factor 4 Bass
1985-present. Solidbody, maple body, bolt-on maple neck, 2 pickups, active electronics.

1980s		$700	$1,000

Factor 4 Bass
1985-present. Solidbody, maple body, bolt-on maple neck, fretless available, 4 strings, 2 pickups, active electronics.

1980s		$900	$1,200

Factor 5-String Bass
1985-ca.1990. Solidbody, bolt-on maple neck, fretless available, 5 strings, 2 pickups, active electronics.

1980s		$900	$1,200

Kustom
1968-present. Founded by Bud Ross in Chanute, Kansas, and best known for the tuck-and-roll amps, Kustom also offered guitars and basses from '68 to '69.

Electric Hollowbody Bass

1968-1969	Various models	$750	$850

MODEL YEAR	FEATURES	EXC. COND. LOW	HIGH

La Baye

1967. Short-lived brand out of Green Bay, Wisconsin and built by the Holman-Woodell factory in Neodesha, Kansas. There was also a guitar model.

Model 2x4 II Bass

1967. Very low production, dual pickups, long-scale, small rectangle solidbody, sometimes referred to as the Bass II.

1967		$1,400	$1,700

Model 2x4 Mini-Bass

1967. Short-scale, 1 pickup, small rectangle solidbody.

1967		$1,200	$1,500

Lado

1973-present. Founded by Joe Kovacic, Lado builds professional and premium grade, production/custom, solidbody basses in Lindsay, Ontario. Some model lines are branded J. K. Lado. They also build guitars.

Lafayette

Ca. 1963-1967. Sold through Lafayette Electronics catalogs. Early Japanese-made guitars and basses from pre-copy era, generally shorter scale beginner instruments. Many made by Guyatone, some possibly by Teisco.

Lakland

1994-present. Professional and premium grade, production/custom, solid and hollowbody basses from luthier Dan Lakin in Chicago, Illinois. Lakland basses are built in the U.S. and overseas (Skyline series).

4 - 63 Classic Bass

1994-2002. Offset double-cut alder body, large bass horn, bolt neck.

1994-2002		$1,600	$1,800

4 - 63 Deluxe Bass

1994-2002. Like Classic but with figured maple top on ash body.

1994-2002		$1,800	$2,000

4 - 63 Standard Bass

1994-2002. Like Classic, but with swamp ash body.

1994-2002		$1,600	$1,800

4 - 94 Classic Bass

1994-present. Offset double-cut alder body with maple top, large bass horn, bolt neck.

1990s		$1,600	$1,800

4 - 94 Deluxe Bass

1994-present. Like Classic but with figured maple top on ash body.

1990s		$1,800	$2,000

4 - 94 Standard Bass

1994-present. Like Classic, but with swamp ash body.

1990s		$1,600	$1,800

Joe Osborn Bass

1998-present. Classic offset double-cut, 4- or 5-string, alder or swamp ash body, 2 pickups.

1998-2003		$1,800	$2,000

Larrivee

1968-present. Founded by Jean Larrivee in Toronto and currently located in Vancouver, British Columbia, Larrivee has offered several acoustic basses over the years.

Leach

1980-present. Luthier Harvey Leach builds his premium grade, custom, acoustic basses in Cedar Ridge, California. He also builds guitars.

Lehtela

1993-present. Professional and premium grade, custom/production, solidbody basses built by luthier Ari Lehtela in Charlotte, North Carolina. He also builds guitars.

Linc Luthier

Professional and premium grade, custom/production, electric, acoustic and upright basses built by luther Linc Luthier in Upland, California. He also builds guitars and double-necks.

Lotus

Late-1970-present. Electric basses imported originally by Midco International, and most recently by Musicorp. They also make guitars, banjos and mandolins.

Lowrider Basses

2003-present. Professional grade, production/custom, solidbody basses made in Las Vegas, Nevada by Ed Roman.

LSR Headless Instruments

1988-present. Professional grade, production/custom, solidbody headless basses made in Las Vegas, Nevada by Ed Roman. They also make guitars.

LTD

1995-present. Intermediate grade, production, Korean-made solidbody basses offered by ESP. They also offer guitars.

Lyle

Ca. 1969-1980. Japanese guitars and basses imported by distributor L.D. Heater in Portland, Oregon.

Electric Solidbody Bass

1970s	Various models	$100	$200

Lyon by Washburn

1990s-present. Budget basses sold by mass merchandisers such as Target. They also offer guitars.

Lakland Jerry Scheff signature

Lowrider

Martin B-40

Mollerup Orca 6-string

MODEL YEAR	FEATURES	EXC. COND. LOW	HIGH
Electric Solidbody Bass			
2000s	Various models	$75	$125

Lyric
1996-present. Luthier John Southern builds his professional and premium grade, custom, basses in Tulsa, Oklahoma. He also builds guitars.

Magnatone
Ca. 1937-1971. Founded as Dickerson Brothers, known as Magna Electronics from '47. Produced instruments under own brand and for many others.

Hurricane Bass
1965-1966. Offset double cut solidbody, 1 single-coil, 4-on-a-side tuners, Magnatone logo on guard and headstock, Hurricane logo on headstock.

1965-1966		$300	$375

Mako
1985-1989. Line of solidbody basses from Kaman (Ovation, Hamer). They also offered guitars and amps.

Electric Solidbody Bass

1985-1989	Student bass	$100	$125

Marco Polo
1960- ca.1964. One of the first inexpensive Japanese brands to be imported into the U.S., they also offered guitars.

Solidbody Bass

1960s	Various models	$100	$175

Marling
Ca. 1975. Budget line instruments marketed by EKO of Recanati, Italy; probably made by them, although possibly imported. They also had guitars.

Electric Solidbody Bass
Models include the E.495 (copy of LP), E.485 (copy of Tele), and the E.465 (Manta-style).

1970s		$100	$175

Martin
1833-present. Professional grade, production, acoustic basses made in the U.S. In 1978, Martin re-entered the electric market and introduced their solidbody EB-18 and EB-28 Basses. In the '80s they offered Stinger brand electric basses. By the late '80s, they started offering acoustic basses.

B-40 Acoustic Bass
1989-1996. Jumbo-size, spruce top and Indian rosewood back and sides, mahogany neck, ebony 'board, built-in pickup and volume and tone controls. The B-40B had a pickup.

1989-1996	B-40B	$1,500	$1,700
1989-1996	Without pickup	$1,300	$1,500

B-65 Acoustic Bass
1989-1993. Jumbo-size, spruce top, maple back and sides, mahogany neck, ebony 'board with 23 frets, built-in pickup and volume and tone controls, natural.

1989-1993		$1,300	$1,700

MODEL YEAR	FEATURES	EXC. COND. LOW	HIGH
BC-15E Acoustic Bass			

1999-present. Single cut, sapele or mahogany top, sides, and back, Fishman pickup.

1999-2005		$900	$1,000
EB-18 Bass			

1979-1982. Electric solidbody, neck-thru, 1 pickup, natural.

1979-1982		$550	$650
EB-28 Bass			

1980-1982. Electric solidbody.

1980-1982		$750	$850
SBL-10 Bass			

Stinger brand solidbody, maple neck, 1 split and 1 bar pickup.

1980s		$150	$200

Marvel
1950s-mid-1960s. Brand used for budget guitars and basses marketed by Peter Sorkin Company in New York, New York.

Electric Solidbody Bass

1950s	Various models	$125	$225

Messenger
1967-1968. Built by Musicraft, Inc., Messengers featured a neck-thru metal alloy neck. They also made guitars.

Bass
1967-1968. Metal alloy neck. Messenger mainly made guitars - they offered a bass, but it is unlikely many were built.

1967-1968		$2,200	$2,800

Messenger Upright
Made by Knutson Luthiery, see that listing.

Michael Kelly
2000-present. Intermediate grade, production, acoustic/electric basses imported by Elite Music Brands of Clearwater, Florida. They also offer mandolins and guitars.

Michael Tuttle
2003-present. Luthier Michael Tuttle builds his professional and premium grade, custom, solid and hollow body basses in Saugus, California. He also builds guitars.

Microfrets
1967-1975, 2004-present. Professional grade, production, electric basses built in Myersville, Maryland. They also build guitars.

Husky Bass
1971-1974/75. Double-cut, 2 pickups, two-on-a-side tuners.

1971-1975		$550	$650

Rendezvous Bass
1970. One pickup, orange sunburst.

1970		$600	$700

MODEL YEAR	FEATURES	EXC. COND. LOW	HIGH

Signature Bass
1969-1975. Double-cut, 2 pickups, two-on-a-side tuners.

1969-1975		$700	$850

Stage II Bass
1969-1975. Double-cut, 2 pickups, two-on-a-side tuners.

1969-1975		$700	$850

Thundermaster Bass
1969		$700	$850

Mike Lull Custom Guitars
1995-present. Professional and premium grade, production/custom, basses built by luthier Mike Lull in Bellevue, Washington. He also builds guitars.

Mitre
1983-1985. Bolt-neck solidbody basses made in Aldenville (or East Longmeadow), Massachusetts. They also built guitars.

MJ Guitar Engineering
1993-present. Luthier Mark Johnson builds his professional grade, production/custom, chambered basses in Rohnert Park, California. He also builds guitars.

Modulus
1978-present. Founded by aerospace engineer Geoff Gould, Modulus currently offers professional and premium grade, production/custom, solidbody basses built in California. They also build guitars.

Bassstar SP-24 Active Bass
1981-ca. 1990. EMG J pickups, active bass and treble circuits.

1980s		$1,100	$1,400

Flea 4 Bass/Flea Signature
1997-2003. Offset double-cut alder solidbody, also offered as 5-string.

1997-2003		$1,100	$1,700

Genesis Series Bass
1997-1998, 2003-present. Offset double-cut, 2 pickups, 4- or 5-string.

2003-2004	Various models	$800	$1,200

Quantum-4 Series Bass
1982-present. Offset double-cut, 2 pickups, 35" scale.

1982-2000		$1,400	$1,750

Quantum-5 Series Bass
1982-present. 5-String version.

1982-2000		$1,500	$1,800

Quantum-6 Series Bass
1982-present. 6-string version.

1982-2000		$1,600	$1,850

Mollerup Basses
1984-present. Luthier Laurence Mollerup builds his professional grade, custom/production, electric basses and electric double basses in Vancouver, British Columbia. He has also built guitars.

Moon
1979-present. Professional grade, production/custom, basses made in Japan. They also build guitars.

Moonstone
1972-present. Luthier Steve Helgeson builds his premium grade, production/custom, acoustic and electric basses in Eureka, California. He also builds guitars.

Explorer Bass
1980-1983. Figured wood body, neck-thru.

1980-1983		$1,500	$2,000

Morales
Ca.1967-1968. Guitars and basses made in Japan by Zen-On and not heavily imported into the U.S.

Electric Solidbody Bass
1967-1968	Various models	$125	$250

Morgan Monroe
1999-present. Intermediate grade, production, acoustic/electric basses made in Korea and distributed by SHS International of Indianapolis, Indiana. They also offer mandolins, guitars, banjos, and fiddles.

Mosrite
Semie Moseley's Mosrite offered various bass models throughout the many versions of the Mosrite company.

Brut Bass
Late-1960s. Assymetrical body with small cutaway on upper treble bout.

1960s		$950	$1,050

Celebrity Bass
1965-1969. ES-335-style semi-thick double-cut body with F-holes, 2 pickups.

1965-1966	Custom color	$1,100	$1,500
1965-1967	Sunburst	$900	$1,100
1968	Red	$900	$1,100
1969	Sunburst or red	$800	$1,000

Joe Maphis Bass
1966-1969. Ventures-style body, hollow without F-holes, 2 pickups, natural.

1966-1969		$1,000	$1,400

Ventures Bass
1965-1972. Two pickups.

1965	Blue or red	$2,900	$3,100
1965	Sunburst	$2,700	$2,900
1966	Black	$2,800	$3,000
1966	Sunburst	$2,500	$2,700
1967-1968	Blue Metallic	$2,700	$3,000
1967-1968	Red Sparkle	$2,500	$2,800
1967-1968	Sunburst	$2,200	$2,600
1969	Sunburst	$2,000	$2,400
1970-1972	Sunburst	$1,400	$1,600

Mike Hall bass

1960s Mosrite Ventures

1979 Music Man Sabre Bass

National 85

MODEL YEAR	FEATURES	EXC. COND. LOW	HIGH

V-II Bass
1973-1974. Ventures-style, 2 humbuckers, sunburst.

1973-1974		$1,300	$1,500

MTD
1994-present. Intermediate, professional, and premium grade, production/custom, electric basses built by luthier Michael Tobias (who founded Tobias Basses in '77) in Kingston, New York. Since '00, he also imports basses built in Korea to his specifications.

Music Man
1972-present. Intermediate and professional grade, production, electric basses. They also build guitars.

Cutlass I/Cutlass II Bass
1982-1987. Ash body, graphite neck, string-thru-body.

1982-1984	CLF era Cutlass I	$1,400	$1,600
1982-1984	CLF era Cutlass II	$1,700	$2,000
1984-1987	Ernie Ball era Cutlass I	$1,100	$1,300
1984-1987	Ernie Ball era Cutlass II	$1,300	$1,500

Sabre Bass
1978-ca.1991. Double-cut solidbody bass, 3-and-1 tuning keys, 2 humbucking pickups, on-board preamp, natural.

1978-1979	CLF era	$1,100	$1,300
1980-1984	CLF era	$1,000	$1,200
1984-1991	Ernie Bass era	$800	$1,000

Stingray Bass
1976-present. Offset double-cut solidbody, 1 pickup, 3-and-1 tuners, string-thru until '80, various colors. In '05, additional pickup options available.

1976-1979	CLF era	$2,100	$2,500
1980-1984	CLF era	$1,900	$2,200
1984-1989	Ernie Ball era	$1,000	$1,900
1990-1999		$700	$900
2000-2005		$700	$900

Stingray 20th Anniversary Bass
1992. 1400 made, flamed maple body.

1992		$1,750	$1,850

Stingray 5-String Bass
1987-present. Active electronics, birdseye maple bolt neck, 1 humbucking pickup, 3-band EQ. In '05, additional pickup options available.

1987-2003		$900	$1,200

Musicvox
1996-present. Intermediate grade, production, Korean-made retro-vibe guitars and basses from Matt Eichen of Cherry Hill, New Jersey.

Nady
1976-present. Wireless sound company Nady Systems offered guitars and basses with built-in wireless systems for 1985-'87. The neck-thru bass was made by Fernandes in Japan and was only available for about a year.

Nashguitars
2001-present. Luthier Bill Nash builds his professional grade, production/custom, solidbody basses in Olympia, Washington. He also builds guitars.

Timewarp Bass Series
2001-present.

2001-2005	J and P styles	$400	$600

National
Ca. 1927-present. National offered electric basses in the '60s when Valco owned the brand.

N-850 Bass
1967-1968. Semi-hollow double-cut, art deco f-holes, 2 pickups, block markers, bout control knobs, sunburst.

1967-1968		$700	$800

Val-Pro 85 Bass
1961-1962. Res-O-Glas body shaped like the U.S. map, 2 pickups, snow white, renamed National 85 in '63.

1961-1962		$1,000	$1,200

National Reso-Phonic
1988-present. Professional grade, production/custom, acoustic and acoustic/electric resonator basses built in San Luis Obispo, California. They also build guitars and ukes.

New York Bass Works
Luthier David Segal builds his professional and premium grade, production/custom, electric basses in New York.

Noble
Ca. 1950-ca. 1969. Guitars and basses distributed by Don Noble and Company of Chicago. Made by other companies.

Norma
Ca.1965-1970. Guitars and basses imported from Japan by Chicago's Strum and Drum.

Electric Solidbody Bass

1960s	Various models	$150	$225

Northworthy
1987-present. Professional and premium grade, production/custom, acoustic and electric basses built by luthier Alan Marshall in Ashbourne, Derbyshire, England. He also builds guitars and mandolins.

Novax
1989-present. Luthier Ralph Novak builds his fanned-fret professional grade, production/custom, solidbody basses in San Leandro, California. He also builds guitars.

O'Hagan
1979-1983. Designed by Jerol O'Hagan in St. Louis Park, Minnesota. He also offered guitars.

MODEL YEAR	FEATURES	EXC. COND. LOW	HIGH

Electric Solidbody Basses
1979-1983. Models include the Shark Bass, Night-Watch Bass, NightWatch Regular Bass, and the Twenty Two Bass.

1980s		$350	$550

Old Kraftsman
1930s-1960s. Brand used by the Spiegel Company. Guitars and basses made by other American manufacturers.

Electric Solidbody Bass

1950s	Various models	$200	$400

Oncor Sound
1980-ca. 1981. This Salt Lake City-based company made both a guitar and a bass synthesizer.

Ovation
1966-present. Intermediate and professional grade, production, acoustic/electric basses. Ovation offered electric solidbody basses early on and added acoustic basses in the '90s.

Celebrity Series Bass
1990s-2000s. Deep bowl back, cutaway, acoustic/electric.

1990-2000s		$350	$400

Magnum Series Bass
1974-1980. Magnum I is odd-shaped mahogany solidbody, 2 pickups, mono/stereo, mute, sunburst, red or natural. Magnum II is with battery-powered preamp and 3-band EQ. Magnum III and IV had a new Strat-style body.

1974-1978	Magnum I	$500	$600
1974-1978	Magnum II	$550	$650
1978-1980	Magnum III	$500	$600
1978-1980	Magnum IV	$550	$650

Typhoon II/Typhoon III Bass
1968-1971. Ovation necks, but bodies and hardware were German imports. Semi-hollowbody, 2 pickups, red or sunburst. Typhoon II is 335-style and III is fretless.

1968-1971	Typhoon II	$500	$700
1968-1971	Typhoon III	$550	$750

PANaramic
1961-1963. Guitars and basses made in Italy by the Crucianelli accordion company and imported by PANaramic accordion. They also offered amps made by Magnatone.

Electric Bass
1961-1963. Double-cut solidbody, 2 pickups, dot markers, sunburst.

1961-1963		$500	$600

Parker
1992-present. Premium grade, production/custom, solidbody electric basses. They also build guitars.

Patrick Eggle Guitars
1991-present. Solidbody electric basses built in Birmingham, England. They also build guitars.

Paul Reed Smith
1985-present. PRS added basses in '86, but by '92 had dropped the models. In 2000 PRS started again offering professional and premium grade, production, solidbody electric basses. Bird inlays can add $100 or more to the values of PRS basses listed here.

Bass-4
1986-1992. Set neck, 3 single-coil pickups, hum-cancelling coil, active circuitry, 22-fret Brazilian rosewood 'board. Reintroduced (OEB Series) in 2000s.

1986-1987		$1,500	$2,000
1988-1992		$1,200	$1,700
2000s	OEB Series	$1,300	$1,900

Bass-5
1986-1992. Five-string, set-neck, rosewood 'board, 3 single-coil pickups, active electronics. Options include custom colors, bird inlays, fretless 'board.

1986-1987		$1,500	$2,000
1988-1992		$1,200	$1,700

CE Bass 4
1986-1991. Solidbody, maple bolt neck, alder body, rosewood 'board, 4-string.

1986-1987		$1,100	$1,300
1988-1991		$900	$1,100

CE Bass 5
1986-1991. Five-string solidbody, maple bolt neck, alder body, rosewood 'board.

1986-1987		$1,200	$1,500
1988-1991		$1,100	$1,300

Curly Bass-4
1986-1992. Double-cut solidbody, curly maple top, set maple neck, Brazilian rosewood 'board (ebony on fretless), 3 single-coil and 1 hum-cancelling pickups, various grades of maple tops, moon inlays.

1986-1987		$1,700	$2,300
1988-1992		$1,600	$2,000

Curly Bass-5
1986-1992. Five-string version of Curly Bass-4.

1986-1987		$1,900	$2,500
1988-1992		$1,800	$2,200

Peavey
1965-present. Intermediate and professional grade, production/custom, electric basses. They also build guitars and amps. Hartley Peavey's first products were guitar amps and he added guitars and basses to the mix in '78.

Axcelerator Bass
1994-1998. Offset double-cut, long thin horns, 2 humbuckers, stacked control knobs, bolt neck, dot markers.

1994-1998		$275	$350

Cirrus Series Bass
1998-present. Offset double-cut, active electronics, in 4-, 5-string, and custom shop versions.

1998-2003	Cirrus 4	$700	$750
1998-2003	Cirrus 5	$700	$750

1968 Ovation K-1240

PRS Curly Bass 4

1983 Peavey T-45

Pedulla Buzz 4

MODEL YEAR	FEATURES	EXC. COND. LOW	HIGH

Dyna-Bass
1987-1993. Double-cut solidbody, active electronics, 3-band EQ, rosewood 'board, opaque finish.

1987-1993		$225	$325

Dyna-Bass Limited
1987-1990. Neck-thru-body, ebony 'board, flamed maple neck/body construction, purple heart strips, mother-of-pearl inlays.

1987-1990		$400	$600

Forum Bass
1994-1995. Double-cut solidbody, rosewood 'board, dot inlays, 2 humbuckers.

1994-1995		$250	$350

Forum Plus Bass
1994. Forum Bass with added active electronics.

1994		$275	$375

Foundation Bass
1984-2002. Double-cut solidbody, 2 pickups, maple neck.

1984-2002		$225	$325

Foundation S Active Bass
1987-1991. Similar to Foundation S Bass with added active circuitry, provides low-impedance output, 2 pickups.

1987-1991		$250	$350

Foundation S Bass
1986-1991. Two split-coil pickups, maple body, rosewood 'board, black hardware, black painted headstock.

1986-1991		$150	$225

Fury Bass
1986-1999. Double-cut solidbody, rosewood 'board, 1 split-coil humbucker.

1986-1999		$150	$200

Fury Custom Bass
1986-1993. Fury Bass with black hardware and narrow neck.

1986-1993		$250	$300

Grind Series Bass
2001-present. Offset double-cut, neck-thru, long bass horn, 2 pickups, 4-, 5-, or 6-string.

2001-2004	Grind 4	$200	$250
2001-2004	Grind 5	$225	$275

Millenium Series Bass
2001-present. Offset double-cut, agathis bodies, maple tops, in 4- or 5-string.

2001-2004		$150	$200

Patriot Bass
1984-1988. General J-Bass styling with larger thinner horns, 1 single-coil, maple neck.

1984-1988		$150	$200

Patriot Custom Bass
1986-1988. Patriot with rosewood neck, matching headstock.

1986-1988		$250	$300

RJ-4 Bass
1989-1991. Randy Jackson Signature model, neck-thru-body, 2 split-coil active pickups, ebony 'board, mother-of-pearl position markers.

1989-1991		$350	$450

Rudy Sarzo Signature Bass
1988-1993. Double-cut solidbody, active EQ, ebony 'board, 2 pickups.

1988-1993		$350	$500

T-20FL Bass
1980s. Fretless solidbody, 1 pickup.

1980s		$225	$300

T-40/T-40FL Bass
1978-1987. Double-cut solidbody, 2 pickups. T-40FL is fretless.

1978-1987	T-40	$225	$300
1978-1987	T-40FL	$225	$300

T-45 Bass
1982-1986. T-40 with 1 humbucking pickup, and a mid-frequency rolloff knob.

1982-1986		$250	$350

TL Series Bass
1988-1998. Neck-thru-body, gold hardware, active humbuckers, EQ, flamed maple neck and body, 5-string (TL-Five) or 6 (TL-Six).

1988-1998	TL-Five	$550	$700
1989-1998	TL-Six	$750	$800

Pedulla
1975-present. Professional and premium grade, production/custom, electric basses made in Rockland, Massachusetts. Founded by Michael Pedulla, Pedulla offers various upscale options which affect valuation so each instrument should be evaluated on a case-by-case basis. Unless specifically noted, the following listings have standard to mid-level features. High-end options are specifically noted; if not, these options will have a relatively higher value than those shown here.

Buzz-4/Buzz-5 Bass
1984-present. Double-cut neck-thru solidbody, fretless, long-scale, maple neck and body wings, 2 pickups, preamp, some with other active electronics, various colors, 4-, 5-, 6-, 8-string versions.

1984-1999		$1,300	$1,500

Interceptor Bass
1980s. Double-cut, maple/walnut laminated neck-thru.

1980s		$1,000	$1,300

MVP Series Bass
1984-present. Fretted version of Buzz Bass, standard or flame top, 4-, 5-, 6-, 8-string versions.

1980s	MVP-4 flame top	$1,300	$1,400
1980s	MVP-4 standard top	$1,100	$1,200
1980s	MVP-5	$1,100	$1,200
1980s	MVP-6	$1,200	$1,300

Orsini Wurlitzer 4-String Bass
Mid-1970s. Body style similar to late-'50s Gibson double-cut slab body SG Special, neck-thru, 2 pickups, natural. Sold by Boston's Wurlitzer music store chain.

1970s		$1,300	$1,500

MODEL YEAR	FEATURES	EXC. COND. LOW	HIGH

Quilt Ltd. Bass
Neck-thru-body with curly maple centerstrip, quilted maple body wings, 2 Bartolini pickups, available in fretted or fretless 4- and 5-string models.

1987		$1,100	$1,400

Rapture 4/5 Series Bass
1995-present. Solidbody with extra long thin bass horn and extra short treble horn, 4- or 5-string, various colors.

1995-1999		$1,000	$1,200

Series II Bass
1987-1992. Bolt neck, rosewood 'board, mother-of-pearl dot inlays, Bartolini pickups.

1987-1992		$600	$900

Thunderbass 4/5 Series Bass
1993-present. Solidbody with extra long thin bass horn and extra short treble horn, 4- or 5-string, standard features or triple A top.

1993-1999	AAA top	$1,800	$2,000
1993-1999	Standard features	$1,400	$1,600
2000-2005	AAA top	$1,900	$2,000

Penco
Ca. 1974-1978. Generally high quality Japanese-made copies of classic American bass guitars. They also made guitars, mandolins and banjos.

Pensa (Pensa-Suhr)
1982-present. Premium grade, production/custom, solidbody basses built in the U.S. They also build guitars.

Phantom Guitar Works
1992-present. Intermediate grade, production/custom, solid and hollowbody basses assembled in Clatskanie, Oregon. They also build guitars and the MandoGuitar.

Phantom Bass
1995-present. Classic 5-sided Phantom body shape, 2 humbuckers.

1995-2000		$350	$450

Pieper
2005-present. Premium grade, production/custom, solidbody basses with interchangable necks built by luthier Robert Pieper in New Haven, Connecticut. He also builds guitars.

Premier
Ca.1938-ca.1975, 1990s-present. Budget and intermediate grade, production, import basses. They also offer guitars. Originally American-made instruments, but by the '60s imported parts were being used. Current models are imports.

Bantam Bass
1950-1970. Small body, single-cut short-scale archtop electric, torch headstock inlay, sparkle 'guard, sunburst.

1950-1970		$450	$600

Electric Solidbody Bass

1960s	Various models	$300	$400

Prestige
Professional grade, production, acoustic and electric basses from Vancouver, British Columbia. They also offer guitars.

Rarebird Guitars
1978-present. Luthier Bruce Clay builds his professional grade, production/custom, electric solidbody and hollowbody basses originally in Arvada, Colorado, but since '05 in Santa Fe, New Mexico. He also builds guitars.

Rat Fink
2002-present. Lace Music Products offered these intermediate grade, production, basses and guitars, featuring the artwork of Ed "Big Daddy" Roth until '05. They still offer amps.

Regal
Ca. 1884-1966, 1987-present. Intermediate grade, production, acoustic wood body resonator basses from Saga. They also build guitars.

Renaissance
1978-1980. Plexiglass solidbody electric guitars and basses made in Malvern, Pennsylvania.

Plexiglas Bass
1978-1980. Plexiglas bodies and active electronics, models include the DPB bass (double-cut, 1 pickup, '78-'79), SPB (single-cut, 2 pickups, '78-'79), T-100B (Bich-style, 1 pickup, '80), S-100B (double-cut, 1 pickup, '80), and the S-200B (double-cut, 2 pickups, '80).

1978-1980		$450	$650

Renaissance Guitars
1994-present. Professional grade, custom, acoustic and solidbody basses built by luthier Rick Turner in Santa Cruz, California. He also builds guitars and ukuleles.

Reverend
1996-present. Reverend built electric basses in Warren, Michigan, from '98 to '04. They continue to build guitars.

Rumblefish
1998-2004. Offset double-cut, J-style neck and bridge pickups, 2 volumes, 1 master tone.

1998-2004		$550	$650

Rick Turner
1979-1981, 1990-present. Rick Turner has a long career as a luthier, electronics designer and innovator. He also makes the Renaissance line of guitars in his shop in Santa Cruz, California.

Rickenbacker
1931-present. Professional grade, production/custom, electric basses. They also build guitars. Rickenbacker introduced their first electric bass in '57 and has always been a strong player in the bass market.

Phantom BW

Reverend Rumblefish PJ

Rickenbacker 4001 V63

1979 Rickenbacker 4005

MODEL YEAR	FEATURES	EXC. COND. LOW	HIGH

Model 1999 (Rose-Morris) Bass
1964-1967. Export made for English distributor Rose-Morris of London, built along the lines of the U.S. Model 4000 Bass but with small differences that are considered important in the vintage guitar market.

1964-1967		$2,500	$5,500

Model 2030/2020 Hamburg Bass
1984-1997. Double-cut, 2 pickups, active electronics, changed to Model 2020 in '92.

1984-1989		$600	$750
1990-1997		$550	$700

Model 2030GF (Glenn Frey)
1992-1995. Limited Edition, double-cut, 2 humbuckers, Jetglo finish.

1992-1995		$850	$1,150

Model 2050/2060 El Dorado
1984-1997. Double-cut bound body, bound rosewood 'board, gold hardware, 2 pickups, active, changed to Model 2060 in '92.

1984-1997		$700	$900

Model 3000 Bass
1975-1984. Rounded double-cut, 30" scale, 1 pickup, brown sunburst.

1975-1984		$1,000	$1,500

Model 3001 Bass
1975-1984. Same as Model 3000 but with longer 33-1/2" scale, Wine Red.

1975-1984		$750	$1,075

Model 3261 (Rose-Morris Slim-Line) Bass
1967. Export model made for English distributor Rose-Morris, built along the lines of a U.S. equivalent Model 4005 Bass.

1967		$3,500	$6,500

Model 4000 Bass
1958-1985. Cresting wave body and headstock, 1 horseshoe pickup (changed to regular pickup in '64), neck-thru-body.

1958-1959	Autumnglo, Mapleglo	$5,000	$10,000
1960	Fireglo	$4,900	$9,500
1960	Mapleglo	$4,500	$6,000
1961-1965	Fireglo	$4,200	$5,500
1961-1965	Mapleglo	$4,200	$6,000
1967-1969	Various colors	$2,600	$4,200
1970-1972	Various colors	$1,700	$3,000
1973-1979	Various colors	$1,200	$1,900
1980-1985	Various colors	$1,100	$1,500

Model 4001 Bass
1961-1965, 1968-1986. Fancy version of 4000, 1 horseshoe magnet pickup (changed to regular pickup in '64) and 1 bar magnet pickup, triangle inlays, bound neck.

1961-1965	Fireglo	$4,500	$6,000
1963-1965	Mapleglo	$4,500	$6,500
1967-1969	Various colors	$2,800	$4,400
1970-1972	Various colors	$1,800	$3,100
1973-1979	Various colors	$1,400	$2,000
1980-1986	Various colors	$1,300	$1,700

Model 4001 C64S Bass
2004. Recreation of Paul McCartney's 4001.

2004		$1,700	$2,100

MODEL YEAR	FEATURES	EXC. COND. LOW	HIGH

Model 4001 CS Bass
1991-1997. Chris Squire signature model.

1991-1997	With certificate	$3,700	$5,000
1991-1997	Without certificate	$3,600	$4,000

Model 4001 FL Bass
1968-1986. Fretless version of 4001 Bass, special order in '60s, various colors.

1968-1970s		$1,000	$2,700

Model 4001 V63 Bass
1984-2000. Vintage '63 reissue of Model 4001, horseshoe-magnet pickup, Mapleglo.

1984-2000		$1,800	$2,250

Model 4001-S Bass
1964-1985. Same as Model 4000, but with 2 pickups, export model.

1980-1985		$1,100	$1,400

Model 4002 Bass
1967-1985. Cresting wave body and headstock, 2 humbuckers, black 'guard, checkerboard binding.

1980-1985		$2,800	$5,000

Model 4003 Bass
1979-present. Similar to Model 4001, split 'guard, deluxe features.

1979-1989		$1,400	$1,800
1990-1999		$1,000	$1,200
2000-2004		$975	$1,150

Model 4003 FL Bass
1979-present. Fretless version.

1980s		$1,000	$1,100

Model 4003-S Bass
1986-2003. Standard feature version of 4003.

1986-2003		$1,100	$1,300

Model 4003-S/5 Bass
1986-2003. 5-string 4003-S.

1986-2003		$1,100	$1,700

Model 4003-S/8 Bass
1986-2003. 8-string 4003-S.

1986-2003		$2,200	$3,200

Model 4003S/SPC Blackstar Bass
1989. Black version, black finish, 'board, knobs, and hardware. Also offered as 5-string.

1989		$2,500	$4,000

Model 4003S Redneck Bass
Late 1980s. Red body, 'board and headstock, black hardware.

1980s		$2,000	$3,000

Model 4003S Tuxedo Bass
1987. White body with black 'guard and hardware. 100 made.

1987		$1,400	$2,000

Model 4004C Cheyenne/Cheyenne II
1993-present. Cresting wave, maple neck-thru-body with walnut body and head wings, gold hardware, dot inlay. Replaced by maple top 4004Cii Cheyenne II in '00.

1993-1999		$1,200	$1,400
2000-2004	Cheyenne II	$1,200	$1,400

MODEL YEAR	FEATURES	EXC. COND. LOW	HIGH
Model 4005 Bass			
1965-1984. New style double-cut semi-hollowbody, 2 pickups, R tailpiece, cresting wave headstock.			
1965-1969	Various colors	$4,500	$6,500
1970-1979	Various colors	$3,500	$4,500
1980-1984	Various colors	$3,500	$4,000
Model 4005-6 Bass			
1965-1977. Model 4005 with 6 strings.			
1965-1969		$5,000	$12,000
1970-1977		$4,000	$8,000
Model 4005-8 Bass			
Late-1960s. Eight-string Model 4005.			
1968-1969	Fireglo, Mapleglo	$5,000	$15,000
Model 4005 L (Lightshow) Bass			
1970-1975. Model 4005 with translucent top with lights in body that lit up when played, needed external transformer.			
1970-1975		$10,000	$20,000
Model 4005 WB Bass			
1966-1983. Old style Model 4005 with white-bound body.			
1966	Mapleglo	$4,800	$6,500
1967-1969	Various colors	$4,800	$6,500
Model 4008 Bass			
1975-1983. Eight-string, cresting wave body and headstock.			
1975-1983		$1,400	$2,000
Model 4080 Doubleneck Bass			
1975-1992. Bolt-on 6- and 4-string necks.			
1975-1979	Jetglo or Mapleglo	$2,500	$3,500
1980-1992		$2,000	$3,000

Ritter

Production/custom, solidbody basses built by luthier Jens Ritter in Wachenheim, Germany.

RKS

2003-present. Professional and premium grade, production/custom, solidbody basses designed by Ravi Sawhney and guitarist Dave Mason and built in Thousand Oaks, California. They also build guitars.

Rob Allen

1997-present. Professional grade, production/custom, lightweight basses made by luthier Robert Allen in Santa Barbara, California.

Robin

1982-present. Founded by David Wintz and located in Houston, Texas, Robin built basses until 2000. Most basses were Japanese-made until '87; American production began in '88. They continue to build guitars and also make Metropolitan (since 1996) and Alamo (since 2000) brand guitars.

MODEL YEAR	FEATURES	EXC. COND. LOW	HIGH
Freedom Bass			
1984-1986. Offset double-cut, active treble and bass EQ controls, 1 pickup.			
1984-1986		$500	$550

MODEL YEAR	FEATURES	EXC. COND. LOW	HIGH
Freedom Bass I Passive			
1986-1989. Non-active version of Freedom Bass, I humbucker. Passive dropped from name in '87.			
1986-1989		$500	$550
Medley Bass			
1984-1989. Reverse headstock, deep cutaways, 2 pickups.			
1984-1989		$400	$600
Ranger Bass			
1984-1997. Vintage style body with P-style and J-style pickup configuration, dot markers, medium scale from '84 to '89 and long scale from '90 to '97.			
1984-1987	Japan	$400	$500
1988-1997	USA	$600	$800

Rock Bass

2002-present. Chinese-made, intermediate and professional grade, production, bolt neck solidbody basses from the makers of Warwick basses.

Rogue

2001-present. Budget and intermediate grade, production, solidbody and acoustic/electric basses. They also offer guitars, mandolins, banjos, effects and amps.

Roland

Best known for keyboards, effects, and amps, Roland offered synthesizer-based guitars and basses from 1977 to '86.

Roman & Blake Basses

1977-2003. Professional grade, production/custom, solidbody bass guitars made in Warren, Connecticut by Ed Roman.

Roman & Lipman Guitars

1989-2000. Production/custom, solidbody basses made in Danbury, Connecticut by Ed Roman. They also made guitars.

Roman USA Basses

2000-present. Professional grade, production/custom, solidbody basses made in Las Vegas, Nevada by Ed Roman.

Rono

1967-present. Luthier Ron Oates builds his professional and premium grade, production/custom, acoustic and solidbody basses in Boulder, Colorado. He also builds guitars and mandolins.

S101

2002-present. Budget and intermediate grade, production, solidbody basses imported from China. They also offer guitars, mandolins, and banjos.

Robin Freedom

Robin S101 5-string

BASSES

1977 S.D. Curlee

1960s Silvertone bass

MODEL		EXC. COND.	
YEAR	FEATURES	LOW	HIGH

Sadowsky

1980-present. Professional and premium grade, production/custom, solidbody basses built by luthier Roger Sadowsky in Brooklyn, New York. He also builds guitars. In '96, luthier Yoshi Kikuchi started building Sadowsky Tokyo instruments in Japan; those basses are now available in the U.S.

Samick

1958-2001, 2002-present. Budget, intermediate, and professional grade, production, imported acoustic and electric basses. They also offer guitars, mandolins, ukes and banjos.

Schecter

1976-present. Intermediate and professional grade, production/custom, electric basses made in the U.S. and overseas. They also offer guitars. Schecter Custom Shop basses are made in Burbank, California and their Diamond Series is made in South Korea.

Bass

1980s	Various models	$250	$450

S.D. Curlee

1975-1982. S.D. Curlee guitars and basses were made in Illinois; S.D. Curlee International instruments were made in Japan.

Electric Solidbody Bass

1970s	Various models	$400	$600

Shergold

1968-1992. Founded by Jack Golder and Norman Houlder, Shergold originally made guitars for other brands. In '75, they started building guitars and basses under their own name. By '82, general guitar production was halted but custom orders were filled through '90. In '91, general production was again started but ended in '92 when Golder died.

Shifflett

1990-present. Luthier Charles Shifflett builds his premium grade, custom, acoustic basses in High River, Alberta. He also guitars and banjos.

Silvertone

1941- ca.1970, present. Brand used by Sears. Instruments were U.S.-made and imported.

Bass VI

One lipstick pickup.

1960s		$650	$1,000

Hornet

1960s. Fender-shape, 1 lipstick pickup.

1960s		$300	$400

Simmons

2002-present. Luthier David L. Simmons builds his professional grade, production/custom, 4- and 5-string basses in Hendersonville, North Carolina.

MODEL		EXC. COND.	
YEAR	FEATURES	LOW	HIGH

Sinister

2003-present. Intermediate and professional grade, custom/production, solidbody basses built for Sinister Guitars by luthier Jon Kammerer.

Slammer

1990-present. Budget and intermediate grade, production, basses imported by Hamer. They also offer guitars.

Smith

1978-present. Professional and premium grade, production/custom, electric basses built by luthier Ken Smith in Perkasie, Pennsylvania. Earlier models had Ken Smith on the headstock, recent models have a large S logo. He also designs the imported KSD line of basses.

American-Made Bass

1978-2000	Various models	$1,200	$3,000

B.T. Custom VI Bass

1985-present. Six strings, double-cut, neck-thru-body.

1985-1999		$2,000	$3,500

Imported Bass

1990s	Various models	$700	$800

Specimen Products

1984-present. Luthier Ian Schneller builds his professional and premium grade, production/custom, aluminum and wood body basses in Chicago, Illinois. He also builds guitars, ukes, amps and speaker cabs.

Spector/Stuart Spector Design

1975-1990 (Spector), 1991-1998 (SSD), 1998-present (Spector SSD). Imtermediate, professional, and premium grade, production/custom, basses made in the U.S., the Czech Republic, Korea, and China. Stuart Spector's first bass was the NS and the company quickly grew to the point where Kramer acquired it in '85. After Kramer went out of business in '90, Spector started building basses with the SSD logo (Stuart Spector Design). In '98 he recovered the Spector trademark.

Bob Series Bass

1996-1999. Offset deep double-cut swamp ash or alder body, bolt neck, various colors, SSD logo on headstock, 4-string (Bob 4) or 5 (Bob 5).

1996-1999	Bob 4	$800	$1,000
1996-1999	Bob 5	$900	$1,100

NS Series Bass

1977-present. Offset double-cut solidbody, neck-thru, 1 pickup (NS-1, made into '80s) or 2 (NS-2), gold hardware.

1977-1984	NS-1	$1,400	$1,600
1977-1984	NS-2	$1,500	$1,800
1985-1990	NS-1, NS-2 (Kramer era)	$1,000	$1,300
1990-2000	NS-2, NS-2 (SSD era)	$1,100	$1,300

MODEL YEAR	FEATURES	EXC. COND. LOW	HIGH

St. Moritz

1960s. Japanese imports, generally shorter-scale, beginner basses. They also had guitars.

Stambaugh

1995-present. Luthier Chris Stambaugh builds his professional grade, custom/production, solidbody basses in Stratham, New Hampshire. He also builds guitars.

Standel

1952-1974, 1997-present. Amp builder Bob Crooks offered instruments under his Standel brand name three different times during the '60s. See Guitar section for production details. See Amp section for more company info.

Custom Deluxe Solidbody 401 Bass

1967-1968. Custom with higher appointments, various colors.

1967-1968		$1,000	$1,200

Custom Deluxe Thinbody 402 Bass

1967-1968. Custom with higher appointments, various colors.

1967-1968		$1,100	$1,300

Custom Solidbody 501 Bass

1967-1968. Solidbody, 1 pickup, various colors.

1967-1968		$800	$900

Custom Thinbody 502 Bass

1967-1968. Thin solidbody, 2 pickups, various colors.

1967-1968		$900	$1,000

Steinberger

1979-present. Steinberger offers budget and intermediate grade, production, electric basses. They also offer guitars.

Q-4 Bass

1990-1991. Composite neck, Double Bass system, headless with traditional-style maple body, low-impedance pickups.

1990-1991		$700	$1,000

Q-5 Bass

1990-1991. Five-string version of Q Bass.

1990-1991		$800	$1,100

XL-2 Bass

1984-1993. Rectangular composite body, 4-string, headless, 2 pickups.

1984-1989	Black	$1,300	$1,700
1990-1993	Red	$1,100	$1,400

XL-2GR Bass

1985-1990. Headless, Roland GR synthesizer controller.

1985-1990		$1,100	$1,700

XM-2 Bass

1986-1992. Headless, double-cut maple body, 4-string, 2 low-impedance pickups, optional fretted, lined fretless or unlined fretless, black, red or white.

1986-1992		$1,100	$1,400

Stevenson

1999-present. Luthier Ted Stevenson, of Lachine, Quebec, added professional grade, production/custom, basses to his product line in '05. He also builds guitars and amps.

Stewart Basses

2000-present. Luthier Fred Stewart builds his premium grade, custom/production, solidbody basses in Charlton, Maryland. He has also built guitars since '94.

Stinger

See Martin listing.

Stonetree

1996-present. Luthier Scott Platts builds his professional and premium grade, custom/production, solidbody basses in Saratoga, Wyoming. He also builds guitars.

Suhr Guitars

1997-present. In '03, luthier John Suhr added professional grade, production/custom, solidbody basses, to his instrument line built in Lake Elsinore, California. He also builds guitars.

Supro

1935-1968, 2004-present. Supro was a budget brand for the National Dobro Company. Supro offered only two bass models in the '60s. Amp builder Bruce Zinky revived the Supro name for a guitar and amp model.

Pocket Bass

1960-1968. Double-cut, neck pickup and bridge mounted pickup, semi-hollow, short-scale, black.

1960-1968		$600	$750

Taurus Bass

1967-1968. Asymmetrical double-cut, neck pickup and bridge mounted pickup.

1967-1968		$400	$500

SX

See listing for Essex.

Tacoma

1995-present. Professional grade, production, acoustic basses produced in Tacoma, Washington. They also build acoustic guitars and mandolins.

Takamine

1962-present. Intermediate, professional and premium grade, production, acoustic and acoustic/electric basses. They also make guitars. They offered solidbody electrics for '83-'84.

Taylor

1974-present. Professional and premium grade, production, acoustic basses built in El Cajon, California. They also build guitars.

Spector Spectorcore 4

Stambaugh Standard

Timtone Boomtown Bass

Tobias Signature 6-string0

MODEL YEAR	FEATURES	EXC. COND. LOW	HIGH

AB1 Bass
1996-2003. Acoustic/electric, sitka spruce top, imbuia walnut back and sides, designed for 'loose' woody sound.

1996-2003		$1,300	$1,600

AB2 Bass
1996-2003. Acoustic/electric, all imbuia walnut body.

1996-2003		$1,300	$1,600

AB3 Bass
1998-2003. Acoustic/electric, sitka spruce top, maple back and sides.

1998-2003		$1,400	$1,700

Teisco
1946-1974, 1994-present. The Japanese Teisco line started offering basses in '60.

EB-100 Bass
1968-1969. One pickup, white 'guard, blue.

1968-1969		$125	$225

EP-200 B Bass
1968-1969. Semi-hollowbody.

1968-1969		$200	$250

Tele-Star
1965-ca.1972. Guitars and basses imported from Japan by Tele-Star Musical Instrument Corporation of New York. Primarily made by Kawai, many inspired by Burns designs, some in cool sparkle finishes.

Electric Solidbody Bass

1960s	Various models	$100	$250

Timtone Custom Guitars
1993-2006. Luthier Tim Diebert built his premium grade, custom, solidbody and chambered-body basses in Grand Forks, British Columbia. He also built guitars and lap steels.

Tobias
1977-present. Founded by Mike Tobias in Orlando, Florida. Moved to San Francisco for '80-'81, then to Costa Mesa, eventually ending up in Hollywood. In '90, he sold the company to Gibson which moved it to Burbank. The first Tobias made under Gibson ownership was serial number 1094. The instruments continued to be made by the pre-Gibson crew until '92, when the company was moved to Nashville. The last LA Tobias/Gibson serial number is 2044. Mike left the company in '92 and started a new business in '94 called MTD where he continues to make electric and acoustic basses. In '99, production of Tobias basses was moved overseas. In late '03, Gibson started again offering U.S.-made Tobias instruments; they are made in Conway, Arkansas, in the former Baldwin grand piano facility. Currently Tobias offers imported and U.S.-made, intermediate and professional grade, production, acoustic and electric basses.

MODEL YEAR	FEATURES	EXC. COND. LOW	HIGH

Basic B-4 Bass
1984-1999. 30", 32", or 34" scale, neck-thru-body in alder, koa or walnut, 5-piece laminated neck.

1984-1992		$1,800	$2,000

Classic C-4 Bass
1978-1999. One or 2 pickups, active or passive electronics, 2-octave rosewood 'board, available in short-, medium-, and long-scale models.

1978-1992		$2,000	$2,300

Classic C-5 Bass
1985-1999. 30", 32" or 34" scale, alder, koa or walnut body, bookmatched top, ebony or phenolic 'board, hardwood neck.

1985-1992		$2,000	$2,300

Classic C-6 Bass
Ca. 1986-1999. Flamed maple and padauk neck, alder body, padauk top, ebony 'board, active electronics, 32" or 34" scale.

1986-1992		$2,200	$2,500

Growler GR-5 Bass
1996-1999. 5-string, offset double-cut, bolt neck, various colors.

1996-1999		$900	$1,000

Killer Bee KB-5 Bass
1991-1999. Offset double-cut, swamp ash or lacewood body, various colors.

1991-1999		$1,500	$1,700

Model T Bass
1989-1991. Line of 4- and 5-string basses, 3-piece maple neck-thru-body, maple body halves, active treble and bass controls. Fretless available.

1989-1991		$1,200	$1,400

Signature S-4 Bass
1978-1999. Available in 4-, 5-, and 6-string models, chrome-plated milled brass bridge.

1978-1992		$2,000	$2,300

Standard ST-4 Bass
1992-1995. Japanese-made, 5-piece maple neck-thru, swamp ash body wings.

1992-1995		$1,100	$1,300

Toby Deluxe TD-4 Bass
1994-1996. Offset double-cut, bolt neck.

1994-1996		$550	$650

Toby Deluxe TD-5 Bass
1994-1996. 5-string version.

1994-1996		$575	$675

Toby Pro 6 Bass
1994-1996. Solidbody 6-string, Toby Pro logo on truss rod cover, neck-thru body.

1994-1996		$600	$700

Tokai
1947-present. Tokai started making guitars and basses around '70 and by the end of that decade they were being imported into the U.S. Today Tokai offers electrics, acoustics, and electric basses made in Japan and Korea.

Vintage Bass Copies
1970s-1980s. Tokai offered near copies of classic U.S. basses.

1970s		$550	$700

BASSES

MODEL YEAR	FEATURES	EXC. COND. LOW	HIGH

Tonemaster

1960s. Guitars and basses, imported from Italy, with typical '60s Italian sparkle plastic finish and push-button controls, bolt-on neck.

Electric Bass

1960s	Sparkle finish	$400	$600

ToneSmith

1997-present. Luthier Kevin Smith builds his professional and premium grade, production/custom, semi-hollow body basses in Rogers, Minnesota. He also builds guitars.

Traben

2004-present. Intermediate grade, production, solidbody basses imported by Elite Music Brands of Clearwater, Florida.

Traveler Guitar

1992-present. Intermediate grade, production, travel size electric basses made in Redlands, California. They also make guitars.

Travis Bean

1974-1979, 1999. The unique Travis Bean line included a couple of bass models. Travis Bean announced some new instruments in '99, but general production was not resumed.

TB-2000 Bass

Aluminum neck, T-slotted headstock, longer horned, double-cut body, 2 pickups, 4 controls, dot markers, various colors.

1970s		$2,000	$3,000

TB-4000 (Wedge Vee) Bass

1970s. Bass version of Bean's Wedge guitar, few made.

1970s		$3,000	$4,000

Trinity River

Acoustic basses from Stenzler Musical Instruments of Ft. Worth, Texas. They also offer guitars, mandolins, and fiddles.

True Tone

1960s. Western Auto retailed this line of basses, guitars and amps which were manufactured by Chicago builders makers like Kay. The brand was most likely gone by '68.

Electric Basses

1960s		$150	$350

Tyler

Luthier James Tyler builds his professional and premium grade, custom/production, solidbody basses in Van Nuys, California. He also builds guitars.

Unique Guitars

2003-present. Professional and premium grade, production/custom, solidbody basses built by luthier Joey Rico in California. He also builds guitars.

Univox

1964-1978. Univox started out as an amp line and added guitars and basses around '69. Guitars were imported from Japan by the Merson Musical Supply Company, later Unicord, Westbury, New York. Generally mid-level copies of American designs.

Badazz Bass

1971-ca. 1975. Based on the Guild S-100.

1971-1977		$275	$400

Bicentennial

1976. Carved eagle in body, matches Bicentennial guitar (see that listing), brown stain, maple 'board.

1976		$550	$900

Hi Flyer Bass

1969-1977. Mosrite Ventures Bass copy, 2 pickups, rosewood 'board.

1969-1977		$400	$500

'Lectra (Model 1970F) Bass

1969-ca. 1973. Violin bass, walnut.

1969-1973		$350	$450

Model 3340 Semi-Hollow

1970-1971. Copy of Gibson EB-0 semi-hollow bass.

1970-1971		$300	$400

Precisely Bass

1971-ca. 1975. Copy of Fender P-Bass.

1971-1975		$300	$400

Stereo Bass

1976-1977. Rickenbacker 4001 Bass copy, model U1975B.

1976-1977		$400	$500

Vaccaro

1997-2002. They offered intermediate and professional grade, production/custom, aluminum-necked basses built in Asbury Park, New Jersey. They also built guitars.

Valley Arts

Ca. 1977-present. Professional and premium grade, production/custom, solidbody basses built in Nashville, Tennessee. They also make guitars.

Vantage

1977-present. Intermediate grade, production, electric basses imported from Korea (from Japan until '90). They also offer guitars.

Veillette

1991-present. Luthiers Joe Veillette and Martin Keith build their professional and premium grade, production/custom, electric basses in Woodstock, New York. They also build guitars and mandolins.

Veillette-Citron

1975-1983. Founded by Joe Veillette and Harvey Citron who met at the NY College School of Architecture in the late '60s. Joe took a guitar building course from Michael Gurian and by the Summer of '76, he and Harvey started producing neck-thru solidbody guitars and basses. Veillette and Citron both are back building instruments.

1960 True Tone Bass

Univox Hi Flyer

1968 Vox Constellation

Warwick Streamer Stage 1

MODEL YEAR	FEATURES	EXC. COND. LOW	HIGH

Vengeance Guitars & Graphixs

2002-present. Luthier Rick Stewart builds his professional and premium grade, custom/production, solidbody basses in Arden, North Carolina. He also builds guitars.

Ventura

1970s. Import classic bass copies distributed by C. Bruno (Kaman). They also had guitars.

Versoul, LTD

1989-present. Production/custom acoustic/electric and solidbody basses built by luthier Kari Nieminen in Helsinki, Finland. He also builds guitars and sitars.

Vox

1957-1972, 1982-present. The first Vox products were amplifiers brought to market in '58 by Tom Jennings and Dick Denny. By '61 they had added instruments to the line. Guitars and basses bearing the Vox name were offered from 1961-'69 (made in England, Italy), '82-'85 (Japan), '85-'88 (Korea), and for '98-2001 (U.S.). Special thanks to Jim Rhoads of Rhoads Music in Elizabethtown, Pennsylvania, for help on production years of these models.

Apollo IV Bass
1967-1969. Single-cut hollowbody, bolt maple neck, 1 pickup, on-board fuzz, booster, sunburst.

1967-1969		$750	$900

Astro IV Bass
1967-1969. Two pickups.

1967-1969		$750	$900

Clubman Bass
1961-1966. Double-cut 2-pickup solidbody, red.

1961-1966		$400	$500

Constellation IV Bass
1967-1968. Teardrop-shaped body, 2 pickups, 1 f-hole, 1 set of controls, treble, bass and distortion boosters.

1967-1968		$700	$900

Cougar Bass
1963-1967. Double-cut semi-hollow body, 2 f-holes, 2 pickups, 2 sets of controls, sunburst.

1963-1967		$700	$800

Delta IV Bass
1967-1968. Five-sided body, 2 pickups, 1 volume and 2 tone controls, distortion, treble and bass boosters.

1967-1968		$900	$1,100

Mark IV Bass
1963-1969. Teardrop-shaped body, 2 pickups, 1 set of controls, sunburst.

1963-1969		$1,000	$1,200

Panther Bass
1967-1968. Double-cut solidbody, 1 slanted pickup, rosewood 'board, sunburst.

1967-1968		$450	$550

MODEL YEAR	FEATURES	EXC. COND. LOW	HIGH

Phantom IV Bass
1963-1969. Five-sided body, 2 pickups, 1 set of controls.

1963-1964	English made	$1,700	$2,000
1965-1969	Italian made	$1,200	$1,400

Saturn IV Bass
1967-1968. Single-cut, 2 F-holes, 1 set of controls, 1 pickup.

1967-1968		$600	$800

Sidewinder IV Bass (V272)
1967-1968. Double-cut semi-hollow body, 2 f-holes, 2 pickups, 1 set of controls, treble, bass, and distortion boosters.

1967-1968		$700	$900

Stinger Bass
1968. Teardrop-shaped, boat oar headstock.

1968		$700	$900

Wyman Bass
1966. Teardrop-shaped body, 2 pickups, 1 F-hole, 1 set of controls, sunburst.

1966		$950	$1,150

Wandre (Davoli)

Ca. 1956/57-1969. Italian-made guitars and basses.

Warrior

1995-present. Professional and premium grade, production/custom, solidbody basses built by luthier J.D. Lewis in Roseville, Georgia. He also builds guitars.

Warwick

1982-present. Professional and premium grade, production/custom, electric and acoustic basses made in Markneukirchen, Germany; founded by Hans Peter Wilfer, whose father started Framus guitars. They also build amps.

Corvette Standard Bass
1997-present. Offset double-cut, bubinga body, offered in 4-, 5-, and 6-string.

1997-2004		$600	$750

Jack Bruce Signature Bass
1990-1991, 2001. Based on Thumb Bass, '01 version a limited edition with 50 fretted and 50 unfretted made.

1990-1991		$1,500	$1,800

Streamer I-5 Bass
1984-present. Five-string, gold hardware, active electronics.

1984-1990s		$1,400	$1,600

Thumb/Thumb-5 Bass
1980s-present. Walnut, neck-thru, double-cut solidbody, 2 pickups.

1980-1990s		$1,300	$1,500

Triumph Electric Upright
1996-present. Reissue of Framus bean pole Triumph Upright Electric bass.

1996-2002		$1,100	$2,000

BASSES

MODEL YEAR	FEATURES	EXC. COND. LOW	HIGH

Washburn

1974-present. Intermediate and professional grade, production, acoustic and electric basses. Washburn instruments were mostly imports early on, U.S. production later, currently a combination of both. Washburn also offers guitars, mandolins, and amps.

Electric Bass

1980-2000s Various models		$250	$500

Watkins

1957-present. Watkins Electric Music (WEM) was founded by Charlie Watkins. Their first commercial product was the Watkins Dominator amp in '57. They made the Rapier line of guitars and basses from the beginning. Watkins offered guitars and basses up to '82.

Rapier Bass

1957-1982. 2 pickups, red.

1960s		$400	$550

Wechter

1984-present. Professional grade, production/custom acoustic basses built by luthier Abe Wechter in Paw Paw, Michigan. He also offers U.S-made and import guitars.

Wendler

1999-present. Luthier Dave Wendler, of Ozark Instrument Building, builds his intermediate and professional grade, production/custom, solidbody, electro-acoustic basses in Branson, Missouri. He also builds guitars.

Westbury-Unicord

1978-ca. 1983. Japanese guitars and basses imported by Unicord.

Westone

1970s-1990, 1996-2001. Guitars and basses originally imported from Japan by St. Louis Music. Name revived from '96 to '01, by England's FCN Music.

Wilson Brothers Guitars

2004-present. Production electric basses. They also build guitars. Founded by Ventures guitarist Don Wilson.

Winston

Ca. 1963-1967. Guitars and basses imported by Buegeleisen & Jacobson of New York.

Wurlitzer

1970s. Private branded by Pedulla for the Wurlitzer music store chain. Manufacturer and retailer were both based in Massachusetts. Refer to Pedulla listing.

Yamaha

1946-present. Budget, intermediate, professional and premium grade, production, electric basses. They also build guitars. Yamaha began producing solidbody instruments in '66.

Attitude Custom Bass

1990-1994. Part of the Sheehan Series, champagne sparkle.

1990-1994		$700	$800

Electric Bass

1960-1990s Various models		$225	$550

Zemaitis

1960-1999, 2004-present. Tony Zemaitis began selling his guitars and basses in '60 and he retired in '99. He emphasized simple lightweight construction and his instruments are known for hand engraved metal fronts. Each hand-built custom guitar was a unique instrument. Approximately 10 custom guitars were built each year. In '04, Japan's Kanda Shokai, with the endorsement of Tony Zemaitis, Jr., started building the guitars again.

Electric Bass

1970s	Heart hole		
	(4 made)	$28,000	$30,000
1980s	1/2 metal		
	& spruce	$14,000	$16,000
1980s	Metal-front		
	4-string	$18,000	$25,000

Zen-On

1946-ca.1968. Japanese-made. By '67 using the Morales brandname. Not heavily imported into the U.S., if at all (see Morales).

Electric Solidbody Bass

1950s	Various models	$150	$250

Zeta

1982-present. Professional and premium grade, production/custom, acoustic, electric and upright basses, with MIDI options, made in Oakland, California. They also make guitars, amps and mandolins.

Zim-Gar

1960s. Japanese guitars and basses imported by Gar-Zim Musical Instrument Corporation of Brooklyn, New York.

Electric Solidbody Bass

1960s	Various models	$150	$250

Zolla

1979-present. Professional grade, production/custom, electric basses built by luthier Bill Zolla in San Diego, California. Zolla also builds guitars, necks and bodies.

BZ-1 Bass

1988-present. Offset double-cut solidbody, 2 pickups, offered in 4-, 5-, and 6-string versions.

1980s		$500	$600

Wechter 9400

Zemaitis GZB-2500

BASSES

Zon Sonus Classic

Zon Tribute

MODEL YEAR	FEATURES	EXC. COND. LOW	HIGH

Zon

1981-present. Luthier Joe Zon builds his professional and premium grade, production/custom, solidbody basses in Redwood City, California. Zon started the brand in Buffalo, New York and relocated to Redwood City in '87. He has also built guitars.

Legacy Elite VI Bass

1989-present. Six-string, 34" scale carbon-fiber neck, Bartolini pickups, ZP-2 active electronics.

MODEL YEAR	FEATURES	EXC. COND. LOW	HIGH
1990s		$1,000	$1,200

MODEL YEAR	FEATURES	EXC. COND. LOW	HIGH

Scepter Bass

1984-1993. Offset body shape, 24 frets, 1 pickup, tremolo.

1984-1993		$900	$1,100

ZZ Ryder

Solidbody electric basses from Stenzler Musical Instruments of Ft. Worth, Texas. They also offer guitars.

Amps

MODEL YEAR	FEATURES	EXC. COND. LOW	HIGH

65Amps London

Acoustic 125

1977 Acoustic 135

65amps

2004-present. Founded by Peter Stroud and Dan Boul, 65 builds tube guitar head and combo amps and speaker cabs in Valley Village, California.

Ace Tone

Late-1960-1970s. Made by Sakata Shokai Limited of Osaka, Japan, early importer of amps and effects pedals. Later became Roland/Boss.

B-9 Amp

Late-1960s-early-1970s. Solid-state bass amp head.

1960-1970s		$100	$175

Mighty-5 Amp

Late-1960s-early-1970s. Tubes, 50-watt head.

1960-1970s		$125	$225

Acoustic

Ca.1965-ca.1990, 2001-2005. The Acoustic Control Corp., of Los Angeles, California, was mostly known for solidstate amplifiers. Heads and cabinets were sold separately with their own model numbers, but were also combined (amp sets) and marketed under a different model number (for example, the 153 amp set was the 150b head with a 2x15" cabinet). The brand was revived by Samick in '01 for a line of amps.

114 Amp

Ca.1977-mid-1980s. Solidstate, 50 watts, 2x10", reverb, master volume.

1978-1984		$225	$375

115 Amp

1977-1978. Solidstate, 1x12", 50 watts, reverb, master volume.

1977-1978		$250	$400

116 Bass Amp

1978-mid-1980s. Solidstate, 75 watts, 1x15", power boost switch.

1978-1984		$275	$400

120 Amp Head

1977-mid-1980s. Solidstate head, 125 watts.

1977-1984		$225	$300

123 Amp

1977-1984. 1x12" combo.

1977-1984		$175	$250

124 Amp

1977-mid-1980s. Solidstate, 4x10", 5-band EQ, 100 watts, master volume.

1977-1984		$300	$400

125 Amp

1977-mid-1980s. Solidstate, 2x12", 5-band EQ, 100 watts, master volume.

1977-1984		$300	$400

126 Bass Amp

1977-mid-1980s. Solidstate, 100 watts, 1x15", 5-band EQ.

1977-1984		$275	$375

134 Amp

1972-1976. Solidstate, 100-125 watts, 4x10" combo.

1972-1976	125 watts	$300	$400

135 Amp

1972-1976. Solidstate, 125 watts, 2x12" combo, reverb, tremolo.

1972-1976		$300	$450

136 Amp

1972-1976. Solidstate, 125 watts, 1x15" combo.

1972-1976		$300	$450

140 Bass Head

1972-1976. Solidstate, 125 watts, 2 channels.

1972-1976		$200	$275

150 Amp Head

1960s-1976. Popular selling model, generally many available in the used market. Solidstate, 110 watts until '72, 125 watts after.

1968-1976		$225	$275

150b Bass Head

1960s-1971. Bass amp version of 150 head.

1968-1971		$200	$250

153 Bass Amp Set

1960s-1971. 150b head (bass version of 150) with 2x15" 466 cabinet, 110 watts.

1968-1971		$325	$450

165 Amp

1979-mid-1980s. All tube combo, switchable to 60 or 100 watts, brown tolex.

1979-1984		$325	$450

220 Bass Head

1977-1980s. Solidstate, 5-band EQ, either 125 or 160 watts, later models 170 or 200 watts, black tolex.

1977-1984	170 or 200 watts	$225	$300

230 Amp Head

1977-1980s. Solidstate head, 125/160 watts, 5-band EQ.

1977-1984		$225	$300

260 Amp Head

1960s-1971. Solidstate, 275 watt, stereo/mono.

1968-1971		$325	$350

270 Amp Head

1970s. 400 watts.

1970s		$325	$450

320 Bass Head

1977-1980s. Solidstate, 5-band EQ, 160/300 watts, 2 switchable channels, black tolex.

1977-1984		$325	$450

360 Bass Head

1960s-1971. One of Acoustic's most popular models, 200 watts. By '72, the 360 is listed as a "preamp only."

1968-1971		$425	$550

370 Bass Head

1972-1977. Solidstate bass head, 365 watts early on, 275 later.

1972-1977	275 or 365 watts	$325	$450

402 Cabinet

1977-1980s. 2x15" bass cab, black tolex, black grille.

1977-1984		$225	$275

450 Amp Head

1974-1976. 170 watts, 5-band EQ, normal and bright inputs.

1974-1976		$225	$275

AMPS

MODEL YEAR	FEATURES	EXC. COND. LOW	HIGH

455 Amp Set
1974-1976. 170 watt 450 head with 4x12" cabinet, black.

1970s	Black	$450	$550

470 Amp Head
1974-1977. 170 watt, dual channel.

1974-1977		$250	$450

G20-110 Amp
1981-mid-1980s. Solidstate, 20 watts, 1x10". The G series was a lower-priced combo line.

1981-1985		$100	$175

G20-120 Amp
1981-mid-1980s. Solidstate, 20 watts, 1x12".

1981-1985		$100	$200

G60-112 Amp
1981-mid-1980s. Solidstate, 60 watts, 1x12".

1981-1985		$125	$250

G60-212 Amp
1981-mid-1980s. Solidstate, 60 watts, 2x12".

1981-1985		$150	$175

G60T-112 Amp
1981-1987. Tube, 60 watts, 1x12".

1981-1985		$300	$350

Tube 60 Amp
1986-1987. Combo, 60 watts, 1x12", spring reverb, bright switch, master volume control, effects loop.

1986-1987		$300	$350

ADA

1977-2002. ADA (Analog/Digital Associates) was located in Berkeley, California, and introduced its Flanger and Final Phase in '77. The company later moved to Oakland and made amplifiers, high-tech signal processors, and a reissue of its original Flanger.

Aguilar

1995-present. U.S.-made tube and solidstate amp heads, cabinets, and pre-amps from New York City, New York.

Aiken Amplification

2000-present. Tube amps, combos, and cabinets built by Randall Aiken originally in Buford, Georgia, and since '05 in Pensacola, Florida.

Aims

1970s. Aims amps were manufactured and distributed by Randall Instruments in the mid-'70s. They also offered guitars and basses.

Airline

Ca.1958-1968. Brand for Montgomery Ward, built by Kay, Harmony, and Valco.

Small to Mid Tube Amp

1960s	Various models	$150	$300

Mid to Large Tube Amp

1960s	Various models	$300	$450

Alamo

1947-1982. Founded by Charles Eilenberg, Milton Fink, and Southern Music, San Antonio, Texas, and distributed by Bruno and Sons. Alamo started producing amps in '49 and the amps were all-tube until '73; solidstate preamp and tube output from '73 to ca. '80; all solidstate for ca. '80 to '82.

Birch "A" Combo Amp
1949-1962. Birch wood cabinets with A-shaped grill cutout, 2 to 5 tubes. Models include the Embassy Amp 3, Jet Amp 4, Challenger Amp 2, Amp 5, and the Montclair.

1949-1962		$150	$300

Bass Tube Amp
1960-1972. Leatherette covered, all tube, 20 to 35 watts, 15" speakers, combo or piggyback, some with Lansing speaker option. Models include the Paragon Special, Paragon Bass, Piggyback Band, Piggyback Bass, Fury Bass, and Paragon Bass (piggyback).

1960-1972		$175	$325

Bass Solidstate Preamp-Tube Output Amp
1973-ca.1979. Solidstate preamp section with tube output section, 35 or 40 watts, 15" speakers, combo or piggyback. Models include the Paragon Bass, Paragon Bass Piggyback, Paragon Country Western Bass, Paragon Super Bass, and the Fury Bass.

1973-1979		$125	$250

Small Tube Amp
1960-1972. Leatherette covered, all tube, 3 to 10 watts, 6" to 10" speakers, some with tremolo. Models include the Jet, Embassy, Challenger, Capri, Fiesta, Dart, and Special.

1960-1972		$175	$325

Mid-power Tube Amp
1960-1970. Leatherette covered, all tube, 15 to 30 watts, 12" or 15" speakers, some with tremolo and reverb, some with Lansing speaker option. Models include Montclair, Paragon, Paragon Band, Titan, and Futura.

1960-1970		$225	$500

Twin Speaker Piggyback Tube Amp
1962-1972. Leatherette covered, all tube, up to 45 watts, 8", 10", 12" or 15" speaker configurations, some with tremolo and reverb, some with Lansing speaker option. Models include the Electra Twin Ten, Century Twin Ten, Futuramic Twin Eight, Galaxie Twin Twelve, Galaxie Twin Twelve Piggyback, Piggyback Super Band, Alamo Pro Reverb Piggyback, Futura, Galaxie Twin Ten, Twin-Ten, and Band Piggyback.

1962-1972		$350	$550

Small Solidstate Preamp-Tube Output Amp
1973-ca.1979. Solidstate preamp section with tube output section, 3 to 12 watts, 5" to 12" speaker, some with reverb. Models include the Challenger, Capri, Special, Embassy, Dart, and Jet.

1973-1979		$75	$150

Aguilar DB 728

'60s Alamo

1962 Alamo 2566 Century Twin Ten

AMPS

Alesis Wildfire 60

Allen Old Flame

Alessandro Boxer

MODEL YEAR	FEATURES	EXC. COND. LOW	HIGH

Mid-power Solidstate Preamp-Tube Output Amp

1973-ca.1979. Solidstate preamp section with tube output section, 25 watts, 12" speaker, with reverb and tremolo. Models include the Montclair.

1973-1979		$125	$200

Twin Speaker Combo (Tube/Hybrid) Amp

1973-ca.1979. Solidstate preamp section with tube output section, 20 or 70 watts, 10", 12" and 15" speaker configurations, some with reverb and tremolo. Models include the 70-watt Paragon Super Reverb Piggybacks, the 45-watt Futura 2x12, and the 20-watt Twin-Ten.

1973-1979		$200	$300

Solidstate Amp

Ca.1980-1982. All solidstate.

1980-1982		$50	$125

Alden

Small budget grade solidstate guitar and bass amps from Muse, Inc. of China.

Alesis

1992-present. Alesis has a wide range of products for the music industry, including digital modeling guitar amps. They also offer guitar effects.

Alessandro

1998-present. Tube amps built by George Alessandro in Huntingdon Valley, Pennsylvania. Founded in '94 as the Hound Dog Corporation, in '98 the company name was changed to Alessandro. The Redbone ('94) and the Bloodhound ('96) were the only models bearing the Hound Dog mark. Serial numbers are consecutive regardless of model (the earliest 20-30 did not have serial numbers). In '98, the company converted to exotic/high-end components and the name changed to Alessandro High-End Products. In '01, he added the Working Dog line.

Allen Amplification

1998-present. Tube combo amps, heads and cabinets built by David Allen in Walton, Kentucky. He also offers the amps in kit form and produces replacement and upgrade transformers and a tube overdrive pedal.

Aloha

Late-1940s. Electric lap steel and amp Hawaiian outfits made for the Dallas-based Aloha.

Ampeg

1949-present. Ampeg was originally primarily known for their bass amps. In the eastern U.S., Ampeg was Fender's greatest challenger in the '60s and '70s bass amplifier market. St. Louis Music currently offers a line of Ampeg amps.

Amp Covering Dates

Wood veneer	1946-1949.
Smooth brown	1949-1952.
Dot tweed	1952-1954.

MODEL YEAR	FEATURES	EXC. COND. LOW	HIGH

Tweed	1954-1955.		
Rough gray	1957-1958.		
Rough tan	1957-1958.		
Cream	1957-1958.		
Light blue	1958.		
Navy blue	1958-1962.		
Blue check	1962-1967.		
Black pebble	1967.		
Smooth black	1967-1980.		
Rough black	1967-1985.		

AC-12 Amp

1970. 20 watts, 1x12", accordion amp that was a market failure and dropped after 1 year.

1970		$350	$450

AP-3550 Amp

1992-1993. Rackmount solidstate head, 350 watts or 200 watts, black metal.

1992-1993	350 watts	$225	$275

AP-6500 Amp

1992-1993. 650 watts per channel, solidstate power amp, used with bass preamp.

1992-1993		$300	$450

B-2 Bass Amp

1994-2000. Solidstate, 200 watts, 1x15" combo or 4x8" combo, black vinyl, black grille, large A logo.

1994-2000	1x15"	$500	$700

B-2 R Bass Head

1994-2005. 200 watts, rackmount, replaced by 450 watt B2RE.

1994-2005		$300	$500

B-3 Amp

1995-2001. Solidstate head, 150 watts, 1x15".

1995-2000		$400	$550

B-12 N Portaflex Amp

1961-1965. 25 watts, 2x12", 2 6L6 power tubes.

1961-1965		$1,000	$1,500

B-12 XT Portaflex Amp

1965-1969. Tube, 50 watts, 2x12", reverb, vibrato, 2x7027A power tubes.

1965-1969		$900	$1,400

B-15 N (NB, NC, NF) Portaflex Amp

1960-1970. Introduced as B-15 using 2 6L6 power tubes, B-15 N in '61, B-15 NB in '62, B-15 NC with recti- fier tube in '64, B-15 NF with fixed-bias 2 6L6 power tubes and 30 watts in '67, 1x15".

1960-1965		$1,000	$1,500
1966-1970		$900	$1,400

B-15 R Portaflex Amp (reissue)

1990s. Reissue of '65 Portaflex 1x15", blue check.

1990s		$750	$850

B-15 S Portaflex Amp

1971-1977. 60 watts, 2x7027A power tubes, 1x12".

1971-1977		$950	$1,050

B-18 N Portaflex Amp

1964-1969. Bass, 50 watts, 1x18".

1964-1965		$1,050	$1,200
1966-1969		$950	$1,100

B-25 Amp

1969 only. 55 watts, 2 7027A power tubes, 2x15", no reverb, guitar amp.

1969		$900	$1,050

MODEL YEAR FEATURES	EXC. COND. LOW	HIGH

B-25 B Bass Amp
1969-1980. Bass amp, 55 watts, 2 7027A power tubes, 2x15".

1969-1980	$900	$1,050

B-50 R Rocket Bass Amp (reissue)
1996-2005. 50 watts, 1x12" combo, vintage-style blue check cover.

1996-2005	$225	$300

B-100 R Rocket Bass Amp (reissue)
1996-2005. Solidstate, 100 watts, 1x15" combo bass amp, vintage-style blue check cover.

1996-2005	$275	$350

B-115 Amp
1973-1980. 120 watts, solidstate, 1x15" combo.

1973-1980	$350	$450

B-410 Bass Amp
1973-1980. Solidstate, 120 watts, 4x10", black vinyl, black grille.

1973-1980	$400	$475

B-3158 B Bass Amp
1995-2000. Solidstate combo, 100 watts, 1x15" and 1x8", black vinyl.

1995-2000	$525	$600

BT-15 Amp
1966-1968. Ampeg introduced solidstate amps in '66, the same year as Fender. Solidstate, 50 watts, 1x15", generally used as a bass amp. The BT-15D has 2 1x15" cabinets. The BT-15C is a 2x15" column portaflex cabinet.

1966-1968	$350	$450

BT-18 Amp
1966-1968. Solidstate, 50 watts, 1x18", generally used as a bass amp. The BT-18D has dual 1x18" cabinets. The BT-18C is a 2x18" column portaflex cabinet.

1966-1968	$325	$425

ET-1 Echo Twin Amp
1961-1964. Tube, 30 watts, 1x12", stereo reverb.

1961-1964	$700	$800

ET-2 Super Echo Twin Amp
1962-1964. Tube, 2x12", 30 watts, stereo reverb.

1962-1964	$800	$900

G-12 Gemini I Amp
1964-1971. Tube, 1x12", 22 watts, reverb.

1964-1971	$550	$675

G-15 Gemini II Amp
1965-1968. Tube, 30 watts, 1x15", reverb.

1965-1968	$575	$700

G-18 Amp
1977-1980. Solidstate, 1 channel, 10 watts, 1x8", volume, treble, and bass controls,

1977-1980	$120	$130

G-110 Amp
1978-1980. Solidstate, 20 watts, 1x10", reverb, tremolo.

1978-1980	$200	$250

G-115 Amp
1979-1980. Solidstate, 175 watts, 1x15" JBL, reverb and tremolo, designed for steel guitar.

1979-1980	$250	$300

G-212 Amp
1973-1980. Solidstate, 120 watts, 2x12".

1973-1980	$300	$350

GS-12 Rocket 2 Amp
1965-1968. This name replaced the Reverberocket 2 (II), 15 watts, 1x12".

1965-1968	$625	$675

GS-12-R Reverberocket 2 Amp
1965-1969. Tube, 1x12", 18 watts, reverb. Called the Reverberocket II in '68 and '69, then Rocket II in '69.

1965-1969	$625	$675

GS-15-R Gemini VI Amp
1966-1967. 30 watts, 1x15", single channel, considered to be "the accordion version" of the Gemini II.

1966-1967	$625	$675

GT-10 Amp
1971-1980. Solidstate, 15 watts, 1x10", basic practice amp with reverb.

1971-1980	$200	$250

GV-22 Gemini 22 Amp
1969-1972. Tube, 30 watts, 2x12".

1969-1972	$625	$675

J-12 A Jet Amp
1964. Jet Amp with 7591A power tubes.

1964	$300	$450

J-12 D Jet Amp
1966. Jet Amp with new solidstate rectifier.

1966	$300	$450

J-12 Jet Amp
1958-1964, 1967-1972. 20 watts, 1x12", 6V6GT power tubes. Second addition, also known as the Jet II, was like the J-12 D Jet but with 12AX7s.

1958-1963	$300	$450
1967-1972 Model reappears	$300	$400

J-12 T Jet Amp
1965. J-12 A with revised preamp.

1965	$300	$450

M-12 Mercury Amp
1957-1965. 15 watts, 2 channels, Rocket 1x12".

1957-1959	$550	$625
1960-1965	$550	$600

M-15 Big M Amp
1959-1965. 20 watts, 2x6L6 power, 1x15".

1959	$600	$675
1960-1965	$600	$650

Model 815 Bassamp Amp
1955. 15 watt combo, 1 channel.

1955	$600	$800

Model 820 Bassamp Amp
1956-1958. 20 watt combo, 1 channel.

1956-1958	$650	$850

Model 822 Bassamp Amp
1957-1958. 2 channel 820.

1957-1958	$675	$875

Model 830 Bassamp Amp
1956-1958. 30 watt combo.

1956-1958	$700	$900

Model 835 Bassamp Amp
1959-1961. 35 watt 1x15" combo, 2 channels.

1959-1961	$850	$950

Ampeg B-15-N

1960s Ampeg GV-22

1959 Ampeg J-12 Jet

AMPS

1965 Ampeg R-12-R-T Reverberocket

Ampeg Reverbojet 275

Ampeg SVT

MODEL YEAR	FEATURES	EXC. COND. LOW	HIGH
R-12 Rocket Amp	*1957-1963. 12 watts, 1x12", 1 channel.*		
1957-1963		$625	$675
R-12 B Rocket Amp	*1964. 12 watts, 1x12", follow-up to the R-12 Rocket.*		
1964		$625	$675
R-12 R Reverberocket Amp	*1961-1963. Rocket with added on-board reverb.*		
1961-1963		$625	$675
R-12 R Reverberocket Amp (reissue)	*1996-present. 50 watts, 2xEL34 power tubes, 1x12" (R-212R is 2x12").*		
1996-1999		$375	$400
R-12 R-B Reverberocket Amp	*1964. 7591A power tubes replace R-12-R 6V6 power tubes.*		
1964		$625	$675
R-12 R-T Reverberocket Amp	*1965. 7591A or 7868 power tubes, revised preamp.*		
1965		$625	$675
R-212 R Reverberocket Combo 50 Amp (reissue)	*1996-present. 50 watts, 2x12", all tube reissue, vintage-style blue check cover, vintage-style grille.*		
1996-1999		$400	$425
SB-12 Portaflex Amp	*1965-1971. 22 watts, 1x12", designed for use with Ampeg's Baby Bass, black.*		
1965-1971		$750	$800
SBT Amp	*1969-1971. 120 watts, 1x15", bass version of SST Amp.*		
1969-1971		$700	$850
SE-412 Cabinet	*1996-1999. 4x12" speakers.*		
1996-1999		$275	$350
SJ-12 R/RT Super Jet Amp	*1996-present. 50 watts, tube, 1x12", SJ-12 RT has tremolo added.*		
1996-1999		$275	$350
SS-35 Amp	*1987-1992. Solidstate, 35 watts, 1x12", black vinyl, black grille, large A logo.*		
1987-1992		$200	$275
SS-70 Amp	*1987-1990. Solidstate, 70 watts, 1x12".*		
1987-1990		$350	$425
SS-70 C Amp	*1987-1992. Solidstate, 70 watts, 2x10", chorus, black vinyl.*		
1987-1992		$350	$425
SVT Bass Head Amp	*1969-1985. 300 watt head only.*		
1969	Stones World-Tour assoc.	$2,200	$2,500
1970-1972		$1,700	$2,200
1970-1972	w/ set of NOS tubes	$700	$1,000
1970-1972	w/set of new tubes	$700	$800
1973-1979		$1,500	$1,700
1980-1985		$1,400	$1,600

MODEL YEAR	FEATURES	EXC. COND. LOW	HIGH
SVT Bass Cabinets	*1969-1985. Two 8x10" cabs only.*		
1969		$800	$1,200
1970-1985		$700	$1,100
SVT Bass Amp Set	*1969-1985. 300 watt head with matching dual 8x10" cabs.*		
1969	Stones World-Tour assoc.	$3,400	$4,000
1970-1972	Original matching set	$3,000	$3,500
1973-1979	Original matching set	$2,500	$3,000
1980-1985	Original matching set	$2,000	$2,500
SVT-II Bass Head	*1989-1994. Rackmount, 300 watts, tube.*		
1989-1994		$1,000	$1,200
SVT-2 Pro Bass Head Amp	*1992-present. 300 watts, rackmount, Tube preamp and MOS-FET power section, black metal.*		
1992-2003		$900	$1,000
SVT-3 Pro Bass Head Amp	*1993-present. Tube preamp and MOS-FET power section, 450 watts, rack-mountable, black metal.*		
1993-2003		$650	$750
SVT-4 Pro Bass Head Amp	*1997-present. Hybrid rack-mountable, all tube preamp, MOS-FET power section yielding, 1600 watts.*		
1997-2003		$725	$775
SVT-100 T Bass Combo Amp	*1990-1992. Solidstate, ultra-compact bass combo, 100 watts, 2x8".*		
1990-1992		$400	$450
SVT-200 T Head Amp	*1987 only. Solidstate, 200 watts to 8 ohms or 320 watts to 4 ohms.*		
1987		$400	$500
SVT-350 Head Amp	*1995-present. Solidstate head, 350 watts, graphic EQ.*		
1995-2000		$400	$500
SVT-400 Head Amp	*1987-1997. Solidstate, 400 watts per side, rack-mountable head with advanced (in '87) technology.*		
1987-1997		$400	$550
SVT-AV Anniversary Edition Amp			
2001		$1,050	$1,150
V-2 Head Amp	*1971-1980. 60 watt tube head.*		
1971-1980		$400	$475
V-2 Amp Set	*1971-1980. 60 watt head with 4x12" cab, black tolex.*		
1971-1980		$700	$900
V-4 B Bass Head Amp	*1972-1980. Bass version of V-4 without reverb.*		
1972-1980		$600	$650
V-4 Cabinet	*1970s. Single 4x12" cabinet only.*		
1970-1980		$350	$450

MODEL		EXC. COND.	
YEAR	**FEATURES**	**LOW**	**HIGH**

V-4 Amp Stack
1970-1980. 100 watts, with dual 4x12" cabs.

| 1970-1980 | Head and cabs | $1,000 | $1,200 |
| 1970-1980 | Head only | $600 | $650 |

V-7 SC Amp
1981-1985. Tube, 100 watts, 1x12", master volume, channel switching, reverb.

| 1981-1985 | | $600 | $650 |

VH-70 Amp
1991-1992. 70 watts, 1x12" combo with channel switching.

| 1991-1992 | | $300 | $350 |

VH-140 C Amp
1992-1995. Varying Harmonics (VH) with Chorus (C), two 70-watt channel stereo, 2x12".

| 1992-1995 | | $350 | $400 |

VH-150 Head Amp
1991-1992. 150 watts, channel-switchable, reverb.

| 1991-1992 | | $325 | $375 |

VL-502 Amp
1991-1995. 50 watts, channel-switchable, all tube.

| 1991-1995 | | $400 | $450 |

VL-1001 Head Amp
1991-1993. 100 watts, non-switchable channels, all tube.

| 1991-1993 | | $350 | $400 |

VL-1002 Head Amp
1991-1995. 100 watts, channel-switchable, all tube.

| 1991-1995 | | $400 | $450 |

VT-22 Amp
1970-1980. 100 watt combo version of V-4, 2x12".

| 1970-1980 | | $700 | $900 |

VT-40 Amp
1971-1980. 60 watt combo, 4x10".

| 1971-1980 | | $700 | $900 |

VT-60 Combo Amp
1989-1991. Tube, 6L6 power, 60 watts, 1x12".

| 1989-1991 | | $500 | $600 |

VT-60 Head Amp
1989-1991. Tube head only, 6L6 power, 60 watts.

| 1989-1991 | | $400 | $500 |

VT-120 Combo Amp
1989-1992. Tube, 6L6 power, 120 watts, 1x12", also offered as head only.

| 1989-1992 | | $550 | $650 |

VT-120 Head Amp
1989-1992. 120 watts, 6L6 tube head.

| 1989-1992 | | $400 | $500 |

Anderson Amplifiers

1993-present. Tube amps and combos built by Jack Anderson in Gig Harbor, Washington.

Area 51

2003-present. Tube combo amps made in Kemper, Texas until '06, and currently in Newaygo, Michigan, by Dan Albrecht. They also build effects.

Aria/Aria Pro II

1960-present. The Japanese instrument builder offered a range of amps from around '79 to '89.

Ashdown Amplification

1999-present. Founded in England by Mark Gooday after he spent several years with Trace Elliot, Ashdown offers amps, combos, and cabinets.

Audiovox

Ca.1935-ca.1950. Paul Tutmarc's Audiovox Manufacturing, of Seattle, Washington, was a pioneer in electric lap steels, basses, guitars and amps.

Auralux

2000-present. Founded by Mitchell Omori and David Salzmann, Auralux builds effects and tube amps in Highland Park, Illinois.

Bacino

2002-present. Tube combo amps, heads and cabinets built by Mike Bacino in Arlington Heights, Illinois.

Bad Cat Amplifier Company

1999-present. Founded in Corona, California by James and Debbie Heidrich, Bad Cat offers class A combo amps, heads, cabinets and effects.

Baldwin

Piano maker Baldwin offered amplifiers from 1965 to '70. The amps were solidstate with organ-like pastel-colored pushbutton switches.

Exterminator Amp
1965-1970. Solidstate, 100 watts, 2x15"/2x12"/2x7", 4' vertical combo cabinet, reverb and tremolo, Supersound switch and slide controls.

| 1965-1970 | | $525 | $625 |

Model B1 Bass Amp
1965-1970. Solidstate, 45 watts, 1x15"/1x12", 2 channels.

| 1965-1970 | | $225 | $275 |

Model B2 Bass Amp
1965-1970. Solidstate, 35 watts, 1x15", 2 channels.

| 1965-1970 | | $200 | $250 |

Model C1 Custom (Professional) Amp
1965-1970. Solidstate, 45 watts, 2x12", reverb and tremolo, Supersound switch and slide controls.

| 1965-1970 | | $275 | $325 |

Model C2 Custom Amp
1965-1970. Solidstate, 40 watts, 2x12", reverb and tremolo.

| 1960s | | $250 | $300 |

Barcus-Berry

1964-present. Pickup maker Barcus-Berry offered a line of amps from '75 to '79.

Ampeg SVT-4 Pro

Bacino

Bad Cat Mini Cat

AMPS

Blue Tone Pro 30M

Callaham EL34 Amp

Carr Mercury

MODEL YEAR	FEATURES	EXC. COND. LOW	HIGH

Barth

1960s. Products of the Paul Barth's Barth Musical Instrument Company. Barth was also a cofounder of Rickenbacker.

Studio Deluxe 958 Amp
1960s. Small practice combo amp.

1960s		$250	$350

Basson

2001-present. Speaker cabinets for guitar, bass and PA made by Victor Basson in Carlsbad, California.

Bedrock

1984-1997. Tube amp company founded by Brad Jeter and Ron Pinto in Nashua, New Hampshire. They produced 50 amps carrying the brand name Fred before changing the company name to Bedrock in '86. Around '88, Jay Abend joined the company, eventually becoming President. In '88, Evan Cantor joined the company as an amp designer. In '90, Jeter left Bedrock and, shortly after, Pinto and Abend moved the company to Farmington, Massachusetts. The company closed in '97.

Behringer

1989-present. Founded in Germany by Uli Behringer, offering a full line of professional audio products. In '98 they added tube, solidstate, and modeling amps. They also offer effects and guitars.

BigDog Amps

2005-present. Tube head and combo amps and speaker cabinets built in Galveston, Texas, by Steve Gaines.

Blue Tone Amplifiers

2002-present. Founded by Alex Cooper in Worcestershire, England, Blue Tone offers professional grade, production amps employing their virtual valve technology.

Bogen

1960s. Power and PA tube amps not built for guitar but used by some 1960s/1970s bands.

Bogner

1988-present. Tube combos, amp heads, and speaker cabinets from builder Reinhold Bogner of North Hollywood, California.

Brand X

2004-present. Small solidstate combo amps from Fender Musical Instruments Corporation.

Bruno (Tony)

1995-present. Tube combos, amp heads, and speaker cabinets from builder Tony Bruno of Cairo, New York.

Budda

1995-present. Amps, combos, and cabinets built by Jeff Bober and Scot Sier in San Francisco, California. They also produce effects pedals.

Burriss

2001-present. Bob Burriss builds custom and production guitar and bass tube amps, bass preamps and speaker cabinets in Lexington, Kentucky. He also builds effects.

Callaham

1989-present. Tube amp heads built by Bill Callaham in Winchester, Virginia. He also builds solidbody electric guitars.

Carl Martin

1993-present. In '05, the Denmark-based guitar effects company added tube combo amps.

Carlsbro

1959-present. Guitar, bass, and keyboard combo amps, heads and cabinets from Carlsbro Electronics Limited of Nottingham, England. They also offer PA amps and speaker cabinets.

Carr Amplifiers

1998-present. Steve Carr started producing amps in his Chapel Hill, North Carolina amp repair business in '98. The company is now located in Pittsboro, North Carolina, and makes tube combo amps, heads, and cabinets.

Hammerhead Amp
2000-present. Class A, 2 EL34 power tubes, 25 watts with 1x12", 25 watts with 2x10" or 25 watts with 2x12".

2000-2002	1x12"	$950	$1,050
2000-2002	2x10"	$1,000	$1,200
2003	2x12"	$1,150	$1,250

Imperial Combo Amp
2002-2004. 60 watts, with 1x15", 2x12" or 4x10".

2002-2004	1x15"	$1,450	$1,650
2002-2004	2x12"	$1,500	$1,700
2002-2004	4x10"	$1,600	$1,800

Mercury Combo Amp
2003-2005. 1x12", combo, 8 watts, reverb, built-in attenuator.

2003-2005	Standard color	$1,600	$1,700
2003-2005	2-tone color	$1,800	$1,900

Rambler Combo Amp
1999-present. Class A, 2x6L6 power tubes, 28 watts with 1x12", 2x10", 2x12" or 1x15" speakers.

1999-2003	1x12"	$1,300	$1,500
1999-2003	1x15"	$1,350	$1,550
1999-2003	2x10"	$1,400	$1,600
1999-2003	2x12"	$1,450	$1,650

Slant 6V (Dual 6V6) Amp
1998-present. 40 watts, 2 channel, combo amp, 2x12" or 1x15", also available as a head.

1998-2002		$1,600	$1,700

MODEL YEAR	FEATURES	EXC. COND. LOW	HIGH

Carvin

1946-present. Founded in Los Angeles by Lowell C. Kiesel who sold guitars and amps under the Kiesel name until late-'49, when the Carvin brand is introduced. They added small tube amps to their product line in '47 and today offer a variety of models. They also build guitars and basses.

Chicago Blues Box/Butler Custom Sound

2001-present. Tube combo amps built by Dan Butler of Butler Custom Sound in Elmhurst, Illinois.

Clark Amplification

1995-present. Tweed-era replica tube amplifiers from builder Mike Clark, of Cayce, South Carolina. He also makes effects.

Beaufort Amp

1992-present. Classic tweed Fender 5E3 circuit, 1x12", 18 watts.

| 1992-2004 | Non-reverb | $1,000 | $1,200 |
| 1992-2004 | Reverb | $1,100 | $1,400 |

Lil' Bit Amp

1992-present. Tweed Champ circuit, 1x8".

| 1992-2004 | | $750 | $850 |

Tyger Amp

2000-present. Classic tweed Fender 5E7 Bandmaster circuit, 3x10", 35 watts. Also available with optional 3-knob reverb and 3-position power attenuator.

| 2000-2004 | Non-reverb | $1,100 | $1,400 |
| 2000-2004 | Reverb | $1,200 | $1,600 |

CMI

1976-1977. Amps made by Marshall for Cleartone Musical Instruments of Birmingham, England. Mainly PA amps, but two tube heads and one combo amp were offered.

CMI Electronics

Late-1960s-1970s. CMI branded amplifiers designed to replace the Gibson Kalamazoo-made amps that ceased production in '67 when Gibson moved the electronics lab to Chicago, Illinois.

Sabre Reverb 1

Late-1960s-early-1970s. Keyboard amp, 1x15" and side-mounted horn, utilized mid- to late-'60s cabinets and grilles, look similar to mid-late '60s Gibson black tolex and Epiphone gray amp series, black or gray tolex and silver grille.

| 1970 | | $125 | $175 |

Comins

1992-present. Archtop luthier Bill Comins, of Willow Grove, Pennsylvania, introduced a Comins combo amp, built in collaboration with George Alessandro, in '03.

Coral

1967-1969. In '66 MCA bought Danelectro and in '67 introduced the Coral brand of guitars, basses

and amps. The amp line included tube, solidstate, and hybrid models ranging from small combo amps to the Kilowatt (1000 Watts of Peak Power!), a hybrid head available with two 8x12" cabinets.

Cornell/Plexi

Amps based on the '67 Marshall plexi chassis built by Denis Cornell in the United Kingdom. Large Plexi logo on front.

Cosmosound

Italy's Cosmosound made small amps with Leslie rotating drums in the late '60s and '70s. They also made effects pedals.

Crafter USA

1986-present. Giant Korean guitar and bass manufacturer Crafter also builds an acoustic guitar amp.

Crate

1979-present. Solidstate and tube amplifiers distributed by St. Louis Music.

Solidstate Amp

Various student to mid-level amps, up to 150 watts.

| 1970s | | $50 | $175 |
| 1980s | | $50 | $175 |

Vintage Club 3112/VC-3112

1994-2001. 30 watts, tube, 1x12".

| 1994-2001 | | $325 | $375 |

Vintage Club 50/VC-50 Amp

1994-1999. 50-watt tube head.

| 1994-1999 | | $275 | $325 |

Vintage Club 5212/VC-5212 Amp

1994-2001. 50 watts, 2x12", tube.

| 1994-2001 | | $350 | $400 |

Vintage Club 5310/VC-5310 Amp

1994-1997. 50 watts, tube, 3x10".

| 1994-1997 | | $350 | $400 |

Cruise Audio Systems

1999-present. Founded by Mark Altekruse, Cruise offers amps, combos, and cabinets built in Cuyahoga Falls, Ohio

Da Vinci

Late-1950s-early-1960s. Another one of several private brands (for example, Unique, Twilighter, Titano, etc.) that Magnatone made for teaching studios and accordion companies.

Model 250 Amp

1958-1962. Similar to Magnatone Model 250 with about 20 watts and 1x12".

| 1958-1962 | | $600 | $700 |

Danelectro

1946-1969, 1997-present. Founded in Red Bank, New Jersey, by Nathan I. "Nate" or "Nat" Daniel. His first amps were made for Montgomery Ward in '47, and in '48 he began supplying Silvertone Amps

Chicago Blues Box Kingston

Cruise MQ4212

Danelectro Commando

AMPS

Danelectro Model 78 Maestro

Demeter TGA-2.1 Inverter

Dinosaur DG-200R

MODEL YEAR	FEATURES	EXC. COND. LOW	HIGH

for Sears. His own amps were distributed by Targ and Dinner as Danelectro and S.S. Maxwell brands. In '96, the Evets Corporation, of San Clemente, California, reintroduced the Danelectro brand on effects, amps, basses and guitars. In early '03, Evets discontinued the guitar and amp lines, but still offers effects.

Cadet Amp

Tube, 6 watts, 1x6".

1955-1959		$225	$275
1960-1963		$175	$225
1964-1966		$150	$200
1967-1969		$125	$175

Centurion Model 275 Amp

2 6V6 power tubes for approximately 15-18 watts, 1x12", gray cover.

1959-1960		$275	$375

Corporal Model 132 Amp

Early-1960s. Low power, 2x8".

1960s		$300	$400

DM-10 Amp

Five watts, 1x6".

1960s		$150	$200

DM-25 Amp

35 watts, 1x12", reverb and tremolo.

1960s		$350	$450

DS-50 Amp

1967-1969. 50 watts, 3x10" piggyback set, reverb and tremolo, suitable for bass accordion.

1967-1969		$400	$500

DS-100 Amp

1967-1969. 100 watts, piggyback, 6x10" Jensens, reverb, tremolo, suitable for bass accordion.

1967-1969		$500	$600

Model 68 Special Amp

1950s. 20 watts, 1x12", light tweed-fabric cover, light grille, leather handle, script Danelectro plexi-plate logo.

1950s		$450	$500

Model 89 (Series D)

1x15" combo, blond tweed, rounded front D cabinet.

1954-1957		$500	$550

Model 98 Twin 12 Amp (Series D)

1954-ca.1957. Blond tweed-style cover, brown control panel, 2x12", vibrato speed and strength, rounded front Series D.

1954-1957		$600	$800

Model 217 Twin 15 Amp

1960s. Combo amp, 100 watts, 2x15" Jensen C15P speakers, black cover, white-silver grille, 2 channels with tremolo.

1962		$500	$600

Viscount Model 142 Amp

Late-1950s. Combo amp, lower watts, 1x12", light cover, brown grille, vibrato.

1959		$450	$500

Dean

1976-present. Acoustic, electric, and bass amps made overseas. They also offer guitars, banjos, mandolins, and basses.

MODEL YEAR	FEATURES	EXC. COND. LOW	HIGH

Dean Markley

The string and pickup manufacturer added a line of amps in 1983. Distributed by Kaman, they now offer combo guitar and bass amps and PA systems.

K Series Amp

1980s. All solidstate, various models include K-15 (10 watts, 1x6"), K-20/K-20X (10 to 20 watts, 1x8", master volume, overdrive switch), K-50 (25 watts, 1x10", master volume, reverb), K-75 (35 watts, 1x12", master volume, reverb).

1980s	K-15, 20, 20X	$25	$50
1980s	K-50	$30	$55
1980s	K-75	$35	$60

Decca

Mid-1960s. Small student-level amps made in Japan by Teisco and imported by Decca Records. They also offered guitars and a bass.

Demeter

1980-present. James Demeter founded the company as Innovative Audio and renamed it Demeter Amplification in '90. Located in Van Nuys, California. First products were direct boxes and by '85, amps were added. Currently they build amp heads, combos, and cabinets. They also have pro audio gear and guitar effects.

Diaz

Early-1980s-2002. Cesar Diaz restored amps for many of rock's biggest names, often working with them to develop desired tones. Along the way he produced his own line of high-end custom amps and effects. Diaz died in '02; his family announced plans to resume production of effects in '04.

Dickerson

1937-1947. Dickerson was founded by the Dickerson brothers in 1937, primarily for electric lap steels and small amps. Instruments were also private branded for Cleveland's Oahu company, and for the Gourley brand. By '47, the company changed ownership and was renamed Magna Electronics (Magnatone).

Oasis Amp

1940s-1950s. Blue pearloid cover, 1x10", low wattage, Dickerson silk-screen logo on grille with Hawaiian background.

1940s	Blue pearloid	$200	$325

Dinosaur

2004-present. Student/budget level amps and guitar/amp packs, imported by Eleca International.

Divided By Thirteen

Fred Taccone builds his tube amp heads and cabinets in the Los Angeles, California area. He also builds effects.

MODEL YEAR	FEATURES	EXC. COND. LOW	HIGH

Dr. Z

1988-present. Mike Zaite started producing his Dr. Z line of amps in the basement of the Music Manor in Maple Heights, Ohio. The company is now located in its own larger facility in the same city. Dr. Z offers combo amps, heads and cabinets.

DST Engineering

2001-present. Jeff Swanson and Bob Dettorre build their amp combos, heads and cabinets in Beverly, Massachusetts. They also build reverb units.

Duca Tone

The Duca Tone brand was distributed by Lo Duca Brothers, Milwaukee, Wisconsin, which also distributed EKO guitars in the U.S.

Tube Amp
12 watts, 1x12".

1950s		$500	$600

Dumble

1963-present. Made by Howard Alexander Dumble, an early custom-order amp maker from California. Initial efforts were a few Mosrite amps for Semie Moseley. First shop was in '68 in Santa Cruz, California.

Overdrive Special Amp and Cabinet
100 watts, 1x12", known for durability, cabinets vary.

1970s	Black	$15,000	$24,000
1980s	Black	$15,000	$24,000
1990s	Black	$15,000	$24,000

Earth Sound Research

1970s. Earth Sound was a product of ISC Audio of Farmingdale, New York, and offered a range of amps, cabinets and PA gear starting in the '70s. They also made Plush amps.

2000 G Half-Stack Amp
1970s. 100 watts plus cab.

1970s		$400	$550

Original 2000 Model 340 Amp
1970s. Black Tolex, 400-watt head and matching 2x15" cab.

1970s		$350	$475

Super Bass/B-2000 Amp
1970s. Tuck & roll black cover, 2 channels - super and normal, volume, bass, mid range, and treble tone controls, no reverb or trem.

1970s	Cabinet	$200	$275
1970s	Head only	$200	$275

Traveler Amp
1970s. Vertical cab solidstate combo amp, 50 watts, 2x12 offset, black tolex.

1977		$200	$275

Eden

1976-present. Founded by David Nordschow in Minnesota as a custom builder, Eden now offers a full line of amps, combos, and cabinets for the bassist, built in Mundelein, Illinois. In '02, the brand became a division of U.S. Music Corp (Washburn, Randall). They also produce the Nemesis brand of amps.

Egnater

1980-present. Tube amps, combos, preamps and cabinets built in Michigan by Bruce Egnater.

EKO

1959-1985, 2000-present. In '67 EKO added amps to their product line, offering three piggyback and four combo amps, all with dark covering, dark grille, and the EKO logo. The amp line may have lasted into the early '70s. Since about 2000, EKO Asian-made, solidstate guitar and bass amps are again available. They also make basses and guitars.

Eleca

2004-present. Student level imported combo amps, Eleca logo on bottom center of grille.

Electar

1996-present. The Gibson owned Electar brand offers tube and solidstate amps, PA gear and wireless systems. Epiphone had a line of Electar amps in the 1930s.

Electro-Harmonix

1968-1981, 1996-present. Electro-Harmonix offered a few amps to go with its line of effects. See Effects section for more company info.

Freedom Brothers Amp
Introduced in 1977. Small AC/DC amp with 2x5 1/2" speakers. E-H has reissued the similar Freedom amp.

1977		$175	$300

Mike Matthews Dirt Road Special Amp
25 watts, 1x12" Celestion, built-in Small Stone phase shifter.

1977		$175	$300

Elk

Late-1960s. Japanese-made by Elk Gakki Co., Ltd. Many were copies of American designs. They also offered guitars and effects.

Custom EL 150L Amp
Late-1960s. Piggyback set, all-tube with head styled after very early Marshall and cab styled after large vertical Fender cab.

1968		$350	$425

Guitar Man EB 105 (Super Reverb) Amp
Late-1960s. All-tube, reverb, copy of blackface Super Reverb.

1968		$300	$375

Twin Amp 6/Twin Amp 50 EB202
Late-1960s. All-tube, reverb, copy of blackface Dual Showman set (head plus horizontal cab).

1968		$350	$425

Dr. Z Maz 18

DST MarWatt

Eden WT800 Time Traveler

AMPS

Emery Sound Microbaby

1966 Epiphone EA-14 RVT Ensign

Epiphone Electar Zephyr

MODEL YEAR	FEATURES	EXC. COND. LOW	HIGH

Viking 100 VK 100 Amp
Late-1960s. Piggyback set, head styled after very early Marshall and cab styled after very large vertical Fender cab.

| 1968 | | $350 | $425 |

Elpico
1960s. Made in Europe, PA tube amp heads sometimes used for guitar.

PA Power Tube Amp
1960s. Tubes, 20-watt, metal case, 3 channels, treble and bass control, 2 speaker outs on front panel, Elpico logo on front, small Mexican characterization logo on front.

| 1960s | | $350 | $500 |

Emery Sound
1997-present. Founded by Curt Emery in El Cerrito, California, Emery Sound specializes in custom-made low wattage tube amps.

Epiphone
1928-present. Epiphone offered amps into the mid-'70s and reintroduced them in '91 with the EP series. Currently they offer tube and solidstate amps.

E-30 B Amp
1972-1975. Solidstate model offered similarly to Gibson G-Series (not GA-Series), 30 watts, 2x10", 4 knobs.

| 1972-1975 | | $175 | $225 |

E-60 Amp
1972-1975. Solidstate, 3 watts, 1x10", volume and tone knobs.

| 1972-1975 | | $80 | $110 |

E-60 T Amp
1972-1975. E-60 with tremolo, volume, tone, and tremolo knobs.

| 1972-1975 | | $80 | $115 |

E-70 Amp
1971-1975. Solidstate, tremolo, 1x10", 3 knobs.

| 1971-1975 | | $90 | $135 |

E-1051 Amp
1970s. Tube practice amp, 1x10".

| 1970s | | $175 | $200 |

EA-12 RVT Futura Amp
1962-1967. Low- to mid-power, 4x8", '60s gray tolex, light grille.

| 1962-1967 | | $700 | $850 |

EA-14 RVT Ensign Amp
1965-1969. Gray tolex, silver-gray grille, 50 watts, 2x12", split C logo.

| 1965-1969 | | $500 | $600 |

EA-15 RVT Zephyr Amp
1961-1965. 14 or 20 watts, 1x15", gray tolex, light grille, split C logo on panel, tremolo and reverb, script Epiphone logo lower right grille.

| 1961-1965 | | $450 | $550 |

EA-16 RVT Regent Amp
1965-1969. 25 watts, 1x12", gray vinyl, gray grille, tremolo, reverb. Called the Lancer in first year.

| 1965-1969 | | $450 | $550 |

EA-22RVT Mighty Mite Amp
1965-ca. 1966. 1x12", mid-level power, stereo, reverb, vibrato, old style rear mounted control panel.

| 1965-1966 | | $850 | $950 |

EA-26 RVT Electra Amp
1965-1969. Gray tolex, reverb, tremolo, footswitch, 1x12".

| 1965-1969 | | $400 | $500 |

EA-32 RVT Comet Amp
1965-1967. 1x10", tremolo, reverb.

| 1965-1967 | | $350 | $450 |

EA-33 RVT Galaxie Amp
1963-1964. Gray tolex, gray grille, 1x10".

| 1963-1964 | | $450 | $500 |

EA-35 Devon Amp
1961-1963. 1x10" until '62, 1x12" with tremolo in '63.

| 1961-1963 | | $350 | $400 |

EA-50 Pacemaker Amp
1961-1969. 1x8" until '62, 1x10" after. EA-50T with tremolo added in '63. Non-tremolo version dropped around '67.

| 1961-1969 | | $250 | $375 |

EA-300 RVT Embassy Amp
1965-1969. 90 watts, 2x12", gray vinyl, gray grille, tremolo, reverb.

| 1965-1969 | | $600 | $700 |

EA-500T Panorama
1963-1967. 65 watts, head and large cabinet, tremolo, 1x15" and 1x10" until '64, 1x15" and 2x10" after.

| 1964-1967 | | $350 | $650 |

EA-600 RVT Maxima Amp
1966-1969. Solidstate Epiphone version of Gibson GSS-100, gray vinyl, gray grille, two 2x10" cabs and hi-fi stereo-style amp head.

| 1966-1969 | | $525 | $600 |

Zephyr Amp
1939-1957. Maple veneer cabinet, E logo on front, 1x12" until '54, 1x15" after.

| 1939-1957 | | $500 | $750 |

Excelsior
The Excelsior Company started offering accordions in 1924 and had a large factory in Italy by the late '40s. They started building guitars and amps around '62. By the early '70s they were out of the guitar business.

Americana Stereophonic High Fidelity
Late 1960s. 50 watts, 1x15", 2x8", 2x3x9" ovals, 2xEL34 power, tube rectifier, large Excelsior logo and small Excelsior The House of Music logo, guitar and accordion inputs, stereo reverb and vibrato.

| 1968-1969 | | $900 | $1,100 |

Fender
1946-present. Leo Fender developed many ground-breaking instruments, but Leo's primary passion was amplifiers, and of all his important contributions to musicians, none exceed those he made to the electric tube amplifier.

AMPS

Tweed Fender amp circuits are highly valued because they defined the tones of rock and roll. Blackface models remained basically the same until mid-'67. Some silverface circuits remained the same as the blackface circuits, while others were changed in the name of reliability. Price Guide values are for all original, excellent condition amps. Small differences in an amp's condition can generate larger differences in selling prices. Non-original speakers will significantly reduce a pre-'68 amp's value. Reconed speakers will reduce the value, but a reconed speaker is preferable to a replacement speaker. Multi-speaker amps generally have matching speaker codes. Different speaker codes require explanation. Fender leather handles are often broken and replaced. A replacement handle drops the value of an amp. Grille cloths should have no tears and a single tear can drop the value of an amp. Each Tweed amp should be evaluated on a case-by-case basis, and it is not unusual for a Tweed amp to have a wide range of values. Alnico speaker replacement is more significant than ceramic speaker replacement. Fender converted to ceramic about '62.

Speaker replacement is of less concern in post-'70 Fender amps.

From 1953 to '67, Fender stamped a two-letter date code on the paper tube chart glued inside the cabinet. The first letter was the year (C='53, D='54, etc.) with the second the month (A=January, etc.).

The speaker code found on the frame of an original speaker will identify the manufacturer, and the week and year that the speaker was assembled. The speaker code is typically six (sometimes seven) digits. The first three digits represent the Electronics Industries Association (E.I.A.) source code which identifies the manufacturer. For example, a speaker code 220402 indicates a Jensen speaker (220), made in '54 (4) during the second week (02) of that year. This sample speaker also has another code stamped on the frame. ST654 P15N C4964 indicates the model of the speaker, in this case it is a P15N 15" speaker. The sample speaker also had a code stamped on the speaker cone, 4965 1, which indicates the cone number. All of these codes help identify the originality of the speaker. The value ranges provided in the Guide are for amps with the original speaker and original speaker cone.

Most Fender speakers from the '50s will be Jensens (code 220). By the late-'50s other suppliers were used. The supplier codes are: Oxford (465), C.T.S. (137), Utah (328). JBL speakers were first used in the late-'50s Vibrasonic, and then in the Showman series, but JBL did not normally have a E.I.A. source code. An amp's speaker code should be reconciled with other dating info when the amp's original status is being verified.

General Production Eras
Diagonal tweed era
Brown tolex era
Blackface era
Silverface era with raised Fender logo with
underlining tail
Silverface era with raised Fender logo without
underlining tail
Silverface era with raised Fender logo with
small MADE IN USA designation
Nameplate and Logo Attribution
Fender nameplate with city but without model
name (tweed era)
Fender nameplate without city or model name
(tweed era)
Fender nameplate with model name noted
(tweed era)
Fender flat logo (brown era)
Fender script raised logo (blackface era)

MODEL YEAR	FEATURES	EXC. COND. LOW	HIGH

30 Amp
1980-1981. Tube combo amp, 30 watts, 2x10" or 1x12".

1980-1981		$525	$675

75 Amp
1980-1982. Tube, 75 watts, offered as a 1x15" or 1x12" combo, or as head and 4x10" or 2x12" cab.

1980-1982		$550	$700

85 Combo Amp
1988-1992. Solidstate, 85 watt 1x12" combo, black cover, silver grille.

1988-1992		$250	$300

800 Pro Bass Head Amp
2004-present. Rack-mountable, 800 watts, 5-band EQ.

2004		$500	$550

Acoustasonic 30/30 DSP Amp
2000-present. Small combo, brown tolex, wheat grille. Upgrade model includes DSP (Digital Signal Processor) effects.

2000-2004	30	$225	$275
2000-2004	30 DSP	$350	$400

Acoustasonic Junior/Junior DSP Amp
1998-present. 2x40 watts, 2x8", Piezo horn.

1998-2003		$300	$350

Acoustasonic SFX/SFX II Amp
1998-present. SFX technology, 32 stereo digital presents, 2x80 watts, 1x10" and 1x8", Piezo horn.

1998-2002		$400	$450

AmpCan Amp
1997-present. Cylindrical can-shaped battery powered portable amp.

1997-2004		$100	$140

Bandmaster Amp
1953-1974. Wide-panel 1x15" combo '53-'54, narrow-panel 3x10" combo '55-'60, tolex '60, brownface with 1x12" piggyback speaker cabinet '61, 2x12" '62, blackface '62-'67, silverface '68-'74.

The Fender tweed 4x10" Bassman and tweed 3x10" Bandmaster amps are highly sensitive to condition. Because there are so few that are truly excellent, the price ranges listed may be misleading. Most Bassman amps are at best very good minus (VG-) because their tweed is so damaged and stained. It is also rare to find the original speakers, and if the frames are original, they have often been reconed. 4x10" Bassman and 3x10" Bandmasters that are excellent plus plus

Fender Amp Can

Fender Acoustasonic SFX II

Fender Bandmaster (5E7)

AMPS

1964 Fender Bandmaster head

Late-'50s Fender Bassman

Fender Blues Junior

MODEL YEAR	FEATURES	EXC. COND. LOW	HIGH

(Exc++) may have price ranges that are much higher than the values listed. It is estimated that 90% of the vintage 4x10" Bassman are really only VG or less. Because of the extreme condition factor for these tweed amps, the prices below include amps in very good (VG) condition. Therefore the condition for these listed amps is VG to Exc. Exc+ will be more than the values listed here. As per other high-end collectible, each amp should be taken on a case by case basis.

1953-1954	Tweed, 1x15"	$4,600	$5,000
1955-1958	Tweed, 3x10"	$6,500	$8,500
1959-1960	Matching trio of orig P10Rs	$1,600	$1,700
1959-1960	Tweed, 3x10"	$6,700	$10,000
1960	Brown tolex, 3x10"	$5,500	$7,500
1961	Rough white & oxblood, 1x12"	$2,300	$2,400
1961-1962	Rough white & oxblood, 2x12"	$2,200	$2,300
1963-1964	Smooth white & gold, 2x12"	$2,000	$2,100
1964-1967	Black tolex, 2x12"	$1,400	$1,600
1967-1969	Silverface, 2x12"	$900	$1,000
1970-1974	Silverface, 2x12"	$600	$800

Bandmaster Head Amp
1961-1975. Non-reverb model.

1961-1962	Rough white tolex	$1,000	$1,300
1963-1964	Smooth white tolex	$900	$1,200
1964-1967	Blackface, black tolex	$600	$800
1967-1969	Silverface	$400	$500
1970-1971	Silverface, black tolex	$350	$400

Bandmaster Cabinet
1961-1975. 2x12" speakers.

1961-1963	Blond tolex	$750	$950
1964-1967	Blackface horizontal	$425	$550
1967-1970	Silverface vertical	$300	$350

Bandmaster Reverb Amp
1968-1980. 45 watt silverface head with 2x12" cabinet.

| 1968-1972 | | $950 | $1,100 |
| 1973-1980 | | $850 | $1,000 |

Bandmaster Reverb Head Amp
1968-1980. Reverb, 45 watts.

| 1968-1972 | | $550 | $700 |
| 1973-1980 | | $450 | $600 |

Bantam Bass Amp
1969-1971. 50 watts, large unusual 1x10" Yamaha speaker.

| 1969-1971 | Original speaker | $450 | $650 |

Bassman Amp
1952-1971. Tweed TV front combo, 1x15" in '52, wide-panel '53-'54, narrow-panel and 4x10" '54-'60, tolex brownface with 1x12" in piggyback cabinet '61, 2x12" cabinet '61-'62, blackface '63-'67, silverface '67-'71, 2x15" cabinet '68-'71. Renamed the Bassman 50 in '72.

The Fender tweed 4x10" Bassman and tweed 3x10" Bandmaster amps are highly sensitive to condition. Because there are so few that are truly excellent, the

MODEL YEAR	FEATURES	EXC. COND. LOW	HIGH

price ranges listed may be misleading. Most Bassman amps are at best very good minus (VG-) because their tweed is so damaged and stained. It is also rare to find the original speakers, and if the frames are original, they have often been reconed. 4x10" Bassmans and 3x10" Bandmasters that are excellent plus plus (Exc++) may have price ranges that are much higher than the values listed. It is estimated that 90% of the vintage 4x10" Bassman are really only VG or less. Because of the extreme condition factor for these tweed amps, the prices below include amps in very good (VG) condition. Therefore the condition for these listed amps is VG to Exc. Exc+ will be more than the values listed here. As per other high-end collectibles, each amp should be taken on a case by case basis.

1952	TV front, 1x15"	$4,500	$5,000
1953-1954	Wide panel, 1x15"	$4,500	$5,000
1955-1957	Tweed, 4x10", 2 inputs	$6,700	$8,500
1957-1958	Tweed, 4x10", 4 inputs	$6,700	$9,000
1959-1960	Tweed, 4x10", 4 inputs	$6,900	$10,000
1961	White 1x12", 6G6, tube rectifier	$2,500	$3,000
1962	White 1x12", 6G6A, s.s. rectifier	$2,300	$2,700
1963-1964	Smooth white 2x12", 6G6A/B	$2,100	$2,500
1965-1966	AA165/AB165, black knobs	$1,500	$1,800
1967-1969	Silverface lg. vertical 2x15"	$900	$1,100
1970-1971	Silverface 2x15"	$650	$800

Bassman Amp Parts
The cost of replacement partss for the '59-'60 models.

1959-1960	4 matching orig P10Q speakers	$1,800	$1,900
1959-1960	New tubes	$100	$120
1959-1960	NOS tubes	$275	$475

Bassman Head Amp
1961-1971. Bassman head only, no cabinet.

1961	White, 6G6, tube	$1,400	$1,600
1962	White, 6G6A, s.s.	$1,100	$1,300
1963-1964	Smooth white, 6G6A/B	$1,100	$1,300
1964	Blackface AA864, white knobs	$600	$750
1965-1967	AA165/AB165, black knobs	$550	$700
1967-1969	Silverface	$500	$550
1970-1971	Silverface, black tolex	$450	$500

Bassman Cabinet
1961-early-1967. Blackface, 2x12" small horizontal cab, replaced in '67 with larger silverface vertical cab.

1961-1963	Blond tolex	$750	$950
1964-1967	Blackface	$450	$550
1967-1970	Silverface verticle	$300	$350

The *Vintage Guitar Price Guide* shows low to high values for items in all-original excellent condition, and, where applicable, with original case or cover.

MODEL YEAR	FEATURES	EXC. COND. LOW	HIGH

Bassman '59 Reissue Amp

1990-present. Tube, 45 watts, 4x10", tweed covering.

1990s		$650	$700

Bassman 10 Amp

1972-1982. 4x10" combo, silverface and 50 watts for '72-'80, blackface and 70 watts after.

1972-1980	50 watts	$450	$525
1981-1982	70 watts	$475	$550

Bassman 20 Amp

1982-1985. Tubes, 20 watts, 1x15".

1982-1985		$250	$350

Bassman 25 Amp

2000-2005. Wedge shape, 1x10", 25 watts, 3-band EQ.

2000-2005		$125	$175

Bassman 50 Amp

1972-1977. 50 watts, with 2x12" cab.

1972-1977		$450	$500
1972-1977	Head only	$350	$400

Bassman 60 Amp

1972-1976, 2000-2005. 60 watts, 1x12". Name reused on solidstate compact combo.

1972-1976		$450	$550
2000-2005	Combo	$200	$225

Bassman 70 Amp

1977-1979. 70 watts, 2x15" cab.

1977-1979		$550	$650
1977-1979	Head only	$400	$450

Bassman 100 Amp

1972-1977, 2000-present. Tube, 100 watts, 4x12", name reused on solidstate combo amp.

1972-1977		$550	$650
1972-1977	Head only	$400	$450

Bassman 135 Amp

1978-1983. Tube, 135 watts, 4x10".

1978-1983		$550	$650
1978-1983	Head only	$400	$450

Bassman 150 Combo Amp

2005-present. Solidstate 1x12" combo, 150 watts.

2005		$325	$350

Bassman 300 Head Amp

2002-2003. All tube, 300 watts, black cover, black metal grille.

2002-2003		$675	$750

Bassman 400 Combo Amp

2000-2004. Solidstate, 350 watts with 2x10" plus horn, combo, black cover, black metal grille.

2000-2004		$500	$600

Bassman Bassbreaker (Custom Shop) Amp

1998-2003. Classic Bassman 4x10" configuration. Not offered by 2004 when the '59 Bassman LTD was introduced.

1998-2003	2x12"	$775	$850
1998-2003	4x10"	$775	$850

Blues De Ville Amp

1993-1996. All tube Tweed Series, 60 watts, 4x10" (optional 2x12" in '94), reverb, high-gain channel, tweed cover (blond tolex optional '95 only).

1993-1996	Tweed, 4x10"	$450	$550

1994-1996	Tweed, 2x12"	$450	$525
1995	Blond tolex, 4x10"	$500	$600

Blues Deluxe Amp

1993-1996. All tube Tweed Series, 40 watts, 2 5881 output tubes, reverb, 1x12", tweed covering (blond tolex optional '95 only).

1993-1996	Tweed	$300	$400
1995	Blond	$375	$425

Blues Junior Amp

1995-present. All tube, 15 watts, 1x10", spring reverb, tweed in '95, black tolex with silver grille '96 on.

1995-2005		$300	$350
2000-2005	Hardwood cab option	$525	$575

Bronco Amp

1968-1974, 1993-2001. 1x 8" speaker, all tube, 5 watts until '72, 6 watts for '72-'74, ('90s issue is 15 watts), solidstate, tweed covering (blond tolex was optional for '95 only).

1968-1974		$325	$375
1993-2001	15 watts, no reverb	$100	$150

Bullet/Bullet 150 Amp

1994-2005. Solidstate, 15 watts, 1x8", with or without reverb.

1994-2005	With reverb	$100	$125
1994-2005	Without reverb	$75	$100

Capricorn Amp

1970-1972. Solidstate, 105 watts, 3x12".

1970-1972		$175	$300

Champ Amp

1953-1982. Renamed from the Champion 600. Tweed until '64, black tolex after, 3 watts in '53, 4 watts '54-'64, 5 watts '65-'71, 6 watts '72-'82, 1x6" until '57, 1x8" after.

1953-1954	Wide panel, 1x6"	$850	$1,000
1955-1956	Narrow panel, tweed, 1x6"	$900	$1,100
1956-1964	Narrow panel, tweed, 1x8"	$1,000	$1,300
1964	Old cab, black, 1x8", last F51	$900	$1,000
1964-1967	New cab, black tolex, 1x8", AA764	$500	$600
1968-1972	Silverface, 1x8"	$350	$400
1973-1982	Silverface, 1x8"	$275	$325

Champ Amp Tubes

The cost of replacement tubes for the '56-'64 models.

1956-1964	New tubes	$45	$55
1956-1964	NOS tubes	$85	$100

Champ II Amp

1982-1985. 18 watts, 1x10".

1982-1985		$350	$425

Champ 12 Amp

1986-1992. Tube, 12 watts, overdrive, reverb, 1x12".

1986-1992	Black	$300	$325
1986-1992	Red, white, gray or snakeskin	$350	$400

Fender Bassman 100

1960 Fender Champ

Fender Champ 12

AMPS

Fender Champ (5E1)

Fender Concert (6G12)

Fender Concert II 112

MODEL YEAR	FEATURES	EXC. COND. LOW	HIGH

Champ 25 SE Amp
1992-1993. Hybrid solidstate and tube combo, 25 watts, 1x12".

1992-1993		$175	$200

Champion 30/30 DSP Amp
1999-2003. Small solidstate combo, 30 watts, 1x8", reverb.

1999-2003		$125	$150

Champion 110 Amp
1993-2000. Solidstate, 25 watts, 1x10", 2 channels, black tolex, silver grille.

1993-2000		$125	$175

Champion 300 Amp
2004-present. 30 watt solidstate combo, Dyna-Touch Series, DSP effects.

2004-2005		$170	$180

Champion 600 Amp
1949-1953. Replaced the Champion 800, 3 watts, 1x6", 2-tone tolex, TV front. Replaced by the Champ.

1949-1953		$800	$1,050

Concert Amp
1960-1965, 1992-1995. Introduced with 40 watts and 4x10", brown tolex until '63, blackface '63-'65. In '62 white tolex was ordered by Webbs Music (CA) instead of the standard brown tolex. A wide range is noted for the rare white tolex, and each amp should be valued on a case-by-case basis. In '60, the very first brown tolex had a pink tint but only on the first year amps. Reissued in '92 with 60 watts and a 1x12".

1960	Brown (pink) tolex	$1,900	$2,400
1961-1963	Brown tolex	$1,900	$2,200
1962	White tolex (Webb Music)	$2,000	$3,000
1963-1965	Blackface	$1,800	$2,000

Concert 112 Amp
1982-1985. Tube, 60 watts, 1x12".

1982-1985		$550	$700

Concert 210 Amp
1982-1985. Tube, 60 watts, 2x10".

1982-1985		$575	$725

Concert 410 Amp
1982-1985. Tube, 60 watts, 4x10".

1982-1985		$600	$750

Concert Reverb (Pro Tube Series) Amp
2002-2005. 4x10" combo, reverb, tremolo, over-drive.

2002-2005		$875	$975

Cyber Champ Amp
2004-2005. 65 watts, 1x12", Cyber features, 21 presets

2004-2005		$225	$275

Cyber Deluxe Amp
2002-2005. 65 watts, 1x12", Cyber features, 64 presets.

2002-2005		$400	$450

Cyber Twin Combo Amp
2001-present. Hybrid tube/solidstate modeling amp, 2x65 watts, 2x12".

2001-2003		$600	$750

MODEL YEAR	FEATURES	EXC. COND. LOW	HIGH

Deco-Tone (Custom Shop) Amp
2000. Art-deco styling, all tube, 15 watts, 1x12", round speaker baffle opening, uses 6BQ5/ES84 power tubes.

2000		$900	$1,000

Deluxe Amp
1948-1981. Name changed from Model 26 ('46-'48). 10 watts (15 by '54 and 20 by '63), 1x12", TV front with tweed '48-'53, wide-panel '53-'55, narrow-panel '55-'60, brown tolex with brownface '61-'63, black tolex with blackface '63-'66.

1948-1952	Tweed, TV front	$1,800	$2,300
1953-1954	Wide panel	$2,000	$2,500
1955-1956	Narrow panel, smaller cab	$2,700	$3,300
1956-1960	Narrow panel, slightly larger cab	$2,700	$3,300
1961-1963	Brown tolex	$1,600	$1,800
1964-1966	Black tolex	$1,200	$1,600

Deluxe Amp Parts
Cost of replacement parts for the '55-'56 Deluxe.

1955-1956	New tubes	$45	$75
1955-1956	NOS tubes	$170	$225
1955-1956	Orig P12R Bluebell speaker	$275	$325
1955-1956	Re-coned P12R	$225	$275
1955-1956	Orig. output trans.	$200	$250
1955-1956	Rewind orig. output tran	$200	$250
1955-1956	Orig. power trans.	$250	$300
1955-1956	Rewind orig. power tran	$250	$300
1955-1956	New output or power trans.	$65	$100

Deluxe Reverb Amp
1963-1981. 1x12", 20 watts, blackface '63-'67, silverface '68-'80, blackface with silver grille option introduced in mid-'80. Replaced by Deluxe Reverb II. Reissued as Deluxe Reverb '65 Reissue.

1963-1967	Blackface	$2,100	$2,200
1968-1972	Silverface	$1,300	$1,500
1973-1980	Silverface	$1,200	$1,500
1980-1981	Blackface	$1,200	$1,500

Deluxe Reverb Amp Parts
Cost of replacement parts for the '63-'67 Deluxe Reverb.

1963-1967	New tubes	$170	$200
1963-1967	NOS tubes	$365	$475
1963-1967	Orig 12K5-2 Oxford speaker	$175	$275

Deluxe Reverb (Solidstate) Amp
1966-1969. Part of Fender's early solidstate series.

1966-1969		$250	$325

Deluxe Reverb '65 Reissue Amp
1993-present. Blackface reissue, 22 watts, 1x12".

1993-1999	Blond (limited production)	$575	$675
1993-2005	Black tolex	$550	$650

MODEL YEAR	FEATURES	EXC. COND. LOW	HIGH

Deluxe Reverb II Amp
1982-1986. Updated Deluxe Reverb with 2 6V6 power tubes, all tube preamp section, black tolex, blackface, 20 watts, 1x12".

1982-1986		$625	$700

Deluxe 85 Amp
1988-1993. Solidstate, 65 watts, 1x12", black tolex, silver grille, Red Knob Series.

1988-1993		$250	$300

Deluxe 90 Amp
1999-2003. Solidstate, 90 watts, 1x12" combo, DSP added in '02.

1999-2002		$200	$225
2002-2003	DSP option	$250	$275

Deluxe 112 Amp
1992-1995. Solidstate, 65 watts, 1x12", black tolex with silver grille.

1992-1995		$175	$275

Deluxe 112 Plus Amp
1995-2000. 90 watts, 1x12", channel switching.

1995-2000		$200	$300

Deluxe 900 Amp
2004-present. Solidstate, 90 watts, 1x12" combo, DSP effects.

2004-2005		$350	$375

Dual Professional Amp
1994-2002. Custom Shop amp, all tube, point-to-point wiring, 100 watts, 2x12" Celestion Vintage 30s, fat switch, reverb, tremolo, white tolex, oxblood grille.

1994-2002		$1,400	$1,600

Dual Showman Amp
1962-1969. Called the Double Showman for the first year. White tolex (black available from '64), 2x15", 85 watts. Reintroduced '87-'94 as solidstate, 100 watts, optional speaker cabs.

1962	Rough blond and oxblood	$4,000	$4,700
1963	Smooth blond and wheat	$3,000	$3,400
1964-1967	Black tolex, horizontal cab	$2,200	$2,500
1968	Blackface, large vertical cab	$1,100	$1,500
1968-1969	Silverface	$900	$1,200

Dual Showman Head Amp
1962-1969. Dual Showman head with output transformer for 2x15" (versus single Showman's 1x15" output ohms), blackface '62-'67, the late-'67 model logo stipulated "Dual Showman" while the '62-early-'67 head merely stated Showman (could be a single Showman or Dual Showman), '68-'69 silverface.

1962-1963	Blond	$1,700	$2,000
1964-1968	Dual Showman blackface	$1,200	$1,300
1968-1969	Silverface	$550	$650

Dual Showman Reverb Amp
1968-1981. Black tolex with silver grille, silverface, 100 watts, 2x15".

1968-1972		$1,100	$1,200
1973-1981		$1,000	$1,100

Dual Showman Reverb Head Amp
1968-1981. Amp only.

1968-1972	Includes TFL5000 series	$750	$825
1973-1981		$650	$750

Frontman Series Amp
1997-present. Student combo amps, models include 15/15B/15G/15R (15 watts, 1x8"), 25R (25 watts, 1x10", reverb).

1997-2004	15/15B/15G/15R	$50	$75
1997-2004	25R	$60	$90
2005	15 DSP w/15 FX selections	$125	$140
2005-2006	15G/15R	$75	$100

H.O.T. Amp
1990-1996. Solidstate, 25 watts, 1x10", gray carpet cover (black by '92), black grille.

1990-1996		$75	$90

Harvard (Tube) Amp
1956-1961. Tweed, 10 watts, 1x10", 2 knobs volume and roll-off tone, some were issued with 1x8". Reintroduced as a solidstate model in '80.

1956-1961		$1,400	$1,800

Harvard (Solidstate) Amp
1980-1983. Reintroduced from tube model, black tolex with blackface, 20 watts, 1x10".

1980-1983		$75	$150

Harvard Reverb Amp
1981-1982. Solidstate, 20 watts, 1x10", reverb, replaced by Harvard Reverb II in '83.

1981-1982		$125	$200

Harvard Reverb II Amp
1983-1985. Solidstate, black tolex with blackface, 20 watts, 1x10", reverb.

1983-1985		$125	$200

Hot Rod De Ville 212 Amp
1996-present. Updated Blues De Ville, tube, 60 watts, black tolex, 2x12".

1996-2000		$450	$550
2001-2006	Black tolex	$575	$600

Hot Rod De Ville 410 Amp
1996-present. Tube, 60 watts, black tolex, 4x10".

1996-2000		$450	$550
2001-2006	Black tolex	$400	$550
2001-2006	Ltd. Ed. brown tolex	$500	$600

Hot Rod Deluxe Amp
1996-present. Updated Blues Deluxe, tube, 40 watts, 1x12", black tolex. Various covering optional by '98, also a wood cab in 2003.

1996-2000	Black tolex	$375	$475
1996-2000	Blond tolex or tweed option	$400	$475
1996-2001	Brown option	$375	$475
2001-2006	Black tolex	$450	$475
2003	Wood cab	$700	$775

J.A.M. Amp
1990-1996. Solidstate, 25 watts, 1x12", 4 preprogrammed sounds, gray carpet cover (black by '92).

1990-1996		$85	$100

1955 Fender Deluxe

Fender Dual Showman Reverb

Fender Harvard

AMPS

'70s Fender Musicmaster Bass

1957 Fender Princeton Amp

Fender Princeton 650

MODEL YEAR	FEATURES	EXC. COND. LOW	HIGH
Jazz King Amp			
2005-present. 140 watt solidstate 1x15" combo,			
2005		$500	$550
Libra Amp			
1970-1972. Solidstate, 105 watts, 4x12" JBL speakers, black tolex.			
1970-1972		$275	$400
London 185 Amp			
1988-1992. Solidstate, 160 watts, black tolex.			
1988-1992	Head only	$175	$200
London Reverb 112 Amp			
1983-1985. Solidstate, 100 watts, black tolex, 1x12".			
1983-1985		$225	$350
London Reverb 210 Amp			
1983-1985. Solidstate, 100 watts, black tolex, 2x10".			
1983-1985		$250	$375
London Reverb Head Amp			
1983-1985. Solidstate head, 100 watts.			
1983-1985		$150	$275
M-80 Amp			
1989-1994. Solidstate, 90 watts, 1x12". The M-80 series were also offered as head only amp.			
1989-1993		$150	$275
M-80 Bass Amp			
1991-1994. Solidstate, bass and keyboard amp, 160 watts, 1x15".			
1991-1994		$150	$275
M-80 Chorus Amp			
1990-1994. Solidstate, stereo chorus, 2 65-watt channels, 2x12", 90 watts.			
1990-1994		$250	$300
M-80 Pro Amp			
1992. Rackmount version of M-80, 90 watts.			
1992		$125	$175
Model 26 Amp			
1946-1947. Tube, 10 watts, 1x10", hardwood cabinet. Sometimes called Deluxe Model 26, renamed Deluxe in '48.			
1946-1947		$1,500	$2,500
Montreux Amp			
1983-1985. Solidstate, 100 watts, 1x12", black tolex with silver grille.			
1983-1985		$225	$350
Musicmaster Bass Amp			
1970-1983. Tube, 12 watts, 1x12", black tolex.			
1970-1972	Silverface	$225	$325
1973-1980	Silverface	$225	$300
1981-1983	Blackface	$225	$300
PA-100 Amp			
100 watts.			
1970s		$350	$450
Performer 650 Amp			
1993-1995. Solidstate hybrid amp with single tube, 70 watts, 1x12".			
1993-1995		$250	$300
Performer 1000 Amp			
1993-1995. Solidstate hybrid amp with a single tube, 100 watts, 1x12".			
1993-1995		$250	$300

MODEL YEAR	FEATURES	EXC. COND. LOW	HIGH
Princeton Amp			
1948-1979. Tube, 4.5 watts (12 watts by '61), 1x8" (1x10" by '61), tweed '48-'61, brown '61-'63, black with blackface '63-'69, silverface '69-'79.			
1948-1953	TV front	$1,000	$1,200
1953-1954	Wide panel	$1,000	$1,200
1955-1956	Narrow panel, sm. Box	$1,100	$1,300
1956-1961	Narrow panel, lg. box	$1,100	$1,300
1961-1963	Brown, 6G2	$1,000	$1,150
1963-1964	Black, 6G2	$700	$850
1964-1966	Black, AA964	$675	$800
1968-1969	Silverface, alum. grille trim	$475	$550
1969-1970	Silverface, no grille trim	$450	$500
1971-1979	Silverface	$425	$475
Princeton Reverb Amp			
1964-1981. Tube, black tolex, blackface until '67, silverface after.			
1964-1967	Blackface	$1,400	$1,800
1968-1981	Silverface or blackface	$800	$1,000
Princeton Chorus Amp			
1988-1996. Solidstate, 2x10", 2 channels at 25 watts each, black tolex. Replaced by Princeton Stereo Chorus in '96.			
1988-1996		$225	$275
Princeton Reverb II Amp			
1982-1985. Tube amp, 20 watts, 1x12", black tolex, silver grille, distortion feature.			
1982-1985		$550	$600
Princeton 65 Amp			
1999-2003. Combo 1x2", reverb, blackface, DSP added in '02.			
1999-2003		$175	$275
Princeton 112/112 Plus Amp			
1993-1997. Solidstate, 40 watts (112) or 60 watts (112 Plus), 1x12", black tolex.			
1993-1994	40 watts	$175	$225
1995-1997	60 watts	$175	$225
Princeton 650 Amp			
2004-present. Solidstate 65 watt 1x12" combo, DSP effects.			
2004-2006		$300	$325
Pro Amp			
1947-1965. Called Professional '46-'48. 15 watts (26 by '54 and 25 by '60), 1x15", tweed TV front '48-'53, wide-panel '53-'54, narrow-panel '55-'60, brown tolex and brownface '60-'63, black and blackface '63-'65.			
1947-1953	Tweed, TV front	$3,000	$4,000
1953-1954	Wide panel	$3,100	$4,000
1955	Narrow panel (old chassis)	$3,200	$4,000
1955-1959	Narrow panel (new chassis)	$3,500	$4,500
1960-1965	Brown or brown tolex	$1,800	$2,000

MODEL YEAR	FEATURES	EXC. COND. LOW	HIGH

Pro Reverb (solidstate) Amp
1967-1969. Fender's first attempt at solidstate design, the attempt was unsuccessful and many of these models will overheat and are known to be unreliable. 50 watts, 2x12", upright vertical combo cabinet.

1967-1969		$275	$350

Pro Reverb Amp
1965-1982. Tube, black tolex, 40 watts (45 watts by '72, 70 watts by '81), 2x12", blackface '65-'69 and '81-'83, silverface '69-'81.

1965-1967	Blackface	$1,900	$2,100
1968-1982	Silverface or blackface	$1,100	$1,400

Pro Reverb Reissue (Pro Series) Amp
2002-2005. 50 watts, 1x12", 2 modern designed channels - clean and high gain.

2002-2005		$700	$900

Pro 185 Amp
1989-1991. Solidstate, 160 watts, 2x12", black tolex.

1989-1991		$250	$300

Pro Junior Amp
1994-present. All tube, 2xEL84 tubes, 15 watts, 1x10" Alnico Blue speaker, tweed until '95, black tolex '96 on.

1994-1999		$275	$350
2000-2006		$225	$250

Prosonic Amp
1996-2001. Custom Shop combo, 60 watts, 2 channels, 3-way rectifier switch, 2x10" Celestion or separate cab with 4x12", tube reverb, black, red or green.

1996-2001		$700	$850

Prosonic Head Amp
1996-2001. Amp head only version.

1996-2001		$700	$750

Quad Reverb Amp
1971-1978. Black tolex, silverface, 4x12", tube, 100 watts.

1971-1978		$700	$900

R.A.D. Amp
1990-1996. Solidstate, 20 watts, 1x8", gray carpet cover until '92, black after.

1990-1996		$60	$70

R.A.D. Bass Amp
1992-1994. 25 watts, 1x10", renamed BXR 25.

1992-1994		$60	$70

Roc-Pro 1000 Amp
1997-2001. Hybrid tube combo or head, 100 watts, 1x12", spring reverb, 1000 logo on front panel.

1997-2001	Combo	$250	$300
1997-2001	Head only	$225	$250

Rumble Bass Head Amp
1994-1998. Custom Shop tube amp, 300 watts.

1994-1998		$2,100	$2,200

Rumble Series Amp
2003-present. Solidstate bass amps, include Rumble 15 (15 watts, 1x8"), 25 (25 watts, 1x10"), 60 (60 watts, 1x12"), and 100 (100 watts, 1x15").

2003-2004	Rumble 25	$100	$125
2003-2006	Rumble 15	$75	$100

Scorpio Amp
1970-1972. Solidstate, 56 watts, 2x12", black tolex.

1970-1972		$225	$350

SFX Keyboard 200 Amp
1998-1999. Keyboard combo amp, digital effects, black tolex.

1998-1999		$225	$275

SFX Satellite Amp
1997-2001. Hybrid tube combo or head, 100 watts, 1x12", spring reverb.

1998-2000		$200	$250

Showman 12 Amp
1960-1966. Piggyback cabinet with 1x12", 85 watts, blond tolex (changed to black in '64), maroon grille '61-'63, gold grille '63-'64, silver grille '64-'67.

1960-1962	Rough blond and oxblood	$3,800	$4,300
1963-1964	Smooth blond and gold	$2,900	$3,500
1964-1966	Black	$2,000	$2,400

Showman 15 Amp
1960-1968. Piggyback cabinet with 1x15", 85 watts, blond tolex (changed to black in '64), maroon grille '61-'63, gold grille '63-'64, silver grille '64-'67.

1960-1962	Rough blond and oxblood	$3,800	$4,300
1963-1964	Smooth blond and gold	$2,900	$3,500
1964-1967	Blackface	$2,000	$2,400
1967-1968	Silverface	$900	$1,100

Showman 112 Amp
1983-1987. Solidstate, 2 channels, 200 watts, reverb, 4 button footswitch, 5-band EQ, effects loop, 1x12".

1983-1987		$325	$425

Showman 115 Amp
1983-1987. Solidstate, 1x15", 2 channels, reverb, EQ, effects loop, 200 watts, black tolex.

1983-1987		$325	$425

Showman 210 Amp
1983-1987. Solidstate, 2 channels, reverb, EQ, effects loop, 2x10", 200 watts, black tolex.

1983-1987		$350	$450

Showman 212 Amp
1983-1987. Solidstate, 2 channels, reverb, EQ, effects loop, 2x12", 200 watts, black tolex.

1983-1987		$350	$475

Sidekick 10 Amp
1983-1985. Small solidstate Japanese or Mexican import, 10 watts, 1x8".

1983-1985		$50	$75

Sidekick 100 Bass Head Amp
1986-1993. 100 watt bass head.

1986-1993		$80	$100

Sidekick Bass 30 Amp
1983-1985. Combo, 30 watts, 1x12".

1983-1985		$60	$80

Sidekick Reverb 15 Amp
1983-1985. Small solidstate import, reverb, 15 watts.

1983-1985		$70	$80

Fender Pro Junior

Fender Rumble 100

1980s Fender Showman Amp

1959 Fender Super Amp

1960 Fender Super Amp

1969 Fender Super Reverb

MODEL YEAR	FEATURES	EXC. COND. LOW	HIGH

Sidekick Reverb 20 Amp
1983-1985. Small solidstate Japanese or Mexican import, 20 watts, reverb, 1x10".

| 1983-1985 | | $80 | $90 |

Sidekick Reverb 30 Amp
1983-1985. Small solidstate Japanese or Mexican import, 30 watts, 1x12", reverb.

| 1983-1985 | | $90 | $110 |

Sidekick Reverb 65 Amp
1986-1988. Small solidstate Japanese or Mexican import, 65 watts, 1x12".

| 1986-1988 | | $100 | $125 |

Squire SKX 15/15R Amp
1990-1992. Solidstate, 15 watts, 1x8", model 15R with reverb.

| 1990-1992 | Non-reverb | $40 | $50 |
| 1990-1992 | Reverb | $55 | $65 |

Stage 100/Stage 1000 Amp
1999-present. Solidstate, 1x12", combo or head only options, 100 watts, blackface. Head unit available 2004 only.

| 1999-2004 | Combo | $250 | $300 |
| 2004 | Head only | $175 | $200 |

Stage 1600 DSP Amp
2004-present. Solidstate, 160 watts, 2x12" combo, 16 digital effects (DSP).

| 2004-2006 | | $350 | $375 |

Stage Lead/Lead II Amp
1983-1985. Solidstate, 100 watts, 1x12", reverb, channel switching, black tolex. Stage Lead II has 2x12".

| 1983-1985 | 1x12" | $225 | $300 |
| 1983-1985 | 2x12" | $250 | $325 |

Steel-King Amp
2004-present. Designed for pedal steel, 200 watts, solidstate, 1x15".

| 2004-2005 | | $450 | $550 |

Studio Lead Amp
1983-1986. Solidstate, 50 watts, 1x12", black tolex.

| 1983-1986 | | $225 | $300 |

Super Amp
1947-1963, 1992-1997. Introduced as Dual Professional in 1946, renamed Super '47, 2x10" speakers, 20 watts (30 watts by '60 with 45 watts in '62), tweed TV front '47-'53, wide-panel '53-'54, narrow-panel '55-'60, brown tolex '60-'64. Reintroduced '92-'97 with 4x10", 60 watts, black tolex.

1947-1952	Tweed, TV front	$3,500	$4,000
1953-1954	Tweed, wide panel	$3,700	$4,000
1955	Tweed, narrow panel, 6L6	$5,500	$6,000
1956-1957	Tweed,narrow panel, 5E4, 6V6	$5,000	$5,500
1957-1960	Tweed, narrow panel, 6L6	$5,500	$7,000
1960	Pink/brown metal knobs	$2,700	$3,300
1960	Pink/brown reverse knobs	$2,700	$3,200
1960-1962	Brown, oxblood grille, 6G4	$2,400	$2,800

MODEL YEAR	FEATURES	EXC. COND. LOW	HIGH
1962-1963	Brown, tan/wheat grille, 6G4	$2,000	$2,400

Super (4x10") Amp
1992-1997. 60 watts, 4x10", black tolex, silver grille, blackface control panel.

| 1992-1997 | | $600 | $700 |

Super 60 Amp
1989-1993. Red Knob series, 1x12", 60 watts, earlier versions with red knobs, later models with black knobs, offered in optional covers such as red, white, gray or snakeskin.

| 1989-1993 | | $300 | $400 |

Super 112 Amp
1990-1993. Red Knob series, 1x12", 60 watts, earlier versions with red knobs, later models with black knobs, originally designed to replace the Super60 but the Super60 remained until '93.

| 1990-1993 | | $300 | $400 |

Super 210 Amp
1990-1993. Red Knob series, 2x10", 60 watts, earlier versions with red knobs, later models with black knobs.

| 1990-1993 | | $325 | $425 |

Super Champ Amp
1982-1986. Black tolex, 18 watts, blackface, 1x10".

| 1982-1986 | | $700 | $1,000 |

Super Champ Deluxe Amp
1982-1986. Solid oak cabinet, 18 watts, upgrade 10" Electro-Voice speaker, see-thru brown grille cloth.

| 1982-1986 | | $850 | $1,150 |

Super Reverb Amp
1963-1982. 4x10" speakers, blackface until '67 and '80-'82, silverface '68-'80.

1963-1967	Blackface	$2,000	$2,100
1968	Silverface, AB763	$1,300	$1,500
1969-1970	Silverface	$1,100	$1,300
1970-1972	Silverface, AA270	$1,050	$1,300
1973-1980	Silverface, no MV	$1,000	$1,200
1981-1982	Blackface	$1,000	$1,200

Super Reverb '65 Reissue Amp
2001-present. 45 watts, all tube, 4x10", blackface cosmetics.

| 2001-2005 | | $725 | $775 |

Super Six Reverb Amp
1970-1979. Large combo amp based on the Twin Reverb chassis, 100 watts, 6x10", black tolex.

| 1970-1979 | | $700 | $900 |

Super Twin (Non-reverb) Amp
1975-1976. 180 watts (6 6L6 power tubes), 2x12", distinctive dark grille.

| 1975-1976 | | $400 | $500 |

Super Twin (with reverb) Amp
1976-1980. 180 watts (6 6L6 power tubes), 2x12", distinctive dark grille.

| 1976-1980 | | $500 | $800 |

Taurus Amp
1970-1972. Solidstate, 42 watts, 2x10" JBL, black tolex, silver grille, JBL badge.

| 1970-1972 | | $225 | $300 |

AMPS

Tonemaster Head Amp
1993-2002. Custom Shop, hand-wired high-gain head, 100 watts, 2 channels, effects loop, blond tolex.

1993-1999		$900	$1,000

Tonemaster 212 Cabinet
1993-2002. Custom Shop extension cabinet for Tonemaster head, blond tolex, Oxblood grille, 2x12" Celestion Vintage 30.

1993-1999		$375	$450

Tonemaster 412 Cabinet
1993-2002. 4x12" Celestion Vintage 30 version.

1993-1999		$425	$500

Tonemaster Set Amp
1993-2002. Custom Shop, hand-wired head with Tonemaster 2x12" or 4x12" cabinet.

1993-1999	Blond and oxblood	$1,400	$1,500
1993-1999	Custom color red	$1,500	$1,600

Tremolux Amp
1955-1966. Tube, tweed, 1x12" '55-'60, white tolex with piggyback 1x10" cabinet '61-'62, 2x10" '62-'64, black tolex '64-'66.

1955-1960	Tweed, 1x12", narrow panel	$2,500	$3,300
1961	Rough white and oxblood, 1x10"	$2,200	$2,800
1961-1962	Rough white and oxblood, 2x10"	$2,000	$2,500
1962-1963	Rough white and wheat, 2x10"	$1,800	$2,300
1963-1964	Smooth white and gold, 2x10"	$1,800	$2,200
1964-1966	Black tolex, 2x10"	$1,400	$1,800

Twin Amp
1952-1963, 1996-present. Tube, 2x12"; 15 watts, tweed wide-panel '52-'55; narrow-panel '55-'60; 50 watts '55-'57; 80 watts '58; brown tolex '60; white tolex '61-'63. Reintroduced in '96 with black tolex, spring reverb and output control for 100 watts or 25 watts.

1952-1954	Tweed, wide panel	$5,500	$6,000
1955-1957	Tweed, 50 watts	$7,000	$10,000
1958-1959	Tweed, 80 watts	$8,000	$12,000
1960	Brown tolex, 80 watts	$7,000	$11,000
1960-1962	Rough white and oxblood	$6,000	$8,000
1963	Smooth white and gold	$5,500	$7,500

Twin '57 Reissue Amp
2004. Custom Shop '57 tweed, low power dual rectifier model, 40 watts, 2x12", authentic tweed lacquering.

2004		$1,100	$1,200

Twin Reverb Amp
1963-1982. Black tolex, 85 watts (changed to 135 watts in '81), 2x12", blackface '63-'67 and '81-'82, silverface '68-'81, blackface optional in '80-'81 and standard in '82. Reverb reintroduced as Twin in '96.

1963-1967	Blackface	$2,000	$2,600
1968-1972	Silverface, no master vol.	$1,000	$1,200
1973-1975	Silverface, master vol.	$800	$975
1976-1980	Silverface, push/pull	$650	$900
1980-1982	Blackface	$650	$900

Twin Reverb (Solidstate) Amp
1966-1969. 100 watts, 2x12", black tolex.

1966-1969		$325	$500

Twin Reverb '65 Reissue Amp
1992-present. Black tolex, 2x12", 85 watts.

1992-2002	High or low output	$700	$800

Twin Reverb II Amp
1983-1985. Black tolex, 2x12", 105 watts, channel switching, effects loop, blackface panel, silver grille.

1983-1985		$700	$750

Twin "The Twin"/"Evil Twin" Amp
1987-1992. 100 watts, 2x12", red knobs, most black tolex, but white, red and snakeskin covers offered.

1987-1992		$450	$700

Ultimate Chorus DSP Amp
1995-2001. Solidstate, 2x65 watts, 2x12", 32 built-in effect variations, blackface cosmetics.

1995-2001		$350	$375

Ultra Chorus Amp
1992-1994. Solidstate, 2x65 watts, 2x12", standard control panel with chorus.

1992-1994		$300	$325

Vibrasonic Amp
1959-1963. First amp to receive the new brown tolex and JBL, 1x15", 25 watts.

1959-1963		$2,000	$2,200

Vibrasonic Custom Amp
1995-1997. Custom Shop designed for steel guitar and guitar, blackface, 1x15", 100 watts.

1995-1997		$650	$800

Vibro-Champ Amp
1964-1982. Black tolex, 4 watts, (5 watts '69-'71, 6 watts '72-'80), 1x8", blackface '64-'68 and '82, silverface '69-'81.

1964-1967	Blackface, AA764	$550	$675
1968-1982	Silverface or blackface	$350	$450

Vibro-King Amp
1993-present. Custom Shop combo, blond tolex, 60 watts, 3x10", vintage reverb, tremolo, single channel, all tube.

1993-1999		$1,300	$1,400

Vibro-King 212 Cabinet
1993-present. Custom Shop extension cabinet, blond tolex, 2x12" Celestion GK80.

1993-1999		$400	$500

Vibrolux Amp
1956-1964. Narrow-panel, 10 watts, tweed with 1x10" '56-'61, brown tolex and brownface with 1x12" and 30 watts '61-'62, black tolex and blackface '63-'64.

1956-1961	Tweed, 1x10"	$1,900	$2,300
1961-1962	Brown tolex, 1x12", 2x6L6	$2,100	$2,400
1963-1964	Black tolex, 1x12"	$2,000	$2,200

Fender Super Amp (6G4A)

Fender Twin Amp

Fender Vibrolux

1963 Fender Vibroverb Amp

Fuchs OD Supreme

Gabriel Sound Garage Voxer 18

MODEL YEAR	FEATURES	EXC. COND. LOW	HIGH

Vibrolux Reverb Amp

1964-1982. Black tolex, 2x10", blackface and 35 watts '64-'69, silverface and 40 watts '70-'79. Reissued in '96 with blackface and 40 watts.

1964-1967	Blackface	$2,400	$2,500
1968-1972	Silverface	$1,200	$1,500
1973-1980	Silverface or blackface	$1,100	$1,400

Vibrolux Reverb (Solidstate) Amp

1967-1969. Fender CBS solidstate, 35 watts, 2x10", black tolex.

1967-1969		$275	$350

Vibrolux Reverb Reissue Amp

1996-present. 40 watts, 2x10", all tube, black or blond tolex.

1996-1999	Blond and tan	$750	$900
1996-2003	Black and silver	$650	$800

Vibrolux Custom Reverb Amp

1995-present. Part of Professional Series, Custom Shop designed, standard factory built, 40 watts, 2x10", tube, black tolex, silver grille, white knobs.

1995-2004		$700	$800

Vibrosonic Reverb Amp

1972-1981. Black tolex, 100 watts, 1x15", silverface.

1972-1981		$700	$800

Vibroverb Amp

1963-1964. Brown tolex with 35 watts, 2x10" and brownface '63, black tolex with 1x15" and blackface '64-'65.

1963	Brown tolex, 2x10"	$6,700	$8,200
1964	Black tolex, 1x15"	$3,300	$4,100

Vibroverb '63 Reissue Amp

1990-1995. Reissue of 1963 Vibroverb, 40 watts, 2x10", reverb, vibrato, brown tolex.

1990-1995		$700	$750

Vibroverb '64 Custom Shop Amp

2003-present. Reissue of 1964 Vibroverb with 1x15" blackface specs.

2003-2004		$1,500	$1,750

Yale Reverb Amp

1983-1985. Solidstate, black tolex, 50 watts, 1x12", silverface.

1983-1985		$200	$275

Flot-A-Tone

Ca.1946-early 1960s. Flot-A-Tone was located in Milwaukee, Wisconsin, and made a variety of tube guitar and accordion amps.

Small Amp

1x8" speaker.

1962		$300	$400

Large Amp

Four speakers.

1960s		$500	$800

Framus

1946-1977, 1996-present. Tube guitar amp heads, combos and cabinets made in Markneukirchen, Germany. They also build guitars, basses, mandolins and banjos. Begun as an acoustic instrument manufacturer, Framus added electrics in the mid-'50s. In the '60s, Framus instruments were imported into the U.S. by Philadelphia Music Company. The brand was revived in '96 by Hans Peter Wilfer, the president of Warwick, with production in Warwick's factory in Germany. Distributed in the U.S. by Dana B. Goods.

Fred

1984-1986. Before settling on the name Bedrock, company founders Brad Jeter and Ron Pinto produced 50 amps carrying the brand name Fred in Nashua, New Hampshire.

Fuchs Audio Technology

2000-present. Andy Fuchs started the company, located in Bloomfield, New Jersey, in '99 to rebuild and modify tube amps. In 2000 he started production of his own brand of amps, offering combos and heads from 10 to 150 watts. They also custom build audiophile and studio tube electronics.

Fulton-Webb

Ca.1977-present. Steve Fulton and Bill Webb build their tube amp heads, combos and cabinets in Austin, Texas.

Gabriel Sound Garage

2004-present. Gabriel Bucataru builds his tube amp heads and combos in Arlington Heights, Illinois.

Gallien Krueger

1969-present. Gallien-Krueger has offered a variety of bass and guitar amps, combos and cabinets and is located in San Jose, California.

200G Amp

1980s. Solidstate, black tolex, black grille.

1980s		$250	$350

212GS/212LC Amp

1986-ca.1989. 140-watt mono or 70-watt stereo, 2x12", black carpet.

1986-1989		$350	$450

250ML Amp

Small practice amp, 2x4 1/2", chorus and echo.

1986-1989		$300	$350

700RB Bass Amp

Late 1990s. Rackmount, 380 watts.

1999		$275	$300

2100CEL Digital Stereo Guitar Combo Amp

1989-1991. 200 watts (100 per channel), 2x8", EQ, compression, chorus and reverb.

1989-1991		$350	$450

Garcia

2004-present. Tube amp heads and speaker cabinets built by Matthew Garcia in Myrtle Beach, South Carolina. He also builds effects.

AMPS

MODEL YEAR	FEATURES	EXC. COND. LOW	HIGH

Garnet

Mid 1960s-1989. In the mid '60s, "Gar" Gillies started the Garnet Amplifier Company with his two sons, Russell and Garnet, after he started making PA systems in his Canadian radio and TV repair shop. The first PA from the new company was for Chad Allen & the Expressions (later known as The Guess Who). A wide variety of tube amps were offered and all were designed by Gar, Sr. The company also produced the all-tube effects The Herzog, H-zog, and two stand-alone reverb units designed by Gar in the late '60s and early '70s. The company closed in '89, due to financial reasons caused largely by a too rapid expansion. Gar still repairs and designs custom amps.

GDS Amplification

1998-present. Tube amps, combos and speaker cabinets from builder Graydon D. Stuckey of Flint, Michigan. GDS also offers amp kits.

Genesis

Genesis was a 1980s line of student amps from Gibson.

B40 Amp
1984-late-1980s. Bass combo with 40 watts.

1984-1989		$100	$150

G Series Amps
1984-late-1980s. Small combo amps.

1984-1989	G10 (10 watts)	$50	$100
1984-1989	G25 (25 watts)	$75	$125
1984-1989	G40R		
	(40 watts, reverb)	$125	$175

Genz Benz

1983-present. Founded by Jeff and Cathy Genzler and located in Scottsdale, Arizona, the company offers guitar, bass, and PA amps and speaker cabinets. In late 2003, Genz Benz was acquired by Kaman (Ovation, Hamer, Takamine).

George Dennis

1991-present. Founded by George Burgerstein, original products were a line of effects pedals. In '96 they added a line of tube amps. The company is located in Prague, Czech Republic.

Gerhart

2000-present. Production/custom, amps and cabinets from builder Gary Gerhart of West Hills, California. He also offers an amp in kit form.

Germino

2002-present. Tube amps, combos and cabinets built by Greg Germino in Graham, North Carolina.

Gibson

1880s (1902)-present. Gibson has offered a variety of amps since the mid-'30s to the present under the Gibson brandname and others. The price ranges listed are for excellent condition, all original amps though tubes may be replaced with affecting value. Many Gibson amps have missing or broken logos. The prices listed are for amps with fully intact logos. A broken or missing logo can diminish the value of the amp. Amps with a changed handle, power cord, and especially a broken logo should be taken on a case-by-case basis.

Atlas IV Amp
1963-1967. Piggyback head and cab, introduced with trapezoid shape, changed to rectangular cabs in '65-'66 with black cover, simple circuit with 4 knobs, no reverb or tremolo, mid-power with 2 6L6, 1x15".

1963-1965	Brown	$500	$700
1966-1967	Black	$500	$700

Atlas Medalist Amp
1964-1967. Combo version with 1x15".

1964-1967		$500	$700

B-40 Amp
1972-1975. 40 watts, 1x12".

1972-1975		$200	$300

BR-1 Amp
1945-1949. 15 watts, 1x12" field-coil speaker, brown leatherette cover, rectangular metal grille with large G.

1945-1949		$400	$500

BR-3 Amp
1946-1947. 12 watts, 1x12" Utah field-coil speaker (most BR models used Jensen speakers).

1946-1947		$350	$450

BR-4 Amp
1946-1947. 14 watts, 1x12" Utah field-coil speaker (most BR models used Jensen speakers).

1946-1947		$400	$500

BR-6 Amp
1946-1956. 10 to 12 watts, 1x10", brown leatherette, speaker opening split by cross panel with G logo, bottom mounted chassis with single on-off volume pointer knob.

1946-1947	Verticle cab	$350	$450
1948-1956	Horizontal cab	$300	$350

BR-9 Amp
1948-1953. Cream leatherette, 10 watts, 1x8". Originally sold with the BR-9 lap steel. Renamed GA-9 in '54.

1948-1953		$300	$350

Duo Metalist Amp
1967-1968. Upright vertical combo cab, tubes, faux wood grain panel, mid-power, 1x12".

1967-1968		$300	$400

EH-100 Amp
1936-1941. Electric-Hawaiian companion amp, 1x10". AC/DC version called EH-110.

1936-1941		$450	$600

EH-125 Amp
1941-1942. 1x12", rounded shoulder cab, brown cover in '41 and dark green in '42, leather handle.

1941-1942		$600	$750

EH-126 Amp
1941-1942. Experimental model, 6-volt variant of EH-125, about 5 made.

1941-1942		$600	$750

GDS 18W S/C

Gerhart Gilmore

1960s Gibson Atlas

AMPS

Gibson EH-185

'55 Gibson GA-5 Les Paul Junior

Gibson GA-5 Skylark

MODEL YEAR	FEATURES	EXC. COND. LOW	HIGH

EH-135 Amp
1941. Experimental model, alternating and direct current switchable, about 7 made.

1941		$650	$800

EH-150 Amp
1935-1941. Electric-Hawaiian companion amp, 1x12" ('35-'37) or 1x10" ('38-'42). AC/DC version called EH-160.

1935	13 3/4" sq. cab	$700	$900
1936-1937	14 3/4" sq. cab	$700	$900
1937-1942	15 3/8" round cab	$700	$900

EH-185 Amp
1939-1942. 1x12", tweed cover, black and orange vertical stripes, marketed as companion amp to the EH-185 Lap Steel. AC/DC version called EH-195.

1939-1942		$750	$950

EH-195 Amp
1939-1942. EH-185 variant with vibrato.

1939-1942		$900	$1,100

EH-250 Amp
1940-1942. Upgraded natural maple cabinet using EH-185 chassis, very few made, evolved into EH-275.

1940-1942		$950	$1,150

EH-275 Amp
1940-1942. Similar to EH-185 but with maple cab and celluloid binding, about 30 made.

1940-1942		$950	$1,150

Falcon Medalist (Hybrid) Amp
1967. Transitional tube 1x12" combo amp from GA-19 tube Falcon to the solidstate Falcon, Falcon logo and Gibson logo on front panel, brown control panel, dark cover and dark grille, vertical combo cabinet.

1967		$300	$400

Falcon Medalist (Solidstate) Amp
1968-1969. Solidstate combo, 15 watts, 1x12".

1968-1969		$300	$400

G-10 Amp
1972-1975. Solidstate, 10 watts, 1x10", no tremolo or reverb.

1972-1975		$75	$125

G-20 Amp
1972-1975. Solidstate with tremolo, 1x10", 10 watts.

1972-1975		$125	$200

G-25 Amp
1972-1975. 25 watts, 1x10".

1972-1975		$150	$225

G-35 Amp
1975. Solidstate, 30 watts, 1x12".

1975		$200	$275

G-40/G-40 R Amp
1972. Solidstate with tremolo and reverb, 40 watts, 1x12" (G-40) and 2x10" (G-40 R).

1972-1974	G-40 R	$250	$325
1972-1975	G-40	$225	$300

G-50/G-50 A/G-50 B Amp
1972, 1975. Solidstate with tremolo and reverb, models G-50 and 50 A are 1x12", 40 watts, model 50 B is a bass 1x15", 50 watts.

1972	G-50	$250	$325
1975	G-50 A & B	$250	$325

G-55 Amp
1975. 50 watts, 1x12".

1975		$250	$325

G-60 Amp
1972. Solidstate with tremolo and reverb, 1x15", 60 watts.

1972		$250	$325

G-70 Amp
1972. Solidstate with tremolo and reverb, 2x12", 60 watts.

1972		$300	$350

G-80 Amp
1972. Solidstate with tremolo and reverb, 4x10", 60 watts.

1972		$350	$400

G-100 A/G-100 B Amp
1975. 100 watts, model 100 A is 2x12" and 100 B is 2x15".

1975	A & B	$350	$400

G-105 Amp
1975 Solidstate, 100 watts, 2x12", reverb.

1975		$350	$400

G-115 Amp
1975. 100 watts, 4x10".

1975		$375	$450

GA-5 Les Paul Jr. Amp
1954-1957. Tan fabric cover (Mottled Brown by '47), 7" oval speaker, 4 watts. Renamed Skylark in '58.

1954		$450	$550
1955-1957		$350	$500

GA-5 Skylark Amp
1957-1968. Gold cover (brown by '63 and black by '66), 1x8" (1x10" from '64 on), 4.5 watts (10 watts from '64 on), tremolo. Often sold with the Skylark Lap Steel.

1957-1962	Gold, 4.5 watts, 1x8"	$300	$400
1963	Brown, 4.5 watts, 1x8"	$325	$350
1964	Brown, 10 watts, 1x10"	$325	$350
1965-1967	Black, 10 watts, 1x10"	$325	$350
1968	Skylark, last version	$250	$300

GA-5 T Skylark Amp
1960-1967. Tremolo, 4.5 watts, gold covering and 1x8" until '63, brown '63-'64, black and 1x10" after.

1961-1962	Gold, 4.5 watts, 1x8"	$325	$425
1963	Brown, 4.5 watts, 1x8"	$350	$375
1964	Brown, 10 watts, 1x10"	$350	$375
1965-1967	Black, 10 watts, 1x10"	$325	$350

GA-5 Les Paul Jr. (Goldtone Series) Amp
2004. Class A, 6 watts, 1x8".

2004		$250	$350

GA-6 Amp
1956-1960. Replaced the BR-6, 8 to 12 watts, 1x12", has Gibson 6 above the grille. Renamed GA-6 Lancer in '60.

1956-1960		$350	$525

AMPS

AMPS

GA-6 Lancer Amp
1960-1962. Renamed from GA-6, 1x12", tweed cover, 3 knobs, 14 watts.

1960-1962		$600	$700

GA-7 Amp
1955-1957. Described as "Les Paul TV Model", a basic old style GA-5 with different graphics, 4 watts, small speaker.

1955-1957		$350	$500

GA-8 Gibsonette Amp
1952-1962. Tan fabric cover (gold by '58), 1x10", 8 watts (9 watts by '58). Name changed to GA-8 Discoverer in '62.

1952-1962		$350	$525

GA-8 Discoverer Amp
1962-1964. Renamed from GA-8 Gibsonette, gold fabric cover, 1x12", 10 watts.

1962-1964		$350	$525

GA-8 T Discoverer Amp
1960-1967. Gold fabric cover, 1x10", 9 watts (tan cover, 1x12" and 15 watts by '63), tremolo.

1960-1962	Tweed, 9 watts, 1x10"	$400	$575
1963-1964	Brown, 15 watts, 1x12"	$350	$450
1965-1967	Black, 15 watts, 1x12"	$300	$400

GA-9 Amp
1954-1961. Renamed from BR-9, tan fabric cover, 8 watts, 1x10". Often sold with the BR-9 Lap Steel.

1954-1957		$350	$450
1958-1961	Tweed, 6V6s	$400	$500

GA-14 Titan Amp
1959-1961. About 15 watts using 2x6V6 power tubes, 1x10", tweed cover.

1959-1961		$500	$600

GA-15 RV (Custom Shop) Amp
2002. Custom Shop built, 15 watts, 1x12", quilted maple cabinet in natural finish, companion amp to Custom Shop L-5C or Super 400 set.

2002	.	$1,700	$2,000

GA-15 RV Goldtone Amp
1999-2004. 15 watts, Class A, 1x12", spring reverb.

1999-2004		$325	$400

GA-15 RVT Explorer amp
1965-1967. Tube, 1x10", tremolo, reverb, black vinyl.

1965-1967		$350	$400

GA-17 RVT Scout Amp
1963-1965. Low power, 1x12", reverb and tremolo.

1963-1964	Brown	$350	$525
1965	Black	$300	$475

GA-18 Explorer Amp
1959. Tube, 14 watts, 1x10". Replaced in '60 by the GA-18 T Explorer.

1959		$550	$650

GA-18 T Explorer Amp
1959-1964. Tweed, 14 watts, 1x10", tremolo.

1959-1962		$600	$700
1963-1964		$325	$500

GA-19 RVT Falcon Amp
1961-1966. One of Gibson's best selling amps. Initially tweed covered, followed by smooth brown, textured brown, and black. Each amp has a different tone. One 12" Jensen with deep-sounding reverb and tremolo.

1961-1962	Tweed, 6V6	$650	$750
1962-1963	Smooth brown	$500	$575
1964	Textured brown	$450	$500
1965-1966	Black	$400	$450

GA-20 RVT Minuteman Amp
1965-1967. Black, 14 watts, 1x12", tube, reverb, tremolo.

1965-1967		$400	$550

GA-20 T/Ranger Amp
1956-1962. Tube, 16 watts, tremolo, 1x12". Renamed Ranger in '60.

1956-1958	2-tone	$650	$800
1959-1962	Tweed	$700	$850
1960-1962	Ranger	$500	$600

GA-20/GA-20 Crest Amp
1950-1962. Brown leatherette (2-tone by '55 and tweed by '60), tube, 12 watts early, 14 watts later, 1x12". Renamed Crest in '60.

1952-1954	Brown, 14 watts	$600	$750
1955-1958	2-tone, 14 watts	$650	$775
1959-1962	Tweed/Crest, 14 watts	$700	$800

GA-25 Amp
1947-1948. Brown, 1x12" and 1x8", 15 watts. Replaced by GA-30 in '48.

1947-1948		$450	$550

GA-25 RVT Hawk Amp
1963-1968. Reverb, tremolo, 1x15".

1963	Smooth brown	$450	$550
1964	Rough brown	$350	$525
1965-1967	Black	$325	$500
1968	Hawk, last version	$225	$325

GA-30 Amp
1948-1961. Brown until '54, 2-tone after, tweed in '60, 1x12" and 1x8", 14 watts. Renamed Invader in '60.

1948-1954	Brown	$650	$750
1955-1958	2-tone	$700	$800
1959	Tweed	$750	$850

GA-30 RV Invader Amp
1960-1961. Tweed, 1x12" and 1x8", 14-16 watts, reverb but no tremolo.

1960-1961		$1,000	$1,200

GA-30 RVT Invader Amp
1962-1967. Updated model with reverb and tremolo, dual speakers 1x12" and 1x8", first issue in tweed.

1962	Tweed	$850	$1,200
1963	Smooth brown	$650	$700
1964-1965	Rough brown	$600	$650
1966-1967	Black	$550	$600

GA-30 RVH Goldtone Head Amp
1999-2004. 30 watts, Class A head, reverb.

1999-2004		$750	$850

Gibson GA-15

1965 Gibson GA-19RVT Falcon

Gibson GA-30

Gibson GA-40 Les Paul Amp

'54 Gibson GA-40
Les Paul Amp

1959 Gibson GA-55V

MODEL YEAR	FEATURES	EXC. COND. LOW	HIGH

GA-30 RVS (Stereo) Goldtone Amp
1999-2004. 15 watts per channel, Class A stereo, 2x12", reverb.

1999-2004		$850	$900

GA-35 RVT Lancer Amp
1966-1967. Black, 1x12", tremolo, reverb.

1966-1967		$450	$550

GA-40 Les Paul Amp
1952-1960. Introduced in conjunction with the Les Paul Model guitar, 1x12" Jensen speaker, 14 watts on early models and 16 watts later, recessed leather handle using spring mounting (the handle is easily broken and an unsimilar replacement handle is more common than not). Two-tone leatherette covering, '50s checkerboard grille ('52-early-'55), Les Paul script logo on front of the amp ('52-'55), plastic grille insert with LP monogram, gold Gibson logo above grille. Cosmetics changed dramatically in early/mid-'55. Renamed GA-40 T Les Paul in '60.

1952-1955	Brown 2-tone, LP grille	$1,200	$1,500
1955-1956	Mottled Gray 2-tone	$1,150	$1,450
1957-1959	2-tone	$1,150	$1,450
1959-1960	Tweed	$1,200	$1,600

GA-40 T Les Paul Amp
1960-1965. Renamed from GA-40 Les Paul, 1x12", 16 watts, tremolo. Renamed Mariner in '65-'67.

1961	Tweed	$1,200	$1,600
1962-1963	Smooth brown	$650	$700
1964-1965	Rough brown	$500	$550

GA-45 RVT Saturn Amp
1965-1967. 2x10", mid power, tremolo, reverb.

1965-1967		$500	$600

GA-50/GA-50 T Amp
1948-1955. Brown leatherette, 25 watts, 1x12" and 1x8", GA-50 T with tremolo.

1948-1955	GA-50	$1,200	$1,800
1948-1955	GA-50 T	$1,300	$1,900

GA-55/GA-55 V Amp
1954-1958. 2x12", 20 watts, GA-55 V with vibrato.

1954-1958	GA-55	$1,500	$1,700
1954-1958	GA-55 V	$1,800	$2,000

GA-55 RVT Ranger Amp
1965-1967. Black cover, 4x10", tremolo, reverb.

1965-1967		$600	$700

GA-70 Country and Western Amp
1955-1958. 25 watts, 1x15", 2-tone, longhorn cattle western logo on front, advertised to have extra bright sound.

1955-1958		$1,500	$1,700

GA-75 Amp
1950-1955. Mottled Brown leatherette, 1x15", 25 watts.

1950-1955		$1,000	$1,200

GA-75 Recording Amp
1964-1967. 2x10" speakers, no reverb or tremolo, 2 channels, dark cover, gray grille.

1964-1967		$550	$650

GA-75 L Recording Amp
1964-1967. 1x15" Lansing speaker, no reverb or tremolo, 2 channels, dark cover, gray grille.

1964-1967		$550	$650

GA-77/Vanguard Amp
1954-1960. Brown tolex, 1x15" JBL, 25 watts, 2 6L6 power tubes, near top-of-the-line for the mid-'50s. Renamed Vanguard in '60.

1954-1958	2-tone	$1,100	$1,400
1959-1960	Tweed	$1,300	$1,500
1960-1962	Vanguard, no reverb	$1,100	$1,400

GA-77 RET Amp
1964-1967. 2x10" speakers, reverb, echo, tremolo.

1964-1967		$550	$650

GA-78 Bell Stereo Amp
1960. Gibson-branded amp made by Bell, same as GA-79 series, Bell 30 logo on front, 30 watts, 2x10" wedge cab.

1960		$2,000	$2,400

GA-79 RV Amp
1960-1962. Stereo-reverb, 2x10", 30 watts.

1960-1961	Tweed	$2,500	$2,800
1962	Gray tolex	$2,300	$2,600

GA-79 RVT Multi-Stereo Amp
1961-1967. Introduced as GA-79 RVT, Multi-Stereo was added to name in '61. Stereo-reverb and tremolo, 2x10", tweed (black and brown also available), 30 watts.

1961-1962	Tweed	$2,300	$2,800
1963-1964	Textured brown	$2,000	$2,400
1965-1967	Black	$1,500	$2,000

GA-80/GA-80 T/Vari-Tone Amp
1959-1961. 25 watts, 1x15", 2 channels, described as "6-in-1 amplifier with improved tremolo," 6 Vari-Tone pushbottons which give "six distinctively separate sounds," 7 tubes, tweed cover.

1959-1961		$1,300	$1,600

GA-83 S Stereo-Vibe Amp
1959-1961. Interesting stereo amp with front baffle mounted 1x12" and 4x8" side-mounted speakers (2 on each side), 35 watts, Gibson logo on upper right corner of the grille, tweed cover, brown grille (late '50s Fender-style), 3 pointer knobs and 3 round knobs, 4 inputs.

1959-1961		$2,400	$2,600

GA-85 Bass Reflex Amp
1957-1958. Removable head, 25 watts, 1x12", very limited production.

1957-1958		$650	$850

GA-90 High Fidelity Amp
1953-1960. 25 watts, 6x8", 2 channels, advertised for guitar, bass, accordion, or hi-fi.

1953-1960		$1,100	$1,400

GA-95 RVT Apollo Amp
1965-1967. 90 watts, 2x12", black vinyl, black grille, tremolo, reverb.

1965-1967		$600	$700

GA-100 Bass Amp
1960-1963. Tweed, 35 watts, 1x12" cabinet, tripod was available for separate head.

1960-1963		$800	$1,000

AMPS

MODEL YEAR	FEATURES	EXC. COND. LOW	HIGH

GA-200 Rhythm King Amp

1957-1962. Introduced as GA-200, renamed Rhythm King in '60, 2-channel version of GA-400. Bass amp, 60 watts, 2x12".

1957-1959	2-tone	$1,700	$1,850
1959-1962	Tweed	$1,700	$1,850

GA-400 Super 400 Amp

1957-1962. 60 watts, 2x12", 3 channels, same size as GA-200 cab, 1 more tube than GA-200.

1957-1959	2-tone	$1,750	$1,900
1959-1962	Tweed	$1,750	$1,900

GSS-50 Amp

1966-1967. Solidstate, 50 watts, 2x10" combo, reverb and tremolo, black vinyl cover, silver grille, no grille logo.

1966-1967		$425	$500

GSS-100 Amp

1966-1967. Solidstate, 100 watts, two 24"x12" 2x10" sealed cabs, black vinyl cover, silver grille, 8 black knobs and 3 red knobs, slanted raised Gibson logo. Speakers prone to distortion.

1966-1967		$450	$500

Hawk Amp

1968-1969. Solidstate, upright vertical cab, faux wood grain front panel, 15 watts, 1x10".

1968-1969		$150	$200

LP-1/LP-2 Amp Set

1970. Les Paul model, piggyback amp and cab set, LP-1 head and LP-2 4x12" plus 2 horns cab, large vertical speaker cabinet, rather small compact 190 watt solidstate amp head.

1970		$300	$425

Medalist 2/12 Amp

1968-1970. Vertical cabinet, 2x12", reverb and temolo.

1968-1970		$400	$450

Medalist 4/10 Amp

1968-1970. Vertical cabinet, 4x10", reverb and tremolo.

1968-1970		$450	$550

Mercury I Amp

1963-1965. Piggyback trapezoid-shaped head with 2x12" trapezoid cabinet, tremolo, brown.

1963-1965		$450	$550

Mercury II Amp

1963-1967. Mercury I with 1x15" and 1x10", initially trapezoid cabinets then changed to rectangular.

1963-1964	Brown trapezoid cabs	$450	$550
1965-1967	Black rectangular cabs	$450	$550

Plus-50 Amp

1966-1967. 50 watts, powered extension amplifier. Similar to GSS-100 cabinet of the same era, 2x10" cab, black vinyl cover, silver grille, slant Gibson logo.

1966-1967		$450	$550

Super Thor Bass Amp

1972-1974. Solidstate, part of the new G-Series (not GA-Series), 65 watts, 2x15", black tolex, black grille, upright vertical cab with front control, single channel.

1972-1974		$300	$375

MODEL YEAR	FEATURES	EXC. COND. LOW	HIGH

Thor Bass Amp

1970-1974. Solidstate, smaller 2x10" 50 watt version of Super Thor.

1970-1974		$275	$350

Titan I Amp

1963-1965. Piggyback trapezoid-shaped head and 2x12" trapezoid-shaped cabinet, tremolo.

1963-1965		$450	$550

Titan III Amp

1963-1967. Piggyback trapezoid-shaped head and 1x15" + 2x10" trapezoid-shaped cabinet, tremolo.

1963-1964	Brown	$450	$650
1965-1967	Black	$450	$650

Titan V Amp

1963-1967. Piggyback trapezoid-shaped tube head and 2x15" trapezoid-shaped cabinet, tremolo.

1963-1964	Brown	$450	$650
1965-1967	Black	$450	$650

Titan Medalist Amp

1964-1967. Combo version of Titan Series with 1x15" and 1x10", tremolo only, no reverb, black.

1964-1967		$450	$650

Ginelle

1996-present. Rick Emery builds his tube combo amps in West Berlin, New Jersey.

Goodsell

2004-present. Tube head and combo amps built by Richard Goodsell in Atlanta, Georgia.

Gorilla

1980s-present. Small solidstate entry-level amps, distributed by Pignose, Las Vegas, Nevada.

Compact Practice Student Amp

1980s-present. Solidstate, 10 to 30 watts, compact design.

1980s		$30	$45
1990s		$30	$45
2000s		$35	$50

Goya

1955-1996. Goya was mainly known for acoustics, but offered a few amps in the '60s. The brand was purchased by Avnet/Guild in '66 and by Martin in the late '70s.

Green

1993-present. Amp model line made in England by Matamp (see that brand for listing), bright green covering, large Green logo on the front.

Greer Amplification

1999-present. Tube guitar amps and speaker cabinets built by Nick Greer in Athens, Georgia. He also builds effects.

1962 Gibson GA-200 Rhythm King

Gibson Hawk

Green amp

1964 Gretsch 6164 Variety

1950s Gretsch Model 6169 Electromatic Twin

1959 Gretsch Model 6169 Electromatic Twin Western

MODEL YEAR	FEATURES	EXC. COND. LOW	HIGH

Gregory

1950s-1960s. Private branded amps sold via music wholesalers, by late '60s solidstate models made by Harmony including the 007, C.I.A., Mark Six, Mark Eight, Saturn 80, most models were combo amps with Gregory logo.

Solidstate Amps

1960s		$100	$250

Gretsch

1883-present. In '05, Gretsch again starting offering amps after previously selling them from the 1950s to '73. Initially private branded for them by Valco (look for the Valco oval or rectangular serialized label on the back). Early-'50s amps were covered in the requisite tweed, but evolved into the Gretsch charcoal gray covering. The mid-'50s to early-'60s amps were part of the Electromatic group of amps. The mid-'50s to '62 amps often sported wrap-around and slanted grilles. In '62, the more traditional box style was introduced. In '66, the large amps went piggyback. Baldwin-Gretsch began to phase out amps effective '65, but solidstate amps continued being offered for a period of time. The '73 Gretsch product line only offered Sonax amps, made in Canada and Sho-Bud amps made in the U.S. In '05, they introduced a line tube combo amps made in U.S. by by Victoria Amp Company.

Model 6150 Compact Amp

Early-1950s-1960s. Early amps in tweed, '60s amps in gray covering, no tremolo, single volume knob, no treble or bass knob, 1x8".

1950s	Brown tweed	$325	$375
1960s	Gray	$275	$350

Model 6151/6151 Compact Tremolo Amp

Late-1940s-late-1960s. 1x8", various covers.

1940s		$350	$400
1950s		$375	$425
1960s		$325	$375

Model 6152 Compact Tremolo Reverb Amp

Ca.1964-late-1960s. Five watts, 11x6" elliptical speaker early on, 1x12" later.

1964-1966	Elliptical speaker	$525	$575
1967-1969	Round speaker	$500	$550

Model 6154 Super-Bass Amp

Early-1960s-mid-1960s. Gray covering, 2x12", 70 watts, tube.

1960s		$450	$500

Model 6156 Playboy Amp

Early-1950s-1966. Tube amp, 17 watts, 1x10" until '61 when converted to 1x12", tweed, then gray, then finally black covered.

1950s	Tweed	$450	$550
1960-1962	Tweed, 1x10" or 1x12"	$450	$550
1963-1966	Black or gray, 1x12"	$450	$550

Model 6157 Super Bass (Piggyback) Amp

Mid-late-1960s. 35 watts, 2x15" cabinet, single channel.

1960s		$400	$500

Model 6159 Super Bass/Dual Playboy (Combo) Amp

Mid-late-1960s. 35 watts, tube, 2x12" cabinet, dual channel, black covering. Replaced by 6163 Chet Atkins Piggyback Amp.

1960s		$450	$600

Model 6160 Chet Atkins Country Gentleman Amp

Early-late-1960s. Combo tube amp, 35 watts, 2x12" cabinet, 2 channels. Replaced by 6163 Chet Atkins Piggyback amp with tremolo but no reverb.

1960s		$500	$600

Model 6161 Dual Twin Tremolo Amp

Ca.1962-late-1960s. 19 watts (later 17 watts), 2x10" with 5" tweeter, tremolo.

1960s		$650	$700

Model 6161 Electromatic Twin Amp

Ca.1953-ca.1960. Gray Silverflake covering, two 11x6" speakers, 14 watts, tremolo, wraparound grille '55 and after.

1953-1960		$650	$700

Model 6162 Dual Twin Tremolo & Reverb Amp

Ca.1964-late-1960s. 17 watts, 2x10", reverb, tremolo. Vertical combo amp style introduced in '68.

1964-1967	Horizontal ombo style	$600	$700
1968-1969	Vertical combo style	$450	$600

Model 6163 Chet Atkins (Piggyback) Amp

Mid-late-1960s. 70 watts, 1x12" and 1x15", black covering, tremolo, reverb.

1960s		$500	$600

Model 6164 Variety Amp

Early-mid-1960s. 35 watts, tube, 2x12".

1960s		$500	$600

Model 6165 Variety Plus Amp

Early-mid-1960s. Tube amp, 35 watts, 2x12", reverb and tremolo, separate controls for both channels.

1960s		$600	$700

Model 6166 Fury (Combo) Amp

Mid-1960s. Tube combo amp, 70 watts, 2x12", separate controls for both channels, large metal handle.

1960s		$500	$600

Model 6169 Electromatic Twin Western Finish Amp

Ca.1953-ca.1960. Western finish, 14 watts, 2-11x6" speakers, tremolo, wraparound grill '55 and after.

1950s		$2,000	$3,000

Model 6169 Fury (Piggyback) Amp

Late-1960s. Tube amp, 70 watts, 2x12", separate controls for both channels.

1960s		$500	$650

Model 6170 Pro Bass Amp

1966-late-1960s. 25 or 35 watts, depending on model, 1x15", vertical cabinet style (vs. box cabinet).

1966-1969		$350	$450

Model 7154 Nashville Amp

Introduced in 1969. Solidstate combo amp, 4' tall, 75 watts, 2x15", reverb, tremolo, magic echo.

1970s		$475	$550

AMPS

MODEL YEAR	FEATURES	EXC. COND. LOW	HIGH

Model 7155 Tornado PA System Amp
Introduced in 1969. Solidstate piggyback head and cab, 150 watts, 2 column speaker cabs, reverb, tremolo, magic echo.

| 1970s | 2x2x15" | $475 | $550 |
| 1970s | 2x4x15" | $575 | $650 |

Model 7517 Rogue Amp
1970s. Solidstate, 40 watts, 2x12", tall vertical cabinet, front control panel.

| 1970s | | $250 | $275 |

Rex Royal Amp
1950s. Small student compact amp, low power, 1x8", Rex Royal logo on grille, Fred Gretsch logo on back panel, single on-off volume knob.

| 1950s | | $200 | $225 |

Groove Tubes

1979-present. Started by Aspen Pittman in his garage in Sylmar, California, Groove Tubes is now located in San Fernando. GT manufactures and distributes a full line of tubes. In '86 they added amp production and in '91 tube microphones. Aspen is also the author of the Tube Amp Book.

Guild

1952-present. Guild offered amps from the '60s into the '80s. Some of the early models were built by Hagstrom.

Double Twin Amp
1953-1955. 35 watts, 2x12" plus 2 tweeters, 2-tone leatherette covered cab.

| 1953-1955 | | $425 | $625 |

Master Amp
Ca. 1957- Ca. 1957. 2-tone tweed and leatherette combo, tremolo, Guild script logo and smaller block Master logo..

| 1950s | | $350 | $500 |

Maverick Amp
1960s. Dual speaker combo, verticle cab, tremolo, reverb, red/pink control panel, 2-tone black and silver grille.

| 1960s | | $200 | $350 |

Model One Amp
Mid-1970s-1977. 30 watts, 1x12" vertical cab combo, reverb and tremolo.

| 1970s | | $150 | $225 |

Model Two Amp
Mid-1970s-1977. 50 watts, 2x10" vertical cab combo, reverb and tremolo.

| 1977-1978 | | $175 | $250 |

Model Three Amp
Mid-1970s-1977. 60 watts, 1x15" vertical cab combo, for bass, organ and guitar.

| 1977-1978 | | $200 | $275 |

Model Four Amp
Early-1980s. Six watts.

| 1980s | | $100 | $200 |

Model Five Amp
Early-1980s. 10 watts, 6.25" speaker.

| 1980s | | $100 | $175 |

Model Six Amp
Early-1980s. Same as Model Five but with reverb.

| 1980s | | $125 | $200 |

Model Seven Amp
Early-1980s. Small amp for guitar, bass and keyboard, 12 watts.

| 1980s | | $125 | $175 |

Model 50-J Amp
Early-1960s. 14 watts, 1x12", tremolo, blue/gray vinyl.

| 1962-1963 | | $150 | $200 |

Model 66 Amp
1953-1955. 15 watts, 1x12", tremolo, 2-tone leatherette.

| 1953-1955 | | $175 | $275 |

Model 66-J Amp
1962-1963. 20 watts, 1x12", tremolo, blue/gray vinyl.

| 1962-1963 | | $200 | $300 |

Model 98-RT Amp
1962-1963. The only stand-alone reverb amp from Guild in the early '60s, 30 watts, 1x12", blue/gray vinyl.

| 1962-1963 | | $450 | $650 |

Model 99 Amp
1953-1955. 20 watts, 1x12", tremolo, 2-tone leatherette.

| 1953-1955 | | $275 | $350 |

Model 99-J Amp
Early-1960s. 30 watts, 1x12", tremolo, blue/gray vinyl.

| 1962-1963 | | $325 | $400 |

Model 99-U Ultra Amp
Early-1960s. Piggyback 30-watt head with optional 1x12" or 1x15" cab, cab and head lock together, tremolo, blue/gray vinyl.

| 1962-1963 | | $375 | $500 |

Model 100-J Amp
Early-1960s. 35 watts, 1x15", blue/gray vinyl.

| 1962-1963 | | $350 | $425 |

Model 200-S Stereo Combo Amp
Early-1960s. 25 watts per channel, total 50 watts stereo, 2x12", tremolo, blue/gray vinyl, wheat grille.

| 1962-1963 | | $650 | $800 |

Model RC-30 Reverb Converter Amp
Early-1960s. Similar to Gibson GA-1 converter, attaches with 2 wires clipped to originating amp's speaker, 8 watts, 1x10", blue/gray vinyl.

| 1962-1963 | | $300 | $350 |

SuperStar Amp
Ca.1972-ca.1974. 50 watts, all tubes, 1x15" Jensen speakers, vertical combo, reverb, tremolo, black vinyl cover, 2-tone black/silver grille.

| 1972-1974 | | $275 | $400 |

Thunder 1 (Model 11RVT)/T1 Amp
Introduced 1965. Combo with dual speakers and reverb, light tan cover, 2-tone tan grille.

| 1965-1968 | | $400 | $450 |

Groove Tubes Soul-O Single (head)

Guild 66-J

1971 Guild Maverick

Guild Thunderstar

Guytron GT100

Harmony H-80

AMPS

ThunderStar Bass Amp
1960s. Piggyback bass tube head or combo, 50 watts.

MODEL YEAR	FEATURES	EXC. COND. LOW	HIGH
1965-1968		$450	$600

Guyatone

1933-present. Started offering amps by at least the late '40s with their Guya lap steels. In '51 the Guyatone brand is first used on guitars and most likely amps. Guyatone also made the Marco Polo, Winston, Kingston, Kent, LaFayette and Bradford brands.

Guytron

1995-present. Tube amp heads and speaker cabinets built by Guy Hedrick in Columbiaville, Michigan.

Hagstrom

1921-1983. The Swedish guitar maker built a variety of tube and solidstate amps from ca. 1961 into the '70s. They also supplied amps to Guild.

Harmony

1892-1976, late-1970s-present. Harmony was one of the biggest producers of guitars, and offered amps as well. MBT International offered Harmony amps for 2000-'02.

H Series Amp
Harmony model numbers begin with H, such as H-304, all H series models shown are tube amps unless otherwise noted as solidstate.

YEAR	FEATURES	LOW	HIGH
1940-1950s	H-200	$275	$375
1950s	H-204, 18w, 1x12"	$150	$250
1960s	H-303A, 8w, 1x8"	$100	$175
1960s	H-304, low pwr, small spkr	$150	$225
1960s	H-305A, low pwr, small spkr	$150	$250
1960s	H-306A, combo 1x12"	$175	$250
1960s	H306C, piggyback 2x12"	$450	$525
1960s	H-400, 8w, 1x8"	$100	$175
1960s	H-410A, 10w, 1x10"	$150	$225
1960s	H-415, 20w, 2x10"	$200	$275
1960s	H-420, 20w, 1x12"	$175	$250
1960s	H-430, 30w, 2x12"	$225	$300

Small Solidstate Amps
Dark covering, dark grille.

YEAR	LOW	HIGH
1970s	$75	$125

Harry Joyce

1993-2000. Hand-wired British tube amps, combos, and cabinets from builder Harry Joyce. Joyce was contracted to build Hiwatt amps in England during the '60s and '70s. He died on January 11, 2002.

Hartke

1984-present. Guitar and bass amps, combos and cabinets made in the U.S. Founded by Larry Hartke, since the mid-'80s, Hartke has been distributed by Samson Technologies. Hartke also offered basses in the past.

1-15B-XL Cab
1994-present. XL Series, 1x15" rated at 180 watts, larger cab, black cover.

YEAR	FEATURES	LOW	HIGH
1990s		$225	$275

4.5-XL Cab
1994-present. XL Series, 4x10" and 5" driver rated at 400 watts, larger ported cab.

| 1994-2003 | | $325 | $425 |

B 30/B 300 Bass Combo Amp
1999-present. Compact practice amp, 30 watts, 1x10", dark cover. Changed to B 300 in '05.

| 1999-2000 | | $125 | $175 |

HA 1410 Bass Combo Amp
1994-2004. Solidstate, 140 watts, 2x10", dark cover.

| 1994-2004 | | $275 | $350 |

HA 2000 Bass Head Amp
1992-2004. 200 watts, tube preamp, solidstate power section, tube/solidstate switchable.

| 1992-2004 | | $275 | $350 |

HA 3500 Bass Head Amp
1992-present. Solidstate, 350 watts, 10-band graphic EQ, rack mount.

| 1992-1999 | | $350 | $400 |
| 2000-2004 | | $375 | $425 |

Transporter Series Cab
1990s. 1x15" cab rated 150 watts, or 4x10" rated 200-300 watts, black cover, black metal grille.

YEAR	FEATURES	LOW	HIGH
1990s	150 watts, 1x15"	$225	$275
1990s	200-300 watts, 4x10"	$250	$325

Haynes

Haynes guitar amps were built by the Amplifier Corporation of America (ACA) of Westbury, New York. ACA also made an early distortion device powered by batteries. Unicord purchased the company in around 1964, and used the factory to produce its Univox line of amps, most likely discontinuing the Haynes brand at the same time.

Jazz King II Amp
1960s. Solidstate, stereo console-style, 2x12", Haynes logo upper right side.

| 1960s | | $300 | $500 |

Headstrong

2003-present. Tube combo amps built by Wayne Jones in Asheville, North Carolina. They also offer a range of replacement cabinets for vintage amps.

Heritage

2004-present. Founded by Malcolm MacDonald and Lane Zastrow who was formerly involved with Holland amps. Located in the former Holland facility in Brentwood, Tennessee, they build tube combo and piggyback amps.

MODEL YEAR	FEATURES	EXC. COND. LOW	HIGH

Hilgen

1960s. Mid-level amplifiers from Hilgen Manufacturing, Hillside, New Jersey. Dark tolex covering and swiggle-lined light color grille cloth. Examples have been found with original Jensen speakers.

Basso B-2501 Amp

1960s. 25 watts, 1x15" combo, swirl grille, Hilgen crest logo, compact size.

1965		$200	$300

Basso B-2502 Amp

1960s. 25 watts, 1x15" combo, swirl grille, Hilgen crest logo, large cab.

1965		$250	$350

Basso Grande B-2503 Amp

1960s. Brown sparkle cover, piggyback, 2x12".

1965		$300	$400

Champion R-2523 Amp

Mid-1960s. Highest offering in their amp line, piggyback with 2x12" cab, tremolo, reverb, swirl grille cloth.

1965		$450	$550

Galaxie T-2513 Amp

1960s. 25 watts, 1x12" piggyback cabinet, tremolo.

1965		$325	$425

Metero T-2511 Amp

Mid-1960s. Compact 1x12" combo, tremolo.

1965		$250	$350

Pacesetter R-2521 Amp

Mid-1960s. 1x12" combo, tremolo, reverb, swirl grille cloth.

1965		$275	$375

Star T-2512 Amp

1960s. 25 watts, 1x12" combo, tremolo.

1965		$275	$375

Victor R-2522 Amp

Mid-1960s. 1x12" combo, larger cabinet, reverb, tremolo.

1965		$300	$400

HiWatt

Bulldog SA112 Amp

1980s, 1994-present. 50 watts, combo, 1x12".

1980s		$1,100	$1,600
1990s		$700	$1,100

Bulldog SA112FL Amp

1980s-1990s. 100 watts, combo, 1x12".

1980s		$1,100	$1,600
1990s		$700	$1,100

DR-103 Custom 100 Amp Head

1970-late-1980s. Tube head, 100 watts, custom Hiwatt 100 logo on front.

1970-1977		$1,500	$2,200

DR-103 Matching Head and Cab

100-watt head, matching SE4122 or SE4123 4x12" cab(s).

1973	Full stack	$4,400	$6,500
1973	Half stack	$3,000	$4,400

DR-201 Hiwatt 200

1970s. 200-watt amp head, Hiwatt 200 logo on front.

1970s		$2,100	$3,200

DR-201 Matching Head and Cab

200-watt head, matching SE4122 or SE4151 cab(s).

1970s	Full stack	$5,500	$8,000
1970s	Half stack	$4,600	$6,800

DR-405 Hiwatt 400

1970s. 400-watt amp head.

1970s		$3,500	$5,000

DR-405 Matching Head and Cab

400-watt head, matching SE4123, SE 4122, or SE 4129 cabs.

1970s	Full stack	$6,500	$9,000
1970s	SE4122 quad	$10,000	$14,000
1970s	SE4123 quad	$9,000	$13,000
1970s	SE4129 quad	$12,000	$16,000

DR-504 Custom 50 Amp Head

1970-late-1980s, 1995-1999. Tube head amp, 50 watts.

1970s		$1,100	$1,650

DR-504 Matching Head and Cab

50-watt head, matching SE4122 or SE4123 4x12" cab(s).

1970s	Full stack	$4,000	$5,900
1970s	Half stack	$2,600	$3,800

Lead 20 (SG-20) Amp Head

1980s. Tube amp head, 30 watts, black cover, rectangular HiWatt plate logo.

1980s		$800	$1,200

Lead 50R Combo Amp

1980s. Combo tube amp, 50 watts, 1x12", reverb, dark cover, dark grille, HiWatt rectangular plate logo.

1980s		$1,000	$1,500

PW-50 Tube Amp

1989-1993. Stereo tube amp, 50 watts per channel.

1989-1993		$800	$1,200

S50L Amp Head

1989-1993. Lead guitar head, 50 watts, gain, master volume, EQ.

1989-1993		$700	$1,000

SA 112 Combo Amp

1970s. 50 watts, 1x12".

1970s		$1,600	$2,400

SA 212 Combo Amp

1970s. 50 watts, 2x12", low production, uses DR 504 chasis in combo form.

1970s		$1,700	$2,500

SA 412 Combo Amp

1970s. 50 watts, 4x12" combo.

1970s		$2,200	$3,300

SE 2150 Speaker Cab

1970s. Veritcal 2x15" cab.

1970s		$1,800	$2,600

SE 4122 (lead) Speaker Cab

1971- mid-1980s. 4x12" Fane speakers, 300 watts.

1970s		$1,600	$2,400

SE 4123 (bass) Speaker Cab

1970s. Bass version of SE, often used with DR103 head, straight-front cab and stackable, black tolex with gray grille, Hiwatt logo plate in center of grille.

1970s		$1,400	$2,100

Hartke B120

AMPS

Headstrong BL 310

HiWatt Bulldog SA112

Holland Lil' Jimi

Holmes Pro 112

Hughes & Kettner ATS-60

MODEL YEAR	FEATURES	EXC. COND. LOW	HIGH

SE 4129 (bass) Speaker Cab
1970s. SE series for bass, 4x12", often used with DR 201 head.

| 1970s | | $2,200 | $3,300 |

SE 4151 Speaker Cab
1970s. SE series with 4 x 15".

| 1970s | | $2,400 | $3,600 |

Hoffman
1993-present. Tube amps, combos, reverb units, and cabinets built by Doug Hoffman from 1993 to '99, in Sarasota, Florida. Hoffman no longer builds amps, concentrating on selling tube amp building supplies, and since 2001 has been located in Pisgah Forest, North Carolina.

Hohner
1857-present. Matthias Hohner, a clockmaker in Trossingen, Germany, founded Hohner in 1857, making harmonicas. Hohner has been offering guitars and amps at least since the early '70s.

Panther Series Amps
1980s. Smaller combo amps, master volume, gain, EQ.

1980s	P-12 (12w)	$70	$100
1980s	P-20 (20w), -25R (25w)	$75	$125
1980s	PBK-20 bass/keyboard (25w)	$75	$150

Sound Producer Series Amps
1980s. Master volume, normal and overdrive, reverb, headphone jack.

| 1980s | BA 130 bass, SP 35, SP 55 | $75 | $150 |
| 1980s | SP 75 | $100 | $175 |

Holland
1992-2004. Tube combo amps from builder Mike Holland, originally in Virginia Beach, Virginia, and since 2000 in Brentwood, Tennessee. In 2000, Holland took Lane Zastrow as a partner, forming L&M Amplifiers to build the Holland line. The company closed in '04.

Holmes
1970-late 1980s. Founded by Harrison Holmes. Holmes amplifiers were manufactured in Mississippi and their product line included guitar and bass amps, PA systems, and mixing boards. In the early '80s, Harrsion Holmes sold the company to On-Site Music which called the firm The Holmes Corp. Products manufactured by Harrison have an all-caps HOLMES logo and the serial number plate says The Holmes Company.

Performer PB-115 Bass Amp
60 watts, 1x15", black tolex.

| 1982 | | $100 | $150 |

Pro Compact 210S Amp
60 watts, 2x10", 2 channels, active EQ, black tolex.

| 1982 | | $100 | $150 |

MODEL YEAR	FEATURES	EXC. COND. LOW	HIGH

Pro Compact 212S Amp
2x12" version of Pro.

| 1982 | | $125 | $175 |

Rebel RB-112 Bass Amp
35 watts, 1x12", black tolex

| 1982 | | $75 | $125 |

Hondo
1969-1987, 1991-present. Hondo has offered imported amps over the years. 1990s models ranged from the H20 Practice Amp to the H160SRC with 160 watts (peak) and 2x10" speakers.

Amps

| 1970-1990s | Various models | $25 | $75 |

Hound Dog
1994-1998. Founded by George Alessandro as the Hound Dog Corporation. Name was changed to Alessandro in 1998 (see that brand for more info).

Hughes & Kettner
1985-present. Hughes & Kettner offers a line of solidstate and tube guitar and bass amps, combos, cabinets and effects, all made in Germany.

ATS MkII 112 Combo Amp
1990-1993. MOS-FET power amp, 2-stage tube channel, transistorized clean channel, compressor, EQ, reverb. Available with 1x12", 2x12", or 4x12" cabs (GL 112, GL 212, or GL 412).

| 1990-1993 | | $250 | $350 |

ATTAX 50 Stereo Amp
1996-2000. 40 watt 1x12" combo, black vinyl.

| 1996-2000 | | $250 | $350 |

ATTAX 200 Stereo Amp
1994-2000. 200 watt 2x12" combo, black vinyl, tube preamp.

| 1994-2000 | | $375 | $475 |

Duotone Amp
2000-present. 50 watt 1x12" tube combo.

| 2000-2004 | | $850 | $1,000 |

Edition Tube Amp
2001-2002. 20 watt 1x12" tube combo.

| 2001-2002 | | $300 | $450 |

Fortress Bass Preamp
1990-1994. Built-in compressor, EQ, tube preamp section.

| 1990-1994 | | $125 | $175 |

Warp 7 Amp
2002-present. 100 watts, offered as head or 1x12" or 2x12" combo.

| 2002-2004 | Combo | $175 | $225 |
| 2002-2004 | Head | $150 | $200 |

Hurricane
1998-present. Tube guitar and harmonica combo amps built by Gary Drouin in Sarasota, Florida. Drouin started the company with harp master Rock Bottom, who died in September, 2001.

MODEL YEAR	FEATURES	EXC. COND. LOW	HIGH

Ibanez

1932-present. Ibanez added solidstate amps to their product line in '98. They also build guitars, basses and effects.

TA Series Amp

Models include TA35 Troubadour (35 watts, 1x10").

2004-2005	TA35	$175	$200

Idol

Late-1960s. Made in Japan. Dark tolex cover, dark grille, Hobby Series with large Idol logo on front.

Hobby Series Amps

1968	Hobby 10	$75	$90
1968	Hobby 20	$100	$150
1968	Hobby 45	$150	$200
1968	Hobby 100	$175	$250

Impact

1963-early 1970s. Based in London, England, tube amps made by Don Mackrill and Laurie Naiff for Pan Musical Instrument Company and their music stores. About a dozen different models of combos, piggyback half-stacks and PAs were offered.

Imperial

Ca.1963-ca.1970. The Imperial Accordion Company of Chicago, Illinois offered one or two imported small amps in the '60s.

Jack Daniel's

2004-present. Tube guitar amp built by Peavey for the Jack Daniel Distillery. They also offer a guitar model.

Jackson

1980-present. The Jackson-Charvel Company offered amps and cabinets in the late '80s and the '90s.

4x12" Cabinet

1990s. Red cone Jackson speakers in slant cabinet with see-thru metal grille.

1990s		$350	$500

Apogee 50 Combo Amp

1980s. Two channels, lead with boost, 2 speakers.

1980s		$800	$950

JG-2 Head Amp

Tube head, 50 watts, 2-stage preamp, midrange boost, presence, effects loop, EL34 tubes.

1980s		$350	$400

JG-3 Head Amp

Tube head, 100 watts, 2-stage preamp, midrange boost, presence, effects loop, EL34 tubes.

1980s		$375	$425

Reference 100 Head Amp

1990s. 100 watts, 3 channels, welded chromate-conversion aluminum chassis.

1994		$300	$375

Jackson Ampworks

2001-present. Brad Jackson builds his tube amp heads and speaker cabinets in Bedford, Texas.

Jackson-Guldan

1920s-1960s. The Jackson-Guldan Violin Company, of Columbus, Ohio, offered lap steels and small tube amps early on. They also built acoustic guitars.

Jay Turser

1997-present. Smaller, inexpensive imported solidstate guitar and bass amps. They also offer basses and guitars.

Jim Kelly

Early 1980s. High-gain, channel-switching tube amps, compact combos and heads, hardwood cabinets available, made by Active Guitar Electronics in Tustin, California, limited production.

JMI (Jennings Musical Industries)

2004-present. Jennings built the Vox amps of the 1960s. They are back with tube amp heads and cabinets based on some of their classic models.

Johnson

Mid-1990s-present. Line of solidstate amps imported by Music Link, Brisbane, California. Johnson also offers guitars, basses, mandolins and effects.

Johnson Amplification

1997-present. Intermediate and professional grade, production, modeling amps and effects designed by John Johnson, of Sandy, Utah. The company is part of Harman International. In 2002, they quit building amps, but continue the effects line.

JoMama

1994-present. Tube amps and combos under the JoMama and Kelemen brands built by Joe Kelemen in Santa Fe, New Mexico.

Juke

1989-present. Tube guitar and harmonica amps built by G.R. Croteau in Troy, New Hampshire. He also built the Warbler line of amps.

Kafel

2004-present. Jack Kafel builds his tube amp heads in Chicago, Illinois.

Kalamazoo

1933-1942, 1965-1970. Kalamazoo was a brand Gibson used on one of their budget lines. They used the name on amps from '65 to '67.

Hurricane V-30 combo

Jackson JG-3

Juke 1210

AMPS

1962 Kay 703

1963 Kay Vanguard 704

Kendrick K Spot

MODEL YEAR	FEATURES	EXC. COND. LOW	HIGH

Bass Amp
1965-1967. Enclosed back, 2x10", flip-out control panel, not a commonly found model as compared to numerous Model 1 and 2 student amps.

1965-1967		$300	$325

Lap Steel Amp
1940s. Kalamazoo logo on front lower right, low power with 1-6V6, round speaker grille opening, red/brown leatherette.

1940s		$150	$250

Model 1 Amp
1965-1967. No tremolo, 1x10", front control panel, black.

1965-1967		$125	$225

Model 2 Amp
1965-1967. Same as Model 1 with tremolo, black.

1965-1967		$150	$250

Reverb 12 Amp
1965-1967. Black vinyl cover, 1x12", reverb, tremolo.

1965-1967		$250	$400

Kay
Ca.1931-present. Kay origianlly offered amps up to around '68 when the brand changed hands. Currently they offer a couple small solidstate imported amps. They also make basses, guitars, banjos, mandolins, ukes, and violins.

K506 Vibrato 12" Amp
1960s. 12 watts, 1x12", swirl grille, metal handle.

1962		$200	$250

K507 Twin Ten Special Amp
1960s. 20 watts, 2x10", swirl grille, metal handle.

1962		$250	$300

Small Tube Amps

1940s	Wood cabinet	$200	$300
1950s	Various models	$150	$200
1960s	Models K503, K504, K505	$120	$175

Kelemen
1994-present. Tube amps and combos under the JoMama and Kelemen brands built by Joe Kelemen in Santa Fe, New Mexico.

Kendrick
1989-present. Founded by Gerald Weber in Austin, Texas and currently located in Kempfner, Texas. Mainly known for their handmade tube amps, Kendrick also offers guitars, speakers, and effects. At the end of '03, Weber quit taking orders for most production amps, but still builds select models. Gerald writes monthly columns for Vintage Guitar magazine and has authored books and videos on tube amps.

118 Amp
1990s. Narrow panel tweed, 5 watts, 1x8".

1990s		$500	$600

2210 Amp
1993-1995. Tweed combo, 2x10", a few were also made from '98-'03.

1993-1995		$1,200	$1,600

2410 Amp
1989-1995. Combo 4x10", a few were also made from '98-'03.

1989-1995		$1,300	$1,800

4212 Amp
1992-1995. Combo, 2x12", a few were also made from '98-'03.

1992-1995		$1,300	$1,800

Baby Huey Combo Amp
1993-1994. Special custom order, 12 made, all but 2 made from a re-manufactured Vox AC 125 chassis with special custom output transformers, a 2X12" cabinet and a Kendrick Model 1000 Reverb. Not a part of the Kendrick line.

1993-1994		$1,500	$2,000

Black Gold Stereo BG-15 Amp
1998-2003. Class A, 2x15 watt output to separate output transformer and speaker.

1998-2003		$1,000	$1,200

Black Gold BG-35 Amp
1997-2003. 35 watts, 1x12" or 2x10".

1997-2003		$1,000	$1,200

Model 4000 Special Amp Head
1990-1993. Solidstate rectifiers, 4 6L6GC output tubes, switchable to 120 or 60 watts, black tolex, only 25 made.

1990-1993		$800	$950

Sonny Boy Amp
1990s. Compact, 2 6L6 combo.

1990s		$1,000	$1,200

Texas Crude Gusher Amp
1995-1998. 50 watts, 2x12" or 4x10" combo.

1995-1998	2x12"	$1,300	$2,000
1995-1998	4x10"	$1,300	$1,900

The Gusher Combo Amp
1996-1998. 50 watt Texas Gusher combo, 1x15", 2x10", or 4x10", a few were also made from 2002 to '03.

1996-1998		$1,300	$1,900

Kent
Ca.1962-1969. Imported budget line of guitars and amps.

Guitar and Bass Amps
1960s. Various models.

1966	1475, 3 tubes, brown	$50	$60
1966	2198, 3 tubes, brown	$60	$70
1966	5999, 3 tubes, brown	$70	$80
1966	6104, piggyback, 12w	$110	$135
1969	6610, solidstate, small	$25	$30

Kiesel
See Carvin.

Kingston
1958-1967. Economy solidstate amps imported by Westheimer Importing, Chicago, Illinois.

Cat Amps
Mid-1960s. Solidstate Cat Series amps have dark vinyl, dark grilles.

1960s	P-1, 3 watt	$30	$45

MODEL YEAR	FEATURES	EXC. COND. LOW	HIGH
1960s	P-2, 5 watts	$35	$50
1960s	P-3, 8 w, P-8 20 w, both 1x8"	$40	$55

Cougar BA-21 Bass Piggyback Amp
Mid-1960s. Solidstate, 60 watts, 2x12" cab, dark vinyl, light silver grille.

1960s		$70	$150

Cougar PB-5 Bass Combo Amp
Mid-1960s. Solidstate, 15 watts, 1x8".

1960s		$40	$55

Lion 2000 Piggyback Amp
Mid-1960s. Solidstate, 90 watts, 2x12" cab.

1960s		$90	$175

Lion 3000 Piggyback Amp
Mid-1960s. Solidstate, 250 watts, 4x12" cab.

1960s		$120	$200

Lion AP-281 R Piggyback Amp
Mid-1960s. Solidstate, 30 watts, 2x8" cab, dark vinyl cover, light silver grille.

1960s		$55	$90

Lion AP-281 R10 Piggyback Amp
Mid-1960s. Solidstate, 30 watts, 2x10" cab.

1960s		$70	$150

Kitchen-Marshall

1965-1966. Private branded for Kitchen Music by Marshall, primarily PA units with block logos. Limited production.

JTM 45 MKII 45-Watt Head Amp
1965-1966. Private branded for Kitchen Music, JTM 45 Marshall with Kitchen logo plate, 45 watts.

1965-1966		$5,500	$6,500

Slant 4x12 1960 Cab
1965-1966. Slant front 4x12" 1960-style cabinet with gray bluesbreaker grille, very limited production.

1965-1966	Black on green vinyl	$4,500	$5,100

KJL

1995-present. Founded by Kenny Lannes, MSEE, a professor of Electrical Engineering at the University of New Orleans. KLJ makes tube combo amps, heads and an ABY box.

Dirty 30 Amp Head
2004-present. Tube amp head, 15/30 watts, switchable A to AB.

2004		$600	$700

Open Back Cabinet

2000s	2x10"	$325	$375

KMD (Kaman)

1986-ca.1990. Distributed by Kaman (Ovation, Hamer, etc.) in the late '80s, KMD offered a variety of amps and effects.

Koch

All-tube combo amps, heads, effects and cabinets built in The Netherlands.

Komet

2004-present. Tube amp heads built with circuits designed by Ken Fischer of Trainwreck fame.

60-Watt Head Amp
2000s. 2 ECC83s, single channel and input.

2000s		$1,600	$1,900

Kona

2001-present. Budget solidstate amps made in Asia. They also offer guitars, basses and mandolins.

Krank

1996-present. Founded by Tony Dow and offering tube amp heads, combos and speaker cabinets built in Tempe, Arizona. They also build effects. The company greatly upped its distribution in '03.

Kustom

1965-present. Kustom, a division of Hanser Holdings, offers guitar and bass combo amps and PA equipment. Founded by Bud Ross in Chanute, Kansas, who offered tuck-and-roll amps as early as '58, but began using the Kustom brand name in '65. From '69 to '75 Ross gradually sold interest in the company (in the late '70s, Ross introduced the line of Ross effects stomp boxes). The brand changed hands a few times, and by the mid-'80s it was no longer in use. In '89 Kustom was in bankruptcy court and was purchased by Hanser Holdings Incorporated of Cincinnati, Ohio (Davitt & Hanser) and by '94, they had a new line of amps available.

Prices are for excellent condition amps with no tears in the tuck-and-roll cover and no grille tears. A tear in the tuck-and-roll will reduce the value, sometimes significantly.

Kustom model identification can be frustrating as they used series numbers, catalog numbers (the numbers in the catalogs and price lists), and model numbers (the number often found next to the serial number on the amp's back panel). Most of the discussion that follows is by series number (100, 200, 300, etc.) and catalog number. Unfortunately, vintage amp dealers use the serial number and model number, so the best way is to cross-check speaker and amplifier attributes. Model numbers were used primarily for repair purposes and were found in the repair manuals.

In many, but not all cases, the model number is the last digit of the catalog number; for example the catalog lists a 100 series Model 1-15J-1, where the last digit 1 signifies a Model 1 amplifier chassis which is a basic amp without reverb or tremolo. A Model 1-15J-2 signifies a Model 2 amp chassis that has reverb and tremolo. In this example, Kustom uses a different model number on the back of the amp head. For the 1-15J-2, the model number on the back panel of the amp head would be K100-2, indicating a series 100 (50 watts) amp with reverb and tremolo (amp chassis Model 2).

KJL Dirty 30

Krank 100 Watt combo

Kustom 36

Kustom Commander

AMPS

Kustom Hustler

Kustom K-25-C

Amp Chasis Model Numbers ('68-'72)

Model 1 Amp (basic)
Model 2 Amp with reverb
Model 3 Amp with Harmonic Clip and Boost
Model 4 Amp with reverb, tremolo, vibrato, Harmonic Clip and Selective Boost
Model 5 PA with reverb
Model 6 Amp (basic) with Selectone
Model 7 Amp with reverb, tremolo, vibrato, boost (different parts)
Model 8 Amp with reverb, tremolo, vibrato, boost (different parts)

Naugahyde Tuck-&-Roll 200 ('65-'67)

The very first Kustoms did not have the model series on the front control panel. The early logo stipulated Kustom by Ross, Inc. The name was then updated to Kustom Electronics, Inc. 1965-'67 amp heads have a high profile/tall "forehead" area (the area on top of the controls) and these have been nicknamed "Frankenstein models." The '65-'67 catalog numbers were often 4 or 5 digits, for example J695. The first digit represents the speaker type (J = Jensen, etc.), other examples are L995, L1195, L795RV, etc. Some '67 catalog numbers changed to 2 digits followed by 3 digits, like 4-D 140f, or 3-15C (3 CTS speakers), etc. Others sported 5 characters like 4-15J-1, where 4 = 4 speakers, 15 = 15" speakers, J = Jensen, and 1 = basic amp chassis with no effects. The fifth digit indicated amp chassis model number as described above.

Naugahyde Tuck-&-Roll 100/200/400 ('68-'71)

Starting in '68, the Kustom logo also included the model series. A K100, for example, would have 100 displayed below the Kustom name. The model series generally is twice the relative output wattage, for example, the 100 Series is a 50-watt amp. Keep in mind, solidstate ratings are often higher than tube-amp ratings, so use the ratings as relative measurements. Most '68-'70 Kustom catalog numbers are x-xxx-x, for example 1-15L-1. First digit represents the number of speakers, the 2nd and 3rd represent the speaker size, the fourth represents the speaker type (A = Altec Lansing, L = J.B.L., J = Jensen, C = C.T.S. Bass), the fifth digit represents the amp chassis number. The power units were interchangeable in production, so amps could have similar front-ends but different power units (more power and different effect options) and visa versa. Some '68 bass amp catalog numbers were 4 digits, for example 2-12C, meaning two 12" CTS speakers. Again, there were several different numbers used. Kustom also introduced the 200 and 400 amp series and the logo included the series number. The catalog numbers were similar to the 100 series, but they had a higher power rating of 100 equivalent watts (200 series), or 200 equivalent watts (400 series).

Kustom U.S. Naugahyde (tuck-&-roll) covers came in 7 colors: black (the most common), Cascade (blue/green), silver (white-silver), gold (light gold), red, blue, and Charcoal (gray). The market historically shows color options fetching

more. The market has not noticeably distinguished power and features options. Condition and color seem to be the most important. Gold and Cascade may be the rarest seen colors.

Naugahyde Tuck-&-Roll 150/250/300/500/600 (c.'71-c.'75)

The amp heads changed with a slightly slanted control panel and the Kustom logo moved to the right/upper-right portion of the front panel. They continued to be tuck-&-roll offered in the same variety of colors. The sales literature indicated a 150 series had 150 watts, 250 had 250 watts, etc.

Naugahyde Tuck-&-Roll SC (Self Contained) Series

Most SC combo amps were rated at 150 watts, with the 1-12SC listed at 50 watts. They were offered in 7 colors of tuck-and-roll. Again the model numbers indicate the features as follows: 4-10 SC is a 4 x 10", 2-10 SC is a 2x10", etc.

Super Sound Tuck-and-Roll Combo Series

The last tuck-and-roll combo amps with slightly smaller tucks. Amp control panel is noticeably smaller and the Kustom logo is in the right side of the control panel.

Black Vinyl ('75-c.'78)

By '75 ownership changes were complete and the colorful tuck-and-roll was dropped in favor of more traditional black vinyl. The products had a slant Kustom logo spelled-out and placed in a position on the grille similar to a Fender black-face baffle. Models included the I, II, III, and IV Lead amps. Heads with half- and full-stacks were available. Bass amps included the Kustom I, Bass I, II, III, IV, and IV SRO.

Black Vinyl "K" logo ('78-'83)

This era is easily recognized by the prominent capital K logo.

Bass V Amp

1990s. Large Kustom Bass V logo upper right side of amp, 35 watts, 1x12", black vinyl.

MODEL YEAR	FEATURES	EXC. COND. LOW	HIGH
1990s		$75	$125

Challenger Amp

1973-1975. 1x12" speaker.

1973-1975	Black	$300	$400
1973-1975	Color option	$450	$550

Hustler Amp

1973-1975. Solidstate combo amp, 4x10", tremolo, tuck-and-roll.

1973-1975	Black	$350	$400
1973-1975	Color option	$550	$600

K25/K25 C-2 SC Amp

1960s. SC (self-contained) Series, small combo tuck-and-roll, 1x12", solidstate, reverb, black control panel.

1971-1973	Black	$350	$375
1971-1973	Color option	$450	$575

K50-2 SC Amp

1971-1973. Self-contained (SC) small combo tuck-and-roll, 1x12", reverb and tremolo.

1971-1973	Black	$375	$425
1971-1973	Color option	$475	$600

MODEL YEAR	FEATURES	EXC. COND. LOW	HIGH

K100-1 Amp Head
1968-1972. The K100-1 is the basic amp without reverb (suffix 1), 50-watt, solidstate energizer head, offered in black or several color options.

1968-1972	Black	$175	$225
1968-1972	Color option	$300	$350

K100-1 1-15C Bass Amp Set
1968-1972. The K100-1 with 1-15C speaker option with matching 1x15" cab, black tuck-and-roll standard, but several sparkle colors offered, C.T.S. bass reflex speaker.

1968-1972	Black	$350	$400
1968-1972	Color option	$600	$750

K100-1 1-15L-1/1-15A-1/1-15J-1 Amp Set
1968-1972. K100-1 with matching 1x15" cab, black tuck-and-roll standard, but several colors offered, speaker options are JBL, Altec Lansing or Jensen.

1968-1972	Black	$300	$425
1968-1972	Color option	$600	$750

K100-1 1-D140F Bass Amp
1968-1972. K100-1 with matching 1x15" JBL D-140F cab, black tuck-and-roll standard, but several sparkle colors offered.

1968-1972	Black	$350	$450
1968-1972	Color option	$600	$800

K100-1 2-12C Bass Amp Set
1968-1972. K100-1 with matching 2x12" cab, black tuck-and-roll standard, but several sparkle colors offered, C.T.S. bass reflex speakers.

1968-1972	Black	$375	$475
1968-1972	Color option	$650	$800

K100-2 Reverb/Tremolo Amp Head
1968-1972. K100 50-watt solidstate energizer head with added reverb/tremolo, offered in black or several color options.

1968-1972	Black	$250	$300
1968-1972	Color option	$475	$550

K100-2 1-15L-2/1-15A-2/1-15J-2 Amp Set
1968-1972. K100-2 head and matching 1x15" cab, black tuck-and-roll standard, but several sparkle colors offered.

1968-1972	Black	$400	$500
1968-1972	Color option	$650	$850

K100-2 2-12A-2/2-12J-2 Amp Set
1968-1972. K100-2 head with matching 2x12" cab, black tuck-and-roll standard, but several sparkle colors offered.

1968-1972	Black	$450	$550
1968-1972	Color option	$700	$900

K100-5 PA Amp Head
1968-1972. 50 watts, 2 channels with 8 control knobs per channel, reverb, Kustom 100 logo located above the 4 high-impedance mic inputs.

1968-1972	Black	$250	$300
1968-1972	Color option	$400	$475

K100-6 SC Amp
1970-1972. Basic combo amp with selectone, no reverb.

1970-1972	Black	$300	$400

K100-7 SC Amp
1970-1972. Combo amp with reverb, tremolo, vibrato and boost.

1970-1972	Black	$350	$425
1970-1972	Color option	$600	$750

K100-8 SC Amp
1970-1972. Combo amp with reverb, tremolo, vibrato and boost.

1970-1972	Black	$375	$450
1970-1972	Color option	$625	$775

K100C-6 Amp
1968-1970. Kustom 100 logo middle of the front control panel, 1x15" combo, selectone option.

1968-1970	Black	$300	$400

K100C-8 Amp
1968-1970. Kustom 100 logo middle of the front control panel, 4x10" combo, reverb, tremolo, vibrato.

1968-1970	Black	$400	$500

K150-1 Amp Set
1972-1975. Piggyback, 150 watts, 2x12", no reverb, logo in upper right corner of amp head, tuck-and-roll, black or color option.

1972-1975	Color option	$425	$500

K150-2 Amp Set
1972-1975. K150 with added reverb and tremolo, piggyback, 2x12", tuck-and-roll, black or color option.

1972-1975	Color option	$600	$650

K200-1/K200B Bass Amp Head
1966-1972. Head with 100 relative watts, 2 channels, 4 controls and 2 inputs per channel, no effects. K200 heads were also offered with Reverb/Tremolo (suffix 2), Harmonic Clipper & Boost (suffix 3), and Reverb/Trem/Clipper/Boost (suffix 4). 1966 and '67 models have the "high forehead" appearance versus normal appearance by '68.

1966-1967	Black	$250	$300
1966-1967	Color option	$400	$450
1968-1972	Black	$225	$275
1968-1972	Color option	$375	$425

K200-1/K200B Bass Amp Set
1966-1972. K200 head with 2x15" cab.

1966-1972	Black	$350	$450
1966-1972	Color option	$600	$875

K200-2 Reverb/Tremolo Amp and Cab Set
1966-1972. K200-2 head with 2x15" or 3x12" cab, available with JBL D-140F speakers, Altec Lansing (A) speakers, C.T.S. (C), or Jensen (J).

1966-1967	Black	$425	$525
1966-1967	Blue	$675	$875
1966-1967	Cascade	$700	$900
1966-1967	Charcoal	$675	$850
1966-1967	Gold	$700	$900
1966-1967	Red	$675	$900
1966-1967	Silver	$675	$875
1968-1972	Black	$425	$525
1968-1972	Blue	$675	$900
1968-1972	Cascade	$700	$925
1968-1972	Charcoal	$675	$900
1968-1972	Gold	$700	$925
1968-1972	Red	$675	$900
1968-1972	Silver	$675	$900

Kustom K-100

Kustom K-100-1-15

Kustom K-150-7

AMPS

Kustom K250-2-15

Kustom K-400-2

Lab Series K5

MODEL YEAR	FEATURES	EXC. COND. LOW	HIGH

K200-2 Reverb/Tremolo Amp Head
1966-1972. K200 head, with added reverb and tremolo (suffix 2).

1966-1967	Black	$225	$325
1966-1972	Color option	$425	$500
1968-1972	Black	$275	$300

K250 Reverb/Tremolo Amp Head
1971-1975. 250 watts, tuck-and-roll cover, Kustom 250 logo on upper right section of control panel, reverb.

1971-1975	Black	$275	$325
1971-1975	Color option	$400	$500

K250 Amp and Cab Set
1971-1975. K250 head with 2x15", tuck-and-roll cover.

1971-1975	Black	$400	$525
1971-1975	Color option	$675	$900

K300 PA Amp and Speaker Set
1971-1975. Includes 302 PA, 303 PA, 304 PA, 305 PA, head and 2 cabs.

1971-1975	Color option	$725	$925

K400-2 Reverb/Tremolo Amp and Cab Set
1968-1972. 200 relative watts, reverb, tremolo, with 6x12" or 8x12" cab, available with JBL D-140F speakers, Altec Lansing (A), C.T.S. (C), or Jensen (J). The K400 was offered with no effects (suffix 1), with reverb and tremolo (suffix 2), with Harmonic Clipper & Boost (suffix 3), and Reverb/Trem/Clipper/Boost (suffix 4). The 400 heads came with a separate chrome amp head stand.

1968-1972	Black	$450	$550
1968-1972	Color option	$700	$925

KBA-10 Combo Amp
Late-1980s-1990s. Compact solidstate bass amp, 10 watts, 1x8".

1990s		$50	$75

KBA-20 Combo Amp
Late-1980s-early-1990s. KBA series were compact solidstate bass amps with built-in limiter, 20 watts, 1x8".

1989-1990		$50	$75

KBA-30 Combo Amp
Late-1980s-early-1990s. 30 watts, 1x10".

1989-1990		$50	$75

KBA-40 Combo Amp
Late-1980s-early-1990s. 40 watts, 1x12".

1989-1990		$50	$90

KBA-80 Combo Amp
Late-1980s-early-1990s. 80 watts, 1x15".

1989-1990		$100	$125

KBA-160 Combo Amp
Late-1980s-early-1990s. Solidstate bass amp with built-in limiter, 160 watts, 1x15".

1989-1990		$125	$150

KGA-10 VC Amp
1999-present. 10 watts, 1x6.5" speaker, switchable overdrive.

1999-2004		$25	$50

KLA-15 Combo Amp
Late-1980s-early-1990s. Solidstate, overdrive, 15 watts, 1x8".

1989-1990		$50	$100

KLA-20 Amp
Mid-1980s-late-1980s. 1x10", MOS-FET, gain, EQ, reverb, headphone jack.

1986		$50	$100

KLA-25 Combo Amp
Late-1980s-early-1990s. Solidstate, overdrive, reverb, 25 watts, 1x10".

1989-1990		$50	$100

KLA-50 Combo Amp
Late-1980s-early-1990s. Solidstate, overdrive, reverb, 50 watts, 1x12".

1989-1990		$75	$125

KLA-75 Amp
Mid-1980s-late-1980s. 75 watts, reverb, footswitching.

1987		$100	$150

KLA-100 Combo Amp
Late-1980s-early-1990s. Solidstate, reverb, 100-watt dual channel, 1x12".

1989-1990		$125	$175

KLA-185 Combo Amp
Late-1980s-early-1990s. Solidstate, reverb, 185-watt dual channel, 1x12".

1989-1990		$150	$200

KPB-200 Bass Combo Amp
1994-1997. 200 watts, 1x15".

1990s		$225	$275

SC 1-12 SC Amp
1971-1975. 50 watts, 1x12" Jensen speaker.

1971-1975	Black	$350	$400
1971-1975	Color option	$450	$600

SC 1-15 SC Amp
1971-1975. 150 watts, 1x15" C.T.S. speaker.

1971-1975	Black	$350	$400
1971-1975	Color option	$450	$600

SC 1-15AB SC Amp
1971-1975. 150 watts, 1x15" Altec Lansing speaker.

1971-1975	Black	$350	$400
1971-1975	Color option	$450	$600

SC 2-12A SC Amp
1971-1975. 150 watts, 2x12" Altec Lansing speakers.

1971-1975	Black	$400	$450
1971-1975	Color option	$575	$725

SC 2-12J SC Amp
1971-1975. 150 watts, 2x12" Jensen speakers.

1971-1975	Black	$400	$450
1971-1975	Color option	$575	$725

SC 4-10 SC Amp
1971-1975. 150 watts, 4x10" Jensen speakers.

1971-1975	Black	$400	$450
1971-1975	Color option	$575	$725

Lab Series

1977-1980s. Five models of Lab Series amps, ranging in price from $600 to $3,700, were introduced at the '77 NAMM show by Norlin (then owner of Gibson). Two more were added later. The '80s models were Lab Series 2 amps and had a Gibson logo on the upper-left front.

MODEL YEAR	FEATURES	EXC. COND. LOW	HIGH

B120 Amp
Ca.1984. Bass combo, 120 watts, 2 channels, 1x15".
| 1984 | | $125 | $175 |

G120 R-10 Amp
Ca.1984. Combo, 120 watts, 3-band EQ, channel switching, reverb, 4x10".
| 1984 | | $250 | $350 |

G120 R-12 Amp
Ca.1984. Combo, 120 watts, 3-band EQ, channel switching, reverb, 2x12".
| 1984 | | $250 | $350 |

L2 Amp Head
1977-1983. Head, 100 watts, black covering.
| 1977-1983 | | $150 | $225 |

L3 Amp
1977-ca.1983. 60 watt 1x12" combo.
| 1977-1983 | | $200 | $300 |

L4 Amp Head
1977-1983. Solidstate, 200 watts, black cover, dark grille, large L4 logo on front panel.
| 1977-1983 | | $175 | $250 |

L5 Amp
1977-ca.1983. Solidstate, 100 watts, 2x12".
| 1977-1983 | | $400 | $450 |

L7 Amp
1977-1983. Solidstate, 100 watts, 4x10".
| 1977-1983 | | $350 | $450 |

L11 Amp
1977-1983. 200 watts, 8x12", piggyback.
| 1977-1983 | | $400 | $600 |

Lace Music Products
1979-present. Lace Music Products, which was founded by pickup innovator Don Lace Sr., added amplifiers in '96. They also offer amps under the Rat Fink and Mooneyes brands.

Lafayette
Ca.1963-1967. Japanese-made guitars and amps sold through the Lafayette Electronics catalogs.

Small Tube Amp
Japanese-made tube, gray speckle 1x12" with art deco design or black 2x12".
| 1960s | Black | $175 | $225 |
| 1960s | Gray speckle | $175 | $225 |

Laney
1968-present. Founded by Lyndon Laney and Bob Thomas in Birmingham, England. Laney offered tube amps exclusively into the '80s. A wide range of solidstate and tube amps are currently offered.

100-Watt Amp Head
1968-1969. Similar to short head Plexi Marshall amp cab, large Laney with underlined "y" logo plate on upper left front corner, black vinyl cover, grayish grille.
| 1968-1969 | | $1,300 | $2,300 |

EA-120 Amp
1990s. 120 watts, 2x10", dark vinyl cover.
| 1990s | | $375 | $400 |

GC-30 Amp
1990s. Compact combo amp, 30 watts, dark vinyl cover, reverb, dark see-thru grille.
| 1990s | | $225 | $300 |

GS-212 2x12" Cab
1980s-1990s. Rated at 150 watts, 2x12", slant front cab, black vinyl cover, metal grille.
| 1990s | | $250 | $300 |

GS-410 4x10" Cab
1980s-1990s. 4x10" speakers, straight-front cab, black vinyl cover, metal grille.
| 1990s | | $275 | $325 |

GS-412 4x12" Cab
1980s-1990s. Straight-front or slant cab, 4x12" rated at 150 watts, black vinyl cover.
| 1990s | | $350 | $450 |

LC-15 Amp
1990s. Compact practice amp, 15 watts.
| 1990s | | $200 | $250 |

MY-50 Amp Head
All tube head, 50 watts, master volume, 4-stage cascaded preamp, active boosts for treble, middle and bass.
| 1980s | | $250 | $350 |

MY-100 Amp Head
All tube head, 100 watts, master volume, 4-stage cascaded preamp, active boosts for treble, middle and bass.
| 1980s | | $300 | $400 |

Quarter Stack Amp
All tube, 2x12", self-contained, sealed back, foot-switchable reverb and overdrive, effects loop, active tone controls with push/pull switches.
| 1980s | | $350 | $400 |

Legend
1978-1984. From Legend Musical Instruments of East Syracuse, New York, these amps featured cool wood cabinets. They offered heads, combos with a 1x12" or 2x12" configuration, and cabinets with 1x12", 2x12" or 4x12".

A-30 Amp
Late-1970s-early-1980s. Natural wood cabinet, Mesa-Boogie compact amp appearance.
| 1980s | | $350 | $475 |

A-60 Amp
Late-1970s-early-1980s. Mesa-Boogie appearance, wood cabinet and grille, transtube design dual tube preamp with solidstate power section.
| 1980s | | $350 | $475 |

Rock & Roll 50 Combo Amp
1978-1983. Mesa-Boogie-style wood compact combo, either 1x15" or 2x12" options, tube preamp section and solidstate power supply.
| 1978-1979 | 2x12" option | $375 | $425 |
| 1978-1983 | 1x15" option | $350 | $400 |

Super Lead 50 Amp
Late-1970s-early-1980s. Rock & Roll 50-watt model with added bass boost and reverb, 1x12".
| 1978-1983 | | $350 | $400 |

Lace 20-watt

Lace RF20T

Laney TT 50H

Little Lanilei

Louis Electric Bluesbreaker

1958 Maestro

MODEL YEAR	FEATURES	EXC. COND. LOW	HIGH

Super Lead 100 Amp

Late-1970s-early-1980s. Rock & Roll 100-watt model with added bass boost and reverb, 2x12".

| 1978-1983 | | $375 | $425 |

Leslie

Most often seen with Hammond organs, the cool Leslie rotating speakers have been adopted by many guitarists. Many guitar effects have tried to duplicate their sound. And they are still making them.

16 Rotating Speaker Cab

1960s-1970s. 1x10" or 1x12" rotating speaker (requires an amp head), black vinyl cover, silver grille, Leslie 60 logo on grille.

| 1960s | 1 cabinet | $350 | $550 |
| 1970s | 1 cabinet | $300 | $500 |

60 M Rotating Speaker Cabs

1960s-1970s. Two 1x10" rotating speaker cabs with 45-watt amp, black vinyl cover, light silver grille, Leslie logo upper left on grille.

| 1960s | 2 cabinets | $550 | $600 |

103 Amp

Two-speed.

| 1960s | | $225 | $300 |

118 Amp

1x12" Altec speaker.

| 1960s | | $250 | $325 |

125 Amp

Late-1960s. All tube amp with 2-speed rotating 1x12" speaker.

| 1960s | | $225 | $300 |

145 Amp

| 1960s | | $450 | $550 |

Line 6

1996-present. Founded by Marcus Ryle and Michel Doidic and specializing in digital signal processing in both effects and amps.

Little Lanilei

1997-present. Small handmade, intermediate grade, production/custom, amps made by Songworks Systems & Products of San Juan Capistrano, California. They also build a reverb unit and a rotary effect.

Louis Electric Amplifier Co.

1993-present. Founded by Louis Rosano in Bergenfield, New Jersey. Louis produces custom-built tweeds and various combo amps from 35 to 80 watts.

Maestro

Maestro amps are associated with Gibson and were included in the Gibson catalogs. For example, in the '62-'63 orange cover Gibson catalog, tweed Maestro amps were displayed in their own section. Tweed Maestro amps are very similar to Gibson tweed amps. Maestro amps were often associated with accordions in the early-'60s but the amps featured standard guitar inputs. Gibson also used

MODEL YEAR	FEATURES	EXC. COND. LOW	HIGH

the Maestro name on a line of effects.

The price ranges listed are for excellent condition, all original amps though tubes may be replaced without affecting value. The prices listed are for amps with fully intact logos. A broken or missing logo may diminish the value of the amp. Amps with a changed handle, power cord, and especially a broken logo, should be taken on a case-by-case basis.

Amp models in '58 include the Super Maestro and Maestro, in '60 the Stereo Maestro Accordion GA-87, Super Maestro Accordion GA-46 T, Standard Accordion GA-45 T, Viscount Accordion GA-16 T, in '62 the Reverb-Echo GA-1 RT, Reverb-Echo GA-2 RT, 30 Stereo Accordion Amp, Stereo Accordion GA-78 RV.

GA-1 RT Reverb-Echo Amp

1961. Tweed, 1x8".

| 1961 | | $400 | $500 |

GA-2 RT Deluxe Reverb-Echo Amp

1961. Deluxe more powerful version of GA-1 RT, 1x12", tweed.

| 1961 | | $800 | $950 |

GA-15 RV/Bell 15 RV Amp

1961. 15 watts, 1x12", gray sparkle.

| 1961 | | $500 | $650 |

GA-16 T Viscount Amp

1961. 14 watts, 1x10", gray sparkle. Gibson also had a GA-16 Viscount amp from '59-'60.

| 1961 | | $400 | $550 |

GA-45 Maestro Amp

1955-1960. 16 watts, 4x8", 2-tone.

| 1955-1960 | | $700 | $850 |

GA-45 RV Standard Amp

1961. 16 watts, 4x8", reverb.

| 1961 | | $1,000 | $1,200 |

GA-45 T Standard Accordion Amp

1961. 16 watts, 4x8", tremolo.

| 1961 | | $750 | $900 |

GA-46 T Super Maestro Accordion and Bass Amp

1957-1961. Based on the Gibson GA-200 and advertised to be "designed especially for amplified accordions," 60 watts, 2x12", vibrato, 2-tone cover, large Maestro Super logo on top center of grille.

| 1957-1960 | | $1,500 | $1,750 |

GA-78 Maestro Series Amp

1960-1961. Wedge stereo cab, 2x10", reverb and tremolo.

1960-1961	GA-78 RV		
	Maestro 30	$1,900	$2,400
1960-1961	GA-78 RVS	$1,900	$2,400
1960-1961	GA-78 RVT	$1,900	$2,400

Magnatone

Ca.1937-1971. Magnatone made a huge variety of amps sold under their own name and under brands like Dickerson, Oahu (see separate listings), and Bronson. They also private branded amps for several accordion companies or accordion teaching studios. Brands used for them include Da Vinci,

MODEL YEAR	FEATURES	EXC. COND. LOW	HIGH

PAC - AMP, PANaramic, Titano, Tonemaster, Twilighter, and Unique (see separate listings for those brands).

Model 108 Varsity Amp
1948-1954. Gray pearloid cover, small student amp or lap steel companion amp.
1948-1954		$250	$350

Model 110 Melodier Amp
1953-1954. 12 watts, 1x10", brown leatherette cover, light grille.
1953-1954		$350	$400

Model 111 Student Amp
1955-1959. Two to 3 watts, 1x8", brown leatherette, brown grille.
1955-1959		$225	$300

Model 112/113 Troubadour Amp
1955-1959. 18 watts, 1x12", brown leatherette, brown grille, slant back rear control panel.
1955-1959		$400	$500

Model 120B Cougar Bass Amp
1967-1968. Initial Magnatone entry into the solidstate market, superseded by Brute Series in '68, 120 watts, 2x12" solidstate bass piggyback amp, naugahyde vinyl cover with polyester rosewood side panels.
1967-1968		$200	$275

Model 120R Sting Ray Reverb Bass Amp
1967-1968. Initial Magnatone entry into the solidstate market, superseded by Brute Series in '68, 150 watts, 4x10" solidstate combo amp, naugahyde vinyl cover with polyester rosewood side panels.
1967-1968		$200	$275

Model 130V Custom Amp
1969-1971. Solidstate 1x12" combo amp.
1969-1971		$150	$200

Model 150R Firestar Reverb Amp
1967-1968. Initial Magnatone entry into the solidstate market, superseded by Brute Series in '68, 120 watts, 2x12" solidstate combo amp, naugahyde vinyl cover with polyester rosewood side panels.
1967-1968		$250	$300

Model 180 Triplex Amp
Mid-to-late-1950s. Mid-level power using 2 6L6 power tubes, 1x15" and 1x8" speakers.
1950s		$400	$600

Model 192-5-S Troubadour Amp
Early-1950s. 18 watts, 1x12" Jensen Concert speaker, brown alligator covering, lower back control panel, 3 chicken-head knobs, Magnatone script logo on front, Troubadour script logo on back control panel.
1950s		$300	$400

Model 194 Lyric Amp
1947-mid-1950s. 1x12" speaker, old-style tweed vertical cab typical of '40s.
1940s		$300	$400

Model 195 Melodier Amp
1951-1954. Vertical cab with 1x10" speaker, pearloid with flowing grille slats.
1951-1954		$300	$400

Model 196 Amp
1947-mid-1950s. Five to 10 watts, 1x12", scroll grille design, snakeskin leatherette cover.
1940s		$300	$400

Model 199 Student Amp
1950s. About 6 to 10 watts, 1x8", snakeskin leatherette cover, metal handle, slant grille design.
1950s		$225	$350

Model 210 Deluxe Student Amp
1958-1960. 5 watts, 1x8", vibrato, brown leatherette, V logo lower right front on grille.
1958-1960		$300	$350

Model 213 Troubadour Amp
1957-1958. 10 watts, 1x12", vibrato, brown cover, V logo lower right of grille.
1957-1958		$550	$600

Model 240 SV Magna-Chordion Amp
1967-1968. Initial Magnatone entry into the solidstate market, superseded by Brute Series in '68, 240 watts, 2x12" solidstate stereo accordion or organ amp, naugahyde vinyl cover, polyester rosewood side panels, input jacks suitable for guitar, reverb and vibrato, lateral combo cab, rear mounted controls.
1967-1968		$275	$325

Model 250 Professional Amp
1958-1960. 20 watts, 1x12", vibrato, brown leatherette with V logo lower right front of grille.
1958-1960		$600	$700

Model 260 Amp
1957-1958. 35 watts, 2x12", brown leatherette, vibrato, V logo lower right front corner of grille.
1957-1958		$950	$1,250

Model 262 Jupiter/Custom Pro Amp
1961-1963. 35 watts, 2x12", vibrato, brown leatherette.
1961-1963		$700	$800

Model 280/Custom 280 Amp
1957-1958. 50 watts, brown leatherette covering, brown-yellow tweed grille, 2x12" plus 2x5" speakers, double V logo.
1957-1958		$1,000	$1,300

Model 280A Amp
1958-1960. 50 watts, brown leatherette covering, brown-yellow tweed grille, 2x12" plus 2x5" speakers, V logo lower right front.
1958-1960		$950	$1,100

Model 410 Diana Amp
1961-1963. Five watts, 1x12", advertised as a 'studio' low power professional amp, brown leatherette cover, vibrato.
1961-1963		$350	$450

Model 413 Centaur Amp
1961-1963. 18 watts, 1x12", brown leatherette cover, vibrato.
1961-1963		$550	$600

Model 415 Clio Bass Amp
1961-1963. 25 watts, 4x8", bass or accordion amp, brown leatherette cover.
1961-1963		$550	$600

Magnatone Model 3802

Magnatone Custom 280

Magnatone 401-A

AMPS

Magnatone Custom 4502

Magnatone 480 Venus

Magnatone Starlite 401-A

MODEL YEAR	FEATURES	EXC. COND. LOW	HIGH

Model 432 Amp
Mid-1960s. Compact student model, wavey-squiggle art deco-style grille, black cover, vibrato and reverb.

| 1960s | | $350 | $450 |

Model 435 Athene Bass Amp
1961-1963. 55 watts, 4x10", piggyback head and cab, brown leatherette.

| 1961-1963 | | $700 | $900 |

Model 440 Mercury Amp
1961-1963. 18 watts, 1x12", vibrato, brown leatherette.

| 1961-1963 | | $600 | $750 |

Model 450 Juno/Twin Hi-Fi Amp
1961-1963. 25 watts, 1x12" and 1 oval 5"x7" speakers, reverb, vibrato, brown leatherette.

| 1961-1963 | | $750 | $1,000 |
| 1961-1963 | Extension cab only | $450 | $500 |

Model 460 Victory Amp
1961-1963. 35 watts, 2x12" and 2 oval 5"x7" speakers, early-'60s next to the top-of-the-line, reverb and vibrato, brown leatherette.

| 1961-1963 | | $800 | $1,100 |

Model 480 Venus Amp
1961-1963. 50 watts, 2x12" and 2 oval 5"x7" speakers, early-'60s top-of-the-ine, reverb and stereo vibrato, brown leatherette.

| 1961-1963 | | $900 | $1,200 |

Model M6 Amp
1964 (not seen in '65 catalog). 25 watts, 1x12", black molded plastic 'suitcase' amp.

| 1964 | | $450 | $500 |

Model M7 Bass Amp
1964-1966. 38 watts, 1x15" bass amp, black molded plastic 'suitcase' amp.

| 1964-1966 | | $450 | $500 |

Model M8 Amp
1964-1966. 27 watts, 1x12", reverb and tremolo, black molded plastic 'suitcase' amp.

| 1964-1966 | | $550 | $650 |

Model M9 Amp
1964-1966. 38 watts, 1x15", tremolo, no reverb, black molded plastic 'suitcase' amp.

| 1964-1966 | | $600 | $700 |

Model M10 Amp
1964-1966. 38 watts, 1x15", tremolo, transistorized reverb section, black molded plastic 'suitcase' amp.

| 1964-1966 | | $700 | $800 |

Model M12 Bass Amp
1964-1966. 80 watts, 1x15" or 2x12", mid-'60s top-of-the-line bass amp, black molded plastic 'suitcase' amp.

| 1964-1966 | | $600 | $700 |

Model M14 Amp
1964-1966. Stereo, 75 watts, 2x12" plus 2 tweeters, stereo vibrato, no reverb, black molded plastic 'suitcase' amp.

| 1964-1966 | | $700 | $800 |

Model M15 Amp
1964-1966. Stereo 75 watts, 2x12" plus 2 tweeters, stereo vibrato, transistorized reverb, black molded plastic 'suitcase' amp.

| 1964-1966 | | $750 | $900 |

Model M27 Bad Boy Bass Amp
1968-1971. 150 watts, 2x15" (1 passive), reverb, vibrato, solidstate, vertical profile bass amp, part of Brute Series.

| 1968-1971 | | $250 | $300 |

Model M30 Fang Amp
1968-1971. 150 watts, 2x15" (1 passive), 1 exponential horn, solidstate, vibrato, reverb, vertical profile amp.

| 1968-1971 | | $250 | $300 |

Model M32 Big Henry Bass Amp
1968-1971. 300 watts, 2x15" solidstate vertical profile bass amp.

| 1968-1971 | | $250 | $300 |

Model M35 The Killer Amp
1968-1971. 300 watts, 2x15" and 2 horns, solidstate, vibrato, vertical profile amp.

| 1968-1971 | | $275 | $325 |

Model MP-1 (Magna Power I) Amp
1966-1967. 30 watts, 1x12", dark vinyl, light grille, Magnatone-Estey logo on upper right of grille.

| 1966-1967 | | $350 | $400 |

Model MP-3 (Magna-Power 3) Amp
1966-1967. Mid-power, 2x12", reverb, dark vinyl, light grille, Magnatone-Estey logo on upper right of grille.

| 1966-1967 | | $425 | $525 |

Model PS150 Amp
1968-1971. Powered slave speaker cabinets, 150 watts, 2x15" linkable cabinets.

| 1968-1971 | | $175 | $225 |

Model PS300 Amp
1968-1971. Powered slave speaker cabinets, 300 watts, 2x15" (1 passive) linkable cabinets.

| 1968-1971 | | $175 | $225 |

Small Pearloid Amp
1947-1955. Pearloid (MOTS) covered low- and mid-power amps generally associated with pearloid lap steel sets.

| 1947-1955 | | $250 | $325 |

Starlet Amp
1951-1952. Student model, 1x8", pearloid cover.

| 1951-1952 | | $300 | $350 |

Starlite Model 401 Amp
Magnatone produced the mid-'60s Starlite amplifier line for the budget minded musician. Each Starlite model prominently notes the Magnatone name. The grilles show art deco wavy circles. Magnatone 1960-'63 standard amps offer models starting with 12" speakers. Starlight models offer 10" and below. Model 401 has 15 watts, 1x8" and 3 tubes.

| 1960s | | $200 | $250 |

Starlite Model 411 Amp
Mid-1960s. 15 watts, 1x8", 5 tubes, tremolo (not advertised as vibrato), art deco wavy grille.

| 1960s | | $200 | $250 |

Starlite Model 441A Bass Amp
Early-mid-1960s. Lower power with less than 25 watts, 1x15", tube amp.

| 1960s | | $375 | $425 |

Starlite Model Custom 421 Amp
Early-mid-1960s. Tube amp, 25 watts, 1x10".

| 1960s | | $350 | $400 |

MODEL YEAR	FEATURES	EXC. COND. LOW	HIGH

Starlite Model Custom 431 Amp
Early-mid-1960s. Tube amp, 30 watts, 1x10", vibrato and reverb.

1960s		$425	$500

Mako
1985-1989. Line of solidstate amps from Kaman (Ovation, Hamer). They also offered guitars and basses.

Marlboro Sound Works
1970-1980s. Economy solidstate amps imported by Musical Instruments Corp., Syosset, New York. Initially, Marlboro targeted the economy compact amp market, but quickly added larger amps and PAs.

3GA-2 Amp
1970s. 3 watts, 1x8".

1970s		$15	$20

GA-3 Amp
1970s. 3 watts, 1x8", trem.

1970s		$20	$30

GA-20B Amp
1970s. Bass/keyboard amp, 25 watts, 1x12".

1970s		$30	$70

GA-20R Amp
1970s. 25 watts, 1x12", trem, reverb.

1970s		$30	$70

GA-40R Amp
1970s. 30 watts, 1x12", trem, reverb.

1970s		$60	$100

Model 1200R Head Amp
1970s. 60 watts, reverb.

1970s		$60	$100

Model 520B Amp
1970s. 25 watts, 1x15", bass/keyboard amp.

1970s		$60	$100

Model 560A Amp
1970s. 45 watts, 2x10".

1970s		$60	$100

Model 760A Amp
1970s. Guitar/bass/keyboard, 60 watts, 1x15".

1970s		$60	$100

Model 1500B Bass Head Amp
1970s. 60 watts.

1970s		$60	$100

Model 2000 Bass Amp Set
1970s. 1500B head and 1x12" cab.

1970s		$60	$100

Marshall
1962-present. Drummer Jim Marshall started building bass speaker and PA cabinets in his garage in 1960. He opened a retail drum shop for his students and others and soon added guitars and amps. When Ken Bran joined the business as service manager in '62, the two decided to build their own amps. By '63 they had expanded the shop to house a small manufacturing space and by late that year they were offering the amps to other retailers. Marshall also made amps under the Park, CMI, Narb, Big M,

and Kitchen-Marshall brands. Marshall continues to be involved in the company.

Mark I, II, III and IVs are generally '60s and '70s and also are generally part of a larger series (for example JTM), or have a model number that is a more specific identifier. Describing an amp only as Mark II can be misleading. The most important identifier is the Model Number, which Marshall often called the Stock Number. To help avoid confusion we have added the Model number as often as possible. In addition, when appropriate, we have included the wattage, number of channels, master or no-master info in the title. This should help the reader more quickly find a specific amp. Check the model's description for such things as two inputs or four inputs, because this will help with identification. Vintage Marshall amps do not always have the Model/Stock number on the front or back panel, so the additional identifiers should help. The JMP logo on the front is common and really does not help with specific identification. For example, a JMP Mark II Super Lead 100 Watt description is less helpful than the actual model/stock number. Unfortunately, many people are not familiar with specific model/stock numbers. VG has tried to include as much information in the title as space will allow.

Marshall amps are sorted as follows
AVT Series - new line for Marshall
Club and Country Series (Rose-Morris)-introduced in '78
JCM 800 Series - basically the '80s
JCM 900 Series - basically the '90s
JCM 2000 Series - basically the '00s
JTM Series
Micro Stack Group
Model Number/Stock Number (no specific series, basically the '60s, '70s) - including Artist and Valvestate models (Valvestate refers to specific Model numbers in 8000 Series)
Silver Jubilee Series

AVT 20 Combo Amp
2001-present. Solidstate, 20 watts, 12AX7 preamp tube, 1x10", Advanced Valvestate Technology (AVT) models have black covering and grille, and gold panel.

2001-2004		$175	$250

AVT 50/50H Amp
2001-present. Solidstate, 50 watts, head only or 1x12" combo.

2001-2004	Combo	$350	$375
2001-2004	Head	$300	$350

AVT 100 Combo Amp
2001-present. Solidstate, 100 watts, tube preamp, 1x12".

2001-2004		$450	$525

AVT 150 Series Amp
2001-present. Solidstate, additional features over AVT 100. Combo (100 watts, 1x12"), Half-Stack (150 watts, 4x12") and Head only (150 watts).

2001-2004	Combo	$650	$700
2001-2004	Half-Stack	$875	$925
2001-2004	Head	$475	$575

Marlboro 560A

Marshall AVT-50

Marshall AVT-150

AMPS

Marshall AVT-275

Marshall Club and Country 4140

Marshall JCM 2000 TSL 100

MODEL YEAR	FEATURES	EXC. COND. LOW	HIGH

AVT 275 Combo Amp

2001-present. Solidstate DFX stereo, 75 watts per side, 2x12".

| 2001-2004 | | $650 | $725 |

AVT 412/412A Cab

2001-present. Slant half-stack 4x12" cab, 200-watt load, 25-watt Celestions.

| 2001-2004 | | $300 | $375 |

AVT 412B Cab

2001-present. Straight-front half-stack 4x12" cab, 200-watt load.

| 2001-2004 | | $300 | $375 |

Club and Country Model 4140 Amp

1978-1982. Tubes, 100 watts, 2x12" combo, Rose-Morris era, designed for the country music market, hence the name, brown vinyl cover, straw grille.

| 1978-1982 | | $800 | $900 |

Club and Country Model 4145 Amp

1978-1982. Tubes, 100 watts, 4x10" combo, Rose-Morris era, designed for the country music market, hence the name, brown vinyl, straw grille.

| 1978-1982 | | $800 | $900 |

Club and Country Model 4150 Bass Amp

1978-1982. Tubes, 100 watts, 4x10" bass combo, Rose-Morris era, designed for the country music market, hence the name, brown vinyl cover, straw grille.

| 1978-1982 | | $700 | $800 |

DSL 201 Amp

1999-2002. 20 watts, 1x12" tube combo.

| 1999-2002 | | $375 | $425 |

JCM 800 Model 1959 Amp Head

1981-1991. 100 watts.

| 1981-1991 | | $900 | $1,000 |

JCM 800 Model 1987 Amp Head

1981-1991. 50 watts.

| 1981-1991 | | $850 | $950 |

JCM 800 Model 2000 Amp Head

1981-1982. 200 watts.

| 1981-1982 | | $900 | $1,000 |

JCM 800 Model 2001 Amp Head

1981-1982. Bass head amp, 300 watts.

| 1981-1982 | | $900 | $1,000 |

JCM 800 Model 2203 Amp Head

1981-1990. 100 watts, master volume, reissued in '02..

| 1981-1990 | | $900 | $1,000 |

JCM 800 Model 2204 Amp Head

1981-1990. 50 watts, 1 channel, 2 inputs, master volume, front panel says JCM 800 Lead Series.

| 1981-1990 | | $900 | $1,000 |

JCM 800 Model 2204S Amp Head

1986-1987. Short head, 50 watts.

| 1986-1987 | | $900 | $1,000 |

JCM 800 Model 2205 Amp Head

1983-1990. 50 watts, split channel (1 clean and 1 distortion), switchable, both channels with reverb, front panel reads JCM 800 Lead Series.

| 1983-1990 | | $900 | $1,000 |

JCM 800 Model 2205 Limited Edition Full Stack Amp

Late-1980s. 50-watt head, 1960A slant and 1960B straight front 4x12" cabs.

| 1988 | Red tolex | $1,700 | $1,900 |

JCM 800 Model 2210 Amp Head

1983-1990. 100 watts.

| 1983-1990 | | $950 | $1,100 |

JCM 800 Model 4010 Combo Amp

1981-1990. 50 watts, 1x12", reverb, single channel master volume.

| 1981-1990 | | $850 | $1,050 |

JCM 800 Model 4103 Combo Amp

1981-1990. Lead combo amp, 100 watts, 2x12".

| 1981-1990 | | $900 | $1,100 |

JCM 800 Model 4104 Combo Amp

1980-1990. Tube lead amp, 50 watts, 2x12".

| 1980-1990 | Black | $900 | $1,100 |
| 1980-1990 | White option | $1,100 | $1,200 |

JCM 800 Model 4210 Combo Amp

1982-1990. 50 watts, 1x12" tube combo, split-channel, single input, master volume.

| 1982-1990 | | $600 | $800 |

JCM 800 Model 4211 Combo Amp

1983-1990. Lead combo amp, 100 watts, 2x12".

| 1983-1990 | | $650 | $850 |

JCM 800 Model 5005 Combo Amp

1983-1990. Solidstate combo amp, 12 watts, master volume, 1x10".

| 1983-1990 | | $300 | $400 |

JCM 800 Model 5010 Combo Amp

1983-1990. Solidstate combo amp, 30 watts, master volume, 1x12".

| 1983-1990 | | $350 | $400 |

JCM 800 Model 5150 Combo Amp

1987-1991. Combo amp, 150 watts, specially designed 12" Celestion speaker, split channel design, separate clean and distortion channels, presence and effects-mix master controls.

| 1987-1991 | | $500 | $550 |

JCM 800 Model 5212 Combo Amp

1986-1991. 2x12" split channel reverb combo.

| 1986-1991 | | $500 | $550 |

JCM 800 Model 5213 Combo Amp

1986-1991. MOS-FET solidstate combo, 2x12", channel-switching, effects loop, direct output, remote footswitch.

| 1986-1991 | | $400 | $450 |

JCM 800 Model 5215 Combo Amp

1986-1991. MOS-FET solidstate, 1x15", Accutronics reverb, effects loop.

| 1986-1991 | | $450 | $500 |

JCM Slash Signature Model 2555SL Amp Set

1996. Based on JCM 800 with higher gain, amp and cab set, JCM Slash Signature logo on front panel, single channel, Slash Signature 1960AV 4x12" slant cab, black.

| 1996 | | $1,650 | $1,750 |

AMPS

MODEL YEAR	FEATURES	EXC. COND. LOW	HIGH

JCM 900 2100 Mark III Amp Head
1990-1993. FX loop, 100/50-watt selectable lead head.

1990-1993		$700	$800

JCM 900 2100 SL-X Amp Head
1992-1998. Hi-gain 100 watt head amp, additional 12AX7 preamp tube.

1992-1998		$700	$800

JCM 900 2500 SL-X Amp Head
1990-2000. 50 watt version of SL-X.

1992-1998		$700	$800

JCM 900 4100 Dual Reverb Amp Head
1990-2000. 100/50 switchable head, JCM 900 on front panel, black with black front.

1990-2000		$800	$900

JCM 900 4101 Combo Amp
1990-2000. All tube, 100 watts, 1x12" combo.

1990-2000		$725	$850

JCM 900 4102 Combo Amp
1990-2000. Combo amp, 100/50 watts switchable, 2x12".

1990-2000		$750	$850

JCM 900 4500 Amp Head
1990-2000. All tube, 2 channels, 50/25 watts, EL34 powered, reverb, effects loop, compensated recording out, master volume, black.

1990-2000		$650	$750

JCM 900 4501 Dual Reverb Combo Amp
1990-2000. 50/25 switchable, 1x12".

1990-2000		$750	$850

JCM 900 4502 Combo Amp
1990-2000. 50/25 switchable, 2x12".

1990-2000		$800	$900

JCM 2000 Series Amps
1998-present. TSL is Triple Super Lead with 3 channels, DSL is Dual Single Lead.

1998-2003	DSL 50 head, 50 w	$800	$850
1998-2003	TSL 100 head	$950	$1,050
2000-2004	DSL 401 1x12 tube combo	$400	$600

JTM 45 Amp Head
1962-1964. Amp head, 45 watts. The original Marshall amp. Became the Model 1987 45-watt for '65-'66.

1962-1964		$12,000	$15,000

JTM 45 MK IV Model 1961 4x10 Combo Amp
1965-1966. 45 watts, 4x10", tremolo, JTM 45 MK IV on panel, Bluesbreaker association.

1965-1966		$9,000	$11,000

JTM 45 MK IV Model 1962 2x12 Combo Amp
1965-1966. 45 watts, 2x12", tremolo, JTM 45 MK IV on panel, Bluesbreaker association.

1965-1966		$11,000	$13,000

JTM 45 Model 1987 Mark II Lead Amp Head
1965-1966. Replaced JTM 45 Amp ('62-'64), but was subsequently replaced by the Model 1987 50-watt Head during '66.

1965-1966		$7,000	$7,900

JTM 45 Amp (Model 1987) Amp Head Reissue
1989-1999. Black/green tolex.

1988-1999		$750	$850

JTM 45 Offset Limited Edition Amp Set Reissue
Introduced in 2000. Limited run of 300 units, old style cosmetics, 45-watt head and offset 2x12" cab, dark vinyl cover, light gray grille, rectangular logo plate on front of amp and cab, Limited Edition plate on rear of cab, serial number xxx of 300.

2000		$3,000	$3,500

JTM 50 MK IV Model 1961 4x10 Amp
1965-1972. 50 watts, 4x10", Bluesbreaker association, tremolo, JTM 50 MK IV on front panel to '68, plain front panel without model description '68-'72.

1966-1967		$9,500	$10,000
1968		$8,500	$9,000
1969		$6,500	$8,000
1970		$5,500	$7,000
1971-1972		$4,500	$5,000

JTM 50 MK IV Model 1962 2x12 Amp
1966-1972. 50 watts, 2x12", tremolo, Bluesbreaker association, JTM 50 MK IV on front panel to '68, plain front panel without model description '68-'72.

1966-1967		$11,000	$15,000
1968	Plain panel	$10,000	$14,000
1969	Plain panel	$8,000	$12,000
1970	Plain panel	$6,000	$10,000
1971-1972	Plain panel	$5,000	$6,500

JTM 50 Model 1963 PA Amp Head
1965-1966. MK II PA head, block logo.

1965-1966		$4,000	$6,000

JTM 50 Amp (Model 1962) Bluesbreaker Reissue
1989-present. 50 watts, 2x12", Model 1962 reissue Bluesbreaker.

1989-1999		$900	$950

JTM 60 Mini Half-Stack Amp
1996. 60 watts, 4x10".

1996		$650	$775

JTM 310 Amp
1995-1997. Tube combo, reverb, 30 watts, 2x10", effects loops, 5881 output sections, footswitchable high-gain modes.

1995-1997		$525	$625

JTM 612 Combo Amp
1995-1997. Tube combo amp, 60 watts, 1x12", EQ, reverb, effects loop.

1995-1997		$525	$625

MG 15MS/MSII (Micro Stack) Amp
1999-2004. 15-watt head, 1x8" slant cab and 1x8" straight cab. MSII, introduced in '02, has 10" speakers.

1999-2004		$275	$325

MG 15 RCD Amp
2000-present. Solidstate, 15 watts, 1x8".

2000-2004		$90	$100

MG100 RCD Amp Head
2000-present. Valvestate Series, made in Korea, 100 watts.

2000-2004		$275	$300

1962 Marshall JTM 45

Marshall JTM 45 Mk II Lead

Marshall Super Tremolo Mk IV

AMPS

Marshal 3005 Silver Jubilee

Marshall 1959 Super Lead

Marshall 1959 SLP Reissue

AMPS

MODEL YEAR	FEATURES	EXC. COND. LOW	HIGH
Micro Stack 3005 Amp			
1986-1991. Solidstate head, 12 watts, 2 1x10" stackable cabs (one slant, one straight). Standard model is black, but was also offered in white, green, red, or the silver Silver Jubilee version with Jubilee 25/50 logo.			
1986-1991	Black	$300	$525
1986-1991	Green, red, white	$400	$600
1986-1991	Head only, black	$150	$175
1987-1989	Silver Jubilee/silver	$450	$650
Mini-Stack 3210 MOS-FET Amp Head with 2x4x10"			
1984-1991. Model 3210 MOS-FET head with two 4x10" cabs, designed as affordable stack.			
1984-1991		$300	$500
Model 1710 Bass Cab			
1990s. 1x15" speaker.			
1990s		$300	$350
Model 1930 Popular Combo Amp			
1969-1973. 10 watts, 1x12", tremolo.			
1969-1973		$2,500	$3,500
Model 1935/1935A/1935B Bass Cab			
1967-1986. 4x12" bass Cab, A slant front, B straight front, models 1935.			
1967-1970	75 w, black	$2,000	$2,500
1970-1979	100 w, black	$800	$2,000
1979-1983	260 w, black	$650	$900
1983-1986	280 w, black	$650	$900
Model 1936 2x12" Cab			
1981-present. 2x12" speakers, extension straight-front cab, black.			
1981-1999		$300	$350
Model 1937 Bass Cab			
1981-1986. 4x12", 140 watts.			
1981-1986		$600	$800
Model 1958 18-Watt Lead Amp			
1965-1968. 18 watts, 2x10" combo, Bluesbreaker cosmetics.			
1965		$7,500	$8,500
1966		$7,000	$7,500
1967		$6,500	$7,000
1968		$5,500	$6,500
Model 1958 20-Watt Lead Amp			
1968-1972. 20 watts, 2x10" combo, tremolo.			
1968		$5,500	$6,500
1969		$5,000	$5,500
1970		$4,500	$5,000
1971-1972		$4,000	$4,500
Model 1959 Super Lead Amp			
1966-1981. Two channels, 100 watts, 4 inputs, no master volume. Plexiglas control panels until mid-'69, aluminum after. See Model T1959 for tremolo version. Early custom color versions are rare and more valuable.			
1966-1969	Black, plexi	$5,500	$7,000
1966-1969	Custom color, plexi	$8,000	$10,500
1969-1970	Black, aluminum	$3,700	$5,000
1969-1970	Custom color, aluminum	$5,000	$6,500
1971-1972	Black, hand-wired, small box	$2,000	$2,500

MODEL YEAR	FEATURES	EXC. COND. LOW	HIGH
1971-1972	Custom color, hand-wired	$3,000	$4,000
1973-1975	Black, printed C.B., large box	$1,400	$2,000
1973-1975	Custom color, printed C.B.	$1,700	$2,200
1976-1979	Black	$1,400	$1,800
1976-1979	Custom color	$1,700	$2,200
1980-1981	Black	$1,200	$1,500
1980-1981	Custom color	$1,500	$2,000
Model T1959 Super Lead (Trem) Amp Head			
1966-1973. Head amp, 100 watts, plexi until mid-'69, aluminum after. Tremolo version of the Model 1959 Amp.			
1966-1969	Black, plexi	$5,500	$7,000
1967-1969	Custom color, plexi	$8,000	$10,500
1969-1970	Black, aluminum	$3,700	$5,000
1969-1970	Custom color, aluminum	$5,000	$6,500
1971-1973	Black, hand-wired, small box	$2,000	$2,500
1971-1973	Custom color, hand-wired	$3,000	$4,000
Model T1959 Tubes & Speakers			
The cost of replacement tubes and speakers for the '66-'69 models.			
1966-1969	New tubes	$140	$160
1966-1969	NOS original tubes	$700	$900
1966-1969	Orig. quad G12M 20w speakers	$1,600	$2,000
Model 1959 Super Lead Matching Half Stack Set			
1966-1981 option. 100 watt head and matching color 4x12" cabinet. Plexiglass control panels made from '65 to mid-'69, followed by aluminum panel. Matching set requires that the head and cab are the exact matching set that came out of the factory as a set. A mismatched set that is of similar color but not built as a set is not applicable for this pricing. As is the case with all vintage amps, the speakers must be the factory original (untouched) speakers.			
1966-1969	Black, plexi, weave	$10,000	$15,000
1966-1969	Custom color, plexi, weave	$14,000	$20,000
1969-1970	Black, aluminum, weave	$7,000	$12,000
1969-1970	Custom color, aluminum, weave	$8,000	$14,000
1971-1972	Black, hand-wired, weave	$5,000	$6,000
1971-1972	Custom color, hand-wired, weave	$6,500	$7,500
1973-1975	Black, printed C.B., large box, checkerboard	$3,000	$4,000
1973-1975	Custom color, printed C.B., large box, checkerboard	$5,000	$6,000
1976-1979	Black	$2,500	$3,000
1976-1979	Custom color	$4,000	$5,000

MODEL YEAR	FEATURES	EXC. COND. LOW	HIGH
1980-1981	Black	$2,100	$2,500
1980-1981	Custom color	$3,500	$4,000

Model 1959 Super Lead Matching Full Stack Set

1966-1981 option. Head with 100 watts and matching color slant and straight front 4x12" cabinets.

1966-1969	Black, plexi, weave	$13,000	$19,000
1966-1969	Custom color, plexi, weave	$19,000	$26,000
1969-1970	Black, aluminum, weave	$9,500	$15,000
1969-1970	Custom color, aluminum, weave	$12,000	$17,500
1971-1972	Black, hand-wired, small box, weave	$7,500	$9,000
1971-1972	Custom color, hand-wired, weave	$9,500	$11,000
1973-1975	Black, printed CB, large box, checkerboard	$4,500	$6,000
1973-1975	Custom color, CB, checkerboard	$7,000	$8,500
1976-1979	Black	$3,500	$4,500
1976-1979	Custom color	$6,000	$7,500
1980-1981	Black	$3,100	$3,500
1980-1981	Custom color	$4,500	$5,000

Model 1959 SLP Reissue Amp Head

1992-present. SLP refers to Super Lead Plexi.

1990s	Black vinyl	$900	$1,000
1990s	Purple vinyl	$1,100	$1,400
1990s	White limited edition	$1,000	$1,300
2000-2004	Black vinyl	$900	$1,000

Model 1959 SLP Reissue Amp Set

1992-present. 100 watt Super Lead head and matching 4x12" slant cab.

1990s	Purple, full-stack, 2x4x12"	$2,500	$3,500
1990s	Purple, half-stack, 1x4x12"	$2,000	$2,800

Model 1959HW

2005-present. Hand-wired, 100 watts, 4x12" slant front 1960HW cab (1/2 stack).

2005-2006	Head & half stack	$2,850	$3,250
2005-2006	Head only	$2,000	$2,200

Model 1960 4x12 Speaker Cabinet

1964-1979. Both straight and slant front. The original Marshall 4x12" cab designed for compact size with 4x12" speakers. First issue in '64/'65 is 60-watt cab, from '65-'70 75 watts, from '70-'79 100 watts. After '79, model numbers contained an alpha suffix: A for slant front, B straight.

1966-1970	Black, weave	$2,700	$3,000
1966-1970	Custom color, weave	$4,700	$5,100
1971-1972	Black, weave	$2,200	$2,500
1971-1972	Custom color, weave	$2,700	$3,000
1973-1975	Black, checkerboard	$1,100	$1,300
1973-1975	Custom color, checkerboard	$2,200	$2,500
1976-1979	Black	$900	$1,100
1976-1979	Custom color	$1,800	$2,200

Model 1960A/1960B 4x12 Cabinet

1980-1983 (260 watts), '84-'86 (280 watts, JCM 800 era), '86-'90 (300 watts, JCM 800 era). A for slant front, B straight.

1980-1983	Black	$700	$900
1980-1983	Custom color	$900	$1,700
1984-1986	Black	$650	$800
1984-1986	Custom color	$900	$1,700
1986-1990	Black	$575	$700
1986-1990	Custom color	$750	$1,700

Model 1960A/1960B JCM 900 4x12 Cabinet

1990-2000. JCM 900 Series updated to 300 watts, stereo-mono switching, A slant, B straight.

1990-2000		$550	$600

Model 1960AHW 4x12 Slant Cab

2005-present. Half stack slant front cab for HW series.

2005-2006		$800	$900

Model 1960AV/1960BV 4x12 Cabinet

1990-present. JCM 900 updated, stereo/mono switching, A slant, B straight front.

1990-2006	Black vinyl, black grille	$600	$700
1990s	Red vinyl, tan grille	$800	$900

Model 1960AX/1960BX 4x12 Cabinet

1990-present. Cab for Model 1987X and 1959X reissue heads, A slant, B straight.

1990-1999		$625	$700

Model 1960TV 4x12 Slant Cabinet

1990-present. Extra tall for JTM 45, mono, 100 watts.

1990-2000		$600	$700

Model 1964 Lead/Bass 50-Watt Amp Head

1973-1976. Head with 50 watts, designed for lead or bass.

1973-1976		$1,200	$1,400

Model 1965A/1965B Cabinet

1984-1991. 140 watt 4x10" slant front (A) or straight front (B) cab.

1984-1991		$325	$400

Model 1966 Cabinet

1985-1991. 150 watt 2x12" cab.

1985-1991		$300	$350

Model 1967 Pig 200-Watt Amp Head

1967-early-1968 only. Head with 200 watts. The control panel was short and stubby and nicknamed the 'Pig', the 200-watt circuit was dissimilar (and unpopular) to the 50-watt and 100-watt circuits.

1967-1968		$3,000	$3,500

Model 1967 Major 200-Watt Amp Head

1968-1974. 200 watts, the original Marshall 200 'Pig' was not popular and revised into the 200 'Major'. The new Major 200 was similar to the other large amps and included 2 channels, 4 inputs, but a larger amp cab.

1968		$3,000	$4,000
1969		$2,300	$3,300
1970		$2,000	$3,000
1971-1974		$1,500	$2,500

Marshall 1960A slant cab

Marshall 1959 HW stack

1972 Marshall 1967 Major

AMPS

Marshall 2060 Mercury

Marshall 1974x

Marshall 3203 Artist

MODEL YEAR	FEATURES	EXC. COND. LOW	HIGH

Model 1968 100-Watt Super PA Amp Head

1968-1975. PA head with 100 watts, 2 sets of 4 inputs (identifies PA configuration), often used for guitar.

1966-1969	Plexi	$3,000	$3,500
1969-1972	Aluminum	$2,000	$3,000

Model 1973 Amp

1965-1968. Tube combo, 18 watts, 2x12".

1965		$9,000	$11,000
1966		$8,000	$10,000
1967		$7,000	$9,000
1968		$5,000	$8,000

Model 1973 JMP Lead & Bass 20 Amp

1973 only. Front panel: JMP, back panel: Lead & Bass 20, 20 watts, 1x12" straight front checkered grille cab, head and cab black vinyl.

1973		$2,000	$2,500

Model 1974 Amp

1965-1968. Tube combo, 18 watts, 1x12".

1965		$5,500	$7,000
1966		$5,500	$6,500
1967		$5,000	$6,000
1968		$4,000	$5,000

Model 1974X Amp

2004. Reissue of 18-watt, 1x12" combo.

2004	1974CX ext. cab	$400	$450
2004	Combo amp	$1,600	$1,800

Model 1987 50-Watt Amp Head

1966-1981. Head amp, 50 watts, plexiglas panel until mid-'69, aluminum panel after.

1966-1969	Black, plexi	$5,000	$6,000
1966-1969	Custom color, plexi	$7,500	$8,500
1969-1970	Black, aluminum	$3,500	$4,500
1969-1970	Custom color, aluminum	$4,500	$6,000
1971-1972	Custom color, hand-wired	$2,500	$3,500
1971-1972	Hand-wired, small box	$1,700	$2,700
1973-1975	Black, printed C.B., large box	$1,300	$1,700
1973-1975	Custom color, printed C.B.	$1,500	$2,000
1976-1979	Black	$1,200	$1,600
1976-1979	Custom color	$1,400	$1,900
1980-1981	Black	$1,100	$1,400
1980-1981	Custom color	$1,200	$1,800

Model 1987 50-Watt Matching Set

Head and matching 4x12" cab, plexiglas control panels from '65 to mid-'69, aluminum panel after.

1966-1969	Black, plexi	$11,000	$17,000
1966-1969	Custom color, plexi	$17,000	$24,000
1969-1970	Black, aluminum	$7,500	$13,000
1969-1970	Custom color, aluminum	$10,000	$15,000
1971-1972	Black, hand-wired, small box	$5,500	$7,000
1971-1972	Custom color, hand-wired	$7,500	$9,000

MODEL YEAR	FEATURES	EXC. COND. LOW	HIGH
1973-1975	Black, printed C.B., large box	$3,500	$5,000
1973-1975	Custom color, printed C.B.	$6,000	$7,000
1976-1979	Black	$3,000	$4,000
1976-1979	Custom color	$4,000	$5,000
1980-1981	Black	$2,500	$3,000
1980-1981	Custom color	$3,500	$4,500

Model 1987 50-Watt Matching Full Stack Set

1966-1981. Head and two matching 4x12" cabs.

1976-1979	Custom color	$5,000	$5,500

Model 1992 Super Bass Amp Head

1966-1981. 100 watts, plexi panel until mid-'69 when replaced by aluminum front panel, 2 channels, 4 inputs.

1966-1969	Black, plexi	$5,000	$6,000
1966-1969	Custom color, plexi	$7,500	$8,500
1969-1970	Black, aluminum	$3,500	$4,500
1969-1970	Custom color, aluminum	$4,500	$6,000
1971-1972	Black, hand-wired, small box	$1,700	$2,700
1971-1972	Custom color, hand-wired	$2,500	$3,500
1973-1975	Black, printed C.B., large box	$1,300	$1,700
1973-1975	Custom color, printed C.B.	$1,500	$2,000
1976-1979	Black	$1,200	$1,600
1976-1979	Custom color	$1,400	$1,900
1980-1981	Black	$1,100	$1,400
1980-1981	Custom color	$1,200	$1,800

Model 2040 Artist 50-Watt Combo Amp

1971-1978. 50 watts, 2x12" Artist/Artiste combo model with a different (less popular?) circuit.

1971-1978		$2,000	$2,200

Model 2041 Artist Head and Cab Set

1971-1978. 50 watts, 2x12" half stack Artist/Artiste cab with a different (less popular?) circuit.

1971-1978		$2,000	$2,200

Model 2046 Specialist 25-Watt Combo Amp

1972-1973. 25 watts, 1x15" speaker, limited production due to design flaw (amp overheats).

1972-1973		$800	$900

Model 2060 Mercury Combo Amp

1972-1973. Combo amp, 5 watts, 1x12", available in red or orange covering.

1972-1973	Red	$1,200	$1,800

Model 2061 20-Watt Lead/Bass Amp Head

1968-1973. Lead/bass head, 20 watts, plexi until '69, aluminum after. Reissued in '04 as the Model 2061X.

1968-1969	Black, plexi	$3,000	$4,000
1969-1973	Black, aluminum	$2,000	$3,000

Model 2061X 20-Watt Lead/Bass Amp Head

2004. Reissue of 2061 amp head, 20 watts.

2004		$1,000	$1,250

The *Vintage Guitar Price Guide* shows low to high values for items in all-original excellent condition, and, where applicable, with original case or cover.

MODEL		EXC. COND.	
YEAR	FEATURES	LOW	HIGH

Model 2078 Combo Amp
1973-1978. Solidstate, 100 watts, 4x12" combo, gold front panel, dark cover, gray grille.

1973-1978		$1,000	$1,100

Model 2103 100-Watt 1-Channel Master Combo Amp
1975-1981. One channel, 2 inputs, 100 watts, 2x12", first master volume design, combo version of 2203 head.

1975-1981		$1,400	$1,700

Model 2104 50-Watt 1-Channel Master Combo Amp
1975-1981. One channel, 2 inputs, 50 watts, 2x12", first master volume design, combo version of 2204 head.

1975-1981		$1,300	$1,600

Model 2144 Master Reverb Combo Amp
1978 only. Master volume similar to 2104 but with reverb and boost, 50 watts, 2x12".

1978		$1,500	$1,600

Model 2159 100-Watt 2-Channel Combo Amp
1977-1981. 100 watts, 2 channels, 4 inputs, 2x12" combo version of Model 1959 Super Lead head.

1977-1981		$1,500	$2,000

Model 2203 Lead Amp Head
1975-1981. Head amp, 100 watts, 2 inputs, first master volume model design, often seen with Mark II logo.

1975-1981		$1,000	$1,200

Model 2204 50-Watt Amp Head
1975-1981. Head amp, 50 watts with master volume.

1975-1981		$1,000	$1,200

Model 3203 Artist Amp Head
1986-1991. Tube head version of earlier '84 Model 3210 MOS-FET, designed as affordable alternative, 30 watts, standard short cab, 2 inputs separated by 3 control knobs, Artist 3203 logo on front panel, black.

1986-1991		$350	$500

Model 3210 MOS-FET Amp Head
1984-1991. MOS-FET solidstate head, refer Mini-Stack listing for 3210 with 4x10" stacked cabinets. Early-'80s front panel: Lead 100 MOS-FET.

1984-1991		$250	$350

Model 3310 100-Watt Lead Amp
1988-1991. Solidstate, 100 watts, lead head with channel switching and reverb.

1988-1991		$550	$600

Model 4001 Studio 15 Amp
1985-1992. 15 watts using 6V6 (only model to do this up to this time), 1x12" Celestion Vintage 30 speakers.

1985-1992		$650	$700

Model 4203 Artist 30 Combo Amp
1986-1991. 30-watt tube hybrid combo, 1x12", channel switching.

1986-1991		$500	$750

Model 5002 Combo Amp
1984-1991. Solidstate combo amp, 20 watts, 1x10", master volume.

1984-1991		$150	$200

Model 5005 Combo Amp
1984-1991. Solidstate, 12 watts, 1x10", practice amp with master volume, headphones and line-out.

1984-1991		$125	$175

Model 5302 Keyboard Amp
1984-1988. Solidstate, 20 watts, 1x10", marketed for keyboard application.

1984-1988		$125	$175

Model 5502 Bass Amp
1984-ca.1992. Solidstate bass combo amp, 20 watts, 1x10" Celestion.

1984-1992		$125	$175

Model 6100 30th Anniversary Amp Head
1992-1995. All tube, 3 channels, 100 watts, EQ, gain, contour, full and half power modes, blue vinyl covering, front panel: 6100 LM Anniversary Series. Listed as JCM 900 6100 in '95.

1992-1995		$900	$1,100

Model 6100 30th Anniversary Amp Set
1992-1995. Matching head with 100/50/25 watts and 4x12" cabinet (matching colors), first year was blue tolex.

1992	Blue tolex	$2,000	$2,500
1993-1995	Purple tolex	$1,800	$2,300

Model 6101 LE Combo Amp
1992-1995. 1x12", 100/50/25 switchable watts, blue/purple cover, limited edition.

1992-1995		$1,300	$1,400

Model 8008 Valvestate Rackmount Amp
1991-2001. Valvestate solidstate rack mount power amp with dual 40-watt channels.

1991-2001		$275	$375

Model 8010 Valvestate VS15 Combo Amp
1991-1997. Valvestate solidstate, 10 watts, 1x8", compact size, black vinyl, black grille.

1991-1997		$100	$150

Model 8040 Valvestate 40V Combo Amp
1991-1997. Valvestate solidstate with tube preamp, 40 watts, 1x12", compact size, black vinyl, black grille.

1991-1997		$275	$325

Model 8080 Valvestate 80V Combo Amp
1991-1997. Valvestate solidstate with tube 12AX7 preamp, 80 watts, 1x12", compact size, black vinyl, black grille.

1991-1997		$275	$350

Model 8100 100-Watt Valvestate VS100H Amp Head
1991-2001. Valvestate solidstate head, 100 watts.

1991-2001		$300	$375

Model 8200 200-Watt Valvestate Amp Head
1991-1998. Valvestate solidstate reverb head, 2x100-watt channels.

1991-1998		$350	$425

1985 Marshall 3210 head

AMPS

Marshall 4101

Marshall 8100 VSH100H head

Marshall Model 2553 50/25 Silver Jubilee

Marshall MS-2

Matamp 1224

MODEL YEAR	FEATURES	EXC. COND. LOW	HIGH

Model 8240 Valvestate Stereo Chorus Amp
1992-1996. Valvestate, 80 watts (2x40 watts stereo), 2x12" combo, reverb, chorus.

| 1992-1996 | | $375 | $450 |

Model 8280 2x80-Watt Valvestate Combo Amp
1991-1996. Valvestate solidstate, 2x80 watts, 2x12".

| 1991-1996 | | $425 | $500 |

MS-2/R/C Amp
1990-present. One watt, battery operated, miniature black half-stack amp and cab. Red MS-2R and checkered speaker grille and gold logo MS-2C added in '93.

| 1990-2003 | | $25 | $30 |

MS-4 Amp
1998-present. Full-stack version of MS-2, black.

| 1998-2003 | | $35 | $50 |

Silver Jubilee Model 2550 50/25 (Tall) Amp Head
1987-1989. 50/25 switchable tall box head for full Jubilee stack.

| 1987-1989 | | $1,200 | $1,500 |

Silver Jubilee Model 2553 50/25 (Short) Amp Head
1987-1989. 50/25 switchable small box head for mini-short stack.

| 1987-1989 | | $1,000 | $1,300 |

Silver Jubilee Model 2553 (short) 2556A (mini)
1987-1989. Short box, 100/50 watt, two 2x12".

| 1987-1989 | | $1,900 | $2,550 |

Silver Jubilee Model 2554 1x12 Combo Amp
1987-1989. 50/25 watts, 1x12" combo using 2550 chasis.

| 1987-1989 | | $1,300 | $1,600 |

Silver Jubilee Model 2555 Amp with Full Stack
1987-1989. Silver vinyl covering, chrome control panel, 100/50 watts with 2 2551A 4x12" cabinets.

| 1987-1989 | | $2,400 | $2,900 |

Silver Jubilee Model 2555 Amp with Half Stack
1987-1989. 100/50 watts, one 4x12".

| 1987-1989 | | $1,700 | $2,200 |

Silver Jubilee Model 2556 4x12 Cab
1987-1989. Cab with 4x12" speakers in 3 brand name options.

| 1987-1989 | | $550 | $750 |

Silver Jubilee Model 2556A/AV 2x12 Cab
1987-1989. Cab with 2x12" speakers with 3 brand name options.

| 1987-1989 | | $450 | $650 |

Silver Jubilee Model 2558 2x12 Combo Amp
1987-1989. 50/25 watts, 2x12" combo using 2550 chasis.

| 1987-1989 | | $1,400 | $1,900 |

MODEL YEAR	FEATURES	EXC. COND. LOW	HIGH

TSL 122 Triple Super Lead Combo Amp
1998-present. 100 watts, 3 channels, 2x12" combo.

| 1998-2004 | | $1,000 | $1,200 |

Martin
Martin has dabbled in amps a few times, under both the Martin and Stinger brand names.

Stinger FX-1 Amp
1988-1990. 10 watts, EQ, switchable solidstate tube-synth circuit, line out and footswitch jacks.

| 1988 | | $100 | $150 |

Stinger FX-1R Amp
1988-1990. Mini-stack amp, 2x10", 15 watts, dual-stage circuitry.

| 1989 | | $125 | $200 |

Stinger FX-6B Amp
1989-1990. Combo bass amp, 60 watts, 1x15".

| 1989 | | $125 | $200 |

Matamp
1966-present. Tube amps, combos and cabinets built In Huddersfield, England, bearing names like Red, Green, White, Black, and Blue. German-born Mat Mathias started building amps in England in '58 and designed his first Matamp in '66. From '69 to '73, Mathias also made Orange amps. In '89, Mathias died at age 66 and his family later sold the factory to Jeff Lewis.

Green GT-120 Stack
1990s. 120 watt GT head with 4x12" straight front cab.

| 1993-1999 | | $1,500 | $2,000 |

Matchless
1989-1999, 2001-present. Founded by Mark Sampson and Rick Perrotta in California. Circuits based on Vox AC-30 with special attention to transformers. A new Matchless company was reorganized in 2001 by Phil Jamison, former head of production for the original company.

Brave 40 112 Amp
1997-1999. 40 watts class A, 1x12", footswitchable between high and low inputs.

| 1997-1999 | | $1,250 | $1,400 |

Brave 40 212 Amp
1997-1999. 2x12" version of Brave.

| 1997-1999 | | $1,450 | $1,600 |

Chief Amp Head
1995-1999. 100 watts class A, head.

| 1995-1999 | | $2,250 | $2,500 |

Chief 212 Amp
1995-1999. 100 watts class A, 2x12", reverb.

| 1995-1999 | | $2,600 | $2,900 |

Chief 410 Amp
1995-1999. 100 watts class A, 4x10", reverb.

| 1995-1999 | | $2,600 | $2,900 |

Chieftain Amp Head
1995-1999. 40 watts class A head.

| 1995-1999 | | $1,600 | $1,800 |

MODEL YEAR	FEATURES	EXC. COND. LOW	HIGH
Chieftain 112 Amp			
1995-1999. 40 watts class A, 1x12", reverb.			
1995-1999		$2,300	$2,500
Chieftain 210 Amp			
1995-1999. 40 watts class A, 2x10", reverb.			
1995-1999		$2,600	$2,800
Chieftain 212 Amp			
1995-1999. 40 watts class A, 2x12", reverb.			
1995-1999		$2,700	$2,900
Chieftain 410 Amp			
1995-1999. 40 watts class A, 4x10", reverb.			
1995-1999		$2,800	$3,000
Clipper 15 112 Amp			
1998-1999. 15 watts, single channel, 1x12".			
1998-1999		$900	$1,000
Clipper 15 210 Amp			
1998-1999. 15 watts, single channel, 2x10".			
1998-1999		$900	$1,000
Clubman 35 Amp Head			
1993-1999. 35 watts class A head.			
1993-1999		$1,700	$1,900
DC-30 Standard Cabinet			
1991-1999. 30 watts, 2x12", with or without reverb.			
1991-1999	Non-reverb	$2,790	$3,100
1991-1999	With reverb	$2,880	$3,200
DC-30 Exotic Wood Cabinet Option			
1995-1999. 30 watts, 2x12", gold plating, limited production.			
1995-1999	Non-reverb	$4,770	$5,300
1995-1999	With reverb	$5,220	$5,800
EB115 Bass Cabinet			
1997-1999. 1x15" bass speaker cabinet.			
1997-1999		$400	$450
EB410 Bass Cabinet			
1997-1999. 4x10" bass speaker cabinet.			
1997-1999		$450	$500
ES/1012 Cabinet			
1993-1999. 2x10" and 2x12" speaker cabinet.			
1993-1999		$650	$750
ES/210 Cabinet			
1993-1999. 2x10" speaker cabinet.			
1993-1999		$500	$600
ES/410 Cabinet			
1993-1999. 4x10" speaker cabinet.			
1990s		$600	$700
ES/412 Cabinet			
1993-1999. 4x12" speaker cabinet.			
1993-1999		$650	$750
ES/D Cabinet			
1993-1999. 2x12" speaker cabinet.			
1993-1999		$550	$650
ES/S Cabinet			
1991-1999. 1x12" speaker cabinet.			
1991-1999		$450	$550
HC-30 Amp Head			
1991-1999. The first model offered by Matchless, 30 watts class A head.			
1991-1999		$2,100	$2,400
Hurricane Amp Head			
1997. 15 watts class A head.			
1997		$1,100	$1,200

MODEL YEAR	FEATURES	EXC. COND. LOW	HIGH
Hurricane 112 Amp			
1994-1997. 15 watts class A, 1x12".			
1994-1997		$1,300	$1,400
Hurricane 210 Amp			
1996-1997. 15 watts class A, 2x10".			
1996-1997		$1,300	$1,400
JJ-30 112 John Jorgensen Amp			
1997-1999. 30 watts, DC-30 chasis with reverb and tremolo, 1x12" Celestion 30, offered in white, blue, gray sparkle tolex or black.			
1997-1999		$4,000	$5,000
Lightning 15 Amp Head			
1997. 15 watts class A head.			
1997		$1,100	$1,200
Lightning 15 112 Amp			
1994-1999. 15 watts class A, 1x12".			
1994-1999	Non-reverb	$1,300	$1,500
1997-1999	With reverb	$1,600	$1,800
Lightning 15 210 Amp			
1996-1997. 15 watts class A, 2x10".			
1996-1997	Non-reverb	$1,700	$1,900
1997	With reverb	$1,800	$2,100
Lightning 15 212 Amp			
1996-1997. 15 watts class A, 2x12".			
1996-1997	Non-reverb	$1,800	$2,000
1997	With reverb	$2,000	$2,300
SC-30 Standard Cabinet Amp			
1991-1999. 30 watts class A, 1x12".			
1991-1999	Non-reverb	$2,500	$2,800
1991-1999	With reverb	$2,800	$3,100
SC-30 Exotic Wood Cabinet Amp			
1995-1999. 30 watts class A, 1x12", gold plating, limited production.			
1995-1999	Non-reverb	$4,500	$5,000
1995-1999	With reverb	$5,000	$5,500
Skyliner Reverb 15 112 Amp			
1998-1999. 15 watts, 2 channels, 1x12".			
1998-1999		$1,000	$1,100
Skyliner Reverb 15 210 Amp			
1998-1999. 15 watts, 2 channels, 2x10".			
1998-1999		$1,000	$1,100
Spitfire 15 Amp Head			
1997. 15 watts, head.			
1997		$1,000	$1,100
Spitfire 15 112 Amp			
1994-1997. 15 watts, 1x12".			
1994-1997		$1,100	$1,200
Spitfire 15 210 Amp			
1996-1997. 15 watts, 2x10".			
1996-1997		$1,300	$1,400
Starliner 40 212 Amp			
1999. 40 watts, 2x12".			
1999		$1,400	$1,600
Superchief 120 Amp Head			
1994-1999. 120 watts, class A head.			
1994-1999		$1,800	$2,000
TC-30 Standard Cabinet			
1991-1999. 30 watts, 2x10" class A, low production numbers makes value approximate with DC-30.			
1991-1999	Non-reverb	$2,500	$2,800
1991-1999	With reverb	$3,000	$3,300

Matchless Chief 410

Matchless Lightning 15

Matchless Spitfire 112

AMPS

To get the most from this book, be sure to read "Using *The Guide*" in the introduction.

AMPS

1997 Matchless Thunderchief

Maven Peal Zeetz 0.5>50

Mesa-Boogie F-30

MODEL YEAR	FEATURES	EXC. COND. LOW	HIGH

TC-30 Exotic Wood Cabinet Option
1991-1999. 30 watts, 2x10" class A, limited production.

| 1991-1999 | Non-reverb | $4,800 | $5,300 |
| 1991-1999 | With reverb | $5,200 | $5,800 |

Thunderchief Bass Amp Head
1994-1999. 200 watts, class A bass head.

| 1994-1999 | | $1,100 | $1,700 |

Thunderman 100 Bass Combo Amp
1997-1998. 100 watts, 1x15" in portaflex-style flip-top cab.

| 1997-1998 | | $1,400 | $1,900 |

Tornado 15 112 Amp
1994-1995. Compact, 15 watts, 1x12", 2-tone covering, simple controls--volume, tone, tremolo speed, tremolo depth.

| 1994-1995 | | $900 | $1,000 |

Maven Peal
1999-present. Amps, combos and cabinets built by David Zimmerman in Plainfield, Vermont (the name stands for "expert sound"). Serial number format is by amp wattage and sequential build; for example, 15-watt amp 15-001, 30-watt 30-001, and 50-watt 50-001with the 001 indicating the first amp built. S = Silver Series, no alpha = Gold Series.

Mega Amplifiers
Budget and intermediate grade, production, solidstate and tube amps from Guitar Jones, Inc. of Pomona, California.

Merlin
Rack mount bass heads built in Germany by Musician Sound Design. They also offer the MSD guitar effects.

Mesa-Boogie
1971-present. Founded by Randall Smith in San Francisco, California. Circuits styled on high-gain Fender-based chassis designs, ushering in the compact high-gain amp market. The following serial number information and specs courtesy of Mesa Engineering.

.50 Caliber/.50 Caliber+ Amp Head
Jan. 1987-Dec. 1988, 1992-1993. Serial numbers: SS3100 - SS11,499. Mesa Engineering calls it Caliber .50. Tube head amp, 50 watts, 5-band EQ, effects loop. Called the .50 Caliber Plus in '92 and '93.

| 1987-1988 | Caliber | $450 | $500 |
| 1992-1993 | Caliber+ | $450 | $500 |

.50 Caliber+ Combo Amp
Dec. 1988-Oct.1993. Serial numbers FP11,550 - FP29,080. 50 watts, 1x12" combo amp.

| 1988-1993 | | $500 | $600 |

20/20 Amp
Jun. 1995-present. Serial numbers: TT-01. 20-22 watts per channel.

| 1995-2004 | | $550 | $650 |

50/50 (Fifty/Fifty) Amp
May 1989-2001. Serial numbers: FF001-. 100 watts total power, 50 watts per channel, front panel reads Fifty/Fifty, contains 4 6L6 power tubes.

| 1989-2001 | | $600 | $700 |

395 Amp
Feb. 1991-Apr. 1992. Serial numbers: S2572 - S3237.

| 1991-1992 | | $600 | $650 |

Bass 400/Bass 400+ Amp Head
Aug. 1989-Aug. 1990. Serial numbers: B001-B1200. About 500 watts using 12 5881 power tubes. Replaced by 400+ Aug.1990-present, serial numbers: B1200- . Update change to 7-band EQ at serial number B1677.

| 1989-1990 | Bass 400 | $700 | $900 |
| 1990-1999 | Bass 400+ | $700 | $900 |

Blue Angel Series Amp
Jun. 1994-2004. Serial numbers BA01-. Lower power combos.

| 1994-2004 | 4x10" | $600 | $700 |

Buster Bass Amp Head
Dec. 1997-Jan. 2001. Serial numbers: BS-1-999. 200 watts via 6 6L6 power tubes.

| 1997-2001 | | $550 | $650 |

Buster Bass Combo Amp
1999-2001. 200 watts, 2x10", wedge cabinet, black vinyl, metal grille.

| 1999-2001 | | $600 | $725 |

Coliseum 300 Amp
Oct. 1997-2000. Serial numbers: COL-01 - COL-132. 200 watts/channel, 12 6L6 power tubes, rack mount.

| 1997-2000 | | $900 | $1,000 |

D-180 Amp Head
Jul. 1982-Dec. 1985. Serial numbers: D001-D681. All tube head amp, 200 watts, preamp, switchable.

| 1982-1985 | | $600 | $700 |

DC-3 Amp
Sep. 1994-Jan. 1999. Serial numbers: DC3-001 - DC3-4523. 35 watts, 1x12".

| 1994-1999 | | $550 | $750 |

DC-5 Amp
Oct. 1993-Jan. 1999. Serial numbers: DC1024 - DC31,941. 50-watt head, 1x12" combo.

| 1993-1999 | | $650 | $800 |

DC-10 Amp Head
May 1996-Jan. 1999. Serial numbers: DCX-001 - DCX-999. Dirty/Clean (DC) 60 or 100 watts (6L6s).

| 1996-1999 | | $700 | $850 |

Diesel Bass Cabinets
1994-2003. Designation for regular vinyl covered bass cabs after heavy-duty RoadReady cab option becomes available. Replaced by PowerHouse series.

| 1994-2003 | 1x15" bass cab | $300 | $400 |

F-50 Amp
2002-present. Combo, 50 watts, 1x12", AB 2 6L6 power.

| 2002-2004 | | $800 | $850 |

MODEL YEAR	FEATURES	EXC. COND. LOW	HIGH

Formula Preamp
Jul. 1998-2002. Serial numbers: F-01. Used 5 12AX7 tubes, 3 channels.

1998-2000		$450	$550

Heartbreaker Amp
Jun. 1996-2001. Serial numbers: HRT-01. 60 to 100 watts switchable, 2x12" combo, designed to switch-out 6L6s, EL34s or the lower powered 6V6s in the power section, switchable solidstate or tube rectifier.

1996-2001		$1,050	$1,150

Lonestar Series Amp
2004-present. Designed by founder Randall Smith with Doug West with focus on boutique-type amp. Class A (EL84) or AB (4 6L6) circuits, long or short head, 1x12" combo, 2x12" combo, and short head 4x10" cab, and long head 4x12" cab.

2004-2006	1x12" combo	$1,100	$1,400
2004-2006	2x12" combo	$1,200	$1,500
2004-2006	4x12"	$600	$750
2004-2006	Head, class A	$1,050	$1,300
2004-2006	Head, Class AB	$1,000	$1,250

M-180 Amp
Apr. 1982-Jan. 1986. Serial numbers: M001-M275.

1982-1986		$550	$650

M-2000 Amp
Jun. 1995-2003. Serial numbers: B2K-01.

1995-2003		$600	$700

Mark I Combo (Model A) Amp
1971-1978. The original Boogie amp, not called the Mark I until the Mark II was issued, 60 or 100 watts, 1x12", Model A serial numbers: 1-2999, very early serial numbers 1-299 had 1x15".

1971-1972	1x15"	$900	$1,150
1971-1978	1x12"	$900	$1,150

Mark I Reissue Amp
Nov. 1989-present. Serial numbers: H001- . 100 watts, 1x12", reissue features include figured maple cab and wicker grille.

2000-2004		$650	$800

Mark II Combo Amp
1978-1980. Late-'78 1x12", serial numbers: 3000-5574. Effective Aug.'80 1x15", serial numbers: 300-559 until Mark II B replaced.

1978-1980	1x12"	$900	$1,150
1978-1980	1x15"	$900	$1,150

Mark II B Amp Head
Head only.

1981-1983		$700	$900

Mark II B Combo Amp
1980-1983. Effective Aug. '80 1x12" models, serial numbers 5575 - 110000. May '83 1x15" models, serial numbers 560 - 11000. The 300 series serial numbers K1 - K336.

1981-1983	1x12"	$900	$1,150
1981-1983	1x15"	$900	$1,150

Mark II C/Mark II C+ Amp
May 1983-Mar. 1985. Serial numbers 11001 - 14999 for 60 watts, 1x15", offered with optional white tolex cover. 300 series serial numbers after C+ are in the series K337 - K422.

1983-1985		$1,200	$1,600
1983-1985	White tolex	$1,200	$1,600

Mark II C+ Head Amp
1983-1985. 60-watt head.

1983-1985		$700	$1,000

Mark III Amp Head
1985-1999. 100 watts, black vinyl.

1985-1990		$850	$1,000
1990-1999	Graphic EQ model	$950	$1,050

Mark III 1x12 Cab
Late-1980s-early-1990s. Typically sized 1x12" extension cab with open half back, black vinyl, black grille, not strictly for Mark III, usable for any Boogie with matching output specs, rated for 90 watts.

1988-1990s		$300	$400

Mark III 4x12 Cab
Late-1980s-early-1990s. Half stack 4x12" slant cab with open half back or straight-front cab, not strictly for Mark III, usable for any Boogie with matching output specs, often loaded with Celestion Vintage 30s, small weave grille (not see-thru crossing strips).

1988-1990s	Slant or straight	$650	$750

Mark III Combo Amp
Mar. 1985-Feb. 1999. Serial numbers: 15,000 - 28,384. 300 series serialization K500- . Graphic equalizer only Mark III since Aug.'90, 100 watts, 1x12" combo. Custom cover or exotic hardwood cab will bring more than standard vinyl cover cab.

1985-1990	Black	$900	$1,100
1985-1990	Custom color	$1,000	$1,800
1985-1991	Custom hardwood cab	$1,000	$2,000
1990-1999	Graphic EQ, hardwood cab	$1,000	$2,000
1990-1999	Graphic EQ, standard cab	$900	$1,100

Mark IV Head and Half Stack Amp Set
1991-present. Mark IV head and matching 4x12" slant half stack cab.

1991-2004		$1,700	$1,900

Mark IV/Mark IV B Combo Amp
May 1990-present. Changed to Model IV B Feb.'95, serial numbers: IV001. Clean rhythm, crunch rhythm and lead modes, 40 watts, EQ, 3-spring reverb, dual effects loops, digital footswitching.

1991-1999		$1,300	$1,500
1991-1999	Custom hardwood cab	$1,400	$1,900
2000-2004		$1,300	$1,500

Mark IV (rack mount) Amp Head
1999-present.

1999-2004		$1,300	$1,500

Maverick Amp Head
1994-present. 35 watts, Dual Rectifier head, white/blond vinyl cover.

1994-2004		$600	$750

Maverick Half Stack Amp Set
Apr. 1994-present. Serial numbers: MAV001- . 35 watts, Dual Rectifier head and half stack cab set.

1994-2004		$1,250	$1,450

Mesa-Boogie Mk 1

Mesa-Boogie Mk II B

Mesa-Boogie Mk IV B reissue

AMPS

Mesa-Boogie Nomad 45

Mesa-Boogie Nomad 100

*1984 Mesa-Boogie
Son of Boogie*

MODEL YEAR	FEATURES	EXC. COND. LOW	HIGH

Maverick Combo Amp
1997-present. Dual channels, 4 EL84s, 35 watts, 1x12" or 2x12" combo amp, 5AR4 tube rectifier, cream vinyl covering. Serial number: MAV. Also available as head.

1997-2004	1x12"	$650	$850
1997-2004	2x12"	$700	$900

M-Pulse 360 Amp
Jul. 2001-2005. Serial numbers: MP3-01- . Rack mount, silver panel.

2001-2004		$650	$750

M-Pulse 600 Amp
Apr. 2001-present. Serial numbers: MP6-01- . Rack mount bass with 600 watts, tube preamp.

2001-2004		$800	$950

Nomad 45 Combo Amp
Jul. 1999-present. Serial numbers: NM45-01. 45 watts, 1x12, 2x12" or 4x10" combo, dark vinyl cover, dark grille.

1999-2004	1x12"	$750	$850
1999-2004	2x12"	$800	$900
1999-2004	4x10"	$900	$1,000

Nomad 55 Combo Amp
Jul. 1999-2004. Serial numbers: NM55-01. 55 watts, 1x12", 2x12" or 4x10" combo.

1999-2004	1x12"	$900	$1,000
1999-2004	2x12"	$1,000	$1,100

Nomad 100 Amp Head
Jul. 1999-present. 100 watts, black cover, black grille.

1999-2004		$850	$1,000

Nomad 100 Combo Amp
Jul. 1999-present. 100 watts, 1x12" or 2x12" combo, black cover, black grille.

1999-2004	1x12"	$1,000	$1,100
1999-2004	2x12"	$1,100	$1,200

Powerhouse Series Bass Cabinets
2004-present.

2004-2005	1x15", 400 watts	$350	$400
2004-2005	2x10", 600 watts	$400	$450
2004-2005	4x10", 600 watts	$450	$500

Princeton Boost Fender Conversion
1970. Fender Princeton modified by Randall Smith, Boogie badge logo instead of the Fender blackface logo on upper left corner of the grille. About 300 amps were modified and were one of the early mods that became Mesa-Boogie.

1970		$2,000	$2,500

Quad Preamp
Sep. 1987-1992. Serial numbers: Q001-Q2857. Optional Quad with FU2-A footswitch Aug.'90-Jan.'92, serial numbers: Q2022 - Q2857.

1987-1992	Without footswitch	$450	$550
1990-1992	With footswitch	$600	$650

Recto Recording Preamp
2004-present. Rack mount preamp.

2004		$800	$850

Rect-O-Verb Combo Amp
Dec.1998-present. Serial numbers R50- . 50 watts, 1x12", black vinyl cover, black grille.

1998-2004		$900	$975

Rect-O-Verb I Amp Head
Dec. 1998-2001. Serial numbers: R50-. 50 watts, head with 2 6L6 power tubes, upgraded Apr.'01 to II Series.

1998-2001		$600	$800

Rect-O-Verb II Amp Head
Apr. 2001-present. Upgrade, serial number R5H-750.

2001-2004		$600	$800

Rect-O-Verb II Combo Amp
April 2001-pressent. Upgrade R5H-750, 50 watts, AB, 2 6L6, spring reverb.

2001-2004		$925	$1,000

Rect-O-Verb/Recto Cab
1998-2001. Slant front 4x12" or 2x12" option cab, black cover, dark grille.

1998-2001	2x12" option	$450	$525
1998-2001	4x12" slant front	$575	$675

Road King Combo Amp
2002-present. 2x12" combo version.

2002-2004		$1,700	$1,900

Road King Dual Rectifier Amp Head
2002-present. Tube head, various power tube selections based upon a chasis which uses 2 EL34s and 4 6L6, 2 5U4 dual rectifier tubes or silicon diode rectifiers, 50 to 120 watts.

2002-2004		$2,300	$2,600

RoadReady Bass Cabinets
1994-present. Heavy-duty road case bass cabinets with metal grilles, casters and metal corners.

1994-2004	1x15"	$350	$450
1994-2004	2x12"	$450	$550

Rocket 440 Amp
Mar. 1999-Aug. 2000. Serial numbers: R440-R44-1159. 45 watts, 4x10".

1999-2000		$650	$750

Satellite/Satellite 60 Amp
Aug. 1990-1999. Serial numbers: ST001-ST841. Uses either 6L6s for 100 watts or EL34s for 60 watts, dark vinyl, dark grille.

1990-1999		$450	$650

Solo 50 Rectifier Series I Amp Head
Nov. 1998-Apr. 2001. Serial numbers: R50. 50-watt head.

1998-2001		$950	$1,100

Solo 50 Rectifier Series II Amp Head
Apr. 2001. Upgrade, serial numbers: S50-S1709. Upgrades preamp section, head with 50 watts.

2001		$950	$1,100

Son Of Boogie Amp
May 1982-Dec.1985. Serial numbers: S100-S2390. 60 watts, 1x12", considered the first reissue of the original Mark I.

1982-1985		$650	$750

Stereo 290 (Simul 2-Ninety) Amp
Jun. 1992-present. Serial numbers: R0001- . Dual 90-watt stereo channels, rack mount.

1992-2004		$800	$850

MODEL YEAR	FEATURES	EXC. COND. LOW	HIGH

Stereo 295 Amp
March 1987-May 1991. Serial numbers: S001-S2673. Dual 95-watt class A/B stereo channels, rack mount. Selectable 30 watts Class A (EL34 power tubes) power.

1987-1991		$600	$650

Stilleto Series Amp Heads
2004-present. Series includes the Deuce (50 or 100 watts, 4 EL-34s) and Trident (50 or 150 watts, 6 EL-34s).

2004-2005	Deuce\Trident	$1,100	$1,300

Strategy 400 Amp
Mar.1987-May 1991. Serial numbers: S001-S2627. 400 to 500 watts, power amplifier with 12 6L6 power tubes.

1987-1991		$750	$850

Strategy 500 Amp
June 1991-April 1992. S2,552- . Rack mount, 500 watts, 4 6550 power tubes.

1991-1992		$900	$1,000

Studio Preamp
Aug. 1988-Dec. 1993. Serial numbers: SP000-SP7890. Tube preamp, EQ, reverb, effects loop.

1988-1993		$400	$500

Studio .22/Studio .22+ Amp
Nov. 1985-1988. Serial numbers: SS000-SS11499, black vinyl, black grille, 22 watts, 1x12". Replaced by .22+ Dec. 1988-Aug. 1993. Serial numbers: FP11,500 - FP28,582. 22 watts.

1985-1988		$450	$650
1988-1993		$450	$650

Studio Caliber DC-2 Amp
Apr. 1994-Jan. 1999. Serial numbers: DC2-01 - DC2-4247 (formerly called DC-2). 20 watts, 1x12" combo, dark vinyl, dark grille.

1994-1999		$500	$575

Subway/Subway Blues Amp
Sep. 1994-Aug. 2000. Serial numbers: SB001-SB2515. 20 watts, 1x10".

1994-2000		$600	$650

Subway Reverb Rocket Amp
Jun. 1998-Aug. 2001. Serial numbers: RR1000-RR2461. 20 watts, 1x10".

1998-2001		$600	$650

Subway Rocket (no reverb) Amp
Jan. 1996-Jul. 1998. Serial numbers: SR001-SR2825. No reverb, 20 watts, 1x10".

1996-1998		$575	$625

Trem-O-Verb Dual Rectifier Amp Head
Jun. 1993-Jan. 2001. 100-watt head version.

1993-2001		$1,000	$1,200
1993-2001	Rack mount version	$1,000	$1,200

Trem-O-Verb Dual Rectifier Cab
Late-1980s-early-1990s. Half stack 4x12" slant cab with open half back, or straight-front cab, 2x12" straight-front option, not strictly for this model, useable for any Boogie with matching output specs, often loaded with Celestion Vintage 30s, small weave grille (not see-thru

1988-1990s	2x12" straight cab option	$500	$575
1988-1990s	4x12" slant or straight	$600	$600

Trem-O-Verb Dual Rectifier Half Stack Amp
Jun. 1993-Jan. 2001. 100 watts, head with matching 4x12" slant cab.

1993-2001		$1,700	$2,000

Trem-O-Verb Dual Rectifier Combo Amp
Jun. 1993-Jan. 2001. Serial numbers: R- to about R-21210. 100 watts, 2x12" Celestion Vintage 30.

1993-2001		$1,200	$1,400

Triaxis Preamp
Oct. 1991-present. Serial numbers:T0001-. 5 12AX7 tube preamp, rack mount.

1991-2004		$1,000	$1,400

Triple Rectifier Amp Head
1997-present. Three-channel amp head.

1997-2004		$1,250	$1,500

V-Twin Rackmount Amp
May 1995-Jun. 1998. Serial numbers: V2R-001 to V2R-2258.

1995-1998		$450	$500

Walk About M-Pulse Bass Amp Head
Sep. 2001-present. Serial numbers: WK-01-. Lightweight 13 pounds, 2 12AX7s + 300 MOS-FET.

2001-2004		$600	$700

Meteoro
1986-present. Guitar, bass, harp and keyboard combo amps, heads, and cabinets built in Brazil. They also build effects.

Mission Amps
1996-present. Bruce Collins' Mission Amps, located in Arvada, Colorado, produces a line of custom-made combo amps, heads, and cabinets.

Mojave Amp Works
2002-present. Tube amp heads and speaker cabinets by Victor Mason in Apple Valley, California.

Montgomery Ward
Amps for this large retailer were sometimes branded as Montgomery Ward, but usually as Airline (see that listing).

Higher Power 1x12" Combo Amp
1950s. 1x12", about 2 6L6 power tubes, includes brown covered Maestro C Series with cloverleaf grille.

1950s		$200	$300

Lower Power 1x12" Combo Amp
1950s. 1x12" speaker, around 12 watts, includes Model 8439.

1950s		$200	$250

Mooneyes
Budget solid state amp line from Lace Music Products. They also offer amps under the Rat Fink and Lace brands. Lace has a Mooneyes guitar model line.

*Mesa-Boogie
Son of Boogie combo*

Mojave Scorpion

Mooneyes ME-10

AMPS

Music Man 212 Sixty Five

Music Man 410 Sixty Five

Early-'50s National/Valco

MODEL YEAR	FEATURES	EXC. COND. LOW	HIGH

Morley
Late-1960s-present. The effects company offered an amp in the late '70s. See Effects section for more company info.
Bigfoot Amp
1979-ca.1981. Looks like Morley's '70s effects pedals, produced 25 watts and pedal controlled volume. Amp only, speakers were sold separately.

1979-1981		$150	$250

Mountain
Mountain builds a 9-volt amp in a wood cabinet. Originally built in California, then Nevada; currently being made in Vancouver, Canada.

Multivox
Ca.1946-ca.1984. Multivox was started as a subsidiary of Premier to manufacture amps, and later, effects.
New York 1st AVE Amp
1982. 15 watts, 1x8".

1982		$50	$80

New York 6th AVE Amp
1982. 60 watts, 1x12".

1982		$80	$110

Music Man
1972-present. Music Man made amps from '73 to '83. The number preceding the amp model indicates the speaker configuration. The last number in model name usually referred to the watts. RD indicated "Reverb Distortion." RP indicated "Reverb Phase." Many models were available in head-only versions and as combos with various speaker combinations.
110 RD Fifty Amp
1980-1983. 50 watts, 1x10", reverb, distortion.

1980-1983		$550	$600

112 RD Fifty Amp
1980-1983. 50 watts, 1x12", reverb, distortion.

1980-1983		$575	$625

112 RD Sixty Five Amp
1978-1983. 65 watts, 1x12", reverb, distortion.

1978-1983		$575	$625

112 RD One Hundred Amp
1978-1983. 100 watts, 1x12", reverb, distortion.

1978-1983		$575	$625

112 Sixty Five Amp
1973-1981. Combo amp, 65 watts, 1x12", reverb, tremolo.

1973-1981		$550	$600

112 RP Sixty Five Amp
1978-1983. 65 watts, 1x12", reverb, built-in phaser.

1978-1983		$525	$600

112 RP One Hundred Amp
1978-1983. Combo amp, 100 watts, 1x12", reverb, built-in phaser.

1978-1983		$525	$600

115 Sixty Five Amp
1973-1981. Combo amp, 65 watts, 1x15", reverb, tremolo.

1973-1981		$525	$600

210 HD130 Amp
1973-1981. 130 watts, 2x10", reverb, tremolo.

1973-1981		$550	$700

210 Sixty Five Amp
1973-1981. 65 watts, 2x10", reverb, tremolo.

1973-1981		$550	$700

212 HD130 Amp
1973-1981. 130 watts, 2x12", reverb, tremolo.

1973-1981		$550	$700

212 Sixty Five Amp
1973-1981. 65 watts, 2x12", reverb, tremolo.

1973-1981		$550	$700

410 Sixty Five Amp
1973-1981. 65 watts, 4x10", reverb, tremolo.

1973-1981		$550	$700

410 Seventy Five Amp
1982-1983. 75 watts, 4x10", reverb, tremolo.

1982-1983		$550	$700

HD-130 Amp
1973-1981. Head amp, 130 watts, reverb, tremolo.

1973-1981		$400	$600

RD Fifty Amp
1980-1983. Head amp, 50 watts, reverb, distortion.

1980-1983		$350	$450

Sixty Five Amp
1973-1981. Head amp, 65 watts, reverb, tremolo.

1973-1981		$350	$450

National
Ca.1927-present. National/Valco amps date back to the late-'30s. National introduced a modern group of amps about the same time they introduced their new Res-O-Glas space-age guitar models in '62. In '64, the amp line was partially redesigned and renamed. By '68, the Res-O-Glas models were gone and National introduced many large vertical and horizontal piggyback models which lasted until National's assets were assigned during bankruptcy in '69. The National name went to Chicago importer Strum N' Drum who then advertised "National is back and better than ever." Initially, Strum N' Drum had one amp, the National GA 950 P Tremolo/Reverb piggyback.
Chicago 51 Aztec/Valco Amp
Late-1940s-early-1950s. Low- to mid-power, 2x6L6, 3 oval Rola speakers, 3 baffle openings (1 for each speaker), tweed cover.

1940-1950s		$300	$500

Chicago/Valco 51 Amp
1950s. Vertical tweed cabinet, metal preamps tubes, late-1940s-early-'50s technology, 1x12".

1950s		$300	$500

Glenwood 90 (Model N6490TR) Amp
1962-1967. 35 watts, 2x12", tremolo (not listed as vibrato) and reverb.

1964-1967		$550	$650

MODEL YEAR	FEATURES	EXC. COND. LOW	HIGH

Glenwood Vibrato (Model N6499VR) Amp
1964-1967. 70 watts, 2x12", vibrato and reverb.

1964-1967		$600	$700

Model 75
Vertical tweed combo cabinet, volume and tone knobs, 3 inputs.

1940s		$425	$475

Model 100 Amp
Tube amp, 40 watts, 1x12".

1940		$400	$500

Model GA 950-P Tremolo/Reverb Piggyback Amp
1970s. Strum N' Drum/National model, solidstate, 50 watts, 2-channel 2x12" and 1x7" in 32" tall vertical cabinet, black.

1970s		$175	$250

Model N6800 - N6899 Piggyback Amps
1968-1969. National introduced a new line of tube amps in '68 and most of them were piggybacks. The N6895 was sized like a Fender piggyback Tremolux, the N6875 and N6878 bass amps were sized like a '68 Fender large cab piggyback with a 26" tall vertical cab, the N6898 and N6899 were the large piggyback guitar amps. These amps feature the standard Jensen speakers or the upgrade JBL speakers, the largest model was the N6800 for PA or guitar, which sported 3x70-watt channels and 2 column speakers using a bass 2x12" + 1x3" horn cab and a voice-guitar 4x10" + 1x3" horn cab.

1968-1969	Various tube models	$200	$375

Model N6816 (Model 16) Amp
1968-1969. Valco-made tube amp, 6 watts, 1x10" Jensen speaker, 17" vertical cab, tremolo, no reverb, black vinyl cover and Coppertone grille, National spelled out on front panel.

1968-1969		$125	$175

Model N6820 Thunderball Bass Amp
1968-1969. Valco-made tube amp, about 35 watts, 1x15" Jensen speaker, 19" vertical cab, black vinyl cover and Coppertone grille, National spelled out on front panel.

1968-1969		$150	$200

Model N6822 (Model 22) Amp
1968-1969. Valco-made, 6 watts tube (4 tubes) amp, 1x12" Jensen speaker, 19" vertical cab, tremolo and reverb, black vinyl cover and Coppertone grille, National spelled out on front panel.

1968-1969		$150	$200

National Dobro Amp
1930s. Sold by the National Dobro Corp. when the company was still in Los Angeles (they later moved to Chicago). National Dobro plate on rear back panel, suitcase style case that flips open to reveal the speaker and amp, National logo on outside of suitcase. The noted price is for an all-original amp in excellent condition (this would be a rare find), there are other 1930s models included in the price range below.

1930s	Model B, not suitcase	$300	$400
1930s	Suitcase style	$400	$700

Sportman Amp

1950s		$400	$450

Student Practice Amp
1970s. Strum N' Drum era, small solidstate, single control.

1970s		$25	$35

Studio 10 Amp
1962-1967. Five watts, 1x3", 3 tubes, 1 channel, 1 volume control, no tone control, no reverb or tremolo.

1962-1963		$350	$450
1964-1967	N6410 Model	$350	$450

Westwood 16 (Model N6416T) Amp
1964-1967. Five watts using 1 6V6 power, 2 12AX7 preamp, 1 5Y3GT rectifier, tremolo, 2x8", dark vinyl cover, silver grille.

1964-1967		$400	$475

Westwood 22 (Model N6422TR) Amp
1964-1967. 5 watts, 2x8", reverb and tremolo, 1 channel, 6 tubes.

1964-1967		$400	$475

Naylor Engineering
1994-present. Joe Naylor and Kyle Kurtz founded the company in East Pointe, Michigan, in the early '90s, selling J.F. Naylor speakers. In '94 they started producing amps. In '96, Naylor sold his interest in the business to Kurtz and left to form Reverend Guitars. In '99 David King bought the company and moved it to Los Angeles, California, then to Dallas, Texas. Currently Naylor builds tube amps, combos, speakers, and cabinets.

Nemesis
From the makers of Eden amps, Nemesis is a line of made-in-the-U.S., FET powered bass combos and extension cabinets. The brand is a division of U.S. Music Corp.

NC-200 Combo Amp
1990s. Compact style cabinet with 200 watts, solidstate, 2x10", black cover, black grille.

1997		$400	$450

NC-200P Combo Amp
1990s. Compact transporter-style cabinet with 200 watts, solidstate, 4x10", black cover, black grille.

1997		$450	$500

Nobel
1950-1960s. From Don Noble and Company, of Chicago, Illinois, owned by Strum N' Drum by mid-'60s.

Mid-Size Tube Amp
1950s. Low- to mid-power tube amp, Noble logo on front.

1950s		$325	$400

Norma
1965-1970. Economy solidstate line imported and distributed by Strum N' Drum, Wheeling (Chicago), Illinois. As noted in the National section, Strum N' Drum acquired the National brand in the '70s. Low values reflect the market's low demand for an import solidstate amp.

Naylor Super-Drive Sixty

National Glenwood 90

Nemesis NC-115

AMPS

Oahu Holiday

'70s Oliver 6200R Uniflex

Overbuilt Napoleon

MODEL YEAR	FEATURES	EXC. COND. LOW	HIGH
GA-725 B Amp			
1969-1970. Bass amp, 38 watts, 1x10".			
1969-1970		$60	$85
GA-918 T Amp			
1969-1970. 24 watts, 1x12", tremolo and reverb.			
1969-1970		$70	$95
GA-93 Amp			
1969-1970. 6 watts, 1x6".			
1969-1970		$55	$75
GA-97 T Amp			
1969-1970. 13 watts, 1x8", tremolo.			
1969-1970		$60	$85
GA-930 P (piggyback) Amp			
1969-1970. 40 watts, 2x12", piggyback.			
1969-1970		$80	$125
GA-6240 Amp			
1969-1970. 50 watts.			
1969-1970		$80	$125
GAP-2 Amp			
1969-1970. 3 watts, 1x4".			
1969-1970		$55	$75

Oahu

The Oahu Publishing Company and Honolulu Conservatory, based in Cleveland, Ohio, started with acoustic Hawaiian and Spanish guitars, selling large quantities in the 1930s. As electric models became popular, Oahu responded with guitar/amp sets. The brand has been revived on a line of U.S.-made tube amps.

Small Guitar/Lab Steel Amps

1950s	Various colors	$250	$350

Oliver

Ca.1966-late-1970s. The Oliver Sound Company, Westbury, New York, was founded by former Ampeg engineer, Jess Oliver, after he left Ampeg in '65. Tube amp designs were based upon Oliver's work at Ampeg. The Oliver Powerflex Amp is the best-known design, and featured an elevator platform that would lift the amp head out of the speaker cabinet.

Model G-150R Combo Amp

2 6L6 power tubes, reverb, tremolo, black tolex with black grille, silver control panel, 40 watts, 1x15".

1970s		$475	$600

Model P-500 Combo Amp

All tube combo with 15" motorized amp chassis that rises out of tall lateral speaker cabinet as amp warms up.

1960s		$600	$700

Orbital Power Projector Amp

Late-1960s-early-1970s. Rotating speaker cabinet with horn, Leslie-like voice.

1970s		$600	$700

Sam Ash Oliver Amp Head

Late-1960s-early-1970s. Private branded for Sam Ash Music, about 30 watts using the extinct 7027A power tubes, Sam Ash script logo on front grille.

1960s		$175	$300

Orange

1969-1981, 1995-present. Orange amps and PAs were made in England by Cliff Cooper and Matthew Mathias. The Orange-colored amps were well-built and were used by many notable guitarists. Since '95, Cliff Cooper is once again making Orange amplifiers in England, with the exception of the small Crush Practice Combo amps, which are made in Korea.

Model OR-80 Amp w/4x12 Bottom.

1970s. 80 watts, 4x12" straight-front cab with Orange crest on grille, orange vinyl and light orange grille.

1970s		$2,800	$3,200

Model OR-80 Combo Amp

1970s. About 80 watts, 2x12" combo.

1970s		$2,400	$2,600

Model OR-120 Graphic Overdrive Amp Head

1970s. 120 watts.

1970s		$2,000	$2,200

Model OR-120 Graphic Head Amp and Half Stack

1970s. 120 watts, 4x12" straight front cab with Orange crest on grille, orange vinyl and light orange grille.

1970s		$3,000	$3,500

Model OR-200 212 Twin Amp

1970s. 120 watts, 2x12" combo, orange vinyl, dark grille, Orange crest on grille, reverb and vibrato, master volume.

1970s		$2,500	$3,000

Orpheum

Late-1950s-1960s. Student to medium level amps from New York's Maurice Lipsky Music.

Small/Mid-Size Amps

Late-1950s-1960s. U.S.-made, 2 6V6 power tubes, Jensen P12R 12" speaker, light cover with gray swirl grille.

1959		$175	$225

Ovation

1966-present. Kaman made few amps under the Ovation name. They offered a variety of amps under the KMD brand from '85 to around '94.

Little Dude Amp

1969-ca.1971. Solidstate combo, 100 watts, 1x15" and horn, matching slave unit also available.

1970s		$175	$250

The Kat (Model 6012) Amp

1970s. Solidstate, 2x12" combo.

1970s		$175	$250

Overbuilt Amps

1999-present. Tube amps and combos built by Richard Seccombe in West Hills, California.

PAC-AMP (Magnatone)

Late-1950s-early-1960s. Private branded by Magnatone, often for accordion studios.

MODEL YEAR	FEATURES	EXC. COND. LOW	HIGH

Model 280-A Amp
1961-1963. About 50 watts, 2x12" + 2x5", brown leatherette, light brown grille, stereo vibrato, PAC-AMP nameplate logo.

1961-1963		$700	$850

PANaramic (Magnatone)
1961-1963. Private branded equivalent of '61-'63 Magnatone brown leatherette series, large PANaramic logo. Many Magnatone private brands were associated with accordion companies or accordian teaching studios. PANaramic was a brand name of PANaramic accordion. They also made guitars.

Model 260/262-style Amp
1961-1963. 35 watts, 2x12", gray vinyl and light grille, vibrato, large PANaramic logo.

1961-1963		$700	$850

Model 413-style Amp
1961-1963. 18 watts, 1x12", black leatherette cover, light silver grille, vibrato, large PANaramic logo.

1961-1963		$550	$650

Model 450-style Amp
1961-1963. 20 watts, 1x12", reverb and vibrato, reverb not generally included in an early-'60s 1x12" Magnatone amp, dark vinyl, dark cross-threaded grille, large PANaramic logo.

1961-1963		$750	$1,000

Paris
Master Series Amps
1960s. Compact solid-state combo, 1x12", slanted Paris logo front upper left side of grille, black tolex-style cover, silver grille (like Fender blackface), rear mounted slanted control panel.

1960s		$100	$150

Park
1965-1982, 1992-2000. Park amps were made by Marshall from '65 to '82. In the '90s, Marshall revived the name for use on small solidstate amps imported from the Far East.

G Series Amp
1990s. Student compact amps, models include G-10 (10 watts, 1x8"), G-25R (25 watts, reverb) and GB-25 (25 watts, 1x12" bass).

1990s	G-10	$40	$85
1990s	G-25R	$90	$110
1990s	GB-25	$85	$105

Model 75 1960 4x12 slant cab
Early 1970s. Similar to Marshall 1960 4x12" cab.

1970-1971	.	$1,800	$2,000

Model 75 Amp Head
1967-1971. Head amp, 50 watts, 2xKT88s, small-box plexi (later aluminum), black tolex.

1967-1969	Plexi	$4,000	$5,000
1969-1971	Aluminum	$3,000	$4,000

Model 1206 50-Watt Amp Head
1981-1982. 50 watts, based upon JCM 800 50-watt made at the same time period.

1981-1982		$800	$1,100

Model 1213 100-Watt Reverb Combo Amp
1970s. 100 watts, 2x12", reverb, dark vinyl, light grille, Park logo on front with elongated P.

1970s		$1,400	$1,600

Model 1228 50-Watt Lead Head Amp
1970s. 50 watts, based upon Marshall 50-watt made at the same time period.

1970s		$1,300	$1,500

Model 2046 25-Watt Combo Amp
1970s. 25 watts, 1x15", '70s era blue grille cloth, black tolex, large P Park logo upper center of grille.

1970s		$1,100	$1,300

Park G10

Paul Reed Smith
1985-present. In the late '80s, PRS offered two amp models. Only 350 amp units shipped. Includes HG-70 Head and HG-212 Combo. HG stands for Harmonic Generator, effectively a non-tube, solid-state amp.

HG-70 Amp Head
1989-1990. 70 watts, reverb, effects loop, noise gate. Options include 150-watt circuitry and 4x12" straight and slant cabinets, gray-black.

1989		$500	$550

4x12" Straight-Front Cab
1989. Straight-front 4x12" black vinyl cab with silver grille, PRS logo front lower right of grille.

1989		$500	$550

HG-212 Amp
1989-1990. Combo, 70 watts, 2x12", reverb, effects loop, noise gate. Options include 150-watt circuitry and 4x12" straight and slant cabinets, gray-black.

1989		$550	$650

Peavey
1965-present. Hartley Peavey's first products were guitar amps. He added guitars to the mix in '78. Headquartered in Meridan, Mississippi, Peavey continues to offer a huge variety of guitars, amps, and PAs.

5150 212 Combo Amp
1995-2004. Combo version of 5150 head, 60 watts, 2x12", large 5150 logo on front panel, small Peavey logo on lower right of grille.

1995-2004		$575	$650

5150 EVH Head and Cab Amp Set
1995-2004. Half stack 5150 head and 4x12" cab, large 5150 logo on front of amp.

1995	Head and cab	$1,100	$1,300
1995	Head only	$700	$900
1996-2004	Cab only	$325	$375
1996-2004	Head and cab	$950	$1,150
1996-2004	Head only	$600	$750

Alphabass Amp
1988-1990. Rack mount all tube, 160 watts, EQ, includes 2x15" Black Widow or 2x12" Scorpion cabinet.

1988-1990		$300	$350

PRS HG-212

Peavey 5150 2x12"

1977 Peavey Backstage 30

Peavey Bandit

Peavey Classic 50/212

MODEL YEAR	FEATURES	EXC. COND. LOW	HIGH

Artist Amp
Introduced in 1975 as 120 watts, 1x12", bright and normal channels, EQ, reverb, master volume.

1970s		$225	$275

Artist 110 Amp
TransTubes, 10 watts.

1990s		$125	$150

Artist 250 Amp
1990s. 100 watts, 1x12", solidstate preamp, 4 6L6 power tubes.

1990s		$200	$250

Artist VT Amp
1990s. Combo amp, 120 watts, 1x12".

1990s		$225	$300

Audition 20 Amp
1980s-1990s. 20 watts, single speaker combo.

1980-1990s		$75	$100

Audition 30 Amp
1980s-1990s. 30 watts, 1x12" combo amp, channel switching.

1980-1990s		$90	$125

Audition 110 Amp
1990s. 25 watts, 1x10" combo, 2 channels.

1990s		$100	$125

Audition Chorus Amp
2x10-watt channels, 2x6", channel switching, post gain and normal gain controls.

1980s		$125	$175

Audition Plus Amp
1980s. Solidstate, 20 watts, 1x10".

1980s		$100	$125

Backstage Amp
1977-mid-1980s. Master gain control, 18 watts, 1x10", 3-band EQ.

1977-1984		$50	$100

Backstage 30 Amp
30 watts, 1x8".

1980s		$75	$100

Backstage 110 Amp
Repackaged and revoiced in 1988, 65 watts, 1x10", Peavey SuperSat preamp circuitry, new power sections.

1980s		$100	$125

Backstage Chorus 208 Amp
1990s. 150 watts, 2x8", reverb, channel switching.

1990s		$150	$200

Backstage Plus Amp
1980s. 35 watts, 1x10" combo, reverb, saturation effect.

1980s		$100	$125

Bandit 75 Amp
Redesigned and renamed Bandit 112 in 1988. Channel switching, 75 watts, 1x12", 4-band EQ, reverb, post-effects loop, Superstat.

1980s	.	$200	$250

Bandit 112/Bandit II 112 Amp
1988-2001. 80 watts, 1x12", active EQ circuit for lead channel, active controls.

1980s	Bandit	$200	$300
1990s	Bandit II	$200	$300

Basic 112 Bass Amp
2000s. 75 watts, 1x12" bass combo, 2000-era red border control panel.

2000s		$200	$225

Basic 40 Amp
40 watts, 1x12".

1980s		$125	$150

Basic 60 Amp
1988-1995. Solidstate combo amp, 50-60 watts, 1x12", 4-band EQ, gain controls.

1988-1995	Black	$175	$200

Blazer 158 Amp
1995-present. 15 watts, 1x8", clean and distortion, now called the TransTube Blazer III.

1995-2000		$75	$100

Bluesman Amp
1992. Tweed, 1x12" or 1x15".

1992		$300	$400

Bravo 112 Amp
1988-1994. All tube reverb, 25 watts, 1x12", 3-band EQ, 2 independent input channels.

1988-1994		$250	$350

Classic 20 Amp
Small tube amp with 2xEL84 power tubes, 1x10", tweed cover.

1990s		$250	$300

Classic 30 Amp
1994-present. Tweed, 30 watts, 1x12", EL84 tubes.

1994-1999		$350	$400

Classic 50/212 Amp
1990-present. Combo, 50 watt, 2x12", 4 EL84s, 3 12AX7s, reverb, high-gain section.

1990-2004		$425	$475

Classic 50/410 Amp
1990-present. Combo amp, 4x10", EL84 power, reverb, footswitchable high-gain mode.

1990s		$450	$500

Classic 120 Amp
1988-ca.1990. Tube, 120 watts.

1988-1990		$350	$375

DECA/750 Amp
1989-ca.1990. Digital, 2 channels, 350 watts per channel, distortion, reverb, exciter, pitch shift, multi-EQ.

1989-1990		$275	$325

Decade Amp
1970s. Practice amp, 10 watts, 1x8", runs on 12 volt or AC.

1970s		$40	$60

Delta Blues Amp
1995-present. 30 watts, tube combo, 4 EL84 tubes, 1x15" or 2x8", tremolo, large-panel-style cab, blond tweed.

1995-2000		$400	$450

Deuce Head Amp
1972-1980s. Tube head, 120 watts.

1972-1980		$200	$250

Deuce Amp
1972-1980s. 120 watts, tube amp, 2x12" or 4x10".

1972-1980		$275	$350

MODEL YEAR	FEATURES	EXC. COND. LOW	HIGH

Ecoustic 112 Amp
100 watts, 1x12" acoustic and mic amp, guitar input and mic input, brown vinyl, brown grille.
| 2000s | | $200 | $250 |

Encore 65 Amp
1990s. Compact solidstate amp, 1x12", reverb, channel switching.
| 1990s | | $200 | $225 |

Envoy 110 Amp
1988-2001. Solidstate, 40 watts, 1x10", patent-applied-for circuitry, TransTubes.
| 1988-2001 | | $125 | $175 |

Heritage VTX Amp
1980s. 130 watts, 4 6L6s, solidstate preamp, 2x12" combo.
| 1980s | | $200 | $250 |

Jazz Classic Amp
Solidstate, 210 watts, 1x15", electronic channel switching, 6-spring reverb.
| 1980s | | $200 | $250 |

KB-100 Amp
Keyboard amp, 1x15".
| 1980s | | $225 | $275 |

LTD Amp
1975-1980s. Solidstate, 200 watts, 1x12" Altec or 1x15" JBL.
| 1975-1982 | | $200 | $250 |

Mace Amp Head
1976-1980s. Tube, 180 watts.
| 1980s | | $275 | $300 |

MegaBass Amp
Rack mount preamp/power amp, 200 watts per 2 channels, solidstate, EQ, effects loop, chorus.
| 1980s | | $250 | $300 |

Microbass Amp
2000s. 20 watts, 1x8" practice amp, made in China.
| 2000s | | $75 | $100 |

Minx 110 Bass Amp
1988-present. Solidstate, 35 watts RMS, 1x10" heavy-duty speaker.
| 1988-1999 | | $125 | $150 |

Musician Amp Head
Introduced in 1965 as 120 watt head, upped to 210 watts in '72.
| 1970s | | $175 | $225 |

Nashville 400 Steel Guitar Amp
210 watts, 1x15" solidstate steel guitar combo amp.
| 1990s | | $275 | $325 |

Nashville 1000 Steel Guitar Amp
1x15" speaker, solidstate steel guitar combo amp.
| 1990s | | $300 | $350 |

Pacer Amp
1974-1980s. Master volume, 45 watts, 1x12", 3-band EQ.
| 1974-1985 | | $125 | $150 |

ProBass 1000 Amp
Rack mount, effects loops, preamp, EQ, crossover, headphone output.
| 1980s | | $175 | $200 |

Rage/Rage 158 Amp
1980s-1990s. Compact practice amp, 15 watts, 1x8".
| 1980s | | $90 | $110 |

Reno 400 Amp
Solidstate, 200 watts, 1x15" with horn, 4-band EQ.
| 1980s | | $200 | $250 |

Renown 112 Amp
1989-1994. Crunch and lead SuperSat, 160 watts, 1x12", master volume, digital reverb, EQ.
| 1989-1994 | | $200 | $250 |

Renown 212 Amp
1989-1994. Crunch and lead SuperSat, 160 watts, 2x12", master volume, digital reverb, EQ.
| 1989-1994 | | $225 | $275 |

Renown 400 Amp
Combo, 200 watts, 2x12", channel switching, Hammond reverb, pre- and post-gain controls.
| 1980s | | $275 | $325 |

Revolution 112 Amp
2000s. 100 watts, 1x12" combo, black vinyl, black grille.
| 2000s | | $225 | $275 |

Session 500 Amp
1980s. 250 watts, 1x15", standard black with metal panels appearance.
| 1980s | | $350 | $475 |

Special 112 Amp
160 watts, 1x12", channel-switching, effects loops, EQ. In 1988, available in wedge-shaped enclosures slanted back 30 degrees.
| 1980s | | $275 | $300 |

Special 130 Amp
1980s. 1x12", 130 watts, transtube, solidstate series.
| 1980s | | $275 | $300 |

Special 212 Amp
1990s. 160 watts, 2x12", transtube, solidstate series.
| 1990s | | $325 | $350 |

Studio Pro 112 Amp
Repackaged and revoiced in 1988. Solidstate, 65 watts, 1x12", Peavey SuperSat preamp circuitry, new power sections
| 1980s | | $200 | $275 |

TKO-65 Bass Amp
1987-1995. Solidstate, 65 watts, 1x15".
| 1987-1995 | | $175 | $225 |

TKO-75 Bass Amp
1987-1995. Solidstate, 75 watts, 1x15", EQ, compression and pre-/post-gain controls.
| 1987-1995 | | $200 | $250 |

TNT-150 Bass Amp
Solidstate, 150 watts, 1x15", EQ, compression, chorus. In 1988, available in wedge-shaped enclosures slanted 30 degrees.
| 1980s | | $225 | $275 |

Triple XXX Amp Head
2001- Present. Tube head, 120 watts.
| 2001-2005 | | $625 | $650 |

Peavey Delta Blues

Peavey Musician (head)

Peavey Special 112

To get the most from this book, be sure to read "Using *The Guide*" in the introduction.

Penn Signature amp

Pignose Hog

Randall R6-200 ES

MODEL YEAR	FEATURES	EXC. COND. LOW	HIGH
Triumph 60 Combo Amp			
Tube head, effects loop, reverb, 60 watts, 1x12", multi-stage gain.			
1980s		$200	$250
Triumph 120 Amp			
Tube, 120 watts, 1x12", 3 gain blocks in preamp, low-level post-effects loop, built-in reverb.			
1989-1990		$250	$300
Ultra 112 Amp			
1998-2002. 60 watts, 1x12", all tube, 2 6L6 power, black, black grille.			
1998-2002		$325	$375
Ultra 410 Amp			
1998-2002. 60 watts, 4x10".			
1998-2002		$375	$475
Vegas 400 Amp			
1980s. 210 watts, 1x15", reverb, compression feature, parametric EQ. Some musicians prefer as a steel guitar amp.			
1980s		$425	$500
Vintage Amp			
2000s. 100 watts, 6x10", tweed combo amp.			
2000s		$550	$650
Wiggy 212 Amp			
2001-present. 100-watt head in mono (2x75-watt in stereo) with matching 2x12" cab, 2 EQ systems including 5-band sliders, rounded amp head cabinet.			
20001-2005		$650	$700

Penn

1994-present. Tube amps, combos, and cabinets built by Billy Penn, originally in Colts Neck, New Jersey, currently in Long Branch, New Jersey.

Pignose

1972-present. Made in the U.S. Pignose Industries was started by people associated with the band Chicago, including guitarist Terry Kath, with help from designers Wayne Kimball and Richard Erlund.

MODEL YEAR	FEATURES	EXC. COND. LOW	HIGH
7-100 Practice Amp			
1972-present. The original Pignose, 7"x5"x3" battery-powered portable amplifier, 1x5".			
1972-1999		$50	$75
30/60 Amp			
1978-ca.1987. Solidstate, 30 watts, 1x10", master volume.			
1978-1987		$125	$175
60R Studio Reverb Amp			
Solidstate, 30 watts.			
1980		$175	$225

Plush

Late 1960s-early 1970s. Roll and tuck covered tube amps made by the same company that made Earth Sound Research amps in Farmingdale, New York.

MODEL YEAR	FEATURES	EXC. COND. LOW	HIGH
Tube Amplifiers			
Early 1970s. Roll and tuck covers, all tube heads and combos including the 450 Super 2x12" combo, 1000/P1000S head, and 1060S Royal Bass combo.			
1971-1972		$200	$450

Polytone

1960s-present. Made in North Hollywood, California, Polytone offers compact combo amps, heads, and cabinets and a pickup system for acoustic bass.

MODEL YEAR	FEATURES	EXC. COND. LOW	HIGH
Mega-Brute Amp			
1990s. Black vinyl, black screen-style grille.			
1990s		$300	$350
Mini-Brute III Bass Amp			
1990s. 80 watts, 1x15", footswitchable reverb and distortion.			
1990s		$300	$350
Mini-Brute IV Amp			
1980s-1990s. 100 watts, 1x15", footswitchable reverb and distortion.			
1980-1990s		$400	$450
Mini-Brute V Amp			
100 watts, 2x10", footswitchable reverb and distortion.			
1980s		$425	$475
RMS Pro Series Bass Amp			
Rack mount, 240 watts, 2 power amps, 2 preamps, crossover for bi-amping.			
1985		$425	$500

Premier

Ca.1938-ca.1975. Produced by Peter Sorkin Music Company in Manhattan. First radio-sized amplifiers introduced by '38. After World War II, established Multivox subsidiary to manufacture amplifiers ca.'46. By mid-'50s at least, the amps featured lyre grilles. Dark brown/light tan amp covering by '60. By '64 amps covered in brown woodgrain and light tan. Multivox amps were made until around '84.

MODEL YEAR	FEATURES	EXC. COND. LOW	HIGH
B-160 Club Bass Amp			
1960s. 15 to 20 watts, 1x12" Jensen speaker, '60s 2-tone brown styling, 6V6 tubes.			
1963-1968		$400	$450
Model 50 Combo Amp			
1940s-1960s. Four to 5 watts, 1x8" similar to Fender Champ circuit with more of a vertical cab.			
1950s		$350	$400
Model 76 Combo Amp			
1950s. Suitcase latchable cabinet that opens out into 2 wedges, Premier 76 logo on amp control panel, 2-tone brown, lyre grille, 1x12".			
1950s		$500	$700
Model 88N Combo Amp			
1950s-early-1960s. Rectangular suitcase cabinet, 2-tone tan and brown, Premier and lyre logo, 25 watts, 1x12".			
1950s		$500	$700
1960s		$500	$700
Model 100R Amp			
Combo amp, 1x12", reverb and tremolo.			
1960s		$450	$500
Twin 8 Amp			
1960s. 20 watts, 2x8", tremolo, reverb.			
1964-1966		$550	$600

AMPS

MODEL		EXC. COND.	
YEAR	FEATURES	LOW	HIGH

Twin 12 T-12R Amp
Late-1950s. Early reverb amp with tremolo, 2x12", rectangular cabinet typical of twin 12 amps (Dano and Fender), brown cover.

1950s		$600	$700

Quantum
1980s. Economy amps distributed by DME, Indianapolis, Indiana.

Q Terminator Economy Amps
1980s. Economy solidstate amps ranging from 12 to 25 watts and 1x6" to 1x12".

1980s		$25	$75

Randall
1960s-present. Randall Instruments was originally out of California and is now a division of U.S. Music Corp. They have offered a range of tube and solidstate combo amps, heads and cabinets over the years.

Guitar and Bass amps
1980s-1990s. Mostly solidstate amps.

1980-1990s	Intermediate-grade	$250	$400
1980-1990s	Student-grade	$100	$250

Rat Fink
2002-present. Solidstate amp line from Lace Music Products. They also sold guitars and basses under this brand and offer amps under the Mooneyes and Lace brands.

Red Bear
1994-1997. Tube amps designed by Sergei Novikov and built in St. Petersburg, Russia. Red Bear amps were distributed in the U.S. under a joint project between Gibson and Novik, Ltd. Novik stills builds amps under other brands.

MK 60 Lead Tube Amp
1994-1997. Head with 4x12" half stack, Red Bear logo on amp and cab.

1994-1997		$700	$800

Reeves Amplification
2002-present. Started by Bill Jansen, Reeves builds tube amps, combos, and cabinets based on the classic British designs of Dan Reeves.

Reverend
1996-present. Joe Naylor started building amps under the Naylor brand in '94. In '96 he left Naylor to build guitars under the Reverend brand. From '01 to '05, Reverend offered tube amps, combos, and cabinets built in Warren, Michigan, that Naylor co-designed with Dennis Kager.

Rex
1930s-1950s, 1960s. Generally beginner-grade instruments and amps made by Harmony and Kay and sold through Fred Gretsch distributors. In the '60s, there were Italian-made electrics bearing the Rex brand. See Gretsch for listings.

Rickenbacker
1931-present. Rickenbacker made amps from the beginning of the company up to the late '80s. Rickenbacker had many different models, from the small early models that were usually sold as a guitar/amp set, to the large, very cool, Transonic.

Electro-Student Amp
Late-1940s. Typical late-'40s vertical combo cabinet, 1x12" speaker, lower power using 5 tubes, bottom mounted chassis, dark gray leatherette cover.

1948-1949		$250	$300

Model M-8 Amp
Gray, 1x8".

1950s		$250	$350
1960s		$250	$325

Model M-11 Amp
1950s. 12-15 watts, 1x12", 2x6V6 power.

1959		$350	$550

Model M-12 Amp
1950s. 12-15 watts, 1x12", M-12 logo on back panel, brown leatherette.

1950s		$350	$550

Professional Model 200-A Amp

1938		$300	$400

RB30 Amp
1986. Bass combo amp, 30 watts, tilted control panel, 1x12".

1986		$125	$175

RB60 Amp
1986. Bass combo amp, 60 watts, tilted control panel, 1x15".

1986		$200	$250

RB120 Amp
1986. Bass combo amp, 120 watts, tilted control panel, 1x15".

1986		$225	$300

Supersonic Model B-16
4x10" speakers, gray cover.

1960s		$650	$800

TR14 Amp
1978-ca.1982. Solidstate, 1x10", reverb, distortion.

1978-1982		$175	$225

TR35B Bass Amp
1970s. Solid-state, mid-power, 1x15".

1970s		$200	$250

TR75G Amp
1978-ca.1982. 75 watts, 2x12", 2 channels.

1978-1982		$150	$200

TR75SG Amp
1978-ca.1983. 1x10" and 1x15" speakers.

1978-1982		$200	$250

TR100G Amp
1978-ca.1982. Solidstate, 100 watts with 4x12", 2 channels.

1978-1982		$250	$300

Transonic Amp
1967-1970. Trapezoid shape, 2x12", head and cabinet, Rick-O-Select.

1967-1970		$850	$1,200

Randall RM50

Reeves Custom 18

Reverend Goblin

AMPS

Rivera Fandango 2x12"

Roccaforte 80 watt

1996 Roland BC-60

MODEL YEAR	FEATURES	EXC. COND. LOW	HIGH

Rivera

1985-present. Amp designer and builder Paul Rivera modded and designed amps for other companies before starting his own line in California. He offers heads, combos, and cabinets.

Chubster 40 Amp
2000-present. 40 watts, 1x12" combo, burgundy tolex, light grille.

2000-2003		$800	$900

Clubster 45 Amp
2005-present. 45 watts, 1x12" combo.

2005		$750	$800

Fandango 212 Combo Amp
2001-present. 55 watts, 2x12" tube amp.

2001-2002		$900	$1,100

Knuckle Head 55 Amp
1995-2002. 55 watts, head amp, replaced by reverb model.

1995-2002		$700	$900

Knuckle Head 100 Amp
1995-2002. 100 watt head, head amp, replaced by reverb model.

1995-2002		$750	$950

Los Lobottom/Sub 1
1999-2004. 1x12" cabinet with 300-watt powered 12" subwoofer.

1999-2004		$500	$600

M-60 Head Amp
1990-present. 60 watts, head amp.

1990-2004		$550	$650

M-60 112 Combo Amp
1989-present. 60 watts, 1x12".

1989-2004		$650	$750

M-100 Head Amp
1990-present. 100 watts, head amp.

1990-2004		$600	$700

M-100 212 Combo Amp
1990-present. 100 watts, 2x12" combo.

1990-2004		$700	$850

Quiana 112 Combo Amp
2000-present. Combo, 55 watts, 1x12".

2000-2004		$800	$1,000

R-30 112 Combo Amp
1993-present. 30 watts, 1x12", compact cab, black tolex cover, gray-black grille.

1993-2004		$550	$750

R-100 212 Combo Amp
1993-present. 100 watts, 2x12".

1993-2004		$700	$850

Suprema R-55 112/115 Combo Amp
2000-present. Tube amp, 55 watts, 1x12" (still available) or 1x15" ('00-'01).

2000-2004 1x12"		$800	$1,000
2000-2004 1x15"		$850	$1,050

TBR-1 Amp
1985-1999. First Rivera production model, rack mount, 60 watts.

1985-1999		$600	$850

Roccaforte Amps

1993-present. Tube amps, combos, and cabinets built by Doug Roccaforte in San Clemente, California.

Rodgers

1993-present. Custom tube amps and cabinets built by Larry Rodgers in Naples, Florida.

Rogue

2001-present. Student-level solidstate import (Korea) compact amps. They also offer guitars, mandolins, banjos, effects and basses.

CG Series
2000s. Solidstate, 20-100 watts.

2000s		$30	$150

Roland

Japan's Roland Corporation's products include amplifiers and keyboards and, under the Boss brand, effects.

AC-100 Amp
1995-present. Acoustic amp, 50 watts, 1x12" and 2x5", chorus, reverb, EQ, effects loop.

1995-2000		$250	$350

Bolt 60 Amp
Early 1980s. Solidstate/tube, 1x12".

1980s		$250	$275

Cube 20 Amp
1978-1982. Portable, 1x8", normal and overdrive channels, headphone jack.

1978-1982		$100	$200

Cube 40 Amp
1978-1980s. Portable, 1x10", normal and overdrive channels, 40 watts.

1978-1983		$125	$225

Cube 60/60B Amp
1978-1980s, 2004-present for Cube 60. 1x12", 60 watts, Cube 60 combo or Cube 60B combo bass amp.

1978-1983	Cube 60/60B	$175	$275

Cube 100 Amp
1978-1982. 100 watts, combo, 1x12".

1978-1982		$200	$300

Jazz Chorus Amp Series
1976-present. Includes the JC-50 (1980s. 50 watts, 1x12"), JC-55 ('87-'94, 50 watts, 2x8"), JC-77 ('87-'94, 80 watts, 2x10"), JC-90 (2x10") and the JC-120 ('76-present, 120 watts, 2x12").

1980s	JC-50	$300	$375
1987-1994	JC-55	$300	$375
1987-1994	JC-77/90	$375	$475
1987-2005	JC-120	$425	$500

Spirit 30 Amp
1982-late 1980s. Compact, 30 watts, 1x12".

1980s		$175	$275

VGA3 V-Guitar Amp
2003-present. GK digital modeling amp, 50 watts, 1x12" combo.

2003-2004		$275	$350

AMPS

MODEL		EXC. COND.	
YEAR	FEATURES	LOW	HIGH

VGA5 V-Guitar Amp
2001-2004. GK digital modeling amp, 65 watts, 1x12".
| 2001-2004 | | $350 | $400 |

VGA7 V-Guitar Amp
2000-present. 65 + 65 watts, 2x12", digital modeling with analog-style controls.
| 2000-2004 | | $400 | $500 |

Sadowsky
1980-present. In '05, luthier Roger Sadowsky added a bass tube amp head to his line of products built in Brooklyn, New York. He also builds basses and guitars.

Sam Ash
1960s-1970s. Sam Ash Music was founded by a young Sam Ash (formerly Ashkynase - an Austro-Hungarian name) in 1924. Ash's first store was in Brooklyn, New York, and by '66 there were about four Ash stores. During this time Ash Music private branded their own amp line which was built by Jess Oliver of Oliver Amps and based upon Oliver's Ampeg designs.

Sam Ash Mark II Pro Combo Amp
1960s. 2x12" with reverb combo amp.
| 1960s | | $275 | $350 |

Sano
1944-ca. 1970. Combo, heads and cabinets made in Irvington, New Jersey. Founded by Joseph Zon-Frilli, Louis Iorio, and Nick Sano, with initial offerings of accordion pickups, amplifiers, and all-electric accordions. Sano patented his accordion pickup in '44 and also developed a highly acclaimed stereophonic pickup accordion and matching amp. By '66 the Sano Corporation augmented their all-tube accordion amps with new solidstate circuitry models. In the mid-'60s they offered a new line of amps specifically designed for the guitar and bass market. Sano amps are generally low-gain, low power amplifiers. They also marketed reverb units and guitars.

Model 160R
1960s. Low power, around 15 watts, 1x12", reverb, trem, all-tube 2xEL84 power.
| 1960s | | $175 | $300 |

Savage
1994-present. Tube combos, amp heads and cabinets built by Jeff Krumm at Savage Audio, originally in Savage, Minnesota, and currently in Burnsville, Minnesota.

Sceptre
1960s. Canadian-made. Sceptre script logo on upper left side of grille ('60s Fender-style and placement).

Signet Amp
1960s. Low power, 1x10", Class-A 6V6 power, Signet model name on front panel.
| 1960s | | $125 | $200 |

Selmer
1960s. The Selmer UK distributor offered mid- to high-level amps.

Futurama Corvette Amp
1960s. Class A low power 1x8", volume and tone controls, plus amplitude and speed tremolo controls, large script Futurama logo on front of amp, Futurama Corvette and Selmer logo on top panel.
| 1960s | | $450 | $500 |

Mark 2 Treble and Bass Head Amp
1960s. About 30 watts (2xEL34s), requires power line transformer for U.S. use, large Selmer logo on grille.
| 1960s | | $550 | $700 |

Zodiac Twin Thirty Amp
1960s. Combo amp, gray snakeskin tolex cover.
| 1960s | | $2,500 | $3,000 |

Seymour Duncan
Pickup maker Seymour Duncan, located in Santa Barbara, California, offered a line of amps from around 1984 to '95.

84-40/84-50 Amp
1989-1995. Tube combo, 2 switchable channels, 1x12", includes the 84-40 ('89-'91, 40 watts) and the 84-50 ('91-'95, 50 watts).
| 1989-1991 | 84-40 | $300 | $400 |
| 1991-1995 | 84-50 | $325 | $425 |

Bass 300 x 2 Amp
1986-1987. Solidstate, 2 channels (300 or 600 watts), EQ, contour boost switches, effects loop.
| 1986-1987 | | $300 | $400 |

Bass 400 Amp
1986-1987. Solidstate, 400 watts, EQ, contour boost, balanced line output, effects loop.
| 1986-1987 | | $300 | $375 |

Convertible 100 Amp
1986-1987. Solidstate, 60 watts, effects loop, spring reverb, EQ, switchable preamp modules.
| 1986-1987 | Head | $325 | $400 |

Convertible 2000 Amp
1988-1995. Solidstate, 100 watts, holds 5 interchangeable modules, 1x12", 2 switchable channels.
| 1988-1995 | | $450 | $525 |

KTG-2075 Stereo Amp
1989-1993. Part of the King Tone Generator Series, 2 channels with 75 watts per channel.
| 1989-1993 | | $225 | $300 |

Sho-Bud
Introduced and manufactured by the Baldwin/Gretsch factory in 1970. Distributed by Kustom/Gretsch in the '80s. Models include D-15 Model 7838, S-15 Model 7836, Twin Tube Model 7834, and Twin Trans Model 7832.

D15 Sho-Bud Double Amp
Introduced in 1970. Solidstate, 100 watts. D-15 is 2 channels, S-15 is 1 channel, both with 1x15" JBL speaker.
| 1970s | | $300 | $375 |

Savage Macht6

Savage Gläs 30

Selmer

AMPS

Siegmund Midnight Blues Breaker Custom

Silvertone Model 1482

Silvertone Model 1484

MODEL YEAR FEATURES	EXC. COND. LOW	HIGH
S15 Sho-Bud Single Amp		
Introduced in 1972. 100 watts, 1x15" JBL, solidstate single channel combo.		
1970s	$250	$325
Sho-Bass Amp		
Introduced in 1972. 100 watts, 1x15", solidstate combo, black grille, black vinyl cover.		
1970s	$250	$325
Twin Trans Amp		
Introduced in 1972. 100 watts, solidstate combo, 2x12", reverb, black vinyl cover, dark grille, Sho-Bud script logo front upper right.		
1970s	$450	$525
Twin Tube Amp		
Introduced in 1972. 100 watt tube combo, 4 6L6s, 2x12", reverb, black vinyl cover, dark grille.		
1970s	$700	$750

Siegmund Guitars & Amplifiers

1993-present. Chris Siegmund builds his tube amp heads, combos and cabinets in Los Angeles, California. He founded the company in Seattle, moving it to Austin, Texas for '95-'97. He also builds effects pedals and guitars.

Silvertone

1941-ca.1970, present. Brand used by Sears. All Silvertone amps were supplied by American companies up to around '66.

MODEL YEAR FEATURES	EXC. COND. LOW	HIGH
Model 100 Amp		
Mid-late-1960s. Solidstate, piggyback amp and 2x12" cabinet with gold-label Jensen speakers.		
1960s	$350	$400
Model 150 Amp		
Mid-late-1960s. Solidstate, piggyback amp and 6x10" cabinet with gold-label Jensen speakers.		
1960s	$450	$550
Model 1331 Amp		
Ca.1954-ca.1957. Danelectro-made, luggage tweed, rounded front, a whole series made this style.		
1954-1957	$300	$350
Model 1336 (early Twin Twelve) Amp		
Ca.1954-ca.1957. Danelectro-made, luggage tweed, rounded front.		
1954-1957	$600	$700
Model 1340 (Student Model) Amp		
Early-1950s. Tan cover, brown grille with Silvertone logo, brown sides.		
1950s	$150	$200
Model 1346 (Twin Twelve) Amp		
Ca.1958-ca.1961. Danelectro-made, brown control panel, 2x12", 4 6L6s, vibrato, leather handle, tan smooth leatherette cover, 2 speaker baffle openings.		
1958-1961	$600	$700
Model 1391 Amp		
1950s. Blond-tan tweed-cloth cover, brown grille, single small speaker, leather handle.		
1950s	$175	$225

MODEL YEAR FEATURES	EXC. COND. LOW	HIGH
Model 1392 Amp		
1950s. Student amp with tremolo, 5 control knobs, brown cover and brown grille.		
1950s	$225	$300
Model 1422 40XL Amp		
1960s. Tube combo, low-mid power, 1x12", tremolo, reverb, vertical cab, 2 channels.		
1960s	$300	$350
Model 1432 Amp		
Late-1950s. 1x12", low- to mid-power, 2 6L6s, late-'50s overhanging top style cabinet.		
1950s	$225	$300
Model 1433 Combo Amp		
Late-1950s. Tube, 30 watts, 2 6L6s, 1x15", gray cover cabinet with pronounced overhanging top, light colored grille.		
1950s	$500	$600
Model 1451 Amp		
Late-1950s. Three or 4 watts, 3 tubes, 1x6" or 1x8" speaker, brown sparkle cover, wheat grille, by Danelectro.		
1950s 1x6"	$150	$200
Model 1457 Amp-In-Case (case only)		
1960s. The amp-in-case with the electric Silvertone guitar, this is the higher powered model with tremolo and higher quality speaker.		
1965 Amp only (no guitar)	$125	$150
Model 1459 Amp		
1960s. Four watts, 1x6" or 1x8".		
1960s	$150	$200
Model 1463 Bass 35 Amp		
1960s. Solidstate, 2x12", piggyback.		
1960s	$300	$325
Model 1465 Head Amp		
Mid-1960s. Rectangular amp head, solidstate, 50 watts, spotted gray cover, used with Twin 12 bottom.		
1960s	$200	$275
Model 1471 Amp		
1x8" speaker.		
1960s	$150	$200
Model 1472 Amp		
1960s. 15-18 watts, 2 6V6s provide mid-level power, 1x12", front controls mounted vertically on front right side, dark cover with silver grille, large stationary handle, tremolo.		
1962-1963	$300	$350
Model 1473 Amp		
1960s. Mid-power, tubes, 1x15" combo.		
1960s	$300	$350
Model 1474 Amp		
1960s. Mid-power, mid-level, dual speakers, tube combo amp, gray tolex, gray grille.		
1960s	$425	$500
Model 1481 Amp		
1960s. Low-power, student amp, 1x6", gray cover, light grille, 2 controls.		
1960s	$125	$175

MODEL YEAR	FEATURES	EXC. COND. LOW	HIGH

Model 1482 Amp
1960s. Low-power, 1x12" combo, gray tolex, silver grille, control panel mounted on right side vertically, tremolo.

1960s		$300	$400

Model 1483 Piggyback Amp
1960s. Mid-power, 1x15" tube amp, gray tolex and gray grille.

1960s		$500	$550

Model 1484 Twin Twelve Amp
1960s. Medium-power, 2x12" piggyback tube amp, classic Silvertone colors--gray cover with light grille.

1966		$600	$700

Skip Simmons
1990-present. Custom and production tube combo amps built by Skip Simmons in Dixon, California.

SMF
Mid-1970s. Amp head and cabinets from Dallas Music Industries, Ltd., of Mahwah, New Jersey. Offered the Tour Series which featured a 150 watt head and 4x12" bottoms with metal speaker grilles and metal corners.

SMF (Sonic Machine Factory)
2002-present. Tube amps and cabinets designed by Mark Sampson (Matchless, Bad Cat, Star) and Rick Hamel (SIB effects) and built in California.

Smicz Amplification
Tube combos and extension cabinets built by Bob Smicz in Bristol, Connecticut.

Smith Custom Amplifiers
2002-present. All tube combo amps, heads and speaker cabinets built by Sam Smith in Montgomery, Alabama.

Smokey
1997-present. Mini amps often packaged in cigarette packs made by Bruce Zinky in Flagstaff, Arizona. He also builds Zinky amps and effects and has revived the Supro brand on a guitar and amp.

Snider
1999-present. Jeff Snider has been building various combo tube amps in San Diego, California, since '95. In '99 he started branding them with his last name.

Soldano
1987-present. Made in Seattle, Washington by amp builder Mike Soldano, the company offers a range of all-tube combo amps, heads and cabinets. They also offer a reverb unit.

Astroverb 16 Combo Amp
1997-present. Atomic with added reverb.

1997-2002		$700	$800

Atomic 16 Combo Amp
1996-2001. Combo, 20 watts, 1x12".

1996-2001		$600	$700

Decatone Amp
1998-2002. 2x12" 100-watt combo, rear mounted controls, still available as a head.

1998-2002	No footswitch	$1,600	$1,800
1998-2002	With Decatrol footswitch	$2,000	$2,100

HR 50/Hot Rod 50 Amp Head
1992-present. 50-watt single channel head.

1992-2002		$800	$950

HR 100/Hot Rod 100 Amp Head
1994-2001. 100-watt single channel head.

1994-2001		$950	$1,100

Lucky 13 Combo Amp
2000-present. 100 watts (50 also available), 2x12" combo.

2000-2002		$1,000	$1,200

SLO-100 Super Lead Overdrive 100-Watt Amp
1988-present. First production model, super lead overdrive, 100 watts, snakeskin cover head amp, 4x12" cabinet.

1988-1999	Head	$1,900	$2,300
1990s	w/ cab	$2,600	$2,900

Sonax
Introduced in 1972. Budget line of solidstate amps offered by Gretsch/Baldwin, made by Yorkville Sound (Traynor) in Toronto, Canada. Introduced with dark grille and dark cover.

530-B Bass Amp
30 watts, 1x12".

1970s		$125	$200

550-B Bass Amp
50 watts, 1x15".

1970s		$150	$225

720-G Amp
Student amp, 20 watts, 2x8", reverb.

1970s		$200	$275

730-G Amp
30 watts, 2x10", reverb and tremolo.

1970s		$300	$375

750-G Amp
50 watts, 2x12", reverb and tremolo.

1970s		$375	$425

770-G Amp
75 watts, 4x10", reverb and tremolo.

1970s		$425	$475

Songworks Systems
See listing under Little Lanilei.

Sonny Jr.
1996-present. Harmonica amplifiers built by harmonica player Sonny Jr. in conjunction with Cotton Amps in Tolland, Connecticut.

Sonic Machine Factory 15 Watter

Snider combo

Soldano Lucky 13

AMPS

Specimen Horn Amp

Speedster 25-Watt Deluxe

Standel Custom

MODEL YEAR	FEATURES	EXC. COND. LOW	HIGH

Sound City

Made in England from the late-1960s to the late-'70s, the tube Sound City amps were Marshall-looking heads and separate cabinets. They were imported, for a time, into the U.S. by Gretsch.

50 PA Plus Amp
Late-1960s-late-1970s. Similar to 50 Plus but with 4 channels.

1970s		$500	$800

50 Plus/50R Amp Head
Late-1960s-late-1970s. Head amp, labeled 50 Plus or 50 R.

1960s		$500	$900
1970s		$500	$900

120/120R Amp Head
Early-late-1970s. The 120-watt head replaced the late-1960s 100-watt model.

1970s	120 no reverb	$600	$1,000
1970s	With reverb	$700	$1,000

Concord Combo Amp
80 watts, 2x12" Fane speakers, cream, basketweave grille.

1968	Cream	$600	$1,000

L-80 Cabinet
1970s. 4x10" cabinet.

1970s		$550	$600

X-60 Cabinet
1970s. 2x12" speaker cabinet.

1970s		$500	$550

Sound Electronics

Sound Electronics Corporation introduced a line of amplifiers in 1965 that were manufactured in Long Island. Six models were initially offered, all with tube preamps and solidstate power sections. Their catalog did not list power wattages but did list features and speaker configurations. The initial models had dark vinyl-style covers and sparkling silver grille cloth. The amps were combos with the large models having vertical cabinets, silver script Sound logo on upper left of grille. The larger models used JBL D120F and D130F speakers. Stand alone extension speakers were also available.

Various Model Amps
Mid-1960s. Includes X-101, X-101R, X-202 Bass/Organ, X-404 Bass and Organ, X-505R amps, hi-fi chassis often using 7868 power tubes.

1965		$350	$500

Sovtek

1992-2000. Sovtek amps were products of Mike Matthews of Electro-Harmonix fame and his New Sensor Corporation. The guitar and bass amps and cabinets were made in Russia.

Mig 50 Head Amp
1994-2000. Tube head, 50 watts.

1994-2000		$300	$350

Mig 60 Head Amp
1994-2000. Tube head, 60 watts, point-to-point wiring.

1994-2000		$350	$375

Mig 100 Head Amp
1992-2000. Tube head, 100 watts.

1992-2000		$375	$425

Mig 100B Head Amp
1996-2000. Bass tube head, 100 watts.

1996-2000		$350	$400

Specimen Products

1984-present. Luthier Ian Schneller added tube amps and speaker cabinets in '93. He also builds guitars, basses and ukes.

Speedster

1995-2000, 2003-present. Founded by Lynn Ellsworth, offering tube amps and combos designed by Bishop Cochran with looks inspired by dashboards of classic autos. In '03, Joe Valosay and Jevco International purchased the company and revived the brand with help from former owner Cory Wilds. Amps were originally built by Soldano, but are now built by Speedster in Gig Harbor, Washington.

St. George

1960s. There were Japanese guitars bearing this brand, but these amps may have been built in California.

Mid-Size Tube Amp
1965. Low power, 1x10" Jensen, 2 5065 and 2 12AX7 tubes.

1960s		$200	$275

Standel

1952-1974, 1997-present. Bob Crooks started custom building amps part time in '52, going into full time standard model production in '58 in Temple City, California. In '61 Standel started distributing guitars under their own brand and others (see Guitar section for more instrument details).

By late '63 or '64, Standel had introduced solidstate amps, two years before Fender and Ampeg introduced their solidstate models. In '67 Standel moved to a new, larger facility in El Monte, California. In '73 Chicago Musical Instruments (CMI), which owned Gibson at the time, bought the company and built amps in El Monte until '74. In '97 the Standel name was revived by Danny McKinney who, with the help of original Standel founder Bob Crooks and Frank Garlock (PR man for first Standel), set about reissuing some of the early models.

A-30 B Artist 30 Bass Amp
1964-early-1970s. Artist Series, the original Standel solidstate series, 80 watts, 2x15".

1964-1969		$300	$400

A-30 G Artist 30 Guitar Amp
1964-early-1970s. Artist Series, the original Standel solidstate series, 80 watts, 2x15".

1964-1969		$350	$450

AMPS

MODEL		EXC. COND.	
YEAR	FEATURES	LOW	HIGH

A-48 G Artist 48 Guitar Amp
1964-early-1970s. Artist Series, the original Standel solidstate series, 80 watts, 4x12".
| 1964-1974 | | $450 | $550 |

A-60 B Artist 60 Bass Amp
1964-early-1970s. Artist Series, the original Standel solidstate series, 160 watts, 4x15".
| 1964-1974 | | $400 | $500 |

A-60 G Artist 60 Guitar Amp
1964-early-1970s. Artist Series, the original Standel solidstate series, 160 watts, 4x15".
| 1964-1974 | | $450 | $550 |

A-96 G Artist 96 Guitar Amp
1964-early-1970s. Artist Series, the original Standel solidstate series, 160 watts, 8x12".
| 1964-1974 | | $500 | $700 |

C-24 Custom 24 Amp
Late-1960s-1970s. Custom Slim Line Series, solidstate, 100 watts, 2x12", dark vinyl, dark grille.
| 1970s | | $375 | $425 |

I-30 B Imperial 30 Bass Amp
1964-early-1970s. Imperial Series, the original Standel solidstate series, 100 watts, 2x15".
| 1960s | | $400 | $450 |

I-30 G Imperial 30 Guitar Amp
1964-early-1970s. Imperial Series, the original Standel solidstate series, 100 watts, 2x15".
| 1960s | | $450 | $500 |

Model 10L8/15L12/25L15
1953-1958. Early custom made tube amps made by Bob Crooks in his garage, padded naugahyde cabinet with varying options and colors. There are a limited number of these amps, and brand knowledge is also limited, therefore there is a wide value range. Legend has it that the early Standel amps made Leo Fender re-think and introduce even more powerful amps.
| 1953-1958 | | $2,500 | $3,500 |

S-10 Studio 10 Amp
Late-1960s-1970s. Studio Slim Line Series, solidstate, 30 watts, 1x10", dark vinyl, dark grille.
| 1970s | | $300 | $350 |

S-50 Studio 50 Amp
Late-1963 or early-1964-late-1960s. Not listed in '69 Standel catalog, 60 watts, gray tolex, gray grille, piggyback.
| 1964 | | $400 | $500 |

Star
2004-present. Tube amps, combos and speaker cabinets built by Mark Sampson in the Los Angeles, California area. Sampson has also been involved with Matchless, Bad Cat, and SMF amps.

Starlite
Starlite was a budget brand made and sold by Magnatone. See Magnatone for listings.

Stella Vee
1999-present. Jason Lockwood builds his combo amps, heads, and cabinets in Lexington, Kentucky.

Stevenson
1999-present. Luthier Ted Stevenson, of Lachine, Quebec, added amps to his product line in '05. He also builds basses and guitars.

Stinger
Budget line imported by Martin.

Stramp
1970s. Stramp, of Hamburg, Germany, offered audio mixers, amps and compact powered speaker units, all in aluminum flight cases.
Solidstate Amp
1970s. Solid-state amp head in metal suitcase with separate Stramp logo cabinet.
| 1970s | | $450 | $550 |

Sunn
1965-2002. Started in Oregon by brothers Conrad and Norm Sundhold (Norm was the bass player for the Kingsman). Sunn introduced powerful amps and extra heavy duty bottoms and was soon popular with many major rock acts. Norm sold his interest to Conrad in '69. Conrad sold the company to the Hartzell Corporation of Minnesota around '72. Fender Musical Instruments acquired the brand in '85 shortly after parting ways with CBS and used the brand until '89. They resurrected the brand again in '98, but quit offering the name in '02.

200S/215B Amp & Cab Set
Late-1960s. 60 watts, 2 6550s, large verticle cab with 2x15" speakers.
| 1969 | | $700 | $1,000 |

601-L Cab
1980s. 6x10" plus 2 tweeters cab.
| 1980s | | $300 | $350 |

Alpha 115 Amp
1980s. MOS-FET preamp section, 1x15", clean and overdrive.
| 1980s | | $200 | $250 |

Alpha 212 R Amp
1980s. MOS-FET preamp section, 2x12", reverb.
| 1980s | | $200 | $250 |

Beta Bass Amp
1978-1980s. 100 watts, solidstate, large "beta bass" logo, 1x15" combo or head only.
| 1970s | Combo | $450 | $500 |
| 1970s | Head | $400 | $425 |

Beta Lead Amp
1978-1980s. Solidstate, 100 watts, as 2x12" or 4x10" combo or head only.
| 1970s | Combos | $500 | $550 |
| 1970s | Head | $400 | $425 |

Concert Bass Head Amp
1970s. Solidstate, 200 watts.
| 1970s | | $200 | $250 |

Concert 215S Bass Amp Set
1970s. Solidstate head, 200 watts, Model 215S tall vertical cabinet with 2x12" Sunn label speakers, dark vinyl cover, silver sparkle grille.
| 1970s | | $500 | $550 |

Standel 100 UL15

Star Gain Star

1969 Sunn 100S

AMPS

1966 Supro Thunderbolt

1950s Supro Comet

SWR Goliath Junior III cab

MODEL YEAR	FEATURES	EXC. COND. LOW	HIGH

Concert Lead 610S Amp Set
1970s. Solidstate, 200 watts, 6x10" piggyback, reverb and built-in distortion.

1970s		$500	$550

Model T Head Amp
1970s. 100 watt head.

1970s		$650	$800

Model T Amp Reissue
1990s. Reissue of '70s Model T, 100 watts, with 4x12" cab.

1990s	Head	$600	$650
1990s	Head & cab	$900	$1,100

SB-200 Amp
1985. 200 watts, 1x15", 4-band EQ, master volume, compressor.

1985		$300	$375

Sceptre Head Amp
1968-1970s. Head amp, 60 watts, 6550 power tubes, tremolo, reverb.

1970s		$400	$550

Sentura Amp Head
1970s. Rectifier and power tubes, I and II versions.

1970s	I & II	$400	$550

Solarus Amp
1967-1970s. Tube amp (EL34s), 40 watts (upgraded to 60 watts in '69), 2x12", reverb, tremolo.

1970s		$500	$600

Sonoro Head Amp
Early-1970s. 60 watts, 2 6550s.

1970s		$400	$550

Sorado Amp and Cab
1970s. 50 watts, tubes, 2x15" matching cab.

1970s		$800	$1,000

SPL 7250 Amp
Dual channels, 250 watts per channel, forced air cooling, switch-selectable peak compressor with LEDs.

1989		$300	$350

Supertone
1914-1941. Supertone was a brand used by Sears for their musical instruments. In the '40s Sears started using the Silvertone name on those products. Amps were made by other companies.

Amp

1930s		$200	$250

Supro
1935-1968, 2004-present. Supro was a budget brand of the National Dobro Company, made by Valco in Chicago, Illinois. Amp builder Bruce Zinky revived the Supro name for a guitar and amp model.

Bantam 1611S Amp
1961-1964. Four watts, 3 tubes, 1x 8" Jensen, petite, Spanish Ivory fabric cover, gold weave saran wrap grille.

1961-1964		$250	$300

MODEL YEAR	FEATURES	EXC. COND. LOW	HIGH

Combo 1696T Amp
1961-1964. 24 watts, 6 tubes, 1x15" Jensen, Rhino-Hide covering in black and white, light grille, tremolo.

1961-1964		$400	$450

Comet 1610B Amp
1957-1959. Grey Rhino-Hide, 1x10".

1957-1959		$300	$350

Corsica Amp
Mid-1960s. Redesigned vertical combo amp, reverb, tremolo, blue control panel, black tolex, silver grille.

1965-1967		$500	$550

Dual-Tone 1624T Amp
1961-1964. 17 watts, 1x12", 6 tubes, organ tone tremolo.

1961-1964		$500	$550

Dual-Tone S6424T Amp
1964-1965. 17 watts, 6 tubes, 1x12" Jensen, restyled in '64, tremolo, Trinidad Blue vinyl fabric cover, light color grille.

1964-1965	Trinidad Blue	$500	$550

Royal Reverb 1650TR Amp
1963-1964. 17 watts, 15 tubes, 2x10" Jensens, catalog says "authentic tremolo and magic-reverberation."

1963-1964		$550	$600

Super 1606S Amp
1961-1964. 4.5 watts, 3 tubes, 1x8", black and white fabric cover, light saran wrap grille.

1961-1964		$275	$325

Thunderbolt S6420(B) Bass Amp
1964-1967. 35 watts, 1x15" Jensen, introduced in the '64 catalog as a no frills - no fancy extra circuits amp. Sometimes referred to as the "Jimmy Page amp" based on his use of this amp in his early career.

1964-1967		$650	$950

Thunderbolt S6920 Amp
1967-1968. Redesign circuit replaced S6420B, 35 watts, 1x12".

1967-1968		$325	$375

Tremo-Verb S6422 TR Amp
1964-1965. Lower power using 4 12AX7s, 1 5Y3GT, and 1 6V6, 1x10", tremolo and reverb.

1964-1965	Persian Red vinyl cover	$650	$800

Trojan Tremolo 1616T/S6416T Amp
1961-1966. 5 watts, 4 tubes, 1 11"x6" oval (generally Rolla) speaker, '61-'64 black and white fabric cover and saran wrap grille, '64-'66 new larger cab with vinyl cover and light grille.

1961-1966	Trinidad Blue vinyl cover	$300	$350

Vibra-Verb S6498VR Amp
1964-1965. "Supro's finest amplifier," 2x35-watt channels, 1x15" and 1x10" Jensens, vibrato and reverb.

1964-1965		$650	$800

Swanpro Amps
2004-present. Robert Swanson builds his tube combo and head amps and cabinets in Denver, Colorado.

MODEL YEAR	FEATURES	EXC. COND. LOW	HIGH

SWR Sound

1984-present. Founded by Steve W. Rabe in '84, with an initial product focus on bass amplifiers. Fender Musical Instruments Corp. acquired SWR in June, 2003.

Baby Blue Studio Bass System

1990-2003. Combo, all tube preamp, 150 watts solidstate power amp, 2x8", 1x5" cone tweeter, gain, master volume, EQ, effects-blend.

1990-2003		$450	$600

Basic Black Amp

1992-1999. Solidstate, 100 watts, 1x12", basic black block logo on front, black tolex, black metal grille.

1992-1999		$350	$450

Goliath III Cab

1996-present. Black tolex, black metal grille, includes the Goliath III Jr. (2x10") and the Goliath III (4x10").

1996-2004	2x10"	$250	$350
1996-2004	4x10"	$400	$550

Strawberry Blonde Amp

1998-present. 80 watts, 1x10" acoustic instrument amp.

1998-2003		$300	$350

Studio 220 Bass Amp

1988-1995. 220 watt solidstate head, tube preamp

1988-1995		$275	$325

Workingman's 15 Bass Amp

1995-2005. Combo amp, 1x15", 160 watts, replaced by WorkingPro 15.

1995-2002		$350	$400

Takt

Late-1960s. Made in Japan, tube and solidstate models.

GA Series Amps

1968. GA-9 (2 inputs and 5 controls, 3 tubes), GA-10, GA-11, GA-12, GA-14, GA-15.

1968	GA-14/GA-15	$50	$75
1968	GA-9 through GA-12	$25	$50

Talos

2004-present. Doug Weisbrod and Bill Thalmann build their tube amp heads, combo amps, and speaker cabinets in Springfield, Virginia. They started building and testing prototypes in '01.

Tech 21

1989-present. Long known for their SansAmp tube amplifier emulator, Tech 21 added solidstate combo amps, heads and cabinets in '96.

Teisco

1946-1974, 1994-present. Japanese brand first imported into the U.S. around '63. Teisco offered both tube and solidstate amps.

Checkmate 50 Amp

Late-1950s-early-1960s. Tubes, 2 6L6s, 50 watts, 2x12" open back, reverb, tremolo, piggyback, gray tolex cover, light gray grille.

1960s		$350	$400

Checkmate CM-100 Amp

Late-1960s. Tubes, 4x6L6 power, 100 watts, piggyback with Vox-style trolley stand.

1960s		$250	$350

Checkmate CM-15 Amp

Late-1960s. Tubes, 15 watts.

1960s		$50	$75

Checkmate CM-20 Amp

Late-1960s. Tubes, 20 watts.

1960s		$75	$100

Checkmate CM-25 Amp

Late-1960s. Tubes, 25 watts.

1960s		$100	$125

Checkmate CM-60 Amp

Late-1960s. Tubes, 60 watts, piggyback amp and cab with wheels.

1960s		$150	$200

Checkmate CM-66 Amp

Late-1960s. Solidstate, dual speaker combo, Check Mate 66 logo on front panel.

1960s		$50	$75

King 1800 Amp

Late-1960s. Tubes, 180 watts, piggyback with 2 cabinets, large Teisco logo on cabinets, King logo on lower right side of one cabinet.

1960s		$350	$450

Teisco 8 Amp

Late-1960s. Five watts

1960s		$25	$50

Teisco 10 Amp

Late-1960s. Five watts.

1960s		$25	$50

Teisco 88 Amp

Late-1960s. Eight watts.

1960s		$50	$75

THD

1987-present. Tube amps and cabinets built in Seattle, Washington, founded by Andy Marshall.

Titano (Magnatone)

1961-1963. Private branded by Magnatone, often for an accordion company or accordion studio, uses standard guitar input jacks.

Model 262 R Custom Amp

1961-1963. 35 watts, 2x12" + 2x5", reverb and vibrato make this one of the top-of-the-line models, black vinyl, light silver grille.

1961-1963		$1,000	$1,200

Model 415 Bass Amp

1961-1963. 25 watts, 4x8", bass or accordion amp, black cover, darkish grille.

1961-1963		$550	$600

Tone King

1993-present. Tube amps, combos, and cabinets built by Mark Bartel in Baltimore, Maryland. The company started in New York and moved to Baltimore in '94.

Talos Basic

Teisco Checkmate 17

Tone King Galaxy

Top Hat Club Royale T-20 CR

Trainwreck Express

Traynor PM-100

Tonemaster (Magnatone)

Late-1950s-early-1960s. Magnatone amps private branded for Imperial Accordion Company. Prominent block-style upper-case Tonemaster logo on front panel, generally something nearly equal to Magnatone equivalent. This is just one of many private branded Magnatones. Covers range from brown to black leatherette and brown to light silver grilles.

Model 214 (V logo) Amp
1959-1960. Ten watts, 1x12", vibrato, brown leatherette, V logo lower right corner front, large TONEMASTER logo.

1959-1960	$550	$600

Model 260 Amp
1961-1963. About 30 watts, 2x12", vibrato, brown leatherette and brown grille, large TONEMASTER logo on front.

1961-1963	$700	$800

Model 380 Amp
1961-1963. 50 watts, 2x12" and 2 oval 5"x7" speakers, vibrato, no reverb.

1961-1963	$800	$1,000

Top Hat Amplification

1994-present. Mostly Class A guitar amps built by Brian Gerhard originally in Anaheim, California, and since '05 in Fuquay-Varina, North Carolina. They also make an overdrive pedal.

Ambassador 100 TH-A100 Head Amp
Jan.1999-present. 100 watts, Class AB, 4 6L6s, reverb, dark green vinyl cover, white chicken-head knobs.

1999-2004	$1,100	$1,250

Ambassador T-35C 212 Amp
1999-present. 35 watts, 2x12" combo, reverb, master volume, blond cover, tweed-style fabric grille.

1999-2004	$1,100	$1,250

Club Deluxe Amp
1998-present. 20 watts, 6V6 power tubes, 1x12".

1988-2004	$975	$1,100

Club Royale TC-R2 Amp
Jan.1999-present. 20 watts, Class A using EL84s, 2x12".

1999-2003	$1,025	$1,200

Emplexador 50 TH-E50 Head Amp
Jan.1997-present. 50 watts, Class AB vint/high-gain head.

1997-2003	$1,300	$1,600

King Royale Amp
1996-present. 35 watts, Class A using 4 EL84s, 2x12".

1996-2003	$1,200	$1,400

Portly Cadet TC-PC Amp
Jan.1999-present. Five watts, 6V6 power, 1x8", dark gray, light gray grille.

1999-2003	$500	$600

Prince Royale TC-PR Amp
Jan.2000-2002. Five watts using EL84 power, 1x8", deep red, light grille.

2000-2003	$550	$650

Super Deluxe TC-SD2 Amp
Jan.2000-present. 30 watts, Class A, 7591 power tubes, 2x12".

2000-2003	$1,000	$1,200

Torres Engineering

Founded by Dan Torres, the company builds tube amps, combos, cabinets and amp kits in San Mateo, California. Dan wrote monthly columns for Vintage Guitar magazine for many years and authored the book Inside Tube Amps.

Trace Elliot

1978-present. Founded in a small music shop in Essex, England. Currently owned by Gibson.

TA100R Acoustic Guitar Amp
1990-present. Compact lateral-style cab with 4x5", 100 watts, with reverb, dark vinyl cover, dark grille.

1990s	$550	$600

TA35CR Acoustic Guitar Amp
1994-1995. Compact lateral-style cab with 2x5", 35 watts, with reverb and chorus, dark vinyl cover, dark grille.

1994-1995	$300	$400

Vellocette Amp
1996-1998. 15 watt, tube, Class A, 1x10", green cover, round sound speaker hole.

1996-1998	$400	$500

Trainwreck

1983-present. Founded by Ken Fischer. Limited production, custom-made amps that are generally grouped by model. Models include the Rocket, Liverpool and Express, plus variations on those themes. Each amp's value should be evaluated on a case-by-case basis. Ken wrote many amp articles for Vintage Guitar.

Custom Built Amp

1980s	High-end model	$14,000	$17,000

Traynor

1963-present. Started by Pete Traynor and Jack Long in Canada and made by Yorkville Sound.

Guitar Mate Reverb YGM3 Amp
1969-1979. 40 watts, 1x12", tube amp, black tolex, gray grille.

1969-1979	$400	$450

Mark II Bass Master Amp
1970s.

1970s	$400	$450

Mark III (YGL-3) Amp
1971-1979. All tube, 80 watts, 2x12" combo, reverb, tremolo.

1971-1979	$450	$500

YBA3 Custom Special Bass Amp Set
1967-1972. Tube head with 130 watts and 8x10" large vertical matching cab, dark vinyl cover, light grille.

1967-1972	$650	$700

True Tone

1960s. Guitars and amps retailed by Western Auto, manufactured by Chicago guitar makers like Kay.

MODEL YEAR	FEATURES	EXC. COND. LOW	HIGH

Hi-Fi 4 (K503 Hot-Line Special) Amp
1960s. Four watts from 3 tubes, gray cabinet, gray grille, metal handle, similar to K503.

1960s		$100	$175

Vibrato 704 Amp
1960s. Solidstate, 10 watts, 1x8", white sides and gray back, gray grille.

1960s		$125	$200

Vibrato 706 Amp
1960s. Solidstate, 15 watts, 1x15", white sides and gray back, brown grille.

1960s		$150	$250

Tube Works
1987-2004. Founded by B.K. Butler in Denver, Tube Works became a division of Genz Benz Enclosures of Scottsdale, Arizona in 1997. Tube Works' first products were tube guitar effects and in '91 they added tube/solidstate amps, cabinets, and DI boxes to the product mix. In '04, Genz Benz dropped the brand.

Twilighter (Magnatone)
Late-1950s-early-1960s. Magnatone amps private branded for LoDuca Brothers. Prominent block-style capital TWILIGHTER logo on front panel, generally something nearly equal to Magnatone equivalent. This is just one of many private branded Magnatones. Covers range from brown to black leatherette, and brown to light silver grilles.

Model 213 Amp
1961-1963. About 20 watts, 1x12", vibrato, brown leatherette and brown grille.

1961-1963		$550	$650

Model 260R Amp
1961-1963. About 18 to 25 watts, 1x12", vibrato, brown leatherette cover.

1961-1963		$600	$700

Model 280A Amp
Late-1950s-early-1960s. About 35 watts, 2x12", vibrato, brown leatherette cover.

1961-1963		$700	$800

Two-Rock
1999-present. Tube guitar amp heads, combos and cabinets built by Joe Mloganoski and Bill Krinard (K&M Analog Designs) originally in Cotati, California, currently in Rohnert Park. They also build speakers.

UltraSound
A division of UJC Electronics, UltraSound builds acoustically transparent amps, designed by Greg Farres for the acoustic guitarist, in Adel, Iowa.

Unique (Magnatone)
1961-1963. Private branded, typically for an accordion company or accordion studio, uses standard guitar input jacks.

Model 260R Amp
1961-1963. Based on Magnatone 260 Series amp, 35 watts, 2x12" but with reverb, black vinyl-style cover with distinctive black diamond-check pattern running through the top and sides.

1961-1963		$800	$1,000

Model 460 Amp
1961-1963. 35 watts, 2x12" and oval 5"x7" speakers, reverb and vibrato make it one of the top models, black vinyl, black grille.

1961-1963		$850	$1,050

Univox
1964-ca.1978. From '64 to early-'68, these were American-made tube amps with Jensen speakers. By '68, they were using Japanese components in American cabinets, still with Jensen speakers. Electronics were a combination of tube and transistors during this time; this type lasted until the mid-'70s. Around '71, Univox introduced a line of all solidstate amps, as well.

Bass Model U130B Amp
1976-1978. 130 watts, 1x15".

1976		$150	$250

Lead Model Tube Amp
1960s. Tube amp, 2x10" or 2x12".

1965-1969		$300	$375

Lead Model 65/U65RD Amp
1976-1978. Solidstate, 65 watts, reverb, 1x12" or 2x12"in a vertical cabinet.

1976-1978		$100	$200

Lead Model U130L Amp
1976-1978. Solidstate.

1976		$150	$250

Valco
Valco, from Chicago, Illinois, was a big player in the guitar and amplifier business. Their products were private branded for other companies like National, Supro, Airline, Oahu, and Gretsch.

Vega
1903-present. The original Boston-based company was purchased by C.F. Martin in '70. In '80, the Vega trademark was sold to a Korean company.

A-49 Amp
1960s. Six watts, 1x8", tubes, tan cover.

1960s		$175	$225

Super Amp
Early 1950s. 1 6L6, 1x10", vertical combo amp typical of the era.

1950s		$300	$350

Vesta Fire
1980s. Japanese imports by Shiino Musical Instruments Corp.; later by Midco International. Mainly known for effects pedals.

Power Amps

1980s	PT-I	$100	$175
1980s	PT-II	$150	$225

Tube Works 6150 DFX

Two-Rock Jet

Univox U130B

AMPS

VHT Pitbull Super 30

Victor MA-25

Victoria Regal

MODEL YEAR	FEATURES	EXC. COND. LOW	HIGH
Preamps			
1980s	J-I, J-II	$50	$125

VHT

1989-present. Founded by Steven M. Fryette, VHT builds amps, combos, and cabinets in Burbank, California.

Pittbull Classic Combo C-100-CL

1992-1994. 4 EL34s, 2x12", 100/50/25 watt. Name changed to Pittbull 100 CL.

1992-1994		$1,300	$1,500

Pittbull Fifty-Twelve Amp

1994-1999. 50 watts, all tube preamp section, 1x12", 2x12" version still available.

1994-1999		$800	$1,300

Victor

Late-1960s. Made in Japan.

MA-25 Amp

Late-1960s. Student model, light cover, dark grille, solidstate, 6 controls, 2 inputs, script Victor logo.

1960s		$75	$125

Victoria

1994-present. Tube amps, combos, and reverb units built by Mark Baier in Naperville, Illinois.

Double Deluxe Amp

1994-present. 35 watts, 2x12".

1994-2004		$1,200	$1,300

Model 518 Amp

1994-present. Tweed, 1x8".

1994-2004		$600	$700

Model 5112 Amp

2001-present. 5 watts, 5F1 circuit, 1x12".

2001-2004		$700	$800

Model 20112 Amp

1994-present. 20 watts, 1x12", tweed.

1994-2004		$800	$900

Model 35210 Amp

1994-present. 35 watts, 2x10", tweed.

1994-2004		$1,000	$1,200

Model 35212-T Amp

1990s. 35 watts, 2x12".

1990s		$1,200	$1,300

Model 35310-T Amp

1994-present. 35 watts, 3x10".

1994-2004		$1,300	$1,500

Model 45410-T Amp

1994-present. 45 watts, 4x10" combo.

1994-2004	Tweed	$1,300	$1,500

Model 50212-T Amp

2002-present. 50 watts, 2x12" combo.

2002-2003		$1,300	$1,500

Model 80212 Amp

1994-present. 80 watts, 2x12", tweed.

1994-2004		$1,300	$1,500

Victoriette Amp

2001-present. 20 watts, 1x12" or 2x10", reverb, tremolo in '01.

2001-2004	2x10"	$1,100	$1,300

Victorilux Amp

2001-present. 35 watts, 2x12", 3x10" or 1x15", EL84s, reverb, tremolo.

2001-2004		$1,300	$1,500

Vivi-Tone

1933-ca.1936. Founded in Kalamazoo, Michigan, by former Gibson designer Lloyd Loar and others, Vivi-Tone built small amps to accompany their early electric solidbody guitars. They possibly also built basses and mandolins.

V-M (Voice of Music) Corp.

1944-1977. Started out building record changers in Benton Harbor, Michigan. By the early '50s had added amplified phonographs, consoles, and tape recorders as well as OEM products for others. Their portable PA systems can be used for musical instruments. Products sport the VM logo.

Small Portable Amp

1950s. Standard phono input for instrument, phono and microphone controls, wood combo cabinet, 1x10" or 1x12" Jensen.

1950s		$250	$350

Voltmaster

Trapezoid-shaped combo amps and reverb units made in Plano, Texas, in the late 1990s.

Voodoo

1998-present. Tube amp heads and speaker cabinets built in Lansing, New York by Trace Davis, Anthony Cacciotti, and Mike Foster.

Vox

1957-1972, 1982-present. Tom Jennings and Dick Denney combined forces in '57 to produce the first Vox product, the 15-watt AC-15 amplifier. The short period between '63-'65 is considered to be the Vox heyday. Vox produced tube amps in England and also the U.S. from '64 to the early part of '66. English-made tube amps were standardized between '60 and '65. U.S.-made Vox amps in '66 were solidstate. In the mid-'60s, similar model names were sometimes used for tube and solidstate amps. In '93 Korg bought the Vox name and current products are built by Marshall.

A Vox amp stand is correctly called a trolley and those amps that originally came with one are priced including the original trolley, and an amp without it trolley will be worth less than the amount shown. Smaller amps were not originally equipped with a trolley.

AC-4 Amp

1958-1965. Made in England, early Vox tube design, 3.5 watts, 1x8", tremolo.

1958-1965		$1,500	$1,600

AC-10 Amp

1960-1965. Made in England, 12 watts, 1x10", tremolo, this tube version not made in U.S. ('64-'65).

1960-1965		$2,000	$2,500

MODEL YEAR	FEATURES	EXC. COND. LOW	HIGH

AC-10 Twin Amp
1960-1965. Made in England, also made in U.S. '64-'65, 12 watts (2xEL84s), 2x10".

1960-1965		$2,500	$3,000

AC-15 Twin Amp
1958-1965. Tube, 2x12", 18 watts.

1958-1965	Black Tolex	$3,500	$4,000
1960-1965	Custom colors	$4,200	$4,500

AC-15 TBX
1996-2000. 15 watts, top boost, 1x12" Celestion (lower cost Eminence available).

1996-2000		$900	$950

AC-30 Super Twin Head Amp
1960-1965. Made in England, 30-watt head.

1960-1963	Custom color	$3,500	$4,000
1960-1965	With footswitch	$2,800	$3,100

AC-30 Twin/AC-30 Twin Top Boost Amp
1960-1965. Made in England, 30-watt head, 36 watts 2x12", Top Boost includes additional treble and bass, custom colors available in '60-'63.

1960-1963	Custom colors	$5,000	$5,500
1960-1965		$4,000	$4,500

AC-30 Reissue Models
1980s-1990s. Standard reissue and Limited edtion models with identification plate on the back of the amp. Models include the AC-30 Reissue and Reissue custom color (1980s-1990s), AC-30 25th Anniv. (1985-1986), AC-30 30th Anniv. (1991), AC-30 Collector Model (1990s, mahogany cabinet) and the AC-30HW Hand Wired (1990s).

1980s	Reissue	$1,300	$1,600
1985-1986	25th Anniv.	$1,400	$1,700
1990s	Collector Model	$2,000	$2,300
1990s	Hand wired	$2,000	$2,800
1990s	Reissue	$1,200	$1,300
1990s	Reissue custom color	$1,600	$1,700
1991	30th Anniv.	$2,000	$2,300

AC-50 Head Amp
1960-1965. Made in England, 50-watt head, U.S. production '64-'65 tube version is Westminster Bass, U.S. post-'66 is solidstate.

1960-1965		$1,600	$1,800

Berkeley II V108 (tube) Amp
1964-1966. U.S.-made tube amp, revised '66-'69 to U.S.-made solidstate model V1081, 18 watts, 2x10" piggyback.

1964-1966		$1,400	$1,500

Berkeley II V1081 (solidstate) Amp
1966-1969. U.S.-made solidstate model V1081, 35 watts, 2x10" piggyback, includes trolley stand.

1966-1969		$800	$900

Berkeley III (solidstate) Amp
1966-1969. Berkeley III logo on top panel of amp.

1966-1969		$800	$900

Buckingham Amp
1966-1969. Solidstate, 70 watts, 2x12" piggyback, includes trolley stand.

1966-1969		$900	$1,000

Cambridge 15 Amp
1999-2001. 15 watts, 1x8", tremolo.

1999-2001		$125	$175

Cambridge 30 Reverb Amp
1999-2002. 30 watts, 1x10", tremolo and reverb.

1999-2002		$175	$275

Cambridge 30 Reverb Twin 210 Amp
1999-2002. 30 watts hybrid circuit, 2x10", reverb.

1999-2002		$275	$375

Cambridge Reverb (tube) V103 Amp
1964-1966. U.S-made tube version, 18 watts, 1x10", a Pacemaker with reverb, superceded by solidstate Model V1031 by '67.

1964-1966		$1,200	$1,300

Cambridge Reverb (solidstate) V1031 Amp
1966-1969. Solidstate, 35 watts, 1x10", model V1031 replaced tube version V103.

1966-1969		$650	$700

Churchill PA V119 Head and V1091 Cab Set
Late-1960s. PA head with multiple inputs and 2 column speakers.

1960s	PA head only	$400	$500
1960s	Head and cabs	$900	$1,000

Climax V-125/V-125 Lead Combo Amp
1970-1991. Solidstate, 125 watts, 2x12" combo, 5-band EQ, master volume.

1970-1991		$500	$700

Defiant Amp
1966-1969. Made in England, 50 watts, 2x12" + Midax horn cabinet.

1966-1969		$1,600	$1,800

Escort Amp
Late 1960s-1983. 2.5 watt battery-powered portable amp.

1968-1986		$375	$450

Essex Bass V1042 Amp
1965-1969. U.S.-made solidstate, 35 watts, 2x12".

1965-1969		$700	$850

Foundation Bass Amp
1966-1969. Tube in '66, solidstate after, 50 watts, 1x18", made in England only.

1966	Tubes	$1,800	$2,200
1967-1969		$550	$650

Kensington Bass V1241 Amp
1965-1969. U.S.-made solidstate bass amp, 22 watts, 1x15", G-tuner.

1965-1969		$400	$600

Pacemaker (tube) V102 Amp
1964-1965. U.S.-made tube amp, 18 watts, 1x10", replaced by solidstate Pacemaker model V1021.

1964-1965		$850	$900

Pacemaker (solidstate) V1021 Amp
1966-1969. U.S.-made solidstate amp, 35 watts, 1x10", replaced Pacemaker model V102.

1967-1969		$350	$450

Pathfinder (tube) V101 Amp
1964-1965. U.S.-made tube amp, 4 watts, 1x18", '66-'69 became U.S.-made solidstate V1011.

1964-1965		$850	$900

1963 Vox AC-2

Vox AC-50 Super Twin

Vox Pathfinder

Vox Super Beatle

Watkins Dominator

Warwick Quad IV

MODEL YEAR	FEATURES	EXC. COND. LOW	HIGH

Pathfinder (solidstate) V1011 Amp

1966-1969. U.S.-made solidstate, 25 watts peak power, 1x8".

1966-1969		$300	$400

Pathfinder 10 Amp

2002-present. Compact practice amp with 1960s cosmetics, 10 watts, 6.5" speaker.

2002-2004		$65	$90

Pathfinder 15 Amp

1998-present. 1960s cosmetics, 15 watts, 1x8".

1998-2004		$65	$90

Royal Guardsman V1131/V1132 Amp

1966-1969. U.S.-made solidstate, 50 watts piggyback, 2x12" + 1 horn, the model below the Super Beatle V1141/V1142.

1966-1969		$1,200	$1,500

Scorpion (solidstate) Amp

1968. Solidstate, 60 watts, 4x10" Vox Oxford speaker.

1968		$500	$700

Super Beatle V1141/V1142 Amp

1966-1967. U.S.-made 120 watt solidstate, 4x12" + 2 horns, with distortion pedal (V1141), or without (V1142).

1966-1967		$2,000	$2,300

Viscount V1151/V1152 Amp

1966-1969. U.S.-made solidstate, 70 watts, 2x12" combo.

1966-1969		$700	$800

Westminster V118 Bass Amp

1966-1969. Solidstate, 120 watts, 1x18".

1966-1969		$600	$650

V-Series

See Crate.

Wabash

1950s. Private branded amps distributed by the David Wexler company.

Model 1158 Amp

Danelectro-made, 1x15", 2x6L6 power tubes.

1955	Tweed	$200	$300

Warbler

See listing under Juke amps.

Warwick

1982-present. Combos, amp heads and cabinets from Warwick Basses of Markneukirchen, Germany.

Washburn

1974-present. Imported guitar and bass amps. Washburn also offers guitars, mandolins, and basses.

Watkins

1957-present. England's Watkins Electric Music (WEM) was founded by Charlie Watkins. Their first commercial product was the Watkins Dominator (wedge Gibson stereo amp shape) in '57, followed by the Copicat Echo in '58. They currently build accordion amps.

Clubman

1960s. Small combo amp with typical Watkins styling, blue cover, white grille.

1960s		$400	$500

Dominator V-Front Amp

Late-1950s-1960s, 2004. 18 watts, 2x10", wedge cabinet similar to Gibson GA-79 stereo amp, tortoise and light beige cab, light grille, requires 220V step-up transformer. Was again offered in '04.

1959-1962		$1,200	$1,400

Webcor

1940s-1950s. The Webster-Chicago Company built recording and audio equipment including portable amplifiers suitable for record turntables, PAs, or general utility. Low power with one or two small speakers.

Small Amplifier

1950s	1 or 2 speakers	$175	$200

West Laboratories

1965-1970s, 2005-present. Founded by David W. West in Flint, Michigan, moved to Lansing in '68. The '71 catalog included three tube and two solid-state amps, speaker cabinets, as well as Vocal Units and Mini Series combo amps. Amps were available as heads, piggyback half-stacks and full-stacks, with the exception of the combo Mini Series. The Fillmore tube amp head was the most popular model. West equipment has a West logo on the front and the cabinets also have a model number logo on the grille. David West reestablished his company in 2005, located in Okemos, Michigan, with models offered on a custom order basis, concentrating on lower power EL84 designs.

Avalon Head Amp

50 watts, 2 6CA7 output tubes.

1971		$400	$600

Fillmore Head Amp

200-watts, 4 KT88 output tubes.

1971		$1,500	$3,000

Grande Head Amp

100 watts, 2 KT88 output tubes.

1971		$700	$900

White

1955-1960. The White brand, named after plant manager Forrest White, was established by Fender to provide steel and small amp sets to teaching studios that were not Fender-authorized dealers. The amps were sold with the matching steel guitar. See Steel section for pricing.

White (Matamp)

See Matamp listing.

MODEL YEAR	FEATURES	EXC. COND. LOW	HIGH

Working Dog

2001-present. Lower cost tube amps and combos built by Alessandro High-End Products (Alessandro, Hound Dog) in Huntingdon Valley, Pennsylvania.

Yamaha

1946-present. Yamaha started building amps in the '60s and offered a variety of guitar and bass amps over the years. The current models are solidstate bass amps. They also build guitars, basses, effects, sound gear and other instruments.

Budokan HY-10G II Amp
1987-1992. Portable, 10 watts, distortion control, EQ.

1987-1992		$75	$100

G50-112 Amp
1983-1992. 50 watts, 1x12".

1983-1992		$200	$300

G100-112 Amp
1983-1992. 100 watts, 1x12" combo, black cover, striped grille.

1983-1992		$200	$300

G100-212 Amp
1983-1992. 100, 2x12" combo, black cover, striped grille.

1983-1992		$250	$350

JX30B Amp
1983-1992. Bass amp, 30 watts.

1983-1992		$150	$250

TA-20 Amp
1968-1972. Upright wedge shape with controls facing upwards, solidstate.

1968-1972		$125	$225

TA-25 Amp
1968-1972. Upright wedge shape with controls facing upwards, 40 watts, 1x12", solidstate, black or red cover.

1968-1972		$150	$250

TA-30 Amp
1968-1972. Upright wedge shape, solidstate.

1968-1972		$175	$275

TA-50 Amp
1971-1972. Solidstate combo, 80 watts, 2x12", includes built-in cart with wheels, black cover.

1971-1972		$200	$300

TA-60 Amp
1968-1972. Upright wedge shape, solidstate, most expensive of wedge-shape amps.

1968-1972		$225	$275

VR4000 Amp
1988-1992. 50-watt stereo, 2 channels, EQ, stereo chorus, reverb and dual effects loops.

1988-1992		$250	$350

VR6000 Amp
1988-1992. 100-watt stereo, 2 channels which can also be combined, EQ, chorus, reverb and dual effects loops.

1988-1992		$350	$450

VX-15 Amp
1988-1992. 15 watts.

1988-1992		$100	$200

VX-65D Bass Amp
1984-1992. 80 watts, 2 speakers.

1984-1992		$150	$225

YBA-65 Bass Amp
1972-1976. Solidstate combo, 60 watts, 1x15".

1972-1976		$150	$225

YTA-25 Amp
1972-1976. Solidstate combo, 25 watts, 1x12".

1972-1976		$150	$225

YTA-45 Amp
1972-1976. Solidstate combo, 45 watts, 1x12".

1972-1976		$150	$225

YTA-95 Amp
1972-1976. Solidstate combo, 90 watts, 1x12".

1972-1976		$150	$250

YTA-100 Amp
1972-1976. Solidstate piggyback, 100 watts, 2x12".

1972-1976		$200	$300

YTA-110 Amp
1972-1976. Solidstate piggyback, 100 watts, 2x12" in extra large cab.

1972-1976		$200	$300

YTA-200 Amp
1972-1976. Solidstate piggyback, 200 watts, 4x12".

1972-1976		$250	$350

YTA-300 Amp
1972-1976. Solidstate piggyback, 200 watts, dual cabs with 2x12" and 4x12".

1972-1976		$400	$450

YTA-400 Amp
1972-1976. Solidstate piggyback, 200 watts, dual 4x12".

1972-1976		$400	$450

Zapp

Ca.1978-early-1980s. Zapp amps were distributed by Red Tree Music, Inc., of Mamaroneck, New York.

Z-10 Amp
1978-1980s. Small student amp, 8 watts.

1979-1982		$25	$75

Z-50 Amp
1978-1980s. Small student amp, 10 watts, reverb, tremelo.

1978-1982		$50	$75

Zeta

1982-present. Solid state amps with MIDI options, made in Oakland, California. They also make basses, violins and mandolins.

Zinky

1999-present. Tube head and combo amps and cabinets built by Bruce Zinky in Flagstaff, Arizona. He also builds the mini Smokey amps (since '97), effects, and has revived the Supro brand on a guitar and amp.

Working Dog Rottweiler

AMPS

Zeta AP-12

Zinky 25-Watt

Effects

ADA Flanger

ADA TFX4 Time Effects

Alesis Guitar FX

MODEL YEAR	FEATURES	EXC. COND. LOW	HIGH

Ace-Tone

1968-1972. Effects from Ace Electronic Industry, which was a part of Sakata Shokai Limited of Osaka, Japan, and and also made organs, amps, etc. Their Ace-Tone effects line was available from '68-'72 and was the precedessor to Roland and Boss.

Fuzz Master FM-1

Distortion and overdrive.

| 1968-1972 | | $125 | $225 |

Wah Master WM-1

Filter wah.

| 1968-1972 | | $125 | $225 |

Acoustyx

1977-1982. Made by the Highland Corporation of Vermont.

Image Synthesizer IS-1

1977-1982.

| 1977-1982 | | $50 | $60 |

Phase Five

1977-ca.1982. Used 6 C cell batteries!

| 1977-1982 | | $50 | $60 |

ADA

1975-2002. ADA is an acronym for Analog/Digital Associates. The company was located in Berkeley, California, and introduced its Flanger and Final Phase in '77. The company later moved to Oakland and made amplifiers, high-tech signal processors, and a reissue of its original Flanger.

Final Phase

1977-1979. Reissued in '97.

| 1977-1979 | | $400 | $450 |

Flanger

1977-1983, 1996-2002. Reissued in '96.

1977-1979	With control pedal	$400	$450
1977-1979	Without control pedal	$350	$400
1980-1983		$250	$300
1996-2002		$80	$100

MP-1

1987-1995. Tube preamp with chorus and effects loop, MIDI.

| 1987-1995 | Without optional foot controller | $150 | $200 |

MP-2

Ca.1988-1995. Tube preamp with chorus, 9-band EQ and effects loop, MIDI.

| 1988-1995 | | $225 | $275 |

Pitchtraq

1987. Programmable pitch transposer including octave shifts.

| 1987 | | $225 | $275 |

Stereo Tapped Delay STD-1

Introduced in 1981.

| 1980s | | $150 | $200 |

TFX4 Time Effects

Introduced in 1982, includes flanger, chorus, doubler, echo.

| 1980s | | $150 | $200 |

Aguilar

The New York, New York amp builder also offers a line of tube and solidstate pre-amps.

Akai

1984-present. In '99, Akai added guitar effects to their line of electronic samplers and sequencers for musicians.

Headrush E1

1999-2005. Delay, tape echo simulations, looping recorder.

| 1999-2005 | | $180 | $190 |

Alamo

1947-1982. Founded by Charles Eilenberg, Milton Fink, and Southern Music, San Antonio, Texas. Distributed by Bruno & Sons. Mainly known for guitars and amps, Alamo did offer a reverb unit.

Reverb Unit

1965-ca.1979. Has a Hammond reverb system, balance and intensity controls. By '73 the unit had 3 controls - mixer, contour, and intensity.

| 1965-1970 | | $275 | $350 |

Alesis

1992-present. Alesis has a wide range of products for the music industry, including digital processors and amps for guitars.

Effects Processors

1992-present. Various digital processors for reverb, echo, etc.

| 1990s | | $125 | $200 |

Allen Amplification

1998-present. David Allen's company, located in Richwood, Kentucky, mainly produces amps, but they also offer a tube overdrive pedal.

Altair Corp.

1977-1980s. Company was located in Ann Arbor, Michigan.

Power Attenuator PW-5

1977-1980. Goes between amp and speaker to dampen volume.

| 1977-1980 | | $100 | $125 |

Amdek

Mid-1980s. Amdek offered many electronic products over the years, including drum machines and guitar effects. Most of these were sold in kit form so quality of construction can vary.

Delay Machine DMK-200

1983. Variable delay times.

| 1983 | | $100 | $125 |

Octaver OCK-100

1983. Produces tone 1 or 2 octaves below the note played.

| 1983 | | $100 | $125 |

MODEL YEAR	FEATURES	EXC. COND. LOW	HIGH

Ampeg

Ampeg entered the effects market in the late-1960s. Their offerings in the early-'60s were really amplifier-outboard reverb units similar to the ones offered by Gibson (GA-1). Ampeg offered a line of imported effects in '82-'83, known as the A-series (A-1 through A-9), and reintroduced effects to their product line in '05.

Analog Delay A-8
1982-1983. Made in Japan.
1982-1983 $75 $125

Chorus A-6
1982-1983. Made in Japan.
1982-1983 $50 $75

Compressor A-2
1982-1983. Made in Japan.
1982-1983 $50 $75

Distortion A-1
1982-1983. Made in Japan.
1982-1983 $50 $75

Echo Jet (EJ-12) Reverb
1963-1965. Outboard, alligator clip reverb unit with 12" speaker, 12 watts, technically a reverb unit. When used as a stand-alone amp, the reverb is off. Named EJ-12A in '65.
1963-1965 $350 $400

Echo Satellite (ES-1)
1961-1963. Outboard reverb unit with amplifier and speaker alligator clip.
1961-1963 $325 $375

Flanger A-5
1982-1983. Made in Japan.
1982-1983 $50 $75

Multi-Octaver A-7
1982-1983. Made in Japan.
1982-1983 $50 $100

Over Drive A-3
1982-1983. Made in Japan.
1982-1983 $50 $75

Parametric Equalizer A-9
1982-1983. Made in Japan.
1982-1983 $45 $70

Phaser A-4
1982-1983. Made in Japan.
1982-1983 $50 $75

Phazzer
1975-1977.
1975-1977 $50 $75

Scrambler Fuzz
1969. Distortion pedal. Reissued in '05.
1969 $75 $150

Amplifier Corporation of America

Late '60s company that made amps for Univox and also marketed effects under their own name.

Analog Man

1994-present. Founded by Mike Piera in '94 with full-time production by 2000. Located in Bethel, Connecticut, producing chorus, compressor, fuzz, and boost pedals by '03.

Aphex Systems

1975-present. Founded in Massachusetts by Marvin Caesar and Curt Knoppel, to build their Aural Exciter and other pro sound gear. Currently located in Sun Valley, California, and building a variety of gear for the pro audio broadcast, pro music and home-recording markets.

Apollo

Ca.1967-1972. Imported by St. Louis Music, includes Fuzz Treble Boost Box, Crier Wa-Wa, Deluxe Fuzz.

Crier Wa-Wa
Ca.1967-1972.
1967-1972 $100 $200

Fuzz/Deluxe Fuzz
Ca.1967-1972. Includes the Fuzz Treble Boost Box and the Deluxe Fuzz.
1967-1972 $150 $250

Arbiter

Ivor Arbiter and Arbiter Music, London, began making the circular Fuzz Face stompbox in 1966. Other products included the Fuzz Wah and Fuzz Wah Face. In '68 the company went public as Arbiter and Western, later transitioning to Dallas-Arbiter. Refer to Dallas-Arbiter for listings.

Area 51

2003-present. Guitar effects made in Newaygo, Michigan, by Dan Albrecht. They also build amps.

Aria

1960-present. Aria provided a line of effects, made by Maxon, in the mid-'80s.

Analog Delay AD-10
1983-1985. Dual-stage stereo.
1983-1985 $65 $75

Chorus ACH-1
1986-1987. Stereo.
1986-1987 $40 $50

Chorus CH-5
1985-1987.
1985-1987 $40 $50

Chorus CH-10
1983-1985. Dual-stage stereo.
1983-1985 $40 $50

Compressor CO-10
1983-1985.
1983-1985 $40 $50

Digital Delay ADD-100
1984-1986. Delay, flanging, chorus, doubling, hold.
1984-1986 $65 $75

Digital Delay DD-X10
1985-1987.
1985-1987 $65 $75

Distortion DT-5
1985-1987.
1985-1987 $40 $50

Ampeg Scrambler Fuzz

*Analog Man
Black Cat Superfuzz*

Aria CH-10 Chorus

EFFECTS

Arion Phase Shifter RE-100

EFFECTS

Arion Stereo Delay SAD-3

Austone Soul-O-Stomp

MODEL YEAR	FEATURES	EXC. COND. LOW	HIGH
Distortion DT-10			
1983-1985. Dual-stage.			
1983-1985		$40	$50
Flanger AFL-1			
1986. Stereo.			
1986		$50	$60
Flanger FL-5			
1985-1987.			
1985-1987		$50	$60
Flanger FL-10			
1983-1985. Dual-stage stereo.			
1983-1985		$50	$60
Metal Pedal MP-5			
1985-1987.			
1985-1987		$40	$50
Noise Gate NG-10			
1983-1985.			
1983-1985		$30	$40
Over Drive OD-10			
1983-1985. Dual-stage.			
1983-1985		$40	$50
Parametric Equalizer EQ-10			
1983-1985.			
1983-1985		$40	$50
Phase Shifter PS-10			
1983-1984. Dual-stage.			
1983-1984		$50	$60
Programmable Effects Pedal APE-1			
1984-1986. Compression, distortion, delay, chorus.			
1984-1986		$50	$60

Arion

1984-present. Arion offers a wide variety of budget imported effects.

Guitar and Bass Effects

1984-present. Various models.

1984-2004		$15	$45

Asama

1970s-1980s. This Japanese company offered solidbody guitars with built-in effects as well as stand-alone units. They also offered basses, drum machines and other music products.

Astrotone

Late 1960s. By Universal Amp, which also made the Sam Ash Fuzzz Boxx.

Fuzz

1966. Introduced in '66, same as Sam Ash Fuzzz Boxx.

1966		$175	$275

ATD

Mid-1960s-early 1980s. Made by the All-Test Devices corporation of Long Beach, New York. In the mid-'60s, Richard Minz and an associate started making effects part-time, selling them through Manny's Music in New York. They formed All-Test and started making Maestro effects and transducer pickups for CMI, which owned Gibson at the time.

By '75, All-Test was marketing effects under their own brand. All-Test is still making products for other industries, but by the early to mid-'80s they were no longer making products for the guitar.

PB-1 Power Booster

1976-ca.1980.

1979-1980		$50	$60

Volume Pedal EV-1

1979-ca.1980.

1979-1980		$30	$40

Wah-Wah/Volume Pedal WV-1

1979-ca.1981.

1979-1981		$50	$60

Audio Matrix

1978-1984. Effects built by B.K Butler in Escondido, California. He later designed the Tube Driver and founded Tube Works in 1987. He nows operates Butler Audio, making home and auto hybrid tube stereo amps.

Mini Boogee B81

1981. Four-stage, all-tube preamp, overdrive, distortion.

1981		$100	$135

Audioworks

1980s. Company was located in Niles, Illinois.

F.E.T. Distortion

1982.

1980s		$40	$55

Auralux

2000-present. Founded by Mitchell Omori and David Salzmann, Auralux builds effects and tube amps in Highland Park, Illinois.

Austone Electronics

1997-present. Founded by Jon Bessent and Randy Larkin, Austone offers a range of stomp boxes, all made in Austin, Texas.

Overdrive and Fuzz Pedals

1997-present. Various overdrive and fuzz boxes.

1997-2004		$125	$175

Automagic

1998-present. Wah pedals and distortion boxes made in Germany by Musician Sound Design.

Avalanche

Brianizer

Late-1980s. Leslie effect, dual rotor, adjustable speed and rates.

1980s		$75	$90

Axe

1980s. Early '80s line of Japanese effects, possibly made by Maxon.

B & M

1970s. A private brand made by Sola/Colorsound for Barns and Mullens, a U.K. distributor.

MODEL YEAR	FEATURES	EXC. COND. LOW	HIGH

Fuzz Unit
1970s. Long thin orange case, volume, sustain, tone knobs, on-off stomp switch.

1970s		$275	$325

Bad Cat Amplifier Company
2000-present. Amp company Bad Cat, of Corona, California, also offers guitar effects.

Baldwin
1965-1970. The piano maker got into the guitar market when it acquired Burns of London in '65, and sold the guitars in the U.S. under the Baldwin name. They also marketed a couple of effects at the same time.

Bartolini
The pickup manufacturer offered a few effects from around 1982 to '87.

Tube-It
1982-ca.1987. Marshall tube amplification simulator with bass, treble, sustain controls.

1982-1987	Red case	$80	$90

Basic Systems' Side Effects
1980s. This company was located in Tulsa, Oklahoma.

Audio Delay
1986-ca.1987. Variable delay speeds.

1986-1987		$75	$100

Triple Fuzz
1986-ca.1987. Selectable distortion types.

1986-1987		$50	$60

BBE
1985-present. BBE, owner of G & L Guitars and located in California, manufactures rack-mount effects and added a new line of stomp boxes in '05.

601 Stinger
1985-ca.1989.

1985-1989		$55	$65

Behringer
1989-present. The German professional audio products company added modeling effects in '01 and guitar stomp boxes in '05. They also offer guitars and amps.

Beigel Sound Lab
1980. Music product designer Mike Beigel helped form Musitronics Corp, where he made the Mu-Tron III. In 1978 he started Beigel Sound Lab to provide product design in Warwick, New York, where in '80 he made 50 rack-mount Enveloped Controlled Filters under this brand name.

Bell Electrolabs
1970s. This English company offered a line of effects in the '70s.

MODEL YEAR	FEATURES	EXC. COND. LOW	HIGH

Vibrato

1970s		$150	$200

Bennett Music Labs
Effects built in the U.S. by Bruce Bennett.

Bigsby
Bigsby has been making volume and tone pedals since the 1950s. They currently offer a volume pedal.

Foot Volume and Tone Control

1950s		$125	$175

Binson
Late 1950s-1982. Binson, of Milan, Italy, made several models of the Echorec, using tubes or transistors. They also made units for Guild, Sound City and EKO.

Echorec
Ca.1960-1979. Four knob models with 12 echo selections, 1 head, complex multitap effects, settings for record level, playback and regeneration. Includes B1, B2, Echomaster1, T5 (has 6 knobs), T5E, and Baby. Used a magnetic disk instead of tape. Guild later offered the "Guild Echorec by Binson" which is a different stripped-down version.

1960s	Tube, gold case	$500	$700

Bixonic
1995-present. Originally distributed by Sound-Barrier Music, Bixonic is currently distributed by Godlyke, Inc.

Expandora EXP-2000
1995-2000. Analog distortion, round silver case, internal DIP switches.

1995-2000		$175	$200

Blackbox Music Electronics
2000-present. Founded by Loren Stafford and located in Minneapolis, Minnesota, Blackbox offers a line of effects for guitar and bass.

Blackstone Appliances
1999-present. Distortion effects crafted by Jon Blackstone in New York, New York.

Bon, Mfg
Bon was located in Escondido, California.

Tube Driver 204
1979-ca.1981.

1979-1981		$100	$150

Boss
1976-present. Japan's Roland Corporation first launched effect pedals in '74. A year or two later the subsidiary company, Boss, debuted its own line. They were marketed concurrently at first but gradually Boss became reserved for effects and drum machines while the Roland name was used on amplifiers and keyboards. Boss still offers a wide line of pedals.

Bad Cat 2-Tone

Bixonic Expandora

Blackbox Quicksilver

Boss Acoustic Simulator AC-2

Boss Digital Delay DD-3

Boss ME-50

MODEL YEAR	FEATURES	EXC. COND. LOW	HIGH
Acoustic Simulator AC-2			
1997-present. Four modes that emulate various acoustic tones.			
1997-2005		$55	$65
Auto Wah AW-2			
1991-1999.			
1991-1999		$45	$55
Bass Chorus CE-2B			
1987-1995.			
1987-1995		$45	$55
Bass Equalizer GE-7B			
1987-1995. Seven-band, name changed to GEB-7 in '95.			
1987-1995		$45	$55
Bass Flanger BF-2B			
1987-1994.			
1987-1994		$45	$55
Bass Limiter LM-2B			
1990-1994.			
1990-1994		$40	$45
Bass Overdrive ODB-3			
1994-present.			
1994-2005		$45	$55
Blues Driver BD-2			
1995-present.			
1995-2005		$45	$55
Chorus Ensemble CE-1			
1976-1984. Vibrato and chorus.			
1976-1984		$150	$250
Chorus Ensemble CE-2			
1979-1982.			
1979-1982		$50	$100
Chorus Ensemble CE-3			
1982-1992.			
1982-1992		$50	$100
Chorus Ensemble CE-5			
1991-present.			
1991-2005		$50	$100
Compressor Sustainer CS-1			
1978-1982.			
1978-1982		$75	$100
Compressor Sustainer CS-2			
1981-1986.			
1981-1986		$75	$100
Compressor Sustainer CS-3			
1986-present.			
1986-2004		$75	$100
Delay DM-2			
1981-1984. Analog, hot pink case.			
1981-1984		$175	$250
Delay DM-3			
1984-1988.			
1984-1988		$150	$200
Digital Delay DD-2			
1983-1986.			
1983-1986		$125	$175
Digital Delay DD-3			
1986-present. Up to 800 ms of delay.			
1986-1989		$125	$175
1990-2005		$100	$150

MODEL YEAR	FEATURES	EXC. COND. LOW	HIGH
Digital Delay DD-5			
1995-2005. Up to 2 seconds of delay.			
1995-2005		$100	$150
Digital Delay DD-6			
2003-present. Up to 5 seconds of delay			
2003-2005		$60	$75
Digital Dimension C DC-2			
1985-1989. Two chorus effects and tremolo.			
1985-1989		$140	$150
Digital Metalizer MZ-2			
1987-1992.			
1987-1992		$85	$95
Digital Reverb RV-2			
1987-1990.			
1987-1990		$100	$150
Digital Reverb/Delay RV-3			
1994-2004.			
1994-2004		$100	$125
Digital Reverb RV-5			
2003-present. Dual imput and dual output, four control knobs, silver case.			
2003-2005		$65	$100
Digital Sampler/Delay DSD-2			
1985-1986.			
1985-1986		$125	$175
Digital Space-DDC-3/Digital Dimension DC-3			
1988-1993. Originally called the Digital Space-D, later changed to Digital Dimension. Chorus with EQ.			
1988-1993		$135	$185
Digital Stereo Reverb RV-70			
1994-1995. Rack mount, MIDI control, reverb/delay, 199 presets.			
1994-1995		$135	$185
Distortion DS-1			
1978-1989, 1990s-2000s.			
1978-1989		$55	$65
1990-1999		$35	$55
2000-2004		$25	$30
Dr. Rhythm DR-55			
1979-1989. Drum machine.			
1979-1989		$150	$200
Dual Over Drive SD-2			
1993-1998.			
1993-1998		$50	$60
Dynamic Wah AW-3			
2000-present. Auto wah with humanizer, for guitar or bass.			
2000-2005		$55	$65
Dynamic Filter FT-2			
1986-1988. Auto wah.			
1986-1988		$75	$100
Enhancer EH-2			
1990-1998.			
1990-1998		$40	$50
Flanger BF-1			
1977-1980.			
1977-1980		$60	$75

MODEL YEAR FEATURES	EXC. COND. LOW	HIGH
Flanger BF-2		
1980-2002.		
1980-1989	$60	$75
1990-2002	$45	$60
Foot Wah FW-3		
1992-1996.		
1992-1996	$50	$60
Graphic Equalizer GE-6		
1978-1981. Six bands.		
1978-1981	$50	$75
Graphic Equalizer GE-7		
1981-present. Seven bands.		
1982-1989	$75	$100
1990-2005	$50	$70
Graphic Equalizer GE-10		
1976-1985. 10-band EQ for guitar or bass.		
1976-1985	$100	$125
Harmonist HR-2		
1994-1999. Pitch shifter.		
1994-1999	$75	$100
Heavy Metal HM-2		
1983-1991. Distortion.		
1983-1991	$35	$45
Hyper Fuzz FZ-2		
1993-1997.		
1993-1997	$50	$75
Hyper Metal HM-3		
1993-1998.		
1993-1998	$40	$50
Limiter LM-2		
1987-1992.		
1987-1992	$30	$40
Line Selector LS-2		
1991-present. Select between 2 effects loops.		
1991-2005 With adapter	$50	$75
Mega Distortion MD-2		
2003-present.		
2003-2005	$50	$60
Metal Zone MT-2		
1991-present. Distortion and 3-band EQ.		
1991-2005	$50	$75
Multi Effects ME-5		
1988-1991. Floor unit.		
1988-1991	$75	$125
Multi Effects ME-6		
1992-1997.		
1992-1997	$75	$125
Multi Effects ME-8		
1996-1997.		
1996-1997	$75	$125
Multi Effects ME-30		
1998-2002.		
1998-2002	$75	$125
Multi Effects ME-50		
2003-present. Floor unit.		
2003-2005	$175	$200
Noise Gate NF-1		
1979-1988.		
1979-1988	$45	$55

MODEL YEAR FEATURES	EXC. COND. LOW	HIGH
Noise Suppressor NS-2		
1987-present.		
1987-2005	$45	$55
Octaver OC-2/Octave OC-2		
1982-2005. Originally called the Octaver.		
1982-2005	$60	$75
Overdrive OD-1		
1977-1985.		
1977-1979	$100	$175
1980-1985	$75	$150
Overdrive OD-3		
1997-present.		
1997-2005	$50	$75
Parametric Equalizer PQ-4		
1991-1997.		
1991-1997	$50	$75
Phaser PH-1		
1977-1981.		
1977-1981	$75	$100
Phaser PH-1R		
1982-1985. Resonance control added to PH-1.		
1982-1985	$75	$125
Pitch Sifter/Delay PS-2		
1987-1993.		
1987-1993	$100	$125
Reverb Box RX-100		
1981-mid-1980s.		
1981-1985	$75	$100
Rocker Distortion PD-1		
1980-mid-1980s. Variable pedal using magnetic field.		
1980-1985	$50	$75
Rocker Volume PV-1		
1981-mid-1980s.		
1980-1985	$50	$60
Rocker Wah PW-1		
1980-mid-1980s. Magnetic field variable pedal.		
1980-1985	$60	$70
Slow Gear SG-1		
1979-1982. Violin swell effect, automatically adjusts volume.		
1979-1982	$275	$325
Spectrum SP-1		
1977-1981. Single-band parametric EQ.		
1977-1981	$275	$325
Super Chorus CH-1		
1989-present.		
1989-2005	$50	$75
Super Distortion & Feedbacker DF-2		
1984-1994. Also labeled as the Super Feedbacker & Distortion.		
1984-1994	$100	$125
Super Over Drive SD-1		
1981-present.		
1981-1989	$50	$90
1990-2005	$35	$55
Super Phaser PH-2		
1984-2001.		
1984-1989	$50	$90
1990-2001	$35	$55

Boss Noise Gate NF-1

Boss Phase Shifter PH-3

Boss Super Chorus CH-1

Boss FV-50L

Carl Martin Hydra

Catalinabread Super Chili Picoso

MODEL YEAR	FEATURES	EXC. COND. LOW	HIGH
Super Shifter PS-5			
1999-present. Pitch shifter/harmonizer.			
1999-2005		$100	$125
Touch Wah TW-1/T Wah TW-1			
1978-1987. Auto wah, early models were labeled as Touch Wah.			
1978-1987		$100	$125
Tremolo TR-2			
1997-present.			
1997-2005		$70	$80
Tremolo/Pan PN-2			
1990-1995.			
1990-1995		$125	$150
Turbo Distortion DS-2			
1987-present.			
1987-2005		$75	$125
Turbo Overdrive OD-2			
1985-1994. Called OD-2R after '94, due to added remote on/off jack.			
1985-1994		$75	$125
Vibrato VB-2			
1982-1986. True pitch-changing vibrato, warm analog tone, 'rise time' control allows for slow attach, 4 knobs, aqua-blue case.			
1982-1986		$375	$425
Volume FV-50H			
1987-1997. High impedance, stereo volume pedal with inputs and outputs.			
1987-1997		$50	$60
Volume FV-50L			
1987-1997. Low impedance version of FV-50.			
1987-1997		$40	$50
Volume Pedal FV-100			
Late-1980s-1991. Guitar volume pedal.			
1987-1991		$40	$50

Bruno

1834-present. Music Disributor Bruno and Sons had a line of Japanese-made effects in the early '70s.

Budda

1995-present. Wahs and distortion pedals by Jeff Bober and Scott Sier in San Francisco, California. They also build amps.

Burriss

Guitar effects from Bob Burriss of Lexington, Kentucky. He also builds amps.

Carl Martin

1993-present. Line of effects from Søren Jongberg and East Sound Research of Denmark. In '06 they added their Chinese-made Vintage Series. They also build amps.

Carlsbro

1959-present. English amp company Carlsbro Electronics Limited offered a line of effects from '77 to '81.

MODEL YEAR	FEATURES	EXC. COND. LOW	HIGH

Carrotron

Late-1970s-mid-1980s. Carrotron was out of California and offered a line of effects.

MODEL YEAR	FEATURES	EXC. COND. LOW	HIGH
Noise Fader C900B1			
1980-1982.			
1980-1982		$50	$60
Preamp C821B			
1981-ca.1982.			
1981-1982		$55	$65

Carvin

1946-present. Carvin introduced its line of Ground Effects in '02 and discontinued them in '03.

Castle Instruments

Early 1980s. Castle was located in Madison, New Jersey, and made rack-mount and floor phaser units.

MODEL YEAR	FEATURES	EXC. COND. LOW	HIGH
Phaser III			
1980-1982. Offered mode switching for various levels of phase.			
1980-1982		$100	$175

Catalinbread

2003-present. Nicholas Harris founded Catalinbread Specialized Mechanisms of Music in Seattle, Washington, in '02 to do mods and in '03 added his own line of guitar effects.

Cat's Eye

2001-present. Dean Solorzano and Lisa Kroeker build their analog guitar effects in Oceanside, California.

Chandler

1984-present. Located in California, Chandler Musical Instruments offers instruments, pickups, and pickguards, as well as effects.

MODEL YEAR	FEATURES	EXC. COND. LOW	HIGH
Digital Echo			
1992-2000. Rackmount, 1 second delay, stereo.			
1992-2000		$350	$450
Tube Driver			
1986-1991. Uses a 12AX7 tube. Not to be confused with the Tube Works Tube Driver.			
1980s	Large Box	$200	$250
1980s	Rackmount	$75	$125
1990s	Rackmount	$75	$125

Chapman

1970-present. From Emmett Chapman, maker of the Stick.

MODEL YEAR	FEATURES	EXC. COND. LOW	HIGH
Patch of Shades			
1981, 1989. Wah, with pressure sensitive pad instead of pedal. 2 production runs.			
1980s		$50	$75

Chicago Iron

1998-present. Faithful reproductions of classic effects built by Kurt Steir in Chicago, Illinois.

EFFECTS

MODEL YEAR	FEATURES	EXC. COND. LOW	HIGH

Chunk Systems

1996-present. Guitar and bass effects pedals built by Richard Cartwright in Sydney, Australia.

Clark

1960s. Built in Clark, New Jersey, same unit as the Orpheum Fuzz and the Mannys Music Fuzz.

SS-600 Fuzz

1960s. Chrome-plated, volume and tone knobs, toggle switch.

| 1960s | | $150 | $200 |

Clark Amplification

1995-present. Amplifier builder Mike Clark, of Cayce, South Carolina, offers a reverb unit and started building guitar effects as well, in '98.

Colorsound

1967-present. Colorsound effects were produced by England's Sola Sound, which was founded in '62 by former Vox associate Larry Macari and his brother Joe. The first product was a fuzzbox called the Tone Bender, designed by Gary Hurst and sold at Macari's Musical Exchange stores. The first readily available fuzz in Britain, it was an instant success. In '67, the Colorsound brand was launched. In the late-'60s, wah and fuzz-wah pedals were added, and by the end of the '70s, Colorsound offered 18 different effects, an amp, and accessories. Few early Colorsound products were imported into the U.S., so today they're scarce. Except for the Wah-Wah pedal, Colorsound's production stopped in the early '80s, but in '96 most of their early line was reissued by Dick Denny of Vox fame. Denny died in 2001. Since then, Anthony and Steve Macari build Colorsound effects in London. Mutronics offered a licensed rack mount combination of 4 classic Colorsound effects for a short time in the early 2000s.

Flanger

| 1970s | | $100 | $200 |

Fuzz Phazer

Introduced in 1973.

| 1970s | | $150 | $225 |

Jumbo Tonebender

1974-early 1980s. Replaced the Tonebender fuzz, with wider case and light blue lettering.

| 1979 | | $150 | $250 |

Octivider

Introduced in 1973.

| 1970s | | $150 | $225 |

Overdriver

Introduced in 1972, Controls for drive, treble and bass.

| 1970s | | $150 | $225 |

Phazer

Introduced in 1973. Magenta/purple-pink case, slanted block Phazer logo on front.

| 1970s | | $150 | $225 |

Ring Modulator

Introduced in 1973. Purple case, Ring Modulator name with atom orbit slanted block logo on case.

| 1970s | | $250 | $275 |

Supa Tonebender Fuzz

1977-early 1980s. Sustain and volume knobs, tone control and toggle. Same white case as Jumbo Tonebender, but with new circuit.

| 1970s | | $150 | $225 |

Supa Wah-Swell

1970s. Supa Wah-Swell in slanted block letters on the end of the pedal, silver case.

| 1970s | | $150 | $225 |

Supaphase

| 1970s | | $150 | $225 |

Supasustain

| 1960s | | $125 | $200 |

Tremolo

| 1970s | | $150 | $200 |

Tremolo Reissue

1996-present. Purple case.

| 1996-2005 | | $100 | $125 |

Wah Fuzz Straight

Introduced in 1973. Aqua-blue case, Wah-Fuzz-Straight in capital block letters on end of wah pedal.

| 1970s | | $175 | $250 |

Wah Fuzz Swell

Introduced in 1973. Yellow case, block letter Wah Fuzz Swell logo on front, three control knobs and toggle.

| 1970s | | $250 | $350 |

Wah Swell

1970s. Light purple case, block letter Wah-Swell logo on front.

| 1970s | | $225 | $275 |

Wah Wah

1970s. Dark gray case, Wah-Wah in capital block letters on end of wah pedal.

| 1975 | | $300 | $350 |

Wah Wah Reissue

1996-2005. Red case, large Colorsound letter logo and small Wah Wah lettering on end of pedal.

| 1996-2005 | | $75 | $100 |

Wah Wah Supremo

1970s. Silver/chrome metal case, Wah-Wah Supremo in block letters on end of wah pedal.

| 1975 | | $425 | $475 |

Companion

1970s. Private branded by Shinei of Japan, which made effects for others as well.

Wah pedal

| 1970s | | $125 | $175 |

Conn

Ca.1968-ca.1978. Band instrument manufacturer and distributor Conn/Continental Music Company, of Elkhart, Indiana, imported guitars and effects from Japan.

Strobe ST-8 Tuner

Late-1960s. Brown case.

| 1968 | | $215 | $225 |

Chandler Tube Driver

Chunk Systems Fuzz Bass FZ002

Colorsound Sustain Module

EFFECTS

Dallas Arbiter Fuzz Face

Dan Armstrong Orange Squeezer

Danelectro Chicken Salad

MODEL YEAR	FEATURES	EXC. COND. LOW	HIGH

Coron
1970s-1980s. Japanese-made effects, early ones close copies of MXR pedals.

Cosmosound
Italy's Cosmosound made small amps with Leslie drums and effects pedals in the late '60s and '70s.

Crowther Audio
1976-present. Guitar effects built by Paul Crowther, who was the original drummer of the band Split Enz, in Auckland, New Zealand. His first effect was the Hot Cake.

Crybaby
See listing under Vox for early models, and Dunlop for recent versions.

CSL
Sola Sound made a line of effects for C. Summerfield Ltd., an English music company.

Dallas Arbiter
Dallas Arbiter, Ltd. was based in London and it appeared in the late-1960s as a division of a Dallas group of companies headed by Ivor Arbiter. They also manufactured Sound City amplifiers and made Vox amps from '72 to '78. The Fuzz Face is still available from Jim Dunlop.

Fuzz Face
Introduced in 1966. The current reissue of the Dallas Arbiter Fuzz Face is distributed by Jim Dunlop USA.

1968-1969	Red	$475	$600
1970	Red	$350	$400
1970-1976	Blue	$325	$400
1977-1980	Blue	$250	$300
1981	Grey, reissue	$150	$225
1990-1999	Red, reissue	$60	$65
2000-2003	Red, reissue	$65	$70

Fuzz Wah Face

1970s	Black	$200	$275
1990s	Reissue copy	$55	$65

Sustain

1970s		$175	$275

Treble & Bass Face

1960s		$200	$300

Trem Face
Ca.1970-ca.1975. Reissued in '80s, round red case, depth and speed control knobs, Dallas-Arbiter England logo plate.

1970-1975	Red	$250	$325

Wah Baby
1970s. Gray speckle case, Wah Baby logo caps and small letters on end of pedal.

1970s		$250	$350

Dan Armstrong
In 1976, Musitronics, based in Rosemont, New Jersey, introduced 6 inexpensive plug-in effects designed by Dan Armstrong. Perhaps under the influence of John D. MacDonald's Travis McGee novels, each effect name incorporated a color, like Purple Peaker. Shipping box labeled Dan Armstrong by Musitronics. They disappeared a few years later but were reissued by WD Products in '91. Since '03, Vintage Tone Project has offered the Dan Armstrong Orange Crusher. Dan Armstrong died in '04.

Blue Clipper
1976-1981. Fuzz, blue-green case.

1976-1981		$90	$100

Green Ringer
1976-1981. Ring Modulator/Fuzz, green case.

1970s		$90	$100

Orange Squeezer
1976-1981. Compressor, orange case.

1976-1981		$90	$100

Purple Peaker
1976-1981. Frequency Booster, light purple case.

1976-1981		$90	$100

Red Ranger
1976-1981. Bass/Treble Booster, light red case.

1976-1981		$90	$100

Yellow Humper
1976-1981. Yellow case.

1976-1981		$90	$100

Danelectro
1946-1969, 1996-present. The Danelectro brand was revived in '96 with a line of effects pedals. They also offer the Wasabi line of effects. Prices do not include AC adapter, add $10 for the Zero-Hum adapter.

Chicken Salad Vibrato
2000-present. Orange case.

2000-2005		$20	$25

Cool Cat Chorus
1996-present.

1996-2005		$30	$40

Corned Beef Reverb
2000-present. Blue-black case

2000-2005		$15	$20

Daddy-O Overdrive
1996-present. White case.

1996-2005		$30	$40

Dan Echo
1998-present.

1998-2005		$40	$45

Fab Tone Distortion
1996-present.

1996-2005		$30	$40

Reverb Unit

1965		$200	$300

Davoli
1960s-1970. Davoli was an Italian pickup and guitar builder and is often associated with Wandre guitars.

TRD
1970s. Solidstate tremolo, reverb, distortion unit.

1970s		$175	$225

EFFECTS

MODEL YEAR	FEATURES	EXC. COND. LOW	HIGH

Dean Markley

The string and pickup manufacturer offered a line of effects from 1976 to the early-'90s.

Overlord Classic Tube Overdrive
1988-1991. Uses a 12AX7A tube, AC powered.

1988-1991		$60	$80

Overlord III Classic Overdrive
1990-1991. Battery-powered version of Overlord pedal. Black case with red letters.

1990-1991		$40	$70

Voice Box 50 (watt model)
1976-1979.

1976-1979		$75	$125

Voice Box 100 (watt model)
1976-1979, 1982-ca.1985.

1976-1979		$75	$125

Voice Box 200 (watt model)
1976-1979.

1976-1979		$75	$125

DeArmond

In 1947, DeArmond may have introduced the first actual signal-processing effect pedal, the Tremolo Control. They made a variety of effects into the '70s, but only one caught on - their classic volume pedal. DeArmond is primarily noted for pickups.

Pedal Phaser Model 1900
1974-ca.1979.

1974-1979		$75	$125

Square Wave Distortion Generator
1977-ca.1979.

1977-1979		$100	$150

Thunderbolt B166
1977-ca.1979. Five octave wah.

1977-1979		$50	$100

Tone/Volume Pedal 610
1978-ca.1979.

1978-1979		$75	$125

Tornado Phase Shifter
1977-ca.1979.

1977-1979		$100	$125

Tremolo Control Model 60A/60B
The Model 60 Tremolo Control dates from 1947 to the early-1950s. Model 60A dates from mid- to late-'50s. Model 60B, early-'60s.

1950s	60A	$300	$375
1960s	60B	$100	$250

Twister 1930
1980. Phase shifter.

1980		$100	$125

Volume Pedal 1602
1978-ca.1980s.

1970s		$40	$60

Volume Pedal 1630
1978-1980s. Optoelectric.

1970s		$40	$60

Volume Pedal Model 602
1960s.

1960s		$40	$70

Weeper Wah Model 1802
1970s. Weeper logo on foot pedal.

1970s		$100	$125

DeltaLab Research

Late 1970s-early 1980s. DeltaLab, which was located in Chelmsford, Massachusetts, was an early builder of rackmount gear.

DL-2 Acousticomputer
1980s. Delay.

1980s		$75	$125

DL-4 Time Line
1980s. Delay.

1980s		$75	$125

DL-5
1980s. Various digital processing effects, blue case, rackmount.

1980s		$175	$225

DLB-1 Delay Control Pedal
1980s. Controls other DeltaLab pedals, chrome, Morley-looking pedal.

1980s		$50	$75

Electron I ADM/II ADM
1980s. Blue case, rackmount effects. Models include the Electron I ADM, and the Electron II ADM.

1980s	Electron I ADM	$50	$75
1980s	Electron II ADM	$75	$125

Demeter

1980-present. Amp builder James Demeter and company, located in Van Nuys, California, also build guitar effects.

Denio

Line of Japanese-made Boss lookalikes sold in Asia and Australia.

Diaz

Early 1980s-2002, 2004-present. Line of effects from the "amp doctor" Cesar Diaz. Diaz died in '02; in '04, his family announced plans to resume production.

DigiTech

The DigiTech/DOD company is in Utah and the effects are made in the U.S.A. The DigiTech name started as a line under the DOD brand in the early 1980s; later spinning off into its own brand. They also produce vocal products and studio processors and are now part of Harman International Industries.

Digital Delay PDS 1000
1985-ca.1989. One second delay.

1985-1989		$100	$150

Digital Delay and Sampler PDS 2000
1985-1991. 2 second delay.

1985-1991		$125	$175

Digital Delay PDS 2700 Double Play
1989-1991. Delay and chorus

1989-1991		$125	$175

Dean Markley Overlord

DeArmond Weeper Wah

Digitech PDS 2730 Hot Box

EFFECTS

EFFECTS

Digitech Reverberator XP400

DOD A-B Box 270

DOD Envelope Filter FX25B

MODEL YEAR	FEATURES	EXC. COND. LOW	HIGH
Digital Stereo Chorus/Flanger PDS 1700			
1986-1991.			
1986-1991		$100	$150
Echo Plus 8 Second Delay PDS 8000			
1985-1991.			
1985-1991		$175	$200
Guitar Effects Processor RP 1			
1992-1996. Floor unit, 150 presets.			
1992-1996		$100	$150
Guitar Effects Processor RP 3			
1998-2003. Floor unit.			
1998-2003		$110	$150
Guitar Effects Processor RP 5			
1994-1996. Floor unit, 80 presets.			
1994-1996		$120	$175
Guitar Effects Processor RP 6			
1996-1997. Floor unit.			
1996-1997		$125	$200
Guitar Effects Processor RP 10			
1994-1996. Floor unit, 200 presets.			
1994-1996		$125	$175
Guitar Effects Processor RP 14D			
1999. Floor unit with expression pedal, 1x12AX7 tube, 100 presets.			
1999		$300	$350
Guitar Effects Processor RP 100			
2000-present.			
2000-2005		$100	$125
Guitar Effects Processor RP 200			
2001-present. 140 presets, drum machine, Expression pedal.			
2001-2005		$100	$125
Hot Box PDS 2730			
1989-1991. Delay and distortion			
1989-1991		$100	$125
Modulator Pedal XP 200			
1996-2002. Floor unit, 61 presets.			
1996-2002		$100	$125
Multi Play PDS 20/20			
1987-1991. Multi-function digital delay.			
1987-1991		$125	$150
Pedalverb Digital Reverb Pedal PDS 3000			
1987-1991.			
1987-1991		$100	$125
Programmable Distortion PDS 1550			
1986-1991.			
1986-1991	Yellow case	$50	$75
Programmable Distortion PDS 1650			
1989-1991.			
1989-1991	Red case	$50	$75
Rock Box PDS 2715			
1989-1991. Chorus and distortion.			
1989-1991		$50	$75
Two Second Digital Delay PDS 1002			
1987-1991.			
1987-1991		$100	$125
Whammy Pedal WP I			
1990-1993. Original Whammy Pedal, red case, reissued as WP IV in '00.			
1990-1993		$375	$475

MODEL YEAR	FEATURES	EXC. COND. LOW	HIGH
Whammy Pedal WP II			
1994-1997. Can switch between 2 presets, black case.			
1994-1997		$200	$275
Whammy Pedal Reissue			
2000-present. Reissue version of classic WP-1 with added dive bomb and MIDI features.			
2000-2005		$125	$150

DiMarzio

The pickup maker offered a couple of effects in the late-1980s to the mid-'90s.

Metal Pedal			
1987-1989.			
1987-1989		$50	$75
Very Metal Fuzz			
Ca.1989-1995. Distortion/overdrive pedal.			
1989-1995		$50	$75

Divided By Thirteen

Fred Taccone builds his stomp box guitar effects in the Los Angeles, California area. He also builds amps.

DOD

DOD Electronics started in Salt Lake City, Utah in 1974. Today, they're a major effects manufacturer with dozens of pedals made in the U.S. They also market effects under the name DigiTech and are now part of Harman International Industries.

6 Band Equalizer EQ601			
1977-1982.			
1977-1982		$50	$70
AB Box 270			
1978-1982.			
1978-1982		$30	$35
American Metal FX56			
1985-1991.			
1985-1991		$40	$50
Analog Delay 680			
1979-1982			
51979-1982		$125	$150
Attacker FX54			
1992-1994. Distortion and compressor.			
1992-1994		$40	$50
Bass Compressor FX82			
1987-ca.1989.			
1987-1989		$40	$50
Bass EQ FX42B			
1987-1996.			
1987-1996		$40	$50
Bass Grunge FX92			
1995-1996.			
1995-1996		$40	$50
Bass Overdrive FX91			
1998-present.			
1998-2005		$40	$50
Bass Stereo Chorus FX62			
1987-1996.			
1987-1996		$50	$60

MODEL YEAR FEATURES	EXC. COND. LOW	HIGH
Bass Stereo Chorus Flanger FX72		
1987-1997.		
1987-1997	$50	$60
Bi-FET Preamp FX10		
4 *1982-1996.*		
1982-1996	$30	$40
Buzz Box FX33		
1994-1996. Grunge distortion.		
1994-1996	$45	$60
Chorus 690		
1980-ca.1982. Dual speed chorus.		
1980-1982	$75	$100
Classic Fuzz FX52		
1990-1997.		
1990-1997	$35	$45
Classic Tube FX53		
1990-1997.		
1990-1997	$45	$55
Compressor 280		
1978-ca.1982.		
1978-1982	$45	$55
Compressor FX80		
1982-1985.		
1982-1985	$45	$55
Compressor Sustainer FX80B		
1986-1996.		
1986-1996	$45	$55
Death Metal FX86		
1994-present. Distortion.		
1994-2005	$35	$50
Delay FX90		
1984-ca.1987.		
1984-1987	$75	$100
Digital Delay DFX9		
1989-ca.1990.		
1989-1990	$65	$90
Digital Delay Sampler DFX94		
1995-1997.		
1995-1997	$75	$100
Distortion FX55		
1982-1986. Red case.		
1982-1986	$35	$45
Edge Pedal FX87		
1988-1989.		
1988-1989	$25	$45
Envelope Filter 440		
1981-ca.1982.Reissued in '95.		
1981-1982	$65	$75
Envelope Filter FX25		
1982-1997. Replaced by FX25B.		
1982-1987	$45	$65
Envelope Filter FX25B		
1981-1987.		
1982-1987	$45	$65
Equalizer FX40		
1982-1986.		
1982-1986	$40	$55
Equalizer FX40B		
1987-present. Eight bands for bass.		
1987-2005	$40	$55

MODEL YEAR FEATURES	EXC. COND. LOW	HIGH
Fet Preamp 210		
1981-ca.1982.		
1981-1982	$40	$55
Flanger 670		
1981-1982.		
1981-1982	$75	$100
Gate Loop FX30		
1980s	$30	$40
Graphic Equalizer EQ-610		
1980-ca.1982. Ten bands.		
1980-1982	$50	$65
Graphic Equalizer EQ-660		
1980-ca.1982. Six bands.		
1980-1982	$40	$55
Grunge FX69		
1993-present. Distortion.		
1993-2005	$35	$50
Hard Rock Distortion FX57		
1987-1994. With built-in delay.		
1987-1994	$35	$50
Harmonic Enhancer FX85		
1986-ca.1989.		
1986-1989	$35	$50
I. T. FX100		
1997. Intergrated Tube distortion, produces harmonics.		
1997	$50	$60
Ice Box FX64		
1996-present. Chorus, high EQ.		
1996-2005	$25	$35
Juice Box FX51		
1996-1997.		
1996-1997	$30	$40
Master Switch 225		
1988-ca.1989. A/B switch and loop selector.		
1988-1989	$30	$40
Meat Box FX32		
1994-1996.		
1994-1996	$40	$50
Metal Maniac FX58		
1990-1996.		
1990-1996	$40	$50
Metal Triple Play Guitar Effects System TR3M		
1994.		
1994	$40	$50
Metal X FX70		
1993-1996.		
1993-1996	$40	$50
Milk Box FX84		
1994-present.		
1994-2005	$40	$50
Mini-Chorus 460		
1981-ca.1982.		
1981-1982	$50	$75
Mixer 240		
1978-ca.1982.		
1978-1982	$25	$35

DOD Death Metal FX86

DOD Equalizer FX40B

DOD Mixer 240

To get the most from this book, be sure to read "Using *The Guide*" in the introduction.

DOD Noise Gate FX30

DOD Phasor 595-A

Dunlop Rotovibe

MODEL YEAR	FEATURES	EXC. COND. LOW	HIGH
Momentary Footswitch			
Introduced in 1987. Temporally engages other boxes.			
1980s		$25	$35
Mystic Blues Overdrive FX102			
1998-present. Medium gain overdrive.			
1998-2005		$25	$30
Noise Gate 230			
1978-1982.			
1978-1982		$30	$40
Noise Gate FX30			
1982-ca.1987.			
1982-1987		$30	$40
Octoplus FX35			
1987-1996. Octaves.			
1987-1996		$40	$45
Overdrive Plus FX50B			
1986-1997.			
1986-1997		$35	$45
Overdrive Preamp 250			
1978-1982, 1995-present. Reissued in '95.			
1978-1982		$80	$100
1995-2002		$30	$45
Overdrive Preamp FX50			
1982-1985.			
1982-1985		$35	$45
Performer Compressor Limiter 525			
1981-1984.			
1981-1984		$55	$60
Performer Delay 585			
1982-1985.			
1982-1985		$60	$75
Performer Distortion 555			
1981-1984.			
1981-1984		$40	$50
Performer Flanger 575			
1981-1985.			
1981-1985		$40	$50
Performer Phasor 595			
1981-1984.			
1981-1984		$45	$55
Performer Stereo Chorus 565			
1981-1985.			
1981-1985	FET switching	$60	$75
Performer Wah Filter 545			
1981-1984.			
1981-1984		$50	$75
Phasor 201			
1981-ca.1982. Reissued in '95.			
1981-1982		$70	$100
Phasor 401			
1978-1981.			
1978-1981		$70	$100
Phasor 490			
1980-ca.1982.			
1980-1982		$70	$100
Phasor FX20			
1982-1985.			
1982-1985		$40	$50

MODEL YEAR	FEATURES	EXC. COND. LOW	HIGH
Psychoacoustic Processor FX87			
1988-1989.			
1988-1989		$40	$50
Punkifier FX76			
1997.			
1997		$40	$50
Resistance Mixer 240			
1978-ca.1982.			
1978-1982		$30	$35
Silencer FX27			
1988-ca.1989. Noise reducer.			
1988-1989		$35	$45
Stereo Chorus FX60			
1982-1986.			
1982-1986		$40	$50
Stereo Chorus FX65			
1986-1996. Light blue case.			
1986-1996		$40	$50
Stereo Flanger FX70			
1982-ca.1985.			
1982-1985		$40	$50
Stereo Flanger FX75			
1986-1987. Silver case with blue trim.			
1986-1987		$45	$55
Stereo Flanger FX75B			
1987-1997.			
1987-1997		$45	$55
Stereo Phasor FX20B			
1986-1999.			
1986-1999		$45	$55
Stereo Turbo Chorus FX67			
1988-1991.			
1988-1991		$40	$50
Super American Metal FX56B			
1992-1996.			
1992-1996		$35	$45
Super Stereo Chorus FX68			
1992-1996.			
1992-1996		$40	$50
Supra Distortion FX55B			
1986-present.			
1986-2005		$30	$40
Thrash Master FX59			
1990-1996.			
1990-1996		$30	$40
Votec Vocal Effects Processor and Mic preamp			
1998-2001.			
1998-2001		$60	$65
Wah-Volume FX-17 (pedal)			
1987-2000.			
1987-2000		$45	$55

Dredge-Tone

Located in Berkeley, California, Dredge-Tone offers effects and electronic kits.

DST Engineering

2001-present. Jeff Swanson and Bob Dettorre build reverb units in Beverly, Massachusetts. They also build amps.

MODEL YEAR	FEATURES	EXC. COND. LOW	HIGH

Dunlop

Jim Dunlop, USA offers the Crybaby, MXR (see MXR), Rockman, High Gain, Heil Sound (see Heil), Tremolo, Jimi Hendrix, Rotovibe and Uni-Vibe brand effects.

Crybaby Bass
1985-present. Bass wah.

1985-2005		$75	$100

Crybaby Wah Pedal 535
1995-present. Multi-range pedal with an external boost control.

1995-2005		$70	$90

Crybaby Wah-Wah GCB-95
1982-present. Dunlop began manufacturing the Crybaby in '82.

1982-1989		$55	$75
1990-1999		$45	$70
2000-2005		$40	$50

High Gain Volume + Boost Pedal
1983-1996.

1983-1996		$35	$45

High Gain Volume Pedal
1983-present.

1983-2005		$40	$50

Jimi Hendrix Fuzz (Round)
1987-1993.

1987-1993		$50	$75

Rotovibe JH-4S Standard
1989-1998. Standard is finished in bright red enamel with chrome top.

1989-1998		$125	$150

Tremolo Volume Plus TVP-1
1995-1998. Pedal.

1995-1998		$125	$140

Uni-Vibe UV-1
1995-present. Rotating speaker effect.

1995-1999		$175	$225
2000-2005		$175	$200

Dynacord

1950-present. Dynacord is a German company that makes audio and pro sound amps, as well as other electronic equipment and is now owned by TELEX/EVI Audio (an U.S. company), which also owns the Electro-Voice brand. In the '60s they offered tape echo machines. In '94 a line of multi-effects processors were introduced under the Electro-Voice/Dynacord name, but by the following year they were just listed as Electro-Voice.

EchoCord
Introduced in 1959. Tape echo unit.

1960s		$275	$350

Dyno

See Dytronics.

Dytronics

Mid-1970s-early 1980s. The Japanese Dytronics company made a chorus rackmount unit for electric piano called the Dyno My Piano with flying piano keys or a lightning bolt on the front.

Another version was called the Tri-Stereo Chorus and a third, called the Songbird, had a bird's head on the front.

CS-5/Dyno My Piano Tri Chorus/Songbird
1970s. Tri-Stereo Chorus, 3 individual chorus settings which can be used all at once. Sold under all 3 brands/models.

1970s		$2,500	$3,000

EBow

See Heet Sound Products.

Ecco Fonic

The Ecco Fonic was distributed by Fender in 1958-'59.

Echo Unit
1958-1959. Reverb unit.

1958-1959	With Brown case	$300	$350

Echoplex

The Echoplex tape echo units were first sold under the Maestro brand. After Maestro dropped the Echoplex, it was marketed under the Market Electronics name from the late-'70s to the early-'80s. In the later '80s, Market Electronics was dropped from the ads and they were marketed under the Echoplex brand. Both the Market and Echoplex brands are listed here; for earlier models see Maestro. In '94, Gibson's Oberheim division introduced a rackmount unit called the Echoplex. In '01, it was relabeled as Gibson.

Echoplex EP3
1984-ca. 1988. Solidstate version.

1984-1988		$350	$425

Echoplex EP4
1984-1991. Solidstate version.

1984-1991		$350	$425

Echoplex EP6T
1980-ca.1988. All-tube reissue of the EP2.

1980-1988		$400	$475

Effector 13

2002-present. Ever Was builds his guitar effects in Minneapolis, Minnesota. He was located in Austin, Texas until mid-'04.

EFX

1980s. Brand name of the Los Angeles-based EFX Center; they also offered a direct box and a powered pedal box/board.

Switch Box B287
1984. Dual effects loop selector.

1984		$25	$35

EKO

1959-1985, 2000-present. In the '60s and '70s EKO offered effects made by EME and JEN Elettronica, which also made Vox effects.

Dunlop Jimi Hendrix Fuzz Wah

Echoplex EP-4

Effector 13 Disaster Fuzz

EFFECTS

Electra Metal 698HM

E-H Bassballs

E-H Black Finger

MODEL YEAR	FEATURES	EXC. COND. LOW	HIGH

Electra

1971-1984. A guitar brand imported by St. Louis Music, Electra offered a line of effects in the late '70s.

Chorus 504CH
Ca.1975-ca.1980.

| 1975-1980 | | $55 | $75 |

Compressor 502C/602C
1975-1980.

| 1975-1980 | | $45 | $55 |

Distortion 500D
Ca.1976-ca.1980.

| 1976-1980 | | $55 | $75 |

Flanger (stereo) 605F
Ca.1975-ca.1980.

| 1975-1980 | | $55 | $75 |

Fuzz Wah
Ca.1975-ca.1980.

| 1975-1980 | | $75 | $125 |

Pedal Drive 515AC
Ca.1976-ca.1980. Overdrive.

| 1975-1980 | | $40 | $50 |

Phaser Model 501P
4 *Ca.1976-ca.1980.*

| 1975-1980 | | $50 | $60 |

Phaser Model 875
1975-ca.1980.

| 1975-1980 | | $50 | $60 |

Roto Phase I
1975-ca.1980. Small pocket phaser.

| 1975-1980 | | $70 | $85 |

Roto Phase II
1975-ca.1980. Pedal phasor.

| 1975-1980 | | $80 | $95 |

Electro-Harmonix

1968-1984, 1996-present. Founded by Mike Matthews in New York City, the company initially produced small plug-in boosters such as the LPB-1. In '71, they unveiled the awe-inspiring Big Muff Pi fuzz and dozens of innovative pedals followed. After years of disputes, the nonunion E-H factory became the target of union organizers and a '81 union campaign, combining picketing and harrying of E-H employees, brought production to a halt. Matthews' financier then cut his funding, and in early '82, E.H. filed for bankruptcy. Later that year, Matthews was able to reopen and continue through '84. In '96, he again began producing reissues of many of his classic effects as well as new designs.

3 Phase Liner
1981.

| 1981 | | $50 | $60 |

5X Junction Mixer
1977-1981.

| 1977-1981 | | $30 | $40 |

10 Band Graphic Equalizer
1977-1981. Includes footswitch.

| 1977-1981 | | $60 | $70 |

16-Second Digital Delay
Early-1980s, 2004-present. An updated version was reissued in '04.

1980s	With foot controller	$650	$800
1980s	Without foot controller	$500	$650
1990s		$325	$500
2004-2005		$275	$375

Attack Equalizer
1975-1981. Active EQ, a.k.a. "Knock Out."

| 1975-1981 | | $150 | $200 |

Attack/Decay
1980-1981. Tape reverse simulator.

| 1980-1981 | | $200 | $225 |

Bad Stone Phase Shifter
1975-1981.

| 1970s | Three knobs | $200 | $250 |
| 1970s | Two knobs, color switch | $175 | $225 |

Bass Micro-Synthesizer
1981-1984, 1999-present. Analog synthesizer sounds.

| 1981-1984 | | $225 | $300 |
| 1999-2005 | | $150 | $175 |

Bassballs
1978-1984, 1998-present. Bass envelope filter/distortion.

| 1978-1984 | | $200 | $225 |

Big Muff Pi
1971-1984. Sustain, floor unit, issued in 3 different looks, as described below.

1970s	Earlier black graphics, knobs in triangle pattern	$325	$375
1970s	Later red/black graphics, 1/2" letters	$150	$225
1980s	Red/black graphics, logo in 1" letters	$125	$200

Big Muff Pi (reissue)
1996-present. Originally made in Russia, but currently both Russian- and U.S.-made versions are available.

| 1996-2005 | Russian-made | $40 | $45 |

Big Muff Sovtek
2000s. Big Muff Pi, Electro Harmonix, and Sovtek logos on an olive green case.

| 2000s | | $100 | $125 |

Black Finger Compressor Sustainer
1977, 2003-present. Original has 3 knobs in triangle pattern.

| 1977 | | $125 | $225 |
| 2003-2005 | | $75 | $100 |

Clap Track
1980-1984. Drum effect.

| 1980-1984 | | $40 | $60 |

Clone Theory
1977-1981. Chorus effect.

| 1977-1981 | The Clone Theory logo | $150 | $175 |

Crash Pad
1980-1984. Percussion synth.

| 1980-1984 | | $40 | $60 |

MODEL		EXC. COND.	
YEAR	FEATURES	LOW	HIGH

Crying Tone Pedal
1976-1978. Wah-wah.

1976-1978		$175	$225

Deluxe Big Muff Pi
1978-1981. Sustain, AC version of Big Muff Pi, includes a complete Soul Preacher unit.

1978-1981	Red graphics	$125	$200

Deluxe Electric Mistress Flanger
1977-1983, 1996-present. AC.

1977-1979		$150	$250
1980-1983		$125	$175

Deluxe Memory Man
1977-1983, 1996-present. Echo and delay, featured 4 knobs '77-'78, from '79-'83 it has 5 knobs and added vibrato and chorus.

1977-1978	Four knobs	$225	$300
1979-1983	Five knobs	$200	$275
1996-2005		$150	$165

Deluxe Octave Multiplexer
1977-1981.

1977-1981		$200	$250

Digital Delay/Chorus
1981-84. With digital chorus.

1981-1984		$250	$300

Digital Rhythm Matrix DRM-15
1981-1984.

1981-1984		$225	$250

Digital Rhythm Matrix DRM-16
1979-1983.

1979-1983		$225	$250

Digital Rhythm Matrix DRM-32
1981-1984.

1981-1984		$225	$250

Doctor Q Envelope Follower
1976-1983, 2001-present. For bass or guitar.

1976-1983		$150	$200
2001-2005		$30	$35

Domino Theory
1981. Sound sensitive light tube.

1981		$50	$100

Echo 600
1981.

1981		$175	$225

Echoflanger
1977-1982. Flange, slapback, chorus, filter.

1977-1982		$200	$250

Electric Mistress Flanger
1976-1984.

1976-1984		$175	$275

Electronic Metronome
1978-1980.

1978-1980		$25	$30

Frequency Analyzer
1977-1984, 2001-present. Ring modulator.

1977-1984		$200	$250

Full Double Tracking Effect
1978-1981. Doubling, slapback.

1978-1981		$100	$150

Fuzz Wah
Introduced around 1974.

1970s		$175	$225

MODEL		EXC. COND.	
YEAR	FEATURES	LOW	HIGH

Golden Throat
1977-1984.

1977-1984		$300	$400

Golden Throat Deluxe
1977-1979. Deluxe has a built-in monitor amp.

1977-1979		$300	$400

Golden Throat II
1978-1981.

1978-1981		$150	$225

Guitar Synthesizer
1981. Sold for $1,495 in May '81.

1981		$225	$300

Hog's Foot Bass Booster
1977-1980.

1977-1978		$70	$90

Holy Grail
2002-present. Digital reverb.

2002-2005		$80	$90

Hot Foot
1977-1978. Rocker pedal turns knob of other E-H effects.

1977-1978	Gold case, red graphics	$75	$100

Hot Tubes
1978-1984, 2001-present. Overdrive.

1978-1984		$125	$200

Linear Power Booster LPB-1
1968-1983.

1976-1979		$55	$80
1980-1983		$45	$75

Linear Power Booster LPB-2
Ca.1968-1983.

1968-1983		$90	$100

Little Big Muff Pi
1976-1980, 2006-present. Sustain, 1-knob floor unit.

1976-1980		$150	$175

Memory Man
1976-1984, 1999-present. Analog delay, newer version in stereo.

1976-1979		$250	$300
1980-1984		$150	$250

Micro Synthesizer
1978-1984, 1998-present. Mini keyboard phaser.

1978-1979		$225	$250
1978-1984		$225	$250
1998-2005		$150	$170

Mini Q-Tron
2002-present. Battery-operated smaller version of Q-Tron envelope follower

2002-2005		$40	$45

Mini-Mixer
1978-1981. Mini mic mixer, reissued in '01.

1978-1981		$30	$40

MiniSynthesizer
1981-1983. Mini keyboard with phaser.

1981-1983		$300	$400

MiniSynthesizer With Echo
1981.

1981		$375	$500

E-H Deluxe Memory Man

E-H Frequency Analyzer

E-H Hot Foot

EFFECTS

To get the most from this book, be sure to read "Using *The Guide*" in the introduction.

E-H Octave Multiplexer

E-H Pulsar

E-H Small Clone EH4600

MODEL YEAR	FEATURES	EXC. COND. LOW	HIGH
Mole Bass Booster	*1968-1978.*		
1968-1969		$60	$80
1970-1978		$40	$60
Muff Fuzz Crying Tone	*1977-1978. Fuzz, wah.*		
1977-1978		$150	$250
Octave Multiplexer Floor Unit	*1976-1980.*		
1976-1980		$175	$275
Octave Multiplexer Pedal	*1976-1977, 2001-present.*		
1976-1977		$150	$250
2001-2005		$40	$45
Panic Button	*1981. Siren sounds for drum.*		
1981		$30	$40
Poly Chorus/Stereo Poly Chorus	*1981, 1999-present. Same as Echoflanger.*		
1981		$175	$200
1999-2005		$125	$150
Polyphase	*1979-1981. With envelope.*		
1979-1981		$175	$225
Pulsar	*2004-present. Variable wave form tremolo.*		
2004		$45	$55
Pulse Modulator	*Ca.1968 -ca.1972. Triple tremolo.*		
1968-1969		$250	$325
1970-1972		$200	$250
Q-Tron	*1997-present. Envelope controlled filter.*		
1997-2003		$125	$175
Q-Tron +	*1999-present. With added effects loop and Attack Response switch.*		
1999-2003		$70	$80
Queen Triggered Wah	*1976-1978. Wah/Envelope Filter.*		
1976-1978		$125	$150
Random Tone Generator RTG	*1981.*		
1981		$40	$60
Rhythm 12 (rhythm machine)	*1978.*		
1978		$75	$125
Rolling Thunder	*1980-1981. Percussion synth.*		
1980-1981		$40	$50
Screaming Bird Treble Booster	*Ca.1968-1980. In-line unit.*		
1968-1980		$75	$100
Screaming Tree Treble Booster	*1977-1981. Floor unit.*		
1977-1981		$100	$150
Sequencer Drum	*1981. Drum effect.*		
1981		$40	$50

MODEL YEAR	FEATURES	EXC. COND. LOW	HIGH
Slapback Echo	*1977-1978. Stereo.*		
1977-1978		$150	$200
Small Clone	*1983-1984, 1999-present. Analog chorus, depth and rate controls, purple face plate, white logo.*		
1983-1984		$150	$200
1999-2005		$35	$40
Small Stone Phase Shifter	*1975-1984, 1996-present. Both Russian and U.S. reissues were made.*		
1975-1979		$175	$225
1980-1984		$125	$175
Soul Preacher	*1977-1983. Compressor sustainer.*		
1977-1983		$100	$150
Space Drum/Super Space Drum	*1980-1981. Percussion synthesizer.*		
1980-1981		$125	$175
Switch Blade	*1977-1983. A-B Box.*		
1977-1983		$45	$55
Talking Pedal	*1977-1978. Creates vowel sounds.*		
1977-1978		$350	$550
The Silencer	*1976-1981. Noise elimination.*		
1976-1981		$60	$80
The Wiggler	*2002-present. All-tube modulator including pitch vibrato and volume tremolo.*		
2002-2005		$100	$110
The Worm	*2002-present. Wah/Phaser.*		
2002-2005		$55	$65
Tube Zipper	*2001-present. Tube (2x12AX7) envelope follower.*		
2001-2005		$100	$120
Vocoder	*1978-1981. Modulates voice with instrument.*		
1978-1981	Rackmount	$425	$525
Volume Pedal	*1978-1981.*		
1978-1981		$45	$65
Y-Triggered Filter	*1976-1977.*		
1976-1977		$140	$160
Zipper Envelope Follower	*1976-1978. The Tube Zipper was introduced in 2001.*		
1976-1978		$200	$300

Elk

Late-1960s. Japanese company Elk Gakki Co., Ltd. mainly made guitars and amps, but did offer effects as well.

Elka

In the late '60s or early '70s, Italian organ and synthesizer company Elka-Orla (later just Elka) offered a few effects, likely made by JEN Elettronica (Vox, others).

EFFECTS

MODEL YEAR	FEATURES	EXC. COND. LOW	HIGH

EMMA Electronic

Line of guitar effects built in Denmark.

ReezaFRATzitz RF-1

2004-present. Overdrive and distortion, red case.

2004-2005		$80	$95

EMS

1969-1979. Peter Zinnovieff's English synth company (Electronic Music Studios) also offered a guitar synthesizer. The company has reopened to work on original EMS gear.

Epiphone

Epiphone pedals are labeled "G.A.S Guitar Audio System" and were offered from around 1988 to '91.

Pedals

Various models with years available.

1988-1989	Chorus EP-CH-70	$35	$45
1988-1989	Delay EP-DE-80	$45	$60
1988-1991	Compressor EP-CO-20	$35	$40
1988-1991	Distortion EP-DI-10	$35	$45
1988-1991	Flanger EP-FL-60	$40	$55
1988-1991	Overdrive EP-OD-30	$35	$45

Ernie Ball

Ernie Ball owned a music store in Tarzana, California, when he noticed the demand for a better selection of strings. The demand for his Slinky strings grew to the point where, in '67, he sold the store to concentrate on strings. He went on to produce the Earthwood brand of guitars and basses from '72-'85. In '84, Ball purchased the Music Man company.

Volume Pedal

1977-present.

1977-2005		$35	$65

Euthymia Electronics

Line of guitar effects built by Erik Miller in Alameda, California.

Eventide

1971-present. This New Jersey electronics manufacturer has offered studio effects since the late '70s.

EXR

The EXR Corporation was located in Brighton, Michigan.

Projector

1983-ca.1984. Psychoacoustic enhancer pedal.

1983-1984		$65	$75

Projector SP III

1983-ca.1984. Psychoacoustic enhancer pedal, volume pedal/sound boost.

1983-1984		$65	$70

Farfisa

The organ company offered effects pedals in the 1960s. Their products were manufactured in Italy by the Italian Accordion Company and distributed by Chicago Musical Insturments.

Model VIP 345 Organ

Mid-1960s. Portable organ with Syntheslalom used in the rock and roll venue.

1960s		$500	$600

Repeater

1969		$100	$150

Sferasound

1960s. Vibrato pedal for a Farfisa Organ but it works well with the guitar, gray case.

1960s		$275	$375

Wah/Volume

1969		$100	$150

Fender

Although Fender has flirted with effects since the 1950s (the volume/volume-tone pedal and the EccoFonic), it concentrated mainly on guitars and amps. Fender effects ranged from the sublime to the ridiculous, from the tube Reverb to the Dimension IV. Presently they offer a reverb unit.

Blender Fuzz

1968-1977. Battery operated fuzz and sustain. In '05, Fender issued the Blender Custom.

1968-1969		$350	$375
1970-1977		$275	$300

Contempo Organ

1967-1968. Portable organ, all solidstate, 61 keys including a 17-key bass section, catalog shows with red cover material.

1967-1968		$525	$550

Dimension IV

1968-1970. Multi-effects unit using an oil-filled drum.

1968-1970		$150	$200

Echo-Reverb

1966-1970. Solidstate, echo-reverb effect produced by rotating metal disk, black tolex, silver grille.

1966-1970		$175	$300

Electronic Echo Chamber

1962-1968. Solidstate tape echo, up to 400 ms of delay, rectangle box with 2 controls '62-'67, slanted front '67-'68.

1962-1968		$275	$325

Fuzz-Wah

1968-1984. Has Fuzz and Wah switches on sides of pedal '68-'73, has 3 switches above the pedal '74-'84.

1968-1973	Switches on side	$175	$225
1974-1984	Switches above	$150	$200

Phaser

1975-1977. AC powered.

1975-1977		$125	$175

Reverb Unit

1961-1966, 1975-1978. Fender used a wide variety of tolex coverings in the early-'60s as the coverings matched those on the amps. Initially, Fender used rough blond tolex, then rough brown tolex, followed by smooth white or black tolex.

1961	Blond Tolex, Oxblood grille	$1,100	$1,350

Eventide H8000

Ernie Ball Volume Pedal

Fender Blender

EFFECTS

Fender Electronic Echo Chamber

Flip Tube Echo

Foxx Tone Machine

MODEL YEAR	FEATURES	EXC. COND. LOW	HIGH
1961	Brown Tolex	$900	$1,200
1962	Blond Tolex, Oxblood grille	$1,100	$1,300
1962	Brown Tolex, Wheat grille	$800	$1,100
1963	Brown Tolex	$800	$1,050
1963	Rough Blond Tolex	$900	$1,100
1963	Smooth White Tolex	$1,000	$1,200
1964	Brown Tolex, gold grille	$800	$1,050
1964	Smooth White Tolex	$1,000	$1,200
1964-1966	Black Tolex	$800	$1,050
1966	Solidstate, flat cabinet	$200	$350
1975-1978	Tube reverb reinstated	$500	$600

Reverb Unit Reissue Models
1994-present. Reissue spring/tube Reverb Units with various era cosmetics as listed below.

1990s	'63 brown tolex	$275	$325
1990s	'63 white (limited run)	$325	$375
1990s	Blackface	$325	$350
1990s	Tweed (limited run)	$350	$400

Tone and Volume Foot Pedal
1954-1984.

1960s		$125	$175

Vibratone
1967-1972. Leslie-type speaker cabinet made specifically for the guitar, 2-speed motor.

1960s		$750	$850

FlexiSound
FlexiSound products were made in Lancaster, Pennsylvania.

F. S. Clipper
1975-ca.1976. Distortion, plugged directly into guitar jack.

1975-1976		$55	$65

The Beefer
1975. Power booster, plugged directly into guitar jack.

1975		$40	$50

Flip
Line of tube effects by Guyatone and distributed in the U.S. by Godlyke Distributing.

TD-X Tube Echo
2004-present. Hybrid tube power delay pedal.

2004		$90	$100

FM Acoustics
Made in Switzerland.

E-1 Pedal
1975. Volume, distortion, filter pedal.

1975		$70	$80

Foxx
Foxx pedals are readily identifiable by their fur-like covering. They slunk onto the scene in 1971 and were extinct by '78. Made by Hollywood's Ridinger Associates, their most notable product was the Tone Machine fuzz. Foxx-made pedals also have appeared under various brands such as G and G, Guild, Yamaha and Sears Roebuck, generally without fur. Since 2005, reissues of some of the classic Foxx pedals are being built in Provo, Utah.

Clean Machine
1974-1978.

1974-1978		$250	$275

Down Machine
1971-1977. Bass wah.

1971-1977	Blue case	$250	$275

Foot Phaser
1975-1977, 2006-present.

1975-1977		$300	$650

Fuzz and Wa and Volume
1974-1978, 2006-present.

1974-1978		$300	$350

Guitar Synthesizer I
1975.

1975		$300	$350

O.D. Machine
1972-ca.1975.

1972-1975		$150	$200

Phase III
1975-1978.

1975-1978		$100	$150

Tone Machine
1971-1978, 2005-present. Fuzz with Octave.

1971-1978		$400	$475

Wa and Volume
1971-1978.

1971-1978		$200	$225

Wa Machine
1971-ca.1978.

1971-1978		$150	$200

Framptone
2000-present. Founded by Peter Frampton, Framptone offers hand-made guitar effects.

Frantone
1994-present. Effects and accessories hand built in New York City.

Fulltone
1991-present. Fulltone effects are based on some of the classic effects of the past. Fulltone was started in Los Angeles, California by Michael Fuller who says the company was born out of his love for Jimi Hendrix and fine vintage pedals.

Deja Vibe
1991-2002. UniVibe-type pedal, later models have a Vintage/Modern switch. Stereo version also available. Now offerered in Mini version.

1991-2004	Mono	$175	$200

MODEL YEAR	FEATURES	EXC. COND. LOW	HIGH
Deja Vibe II			
1997-present. Like Deja Vibe but with built-in speed control. Stereo version also available.			
1997-2005	Mono	$200	$225
Distortion Pro			
2002-present. Red case, volume and distortion knobs with four voicing controls.			
2002-2005		$125	$150
Fat Boost			
2001-present. Clean boost, silver-sparkle case, volume and drive knobs.			
2001-2005		$125	$135
Full-Drive 2			
1995-present. Blue case, four control knobs.			
1995-2005		$120	$145
Octafuzz			
1996-present. Copy of the Tycobrahe Octavia.			
1996-2005		$85	$100
Soul Bender			
1994-present. Volume, tone and dirt knobs.			
1994-2005		$100	$125
Supa-Trem			
1995-present. Black case, white Supa-Trem logo, rate and mix controls.			
1995-2005		$100	$125
Tube Tape Echo TTE			
2004-present. EchoPlex style using tape.			
2004-2005		$725	$850

Furman Sound

1993-present. Located in Petaluma, California, Furman makes audio and video signal processors and AC power conditioning products for music and other markets.

MODEL YEAR	FEATURES	EXC. COND. LOW	HIGH
LC-2 Limiter Compressor			
1990s. Rackmount unit with a black suitcase and red knobs.			
1990s		$40	$50
PQ3 Parametric EQ			
1990s. Rackmount preamp and equalizer.			
1998-1999		$110	$150
PQ6 Parametric Stereo			
1990s		$135	$175
RV1 Reverb Rackmount			
1990s		$110	$150

Garcia

2004-present. Guitar effects built by Matthew Garcia in Myrtle Beach, South Carolina. He also builds amps.

George Dennis

1991-present. Founded by George Burgerstein, original products were a line of effects pedals. In '96 they added a line of tube amps. The company is located in Prague, Czech Republic.

Gibson

Gibson did offer a few effects bearing their own name, but most were sold under the Maestro name (see that listing).

MODEL YEAR	FEATURES	EXC. COND. LOW	HIGH
Echoplex Digital Pro			
1994-present. Rackmount unit with digital recording, sampling and digital delay. Labeled as just Echoplex until '01 when Gibson name added.			
1994-2005		$700	$850
GA-3RV Reverb Unit			
1964-1967. Small, compact, spring reverb unit, black tolex, gray grille.			
1964-1967		$325	$400
GA-4RE Reverb-Echo Unit			
1964-1967. Small, compact, lightweight accessory reverb-echo unit that produces complete reverberation and authentic echo, utilizes Gibson's "electronic memory" system for both reverb and echo, black tolex, gray grille.			
1964-1967		$450	$550

Godbout

Sold a variety of effects do-it-yourself kits in the 1970s. Difficult to value because quality depends on skills of builder.

MODEL YEAR	FEATURES	EXC. COND. LOW	HIGH
Effects Kits			
1970s		$20	$30

Goodrich Sound

Late-1970s. Goodrich was located in Grand Haven, Michigan.

MODEL YEAR	FEATURES	EXC. COND. LOW	HIGH
Match Box 33670 Line Boost			
Early-1980s. Small rectangular in and out box with control knob.			
1980s		$45	$55
Volume Pedal 6122			
1979-ca.1980. Uses a potentiometer.			
1970s		$45	$55
Volume Pedal 6400ST			
1979-ca.1980. Uses a potentiometer.			
1970s		$45	$55
Volume Pedal 6402			
1979-ca.1980. Uses photocell.			
1970s		$45	$55

Greer Amplication

1999-present. Guitar stomp box effects built by Nick Greer in Athens, Georgia. He also builds amps.

Gretsch

Gretsch has offered a limited line of effects from time to time.

MODEL YEAR	FEATURES	EXC. COND. LOW	HIGH
Controfuzz			
Mid-1970s. Distortion.			
1970s		$150	$225
Deluxe Reverb Unit Model 6149			
1963-1969. Similar to Gibson's GA-1 introduced around the same time.			
1963-1969		$400	$500
Expandafuzz			
Mid-1970s. Distortion.			
1970s		$150	$200

Fulltone Choralflange

George Dennis Elite Wah

Gretsch Expandafuzz

EFFECTS

Heil Sound Talk Box

Guyatone Silver Machine

Hohner Tri-Dirty Booster

MODEL YEAR	FEATURES	EXC. COND. LOW	HIGH

Reverb Unit Model 6144 Preamp Reverb
1963-1967. Approximately 17 watts, preamp functionality, no speaker.

1963-1967		$250	$350

Tremofect
Mid-1970s. Tremolo effect, 3-band EQ, speed, effect, bass, total, and treble knobs.

1970s		$225	$300

Guild
Guild marketed effects made by Binson, Electro-Harmonix, Foxx, WEM and Applied in the 1960s and '70s.

Copicat
1960s-1979. Echo.

1970s		$300	$400

DE-20 Auto-Rhythm Unit
1971-1974. 50 watt rhythm accompaniment unit. Included 20 rhythms and a separate instrument channel with its own volume control. 1x12" plus tweeter.

1971-1974		$200	$300

Echorec (by Binson)
Ca.1960-1979. This was different stripped-down version of the Binson Echorec.

1960s		$375	$475

Foxey Lady Fuzz
1968-1977. Distortion, sustain.

1968-1975	Two knobs, made by E-H	$200	$250
1976-1977	3 knobs in row, same as Big Muff	$150	$200

Fuzz Wah FW-3
1975-ca.1979. Distortion, volume, wah, made by Foxx.

1970s		$150	$175

HH Echo Unit
1976-ca.1979.

1970s		$200	$300

VW-1
1975-ca.1979. Volume, wah, made by Foxx.

1970s		$200	$250

Guyatone
1998-present. Imported stomp boxes, tape echo units and outboard reverb units distributed by Godlyke Distributing.

HAO
Line of guitar effects built in Japan by J.E.S. International, distributed in the U.S. by Godlyke.

Heathkit
1960s. Unassembled kits sold at retail.

TA-28 Distortion Booster
1960s. Fuzz assembly kit, heavy '60s super fuzz, case-by-case quality depending on the builder.

1960s		$140	$150

Heavy Metal Products
Mid-1970s. From Alto Loma, California, products for the heavy metal guitarist.

MODEL YEAR	FEATURES	EXC. COND. LOW	HIGH

Raunchbox Fuzz
1975-1976.

1975-1976		$75	$100

Switchbox
1975-1976. A/B box.

1975-1976		$25	$35

Heet Sound Products
1974-present. The E Bow concept goes back to '67, but a hand-held model wasn't available until '74. Made in Los Angeles, California.

E Bow
1974-1979, 1985-1987, 1994-present. The Energy Bow, hand-held electro-magnetic string driver.

1974-1979		$50	$60

E Bow for Pedal Steels
1979. Hand-held electro-magnetic string driver.

1979		$35	$55

Heil Sound
1960-present. Founded by Bob Heil, Marissa, Illinois. Created the talk box technology as popularized by Peter Frampton. In the '60s and '70s Heil was dedicated to innovative products for the music industry. In the late-'70s, innovative creations were more in the amateur radio market, and by the '90s Heil's focus was on the home theater market. The Heil Sound Talkbox was reissued by Jim Dunlop USA in '89.

Talk Box
1976-ca.1980, 1989-present. Reissued by Dunlop.

1976-1980		$100	$125
1989-1999		$75	$85
2000-2005		$70	$80

High Gain
See listing under Dunlop.

Hohner
Hohner offered effects in the late-1970s.

Dirty Booster
1977-ca.1978. Distortion.

1977-1978		$55	$65

Dirty Wah Wah'er
1977-ca.1978. Adds distortion.

1977-1978		$65	$75

Fuzz Wah
1970s. Morley-like volume pedal with volume knob and fuzz knob, switch for soft or hard fuzz, gray box with black foot pedal.

1970s		$65	$75

Multi-Exciter
1977-ca.1978. Volume, wah, surf, tornado, siren.

1977-1978		$60	$70

Tape Echo/Echo Plus
1970s. Black alligator suitcase.

1970s		$200	$300

Tri-Booster
1977-ca.1978. Distortion, sustain.

1977-1978		$55	$65

MODEL YEAR	FEATURES	EXC. COND. LOW	HIGH

Vari-Phaser
1977-ca.1978.
| 1977-1978 | | $55 | $65 |

Vol-Kicker Volume Pedal
1977-ca.1978.
| 1977-1978 | | $30 | $40 |

Wah-Wah'er
1977-ca.1978. Wah, volume.
| 1977-1978 | | $55 | $65 |

HomeBrew Electronics
2001-present. Stomp box effects hand made by Joel and Andrea Weaver in Glendale, Arizona.

Ibanez
Ibanez effects were introduced ca. 1974, and were manufactured by Japan's Maxon Electronics. Although results were mixed at first, a more uniform and modern product line, including the now legendary Tube Screamer, built Ibanez's reputation for quality. They continue to produce a wide range of effects.

60s Fuzz FZ5 (Soundtank)
1991-1992, 1996-1998. Fuzz with level, tone and distortion controls, black plastic case, green label.
| 1990s | | $30 | $35 |

7th Heaven SH7 (Tone-Lok)
2000-2004. Lo, high, drive and level controls, gray-silver case, blue-green label.
| 2000-2004 | | $25 | $35 |

Acoustic Effects PT-4
1993-1998. Acoustic guitar multi-effect with compressor/limiter, tone shaper, stereo chorus, digital reverb, with power supply.
| 1993-1998 | | $75 | $100 |

Analog Delay 202 (Rack Mount)
1981-1983. Rack mount with delay, doubling, flanger, stereo chorus, dual inputs with tone and level.
| 1981-1983 | | $200 | $250 |

Analog Delay AD9
1982-1984. 3 control analog delay, Hot Pink metal case.
| 1982-1984 | | $200 | $275 |

Analog Delay AD-80
1980-1981. Pink case.
| 1980-1981 | | $200 | $300 |

Analog Delay AD99
1996-1998. Reissue, 3 control knobs and on/off switch, winged-hand logo, black case.
| 1996-1998 | | $125 | $150 |

Analog Delay AD-100 (Table Unit)
1981-1983. Stand-alone table/studio unit (not rack mount) with power cord.
| 1981-1983 | | $200 | $250 |

Auto Filter AF9
1982-1984. Replaces AF201 model.
| 1982-1984 | | $175 | $200 |

Auto Filter AF201
1981. Two min-max sliders, 3 mode toggle switches, orange metal case.
| 1981 | | $175 | $200 |

Auto Wah AW5 (SoundTank)
1994-1999. Plastic case SoundTank series.
| 1994-1999 | | $35 | $45 |

Auto Wah AW7 (Tone-Lok)
2000-present. Silver case.
| 2000-2005 | | $25 | $35 |

Bass Compressor BP10
1986-1991.
| 1986-1991 | | $70 | $80 |

Bi-Mode Chorus BC-9
1984. Dual channel for 2 independent speed and width settings.
| 1984 | | $75 | $100 |

Chorus CS-505
1980-1981. Speed and depth controls, gray-blue case, stereo or mono input, battery or external power option.
| 1980-1981 | | $100 | $125 |

Chorus Flanger CF7 (Tone-Lok)
1999-present. Speed, depth, delay, regeneration controls, mode and crazy switches.
| 1999-2005 | | $40 | $45 |

Classic Flange FL99
1997-1999. Analog reissue, silver metal case, winged-hand artwork, 4 controls, 2 footswitch buttons.
| 1997-1999 | | $90 | $110 |

Classic Phase PH99
1995-1999. Analog reissue, silver metal case, winged-hand artwork, speed, depth, feedback, effect level controls, intense and bypass footswitches.
| 1995-1999 | | $90 | $110 |

Compressor CP-5 (SoundTank)
1991-1998.
| 1991-1998 | | $25 | $35 |

Compressor Limiter CP9
1982-1984.
| 1982-1984 | | $100 | $125 |

Compressor CP10
1986-1992.
| 1986-1992 | | $75 | $80 |

Compressor CP-830
1975-1979.
| 1975-1979 | | $100 | $125 |

Compressor II CP-835
1980-1981.
| 1980-1981 | | $100 | $125 |

Delay Champ CD10
1986-1989. Red case, 3 knobs.
| 1986-1989 | | $125 | $150 |

Delay Echo DE-7 (Tone-Lok)
1999-present. Stereo delay/echo.
| 1999-2005 | | $45 | $55 |

Delay Harmonizer DM-1000
1983-1984. Rack mount, with chorus, 9 control knobs.
| 1983-1984 | | $175 | $225 |

HomeBrew Compressor Retro

Ibanez Classic Phase PH-99

Ibanez DE7 Delay/Echo

EFFECTS

EFFECTS

Ibanez Flanger FL-9

Ibanez LA Metal LM7

Ibanez UE-300

MODEL YEAR FEATURES	EXC. COND. LOW	HIGH
Delay III DDL20 Digital Delay		
1988-1989. Filtering, doubling, slap back, echo S, echo M, echo L, Seafoam Green coloring on pedal.		
1988-1989	$100	$125
Delay PDD1 (DPC Series)		
1988-1989. Programmable Digital Delay (PDD) with display screen.		
1988-1989	$125	$150
Digital Chorus DSC10		
1990-1992. 3 control knobs and slider selection toggle.		
1990-1992	$75	$100
Digital Delay DL5 (SoundTank)		
1991-1998.		
1991-1998	$40	$50
Digital Delay DL10		
1989-1992. Digital Delay made in Japan, blue case, 3 green control knobs, stompbox.		
1989-1992	$100	$125
Distortion DS7 (Tone-Lok)		
2000-present. Drive, tone, and level controls.		
2000-2005	$45	$50
Distortion Charger DS10		
1986-1989.		
1986-1989	$70	$90
Echo Machine EM5 (SoundTank)		
1996-1998. Simulates tape echo.		
1996-1998	$50	$60
Fat Cat Distortion FC10		
1987-1989. 3-knob pedal with distortion, tone, and level controls.		
1987-1989	$50	$75
Flanger FFL5 (Master Series)		
1984-1985. Speed, regeneration, width, D-time controls, battery or adapter option.		
1984-1985	$70	$90
Flanger FL5 (SoundTank)		
1991-1998.		
1991-1998	$30	$40
Flanger FL9		
1982-1984. Yellow case.		
1982-1984	$100	$150
Flanger FL-301		
1979-1982. Mini flanger, 3 knobs, called the FL-301 DX in late '81-'82.		
1979-1982	$100	$125
Flanger FL-305		
1976-1979. Five knobs.		
1976-1979	$100	$125
Flying Pan FP-777		
1976-1979. Auto pan/phase shifter, 4 control knobs, phase on/off button, pan on/off button, silver metal case with blue trim and Flying Pan winged-hand logo.		
1976-1979	$500	$800
Fuzz FZ7 (Tone-Lok)		
2000-present. Drive, tone and level controls, gray-silver case, blue-green FZ7 label.		
2000-2005	$50	$55

MODEL YEAR FEATURES	EXC. COND. LOW	HIGH
Graphic Bass EQ BE10		
1986-1992. Later labeled as the BEQ10.		
1986-1992	$60	$80
Graphic EQ GE9		
1982-1984. Six EQ sliders, 1 overall volume slider, turquoise blue case.		
1982-198	$60	$80
Graphic EQ GE10		
1986-1992. Eight sliders.		
1986-1992	$60	$80
Graphic Equalizer GE-601 (808 Series)		
1980-1981. 7-slider EQ, aqua blue metal case.		
1980-1981	$75	$100
Guitar Multi-Processor PT5		
1993-1997. Floor unit, programmable with 25 presets and 25 user presets, effects include distortion, chorus, flanger, etc, green case.		
1993-1997	$100	$125
LA Metal LM7		
1988-1989. Silver case.		
1988-1989	$55	$65
LoFi LF7 (Tone-Lok)		
2000-present. Filter, 4 knobs.		
2000-2005	$25	$35
Metal Charger MS10		
1986-1992. Distortion, level, attack, punch and edge control knobs, green case.		
1986-1992	$55	$65
Metal Screamer MSL		
1985. 3 control knobs.		
1985	$55	$65
Modern Fusion MF-5 (SoundTank)		
1990-1991. Level, tone and distortion controls.		
1990-1991	$50	$55
Modulation Delay PDM1		
1988-1989. Programmable Digital Modulation pedal.		
1988-1989	$100	$125
Modulation Delay DM1000		
1983-1984. Rack mount with delay, reverb, modulation.		
1983-1984	$100	$125
Modulation Delay DM500		
1983-1984. Rack mount.		
1983-1984	$75	$100
Mostortion MT10		
1990-1992. Mos-FET circuit distortion pedal, 5 control knobs, green case.		
1990-1992	$50	$60
Multi-Effect UE-300 (floor unit)		
1983-1984. Floor unit, 4 footswitches for super metal, digital delay, digital stereo chorus, and master power, 3 delay modes.		
1983-1984	$275	$350
Multi-effect UE-300B (floor unit)		
1983-1984. Floor unit for bass.		
1983-1984	$275	$350
Multi-Effect UE-400 (rackmount)		
1980-1984. Rack mount with foot switch.		
1980-1984	$300	$375

MODEL YEAR FEATURES	EXC. COND. LOW	HIGH
Multi-Effect UE-405 (rackmount)		
1981-1984. Rack mount with analog delay, parametric EQ, compressor/limiter, stereo chorus and loop.		
1981-1984	$300	$375
Noise Buster NB10		
1988-1989. Eliminates 60-cycle hum and other outside signals, metal case.		
1988-1989	$70	$75
Overdrive OD-850		
1975-1979.		
1975-1979	$300	$400
Overdrive II OD-855		
1977-1979. Distortion, tone, and level controls, yellow/green case, large Overdrive II logo.		
1977-1979	$300	$400
Pan Delay DPL10		
1990-1992. Royal Blue case, 3 green control knobs.		
1990-1992	$100	$125
Parametric EQ PQ9		
1982-1984.		
1982-1984	$85	$100
Parametric EQ PQ401		
1981. 3 sliders, dial-in knob, light aqua blue case.		
1981	$95	$145
Phase Tone II PT-707		
1976-1979. Blue box, 1 knob, script logo for first 2 years.		
1976-1979	$100	$130
Phase Tone PT-909		
1979-1982. Blue box, 3 knobs, early models with flat case (logo at bottom or later in the middle) or later wedge case.		
1979-1982	$140	$150
Phase Tone PT-999		
1975-1979. Script logo, 1 knob, round footswitch, becomes PT-909.		
1975-1979	$125	$150
Phase Tone PT-1000		
1974-1975. Morley-style pedal phase, light blue case, early model of Phase Tone.		
1974-1975	$200	$300
Phaser PH5 (SoundTank)		
1991-1998		
1991-1998	$25	$35
Phaser PH7 (Tone-Lok)		
1999-present. Speed, depth, feedback and level controls.		
1999-2005	$40	$45
Phaser PT9		
1982-1984. Three control knobs, red case.		
1982-1984	$75	$100
Powerlead PL5 (SoundTank)		
1991-1998. Metal case '91, plastic case '91-'98.		
1991 Metal	$30	$45
1991-1998 Plastic	$20	$25
Renometer		
1976-1979. 5-band equalizer with preamp.		
1976-1979	$75	$100

MODEL YEAR FEATURES	EXC. COND. LOW	HIGH
Rotary Chorus RC99		
1996-1999. Black or silver cases available, requires power pack and does not use a battery.		
1996-1999 Black case	$100	$125
Session Man SS10		
1988-1989. Distortion, chorus.		
1988-1989	$70	$80
Session Man II SS20		
1988-1989. 4 controls + toggle, light pink-purple case.		
1988-1989	$70	$80
Slam Punk SP5 (SoundTank)		
1996-1999.		
1996-1999	$40	$45
Smash Box SM7 (Tone-Lok)		
2000-present.		
2000-2005	$35	$40
Sonic Distortion SD9		
1982-1984.		
1982-1984	$75	$100
Standard Fuzz (No. 59)		
1974-1979. Two buttons (fuzz on/off and tone change).		
1974-1979	$175	$200
Stereo Box ST-800		
1975-1979. One input, 2 outputs for panning, small yellow case.		
1975-1979	$175	$225
Stereo Chorus CSL (Master Series)		
1985-1986.		
1985-1986	$70	$90
Super Chorus CS5 (SoundTank)		
1991-1998.		
1991-1998	$25	$35
Stereo Chorus CS9		
1982-1984.		
1982-1984	$75	$100
Super Metal SM-9		
1984. Distortion.		
1984	$75	$95
Super Stereo Chorus SC-10		
1986-1992.		
1986-1992	$75	$100
Super Tube Screamer ST9		
1984-1985. 4 knobs, light green metal case.		
1984-1985	$225	$300
Super Tube STL		
1985.		
1985	$75	$95
Swell Flanger SF10		
1986-1992. Speed, regeneration, width and time controls, yellow case.		
1986-1992	$50	$55
Trashmetal TM5 (SoundTank)		
1990-1998. Tone and distortion pedal, 3 editions (1st edition, 2nd edition metal case, 2nd edition plastic case).		
1990-1998	$20	$25
Tremolo Pedal TL5 (SoundTank)		
1995-1998.		
1995-1998	$50	$100

Ibanez Phat Head PD7

Ibanez Phase Tone PT-909

Ibanez Super Metal SM-9

EFFECTS

Ibanez TS5 Tube Screamer

Ibanez TS-808

Jacques Fuse Blower

MODEL YEAR	FEATURES	EXC. COND. LOW	HIGH

Tube King TK999
1994-1995. Has a 12AX7 tube and 3-band equalizer.

| 1994-1995 | Includes power pack | $150 | $200 |

Tube King TK999US
1996-1998. Has a 12AX7 tube and 3-band equalizer, does not have the noise switch of original TK999. Made in the U.S.

| 1996-1998 | Includes power pack | $150 | $200 |

Tube Screamer TS5 (SoundTank)
1991-1998.

| 1991-1998 | | $25 | $30 |

Tube Screamer TS7 (Tone-Lok)
1999-present. 3 control knobs.

| 1999-2005 | | $35 | $40 |

Tube Screamer TS9
1982-1984, 1993-present. Reissued in '93

| 1982-1984 | | $150 | $200 |
| 1993-2005 | | $75 | $100 |

Tube Screamer Classic TS10
1986-1993.

| 1986-1993 | | $200 | $225 |

Tube Screamer TS-808
1980-1982, 2004-present. Reissued in '04.

| 1980-1981 | | $575 | $700 |

Turbo Tube Screamer TS9DX
1998-present. Tube Screamer circuit with added 3 settings for low-end.

| 1998-2005 | | $70 | $85 |

Twin Cam Chorus TC10
1986-1989. Four control knobs, light blue case.

| 1986-1989 | | $75 | $100 |

Virtual Amp VA3 (floor unit)
1995-1998. Digital effects processor.

| 1995-1998 | | $55 | $75 |

VL10
1987-1997. Stereo volume pedal.

| 1987-1997 | | $50 | $75 |

Wah Fuzz Standard (Model 58)
1974-1981. Fuzz tone change toggle, fuzz on toggle, fuzz depth control, balance control, wah volume pedal with circular friction pads on footpedal.

| 1974-1981 | | $225 | $300 |

Wah WH10
1988-1997.

| 1988-1997 | | $50 | $75 |

Intersound
Made by Intersound, Inc. of Boulder, Colorado.

Reverb-Equalizer R100F
1977-1979. Reverb and 4-band EQ, fader.

| 1977-1979 | | $75 | $100 |

J. Everman
2000-present. Analog guitar effects built by Justin J. Everman in Richardson, Texas.

Jacques
One-of-a-kind handmade stomp boxes and production models made in France. Production models are distributed in the U.S. by Godlyke Distributing.

MODEL YEAR	FEATURES	EXC. COND. LOW	HIGH

Jan-Mar Industries
Jan-Mar was located in Hillsdale, New Jersey.

The Talker
1976. 30 watts.

| 1976 | | $75 | $125 |

The Talker Pro
1976. 75 watts.

| 1976 | | $100 | $150 |

Jax
1960s-1970. Japanese imports made by Shinei.

Fuzz Master

| 1960s | | $100 | $150 |

Vibrachorus
Variant of Univibe.

| 1969 | | $750 | $1,000 |

Wah-Wah

| 1960s | | $100 | $150 |

Jersey Girl
1991-present. Line of guitar effects pedals made in Japan. They also build guitars.

Jet Sounds LTD
1977. Jet was located in Jackson, Mississippi.

Hoze Talk Box
1977. Large wood box, 30 watts.

| 1977 | | $90 | $125 |

JHD Audio
1974-1990. Hunt Dabney founded JHD in Costa Mesa, California, to provide effects that the user installed in their amp. Dabney is still involved in electronics and builds the BiasProbe tool for tubes.

SuperCube/SuperCube II
1974-late 1980s. Plug-in sustain mod for Fender amps with reverb, second version for amps after '78.

| 1970s | | $50 | $75 |

Jimi Hendrix
See listing under Dunlop.

John Hornby Skewes & Co.
Mid-1960s-present. Large English distributor of musical products which has also made their own brands, or self-branded products from others, over the years.

Johnson
Mid-1990s-present. Budget line of effects imported by Music Link, Brisbane, California. Johnson also offers guitars, amps, mandolins and basses.

Johnson Amplification
1997-present. Modeling amps and effects designed by John Johnson, of Sandy, Utah. The company is part of Harman International. In '02, they quit building amps, but continue the effects line.

MODEL YEAR	FEATURES	EXC. COND. LOW	HIGH

Jordan

1960s. Jordan effects were distributed by Sho-Bud of Nashville, Tennessee.

Boss Tone Fuzz

1968-1969. Tiny effect plugged into guitar's output jack.

1968-1969		$100	$125

Compressor J-700

1960s		$75	$100

Creator Volume Sustainer

1960s		$125	$175

Gig Wa-Wa Volume

1960s		$125	$150

Phaser

Black case, yellow knobs.

1960s	Black case	$125	$150

Kay

1931-present. Kay was once one of the largest instrument producers in the world, offering just about everything for the guitarist, including effects.

Effects Pedals

1970s. Includes the Wah, Graphic Equalizer GE-5000, Rhythmer, and Tremolo.

1970s		$50	$75

Keeley

2001-present. Line of guitar effects designed and built by Robert Keeley in Edmond, Oklahoma. Keeley Electronics also offers a range of custom modifications for other effects.

Kendrick

1989-present. Texas' Kendrick offers guitars, amps, and effects.

ABC Amp Switcher

1990s.

1990s		$100	$140

Buffalo Pfuz

1990s.

1990s		$70	$100

Model 1000 Reverb

1991-2003. Vintage style, 3 knobs: dwell, tone, and mix, brown cover, wheat grille with art deco shape.

1991-2003		$400	$450

Power Glide Attenuator

1998-present. Allows you to cut the output before it hits the amp's speakers, rack mount, metal cab.

1998-2003		$180	$200

Kent

1961-1969. This import guitar brand also offered a few effects.

Kern Engineering

Located in Kenosha, Wisconsin, Kern offers pre-amps and wah pedals.

Klon

1994-present. Originally located in Brookline, Massachusetts, and now located in Cambridge, Massachusetts, Klon was started by Bill Finnegan after working with two circuit design partners on the Centaur Professional Overdrive.

Centaur Professional Overdrive

1994-present. Gold case.

1990s		$400	$650

KMD (Kaman)

1986-ca. 1990. Distributed by Kaman (Ovation, Hamer, etc.) in the late '80s.

Effects Pedals

1986-1990	Analog Delay	$65	$90
1986-1990	Overdrive	$30	$45
1987-1990	Distortion	$30	$45
1987-1990	Flanger	$30	$50
1987-1990	Phaser	$30	$50
1987-1990	Stereo Chorus	$30	$50

Korg

Most of the Korg effects listed below are modular effects. The PME-40X Professional Modular Effects System holds four of them and allows the user to select several variations of effects. The modular effects cannot be used alone. This system was sold for a few years starting in 1983. Korg currently offers the Toneworks line of effects.

PEQ-1 Parametric EQ

1980s. Dial-in equalizer with gain knob, band-width knob, and frequency knob, black case.

1980s		$40	$50

PME-40X Professional Modular Effects System

1983-ca.1986. Board holds up to 4 of the modular effects listed below.

1983-1986		$125	$150

PME-40X Modular Effects

1983-1986	KAD-301		
	Analog Delay	$60	$70
1983-1986	KCH-301		
	Stereo Chorus	$25	$35
1983-1986	KCO-101 Compressor	$45	$55
1983-1986	KDI-101 Distortion	$45	$55
1983-1986	KDL-301		
	Dynamic Echo	$90	$110
1983-1986	KFL-401		
	Stereo Flanger	$40	$50
1983-1986	KGE-201 Graphic EQ	$25	$35
1983-1986	KNG-101 Noise Gate	$25	$35
1983-1986	KOD-101 Over Drive	$45	$55
1983-1986	KPH-401 Phaser	$45	$55
1983-1986	OCT-1 Octaver	$70	$80

SSD 3000 Digital Delay

1980s. Rack mount, SDD-3000 logo on top of unit.

1980s		$600	$850

Krank

1996-present. Tempe, Arizona, amp builder Krank also builds effects pedals.

Jan-Mar The Talker

Keeley Compressor

Klon Centaur

Line 6 MM-4

Lock & Rock Sour Boost

Maestro Boomerang

MODEL YEAR	FEATURES	EXC. COND. LOW	HIGH

Laney

1968-present. Founded by Lyndon Laney and Bob Thomas in Birmingham, England, this amp builder also offered a reverb unit.

Reverberation Unit

1968-1969. Sleek reverb unit, plexi-style front panel, black vinyl cover.

1968-1969		$300	$400

Lehle

2001-present. Loop switches from Burkhard Georg Lehle of Lehle Gitarrentechnik in Voerde, Germany.

D.Loop Signal Router

2004		$150	$175

Line 6

1996-present. Effects from Marcus Ryle and Michel Doidic who were product line designers prior to forming their own design company. A sixth company telephone line was added to their product design business to handle their own product line, thus Line 6. They also produce amps and guitars. All prices include Line 6 power pack if applicable.

DL-4 Delay Modeler

1999-present. Green case.

1999-2005		$175	$225

DM-4 Distortion Modeler

1999-present. Yellow case.

1999-2005		$100	$125

FM-4 Filter Modeler

2001-present. Purple case.

2001-2005		$175	$225

MM-4 Modulation Modeler

1999-present. Aqua blue case.

1999-2005		$150	$185

POD 2.0

2001-present. Updated version of the original Amp modeler.

2001-2005		$150	$200

Little Lanilei

1997-present. Best known for their small hand-made amps, Songworks Systems & Products of San Juan Capistrano, California, also offers effects bearing the Little Lanilei name.

Lock & Rock

2003-present. Line of floor pedal guitar and microphone effects produced by Brannon Electronics, Inc. of Houston, Texas.

Loco Box

1982-1983. Loco Box was a brand of effects distributed by Aria Pro II for a short period starting in '82. It appears that Aria switched the effects to their own brand in '83.

Effects

1982-1983	Analog Delay AD-01	$35	$45
1982-1983	Chorus CH-01	$55	$65

MODEL YEAR	FEATURES	EXC. COND. LOW	HIGH
1982-1983	Compressor CM-01	$35	$45
1982-1983	Distortion DS-01	$40	$55
1982-1983	Flanger FL-01	$35	$45
1982-1983	Graphic Equalizer GE-06	$25	$35
1982-1983	Overdrive OD-01	$40	$50
1982-1983	Phaser PH-01	$45	$55

Lovepedal

2000-present. Sean Michael builds his preamps and guitar stomp boxes in Detroit, Michigan.

Lovetone

1995-present. Hand-made analog effects from Oxfordshire, England.

Ludwig

Drum builder Ludwig offered a guitar synth in the 1970s.

Phase II Guitar Synth

1970-1971. Oversized synth, mushroom-shaped footswitches.

1970-1971	Vertical silver case	$450	$600

M.B. Electronics

Made in San Francisco, California.

Ultra-Metal UM-10

1985. Distortion.

1985		$35	$40

Maestro

Maestro was a Gibson subsidiary; the name appeared on 1950s accordian amplifiers. The first Maestro effects were the Echoplex tape echo and the FZ-1 Fuzz-Tone, introduced in the early-'60s. Maestro products were manufactured by various entities such as Market Electronics, All-Test Devices, Lowrey and Moog Electronics. In the late-'60s and early-'70s, they unleashed a plethora of pedals; some were beautiful, others had great personality. The last Maestro effects were the Silver and Black MFZ series of the late-'70s.

Bass Brassmaster BB-1

1971-ca.1974. Added brass to your bass.

1971-1974		$450	$650

Boomerang

Ca.1969-ca.1972.　Wah pedal made by All-Test Devices.

1969-1972		$175	$200

Boomerang BG-2

1972-ca.1976.　Wah pedal made by All-Test Devices.

1972-1976		$100	$125

Echoplex EP-1

1962/63-mid-1960s. Original model, smaller box, tube, separate controls for echo volume and instrument volume, made by Market Electronics. Though not labeled as such, it is often referred to as the EP-1 by collectors.

1960s	Earlier small Green box	$800	$900

MODEL YEAR	FEATURES	EXC. COND. LOW	HIGH

Echoplex EP-2
Mid-1960s-ca.1970. Larger box than original, tube, single echo/instrument volume control, made by Market Electronics. Around '70, the EP-2 added a Sound-On-Sound feature.

1960s	Larger Green box	$800	$900

Echoplex EP-3
Ca.1970-1977. Solidstate, made by Market Electronics, black box.

1970-1977		$400	$550

Echoplex IV (EP-4)
1977-1978. Solidstate, last version introduced by Maestro. See brands Market Electronics and Echoplex for later models.

1977-1978		$375	$500

Echoplex Groupmaster
Ca.1970-ca.1974. Two input Echoplex, solidstate.

1970-1977		$500	$700

Echoplex Sireko ES-1
Ca.1971-mid-1970s. A budget version of the Echoplex, solidstate, made by Market.

1971-1975		$200	$300

Envelope Modifier ME-1
1971-ca.1976. Tape reverse/string simulator, made by All-Test.

1971-1976		$150	$225

Filter Sample and Hold FSH-1
1975-ca.1976.

1975-1976		$475	$700

Full Range Boost FRB-1
1971-ca.1975. Frequency boost with fuzz, made by All-Test.

1971-1975		$150	$200

Fuzz MFZ-1
1976-1979. Made by Moog.

1976-1979		$150	$200

Fuzz Phazzer FP-1
1971-1974.

1971-1974		$200	$300

Fuzz Tone FZ-1
1962-1963. Brown, uses 2 AA batteries.

1962-1963		$175	$225

Fuzz Tone FZ-1A
1965-1967. Brown, uses 1 AA battery.

1965-1967		$175	$225

Fuzz Tone FZ-1A (reissue)

2000s		$65	$70

Fuzz Tone FZ-1B
Late-1960s- early-1970s. Black, uses 9-volt battery.

1970s		$150	$250

Fuzztain MFZT-1
1976-1978. Fuzz, sustain, made by Moog.

1976-1978		$200	$250

Mini-Phase Shifter MPS-2
1976. Volume, speed, slow and fast controls.

1976		$110	$125

Octave Box OB-1
1971-ca.1975. Made by All-Test Devices.

1971-1975		$225	$300

Parametric Filter MPF-1
1976-1978. Made by Moog.

1970s		$185	$200

Phase Shifter PS-1
1971-1975. With or without 3-button footswitch, made by Oberheim.

1971-1975	With footswitch	$250	$300
1971-1975	Without footswitch	$150	$250

Phase Shifter PS-1A
1976.

1976		$150	$250

Phase Shifter PS-1B
1970s.

1970s		$150	$250

Phaser MP-1
1976-1978. Made by Moog.

1976-1978		$100	$120

Repeat Pedal RP-1

1970s		$200	$300

Rhythm King MRK-2
1971-ca.1974. Early drum machine.

1972		$200	$300

Rhythm Queen MRQ-1
Early 1970s. Early rhythm machine.

1970s		$125	$150

Rhythm'n Sound G-2
Ca.1969-1970s. Multi-effect unit.

1969-1975		$200	$300

Ring Modulator RM-1
1971-1975.

1971-1975	With MP-1 control pedal	$650	$700
1971-1975	Without control pedal	$550	$600

Rover Rotating Speaker
1971-ca.1973. Rotating Leslie effect that mounted on a large tripod.

1971-1973		$750	$900

Stage Phaser MPP-1
1976-1978. Had slow, fast and variable settings, made by Moog.

1976-1978		$175	$225

Super Fuzztone FZ-1S

1971-1975		$200	$300

Sustainer SS-2
1971-ca.1975. Made by All-Test Devices.

1971-1975		$100	$150

Theramin TH-1
1971-mid-1970s. Device with 2 antennae, made horror film sound effects. A reissue Theremin is available from Theremaniacs in Milwaukee, Wisconsin.

1971-1975		$800	$1,000

Wah-Wah/Volume WW-1
1970s. Wah-Wah Volume logo on end of pedal, green foot pad.

1971-1975		$150	$250

Maestro Fuzztain

Mestro Fuzz-Tone FZ-1A

Maestro Theremin

EFFECTS

Magnatone RVB-1

Matchless Coolbox

Moonrock

MODEL YEAR	FEATURES	EXC. COND. LOW	HIGH

Magnatone

1937-1970s. Magnatone built very competitive amps from '57 to '66. In the early-'60s, they offered the RVB-1 Reverb Unit. The majority of Magnatone amps pre-'66 did not have on-board reverb.

Model RVB-1 Reverb Unit

1961-1966. Typical brown leatherette cover, square box-type cabinet. From '64-'66, battery operated, solidstate version of RVB-1, low flat cabinet.

1961-1963		$275	$400
1964-1966	Battery and solidstate	$200	$300

Mannys Music

Issued by the New York-based retailer.

Fuzz

1960s. Same unit as the Orpheum Fuzz and Clark Fuzz.

1960s		$225	$325

Market Electronics

Market, from Ohio, made the famous Echoplex line. See Maestro section for earlier models and Echoplex section for later versions.

Marshall

1962-present. The fuzz and wah boom of the '60s led many established manufacturers, like Marshall, to introduce variations on the theme. They got back into stomp boxes in '89 with the Gov'nor distortion, and currently produce several distortion/overdrive units.

Blues Breaker

1992-1999. Replaced by Blues Breaker II in 2000.

1992-1999		$100	$130

Blues Breaker II Overdrive

2000-present. Overdrive pedal, 4 knobs.

2000-2005		$50	$65

Drive Master

1992-1999.

1992-1999		$70	$75

Guv'nor

1989-1991. Distortion, Guv'nor Plus introduced in 1999.

1989-1991		$75	$100

Jackhammer

1999-present. Distortion pedal.

1999-2005		$55	$65

PB-100 Power Brake

1993-1995. Speaker attenuator for tube amps.

1993-1995		$190	$230

Shred Master

1992-1999.

1992-1999		$75	$100

Supa Fuzz

Late-1960s. Made by Sola Sound (Colorsound).

1967		$300	$400

Supa Wah

Late-1960s. Made by Sola Sound (Colorsound).

1969		$300	$425

MODEL YEAR	FEATURES	EXC. COND. LOW	HIGH

Vibratrem VT-1

1999-present. Vibrato and tremolo.

1999-2005		$75	$85

Matchless

1989-1999, 2001-present. Matchless amplifiers offered effects in the '90s.

AB Box

1990s. Split box for C-30 series amps (DC 30, SC 30, etc.)

1990s		$175	$300

Coolbox

1997-1999. Tube preamp pedal.

1997-1999		$275	$350

Dirtbox

1997-1999. Tube-driven overdrive pedal.

1997-1999		$225	$350

Echo Box

1997-1999. Limited production because of malfunctioning design which included cassette tape. Black case, 8 white chickenhead control knobs.

1990s	Original unreliable status	$300	$400
1990s	Updated working order	$700	$850

Hotbox/Hotbox II

1995-1999. Higher-end tube-driven preamp pedal.

1995-1999		$375	$425

Mix Box

1997-1999. 4-input tube mixer pedal.

1997-1999		$375	$425

Reverb RV-1

1993-1999. 5 controls, tube reverb tank.

1993-1999	Various colors	$1,000	$1,300

Split Box

1990s. Tube AB box.

1997	Standard AB	$275	$325

Tremolo/Vibrato TV-1

1993-1995. Tube unit.

1993-1995		$350	$400

Maxon

1970s-present. Maxon was the original manufacturer of the Ibanez line of effects. Currently offering retro '70s era stomp boxes distributed in the U.S. by Godlyke.

AD-9 Analog Delay

2001-present. Purple case.

2001-2005		$225	$275

CS-550 Stereo Chorus

2000-present. Light blue case.

2000-2005		$100	$130

OD-820 Over Drive Pro

2001-present.

2001-2005		$140	$175

Mesa-Boogie

1971-present. Mesa added pre-amps in the mid '90s.

MODEL YEAR	FEATURES	EXC. COND. LOW	HIGH
V-Twin Preamp Pedal			
Dec. 1993-2004. Serial number series: V011-. 100 watts, all tube preamp, floor unit, silver case.			
1993-1999		$225	$275
2000-2004	Updated bottom tone adj.	$275	$325
V-Twin Bottle Rocket			
2000-2004.			
2000-2004		$100	$150

Meteoro

1986-present. Guitar effects built in Brazil. They also build guitar and bass amps.

Mica

Early 1970s. These Japanese-made effects were also sold under the Bruno and Marlboro brand names.

MODEL YEAR	FEATURES	EXC. COND. LOW	HIGH
Tone Fuzz			
Silver case, black knobs.			
1970s		$200	$250
Tone Surf Wah Siren			
1970s. Wah pedal.			
1970s		$150	$175
Wailer Fuzz			
1970		$75	$100
Wau Wau Fuzz			
1970s. Wau Wau Fuzz logo on end of pedal, black.			
1970s		$150	$175

Moog/Moogerfooger

Robert Moog, of synth fame, introduced his line of Moogerfooger analog effects in 1998.

MODEL YEAR	FEATURES	EXC. COND. LOW	HIGH
Misc. Effects			
2004	MF-105 MuRF	$250	$275
2004	Theremin	$250	$275

Moonrock

2002-present. Fuzz/distortion unit built by Glenn Wylie and distributed by Tonefrenzy.

Morley

Late-1960s-present. Founded by brothers Raymond and Marvin Lubow, Morley has produced a wide variety of pedals and effects over the years, changing with the trends. In '89, the brothers sold the company to Accutronics (later changed to Sound Enhancements, Inc.) of Cary, Illinois.

MODEL YEAR	FEATURES	EXC. COND. LOW	HIGH
ABY Switch Box			
1981-ca.1985. Box.			
1981-1985		$25	$35
Auto Wah PWA			
1976-ca.1985.			
1976-1985		$25	$35
Bad Horsie Steve Vai Signature Wah			
1997-present			
1997-2005		$65	$70
Black Gold Stereo Volume BSV			
1985-1991.			
1985-1991		$25	$35

MODEL YEAR	FEATURES	EXC. COND. LOW	HIGH
Black Gold Stereo Volume Pan BSP			
1985-1989.			
1985-1989		$30	$40
Black Gold Volume BVO			
1985-1991.			
1985-1991		$25	$35
Black Gold Wah BWA			
1985-1991.			
1985-1991		$30	$40
Black Gold Wah Volume BWV			
1985-1989.			
1985-1989		$30	$40
Chrystal Chorus CCB			
1996-1999. Stereo output.			
1996-1999		$25	$30
Deluxe Distortion DDB			
1981-1991. Box, no pedal.			
1981-1991		$40	$60
Deluxe Flanger FLB			
1981-1991. Box, no pedal.			
1981-1991		$55	$65
Deluxe Phaser DFB			
1981-1991. Box, no pedal.			
1981-1991		$40	$60
Distortion One DIB			
1981-1991. Box, no pedal.			
1981-1991		$35	$45
Echo Chorus Vibrato ECV			
1982-ca.1985.			
1982-1985		$150	$225
Echo/Volume EVO-1			
1974-ca.1982.			
1974-1982		$150	$225
Electro-Pik-a-Wah PKW			
1979-ca.1982.			
1979-1982		$55	$65
Emerald Echo EEB			
1996-1999. 300 millisecond delay.			
1996-1999	Green case	$40	$50
Jerry Donahue JD-10			
1995-1997. Multi-effect, distortion, overdrive.			
1995-1997		$80	$90
Power Wah PWA/PWA II			
1992-2006. Wah with boost. Changed to II in '98.			
1992-2006		$40	$50
Power Wah PWO			
Ca.1969-1984, 2006-present.			
1969-1984		$60	$70
Power Wah/Boost PWB			
Introduced in 1973, doubles as a volume pedal.			
1970s		$70	$80
Power Wah/Fuzz PWF			
Ca.1969-ca.1984.			
1969-1984		$75	$125
Pro Compressor PCB			
1978-1984. Stomp box without pedal, compress-sustain knob and output knob.			
1978-1984		$45	$55
Pro Flanger PFL			
1978-1984.			
1978-1984		$100	$125

Moogerfooger MF-105 MuRF

Morley ABY

Morley Jerry Donahue JD10

Morley Volume Boost VBO

Mosferatu Zendrive

Multivox Basky II

MODEL YEAR	FEATURES	EXC. COND. LOW	HIGH
Pro Phaser PFA	*1975-1984.*		
1975-1984		$100	$125
Rotating Sound Power Wah Model RWV	*1974-1982.*		
1974-1982		$325	$375
Select-Effect Pedal SEL	*Lets you control up to 5 other pedals.*		
1980s		$20	$30
Slimline Echo Volume 600	*1983-1985. 20 to 600 ms delay.*		
1983-1985		$45	$55
Slimline Echo Volume SLEV	*1983-1985. 20 to 300 ms delay.*		
1983-1985		$50	$60
Slimline Variable Taper Stereo Volume SLSV	*1982-1986.*		
1982-1986		$70	$100
Slimline Variable Taper Volume SLVO	*1982-1986.*		
1982-1986		$35	$50
Slimline Wah SLWA	*1982-1986. Battery operated electro-optical.*		
1982-1986		$55	$75
Slimline Wah Volume SLWV	*1982-ca.1986. Battery operated electro-optical.*		
1982-1986		$55	$75
Stereo Chorus Flanger CFL	*1980-ca. 1986. Box, no pedal.*		
1980-1986		$60	$70
Stereo Chorus Vibrato SCV	*1980-1991. Box, no pedal.*		
1980-1991		$80	$100
Stereo Volume CSV	*1980-ca. 1986. Box, no pedal.*		
1980-1986		$30	$45
Volume Compressor VCO	*1979-1984.*		
1979-1984		$30	$45
Volume Phaser PFV	*1977-1984. With volume pedal.*		
1977-1984		$125	$150
Volume VOL	*1975-ca.1984.*		
1975-1979		$30	$45
1980-1984		$25	$40
Volume XVO	*1985-1988.*		
1985-1988		$25	$40
Volume/Boost VBO	*1974-1984.*		
1974-1984		$50	$60
Wah Volume CWV	*1987-1991. Box, no pedal.*		
1987-1991		$65	$80
Wah Volume XWV	*1985-ca.1989.*		
1985-1989		$65	$80

MODEL YEAR	FEATURES	EXC. COND. LOW	HIGH
Wah/Volume WVO	*1977-ca.1984.*		
1977-1984		$80	$100

Mosferatu
Line of guitar effects pedals built by Hermida Audio Technology.

Mosrite
Semie Moseley's Mosrite company dipped into effects in the 1960s.
Fuzzrite

1966		$175	$225

Multivox
New York-based Multivox offered a variety of effects in the 1970s and '80s.
Big Jam Effects
Multivox offered the Big Jam line of effects from 1980 to ca. '83.

1980-1983	6-Band EQ, Compressor, Phaser, Spit-Wah	$40	$50
1980-1983	Analog Echo/Reverb	$100	$125
1980-1983	Bi-Phase 2, Flanger, Jazz Flanger	$50	$60
1980-1983	Chorus	$45	$55
1980-1983	Distortion	$70	$80
1980-1983	Octave Box	$40	$55
1981-1983	Noise Gate, Parametric EQ	$35	$45
1981-1983	Space Driver, Delay	$60	$70
1982-1983	Volume Pedal	$30	$35

Full Rotor MX-2
1978-ca.1982. Leslie effect.

1978-1982		$300	$350

Little David LD-2
Rotary sound effector in mini Leslie-type case.

1970s	With pedal	$375	$450
1970s	Without pedal	$325	$375

Multi Echo MX-201
Tape echo unit, reverb.

1970s		$200	$250

Multi Echo MX-312
Tape echo unit, reverb.

1970s		$225	$300

Rhythm Ace FR6M
27 basic rhythms.

1970s		$60	$80

Mu-tron
1972-ca.1981. Made by Musitronics (founded by Aaron Newman), Rosemont, New Jersey, these rugged and unique-sounding effects were a high point of the '70s. The Mu-Tron III appeared in '72 and more products followed, about 10 in all. Musitronics also made the U.S. models of the Dan Armstrong effects. In '78 ARP synthesizers bought Musitronics and sold Mutron products to around '81. A reissue of the Mu-Tron III was made available in '95 by NYC Music Products and distributed by Matthews and Ryan Musical Products.

MODEL YEAR	FEATURES	EXC. COND. LOW	HIGH
Bi-Phase			
1975-ca.1981. Add $50-$75 for Opti-Pot pedal.			
1975-1981	With 2-button footswitch	$700	$950
C-100 OptiPot Control Pedal			
1975-1981	Blue case	$550	$700
C-200 Volume-Wah			
1970s		$300	$400
Flanger			
1977-ca.1981.			
1977-1981		$400	$450
III Envelope Filter			
1972-ca.1981. Envelope Filter.			
1972-1981		$600	$650
Micro V			
Ca.1975-ca.1977. Envelope Filter.			
1970s		$200	$250
Octave Divider			
1977-ca.1981.			
1977-1981		$700	$750
Phasor			
Ca.1974-ca.1976. Two knobs.			
1974-1976		$200	$300
Phasor II			
1976-ca.1981. Three knobs.			
1976-1981		$200	$300

MXR

1972-present. MXR Innovations launched its line of pedals in '72. Around '77, the Rochester, New York, company changed lettering on the effects from script to block, and added new models. MXR survived into the mid-'80s. In '87, production was picked up by Jim Dunlop. Reissues of block logo boxes can be differentiated from originals as they have an LED above the switch and the finish is slightly rough; the originals are smooth.

MODEL YEAR	FEATURES	EXC. COND. LOW	HIGH
6 Band Equalizer			
1975-1982.			
1975-1979		$70	$85
1980-1982		$60	$70
6 Band Equalizer M-109 (reissue)			
1987-present. Reissued by Jim Dunlop.			
1987-2005		$30	$40
10 Band Graphic Equalizer			
1975-1981, 2004-present.			
1975-1981	With AC power cord	$80	$100
Analog Delay			
1975-1981. Green case, power cord.			
1975-1979	Earlier 2-jack model	$300	$325
1980-1981	Later 3-jack model	$150	$200
Blue Box			
1972-ca.1978. Octave pedal, M-103.			
1970s	Earlier script logo	$300	$375
1970s	Later block logo	$175	$250
Blue Box (reissue)			
1995-present. Reissued by Jim Dunlop. Produces 1 octave above or 2 octaves below.			
1995-2005		$40	$45

MODEL YEAR	FEATURES	EXC. COND. LOW	HIGH
Commande Overdrive			
1981-1983. The Commande series featured plastic housings and electronic switching.			
1981-1983		$40	$50
Commande Phaser			
1981-1983.			
1981-1983		$100	$110
Commande Preamp			
1981-1983.			
1981-1983		$40	$50
Commande Stereo Chorus			
1981-1983.			
1981-1983		$60	$70
Commande Stereo Flanger			
1982-1983.			
1982-1983		$70	$80
Commande Sustain			
1981-1983.			
1981-1983		$60	$70
Commande Time Delay			
1981-1983.			
1981-1983		$70	$80
Distortion +			
1972-1982.			
1970s	Earlier script logo	$185	$225
1970s	Later block logo	$85	$110
1980s	Block logo	$80	$95
Distortion + (Series 2000)			
1983-1985.			
1983-1985		$60	$70
Distortion + M-104 (reissue)			
1987-present. Reissued by Jim Dunlop.			
1987-1990		$55	$65
1991-2005		$45	$55
Distortion II			
1981-1983.			
1981-1983	With AC power cord	$140	$150
Double Shot Distortion M-151			
2003-2005. 2 channels.			
2003-2005		$65	$75
Dyna Comp			
1972-1982. Compressor.			
1970s	Earlier script logo, battery	$175	$200
1970s	Later block logo, battery	$90	$120
1980s	Block logo, battery	$65	$80
Dyna Comp (Series 2000)			
1982-1985.			
1982-1985		$65	$75
Dyna Comp M-102 (reissue)			
1987-present. Reissued by Jim Dunlop.			
1987-2005		$35	$40
Envelope Filter			
1976-1983.			
1976-1983		$125	$225

Mu-Tron Phasor II

MXR Analog Delay

MXR Distortion +

EFFECTS

MXR Wylde Overdrive

Nobels TR-X Vintage Tremolo

Olson Reverberation Amplifier RA-844

MODEL YEAR	FEATURES	EXC. COND. LOW	HIGH
Flanger			
1976-1983, 1997-present. Analog, reissued by Dunlop in '97.			
1976-1979	AC power cord, 2 inputs	$175	$225
1980-1983	AC power cord	$100	$150
1997-2004	Dunlop reissue	$60	$70
Flanger/Doubler			
1979	Rack mount	$150	$175
Limiter			
1980-1982. AC, 4 knobs.			
1980-1982	AC power cord	$125	$200
Loop Selector			
1980-1982. A/B switch for 2 effects loops.			
1980-1982		$50	$60
Micro Amp			
1978-1983, 1995-present. Variable booster, white case, reissued in '95.			
1978-1983		$75	$100
1995-2005	M-133 reissue	$40	$45
Micro Chorus			
1980-1983. Yellow case.			
1980-1983		$125	$175
Micro Flanger			
1981-1982.			
1981-1982		$100	$150
Noise Gate Line Driver			
1974-1983.			
1970s	Script logo	$75	$125
1980s	Block logo	$75	$100
Omni			
1980s. Rack unit with floor controller, compressor, 3-band EQ, distortion, delay, chorus/flanger.			
1980s		$425	$475
Phase 45			
Ca.1976-1982.			
1970s	Script logo, battery	$125	$175
1980s	Block logo, battery	$75	$125
Phase 90			
1972-1982.			
1970s	Earlier script logo	$325	$400
1970s	Later block logo	$200	$275
1980s	Block logo	$150	$200
Phase 90 M-101 (reissue)			
1987-present. Reissued by Jim Dunlop.			
1987-1989	Block logo	$60	$85
1990-2005	Block or script logo	$50	$75
Phase 100			
1974-1982.			
1970s	Earlier script logo	$250	$325
1970s	Later block logo, battery	$175	$275
Phaser (Series 2000)			
1982-1985. Series 2000 introduced cost cutting die-cast cases.			
1982-1985		$60	$85
Pitch Transposer			
1980s		$400	$475
Power Converter			
1980s		$45	$60

MODEL YEAR	FEATURES	EXC. COND. LOW	HIGH
Smart Gate M-135			
2002-present. Noise-gate, single control, battery powered.			
2002-2004		$60	$70
Stereo Chorus			
1978-1985. With AC power cord.			
1978-1979		$175	$275
1980-1985		$150	$200
Stereo Chorus (Series 2000)			
1983-1985. Series 2000 introduced cost cutting die-cast cases.			
1983-1985		$55	$75
Stereo Flanger (Series 2000)			
1983-1985. Series 2000 introduced cost cutting die-cast cases, black with blue lettering.			
1983-1985		$60	$80
Super Comp M-132			
2002-present. 3 knobs.			
2002-2005		$40	$55

Nobels

1997-present. Effects pedals from Nobels Electronics of Hamburg, Germany. They also make amps.

ODR-1
1997-present. Overdrive.

1997-2005		$30	$40

TR-X Tremolo
1997-present. Tremolo effect using modern technology, purple case.

1997-2005		$30	$40

Nomad
Fuzz Wah
1960s. Import from Japan, similar looking to Morley pedal with depth and volume controls and fuzz switch, silver metal case and black foot pedal.

1960s		$75	$125

Olson

Olson Electronics was in Akron, Ohio.

Reverberation Amplifier RA-844
1967. Solidstate, battery-operated, reverb unit, depth and volume controls, made in Japan.

1967		$100	$150

Ovation

Ovation ventured into the solidstate amp and effects market in the early '70s.

K-6001 Guitar Preamp
1970s. Preamp with reverb, boost, tremolo, fuzz, and a tuner, looks something like a Maestro effect from the '70s, reliability may be an issue.

1970s		$100	$125

PAIA

1967-present. Founded by John Paia Simonton in Edmond, Oklahoma, specializing in synthesizer and effects kits. PAIA did make a few complete products but they are better known for the various electronic kit projects they sold. Values on kit

MODEL YEAR	FEATURES	EXC. COND. LOW	HIGH

projects are difficult as it depends on the skills of the person who built it.

Roctave Divider 5760
Kit to build analog octave divider.

1970s		$70	$85

Park
1965-1982, 1992-2000. Sola/Colorsound made a couple of effects for Marshall and their sister brand, Park. In the '90s, Marshall revived the name for use on small solidstate amps.

Pax
1970s. Imported Maestro copies.

Fuzz Tone Copy
1970s		$125	$150

Octave Box Copy
1970s. Dual push-buttons (normal and octave), 2 knobs (octave volume and sensitivity), green and black case.

1970s		$125	$150

Pearl
Pearl, located in Nashville, Tennessee, and better known for drums, offered a line of guitar effects in the 1980s.

Analog Delay AD-08
1983-1985. Four knobs.

1983-1985		$100	$150

Analog Delay AD-33
1982-1984. Six knobs.

1982-1984		$175	$225

Chorus CH-02
1981-1984. Four knobs.

1981-1984		$75	$100

Chorus Ensemble CE-22
1982-1984. Stereo chorus with toggling between chorus and vibrato, 6 knobs.

1982-1984		$125	$175

Compressor CO-04
1981-1984.

1981-1984		$50	$75

Distortion DS-06
1982-1986.

1982-1986		$40	$60

Flanger FG-01
1981-1986. Clock pulse generator, ultra-low frequency oscillator.

1981-1986		$75	$100

Graphic EQ GE-09
1983-1985.

1983-1985		$40	$55

Octaver OC-07
1982-1986.

1982-1986		$100	$300

Overdrive OD-05
1981-1986.

1981-1986		$75	$100

Parametric EQ PE-10
1983-1984.

1983-1984		$45	$60

Phaser PH-03
1981-1984. Four knobs.

1981-1984		$75	$100

Phaser PH-44
1982-1984. Six knobs.

1982-1984		$150	$175

Stereo Chorus CH-22
1982-1984.

1982-1984	Blue case	$75	$125

Thriller TH-20
1984-1986. Exciter.

1984-1986	Black case, four knobs	$175	$225

Peavey
1965-present. Peavey made stomp boxes from '87 to around '90. They offered rack mount gear after that.

Accelerator Overdrive AOD-2
1980s		$30	$35

Biampable Bass Chorus BAC-2
1980s		$30	$35

Companded Chorus CMC-1
1980s		$25	$30

Compressor/Sustainer CSR-2
1980s		$35	$40

Digital Delay DDL-3
1980s		$30	$35

Digital Stereo Reverb SRP-16
1980s		$50	$55

Dual Clock Stereo Chorus DSC-4
1980s		$30	$35

Hotfoot Distortion HFD-2
1980s		$25	$30

PedalDoctor FX
1996-present. Tim Creek builds his production and custom guitar effects in Nashville, Tennessee.

Pedalworx
2001-present. Bob McBroom and George Blekas build their guitar effects in Manorville, New York and Huntsville, Alabama. They also do modifications to wahs.

Pharaoh Amplifiers
1998-present. Builder Matt Farrow builds his effects in Raleigh, North Carolina.

Premier
Ca.1938-ca.1975, 1990-present. Premier offered a reverb unit in the '60s.

Reverb Unit
1961-late-1960s. Tube, footswitch, 2-tone brown.

1960s		$250	$300

Prescription Electronics
1994-present. Located in Portland, Oregon, Prescription offers a variety of hand-made effects.

Pearl CO-04 Compressor

Peavey EDI

Pedalworx Texas Two Step

EFFECTS

ProCo Rat

Red Witch Deluxe Moon Phaser

Rocktek Metalworker

MODEL YEAR	FEATURES	EXC. COND. LOW	HIGH
Dual-Tone			
1998-present. Overdrive and distortion.			
1998-2005		$165	$175
Throb			
1996-present. Tremolo.			
1996-2005		$165	$175
Yardbox			
1994-present. Patterned after the original Sola Sound Tonebender.			
1994-2005		$90	$125

ProCo

1974-present. Located in Kalamazoo, Michigan and founded by Charlie Wicks, ProCo produces effects, cables and audio products.

MODEL YEAR	FEATURES	EXC. COND. LOW	HIGH
Rat			
1979-1987. Fuzztone, large box until '84. The second version was 1/3 smaller than original box. The small box version became the Rat 2. The current Vintage Rat is a reissue of the original large box.			
1979-1984	Large box	$200	$250
1984-1987	Compact box	$100	$150
Rat 2			
1987-present.			
1987-1999		$75	$100
2000-2005		$40	$50
Turbo Rat			
1989-present. Fuzztone with higher output gain, slope-front case.			
1989-2005		$40	$50
Vintage Rat			
1992-2005. Reissue of early-'80s Rat.			
1992-2002		$40	$50

Pro-Sound

The effects listed here date from 1987, and were, most likely, around for a short time.

MODEL YEAR	FEATURES	EXC. COND. LOW	HIGH
Chorus CR-1			
1980s		$25	$40
Delay DL-1			
Analog.			
1980s		$35	$55
Distortion DS-1			
1980s		$20	$35
Octaver OT-1			
1980s		$25	$40
Power and Master Switch PMS-1			
1980s		$15	$25
Super Overdrive SD-1			
1980s		$20	$35

Radial Engineering

1994-present. Radial makes a variety of products in Port Coquitlam, British Columbia, including direct boxes, snakes, cables, splitters, and, since '99, the Tonebone line of guitar effects.

Rapco

The Jackson, Missouri based cable company offers a line of switch, connection and D.I. Boxes.

MODEL YEAR	FEATURES	EXC. COND. LOW	HIGH
The Connection AB-100			
1988-present. A/B box			
1988-1999		$25	$35

Real McCoy Custom

1993-present. Wahs and effects by Geoffrey Teese. His first wah was advertised as "the Real McCoy, by Teese." He now offers his custom wah pedals under the Real McCoy Custom brand. He also used the Teese brand on a line of stomp boxes, starting in '96. The Teese stomp boxes are no longer being made.

Red Witch

2003-present. Analog guitar effects, designed by Ben Fulton, and made in Paekakariki, New Zealand.

Retroman

2002-present. Joe Wolf builds his retro effects pedals in Janesville, Wisconsin.

Reverend

1996-present. Reverend offered its Drivetrain effects from '00 to '04. They also build guitars.

RGW Electronics

2003-present. Guitar effects built by Robbie Wallace in Lubbock, Texas.

Rockman

See listings under Scholz Research and Dunlop.

Rocktek

1986-present. Imports formerly distributed by Matthews and Ryan of Brooklyn, New York; currently handled by D'Andrea USA.

MODEL YEAR	FEATURES	EXC. COND. LOW	HIGH
Various Effects			
1986-present.			
1986-2004	Delay, Super Delay	$30	$40
1986-2004	Distortion, 6 Band EQ, Bass EQ, Chorus, Compressor	$15	$25
1986-2004	Overdrive, Flanger, Metal Worker, Phaser, Vibrator Tremolo	$15	$20

Rocktron

1980s-present. Rocktron is a division of GHS Strings and offers a line of amps, controllers, stomp boxes, and preamps.

MODEL YEAR	FEATURES	EXC. COND. LOW	HIGH
Austin Gold Overdrive			
1997-present. Light overdrive.			
1997-2005		$25	$35
Banshee Talk Box			
1997-present. Includes power supply.			
1997-2005		$65	$80
Hush Rack Mount			
1980s-present.			
2000-2005		$50	$100

MODEL YEAR	FEATURES	EXC. COND. LOW	HIGH

Hush Pedal
1996-present. Pedal version of rackmount Hush.

1996-2005		$25	$35

Rampage Distortion
1996-present. Sustain, high-gain and distortion.

1996-2005		$25	$35

Surf Tremolo
1997-2000.

1997-2000		$60	$80

Tsunami Chorus
1996-present. Battery or optional AC adapter.

1996-2005	Battery power	$40	$50
1996-2005	With power supply	$50	$60

Vertigo Vibe
2003-present. Rotating Leslie speaker effect.

2003-2005	Battery power	$50	$60
2003-2005	With power supply	$60	$70

XDC
1980s. Rack mount stereo preamp, distortion.

1980s		$100	$150

Roger Mayer Electronics

1964-present. Roger Mayer started making guitar effects in England in '64 for guitarists like Jimmy Page and Jeff Beck. He moved to the U.S. in '69 to start a company making studio gear and effects. Until about 1980, the effects were built one at a time in small numbers and not available to the general public. In the '80s he started producing larger quantities of pedals, introducing his rocket-shaped enclosure. He returned to England in '89.

Axis Fuzz
Early 1980s-present.

1987-2005		$125	$150

Classic Fuzz
1987-present. The Fuzz Face.

1987-2005		$175	$200

Metal Fuzz
Early 1980s-1994.

1987-1994		$125	$150

Mongoose Fuzz
Early 1980s-present.

1987-2005		$175	$200

Octavia
Early 1980s-present. Famous rocket-shaped box.

1981-2005		$150	$200

VooDoo-1
Ca.1990-present.

1990-2005		$175	$300

Rogue

2001-present. Budget imported guitar effects. They also offer guitars, basses, mandolins, banjos, ukes and amps.

Roland

Japan's Roland Corporation first launched effect pedals in 1974; a year or two later the subsidiary company, Boss, debuted its own line. They were marketed concurrently at first, but gradually Boss became reserved for compact effects while the

Roland name was used on amplifiers, keyboards, synths and larger processors.

Analog Synth SPV
1970s. Multi-effect synth, rack mount.

1970s		$700	$900

Bee Baa AF-100
1975-ca.1980. Fuzz and treble boost.

1975-1980		$300	$350

Bee Gee AF-60
1975-ca.1980. Sustain, distortion.

1975-1980		$75	$125

Double Beat AD-50
1975-ca.1980. Fuzz wah.

1975-1980		$175	$200

Expression Pedal EV-5
1970s.

1970s		$50	$75

Expression Pedal EV-5 Reissue
2000. Black pedal, blue foot pad.

2000		$25	$30

Guitar Synth Pedal GR-33 and Pickup GK-2A
2000-2005. Requires optional GK-2A pickup, blue case.

2000-2005		$475	$550

Human Rhythm Composer R-8
1980s. Drum machine, key pad entry.

1980s		$250	$350

Human Rhythm Composer R-8 MK II
2000s. Black case.

2000s		$300	$400

Jet Phaser AP-7
1975-ca.1978. Phase and distortion.

1975-1978		$225	$250

Phase Five AP-5
1975-ca.1978.

1975-1978		$200	$225

Phase II AP-2
1975-ca.1980. Brown case.

1975-1980		$150	$175

Space Echo Unit
1974-ca.1980. Tape echo and reverb, various models.

1970s	RE-101, RE-150, RE-201, RE-301	$550	$800
1970s	RE-501	$600	$850

Vocoder SVC-350
Late-1970s-1980s. Vocal synthesis (vocoder) for voice or guitar, rack mount version of VP-330.

1980		$550	$700

Vocoder VP-330 Plus
Late-1970s-1980s. Analog vocal synthesis (vocoder) for voice or guitar, includes 2 1/2 octaves keyboard.

1978-1982		$700	$900

Wah Beat AW-10
1975-ca.1980.

1975-1980		$100	$125

Ross

Founded by Bud Ross, who also established Kustom, in Chanute, Kansas, in the 1970s. Ross produced primarily amplifiers. In about '78, they introduced a line of U.S.-made effects. Later production switched to the Orient.

Rocktron Vertigo Vibe

Roger Mayer Octavia

Roland Jet Phaser AP-7

EFFECTS

Ross Distortion

EFFECTS

Scholz Rockman X100

SIB Mr. Fazeadelic

MODEL YEAR	FEATURES	EXC. COND. LOW	HIGH
10 Band Graphic Equalizer			
1970s		$80	$100
Compressor			
1970s. Gray case.			
1970s		$250	$300
Distortion			
1978-ca.1980. Brown.			
1979-1980		$75	$125
Flanger			
1977-ca.1980. Red.			
1977-1980		$100	$150
Phase Distortion R1			
1979. Purple.			
1979		$100	$125
Phaser			
1978-ca.1980. Orange.			
1978-1980		$80	$100
Stereo Delay			
1978-ca.1980.			
1978-1980		$125	$175

Rotovibe
See listing under Dunlop.

Sam Ash
1960s-1970s. Sam Ash Music was founded by a young Sam Ash (nee Askynase) in '24. Ash's first store was in Brooklyn, and was relocated in '44. By '66, there were about four Ash stores. During this time, Ash Music private branded their own amps and effects.

Fuzzz Boxx			
1966-1967. Red, made by Universal Amplifier Company, same as Astrotone Fuzz.			
1967		$200	$225
Volume Wah			
Italian-made.			
1970s		$175	$200

Sano
1944-ca. 1970. Sano was a New Jersey-based accordion company that built their own amps and a reverb unit. They also imported guitars for a few years, starting in '66.

Schaller
1970s. German-made guitar effects.

Scholz Research
1982-present. Started by Tom Scholz of the band Boston. In '95, Jim Dunlop picked up the Rockman line (see Dunlop).

Power Soak			
1980s		$100	$160
Rockman			
1980s		$70	$130
Rockman X100			
Professional studio processor.			
1980s		$100	$150

MODEL YEAR	FEATURES	EXC. COND. LOW	HIGH
Soloist			
Personal guitar processor.			
1980s		$50	$80

Seamoon
1973-1977, 1997-2002. Seamoon made effects until '77, when Dave Tarnowski bought up the remaining inventory and started Analog Digital Associates (ADA). He reissued the brand in '97.

Fresh Fuzz			
1975-1977. Recently reissued by ADA.			
1975-1977		$150	$200
Funk Machine			
1974-1977. Envelope filter. Recently reissued by ADA.			
1974-1977		$175	$225
Studio Phase			
1975-1977. Phase shifter.			
1975-1977		$75	$125

Sekova
Mid-1960s-mid-1970s. Entry level instruments imported by the U.S. Musical Merchandise Corporation of New York.

Seymour Duncan
In late 2003, pickup maker Seymour Duncan, located in Santa Barbara, California, added a line of stomp box guitar effects.

Shinei
Japanese imports. Shinei also made effects for Univox and probably others.

Fuzz Wah			
1970s		$125	$175
Resly (repeat time) Machine			
Black case, 3 speeds.			
1970s		$400	$500

Sho-Bud
1956-1980. This pedal steel company offered volume pedals as well.

Volume Pedal			
1965		$90	$95

SIB
Effects pedals from Rick Hamel, who helped design SMF amps.

Siegmund Guitars & Amplifiers
1993-present. Los Angeles, California amp and guitar builder Chris Siegmund added effects to his product line in '99.

Snarling Dogs
1997-present. Started by Charlie Stringer of Stringer Industries, Warren, New Jersey in '97. Stringer died in May '99. The brand is now carried by D'Andrea USA.

MODEL YEAR	FEATURES	EXC. COND. LOW	HIGH

Sobbat

1995-present. Line of effects from Kinko Music Company of Kyoto, Japan.

Sola/Colorsound

1965-present. Sola was founded by London's Macari's Musical Exchange in '65. Sola made effects for Vox, Marshall, Park, and B & M and later under their own Colorsound brand. Refer to Colorsound for listings and more company info.

Soldano

1987-present. Seattle, Washington amp builder Soldano also builds a reverb unit.

Songbird

See Dytronics.

South Hawk

Hawk I Fuzz

Year	Features	Low	High
1975		$100	$125

LTD

Year	Features	Low	High
1975	Silver case, slider	$100	$125

Speedster

1995-2000, 2003-present. Speedster added American-made guitar effects pedals to their product line in '04.

Stinger

Stinger effects were distributed by the Martin Guitar Company from 1989 to '90.

Effects

Year	Features	Low	High
1989-1990	CH-70 Stereo Chorus	$25	$55
1989-1990	CO-20 Compressor	$35	$55
1989-1990	DD-90 Digital Delay	$45	$65
1989-1990	DE-80 Analog Delay	$50	$70
1989-1990	DI-10 Distortion	$40	$65
1989-1990	FL-60 Flanger	$40	$65
1989-1990	OD-30 Overdrive	$40	$65
1989-1990	TS-5 Tube Stack	$45	$65

Studio Electronics

1989-present. Synth and midi developer Greg St. Regis' Studio Electronics added guitar pedal effects to their line in '03.

Subdecay Studios

2003-present. Brian Marshall builds his guitar effects in Woodinville, Washington.

Supro

1935-1968. Supro offered a few reverb units in the '60s.

500 R Standard Reverb Unit

1962-1963. Outboard reverb unit.

Year	Features	Low	High
1962-1963		$300	$350

Sweet Sound

1994-present. Line of effects from Bob Sweet, originally made in Trenton, Michigan, currently in Coral Springs, Florida.

Systech (Systems & Technology in Music, Inc)

1975-late-1970s. Systech was located in Kalamazoo, Michigan.

Effects

Year	Features	Low	High
1975-1979	Envelope and Repeater	$75	$125
1975-1979	Envelope Follower	$75	$125
1975-1979	Flanger	$75	$125
1975-1979	Harmonic Energizer	$150	$225
1975-1979	Overdrive Model 1300	$75	$125
1975-1979	Phase Shifter Model 1200	$75	$125

T.C. Electronics

1976-present. Brothers Kim and John Rishøj founded TC Electronic in Risskov, Denmark, and made guitar effects pedals for several years before moving into rack-mounted gear. Currently they offer a wide range of pro audio gear.

Booster + Distortion

Year	Features	Low	High
1980s		$325	$400

Dual Parametric Equalizer

Year	Features	Low	High
1980s		$275	$350

Stereo Chorus/Flanger

Introduced in 1982, and reissued in '91.

Year	Features	Low	High
1980s		$175	$225

Sustain + Equalizer

Year	Features	Low	High
1980s		$225	$300

T.C. Jauernig Electronics

2004-present. Tim Jauernig, of Rothschild, Wisconsin, built effects for several years before launching his T.C. Jauernig brand in '04.

Tech 21

1989-present. Tech 21 builds their SansAmp and other effects in New York City. They also build amps.

Sansamp

1989-present. Offers a variety of tube amp tones.

Year	Features	Low	High
1989	1st year	$125	$175
1990-2005		$100	$125

XXL Pedal

1995-2000, 2005-present. Distortion, fuzz.

Year	Features	Low	High
1995-2000		$50	$75

Teese

Geoffrey Teese's first wah was advertised as "the Real McCoy, by Teese." He now offers his custom wah pedals under the Real McCoy Custom brand. The Teese brand was used on his line of stomp boxes, starting in '96. The Teese stomp boxes are no longer being made.

Thomas Organ

The Thomas Organ Company was heavily involved with Vox from 1964 to '72, importing their instruments into the U.S. and designing and assembling products, including the wah-wah pedal. Both Thomas Organ and JMI, Vox's European distribu-

Sobbat FB-1R Fuzz Breaker

Subdecay Liquid Sunshine

T.C. Jauernig Luxury Drive

EFFECTS

Tycobrahe Parapedal

EFFECTS

Univox Echo-Tech EM-200

T-Rex BetaVibe

MODEL YEAR	FEATURES	EXC. COND. LOW	HIGH

tor, wanted to offer the new effect. The problem was solved by labeling the Thomas Organ wah the Crybaby. The Crybaby is now offered by Dunlop. Refer to Vox listing for Crybaby Stereo Fuzz Wah, Crybaby Wah, and Wah Wah.

ToadWorks
2001-present. Guitar effects built in Spokane, Washington by Ryan Dunn and Doug Harrison.

Tonebone
See Radial Engineering listing.

Top Gear
1960s-1970s. Top Gear was a London music store. Their effects were made by other manufacturers.
Rotator
Leslie effect.

1970s		$100	$175

Top Hat Amplification
1994-present. The Anaheim, California, amp builder also offers effects.

Tremolo
See listing under Dunlop.

T-Rex
2003-present. Made in Denmark and imported by European Musical Imports.

Tube Works
1987-2004. Founded by B.K. Butler (see Audio Matrix) in Denver, Colorado, Tube Works became a division of Genz Benz Enclosures of Scottsdale, Arizona in 1997 which dropped the brand in 2004. They also offered tube/solidstate amps, cabinets, and DI boxes.
Blue Tube
1989-2004. Overdrive bass driver with 12AX7A tube.

1989-2004		$100	$150

Real Tube
Ca.1987-2004. Overdrive with 12AX7A tube.

1987-1999		$100	$150

Tube Driver
1987-2004. With tube.

1987-2004	With tube	$100	$150

Tycobrahe
The Tycobrahe story was over almost before it began. Doing business in 1976-1977, they produced only three pedals and a direct box, one the fabled Octavia. The company, located in Hermosa Beach, California, made high-quality, original devices, but they didn't catch on. Now, they are very collectible.
Octavia
1976-1977. Octave doubler.

1970s		$950	$1,050

Parapedal
1976-1977. Wah.

1976-1977		$750	$950

MODEL YEAR	FEATURES	EXC. COND. LOW	HIGH

Pedalflanger
1976-1977. Blue pedal-controlled flanger.

1976-1977		$750	$950

Uni-Vibe
See listings under Univox and Dunlop.

Univox
Univox was a brand owned by Merson (later Unicord), of Westbury, New York. It marketed guitars and amps, and added effects in the late-'60s. Most Univox effects were made by Shinei, of Japan. They vanished in about '81.
EC-80 A Echo
Early-1970s-ca.1977. Tape echo, sometimes shown as The Brat Echo Chamber.

1970s		$95	$135

EC-100 Echo
Tape, sound-on-sound.

1970s		$105	$145

Echo-Tech EM-200
Disc recording echo unit.

1970s		$130	$170

Micro 41 FCM41 4 channel mixer

1970s		$35	$50

Micro Fazer
1970s. Phase shifter.

1970s		$75	$100

Noise-Clamp EX110

1970s		$45	$55

Phaser PHZ1
AC powered.

1970s		$50	$75

Pro Verb
1970s. Reverb (spring) unit, black tolex, slider controls for 2 inputs, 1 output plus remote output.

1970s		$80	$100

Square Wave SQ150
Introduced in 1976, distortion, orange case.

1970s		$75	$125

Super-Fuzz
1968-1970s. Early transistor effect, made by Shinei.

1971	Gray box, normal bypass switch	$225	$300
1973	Unicord, various colors, blue bypass pedal	$225	$300

Uni-Comp
Compression limiter.

1970s		$50	$100

Uni-Drive

1970s		$150	$200

Uni-Fuzz
1960s. Fuzz tone in blue case, 2 black knobs and slider switch.

1960s		$275	$375

Uni-Tron 5
A.k.a. Funky Filter, envelope filter.

1975		$125	$200

MODEL YEAR	FEATURES	EXC. COND. LOW	HIGH

Uni-Vibe
Introduced around 1969, with rotating speaker simulation, with pedal.

1960s		$1,200	$1,500
1970s		$825	$975

Uni-Wah Wah/Volume
1970s		$100	$125

Vesta Fire
Ca.1981-ca.1988. Brand of Japan's Shiino Musical Instrument Corp.

Effects
1981-1988	Digital Chorus/ Flanger FLCH	$35	$50
1981-1988	Distortion DST	$35	$50
1981-1988	Flanger	$35	$50
1981-1988	Noise Gate	$25	$40
1981-1988	Stereo Chorus SCH	$35	$50

Vintage Tone Project
2003-present. Line of guitar effects made by Robert Rush and company in Lafayette, Colorado. They also build reissues of Dan Armstong's '70s effects.

VooDoo Lab
1994-present. Line of effects made by Digital Music Corp. in California.

Analog Chorus
1997-present.
1997-2005		$100	$120

Bosstone
1994-1999. Based on '60s Jordan Electronics Fuzz.
1994-1999		$70	$75

Microvibe
1996-present. UniVibe swirl effect.
1996-2005		$55	$65

Overdrive
1994-2002. Based on '70s overdrive.
1994-2002		$55	$65

Superfuzz
1999-present.
1999-2005		$75	$90

Tremolo
1995-present.
1995-2005		$55	$75

Vox
1957-present. Vox offered a variety of guitars, amps, organs and effects. Ca. '66, they released the Tone Bender, one of the classic fuzzboxes of all time. A year or so later, they delivered their greatest contribution to the effects world, the first wah-wah pedal. The American arm of Vox (then under Thomas Organ) succumbed in '72. In the U.K., the company was on-again/off-again.

Clyde McCoy Wah-Wah Pedal
Introduced in 1967, reissued in 2001-present. Clyde's picture on bottom cover.
1967	Clyde's picture	$900	$1,000
1968	No picture	$600	$750
2001-2004	Model V-848	$85	$100

Crybaby Wah
Introduced in 1968. The Thomas Organ Company was heavily involved with Vox from '64 to '72, importing their instruments into the U.S. and designing and assembling products. One product developed in conjunction with Vox was the wah-wah pedal. Both Thomas Organ and JMI, Vox's European distributor, wanted to offer the new effect. The problem was solved by labeling the Thomas Organ wah the Crybaby. The original wahs were built by Jen in Italy, but Thomas later made them in their Chicago, Illinois and Sepulveda, California plants. Thomas Organ retained the marketing rights to Vox until '79, but was not very active with the brand after '72. The Crybaby brand is now offered by Dunlop.
1960s	Jen-made	$200	$250
1970	Sepulveda-made	$125	$175

Double Sound
Jen-made, Double Sound model name on bottom of pedal, double sound derived from fuzz and wah ability.
1970s		$200	$250

Flanger
1970s		$200	$250

King Wah
Chrome top, Italian-made.
1970s		$200	$250

Stereo Fuzz Wah
1970s		$150	$200

Tone Bender V-828
1966-1970s. Fuzz box, reissued as the V-829 in '93.
1966	Gray	$300	$400
1969	Black	$250	$350

V-807 Echo-Reverb Unit
Solidstate, disc echo.
1967		$275	$375

V-837 Echo Deluxe Tape Echo
Solidstate, multiple heads.
1967		$350	$450

V-846 Wah
1969-1970s. Chrome top, Italian-made.
1969	Transitional Clyde McCoy	$500	$650
1970s		$300	$400

V-847 Wah
1992-present. Reissue of the original V-846 Wah.
1992-2005		$65	$80

Valvetronix Tonelab
2003-present. Multi-effect modeling processor, 12AX7 tube preamp.
2003-2005		$400	$425

Volume Pedal
Late 1960s. Reissued as the V850.
1960s		$50	$100

Voodoo Lab Tremolo

Vox Clyde McCoy Wah

Vox King Wah

420 **Warmenfat – Zoom**

The Official Vintage Guitar Magazine Price Guide 2007

Warmenfat tube preamp

EFFECTS

Xotic AC Booster

Zoom 506II Bass

MODEL YEAR	FEATURES	EXC. COND. LOW	HIGH

Warmenfat
2004-present. Pre-amps and guitar effects built in Sacramento, California, by Rainbow Electronics.

Wasabi
2003-present. Line of guitar effect pedals from Danelectro.

Washburn
Washburn offered a line of effects from around 1983 to ca. '89.
Effects

1980s	Analog Delay AX:9	$30	$35
1980s	Flanger FX:4	$35	$40
1980s	Phaser PX:8	$40	$45
1980s	Stack in a Box SX:3	$30	$35

Watkins/WEM
1957-present. Watkins Electric Music (WEM) was founded by Charlie Watkins. Their first commercial product was the Watkins Dominator amp in '57, followed by the Copicat Echo in '58.
Copicat Tape Echo
1958-1970s, 1985-present. The Copicat has been reissued in various forms by Watkins.

1960s	Solidstate	$300	$400
1960s	Tube	$700	$1,000

Way Huge Electronics
1995-1998. Way Huge offered a variety of stomp boxes, made in Sherman Oaks, California.

WD Music
Since 1978, WD Music has offered a wide line of aftermarket products for guitar players. In '91, they introduced a line of effects that were copies of the original Dan Armstrong color series (refer to Dan Armstrong listing).
Blue Clipper
1991-present. Fuzz.

1991-2002		$30	$45

Orange Squeezer
1991-present. Signal compressor.

1991-2002	Light Orange case	$40	$50

Purple Peaker
1991-present. Mini EQ.

1991-2002		$40	$50

Westbury
1978-ca.1983. Brand imported by Unicord.
Tube Overdrive
1978-1983. 12AX7.

1978-1983		$150	$200

Whirlwind
1980s. Whirlwind called Rochester, New York, home.
Commander
Boost and effects loop selector.

1980s		$75	$100

Wurlitzer
Wurlitzer offered the Fuzzer Buzzer in the 1960s, which was the same as the Clark Fuzz.

Xotic Effects
2001-present. Hand-wired effects made in Los Angeles, California, and distributed by Prosound Communications.

Yamaha
1946-present. Yamaha has offered effects since at least the early '80s. They also build guitars, basses, amps, and other musical instruments.
Analog Delay E1005
1980s. Free-standing, double-space rack mount-sized, short to long range delays, gray case.

1980s		$160	$180

Yubro
Yubro, of Bellaire, Texas, offered a line of nine effects in the mid- to late-'80s.
Analog Delay AD-800
300 ms.

1980s		$75	$125

Stereo Chorus CH-600

1980s		$50	$75

Zinky
1999-present. Guitar effects built by Bruce Zinky in Flagstaff, Arizona. He also builds amps and has revived the Supro brand on a guitar and amp.

Zoom
Effects line from Samson Technologies Corp. of Syosset, New York.
503 Amp Simulator
1998-2000.

1998-2000		$25	$40

504 Acoustic Pedal
1997-2000. Compact multi-effects pedal, 24 effects, tuner, replaced by II version.

1997-2000		$25	$40

505 Guitar Pedal
1996-2000. Compact multi-effects pedal, 24 effects, tuner, replaced by II version.

1996-2000		$30	$40

506 Bass Pedal
1997-2000. Compact multi-effects bass pedal, 24 effects, tuner, black box, orange panel. Replaced by II version.

1997-2000		$35	$45

507 Reverb
1997-2000.

1997-2000		$25	$40

1010 Player
1996-1999. Compact multi-effects pedal board, 16 distortions, 25 effects.

1996-1999		$40	$75

The *Vintage Guitar Price Guide* shows low to high values for items in all-original excellent condition, and, where applicable, with original case or cover.

Steels and Lap Steels

1960 Alamo Embassy

Asher Ben Harper

STEELS & LAPS

MODEL YEAR	FEATURES	EXC. COND. LOW	HIGH

Airline
Ca. 1958-1968. Name used by Montgomery Ward for instruments built by Kay, Harmony and Valco.

Lap Steel

1960s	Rec-O-Glas/plastic	$500	$600
1960s	Wood	$175	$250

Rocket 6-String Steel
Black and white, 3 legs, Valco-made.

1960s		$325	$375

Student 6 Steel

1950s	Black	$125	$150

Alamo
1947-1982. The first musical instruments built by Alamo, of San Antonio, Texas, were lap steel and amp combos with early models sold with small birch amps.

Hawaiian Lap Steels
1947-ca. 1967. Models include the '50s Challenger and Futuramic Dual Eight, the '50s and early-'60s Embassy (pear-shape) and Jet (triangular), the early-'60s Futuramic Eight and Futuramic Six, and the late-'60s Embassy (triangular Jet).

1950s		$125	$200

Alkire
1939-1950s. Founded by musician and teacher Eddie Alkire, the instruments may have been built by another company.

E-Harp 10-String Steel
1939-1950s. Similar to Epiphone lap steel with Epi-style logo, offered in lap steel or console.

1940s		$650	$800
1950s		$650	$800

Alvarez
Ca. 1966-present. Imported by St. Louis Music from mid-'60s.

Model 5010 Koa D Steel-String

1960s		$275	$325

Aria
1960-present. Aria offered Japanese-made steels and lap steels in the '60s.

Laps Steels

1960s		$275	$350

Asher
1982-present. Intermediate, professional and premium grade, production/custom, solidbody, semi-hollow body and acoustic lap steels built by luthier Bill Asher in Venice, California. He also builds guitars.

Ben Harper Model
1998-2001. Limited edition of 70, electric lap steel version of Weissenborn guitars, mahogany body, 8 tone chambers, koa top and fretboard, natural oil or lacquer finish.

2005		$1,800	$2,200

MODEL YEAR	FEATURES	EXC. COND. LOW	HIGH

Audiovox
Ca. 1935-ca. 1950. Paul Tutmarc's Audiovox Manufacturing, of Seattle, Washington, was a pioneer in electric lap steels, basses, guitars and amps.

Lap Steel

1940s		$900	$1,000

Lap Steel and Amp Set

1940s		$1,250	$1,300

Bigsby
1947-1965. All handmade by Paul Arthur Bigsby, in Downey, California. Bigsby was a pioneer in developing pedal steels and they were generally special order or custom-made and not mass produced. The original instruments were made until '65 and should be valued on a case-by-case basis. Models include the Single Neck pedal steel, Double 8 pedal steel, 8/10 Doubleneck pedal steel, Triple 8 pedal steel (all ca. '47-'65), and the '57-'58 Magnatone G-70 lap steel. A solidbody guitar and a pedal steel based upon the original Paul Bigsby designs were introduced January, 2002.

Triple 8-String Neck Steel
1947-1965. Bigsby steel were generally special order or custom-made and not mass produced. Instruments should be valued on a case-by-case basis.

1947-1959	Natural	$2,500	$5,000

Blue Star
1984-present. Intermediate grade, production/custom, lap steels built by luthier Bruce Herron in Fennville, Michigan. He also builds guitars, mandolins, dulcimers, and ukes.

Bronson
George Bronson was a steel guitar instructor in the Detroit area from the 1930s to the early '50s and sold instruments under his own brand. Most instruments and amps were made by Rickenbacker, Dickerson or Valco.

Melody King Model 52 Lap Steel
Brown bakelite body with 5 gold cavity covers on the top, made by Rickenbacker.

1950s		$550	$700

Carvin
1946-present. Founded by Lowell C. Kiesel who produced lapsteels under the Kiesel brand for 1947-'50. In late '49, he renamed the instrument line Carvin after sons Carson and Galvin. Until '77, they offered lap, console, and pedal steels with up to 4 necks.

Double 6 Steel With Legs

1960s		$650	$750

Double 8 Steel With Legs

1960s	Sunburst	$675	$775

Electric Hawaiian Lap Steel

1950s		$225	$300

MODEL YEAR	FEATURES	EXC. COND. LOW	HIGH

Single 8 With Legs
Large block position markers, 1 pickup, 2 knobs, blond finish.

1960s		$500	$550

Chandler
1984-present. Intermediate grade, production/custom, solidbody Weissenborn-shaped electric lapsteels built by luthiers Paul and Adrian Chandler in Chico, California. They also build guitars, basses and pickups.

Cromwell
1935-1939. Budget model brand built by Gibson and distributed by various mail-order businesses.

Lap Steel
Charlie Christian bar pickup.

1939	Sunburst	$300	$375

Danelectro
1946-1969, 1997-present. Known mainly for guitars and amps, Danelectro did offer a few lap steels in the mid-'50s.

Lap Steels

1950s		$250	$350

Denley
1960s. Pedal steels built by Nigel Dennis and Gordon Huntley in England. They also made steels for Jim Burns' Ormston brand in the '60s.

Dickerson
1937-1948. Founded by the Dickerson brothers in '37, primarily for electric lap steels and small amps. Besides their own brand, Dickerson made instruments for Cleveland's Oahu Company, Varsity, Southern California Music, Bronson, Roland Ball, and Gourley. The lap steels were often sold with matching amps, both covered in pearloid mother-of-toilet-seat (MOTS). By '48, the company changed ownership and was renamed Magna Electronics (Magnatone).

Lap Steel with matching amp
1950s. Gray pearloid with matching amp.

1950s		$450	$550

Dobro
1929-1942, ca.1954-present. Dobro offered lap steels from '33 to '42. Gibson now owns the brand and recently offered a lap steel.

Hawaiian Lap Steel

1933-1942		$350	$450

Lap Steel Guitar and Amp Set
1930s-1940s. Typical pearloid covered student 6-string lap steel and small matching amp (with 3 tubes and 1 control knob).

1933-1942	Pearloid	$450	$550

Dwight
1950s. Private branded instruments made by National-Supro.

Lap Steel
1950s. Pearloid, 6 strings.

1950s	Gray pearloid	$350	$450

Emmons
1970s-present. Owned by Lashley, Inc. of Burlington, North Carolina.

Lashley LeGrande III Steel
2001-present. Double-neck, 8 pedals, 4 knee levers, 25th Anniversary.

2001		$2,000	$3,000

S-10 Pedal Steel
Single 10-string neck pedal steel.

1970s		$950	$1,750

English Electronics
1960s. Norman English had a teaching studio in Lansing, Michigan, where he gave guitar and steel lessons. He had his own private-branded instruments made by Valco in Chicago.

Tonemaster Lap Steel
Cream pearloid, 6 strings, 3 legs, Valco-made.

1960s		$300	$450
1960s	Stringtone pitch changer	$450	$800

Epiphone
1928-present. The then Epiphone Banjo Company was established in '28. Best known for its guitars, the company offered steels from '35 to '58 when Gibson purchased the brand.

Century Lap Steel
1939-1957. Rocket-shaped maple body, 1 pickup, metal 'board, 6, 7 or 8 strings, black finish.

1939-1957		$400	$500

Electar Hawaiian Lap Steel
1935-1937. Wood teardrop-shaped body, bakelite top, black, horseshoe pickup, 6 string.

1935-1937		$500	$600

Electar Model M Hawaiian Lap Steel
1936-1939. Metal top, stair-step body, art deco, black ('36-'37) or gray ('38-'39), 6, 7 or 8 strings.

1936-1939		$400	$500

Kent Hawaiian Lap Steel
1949-1953. Guitar-shaped maple body, 6 strings, lower-end of Epiphone Hawaiian line, Electar script logo below bottom of fretboard.

1949-1953		$325	$400

Solo Console Steel
1939-1954. Maple with white mahogany laminated body, black binding, black metal 'board, 6, 7 or 8 strings.

1939-1954		$450	$600

Triple-Neck Console Steel
1954-1957. neck version of Solo, sunburst or natural finish.

1954-1957		$1,000	$1,500

Chandler Lectraslide

Epiphone Electar Model M

STEELS & LAPS

1948 Fender Princeton

Fender Champion

STEELS & LAPS

MODEL YEAR	FEATURES	EXC. COND. LOW	HIGH
Zephyr Hawaiian Lap Steel			
1939-1957. Maple stair-step body, metal 'board, 6, 7 or 8 strings.			
1939-1949	Black, with white top	$650	$750
1950-1957	Sunburst	$600	$700

Fender

1946-present. Fender offered lap and pedal steels from '46 to '80.

400 Pedal Steel

1958-1976. One 8-string neck with 4 to 10 pedals.

1958-1964		$850	$1,000
1965-1976		$800	$950

800 Pedal Steel

1964-1976. One 10-string neck, 6 to 10 pedals.

1964		$950	$1,200
1965-1976		$900	$1,150

1000 Pedal Steel

1957-1976. Two 8-string necks and 8 or 10 pedals.

1957-1964	Natural or sunburst, 8 or 10 pedals	$1,000	$1,400
1965-1976	Natural, 8 pedals	$1,000	$1,400
1965-1976	Sunburst, 8 or 10 pedals	$900	$1,300

2000 Pedal Steel

1964-1976. Two 10-string necks, 10 or 11 pedals, sunburst.

1964	10 or 11 pedals	$1,300	$1,700
1965-1976	10 or 11 pedals	$1,200	$1,600

Artist Dual 10 Pedal Steel

1976-1981. Two 10-string necks, 8 pedals, 4 knee levers, black or mahogany.

1976-1981		$700	$1,000

Champ Lap Steel

1955-1980. Replaced Champion Lap Steel, tan.

1955-1959		$700	$800
1960-1969		$650	$750
1970-1980		$500	$650

Champion Lap Steel

1949-1955. Covered in what collectors call mother-of-toilet-seat (MOTS) finish, also known as pearloid. Replaced by Champ Lap Steel.

1949-1955	Tan	$700	$800
1949-1955	White or yellow pearloid	$700	$800

Deluxe Steel

1949-1950. Strings-thru-pickup, Roman numeral markers, became the Deluxe 6 or Deluxe 8 Lap Steel in '50.

1946	Wax	$900	$1,100
1947-1950	Blond or Walnut	$900	$1,100

Deluxe 6/Stringmaster Single Steel

1950-1981. Renamed from the Deluxe, 6 strings, 3 legs.

1950-1969	Blond or Walnut	$900	$1,100
1970-1981	Black or White	$750	$1,000

Deluxe 8/Stringmaster Single Steel

1950-1981. Renamed from the Deluxe, 8 strings, 3 legs.

1950-1969	Blond or Walnut	$900	$1,100
1970-1981	Black or White	$750	$1,000

Dual 6 Professional Steel

1950-1981. Two 6-string necks, 3 legs optional, blond or walnut.

1952-1981	Blond	$900	$1,300
1952-1981	Walnut	$900	$1,100

Dual 8 Professional Steel

1946-1957. Two 8-string necks, 3 legs optional, blond or walnut.

1946-1957	Blond	$900	$1,300
1946-1957	Walnut	$900	$1,100

K & F Steel

1945-1946. Made by Doc Kauffman and Leo Fender, strings-thru-pickup.

1945-1946	Black	$1,500	$1,600

Organ Button Steel

1946-1947.

1946-1947	Wax	$950	$1,100

Princeton Steel

1946-1948. Strings-thru-pickup, Roman numeral markers.

1946-1948	Wax	$750	$1,000

Stringmaster Steel (two-neck)

1953-1981. The Stringmaster came in 3 versions, having 2, 3 or 4 8-string necks (6-string necks optional).

1953-1959	Blond (light finish)	$1,500	$2,000
1953-1959	Walnut (dark finish)	$1,200	$1,600
1960-1969	Blond	$1,400	$1,800
1960-1969	Walnut	$1,000	$1,500
1970-1981	Blond or Walnut	$1,000	$1,400

Stringmaster Steel (three-neck)

1953-1981.

1953-1959	Blond (light finish)	$2,300	$2,500
1953-1959	Walnut (dark finish)	$1,800	$2,200
1960-1969	Blond	$2,100	$2,400
1960-1969	Walnut	$1,400	$1,900
1970-1981	Blond	$1,600	$1,800
1970-1981	Walnut	$1,200	$1,500

Stringmaster Steel (four-neck)

1953-1968.

1953-1959	Blond (light finish)	$2,500	$2,900
1953-1959	Walnut (dark finish)	$2,000	$2,500
1960-1968	Blond	$2,200	$2,800
1960-1968	Walnut	$1,700	$2,200

Studio Deluxe Lap Steel

1956-1981. One pickup, 3 legs.

1956-1981	Blond	$750	$900

Framus

1946-1977, 1996-present. Imported into the U.S. by Philadelphia Music Company in the '60s. Brand revived in '96, and distributed in the U.S. by Dana B. Goods.

Deluxe Table Steel 0/7

1970s	White	$300	$350

Student Hawaiian Model 0/4

1970s	Red	$175	$225

G.L. Stiles

1960-1994. Gilbert Lee Stiles made a variety of instruments, mainly in the Miami, Florida area. See Guitar section for more company info.

MODEL		EXC. COND.	
YEAR	FEATURES	LOW	HIGH

Doubleneck Pedal Steel
1970s		$500	$600

Gibson

1902-present. Gibson offered steels from '35-'68.

BR-4 Lap Steel

1947. Guitar-shaped of solid mahogany, round neck, 1 pickup, varied binding.
1947	Sunburst	$450	$550

BR-6 Lap Steel

1947-1960. Guitar-shaped solid mahogany body, square neck (round by '48).
1947-1960		$450	$550

BR-9 Lap Steel

1947-1959. Solidbody, 1 pickup, tan.
1947-1949	Non-adj. Poles	$375	$475
1950-1959	Adj. Poles	$475	$575
1950-1959	Matching Steel and Amp	$700	$900

Century 6 Lap Steel

1948-1968. Solid maple body, 6 strings, 1 pickup, silver 'board.
1948-1968		$550	$650

Century 10 Lap Steel

1948-1955. Solid maple body, 10 strings, 1 pickup, silver 'board.
1948-1955	Black	$550	$650

Console Grand Steel

1938-1942, 1948-1967. Hollowbody, 2 necks, triple-bound body, standard 7- and 8-string combination until '42, double 8-string necks standard for '48 and after.
1938-1942	Sunburst	$1,200	$1,400
1948-1967	Sunburst	$1,200	$1,400

Console Steel (C-530)

1956-1966. Replaced Consolette during '56-'57, double 8-string necks, 4 legs optional.
1956-1966	With legs	$1,000	$1,200

Consolette Table Steel

1952-1957. Rectangular korina body, 2 8-string necks, 4 legs, replaced by maple-body Console after '56.
1952-1957		$1,100	$1,300

EH-100 Lap Steel

1936-1949. Hollow guitar-shaped body, bound top, 6 or 7 strings.
1936-1939		$650	$850
1940-1949		$550	$750

EH-125 Lap Steel

1939-1942. Hollow guitar-shaped mahogany body, single-bound body, metal 'board.
1939-1942	Sunburst	$750	$950

EH-150 Doubleneck Electric Hawaiian Steel

1937-1939. Doubleneck EH-150 with 7- and 8-string necks.
1937-1939		$2,700	$3,000

EH-150 Lap Steel

1936-1943. Hollow guitar-shaped body, 6 to 10 strings available, bound body.
1936	1st offering metal body	$2,500	$3,000
1937-1939	Sunburst	$1,000	$1,200
1940-1943	Sunburst	$900	$1,100

EH-150 Lap Steel Matching Set (guitar and amp)

1936-1942. Both electric Hawaiian steel guitar and amp named EH-150, with matching tweed guitar case.
1936-1939	Guitar with Christian pickup	$2,100	$2,200
1940-1942		$1,700	$1,800

EH-185 Lap Steel

1939-1942. Hollow guitar-shaped curly maple body, triple-bound body, 6, 7, 8 or 10 strings.
1939-1942	Sunburst, lap steel and amp	$2,500	$2,600
1939-1942	Sunburst, lap steel only	$1,400	$1,800

EH-500 Skylark Deluxe Lap Steel

1958-1959. Like Skylark, but with dot markers.
1958-1959		$900	$1,000

EH-500 Skylark Lap Steel

1956-1968. Solid korina body, 8-string available by '58, block markers with numbers.
1956-1968	Natural	$950	$1,000

EH-620 Steel

1955-1967. Eight strings, 6 pedals.
1955-1967	Natural	$800	$1,000

EH-630 Electraharp Steel

1941-1967. Eight strings, 8 pedals (4 in '49-'67). Called just EH-630 from '56-'67.
1941-1967	Sunburst	$1,000	$1,400

EH-820 Steel

1960-1966. Two necks, 8 pedals, Vari-Tone selector.
1960-1966	Cherry	$1,200	$1,600

Royaltone Lap Steel

1950-1952, 1956-1957. Symmetrical wavy body, volume and tone knobs on treble side of pickup, Gibson silk-screen logo, brown pickup bridge cover, updated guitar-shaped body style for '56-'57.
1950-1952	Symmetrical body	$800	$1,000
1956-1957	Guitar-shaped body	$600	$800

Ultratone Lap Steel

1946-1959. Solid maple body, plastic 'board, 6 strings.
1940s	White	$900	$1,000
1950s	Dark Blue or Seal Brown	$900	$1,000

Gold Tone

1993-present. Wayne and Robyn Rogers build their intermediate grade, production/custom lap steels in Titusville, Florida. They also offer basses, mandolins, banjos and banjitars.

Gibson EH-500 Skylark

Gibson Royaltone

STEELS & LAPS

1950s Gretsch Electromatic

Harmony Roy Smeck

MODEL YEAR	FEATURES	EXC. COND. LOW	HIGH

Gourley
See Dickerson listing.

Gretsch
1883-present. Gretsch offered a variety of steels from 1940-'63. Gretsch actually only made 1 model; the rest were built by Valco. Currently they offer 2 lap steel models.

Electromatic Console (6158) Twin Neck Steel
1949-1955. Two 6-string necks with six-on-a-side tuners, Electromatic script logo on end cover plates, 3 knobs, metal control panels and knobs, pearloid covered.

1949-1955		$700	$1,000

Electromatic Standard (6156) Lap Steel
1950-1955.

1950-1955	Brown Pearloid	$500	$600

Electromatic Student (6152) Lap Steel
1949-1955. Square bottom, pearloid cover.

1949-1955	Brown Pearloid	$350	$400

Jet Mainliner (6147) Steel
1955-1963. Single-neck version of Jet Twin.

1955-1963		$500	$600

Jet Twin Console (6148) Steel
1955-1963. Valco-made, 2 6-string necks, six-on-a-side tuners, Jet Black.

1955-1963		$700	$1,000

Guyatone
1933-present. Large Japanese maker. Brands also include Marco Polo, Winston, Kingston, Kent, LaFayette and Bradford. They offered lap steels under various brands from the '30s to the '60s.

Lap Steels

1960s		$250	$300

Table Steels
Three legs, 2 pickups.

1960s		$350	$425

Harmony
1982-1976. Founded by Wilhelm Schultz and purchased by Sears in 1916. The company evolved into the largest producer of stringed instruments in the U.S. in the '30s. They offered electric lap steels by '36.

Lap Steels

1936-1959	Various models	$250	$450
1960s	Painted body	$250	$450
1960s	Pearloid body	$300	$450

Hilo
1920s-1930s. Weissenborn style guitars most likely made by New Jersey's Oscar Schmitt Company.

Hawaiian Steel Guitar
Guitar shaped body, round sound hole, acoustic steel.

1930s		$1,900	$2,100

Jackson-Guldan
1920s-1960s. The Jackson-Guldan Violin Company, of Columbus, Ohio, offered lap steels and small tube amps early on. They also built acoustic guitars.

K & F (Kaufman & Fender)
See listing under Fender.

Kalamazoo
1933-1942, 1946-1947, 1965-1970. Budget brand produced by Gibson in Kalamazoo, Michigan. They offered lap steels in the '30s and '40s.

Lap Steels
1938-1942, 1946-1947.

1938-1942	Matching steel and amp	$600	$800
1938-1947	Steel	$300	$500

Kay
Ca. 1931-present. Huge Chicago manufacturer Kay offered steels from '36 to '60 under their own brand and others.

Lap Steel

1940s		$300	$400
1950s		$300	$400
1960s		$300	$400

Lap Steel with matching amp

1940s	Dark mahogany	$400	$600
1950s	Green	$400	$600

Kiesel
1946-1949. Founded by Lowell Kiesel as L.C. Kiesel Co., Los Angeles, California, but renamed Carvin in '49. Kiesel logo on the headstock.

Bakelite Lap Steel
1946. Small guitar-shaped bakelite body, 1 pickup, 2 knobs, diamond markers.

1946		$300	$500

Lapdancer
2001-present. Intermediate and professional grade, custom/production, lap steels built by luthier Loni Specter in West Hills, California.

Maestro
A budget brand made by Gibson.

Lap Steel
Pearloid, 1 pickup, 6 strings.

1940s		$300	$400
1950s		$300	$400

Magnatone
Ca. 1937-1971. Magnatone offered lap steels from '37 to '58. Besides their own brand, they also produced models under the Dickerson, Oahu, Gourley, and Natural Music Guild brands.

Lap Steel and Amp MOTS Set
Late-1940s-mid-1950s. Matching pearloid acetate covered lap steel and small amp.

1948-1955		$600	$700

MODEL YEAR	FEATURES	EXC. COND. LOW	HIGH

Lyric Doubleneck Lap Steel
Ca.1951-1958. Model G-1745-D-W, 8 strings per neck, hardwood body.

1951-1958		$400	$600

Maestro Tripleneck Steel
Ca.1951-1958. Model G-2495-W-W, maple and walnut, 8 strings per neck, legs.

1951-1958		$800	$1,200

Pearloid (MOTS) Lap Steels
1950s. These were often sold with a matching amp; price here is for lap steel only.

1950s		$200	$400

Marvel
1950-mid 1960s. Budget brand marketed by the Peter Sorkin Company of New York.

Electric Hawaiian Lap Steel

1950s		$150	$250

May Bell
See listing under Slingerland.

McKinney
1950s. Private branded for McKinney Guitars by Supro, blue McKinney Guitar logo on headstock.

Lap Steel
Similar to Supro Comet.

1950s	White Pearloid	$325	$350

Melobar
1970-present. Designed by Walt Smith, of Smith Family Music, Melobar instruments feature a guitar body with a tilted neck, allowing the guitarist to play lap steel standing up. The instrument was developed and first made in Ed and Rudy Dopyera's Dobro factory. Most were available in 6-, 8-, or 10-string versions. Ted Smith took over operations from his father. Ted retired in late 2002.

6-String Electric Steel
1990s. Solidbody cutaway body shape, portable Melobar-style.

1990s		$700	$900

10-String Electric Steel
1970s. Double-cut guitar-shaped body, portable Melobar-style. Similar model currently offered as the Skreemr.

1970s		$900	$1,100

Skreemr Electric Steel
Early 1990s-present. The classic Melobar in a V (Skreemr SK2000) or double-cut (Skreemr) version, available in 6-, 8- and 10-string versions.

1990s	6-string version	$700	$900

V-10 Power-Slide Guitar
1982-early 1990s. Solidbody, V-shaped body, tilted neck, 10 strings (6- or 8-string models were available). Similar model now called the Skreemr SK2000.

1980s		$750	$1,000

X-10 Power-Slide Guitar
1981-early 1990s. Solidbody, futuristic body shape, tilted neck, 10 strings (6- or 8-string models were available). Called the Power-Slide One in early literature.

1980s		$750	$1,000

MSA
1963-1983, 2001-present. Professional and premium grade, production/custom, pedal and lap steel guitars built in Dallas, Texas by Maurice Anderson. The company was dissolved in '83, and reorganized in '01.

Pedal Steels

1962-1983	Various models	$600	$1,200

National
Ca. 1927-present. Founded in Los Angeles as the National String Instrument Corporation in '27, the brand has gone through many ownership changes over the years. National offered lap steels from '35 to '68.

Chicagoan Lap Steel
1948-1961. Gray pearloid, metal hand rest.

1948-1961		$350	$450

Console (Dual 8) Steel
1939-1942. Two 8-string necks, parallelogram markers, black top with white sides.

1939-1942		$900	$1,100

Dynamic Lap Steel
1941-1968. New Yorker-style body, 6 strings, 3 detachable screw-in legs added by '56.

1941-1965	Lap steel	$400	$500
1956-1968	With legs	$500	$600

Electric Hawaiian Lap Steel
1935-1937. Cast aluminum round body, 1 pickup, square neck, 6 or 7 strings.

1935-1937	6 strings	$700	$850
1935-1937	7 strings	$700	$850

Grand Console Steel
1947-1968. 2 or 3 8-string necks, Totem Pole 'board markers, black and white, came with or without legs, National's answer to Fender Stringmaster Series.

1947-1959	Double neck	$600	$800
1947-1959	Triple neck	$800	$1,000
1960-1968	Double neck	$550	$750

New Yorker Lap Steel
1939-1967. Introduced as Electric Hawaiian model in '35, square end body with stair-step sides, 7 or 8 strings, black and white finish.

1939-1949		$650	$800
1950-1959		$550	$650
1960-1967		$450	$550

Princess Lap Steel
1942-1947. Strings-thru-pickup, parallelogram markers, white pearloid.

1942-1947		$350	$450

Rocket One Ten Lap Steel
1955-1958. Rocket-shaped, black and white finish.

1955-1958		$350	$450

Melobar Skreemr

National Reso-Phonic

STEELS & LAPS

1940 Oahu Tonemaster

Rickenbacker seven-string

STEELS & LAPS

MODEL YEAR	FEATURES	EXC. COND. LOW	HIGH
Trailblazer Steel			
1948-1950. Square end, numbered markers, black.			
1948-1950		$350	$450
Triplex Chord Changer Lap Steel			
1949-1958. Maple and walnut body, 2 knobs, natural.			
1949-1958		$350	$450

Nioma

Regal and others (maybe Dickerson?) made instruments for this brand, most likely for a guitar studio or distributor.

MODEL YEAR	FEATURES	EXC. COND. LOW	HIGH
Lap Steel			
1930s	Pearloid	$225	$300

Oahu

1926-1985. The Oahu Publishing Company and Honolulu Conservatory, based in Cleveland, published a very popular guitar study course. They sold instruments to go with the lessons, starting with acoustic Hawaiian and Spanish guitars, selling large quantities in the '30s. As electric models became popular, Oahu responded with guitar-amp sets. Lap steel and matching amp sets were generally the same color; for example, yellow guitar and yellow amp, or white pearloid guitar and white amp. These sets were originally sold to students who would take private or group lessons. The instruments were made by Oahu, Valco, Harmony, Dickerson, and Rickenbacker and were offered into the '50s and '60s.

MODEL YEAR	FEATURES	EXC. COND. LOW	HIGH
Dianna Lap Steel			
1950s. Oahu and Diana logos on headstock, Oahu logo on fretboard, fancy bridge, pleasant unusual sunburst finish.			
1950s		$500	$600
Hawaiian Lap Steel			
1930s	Sunburst	$350	$400
1930s	Tonemaster with decal art	$400	$450
1940s	Pearloid, Supro-made	$300	$400
1950s	Pearloid or painted	$300	$400
K-71 Acoustic Lap Steel			
1930s. Flat top, round sound hole, decals on lower bouts.			
1930s		$250	$500
Lap Steel/Amp Set			
See also Lap Steel Oahu Amp listing in the Guide's amp section.			
1930s	Pearloid, small rectangular amp	$550	$650
1930s	Sunburst, mahogany	$450	$550
1950s	White Valco Amp, 1x10"	$500	$550
1950s	Yellow Valco amp	$500	$550
Lolana			
1950-1951, Late-1950s. Gold hardware, 2 6-string necks. Early model is lap steel, later version a console.			
1950-1951	Lap	$500	$600
1950s	Console	$700	$900

Ormston

1966-1968. Pedal steels built in England by Denley and marketed by James Ormston Burns between his stints with Burns London, which was bought by America's Baldwin Company in '65, and the Dallas Arbiter Hayman brand.

Premier

Ca.1938-ca.1975, 1990s-present. Premier made a variety of instruments, including lap steels, under several brands.

Recording King

Ca. 1930-1943. Brand used by Montgomery Ward for instruments made by Gibson, Regal, Kay, and Gretsch.

MODEL YEAR	FEATURES	EXC. COND. LOW	HIGH
Electric Hawaiian Lap Steel			
1930s		$400	$550
Roy Smeck Model AB104 Steel			
1938-1941. Pear-shaped body, 1 pickup.			
1940s		$400	$550

Regal

Ca. 1884-1954. Regal offered their own brand and made instruments for distributors and mass-merchandisers. The company sold out to Harmony in '54.

MODEL YEAR	FEATURES	EXC. COND. LOW	HIGH
Acoustic Hawaiian			
1930s. Small 13" body, square neck, glued or trapeze bridge, student model.			
1930s	Faux grain painted finish	$175	$375
1930s	Plain birch, sunburst, trap	$125	$175
Electric Hawaiian Lap Steel			
1940s		$175	$275
Octophone Steel			
1930s		$350	$500
Reso-phonic Steel			
1930s. Dobro-style resonator and spider assembly, round neck, adjustable nut.			
1930s		$850	$1,100

Rickenbacker

1931-present. Rickenbacker produced steels from '32 to '70.

MODEL YEAR	FEATURES	EXC. COND. LOW	HIGH
Acadamy Lap Steel			
1946-1947. Bakelite student model, horseshoe pickup, replaced by the Ace.			
1946-1947		$450	$550
Ace Lap Steel			
1948-1953. Bakelite body, 1 pickup.			
1948-1953		$450	$550
DC-16 Steel			
1950-1952. Metal, double 8-string necks.			
1950-1952		$900	$1,200
Electro Doubleneck Steel			
1940-1953. Two bakelite 8-string necks.			
1940-1953		$1,200	$1,400
Electro Tripleneck Steel			
1940-1953. Three bakelite 8-string necks.			
1940-1953		$1,400	$1,500

MODEL YEAR	FEATURES	EXC. COND. LOW	HIGH

Model 59 Lap Steel

1937-1943. Sheet steel body, baked-enamel light-colored crinkle finish, 1 pickup.

| 1937-1943 | | $700 | $750 |

Model 100 Lap Steel

1956-1970. Wood body, 6 strings, block markers, light or silver gray finish.

| 1956-1970 | | $500 | $600 |

Model A-22 "Frying Pan" Steel

1932-1950, 1954-1958. Frying Pan Electro Hawaiian Guitar, cast aluminum body, 1 pickup, slotted peghead.

| 1932-1936 | | $1,500 | $1,700 |

Model B Steel

1935-1955. Bakelite body and neck, 1 pickup, string-thru-body, decorative metal plates, 6 strings.

| 1935-1955 | Black | $925 | $1,000 |

Model BD Steel

1949-1970. Bakelite body, 6 strings, deluxe version of Model B, black.

| 1949-1960 | | $650 | $750 |

Model CW-6 Steel

1957-1961. Wood body, grille cloth on front, 6 strings, 3 legs, renamed JB (Jerry Byrd) model in '61.

| 1957-1961 | Walnut | $650 | $750 |

Model DW Steel

1955-1961. Wood body, double 6- or 8-string necks, optional 3 legs.

| 1955-1961 | 8-string necks | $800 | $1,000 |

Model G Lap Steel

Ca.1948-1957. Chrome-plated ornate version of Silver Hawaiian, gold hardware and trim, 6 or 8 strings.

| 1948-1957 | | $650 | $750 |

Model S/NS (New Style) Steel

1946-early-1950s. Sheet steel body, gray, gray sparkle or grayburst, 1 pickup, also available as a doubleneck.

| 1946-1950 | Gray Sparkle | $550 | $750 |

Model SD Steel

1949-1953. Deluxe NS, sheet steel body, 6, 7 or 8 strings, Copper Crinkle finish.

| 1949-1953 | | $600 | $650 |

Silver Hawaiian Lap Steel

1937-1943. Chrome-plated sheet steel body, 1 horseshoe pickup, 6 strings.

| 1937-1943 | | $1,000 | $1,300 |

Roland Ball

See Dickerson listing.

Sherwood

c.1950s. Private brand made by Chicago manufacturers such as Kay.

Deluxe Lap Steel

1950s. Symmetrical body, bar pickup, volume and tone controls, wood body, sunburst, relatively ornate headstock with script Sherwood logo, vertical Deluxe logo, and lightning bolt art.

| 1950s | | $400 | $450 |

Sho-Bud

1956-1980. Founded by Shot Jackson in Nashville. Distributed by Gretsch. They also had guitar models. Baldwin bought the company in '79 and closed the factory in '80.

Maverick Pedal Steel

Ca. 1970-1980. Beginner model, burl elm cover, 3 pedals.

| 1970-1980 | | $600 | $700 |

Pro I

1970-1980. Three pedals, natural.

| 1970-1975 | Round front pre-1976 | $750 | $900 |
| 1976-1980 | Square front later model | $850 | $1,100 |

Pro II

1973-1980. Birdseye maple, double 10-string necks, natural.

| 1973-1975 | Round front pre-1976 | $850 | $1,000 |
| 1976-1980 | Square front later model | $950 | $1,200 |

Pro III

1975-1980. Metal necks.

| 1975 | Round front | $950 | $1,100 |
| 1976-1980 | Square front later model | $1,050 | $1,200 |

Super Pro

1977-1980. Doubleneck 10 strings, 8 floor pedals, 6 knee levers, Jet Black.

| 1977-1980 | | $2,000 | $2,500 |

Silvertone

1940-1970. Brand name for instruments sold by Sears.

Amp-In-Case Lap Steel

Early 1940s. Lap steel and amp set, amp cabinet doubles as lap case with the lap stored above the amp, amp is long vertical cabinet with brown tweed covering, manufacturer appears to be the same as used by Gibson in the late '30s, low to mid power, 1x10" speaker.

| 1941-1942 | | $700 | $800 |

Six-String Lap Steels

1940s	Valco-made	$350	$500
1950s	Standard finish	$200	$400
1950s	White pearloid	$300	$400
1960s		$200	$400

Slingerland

1916-present. Offered by Slingerland Banjos and Drums. They also sold the May Bell brand. Instruments were made by others and sold by Slingerland in the '30s and '40s.

May Bell Lap Steel

1930s. Guitar-shaped lap steel with May Bell logo. This brand also had '30s Hawaiian and Spanish guitars.

| 1930s | | $250 | $450 |

Rickenbacker A22 "Frying Pan"

Rickenbacker Model B-6

STEELS & LAPS

Slingerland Songster

1930s Supro Hawaiian Electric

MODEL YEAR	FEATURES	EXC. COND. LOW	HIGH

Songster Lap Steel
1930s. Slingerland logo headstock, Songster logo near nut, guitar-shaped body, sunburst maple top, some with figured maple back, 1 pickup, 2 bakelite brown knobs, dot markers.

1930s		$950	$1,050

Stella
Ca. 1899-1974, present. Stella was a brand of the Oscar Schmidt Company. Harmony acquired the brand in '39. The Stella brand has been reintroduced by MBT International.

Electric Hawaiian Lap Steel
1937		$600	$800

Supertone
1914-1941. Brand name for Sears which was replaced by Silvertone. Instruments made by Harmony and others.

Electric Hawaiian Lap Steel
1930s	Various models	$300	$450

Supro
1935-1968, 2004-present. Budget brand of the National Dobro Company. Amp builder Bruce Zinky revived the Supro name for a guitar and amp model.

Clipper Lap Steel
1941-1943. One pickup, bound rosewood 'board, dot inlay, brown pearloid.

1941-1943		$300	$400

Comet Lap Steel
1947-1966. One pickup, attached cord, painted-on 'board, pearloid.

1947-1949	Gray pearloid	$300	$400
1950-1966	White pearloid	$300	$400

Comet Steel (with legs)
1950s-1960s. Three-leg 6-string steel version of the lap steel, 2 knobs, Supro logo on cover plate, 1 pickup.

1960s	Black and White	$600	$750

Console 8 Steel
1958-1960. Eight strings, 3 legs, black and white.

1958-1960		$600	$750

Irene
1940s. Complete ivory pearloid cover including headstock, fretboard and body, Roman numeral markers, 1 pickup, 2 control knobs, hard-wired output cord.

1940s		$350	$450

Jet Airliner Steel
1962-1964. One pickup, totem pole markings, 6 or 8 strings, pearloid, National-made.

1962-1964	Red	$250	$300

Professional Steel
Light brown pearloid.

1950s		$300	$400

Special Steel
1955-1962. Pearloid lap steel, student model, large script Special logo near pickup on early models, red until '57, white after.

1955-1957	Red pearloid	$300	$400
1957-1962	White pearloid	$300	$400

Spectator Steel
1952-1954. Wood body, 1 pickup, painted-on 'board, natural.

1952-1954		$175	$275

Student De Luxe Lap Steel
1952-1955. One pickup, pearloid, large script Student De Luxe logo located near pickup, replaced by Special in '55.

1952-1955	Black and white, or red, pearloid	$300	$400
1952-1955	Natural or white paint	$175	$275

Supreme Lap Steel
1947-1960. One pickup, painted-on 'board, brown pearloid until ca.'55, then red until ca.'58, Tulip Yellow after that.

1947-1960		$275	$375

Supro 60 lap steel and amp-in-case
Late 1930s-early '40s. Supro 60 logo near the single volume knob, long horizontal guitar case which houses a small tube amp and speaker, the case cover folds out to allow for ventilation for the tubes, the amp was made by National Dobro of Chicago.

1939-1941	White pearloid, black amp case	$750	$850

STEELS & LAPS

MODEL YEAR	FEATURES	EXC. COND. LOW	HIGH

Twin Lap Steel
1948-1955. Two 6-string necks, pearloid covering, renamed Console Steel in '55.

1948-1955		$600	$700

Teisco
1946-1974. The Japanese guitar-maker offered many steel models from '55 to around '67. Models offered '55-'61: EG-7L, -K, -R, -NT, -Z, -A, -S, -P, -8L, -NW, and -M. During '61-'67: EG-TW, -O, -U, -L, -6N, -8N, -DB, -DB2, -DT, H-39, H-905, TRH-1, Harp-8 and H-850.

Hawaiian Lap Steels

1955-1967		$150	$400

Timtone Custom Guitars
1993-2006. Luthier Tim Diebert built professional grade, custom, lap steel guitars in Grand Forks, British Columbia. He also built guitars and basses.

True Tone
1960s. Brand name sold by Western Auto (hey, everybody was in the guitar biz back then). Probably made by Kay or Harmony.

Lap Steel
1960s. Guitar-shaped, single-cut, 1 pickup.

1960s		$175	$275

Varsity
See Dickerson listing.

Vega
1903-present. The original Boston-based company was purchased by C.F. Martin in '70. In '80, the Vega trademark was sold to a Korean company. The company was one of the first to enter the electric market by offering products in '36 and offered lap steels into the early '60s.

DG-DB Steel
Two necks, 8 strings.

1950s		$700	$800

Odell Lap Steel
White pearloid.

1950s		$300	$400

Other Lap Steels

1930s		$300	$450
1940s	Art deco-style	$300	$450

Wabash
Brand name of the Wexler Company, which was located on Wabash Avenue in Chicago. They also offered ukes.

Lap Steel (Hawaiian Scene tailpiece)
Natural, 12 frets.

1950s		$225	$325

Wayne
1998-present. Luthiers Wayne and Michael Charvel, of Paradise, California, added intermediate grade, production, lap steel guitars to their line in '04. They also build guitars.

White
1955-1960. The White brand, named after plant manager Forrest White, was established by Fender to provide steel and small amp sets to teaching studios that were not Fender-authorized dealers. A standard guitar was planned, but never produced.

6 String Steel
1955-1956. White finish, block markers, 2 knobs, 3 legs. The 6 String Steel was usually sold with the matching white amp Model 80. Possibly only 1 batch of these was made by Fender in October/November '55.

1955-1956		$700	$900

Matching Steel and Amp Set

1955-1956		$1,400	$1,600

Timtone Lapdog

Wayne lap steel

STEELS & LAPS

Mandolins

Alvarez A800

Andersen Stringed Instruments mando

MODEL YEAR	FEATURES	EXC. COND. LOW	HIGH

Airline

Ca. 1958-1968. Brand for Montgomery Ward. Instruments were built by Kay, Harmony and Valco.

Electric Mandolin (Kay K390)

Early-1960s. In '62 the K390 was advertised as the Kay Professional Electric Mandolin. Venetian shape with sunburst spruce top, curly maple back and sides, tube-style pickup, white 'guard, rope-style celluloid binding.

1962		$350	$550

Mandolin (lower end)

1960s. Acoustic, plainer features.

1960s		$200	$300

Allen

1982-present. Premium grade, production resonators, steel-string flat-tops, and mandolins built by Luthier Randy Allen, Colfax, California.

Alvarez

C.1966-present. An import brand for St. Louis Music, Alvarez currently offers intermediate grade, production, mandolins.

Model A Mandolins

Classic F-style mandolin features, round soundhole or F-holes. Models include the A700 and A910.

1970s		$350	$600

American Conservatory (Lyon & Healy)

Late-1800s-early-1900s. Mainly catalog sales of guitars and mandolins from the Chicago maker. Marketed as a less expensive alternative to the Lyon & Healy Washburn product line.

Arched Back Mandolins

1910s. Flat back with a mild arch, standard appointments, nothing fancy.

1910s		$350	$400

Bowl Back Mandolin Style G2603

Early-1900s. Bowl back-style, 28 rosewood ribs (generally more ribs and use of rosewood ribs versus mahogany indicates higher quality), color corded soundhole and edge inlay, inlaid tortoise shell celluloid guard plate underneath strings and below the soundhole, bent top, butterfly headstock inlay.

1917		$350	$450

Bowl Back Mandolin Style G2604

Early-1900s. Bowl back-style, 42 rosewood ribs (generally more ribs incidated higher quality), extra fancy color corded soundhole and edge inlay around, extra fancy inlaid tortoise shell celluloid guard plate underneath strings and below the soundhole, bent top, butterfly headstock inlay.

1917		$500	$550

Andersen Stringed Instruments

1978-present. Luthier Steve Andersen builds his premium grade, production/custom mandolins in Seattle, Washington. He also builds guitars.

Apitius

1976-present. Luthier Oliver Apitius builds his premium and presentation grade, production/custom, mandolins in Shelburne, Ontario.

Applause

1994-present. Applause currently offers intermediate grade, production, mandolins. Kaman Music's entry-level Ovation-styled import brand added mandolins in '94.

Mandolin

1990s		$100	$250

Aria/Aria Pro II

1960-present. Intermediate grade, production, acoustic and electric mandolins from Aria/Aria Pro II, which added Japanese and Korean mandolins to their line in '76.

AM200 Mandolin

1994-present. Pear-shaped A body, plywood.

1994-2004		$175	$250

AM400 Mandolin

1994-present. F-style, sunburst.

1994-2004		$325	$400

AM600 Mandolin

1994-present. F-style, solid wood.

1994-2004		$350	$400

PM750 Mandolin

1976-ca. 1982. F-style Loar copy, maple plywood body.

1976-1982		$400	$550

Armstrong, Rob

1971-present. Custom mandolins made in Coventry, England, by luthier Rob Armstrong. He also builds basses, flat-tops, and parlor guitars.

Atkin Guitars

1993-present. Luthier Alister Atkin builds his production/custom mandolins in Canterbury, England. He also builds flat-top guitars.

Austin

1999-present. Budget and intermediate grade, production, mandolins imported by St. Louis Music. They also offer guitars, basses and banjos.

Bacon & Day

Established in 1921 by David Day and Paul Bacon, primarily known for fine quality tenor and plectrum banjos in the '20s and '30s.

Mandolin Banjo Orchestra

1920s. Mandolin neck and banjo body with open back, headstock with Bacon logo.

1920s		$350	$500

Senorita Banjo Mandolin

1930s		$400	$550

Silverbell #1 Banjo Mandolin

1920s. Fancy appointments, closed-back resonator.

1920s		$1,000	$1,100

MODEL		EXC. COND.	
YEAR	FEATURES	LOW	HIGH

Bauer (George)

1894-1911. Luthier George Bauer built guitars and mandolins in Philadelphia, Pennsylvania. He also built instruments with Samuel S. Stewart (S.S. Stewart).

Acme Professional (bowl back)
1890s. 29 ribs Brazilian, fancy styling.
1890s $300 $400

Beltone

1920s-1930s. Acoustic and resonator mandolins and banjo-mandolins made by others for New York City distributor Perlberg & Halpin. Martin did make a small number of instruments for Beltone, but most were student-grade models most likely made by one of the big Chicago builders.

Resonator Mandolin
1930s. F-hole top, banjo-style resonator back.
1930s $250 $400

Bertoncini Stringed Instruments

1995-present. Luthier Dave Bertoncini mainly builds flat-top guitars in Olympia, Washington, but has also built mandolins.

Bigsby

Ca. 1947-present. Guitar builder Paul Arthur Bigsby also built 6 electric mandolins.

Blue Star

1984-present. Luthier Bruce Herron builds his intermediate grade, production/custom, electric solidbody mandolins in Fennville, Michigan. He also builds guitars, lap steels, dulcimers, and ukes.

Bohmann

1878-ca.1926. Established by Czechoslavakian-born Joseph Bohmann in Chicago, Illinois.

Fancy Bowl Mandolin
Spruce top, marquetry trimmed, inlay, pearl.
1890 $400 $600

Brandt

Early 1900s. John Brandt started making mandolin-family instruments in Chicago, Illinois around 1898.

Mandola
1900s. Spruce top, rosewood body, scroll headstock, pearl and abalone fretboard binding.
1900 $1,100 $1,300

Presentation Mandolin
Spruce top, tortoise shell-bound.
1900s $700 $1,000

Breedlove

1990-present. Founded by Larry Breedlove and Steve Henderson. Professional and premium grade, production/custom, mandolins made in Tumalo, Oregon. They also produce guitars.

MODEL		EXC. COND.	
YEAR	FEATURES	LOW	HIGH

Alpine Master Class
2000s. O-style body, spruce/maple.
2000s $1,900 $2,100

K-5 Mandolin
Asymmetric carved top, maple body.
1990s $1,600 $1,800

Olympic Mandolin
Solid spruce top, teardrop-shaped, oval soundhole, highly flamed maple back, sunburst.
1990s $1,200 $1,400

Quartz OF/OO Mandolin
2000s. Basic A-style body with f-holes.
2000s $800 $900

Brian Moore

1992-present. Moore offers premium grade, production/custom, semi-hollow electric mandolins. They also build guitars and basses.

Bruno and Sons

1834-present. Established in 1834 by Charles Bruno, primarily as a distributor, Bruno and Sons marketed a variety of brands, including their own; currently part of Kaman. In the '60s or '70s, a Japanese-made solidbody electric mandolin was sold under the Bruno name.

Banjo Mandolin
Open back, 10" model.
1920s $300 $375

Bowl Back Mandolin
1890s-1920s. Brazilian rosewood, spruce, rosewood ribs.
1920s $300 $400

Calace

1825-present. Nicola Calace started The Calace Liuteria lute-making workshop in 1825 on the island of Procida, which is near Naples. The business is now in Naples and still in the family.

Lyre/Harp-Style Mandolin
Late-1800s-early-1900s. Lyre/harp-style, 8 strings, round soundhole, slightly bent top. Condition is important for these older instruments and the price noted is for a fully functional, original or pro-restored example.
1900 $1,000 $1,500

Carvin

1946-present. Carvin offered solidbody electric mandolins from around '56 to the late '60s, when they switched to a traditional pear-shaped electric/acoustic.

MB Mandolins
1956-1968. Solidbody, 1 pickup, single-cut Les Paul shape until '64, double-cut Jazzmaster/Strat shape after. Models include the #1-MB and the #2-MB, with different pickups.
1950s $750 $950

Bertoncini F5M

Carvin 1-MB

MANDOLINS

D'Angelico

MODEL		EXC. COND.	
YEAR	FEATURES	LOW	HIGH

Clifford

Clifford mandolins were manufactured by Kansas City, Missouri instrument wholesalers J.W. Jenkins & Sons. First introduced in 1895, the brand also offered guitars.

Collings

1986-present. Professional and premium grade, production/custom, mandolins built in Austin, Texas. Collings added mandolins to their line in '99. They also build guitars.

MF

1999-present. F-style, carved top and back.

1999-2004		$3,300	$3,500

MF-5 Deluxe

2005. Limited production, varnish finish, hand engraved nickel tailpiece unique to each instrument.

2005		$11,000	$14,000

MT

1999-presnt. A-style, 2 f-holes, carved top and back, matte finish, tortoise-bound top.

1999-2004		$1,500	$1,800

MT2

1999-present. MT with high gloss finish, ivoroid body, neck and headstock binding.

1999-2004		$2,400	$3,000

Conrad

Ca. 1968-1977. Imported from Japan by David Wexler and Company, Chicago, Illinois. Mid- to better-quality copy guitars, mandolins and banjos.

Crafter

2000-present. Line of intermediate grade, production, acoustic and acoustic/electric mandolins from Hohner. They also offer guitars and a bass.

Crestwood

1970s. Copy models imported by La Playa Distributing Company of Detroit.

Mandolin

Includes models 3039 (electric A-style), 3041 (bowl back-style, flower 'guard), 3043 (bowl back-style, plain 'guard), 71820 (A-style), and 71821 (F-style).

1970s		$100	$275

Cromwell

1935-1939. Private branded instruments made by Gibson at their Parsons Street factory in Kalamazoo, Michigan. Distributed by a variety of mail order companies such as Continental, Grossman, and Richter & Phillips.

GM-4 Mandolin

1935-1939. Style A, f-holes, solid wood arched top, mahogany back and sides, block capital letter Cromwell headstock logo, dot markers, elevated 'guard, sunburst.

1935-1939		$700	$800

Dean Bluegrass

MODEL		EXC. COND.	
YEAR	FEATURES	LOW	HIGH

D'Angelico

1932-1964. Handcrafted by John D'Angelico. Models include Excel, Teardrop, and Scroll. Appointments can vary from standard to higher-end so each mandolin should be evaluated on a case-by-case basis.

Mandolin

1932-1949. Various models and appointments.

1932-1949	Plain styling, lower range	$2,200	$3,000
1932-1949	Plain, non-elevated pickguard	$8,000	$10,000
1932-1949	High-end appointments	$22,000	$25,000

D'Aquisto

1965-1995. James D'Aquisto apprenticed under D'Angelico. He started his own production in '65.

Mandolin

1970s. Various models and appointments.

1970s	Only 3 made	$26,000	$30,000

Dean

1976-present. Intermediate grade, production, acoustic and acoustic/electric mandolins made overseas. They also offer guitars, banjos, basses, and amps.

Dearstone

1993-present. Luthier Ray Dearstone builds his professional and premium grade, custom, mandolin-family instruments in Blountville, Tennessee. He also builds guitars and violins.

DeCava Guitars

1983-present. Premium grade, production/custom, mandolins built by luthier Jim DeCava in Stratford, Connecticut. He also builds guitars, ukes, and banjos.

DeGennaro

2003-present. Professional and premium grade, custom/production, acoustic and electric mandolins built by luthier William Degennaro in Grand Rapids, Michigan. He also builds guitars and basses.

DeLucia, Vincenzo

1910s-1920s. Luthier Vincenzo DeLucia built mandolins in Philadelphia, Pennsylvania.

Mandolin

Early-1900s. High quality material, rosewood body, fine ornamentation.

1910s		$900	$1,100

Dennis Hill Guitars

1991-present. Premium grade, production/custom, mandolins built by luthier Dennis Hill in Panama City, Florida. He has also built dulcimers, guitars, and violins.

MANDOLINS

MODEL YEAR	FEATURES	EXC. COND. LOW	HIGH

Ditson

Mandolins made for the Oliver Ditson Company of Boston, an instrument dealer and music publisher. Turn of the century and early-1900s models were bowl back-style with the Ditson label. The '20s Ditson Style A flat back mandolins were made by Martin. Models were also made by Lyon & Healy of Boston, often with a Ditson Empire label.

Style A Mandolin
1920s. Style A flat back made by Martin, mahogany sides and back, plain ornamentation.

1920s		$750	$900

Victory Bowl Back Mandolin
1890s. Brazilian rib bowl back-style with fancy inlays.

1890s		$450	$800

Dobro

1929-1942, 1954-present. Dobro offered mandolins throughout their early era and from the '60s to the mid-'90s.

Mandolin (wood body)
Resonator on wood body.

1930s		$1,000	$1,300
1940s		$1,000	$1,300
1960s		$850	$1,100

Dudenbostel

1989-present. Luthier Lynn Dudenbostel builds his limited production, premium and presentation grade, custom, mandolins in Knoxville, Tennessee. Started with guitars and added mandolins in '96, started full-time building in '95.

F-5 (Loar) Style
1996-2005. About 30 made.

1996-2005		$24,000	$27,000

Eastman

1992-present. Intermediate and professional grade, production, mandolins built in China. Eastman added mandolins in '04. They also build guitars, violins, and cellos.

EKO

1961-1985, 2000-present. The Italian-made EKOs were imported by LoDuca Brothers of Milwaukee. The brand was revived around 2000, but does not currently include mandolins.

Baritone Mandolin
1960s. Baritone mandolin with ornate inlays.

1960s		$350	$400

Octave Mandolin
1960s. Octave mandolin with ornate inlays.

1960s		$350	$400

Epiphone

1928-present. Intermediate grade, production, acoustic mandolins. Epiphone has offered several mandolin-family models over the years. Those from the '30s to the '60s were U.S.-made, the later models imported.

Adelphi Mandolin
1932-1948. A-style body, maple back and sides, f-holes, single-bound top and back.

1945-1946		$600	$1,000

Mandobird VIII
2004-present. Reverse Firebird-style body with mandolin neck, electric.

2004-2005		$125	$175

MM50
1998-present. Import f-style with The Epiphone logo.

1998-2004		$400	$500

Strand Mandolin
1932-1958. Walnut back and sides, F-holes, multibound, sunburst.

1944		$600	$700

Venetian Electric Mandolin
1961-1970. Gibson-made, pear-shaped body, 4 pole P-90 'dog-ear' mounted pickup, volume and tone knobs, dot markers, sunburst finish.

1961-1964		$1,200	$1,700
1965-1970		$1,000	$1,500

Zephyr Mandolin
1939-1958. A-style, electric, F-holes, maple body, 1 pickup, slotted block inlay.

1950s		$500	$700

Esquire

1930s. Student level instruments with painted Esquire logo and painted wood grain.

Mandolins
1930s. Laminate A-style wood body, sunburst.

1930s		$200	$250

Euphonon

1934-1944. Euphonon was a brand of the Larson Brothers of Chicago. The brand was introduced so Larson could compete in the guitar market with the new larger body 14-fret guitar models. Production also included mandolins, and most models were A-style, with teardrop body and flat backs.

Mandolin
1934-1944. Various models and appointments, each mandolin should be evaluated on a case-by-case basis.

1934-1944	Rosewood	$950	$1,250
1934-1944	Rosewood, fancy trim	$2,500	$3,500

Everett Guitars

1977-present. Luthier Kent Everett, of Atlanta, Georgia, mainly builds guitars, but has also built mandolins.

Evergreen Mountain

1971-present. Professional grade, custom, mandolins built by luthier Jerry Nolte in Cove, Oregon. He also builds guitars and basses.

Epiphone Mandobird VIII

Evergreen Mountain

MANDOLINS

Flatiron A-5

Flatiron Festival

MODEL YEAR	FEATURES	EXC. COND. LOW	HIGH

Fairbanks (A.J.)

1875-ca.1920s. Primarily known for banjos, Fairbanks also offered mandolins.

Mandolin

1890-1910. Typical late-1890s bent top-style mandolin, with decorated top and rope-style binding.

1900s		$250	$450

Fender

1946-present. Intermediate grade, production, acoustic and acoustic/electric mandolins. Fender also offered an electric mandolin for 20 years.

Mandolin

1956-1976. Electric solidbody, often referred to as the Mandocaster by collectors.

1956-1957	Blond	$2,700	$3,000
1958-1959	Sunburst	$2,500	$2,700
1960-1961	Sunburst	$2,200	$2,500
1962-1963	Sunburst	$2,200	$2,400
1964-1965	Sunburst	$2,000	$2,200
1966-1970	Sunburst	$1,800	$2,000
1971-1976	Sunburst	$1,700	$1,800

Fine Resophonic

1988-present. Professional grade, production/custom, wood and metal-bodied resophonic mandolins built by luthiers Mike Lewis and Pierre Avocat in Vitry Sur Seine, France. They also build guitars and ukes.

Flatiron

1977-2003. Gibson purchased Flatiron in 1987. Production was in Bozeman, Montana until the end of '96, when Gibson closed the Flatiron mandolin workshop and moved mandolin assembly to Nashville, Tennessee. General production tapered off after the move and Flatirons were available on a special order basis for a time.

Festival Series

F-holes, maple body and neck, carved spruce top, ebony board.

1977-1987	Style A	$1,100	$1,600
1977-1987	Style F	$2,200	$2,500
1988-1995	Style A	$1,000	$1,400
1988-1995	Style F	$2,000	$2,200

Model 1 Mandolin

Oval shape, spruce top, maple body, rosewood board.

1977-1987	Pre-Gibson	$400	$550
1988-1995	Gibson Montana	$350	$500

Model 2 Mandolin

Oval body, curly maple (MC) or birdseye maple (MB) back and sides, spruce top, ebony 'board.

1977-1987	Pre-Gibson	$400	$550
1977-1995	Flamed koa back and sides	$550	$750
1988-1995	Gibson Montana	$350	$500

Model 2MW Mandola

1977-1987	Pre-Gibson	$550	$650
1988-1995	Gibson Montana	$500	$600

MODEL YEAR	FEATURES	EXC. COND. LOW	HIGH

Model 3 Octave Mandolin

Oval shape, birdseye maple (MB) or curly maple (MC) body, spruce top, ebony 'board, longer scale.

1977-1987	Pre-Gibson	$700	$900
1988-1995	Gibson Montana	$650	$800

Performer Series

Spruce top, maple body, nickel hardware.

1977-1987	Style A	$800	$900
1977-1987	Style F	$1,600	$1,800
1988-1995	Cadet	$500	$550
1988-1995	Style A	$750	$800
1988-1995	Style F	$1,500	$1,600

Signature Series

Introduced in the 1996 catalog, flamed maple body and neck, carved spruce top, rosewood or ebony board.

1996-2003	A-5	$1,400	$1,700
1996-2003	A-5 Artist	$1,400	$1,700
1996-2003	A-5 Junior	$1,100	$1,200
1996-2003	F-5 Artist (Modified Fern)	$3,000	$3,700

Fletcher Brock Stringed Instruments

1992-present. Custom mandolin-family instruments made by luthier Fletcher Brock originally in Ketchum, Idaho, and currently in Seattle, Washington. He also builds guitars.

Framus

1946-1977, 1996-present. Founded in Erlangen, Germany by Fred Wilfer. In the '60s, Framus instruments were imported into the U.S. by Philadelphia Music Company. They offered acoustic and electric mandolins. The brand was revived in '96.

12-string mandolin

1960s		$300	$350

Freshwater

1992-present. Luthier Dave Freshwater and family build mandolin family instruments in Beauly, Inverness, Scotland. They also build bouzoukis, dulcimers and harps.

Mandolin/Mandolin Family

2000s. Lateral Freshwater logo on headstock.

2000s		$450	$550

Fylde

1973-present. Luthier Roger Bucknall builds his intermediate and professional, production/custom mandolins and mandolas in Penrith, Cumbria, United Kingdom. He also builds guitars and basses, bouzoukis, and citterns.

Galiano/A. Galiano

New Yorkers Antonio Cerrito and Raphael Ciani offered instruments built by them and others under the Galiano brand during the early 1900s.

Mandolin
Bowl back, some fancy appointments.

MODEL YEAR	FEATURES	EXC. COND. LOW	HIGH
1920s		$300	$400

Giannini
1900-present. Acoustic mandolins built in Salto, SP, Brazil near Sao Paolo. They also build guitars, violas, and cavaquinhos.

Gibson
1890s-present. Orville Gibson created the violin-based mandolin body-style that replaced the bowl back-type. Currently Gibson offers professional, premium and presentation grade, production/custom, mandolins.

Special Designations:

Snakehead headstock: 1922-1927 with production possible for a few months plus or minus.

Lloyd Loar era: Mid-1922-late 1924 with production possible for a few months plus or minus.

A Mandolin
1902-1933. Oval soundhole, snakehead headstock '22-'27, Loar era mid-'22-late-'24.

1902-1909	Orange Top	$1,000	$1,300
1910-1918	Orange Top	$1,200	$1,600
1918-1921	Brown	$1,500	$1,700
1922-1924	Loar era	$2,500	$3,000
1925-1933		$2,300	$2,500

A Jr. Mandolin
1920-1927. The Junior was the entry level mandolin for Gibson, but like most entry level Gibsons (re: Les Paul Junior), they were an excellent product. Oval soundhole, dot markers, plain tuner buttons. Becomes A-0 in '27.

1920-1927	Sheraton Brown	$1,200	$1,500

A-0 Mandolin
1927-1933. Replaces A Jr., oval soundhole, dot inlay, brown finish.

1927-1933		$1,400	$1,600

A-00 Mandolin
1933-1943. Oval soundhole, dot inlay, carved bound top.

1933-1943	Sunburst	$1,500	$1,900

A-1 Mandolin
1902-1918, 1922-1927, 1933-1943. Snakehead headstock '23-'27.

1902-1918	Orange	$1,400	$1,700
1922-1924	Loar era	$2,500	$3,500
1925-1927	Black	$2,400	$2,900
1927	Not snaked	$2,300	$2,700
1927	Snaked	$2,400	$2,900
1932	Re-introduced, oval	$2,300	$2,700
1933-1943	Sunburst, F-holes	$1,900	$2,100

A-2/A-2Z Mandolin
1902-1908, 1918-1922. A-2Z '22-'27. Renamed A-2 '27-'28. Snakehead headstock '23-'27. Lloyd Loar era mid-'22-late-'24.

1902-1908	Orange	$1,800	$2,000
1918-1921	Brown	$2,000	$2,200

1918-1922	White (optional)	$2,300	$2,700
1922-1924	Loar Era	$3,800	$4,300
1925-1928		$2,800	$3,000

A-3 Mandolin
1902-1922. Oval soundhole, single-bound body, dot inlay.

1902-1905		$1,900	$2,300
1906-1922		$2,400	$2,800

A-4 Mandolin
1902-1935. Oval soundhole, single-bound body, dot inlay, snakehead '23-'27.

1902-1917	Various colors	$2,500	$2,700
1918-1921	Dark mahogany	$2,700	$2,900
1922-1924	Loar era	$4,700	$5,300
1925-1935	Various colors	$3,000	$3,500

A-5 Mandolin
1957-1979. Oval soundhole, maple back and sides, dot inlay, scroll headstock, sunburst.

1957-1964		$2,800	$3,000
1965-1969		$2,700	$2,900
1970-1979		$2,300	$2,700

A-5 G Mandolin
1988-1996. Less ornate version of the A-5 L, abalone fleur-de-lis headstock inlay.

1988-1996		$1,700	$2,000

A-5 L/A-5 Mandolin
1988-present. Extended neck, raised 'board, flowerpot headstock inlay, curly maple and spruce, based on custom-made 1923 Loar A-5.

1988-1999		$2,400	$2,700

A-9 Mandolin
2002-present. Spruce top, maple back and sides, black bound top, satin brown finish.

2002-2004		$950	$1,050

A-12 Mandolin
1970-1979. F-holes, long neck, dot inlay, fleur-de-lis inlay, sunburst.

1970-1979		$1,700	$2,000

A-40 Mandolin
1948-1970. F-holes, bound top, dot inlay, natural or sunburst.

1948-1949		$1,000	$1,300
1950-1964		$900	$1,200
1965-1970		$800	$900

A-50 Mandolin
1933-1971. A-style oval bound body, F-holes, sunburst.

1933-1941	Larger 11.25" body	$1,200	$1,400
1942-1965	Smaller 10" body	$1,000	$1,300
1966-1971		$700	$1,000

A-C Century Mandolin
1935-1937. Flat back, bound body, oval soundhole.

1935-1937	Sunburst	$3,000	$3,200

Army and Navy Special Style DY/Army-Navy Mandolin
1918-1922. Lower-end, flat top and back, round soundhole, no logo, round label with model name. Reintroduced as Army-Navy (AN Custom) '88-'96.

1918-1922	Brown stain	$900	$1,000

Gibson A Junior

Gibson A-9

MANDOLINS

Gibson F-4

1927 Gibson F-5

MODEL YEAR	FEATURES	EXC. COND. LOW	HIGH

Bill Monroe Model F Mandolin
1992-1995. Limited run of 200.

| 1992-1995 | Sunburst | $7,000 | $10,000 |

C-1 Mandolin
1932. Flat top, mahogany back and sides, oval soundhole, painted on 'guard, a '32 version of the Army and Navy Special. This model was private branded for Kel Kroydon in the early-'30s.

| 1932 | Natural | $1,000 | $1,100 |

EM-100/EM-125 Mandolin
1938-1943. Initially called EM-100, renamed EM-125 in '41-'43. Style A (pear-shape) archtop body, 1 blade pickup, 2 knobs on either side of bridge, dot markers, tortoise 'guard, sunburst.

| 1938-1940 | EM-100 | $1,700 | $2,000 |
| 1941-1943 | EM-125 | $1,600 | $1,900 |

EM-150 Mandolin
1936-1971. Electric, A-00 body, 1 Charlie Christian pickup early on, 1 P-90 later, bound body, sunburst.

1936-1940	Charlie Christian pickup	$2,400	$2,600
1941-1949	Rectangular pickup	$2,000	$2,200
1949-1965	P-90 pickup	$2,000	$2,200
1966-1971	P-90 pickup	$1,600	$1,800

EM-200/Florentine Mandolin
1954-1971. Electric solidbody, 1 pickup, gold-plated hardware, 2 control knobs, dot markers, sunburst. Called the EM-200 in '60 and '61.

1954-1960	Florentine	$2,500	$2,800
1960-1961	Renamed EM-200	$2,400	$2,700
1962-1971	Renamed Florentine	$2,300	$2,600

F-2 Mandolin
1902-1934. Oval soundhole, pearl inlay, star and crescent inlay on peghead.

1902-1909	3-point	$3,500	$4,000
1910-1917	2-point	$3,500	$4,000
1918-1921	2-point	$4,200	$5,000
1922-1924	Loar era	$5,500	$7,000
1925-1934		$3,700	$4,500

F-3 Mandolin
1902-1908. Three-point body, oval soundhole, scroll peghead, pearl inlayed 'guard, limited production model, black top with red back and sides.

| 1902-1908 | | $3,700 | $5,000 |

F-4 Mandolin
1902-1943. Oval soundhole, rope pattern binding, various colors.

1902-1909	3-point	$4,000	$5,000
1910-1917	2-point	$4,500	$5,000
1918-1921	2-point	$5,500	$6,000
1922-1924	Loar era	$7,000	$9,000
1925-1943		$5,000	$6,000

F-5 Mandolin
1922-1943; 1949-1980. F-holes, triple-bound body and 'guard. The '20s Lloyd Loar era F-5s are extremely valuable. Reintroduced in '49 with single-bound body, redesigned in '70.

| 1922-1924 | Loar no virzi | $130,000 | $160,000 |
| 1922-1924 | Loar with virzi | $120,000 | $135,000 |

MODEL YEAR	FEATURES	EXC. COND. LOW	HIGH
1923	Loar - exact Monroe specs	$150,000	$170,000
1925-1928	Fern, Master-built	$75,000	$80,000
1928-1929	Fern, not Master-built	$65,000	$70,000
1930-1931	Fern peghead inlay	$55,000	$60,000
1932-1935	Fern peghead inlay	$45,000	$55,000
1936-1940	Fern (limited production)	$40,000	$50,000
1940-1943	Fleur-de-lis peghead inlay	$35,000	$45,000
1949	Flower pot, mahogany neck	$10,000	$15,000
1950-1953	Flower pot, maple neck	$8,000	$9,000
1954	Flower pot peghead inlay	$7,500	$8,500
1955-1956	Flower pot peghead inlay	$7,000	$8,000
1957-1959	Flower pot peghead inlay	$6,500	$7,500
1960-1965		$5,000	$6,000
1966-1969	Sunburst	$4,000	$5,000
1970-1980	Sunburst	$3,200	$4,000

F-5 Bella Voce Mandolin
1989. Custom Shop master-built model, high-end materials and construction, engraved tailpiece with Bella Voce F-5, sunburst.

| 1989 | | $8,500 | $9,000 |

F-5G/F-5G Deluxe
1993-present. Two-point style F, Deluxe has a slightly wider neck profile.

| 1993-1999 | | $3,400 | $3,800 |

F-5 L Mandolin
1978-present. Reissue of Loar F-5, gold hardware, fern headstock inlay (flowerpot inlay with silver hardware also offered for '88-'91), sunburst.

| 1978-1984 | Kalamazoo-made | $4,200 | $4,900 |
| 1984-1999 | | $4,900 | $5,100 |

F-5 Master Model
2003-present. F-holes, triple-bound body and guard, red spruce top, maple back and sides, flowerpot inlay.

| 2003-2004 | | $10,000 | $11,000 |

F-5 V Mandolin
1990s. Based on Lloyd Loar's original F-5s of 1922-24, varnish Cremona Brown sunburst finish.

| 1990s | | $6,500 | $7,000 |

F-5 Wayne Benson Signature
2003. Limited edition of 50, solid spruce top, figured maple back, sides and neck, gold hardware, vintage red satin.

| 2003 | | $5,000 | $5,500 |

Sam Bush F-5 Mandolin
2000-present. Artist Series model, carved spruce top, gold hardware, built at Opry Mill plant in Nashville.

| 2000-2002 | | $5,200 | $5,500 |

F-7 Mandolin
1934-1940. F-holes, single-bound body, neck and 'guard, fleur-de-lis peghead inlay, sunburst.

1934-1937	$9,500	$12,000

F-9 Mandolin
2002-present. F-5 style, carved spruce top, no inlays, black bound body.

2002-2004	$1,800	$2,000

F-10 Mandolin
1934-1936. Slight upgrade of the '34 F-7 with extended 'board and upgraded inlay, black finish.

1934-1936	$9,500	$12,000

F-12 Mandolin
1934-1937, 1948-1980. F-holes, bound body and neck, scroll inlay, raised 'board until '37, 'board flush with top '48-on, sunburst.

1934-1937	$9,500	$12,000
1948-1959	$4,000	$4,500
1960-1969	$3,500	$4,000
1970-1980	$2,500	$3,500

H-1 E Mandola
Late-1930s. Limited number built, electric with built-in adjustable bar pickup, sunburst.

1938	$3,700	$3,900

H-1 Mandola
1902-1936. Has same features as A-1 mandolin, but without snakehead headstock.

1902-1908	Orange	$1,900	$2,100
1918-1921	Brown	$2,000	$2,200
1922-1924	Loar era	$3,800	$4,300
1925-1928		$2,700	$2,900

H-2 Mandola
1902-1922. Has same features as A-4 mandolin.

1902-1917	Various colors	$2,400	$2,900
1918-1921	Dark Mahogany	$2,700	$3,400

H-4 Mandola
1910-1940. Same features as F-4 mandolin.

1910-1921		$4,200	$5,200
1922-1924	Loar era	$7,000	$9,000
1925-1940		$5,500	$8,800

H-5 Mandola
1923-1929 (available by special order 1929-1936), 1990-1991. Same features as the high-end F-5 Mandolin. This is a very specialized market and instruments should be evaluated on a case-by-case basis.

1923-1924	Loar ear	$55,000	$65,000
1925-1928	Fern, Master-built	$40,000	$45,000
1928-1929	Fern, not Master-built	$35,000	$40,000
1990-1991	Limited production	$5,000	$5,500

K-1 Mandocello
1902-1943. Same features as H-1 mandola, off & on production, special order available.

1902-1908	Orange	$3,200	$3,700
1918-1921	Brown	$3,700	$4,200
1922-1924	Loar era	$6,000	$8,000
1925-1943		$3,500	$3,800

K-2 Mandocello
1902-1922. Same features as A-4 mandolin.

1902-1917	Black or Red mahogany	$4,000	$4,400
1918-1922		$4,400	$4,800

K-4 Mandocello
1912-1929 (offered as special order post-1929). Same features as F-4 mandolin, sunburst.

1912-1921		$6,500	$7,000
1922-1924	Loar era	$10,000	$15,000
1925-1929		$7,000	$8,000

M-6 (octave guitar)
2002-present. A-style mandolin body, short-scale 6-string guitar neck.

2002-2004	$1,300	$1,400

MB-1 Mandolin Banjo
1922-1923, 1925-1937.

1922-1923	$1,100	$1,300
1925-1937	$1,100	$1,300

MB-2 Mandolin Banjo
1920-1923, 1926-1937.

1920-1937	$1,200	$1,400

MB-3 Mandolin Banjo
1923-1939.

1923-1939	$1,500	$1,700

MB-4 Mandolin Banjo
1923-1932. Fleur-de-lis inlay.

1923-1932	$1,700	$1,800

MB-Junior Mandolin Banjo
Open back, budget level.

1924-1925	$800	$900

Style J Mando Bass
1912-1930 (special order post-1930). A-style body, 4 strings, round soundhole, bound top, dot inlay.

1912-1930	$4,200	$6,200

Style TL-1 Tenor Lute Mandolin

1924-1926	$1,500	$3,000

Gilchrist
1978-present. Premium and presentation grade, custom, mandolins made by luthier Steve Gilchrist of Warrnambool, Australia. Custom ordered but were also initially distributed through Gruhn Guitars, Nashville, Tennessee and then exclusively by Carmel Music Company. Designs are based upon Gibson mandolins built between 1910 and '25.

Model 5 Mandolin
1978-present. Based on the Gibson '22-'24 Loar-era F-5 mandolin, Gilchrist slant logo, spruce top, flamed maple back, sides, and neck, ebony 'board, multiple binding, sunburst.

1978-1995	Sunburst	$18,000	$21,000
1996-2006	Sunburst	$21,000	$23,000

Givens
1962-1992. Luthier R. L. (Bob) Givens handcrafted about 800 mandolins and another 700 in a production shop.

A Mandolin
1962-1975. Early production A-style.

1962-1975	$1,500	$2,500

Gibson K-2 mandocello

Givens A-4

MANDOLINS

Godin A-8

Gold Tone GM-50

MODEL YEAR	FEATURES	EXC. COND. LOW	HIGH

A-3 Mandolin
Mid-1970s-mid-1980s. Distinguished by use of decal (the only model with Givens decal).

| 1975-1988 | | $1,300 | $2,300 |

A-4 Mandolin
1988-1993. No 'board binding, simple block-like multiple-line RL Givens inlay, nicer maple.

| 1988-1993 | | $1,000 | $2,000 |

A-5 Mandolin
1988-1993. Bound 'board, pearl headstock inlay.

| 1988-1993 | | $1,200 | $2,200 |

A-6 (Torch) Mandolin
1988-1992. Torch inlay (the only model with this), gold hardware, snowflake markers.

| 1988-1992 | | $2,300 | $3,300 |

A-6 Custom Mandolin
1991-1992. Elaborate customized A-6 model.

| 1991-1992 | | $3,000 | $4,000 |

F-5 (Fern) Mandolin
1973-1985. Givens' own version with fern ornamentation.

| 1973-1985 | | $3,300 | $4,300 |

F-5 (Loar) Mandolin
1962-1972. Givens' own version based upon the Loar model F-5.

| 1962-1972 | | $3,300 | $4,300 |

F-5 (Torch) Mandolin
1988-1992. Givens F-5 with torch inlay (the only F model with this).

| 1988-1992 | | $5,500 | $7,500 |

F-5 (Wheat Straw) Mandolin
1986-1988. Givens F-5-style with wheat straw ornamentation.

| 1986-1988 | | $4,800 | $6,000 |

G.L. Stiles
1960-1994. Built by Gilbert Lee Stiles in Florida. He also built acoustics, soldibodies, basses, steels, and banjos.

Mandolin

| 1960s | | $400 | $550 |

Godin
1987-present. Intermediate grade, production, acoustic/electric mandolins from luthier Robert Godin. They also build basses and guitars.

A-8 Mandolin
2000-present. Single-cut chambered body, acoustic/electric.

| 2000-2003 | | $450 | $550 |

Gold Tone
1993-present. Wayne and Robyn Rogers build their intermediate grade, production/custom mandolins in Titusville, Florida. They also offer lap steels, basses, banjos and banjitars.

Goya
1955-present. Korean-made mandolins. They also build guitars and banjos. Originally made in Sweden, by the late '70s from Japan, then from Korea.

MODEL YEAR	FEATURES	EXC. COND. LOW	HIGH

Mandolin

1960s	Japan/Korea	$150	$200
1960s	Sweden Built	$200	$300
1970s	Sweden Built	$200	$300

Gretsch
1883-present. Gretsch started offering mandolins by the early 1900s. Currently Gretsch does not offer mandolins.

New Yorker Mandolin
Late 1940s-late 1950s. Teardrop shape, F-holes, arched top and back, spruce top, maple back, sides, and neck, rosewood 'board.

| 1950s | | $500 | $800 |

GTR
1974-1978. GTR (for George Gruhn, Tut Taylor, Randy Wood) was the original name for Gruhn Guitars in Nashville, Tennessee (it was changed in '76). GTR imported mandolins and banjos from Japan. An A-style (similar to a current Gibson A-5 L) and an F-style (similar to mid- to late-'20s F-5 with fern pattern) were offered. The instruments were made at the Moridaira factory in Matsumoto, Japan by factory foreman Sadamasa Tokaida. Quality was relatively high but quantities were limited.

A-Style Mandolin
1974-1978. A5-L copy with GTR logo on headstock.

| 1974-1978 | | $1,400 | $1,600 |

F-Style Mandolin
1974-1978. F-5 Fern copy with slant GTR logo on headstock, handmade in Japan.

| 1974-1978 | Sunburst | $2,400 | $2,600 |

Harmony
1982-1976. Founded by Wilhelm Schultz in 1892, and purchased by Sears in 1916. The company evolved into one of the largest producers of stringed instruments in the U.S. in the '30s.

Baroque H35/H835 Electric Mandolin
Late 1960s-early 1970s. Electric version of Baroque H425 with single pickup and two controls.

| 1969-1970 | H35 | $350 | $400 |
| 1971-1976 | H835 | $300 | $400 |

Baroque H425/H8025 Mandolin
F-style arched body, extreme bass bout pointy horn, close grained spruce top, sunburst.

| 1969-1970 | H425 | $300 | $350 |
| 1971-1976 | H8025 | $250 | $300 |

Lute H331/H0831 Mandolin
1960s-1970s. A-style, flat top and back, student level.

| 1960s | H331 | $100 | $200 |
| 1970s | H8031 | $100 | $200 |

Monterey H410/H417/H8017 Mandolin
1950s-1970s. A-style arched body with f-holes, sunburst.

| 1955-1970 | | $100 | $200 |

MODEL YEAR	FEATURES	EXC. COND. LOW	HIGH

Heiden Stringed Instruments

1974-present. Luthier Michael Heiden builds his premium grade, production/custom mandolins in Chilliwack, British Columbia. He also builds guitars.

Heritage

1985-present. Started by former Gibson employees in Gibson's Kalamazoo, Michigan plant, Heritage offered mandolins for a number of years.

H-5 Mandolin

1986-1990s. F-style scroll body, f-holes.

1980s		$3,000	$4,000

Hofner

1887-present. Hofner has offered a wide variety of instruments, including mandolins, over the years. They currently do not offer a mandolin.

Model 545/E545 Mandolin

1960s. Pear-shaped A-style with catseye F-holes, block-style markers, engraved headstock, Genuine Hofner Original and Made in Germany on back of headstock, transparent brown.

1968-1969	545 (acoustic)	$325	$425
1968-1969	E545 (acoustic-electric)	$425	$475

Hohner

1857-present. Intermediate grade, production, acoustic and acoustic/electric mandolins. They also offer guitars, basses, and ukes.

Hondo

1969-1987, 1991-present. Budget grade, production, imported mandolins. They also offer basses and guitars. Hondo also offered mandolins from around '74 to '87.

Mandolin

1974-1987. Hondo offered F-style, A-style, and bowl back mandolin models.

1970s	Acoustic	$100	$150
1970s	Acoustic-electric	$150	$200

Hopf

1906-present. Professional grade, production/custom, mandolins made in Germany. They also make basses, guitars and flutes.

Howe-Orme

1897-ca. 1910. Elias Howe patented a guitar-shaped mandolin on November 14, 1893 and later partnered with George Orme to build a variety of mandolin family instruments and guitars.

Mandola

1897-early-1900s. Guitar body-style with narrow waist, not the common mandolin F- or S-style body, pressed (not carved) spruce top, mahogany back and sides, flat-top guitar-type trapeze bridge, decalomania near bridge.

1890s	Natural	$1,400	$1,700

Mandolinetto

Guitar body, mandolin neck and tuning, 'guard below oval soundhole, slightly arched top, Brazilian rosewood sides and back, dot/diamond/oval markers.

1890s		$1,800	$1,900

Ibanez

1932-present. Ibanez offered mandolins from '65 to '83. In '04 they again added mandolins to the product line.

Model 513 Mandolin

1974-1979. A-5 copy with double cutaways, oval sound hole, dot markers.

1974-1979	Sunburst	$325	$425

Model 514 Mandolin

1974-1979. Arched back, spruce, rosewood, dot inlays.

1974-1979	Sunburst	$325	$400

Model 524 Artist Mandolin

1974-1978. F-5 Loar copy, solid wood carved top and solid wood carved top and solid wood back.

1974-1978	Sunburst	$750	$950

Model 526 (electric) Mandolin

1974-1978. A-style body, single pickup, two control knobs, sunburst.

1974-1978		$400	$450

Model 529 Artist Mandolin

1982-1983. F-5 Loar era copy, solid wood carved top and solid wood spruce top and solid maple sides and back.

1982-1983	Sunburst	$800	$1,000

Imperial

1890-1922. Imperial mandolins were made by the William A. Cole Company of Boston, Massachusetts.

Bowl Back Mandolin

1890s		$300	$400

J.B. Player

1980s-present. Budget grade, production, imported mandolins. They also offer basses, banjos and guitars.

J.R. Zeidler Guitars

1977-present. Luthier John Zeidler builds his premium grade, custom, mandolins in Wallingford, Pennsylvania. He also builds guitars.

John Le Voi Guitars

1970-present. Production/custom, mandolin family instruments built by luthier John Le Voi in Lincolnshire, United Kingdom. He also builds guitars.

Johnson

Mid-1990s-present. Budget and intermediate grade, production, mandolins imported by Music Link, Brisbane, California. Johnson also offers guitars, amps, basses and effects.

Ibanez M510

Hohner HMA

MANDOLINS

Kalamazoo A-style

1950s Kay K73

MODEL YEAR	FEATURES	EXC. COND. LOW	HIGH

MA Series A-Style Mandolin
Mid-1990s-present. Import, A-style copy, plain Johnson logo on headstock. Several levels offered; the range shown is for all value levels.

1990s		$100	$175

MF Series F-Style Mandolin
Mid-1990s-present. Import, F-style copy, plain Johnson logo on headstock. Several levels offered; the range shown is for all value levels.

1990s	Sunburst	$150	$300

K & S
1992-1998. Mandolins and mandolas distributed by George Katechis and Marc Silber and handmade in Paracho, Mexico. They also offered guitars and ukes.

Kalamazoo
1933-1942, 1946-1947, 1965-1970. Budget brand produced by Gibson in Kalamazoo, Michigan. They offered mandolins until '42.

Kalamazoo/Oriole A-Style Mandolin
1930s. Kalamazoo and Oriole on the headstock, KM/A-style.

1930s		$850	$900

KM-11 Mandolin
1935-1941. Gibson-made, A-style, flat top and back, round soundhole, dot inlay.

1935-1941	Sunburst	$750	$850

KM-21 Mandolin
1936-1940. Gibson-made, A-style, f-holes, arched bound spruce top and mahogany back.

1936-1940	Sunburst	$850	$950

KMB Mandolin/Banjo
1930s. Banjo-mandolin with resonator.

1930s		$450	$500

Kay
1931-present. Located in Chicago, Illinois, the Kay company made an incredible amount of instruments under a variety of brands, including the Kay name. From the beginning, Kay offered several types of electric and acoustic mandolins. In '69, the factory closed, marking the end of American-made Kays. The brand survives today on imported instruments.

K68/K465 Concert Mandolin
1952-1968. Pear-shape, close-grain spruce top, genuine mahogany back and sides. Renamed the K465 in '66. Kay also offered a Venetian-style mandolin called the K68 in '37-'42.

1952-1968	Natural	$200	$250

K73 Mandolin
1939-1952. Solid spruce top, maple back and sides, A-style body, F-holes, cherry sunburst.

1939-1952		$200	$250

K390/K395 Professional Electric Mandolin
1960-1968. Modified Venetian-style archtop, 1 pickup, F-hole, spruce top, curly maple back and sides, sunburst finish. Renamed K395 in '66.

1960-1968		$350	$550

K494/K495 Electric Mandolin
1960-1968. A-style archtop, single metal-covered (no poles) pickup, volume and tone control knobs, the K494 was originally about 60% of the price of the K390 model (see above) in '65. Renamed K495 in '66.

1960-1968	Sunburst	$350	$450

Kay Kraft
1931-1937. First brand name of the newly formed Kay Company. Brand replaced by Kay in '37.

Mandolin
1931-1937. Kay Kraft offered Venetian- and teardrop-shaped mandolins.

1931-1937		$275	$350

Kel Kroydon (by Gibson)
1930-1933. Private branded budget level made by Gibson.

KK-20 (Style C-1) Mandolin
1930-1933. Flat top, near oval-shaped body, oval soundhole, natural finish, dark finish mahogany back and sides.

1930-1933		$600	$800

Kent
1961-1969. Japanese-made instruments. Kent offered teardrop, A style, and bowlback acoustic mandolins up to '68.

Acoustic Mandolin
1961-1968. Kent offered teardrop, A-style, and bowlback acoustic mandolins up to '68.

1961-1968		$100	$150

Electric Mandolin
1964-1969. Available from '64-'66 as a solidbody electric (in left- and right-hand models) and from '67-'69 an electric hollowbody Venetian-style with F-holes (they called it violin-shaped).

1964-1969		$150	$200

Kentucky (Saga M.I.)
1977-present. Brand name of Saga Musical Instruments currently offering budget, intermediate, and professional grade, production, A- and F-style mandolins.

KM Series

2000s	KM-140 A-style	$100	$125
2000s	KM-150 A-style	$125	$150
2000s	KM-630 F-style	$300	$450
2000s	KM-700 F-style	$375	$425
2000s	KM-800 F-style	$400	$450

Kingston
Ca. 1958-1967. Japanese imports. See Guitar section for more company info.

Acoustic Mandolin

1960s		$125	$175

EM1 Electric Mandolin
1964-1967. Double-cut solidbody electric, 15.75" scale, 1 pickup.

1960s		$125	$200

MODEL		EXC. COND.	
YEAR	FEATURES	LOW	HIGH

Knutsen

1890s-1920s. Luthier Chris J. Knutsen of Tacoma/Seattle, Washington.

Harp Mandolin

1910s. Harp mandolin with tunable upper bass bout with 4 drone strings, and standard mandolin neck. The mandolin version of a harp guitar.

1910s		$4,500	$5,000

Knutson Luthiery

1981-present. Professional and premium grade, custom, acoustic and electric mandolins built by luthier John Knutson in Forestville, California. He also builds guitars and basses.

Kona

2001-present. Budget grade, production, acoustic mandolins made in Asia. They also offer guitars, basses and amps.

La Scala

Ca. 1920s-1930s. A brand of the Oscar Schmidt Company of New Jersey, used on guitars, banjos, and mandolins. These were often the fanciest of the Schmidt instruments.

Lakeside (Lyon & Healy)

Early-1900s. Mainly catalog sales of guitars and mandolins from the Chicago maker. Marketed as a less expensive alternative to the Lyon & Healy Washburn product line.

Style G2016 12-String Mandolin

Early-1900s. 12-string, 18 mahogany ribs with white inlay between, celluloid guard plate, advertised as an inexpensive instrument, possessing a good tone, correct scale, and durable construction.

1917		$300	$400

Lakewood

1986-present. Luthier Martin Seeliger builds his professional grade, production/custom, mandolins in Giessen, Germany. He also builds guitars.

Larson Brothers (Chicago)

1900-1944. Made by luthiers Carl and August Larson and marketed under a variety of names including Stetson, Maurer, and Prairie State.

Bowl Back Mandolin

1900s. Neopolitan-style (bowl back) with 36 Brazilian rosewood ribs, spruce top, engraved rosewood 'guard, fancy abalone trim and headstock inlay.

1900		$450	$650

Flat Back Mandolin

1910s. Brazilian rosewood back and sides, standard appointments, dot markers, rope binding.

1910s		$700	$800

Harp-Mandolin Style 35

1920s. Harp-style body with extended upper bass bout horn without drone strings.

1920		$4,000	$6,500

Laurie Williams Guitars

1983-present. Luthier Laurie Williams builds his premium grade, custom/production, acoustic mandolins on the North Island of New Zealand. He also builds guitars.

Levin

1900-1973. Acoustic mandolins built in Sweden. Levin was best known for their classical guitars, which they also built for other brands, most notably Goya. They also built ukes.

Lotus

Late-1970-present. Acoustic mandolins imported by Musicorp. They also offered banjos and guitars.

Lyon & Healy

1964-ca. 1945. Lyon & Healy was a large musical instrument builder and marketer, and produced under many different brands.

Style A Mandocello

Scroll peghead, symmetrical 2-point body, natural.

1910s		$4,000	$8,000
1920s		$4,000	$8,000

Style A Professional Mandolin

Violin scroll peghead, natural.

1918		$3,000	$4,000

Style B Mandolin

Maple back and sides, 2-point body, natural.

1920		$1,500	$2,000

Style C Mandolin

1920s. Like Style A teardrop Gibson body style, oval soundhole, carved spruce top, carved maple back, natural.

1920s		$1,500	$2,000

Lyra

1920s-1930s. Private brand made by Regal, Lyra name plate on headstock.

Style A (scroll) Mandolin

1920s-1930s. Scroll on upper bass bout.

1925-1935		$400	$450

Maccaferri

1923-1990. Mario Maccaferri made a variety of instruments over his career. He produced award-winning models in Italy and France until he fled to the U.S. due to WW II. He applied the new plastic to a highly successful line of instruments after the war. A mandolin was about the only stringed instument they didn't offer in plastic. His Europe-era instruments are very rare.

Mandolins/Mandolas made by Maccaferri:
1928-ca. '31: No. 1 Mandolone, No. 2 Mandoloncello, No. 3 Mandola Baritono, No. 4 Mandola Tenore, No. 5 Mandola Soprano, No. 6 Mandolino, No. 7 Quartino.

Levin Model 350

Lakewood

MANDOLINS

Martin 2-15

Michael Kelly Evolution

MODEL YEAR	FEATURES	EXC. COND. LOW	HIGH

Martin

1833-present. Martin got into the mandolin market in 1896 starting with the typical bowl back designs. By 1914, Gibson's hot selling, innovative, violin-based mandolin pushed Martin into a flat back, bent top hybrid design. By '29, Martin offered a carved top and carved back mandolin. Most models were discontinued in '41, partially because of World War II. Currently Martin offers only a Backpacker mandolin.

Style 0 Mandolin
1905-1925. Bowl back-style, 18 rosewood ribs, solid peghead.

1905-1925		$800	$900

Style 00 Mandolin
1908-1925. Bowl back-style, 9 rosewood ribs (14 ribs by '24), solid peghead.

1908-1925		$600	$800

Style 000 Mandolin
1914 only. Bowl back, solid peghead, dot inlay, 9 mahogany ribs.

1914		$500	$700

Style 1 Mandolin
1898-1924. Bowl back, German silver tuners, 18 ribs.

1898-1924		$850	$950

Style 2 Mandolin
1898-1924. Bowl back, 26 rosewood ribs, higher appointments than Style 1.

1898-1924		$900	$1,000

Style 2-15 Mandolin
1936-1964. Carved spruce top, maple back and sides, F-hole, single-bound back, solid headstock.

1936-1964		$1,000	$1,400

Style 2-20 Mandolin
1936-1941. Carved spruce triple-bound top and bound maple back and sides, F-hole, dot inlay.

1936-1942		$1,900	$2,100

Style 2-30 Mandolin
1937-1941. Carved spruce top and maple back and sides, multi-bound, F-holes, diamond and square inlays.

1937-1941		$3,000	$3,300

Style 5 Mandolin
1898-1920. Bowl back, vine inlay, abalone top trim.

1898-1899		$2,000	$2,400
1900-1909		$1,900	$2,400
1910-1920		$1,900	$2,400

Style 6 Mandolin
1898-1921. Bowl back, top bound with ivory and abalone, vine or snowflake inlay.

1919	Snowflake inlay	$2,400	$2,700

Style 20S Mandolin
1949-1957. 30 made, special ordered for Carlos DeFilipis, decorative point on each side of body, oval sound hole, carved spruce top, carved curley maple back.

1949-1957		$2,000	$2,300

MODEL YEAR	FEATURES	EXC. COND. LOW	HIGH

Style A Mandolin
1914-1995. Flat back, oval soundhole, dot inlay, solid headstock.

1914-1919		$950	$1,200
1920-1939		$1,000	$1,200
1940-1949		$900	$1,100
1950-1969		$800	$1,000
1970-1995		$700	$900

Style AK Mandolin
1920-1937. Koa wood version of Style A, flat back.

1920-1937		$1,100	$1,400

Style B Mandolin
1914-1946, 1981-1987. Flat back with bent top, spruce top and rosewood back and sides, herringbone back stripe, multi-bound.

1914-1919		$1,000	$1,500
1920-1939		$1,100	$1,500
1940-1946		$1,000	$1,400
1981-1987		$700	$1,000

Style BB Mandola
1917-1921, 1932-1939. Brazilian rosewood, herringbone trim, features like Style B mandolin. This is the only Mandola offered.

1917-1921		$1,500	$2,000

Style C Mandolin
1914-1934. Flat back.

1914-1934		$2,700	$2,800

Style D Mandolin
1914-1916. Flat back.

1914-1916		$4,500	$5,000

Style E Mandolin
1915-1937. Flat back, rosewood back and sides, bent spruce top, Style 45 snowflake fretboard inlay and other high-end appointments. Highest model cataloged.

1915-1919		$4,500	$5,000
1920-1929		$4,000	$4,500
1930-1937		$4,000	$4,500

Maurer

Maurer Mandolins from the 1930s include Style 30 Flat Model, Style 40, Octave Mandola Style 45, Mandocello Style 50, and Mandola Tenor.

Mandolin
Brazilian rosewood, birdseye maple, bowl back.

1930		$1,000	$1,200

May Flower

Ca. 1901-1910. H. J. Flower's Chicago-based May Flower Music Company offered bowl back mandolins that he may or may not have built. There were also May Flower harp guitars built by others.

Bowl Back Mandolin
1901-1910. Mid-level bowl back-style with 19 rosewood ribs and mid-level appointments.

1901-1910		$750	$1,100

MODEL YEAR	FEATURES	EXC. COND. LOW	HIGH

Menzenhauer & Schmidt

1894-1904. Founded by Frederick Menzenhauer and Oscar Schmidt International. Menzenhauer created the guitar-zither in the U.S. He had several patents including one issued in September 1899 for a mandolin-guitar-zither. Control of operations quickly went to Oscar Schmidt.

12-String Mandolin

1890s. Bowl back mandolin with 3 strings per course that were tuned in octaves, designed during an experimental era for mandolin-related instrumetns, 13 rosewood ribs, spruce top, inlays.

1890s		$200	$300

Michael Kelly

2000-present. Intermediate and professional grade, production, imported, acoustic and acoustic/electric mandolins. They also offer guitars and basses.

Michael Lewis Instruments

1992-present. Luthier Michael Lewis builds his premium grade, custom, mandolins in Grass Valley, California. He also builds guitars.

Mid-Missouri

1995-present. Intermediate grade, production, acoustic and electric mandloins and mandolas built by luthier Michael Dulak in Columbia, Missouri.

M Series Mandolin

1995-1999. Teardrop A-style body, solid spruce top, solid maple, mahogany or rosewood back and sides.

1995-1999	M-0	$325	$375
1995-1999	M-1	$375	$425
1995-1999	M-2	$425	$475
1995-1999	M-3	$475	$525
1995-1999	M-4	$525	$675

Mirabella

1997-present. Professional and premium grade, mandolins built by luthier Cristian Mirabella in Babylon, New York. He also builds guitars and ukes.

Monteleone

1971-present. Primarily a guitar maker, luthier John Monteleone also builds presentation grade, custom, mandolins in West Islip, New York.

Grand Artist Mandola

1979-present. 15 7/8" scale until '90, then 17".

1979-1995		$23,000	$25,000

Grand Artist Mandolin

1977-present. Style F body, spruce top, curly maple back and sides, dot markers, currently offered in a Standard and Deluxe model.

1977-1989		$25,000	$28,000
1990-2003		$23,000	$27,000

Radio Flyer Mandolin

1996-present. Style F body, currently offered in a Standard and Deluxe model.

1996-2000		$29,000	$33,000

Style B Mandolin

1982-present. Long A body style with long F-holes, flamed curly maple back and sides, elongated fretboard over body.

1982-1990	Sunburst	$15,000	$17,000

Moon

1979-present. Intermediate and professional grade, production/custom, acoustics and acoustic/electric mandolins and mandolas built by luthier Jimmy Moon in Glasgow, Scotland. They also build guitars.

Morales

Ca.1967-1968. Japanese-made, not heavily imported into the U.S.

Electric Mandolin

1967-1968.

1967-1968		$225	$300

Morgan Monroe

1999-present. Intermediate and professional grade, production, acoustic mandolins made in Korea and distributed by SHS International of Indianapolis, Indiana. They also offer guitars, basses, banjos, and fiddles.

Mozzani

Late-1800s-early-1900s. Founder Luigi Mozzani was an Italian (Bologna) master luthier and renowned composer and musician. There are original Mozzani-built mandolins and also factory-built instruments made later at various workshops.

Mandolin

Factory-built bowl back model.

1920s		$300	$400

Original Bowl Back Mandolin

Late-1800s-early-1900s. Handcrafted by Luigi Mozzani, about 24 ribs, soundhole ornamentation, snowflake-like markers.

1904		$1,200	$1,500

National

Ca.1927-present. The National brand has gone through many ownership changes and offered resonator mandolins from around 1927 to '41. Currently, National does not offer a mandolin.

Style 0 Mandolin

1931-early-1940s. Metal body with Hawaiian scenes, single-cone resonator.

1930s	Hawaiian scene	$3,000	$4,000

Style 1 Mandolin

1928-1936. Plain metal body, tri-cone resonator.

1928-1936	Single cone	$2,000	$2,500
1928-1936	Tricone version	$3,500	$4,000

Style 2 Mandolin

1928-1936. Metal body with rose engraving, tri-cone resonator.

1928-1936	Single cone	$4,000	$5,000
1928-1936	Tricone version	$6,000	$7,000

Monteleone Grand Artist

National Style 2

MANDOLINS

Nyberg Instruments mandola

Ovation

MODEL YEAR	FEATURES	EXC. COND. LOW	HIGH
Style 3 Mandolin			
1930s	Single cone	$5,000	$6,500
1930s	Tricone version	$6,000	$7,500
Style 97 Mandolin			
1936-1940. Metal body, tri-cone resonator.			
1936-1940		$4,000	$8,000
Triolian Mandolin			
1928-1940. Metal body with palm trees, single-cone resonator.			
1928-1940	Single cone	$1,500	$2,500

Northworthy

1987-present. Professional and premium grade, production/custom, mandolin-family instruments built by luthier Alan Marshall in Ashbourne, Derbyshire, England. He also builds guitars.

Nugget

1970s-present. Luthier Mike Kemnitzer builds his premium grade mandolins in Central Lake, Michigan.

Nyberg Instruments

1993-present. Professional grade, custom, mandolins and mandolas built by luthier Lawrence Nyberg in Hornby Island, British Columbia. He also builds guitars, bouzoukis and citterns.

O'Dell, Doug

See listing under Old Town.

Old Hickory

2005-present. Budget grade, production, imported F- and A-style acoustic mandolins from Musician's Wholesale America, Nashville, Tennessee. They also offer banjos.

MODEL YEAR	FEATURES	EXC. COND. LOW	HIGH
Style A Mandolin			
2005	AC-1 mid-level	$75	$100
2005	FC-100 highest level	$125	$200
2005	M-1 lowest level	$40	$60

Old Kraftsman

1930s-1960s. Brand name used by the Siegel Company on instruments made by Kay and others (even Gibson). Quality was mixed, but some better-grade instruments were offered.

MODEL YEAR	FEATURES	EXC. COND. LOW	HIGH
Mandolin			
1950s		$250	$350

Old Town

1974-present. Luthier Doug O'Dell builds his professional and premium grade, production/custom acoustic and electric mandolins in Ohio.

EM-10 Electric Mandolin
1980s-present. Double-cut, flamed maple top, 1 pickup, 2 control knobs.

MODEL YEAR	FEATURES	EXC. COND. LOW	HIGH
1980s		$1,800	$2,000

Old Wave

1990-present. Luthier Bill Bussmann builds his professional and premium grade, production/custom, mandolins and mandolas in Caballo, New Mexico. He has also built guitars and basses.

Orpheum

1897-1942, 1944-early 1970s, 2001-present. Currently intermediate grade, production, mandolins. They also offer guitars. An old brand often associated with banjos, 1930s branded guitars sold by Bruno and Sons. 1950s branded guitars and mandolins sold by Maurice Lipsky Music, New York, New York.

Electric Mandolin Model 730 E
1950s. Private branded for Maurice Lipsky. Cataloged as a student model designed for ensemble playing. A-style body, single neck bar pickup, 2 side-mounted knobs, spruce top, maple back and sides, dot markers, sunburst.

MODEL YEAR	FEATURES	EXC. COND. LOW	HIGH
1950s		$500	$650

Model No. 2 Mandolin-Banjo
1920s. Mandolin neck on small banjo body, fancy headstock and fretboard inlay, carved heel.

MODEL YEAR	FEATURES	EXC. COND. LOW	HIGH
1920s		$500	$600

Oscar Schmidt

1879-ca. 1939, 1979-present. Currently offering budget and intermediate grade, production, mandolins. They also offer guitars, banjos, and autoharps. The original Schmidt company offered innovative mandolin designs during the 1900-'30 mandolin boom.

Mandolin Harp Style B
1890s. More zither-autoharp than mandolin, flat autoharp body with soundhole.

MODEL YEAR	FEATURES	EXC. COND. LOW	HIGH
1890s		$100	$125

Sovereign Mandolin
1920s. Bowl back, bent top, rope-style binding, mahogany ribs, dot inlay, plain headstock.

MODEL YEAR	FEATURES	EXC. COND. LOW	HIGH
1920s	Natural	$175	$300

Ovation

1966-present. Known for innovative fiberglass-backed bowl back acoustic and acoustic/electric guitars, Ovation added mandolins in '94 and currently offers intermediate and professional grade, production, mandolins.

Celebrity Mandolin
1994-present. Single-cut, small Ovation body, Ovation headstock.

MODEL YEAR	FEATURES	EXC. COND. LOW	HIGH
1990s	Red Sunburst	$400	$500

P. W. Crump Company

1975-present. Luthier Phil Crump builds his custom mandolin-family instruments in Arcata, California. He also builds guitars.

MODEL YEAR	FEATURES	EXC. COND. LOW	HIGH

Paris Swing

2005-present. Intermediate grade, production, imported acoustic mandolins from The Music Link, which also offers instruments under the Johnson and other brands.

Penco

Ca. 1974-1978. Japanese-made copies of classic American mandolins. They also made guitars, basses and banjos.

Phantom Guitar Works

1992-present. Intermediate grade, production, solidbody MandoGuitars assembled in Clatskanie, Oregon. They also build guitars and basses.

Phoenix

1990-present. Premium grade, production/custom, mandolins built by luthier Rolfe Gerhardt (formerly builder of Unicorn Mandolins in the '70s) in South Thomaston, Maine. Gerhard's Phoenix company specializes in a 2-point Style A (double-cut) body style.

Bluegrass (double-point) Mandolin

1990-present. Double-point shallow body voiced for bluegrass music, adirondack spruce top, figured maple body.

1990s	Sunburst	$2,000	$2,500

Premier

Ca.1938-ca.1975, 1990s-present. Brand produced by Peter Sorkin Music Company in New York City. Around '57 the company acquired Strad-O-Lin and many of their mandolins were offered under that brand. By '75, the Premier brand went into hiatus. The Premier brand currently appears on Asian-made solidbody guitars and basses.

Ramsey

1990s. Built by luthier John Ramsey of Colorado Springs, Colorado.

Randy Wood Guitars

1968-present. Premium and presentation grade, custom/production, mandolins, mandolas, and mandocellos built by luthier Randy Woods in Bloomingdale, Georgia. He also builds guitars and banjos.

Ratliff

1982-present. Professional and premium grade, production/custom, mandolin family instruments built in Church Hill, Tennessee.

R-5 Mandolin

1990s-present. F-5 style, carved spruce top, figured maple back and sides.

1995-2004		$2,000	$2,500

Recording King

1929-1943. Montgomery Ward house brand. Suppliers include Gibson, Kay, Regal, and Gretsch.

Mandolin (Gibson-made)

1929-1940. A-style body.

1930s	Sunburst	$450	$600

Regal

Ca.1884-1954. Large Chicago-based manufacturer which made their own brand name and others for distributors and mass merchandisers. Absorbed by the Harmony Company in 1955.

Mandolin

1920s	Flat-top A-style	$375	$500
1930s	Sunburst, standard model	$375	$500
1930s	Ultra Grand Deluxe model	$700	$1,000

Octophone Mandolin

1920s. Octave mandolin, long body with double points, round soundhole.

1920s		$700	$1,000

Resonator Mandolin

1950s		$400	$500

Rigel

1990-2006. Professional and premium grade, production/custom mandolins and mandolas built by luthier Pete Langdell in Hyde Park, Vermont.

A-Plus Series

1990s-present. A-style body, carved spruce top, maple back and sides, dot markers.

1990s	A-Plus (f-holes)	$1,000	$1,400
1990s	A-Plus (oval soundhole)	$1,000	$1,100

Classic S

2000s	Double cutaway, f-holes	$1,500	$2,000

Model G-110 Mandolin

1990-present. Maple neck, back and sides, red spruce top, f-holes.

1990s	Sunburst	$2,000	$2,300

Roberts

1980s. Built by luthier Jay Roberts of California.

Tiny Moore Jazz 5 Mandolin

1980s. Based on Bigsby design of the early-1950s as used by Tiny Moore, five-string electric.

1985	Sunburst	$1,600	$1,800

Rogue

2001-present. Budget grade, production, imported mandolins. They also offer guitars, basses, ukes, banjos, effects and amps.

Rono

1967-present. Luthier Ron Oates builds his professional grade, production/custom, electric mandolins in Boulder, Colorado. He also builds basses and guitars.

Regal Fancy Scroll

Rigel A-Plus Oval Deluxe

MANDOLINS

Sawchyn Custom A-Style

Tacoma M-3

MODEL YEAR	FEATURES	EXC. COND. LOW	HIGH

Samick
1958-2001, 2002-present. Budget and intermediate grade, production, imported acoustic and acoustic/electric mandolins. They also offer guitars, basses, ukes and banjos.

Sammo
1920s. Labels in these instruments state they were made by the Osborne Mfg. Co. with an address of Masonic Temple, Chicago, Illinois. High quality and often with a high degree of ornamentation. They also made ukes and guitars.

Sawchyn
1972-present. Intermediate and professional grade, production/custom, mandolins built by luthier Peter Sawchyn in Regina, Saskatchewan. He also builds flat-top and flamenco guitars.

Sekova
Mid-1960s-mid-1970s. Entry level, imported by the U.S. Musical Merchandise.
Electric Mandolin
1960s-1970s. Kay-Kraft-style hollowbody with F-holes, 1 pickup and Sekova logo on the headstock.

1965-1970s		$200	$300

Silvertone
1941-ca.1970. Brand name used by Sears on their musical instruments.
Mandolin
Arched top and back.

1940s	Sunburst	$175	$300
1950s	Sunburst	$175	$300

Smart Musical Instruments
1986-present. Premium and presentation grade, custom, mandolin family instruments built by luthier A. Lawrence Smart in McCall, Idaho. He also builds guitars.

Sovereign
Ca. 1899-ca. 1938. Sovereign was originally a brand of the Oscar Schmidt company of New Jersey. In the late '30s, Harmony purchased several trade names from the Schmidt Company, including Sovereign. Sovereign then ceased as a brand, but Harmony continued using it on a model line of Harmony guitars.
Mandolins
1920s. Old-style bent top.

1920s		$250	$400

S. S. Stewart
1878-1904. S.S. Stewart of Philadelphia was primarily known for banjos. Legend has it that Stewart was one of the first to demonstrate the mass production assembly of stringed instruments.
Mandolin Banjo
Early-1900s. Mandolin neck and a very small open back banjo body, star inlay in headstock.

1900s		$325	$450

Stahl
William C. Stahl instruments were made (per their literature they were not manufactured) in Milwaukee, Wisconsin, in the early-1900s. Models included Style 4 (22 ribs) to Style 12 Presentation Artist Special. The more expensive models were generally 44-rib construction.
Arched Back Presentation
1910s. Brazilian rosewood back and sides, very fancy abalone appointments.

1910s		$2,000	$4,000

Bowl Back Mandolin (deluxe professional model)
Rosewood, 40 ribs.

1910s		$800	$1,200

Bowl Back Mandolin (mid-level)
Pearl floral design on 'guard, 32 ribs.

1910s		$350	$550

Stathopoulo
1903-1916. Original design instruments, some patented, by Epiphone company founder A. Stathopoulo.
A-Style Mandolin
1903-1916. A-style with higher-end appointments, bent-style spruce top, figured maple back and sides.

1912		$800	$1,200

Stefan Sobell Musical Instruments
1982-present. Luthier Stefan Sobell builds his premium grade, production/custom, mandolins in Hetham, Northumberland, England. He also builds guitars, citterns and bouzoukis.
10-String Mandolin

1988		$2,700	$3,700

Stella
Ca. 1899-1974, present. Stella was a brand of the Oscar Schmidt Company which was an early contributor to innovative mandolin designs and participated in the 1900-'30 mandolin boom. Pre-World War II Stella instruments were low-mid to mid-level instruments. In '39, Harmony purchased the Stella name and '50s and '60s Stella instruments were student grade, low-end instruments. The Stella brand has been reintroduced by MBT International.
Banjo-Mandolin
1920s. One of several innovative designs that attempted to create a new market, 8-string mandolin neck with a banjo body, Stella logo normally impressed on the banjo rim or the side of the neck.

1920s		$150	$275

Bowl Back Mandolin
1920s. Typical bowl back, bent top-style mandolin with models decalomania, about 10 (wide) maple ribs, dot markers.

1920s		$100	$225

MODEL YEAR	FEATURES	EXC. COND. LOW	HIGH

Pear-Shape Mandolin
1940s-1960s. Harmony-made lower-end mandolins, pear-shaped (Style A) flat back, oval soundhole.

1940s	Natural	$175	$250
1950s		$175	$250
1960s	Sunburst	$175	$250

Sterling
Early-1900s. Distributed by wholesalers The Davitt & Hanser Music Co.

Stiver
Professional and premium grade, custom/production, mandolins built by luthier Lou Stiver in Pennsylvania.

Strad-O-Lin
Ca.1920s-ca.1960s. The Strad-O-Lin company was operated by the Hominic brothers in New York, primarily making mandolins for wholesalers. In the late '50s, Multivox/Premier bought the company and used the name on mandolins and guitars.

Baldwin Electric Mandolin
1950s. A-Style, single pickup, tone and volume knobs, spruce top, maple back and sides, Baldwin logo on headstock.

1950s	Natural	$400	$500

Junior A Mandolin
1950s. A-Style, Stradolin Jr. logo on headstock, dot markers.

1950s	Sunburst	$350	$450

Stromberg-Voisinet
1921-ca.1932. Marketed Stromberg (not to be confused with Charles Stromberg of Boston) and Kay Kraft brands, plus instruments of other distributors and retailers. Became the Kay Musical Instrument Company. By the mid-'20s, the company was making many better Montgomery Ward guitars, banjos and mandolins, often with lots of pearloid. The last Stromberg acoustic instruments were seen in '32.

Mandolin
1921-1932. Vague two point A-style.

1921-1932		$250	$350

Superior
1987-present. Intermediate grade, production/custom mandolin-family instruments made in Mexico for George Katechis Montalvo of Berkeley Musical Instrument Exchange. They also offer guitars.

Supertone
1914-1941. Brand used by Sears before they switched to Silvertone. Instruments made by other companies.

Mandolin
Spruce top, mahogany back and sides, some with decalomania vine pattern on top.

1920s		$250	$350
1930s	Decalomania vine pattern	$250	$350

Supro
1935-1968, 2004-present. Budget line from the National Dobro Company. Amp builder Bruce Zinky revived the Supro name for a guitar and amp model.

T30 Electric Mandolin

1950s		$450	$550

T. H. Davis
1976-present. Premium grade, custom, mandolins built by luthier Ted Davis in Loudon, Tennessee. He also builds guitars.

Tacoma
1995-present. Intermediate, professional and premium grade, production, mandolins made in Tacoma, Washington. They also build guitars and basses.

M-1/M-1E Mandolin
1999-present. Solid spruce top, mahogany back and sides, typical Tacoma body-style with upper bass bout soundhole.

1999-2004	M-1 acoustic	$300	$350
1999-2004	M-1E acoustic/electric	$350	$400

M-3E Mandolin
1999-present. Acoustic/electric, upper bass bout sound hole.

1999-2004		$550	$600

Tennessee
1970-1993, 1996-present. Luthier Mark Taylor builds his professional and premium grade, production/custom, mandolins in Old Hickory, Tennessee. He also builds guitars, mandolins, banjos and the Tut Taylor brand of resophonic guitars.

Timeless Instruments
1980-present. Luthier David Freeman builds his intermediate grade, mandolins in Tugaske, Saskatchewan. He also builds guitars and dulcimers.

Triggs
1992-present. Luthiers Jim Triggs and his son Ryan build their professional and premium grade, production/custom, mandolins in Kansas City, Kansas. They also build guitars. They were located in Nashville, Tennessee until '98.

Trinity River
Mandolins from Stenzler Musical Instruments of Ft. Worth, Texas. They also offer guitars, basses, and fiddles.

Unicorn
1970s-late 1980s. Luthier Rolfe Gerhardt (currently luthier for Phoenix Mandolins) founded Unicorn in the mid-'70s. Gerhardt built 149 mandolins before selling Unicorn to Save Sjnko in '80. Sinko closed Unicorn in the late-'80s.

F-5 Style Mandolin

1976-1980	Sunburst	$1,000	$2,000

Stella pear-shape

Triggs mando

MANDOLINS

Vega bowl mandolin

Vivitone Electric

MODEL YEAR	FEATURES	EXC. COND. LOW	HIGH

Vega

1903-present. The original Boston-based company was purchased by C.F. Martin in '70. In '80, the Vega trademark was sold to a Korean company. Vega means star and a star logo is often seen on the original Vega instruments.

Lansing Special Bowl Mandolin

Spruce top, abalone, vine inlay.

1890s		$500	$650

Little Wonder Mandolin Banjo

Maple neck, resonator.

1920s		$450	$600

Mando Bass Mandolin

1910s-1920s. Large upright bass-sized instrument with bass tuners, body-style similar to dual-point A-style, scroll headstock.

1920s		$2,500	$4,000

Mandolin Cittern

1910s. 10-string (five double strings tuned in 5ths), vague A-style with oval soundhole and cylinder back, natural.

1910s		$2,000	$2,200

Style 202 Lute Mandolin

Early-1900s. Basic A-style with small horns, natural spruce top, mahogany sides and cylinder back, dot markers.

1910s		$800	$900

Style 205 Cylinder Back Mandolin

1920s		$900	$1,000

Style A Mandolin

1910s		$500	$650

Style F Mandolin

1910s. Scroll upper bass bout, oval soundhole, Vega and torch inlay in headstock.

1910s		$900	$1,000

Style K Mandolin Banjo

1910s		$350	$550
1920s		$350	$550
1930s		$350	$550

Style L Banjo Mandolin

1910s. Open back banjo body and mandolin 8-string neck.

1910s		$800	$900

Super Deluxe Mandolin

1939	Sunburst	$700	$800

Tubaphone Style X Mandolin Banjo

1923		$700	$800

MODEL YEAR	FEATURES	EXC. COND. LOW	HIGH

Veillette

1991-present. Luthiers Joe Veillette and Martin Keith build their professional grade, production/custom, mandolins in Woodstock, New York. They also builds basses and guitars.

Vinaccia

Italian-made by Pasquale Vinaccia, luthier.

Bowl Back Mandolin

High-end appointments and 'guard, 30 rosewood ribs.

1900-1920s		$2,000	$3,000

Vivi-Tone

1933-ca. 1936. Lloyd Loar's pioneering guitar company also built early electric mandolins and mandocellos in Kalamazoo, Michigan.

Electric Mandocello

1933-1935. Traditonal guitar-arch body, Vivi-Tone silkscreen logo on headstock.

1933-1935		$5,500	$6,500

Electric Mandola

1933-1935. Traditonal European teardrop/pear-shaped top, Vivi-Tone silkscreen logo on headstock.

1933-1935		$4,500	$5,500

Electric Mandolin

1933-1935. Vivi-Tone silkscreen logo on headstock.

1933-1935		$4,000	$5,000

Ward

Depression era private brand made by Gibson's Kalamazoo factory.

Style A Mandolin

1930s. Style A body with round soundhole and flat top and back, dot markers, mahogany back and sides, silkscreened Ward logo.

1935	Sunburst	$325	$400

Washburn (Lyon & Healy)

1880s-ca.1949. Washburn was founded in Chicago as one of the lines for Lyon & Healy to promote high quality stringed instruments, ca. 1880s. The rights to Washburn were sold to Regal which built Washburns by the mid-'30s until until ca. '49. In '74 the brand resurfaced.

MODEL YEAR	FEATURES	EXC. COND. LOW	HIGH

Bowl Back Mandolin

Lyon and Healy sold a wide variety of bowl back mandolins, Brazilian ribs with fancy inlays and bindings.

1890s	Fancy inlays and bindings	$500	$1,000
1890s	Plain appointments	$300	$400
1900s	Fancy inlays and bindings	$500	$1,000
1900s	Plain appointments	$300	$400
1910s	Standard appointments	$300	$400

Style A Mandolin

Brazilian rosewood.

1920s		$900	$1,000

Style E Mandolin

1915-1923. Brazilian rosewood.

1915-1923		$1,000	$1,200

Washburn (Post 1974)

1974-present. Currently, Washburn offers imported intermediate and professional grade, production, mandolins.

Mandolin/Mandolin family

1974-present.

1974-2005		$300	$600

Washington

Washington mandolins were manufactured by Kansas City, Missouri instrument wholesalers J.W. Jenkins & Sons. First introduced in 1895, the brand also offered guitars.

Weber

1996-present. Intermediate, professional, and premium grade, production/custom, mandolins, mandolas, and mandocellos. Many former Flatiron employees, including Bruce Weber, formed Sound To Earth, Ltd., to build Weber instruments when Gibson moved Flatiron from Bozeman, Montana, to Nashville. Originally in Belgrade, Montana, and since '04, in Logan, Montana. They also build guitars.

Aspen #1

1997-present. Teardrop A-style, solid spruce top, maple sides and back, mahogany neck.

1997-2000		$775	$850

Aspen #2

1997-present. Like #1, but with maple neck.

1997-2000		$950	$1,000

Beartooth

1997-present. Teardrop A-style, solid spruce top, curly maple sides, back, and neck.

1997-2000		$1,700	$1,800

Yellowstone

1997-present. F-style, solid spruce top, curly maple sides, back, and neck.

1997-2000	Sunburst	$1,900	$2,200

Weymann

1864-1940s. H.A. Weymann & Sons was a musical instrument distributor located in Philadelphia. They also built their own instruments.

Keystone State Banjo Mandolin

Maple rim and back, ebony fretboard.

1910s		$300	$400

Model 20 Mando-Lute

1920s. Lute-style body, spruce top, flamed maple sides and back, rope binding, deluxe rosette.

1920s	Natural	$1,000	$1,100

Model 40 Mandolin Banjo

1910s-1920s. Mandolin neck on a open banjo body with a larger sized 10" head.

1920s	10" or 11" rim	$450	$600

Wurlitzer

The old Wurlitzer company would have been considered a mega-store by today's standards. They sold a wide variety of instruments, gave music lessons, and operated manufacturing facilities.

Mandolin

Koa.

1920		$500	$700

Mandolin Banjo

1900s. Mandolin neck on open back banjo body, plain-style.

1900s		$200	$275

Yosco

1900-1930s. Lawrence L. Yosco was a New York City luthier building guitars, round back mandolins and banjos under his own brand and for others.

Zeta

1982-present. Professional grade, production, acoustic/electric mandolins made in Oakland, California. They also make basses, amps and violins.

Weber Style Yellowstone

Wurlitzer Mandolin Banjo

MANDOLINS

Ukuleles

T.V. PAL
Uke

Aero Uke

Dobro resonator

ca. 1916 Earnest Kaai

Aero Uke

1920s. Never branded, but almost certainly produced by Chicago's Stromberg-Voisenet Company, the precursor of Kay, the Aero Uke is an instrument quite unlike any other. With its spruce-capped body resembling an old-timey airplane wing and a neck and headstock that approximate a plane's fuselage, this clever '20s offering cashed in on the Lindbergh craze (like the Harmony Johnny Marvin model with its airplane-shaped bridge), and must have been a big hit at parties.

Aero Uke
Airplane body.

MODEL YEAR	FEATURES	EXC. COND. LOW	HIGH
1927	Black deco on wing	$1,800	$2,000
1927	Gold deco on wing	$2,000	$2,200

Aloha

1935-1960s. The Aloha brand turns up on numerous vastly different ukes. In fact, the variety of features exhibited by Aloha ukuleles leads the modern observer to believe that the ukes that bear this headstock decal were made by as many as a dozen different manufacturers, each with access to the same logo. Many were undoubtedly Island-made, with all koa bodies and some with fancy rope binding; others bear unmistakable mainland traits. Some of these have a more traditional look and are stamped Akai inside the soundhole, while still others, strongly resembling mainland C.F. Martins in design, typically sport a decal of the Sam F. Chang curio shop on the reverse of the headstock.

Akai Soprano Ukulele
Koa construction.

MODEL YEAR	FEATURES	EXC. COND. LOW	HIGH
1930s		$400	$500

Soprano Ukulele
Koa body, plain.

MODEL YEAR	FEATURES	EXC. COND. LOW	HIGH
1950s		$400	$500

Applause

1976-present. Kaman Music's entry-level Ovation-styled import brand Applause currently offers budget and intermediate grade, production, soprano and tenor ukuleles.

Bear Creek Guitars

1995-present. Intermediate and professional grade ukuleles built by luthier Bill Hardin in Kula, Hawaii. He also builds guitars.

Beltona

1990-present. Production metal body resonator ukuleles made in New Zealand by Steve Evans and Bill Johnson. Beltona was originally located in England. They also build guitars.

Blue Star

1984-present. Intermediate grade, production/custom, acoustic and electric ukuleles built by luthier Bruce Herron in Fennville, Michigan. He also builds guitars, mandolins, dulcimers and lap steels.

Bruno

1834-present. This New York distributor certainly subcontracted all of its ukulele production to other manufacturers, and as a result you'd be hard pressed to find two identical Bruno ukes.

Soprano Ukulele

MODEL YEAR	FEATURES	EXC. COND. LOW	HIGH
1920s	Koa, rope soundhole	$300	$400
1930s	Koa, rope bound body	$350	$400

DeCava Guitars

1983-present. Professional grade, production/custom, ukuleles built by luthier Jim DeCava in Stratford, Connecticut. He also builds guitars, banjos, and mandolins.

Del Vecchio Dinamico

With a design patterned after the pioneering work of Dobro and National, this Brazilian company produced a full line of resonator instruments, all constructed of native Brazilian rosewood, from the 1950s onward.

Resonator Ukulele
Brazilian rosewood.

MODEL YEAR	FEATURES	EXC. COND. LOW	HIGH
1950s		$700	$850

Ditson

1916-1930. Don't be fooled. While some of the ukes that were commissioned by this East Coast music publisher and chain store were actually manufactured by C.F. Martin, Martin was by no means the sole supplier. The Martin-made instruments often bear a Martin brand as well as a Ditson one, or, barring that, at least demonstrate an overall similarity to the rest of the ukes in the regular Martin line, both inside and out. The most telling and desirable feature of these Martin-made Ditsons is a dreadnaught-style wide waisted body design.

Soprano Ukulele

MODEL YEAR	FEATURES	EXC. COND. LOW	HIGH
1922	as Martin Style 1 K	$1,500	$2,500
1922	as Martin Style 1 M	$1,000	$1,200
1922	as Martin Style 2 K	$2,000	$3,000
1922	as Martin Style 2 M	$1,300	$1,400
1922	as Martin Style 3 K	$2,500	$3,500
1922	as Martin Style 3 M	$2,500	$3,000
1922	as Martin Style 5 K	$7,000	$10,000
1922	as Martin Style O	$800	$900

Dobro

1929-1942, ca. 1954-present. The ukulele version of the popular amplifying resonator instruments first produced in California, the Dobro uke was offered in 2 sizes (soprano and tenor), 2 styles (f-holes and screen holes), and 2 colors (brown and black). Models with Dobro headstock decals are often outwardly indistinguishable from others bearing either a Regal badge or no logo at all, but a peek inside often reveals the presence of a sound well in the belly of the former, making them the more desirable of the two.

MODEL YEAR	FEATURES	EXC. COND. LOW	HIGH

Resonator Ukulele
Wood body.

1930s	F-holes, Regal-made	$500	$900
1930s	Screen holes	$700	$1,000

Douglas Ching

1976-present. Luthier Douglas J. Ching builds his professional grade, production/custom, ukuleles currently in Chester, Virginia, and previously in Hawaii ('76-'89) and Michigan ('90-'93). He also builds guitars, lutes and violins.

Earnest Kaai

Hawaiian Earnest Kaai was many things (teacher, songbook publisher, importer/exporter) during the early part of the 20th century, but ukulele manufacturer was certainly one job that he couldn't add to his resume. Still, scads of ukes proudly bear his name, in a variety of different styles and variations. Even more puzzling is the fact that while some appear to actually have been island-made, an equal number bear the telltale signs of mainland manufacture.

Soprano Ukulele
Koa body.

1920	Rope bound top/back	$500	$700
1925	Abalone trim top, paper label	$800	$1,000
1925	Unbound, decal logo	$300	$500
1930	Rope bound soundhole only	$400	$600

Favilla

1890-1973. The small New York City family-owned factory that produced primarily guitars also managed to offer some surprisingly high quality ukes, the best of which rival Martin and Gibson for craftsmanship and tone. As a result, Favilla ukuleles are a real value for the money.

Baritone Ukulele
Plain mahogany body.

1950s		$400	$700

Soprano Ukulele

1950s	Mahogany body, triple bound	$500	$700
1950s	Plain mahogany body	$400	$600
1950s	Teardrop-shaped, birch body	$400	$700
1950s	Teardrop-shaped, stained blue	$400	$700

Fender

Fender offered Regal-made ukuleles in the 1960s, including the R-275 Baritone Ukulele.

Fin-der

1950s. The pitch of this short-lived plastic ukulele was apparently the ease of learning, since the included instructional brochure helped you to "find" your chords with the added help of rainbow of color-coded nylon strings.

Diamond Head Ukulele
Styrene plastic, in original box.

1950s		$150	$200

Fine Resophonic

1988-present. Intermediate and professional grade, production/custom, wood and metal-bodied resophonic ukuleles built by luthiers Mike Lewis and Pierre Avocat in Vitry Sur Seine, France. They also build guitars and mandolins.

Flamingo

1950s. If swanky designs and hot-foil stamped into the surface of these '50s swirly injection molded polystyrene ukes didn't grab you, certainly the built-in functional pitch pipe across the top of the headstock would. And I ask you, who can resist a ukulele with a built-in tuner?

Soprano Ukulele

1955	Brown top, white 'board	$125	$150
1955	White top, brown 'board	$125	$150

Gibson

1890s (1902)-present. A relative late-comer to the uke market, Gibson didn't get a line off the ground until 1927, fully 9 years after Martin had already been in production. Even then they only produced 3 soprano styles and 1 tenor version. Worse still, they never made any ukes in koa, sticking to the easier-to-obtain mahogany.

Nonetheless, Gibson ukuleles exhibit more unintentional variety than any other major maker, with enough construction, inlay, binding, and cosmetic variations to keep collectors buzzing for many a year to come. In general, the earliest examples feature a Gibson logo in script, later shortened to just Gibson. Post-war examples adopted the more square-ish logo of the rest of the Gibson line, and, at some point in the late '50s, began sporting ink-stamped serial numbers on the back of the headstock like their guitar and mandolin brethren.

ETU 1 Ukulele
Electric tenor, unbound body, square black pickup, 88 made.

1949		$3,000	$4,500

ETU 3 Ukulele
Electric tenor, triple bound body, square pickup, rare.

1953		$5,000	$6,500

TU-1 Ukulele
Tenor, called the TU until 1 added in 1949, mahogany body, sunburst finish.

1930s		$750	$1,000

Uke-1 Ukulele
Soprano, plain mahogany body.

1927		$600	$750
1951	Red SG guitar-like finish	$600	$750

Favilla

Flamingo

Gibson Uke 1

UKULELES

Gibson Uke 2

Graziano Concert

1920s Harmony Roy Smeck Vita

MODEL YEAR	FEATURES	EXC. COND. LOW	HIGH
Uke-2 Ukulele			
Soprano, mahogany body.			
1934	Triple bound	$700	$900
Uke-3 Ukulele			
Soprano, dark finish, diamonds and squares inlay.			
1933		$1,200	$1,500

Graziano

1969-present. Luthier Tony Graziano has been building ukuleles almost exclusively since '95 in his Santa Cruz shop. Like many, he sees the uke as the instrument of the new millennium, and his entirely handmade, custom orders can be had in a variety of shapes, sizes, and woods.

Gretsch

1883-present. The first (and most desirable) ukuleles by this New York manufacturer were actually stamped with the name Gretsch American or with interior brass nameplates. Subsequent pieces, largely inexpensive laminate-bodied catalog offerings, are distinguished by small round Gretsch headstock decals, and a lack of any kerfed linings inside the bodies.

MODEL YEAR	FEATURES	EXC. COND. LOW	HIGH
Plain Soprano Ukulele			
Natural mahogany body, no binding.			
1950s		$100	$150
Round Ukulele			
Round body, blue to green sunburst.			
1940		$150	$200
Soprano Ukulele			
1940s	Koa wood body, fancy 'board inlay	$650	$750
1940s	Mahogany body, fancy 'board inlay	$600	$750
1940s	Unbound body, engraved rose in peghead	$800	$900
1950s	Darker finish, bordered in dark binding	$250	$450

Guild

1952-present. By rights this fine East Coast shop should have produced a full line of ukes to complement its impressive flat and carved-top guitar offerings. Alas, a lone baritone model was all that they could manage. And it's a darned shame, too.

MODEL YEAR	FEATURES	EXC. COND. LOW	HIGH
B-11 Baritone Ukulele			
1963-1976. Mahogany body, rosewood 'board.			
1960s		$400	$600

Harmony

1892-1976, late 1970s-present. This manufacturer surely produced more ukuleles than all other makers put together. Their extensive line ran the gamut from artist endorsed models and ukes in unusual shapes and materials, to inexpensive but flashy creations adorned with eye-catching decals and silk screening. The earliest examples have a small paper label on the back of the headstock, and a branded logo inside the body. This was replaced by a succession of logo decals applied to the front of the headstock, first gold and black, later green, white, and black. By the '60s Harmony had become so synonymous with ukulele production that they were known around their Chicago locale as simply "the ukulele factory," as in, "Ma couldn't come to the bar-b-que on-a-counta she got a job at the ukulele factory."

MODEL YEAR	FEATURES	EXC. COND. LOW	HIGH
Baritone Ukulele			
Bound mahogany body.			
1960s		$250	$350
Concert Ukulele			
Mahogany body, bound, concert-sized.			
1935		$250	$300
Harold Teen Ukulele			
Carl Ed cartoon decals on front.			
1930	Gray-blue	$300	$500
1930	Red	$200	$400
1930	Yellow	$300	$550
Johnny Marvin Tenor Ukulele			
Sports an airplane bridge.			
1930s	Flamed koa	$550	$800
1930s	Sunburst mahogany	$400	$550
Roy Smeck Concert Ukulele			
Concert-sized, sunburst spruce top.			
1935		$400	$500
Roy Smeck Ukulele			
Mahogany body.			
1955	Plastic 'board	$150	$200
1955	Wood 'board	$350	$450
Roy Smeck Vita Ukulele			
Pear-shaped body, seal-shaped F-holes.			
1926		$550	$750
Tiple			
Multicolored binding, 10 steel strings.			
1935		$600	$850
Ukulele			
1930	Koa body, unbound	$250	$500
1935	Plain mahogany body, unbound	$300	$400

Hilo Bay Ukuleles

2003-present. Intermediate grade, production, tenor ukuleles made in Cebu City, Philippines for Hilo Guitars and Ukuleles of Hilo, Hawaii.

Johnson

Mid-1990s-present. Budget ukuleles imported by Music Link of Brisbane, California. They also offer guitars, amps, mandolins and effects. Most notable of the Johnson ukes are the National metal-bodied uke copies, which come surprisingly close to the look and feel of the originals, at an unfathomably low price.

K & S

1992-1998. Ukes distributed by George Katechis and Marc Silber and handmade in Paracho, Mexico. They also offered guitars. In '98, Silber started marketing the ukes under the Marc Silber Guitar Company brand and Katechis continued to offer instruments under the Casa Montalvo brand.

Kamaka

Part of the second wave of ukulele builders on the Hawaiian islands (after Nunes, Dias, and Santos) Kamaka distinguished itself first with ukes of extremely high quality, subsequently with the most enduring non-guitar-derived designs, the Pineapple Uke, patented in 1928. Kamaka is the only maker which has been in continuous production for nearly a hundred years, offering Hawaiian-made products from native woods in virtually every size and ornamentation. In the early '70s, Kamaka began rubber stamping the full date of manufacture on the end of the neck block of each uke, visible right through the sound hole. Now don't you wish that every manufacturer did that?

Baritone Uke
Koa body, extended 'board.

MODEL YEAR	FEATURES	EXC. COND. LOW	HIGH
1990		$700	$1,000

Concert Uke
Koa body, extended rosewood 'board.

1975		$350	$600

Lili'u Uke
Concert-sized koa body.

1965	8 strings	$600	$750
1985	6 strings	$600	$750

Pineapple Uke

1925	Pineapple art painted onto top or back	$2,000	$3,000
1930	Monkeypod wood, plain, unbound	$1,000	$1,200
1930	Rope bound top only, koawood body	$2,000	$3,000
1935	Rope bound soundhole only	$1,200	$1,500
1960	Koa body, unbound, 2 Ks logo	$600	$700
1970	Koa body, extended rosewood 'board	$500	$700

Tenor Uke
Koa body, extended rosewood 'board.

1955		$400	$750

Kay

1931-present. Kay offered banjo ukuleles in the 1920s and again in the late '50s; they offered ukuleles from '66-'68 and currently offer budget grade, production, imported ukuleles. They also make amps, guitars, banjos, mandolins, basses, and violins.

Kent

1961-1969. Large, student quality ukes of laminated construction were offered by this Japanese concern throughout the '60s.

Baritone Ukulele
Mahogany body, bound top, bound back.

MODEL YEAR	FEATURES	EXC. COND. LOW	HIGH
1960s		$150	$200

Knutsen

1890s-1920s. While Christopher Knutsen was the inventor of flat-topped harp instruments featuring an integral sound chamber on the bass side of the body, he almost certainly left the manufacturing to others. Striking in both concept and design, Knutsen products nonetheless suffer from compromised construction techniques.

Harp Taro Patch
Koa body, large horn chamber, 8 strings, unbound.

1915		$3,500	$5,000

Harp Uke
Koa body, large horn chamber.

1915	Bound	$2,500	$4,000
1915	Unbound	$2,000	$3,000

Kumalae

Along with Kamaka, Kumalae was also of the second wave of Hawaiian uke makers. Jonah Kumalae's company quickly snagged the prestigious Gold Award at the Pan Pacific Exhibition in 1915, and the headstock decals and paper labels aren't about to let you forget it, either. Many assume that these all date from exactly that year, when in fact Kumalaes were offered right up through the late 1930s.

Soprano Ukulele
Figured koa body.

1919	Bound top, back, 'board	$750	$1,000
1920	Rope bound top/back	$600	$750
1927	As 1919 but with fiddle-shaped peghead	$1,000	$1,500
1930	Unbound body	$650	$800
1933	Rope bound soundhole only	$650	$800

Tenor Ukulele
Koa body, unbound top and back.

1930		$800	$1,000

Lanikai

2000-present. Line of budget and intermediate grade, production, koa or nato wood, acoustic and acoustic/electric, ukuleles distributed by Hohner.

Larrivee

1968-present. This mainstream guitar manufacturer has an on-again off-again relationship with the ukulele, having occasionally produced some superb examples in various sizes, woods and degrees of ornamentation. They introduced 3 ukulele models in '00. They also build guitars.

Kamaka Pineapple Uke Style-1

Kumalae Style 1

Larrivee US-01KA

UKULELES

Leonardo Nunes

1920s Lyon & Healey Leland

Magic Fluke Uke

UKULELES

MODEL YEAR	FEATURES	EXC. COND. LOW	EXC. COND. HIGH

Le Domino

This line of striking ukuleles turned the popularity of domino playing into a clever visual motif, displaying not only tumbling dominos on their soundboards and around their soundholes, but 'board markers represented in decal domino denominations (3, 5, 7, 10, 12, etc.). The ukuleles were, in fact, produced by at least 2 different companies - Stewart and Regal - but you can scarcely tell them apart.

Concert Ukukele
Concert size, black-finish, white bound, dominos.

1932		$1,200	$1,500

Soprano Ukukele
Domino decals.

1930	Black finish, white bound	$500	$750
1940	Natural finish, unbound	$150	$250

Leonardo Nunes

Leonardo was the son of Manuel, the self-professed inventor of the Ukulele. Whether actually the originator or not, Manuel was certainly on the ship that brought the inventor to the islands in 1879. Leonardo, instead of joining up and making it Manuel & Son, set out on his own to produce ukes that are virtually indistinguishable from pop's. All constructed entirely of koa, some exhibit considerable figure and rope binding finery, making them as highly desirable to collectors as Manuel's.

Radio Tenor Ukulele
Koa body, bound top, back and neck.

1935		$1,750	$2,000

Soprano Ukulele
Figured koa body.

1919	Bound top/back/'board	$800	$1,100
1920	Rope bound top/back	$800	$1,000
1927	Bound body/'board/head	$1,500	$1,600
1930	Unbound body	$600	$750
1933	Rope bound soundhole only	$700	$800

Taro Patch Fiddle
Koa body, unbound top and back.

1930		$1,600	$2,000

Tenor Ukulele
Koa body, unbound top and back.

1930		$900	$1,100

Levin

1900-1973. Ukuleles built in Sweden. Levin was best known for their classical guitars, which they also built for other brands, most notably Goya. They also built mandolins.

Loprinzi

1972-present. Intermediate and professional grade, production/custom, ukuleles built in Clearwater, Florida. They also build guitars.

Lyon & Healy

1880s-ca.1949. During different periods several different makers constructed ukes bearing this stamp – often with an additional Washburn tag as well. After initial production by Lyon & Healy, instrument manufacture then apparently bounced between Regal, Stewart, and Tonk Brothers all within a span of only a few short years. Adding to the confusion, ukes surface from time to time bearing no maker's mark that can be reasonably attributed to Lyon & Healy. Suffice it to say that the best of these ukes, those displaying the highest degrees of quality and ornamentation, rival Gibson and Martin for collectability and tone and beauty.

Bell-shaped Ukulele
Mahogany body.

1927		$1,500	$2,000

Camp Ukulele
Round nissa wood body, black binding.

1935		$150	$250

Concert Ukulele
Mahogany body, bound top and back.

1930		$2,000	$2,500

Shrine Ukulele
Triangular body.

1927	Koa, Abalone *binding*	$2,500	$4,500
1930	Mahogany, *green binding*	$1,100	$1,500
1933	Koa, *green binding*	$2,000	$3,000

Soprano Ukulele (Mahogany body)

1930	Unbound	$600	$750
1932	Bound top/back	$600	$750

Soprano Ukulele (Koa body)

1927	Bound top, pearl rosette	$2,500	$3,000
1934	Bound top/back	$900	$1,200
1935	Pearl bound top/back	$6,500	$7,500

Tenor Ukulele
Mahogany body, bound top and back.

1933		$2,000	$2,500

Maccaferri

1923-1990. Between the time he designed the Selmer guitar that became instantly synonymous with Django's gypsy jazz and his invention of the plastic clothespin, guitar design genius and manufacturing impresario Mario Maccaferri created a line of stringed instruments revolutionary for their complete plastic construction. The ukuleles were by far the greatest success, and most bore the tiny Maccaferri coat of arms on their tiny headstock.

Baritone Ukulele
Polystyrene cutaway body.

1959		$150	$200

Islander Ukulele
Polytyrene plastic body, crest in peghead.

1953		$150	$200

MODEL YEAR	FEATURES	EXC. COND. LOW	HIGH

Playtune Ukulele
Polystyrene body.

1956		$150	$200

TV Pal Deluxe Ukulele
Extended 'board.

1960		$150	$200

TV Pal Ukulele
Polystyrene plastic body.

1955		$150	$200

Magic Fluke Company

1999-present. Budget grade, production, ukuleles made in New Hartford, Connecticut. With a clever design, exceptional quality, dozens of catchy finishes, and surprisingly affordable prices, it's little wonder that these little wonders have caught on. Riding – if not almost single-handedly driving – the coming third wave of uke popularity (the '20s and '50s were the first and second), Dale and Phyllis Webb of the Magic Fluke, along with Phyllis' brother, author Jumpin' Jim Beloff, are downright ukulele evangelists. The Fluke is the first new uke that you're not afraid to let the kid's monkey with.

Manuel Nunes

The self-professed father of the ukulele was at least one of the first makers to produce them in any quantity. Beginning after 1879, when he and the first boat load of Portuguese settlers landed in Hawaii, until at least the 1930s, Manuel and his son Leonardo (see Leonardo Nunes section) produced some of the most beautiful and superbly crafted ukes offered by any Island maker.

Soprano Ukulele
Koa body.

1919	Figured koa body, bound top, back, 'board	$1,500	$2,000
1920	Rope bound top/back	$900	$1,200
1927	Bound body, 'board/head	$1,500	$2,000
1930	Unbound body	$900	$1,200
1933	Rope bound soundhole only	$900	$1,200

Taro Patch Fiddle
Koa body.

1930	Rope bound top/back	$2,000	$2,500
1930	Unbound top/back	$1,500	$2,000

Tenor Ukulele
Koa body, unbound top and back.

1930		$1,000	$1,250

Marc Silber Guitar Company

1998-present. Mexican-made ukes from designer Marc Silber of Berkley, California. He also offers guitars. His Frisco Uke takes its inspiration from the inimitable Roy Smeck Vita Uke (see Harmony), but without the whimsy of the original.

Martin

1833-present. The C.F. Martin Company knew they wanted in on the uke craze, and toyed with some prototypes as early as 1907 or so, but didn't get around to actually getting serious until '16. The first of these were characterized by rather more primitive craftsmanship (by stringent Martin standards), bar frets, and an impressed logo in the back of the headstock. By '20, koa became available as a pricey option, and by the early '30s, regular frets and the familiar Martin headstock decal had prevailed. Martin single-handedly created the archetype of the mainland uke and the standard by which all competitors are measured.

Martin has recently re-entered the ukulele market with its budget Mexican-made model S-0, the Backpacker Uke, as well as a limited edition of the ornate, and pricey 5K.

Style 0 Ukulele
Unbound mahogany body.

1920	Wood pegs	$500	$750
1953	Patent pegs	$500	$750

Style 1 Taro Patch
Mahogany body, 8 strings, rosewood bound.

1933		$1,250	$1,750

Style 1 Ukulele
Mahogany body.

1940	Rosewood bound top only	$650	$800
1950	Tortoise bound top only	$650	$800
1960s	Tortoise bound top only	$600	$800

Style 1-C Concert Ukulele
Concert-sized mahogany body, bound top.

1950		$1,200	$1,500

Style 1-C K Concert Ukulele
Concert-sized koa body, bound top.

1950		$2,500	$3,500

Style 1-K Taro Patch
Style 1 with koa wood body.

1940		$1,500	$2,500

Style 1-K Ukulele
Koa body, rosewood bound top.

1922	Wood pegs	$1,500	$2,000
1939	Patent pegs	$1,500	$2,000

Style 1-T Tenor Ukulele
Tenor-sized mahogany body, bound top only.

1940		$1,500	$2,000

Style 2 Taro Patch
Mahogany body, 8 strings, ivoroid bound.

1931		$1,500	$2,000

Style 2 Ukulele
Mahogany body, ivoroid bound top and back.

1922		$1,000	$1,200
1935		$1,000	$1,200
1961		$1,000	$1,200

Style 2-K Taro Patch
Style 2 with koa wood body.

1937		$1,700	$2,500

Marc Silber Frisco

Martin Style O

Martin Style 2-K

UKULELES

Michael Dunn Harp Uke

National Concert uke

Pegasus Artist Series tenor 6-string

MODEL YEAR	FEATURES	EXC. COND. LOW	HIGH
Style 2-K Ukulele			
Figured koa body, bound top and back.			
1923		$2,000	$2,500
1939	Patent pegs	$2,000	$2,500
Style 3 Taro Patch			
Mahogany body, 8 strings, multiple bound.			
1941		$2,000	$3,500
Style 3 Ukulele			
Mahogany body.			
1925	Kite inlay in headstock	$2,000	$3,000
1940	B/W lines in ebony 'board	$2,000	$3,000
1950	Extended 'board, dots	$2,000	$3,000
Style 3-C K Concert Ukulele			
Same specs as 3K, but in concert size.			
1930		$10,000	$15,000
Style 3-K Taro Patch			
Style 3 with koa wood body.			
1929		$3,000	$4,500
Style 3-K Ukulele			
Figured koa body.			
1924	Bow-tie 'board inlay	$4,000	$5,000
1932	B/W lines, diamonds, squares	$4,000	$5,000
1940	B/W lines and dot inlay	$4,000	$5,000
Style 5-K Ukulele			
Highly figured koa body, all pearl trimmed.			
1926		$10,000	$15,000
Style 5-M Ukulele			
1941. Same as 5K, but mahogany body.			
1941		$15,000	$25,000
Style 51 Baritone Ukulele			
Mahogany body, bound top and back.			
1966		$1,200	$1,500
Style T-15 Tiple			
Mahogany body, 10 metal strings, unbound.			
1971		$700	$900
Style T-17 Tiple			
Mahogany body, unbound top and back.			
1950		$850	$1,000
Style T-28 Tiple			
Rosewood body, bound top and back.			
1969		$1,200	$1,500

Michael Dunn Guitars

1968-present. Luthier Michael Dunn builds a Knutsen-style harp uke in New Westminster, British Columbia. He also builds guitars.

Mirabella

1997-present. Professional grade, custom ukuleles built by luthier Cristian Mirabella in Babylon, New York. He also builds mandolins and guitars.

National

Ca. 1927-present. To capitalize on the success of their amplifying guitars, the Dopyera brothers introduced metal-bodied ukuleles and mandolins as well. Large, heavy, and ungainly by today's standards, these early offerings nonetheless have their charms. Their subsequent switch to a smaller body shape produced an elegant and sweet-sounding resonator uke that soon became much sought after.

MODEL YEAR	FEATURES	EXC. COND. LOW	HIGH
Style 1 Ukulele			
Nickel body.			
1928	Tenor, 6" resonator	$2,000	$4,000
1933	Soprano	$2,000	$4,000
Style 2 Ukulele			
Nickel body, engraved roses.			
1928	Tenor	$3,500	$5,000
1931	Soprano	$3,500	$5,000
Style 3 Ukulele			
Nickel body, lilies-of-the-valley.			
1929	Tenor	$4,000	$6,000
1933	Soprano	$5,000	$8,000
Style O Ukulele			
Metal body, soprano size, sandblasted scenes.			
1931		$2,000	$3,000
Triolian Ukulele			
1928	Tenor, sunburst painted body	$1,500	$2,000
1930	Soprano, sunburst painted body	$1,500	$2,000
1934	Soprano, wood-grained metal body	$1,000	$1,500

National Reso-Phonic

1988-present. Successors to the National name, with the designs and patented amplifying resonator assemblies of the original National models, they offer professional grade, production, single cone ukuleles from their shop in San Luis Obispo, California. They also build guitars and basses.

Oscar Schmidt

1879-ca. 1939, 1979-present. The same New Jersey outfit responsible for Leadbelly's 12-string guitar offered ukes as well during the same period. Many of these were odd amalgams of materials, often combining koa, mahogany, and spruce in the same instrument. Since 1979, when the name was acquired by the U.S. Music Corp. (Washburn, Randall, etc.), they have offered a line of budget grade, production, Asian-made ukes. They also offer guitars, mandolins, and banjos.

MODEL YEAR	FEATURES	EXC. COND. LOW	HIGH
Soprano Ukulele			
Spruce top, bound mahogany body.			
1930		$200	$450

Pegasus Guitars and Ukuleles

1977-present. Professional grade, custom, ukulele family instruments built by luthier Bob Gleason in Kurtistown, Hawaii, who also builds steel-string guitars.

UKULELES

MODEL YEAR	FEATURES	EXC. COND. LOW	HIGH

Polk-a-lay-lee

1960s. These inexplicably shaped oddities were produced by Petersen Products of Chicago ca. the mid-'60s, and anecdotal Midwestern lore has it that their intent was to be offered as giveaways for the Polk Brothers, a local appliance chain. This may be how they ended up, although the gargantuan original packaging makes no reference to any such promotion. The box does call out what the optional colors were. Many have noted the striking resemblance to the similarly named wares of the Swaggerty company (see Swaggerty) of California, who also offered brightly colored plywood-bodied ukes in comically oversized incarnations, but who was copying whom has yet to be determined.

Ukulele
Long boat oar body, uke scale, brown, natural, red, or black.

1965		$300	$400

Regal

Ca. 1884-1966, 1987-present. Like the other large 1930s Chicago makers, Harmony and Lyon & Healy, the good ukes are very, very good, and the cheap ukes are very, very cheap. Unlike its pals, however, Regal seems to have produced more ukuleles in imaginative themes, striking color schemes, and in more degrees of fancy trim, making them the quintessential wall-hangers. And lucky for you, there's a vintage Regal uke to suit every décor.

Carson Robison Ukulele
Top sports painted signature, cowboy scene.

1935		$750	$1,000

Jungle Ukulele
Birch body, covered in leopard skin fabric.

1950		$500	$900

Resonator Ukulele
Black body, F-holes, see Dobro uke.

1934		$800	$1,000

Soprano Ukulele (birch)
Birch body.

1931	Brown sunburst	$175	$300
1931	Nautical themes, various colors	$175	$250
1945	Painted body, victory themes	$700	$1,000

Soprano Ukulele (koa)
Koa body, multicolored rope bound top.

1930		$300	$500

Soprano Ukulele (mahogany)
Mahogany body.

1930	Multiple bound top	$500	$800
1935	Spruce top, inlays	$350	$700
1940	Extended 'board	$250	$300

Tiple Ukulele

1930	Birch body stained dark, black binding	$300	$450
1935	Spruce top, mahogany body, fancy binding	$400	$550

Wendall Hall Red Head Ukulele
Koa body, celebrity decal on headstock.

1935		$600	$700

Renaissance Guitars

1994-present. In '05 luthier Rick Turner added a line of acoustic and acoustic/electric ukuleles built in Santa Cruz, California. He also builds guitars and basses.

Rogue

2001-present. Budget grade, production, imported ukuleles. They also offer guitars, basses, mandolins, banjos, effects and amps.

S. S. Stewart

Not much is known about the ukuleles of this Philadelphia firm, except that they were most certainly sub-contracted from another maker or makers.

Soprano Ukulele
Mahogany body, bound top and back.

1927		$300	$500

Samick

1958-2001, 2002-present. Budget grade, production, imported ukuleles. They also offer guitars, basses, mandolins and banjos.

Sammo

Flashy internal paper labels trumpet that these ukes (mandolins and guitars, too) were products of the Osborne Mfg. Co. Masonic Temple, Chicago-Illinois and what the heck any of that means is still open to modern speculation. Your guess is as good as mine. Still, the high quality and often opulent degree of ornamentation that the instruments exhibit, coupled with even the vaguest implication that they were made by guys wearing fezzes and/or men who ride around in tiny cars at parades is all the reason we need to buy every one we see.

Soprano Ukulele

1925	Figured maple body, 5-ply top, back binding	$500	$700
1925	Unbound koa body, fancy headstock shape	$500	$700

Silvertone

1941-ca. 1970, present. Silvertone was the house brand of Sears & Roebuck and most (if not all) of its ukes were manufactured for them by Harmony.

Soprano Ukulele
Mahogany body, Harmony-made.

1950	Sunburst	$150	$250
1950	Unbound	$150	$250
1955	Bound	$150	$250
1960	Green	$150	$250

Petersen Polk-A-Lay-Lee

Regal Jungle Uke

Silvertone

UKULELES

Slingerland uke

Specimen Products aluminum uke

Supertone Cheerleader

MODEL YEAR	FEATURES	EXC. COND. LOW	HIGH

Slingerland

Banjo ukuleles bearing this brand (see Slingerland Banjo uke section below) were certainly made by the popular drum company (banjos being little more than drums with necks, after all). Slingerland standard ukuleles, on the other hand, bear an uncanny resemblance to the work of the Oscar Schmidt company.

Soprano Ukulele
Koa body, rope bound top and soundhole.

1920		$300	$500

Specimen Products

1984-present. Luthier Ian Schneller builds his professional grade, production/custom, ukuleles in Chicago, Illinois. He also builds guitars, basses, amps and speaker cabs. Schneller has built some of the most offbeat, endearing - and high quality - custom ukuleles available.

Sterling

The miniscule reference buried deep within the headstock decal to a T.B. Co. can only mean that the Sterling ukulele somehow fits into the mind-numbing Tonk Bros./Lyon & Healy/Regal/S.S. Stewart manufacturing puzzle. Nonetheless, the brand must have been reserved for the cream of the crop, since the Sterling ukes that surface tend to be of the drop-dead-gorgeous variety.

Soprano Ukulele
Flamed koa, multiple fancy binding all over.

1935		$2,500	$3,000

Stetson

Popular misconception - to say nothing of wishful thinking and greed - has it that all instruments labeled with the Stetson brand were the work of the Larson Brothers of Chicago. While a few Stetson guitars and a very few mandolins may be genuine Larson product, the ukuleles surely were made elsewhere.

Soprano Ukulele
Mahogany body, single bound top and back.

1930		$250	$400

Supertone

1914-1940s. For whatever reason, Supertone was the name attached to Sears' musical instruments before the line became Silvertone (see above). These, too, were all Harmony-made.

Soprano Ukulele (koa)
Koa body, Harmony-made.

1935	Rope bound	$250	$500
1943	Unbound	$150	$400

Soprano Ukulele (mahogany)
Mahogany body, Harmony-made.

1930	Unbound	$200	$350
1940	Bound	$200	$350

Swaggerty

Not enough is known of this West Coast company, except that their product line of unusually shaped 4 stringed novelty instruments oddly mirrors those made by Petersen Products in Chicago at the same time (see Polk-a-lay-lee). The two companies even seem to have shared plastic parts, such as 'boards and tuners. Go figure.

Kook-a-lay-lee Ukulele
Green plywood body, twin necks.

1965		$300	$500

Surf-a-lay-lee Ukulele
Plywood body, long horn, green, yellow, or orange.

1965		$250	$400

Tabu

The Tabu brand on either the back of a ukulele's headstock or inside its soundhole was never an indication of its original maker. Rather, it was intended to assure the purchaser that the uke was, indeed of bona fide Hawaiian origin. So rampant was the practice of mainland makers claiming Island manufacture of their wares that in the late 'teens Hawaii launched a campaign to set the record straight, and – lucky for you – a nifty little brand was the result. The Tabu mark actually was used to mark the ukes of several different makers.

Soprano Ukulele
Figured koa body.

1915	Rope bound	$700	$1,000
1915	Unbound	$500	$800

Turturro

Unlike manufacturers like Regal and Harmony who were content to produce novelty ukes by merely spray painting or applying decals with eye-catching motifs, New York manufacturer Nicola Turturro issued novelty ukuleles from his own patented designs. The most well-known is the Turnover Uke, a playable two-sided contraption strung as a four string uke on one side, and an eight string mandolin on the other.

Peanut Ukulele
Ribbed peanut shaped body.

1928		$300	$500

Turnover Ukulele
Two-sided uke and mandolin.

1926		$500	$700

Vega

Famous for their banjos, the Vega name was applied to a sole baritone uke, tied with the endorsement of 1950s TV crooner Arthur Godfrey.

Arthur Godfrey Baritone Ukulele
Mahogany body, unbound.

1955		$500	$700

Washburn

See Lyon & Healy.

UKULELES

MODEL		EXC. COND.	
YEAR	FEATURES	LOW	HIGH

Weissenborn

1910s-1937. The mainland maker famous for their hollow-necked Hawaiian guitars was responsible for several uke offerings over the course of its 20-or-so-year run. Like their 6-stringed big brothers, they were the closest thing to Island design and detail to come from the mainland.

Soprano Ukulele

1920	Rope bound	$1,500	$2,000
1920	Unbound	$1,500	$2,000

Weymann

Renowned for fine tenor banjos, Weyman affixed their name to a full line of soprano ukes of varying degrees of decoration, quite certainly none of which were made under the same roof as the banjos. Most were C.F. Martin knock-offs.

Soprano Ukulele

1925	Mahogany, unbound	$500	$700
1930	Koa, fancy pearl vine 'board inlay	$1,500	$2,000

Banjo Ukuleles
Bacon

This legendary Connecticut banjo maker just couldn't resist the temptation to extend their line with uke versions of their popular banjos. As with Gibson, Ludwig, Slingerland, and Weyman, the banjo ukuleles tended to mimic the already proven construction techniques and decorative motifs of their regular banjo counterparts. In materials, finish, and hardware, most banjo ukes share many more similarities with full sized banjos than differences. The banjo ukes were simply included as smaller, plainer, variations of banjos, much as concert, tenor, and baritone options fleshed out standard ukulele lines.

Banjo Ukulele
Walnut rim, fancy 'board inlays.

1927		$1,000	$1,200

Silver Bell Banjo Ukulele
Engraved pearloid 'board and headstock.

1927		$1,500	$2,000

Dixie

With chrome plated all-metal design, there's only one word for these banjo ukes, "shiny." Their bodies, necks, and frets are die cast together in zinc (think Hot Wheels cars and screen door handles), the Dixie must have made the perfect indestructible instrument for Junior's birthday back in the 1960s. Similar to one made by Werko.

Banjo Ukulele
One-piece, all-metal construction.

1960		$150	$300

Gibson
BU-1 Banjo Uke
Small 6" head, flat panel resonator.

1928		$300	$550

BU-2 Banjo Uke
8" head, dot inlay.

1930		$500	$750

BU-3 Banjo Uke
8" head, diamond and square inlay.

1935		$1,000	$1,250

BU-4 Banjo Uke
8" head, resonator and flange.

1932		$1,000	$1,500

BU-5 Banjo Uke
8" head, resonator and flange, gold parts.

1937		$1,500	$2,500

Le Domino
Banjo Ukulele
Resonator, decorated as Le Domino uke.

1933		$350	$500

Ludwig

The Ludwig was then, and is today, the Cadillac of banjo ukes. British banjo uke icon George Formby's preference for Ludwig continues assuring their desirability, while the fact that they were available in only a couple of models, for a few short years, and in relatively small production numbers only adds to the mystique.

Banjo Uke

1928	Flange w/ crown holes, nickel or gold plated parts	$3,000	$4,000
1930	Ivoroid headstock overlay w/ art deco detail	$2,000	$2,500

Wendell Hall Professional Banjo Uke
Walnut resonator, flange with oval holes.

1927		$1,500	$2,000

Lyon & Healy
Banjo Uke
Walnut neck and resonator, fancy pearl inlay.

1935		$1,500	$2,000

Paramount

1920s-1942, Late 1940s. The William L. Lange Company began selling Paramount banjos, guitar banjos and mandolin banjos in the early 1920s. Gretsch picked up the Paramount name and used it on guitars for a time in the late '40s.

Banner Blue Banjo Uke
Brass hearts 'board inlay, walnut neck.

1933		$1,000	$1,250

Regal
Banjo Ukulele
Mahogany rim, resonator, fancy rope bound.

1933		$300	$500

Weissenborn

Gibson BU 3

Ludwig Banjo Uke

UKULELES

Richter banjo uke

MODEL YEAR	FEATURES	EXC. COND. LOW	HIGH

Richter

Allegedly, this Chicago company bought the already-made guitars, ukes, and mandolins of other manufacturers, painted and decorated them to their liking and resold them. True or not, they certainly were cranked out in a bevy of swanky colors.

Banjo Uke

Chrome plated body, 2 f-holes in back.

1930		$250	$350
1930	Entire body/neck painted	$250	$350

Slingerland

May Bell Banjo Uke

Walnut resonator with multicolored rope.

1935		$400	$600

MODEL YEAR	FEATURES	EXC. COND. LOW	HIGH

Werco

These Chicago-made banjo ukuleles had construction similar to the Dixie brand, and except for the addition of a swank layer of blue sparkle drum binding on the rim, you would be hard pressed to tell them apart.

Banjo Uke

Chrome-plated metal body and neck.

1960		$150	$300

Weymann

Banjo Uke

Maple rim, open back, ebony 'board.

1926		$1,000	$1,200

UKULELES

Banjos

Bacon & Day Silver Bell #1

Deering Maple Brothers

MODEL YEAR	FEATURES	EXC. COND. LOW	HIGH

Bacon & Day

1921-1967. David Day left Vega to join up with Fred Bacon in '21. Gretsch purchased Bacon & Day in '40, and ran the Bacon line until '67.

Blue Bell

| 1922-1939 | Tenor | $1,400 | $1,600 |

Blue Ribbon 17

| 1933-1939 | Tenor | $450 | $850 |

Ne Plus Ultra

1920s	Tenor	$8,000	$10,000
1930s	Tenor	$8,000	$10,000
1950s	Tenor	$2,600	$3,000
1960s	Tenor	$2,600	$3,000

Senorita

| 1930 | Plectrum, pearloid, resonator | $1,100 | $1,200 |
| 1950s | 4-string | $500 | $700 |

Silver Bell #1

| 1922-1939 | Tenor | $1,800 | $2,500 |

Silver Bell Montana #1

| 1933-1939 | Tenor | $2,100 | $2,400 |

Sultana #1

| 1933-1939 | Tenor | $2,300 | $2,500 |

Super

| 1920-1923 | Tenor | $950 | $1,250 |
| 1927 | 5-string, fancy appt., flamed resonator | $3,400 | $3,700 |

Barratt

1890s. Made by George Barratt in Brooklyn, New York.

5-string

Victorian era.

| 1890s | | $350 | $450 |

Benary and Sons

1890-1899. Manufactured by the James H. Buckbee Co. for music instrument wholesaler Robert Benary.

Celebrated Benary

1890-1899. 5-string, open back, plain appointments.

| 1890-1899 | | $500 | $600 |

Boucher

1830s-1850s. William Boucher's operation in Baltimore is considered to be one of the very first banjo-shops. Boucher and the Civil War era banjos are rare. The price range listed is informational guidance pricing only. The wide range reflects conservative opinions. 150 year old banjos should be evaluated per their own merits.

Boucher banjos

| 1840s | | $3,000 | $15,000 |

Buckbee

1863-1897. James H. Buckbee Co. of New York was the city's largest builder. The company did considerable private branding for companies such as Benery, Dobson, and Farland.

Buckbee 5-string

1890-1897. 5-string, open back, plain appointments.

| 1890-1897 | Higher-level models | $600 | $800 |
| 1890-1897 | Lower-level models | $400 | $600 |

Cole

1890-1919. W.A. Cole, after leaving Fairbanks & Cole, started his own line in 1890. He died in 1909 but the company continued until 1919.

Eclipse

| 1890-1919 | Flower inlays, dots | $1,700 | $2,500 |
| 1890-1919 | Man-in-the-moon inlays | $2,500 | $3,800 |

Deering

1975-present. Greg and Janet Deering build their banjos in Spring Valley, California. In 1978 they introduced their Basic and Intermediate banjos. They also offer banjos under the Vega and Goodtime brands.

Ditson

1916-1930. The Oliver Ditson Company of Boston offered a variety of musical instruments.

Tenor Banjo

1920. 4-string, resonator with typical appointments.

| 1920 | | $600 | $700 |

Dobson, George

1870-1890. Marketed by George C. Dobson of Boston, Massachusetts. Brothers Henry, George, and Edgar Dobson were banjo teachers and performers. They designed banjos that were built for them by manufactures such as Buckbee of New York.

Matchless

| 1880s | 5-string | $600 | $800 |

Epiphone

1873-present. Epiphone introduced banjos in the early 1920s, if not sooner, offering them up to WW II. After Gibson bought the company in '57, they reintroduced banjos to the line, which they still offer.

EB-44 Campus

1960s. Long neck, folk-era 5-string banjo.

| 1960s | | $700 | $800 |

Electar (electric) Tenor Banjo

1930s. Maple body, 1 pickup, 3 knobs.

| 1930s | | $1,350 | $1,450 |

Recording A

Ca. 1925-ca. 1935. Epiphone Recording logo on headstock, flamed maple neck and resonator, fancy pearl inlay markers

| 1920s | Tenor | $2,000 | $2,200 |

Recording B

Ca. 1925-ca. 1935.

| 1930s | Tenor | $2,200 | $2,500 |

MODEL YEAR	FEATURES	EXC. COND. LOW	HIGH

Recording Concert C Special
1930s. Tenor, maple body, fancy appointments, resonator.

1930s		$3,200	$3,500

TB-100
Mid 1960s.

1960s	Tenor	$800	$900

Fairbanks/Vega Fairbanks/ A.C. Fairbanks
1875-1919. From 1875 to 1880, A. C. Fairbanks built his own designs in Boston. In 1880, W. A. Cole joined the company, starting Fairbanks & Cole, but left in 1890 to start his own line. The company went by Fairbanks Co. until it was purchased by Vega in 1904. The banjos were then branded Vega Fairbanks until 1919.

Acme (F & C)
1880-1890. 5-string, open back, fancy markers.

1880-1890		$900	$1,000

Electric No. 3
1890s	5-string	$7,000	$7,500

Senator No. 1/Fairbanks 3
1900s	5-string	$1,400	$1,500

Vega Lady's Banjo
1913		$800	$900

Whyte Laydie #2
1901-1904	5-string	$3,300	$3,700

Whyte Laydie #7
1901-1904		$7,500	$9,000
1909		$8,000	$9,000
1921		$8,000	$9,000

Farland
Ca. 1890-1920s. Buckbee and others made instruments for New York banjo teacher and performer A. A. Farland.

Concert Grand
1900-1920	5-string	$1,000	$1,400

Fender
1946-present. Fender added banjos to their product mix in the late 1960s, and continues to offer them.

Allegro (Tenor or 5-string)
Late 1960s-1970s.

1960s		$800	$900

Leo Deluxe
1970s

1970s		$1,600	$1,700

Framus
1946-1977, 1996-present. The new Framus company, located in Markneukirchen, Germany, continues to offer banjos.

5-string Model
1960s		$150	$300

Gibson
1890s (1902)-present. Gibson started making banjos in 1918, and continues to manufacture them. Vega and Gibson were the only major manufacturing companies that offered banjos in their product catalog in the '50s.

    RB prefix = regular banjo (5-string)
    TB prefix = tenor banjo (4-string, tenor tuning)
    PB prefix = plectrum banjo (4-string, plectrum tuning)

All American
1930-1937. Tenor banjo, fancy appointments, historic art, gold hardware.

1930-1937		$13,000	$18,000

Bella Voce
1927-1931. Tenor banjo, fancy appointments, flower-pattern art, gold hardware.

1927-1931		$11,000	$16,000

Earl Scruggs Standard
1984-present. 5-string, high-end appointments, Standard added to model name in '92.

1980s		$2,500	$2,800
1990s		$2,700	$3,000
2000s		$2,800	$3,000

ETB Electric Tenor Banjo
1939-1942. Electric Tenor Banjo, Charlie Christian pickup.

1939-1942	Christian pickup	$1,850	$2,450

Florentine Plectrum
1925-1930	2 piece flange	$11,000	$16,000

Florentine Tenor
1927-1937. High-end appointments, gold hardware.

1927-1937		$9,000	$14,000

Granada Earl Scruggs
With high-end replacement tone ring.

1988-1999		$3,500	$4,000

Granada RB
1925-1939. 5-string banjo with either a 2 piece flange (1925-1930), or a 1 piece flange (1933-1939).

1925-1930		$25,000	$30,000
1933-1939	Flat head tone ring	$135,000	$200,000

Granada TB
1925-1939. Tenor banjo with either a 2 piece flange (1925-1930), or a 1 piece flange (1933-1939).

1925-1930		$20,000	$27,000
1933-1939	Flat head tone ring	$100,000	$150,000

PB-3
1923-1937. Laminated maple resonator Mastertone model, plectrum neck and tuning.

1925-1927		$2,000	$2,400

PB-4
1925-1940. Plectrum banjo with either a 2 piece flange (1925-1932), or a 1 piece flange (1933-1940).

1925-1927	Ball bearing tone ring	$2,500	$3,500
1928-1932	Archtop	$3,500	$4,000
1933-1940	Archtop	$8,000	$12,000
1933-1940	Flat head tone ring	$60,000	$80,000

Fender FB59

1927 Gibson Granada

BANJOS

Gibson RB-3

Gretsch tenor

MODEL YEAR	FEATURES	EXC. COND. LOW	HIGH
RB Jr.			
1924-1925. 5-string, budget line, open back.			
1924-1925		$1,200	$1,300
RB-00			
1932-1942.			
1932-1942		$2,000	$2,100
RB-1			
1922-1940.			
1930-1932	1 piece flange	$1,900	$3,100
1933-1939	Diamond flange	$2,500	$2,800
1933-1939	w/ high-end replacement tone ring	$4,000	$4,500
RB-2			
1933-1939		$8,000	$9,000
RB-3			
1923-1937, 1988-present.			
1988-1999		$2,000	$2,500
2000-2005		$2,000	$3,000
RB-4			
1922-1937. 5-string banjo with either a 2 piece flange (1925-1931), or a 1 piece flange (1933-1937). Trap or non-trap door on earlier models (1922-1924).			
1922-1924	Trap or non-trap door	$2,000	$3,500
1925-1931	Archtop, resonator	$17,000	$23,000
1933-1937	Archtop	$30,000	$40,000
1933-1937	Flat head tone ring	$75,000	$125,000
RB-6			
1927-1937. 5-string banjo with fancy appointments.			
1927-1933	Archtop	$15,000	$25,000
RB-11			
1931-1942.			
1933-1939		$5,300	$5,700
RB-100			
1948-1979.			
1970-1979		$1,000	$1,200
RB-170			
1960-1973. 5-string, no resonator, dot markers, decal logo, multi-ply maple rim.			
1960-1973		$1,000	$1,200
RB-175			
1962-1973. 2000s. Open back, long neck typical of banjos of the 1960s. Models include the RB-175, RB-175 Long Neck, RB-175 Folk.			
1962-1964	RB-175/Long Neck	$1,100	$1,400
1965-1969	Folk	$1,000	$1,300
1970-1973	RB-175	$900	$1,100
RB-250			
1954-present.			
1964-1968	Flat head tone ring	$2,000	$2,200
1970s	Mastertone	$1,600	$2,000
1980s	Mastertone	$1,600	$2,000
RB-800			
1964-1986.			
1971-1986		$2,600	$3,000

MODEL YEAR	FEATURES	EXC. COND. LOW	HIGH
TB			
1918-1923. Renamed TB-4.			
1919		$1,000	$1,300
TB-00			
1932-1942.			
1939		$2,500	$2,800
TB-1			
1922-1939. Tenor banjo with a 1 piece flange.			
1922-1924	Trap door	$750	$850
1925	No resonator	$750	$850
1926	Maple resonator, shoe-plate	$750	$1,100
1933-1939	Simple hoop tone ring	$2,900	$3,200
TB-1 Conversion			
1922-1939. TB-1 with a 5-string conversion and a flat head tone ring.			
1933-1939		$3,400	$3,800
TB-2			
1920-1937.			
1922-1928	Wavy flange	$600	$700
1933-1939	Pearloid board	$3,400	$4,000
TB-3			
1927-1939. Tenor banjo with either a 2 piece flange (1927-1931), or a 1 piece flange (1933-1939).			
1925-1926	Ball-bearing tone ring	$2,200	$3,000
1927-1931	40 or no hole ring	$3,000	$4,000
1933-1939	40 or no hole ring	$8,000	$10,000
1933-1939	Flat head tone ring	$50,000	$70,000
1933-1939	Wreath, archtop	$15,000	$18,000
TB-4			
1923-1937.			
1923-1924	Trap door	$1,500	$1,800
TB-5			
1923-1929.			
1922-1924	Trap door	$1,800	$2,000
TB-11			
1931-1942.			
1933-1939		$3,200	$3,600
TB-11 Conversion			
1933-1939. TB-11 with a 5-string conversion and a flat head tone ring.			
1933-1939		$3,800	$4,200
TB-100			
1948-1979.			
1963-1967		$900	$1,300
TB-250			
1954-1996.			
1970s	Mastertone	$1,500	$2,000

Gretsch

1883-present. Gretsch offered banjos in the '20s and again in the '50s and '60s.

Broadkaster Banjo

1932-1939. Tenor or 5-string banjo with pearloid head and board.

1932-1939	5-string	$700	$1,300
1932-1939	Tenor	$475	$800

The *Vintage Guitar Price Guide* shows low to high values for items in all-original excellent condition, and, where applicable, with original case or cover.

MODEL YEAR	FEATURES	EXC. COND. LOW	HIGH

Orchestella
1925-1929. Tenor or 5-string banjo with gold engravings.

1925-1929	5-string	$2,800	$3,300
1925-1929	Tenor	$900	$1,100

Tenor short-scale
1925-1929	Plain styling	$200	$300
1950s	Plain styling	$250	$300

GTR
1974-1978. GTR (for George Gruhn, Tut Taylor, Randy Wood) was the original name for Gruhn Guitars in Nashville, and they imported mandolins and banjos from Japan.

GTR 5-string banjo copy
1970s		$1,000	$1,100

Harmony
1892-1976, late 1970s-present. Huge, Chicago-based manufacturer of fretted instruments, mainly budget models under the Harmony name or for many other American brands and mass marketers.

Electro
1950s. Electric banjo, wood body, 1 pickup.
1950s		$600	$800

Kalamazoo
1933-1942, 1965-1970. Budget brand built by Gibson. Made flat-tops, solidbodies, mandolins, lap steels, banjos and amps.

Kalamazoo banjos
1935-1940	Plectrum, KPB	$400	$900
1935-1941	5-string, KRB	$500	$1,000

Kay
Ca. 1931 (1890)-present. Kay was a huge manufacturer and built instruments under their name and for a large number of other retailers, jobbers, and brand names.

Student Tenor Banjo
1950s		$250	$350

Kel Kroydon (by Gibson)
1930-1933. Private branded instruments made by Gibson.

Kel Kroyden banjo
1930-1933	Conversion	$3,600	$3,900
1930-1933	Tenor	$2,500	$3,500

Keystone State
1920s. Brand of banjos built by Weymann.

Style 2
1920s. Tenor, resonator, fancy appointments.
1920s		$1,100	$1,300

Lange
1920s-1942, Late 1940s. The William L. Lange Company began selling Paramount banjos, guitar banjos and mandolin banjos in the early 1920s. Gretsch picked up the Paramount name and used

it on acoustics and electrics for a time in the late '40s. See Paramount for more listings.

Tourraine Deluxe
1920s	Tenor	$400	$500

Leedy
1989- Founded in Indianapolis by U. G. Leedy, the company started making banjos in 1924. Leedy was bought out by C. G. Conn in '30.

Solotone
1924-1930	Tenor	$800	$1,200

Ludwig
The Ludwig Drum Company was founded in 1909. They saw a good business opportunity and entered the banjo market in '21. When demand for banjos tanked in '30, Ludwig dropped the line and concentrated on its core business.

Bellevue
1920s. Tenor, closed-back banjo with fancy appointments.
1920s		$800	$1,200

Big Chief
1930. Carved and engraved plectrum banjo.
1930		$7,500	$9,500

Capital
1920s. Tenor banjo, resonator and nice appointments.
1920s		$900	$1,300

Commodore
1930s. Tenor or plectrum, with gold hardware and fancy appointments.
1930s	Tenor	$1,500	$1,800
1932	Plectrum	$2,300	$2,500

Deluxe
1930s. Engraved tenor, with gold hardware.
1930s		$2,800	$3,300

Dixie
1930s	Tenor	$400	$500

Kenmore Plectrum Banjo
1920s	Open back	$600	$750

Kenmore Tenor Banjo
1920s	Resonator	$450	$600

Kingston
1924-1930	Tenor	$600	$800

Standard Art Tenor Banjo
1924-1930. Tenor banjo with fancy appointments.
1924-1930		$3,900	$4,500

The Ace
1920s. Tenor banjo, resonator and nickel appointments.
1920s		$1,100	$1,400

Morrison
Ca. 1870-ca. 1915. Marketed by New Yorker James Morrison, made by Morrison or possibly others like Buckbee. After 1875, his instruments sported the patented Morrison tone ring.

5-string
1885-1890		$700	$800

GTR five-string

Kay KBJ24

Orpheum 22-fret

Paramount Aristrocrat tenor

MODEL YEAR	FEATURES	EXC. COND. LOW	HIGH

ODE/Muse

1961-1980. Founded by Charles Ogsbury in Boulder, Colorado, purchased by Baldwin in '66 and moved to Nashville, Gretsch took over in '76. Muse was a retail store brand of banjos produced by ODE from '61 to '66. In '71, Ogsbury started the OME Banjo Company in Colorado.

Model C

1976-1980. 5-string banjo, resonator and fancy markers.

1976-1980		$1,400	$2,000

Model D

1970s-1980. 5-string banjo, resonator and gold engravings.

1970s		$2,100	$2,800

Orpheum

1897-1922. Lange and Rettberg purchased the J.H. Buckbee banjo factory in 1897 and started making banjos under the Orpheum label. William Lange took control in 1922 and changed the name to Paramount.

Model #2

1920-1922	5-string	$2,800	$3,000
1920-1922	Tenor	$1,000	$1,500

Model #3

1915	5-string	$3,500	$3,750

Paramount

1921-1935. William Lange and his Paramount company are generally accredited with commercializing the first modern flange and resonator in 1921.

Aristocrat

1921-1935	Plectrum	$1,500	$2,200
1921-1935	Tenor	$1,300	$1,900

Aristocrat Special

1921-1935. Plectrum banjo with fancy appointments.

1921-1935		$2,000	$3,000

Artists Supreme

1930s. High-end appointments, 19-fret tenor, engraved gold-plated hardware.

1930s	Tenor	$5,000	$6,000

Junior

1921-1935	Plectrum	$800	$1,100
1921-1935	Tenor, resonator	$700	$950

Leader

1921-1935	Plectrum	$1,000	$1,300
1921-1935	Tenor	$850	$1,100

Style 1

1921-1935	Plectrum	$475	$675
1921-1935	Tenor	$400	$600

Style 2

1921-1935. Tenor banjo, resonator and plain appointments.

1921-1935		$500	$650

MODEL YEAR	FEATURES	EXC. COND. LOW	HIGH

Style A

1921-1935. Models include the Style A Tenor, Plectrum, and the 5-string (with resonator and fancy appointments).

1921-1935	5-string	$2,300	$2,500
1921-1935	Plectrum	$1,400	$1,700
1921-1935	Tenor	$1,300	$1,600

Style B

1921-1935. Models include the Style B Tenor, and the Plectrum (with resonator and fancy appointments).

1921-1935	Plectrum	$1,400	$1,700
1921-1935	Tenor	$1,300	$1,600

Style C

1921-1935. Models include the Style C Tenor, Plectrum, and the 5-string (with resonator and fancy appointments).

1921-1935	5-string	$3,000	$3,800
1921-1935	Plectrum	$1,700	$2,300
1921-1935	Tenor	$1,400	$1,800

Style D

1921-1935	Plectrum	$2,500	$3,500
1921-1935	Tenor	$2,300	$3,300

Style E

1921-1935	Plectrum	$2,600	$3,600
1921-1935	Tenor	$2,400	$3,400

Style F

1921-1935	Plectrum	$3,800	$4,200
1921-1935	Tenor	$3,300	$3,600

Super/Super Paramount

1921-1935	Plectrum	$4,100	$4,800
1921-1935	Tenor	$3,700	$4,200

Trooper

1921-1935	Plectrum	$700	$800
1921-1935	Tenor	$600	$700

Recording King (TML)

2005-present. Intermediate and professional grade, production, banjos imported by The Music Link, which also offers Johnson and other brand instruments. They also have guitars.

S.S. Stewart

1878-1904. S.S. Stewart of Philadelphia is considered to be one of the most important and prolific banjo manufacturers of the late 19th century. It's estimated that approximately 25,000 banjos were made by this company.

American Princess (5-string)

1890s	10" rim	$900	$1,150

Banjeaurine

1890. 5-string banjo, 10" head with and open back.

1890		$1,100	$1,200

Orchestra

1890s	5-string	$1,200	$1,400

Piccolo

1880s	5-string, 7" rim	$1,100	$1,200

Universal Favorite

1892	11" head	$900	$1,100

MODEL YEAR	FEATURES	EXC. COND. LOW	HIGH

Silvertone

1941-ca. 1970, present. Brand of Sears instruments which replaced their Supertone brand in '41. Currently, Samick offers a line of amps under the Silvertone name.

Silvertone 5-string banjo copy

1960s		$300	$400

Slingerland

1930s-mid-1940s. The parent company was Slingerland Banjo and Drums, Chicago, Illinois. The company offered other stringed instruments into the '40s. Slingerland Drums is now owned by Gibson.

Student/economy tenor banjo

1930s. Models include the Tenor, Student, and Maybell series banjos.

1930s		$300	$600

Studio King

1930s. Banjos made by Gibson, most likely for a mail-order house or a jobber.

Studio King banjo

1933-1937	Original 5-string	$2,300	$2,500
1933-1937	Tenor	$1,200	$1,300

Superb

1920s. Private brand made by Epiphone.

Tenor Banjo

Mayfair Tenor, resonator.

1920s		$400	$500

Supertone

1914-1941. Brand used by Sears, Roebuck and Company for instruments made by various American manufacturers, including its own Harmony subsidiary Harmony. In '40, Sears began making a transition to the Silvertone brand.

Prairie Wonder

1925. 5-string, open back banjo.

1925		$300	$600

Thompson & Odell

1875-1998. Boston instrument importers Thompson & Odell started building banjos in the 1880s.

Artist Banjo

1880s	5-string, fretless	$700	$800

Tilton

1850s-late 1800s. Built by William B. Tilton, of New York City. He was quite an innovator and held several instrument-related patents. He also built guitars.

Vega

1903-1980s, 1989-present. Vega of Boston got into the banjo business in 1904 when it purchased Fairbanks. Vega and Gibson were the only major manufacturing companies that offered banjos in their product catalog in the 1950s. The Deering Banjo Company acquired the brand in '89 and uses it on a line of banjos.

Artist Professional #9

1923-1929	Tenor	$2,500	$2,800

Folk Ranger FR-5 Banjo

1960s. 5-string, open back.

1960s		$450	$500

Folk Wonder

1960s	5-string	$850	$1,000

Little Wonder

1920s	Plectrum	$600	$700
1920s	Tenor	$550	$650
1930s	Tenor	$550	$650

Pete Seeger

1958-1966. 5-string, long neck banjo.

1958-1964	Folk era	$2,800	$5,300
1965-1966		$1,500	$3,000

Professional

1960. 5-string banjo with a Tubaphone tone ring.

1960		$1,300	$1,400

Ranger 5-string Banjo

1960s. Standard appointments, dot markers.

1966	5-string	$550	$650

Regent

1920s. 5-string banjo with an open back and dot markers.

1920s		$1,800	$2,000

Style 9

1920s. Tenor banjo with fancy appointments.

1920s		$1,400	$1,500

Style M

1920s. Tenor banjo, models include the Style M and the Style M Tubaphone.

1920s	Style M	$1,900	$2,000
1920s	Tubaphone	$1,100	$1,500

Style X

1926	Tenor	$2,000	$2,800

Tubaphone #3

1918-1929	5-string	$3,500	$4,000
1923-1929	Plectrum	$1,100	$1,400

Tubaphone #9 5-string Banjo

1929		$6,500	$8,000

Tubaphone Deluxe 5-string

1920s. Higher-end appointments, carved heel, Deluxe logo on tailpiece.

1923		$11,000	$13,000

V.I.P. Tenor Banjo

1970s. 4-string, open back, fancy engraved pearl markers, on-board electronics.

1970		$1,800	$1,900

V-45

1970. Plectrum banjo, flat head tone ring, fancy appointments.

1970		$2,800	$3,000

Vegaphone Professional

1960s	5-string	$900	$1,000

Vegavox IV Plectrum Banjo

1960s. IV logo on truss rod cover, high-end appointments, 4-string plectrum neck.

1962		$5,000	$5,500

Whyte Laydie #3

1923-1928	5-string	$3,300	$3,800

S.S. Stewart Thoroughbred

Vega 22-fret plectrum

BANJOS

Washburn 5183 tenor

MODEL YEAR	FEATURES	EXC. COND. LOW	HIGH
Whyte Laydie #7			
1905		$7,000	$8,000
Whyte Laydie Style R			
1930s. Tenor banjo with closed back.			
1930s		$1,200	$1,300

Washburn (Lyon & Healy)

1880s-ca.1949. Washburn was the brand name of Lyon & Healy of Chicago. They made banjos from 1880-1929.

MODEL YEAR	FEATURES	EXC. COND. LOW	HIGH
Irene 5-string			
1920s		$750	$800

Weymann

1864-1940s. The Weymann company was founded in 1864 and got seriously into the banjo manufacturing business in 1917. They manufactured banjos until around 1930.

MODEL YEAR	FEATURES	EXC. COND. LOW	HIGH
Orchestra			
1920s	Style A Plectrum	$750	$1,000
1924-1928	#1 Tenor	$750	$1,000
1924-1928	#2 Tenor	$950	$1,200
Style #6			
1924-1928		$4,000	$5,000

Yosco

1900-1930s. Lawrence L. Yosco was a New York City luthier building guitars, round back mandolins and banjos under his own brand and for others.

MODEL YEAR	FEATURES	EXC. COND. LOW	HIGH
Style 3 Tenor			
1920s		$1,250	$1,400

BIBLIOGRAPHY

'50s Cool: Kay Guitars, by Jay Scott, 1992, Seventh String Press, Inc.

50 Years of Fender, by Tony Bacon, 2000, Miller Freeman Books.

50 Years of Gretsch Electrics, by Tony Bacon, 2005, Backbeat Books.

Acoustic Guitars and Other Fretted Instruments, A Photographic History, by George Gruhn and Walter Carter, 1993, GPI Books.

Acoustic Guitar magazine, various issues, String Letter Publishing.

Acquired of the Angels, by Paul William Schmidt, 1998, Scarecrow Press.

American Basses, by Jim Roberts, 2003, Backbeat Books.

American Guitars, An Illustrated History, by Tom Wheeler, 1992, Harper Collins.

American's Instrument, The Banjo in the Nineteenth Century, by Philip F. Gura and James F. Bollman, 1999, University of North Carolina Press.

Ampeg - The Story Behind The Sound, by Gregg Hopkins and Bill Moore, 1999, Hal Leonard Publishing.

Amps! The Other Half of Rock 'n' Roll, by Ritchie Fliegler, 1993, Hal Leonard publishing.

Analog Man's Guide to Vintage Effects, by Tom Hughes, 2004, Musicians Only Publishing.

The Bass Book, A Complete Illustrated History of Bass Guitars, by Tony Bacon and Barry Moorhouse, 1995, Miller Freeman Books.

The Boss Book, 2001, Hal Leonard Publishing.

The Burns Book, by Paul Day, 1990, PP Publishing and The Bold Strummer.

Classic Guitars U.S.A., by Willie G. Moseley, 1992, Centerstream.

The Classical Guitar Book, by Tony Bacon, et al., 2002, Balafon Books.

The Complete History of Rickenbacker Guitars, by Richard R. Smith, 1987, Centerstream.

Cowboy Guitars, by Steve Evans and Ron Middlebrook, 2002, Centerstream.

Custom Guitars, A Complete Guide to Contempory Handcrafted Guitars, 2000, String Letter Publishing.

The Custom Guitar Shop and Wayne Richard Charvel, by Frank W/m Green, 1999, Working Musician Publications.

A Desktop Reference of Hip Vintage Guitar Amps, by Gerald Weber, 1994, Kendrick Books.

Electric Guitars and Basses, A Photographic History, by George Gruhn and Walter Carter, 1994, GPI Books.

Elektro-Gitarren Made in Germany, by Norbert Schnepel and Helmuth Lemme (German, with English translation), 1987, Musik-Verlag Schnepel-Lemme oHG.

Epiphone: The Complete History, by Walter Carter, 1995, Hal Leonard publishing.

Epiphone: The House of Stathopoulo, by Jim Fisch & L.B. Fred, 1996, Amsco Publications.

The Fender Amp Book, by John Morrish, 1995, Balafon Books and GPI Books.

Fender Amps: The First Fifty Years, by John Teagle and John Sprung, 1995, Hal Leonard Publishing.

The Fender Bass, by Klaus Blasquiz, 1990, Mediapresse.

The Fender Bass, An Illustrated History, by J.W. Black and Albert Molinaro, 2001, Hal Leonard Publishing.

The Fender Book, by Tony Bacon and Paul Day, 1992, Balafon and GPI Books.

Fender: The Sound Heard 'Round the World, by Richard R. Smith, 1995, Garfish Publishing.

The Fender Stratocaster, by Andre Duchossoir, 1988, Mediapresse.

The Fender Telecaster, by Andre Duchossoir, 1991, Hal Leonard Publishing.

G&L: Leo's Legacy, by Paul Bechtoldt, 1994, Woof Associates.

Gibson Electrics, The Classic Years, by A. R. Duchossoir, 1994, Hal Leonard Publishing.

Gibson's Fabulous Flat-Top Guitars, by Eldon Whitford, David Vinopal, and Dan Erlewine, 1994, GPI Books.

Gibson Guitars: 100 Years of An American Icon, by Walter Carter, 1994, W. Quay Hays.

The Gibson Les Paul Book, A Complete History of Les Paul Guitars, by Tony Bacon and Paul Day, 1993 Balafon Books and GPI Books.

The Gibson Super 400, Art of the Fine Guitar, by Thomas A. Van Hoose, 1991, GPI Books.

Gibson Shipping Totals 1948-1979, 1992, J.T.G.

The Gretsch Book, by Tony Bacon & Paul Day, 1996, Balafon Books and GPI Books.

Gruhn's Guide to Vintage Guitars, 2nd Edition, by George Gruhn and Walter Carter, 1999, Miller Freeman Books.

The Guild Guitar Book: The Company and the Instruments 1952-1977, by Hans Moust, 1995, GuitArchives Publications.

Guitar Identification: Fender-Gibson-Gretsch-Martin, by Andre Duchossoir, 1983, Hal Leonard Publishing Corporation.

Guitar People, by Willie G. Moseley, 1997, Vintage Guitar Books.

Guitar Player magazine, various issues, Miller Freeman.

Guitar Stories, Vol. I, by Michael Wright, 1994, Vintage Guitar Books.

Guitar Stories, Vol. II, by Michael Wright, 2000, Vintage Guitar Books.

Guitar World magazine, various issues, Harris Publications.

The Guitars of the Fred Gretsch Company, by Jay Scott, 1992, Centerstream.

Guitars From Neptune, A Definitive Journey Into Danelectro-Mania, by Paul Bechtoldt, 1995, Backporch Publications.

Guitar Graphics, Vol. 1 (Japanese), 1994, Rittor Music Mooks.

The Guru's Guitar Guide, by Tony Bacon and Paul Day, 1990, Track Record and The Bold Strummer.

The History and Artistry of National Resonator Instruments, by Bob Brozman, 1993, Centerstream.

The History of Marshall, by Michael Doyle, 1993, Hal Leonard Publishing.

The History of the Ovation Guitar, by Walter Carter, 1996, Hal Leonard publishing.

The History of Yamaha Guitars, by Mark Kasulen & Matt Blackett, 2006, Hal Leonard Corporation.

Ibanez, the Untold Story, by Paul Specht, Michael Wright, and Jim Donahue, 2005, Hoshino (U.S.A.) Inc.

The Martin Book, by Walter Carter, 1995, Balafon Books and GPI Books.

Martin Guitars, A History, by Mike Longworth, 1988, 4 Maples Press.

Martin Guitars: An Illustrated Celebration of America's Premier Guitarmaker, by Jim Washburn & Richard Johnston, 1997, Rodale Press, Inc.

Musicial Merchandise Review magazine, various issues, Symphony Publishing.

The Music Trades magazine, various issues, Music Trades Corporation.

The Official Vintage Guitar Magazine Price Guide, all editions.

The PRS Guitar Book, by Dave Burrluck, 1999, Outline Press, London.

The Rickenbacker Book, by Tony Bacon & Paul Day, 1994, Balafon Books and GFI Books.

Six Decades of the Fender Telecaster, by Tony Bacon, 2005, Backbeat Books.

Stellas & Stratocasters, by Willie G. Moseley, 1994, Vintage Guitar Books.

Stompbox, by Art Thompson, 1997, Miller Freeman Books.

The Tube Amp Book, 4th Edition, by Aspen Pittman, 1993, Groove Tubes.

The Ultimate Guitar Book, by Tony Bacon and Paul Day, 1991, Alfred A. Knopf.

Vintage Guitar magazine, various issues, Vintage Guitar, Inc.

VG Classics magazine, various issues, Vintage Guitar, Inc.

The Vox Story, A Complete History of the Legend, by David Peterson and Dick Denney, 1993, The Bold Strummer, Ltd.

Washburn: Over One Hundred Years of Fine Stringed Instruments, by John Teagle, 1996, Amsco Publications.

Various manufacturer catalogs, literature, and web sites.

DEALER DIECTORY
A GEOGRAPHICAL GUIDE

AUSTRALIA
Guitar Emporium
Contact: Darren Garth
9 Victoria Avenue
Albert Park, Victoria,
Australia, 3206
Phone 61.3.9696.8032
emporium@ozemail.com.au
www.guitaremporium.com.au

Ric's Vintage Guitars
Contact: Richard Zand-Vliet
Studio 3-13 James St.
Fremantle 6160
West Australia
Phone: international +61 8
9433265
Phone: local 08-94332625
ric@ricsvintageguitars.com
www:ricsvintageguitars.com

CANADA
Capsule Music
Contact: Mark or Peter Kesper
921 Queen St. W.
Toronto, Ontario M6J 1G5
Phone: 416-203-0202
contact@capsulemusic.com
www.capsulemusic.com

Folkway Music
Contact: Mark Stutman
163 Suffolk Street West
Guelph, Ontario N1H 2J7
Phone: 519-763-5524
info@folkwaymusic.com
www.folkwaymusic.com

The Twelfth Fret Inc.
Contact: Grant MacNeill and
  David Wren
2132 Danforth Avenue
Toronto, Ont., Canada M4C 1J9
Phone: 416-423-2132
Fax: 416-423-0012
sales@12fret.com
www.12fret.com

ENGLAND
Ampaholics
Contact: Paul GT
P.O. Box 542
Surrey, GU1 12F, England
Phone: +44-1483-825102
Fax: +44-1483-825102
www.ampaholics.org.uk

Watford Valves & Speakers
Contact: Derek Rocco
Bricket Wood, Street Albans.

Herts. England AL2 3TS
Phone: 44-1923-893270
Fax: 44-1923-679207
sales@watfordvalves.com
www.watfordvalves.com

ITALY
Real Vintage
Contact: Nino Fazio
via Manzoni, 13
98057 Milazzo ME, Italy
Phone: +39-090-40646
realvintage@realvintage.it
www.realvintage.it

UNITED STATES
Alabama
Elite Music Sales
Contact: Brian Hinton
1737 Eastern Blvd.
Montgomery, AL 36117
Phone: 334-215-0215
Fax: 334-215-0216
sales@elitemusicsales.com
www.elitemusicsales.com

Arkansas
Blue Moon Music, Inc.
Contact: Les Haynie
3107 North College Ave.
Fayetteville, AR 72703-2609
Phone: 479-521-8163
blumnmus@aol.com

California
**AA-Ibanez/Gibson Guitar
Collector**
All 1970s - '80s Lawsuit Models
  - L-5s - Byrdlands - Les Pauls
  - ES-335s
Phone: 310-672-2432
bluesfingers@earthlink.net

Buffalo Bros. Guitars
Contact: Steve Mendoza
4901 El Camino Real
Carlsbad, CA 92008
Phone: 760-434-4567
Fax: 760-434-4347
BuffaloBros@aol.com
www.buffalobrosguitars.com

**California Vintage Guitar and
Amps**
5244 Van Nuys Blvd.
Sherman Oaks, CA 91401
Phone: 818-789-8884
www.californiavintageguitaran-
damp.com

Eric Schoenberg Guitars
Contact: Eric
106 Main Street
Tiburon, CA 94920
Phone: 415-789-0846
eric@om28. com
www.om28.com

Freedom Guitar, Inc.
Contact: Dewey L. Bowen
6334 El Cajon Boulevard
San Diego, CA 92115
Phone: 800-831-5569
Fax: 619-265-1414
info@freedomguitar.com
www.freedomguitar.com

Fretted Americana
23901 Calabasas Rd., Ste 2024
Calabasas, CA 91302
Phone: 818-222-4113
Fax: 818-222-6173
vgm@frettedamericana.com
www.frettedamericana.com

Guitar Center (CA)
7425 Sunset Boulevard
Hollywood, CA 90046
Phone: 323-874-2302, 323-874-1060
Fax: 323-969-9783
www.vintageguitars.net

Guitar Connection, The
Contact: Mike VanVoorhees
633 Rose Ave.
Venice, CA 90291
Phone: 310-396-3009
vanvoorhees9@aol.com
www.theguitarconnection.com

Guitar Heaven (CA)
Contact: Frank Benna
1934 Oak Park Blvd.
Pleasant Hill, CA 94523-4602
Phone: 925-938-5750
guitarheaven@sbcglobal.com
www.guitarheaven.com

Guitar Slam
info@guitarslam.com
www.guitarslam.com

Neal's Music
Contact: Neal and Cathy Shelton
6916 Warner Ave.
Huntington Beach, CA 92647
Phone: 714-842-9965
Fax: 714-901-5383
nealmuzic@aol.com
www.nealsmusic.com

Norman's Rare Guitars
Contact: Norman Harris
18969 Ventura Blvd.
Tarzana, CA 91356-3229
Phone: 818-344-8300
Fax: 818-344-1260
normsgtrs@aol.com
www.normansrareguitars.com

Players Vintage Instruments
P.O. Box 445
Inverness, CA 94937-0445
Phone: 415-669-1107
Fax: 415-669-1102
info@vintageinstruments.com
www.vintageinstruments.com

Soest Guitar Shop
Contact: Steve Soest
760 North Main Street Suite D
Orange, CA 92668
Phone: 714-538-0272
Fax: 714-532-4763
soestguitar@earthlink.net
www.soestguitar.com

Vintage Barn
Contact: Barney Roach
San Diego, CA
Phone: 858-692-1030
www.vintagebarn.biz

Virtual Vintage Guitars
Contact: Jason C. Allen
Phone: 949-635-9797
sales@virtualvintageguitars.com
www.virtualvintageguitars.com

Virtuoso Polish and Cleaner
The Virtuoso Group, Inc.
P.O. Box 9775
Canoga Park, CA 91309-0775
Phone: 818-992-4733
virtuosopolish@sbcglobal.net
www.virtuosopolish.com

Delaware
ACME Guitar Works
Phone: 302-836-5301
www.acmeguitarworks.com

Florida
Andy's Guitars
Contact: Andy
1208 North Monroe Street
Tallahassee, FL 32303
Phone: 850-224-9944
Fax: 850-224-5381
info@andysguitars.com
www.andysguitars.com

Crescent City Music
Contact: Allen Glenn
111 North Summit Street
Crescent City, FL 32112
Phone/Fax: 386-698-2873
Phone: 386-698-2874
ccmusic@crescentcitymusic.biz
www.crescentcitymusic.biz

Kummer's Vintage Instruments
Contact: Timm Kummer
Phone: 954-752-6063
prewar99@aol.com
www.kummersvintage.com

Legends Music, Inc.
Contact: Kent Sonenberg
4340 West Hillsborough Avenue
Tampa, FL 33614
Phone: 813-348-0688
Fax: 813-348-0689
ksonenbl@tampabay.rr.com
www.legendsguitars.com

Georgia
Atlanta Vintage Guitars
Contact: Frank Moates
561 Windy Hill Road
Smyrna, GA 30080
Phone: 770-433-1891
Fax: 770-433-1858
atlantavintage@bellsouth.net
www.atlantavintageguitars.com

Midtown Music
Contact: David Tiller
3326 N. Druid Hills Rd.
Decatur, GA 30033
Phone: 404-325-0515
Fax: 404-252-2243
midtownmusic@mindspring.com
www.midtownmusic.com

Hawaii
Coconut Grove Music
Contact: Fred Oshiro
418 Kuulei Road
Kailua, HI 96734
Phone: 808-262-9977
Fax: 808-263-7052
cgmusic@lava.net
www.coconutgrovemusic.com

Illinois
Ax in Hand
Contact: Damon Henrikson
817 W. Lincoln Hwy, Ste B
DeKalb, IL 60115
Phone: 815-758-8898
Fax: 847-985-0282
guitars@axinhandguitars.com
www.axinhandguitars.com

Chicago Music Exchange
Contact: Scott Silver
3316 N. Lincoln Ave.
Chicago, IL 60657
Phone: 773-525-7773

Fax: 773-477-2775
sales@chicagomusicexchange.com
www.chicagomusicexchange.com

Guitar Adoptions
Contact: Dave Schmidt
Wonder Lake, IL 60097
Phone: 877-241-4580
Fax: 815-653-6501
dave@guitaradoptions.com
www.guitaradoptions.com

Guitar Works Ltd
Contact: Steve or Terry
709 Main Street
Evanston, IL 60202
Phone: 847-475-0855
Fax: 847-475-0715
guitarworksltd@aol.com
www.guitarworksltd.com

Make 'n Music
Contact: Teddy
1455 W. Hubbard St.
Chicago, IL 60622
Phone: 312-455-1970
info@makenmusic.com
www.makenmusic.com

Music Gallery
Contact: Frank
2558 Greenbay Road
Highland Park, IL 60035
Phone: 847-432-6350 / 847-432-8883
MusicGlry@aol.com
www.musicgalleryinc.com

RWK Guitars
P.O. Box 1068
Highland Park, IL 60035
Phone: 847-432-4308
Bob@RWKGuitars.com
www.RWKGuitars.com

Indiana
WeberVST
Speakers, Amp Kits, components,
tools and attenuators
Contact: T.A. Weber
329 E Firmin Street
Kokomo, IN 46902
Phone: 765-452-1249
www.webervst.com
www.weberspeakers.com

Kansas
E.M. Shorts Guitars
Contact: Jon Ray
2525 East Douglas Avenue
Wichita, KS 67211
Phone: 800-835-3006
Fax: 316-684-6858
wbic@wichitaband.com
www.wichitaband.com

Overland Express Guitars
Contact: David Schaefer

10739 West 109th Street
Overland Park, KS 66210
Phone: 913-469-4034
Fax: 913-469-9672
dave@overlandexpress.com
www.overlandexpress.com

Kentucky
Guitar Emporium
1610 Bardstown Road
Louisville, KY 40205
Phone 502-459-4153
Fax: 502-454-3661
guitar-emporium@mindspring.
 com
www.guitar-emporium.com

Louisianna
International Vintage Guitars
Contact: Steve Staples
646 Tchopitoulas St.
New Orleans, LA 70130-3212
Phone: 504-524-4557
Fax: 504-524-4665
guitars@webcorral.com
www.webcorral.com

Maryland
Garrett Park Guitars, Inc.
Contact: Rick Hogue
302 S. Truman Pkway, Ste. F
Annapolis, MD 21401
Phone: 410-571-9660
Fax: 410-573-0502
gpguitars@gmail.com
www.gpguitars.com

Guitar Exchange
Contact: Bruce Sandler
740 Frederick Road
Baltimore, MD 21228
Phone: 410-747-0122
Fax: 410-747-0525

Jim's Guitars Inc.
Contact: Jim Singleton
706 Frederick Rd.
Baltimore, MD 21228-4501
Phone: 866-787-2865
Fax: 410-744-0010
info@jimsguitars.com
www.jimsguitars.com

Nationwide Guitars, Inc.
Contact: Bruce Rickard
P.O. Box 2334
Columbia, MD 21045
Phone: 410-997-7440
Fax: 410-997-7440
nationwideguitars@comcast.net
www.nationwideguitars.com

Southworth Guitars
Contact: Gil Southworth
7845 Old Georgetown Road
Bethesda, MD 20814
Phone: 301-718-1667
Fax: 301-718-0391

southworthguitar@aol.com
www.southworthguitars.com

Massachusetts
Bay State Vintage Guitars
Contact: Craig D. Jones
295 Huntington Avenue, Room 304
Boston, MA 02115
Phone: 617-267-6077

Cold Springs Electrical Works
Contact: Norm Moren
332 Rock Rimmon Road
Belchertown, MA 01007
Phone: 413-323-8869
norm@coldspringselectrical-
 works.com
www.coldspringselectricalworks.
 com

Lucchesi Vintage Instruments
Contact: Frank Lucchesi
108 Cottage St.
Easthampton, MA 01027
Phone: 413-527-6627
info@lucchesivintageinstruments.
 com
www.lucchesivintageinstruments.
 com

Michigan
Elderly Instruments
Contact: Stan Werbin
1100 North Washington
P.O. Box 14210 -VGF
Lansing, MI 48901
Phone: 517-372-7890
Fax: 517-372-5155
elderly@elderly.com
www.elderly.com

Huber & Breese Music
33540 Groesbeck Highway
Fraser, MI 48026
Phone: 586-294-3950
Fax: 586-294-7616
handbmusic@sbcglobal.net
www.huberbreese.com

Lakeshore Guitars
Contact: Rich Baranowski
Troy, MI
Phone: 248-879-7474
richbaranow@aol.com
www.lakeshoreguitars.com

Rockin' Daddy's
Contact: Randy Volin
P.O. Box 210368
Auburn Hills, MI 48321
Fax: 248-420-8499
randy@randyvolin.com
www.rockindaddys.com

Minnesota
Solidbodyguitar.com
Contact: Bruce Barnes
2436 Highway 10

Mounds View, MN 55112
Phone: 763-783-0080
Fax: 763-783-0090
solidbodyguitar@quest.net
www.solidbodyguitar.com

Waterman Guitars
Contact: Tim Waterman
2090 Langston Ln. NE
St. Michael, MN 55376
Phone: 612-716-5983
watermanguitars@gmail.com
www.watermanguitars.com

Willie's American Guitars
254 Cleveland Avenue South
St. Paul, MN 55105
Phone: 651-699-1913
Fax: 651-690-1766
info@williesguitars.com
www.williesguitars.com

Missouri
Eddie's Guitars
Contact: Ed Putney
7362 Manchester Rd.
St. Louis, MO 63143-3108
Phone: 314-781-7500
Fax: 314-781-7510
eddiesguitars@sbcglobal.net
www.eddiesguitars.com

Fly By Night Music
Contact: Dave Crocker
103 South Washington
Neosho, MO 64850-1816
Phone: 417-451-5110
Show number: 800-356-3347
crocker@joplin.com
www.texasguitarshows.com

Hazard Ware Inc./ Killer Vintage
Contact: Dave
P.O. Box 190561
St. Louis, MO 63119
Phone: 314-647-7795, 800-646-7795
Fax: 314-781-3240
www.killervintage.com

Nevada
AJ's Music In Las Vegas
Contact: Peter Trauth
2031 W. Sunset Rd.
Henderson, NV 89014-2120
Phone: 702-436-9300
Fax: 702-436-9302
pete@ajsmusic.com
www.ajsmusic.com

Cowtown Guitars
2797 South Maryland Parkway, Ste. 14
Las Vegas, NV 89109
Phone: 702-866-2600
Fax: 702-866-2520
www.cowtownguitars.com

New Hampshire
Retro Music
Contact: Jeff Firestone
38 Washington Street
Keene, NH 03431
Phone/Fax: 603-357-9732
retromusic@verizon.net
www.retroguitar.com

New Jersey
Golden Age Fretted Instruments
Contact: John Paul Reynolds
309 South Avenue W.
Westfield, NJ 07090
Phone: 908-301-0001
Fax: 908-301-1199
info@goldenageguitars.com
www.goldenageguitars.com

Hoboken Vintage Guitars
Contact: Jim Pasch
164 1st Street
Hoboken, NJ 07030-3544
Phone: 201-222-8977
Fax: 201-222-9127
hoboken@extend.net
www.hobokenvintage.com

Lark Street Music
479 Cedar Lane
Teaneck, NJ 07666
Phone: 201-287-1959
Larkstreet@aol.com
www.larkstreet.com

New Jersey Guitar & Bass Center
Contact: Jay Jacus
995 Amboy Avenue
Edison, NJ 08837
Phone: 732-225-4444
Fax: 732-225-4404
NJGtrBass@aol.com
www.newjerseyguitarandbasscenter.com

Pick of the Ricks
Contact: Chris Clayton
121 Holly St.
Lindenwold, NJ 08021
Phone: 856-782-7300
sales@pickofthericks.com
www.pickofthericks.com

Russo Music Center
Contact: Joe Carroll
1989 Arena Dr.
Hamilton, NJ 08610-2428
Phone: 800-847-8776
joe.c@russomusic.com
www.russomusic.com

New York
Bernunzio Vintage Guitars
Contact: John Bernunzio
875 East Avenue
Rochester, NY 14607
Phone: 585-473-6140

Fax: 585-442-1142
info@bernunzio.com
www.bernunzio.com

Diamond Strings
Contact: Bruce Diamond
20 Shaftsbury Rd.
Rochester, NY 14610
Phone: 585-424-3369
dstrings@rochester.rr.com
diamondstrings.com

Imperial Guitar and Sound-works
Contact: Bill Imperial
99 Route 17K
Newburgh, NY 12550
Phone: 845-567-0111
igs55@aol.com
www.imperialguitar.com

Keyboard Instrument Rentals
Vintage Effects, Guitars and Amps
1697 Broadway Ste 504
New York, NY 10019
Phone: 212-245-0820
Fax: 212-245-8858
keyboardrentals@aol.com

Laurence Wexer Ltd.
Contact: Larry
251 East 32nd Street #11F
New York, NY 10016
Phone: 212-532-2994
info@wexerguitars.com

Ludlow Guitars
164 Ludlow Street
New York, NY 10002
Phone: 212-353-1775
Fax: 212-353-1749
www.ludlowguitars.com

Mandolin Brothers, Ltd.
629 Forest Avenue
Staten Island, NY 10310
Phone: 718-981-3226/8585
Fax: 718-816-4416
mandolin@mandoweb.com
www.mandoweb.com

Michael's Music
Contact: Michael Barnett
29 West Sunrise Highway
Freeport, NY 11520
Phone: 516-379-4111
Fax: 516-379-3058
michaelsmusic@optonline.net
www.michaelsmusic.com

My Generation Guitars
Contact: John DeSilva
Syosset, NY
Phone: 516-993-9893
straightshooter@optonline.net
www.straightshooterguitars.com

Rudy's Music
Contact: Rudy
169 West 48th Street
New York, NY 10036
Phone: 212-391-1699
info@rudysmusic.com
www.rudysmusic.com

Rumble Seat Music
Contact: Eliot Michael
121 West State St.
Ithica, NY 14850
Phone: 607-277-9236
Fax: 607-277-4593
rumble@rumbleseatmusic.com
www.rumbleseatmusic.com

We Buy Guitars
David Davidson
705A Bedford Ave.
Bellmore, NY 11710
Phone: 516-221-0563
Fax: 516-221-0856
webuyguitars1@aol.com
www.webuyguitars.com

We Buy Guitars
Richie Friedman
705A Bedford Ave.
Bellmore, NY 11710
Phone: 516-221-0563
Fax: 516-221-0856
webuyguitars@aol.com
www.webuyguitars.com

We Buy Guitars
Tom Dubas
705A Bedford Ave.
Bellmore, NY 11710
Phone: 516-221-0563
Fax: 516-221-0856
webuyguitars2@aol.com
www.webuyguitars.com

North Carolina
Bee-3 Vintage
Contact: Gary Burnette
25 Arbor Lane
Ashville, NC 28805
Phone: 828-298-2197
bee3vintage@hotmail.com
www.bee3vintage.com

Legato Guitars
Contact: Bill Fender
1121C Military Cutoff Rd. #342
Wilmington, NC 28405
Phone: 910-686-3264
By Appointment Only
legatoguitars@ec.rr.com
www.legatoguitars.com

Maverick Music
Contact: Phil Winfield
8425 Old Statesville Rd., Ste 19
Charlotte, NC 28269-1828
Phone: 704-599-3700
Fax: 704-599-3712

sales@maverick-music.com
www.maverick-music.com

Ohio
DHR Music
PO Box 43209
Cincinnati, OH 45243
Phone: 513-272-8004
Fax: 513-530-0229
dhrmusic@hotmail.com
www.dhrmusic.com

Fretware Guitars
Contact: Dave Hussung
400 South Main
Franklin, OH 45005
Phone: 937-743-1151
Fax: 937-743-9987
guitar@erinet.com
www.fretware.cc

Gary's Classic Guitars
Contact: Gary Dick
Cincinnati, OH
Phone: 513-891-0555
Fax: 513-891-9444
garysclssc@aol.com
www.garysguitars.com

Mike's Music
Contact: Mike Reeder
2615 Vine Street
Cincinnati, OH 45219
Phone: 513-281-4900
Fax: 513-281-4968
www.mikesmusicohio.com

Oklahoma
Strings West
Contact: Larry Briggs
P.O. Box 999
20 E. Main Street
Sperry, OK 74073
Phone: 800-525-7273
Fax: 918-288-2888
larryb@stringswest.com
www.stringswest.com

Oregon
McKenzie River Music
455 West 11th
Eugene, OR 97401
Phone: 541-343-9482
Fax: 541-465-9060
www.McKenzieRiverMusic.com

Pennsylvania
Guitar-Villa – Retro Music
Contact: John Slog
216A Nazareth Pike
Bethlehem, PA 18020
Phone: 610-746-9200
Fax: 610-746-9135
gvilla@guitar-villa.com
www.guitar-villa.com

Guitar-Villa – Retro Music
Contact: John Slog

30 S. Westend Boulevard.
Quakertown, PA 18951
Phone: 215-536-5800
gvilla@guitar-villa.com
www.guitar-villa.com

JH Guitars
Contact: Jim Heflybower
Pennsylvania
Phone: 610-363-9204
Fax: 610-363-8689
JHGuitars@webtv.net
www. jhguitars.com

Vintage Instruments & Frederick W. Oster Fine Violins
Contact: Fred W. Oster
1529 Pine Street
Philadelphia, PA 19102
Phone: 215-545-1100
www.vintage-instruments.com

Rhode Island
PM Blues Guitar Heaven
Contact: Paul Moskwa 401-722-5837, Shawn Reilly 401-724-1144
bluespm@aol.com
www.pmblues.com

Tennessee
Gruhn Guitars
Contact: George Gruhn
400 Broadway
Nashville, TN 37203
Phone: 615-256-2033
Fax: 615-255-2021
gruhn@gruhn.com
www.gruhn.com

Music Room Guitars
Contact: Brad Gibson
5103 Kingston Pike
Knoxville, TN 37919
Phone: 865-584-0041
mrgknox@aol.com

Texas
Charley's Guitar Shop
Contact: Clay and Sheila Powers
2720 Royal Ln. Ste.100
Dallas, TX 75229-4727
Phone: 972-243-4187
Fax: 972-243-5193
shop@charleysguitar.com
www.charleysguitar.com

Eugene's Guitars Plus
Contact: Eugene Robertson
2010 South Buckner Boulevard
Dallas, TX 75217-1823
Phone: 214-391-8677
pluspawnguitars@yahoo.com
www.texasguitarshows.com

Hill Country Guitars
Contact: Kevin Drew Davis
111 Old Kyle Rd. #200
Wimberley, TX 78676-9701

Phone: 512-847-8677
Fax: 512-847-8699
info@hillcountryguitars.com
www.hillcountryguitars.com

Hill Country Guitars
Contact: Kevin Drew Davis
4617 Montrose Blvd., Ste C-190
Houston, TX
Phone: 713-521-5900
houston@hillcountryguitars.com
www.hillcountryguitars.com

Southpaw Guitars
Contact: Jimmy
5813 Bellaire Boulevard
Houston, TX 77081
Phone: 713-667-5791
Fax: 713-667-4091
southpawguitars@sbcglobal.net
www.southpawguitars.com

Texas Amigos Guitar Shows
Arlington Guitar Show (The 4 Amigos)
Contact: John or Ruth Brinkmann
Phone: 800-473-6059
Fax: 817-473-1089
web: www.texasguitarshows.com

Chicago/Austin Guitar Show
Contact: Dave Crocker
Phone: 800-356-3347
Fax: 817-473-1089
crocker@joplin.com
www.texasguitarshows.com

California World Guitar Shows
Contact: Larry Briggs
Phone: 800-525-7273
Fax: 918-288-2888
larryb@stringswest.com
www.texasguitarshows.com

Van Hoose Vintage Instruments
Contact: Thomas Van Hoose
2722 Raintree Drive
Carrollton, TX 75006
Phone: (days) 972-250-2919 or (eves) 972-418-4863
Fax: 972-250-3644
tv0109@flash.net
www.vanhoosevintage.com

Waco Vintage Instruments
Contact: John Brinkman
1275 North Main Street, Ste #4
Mansfield, TX 76063
Phone: 817-473-9144
Guitar Show Phone: 888-473-6059

Utah
Intermountain Guitar and Banjo
Contact: Leonard or Kennard
712 East 100 South

Salt Lake City, UT 84102
Phone: 801-322-4682
Fax: 801-355-4023
guitarandbanjo@earthlink.com
www.guitarandbanjo.net

Virginia
Authentic Guitars
Contact: Michael Hansen
12715-Q Warwick Blvd.
Newport News, VA 23606
Phone: 757-595-4663
www.AuthenticGuitars.com

Authentic Guitars - 2nd Store
Contact: Michael Hansen
4809-1 Courthouse St.
Williamsburg, VA 23188
Phone: 757-220-9911
www.AuthenticGuitars.com

Callaham Vintage Guitars and Amps
Contact: Bill Callaham
108 Ruby Place
Winchester, VA 22603
Phone: 540-955-0294
callaham@callahamguitars.com
www.callahamguitars.com

Vintage Sound
Contact: Bill Holter
P.O. Box 11711
Alexandria, VA 22312
Phone: 703-914-2126
Fax: 703-914-1044
bhvsound@vintagesound.com
www.vintagesound.com

Washington
Emerald City Guitars
Contact: Jay Boone
83 South Washington in Pioneer Square
Seattle, WA 98104
Phone: 206-382-0231
jayboone@emeraldcityguitars.com

Guitarville
Contact: Tommy Steinley
19258 15th Avenue North East
Seattle, WA 98155-2315
Phone: 206-363-8188
Fax: 206-363-0478
gv@guitarville.com
www.guitarville.com

Jet City Guitars LLC
Contact: Allen Kaatz
2212 Queen Anne Ave. N., Box 134
Seattle, WA 98109
Phone: 206-361-1365
ark@jetcityguitars.com
www.jetcityguitars.com

Wisconsin
Bizarre Guitars
Contact: Brian Goff
2501 Waunona Way

Madison, WI 53713
Phone: 608-235-3561
bdgoff@sbcglobal.net

Dave's Guitar Shop
Contact: Dave Rogers
1227 South 3rd Street
La Crosse, WI 54601

Phone: 608-785-7704
Fax: 608-785-7703
davesgtr@aol.com
www.davesguitar.com

MANUFACTURER DIECTORY

A Brown Soun
23 Joseph Ct.
San Rafael, CA 94903
Phone: 415-479-2124
Fax: 415-479-2132
abs@abrown.com
www.abrown.com

Allparts
13027 Brittmoore Park Drive
Houston, TX 77041
Phone: 713-466-6414
allpartgtr@aol.com
www.allparts.com

Analog Man Guitar Effects
Contact: Mike Piera
36 Tamarack Avenue #343
Danbury, CT 06811
Phone: 203-778-6658
AnalogMike@aol.com
www.analogman.com

Antique Electronic Supply
Contact: Brian Campanella
6221 South Maple Avenue
Tempe, AZ 85283
Phone: 480-820-5411
Fax: 800-706-6789
info@tubesandmore.com
www.tubesandmore.com

Area 51 Tube Audio Designs
Contact: Dan Albrecht
5909 S. Evergreen Dr.
Newaygo, MI 49337
(231) 652-5072
sales@area51tubeaudiodesigns.com
www.area51tubeaudiodesigns.com

Bad Cat Amps
Contact: James Heidrich
PMB #406, 2621 Green River Road
Corona, CA 92882
Phone: 909-808-8651
Fax: 909-279-6383
badcatamps@earthlink.net
www.badcatamps.com

Bill Lawrence Pickups
Contact: Bill or Becky Lawrence
1785 Pomona Road, Unit D
Corona, CA 92880
Phone: 951-371-1494
Fax: 951-647-2651
becky@billlawrence.com
billlawrence.com

Budda Amplifiers
Contact: Scot Sier
60 Tehama St., Fl 1
San Francisco, CA 94105-3110
Phone: 415-247-2700
Fax: 415-247-2701
sales@budda.com
www.budda.com

Butler Custom Sound/Chicago Blues Box
1040 N. Dupage
Lombard, IL 60148
Phone: 630-268-2670
www.chicagobluesbox.com

Callaham Vintage Guitars and Amps
Contact: Bill Callaham
108 Ruby Place
Winchester, VA 22603
Phone: (540) 955-0294
callaham@callahamguitars.com
www.callahamguitars.com

Campbell American Guitars
Contact: Dean Campbell
PO Box 460
Westwood, MA 02090
Phone: 617-6220-8153
Fax: 508-785-3577
sales@campbellamerican.com
www.campbellamerican.com

Carr Amplifiers
Contact: Steve
433 West Salisbury St.
Pittsboro, NC 27312
Phone: 919-545-0747
Fax: 919-545-0739
info@carramps.com
www.carramps.com

CE Distribution
Contact: Noreen Cravener
6221 South Maple Avenue
Tempe, AZ 85283
Phone: 480-755-4712
Fax: 480-820-4643
info@cedist.com
www.cedist.com

Chandler Musical Instruments
Contact: Paul
Phone: 530-899-1503
www.chandlerguitars.com
www.pickguards.us

Demeter Amplification
Contact: James Demeter
6990 Kingsbury Rd.
Templeton, CA 93465
Phone: 818-994-7658
Fax: 818-994-0647
info@demeteramps.com
www.demeteramps.com

DLS Effects, Inc.
151 Perinton Parkway
Fairport, NY 14450
www.dlseffects.com

Durham Electronics
Contact: Alan Durham
Phone: 512-581-0663
alan@durhamelectronics.com
www.durhamelectronics.com

Emery Sound
Contact: Curtis Emery
Phone: 510-236-1176
www.emerysound.com

Eric Schoenberg Guitars
Contact: Eric
106 Main Street
Tiburon, CA 94920
Phone: 415-789-0846
eric@om28.com
www.om28.com

Fuchs Audio Technology
Contact: Annette Fuchs
357 Broad Street Rear
Bloomfield, NJ 07003
Phone: 973-680-1200
sales@fuchsaudiotechnology.com
fuchsaudiotechnology.com

Gregg Rogers Guitars
Contact: Gregg or Marcia Rogers
32069 Lyman Hamilton Hwy
Sedro Woolley, WA 98284
Phone: 360-826-4860
Fax: 360-826-4860
grguitars@msn.com
www.GRGuitars.com

Kendrick Amplifiers
Route. 2 P.O. Box 871
Kempner, TX 76539
Phone: 512-932-3130
Fax: 512-932-3135
kendrick@kendrick-amplifiers.com
www.kendrick-amplifiers.com

Lovepedal
Phone: 248-766-8660
www.lovepedal.com

Mercury Magnetics
Contact: Paul Patronette
Chatsworth, CA
Phone: 818-998-7791
Fax: 818-998-7835
sales@mercurymagnetics.com
www.mercurymagnetics.com

Mirabella Guitars & Restorations
Contact: Cris Mirabella
P.O. Box 482
Babylon, NY 11702
Phone: 631-842-3819
Fax: 631-842-3827
mirguitars@aol.com
www.mirabellaguitars.com

Phantom Guitar Works Inc.
Contact: Jack Charles
Phone: 503-728-4825
www.phantomguitars.com

Schaefer Guitars
Contact: Ed Schaefer
4221 West 4th Street
Duluth, MN 55807
Phone: 218-624-7231
sguitars@airmail.net
www.schaeferguitars.com

SD Custom Guitar Works
Atelier de Lutherie SD
6610 Blvd des-Galeries-D'Anjou
(Ste. #02)
Montreal (Anjou), Quebec
Phone: 514-817-8930
info@MontrealCustomGuitars.com
www.MontrealCustomGuitars.com

Top Hat Amplification
Contact Brian Gerhard
5316 Millstone Creek Dr.,
Fuquay-Varina, NC 27526
Phone 919-762-9688
tophatamps@aol.com
www.tophatamps.com

Torres Engineering
Amps Guitars & Pickups
www.torresengineering.com

INDEX

Bold Page numbers indicate first listing

Bold Page numbers indicate first listing

Bold Page numbers indicate first listing

Bold Page numbers indicate first listing

Bold Page numbers indicate first listing

Bold Page numbers indicate first listing

Bold Page numbers indicate first listing